Twentieth-Century Literary Criticism

Guide to Gale Literary Criticism Series

For criticism on	Consult these Gale series
Authors now living or who died after December 31, 1959	*CONTEMPORARY LITERARY CRITICISM* (*CLC*)
Authors who died between 1900 and 1959	*TWENTIETH-CENTURY LITERARY CRITICISM* (*TCLC*)
Authors who died between 1800 and 1899	*NINETEENTH-CENTURY LITERATURE CRITICISM* (*NCLC*)
Authors who died between 1400 and 1799	*LITERATURE CRITICISM FROM 1400 TO 1800* (*LC*) *SHAKESPEAREAN CRITICISM* (*SC*)
Authors who died before 1400	*CLASSICAL AND MEDIEVAL LITERATURE CRITICISM* (*CMLC*)
Authors of books for children and young adults	*CHILDREN'S LITERATURE REVIEW* (*CLR*)
Dramatists	*DRAMA CRITICISM* (*DC*)
Poets	*POETRY CRITICISM* (*PC*)
Short story writers	*SHORT STORY CRITICISM* (*SSC*)
Black writers of the past two hundred years	*BLACK LITERATURE CRITICISM* (*BLC*)
Hispanic writers of the late nineteenth and twentieth centuries	*HISPANIC LITERATURE CRITICISM* (*HLC*)
Native North American writers and orators of the eighteenth, nineteenth, and twentieth centuries	*NATIVE NORTH AMERICAN LITERATURE* (*NNAL*)
Major authors from the Renaissance to the present	*WORLD LITERATURE CRITICISM, 1500 TO THE PRESENT* (*WLC*)

ISSN 0276-8178

Volume 91

Twentieth-Century Literary Criticism

Criticism of the Works of Novelists, Poets, Playwrights, Short Story Writers, and Other Creative Writers Who Lived between 1900 and 1960, from the First Published Critical Appraisals to Current Evaluations

Jennifer Baise
Editor

Thomas Ligotti
Associate Editor

Detroit
New York
San Francisco
London
Boston
Woodbridge, CT

STAFF

Jennifer Baise, *Editor*

Thomas Ligotti, *Associate Editor*

Maria Franklin, *Permissions Manager*
Kimberly F. Smilay, *Permissions Specialist*
Kelly A. Quin, *Permissions Associates*
Sandy Gore, *Permissions Assistant*

Victoria B. Cariappa, *Research Manager*
Andrew Guy Malonis, Barbara McNeil, Gary J. Oudersluys, Maureen Richards, Cheryl L. Warnock, *Research Specialists*
Patricia T. Ballard, Tamara C. Nott, Tracie A. Richardson, *Research Associates*
Phyllis Blackman, Corrine Stocker, *Research Assistant*

Mary Beth Trimper, *Production Director*
Stacy L. Melson, *Buyer*

Gary Leach, *Graphic Artist*
Randy Bassett, *Image Database Supervisor*
Robert Duncan, Michael Logusz, *Imaging Specialists*
Pamela Reed, *Imaging Coordinator*

Library of Congress Catalog Card Number 76-46132
ISBN 0-7876-2021-1
ISSN 0276-8178

Printed in the United States of America
10 9 8 7 6 5 4 3 2 1

Contents

Preface vii

Acknowledgments xi

Ernest Fenollosa 1853-1908 1
American translator

Alfred Kinsey 1894-1956 40
American scientist

Ivan Petrovich Pavlov 1849-1936 83
Russian physiologist

Georges Sorel 1847-1922 172
French social and political theorist

Graham Wallas 1858-1932 351
English political scientist

Literary Criticism Series Cumulative Author Index 409

Literary Criticism Series Topic Index 474

TCLC Cumulative Nationality Index 482

Title Index to *TCLC,* Vol. 91 487

Preface

Since its inception more than fifteen years ago, *Twentieth-Century Literary Criticism* has been purchased and used by nearly 10,000 school, public, and college or university libraries. *TCLC* has covered more than 500 authors, representing 58 nationalities, and over 25,000 titles. No other reference source has surveyed the critical response to twentieth-century authors and literature as thoroughly as *TCLC*. In the words of one reviewer, "there is nothing comparable available." *TCLC* "is a gold mine of information—dates, pseudonyms, biographical information, and criticism from books and periodicals—which many libraries would have difficulty assembling on their own."

Scope of the Series

TCLC is designed to serve as an introduction to authors who died between 1900 and 1960 and to the most significant interpretations of these author's works. The great poets, novelists, short story writers, playwrights, and philosophers of this period are frequently studied in high school and college literature courses. In organizing and reprinting the vast amount of critical material written on these authors, *TCLC* helps students develop valuable insight into literary history, promotes a better understanding of the texts, and sparks ideas for papers and assignments. Each entry in *TCLC* presents a comprehensive survey of an author's career or an individual work of literature and provides the user with a multiplicity of interpretations and assessments. Such variety allows students to pursue their own interests; furthermore, it fosters an awareness that literature is dynamic and responsive to many different opinions.

Every fourth volume of *TCLC* is devoted to literary topics. These topic entries widen the focus of the series from individual authors to such broader subjects as literary movements, prominent themes in twentieth-century literature, literary reaction to political and historical events, significant eras in literary history, prominent literary anniversaries, and the literatures of cultures that are often overlooked by English-speaking readers.

TCLC is designed as a companion series to Gale's *Contemporary Literary Criticism*, which reprints commentary on authors now living or who have died since 1960. Because of the different periods under consideration, there is no duplication of material between *CLC* and *TCLC*. For additional information about *CLC* and Gale's other criticism titles, users should consult the Guide to Gale Literary Criticism Series preceding the title page in this volume.

Coverage

Each volume of *TCLC* is carefully compiled to present:

- criticism of authors, or literary topics, representing a variety of genres and nationalities
- both major and lesser-known writers and literary works of the period
- 6-12 authors or 3-6 topics per volume
- individual entries that survey critical response to each author's work or each topic in literary history, including early criticism to reflect initial reactions; later criticism to represent any rise or decline in reputation; and current retrospective analyses.

Organization of This Book

An author entry consists of the following elements: author heading, biographical and critical introduction, list of principal works, reprints of criticism (each preceded by an annotation and a bibliographic citation), and a bibliography of further reading.

- The **Author Heading** consists of the name under which the author most commonly wrote, followed by birth and death dates. If an author wrote consistently under a pseudonym, the pseudonym will be listed in the author heading and the real name given in parentheses on the first line of the biographical and critical introduction. Also located at the beginning of the introduction to the author entry are any name variations under which an author wrote, including transliterated forms for authors whose languages use nonroman alphabets.

- The **Biographical and Critical Introduction** outlines the author's life and career, as well as the critical issues surrounding his or her work. References to past volumes of *TCLC* are provided at the beginning of the introduction. Additional sources of information in other biographical and critical reference series published by Gale, including *Short Story Criticism, Children's Literature Review, Contemporary Authors, Dictionary of Literary Biography,* and *Something about the Author,* are listed in a box at the end of the entry.

- Some *TCLC* entries include **Portraits** of the author. Entries also may contain reproductions of materials pertinent to an author's career, including manuscript pages, title pages, dust jackets, letters, and drawings, as well as photographs of important people, places, and events in an author's life.

- The **List of Principal Works** is chronological by date of first book publication and identifies the genre of each work. In the case of foreign authors with both foreign-language publications and English translations, the title and date of the first English-language edition are given in brackets. Unless otherwise indicated, dramas are dated by first performance, not first publication.

- Critical essays are prefaced by **Annotations** providing the reader with information about both the critic and the criticism that follows. Included are the critic's reputation, individual approach to literary criticism, and particular expertise in an author's works. Also noted are the relative importance of a work of criticism, the scope of the essay, and the growth of critical controversy or changes in critical trends regarding an author. In some cases, these annotations cross-reference essays by critics who discuss each other's commentary.

- A complete **Bibliographic Citation** designed to facilitate location of the original essay or book precedes each piece of criticism.

- Criticism is arranged chronologically in each author entry to provide a perspective on changes in critical evaluation over the years. All titles of works by the author featured in the entry are printed in boldface type to enable the user to easily locate discussion of particular works. Also for purposes of easier identification, the critic's name and the publication date of the essay are given at the beginning of each piece of criticism. Unsigned criticism is preceded by the title of the journal in which it appeared. Some of the essays in *TCLC* also contain translated material. Unless otherwise noted, translations in brackets are by the editors; translations in parentheses or continuous with the text are by the critic. Publication information (such as footnotes or page and line references to specific editions of works) have been deleted at the editor's discretion to provide smoother reading of the text.

- An annotated list of **Further Reading** appearing at the end of each author entry suggests secondary sources on the author. In some cases it includes essays for which the editors could not obtain reprint rights.

Cumulative Indexes

- Each volume of *TCLC* contains a cumulative **Author Index** listing all authors who have appeared in Gale's Literary Criticism Series, along with cross references to such biographical series as *Contemporary Authors* and *Dictionary of Literary Biography.* For readers' convenience, a complete list of Gale titles included appears on the first page of the author index. Useful for locating authors within the various series, this index is particularly valuable for those authors who are identified by a certain period but who, because of their death dates, are placed in another, or for those authors whose careers span two periods. For example, F. Scott Fitzgerald is found in *TCLC,* yet a writer often associated with him, Ernest Hemingway, is found in *CLC.*

- Each *TCLC* volume includes a cumulative **Nationality Index** which lists all authors who have appeared in *TCLC* volumes, arranged alphabetically under their respective nationalities, as well as Topics volume entries devoted to particular national literatures.

- Each new volume in Gale's Literary Criticism Series includes a cumulative **Topic Index,** which lists all literary topics treated in *NCLC, TCLC, LC 1400-1800,* and the *CLC* yearbook.

- Each new volume of *TCLC,* with the exception of the Topics volumes, includes a **Title Index** listing the titles of all literary works discussed in the volume. In response to numerous suggestions from librarians, Gale has also produced a **Special Paperbound Edition** of the *TCLC* title index. This annual cumulation lists all titles discussed in the series since its inception and is issued with the first volume of *TCLC* published each year. Additional copies of the index are available on request. Librarians and patrons will welcome this separate index; it saves shelf space, is easy to use, and is recyclable upon receipt of the following year's cumulation. Titles discussed in the Topics volume entries are not included *TCLC* cumulative index.

Citing Twentieth-Century Literary Criticism

When writing papers, students who quote directly from any volume in Gale's literary Criticism Series may use the following general forms to footnote reprinted criticism. The first example pertains to materials drawn from periodicals, the second to material reprinted from books.

[1]William H. Slavick, "Going to School to DuBose Heyward," *The Harlem Renaissance Re-examined,* (AMS Press, 1987); reprinted in *Twentieth-Century Literary Criticism,* Vol. 59, ed. Jennifer Gariepy (Detroit: Gale Research, 1995), pp. 94-105.

[2]George Orwell, "Reflections on Gandhi," *Partisan Review,* 6 (Winter 1949), pp. 85-92; reprinted in *Twentieth-Century Literary Criticism,* Vol. 59, ed. Jennifer Gariepy (Detroit: Gale Research, 1995), pp. 40-3.

Suggestions Are Welcome

In response to suggestions, several features have been added to *TCLC* since the series began, including annotations to critical essays, a cumulative index to authors in all Gale literary criticism series, entries devoted to criticism on a single work by a major author, more extensive illustrations, and a title index listing all literary works discussed in the series since its inception.

Readers who wish to suggest authors or topics to appear in future volumes, or who have other suggestions, are cordially invited to write the editors.

Acknowledgments

The editors wish to thank the copyright holders of the criticism included in this volume and the permissions managers of many book and magazine publishing companies for assisting us in securing reproduction rights. We are also grateful to the staffs of the Detroit Public Library, the Library of Congress, the University of Detroit Mercy Library, Wayne State University Purdy/Kresge Library Complex, and the University of Michigan Libraries for making their resources available to us. Following is a list of the copyright holders who have granted us permission to reproduce material in this volume of *TCLC*. Every effort has been made to trace copyright, but if omissions have been made, please let us know.

COPYRIGHTED ESSAYS IN *TCLC*, VOLUME 91, WERE REPRODUCED FROM THE FOLLOWING PERIODICALS:

American Literature, v. 59, May, 1987. Copyright © 1987 by Duke University Press, Durham, NC. Reproduced by permission.—***American Quarterly,*** v. XXIX, Winter, 1977. Copyright 1977, American Studies Association. Reproduced by permission of The Johns Hopkins University Press.—***The American Scholar,*** v. 23, Winter, 1953-54. Copyright © 1953, renewed 1981 by the United Chapters of the Phi Beta Kappa Society. Reproduced by permission of the publishers.—***Contemporary French Civilization,*** v. II, Winter, 1978. Reproduced by permission.—***Critical Quarterly,*** v. 20, Spring, 1978. © Manchester University Press 1978. Reproduced by permission.—*Educational Theory,* v. 18, Spring, 1968. Reproduced by permission.—***Encounter,*** v. XXXIV, February, 1970 for "The Legacy of Georges Sorel: Marxism, Violence, Fascism" by J. L. Talmon. © 1970 by the author.—***History of European Ideas,*** v. 12, 1990; v. 13, 1991. Both reproduced by permission.—***Isis,*** v. 88, June, 1997 for "Pavlov's Physiology Factory" by Daniel P. Todes. Copyright © 1997 by the History of Science Society, Inc. Reproduced by permission of the University of Chicago Press and the author.—***Journal for the Scientific Study of Religion,*** v. 25, Summer, 1986. Reproduced by permission.—***Journal of European Studies,*** v. 7, September, 1977 for "The Question of Sorel" by D. C. Band. © 1977 Science History Publications Ltd.—***Journal of the History of Ideas,*** v. XXXIV, July-September, 1973; v. 47, October-December, 1986. © 1973, 1986. Both reproduced by permission of The Johns Hopkins University Press.—***Paideuma: A Journal Devoted to Ezra Pound Scholarship,*** v. 13, Fall, 1984 for "Misreading the Ideogram: From Fenollosa to Derrida and McLuhan" by Hwa Yol Jung; v. 17, Fall-Winter, 1988 for "Ezra Pound's *Cathay*: Compilation from the Fenollosa Notebooks" by Anne S. Chapple. International © 1984, 1988 by the National Poetry Foundation, Inc. Both reproduced by permission of the publisher and the authors.—***Partisan Review,*** April, 1948 for "The Kinsey Report" by Lionel Trilling. Copyright © 1948, renewed 1976 by Partisan Review. Reproduced by permission of the author's estate.—***Political Science Quarterly,*** v. LXXXIII, March, 1968. Reproduced by permission—***The Political Quarterly,*** v. III, October-December, 1932; v. III, July-September, 1940. Both reproduced by permission.—***The Review of Politics,*** v. XXVI, 1964; v. 41, October, 1979. Copyright 1964, 1979 by the University of Notre Dame. Both reproduced by permission.—***Science & Society,*** v. XXV, Spring, 1961. Reproduced by permission.—***The South Atlantic Quarterly,*** v. XLIX, April, 1950. Copyright © 1950, renewed 1978 by Duke University Press, Durham, NC. Reproduced by permission.—***The Times Literary Supplement,*** n. 4035, July 25, 1980. © The Times Supplements Limited 1980. Reproduced from ***The Times Literary Supplement*** by permission..

COPYRIGHTED ESSAYS IN *TCLC,* VOLUME 91, WERE REPRODUCED FROM THE FOLLOWING BOOKS:

—Berlin, Isaiah. From ***Against the Current: Essays in the History of Ideas.*** The Hogarth Press, 1979. © Isaiah Berlin 1955, 1959, 1968, 1969, 1970, 1971, 1972, 1973, 1974, 1979. Reproduced with permission of Curtis Brown Ltd., London, on behalf of The Isaiah Berlin Literary Trust.—Burnham, James. From ***The Machiavellians: Defenders of Freedom.*** The John Day Company, Inc., 1943. Copyright, 1943, renewed 1970, by James Burnham. Reproduced by permission of HarperCollins Publishers.—Carr, E. H. From ***Studies in Revolution.*** Macmillan & Co., Ltd., 1950. Reproduced by permission of Macmillan, London and Basingstoke.—Fancher, Raymond E. From ***Pioneers of Psychology.*** W. W. Norton & Company, Inc., 1979. Copyright © 1979 by Raymond E. Fancher. Reproduced by permission.—Folsom, Joseph K. From "Kinsey's Challenge to Ethics and Religion," in ***Sexual Behavior in American Society: An Appraisal of the First Two Kinsey Reports.*** Edited by Jerome Himelhoch and Sylvia Fleis Fava. W. W. Norton & Company, Inc., 1955. Copyright © 1955 by W. W. Norton & Co., Inc. Reproduced by permission.—Gross, David. From ***Political Symbolism in Modern Europe: Essays in Honor of George L. Mosse.*** Edited by Seymour Drescher, David Sabean, and Allan Sharlin. Copyright © 1982 by Transaction, Inc. Reproduced by permission.—Orage, A. L. From ***Selected Essays and Critical Writings.*** Stanley Nott, 1935.—Rohrich, Wilfried. From ***Social Protest, Violence, and Terror in Nineteenth- and Twentieth-Century Europe.*** Edited by Wolfgang J. Mommsen and Gerhard Hirschfeld. The Macmillan Press Ltd., 1982. © Wolfgang J. Mommsen and Gerhard Hirschfeld 1982. Reproduced by permission of Macmillan, London and Basingstoke.—Shaw, George Bernard, ***From Bernard Shaw &***

Karl Marx: A Symposium, 1884-1889. Constable and Company Limited, 1944. © George Bernard Shaw, October 24, 1944. Reproduced by permission of the author's estate.—Stanley, John. From an introduction to ***The Illusions of Progress*** by Georges Sorel. Translated by John and Charlotte Stanley. University of California Press, 1969. Copyright © 1969 by The Regents of the University of California. Reproduced by permission.—Stanley, John L. From an introduction to ***Social Foundations of Contemporary Economics*** by Georges Sorel. Translated by John L. Stanley. Transaction Books, 1984. Copyright © 1984 by Transaction, Inc. Reproduced by permission.—Tratner, Michael. From ***Modernism and Mass Politics: Joyce, Woolf, Eliot, Yeats.*** Stanford University Press, 1995. © 1995 by the Board of Trustees of the Leland Stanford Junior University. Reproduced with the permission of the publishers, Stanford University Press.

Ernest Fenollosa

1853-1908

(Full name Ernest Francisco Fenollosa) American translator, art historian, educator, poet, and philosopher.

INTRODUCTION

Fenollosa is considered to be one of the first Western experts in East Asian art and literature, and he is given much credit for providing the impetus for Imagist poetry through his extensive research and cataloging of Japanese and Chinese painting and ideograms. After his death in 1908, Fenollosa's widow, the novelist Mary Fenollosa, completed his two-volume manuscript *Epochs of Chinese and Japanese Art: An Outline History of East Asiatic Design.* Mary Fenollosa named American poet and critic Ezra Pound her husband's literary executor, and Pound's subsequent poetry collection of Japanese translations, *Cathay,* gives credit to Fenollosa. Pound also completed Fenollosa's *Certain Noble Plays of Japan, Noh, or Accomplishment: A Study of the Classical Stage of Japan,* and *The Chinese Written Character as a Medium for Poetry* from Fenollosa's notes and unpublished writings. From his work with Fenollosa's notes and research materials, Pound learned concepts about Chinese and Japanese writing that he would use to formulate the tenets of Imagism and Vorticism. Pound also borrowed many of Fenollosa's ideas concerning Buddhism, to which Fenollosa had converted, and Confucianism for many of his *Cantos.* Fenollosa also was the subject of Van Wyck Brooks's 1962 *Fenollosa and His Circle.*

Biographical Information

Fenollosa was born in Salem, Massachusetts, to an immigrant Spanish musician and the daughter of an East Indian ship owner. He attended Harvard University, graduating in 1874, and spent the next four years continuing his studies at Harvard and at the Museum of Fine Arts in Boston. He accepted a position as a professor of political economy and philosophy at the Imperial University in Tokyo in 1878, where he taught until 1888. From 1889 to 1890 Fenollosa was the concurrent manager of the Academy of Fine Arts in Tokyo and the Imperial Museum. During his stay in Tokyo, Fenollosa increased his knowledge of Japanese culture and art and converted to Buddhism. The escalating Westernization of Japan in the latter nineteenth century threatened to destroy much of traditional Japanese culture and art, and Fenollosa fought this trend by convincing the Boston Museum of Fine Arts to preserve much Japanese art that might have been destroyed otherwise. During this period he also helped to found the Tokyo University of Fine Arts and Music and traveled as a emissary of the Japanese Ministry of Education and the imperial household to study American and European methods of museum curatorship. He was accompanied to the United States by his former student, Okakura Kakuzo, who was also instrumental in introducing East Asian art to the West. Fenollosa returned to the United States in 1890, and became Curator of Oriental Art at Boston's Museum of Fine Arts. In 1897, he returned to Japan to teach English at the Imperial Normal School. Fenollosa accepted a teaching post in 1890 at Columbia University, and spent his remaining years teaching and lecturing on Oriental art, philosophy, and literature. He died in London in 1908.

Major Works

Fenollosa published only two major works in his lifetime: *East and West,* a collection of poetry, and *The Masters of Ukioye,* a study on Japanese painting and catalog for a New York exhibition. Fenollosa's *The Chinese Written Character as a Medium for Poetry,* edited and rewritten by Ezra Pound, has evoked both critical praise and dispute. While such critics as Christine Brooke-Rose are intrigued by Fenollosa's understanding of Chinese characters as a basis for a poetic aesthetic, other critics believe his theories are based upon false etymological assumptions. Fenollosa wrote that Chinese characters present a clear mental picture rather than simply a phonetic symbol for the objects they signify. He argued that creating such a mental image is the true function of poetry and the origin of all written language. Fenollosa described metaphor as "the use of material images to suggest immaterial relations," and suggested that that mental process was the basis for all understanding of the written word. Once the symbols became immediately recognizable, their original symbolic function became forgotten. Fenollosa's best-known writings are his literal translations of Chinese and Japanese poems, which Pound used as the basis for the translations appearing in his *Cathay.* Among the poems Pound revised from Fenollosa's notes are "The River-Merchant's Wife: A Letter" and "The River Song," both poems originally written by the poet Rihaku.

PRINCIPAL WORKS

East and West: The Discovery of America, and Other Poems (poetry) 1893
Epochs of Chinese and Japanese Art: An Outline History of East Asiatic Design (criticism) 1911
Cathay (translations) 1915

"Noh," or Accomplishment: A Study of the Classical Stage of Japan (criticism) 1916
Certain Noble Plays of Japan (criticism) 1916
The Chinese Written Character as a Medium for Poetry (criticism) 1919

CRITICISM

William Morton Payne (essay date 1894)

SOURCE: A review of "East and West: The Discovery of America and Other Poems", by Ernest Fenollosa, in *The Dial,* Vol. XVI, No. 189, May 1, 1894, pp. 272-75.

[*In the following essay, Payne determines that the poet characterizes the West as masculine and the East as feminine.*]

Mr. Fenollosa's [***East and West: The Discovery of America, and Other Poems.***] consists of two long and very ambitious poems, and a number of minor pieces. The titular poem is a sort of versified *Culturgeschichte,* philosophical and mystical, in spirit not unlike Mr. Block's "El Nuevo Mundo," which we reviewed a year or so ago. In this poem, says the author, "I have endeavored to condense my experiences of two hemispheres, and my study of their history." The poem is in five parts. The first considers the early meeting of East and West, brought about by the conquests of Alexander. Then follow **"The Separated East"** and **"The Separated West,"** themes of which the author has conceived in the following terms: "Eastern culture, slowly elaborated, has held to ideals whose refinement seems markedly feminine. For it social institutions are the positive harmonies of a life of brotherhood. Western culture, on the contrary, has held to ideals whose strength seems markedly masculine. For it law is the compromise of Liberty with her own excesses, while conquest, science, and industry are but parallel channels for the overflow of hungry personality. But this one-sidedness has been partly compensated by the religious life of each. The violence of the West has been softened by the feminine faith of love, renunciation, obedience, salvation from without. It is the very impersonality of her great ecclesiastical institute which offers to man a refuge from self. On the other hand, the peaceful impotence of the East has been spurred by her martial faith of spiritual knighthood, self-reliance, salvation from within. The intense individuality of her esoteric discipline upholds the fertile tranquillity of her surface. This stupendous double antithesis seems to me the most significant fact in all history. The future union of the types may thus be symbolized as a twofold marriage." In **"The Present Meeting of East and West,"** the author deals with "the first attempts to assimilate alien ideals," which "have led to the irony of a quadruple confusion, analogous to the disruption of Alexander's conquest." But there is to be another and more intimate union, brought about in some mysterious way by the art of music, and in a manner foreshadowed in some sort by the compositions of Herr Brahms. Here, we must confess, we are unable to follow the argument. And the poem ends with a rapturous song of **"The Future Union of East and West."** This is a good deal of philosophical machinery with which to burden a composition of fifteen hundred lines, and the work is too ambitious to be wholly successful. But it abounds in strong passages, such as the finely imaginative struggle of the archangels, who

"Met as mountains meet, when Titans cast
Pelion on Ossa, and their fragments spurt
Through startled space a jet of asteroids,"

or the stanzas to Hangehow, where (among other things),

"In a tangle of leaves with silken sleeves
Thy poets sing on the terraced beach,
Where the blue-flagged taverns with mossy eaves
Are starred by the pink of the blossoming peach,"

or the following fine epitome of the Viking conquests:

"Now shot from polar coasts see meteors flash,
Long lines of Viking ships, with low black hulls
Like vultures, plunging through the Northern seas,
Hovering like gulls in track of channel storms,
Scouring for prey the long white sunlit cliffs;
Wailing their chant to Odin like wild winds
Surging through organ pipes of naked fjords,
Wooing Valhalla to Northumbrian hills
Or primrose-garnished banks of lovely Seine.
Now, drunk with richer wine of vanquished worlds,
Wielding the cross as once their bolt of Thor,
They skirt with gorgeous sweep Hispania's curves,
Through pillared gateway of the land-locked sea
Set in its rifted coasts of gilded cloud,
A blue enamelled dragon! Now they break,
Those strange Norse champions of a Hebrew god,
The threatening onsets of the Saracen,
Dispersed like storms which strew with wrecks
thy coast,
Nurse of a hundred races, Sicily!"

We should like to quote also the fine description of the destruction of the Summer Palace in 1859, but Mr. Fenollosa's other poems claim our remaining space. Of these, the most important is **"The Discovery of America,"** described as "a symphonic poem," in four movements, and in a great variety of metres. Since both the manner and the matter of the author constantly invite musical comparisons, we will remark that the suggestion of Liszt is here very evident. A passage from the soliloquy of Columbus may be reproduced:

"And yet I knew; and yet I dimly guessed
When as a guileless boy
I climbed the steep Ligurian cliffs in lusty joy,
And gazed far off upon the dimpled breast
Of blue-eyed seas that slumbered in the West.
For was I not compelled
As by a great hand held
To gaze, and gaze, and gaze

Through tender brooding miles of purple haze,
Till soft-winged isles
Seemed lifting orange bosoms to the sun's last
smiles,
And my light will, a feather free,
Was blown like a trembling bird far out to sea
By storm-winds, Alpine-brewed, of passionate
prophecy?"

The poem from which this extract is taken must certainly be reckoned among the most notable inspired by the recent quadri-centennial year. As for Mr. Fenollosa's minor poems, they are always interesting, and often satisfying. We will end our examples with the lines to **"Fuji at Sunrise":**

"Startling the cool gray depths of morning air
She throws aside her counterpane of clouds,
And stands half folded in her silken shrouds
With calm white breast and snowy shoulder bare.
High o'er her head a flush all pink and rare
Thrills her with foregleam of an unknown bliss,
A virgin pure who waits the bridal kiss,
Faint with expectant joy she fears to share.
Lo, now he comes, the dazzling prince of day!
Flings his full glory o'er her radiant breast;
Enfolds her to the rapture of his rest,
Transfigured in the throbbing of his ray.
O fly, my soul, where love's warm transports are;
And seek eternal bliss in yon pink kindling star."

Lest this review would seem to have abrogated the traditional fault-finding function of criticism, we will close by remarking the false quantity in the author's use of "Granicus." But this defect is at least partly atoned for by his getting **"Himálya"** right, which few succeed in doing.

F. W. Williams (essay date 1913)

SOURCE: A review of "Epochs of Chinese and Japanese Art: An Outline History of East Asiatic Designs", by Ernest Fenollosa, in *Yale Review,* Vol. III, No. 1, October, 1913, pp. 197-201.

[*In the following essay, Williams praises the author's scholarship, and agrees with his hypothesis that all art derived from two principle locations in the Mediterranean and the Western Pacific.*]

Twenty years ago the author of these sumptuous volumes, [***Epochs of Chinese and Japanese Art: An Outline History of East Asiatic Design.***], in a lecture before the Yale Art School, threw upon the screen a photograph of Kano Utanosuke's "Eagle on a Pine Branch." "There," he declared, "is one of the greatest paintings by an Asiatic artist. Why do I say only this? It is the greatest painting ever produced by any artist at all!" Fenollosa's voice, while he lived, was that of one crying in the wilderness of Western complacency. As with prophets in all ages, his revelations were set down as the thick-coming fancies of a visionary. He had found a new realm of artistic representation, with ideals and canons of its own, the language of which conveyed almost no meaning to the minds of his countrymen. Some exaggeration was inevitable in the new-born enthusiasm of a man of his temperament; yet if he spoke too strongly he never spoke absurdly. He was admirably fitted by training as well as by temperament for his work as herald and historian of an unknown world of art; and the issue of his propaganda is at length manifest in the slow recognition by Westerners of the fact that the art of the Eastern "barbarians" is not inferior intellectually and in creative power to that of Europeans. Since his death in 1908, the appearance of Laurence Binyon's masterly essay on "Painting in the Far East," and the exhibition by the British Museum of the wonderful Chinese mediæval paintings walled up since the eleventh century in a Buddhist cave at Tun Hwang and discovered by Dr. Stein, have greatly quickened interest in the pictorial art of China, and hastened, perhaps, the opening of a new era in the history of the graphic arts. For breadth of treatment, however, and appreciations based upon profound knowledge, the work before us must be recognized as the most important treatise upon the whole subject that has thus far appeared. Had its author lived longer he might have amended his studies in matters of detail, altered some ascriptions, and even reversed certain estimates; but it is a convincing measure of a conscientious life work that his final interpretation of a great exotic culture—shorn though it is of what he would have considered a necessary revision—rises above all other accounts to a position among the standard books of a generation. Merely as a *tour de force* of creative writing these two quarto volumes deserve a place by themselves in modern literature. Fenollosa's widow, to whom we owe their publication, tells us that they were completed in one magnificent effort in three months—the solid outcome of nearly thirty years of research and valuation devoted to one supreme purpose.

From the standpoint of the historian, Fenollosa's chief contribution to the history of art is, perhaps, his suggestion of the existence of two original centres of art-dispersion, one in the eastern Mediterranean basin and the other about the western edge of the Pacific. From this second basis he derives the underlying ideas and motives of primitive Chinese art; but, to quote his own words, "the special value of this theory of two centres lies in the striking fact that Chinese art is the only large form of world art that has combined in itself creative impulses from both. The key to early Chinese art is as follows:—its earliest motives were influenced by Pacific art, and these were later overlaid by forms of the Græco-Persian. Of course this is quite consistent with the fact that Chinese art, like all great schools, still later must have experienced ferments and achieved powerful reaches of advance from causes operating within." A generalization like this requires the work of many specialists in regions as far apart as Borneo, Alaska, and Peru before it can be accepted as anything more important than a brilliant suggestion; but it offers a working hypothesis that accounts at least for the appearance of the same motives on the earliest Chinese bronzes, on Aleutian totem poles, and on Aztec pottery. While this is not the place to examine the evidence produced to support the contention, it is worth a reference in passing to show how the historian, in studying the origins of a culture state, derives materials, sometimes of unexpected importance, from the conclusions of art critics. If the so-called "Yuëh," aborigines of China before the Chinese, are proved to have employed decorative motives common to primitive Pacific groups, it will clear the way to an understanding of the origins of that mysterious people.

Fenollosa has little to say on the highly controversial subject of the source of the group which brought a higher culture into China from the West. The history of China must have developed far upon the paths of civilization before the period ascribed to the earliest ballads of the Shih Ching, and by this time must have felt the contact of ideas from the other original centre. The subsequent intercourse with the western end of the continent seems often to have been severed; but by Alexander's time it had apparently been flowing in a stream sufficiently strong to imbue the rebellious state of Ch'in with a conception of centralized dominion upon the Achæmenid model and to effect the final overthrow of her primitive feudal system. The influences of Hellenism in the Far East, which have seized upon the imaginations of Western students in recent years, are dismissed rather coolly by Fenollosa, though a diluted and transient impulse may well have found its way thither from Greece. His cautious and sensible judgment in the matter leaves us room to conclude that all the "Hellenism" found in the Buddhistic art of China and Japan can be safely derived from what Persia and Parthia knew of the Mediterranean world.

These are, however, only preliminary and incidental matters in a book which is mainly an *exposé* of the whole course of art development in the Far East. A superficial glance at these volumes will convey to some an impression that they are chiefly concerned with Japanese painters, but the true relations of China's position as teacher of design to the younger country are neither denied nor neglected. What is here done to reveal the glories of Chinese art is all that is possible at this time in an outline treatise. So much has been destroyed of that great output of creative genius that we are compelled to study it principally from paintings and statues preserved in Japan, or from Japanese copies. Even the promise of treasures yet to be revealed when the private collections of China are known abroad, does not offer us hope that many masterpieces of the T'ang and Sung artists have survived the utter destruction of their great capitals. It is in Japan, therefore, that we must study what remains of an epoch which it is one of Fenollosa's chief merits to have first adequately revealed to the world outside. While we may regret his decision to discuss these continental artists under their Japanese rather than their own Chinese names, and thus strengthen the reader's sensation of being concerned with an iconography of the Island Empire, the truth is nowhere suppressed that she has always stood to the older empire intellectually as Rome stood to Greece. To the author's untimely death may be attributed the erratic and inconsistent spelling of certain Chinese names, as well as the occasional misprints which sully the pages of an otherwise impeccable letterpress.

It is, in fact, in correcting the current notion that the Japanese have improved upon and even surpassed the Chinese in art that Fenollosa's work will achieve one of its most important results. Only a few as yet know the real nature of Chinese art; its survival in the trivialities displayed in modern China is actually on a par with that of the plaster images of the Italian hawker to-day as exponents of the glories of Renaissance sculpture. Until lately the Western critic called the East æsthetically sensuous and capricious, given to color and extravagance. Yet we shall see from these volumes that during its great periods, Eastern Asia has, unlike ancient Egypt and Greece, subordinated if not entirely eliminated color in its buildings and pictures. Its painters have understood the art of tone; and with their appreciation of subtle harmonies of tint, rather than of color, their work surpasses in decorative value the work of all Europeans. From this has arisen a tradition, derived perhaps from Chinese caligraphy, that seeks for the beautiful not in transferring nature with its varied hues, shadows, and distances to canvas, but in interpreting nature conventionally upon a flat surface with an eye single to its intimately expressive lines. With us, the painter secures his effect by relief and shading; in their art, which is quite as mature as ours, a more difficult success is obtained by procuring the illusion of perfect modelling by contour alone. As we understand the aims of their painting better, we realize that it is primarily an effort to fill and decorate a surface undisturbed by problems of optics or chiaroscuro, in conformity with laws that regard only what seems to them permanent and essential in the painted subject. It may be long before Western painters surrender their ambition to tell stories and reproduce nature on canvas. When they cease to borrow accidental qualities and superfluous details from the laboratory and the scientific lectureroom, their art will eventually return to its true sphere—the incarnation of sensuous beauty and rhythm, the manifestation of the living spirit of things. How far we have yet to go to comprehend the accepted ideal of the Chinese may be seen from the statement of their six canons of æsthetics:—rhythmic movement, organic structure, conformity with nature, color, arrangement, and finish.

The historical periods of the twenty centuries which Fenollosa has recorded are substantially in accordance with those outlined in standard treatises on the subject. It is in his appreciations and fine interpretations of the influence of art in the various epochs that he surpasses his predecessors. What mystical Buddhism meant to the naïvely refined society of the Fujiwara can only be learned by a study of its literature and art, when the romance and spiritual enthusiasm that still vitalizes Japanese life assumed, perhaps, its most radiant phase. For the core of this wonderful life is chiefly explained by its enthusiasm, he tells us:

> Recent Christian visitors to Japan have observed of this remarkable race that, in spite of modern

> Confucian agnosticism, they seem to be a people "on fire with religion." This passionate idealism nobly displayed itself in the sacrifices of the recent Russian war. It was the same divine flame, but reddened a thousand years ago with a stronger Buddhist tinge, that made Fujiwara lords and ladies feel even the most gorgeous human life to be only a threshold for an actual spiritual life. This intermingling of social and spiritual interests sounds a key-note. To make and administer sound laws, to effect hospital, charitable, and university organization, to play a bird-like part in the variegated paradises of court and villa, to beautify the person and flash poetry as fountains do water, was only to play naturally what the gods wished done upon the hardened circumference of heaven; for, after all, the earth is only an outlying province, and the very best of the flesh-bound souls is in touch with the central molten life of Paradise. Thus men do their most menial functions in the very eyes of the gods, and there becomes practically no difference between a palace and a temple.

This life is as far away from modern Japan as it is from us. Will the world of industrialism ever again return to Utanosuke's "Eagle on a Pine Branch"?

Henry B. Fuller (essay date 1917)

SOURCE: A review of "'Noh,' or Accomplishment: A Study of the Classical Stage of Japan", by Ernest Fenollosa, in *The Dial*, Vol. 63, September 13, 1917, pp. 209-10.

[*In the following essay, Fuller gives a brief overview of the origins, intentions, and structure of Noh drama.*]

To-day's reciprocal obligations in regard to culture continue to multiply. This is one of the pleasure-pains of cosmopolitanism. Mr. Fenollosa's records of his conversations with the reviver of the classical drama of Japan [***"Noh." or Accomplishment: A Study of the Classical Stage of Japan.***] tell how he gave the ancient man a brief account of the classic drama of Greece: "he already knew," adds this Occidental adventurer into the lore of the East, "something about opera." Now, if the Oriental shows a disposition to familiarize himself with Euripides and Puccini—to say nothing of Nietzsche, Tolstoy, Victor Hugo, and Oscar Wilde—shall we not exert ourselves in turn, and show a willingness to go beyond Hokusai and Hiroshige?

The "Noh" drama, as shaped in the fifteenth century and saved through Japan's transition to the new day, is the complete negation of all literalism and of the merely mimetic. It scorns both. It relates to the well-known school of the Danjuros about as the classical school of Chinese painting relates to the color-prints of Ukiyo-ye. It is noble, not plebeian; spiritistic, not realistic: it squares with the fundamental principles of all good art, rather than with the thoughtless passing fashion of any particular day.

Fenollosa, on his death, left a large body of notes and translations concerned with this school of drama. Most of his material was got, first hand, from Umèwaka Minoru, descendant of a long line of esteemed actors, who made it the work of his later years to rescue the ancient and honorable traditions of the classic stage from the shock which, in 1868, inaugurated the era of Meiji. This mass of material passed into the hands of Mr. Pound, whose treatment of it is briefly explained in his "Note." Says he: "The vision and the plan are Fenollosa's. In the prose I had had but the part of literary executor; in the plays my work has been that of translator who has found all the heavy work done for him and who has had but the pleasure of arranging beauty into the words." Gather his method from a passage in one of the fifteen short pieces which the book presents, that called "Nishikigi" (The Love-Charm Wands). Here is Fenollosa's prose:

> It is strange, seeing these town-people here. I might suppose them two married people; and what the lady gives herself the trouble of carrying might be a piece of cloth woven from birds' feathers, and what the man has is a sword, painted red. It is indeed queer merchandise.

Here is Pound's verse:

> Strange indeed, seeing these town-people here,
> They seem like man and wife,
> And the lady seems to be holding something
> Like a cloth woven of feathers,
> While he has a staff or a wooden sceptre
> Beautifully ornate.
> Both of these things are strange;
> In any case, I wonder what they call them.

This play, "Nishikigi," though (like most of the others) largely spiritistic, should easily be intelligible to the Western mind: it has a "love interest" which ought to help us take hold and feel at home. A wandering priest, a standard character in "Noh," meets two ghosts in ancient attire in a remote village. They tell their story. The man, for three years, had offered charm-sticks, those "crimson tokens of love," night after night, and finally died of despair. The woman, oblivious or ignorant, or from mere coquetry, had sat at her weaving within her house. The man was buried in a cave, with all his wands. The woman repented of her cruelty—if such it was—and died also. The two have been dead for a century, and have not yet been united. The priest visits the cave. But the night is too cold for sleep, and he enters upon a ritual before the cave's mouth. His warm respect for the old tale begins to produce its effect. The lovers come to life within the illuminated cavern, a kindly chorus coöperates with the priest, and the lovers finally accomplish a spirit union before the final moment which prophesies a void waste—"a wild place, unlit, and unfilled."

Considering the "Noh" in its essence, the ancient and loyal Japanese historian should have had little difficulty with the Greek drama, whatever headway he may or may not have made with the opera. For the two stages, the two schools, have much in common. Each had an independent growth from miracle plays—one from the plays of the worship of Bacchus, the other from the plays of the worship of Buddha and of the Shinto deities; each prefers to deal with a tale or legend already well known; each accomplishes a wide generalization that rises gravely and scornfully above the petty mimetics and realisms of the day; each employs a chorus; each involves dancing, and each practices a play-sequence,—the Greeks, one of four parts and the Japanese, one of six,—which last presents, as Mr. Pound phrases it, "a complete service of life." The mere dialogue is but one feature among several; the singing and the dancing must always be considered if one is to reach a clear understanding and a complete æsthetic appreciation.

The order, as shown by Fenollosa's notes, is this: a congratulatory piece, or ceremonial address to the gods; a battle-piece, with due mindfulness for the emperors; a "wig-piece"—for females; a spirit-piece, since the spirits form the vague but lasting background of man's transitory and tristful experiences; a moral piece, inculcating the various virtues; lastly, another congratulatory piece, to call down blessings on the lords present, on the actors themselves, and on the scene of their endeavors. Thus the cycle is closed.

Mr. Pound, in his notes and comments, writes with his usual unceremonious directness: if he is sometimes rugged, blunt, and downright, one at least gets a strong sense of primary impact from a man who is duly, even vastly, concerned. And as the volume is made by the Clarks, of Edinburgh, a "serious" house, one notes, with gratification, an almost complete suppression of Mr. Pound's tendency toward typographical wilfulnesses and eccentricities.

Hwa Yol Jung (essay date 1984)

SOURCE: "Misreading the Ideogram: From Fenollosa to Derrida and McLuhan," in *Paideuma: A Journal Devoted to Ezra Pound Scholarship,* Vol. 13, No. 2, Fall, 1984, pp. 211-27.

[*In the following essay, Jung examines the influence of Ralph Waldo Emerson on Fenollosa's aesthetics, and how Jacques Derrida and Marshall McLuhan arrived at the same conclusions as Fenollosa and Ezra Pound.*]

> The main title of this article was originally "Inventing Grammatology." Mr. Burton Hatlen, however, suggested another title: "Misreading the Ideogram." I decided to accept his suggestion partly because I remember the title of Harold Bloom's book *A Map of Misreading* (New York: Oxford University Press, 1975). There are at least two reasons for associating my article with the deep structures of his book: first, his theory of poetry is Vichian and Emersonian, and second, his "primal scene of instruction" *differs* markedly from Derrida's "scene of writing," that is, it contains a significant dose of deconstructive *pharmakon* for Derrida's grammatology.

> *Ex litterarum studiis immortalitatem acquiri.*
>
> —Andrea Alciati

> . . . a linguist deaf to the poetic function of language and a literary scholar indifferent to linguistic problems and unconversant with linguistic methods are equally flagrant anachronisms.
>
> —Roman Jakobson

I

Many years ago T. S. Eliot spoke enthusiastically of Ezra Pound as the "inventor" of Chinese poetry for our time. Eliot had to have in mind the "ideogrammic method" employed, for example, by Pound in *The Cantos* whose alphabetic architecture is marked by the soaring columns of Chinese ideograms which are read hierarchically, from top to bottom. These columns shine like the glittering rays of the "sunrise" (East) visible in and through the tree's branches and leaves in the early morning. The "origin" (*arche*) of Pound's "invention" of Chinese poetry and subsequently of his ideogrammic method is traceable directly to the "etymosinology" of Ernest Fenollosa whose literary executor he was. If Pound is the "inventor" of Chinese poetry for our time, then Fenollosa deserves to be called its "arche-inventor."[1]

In the double sense of philia and phobia, the ebb and flow of Orientalism is nothing new in the *habitus* of Western intellectual and practical thought. Indeed, it has been chameleon-like. Early European Catholic missionaries in Japan expressed their unqualified and unrestrained admiration for the Japanese *kanji* (ideograms) as being superior to Greek and Latin. The degree of difficulty in learning it did not deter or dampen their admiration. The "ontological difference," as it were, between the alphabetic and the ideographic deepened the aura and mystery of those little iconographic pyramids. The newly initiated or neophyte would naturally be enchanted by the "ideogrammic abracadabra" and its "poetic alchemy." This is so despite the judgment of the grammatologist Hegel who, perfectly consonant with his general view of world history, was convinced of the superiority of "abstract" alphabetic writing over "concrete" ideographic writing in the historical development of human linguistic systems. Hegel is worth being noted here because Fenollosa went to Japan to teach philosophy with a favorable disposition for his thought.

Fenollosa's youthful literary environment was the "American Renaissance" whose masters were Emerson, Thoreau, Whitman, Poe, Hawthorne and Melville.[2] The American hypnotic fascination with Egyptian hieroglyphics came from the work of Jean-François Champollion—the Frenchman who deciphered Egyptian hieroglyphics with the aid of the Rosetta stone in the 1830s. We do not have to stretch our imagination too far to connect Egyptian hieroglyphics with Chinese ideograms. The enthusiasm for one can easily be transferred to the other. In Fenollosa's case, his etymosinology has been related to Emerson's conception of nature, language and poetry which we shall explore later. Fenollosa's fascination with Chinese ideograms is certainly comparable to Emerson's enchantment with Egyptian hierogylphics: they all are the "emblems" of nature beyond whose visual veil there are inscrutable "golden secrets" which are not readily decipherable to ordinary people. Whoever unveils or deciphers the emblems of nature is a "magician" of some sort—like an ancient Egyptian scribe.

In the long cherished tradition of the American fascination with the "mysterious" and "exotic" land of Japan, it is not surprising to see the fantastic success of James Clavell's *Shogun* on television as well as in classrooms for teaching modern Japanese history. Conversely, Occidentalism has faced the same kind of fate in the Orient—particularly in Japan. The Japanese, I think, are notorious for their Occidentalism (especially in their linguistic Anglophilianism) since the time of the Meiji Restoration in the last quarter of the nineteenth century, during which time Fenollosa spent his most energetic and productive years in organizing Japanese art and propagating its importance to the indigenous population.[3] Several years ago, the Japanese journalist Takao Tokuoka reported with humor in the editorial column of the *New York Times* the inventive word *towelket*—a shop sign written in Japanese phonetic characters (*kana*)—which is a combination of the two English words *towel* and *blanket* [towelket = towel + (blan)ket]. What born Joyceans the Japanese are! Of course, what I have in mind is Joyce's talent or inventiveness for composing chordal vocabularies in the *Ulysses* and the *Finnegans Wake*. The Joycean "decomposition" or musicalization of the "abcedminded" world or the "popeyed world" of the "scribblative" has its structural parallel to Fenollosa's deconstruction or demystification of Chinese ideograms as emblems. Joyceanism or Joyce's unique stylistics stands out for its tremendous proclivities for making visible words chordal and for thinking in chords after the acoustic model of music, that is, for the production of chordal meanings by obliterating (auditory) content and (visual) form: thornghts (thorn + thoughts), rhythmatick (rhythm + mathematics), paupulation (paucity + population), evoluation (evolution + evaluation), cerebration (cerebrum + celebration), etc.[4] If Fenollosa's etymological deconstruction of Chinese ideograms (*kanji*) is correct, the composition of *towelket* is a result of the natural *habitus* of the Japanese mind—in fact, of the Oriental mind that is accustomed to the vorticism of Chinese ideograms.

From the very outset, it must be said that the importance of Fenollosa's etymosinology cannot be underestimated. It is an *archaeology* of linguistic terms in the sense of tracing backward. Moreover, etymosinology implies the inseparable connection between the Chinese language and culture in their historical patterns.[5] Since time immemorial the Chinese have acknowledged the interrelatedness of external reality and the language that describes it. Things of nature become real for men by acquiring names. From the "rectification of names" (*cheng ming*) emerges the unique conception of language as both performative and intrinsic to our conception of the world and our conduct in it. By defining language as intrinsic to our conception of the world, I mean to stress the idea that language is not merely an object among other objects in the world. For it makes all other objects transparent, that is, an object becomes for man an object by acquiring a name for itself.

II

The main topic of our discussion is Ernest Fenollosa's **An Essay on the Chinese Written Character as a Medium for Poetry** which was posthumously published by Ezra Pound in 1920 in his befittingly titled *Instigations*.[6] To be truthful to the carefully phrased title, there are three important issues to be considered: (1) the nature of poetry (Section II), (2) the conception of Chinese ideograms (Section III), and (3) the question of language as a medium of communication (Section IV). The controversial nature of Fenollosa's essay and Pound's use of Chinese ideograms as a medium for his poetry needs no elaboration—especially the pros and cons by sinologists. What is interesting is the fascination with Chinese grammatology of non-sinologists such as Jacques Derrida and Marshall McLuhan, who are primarily interested in advancing their own theories of language and literature.

Emerson's influence on Fenollosa's conception of poetry seems undeniable and clearly visible. Emerson's essay "The Poet" (1844) is singularly important for our discussion of Fenollosa. There are two issues we must analyze: (1) the relationship between poetry and language; and (2) words as actions.

1. *Poetry and Language.* It is not altogether surprising that many poet-critics have come to the conclusion that poetry is the "first language" of humanity and the poet is the "first man." For Fenollosa, poetry and language grew up together. Long before Emerson and Fenollosa, the Neapolitan philosopher Giambattista Vico, who made no distinction between Egyptian hieroglyphics and Chinese ideograms, propounded the view that not only is poetry inseparable from language but also poetry is the "origin" (*arche*) of language itself. The following passage from "The Poet," one of the most eloquent passages in the entire corpus of Emerson's writings, echoes the Vichian philosophy of language:

> The poets made all the words, and therefore, language is the archives of history, and, if we must say it, a sort of tomb of the muses. For, though the origin of most of our words is forgotten, each word was at first a stroke of genius, and obtained currency, because for the moment it symbolized the world to the first speaker and to the hearer. The etymologist finds the deadest word to have been once a brilliant picture. Language is fossil

> poetry. As the limestone of the continent consists of infinite masses of the shells of animalcules, so language is made up of images, or tropes, which now, in their secondary use, have long ceased to remind us of their poetic origin. But the poet names the thing because he sees it, or comes one step nearer to it than any other.[7]

For Emerson, language is the very special gift of man. It is the milieu that connects *invisible* spirit and *visible* nature: it is the "sign" or "emblem" of nature. In this regard, spirit and material things are inseparably linked. Following Emerson, Fenollosa too comes to the view that Chinese ideograms convert "material images" into "immaterial relations."[8] In this sense, every ideogram is a metaphor whose function is absolutely indispensable to poetry and poetic imagination. For Emerson, the words that express our intellectual or moral facts are rooted directly in "material appearance":

> *Right* originally means *straight; wrong* means *twisted. Spirit* primarily means *wind; transgression,* the crossing of a *line; supercilious,* the *raising of the eye-brow.* We say the *heart* to express emotion, the *head* to denote thought; and *thought* and *emotion* are, in their turn, words borrowed from sensible things, and now appropriated to spiritual nature. Most of the process by which this transformation is made, is hidden from us in the remote time when language was framed; but the same tendency may be daily observed in children. Children and savages use only nouns or names of things, which they continually convert into verbs, and apply to analogous mental acts.[9]

What Emerson saw in hieroglyphics is what Fenollosa saw in Chinese ideograms.

2. *Words as Actions.* According to Emerson, "Words are also actions, and actions are a kind of words."[10] By the same token, the poet is one who can articulate the world in terms of "nouns" and "verbs." In this Emersonian tradition, Fenollosa describes ideograms as "vivid shorthand pictures of actions and processes in nature."[11] Chinese ideograms are the "concrete pictures" of things in nature. As the ideogram is an idea in action, there is no separation between thing and action. Moreover, poetry agrees with science, not with logic since science is something "concrete" whereas logic is something "abstract." Poetry as well as art is concerned not with "the general" and "the abstract" but with "the concrete of nature, not with rows of separate 'particulars,' . . . Poetry is finer than prose because it gives us more concrete truth in the same compass of words."[12] Poetry brings language close to things. Whereas logic considers thought as "a kind of brickyard" and builds "pyramids of attenuated concept" until it reaches the apex called "being," science gets at the "things" themselves which lie at the base of the conceptual pyramid. "Grammar" is the "logic" of language; however, nature knows no grammar. Like nature, the Chinese language too knows no grammar. If, in Chinese, words are the "concrete pictures" of nature, nouns are "things in motion" and verbs "motion in things."

Moreover, ideograms are *performative,* that is, they are *kinetic.* Indeed, Chinese ideography (calligraphy in particular) is a kinetic art: it is the human body in motion.[13] In very significant measure, Chinese ideography is a choreography of human gestures or, to use the phrase of George Herbert Mead, "a conversation of gestures."[14] However, it is not simply "physiographic" or "pictorial," because to be ideographic the "pictures" of human gestures or things must reach the proper level of signs or symbols: as a sign or symbol, the ideogram must have twofold unity of external "indication" and meaningful "ex/pression." Be that as it may, I am always impressed with the fact that such Chinese ideograms as "anger," "sorrow," and "smile" depict the contours of those facial expressions themselves. In this sense, Picasso's *Swimmer* (1929) and *Acrobat* (1930) are two choreographs of the human body in motion or kinegraphs which are approaching ideography or calligraphy. Thus Samuel Beckett is absolutely right when he says that in language as gestures the spoken and the written are identical.[15] R. G. Collingwood too makes the perceptive observation that every language is a specialized from of bodily gesture and thus the dance is the mother of all languages.[16] Similarly, Marshall McLuhan and Harley Parker declare that "In contrast to phonetic letters, the ideograph is a vortex that responds to lines of force. It is a mask of corporate energy."[17] In essence, each ideogram is the frolicking of a thing or body. Speech itself is the dance of the tongue and the lips to the etheral tune of breath. No wonder the ancients—in Greece as well as in China and India—considered music, dance, drama and (oral) poetry as a *familial union* of performing arts. Poetry is the primordial union of the "word" and the "deed." It is of no surprise to know that saying or naming is "performative." For this reason *cheng ming* (the "rectification of names") has such an important niche in the fabric of Chinese and moral thought.[18] Likewise, music too approaches and corresponds to human morality in Chinese thought: its nomos and ethos constitute morality.

III

Fenollosa's conception of the written Chinese characters is based on the idea that they are ideographical, i.e., the highly stylized pictures of things in motion as symbols or ideas. Following Fenollosa, Pound too views the Chinese ideogram not as "the picture of a sound" but as "the picture of a thing."[19] Thus, every ideogram is a kind of *ars poetica* or, better, confirms the Horatian precept *ut pictura poesis.* Nonetheless, Oriental children do not learn how to read, write or decipher the meaning of an ideogram by decomposing or dissecting it into a picture or into a composite of simpler characters or radicals. An ideogram is learned as a whole script or a *Gestalt:* first, how it is pronounced and then how to identify its given meaning or meanings. The Orientals also learn how to write not in terms of a character as the moving picture of a thing but in terms of a number or combination of strokes.[20] This is *not* to say, however, that Fenollosa's and Pound's etymopoetics of the written Chinese characters is valueless, uninteresting or uninformative. On the contrary, I find the "decompositional" or "deconstructive" etymolinguistics rather enlightening and fascinating.[21] Take the following examples of "hypograms" as the corporate insemination of other ideograms (ideograms *upon* and *by* ideograms) provided by Fenollosa himself: "East" is an entangling of "sun" with "tree" (i.e., the sun entangled in the branches of a tree in the early morning or at sunrise); "old" or "ancient" is a composite of "ten" and "mouth" ("ten" *over* "mouth," i.e., presumably referring to what has come down through the mouth for ten generations); and "truth" or "faithfulness" is a composite of "man" and "word" (i.e., man standing *by* his word). Two of my favorite characters are "humanity" and "sage." The former is a composite of "man" and "two" (i.e., two men standing together) and the latter is a composite of "ear," "mouth" and "king." As the "king" is the unifier of heaven, man and earth, the "sage" is the unifier of heaven, man and earth by speaking and hearing truthfully. Furthermore, for the Chinese "nature" is signified by the ideograms: "ten thousand" and "things" (i.e., it *is* "ten thousand things").

Recent grammatology as the literary theory of writing has acquired its preeminence with Jacques Derrida who considers Hegel as the first (Western) philosopher of writing. With *Of Grammatology*[22] he holds the most recent copyright on grammatology and may even be cast as the "visionary father" of a new grammatology. It is a seminal work in the critical philosophy of language in general and of writing in particular—writing in the current French sense of *écriture* as an act autonomous or independent of the spoken or the phonetic. It is a deconstruction of photocentrism or logocentrism and ultimately of the (Western) metaphysics of presence since Plato. It is not wrong to say that Derrida's deconstructive grammatology is leaning toward the superiority of Oriental hieroglyphic or ideographic writing over Occidental alphabetic writing. Near the end of an important chapter "Of Grammatology as a Positive Science" in *Of Grammatology,* Derrida has a passage which refers to Fenollosa's and Pound's etymopoetics. To quote Derrida's passage fully: "This is the meaning of the work of Fenellosa [*sic*] whose influence upon Ezra Pound and his poetics is well-known: this irreducibly graphic poetics was, with that of Mallarmé, the first break in the most entrenched Western tradition. The fascination that the Chinese ideogram exercised on Pound's writing may thus be given all its historical significance."[23] Furthermore, Derrida uses some Chinese ideas in his *Dissemination.*[24]

As Derrida's deconstructive grammatology, like Fenollosa's and Pound's etymopoetics, seeks an absolute interiorization of writing as an autonomous act, and because all three found in Chinese ideography what they regard as a perfect example of such interiorization, it is worth comparing the foundation of their poetics and linguistics. I suggest that this foundation is based on the issue of *sound* and *sense* in language and poetry. It is important to note that Derrida's grammatology, which focuses on the idea of the text and the decipherment of its (conceptual) signification rather than on the voice and sense, is perfectly consistent with his conceptualist thought. In the international symposium "The Languages of Criticism and the Sciences of Man" organized in 1966 by the Johns Hopkins Humanities Center, Derrida denied in no uncertain terms the existence of any perception whatsoever, for "perception is precisely a concept."[25] The contrast between Derrida's grammatology and Chinese writing is in a significant way the same as the contrast between the poetics of Mallarmé and that of Gerard Manley Hopkins. Interestingly enough, Pound himself declares in his *ABC of Reading* that "Music rots when it gets *too far* from the dance. Poetry atrophies when it gets too far from music."[26] The ultimate paradox—I say paradox because such concepts as "trace" and *"différance"* (deferment) indispensable to Derrida's grammatology are "time" concepts—of Derrida's grammatology lies in the fact that when it murders the voice and resurrects the text, it tends to shrink time and stretch space.

Admiring the poetic geniality of Shakespeare and the sense of musical delight—the rich sweetness of sound, rhythm, and melody—Samuel Taylor Coleridge declared: "'The man that hath not music in his soul' can indeed never be a genuine poet."[27] In recent decades it was Roman Jakobson who established systematically for the first time the structural interrelatedness between poetics and linguistics: as poetics is concerned with verbal structure and linguistics is the global science of verbal structure, the former is an integral part of the latter.[28] Similarly, Fenollosa too argued: "My subject is poetry, not language, yet the roots of poetry are in language. In the study of a language so alien in form to ours as is Chinese in its written character, it is necessary to inquire how these universal elements of form which constitute poetics can derive appropriate nutriment."[29] Jakobson further mentions paronomasia as a technique of poetry (in alphabetic writing), that is, the use of words similar in sound which are drawn together in meaning as well: dove-love, light-bright, place-space, name-fame, etc. Of course, the use of homonyms is an important part of Chinese poetry. It is a technique of utilizing the same or similar sounds of multiple characters with different meanings. To accentuate the sound quality of poetry, we can conjecture that man's "first poetry" was a kind of music, while his "first speech" was a kind of song. While T. S. Eliot spoke of the "music of poetry," the composer Igor Stravinsky talked about the "poetry of music" which, when desophisticated, is rooted in folksong or oral poetry.[30] It seems quite natural to discover, therefore, that since time immemorial music has been the nomos and ethos of Chinese culture and its composition and performance correspond to the prescription of human conduct in the "rite" order.[31] It is worth nothing that speaking of the art of Chinese poetry, James J. Y. Liu points out that Western translators and students of Chinese poetry totally ignore its tonal, acoustic, and auditory affects. Though admittedly it is difficult to translate the musical quality of poetry, reading a Chinese poem in translation resembles looking at a beautiful woman through a veil or a landscape through a mist. The "veil" or "mist" of Chinese poetry is monosyllable sound, homonym, rhyme, tone, pitch, alliteration, onomatopoeia, metric, consonance, assonance, etc. In accordance with the singing affect of the Chinese language in general, most Chinese readers *chant* rather than merely read verse aloud; and the Chinese syllables tend to produce a *staccato* affect rather than the *legato* rhythm of English or French verse.[32]

In our critical commentary on Chinese grammatology as well as on grammatology as the study of language as writing, we would be remiss if we were to ignore thirteenth-century Chinese scholar Tai T'ung's *Six Scripts (Lio Shu Ku)*[33] which, he confessed, was a product of thirty years of hard work. The work in question deals with the six cardinal principles of Chinese ideographic writing. In his short but laborious work on Chinese writing, Tai produced what I. A. Richards has called "multiple definitions." One of these principles is the tracing of the phonetic or oral from which the written or chirographic developed in the Chinese language. This is the principle of ideographic writing as the *articulation* of speech. When applied, it becomes a deconstruction of grammatology by rhetoric or the study of language as speech acts. From this perspective, Fenollosa, Pound, and particularly Derrida are not so much wrong as one-sided, however seminal their grammatologies may be. In the first place, one "script" or principle of Chinese writing that Tai discusses is called *pictorial,* because the written characters are really the copies of the physical forms of objects in depiction. In addition, there is another "script" or principle called a "suggestive compound" or, better, an "associative compound" which is a "union of figures" in order to express an idea. These two principles govern Fenollosa's and Pound's analysis of Chinese etymopoetics. The other four "scripts" or principles are called "indicative," "deflected," "adoptive," and "phonetic." Among these six principles of Chinese writing, the most important is the "phonetic" principle for our critical analysis. According to Tai, this principle says that "Written figures spring from spoken sounds."[34] Therefore, it is one-sided to say that Chinese writing in its total structure or configuration is purely grammatology or the study of writing as an autonomous act independent of the phonetic. As a matter of fact, Tai is critical of those "etymologists" who knew nothing of the principle of phonetic composition. Ultimately, Tai proposed the idea of the Chinese language as the *"diatactics"*[35] of the spoken and the written. In other words, (Chinese) writing is the "abstract" form of "concrete" speech. As Tai wrote, "The Sonant Form precedes, the Written Form follows; but as without written signs, spoken sounds could not be represented to the eye, I place first the written form and subjoin the spoken sound. The spoken sound is the *yang* . . . , the written sign the *yin* . . . , the spoken sound is the *warp,* the written sign the *woof:* the spoken sound is the *circle,* the written sign the *square:* the spoken sound is complete, the written sign incomplete."[36] In essence, according to Tai, the principal aim of Chinese writing is simply this: *"to make speech visible."*[37]

IV

Fenollosa is not concerned with defining the concept of language as a medium, although it is a key word in his work in question. Understandably so, because he is concerned primarily with the nature of poetry and how the written Chinese character *is* in itself poetry. The question of language as a medium of communication is a natural result of the development of highly sophisticated communication technologies.[38] Marshall McLuhan must be singled out as a high priest of the "medium" age who heralded the advent of recent electronic communication technologies. For our purpose here, two things must be noted. First, McLuhan is an anti-visualist and his opposition to "typographic" man and culture is vividly evidenced in his *magnum opus, The Gutenberg Galaxy.*[39] For him, typography epitomizes visualism and scales the height of "eye culture" and electronic technology is the second coming of (Homeric) oral culture accompanied by the intimate sense of touch. Oral culture is pre-literate, whereas the advent of electronic technology is post-literate in that it surpasses the world of literacy or writing. Second, McLuhan has, rightly or wrongly, a romantic sense of the Chinese ideogram as a vortex of corporate energy. Not unlike electricity, the Chinese ideogram arouses the sense of touch rather than that of sight. McLuhan reportedly said that the ideal form of his anti-typographic treatise *The Gutenberg Galaxy* would have been ideograms or it would have been written as a galaxy of ideograms. While Derrida is a conceptualist who seems to have been attracted by the "abstract" aspect of Chinese ideography in order to substantiate his philosophical grammatology, McLuhan is, in contrast, a congenital perceptualist who seems to be attracted by the "sensorial" aspect of Chinese ideograms as the medium of communication. No doubt both of them are interested in (Oriental) ideographic writing as opposed to (Occidental) alphabetic writing. For Derrida ideographic writing is purged of phoneticism, while for McLuhan it is anti-visual and tactile. As a philosophical grammatologist, Derrida has no use for writing as a medium of communication. McLuhan's message and flamboyant style are unmistakably clear in the following passage from his interview with *Playboy* in 1969:

> Any culture is an order of sensory preferences, and in the tribal world, the senses of touch, taste, hearing and smell were developed, for very practical reasons, to a much higher level than the strictly visual. Into this world, the phonetic alphabet fell like a bombshell installing sight at the head of the hierarchy of senses. Literacy propelled man from the tribe, gave him an eye for an ear and replaced his integral in-depth communal interplay with visual linear values and fragmented consciousness. As an intensification and amplification of the visual function, the phonetic alphabet diminished the role of the senses of hearing and touch and taste and smell, permeating the discontinuous culture of tribal man and translating its organic harmony and complex synaesthesia into the uniform, connected and visual mode that we still consider the norm of "rational" existence. The whole man became fragmented man; the alphabet shattered the charmed circle and resonating magic of the tribal world, exploding man into an agglomeration of specialized

> and psychically impoverished "individuals," or units; functioning in a world of linear time and Euclidean space.[40]

McLuhan was initially trained in English literature. As we have already noted, he is interested in Chinese ideography as a unique medium of communication, although he has no direct reference to Fenollosa as far as I can determine.[41] However, it is worth noting that in *The Gutenberg Galaxy* McLuhan pays a high tribute to his Canadian predecessor and the pioneering philosopher of the medium, Harold A. Innis, when he acknowledges that it is "a footnote of explanation" to Innis' work. *The Bias of Communication* by Innis[42] pertains to the cross-cultural theory of communication in the fast moving context of history in which the medium or the technology of communication itself is a determining factor. Relying on the work of the French sinologist Marcel Granet, Innis observes that the Chinese are not noted for formulating concepts and doctrines discursively and, by the same token, the Chinese ideogram too is not conducive to abstraction or generality but instead it evokes a multitude of concrete images. Neither time nor space is abstractly conceived by the Chinese: time is circular or round, while space is square. Innis quotes the idea of Fenollosa that poetry, like music, is a *time art.*[43] As we have already noted, Tai too used the circle and the square as metaphors of describing the spoken sound and the written sign, respectively.

For McLuhan as for Innis the idea of language as a medium of communication is singularly important. McLuhan single-handedly sloganized the highly charged idea that "the medium *is* the message." For McLuhan (as for Innis), it is the medium of communication that shapes and controls the structures of the human mind, sensorium and association. "For," McLuhan explains, "the 'content' of a medium is like the juicy piece of meat carried by the burglar to distract the watchdog of the mind."[44] Moreover, the content of any medium is always another medium. For Fenollosa the Chinese written character is a medium or vehicle for poetry, whereas in the language of McLuhan it *is* poetry. A critical point must be made here. Certainly the *way* of language is the unity of meaning and the medium itself which are inextricably linked. To dichotomize the "message" and the "medium" or to reduce one to the other is to misunderstand this inextricable linkage between the two. In a very significant sense, however, language is not merely a *medium* of communication if by the medium we mean the "third factor" that facilitates human communication (i.e., instrumental artifact). For, indeed, it *is* communication. To understand the extent to which language is an instrumental artifact of communication, we must distinguish writing from speaking. Writing is an artifact, whereas speaking is not. Speech becomes an artifact only when it is transcribed in visible marks. To be an artifact, writing must be supplemented by other artifacts (e.g., papyrus, paper, printing, tapes, TV screens). Writing, in essence, is a mediated medium, whereas speaking is an unmediated medium for human communication.

V

Fenollosa's etymolinguistic analysis of Chinese ideograms has produced many ripples and waves in the contemporary philosophy of reading, writing and communication. Whether Chinese ideography is just a grammatology or a unique medium of communication is the question that has been essential to the critical understanding of Derrida's philosophical grammatology and McLuhan's "medium" theory of communication. Whether Fenollosa's influence has been a joy or an anxiety, the important point to be made here is the fact that in its ultimate efficacy misreading is also a form of reading. We have attempted to show that Chinese ideography is not a grammatology as the pure and simple act of writing purged of the phonetic (contra Derrida). Nor is it a medium devoid of symbolic contents (contra McLuhan). First of all, poetry needs music to become alive as does dance. Second, the ideogram is iconographic; that is to say, it is not just physiographic or the mirror-image of a thing in motion as in painting or choreography. As Fenollosa put it, it is the verbal *idea* of action in that it converts "material images" into "immaterial relations": in every ideogram, which is also a metaphor, the pictorial becomes the symbolic. As a proper sign or symbol, every ideogram has a double feature: external "indication" and meaningful "ex/pression." Like the Jaina parable of five blind men each of whom touches only a portion of an elephant and claims that his description of the beast is right and the others are wrong and ignorant, Chinese ideography had had different appeals to and sometimes blinding or hypnotizing effects on different theorists—among whom Derrida and McLuhan are a striking contrast—who siphon from it only what is useful or acceptable for validating and advancing their own theories of language and communication. Their readings are not so much wrong as one-sided.

In the end we need a method of "multiple definitions" after the fashion of Tai T'ung in order to remedy this one-sided reading or misreading, that is, to comprehend the composite picture of Chinese ideography as a whole tapestry with a mosaic of icons woven into it.

NOTES

[1] For a well-researched article on Fenollosa's and Pound's conception of Chinese grammatology, see Achilles Fang, "Fenollosa and Pound," *Harvard Journal of Asian Studies,* 20 (1957): 213-238. Fenollosa belongs to the long genealogy of linguistic sinology rooted in Francis Bacon, Sir Thomas Browne, William Warburton, and Wilhelm Leibniz, A critical genealogy of the ideogrammic method in American poetry as found now is Laszlo K. Géfin, *Ideogram: History of a Poetic Method* (Austin, Tex.: University of Texas Press, 1982). I am grateful to Lloyd Burkhart, my colleague in the English Department, for bringing this book to my attention.

[2] See John T. Irwin, *American Hieroglyphics* (New Haven, Conn.: Yale University Press, 1980). There is

neither mention of Fenollosa nor discussion of Chinese grammatology in the book.

[3] Fenollosa's *magnum opus* is a posthumously published work on the history of Chinese and Japanese art. See *Epochs of Chinese and Japanese Art,* 2 vols. (London: William Heinemann, 1912). He also wrote poetry including "East and West" which celebrates the meeting of the *yin* of the "markedly feminine" East and the *yang* of the "markedly masculine" West. See *East and West, the Discovery of America, and Other Poems* (New York: Thomas Y. Crowell, 1893).

[4] James A. Winn makes an astute observation when he writes that "Pound's fascination with Chinese ideograms, beyond their alleged visual expression, lay in the fact that one ideogram might be made out of several others like a chord out of several notes." *Unsuspected Eloquence* (New Haven, Conn.: Yale University Press, 1981), p. 297.

[5] For discussions of the thesis that Chinese ideography reflects the practically- and concretely-minded attitude, see Hajime Nakamura, *Ways of Thinking of Eastern Peoples,* ed. Philip P. Wiener (Honolulu: East-West Center Press, 1964), pp. 175-294; Herrlee Glessner Creel, *Sinism* (Chicago: Open Court, 1929); and Marcel Granet, *La Pensée Chinoise* (Paris: Editions Albin Michel, 1934).

[6] See Ernest Fenollosa, *The Chinese Written Character as a Medium for Poetry,* ed. Ezra Pound (San Francisco: City Lights Books, 1964). It is no secret that there have been the inseparable ties between painting, calligraphy and poetry, and that painting and calligraphy are the two facets of brushwork. Moreover, the idea of *ch'i* (vital energy) permeates all of these activities. See Mai-mai Sze, *The Tao of Painting* (New York: Bollingen Foundation, 1963), Chap. IV, "The Elements of a Picture," pp. 75-104. In "Water and Ice" the Japanese painter Hiro Kamimura plays with the differentiation of the two graphemes by a single stroke or by the absence and presence of a single stroke. For a recent "interartistic" treatise on painting and literature, see Wendy Steiner, *The Colors of Rhetoric* (Chicago: University of Chicago Press, 1982).

[7] Ralph Waldo Emerson, *Essays: Second Series* (New York: Lovell, Coryell, n.d.), p. 21.

[8] Fenollosa, *The Chinese Written Character,* p. 22.

[9] Ralph Waldo Emerson, *Nature, Addresses, and Lectures,* ed. Robert E. Spiller and Alfred R. Ferguson (Cambridge, Mass.: Harvard University Press, 1979), p. 18.

[10] Emerson, *Essays,* p. 10.

[11] Fenollosa, *The Chinese Written Character,* p. 21.

[12] Ibid., p. 23. Cf. Johannes Lohmann who refers to the Chinese as "the most economical man on earth" and to their language as "equally economical" which is not unlike Fenollosa's conception of poetry. See "M. Heidegger's 'Ontological Difference' and Language," in *On Heidegger and Language,* ed. Joseph J. Kockelmans (Evanston, Ill.: Northwestern University Press, 1972), p. 338.

[13] In this regard, Giambattista Vico made the following, interesting observation: " . . . in all languages the greater part of the expressions relating to inanimate things are formed by metaphor from the human body and its parts and from the human senses and passions. Thus, head for top or beginning; the brow and shoulders of a hill; the eyes of needles and of potatoes; mouth for any opening; the lip of a cup or pitcher; the teeth of a rake, a saw, a comb; the beard of wheat; the tongue of a shoe; the gorge of a river; a neck of land, an arm of the sea; the hands of a clock; heart for center (the Latins used *umbilicus,* navel, in this sense); the belly of a sail; foot for end or bottom; the flesh of fruits; a vein of rock or mineral; the blood of grapes for wine; the bowels of the earth. Heaven or the sea smiles; the wind whistles; the waves murmur; a body groans under a great weight. The farmers of Latium used to say the fields were thirsty, bore fruit, were swollen with grain; and our rustics speak of plants making love, vines going mad, resinous trees weeping. Innumerable other examples could be collected from all languages." *The New Science,* trans. Thomas Goddard Bergin and Max Harold Fisch (Ithaca, N.Y.: Cornell University Press, 1970), p. 88, para. 405.

[14] See Chang Cheng-ming, *L'Ecriture Chinoise et le Geste Humain* (Paris: P. Geuthner, 1937).

[15] Samuel Beckett, "Dante . . . Bruno. Vico . . Joyce," in Samuel Beckett *et al., Our Exagmination Round His Factification for Incamination of Work in Progress* (London: Shakespeare, 1929), p. 11.

[16] R. G. Collingwood, *The Principles of Art* (Oxford, England: Clarendon Press, 1938), pp. 243-244. Cf. Curt Sachs, *World History of the Dance,* trans. Bessie Schonberg (New York: W. W. Norton, 1937), p. 3: "The dance is the mother of the arts. Music and poetry exist in time; painting and architecture in space. But the dance lives at once in time and space."

[17] Marshall McLuhan and Harley Parker, *Through the Vanishing Point* (New York: Harper and Row, 1968), p. 39. The opposite page is filled with the Chinese ideogram *language* or *word* whose "acrobatic" character is represented by printing it upside down! Nevertheless, McLuhan and Parker speak of "an alphabetic ballet of words in rite order" in order to characterize E. E. Cumming's poem "Chanson Innocent" [ibid., pp. 186-187].

[18] For a discussion on this matter, see Hu Shih, *The Development of the Logical Method in Ancient China,* 2nd ed. (New York: Paragon, 1963), Chap. V, "The Rectification of Names and Judgments," pp. 46-52.

[19] Ezra Pound, *ABC of Reading* (New York: New Directions, 1960), p. 21.

[20] I am a Korean by birth and I learned how to read Chinese initially from a Japanese teacher—probably the same way as Fenollosa learned Chinese—and later from my grandfather.

[21] I mean to use the term *deconstruction* in the original sense that Martin Heidegger uses the term *destruction* as "a critical process in which the traditional concepts, which at first must necessarily be employed, are deconstructed down to the sources from which they were drawn." See *The Basic Problems of Phenomenology*, trans. Albert Hofstadter (Bloomington, Ind.: Indiana University Press, 1982), p. 23. Walter J. Ong notes that "With work such as Derrida's, philosophy, which as a formal discipline depends on a certain interiorization of writing, becomes acutely and exquisitely aware of its own chirographic framework, but has not yet much attended to the orality out of which the chirographic has developed historically and in which it is always in some way embedded. It may be worth noting that Derrida's key distinction between *différence* and *différance* (his neologism) is not phonemic, but chirographic." *Interfaces of the Word* (Ithaca, N. Y.: Cornell University Press, 1977), p. 17, n. 1. The American "deconstructionist" Paul de Man plays with the "literal" meaning and the "figurative" meaning of Archie Bunker's rhetoric: Archie Bunker answers "What's the difference?" when his wife Edith asks him whether he wants to have his bowling shoes laced over or laced under. When his answer really means "I don't give a damn what the difference is," the literal meaning of "difference" is denied by the figurative meaning. Since Derrida is an archie de-Bunker (a de-bunker of the *arche* or origin), there is indeed the difference between *différence* and *différance* in his deconstructive grammatology. See Paul de Man, *Allegories of Reading* (New Haven, Conn.: Yale University Press, 1979), pp. 8-9. Of course, the frequently cited example of the idea of "difference" in deconstructive rhetoric is a line from William Butler Yeats' poem "Among School Children": "How can we know the dancer from the dance?" The following Japanese *haiku* is also a play on the imagistic "difference": "The fallen blossom files back to its branch: A butterfly."

[22] Trans. Gayatri Chakravorty Spivak (Baltimore: Johns Hopkins University Press, 1974). The beginning of Derrida's deconstructive grammatology can be traced to his long introduction to his 1962 French translation of Edmund Husserl's "The Origin of Geometry" (1939) where Husserl makes reference to the important function of writing or written expression as making human communications possible without immediate or mediate personal address. For Derrida's 1962 introduction to Husserl's "The Origin of Geometry," see *Edmund Husserl's Origin of Geometry: An Introduction*, ed. David B. Allison and trans. John P. Leavy, Jr. (Stony Brook, N. Y.: Nicolas Hays, 1978). In my judgment, Husserl's critique of the Galilean origin of modern scientism exemplifies phenomenology as philosophical deconstruction. See Edmund Husserl, *The Crisis of European Science and Transcendental Phenomenology*, trans. David Carr (Evanston, Ill.: Northwestern University Press, 1970) which includes "The Origin of Geometry," pp. 353-378. The most redeeming quality of Derrida's grammatology in the context of this paper is this: his rejection of logocentrism or alphabetic writing as the surrogate of speech which is characteristic of Western metaphysics, is also the rejection of Western ethnocentrism or what Edward W. Said calls "Orientalism." See Said, *Orientalism* (New York: Pantheon Books, 1978). In discussing the origin of language, the eighteenth-century seminal Neapolitan thinker Gimabattista Vico agreed with Aristotle in defining grammar as the art of writing rather than speaking. Vico observed that being mute initially, the first nations all originally spoke in writing. Mutes made themselves understood by the use of gestures or objects which were related to the ideas they wished to signify (i.e., by sign languages). In short, they spoke in hieroglyphics or ideographics. As Beckett already noted judiciously in the Vichian tradition, the spoken and the written are the same in language as a system of gestures. See Vico, *The New Science*, especially paras. 429, 225, 401, 434, and 435. Cf. *Vico: Selected Writings*, ed. and trans. Leon Pompa (New York: Cambridge University Press, 1982), p. 233.

[23] *Of Grammatology*, p. 92.

[24] Trans. Barbara Johnson (Chicago: University of Chicago Press, 1981). For the "power" of hierography and ideography, see also his "Scribble (Writing-Power)," *Yale French Studies*, No. 58 (1979): 117-147.

[25] Jacques Derrida, "Structure, Sign, and Play in the Discourse of the Human Sciences," in *The Structuralist Controversy*, ed. Richard Macksey and Eugenio Donato (Baltimore: Johns Hopkins University Press, 1970), p. 272. In *Marxism and Deconstruction* (Baltimore: Johns Hopkins University Press, 1982), Michael Ryan comments that "Deconstruction deals for the most part with how we *conceive* the world" [p. 159]. There is, I think, a profound irony or paradox in a deconstructive interplay between *con*/ception and *per*/ception in their literal and figurative meanings. Whereas the notion of "conception" in Derrida's deconstructive grammatology after the tradition of Hegel becomes disembodied and desexualized, there is an embodied and sexualized way of defining "conception" or "to conceive." In the Vichian tradition, Elizabeth Sewell points out that the body *fertilizes* the process of conceptual thinking with language: in grammar there is a gender as masculine, feminine or neuter and also in grammatical terminology, there are "copula" and "conjugation." In grammar, the body is as much operative as the mind. If, as Sewell maintains, grammar is "a choreography of language and mind," that is, it is bodily and sexual, then Fenollosa's contention as noted earlier that Chinese ideography, like nature, knows no grammar must be examined in a different light. For a discussion of the anatomy of grammar as embodied and sexualized, see Elizabeth Sewell, *The Orphic Voice* (London: Routledge and Kegan Paul, 1960), pp. 34-41. It was Vico who defined man as "only mind, body and speech" and speech as standing somewhere "midway

between mind and body." See Vico, *The New Science*, p. 347, para. 1045 and see also the author's paper "Vico's Rhetoric: A Note on Verene's *Vico's Science of Imagination*," *Philosophy and Rhetoric*, 15 (Summer 1982): 187-202.

[26] Pound, *ABC of Reading*, p. 61.

[27] Samuel Taylor Coleridge, *Biographic Literaria*, 2 vols. (London: Rest Fenner, 1817), II: 14. In *Poetry and the Physical Voice* (London: Routledge and Kegan Paul, 1962), Francis Berry comments that "I am indeed half-persuaded by those who urge that the origin of a poem lies not in sound but in seeing" [p. ix]. In *Six Lectures on Sound and Meaning*, trans. John Mepham (Cambridge, Mass.: MIT Press, 1976), Roman Jakobson advances the idea that "In poetic language, in which the sign as such takes on an autonomous value, . . . sound symbolism (i.e., the symbolic value of phonemes as signifiers] becomes an actual factor and creates a sort of accompaniment to the signified" [p. 113].

[28] See Roman Jakobson, "Closing Statement: Linguistics and Poetics," in *Style in Language*, ed. Thomas A. Sebeok (Cambridge, Mass.: MIT Press, 1960), pp. 350-377.

[29] Fenollosa, *The Chinese Written Character*, p. 6.

[30] The conductor-composer Leonard Bernstein attempts to synthesize music and linguistics (Noam Chomsky's linguistics) in *The Unanswered Question* (Cambridge, Mass.: Harvard University Press, 1976).

[31] See one of the Chinese classics: *I Chi: Book of Rites*, 2 vols., trans. James Legge (New Hyde Park, N. Y.: University Books, 1967), II: 92-131 (Book XVII). Speaking of the locus of the personal as moral performance embodied in the Confucian thought of *li* (rite) and *jen* (humanity), Herbert Fingarette writes: "We would do well to take music, of which Confucius was a devotee, as our model here. We distinguish sensitive and intelligent musical performances from dull and unperceptive ones; and we detect in the performance confidence and integrity, or perhaps hesitation, conflict, 'faking,' 'sentimentalizing.' We detect all this *in* the performance; we do not have to look into the psyche or personality of the performer. It is all 'there,' public. Although it is there *in* the performance, it is apparent to us when we consider the performance not as 'the Beethoven Opus 3' (that is, from the composer perspective), nor as a 'public concert' (the *li* perspective), nor as 'post-Mozartian opus' (the style perspective), but primarily as this particular person's performance (the personal perspective)." *Confucius—The Secular as Sacred* (New York: Harper and Row, 1972), p. 53.

[32] James J. Y. Liu, *The Art of Chinese Poetry* (Chicago: University of Chicago Press, 1962), pp. 20-38. This is also one of the main arguments that George Kennedy advances in "Fenollosa, Pound and the Chinese Character," *Yale Literary Magazine*, 126 (December 1958): 24-36.

[33] Tai T'ung, *The Six Scripts; or, the Principles of Chinese Writing*, trans. L. C. Hopkins (Cambridge, England: University Press, 1954).

[34] Ibid., p. 27.

[35] I borrowed the term *diatactics* from Hayden White which means to modify Hegel's and Marx's notions of dialectic. Diatactics is neither "hypotactical" (Hegelian conceptual overdetermination) nor "paratactical" (Marxian conceptual underdetermination). See *Tropics of Discourse* (Baltimore: Johns Hopkins University Press, 1978), p. 4. I like the term especially because it implies the intimate sense of touch or tactility.

[36] Tai, *The Six Scripts*, p. 33. For an excellent discussion of the Chinese logic of correlations in reference to the theory of language and knowledge, see Chang Tung-sun, "A Chinese Philosopher's Theory of Knowledge," in *Our Language and Our World*, ed. S. I. Hayakawa (New York: Harper, 1959), pp. 299-324.

[37] Tai, *The Six Scripts*, p. 43. See also passages in pp. 4-5, 27, and 31. Cf. Gerard Manley Hopkins, *The Journals and Papers of Gerard Manley Hopkins*, ed. Humphry House (London: Oxford University Press, 1959), p. 267: "verse is speech having a marked figure," it is a "figure of spoken sound."

[38] For discussions on the various "medium" issues, see Edmund Carpenter and Marshall McLuhan (eds.), *Explorations in Communication* (Boston: Beacon Press, 1960).

[39] (Toronto: University of Toronto Press, 1962). For a critical assessment of McLuhan, see the author's paper "The Medium as Technology: A Phenomenological Critique of Marshall McLuhan," in *Phenomenology and the Understanding of Human Destiny*, ed. Stephen Skousgaard (Washington, D.C.: Center for Advanced Research in Phenomenology and University Press of Ameica, 1981), pp. 45-80.

[40] Marshall McLuhan, "Playboy Interview: Marshall McLuhan," *Playboy* (March 1969): 59.

[41] It might be of some relevance to our discussion that Hugh Kenner, a noted scholar on Pound, dedicated his *The Poetry of Ezra Pound* (New York: Kraus Reprint, 1968) to McLuhan: "A catalogue, his jewels of conversation."

[42] (Toronto: University of Toronto Press, 1951) which has a critical introduction by McLuhan. An account of Innis' intellectual achievement is found in Eric A. Havelock, "Harold Innis: A Man of His Times," *Et Cetera*, 38 (Fall 1981): 242-268.

[43] Innis, *The Bias of Communication*, p. 106.

[44] Marshall McLuhan, *Understanding Media* (New York: McGraw-Hill, 1964), p. 18.

Cordell D. K. Yee (essay date 1987)

SOURCE: "Discourse on Ideogrammic Method: Epistemology and Pound's 'Poetics'," in *American Literature*, Vol. 59, No. 2, May, 1987, pp. 242-56.

[*In the following essay, Yee explores the differences between Fenollosa's and Pound's approach to the Chinese ideogrammic method of poetics.*]

> Why is it that none of you study the *Odes?* For the *Odes* will help you to incite people's emotions, to observe their feelings, to keep company, to express your grievances. . . . Moreover, they will widen your acquaintance with the names of birds, beasts, plants and trees.—Confucius

For help in understanding Ezra Pound's "ideogrammic method" one almost inevitably turns to Ernest Fenollosa's essay, **"The Chinese Written Character as a Medium for Poetry."** After all, Fenollosa's essay provides Pound with this illustration of the method in *ABC of Reading* (1934):

> [A Chinese person] is to define red. How can he do it in a picture that isn't painted in red paint?
>
> He puts (or his ancestor put) together the abbreviated pictures of
>
> ROSE CHERRY
>
> IRON RUST FLAMINGO . . .
>
> The Chinese "word" or ideogram for red is based on something everyone KNOWS.[1]

According to Pound, a language written in this way must remain poetic. This claim can be understood in terms of Pound's earlier Imagist theory which held that abstractions were unpoetic: abstract ideas should be suggested through the selection of concrete particulars.[2] The poetic theory advanced in *ABC of Reading* has often been interpreted as advocating something similar. After giving the example of the Chinese ideogram for "red," Pound goes on to say that Fenollosa died before he could proclaim a poetic method (*ABCR*, p. 22). That method, Pound suggests, would have been the ideogrammic method: in Fenollosa's essay the ideogrammic method is "seriously indicated" but not "formulated as a method *to be used*" ("Date Line" [1934], *LE*, p. 77). From the context of *ABC of Reading,* one could easily conclude that Pound would base the method on the structure of the Chinese ideogram; and on the basis of Pound's interpretations of Fenollosa, the ideogrammic method has been equated with various poetic techniques: metaphor, juxtaposition, and image-clustering.[3]

Such interpretations of the ideogrammic method seem to be reinforced by other of Pound's pronouncements—for example, his statement that the method involves "heaping together the necessary components of thought."[4] Here Pound could be interpreted as saying that the ideogrammic method is a compositional technique: a writer expresses a certain idea through an accumulation of particulars.

The problem with this interpretation is that it does not entirely square with Fenollosa's standards. The technique supposedly exemplified in *ABC of Reading* would, according to Fenollosa's way of thinking, result in a pyramid with "being" at the top.[5] In this system, once everything has been subsumed under a pyramid, it becomes impossible to represent change or growth. Furthermore, this logic of classification, as Fenollosa calls it, cannot "deal with any kind of interaction or with any multiplicity of function": "It has no way of bringing together any two concepts which do not happen to stand one under the other and in the same pyramid" (Fenollosa, p. 31).

Confronted with such statements, those who would interpret Pound's ideogrammic method solely as a means of suggesting abstract ideas through the juxtaposition or clustering of particulars are placed in an uncomfortable situation. To accept this interpretation, one must discount the importance of Fenollosa's influence on Pound, since the poetics attributed to Pound seems to contradict Fenollosa. Either Pound is being ironic in his praise for Fenollosa, or his understanding of Fenollosa is superficial. In either case, the claim that Fenollosa is not central to an understanding of Pound's poetic theory and practice gains strength—his Fenollosa connection becomes a "red herring."

Evidence from Pound's letters, however, suggests that his admiration for Fenollosa was genuine. In 1917, for example, Pound wrote to John Quinn that "Fenollosa saw and anticipated a good deal of what has happened in art (painting and poetry) during the last ten years, and his essay is basic for all aesthetics."[6] Moreover, Pound's annotations to Fenollosa's essay suggest that he had read it with some seriousness: he points out parallels in the essay with his own critical writings, for example, his "Vorticism" essay (Fenollosa, p. 27), and between the essay's publication in *Instigations* in 1920 and its publication as a book in 1936, Pound revised some of his editorial comments.[7]

From documentary evidence, one also finds that Pound himself believed that the focus of Fenollosa's essay was not on the structure of the Chinese ideogram but on the justification for a theory of poetic language based on verbs:

> [Y]ou should have a chance to see Fenollosa's big essay on verbs, mostly on verbs. Heaven knows when I shall get it printed. He inveighs against "IS," wants transitive verbs. "Become" is as weak as "is." Let the grime *do* something to the leaves. "All nouns come from verbs." To primitive man, a thing only IS what it *does.* That is Fenollosa, but I think the theory is a very good one for poets to go by. (To Iris Barry, June 1916, *L,* p. 82)

In the essay Fenollosa argues that because the sensibilities of primitive peoples were closer to nature, their languages capture the dynamism of nature better than modern languages do. As an example of primitive language, the Chinese transitive sentence that translates "farmer pounds rice" corresponds exactly to the universal form of action in nature—cause and effect. Language is thus brought close to things. The task of the poet, according to Fenollosa, is to do consciously "what the primitive races did unconsciously," that is, to reveal nature through language (Fenollosa, p. 27). Poetry is, for Fenollosa, a means of attaining knowledge.

Consequently, accounts that go no further than to identify Pound's ideogrammic method with a specific compositional technique or poetic structure are too narrow. Pound looks to Fenollosa's essay for the basis of a method, but one must not be misled by the title of Fenollosa's essay and suppose that Pound's method deals with the structure of Chinese characters. The essay deals with language and its relation to knowledge. Pound's ideogrammic method also involves a theory of knowledge. The method's epistemological basis is implied in Pound's pronouncement in *ABC of Reading* that the ideogrammic method is "the method of science."[8]

By science Pound seems to mean only empirical sciences, such as biology, as distinguished from theoretical sciences like mathematics. One of the constants of his thinking is his insistence on concreteness and hostility to abstraction.[9] As early as 1910 he is praising Dante for his precision and avoidance of abstraction.[10] In "I Gather the Limbs of Osiris" (1911-1912) Pound argues for a method of luminous detail, scholarship based on precision and concision as opposed to scholarship that presents lists of minutiae or expresses sentiment and generalization.[11] In *ABC of Reading,* citing Fenollosa, he upholds similar standards when he opposes abstraction and the method of science: "By contrast to the method of abstraction, or of defining things in more and still more general terms, Fenollosa emphasizes the method of science, 'which is the method of poetry', as distinct from that of 'philosophic discussion,' and is the way the Chinese go about it in their ideograph or abbreviated picture writing" (*ABCR,* p. 20). What is interesting to note in this passage is that Pound directs attention not to the structure of the ideograph, but to the "method of science" that is used to produce it.

In a passage that seems to have been widely overlooked, despite its proximity to Pound's discussion of the ideogram for "red," Pound makes clearer the analogy between the method of science and the method of constructing ideograms. The way in which an ideogram is put together "is very much the kind of thing a biologist does (in a very much more complicated way) when he gets together a few hundred or thousand slides, and picks out what is necessary for his general statement. Something that fits the case, that applies in all of the cases" (*ABCR,* p. 22). The method of science and that of the ideogram, Pound implies, involves a process of induction—discovery of regularities by means of specific observations.[12] For Pound, knowledge is grounded in experience: abstractions, generalizations, have meaning only in reference to "known objects or facts" (*ABCR,* p. 26). Logic is not a source of knowledge: "Ernest Fenollosa attacked, quite rightly, a great weakness in western ratiocination. He pointed out that the material sciences, biology, chemistry, examined collections of fact, phenomena, specimens, and gathered general equations of real knowledge from them, even though the observed data had no syllogistic connection one with another. [Nowt novel, but I think E. F. found it out for himself.]"[13]

The method of science, Pound argues, is also the proper means of studying poetry (*ABCR,* p. 23). He concurs with Fenollosa that the method of science and that of poetry coincide: poetry is a source of knowledge. On what a reader is supposed to gain from reading a poem or examining any work of art, Pound, despite his own call for precision, is vague—at least in *ABC of Reading.* Poetry, like all language, is meant to communicate, he says without providing specific details on what is to be communicated. As Pound himself implies, however, the ideas in *ABC of Reading* follow from his earlier conceptions of poetry (see "Date Line," *LE,* p. 77).

In his early essay "The Serious Artist" (1913), for example, he is already attempting to break down the distinction between poetry and science: "The arts, literature, poesy, are a science, just as chemistry is a science" (*LE,* p. 42). To support this claim, he argues for a particular kind of poetry—that which is a source of data: "The arts give us a great percentage of the lasting and unassailable data regarding the nature of man, of immaterial man, of man considered as a thinking and sentient creature" (*LE,* p. 42). If the function of art is to furnish data, then the value of art is determined by the reliability of the data it contains. Good art, in Pound's view, is art that "bears true witness"; the critic's touchstone is precision.

The ideas expounded in "The Serious Artist" accord with the Imagist program that Pound had promulgated the same year. In order for poets to be scientific, they must put into practice Imagist principles. Directness of presentation ensures that the data contained in a poem is reliable, that the poem is an accurate record of what the poet perceives. Directness of presentation itself is achieved by the elimination of any word that "does not contribute to the presentation" ("A Retrospect" [1918], *LE,* p. 3). Poetry, which is meant to transmit knowledge, must not contain elements, such as abstract or imprecise language, that hinder the direct apprehension of reality. What the poet as scientist strives to do is to close the gap between word and object, between signifier and signified.[14]

To the degree to which it bridges this gap, poetry is scientific and thus a source of knowledge—it mirrors the object of study: in this respect Pound can be seen as elaborating Fenollosa's notion that nature leaves its imprint on language. Poetry written in accordance with Pound's tenets is almost a natural object. Thus the proper way to study poetry is the way a biologist studies life forms—through the examination of specimens, preferably without "the smokescreens erected by half-knowing and half-thinking critics" ("How to Read" [1929], *LE,* p. 23): "it is my firm conviction that a man can learn more about poetry by really knowing and examining a few of the best poems than by meandering about among a great many. At any rate, a great deal of false teaching is due to the assumption that poems known to the critic are of necessity the best" (*ABCR,* p. 43).[15] Pound advises those who would learn about poetry to reach their own conclusions on the basis of their own observations rather than accept the interpretations of others.

The primacy of empirical knowledge in Pound's thinking has other consequences for his poetics. If a poem is to be an immediate source of knowledge, the poet's own interpretations must not mediate between reader and the data presented. The poet is under no obligation to impose a logical arrangement on what a poem presents. Pound makes this clear in *Jefferson and / or Mussolini,* written the same year as *ABC of Reading:* "I am not putting these sentences in monolinear syllogistic arrangement, and I have no intention of using that old form of trickery to fool the reader, any reader, into thinking I have proved anything, or that having read a paragraph of my writing he KNOWS something that he can only *know* by examining a dozen or two dozen facts and putting them all together."[16]

It is the reader's task to discover the relationships between facts—this idea underlies Pound's paratactic style in poetry as well as prose.[17] Syntactical devices used to suggest the relationships between statements and even between parts of sentences—logical connectives, conjunctions, prepositions—impede direct apprehension of what a poem presents. Syntax for Pound is unpoetic, as it is for T. E. Hulme, one of his early associates:

> In prose as in algebra concrete things are embodied in signs or counters which are moved about according to rules, without being visualised at all in the process. There are in prose certain type situations and arrangements of words, which move as automatically into certain other arrangements as do functions in algebra. One only changes the X's and the Y's back into physical things at the end of the process. Poetry, in one aspect at any rate, may be considered as an effort to avoid this characteristic of prose. It is not a counter language, but a visual concrete one. . . . It always endeavours to arrest you, and to make you continuously see a physical thing, to prevent you gliding through an abstract process.[18]

Despite Pound's disclaimers of Hulme's influence, what Hulme says also holds for Pound. Syntax relates words and phrases to other words and phrases, instead of the things to which the words correspond: a reader of conventional prose glides from one statement to the next. Since the function of poetry is to help the reader perceive concrete data, poetic language directs attention to the data by being asyntactical, by not explicitly expressing relationships.[19]

As a result, a piece of writing composed to Pound's specifications may seem formless, disjointed, and alogical. A poet following the ideogrammic method does not impose a unitary structure on the work. Structure, as Pound argues in his "Vorticism" essay, expresses meaning—"Every concept, every emotion, presents itself to the vivid consciousness in some primary form" (*GB,* p. 88)—and to fix structure is to fix meaning. Rigidity of structure would prevent a work of art from attaining the "first intensity," the multiplicity of meaning that "would need a hundred works of any other kind of art to explain it" (*GB,* p. 84).

The ideogrammic method, as far as mode of presentation is concerned, is intended to maximize meaning. Coherence is the result of the reader's interpretive activity: "The ideogrammic method consists of presenting one facet and then another until at some point one gets off the dead and desensitized surface of the reader's mind, onto a part that will register" (*GK,* p. 51). Pound's comparison of the mind to a surface is consistent with his empiricism: for classical empiricist philosophers, the mind is like a "white paper," a *tabula rasa,* on which sense impressions, or simple ideas, are imprinted. Complex ideas are the result of association—the combination of sense impressions into composite wholes or the examination of ideas in such a way as to discover what is common to them.

The process by which the mind operates on simple ideas is similar to the way in which Pound expects the mind to act on a literary work: reading ideogrammically is a process of associating a work's various elements so as to arrive at an understanding of its subjects. For a reader, the ideogrammic method involves the "examination and juxtaposition of particular specimens—e.g. particular works, passages of literature"—as a means of acquiring knowledge ("The Teacher's Mission" [1934], *LE,* p. 61). Here Pound develops Fenollosa's suggestion that his essay points toward a method of not only poetic composition but also "intelligent reading" (Fenollosa, p. 37). Pound's ideogrammic method conflates the two. In his poetic theory, readers collaborate with artists: readers, not only poets, can create order and thus meaning. Insofar as readers have differing experiences, readers will associate a work's elements in differing ways—hence the possibility of multiple patterns of coherence and multiple interpretations: "It may or may not matter that the first knowledge is direct, it remains effortlessly as residuum, as part of my total disposition, it affects every perception of form-colour phenomena subsequent to its acquisition" (*GK,* p. 28).

Besides blurring the distinction between author and reader, the ideogrammic method also raises questions about the status of an artwork. A poet composing ideogrammically presents "facets" until the reader discovers a pattern of coherence, but since readers differ in experience, different readers may require different lengths of time to discover a pattern; some may not discern a pattern by the time they reach the end of a work. A poet could conceivably keep presenting facets to enable all readers to find a pattern. As a consequence, a literary work composed in accordance with the ideogrammic method could theoretically have no formal closure: any perceived pattern of coherence would be provisional, since there would always be the possibility of an addition to the work that would alter one's perception and interpretation of the work. In this sense the ideogrammic method represents an extension of Fenollosa's ideas about the lack of closure:

> [I]n nature there is *no* completeness. . . . The truth is that acts are successive, even continuous; one causes or passes into another. And though we may string never so many clauses into a single compound sentence, motion leaks everywhere, like electricity from an exposed wire. All processes in nature are interrelated; and thus there could be no complete sentence (according to this definition) save one which it would take all time to pronounce. (Fenollosa, p. 15).

Change, lack of fixity, Fenollosa says, is characteristic of nature. According to the ideogrammic method, change can be characteristic of a poetic work. Pound's ideogrammic poetics thus seems more dynamic than his earlier Vorticist poetics. The image, in Pound's "Vorticism" essay, is defined as "a radiant node or cluster . . . a VORTEX, from which, and through which, and into which, ideas are constantly rushing" (*GB,* p. 92). An ideogrammic work's potential for growth makes it possible for these nodes of signification to shift in position as new patterns of coherence are perceived.

The open-endedness implied by the ideogrammic method can be seen in the compositional process of Pound's *Cantos.* He published the work incrementally, each increment altering the nature of the poem.[20] For example, after the first thirty cantos the addition of *Eleven New Cantos*—with materials from early American history—shifted the cultural center of gravity in a work that had seemed focused on European culture. The addition of the "Chinese Cantos" (LII-LXI) again forced one to reconsider the interpretation of the poem as a whole. In the earlier sections of the poem, Chinese materials were concentrated in Canto XIII; with the addition of the "Chinese Cantos," Canto XIII and its concern with Confucian ethics assume greater significance. Pound's incremental publication of the *Cantos* seems to have been calculated to unsettle overarching interpretations: to use Fenollosa's metaphor, Pound discourages the construction of mental pyramids by forcing the interpreter to tear the pyramids down once they are built. The ideogrammic method, together with the *Cantos,* thus implies a view of art as process rather than product or fixed object.

This last conclusion highlights the disparity between the assumptions underlying Pound's poetry and contemporaneous critical theory. While Pound was promoting the ideogrammic method, the New Critics were formulating their theory of art as autonomous object with no necessary connection with anything outside it. One of their assumptions was a distinction between scientific and emotive language: poetry and science are linguistically poles apart. Pound's critical thinking moves in the opposite direction. He attempts to bridge science and poetry. Poetry, like science, has an empirical basis. Science, Pound implies, should not be privileged over poetry. This idea may be the motivation for his coining the term "ideogrammic method." The method is a method of understanding common to both scientific and literary study, not peculiar to science.

Pound's empiricism is also of historical interest because it results in openness rather than the formal and logical completeness associated with the empiricist-based philosophy of the logical positivists. Because of the influence of logical positivism, empiricism is commonly held to stifle creativity. The example of Pound, however, shows that empiricist thought can be receptive to creativity.

According to the exposition given here, Pound's ideogrammic method is grounded in ideas he had formulated well before *ABC of Reading:* his empiricism predates his Imagist phase. Some, however, would argue that Pound had no clear conception of the method until after he had completed the first thirty *Cantos.* Ronald Bush, for example, maintains that as early as 1921 Pound had used the term "ideographic" pejoratively, and did not use the word in a positive sense until 1927.[21] If Bush is correct, then the ideogrammic method is not a reliable means of understanding Pound's *Cantos,* especially the first thirty. But there is a problem in Bush's analysis: he confuses word and idea. Pound's terminology may have changed over the years, but those changes do not necessarily correspond to changes in thinking. Pound himself implies that he is not particularly concerned about consistency in terminology—what is important is that the meaning be understood: "I really do not give an underdone damn about your terminology so long as you understand it and don't mess up the meaning of your words. And (we might add) so long as you, as reader, try to understand the meaning of the text (whatever text) you read" (*J / M,* p. 22).

It is Pound's meanings, his ideas, that have consistency: the key elements of the ideogrammic method are expressed in writings predating his coinage of the term. In fact, he advises readers of the *Cantos* to look to the ideogrammic method, his criticism, and Fenollosa as means of understanding the *Cantos.* Without knowledge of these, Pound implies in a note published in 1933, one cannot begin to appreciate the *Cantos* properly: "The nadir of solemn and elaborate imbecility is reached by Mr. Winter in an American publication where he deplores my 'abandonment of logic in the Cantos,' presumably because he has never read Fenollosa or my prose criticism and has never heard of the ideogramic method, and thinks logic is limited to a few 'forms of logic' which better minds were already finding inadequate to the mental needs of the XIIIth century."[22] Pound, in effect, urges a reconsideration of the boundaries of art. He implies that the *Cantos,* at least, must be seen as a component of a complex of texts. This idea is also consistent with the ideogrammic method. One of Pound's illustrations of the method suggests that an artwork can be properly understood only in relation to other artworks: "Hang a painting by Carlo Dolci beside a Cosimo Tura. You cannot prevent Mr. Buggins from preferring the former, but you can very seriously impede his setting up a false tradition of teaching on the assumption that Tura has never existed, or that the qualities of the Tura are nonexistent or outside the scope of the possible" (*ABCR,* p. 26).

The question then arises as to what knowledge of the ideogrammic method, Pound's criticism, and Fenollosa contributes to an understanding of the *Cantos.* The preceding discussion should at least make clear what the ideogrammic method will not do: it will not yield the meaning or the structure of the *Cantos,* though it will yield multiple meanings and structures. It will not necessarily enable one to make sense of every aspect of the *Cantos.* The open-endedness of a poetic work stems in part from a recognition that not everything presented will "register" on a reader's mind: Pound seems to expect that a reader will be unable to understand every element.

The difficulty of the *Cantos* is intentional. They are not meant to be read in the conventional sense of the word, but to be studied—read ideogrammically by examination and juxtaposition of elements. What relationships readers discover between various elements in the *Cantos* depend on the readers' prior experiences. A reader well-grounded in Chinese philosophy will tend to develop an understanding of the poem by focusing on Pound's allusions to Confucius and Chinese history. A reader familiar with medieval literature will probably find it easier to begin with the poem's correspondences with Dante. To the former, the Chinese characters and their place in Confucian ethics may appear to be centers of signification; to the latter, the moments of illumination may appear to be a more fruitful subject of study.

If the *Cantos* are meant to be studied, one may well ask what one is supposed to gain from studying them. The ideogrammic method, according to the interpretation developed here, subsumes a view of poetry as a source of knowledge, data. One might argue that the *Cantos* hardly comport with such a view of poetry. In the *Cantos* Pound incorporates much literary and documentary material but often in fragments insufficient to provide an accurate understanding of the wholes: one could question, for example, whether the excerpts from John Adams' letters constitute a sound basis for knowledge. The *Cantos,* however, need not be regarded as an attempt to provide data about historical reality. A poem, Pound says, can also provide data about a poet's own internal reality:

> The serious artist is scientific in that he presents the image of his desire, of his hate, of his indifference as precisely that, as precisely the image of his own desire, hate or indifference. The more precise his record the more lasting and unassailable his work of art.
>
> The theorist, and we see this constantly illustrated by the English writers on sex, the theorist constantly proceeds as if his own case, his own limits and predilections were the typical case, or even as if it were the universal. He is constantly urging someone else to behave as he, the theorist, would like to behave. Now art never asks anybody to do anything, or to to think anything, or to be anything. ("The Serious Artist," *LE,* p. 46)

To follow Pound, parts of the *Cantos* may be regarded as recording the poet's own experience, and for Pound one thing at the center of that experience is reading (as the poet suggests in the opening canto by referring to the translation of the *Odyssey* he has used). Much of the *Cantos* seems conditioned by what Pound happened to be reading as he composed them: de Mailla's history of China underlies the "Chinese Cantos," and John Adams' writings the "Adams Cantos" (LXII-LXXI). The *Cantos* may make use of historical materials, but they present one person's experience of them. To a certain degree, then, description of the *Cantos* as "personal epic" seems apt.

Pound's explanation of how the serious artist is scientific may have helped to resolve one difficulty, but one of his remarks in the same passage—on what art should not do—leads to another problem. The *Cantos* seem to contradict some of Pound's tenets: at various points, for example, the "Usura Canto" (XLV), he seems to urge that a reader adopt his way of thinking. By making generalizations for the reader, Pound seems to depart from the requirements of the ideogrammic method. Such discrepancies between theory and practice could be interpreted as evidence that Pound did not take his poetic principles seriously enough to follow them: therefore, the ideogrammic method is not an accurate guide to his practice. The discrepancies, however, are capable of another interpretation: there is an unresolved tension in Pound's poetics. In "The Serious Artist" Pound states that the data presented in poetry are to serve as the basis of ethical knowledge. In order to rectify an unethical situation, the situation must be described accurately—thus Pound's conception of poetry as "diagnosis." But in the same essay he also states that poetry is an "art of cure," implying that a poet can point out how to correct an unethical situation. This implication contradicts Pound's dictum that a poet should not be directive. The overt didacticism in the *Cantos* could be regarded as a manifestation of the same contradiction.

The ideogrammic method would then seem to provide at least a partial understanding of Pound's *Cantos,* and should not be dismissed lightly. One should recognize, however, that the interpretation of the method offered here is provisional: it has been arrived at ideogrammically—through the examination and association of particular passages—and could be revised in light of new evidence. But if the general outlines of this account should prove accurate, prevailing conceptions of the history of literary theory may need rethinking. A poetics that blurs the boundaries between texts, that makes a reader as much a creator of meaning as the author, that tries to fill the breach between science and literature, is commonly placed in a Nietzschean-Heideggerian-Derridean line of descent. Such a poetics also accords with Anglo-American philosophical traditions.

NOTES

[1] *ABC of Reading* (1934; rpt. New York: New Directions, 1960), p. 22; cited hereafter within the text as *ABCR.*

[2] In "A Few Don'ts" (1913) Pound advises poets to go "in fear of abstractions." See *Literary Essays of Ezra Pound,* ed. T. S. Eliot (1954; rpt. New York: New Directions, 1968), p. 5; cited hereafter within the text as *LE.*

[3] Among the many works containing treatments of the ideogrammic method are Hugh Kenner, *The Poetry of Ezra Pound* (1951; rpt. Lincoln: Univ. of Nebraska Press, 1985); Laszlo K. Géfin, *Ideogram: History of a Poetic Method* (Austin: Univ. of Texas Press, 1982); Guy Davenport, *Cities on Hills: A Study of I-XXX of Ezra Pound's Cantos* (Ann Arbor: UMI Research Press, 1983).

[4] *ABC of Economics* (London: Faber, 1933), p. 37.

[5] *The Chinese Written Character as a Medium for Poetry,* ed. Ezra Pound (London: Stanley Nott, 1936), p. 30; cited hereafter within the text as Fenollosa.

[6] *The Selected Letters of Ezra Pound, 1907-1941,* ed. D. D. Paige (1950; rpt. New York: New Directions, 1971), p. 101; cited hereafter within the text as *L.* Even earlier, in June 1915, Pound writes: "Fenollosa has left a most enlightening essay on the written character (a whole basis of aesthetic, in reality) . . . " (To Felix E. Schelling, *L,* p. 61).

[7] Pound also added plates with explanations of Chinese characters. Contrary to common belief, his conception of Chinese writing was not completely pictographic. In a note he added to Fenollosa's essay in 1935, he writes: "Whatever a few of us learned from Fenollosa twenty years ago, the whole Occident is still in crass ignorance of the Chinese art of verbal sonority" (Fenollosa, p. 37).

[8] The argument presented here is in part an effort to elaborate on Herbert N. Schneidau's assertion that "the *Cantos* have their roots in Imagist poetics" (*Ezra Pound: The Image and the Real* [Baton Rouge: Louisiana State Univ. Press, 1969], p. 189), and in part a response to Ian F. A. Bell's *Critic as Scientist: The Modernist Poetics of Ezra Pound* (London: Methuen, 1981). Bell argues that Pound borrows critical terminology from scientific disciplines in an effort to formulate a modernist poetics. This essay locates the intersection of science and Pound's ideas at a level deeper than terminology, and explores the implications of this intersection.

[9] Abstraction, in Pound's usage, means "generalization" or "general concept" rather than "formal scheme," an ordering or structuring of particulars. This distinction becomes clear when one recalls Pound's analogy between great art and analytic geometry in his 1914 essay "Vorticism"—*Gaudier-Brzeska: A Memoir* (1916; rpt. New York: New Directions, 1970), pp. 91-92; cited hereafter within the text as *GB.*

[10] *The Spirit of Romance* (1910; rpt. New York: New Directions, [1953]), p. 126.

[11] *Selected Prose: 1909-1965,* ed. William Cookson (New York: New Directions, 1973), p. 21.

[12] See also "The Serious Artist": "That is to say a good biologist will make a reasonable number of observations of any given phenomenon before he draws a conclusion, thus we read such phrases as 'over 100 cultures from the secretions of the respiratory tracts of over 500 patients and 30 nurses and attendants'. The results of each observation must be precise and no single observation must in itself be taken as determining a general law, although, after experiment, certain observations may be held as typical or normal" (*LE,* p. 46).

[13] *Guide to Kulchur* (1938; rpt. New York: New Directions, 1970), pp.27-28; cited hereafter within the text as *GK.*

[14] Thus Imagist theory represents another defense of poetry against Plato's claim that art cannot be a source of knowledge since it is twice removed from reality—*The Republic,* tr. Francis MacDonald Cornford (Oxford: Oxford Univ. Press, 1941), p. 327 (X.597).

[15] See also *ABC of Reading:* "The proper METHOD for studying poetry and good letters is the method of contemporary biologists, that is careful first-hand examination of the matter, and continual COMPARISON of one 'slide' or specimen with another" (p. 17). Note Pound's emphasis on particularity and directness.

[16] *Jefferson and / or Mussolini: L'Idea Statale; Fascism as I Have Seen It* (London: Stanley Nott, 1935), p. 28; cited hereafter within the text as *J / M.*

[17] This has also been observed by Eva Hesse in "Books behind *The Cantos,*" *Paideuma,* 1 (1972), 144-45.

[18] "Romanticism and Classicism," in *Speculations: Essays on Humanism and the Philosophy of Art,* ed. Herbert Read, 2nd ed. (1936; rpt. London: Routledge & Kegan Paul; New York: Humanities Press, 1965), p. 134. The view that Hulme regards syntax as unpoetic has been expressed previously by Donald Davie in *Articulate Energy: An Inquiry into the Syntax of English Poetry* (London: Routledge & Kegan Paul, 1955), pp. 5-9.

[19] Pound's use of parataxis slows the reading process. As Pound implies in a review of Jean Cocteau's *Poesies 1917-1920,* a reader should pay attention to every word: "Slowness is beauty," Pound says, citing Laurence Binyon—*Dial,* 70 (1921), 110.

[20] The fragments of *Cantos CX-CXVII* suggest that Pound planned further increments: the poem is still unfinished. In this respect Pound's *Cantos* resemble another work built on empiricist ideas—Laurence Sterne's *Tristram Shandy*.

[21] *The Genesis of Ezra Pound's* Cantos (Princeton: Princeton Univ. Press, 1976), pp, 10-11.

[22] "Mr. Ezra Pound's Cantos," *New English Weekly*, 11 May 1933, p. 96.

Anne S. Chapple (essay date 1988)

SOURCE: "Ezra Pound's 'Cathay': Compilation from the Fenollosa Notebooks," in *Paideuma: A Journal Devoted to Ezra Pound Scholarship*, Vol. 17, Nos. 2 & 3, Fall & Winter, 1988, pp. 9-46.

[*In the following essay, Chapple relies on one of Ezra Pound's lesser-known essays on Chinese poetics to illuminate Pound's reliance on Fenollosa's notes to produce the poems published in* Cathay.]

In 1918, three years after *Cathay* appeared, Pound published a little known, two-part essay on Chinese poetry, in which he observed:

> In China a "compiler" is a very different person from a commentator. A compiler does not merely gather together, his chief honour consists in weeding out, and even in revising.[1]

His definition refers to the Chinese poet Rihaku, head of the court office of poetry, but it might just as easily apply to Pound himself as inheritor of the Fenollosa notebooks on Chinese poetry. Like Rihaku, Pound was primarily engaged in "weeding out" many of the poems which had been gathered for him, and then in "revising" those he chose for his collection. *Cathay* was the flower which blossomed out of his efforts. Pound's revisionary endeavors have been the object of concentrated critical attention, but the "weeding" which took place beforehand—that is, the selection process which produced the final volume of poems—has been largely neglected in scholarly treatments of *Cathay*. While the issue of selection and several related aspects of revision hold real interest for Pound scholars, the relevance of an understanding of these processes has not been recognized.

We know that Pound's encounter with Fenollosa's notes resulted in the fourteen (later eighteen) poems of *Cathay*.[2] But why did Pound choose to translate only eighteen out of some one hundred fifty poems he found in the notebooks, and how did he go about making his choices? These problems have been slighted at least in part because Fenollosa's notebooks have been unavailable for so many years; until recently they were sealed for legal reasons. The difficulty has been compounded by the paucity of published material recording Pound's intentions for *Cathay*, his working habits in relation to the notes, and his impressions of the poetry with which he was working. Only a few scattered references to *Cathay* can be found among his published letters, and only a handful more remain among the unpublished D. D. Paige papers at the Pound Center at Yale.[3] The 1918 essay on Chinese poetry probably provides the best published record of Pound's perusal of the notebooks, but it, too, is relatively inexplicit with regard to his selection procedures.

The scarcity of published documentation has limited scholarly investigation of Pound's selection methods to inspired guesswork. The issue has been given brief attention in at least two recent articles, but both treatments represent attempts to deduce Pound's manner of selection from a supposed central theme in the *Cathay* poems. Hugh Kenner claims for the volume an "oriental obliquity of reference to what we are to understand as its true theme."[4] For Kenner, the theme is a natural outgrowth of contemporary historical events: "*Cathay*, April 1915 . . . is largely a war book . . . Its exiled bowmen, deserted women, levelled dynasties, departures for far places, lonely frontier guardsmen and glories remembered from afar, cherished memories, were selected from the diverse wealth in the notebooks by a sensibility responsive to torn Belgium and disrupted London . . . "[5] No written evidence exists to substantiate such claims, however. Pound's letters contain no reference to an intended theme for *Cathay*, nor do the poems themselves necessarily lead us to Kenner's conclusion.

In a more recent article, Sanehide Kodama argues for a thematic unity based on sorrow and loneliness, but points to a biographical, rather than a historical, basis for selection:

> . . . Examination of Fenollosa's notebooks in relation to Pound's "translations" reveals that the Chinese poems Pound selected for *Cathay* were mostly the ones which present sorrowful or lonely figures who speak out as if to overcome their sorrow or loneliness—"Exile's Letter," "Lament of the Frontier Guard," "The River Merchant's Wife: A Letter," "Four Poems of Departure," and "To-Em-Mei's 'The Unmoving Cloud'" . . . All of these are confessions by spiritual exiles of their sufferings and crucial emotional experiences. And that this choice may reflect Pound's own state of mind at the time seems apparent in his scribbled note on the last page of *Cathay* . . . Pound was fully aware that he was beginning to be known as a center of the new poetical movement and that he would have to suffer the slings and arrows of his fortune. His fear that he might be more isolated from both American and English societies seems to be reflected in his selection of the poems in *Cathay*.[6]

Again, no written evidence exists to substantiate Kodama's claims, and the poems themselves need not have any biographical significance for Pound at all.

Alternative critical approaches to Pound's selection methods were not possible until recently, when the legal restrictions on Fenollosa's notes were lifted. Critical examination of the newly available notebooks must call into question theories of selection based strictly on biography or on contemporary historical events. Considered in their entirety, the notebooks provide persuasive evidence for a new argument. Pound's selection methods may be traced to personal tastes which stemmed from his own imagist "doctrine" and earlier, related interests. Pound's unpublished papers on *Cathay,* which include notes, drafts of poems, finished but unpublished poetry, and an incomplete essay on Chinese poetry (all of which are included among the Fenollosa papers at the Beinecke library at Yale) strongly substantiate this new perspective. These findings represent an issue of some significance if we accept Eliot's characterization of Pound as "the inventor of Chinese poetry for our time."[7]

I

Pound turned his attention to the Fenollosa notebooks on Chinese poetry sometime late in 1914.[8] He carefully organized the material he had inherited by following a procedure which was consistent for each of the notebooks. Leafing through the pages with a heavy, black pencil, he numbered each of the approximately one hundred fifty poems he discovered in twelve separate notebooks and folders. After he had read the poems in each notebook, he made long columnar lists on their back or front inside covers. The lists correspond to the numbered poems in each notebook. Beside the numbers of poems which caught his eye, Pound penciled brief jottings: sometimes a single word, sometimes the title of the poem, sometimes a phrase or a line from the poem to help him remember what he'd read. He often employed a "+" to flag poems of particular interest to him. While he was reading the notes, he frequently side-lined or otherwise marked passages which drew his attention. Both the lists and the marginal markings provide a substantial record of his "weeding" activities as he made his mental trek through Fenollosa's material.

The best documentation we have of Pound's preferences, however, is a series of early drafts for many of the poems he examined. He produced drafts for far more poems than he actually finished or incorporated into the *Cathay* volume. Some of them may have served as exercises for him. The drafts Pound abandoned along the way are usually accompanied by notes to himself regarding difficulties with the subject matter, problems with translation, etc.; these constitute a revealing record of his opinions and sentiments while he was compiling *Cathay.* His notes reveal that he worked on poems from all of the notebooks he examined, but several of the notebooks he examined first were much more heavily worked.

Given these forms of evidence for Pound's poetic preferences, it is perhaps advisable to start at the beginning; that is, where Pound started when he was initially confronted with the notebooks. By following the traces of his interest in the material he was reading, it is possible to reconstruct the significant moments of his experience with the poetry. We can do this by examining the penciled markings and marginalia which are scattered throughout the hundreds of pages of Fenollosa's notes.

One would naturally expect Imagist doctrine to be uppermost in Pound's mind at the time he was examining Fenollosa's notes, and our expectations are corroborated. The passages which attracted his attention seem especially relevant to the attitudes of an Imagiste. In the first volume of Professor Mori's lectures, for example, Pound flagged Fenollosa's definition of Fu poetry. A Fu poem "is a poem which expounds the facts of things as they are. Later on it came to mean a very prosy poem, with the object merely of amplifying or analyzing an event, like chronicles."[9] There is a strong similarity here to Pound's own early "diagnostic objectivity" and to his later insistence on "direct treatment of the thing."[10] We may suspect that Fenollosa's definition had real relevance for a poet whose current aim was "to bring poetry up to the level of prose."[11]

A passage marked in the second volume of Mori's lectures speaks to the issue of moralizing or didactic poetry. "Some Chinese critics have condemned S. [Sogioku] because he had not enough moral meaning in his poetry. But this is too pedantic and didactic an idea of poetry."[12] Pound's own poetic principles, "freedom from didacticism" and "never comment: state,"[13] are strikingly similar in tone.

A second passage in the same notebook which compares the poets Sogioku and Kutsugen also caught Pound's attention:

> Kutsugen speaks allegorically, but Sogioku not. S. speaks more of things and people for their sake, not to illustrate loyalty and ideas.[14]

Sogilku's technique accords well with several forms of the famous imagist "don'ts": namely, "go in fear of abstraction," and the related "no metaphors which won't permit examination."[15] The tendency to "speak more of things and people for their own sake, "while somewhat inexplicit, works along the same lines as Pound's principle, "direct treatment of the thing."[16]

A flagged passage on the poet Gan-en-nen [?] criticizes him because his style is "too ornate," because "he uses many, too many, fine words" and because he is "rather too skillful."[17] "Gan," Fenollosa wrote, "is like some artistic manufaction spread with golden dust."[18] Elsewhere, the poet Rikki [?] is criticized because he "seems too much bent to show his wide scholarship—his words seem not to answer to his purpose. So it seems just like a weak man raising a great pot . . . He uses too much artifice, poems become too immaterial." His poems, moreover, are "sleepy and unnatural."[19] Fenollosa's negative observations are closely related to the criticisms implied in several of Pound's imagist dicta: "use absolutely no word that does not contribute to the presentation," "no excessive use of adjectives" and "direct treatment of the thing."[20] The quoted commentary on both Gan and Rikki ("too many fine words," "too much artifice," "unnatural," "too scholarly") imply recommendations analogous to those made in Pound's "Prolegomena" essay and those included in a letter written to Harriet Monroe at roughly the same time Pound was reading the notes:

> [the language of poetry] must be a fine language, departing in no way from speech save by a heightened intensity (i.e. simplicity). There must be no book words, no periphrases, no inversions.[21]

Pound's "no book words," "no periphrases, no inversions," and a language like "speech save for its heightened intensity or simplicity" closely parallel Fenollosa's "too scholarly," "unnatural," "too much artifice" and "too many fine words."

Pound must have remembered Fenollosa's criticisms of Gan and Rikki, for he included the following observation in his 1918 essay of Chinese poetry: "China has produced just as many bad poets as England, just as many dull and plodding moralizers, just as many flaccid and overornate versifiers."[22] The comment is relevant to our discussion here because, by extrapolation, it tells us something about the opposite poetic virtues Pound espoused: "simplicity," presentation "without comment," and poetry "as much like granite as it can be"—all imagist ideas.[23]

While Fenollosa's notes include much negative commentary on bad poets and poetry, they also contain favorable commentary on good poets and several laudatory passages on well-written poems. These, too, drew Pound's attention. In several instances when Fenollosa mentioned a certain simplicity of manner or style, marginal markings attest to Pound's interest. The following anecdote about Hakuakulen is a representative example:

> In contrast to the difficult words of Kantaishi he [Hakuakulen] used the easiest words—very plain—but not vulgar. He wished his poems to be understood, even by children and women. It is said that, when he made poems he took his old maid servant and made her read the poems. If there [was] some word she did not understand, he changed it.[24]

There is a strong similarity between the insistence on simplicity or plainness in the above story and Pound's own demands for "simplicity," for a poetry which doesn't depart from speech, "save by a heightened intensity."[25] As several recent scholars have noted, Pound propagandized frequently for a real language of the times, for "natural speech, the language as spoken," throughout his imagist phase.[26]

Two additional passages marked by Pound in the notes are of interest to us here because they shed light on Pound's attitudes toward certain genres of Chinese poetry. The first treats "senshi," or sennin poetry; these are poems which deal with the immortal gods, spirits, fairies, etc. It is too long to quote here, but the main idea of the story centers on the political suppression of poetry during the reign of Shiko, who ruled after the first emperor of Shin, and before Kogai, the second emperor of Shin. Shiko apparently suppressed the circulation of all poetry he felt might threaten the stability of his military dictatorship. "Senshi," or sennin poems, were the only form of poetry which flourished during the history of his rule. Shiko evidently believed that they were harmless, or, to quote Fenollosa, "too imaginary for harm."[27] Pound had a distaste for them which surfaced in his reaction to a second passage on the theme of other-worldliness.

In the notebook entitled **"Notes from Outside Sources."** Fenollosa reproduced the following criticism of an unknown poet's work by a respected Chinese commentator:

> They [the poems] are effective pieces of art but they lack the aspiration of a sustained sense of human relations with infinity.[28]

Pound penciled a contemptuous comment in the margin next to these lines, to the effect that "a sustained sense of human relations with infinity" is not an admirable quality in poetry, an opinion which is shrilly reiterated in his unpublished essay on Chinese poetry. His manifest disregard of all the Chinese poetry in the notebooks which can be characterized by that "aspiration" expresses his feelings on the matter even more forcefully. Though sennin poetry accounts for approximately one-fifth of the poetry in Fenollosa's notes, it is represented by only one poem in *Cathay*.

II

As Witemeyer has suggested, Pound saw a "harmony between Chinese poetry and the principles of Imagism."[29] The opening lines of Pound's 1918 "Chinese Poetry" essay highlight the similarities between his poetic discipline and certain attributes of Chinese poetry:

> It is because Chinese poetry has certain qualities of vivid presentation; and because certain Chinese poets have been content to set forth their matter without moralizing and without comment that one labours to make a translation, and that I personally am most thankful to the late Ernest Fenollosa for his work in sorting out and gathering many Chinese poems into a form and bulk wherein I can deal with them.[30]

The qualities singled out for attention in this passage, namely "vivid presentation" . . . "without moralizing and without comment," echo the imagist credo: "direct treatment of the thing," "convey an emotion by presenting the object and circumstance of that emotion without comment," as well as related earlier principles: "freedom from didacticism," "never comment: state."[31] Already, then, we have a basis for claiming that Pound is "drawing upon the poetry of the past to put across his own program and standards for the present."[32]

Pound's 1918 essay neatly abstracts for us the five "qualities" of Chinese poetry which engaged his attention. His treatment of those qualities is useful for our purposes here because it organizes Fenollosa's vast body of notes according to principles, principles which relate in every case to Pound's own poetic doctrine. The similarities between these abstracted principles and Pound's own imagist dicta are often subtle, and for that reason they warrant our close attention.

The first of the five qualities Pound identifies in Chinese poetry is a marked reticence, elsewhere referred to as "obscurity." This reticence requires considerable thought on the part of its readers:

> The first great distinction between Chinese taste and our own is that the Chinese *like* poetry that they have to think about, and even puzzle over.[33]

As an illustration, Pound cites his own translation of "The Jewel of Stairs' Grievance." which is accompanied by a prose gloss:

> THE JEWEL STAIRS' GRIEVANCE
>
> The jewelled steps are already quite white with dew,
> It is so late the dew soaks my gauze stockings,
> And I let down the crystal curtain
> And watch the moon through the clear autumn.
>
> Note: Jewel stairs, therefore a palace. Grievance, therefore there is something to complain of. Gauze stockings, therefore a court lady, not a servant who complains. Clear autumn, therefore she has no excuse on account of weather. Also she has come early, for the dew has not merely whitened the stairs, but has soaked her stockings. The poem is especially prized because she utters no direct reproach.[34]

Poetry could hardly be more reticent than this; presentational condensation is carried to an extreme degree here. This poem shows the spareness and concision associated with Imagist poems, but when we look more closely, it is not otherwise clear how the poem relates to Pound's doctrine, of why this poem would appeal to him. Apart from the vivid, concise presentation, the poem seems not to fulfill the requirements for an Imagist poem as Pound defined it. Even the vivid presentation of the poem seems undermined by the attachment of an explanatory prose gloss, which would appear to work against the principles "never comment: state," and "freedom from didacticism."[35] More importantly, the poem doesn't seem to contain a conspicuous "Image," if define "Image" as "that which presents an intellectual and emotional complex in an instant of time."[36] Fenollosa's notes for this poem provide a key to the enigma:

> Gioku kai [refers to the title] means here a place where court ladies are living, one of the imperial mistresses. The subject of the poem [is] that one of them was waiting for the lord to come. The beauty of the poem lies in not a single character being used to explain the idea of waiting and resenting; yet the poem fully expresses the idea. This is how. Thinking that the lord will come, she was coming out to meet him at the entrance to a flight of steps ornamented with gems. She was standing there 'til the very dewiness of night wets her stockings. [dew was thought to grow on things] She lets down her curtain already despairing of his coming. And yet she can see the moon shining so bright outside, and had to think of the possibility of the lord's still coming, because it is so fine a night; and so passes the whole night awake.[37]

The basis for the Pound's choice of this poem, I think, is summarized in Fenollosa's third sentence: "the beauty of the poem lies in not a single character being used to explain the idea of waiting and resenting; yet the poem fully expresses the idea." Pound, it will be noted, reiterates this information in his own prose gloss for the benefit of his western readers. From my perspective, the lack of a "direct reproach" in the poem, and yet the achievement of a full expression of that idea by other means, brings Aldington's famous dictum to mind: "we convey an emotion by presenting the object and circumstance of that emotion without comment."[38] Ironically, Pound is put in the position of having to explain a poem which works without explanation—to comment on a poem which works "without comment"—in its own cultural milieu. The prose gloss appended to the poem is intended to compensate for the cultural differences which prevent our appreciation of the poem, as well as for the passivity of the reader.

Chinese readers would be familiar with the situation presented in Pound's poem, and its emotional burden would follow from their familiarity. Apart from what Fenollosa has noted about the situation in the poem, several things would be apparent to such readers. While the woman is not necessarily a king's concubine, or part of an imperial family, that seems likely given the opulence of her surroundings. In feudal times court concubines were not permitted to talk to male strangers. They were isolated in seraglios where they lacked the freedom to socialize; there was generally no one for them to converse with except the maids. Thus, the women have been neglected. As part of the seraglio, the crystal curtain is a metaphor for the social barriers which forbade women to go out into society and mix with the opposite sex. When the woman rolls up the curtain (as she must in order to be able to let it down again in the poem) her action is a kind of protest; she would like to rid herself of those stifling social prohibitions, to pull down the social barriers which enforce her loneliness. In like manner, when she lowers it again, she tacitly surrenders to her oppressive situation. The woman has a private complaint, but she has no one to unburden herself to. The object of her complaint is probably her male master. As a court concubine, it is likely that she has to compete with too many other women for his attention; perhaps she has difficulty getting along with him; perhaps she has any number of other related problems.[39] The poem leaves all of those alternatives open. At any rate, we recognize that she is a lonely, neglected woman and that she will find no immediate relief, and once we recognize the pathos of her situation, we pity her. Her unhappiness, I think, is comprehensible to western readers, though her situation may seem strange to us.

I would claim that "The Jewel Stairs' Grievance" manages to "convey an emotion by presenting the object and circumstance of that emotion without comment" as other Imagist poems do, but with a difference: the "object and "circumstance" of the emotion are themselves so subtly conveyed that we might easily overlook them and therefore miss the emotion which arises from them. As Pound has written, the poem requires careful examination; it works "by a sort of mathematical process of reduction."[40] But while we can claim that "Grievance" presents "an emotional and intellectual complex," it is still one step away from presenting an Image. Pound's comments on his "In a Station of the Metro" help to clarify the distinction: "In a poem of this sort one is trying to record the precise instant when a thing outward and objective transforms itself, or darts into a thing inward and subjective."[41] The significant difference between "Metro" and "The Jewel Stairs' Grievance" is that "Grievance" does not permit "instantaneous" appreciation of its emotional element: we have to puzzle over the circumstances in order to reach it. When we think about the poem, the external, objective details point us back to the hidden emotional content which makes of this scene an Image.[42] Our emotional response to the poem follows from a consideration of the woman's situation. I think we are in a position, now, to see that what interested Pound in "Grievance" was not simply the puzzle it presented, as he leads us to believe in his Chinese poetry essay, but the solution to the puzzle. "The Jewel Stairs' Grievance" represents a kind of delayed Image.

I can substantiate my argument for Pound's interest in "The Jewel Stairs' Grievance" by examining other, generically similar poems which Pound rejected for use in *Cathay*. Pound came across several Chinese "puzzle" poems in Fenollosa's notes. Among them was a poem Fenollosa noted as being "equally famous" as "The Jewel Stairs' Grievance": #128 in the Rihaku notebook, with which it is often paired in anthologies of Chinese poetry. Pound typed a rough sketch of it but jettisoned the draft before it was finished. His version of the poem reads:

CALM NIGHT THOUGHT

The moon light is on the floor luminous
I thought it was frost, it was so white
Holding up head I look at mountain moon
that makes me lower head
lowering head think of old home[43]

mountain
looking up I find it to be the moon
[alternate line]

Fenollosa's notes for the poem tell us that it describes a traveler in a strange place. Like "The Jewel Stairs' Grievance," the poem is valued for expressing an emotion which remains unstated.[44] In this case the emotion is homesickness, the yearning for one's home town which is so much a part of the traditional Chinese mentality.[45] Fenollosa's notes provide commentary on the poem's mechanism: "the meaning is that, seeing white on ground, thought it was frost. Saw it was moon by looking up. But the moon made me think of my home, because it is same moon that shines there and here." Fenollosa claims that "the transition of thought is very strong, yet very natural."[46] Pound evidently didn't share his enthusiasm; his typescript for the poem ends with a note to himself which reads "gnomic poetry." The note is followed by a silly parody of what Pound must have considered rather obtuse poetry.[47]

Unlike "The Jewel Stairs' Grievance," "calm night thought" represents a train of thought, rather than a scene which might provoke thought; the movement of mind is overtly mapped out for us. The poem does not merely present a situation which is the basis for emotion, but makes the appropriate mental connections for the reader; not much is left to the imagination. Given what we know about Pound's preference for purely "presentational" poetry, it is not surprising that he abandoned this piece. We may tentatively attribute its rejection to its explanatory quality. It could also be true that an expression of homesickness of this kind was not the kind of emotion Pound could grasp. The profound attachment that the Chinese feel for their home town has no precise analog in western society. Pound may have felt that a poem on that subject was inappropriate for western readers.

It is worth noting here that "calm night thought" represents only one of many "lonely traveller" or "lonely exile" poems to be found in the Fenollosa notebooks. A partial list of the others would include #13, 26, 65, 126, 132 and 136. Pound discarded all of them as material for *Cathay*, though he referred to one of them (#136) in his 1918 Chinese Poetry essay. For these reasons, we must question Kodama's theory of thematic unity based on the figure of the lonely exile.

Among the other rejected "puzzle poems" is #56 in Volume 2 of Professor Mori's lectures. In this poem a wife wonders when her absent husband will return. A broken mirror provides a clue: it is equivalent to a half-moon. Each line of the poem is "like a hint or joke," Fenollosa wrote.[48] Like "The Jewel Stairs' Grievance," this poem proceeds according to an almost "mathematical process of reduction." Yet Pound rejected it. Had he merely been interested in poetry he had to dismantle, or in poetry which required logical analysis, this poem would have served him as well or better than the one he chose to incorporate into *Cathay*. What this poem lacked in Pound's mind, I suspect, was the subtle presentation of "an emotional and intellectual complex" which constitutes an Image. Then, again, the emotion expressed in this poem may have seemed too foreign for western audiences to appreciate.

•

In contrast to these "short, obscure" puzzle poems, Pound moves on in his essay to discuss the extreme clarity and simplicity of which Chinese poetry is also capable. His treatment constitutes the second of five sections in the essay. As illustrations of Chinese "clarity and simplicity," he cites his own translations of "South-Folk in Cold Country," "Song of the Bowmen of Shu," and "Lament of the Frontier Guard." According to Pound, these poems possess "a directness and realism such as we find only in early Saxon verse and in the Poema del Cid, and in Homer, or rather in what Homer would be if he wrote without epithet. . . . " "South-Folk in Cold Country" is praised for being "very forthright in its manner."[49] After reprinting his translation of that poem, he adds the following commentary: "there you have no mellifluous circumlocution, no sentimentalizing of men who have never seen a battlefield and who wouldn't fight if they had to. You have war, campaigning as it has always been, tragedy, hardship, no illusions.[50]

These are the war poems which have been so highly praised in scholarly commentary. For Kenner, they represent the focus of the whole volume of poems. Selected by a "sensibility responsive to torn Belgium and disrupted London," they supposedly form the "true theme of *Cathay*." But the fact that these poems were suitable choices for a volume published during war-time—"war poems written in war-time"[51]—was a secondary consideration for Pound. When we look closely at his own commentary (above), it becomes clear that what interested him in these poems was not so much their theme as that they reflected qualities remarkably similar to those the imagists strove for. The poetic attributes Pound praises in these poems—"directness and realism," "forthrightness of manner," "no mellifluous circumlocution," "no sentimentalizing," "no illusions"—echo, once again, the do's and dont's of the imagist program: "direct treatment of the thing," "use absolutely no word that doesn't contribute to the presentation," as well as the demand for a poetry "free from emotional slither," "as much like granite as it can be," whose "force will lie in its truth"—"straight talk."[52] The emphasis in his analysis of the war poems is clearly on poetic technique, not on theme. My guess is that Pound selected them more for their "clarity" and "simplicity" than because they demonstrated any thematic unity.

The Fenollosa notebooks provide further evidence to substantiate my claims. Had Pound wanted to construct a volume of poems strictly around a war theme, that opportunity was certainly open to him. The notebooks contain enough war poems and poems on war-related themes to fill a small volume by themselves, but Pound rejected all but the few he incorporated into *Cathay*. Among those he passed up were a poem by Rihaku entitled "Battle at South Castle" which offered striking parallels with modern warfare, a second poem similar in tone to "North Gate" written upon visiting a battlefield ten years after the fray, a third "saibai" poem with an interesting fern-gathering theme close to that in his own "The Bowmen of Shu," and, finally, a drinking song with a war setting.[53] The poems numbered #16, 20, 22, 48, 67, 69, 72, 115, and 123 are all war poems of one kind or another. Pound showed scant interest in any of them, nor did he show interest in Fenollosa's summary account of "osui" and "kosui," military songs sung in actual battle, or during time of peace, respectively. Two other war poems in summary form, one on war horses entitled "Temba" and another entitled "I Tai Gen," a poem to pray for victory in battle, also failed to spark any interest.

In *The Pound Era* Kenner wrote that "the *Cathay* poems paraphrase an elegiac poetry nobody wrote."[54] His implication here and elsewhere in the book is that Pound's war poetry was radically innovative for its time. Fenollosa's notes, however, paint a different picture of his achievement. The array of war poems in the notebooks offered Pound an opportunity to translate far more innovative war poetry than he actually did, poetry akin to "the genre of war poem that was to come out of the [World War I] trenches later on."[55] Rihaku's "Battle at South Castle," for example, with its mention of rocket fire and rotting corpses, would have provided striking parallels with modern warfare.[56]

A third kind of poetry singled out for attention in Pound's 1918 essay is magical or mythical poetry.

> . . . Chinese poetry is full of fairies and fairy lore. Their lore is "quite Celtic." . . . The desire to be taken away by the fairies, the idea of souls flying with the sea birds, and many other things recently made familiar to us by the Celtic school, crop up in one's Chinese reading . . . [57]

Pound is referring here to the "senshi," or sennin poems, which have already been introduced to the reader. As I mentioned earlier, there is a wealth of such poetry in Fenollosa's notebooks, but Pound demonstrated little interest in most of it. His notes reveal that he worked briefly on several specimens, but abandoned all of them except the "Sennin Poem by Kakuhaku" which he incorporated into *Cathay*. A near-complete draft of one other mythical poem—a particularly vivid representation of a rain god—exists among his notes.[58] Most of the drafts share a highly visual presentation of subject material and plenty of imagery, but are marked by that "aspiration of a sustained sense of human relations with infinity" which Pound apparently found so distasteful. Pound is explicit about his reasons for neglecting fairies and fairy lore in his essay: the ideas associated with sennin poetry "crop up in one's Chinese reading and are so familiar and so well known to us that they seem, often, not worth translating."[59] We have no reason to doubt Pound on this point. His stated claims and his evident distaste for "other-worldly" sentiment explain why he didn't select more from this genre.

The last quality to which Pound calls attention in his 1918 essay is the sensitive treatment of nature in Chinese poetry:

> Especially in their poems of nature and of scenery they seem to excel western writers, both when they speak of their sympathy with the emotions of nature and when they describe natural things.

> For instance, when they speak of mountainous crags with the trees clinging head downward, or of a mountain pool where the flying birds are reflected, and
>
> Lie as if on a screen,
>
> as says Rihaku.[60]

Pound does not illustrate this quality with any complete translations, for reasons which we can only guess. He found many poems in the Fenollosa notebooks which exemplify it, and his notes show that he made drafts of several poems containing images like those above but didn't finish any of them. For example, one page of typescript shows that he worked on the following lines from poem #17:

> Orphan straight are pines and oaks
> They can wear the mask of peach petals[61]

as well as on two lines from poem #113:

> The pine stands, but the peach tree makes pretty
> faces
> The apricots mix with their neighbors[62]

Most of his drafts don't proceed much farther than two or three sketchy lines, however. We can hazard a guess as to what appealed to Pound in these poetic equivalents of "scenes out of . . . marvellous Chinese painting."[63] They are Images, according to Pound's definition of the word.[64] The flying birds reflected in the mountain pool where they "lie as if on a screen" arguably give us an "instantaneous" "sense of sudden liberation; that sense of freedom from time limits and space limits; that sense of sudden growth, which we experience in the presence of the greatest works of art."[65] Momentarily suspended in the pool, the birds transcend time and space limitations as a timeless painting might.

The Chinese sympathy with nature closely coincided with Pound's own theory of the Image as an equation for moods.[66] Both of the examples Pound uses in his essay (as well as the two less successful examples reproduced above) represent a fusion of a natural image with human emotion which makes them closely akin to the Images found in Pound's own poems:

> Petals on a wet, black bough.

or:

> A wet leaf that clings to the threshhold.[67]

It is significant for my argument that most of the poems in the notebooks which present natural images like those reproduced above, make use of them as a means of transition into a more introspective, subjective kind of poetry. Familiar themes associated with such poetry are the passage of time and the mortality of man. The logic behind the transition in these poems is a simple one: man's sympathy with nature moves him to think of the cycle of growth and decay, and ultimately of his own mortality. The drift away from natural, concrete images into a more philosophic or moralistic poetry made this poetry difficult to translate in imagist terms. Pound's well-known preference for an understated, non-discursive poetry makes it seem probable that he abandoned the drafts of several of these poems because they drifted in that fashion. The following typescript, which represents one of Pound's abandoned drafts, richly illustrates the kind of "swerve" into philosophic speculation I have been discussing. The draft is a translation of poem #125, attributed to Rihaku:

> The red sun comes out of the Eastern corner
> as if he sprang from the bottom of the earth
> It crosses heaven and sinks again in the sea
> Who will say where the six dragons of his car will
> come to rest
> Who will date its beginning and ending
> Man, who art not a cardinal spirit
> How shall you think to wander forever with the
> unwearying sun, yourself unwearied
> How shall you desire it
> Yet the grass takes no thought of the wind that
> makes it flourish
> The trees do not hate the autumn of their decline
> Who by brandishing whips will hasten the course
> of the seasons?
> Or of the myriad things that
> without thought arise and decay[68]

The draft is clearly rough and unfinished, but I think we can make a case for the presence of an Image in the first three lines of the poem. The vision of a vast, shimmering, "oriental" sun emerging from the sea with a superhuman vitality arguably "presents an intellectual and emotional complex in an instant of time."[69] The affecting visual splendor of the lines engenders an emotion akin to wonder or awe, at least for this reader. Again, the "emotional complex" arises from the fusion of a natural image with a human attribute (in this case, "springing"). It is my guess that the striking picture presented in the opening lines provided the impetus to sketch out the remaining lines, which are far from clear in Fenollosa's notes. But here, as in so many other cases, the visual clarity of the first few lines rapidly fades into an introspective reverie on the passage of time and man's mortality. Line four begins the movement toward a moralizing philosophy. As Pound's typescript of the poem contains no marginal notations, we can only speculate that he lost interest in the poem when it changed direction. It seems likely that many similar poems in the Fenollosa notebooks shared the same fate, as none of them found their way into *Cathay*.

III

Schneidau has remarked that "imagism was best suited to . . . situations in which reticence is the idiomatic norm."[70] More than any other Chinese poet, perhaps, Rihaku's poems exemplify the reticence which suited Pound's own poetic discipline. That Pound felt a professional affinity with the poet is, I think, easily demonstrable. Rihaku's work is disproportionately represented in Pound's volume with respect to the many other poets included in the Fenollosa notebooks; Kenner has correctly observed that the Rihaku notebooks "furnished the backbone of *Cathay*."[71] The Chinese reticence that Pound so admired is especially apparent in Rihaku's poems of departure. Pound used all of them for his volume, except one: a poem with the unlikely title, "saying good-bye to Uncle Cloud."[72] Pound's relish for these poems stems from a close coincidence between his imagistic theory and Rihaku's. One has only to read Fenollosa's notes for "Separation on the River Kiang" to see how closely Rihaku's poetic techniques accord with Pound's own:

> This poem very simple, yet very famous . . . often studied by Japanese students because it conforms to key idea of Teku poems whose art is to depict some striking feature in order to indicate the whole scene with such skill in arrangement of characters that it is impossible to suggest any change for the better.[73]

Pound must have experienced a shock of recognition when he came upon an idea so close to his own stated technique. Compare Pound's claim that "the artist seeks out the luminous detail and presents it."[74] This poem conforms well to Pound's recommendation that the way to write poetry is to delineate an object or situation with a few essential details that will make its uniqueness leap out at the reader: the perceptual image must be "stripped down" to the essence that constitutes a conceptual image.[75]

The occasion of this poem, according to Fenollosa, was an incident in Rihaku's own life. Moko, a famous poet himself, is planning to travel from Ko-kaku-ro, in Busho, down to Yoshu, by river. Rihaku is bidding him good-bye. The crib notes for the poem read:

> Ko-kaku-ro Mo Ko Ko-Rio
> yellow stork pointing saying name of man going
> name of place goodbye
>
> Ko-jin Ko-kaku-ro
> old acquaintance must leave ____
> An old acquaintance, starting from the west, takes
> leave of K. K. R.
>
> ____________ ____________ 3rd month go
> down name of a province
> In the month of March, when flowers (of
> blossoming trees) are smoky
> (blurrey) he descends (by river) to Yoshu
>
> solitary sail far shadow blue sky terminate
> (If I look from the storied house at his boat) the
> distant shade of the
> solitary sail is visible at the very extremity of
> the blue sky
>
> only see long Kiang heaven limit flow
> river
> (and the moment after)
> I only see the long River flowing into the
> horizon—
> horizon means approximation to Ko-rio[76]

For convenience, I will juxtapose Pound's translation here:

SEPARATION OF THE RIVER KIANG

> Ko-jin goes west from Ko-kaku-ro,
> The smoke-flowers are blurred over the river.
> His lone sail blots the far sky.
> And now I see only the river,
> The long Kiang, reaching heaven.[77]

Comparison of Pound's version of the poem with Fenollosa's crib notes shows that Pound altered little of the original text. Yet, while he only changed a few details in the poem, he still managed to adhere to his own poetic doctrine—evidence for the basic similarities between the two poets. Pound reworked this poem according to imagist principles, but all of the changes made in the original poem serve to strengthen the essential features of the scene, and are thus in keeping with the spirit of the original. In accordance with Pound's love of "precision," he has cut out all words which do not contribute to the presentation. For instance, he makes no mention in his translation of the time of year; the "third month" has been left out. "Smoke-flowers" are enough to suggest Spring. The "blurriness" of the smoke-flowers suggest the distance at which they are seen. They do not intrude upon the inner eye, but serve as an "out of focus" background against which we view the sail, the focal point of attention, in the far sky. The lone sail is the essential feature, "the luminous detail," which serves to focus the whole scene. Captured at the moment of its disappearance, it is an Image through which Pound captures the poignant sadness of separation perfectly. As the "blot" on the horizon fades away, the center of the whole poem dissolves with it, leaving us with a sense of emptiness and loneliness. Pound has used adjectives which contribute to the emotion conveyed by the scene. "Blot" and "blurred" both suggest visual qualities that this scene might share with a painting; the impressionistic quality they lend to the poem adds to its poignant beauty. With a maximum efficiency of expression and the achievement of the "mot juste," then, Pound has produced a beautifully compelling translation.[78] We can best appreciate his accomplishment when we juxtapose Pound's version of the poem with a more accurate, but less inspired translation:

TO SEE HAO-JAN OFF TO YANG-CHOU

> My old friend goes away from the Yellow
> Crane Tower.
> In smoke-flower third month down to
> Yang-chou.
> A lone sail, a distant shade, lost in the blue
> horizon.
> Only the long Yangtze is seen flowing into the sky.[79]

While the similarities between the original text of "Separation on the River Kiang" and Pound's imagist poetics resulted in a fortuitous translation, Pound was not so fortunate with another of the poems of departure. In the case of "Leave-taking Near Shoku," the third of four departure poems in *Cathay*, the original material did not prove to be easily translatable in terms of imagist doctrine. Pound's version of the poem reads:

LEAVE-TAKING NEAR SHOKU

"Sanso, King of Shoku, built roads"

They say the roads of Sanso are steep,
 Sheer as the mountains.

The walls rise in a man's face,
Clouds grow out of the hill
 at his horse's bridle.
Sweet trees are on the paved way of the Shin,
 Their trunks burst through the paving,
And freshets are bursting their ice
in the midst of Shoku, a proud city.
 Men's fates are already set,
There is no need of asking diviners.[80]

Compare Pound's version with the summary introduction and rough translation he was working with in Fenollosa's notes:

> this is a poem on a friend going to Shoku—for some unpleasant cause, perhaps exile . . . The whole tenor of the poem is "You are going to Shoku. They say it is hard and yet do not be alarmed. For it is spring (lovely). (As in nature there is dark and light) so in men's life there is rise as well as fall . . . need not ask fortune teller . . . i.e. you may rise again . . . This poem much praised for its skillful comparison of nature to life. For the 8 lines we have force of mts. passage from Shin province to arrival in Shoku city, also the history of the traveller—very comprehensive.

TAKING LEAVE OF A FRIEND ENTERING SHOKU

We hear it said that Sanso's roads
(wild silkworm in Shoku) (Sanso old king of
 Shoku)

are steep are not easy to go
(because) mts. rise up in the very face of a man
and clouds grow alongside the horse's heads

(But at the same time) (this being springtime)
 Fragrant woods
must be covering up the supported paths of Shin

And spring brooks must be encircling the shoku
 city.

Men's fates are already predetermined

so that you have no need to ask Kumpei
(a famous old sage of Kumpei skilled in divination,
 here used for fortune teller in general)[81]

While Pound followed Fenollosa's rough sketch of the actual lines of the poem fairly closely, he did not incorporate the subtle "comparison of nature to life" (mentioned in the summary) into his poem. There is no intimation of the unpleasant reason for the journey, for which the beauty of spring serves to compensate. No sense of the ups and downs of fortune remains in Pound's poem. In short, there is no clear sense of a contrast between the dark and light sides of nature with which to compare the fortunes of man, and for that reason the last two lines of Pound's translation seem tacked on. By cutting out the subtle suggestions in the early lines, he destroyed the philosophical underpinnings which provide the basis for a natural transition into the maxim of the final lines. Pound probably felt that he had to hold the poem together in some other way. One of the techniques he used was to intensify the sense of natural grandeur throughout the poem. He enhanced the sense of spring freshness by adding a completely new line: "Their trunks burst through the paving." and he attempted to unify the poem in other ways. The phrase "a proud city," which has no precedent in the original text, serves to connect Shoku with the "paved way of the Shin," a road "sheer as the mountains." As Pound depicts it, the paved way seems a natural part of its rugged setting.

Pound has created an authentic sense of spring vitality in his poem, but it is a poem very different from the one he started with. His altered version is held together by a series of luminous details, no one of which serves as a unifying image, as the sail did in "Separation on the River Kiang." Each reader must judge for himself whether or not the last two lines seem naturally integrated with the rest of the poem after Pound altered it, but this reader feels that the poem fails to lend itself as successfully to Pound's imagist poetics as did "Separation on the River Kiang."

IV

Just as Pound's 1918 Chinese poetry essay gives us information about the qualities he admired in Chinese poetry, an unpublished piece of writing on the same topic gives us a strong sense about his aversions. The sentiments expressed in this earlier, fragmentary passage take us a long way toward understanding why Pound rejected many of the poems in the notebooks. While the following is not the entire piece, it is the most comprehensible part of it, and the most relevant for the purposes of this paper:

> China has been a [prey] to every sort of idiocy as has the western world. Confucius with his fine ear for music, his profound sense of all things, told men to read the odes. Snivelling imbeciles of whom there are no fewer in China than with us, presumed that he wished to give the world moral and Fabian instruction. The odes have been [ ] in commentary. As writers in the stultified counter reformation used to put in little prefaces saying the names of greek gods are introduced only as allegory and figure and contain nothing contrary to the holy catholic varieties, so the commentators have belabored pleasing love poems with moral glosses. As the snivellers among us have loaded the song of songs. Religion has been the curse of the world. And Confucius who always refused to discuss the future life with his disciples, placed future life among the subjects which he refused to discuss with his disciples, has not escaped its contamination.
>
> We make out souls not with religion but with reading poems and seeing beautiful pictures. Confucius knew

this long before our honored contemporary had put in the cadence of prose.[82]

Despite the unfinished quality of the sentences, Pound's meaning is quite clear: "moral or Fabian instruction" is a contaminating influence in poetry; love poems ought not to be burdened with moral glosses. He seems to lend his support to Confucius' refusal to discuss the future life, and even to hint at its inappropriateness as subject matter for poetry. The opinions expressed in the passage lead us toward a better understanding of Pound's selective predispositions. They are voiced, directly or indirectly, in his decisions to include or exclude individual poems for *Cathay*. Keeping them in mind as we examine several unfinished drafts of poems, we can begin to understand why he rejected them and why he substantially shortened one of the poems he finally chose to include in *Cathay*.

Among Pound's notes and working drafts is a well-developed draft of a Rihaku poem entitled "Song for the falling kingdom." It reads:

SONG FOR THE FALLING KINGDOM

Homing crows drift in the air at nest time
over the terrace at Koso,
Within, the Go king is drinking with Sei-shi,
The song of his dynasty has not yet run to its end
Nor her dances danced to a finish
The Blue Mountain bathes in the sun
Pale rays still strike the gold urn
and fall slowly into the water.
The autumn moonlight is already tinging the river,
What use is this pleasure tomorrow.[83]

There are various other versions of this poem in Pound's notes, but the above draft is the most complete. The original poem, entitled "crow nesting music," was much longer; Pound cut it drastically to produce a distinctively different piece. Though his version doesn't reflect it, the poem had a moral message and could even be characterized as "deeply admonitory" in tone, according to Fenollosa. The general situation which provided the setting for the poem is as follows: the King is drunk with Seishi, a court concubine. Most of the night has already passed—"the sun has set and dawn is coming on" Fenollosa's notes tell us—but the King wants still more pleasure. He must answer an implicit question, which if voiced would be something like: "I wish to have more, what shall I do about it?" A sundial enters the poem as a subtle reminder of the passage of time. A sophisticated Chinese reader, according to Fenollosa, would recognize the significance of that sundial. It says in essence, "so it is today, so it will be tomorrow and what will be the end of it all but destruction?" Translation: the indulgence of passion will lead to the downfall of the kingdom. Fenollosa adds the following commentary: "in its naturalness there is such deep hidden moral meaning that, to a deep mind, no admonition can be stronger."[84]

In his own version, Pound cut out the moral meaning altogether and substituted what might be called a "carpe diem" theme; in short, he completely reversed its meaning. Perhaps he thought the Chinese message would be lost on western readers, but it seems more likely that Pound objected to the "moral instruction" in the poem. His comments in the passage I quoted at the beginning of this section would seem to substantiate the suspicion. Once Pound had done his revisions on the poem, however, it was no longer clear why this kingdom should be a "falling" one. Additional changes would have produced an entirely new poem, certainly nothing that could justifiably be called a translation, and we may speculate that Pound abandoned it for those reasons.

Pound had better success with another poem on a somewhat analogous theme, now known to us as "A Ballad of the Mulberry Road."[85] The original title for this poem was "highway—on—mulberry tree," or "mulberry tree on the highway." Like "Song for the falling kingdom," it is very long, and Fenollosa only included about half of it in his notes.[86] The bulk of our information on "A Ballad of the Mulberry Road" comes from Vol. 2 of Professor Mori's Lectures. Fenollosa's notes from this source give us some idea of the content of the complete poem:

A young girl named Rafu is in the field to pluck mulberry leaves. Her appearance—dress and face—are minutely described. end of 1st part. Then a noble passes by, riding in a carriage. She refuses. end of 2nd part. (This is minutely narrated, tho not very long.) Then she goes on to speak to the noble of her own husband—so he can't take her now.—this is 3rd part.

Fenollosa's notes continue:

There is a tradition that this Rafu refused this prince, by playing the Kolo; and that her words of refusal and her song of husband were in the Kolo.[87]

Pound and Fenollosa both agreed that the "song of husband" which constitutes the third part of the ballad spoils it. We can speculate that Pound characterized the original poem as a love song "burdened" with tedious moralizing. His having found the ballad in an incomplete form gave him a precedent for reducing it even further, to the form it now takes in *Cathay*. It is interesting, but perhaps not surprising, to note that he cut all didactic and moralizing passages from the poem. Again, we have recourse to the Imagist do's and don'ts to explain his actions ("freedom from didacticism," "presentation" without comment).[88] By excluding those passages, and most of the rest of the poem, from his own version, Pound got rid of the moralizing without distorting the section he chose to translate. Fortunately, the "song of husband" was confined to a separate section of the poem. That had not been the case with "Song for the falling kingdom," where the moral message was intertwined with the whole of the rest of the text. In the end, Pound limited his translation to the first part of the ballad, which contains the detailed description of Rafu's physical appearance. Perhaps what interested him in the poem was what Fenollosa referred to as a "full objective description of details" which "goes all though the story," but is especially strong in the first third of the poem where it is "uncontaminated" by moralizing.[89]

Earlier I mentioned Pound's aversion to poetry which "aspires to a sustained sense of human relations with infinity." His distaste for "otherworldly" poetry helps to explain why Pound abandoned yet another of his drafts. Poem #7 in the Hirai and Shida notebook provided the source for the following typescript:

> Red sun fills heaven and earth
> Firey clouds are heaped up like mountain on
> mountain
> Grasses and trees are parched, twisted
> River and marsh are baked dry
> The light gauze weighs heavy upon me
> The thick tree shade is worn thin,
> Bamboo mats are too hot to touch
> We must wash our summer net dress over and over[90]

Despite the unpolished condition of the draft, it possesses "qualities of vivid presentation" and sets forth its masterial "without moralizing and without comment," attributes Pound praised in his 1918 essay.[91] The lines are terse, uncluttered with unnecessary adjectives, and the images are simple and strong. The scene makes a strong visual impression upon the mind of the reader. One might think the poem would be perfect for Pound's purposes, but when we examine its remaining lines, we begin to guess his probable reasons for abandoning it. The poem takes an abrupt tack into the spiritual realm when the narrator projects her mind into the "beyond." Fenollosa's notes for the last few lines read:

> I direct my mind by going beyond the universe
> There very wide it is lonesome and frank (wide-
> and-hollow)
> i.e. there is nothing to bother or deceive
> There long wind comes over 10,000 miles melt
> away
> and sea sweep toublesome dirt
> sweep away harm
> Then, I reflect that it is my body which-brings me
> sadness
> damage
> Here for the first time then understand that my
> mind is not yet enlightened
> Suddenly entering the gate of sweet dews
> What—like pure cool pleasure
> just there is[92]

The speaker escapes the oppressive heat and discomfort of this world by adopting an other-worldly frame of mind. Commenting on this attitude, Fenollosa writes: "there must be some Buddhist conception here, not merely Confucian . . . possibly derived from Koshi."[93] Here is what Pound made of the same lines of the poem:

> I send my thought out from the world
> I give it space in the open
> Long wind from 10,000 miles
> a sea wind clears off the dust
> Then I reflect that the boredom comes from body
> I know that I am not fully enlightened
> What pleasure have in heavens
> like that of going into the gates drenched with dew
> (detachment)[94]

Pound ends his typescript with the word "detachment," which he links in a penciled scrawl with the word "heavens." Given that clue and what we already know about Pound's distaste for other-worldly sentiment, I think that the "detached" quality of the latter half of the poem spoiled it for Pound and ultimately made it unworkable for him. The trend of his revision was to change the other-worldly preoccupation of the narrator to a more earth-bound reverie: the wind from beyond the universe becomes a sea wind clearing off the dusty earth; the mind going beyond the universe into the void is altered to thoughts given space "in the open"; the body as the source of sadness or harm becomes merely a cause of boredom in Pound's poem. Unfortunately, the allusion to a future life and the religious significance of the last four lines posed a stumbling block for Pound. They would not easily fit into his new scheme for the poem, and he could not omit them without radically altering the meaning of the original. At some point, we may surmise, he decided that he couldn't reconcile his own ideas with the original text and lost interest in the draft.

CONCLUSION

That Imagist doctrine was uppermost in Pound's mind as he sorted through the Fenollosa notes on Chinese poetry seems likely, given the evidence. Pound inherited the Fenollosa notebooks during his Imagist phase, and his poetic principles heavily influenced his selection of poems for the *Cathay* volume. While conformity to Imagist doctrine was probably the most important criterion for selection from the Fenollosa notebooks, other factors entered into his choice of poems, as well. Practical problems like the illegibility of Fenollosa's notes, for example, or the fact that many poems were recorded only in summary form, without sketches of actual lines, must inevitably have affected the selection process. The added fact that many poems were either poorly sketched out or incomplete made it impossible for Pound to translate a substantial proportion of the poems he encountered. He often made lists for himself which noted which poems were fleshed out and which were unfinished, and these likely helped make his choice of poems to translate.

Then, too, coping with the great bulk of the Fenollosa material influenced Pound's selection process. The notebooks he examined first, which happened to be the two Rihaku notebooks (we know this because his numbering sequence begins with them), were much more heavily worked than the other notebooks. Pound drafted parts of almost all of the poems in the first volume of the Rihaku notes, which included poems by Omakitsu, Kutsugen, Rihaku and To-em-mei. It seems likely that he went busily to work on that first notebook and then was overwhelmed by the material. His examination of subsequent notebooks was much more cursory. Evidence for that assertion exists in his misnumbering of poems in later notebooks, his accidental separation of the parts of one poem into several poems which were then separately numbered, etc.

Pound's choices were not primarily made with an eye to any supposed theme for *Cathay,* nor were they made according to what was representative of the Chinese poetry in the notebooks. Many kinds of poetry which were strongly represented in Fenollosa's notes were not included in the *Cathay* volume. Sennin poetry, or poetry on Chinese gods and demons, odes to those gods, poems on Chinese legends or myths, poems with characteristically Chinese sentiments (e.g. travel poems with homesickness as a theme), heavily philosophical poetry, Buddhist or Taoist reveries on man's mortality, poems full of "strange" emotion or seemingly illogical combinations of sentiment, poems praising ancient emperors which make use of what we might consider hyperbolic rhetoric, and other poems which aren't easily assignable to any of the above categories, were not proportionately represented in the *Cathay* volume.

Instead, Pound chose poems which either already exemplified Imagist principles, or which lent themselves easily to translation in Imagist terms. He sought poetry free of "emotional slither" and "didacticism," "presented" "without moralizing and without comment," and, on the other hand, written in language "like speech except for a heightened simplicity," "as much like granite as it can be."

ADDENDUM

The Fenollosa notebooks provide detailed information about the composition of two poems which have, to date, posed problems for commentators. The following passage from Volume 3 of Professor Mori's lectures on Chinese poetry probably furnished Pound with the idea for one of the lines from "The River Song":

> Now these two poets, Sin and So, had important positions under empress—Bu Soleulen [?]—she was a very great lady, a heroine. . . . She called the poets to the palace on every 2nd and 3rd day, and gave them subjects, and made them compose on them at once. She made them compete with each other & she judged . . . [95]

As Kenner and Yip have observed, Pound accidentally ran two separate poems together for his "translation" of the "The River Song," incorporating the title of the second poem into the body of the text as four lines of poetry.[96] the four lines in question read as follows:

> And I have moped in the Emperor's garden,
> awaiting an order-to-write!
> I looked at the dragon-pond, with its willow-
> coloured water
> Just reflecting the sky's tinge,
> And heard the five-score nightingales aimlessly
> singing.[97]

Here is Wailim Yip's translation of the erstwhile title:

> Poem composed at the command of the Emperor in I-chun park on the Dragon-Pond as the willows are in their fresh green and the new orioles are singing in their thousand ways[98]

In Yip's translation, the Emperor commands the composition of poems, but in Pound's, the speaker *awaits* an *order* to write. The idea of waiting to be called to the Emperor's palace could only have come from Fenollosa's notes, and Pound probably altered the first line of the old title in this poem according to what he remembered from the passage he had marked in the notes.

Pound relied more heavily on Fenollosa's notes for his translation of "South-Folk in Cold Country" than has been noted in scholarly commentary to date. When Kenner published Fenollosa's crib notes for the poem, he missed a page of notes which had been opposed to a previous poem in the notebook. Those notes contain a summary account of the history of Genso's conquests in the north, in Siberia, and in Turkestan. Two lines jotted at the bottom of the page read as follows:

> Ko horse neigh against the north wind-
> (in north)
> Etsu birds nest on southern branches
> (in south)[99]

The jottings provided details for Pound's own translation of the same lines:

> The Dai horse neighs against the bleak wind of Etsu,
> The birds of Etsu have no love for En, in the
> north.[100]

Pound's translation of the first of these lines is much as he found it in the notes (_____ horse neighs against the _____ wind), and the second bears the traces of its origin (birds of Etsu; in the north), though "En" was borrowed from material located elsewhere in the notes.

WORKS CITED

Brooks, Van Wyck. *Fenollosa and His Circle.* New York: E. P. Dutton and Co., Inc., 1962.

Chisholm, Lawrence W. *Fenollosa: The Far East and American Culture.* New Haven: Yale University Press, 1963.

De Nagy, N. Christoph. *The Poetry of Ezra Pound: The Pre-Imagist Stage.* Berne, Switzerland: Francke Verlag, 1960.

Eliot, T. S. Introduction. *Selected Poems of Ezra Pound.* London: Faber and Faber, 1928.

Fang, Achilles. "Fenollosa and Pound." *Harvard Journal of Asian Studies* XX (1957): 213-38.

Fenollosa, Ernest. "Notebook—Hirai and Shida," #7. All notebooks were examined at The Pound Center, Beinecke Rare Book and Manuscript Library, Yale University.

———. Notebook 8, ms. Ezra Pound Papers. Yale U, New Haven.

———. Notebook 11 (3 vols.), ms. Ezra Pound Papers. Yale U, New Haven.

———. Notebook 12, ms. Ezra Pound Papers. Yale U, New Haven.

———. Notebook 13, ms. Ezra Pound Papers. Yale U, New Haven.

———. Notebook 14, ms. Ezra Pound Papers. Yale U, New Haven.

———. Notebook 15, ts. Ezra Pound Papers. Yale U, New Haven.

———. Notebook 17, ms. Ezra Pound Papers. Yale U, New Haven.

———. Notebook 19, ms. Ezra Pound Papers. Yale U, New Haven.

———. Notebook 20, ms. Ezra Pound Papers. Yale U, New Haven.

———. Notebook 21, ms. Ezra Pound Papers. Yale U, New Haven.

———. *The Chinese Written Character as a Medium for Poetry*. Ed. Ezra Pound. San Francisco: City Lights Books, 1936, 1968.

Giles, Herbert A. *A History of Chinese Literature*. New York: Frederich Ungar Publishing Co., 1901, 1967.

Harmer, J. B. *Victory in Limbo: Imagism 1908-1917*. New York: St. Martin's Press, 1975.

Hughes, Glenn. *Imagism and the Imagists: A Study in Modern Poetry*. Stanford U: Stanford U P, 1975.

Kenner, Hugh. "Ezra Pound and Chinese." *Agenda* IV (1965): 38-41.

———. *The Pound Era*. Berkeley: University of California Press, 1971.

Kodama, Sanehide. "Cathay and Fenollosa's Notebooks." *Paideuma* (1982): 207-40.

Paige, D. D., ed. *The Letters of Ezra Pound, 1907-1941*. New York: Harcourt, Brace and World, Inc., 1950.

Pound, Ezra. "Contemporania." *Poetry* II (1913): 1-12.

———. "Affirmations IV.—As for Imagisme." *New Age* XVI (1915): 349-50.

———. "Chinese Poetry." *To-Day* III (1918): 54-57, 93-95.

———. *Translations*. Introduction by Hugh Kenner. New York: New Directions, 1963.

———. *Literary Essays of Ezra Pound*. Ed. T. S. Eliot. New York: New Directions, 1968.

Schneidau, Herbert N. *Ezra Pound: The Image and the Real*. Baton Rouge: Louisiana State University Press, 1969.

Waley, Arthur. *Translations from the Chinese*. New York: Alfred A. Knopf, Inc., 1941.

APPENDIX

Source poem: #54, in Volume 2 of Professor Mori's lectures

End of a storm

The cloudy God has yoked his dragons together
He binds back the feathery darkness,
Coming between the blue dragons
Coming between the white tigers
Scattering the rain before him
Riding upon the winds, the soft rains obey him
They rush off whispering one to another
The earth is fragrant behind them.
—Attributed to: Shida Sojo
Ssu-ma Hsiang-ju B.C. 117

Pound's Abandoned Drafts

Samples of Sennin poetry

Source poem: #108, in Volume 1 of the Rihaku notes *By Rihaku*

Five storks flew out of the north west
(by Mt. Koriban)
And soared out of heaven

I saw the magic-man stand in his cloud

On a green cloud saying

I am An ki
The jewel-bright youths stood w him, one at each hand
and playing on purple flutes which were
upon flutes decked with the purple plumes of the phoenix.

Swiftly they went into shadow,

and I heard voice in the whirling wind

I thought: should I question it

Floating as wind, flowing as the stars,

I might have eaten of the golden bright shrub

and lived with the unending movers in heaven

Source poem: #12, in the Hirai and Shida notebook *By Rihaku*

Night. Rosan

Seeking blue lotus building

Alone, leaving the (castled) palace with
battlements turreted

Pure frost, bell in east forest fortified

White water, Tiger Valley, moon

heaven fragrance grows nothing, vacancy

heaven music

Sennin music sounds, not stop

Sit quiet, lonesome, not move,

The universe flows through my body-hairs

The true mind is level and deep

Space quenches the idea of an ending

He does not reach temple. I think. idea, temple unnecessary

Source poem: #104, in Volume 1 of the Rihaku notes *By Rihaku*

blue, blue is the mountain Zai Haku

And the stars make a thick forest above it

An old man with black hair wanders
into its clouds and wraps himself in

the pine snow, sober, unspeaking

He lives in a rock hole, somber

Pound's Unfinished Drafts

Samples of poems demonstrating the Chinese sympathy with nature

Source poem: #19, in the Hirai and Shida notebook *By Rihaku*

Pound's Draft

Jade lotus on secret pool
sun shows like a fish in clear (water) river
Autumn petals cover the green water
The leaves are cross-netted with smoke
Their color leads me out from the world
Odour hard to transmit
I can watch the frost creeping over the flower
Withers this crimson fragrant year
The root has no fixed place
But trusts lake border.

Fenollosa's notes for the poem

The jade blue lotus leaves grow in the mysterious pool
The sun of morning irradiates with its fertility, and clear like fish seen in pure streams
Lotus blossoms cover the green water
The dense leaves seem to be netted (with meshed veins) of blue smoke
Surpassing color leaving vacancy behind, is cut away from this world
To what sort of a thing or man can its transcendant fragrance be transmitted

But while we sit we can see the frost come flying and filling (the flower, as the world)
Withers this crimson fragrant year
The roots which tie the ground do not yet attain a fixed place
So, it is fain to put its trust in the borders of the flower lake.

Pound's Unfinished Drafts

Example of a rejected epistolary poem

Source poem: #142, in Volume 2 of Rihaku notes, with Mori and Argia *By Rihaku*

Pound's Draft

At dawn I went out through the gate of Red Sparrows
Evening I lodge in the isle of white heron
The wave-brightness stirs the moonlike jellyfish
Behind me the stars reflect
Star-gleams enter the city gate
rays, reflections, walk into sparrow gate
wall gate house house over gate
glitters of stars on the gate house
glitter against
To think of the reputed governor of Kinso
is like the sorrow of brooding over the tree with
red jewels
red jewel tree
in vain the spirit enters that dream
Suddenly I feel autumn is in the night
green water comprehends human feeling
it flows north west
I will put the sound of it
set within this gemmed lute
Loneliness will come to your hearing.

Fenollosa's Notes

lodging white heron island write to *Willow River peace*
name of man

In the morning I started by the red sparrow gate
and in the evening, I lodge (in boat) alongside White Heron Island
where the shining waves shift the sea moons (jelly fish)
one sees the stars' reflections enter the storied gate
the finely respected governor of Kinzio
I wished to have seen him and could not see
which is like the sorrow of thinking about a red jewelled tree
only in vain my soul enters into (the) dream (of meeting him)
on the contrary I feel as if it were autumn in night
(here he addresses water)—if you green water could understand human feeling
flow
I will put sound (expressing state of my sorrow) inside my jewelled Koto
In order that my sorrow be carried to you, floating on water

NOTES

[1] Ezra Pound, "Chinese Poetry," *To-Day* III (1918): 54-55.

[2] Hugh Kenner, *The Pound Era* (Berkeley: U of California P, 1971) 198.

[3] D. D. Paige, ed., *The Letters of Ezra Pound, 1907-1941* (New York: Harcourt, Brace & World, Inc., 1950).

[4] Kenner 202.

[5] Kenner 202.

[6] Sanehide Kodama, "*Cathay* and Fenollosa's Notebooks," *Paideuma* (1982): 214.

[7] Kenner 192.

[8] Hugh Witemeyer, *The Poetry of Ezra Pound: Forms and Renewal, 1908-1920* (Berkeley: U of California P, 1969) 146.

[9] Ernest Fenollosa, Notebook II (Vol. 1), ms., Ezra Pound Papers, Yale U, New Haven, 73.

[10] Herbert N. Schneidau, *Ezra Pound: The Image and the Real* (Baton Rouge: Louisiana State University Press, 1969) 4, 7. Compare Pound's claim, "I record symptoms as I see 'em." Also Glenn Hughes, *Imagism and the Imagists: A Study in Modern Poetry* (Palo Alto: Stanford U P, 1975) 26.

[11] Schneidau 10.

[12] Ernest Fenollosa, Notebook 11 (Vol. 2), ms., Ezra Pound Papers, Yale U, New Haven.

[13] Schneidau 7, 26, 27 and Yip 35.

[14] Fenollosa, Notebook 11 (Vol. 2).

[15] Yip 36. Also, Schneidau 7.

[16] Schneidau 7.

[17] Ernest Fenollosa, Notebook II (Vol. 3), ms., Ezra Pound Papers, Yale University, New Haven.

[18] Fenollosa, Notebook 11 (Vol. 3).

[19] Fenollosa, Notebook 11 (Vol. 3).

[20] Schneidau 7.

[21] Schneidau 9.

[22] Pound 54.

[23] Schneidau 6, 7, 9, 23.

[24] Fenollosa, Notebook 11 (Vol. 3).

[25] Schneidau 9.

[26] Schneidau 13-14.

[27] Fenollosa, Notebook 11 (Vol. 2).

[28] Ernest Fenollosa, Notebook 16, ms., Ezra Pound Papers, Yale U, New Haven.

[29] Witemeyer 147.

[30] Pound 54.

[31] Schneidau 7, 26, 27. Also, Wailim Yip, *Ezra Pound's Cathay* (Princeton: Princeton U P, 1969) 35.

[32] Witemeyer 147.

[33] Pound 55.

[34] Ezra Pound, *Translations,* introd. Hugh Kenner (New York: New Directions, 1968) 194.

[35] Schneidau 7, 26, 27. Also, Yip 35.

[36] Hughes 28.

[37] Ernest Fenollosa, Notebook 20, ms., Ezra Pound Papers, Yale U, New Haven. This information and the previous commentary on the significance of "The Jewel Stairs' Grievance" both come from this source.

[38] Schneidau 27.

[39] The information in this paragraph from a personal friend and colleague in mainland China. He is Professor Pan Da'an, of the Chinese Language and Literature Department, Hangzhou University, Hangzhou, Zhejiang, P.R.C.

[40] Pound 55.

[41] Yip 49.

[42] Yip 67.

[43] Ernest Fenollosa, Notebook 15, ts., Ezra Pound Papers, Yale U, New Haven. This notebook contains notes by Pound, including translations, in typescript form. The draft of "calm night thought," the note to himself and the parody may all be found in this notebook. The source poem is #128, in the first volume of Rihaku notes (Notebook 20).

[44] Fenollosa, Notebook 20. The note and following summary both come from this source.

[45] Information from Professor Pan Da'an.

[46] Fenollosa, Notebook 20.

[47] Fenollosa, Notebook 15. The silly parody reads as follows:

When the roast smoked in the oven, belching out
blackness
I was be wildered and knew not what to do
But when I was plunged in the contemplation
of Li Po's beautiful verses
This thought came upon me
When the roast smokes pour water upon it.
[Blast!]

[48] Fenollosa, Notebook 11 (Vol. 2).

[49] Pound 56.

[50] Pound 57.

[51] Kenner 202-203.

[52] Schneidau 6, 7.

[53] Fenollosa, Notebook 11 (Vol. 3) and Notebook 11 (Vol. 1).

[54] Kenner 202.

[55] Kenner 202.

[56] The following are Fenollosa's notes for poem #123, "Battle at South Castle" in Vol. 1 of the Rihaku notes (Notebook 20). The bracketed notes are found on the pages opposing the text of the poem.

This is also a melody that existed in time of Han, being one of the 22 melodies concerning war—war song to be sung in war. This one was famous for its martial air accompanied by sadness. Rihaku borrowed the melody to express the popular feeling of the time, lamenting Genso's making war at once on barbarians north, south and west.

on way to Lanking—to N.W. of Pekin refers to So Ken river

Onion River flows from Onion peaks=Himalaya
Mts.—
so this must mean almost to India
Yoshi is supposed to be the phonetic rendering of
Jews—
therefore somewhere near Arabia
battle castle south

last year battle *mulberry dry source*
name of a place, source of So Ken
River
Last year we fought at the source of the So Ken
River

present year battle *onion river way*
name
This year we fight at the onion river way

wash weapon *row branch sea* upon
waves
line
name
(And we want to) wash the weapons (so used) in
the waves of the Yoshi sea

[Three armies in China, always means a complete
army; left-center-and right]

let free horse heaven mt. snow in grass
region of Tibet
and feed our horses among the snow meadows of
the Tibetan mts.

10,000 miles long time expedition battle
this fighting thousands of miles away in long
expedition

three armies all decay grow old
the three armies have already become spent and
old

[This far describes what Genso has done, and
what he still intends]

[The next two lines describe the enemy. The Huns
were the strongest of the enemies,
so all enemies were identified with them.]

Hun slaves with killing massacring make
till cultivate
barbarians cultivate
The Hun barbarians make of massacre their tillage

ancient come only see white bones yellow
sand field
from ancient time
So that from the oldest time on their rice fields
consisting of yellow sand,
nothing but white bones (were planted) (satire)

dynasty (dynasty) build long wall shun
northern place
Shin house (G. W.) defend
barbarian where
(Thus) the Shin house built a long wall to shut out
these northern hordes

[Their system of fighting was that, on approach of
Huns, the Kan sentinels
were ordered to set off rocket fires]
[So much is description of what must still take
place
warfare once begun against such barbarians, will
last again and again]

dynasty house also is rocket fire burn
Han
And the Han dynasty kept on the system of
fighting against them
rocket fire burn not cease
The rocket fires never ceased burning

make battle not cease time
expedition
The expeditions occur without stop

The setting out for battles

[The next lines express the result of the fighting—
by giving a very vivid picture of what simple
soldiers suffer
(possibly wounded)
(not wounded)

With Rihaku, the thing rolls down as a rock falls
down hill.
In Toshin it is nàtural, but not rapid.
Some of the old songs in which R. based this set
are handed down, and are
fine. They are of 2 sorts, those which R. has
followed closely in thought,
and those of which he has taken only the name, or
introducing idea and worked
it out in his own manner.]

field campaign close fight die
(body to body)
fighting in open field (or)—close striking—(he)
dies

defeated horse shriek same kind
facing heaven lament
moan of meaning
The horse he leaves behind whines in sorrow
looking up to heaven

crow falcon peck at human intestines
(tombi)
(after drop) crow and falcon feed on his intestines

[generalization
very powerful expression [refers to the line on the
smeared soldiers]
2 meanings, pouring armies out, and pouring blood
out
From here is moral comment]

holding in fly up hang on decayed trees
branches
beaks
holding these in beak they fly up and perch on old
tree branches
(hang the intestines there)

soldier fellow smear on grass hay
soldiers (dead grass)
Thus all the soldiers are smeared on grasses and
bushes

commander army vacant such do
general vanity
The general (the Emperor!) does all this to no use

thereupon know weapon "thing" this
evil "utensil"
war here sign that thing
of subject
Hereupon I know this truth of the saying that
warfare is a bad means to employ
[This is a quotation from classics
for instance Roshi says that warfare is an
implement of ill omen,
not to be made use of by a wise man, unless an
unavoidable occasion

This has all along been the theory of the Chinese
about war.

This poem has no complex moral or social
reference—bare lament against Genso

But poetically have been praised by commentators
the two lines, beginning "the Huns"—they call it
clever
(crop consists of bones)

If done by weak hand such a powerful figure
would become too mechanical
(horses & crows picking often painted)]

sage man not can stop and use it
that a sage will use it only on unavoidable
occasion

[end poem]

Pound definitely saw the text for this poem. Several sheets of paper covered with scribbled lines from the poem exit among his notes at the Beinecke, but he evidently abandoned his draft before it was completed. Had Pound merely intended to compile a book of war poems, this one would have been perfect for his purposes. His ultimate reasons for abandoning it cannot be determined, but I suspect that the moralizing quality of the last several lines may have spoiled it for him. They work against his insistence on "freedom from didacticism" and presentation "without comment."

[57] Pound 93.

[58] See Appendix.

[59] Pound 93.

[60] Pound 95. The source poem for this reference is #136 in Volume 2 of the Rihaku notes (Notebook 21). Ernest Fenollosa, Notebook 21, ms., Ezra Pound Papers, Yalė U, New Haven.

[61] Ernest Fenollosa, Notebook 7, ms., Ezra Pound Papers, Yale U, New Haven.

[62] Fenollosa, Notebook 20. The draft notes for this citation and for the previous one, can be found in Notebook 15, "Chinese Poetry: Notes by Pound incl. transla."

[63] Pound 95.

[64] "An 'Image' is that which presents an intellectual and emotional complex in an instant of time. . . . It is the presentation of such a 'complex' instantaneously which gives that sense of sudden liberation; that sense of freedom from time limits and space limits; that sense of sudden growth, which we experience in the presence of the greatest works of art." Schneidau 21.

[65] Schneidau 21.

[66] Witemeyer 150.

[67] Commenting upon his own "In a Station of the Metro," Pound wrote the following: "In a poem of this sort one is trying to record the precise instant when a thing outward

and objective transforms itself, or darts into a thing inward and subjective." Yip 49.

[68] The source poem is #125, in Volume 1 of the Rihaku notes (Notebook 20). Pound's draft may be found in Notebook 15, mentioned previously.

[69] Schneidau 21.

[70] Schneidau 31.

[71] Kenner 198.

[72] Fenollosa, Notebook 21. Fenollosa himself commented, "this poem rather angular—not so smooth."

[73] Fenollosa, Notebook 21. These notes to poem #146 and the following crib notes for the text of the poem both come from this source.

[74] Yip 50.

[75] Schneidau 28.

[76] Fenollosa, Notebook 21.

[77] Pound, *Translations* 198.

[78] Schneidau 20, 24.

[79] Yip 212.

[80] Pound, *Translations* 199.

[81] Both the notes and the text for this poem, poem #148, can be found in the second Volume of the Rihaku notes (Notebook 21).

[82] Pound's essay is filed in a notebook entitled "Translations from Chinese Poetry" (Notebook 19).

[83] The source poem is #122, in Volume 1 of the Rihaku notes (Notebook 20).

[84] This note, and following notes, are taken from Fenollosa's notes to poem #122 in Volume 1 of the Rihaku notes (Notebook 20).

[85] Pound, *Translations*.

[86] Fenollosa's notes to poem #31 in the Okakura and Sogioku notebook (Notebook 17).

[87] Fenollosa's notes to poem #31 in the Okakura and Sogioku notebook (Notebook 17).

[88] Yip 49.

[89] Fenollosa, Notebook 11 (Vol. 2); notes for August 27th, 1901.

[90] The source poem is #7, in the Hirai and Shida notebook (Notebook 7). Pound's draft may be found in Notebook 15.

[91] Pound, "Chinese Poetry" 54.

[92] Fenollosa, text and notes for poem #7, in the Hirai and Shida notebook (Notebook 7).

[93] Fenollosa, text and notes for poem #7, in the Hirai and Shida notebook (Notebook 7).

[94] The source poem is #7, in the Hirai and Shida notebook (Notebook 7). Pound's typescript may be found in Notebook 15.

[95] Fenollosa, Notebook 11 (Vol. 3).

[96] Kenner 204.

[97] Pound, *Translations* 191.

[98] Yip 188.

[99] Fenollosa, Notebook 20 verso 37.

[100] Pound, *Translations* 200.

FURTHER READING

Biography

Brooks, Van Wyck. *Fenollosa and His Circle, with Other Essays in Biography*. New York: E. P. Dutton & Co., 1962, 321 p.

Details Fenollosa's life and passion for Oriental art and literature, and presents essays on Fenollosa's contemporaries Fanny Wright, John Lloyd Stephens, George Catlin, Charles Wilkes, Charles Godfrey Leland, Maurice Prendergast, and Randolph Bourne.

Criticism

Brooker, Peter. "The Lesson of Ezra Pound: An Essay in Poetry, Literary Ideology and Politics." In *Ezra Pound: Tactics for Reading,* edited by Ian F. A. Bell, pp. 221-44. Totowa, N.J.: Barnes & Noble Books, 1982.

Traces the influences on Pound's poetics, finding that Fenollosa is but one and that Guido Cavalcanti and Allen Upward are two more.

Chisholm, Lawrence W. "A Review of *Epochs of Chinese and Japanese Art: an Outline History of East Asiatic Design,* by Ernest Fenollosa." *Journal of Asian Studies* 24, No. 3 (May 1965): 504-05.

Acknowledges the importance of Fenollosa's work, while finding it flawed by the author's lack of training in archaeology and history.

Fang, Achilles. "Fenollosa and Pound." *Harvard Journal of Asiatic Studies* 20, Nos. 1 and 2 (June 1957): 213-38.
Discusses the three Fenollosa works edited posthumously by Ezra Pound, and asserts that Fenollosa's work continued to influence the younger poet throughout Pound's career.

Jin, Songping. "Fenollosa and 'Hsiao Hsueh' Tradition." *Paideuma: A Journal Devoted to Ezra Pound Scholarship* 22, Nos. 1-2 (Spring-Fall 1993): 71-97.
Coins the term "etymorhetoric" to explain Fenollosa's and Pound's intentions for language: etymology used decoratively to serve a rhetorical purpose.

Kodama, Sanehide. "'Cathay' and Fenollosa's Notebooks." *Paideuma: A Journal Devoted to Ezra Pound Scholarship* 11, No. 2 (Fall 1982): 207-40.
Relies on Fenollosa's original notebooks to defend him from charges that they are full of errors, and to assert that Ezra Pound rewrote Fenollosa's translations to match Pound's philosophy.

Londraville, Richard. "Fenollosa and the Legacy of Stone Cottage." *Paideuma: A Journal Devoted to Ezra Pound Scholarship* 22, No. 3 (Winter 1993): 101-08.
Focuses on the influence of Fenollosa's notebooks on Ezra Pound, finding that the results are significantly different than on W. B. Yeats's adaptations of the same material.

Miyaye, Akiko. "Contemplation East and West: A Defense of Fenollosa's Synthetic Language and Its Influence on Ezra Pound." *Paideuma: A Journal Devoted to Ezra Pound Scholarship* 10, No. 3 (Winter 1981): 533-70.
Proposes that Pound's analyses of Fenollosa's theories on Chinese writing are incorrect because Pound failed to understand Fenollosa's Buddhist faith.

Tsukui, Nobuko. *Ezra Pound and Japanese Noh Plays*. Washington, D.C.: University Press of America, 1983, 120 p.
Includes a discussion of Fenollosa and Noh theater.

Zong-Qi, Cai. "Poundian and Chinese Aesthetics of Dynamic Force: A Re-discovery of Fenollosa and Pound's 'Theory of the Chinese Written Character'." *Comparative Literature Studies* 30, No. 2 (1993): 170-87.
Attempts to find a middle ground between acceptance and dismissal of Pound and Fenollosa's theories by critics, and finds that Pound and Fenollosa did overstate their claims for Chinese characters, but that they also captured dynamic qualities of Chinese language.

Alfred Kinsey

1894-1956

(Full name Alfred Charles Kinsey) American scientist.

INTRODUCTION

Kinsey is considered a pioneer in the scientific study of human sexuality, and his two major works—*Sexual Behavior in the Human Male* and *Sexual Behavior in the Human Female*—resulted in much controversy and debate upon their publication. Known collectively as *The Kinsey Report*, these works represent the first attempt to apply scientific methodology to human sexuality. Kinsey combined more than 18,000 interviews with United States citizens of varying economic and racial backgrounds and hypothesized that a person's socioeconomic background contributed to their sexual behavior. Furthermore, Kinsey concluded that human sexuality was far more varied than commonly believed at the time. Kinsey's empirical approach to collecting and translating his data caused many detractors to find his work prurient. However, many of his detractors and supporters both continue to attribute the sexual revolution of the 1960s and 1970s in part to Kinsey's groundbreaking work.

Biographical Information

Born in Hoboken, New Jersey, Kinsey was the son of an instructor at Stevens Institute of Technology and a mother who had little education. Both parents were deeply religious, and passed on their beliefs to Alfred, who suffered from rickets, typhoid, and rheumatic fever. Encouraged by his high school biology teacher, Natalie Roeth, Kinsey conducted nature excursions and collected botanical samples. He wrote his first scientific paper for Roeth, entitled "What Do Birds Do when It Rains?" and corresponded with her throughout his life. After high school, he attended Stevens Institute to study mechanical engineering. Two years later, he transferred to Bowdoin College in Maine, graduating magna cum laude in 1916, and entered Harvard University as an assistant in zoology. Upon his graduation in 1920, Kinsey was named assistant professor of zoology at Indiana University. He was associated with the university for the remainder of his life, and he became a full professor in 1929. During the 1920s and '30s, Kinsey focused his entomological and taxonomical research on the gall wasp, which resulted in the respected works *The Gall Wasp Genus Neuroterus* and *The Gall Wasp Genus Cynips: A Study in the Origin of Species.* He also authored the textbooks *Introduction to Biology* and *Workbook in Biology,* and conducted research expeditions in Mexico and Central America during the 1930s. An assignment to teach a class on marriage in 1938 led Kinsey to begin researching human sexuality. Disappointed that most of the existing source material contained obvious inaccuracies, he designed his own questionnaire, which he believed would provide a scientific, biological basis for the existing conclusions. Shortly thereafter, he began conducting personal interviews with his subjects, finding the data from these interviews to be more easily interpretable than data from questionnaires. His diligence in researching during this period caused his wife to remark of her husband, "I hardly see him at night any more since he took up sex." Soliciting the support of the National Research Council, the Rockefeller Foundation, and Indiana University, Kinsey established the Institute of Sex Research in Bloomington, Indiana. *The Kinsey Report*'s notoriety cost Kinsey his funding from the Rockefeller Foundation, drew attacks from such religious leaders as Billy Graham, and caused him to be labeled a political subversive intent on undermining American morality. He continued his research despite the lack of funding until his death from pneumonia and heart complications in 1956.

Major Works

Applying the same techniques he used to study gall wasps to study human sexuality, Kinsey and his colleagues, Wardell Pomeroy, Paul Gebhard, and Clyde Martin, amassed large quantities of data culled from extensive interviews for *The Kinsey Report.* The first study revealed that extramarital and premarital sex were more common then previously believed, that most males masturbated, that masturbation did not result in mental illness, and that one in three men had at least one homosexual encounter in their lifetime. The female study revealed that frigidity was not as common as previouşly believed and that female erotic response was comparable to the male response; the study included a lengthy, graphic, controversial narrative comparing clitoral and vaginal orgasms. Each interview was classified according to the type of person being interviewed and the sexual behavior they discussed. While some scientists and critics distrust Kinsey's methodology and conclusions, *The Kinsey Report* is widely considered among scientists and sociologists to be an important work due to its frank approach to human sexuality, which dispelled many common misconceptions about sex.

PRINCIPAL WORKS

An Introduction to Biology (textbook) 1926
The Gall Wasp Genus Cynips: A Study in the Origin of the Species (nonfiction) 1930
The Origin of Higher Categories in Cynips (nonfiction) 1936
Sexual Behavior in the Human Male [with W. B. Pomeroy and C. E. Martin] (nonfiction) 1948
Sexual Behavior in the Human Female [with W. B. Pomeroy and C. E. Martin] (nonfiction) 1953

CRITICISM

Sociology and Social Research (essay date 1948)

SOURCE: A review of "Sexual Behavior in the Human Male", by Alfred Kinsey, in *Sociology and Social Research,* Vol. 32, No. 4, March-April, 1948, pp.

[*In the following review of Kinsey's* Sexual Behavior in the Human Male, *the critic commends Kinsey's research and findings, and declares the work necessary for overhauling the nation's previous works on sexuality and marriage.*]

Called by one of the newsweeklies a "shocker in sex" and touted by columnist Winchell, ***Sexual Behavior in the Human Male*** this scientific study of the sexual behavior of the male by three Indiana University scientists promises to become a best seller. One fortunate aspect of this is that it will be read by many who would otherwise avoid it. Certainly, physicians, psychiatrists, judges, administrators of both educational and penal institutions, officials in the Army and Navy, and social scientists will find in it a wealth of vitally useful material.

Presented as the objective factual study of sexual behavior that it is, the book reports the results of a nine-year survey, with 12,000 persons, representing every age, every social level, and several racial groups, who were interviewed by the authors and their staff of assistants. Funds from the Rockefeller Foundation provided a major portion of the cost of the survey. The study should demonstrate what well-conducted, scientifically organized research in the social sciences can do for the community and society. In particular, it reveals the necessity for a re-evaluation and overhauling of sex education, for a more scientific outlook in dealing with sex matters, and for better procedures in advisement on sexual adjustments. Many preconceptions regarding so-called "normal" sex activities are knocked into a cocked hat. It is possible that this study has made obsolete many of the discussions on sex and marital life now found in texts on marriage and the family.

Some of the findings are (1) patterns of sexual behavior reflect largely the pattern of the particular social level to which an individual belongs; (2) codes of morals, social and religious systems, sex laws have been built upon the false assumption that individuals are much alike sexually, and even scientific discussions of sex show little understanding of the range of variation in human behavior; (3) case histories abundantly demonstrate that most individuals who engage in taboo activities make satisfactory social adjustments, the taboo activities being often an expression of what is biologically basic in mammalian and anthropoid behavior and of a deliberate disregard for social convention; (4) only half of the male population shows exclusively heterosexual behavior, and but a few per cent exclusively homosexual; (5) nearly 85 per cent of all males have premarital sexual relations by the time they are 20, with the most active sexual period coming during adolescence; (6) by the age of 15 about 92 per cent of males have had some kind of sexual activity; and (7) prostitution patronage has fallen from about one half to two thirds of what it was thirty years ago.

Finally, the volume is noteworthy because of its revealing methodological notes. The chapter on the use of the interview is one of the most sensible and clear-cut descriptions of that method yet written. Another ten years will elapse before the entire study will be completed. Next to appear will be the results of the survey of the sexual behavior of the female, some of the aspects of which may be detected in the volume at hand.

Lionel Trilling (essay date 1948)

SOURCE: "The Kinsey Report," in *The Liberal Imagination: Essays on Literature and Society,* Harcourt Brace Jovanovich, 1979, pp. 210-28.

[In the following essay, originally published in 1948, Trilling identifies Kinsey's work as an enlightening tool to break down cultural repression of humankind's primal and universal sexual consciousness.]

By virtue of its intrinsic nature and also because of its dramatic reception, the ***Kinsey Report,***[1] as it has come to be called, is an event of great importance in our culture. It is an event which is significant in two separate ways, as symptom and as therapy. The therapy lies in the large permissive effect the Report is likely to have, the long way it goes toward establishing the *community* of sexuality. The symptomatic significance lies in the fact that the Report was felt to be needed at all, that the community of sexuality requires now to be established in explicit quantitative terms. Nothing shows more clearly the extent to which modern society has atomized itself than the isolation in sexual ignorance which exists among us. We have censored the folk knowledge of the most primal things and have systematically dried up the social affections which might naturally seek to enlighten and release. Many cultures, the most primitive and the most complex, have entertained sexual fears of an irrational sort, but probably our culture is unique in strictly isolating the individual in the fears that society has devised. Now, having become somewhat aware of what we have perpetrated at great cost and with little gain, we must assure ourselves by statistical science that the solitude is imaginary. The Report will surprise one part of the population with some facts and another part with other facts, but really all that it says to society as a whole is that there is an almost universal involvement in the sexual life and therefore much variety of conduct. This was taken for granted in any comedy that Aristophanes put on the stage.

There is a further diagnostic significance to be found in the fact that our society makes this effort of self-enlightenment through the agency of science. Sexual conduct is inextricably involved with morality, and hitherto it has been dealt with by those representatives of our cultural imagination which are, by their nature and tradition, committed to morality—it has been dealt with by religion, social philosophy, and literature. But now science seems to be the only one of our institutions which has the authority to speak decisively on the matter. Nothing in the Report is more suggestive in a large cultural way than the insistent claims it makes for its strictly scientific nature, its pledge of indifference to all questions of morality at the same time that it patently intends a moral effect. Nor will any science do for the job—it must be a science as simple and materialistic as the subject can possibly permit. It must be a science of statistics and not of ideas. The way for the Report was prepared by Freud, but Freud, in all the years of his activity, never had the currency or authority with the public that the Report has achieved in a matter of weeks.

The scientific nature of the Report must be taken in conjunction with the manner of its publication. The Report says of itself that it is only a "preliminary survey," a work intended to be the first step in a larger research; that it is nothing more than an "accumulation of scientific fact," a collection of "objective data," a "report on what people do, which raises no question of what they should do," and it is fitted out with a full complement of charts, tables, and discussions of scientific method. A work conceived and executed in this way is usually presented only to an audience of professional scientists; and the publishers of the Report, a medical house, pay their ritual respects to the old tradition which held that not all medical or quasi-medical knowledge was to made easily available to the general lay reader, or at least not until it had been subjected to professional debate; they tell us in a foreword for what limited professional audience the book was primarily intended—physicians, biologists, and social scientists and "teachers, social workers, personnel officers, law enforcement groups, and others concerned with the direction of human behavior." And yet the book has been so successfully publicized that for many weeks it was a national best seller.

This way of bringing out a technical work of science is a cultural phenomenon that ought not to pass without some question. The public which receives this technical report, this merely preliminary survey, this accumulation of data, has never, even on its upper educational levels, been properly instructed in the most elementary principles of scientific thought. With this public, science is authority. It has been trained to accept heedlessly "what science says," which it conceives to be a unitary utterance. To this public nothing is more valuable, more precisely "scientific," and more finally convincing than raw data without conclusions; no disclaimer of conclusiveness can mean anything to it—it has learned that the disclaimer is simply the hallmark of the scientific attitude, science's way of saying "thy unworthy servant."

So that if the Report were really, as it claims to be, only an accumulation of objective data, there would be some question of the cultural wisdom of dropping it in a lump on the general public. But in point of fact it is full of assumption and conclusion; it makes very positive statements on highly debatable matters and it editorializes very freely. This preliminary survey gives some very conclusive suggestions to a public that is quick to obey what science says, no matter how contradictory science may be, which is most contradictory indeed. This is the public that, on scientific advice, ate spinach in one generation and avoided it in the next, that in one decade trained its babies to rigid Watsonian schedules and believed that affection corrupted the infant character, only to learn in the next decade that rigid discipline was harmful and that cuddling was as scientific as induction.

Then there is the question of whether the Report does not do harm by encouraging people in their commitment to mechanical attitudes toward life. The tendency to divorce sex from the other manifestations of life is already a strong one. This truly absorbing study of sex in charts and tables, in data and quantities, may have the effect of strengthening the tendency still more with people who are by no means trained to invert the process of abstraction and to put the fact back into the general life from which it has been taken. And the likely mechanical implications of a statistical study are in this case supported by certain fully formulated attitudes which the authors strongly hold despite their protestations that they are scientific to the point of holding no attitudes whatever.

These, I believe, are valid objections to the book's indiscriminate circulation. And yet I also believe that there is something good about the manner of publication, something honest and right. Every complex society has its agencies which are "concerned with the direction of human behavior," but we today are developing a new element in that old activity, the element of scientific knowledge. Whatever the Report claims for itself, the social sciences in general no longer pretend that they can merely describe what people do; they now have the clear consciousness of their power to manipulate and adjust. First for industry and then for government, sociology has shown its instrumental nature. A government which makes use of social knowledge still suggests benignity; and in an age that daily brings the proliferation of government by police methods it may suggest the very spirit of rational liberalism. Yet at least one sociologist has expressed the fear that sociology may become the instrument of a bland tyranny—it is the same fear that Dostoevski gave immortal expression to in "The Grand Inquisitor." And indeed there is something repulsive in the idea of men being studied for their own good. The paradigm of what repels us is to be found in the common situation of the child who is *understood* by its parents, hemmed in, anticipated and lovingly circumscribed, thoroughly taped, finding it easier and easier to conform internally and in the future to the parents' own interpretation of the external acts of the past, and so, yielding to understanding as never to coercion, does not develop the mystery and wildness of spirit which it is still our grace to believe is the mark of full humanness. The act of understanding becomes an act of control.

If, then, we are to live under the aspect of sociology, let us at least all be sociologists together—let us broadcast what every sociologist knows, and let us all have a share in observing one another, including the sociologists. The general indiscriminate publication of the Report makes sociology a little less the study of many men by a few men and a little more man's study of himself. There is something right in turning loose the Report on the American public—it turns the American public loose on the Report. It is right that the Report should be sold in stores that never before sold books and bought by people who never before bought books, and passed from hand to hand and talked about and also snickered at and giggled over and generally submitted to humor: American popular culture has surely been made the richer by the Report's gift of a new folk hero—he already is clearly the hero of the Report—the "scholarly and skilled lawyer" who for thirty years has had an orgasmic frequency of thirty times a week.

As for the objection to the involvement of sex with science, it may be said that if science, through the Report, serves in any way to free the physical and even the "mechanical" aspects of sex, it may by that much have acted to free the emotions it might seem to deny. And perhaps only science could effectively undertake the task of freeing sexuality from science itself. Nothing so much as science has reinforced the moralistic or religious prohibitions in regard to sexuality. At some point in the history of Europe, some time in the Reformation, masturbation ceased to be thought of as merely a sexual sin which could be dealt with like any other sexual sin, and, perhaps by analogy with the venereal diseases with which the sexual mind of Europe was obsessed, came to be thought of as the specific cause of mental and physical disease, of madness and decay.[2] The prudery of Victorian England went forward with scientific hygiene; and both in Europe and in America the sexual mind was haunted by the idea of *degeneration,* apparently by analogy with the second law of thermodynamics—here is enlightened liberal opinion in 1896: "The effects of venereal disease have been treated at length, but the amount of vitality burned out through lust has never been and, perhaps, never can be adequately measured."[3] The very word *sex,* which we now utter so casually, came into use for scientific reasons, to replace *love,* which had once been indiscriminately used but was now to be saved for ideal purposes, and *lust,* which came to seem both too pejorative and too human: *sex* implied scientific neutrality, then vague devaluation, for the word which neutralizes the mind of the observer also neuterizes the men and women who are being observed. Perhaps the Report is the superfetation of neutrality and objectivity which, in the dialectic of culture, was needed before sex could be free of their cold dominion.

Certainly it is a great merit of the Report that it brings to mind the earliest and best commerce between sex and science—the best thing about the Report is the quality that makes us remember Lucretius. The dialectic of culture has its jokes, and *alma Venus* having once been called to preside protectively over science, the situation is now reversed. The Venus of the Report does not, like the Venus of *De Rerum Natura,* shine in the light of the heavenly signs, nor does the earth put forth flowers for her. She is rather fusty and hole-in-the-corner and no doubt it does not help her charm to speak of her in terms of mean frequencies of 3.2. No *putti* attend her: although Dr. Gregg in his Preface refers to sex as the reproductive instinct, there is scarcely any further indication in the book that sex has any connection with propagation. Yet clearly all things still follow where she leads, and somewhere in the authors' assumptions is buried the genial belief that still without her "nothing comes forth into shining borders of light, nothing joyous and lovely is made." Her pandemic quality is still here—it is one of the great points of the Report how much of every kind of desire there is, how early it begins, how late it lasts. Her well-known jealousy is not abated, and prodigality is still her characteristic virtue: the Report assures us that those who respond to her earliest continue to do so longest.

The Lucretian flocks and herds are here too. Professor Kinsey is a zoologist and he properly keeps us always in mind of our animal kinship, even though he draws some very illogical conclusions from it; and those who are honest will have to admit that their old repulsion by the idea of human-animal contacts is somewhat abated by the chapter on this subject, which is, oddly, the only chapter in the book which hints that sex may be touched with tenderness. This large, recognizing, Lucretian sweep of the Report is the best thing about it and it makes up for much that is deficient and confused in its ideas.

But the Report is something more than a public and symbolic act of cultural revision in which, while the Heavenly Twins brood benignly over the scene in the form of the National Research Council and the Rockefeller Foundation, Professor Kinsey and his coadjutors drag forth into the light all the hidden actualities of sex so that they may lose their dark power and become domesticated among us. It is also an early example of science undertaking to deal head-on with a uniquely difficult matter that has traditionally been involved in valuation and morality. We must ask the question very seriously: how does science conduct itself in such an enterprise?

Certainly it does not conduct itself the way it says it does. I have already suggested that the Report overrates its own objectivity. The authors, who are enthusiastically committed to their method and to their principles, make the mistake of believing that, being scientists, they do not deal in assumptions, preferences, and conclusions. Nothing comes more easily to their pens than the criticism of the subjectivity of earlier writers on sex, yet their own subjectivity is sometimes extreme. In the nature of the enterprise, a degree of subjectivity was inevitable. Intellectual safety would then seem to lie not only in increasing the number of mechanical checks or in more rigorously examining those assumptions which had been brought to conscious formulation, but also in straightforwardly admitting that subjectivity was bound to appear and inviting the reader to be on the watch for it. This would not have guaranteed an absolute objectivity, but it would have made for a higher degree of relative objectivity. It would have done a thing even more important—it would have taught the readers of the Report something about the scientific processes to which they submit their thought.

The first failure of objectivity occurs in the title of the Report, ***Sexual Behavior in the Human Male.*** That the behavior which is studied is not that of the human male but only that of certain North American males has no doubt been generally observed and does not need further comment.[4] But the intention of the word *behavior* requires notice. By *behavior* the Report means behavioristic behavior, only that behavior which is physical. "To a large degree the present study has been confined to securing a record of the individual's overt sexual experiences." This limitation is perhaps forced on the authors by considerations of method, because it will yield simpler data and more manageable statistics, but it is also a limitation which suits their notion of human nature and its effect is to be seen throughout the book.

The Report, then, is a study of sexual behavior in so far as it can be quantitatively measured. This is certainly very useful. But, as we might fear, the sexuality that is measured is taken to be the definition of sexuality itself. The authors are certainly not without interest in what they call attitudes, but they believe that attitudes are best shown by "overt sexual experiences." We want to know, of course, what they mean by an experience and we want to know by what principles of evidence they draw their conclusions about attitudes.

We are led to see that their whole conception of a sexual experience is totally comprised by the physical act and that their principles of evidence are entirely quantitative and cannot carry them beyond the conclusion that the more the merrier. Quality is not integral to what they mean by experience. As I have suggested, the Report is partisan with sex, it wants people to have a good sexuality. But by good it means nothing else but frequent. "It seems safe to assume that daily orgasm would be within the capacity of the average male and that the more than daily rates which have been observed for some primate species could be matched by a large portion of the human population if sexual activity were unrestricted." The Report never suggests that a sexual experience is anything but the discharge of specifically sexual tension and therefore seems to conclude that frequency is always the sign of a robust sexuality. Yet masturbation in children may be and often is the expression not of sexuality only but of anxiety. In the same way, adult intercourse may be the expression of anxiety; its frequency may not be so much robust as compulsive.

The Report is by no means unaware of the psychic conditions of sexuality, yet it uses the concept almost always under the influence of its quantitative assumption. In a summary passage (p. 159) it describes the different intensities of orgasm and the various degrees of satisfaction, but disclaims any intention of taking these variations into account in its record of behavior. The Report holds out the hope to respectable males that they might be as frequent in performance as underworld characters if they were as unrestrained as this group. But before the respectable males aspire to this unwonted freedom they had better ascertain in how far the underworld characters are ridden by anxiety and in how far their sexuality is to be correlated with other ways of dealing with anxiety, such as dope, and in how far it is actually enjoyable. The Report's own data suggest that there may be no direct connection between on the one hand lack of restraint and frequency and on the other hand psychic health; they tell us of men in the lower social levels who in their sexual careers have intercourse with many hundreds of girls but who despise their sexual partners and cannot endure relations with the same girl more than once.

But the Report, as we shall see, is most resistant to the possibility of making any connection between the sexual life and the psychic structure. This strongly formulated attitude of the Report is based on the assumption that the whole actuality of sex is anatomical and physiological; the emotions are dealt with very much as if they were a "superstructure." "The subject's awareness of the erotic situation is summed up by this statement that he is 'emotionally' aroused; but the material sources of the emotional disturbance are rarely recognized, either by laymen or scientists, both of whom are inclined to think in terms of passion, or natural drive, or a libido, which partakes of the mystic[5] more than it does of solid anatomy and physiologic function." Now there is of course a clear instrumental advantage in being able to talk about psychic or emotional phenomena in terms of physiology, but to make a disjunction between the two descriptions of the same event, to make the anatomical and physiological description the "source" of the emotional and then to consider it as the more real of the two, is simply to commit not only the Reductive Fallacy but also what William James called the Psychologist's Fallacy. It must bring under suspicion any subsequent generalization which the Report makes about the nature of sexuality.[6]

The emphasis on the anatomical and physiological nature of sexuality is connected with the Report's strong reliance on animal behavior as a norm. The italics in the following quotation are mine. "*For those who like the term,* it is clear that there is a sexual drive which cannot be set aside for any large portion of the population, by any sort of social convention. *For those who prefer to think in simpler terms of action and reaction,* it is a picture of an animal who, however civilized or cultured, continues to respond to the constantly present sexual stimuli, albeit with some social and physical restraints." The Report obviously finds the second formulation to be superior to the first, and implies with a touch of irony that those who prefer it are on firmer ground.

Now there are several advantages in keeping in mind our own animal nature and our family connection with the other animals. The advantages are instrumental, moral, and poetic—I use the last word for want of a better to suggest the mere pleasure in finding kinship with some animals. But perhaps no idea is more difficult to use with precision than this one. In the Report it is used to establish a dominating principle of judgment, which is the Natural. As a concept of judgment this is notoriously deceptive and has been belabored for generations, but the Report knows nothing of its dangerous reputation and uses it with the naïvest confidence. And although the Report directs the harshest language toward the idea of the Normal, saying that it has stood in the way of any true scientific knowledge of sex, it is itself by no means averse to letting the idea of the Natural develop quietly into the idea of the Normal. The Report has in mind both a physical normality—as suggested by its belief that under optimal conditions men should be able to achieve the orgasmic frequency of the primates—and a moral normality, the acceptability, on the authority of animal behavior, of certain usually taboo practices.

It is inevitable that the concept of the Natural should haunt any discussion of sex. It is inevitable that it should make trouble, but most of all for a scientific discussion that bars judgments of value. Thus, in order to show that homosexuality is not a neurotic manifestation, as the Freudians say it is, the Report adduces the homosexual behavior of rats. But the argument *de animalibus* must surely stand by its ability to be inverted and extended. Thus, in having lost sexual periodicity, has the human animal lost naturalness? Again, the female mink, as we learn from the Report itself, fiercely resists intercourse and must be actually coerced into submission. Is it she who is unnatural or is her defense of her chastity to be taken as a comment on the females, animal or human, who willingly submit or who merely play at escape? Professor Kinsey is like no one so much as Sir Percival in Malory, who, seeing a lion and a serpent in battle with each other, decided to help the lion, "for he was the more natural beast of the two."

This awkwardness in the handling of ideas is characteristic of the Report. It is ill at ease with any idea that is in the least complex and it often tries to get rid of such an idea in favor of another that has the appearance of not going beyond the statement of physical fact. We see this especially in the handling of certain Freudian ideas. The Report acknowledges its debt to Freud with the generosity of spirit that marks it in other connections and it often makes use of Freudian concepts in a very direct and sensible way. Yet nothing could be clumsier than its handling of Freud's idea of pregenital generalized infantile sexuality. Because the Report can show, what is interesting and significant, that infants are capable of actual orgasm, although without ejaculation, it concludes that infantile sexuality is not generalized but specifically genital. But actually it has long been known, though the fact of orgasm had not been established, that infants can respond erotically to direct genital stimulation, and this knowledge does not contradict the Freudian idea that there is a stage in infant development in which sexuality is generalized throughout the body rather than specifically centered in the genital area; the fact of infant orgasm must be interpreted in conjunction with other and more complex manifestations of infant sexuality.[7]

The Report, we may say, has an extravagant fear of all ideas that do not seem to it to be, as it were, immediately dictated by simple physical fact. Another way of saying this is that the Report is resistant to any idea that seems to refer to a specifically human situation. An example is the position it takes on the matter of male potency. The folk feeling, where it is formulated on the question, and certainly where it is formulated by women, holds that male potency is not to be measured, as the Report measures it, merely by frequency, but by the ability to withhold orgasm long enough to bring the woman to climax. This is also the psychoanalytic view, which holds further that the inability to sustain intercourse is the result of unconscious fear or resentment. This view is very strongly resisted by the Report. The denial is based on mammalian behavior—"in many species" (but not in all?) ejaculation follows almost immediately upon intromission; in chimpanzees ejaculation occurs in ten to twenty seconds. The Report therefore concludes that the human male who ejaculates immediately upon intromission "is quite normal [here the word becomes suddenly permissible] among mammals and usual among his own species." Indeed, the Report finds it odd that the term "impotent" should be applied to such rapid responses. "It would be difficult to find another situation in which an individual who was quick and intense in his responses was labeled anything but superior, and that in most instances is exactly what the rapidly ejaculating male probably is, however inconvenient and unfortunate his qualities may be from the standpoint of the wife in the relationship."

But by such reasoning the human male who is quick and intense in his leap to the lifeboat is natural and superior, however inconvenient and unfortunate his speed and intensity may be to the wife he leaves standing on the deck, as is also the man who makes a snap judgment, who bites his dentist's finger, who kicks the child who annoys him, who bolts his—or another's—food, who is incontinent of his feces. Surely the problem of the natural in the human was solved four centuries ago by Rabelais, and in the simplest naturalistic terms; and it is sad to have the issue all confused again by the naïveté of men of science. Rabelais' solution lay in the simple perception of the *natural* ability and tendency of man to grow in the direction of organization and control. The young Gargantua in his natural infancy had all the quick and intense responses just enumerated; had his teachers confused the traits of his natural infancy with those of his natural manhood, he would not have been the more natural but the less; he would have been a monster.

In considering the Report as a major cultural document, we must not underestimate the significance of its petulant protest against the inconvenience to the male of the unjust demand that is made upon him. This protest is tantamount to saying that sexuality is not to be involved in specifically human situations or to be connected with desirable aims that are conceived of in specifically human terms. We may leave out of account any ideal reasons which would lead a man to solve the human situation of the discrepancy—arising from conditions of biology or of culture or of both—between his own orgasmic speed and that of his mate, and we can consider only that it might be hedonistically desirable for him to do so, for advantages presumably accrue to him in the woman's accessibility and responsiveness. Advantages of this kind, however, are precisely the matters of quality in experience that the Report ignores.[8]

And its attitude on the question of male potency is but one example of the Report's insistence on drawing sexuality apart from the general human context. It is striking how small a role woman plays in ***Sexual Behavior in the Human Male.*** We learn nothing about the connection of sex and reproduction; the connection, from the sexual point of view, is certainly not constant yet it is of great interest. The pregnancy or possibility of pregnancy of his mate has a considerable effect, sometimes one way, sometimes the other, on the sexual behavior of the male; yet in the index under *Pregnancy* there is but a single entry—*"fear of."* Again, the contraceptive devices which *Pregnancy, fear of,* requires have a notable influence on male sexuality; but the index lists only *Contraception, techniques.* Or again, menstruation has an elaborate mythos which men take very seriously; but the two indexed passages which refer to menstruation give no information about its relation to sexual conduct.

Then too the Report explicitly and stubbornly resists the idea that sexual behavior is involved with the whole of the individual's character. In this it is strangely inconsistent. In the conclusion of its chapter on masturbation, after saying that masturbation does no physical harm and, if there are no conflicts over it, no mental harm, it goes on to raise the question of the effect of adult masturbation on the ultimate personality of the individual. With a certain confusion of cause and effect which we need not dwell on, it says: "It is now clear that masturbation is relied upon by the upper [social] level primarily because it has insufficient outlet through heterosexual coitus. This is, to a degree, an escape from reality, and the effect upon the ultimate personality of the individual is something that needs consideration." The question is of course a real one, yet the Report strenuously refuses to extend the principle of it to any other sexual activity. It summarily rejects the conclusions of psychoanalysis which make the sexual conduct an important clue to, even the crux of, character. It finds the psychoanalytical view unacceptable for two reasons: (1) The psychiatric practitioner misconceives the relation between sexual aberrancy and psychic illness because only those sexually aberrant people who are ill seek out the practitioner, who therefore never learns about the large incidence of mental health among the sexually aberrant. (2) The emotional illness which sends the sexually aberrant person to find psychiatric help is the result of no flaw in the psyche itself that is connected with the aberrancy but is the result only of the fear of social disapproval of his sexual conduct. And the Report instances the many men who are well adjusted socially and who yet break, among them, all the sexual taboos.

The quality of the argument which the Report here advances is as significant as the wrong conclusions it reaches. "It is not possible," the Report says, "to insist that any departure from the sexual mores, or any participation in socially taboo activities, always, or even usually, involves a neurosis or psychosis, for the case histories abundantly demonstrate that most individuals who engage in taboo activities make satisfactory social adjustments." In this context either "neuroses and psychoses" are too loosely used to stand for all psychic maladjustment, or "social adjustment" is too loosely used to stand for emotional peace and psychic stability. When the Report goes on to cite the "socially and intellectually significant persons," the "successful scientists, educators, physicians," etc., who have among them "accepted the whole range of the so-called abnormalities," we must keep in mind that very intense emotional disturbance, known only to the sufferer, can go along with the efficient discharge of social duties, and that the psychoanalyst could counter with as long a list of distinguished and efficient people who do consult him.

Then, only an interest in attacking straw men could have led the Report to insist that psychoanalysis is wrong in saying that *any* departure from sexual mores, or *any* participation in sexually taboo activities, involves a neurosis or a psychosis, for psychoanalysis holds nothing like this view. It is just at this point that distinctions are needed of a sort which the Report seems not to want to make. For example: the Report comes out in a bold and simple way for the naturalness and normality and therefore for the desirability of mouth-genital contacts in heterosexual love-making. This is a form of sexual expression which is officially taboo enough, yet no psychoanalyst would say that its practice indicated a neurosis or psychosis. But a psychoanalyst would say that a person who disliked or was unable to practice any other form of sexual contact thereby gave evidence of a neurotic strain in his psychic constitution. His social adjustment, in the rather crude terms which the Report conceives of it, might not be impaired, but certainly the chances are that his psychic life would show signs of disturbance, not from the practice itself but from the psychic needs which made him insist on it. It is not the breaking of the taboo but the emotional circumstance of the breaking of the taboo that is significant.

The Report handles in the same oversimplified way and with the same confusing use of absolute concepts the sexual aberrancy which is, I suppose, the most complex and the most important in our cultural life, homosexuality. It rejects the view that homosexuality is innate and that "no modification of it may be expected." But then it goes on also to reject the view that homosexuality provides evidence of a "psychopathic personality." "Psychopathic personality" is a very strong term which perhaps few analysts would wish to use in this connection. Perhaps even the term "neurotic" would be extreme in a discussion which, in the manner of the Report, takes "social adjustment," as indicated by status, to be the limit of its analysis of character. But this does not leave the discussion where the Report seems to want to leave it—at the idea that homosexuality is to be accepted as a form of sexuality like another and that it is as "natural" as heterosexuality, a judgment to which the Report is led in part because of the surprisingly large incidence of homosexuality it finds in the population. Nor does the practice of "an increasing proportion of the most skilled psychiatrists who make no attempt to redirect behavior, but who devote their attention to helping an individual accept himself" imply what the Report seems to want it to, that these psychiatrists have thereby judged homosexuality to be an unexceptionable form of sexuality; it is rather that, in many cases, they are able to effect no change in the psychic disposition and therefore do the sensible and humane next best thing. Their opinion of the etiology of homosexuality as lying in some warp—as our culture judges it—of the psychic structure has not, I believe, changed. And I think that they would say that the condition that produced the homosexuality also produces other character traits on which judgment could be passed. This judgment need by no means be totally adverse; as passed upon individuals it need not be adverse at all; but there can be no doubt that a society in which homosexuality was dominant or even accepted would be different in nature and quality from one in which it was censured.

That the Report refuses to hold this view of homosexuality, or any other view of at least equivalent complexity, leads us to take into account the motives that animate the work, and when we do, we see how very characteristically *American* a document the Report is. In speaking of its motives, I have in mind chiefly its impulse toward acceptance and liberation, its broad and generous desire for others that they be not harshly judged. Much in the Report is to be understood as having been dictated by a recoil from the crude and often brutal rejection which society has made of the persons it calls sexually aberrant. The Report has the intention of habituating its readers to sexuality in all its manifestations; it wants to establish, as it were, a democratic pluralism of sexuality. And this good impulse toward acceptance and liberation is not unique with the Report but very often shows itself in those parts of our intellectual life which are more or less official and institutionalized. It is, for example, far more established in the universities than most of us with our habits of criticism of America, particularly of American universities, will easily admit; and it is to a considerable extent an established attitude with the foundations that support intellectual projects.

That this generosity of mind is much to be admired goes without saying. But when we have given it all the credit it deserves as a sign of something good and enlarging in American life, we cannot help observing that it is often associated with an almost intentional intellectual weakness. It goes with a nearly conscious aversion from making intellectual distinctions, almost as if out of the belief that an intellectual distinction must inevitably lead to a social discrimination or exclusion. We might say that those who most explicitly assert and wish to practice the democratic virtues have taken it as their assumption that all social facts—with the exception of exclusion and economic hardship—must be *accepted,* not merely in the scientific sense but also in the social sense, in the sense, that is, that no judgment must be passed on them, that any conclusion drawn from them which perceives values and consequences will turn out to be "undemocratic."

The Report has it in mind to raise questions about the official restrictive attitudes toward sexual behavior, including those attitudes that are formulated on the statute books of most states. To this end it accumulates facts with the intention of showing that standards of judgment of sexual conduct as they now exist do not have real reference to the actual sexual behavior of the population. So far, so good. But then it goes on to imply that there can be only one standard for the judgment of sexual behavior—that is, sexual behavior as it actually exists; which is to say that sexual behavior is not to be judged at all, except, presumably, in so far as it causes pain to others. (But from its attitude to the "inconvenience" of the "wife in the relationship," we must presume that not all pain is to be reckoned with.) Actually the Report does not stick to its own standard of judgment; it is, as I have shown, sometimes very willing to judge among behaviors. But the preponderant weight of its argument is that a fact is a physical fact, to be considered only in its physical aspect and apart from any idea or ideal that might make it a social fact, as having no ascertainable personal or cultural meaning and no possible consequences—as being, indeed, not available to social interpretation at all. In short, the Report by its primitive conception of the nature of fact quite negates the importance and even the existence of sexuality as a social fact. That is why, although it is possible to say of the Report that it brings light, it is necessary to say of it that it spreads confusion.

NOTES

[1] *Sexual Behavior in the Human Male,* by Alfred C. Kinsey, Wardell B. Pomeroy, and Clyde E. Martin. Philadelphia: Saunders, 1948.

[2] See Abram Kardiner, *The Psychological Frontiers of Society,* p. 32 and the footnote on p. 441.

[3] Article "Degeneration" in *The Encyclopedia of Social Reform.*

[4] The statistical method of the report lies, necessarily, outside my purview. Nor am I able to assess with any confidence the validity of the interviewing methods that were employed.

[5] We must observe how the scientific scorn of the "mystic" quite abates when the "mystic" suits the scientist's purpose. The Report is explaining why the interviews were not checked by means of narcosynthesis, lie-detectors, etc.: "In any such study which needs to secure quantities of data from human subjects, there is no way except to win their voluntary cooperation through the establishment of that intangible thing known as rapport." This intangible thing is established by looking the respondent squarely in the eye. It might be asked why a thing which is intangible but real enough to assure scientific accuracy should not be real enough to be considered as having an effect in sexual behavior.

[6] The implications of the Reductive Fallacy may be seen by paraphrasing the sentence I have quoted in which Professor Kinsey commits it: "Professor Kinsey's awareness of the intellectual situation is summed up by his statement that he 'has had an idea' or 'has come to a conclusion'; but the material sources of his intellectual disturbances are rarely recognized, either by laymen or scientists, both of whom are inclined to think in terms of 'thought' or 'intellection' or 'cognition,' which partakes of the mystic more than it does of solid anatomy or physiologic function." The Psychologist's Fallacy is what James calls "the confusion of his own standpoint with that of the mental fact about which he is making a report." "Another variety of the psychologist's fallacy is the assumption that the mental fact studied must be conscious of itself as the psychologist is conscious of it." *Principles of Psychology,* vol. 1, pp. 196-97.

[7] The Report also handles the idea of sublimation in a very clumsy way. It does not represent accurately what the Freudian theory of sublimation is. For this, however, there is some excuse in the change of emphasis and even in meaning in Freud's use of the word.

[8] It is hard not to make a connection between the Report's strong stand against any delay in the male orgasm and its equally strong insistence that there is no difference for the woman between a clitoral and vaginal orgasm, a view which surely needs more investigation before it is as flatly put as the Report puts it. The conjunction of the two ideas suggests the desirability of a sexuality which uses a minimum of sexual apparatus.

Lawrence S. Kubie (essay date 1948)

SOURCE: "Psychiatric Implications of the Kinsey Report," in *Sexual Behavior in American Society: An Appraisal of the First Two Kinsey Reports,* edited by Jerome Himelhoch and Sylvia Fleis Fava, W. W. Norton & Company, Inc., 1955, pp. 270-93.

[*In the following essay, originally published in 1948, Kubie enumerates the benefits Kinsey's research has for psychoanalysts treating patients with sexual disorders.*]

This is the report of an investigation of the sexual behavior of nearly 5,300 white American males, between the ages of three and ninety years, from several occupational groups, and from many economic, educational, religious, and social strata from the underworld to the topmost levels of society, from crowded urban and sparsely settled rural areas, and from most national stocks and racial groups except the Negro. Not all of these various sub-groups are represented in sufficiently large numbers to satisfy the exacting statistical standards of the investigators. For this reason their goal is ultimately to secure a record of the sex lives of one hundred thousand human beings. Therefore since this report will be supplemented by later reports both on the male and on the patterns of sexual behavior in the female, it should be looked upon as preliminary and tentative. This is a fact which the popular press has largely overlooked, both in its acclaim and in its criticisms.

The courage, patience, humility, and above all the broad humanity of those who for the last ten years have devoted themselves to this colossal undertaking must command profound respect. It is indicative of their attitude that they have said that they never secured the life history of anyone without ending up with a heightened regard and liking for him. Undoubtedly in this lies the secret of their success in securing the intimate details of the sexual lives of so many people from so many different walks of life. The work has been supported by the National Research Council's Committee for Research in Problems of Sex, by Indiana University, and by grants from the medical division of the Rockefeller Foundation. The result is the most important statistical addition which has ever been made to our information on the incidence in a total population of various patterns of overt sexual behavior; and although several important types of behavior are omitted, the report merits detailed study by everyone who is concerned with human nature.

In addition to its broad general implications, to psychoanalysts the facts which have been assembled will be gratifying as an independent verification of basic psychoanalytic concepts concerning infantile sexuality and the presence of polymorphous sexual impulses in all human beings. Furthermore the variations in sexual mores which occur at different intellectual and cultural levels give valuable information about the development of ego-ideals and of super-ego functions in different strata of our society.

Eye-catching summaries of some of the more startling findings have already appeared in the popular press. Although there is considerable danger that erroneous conclusions may be drawn from these summaries (a danger which will be discussed below), it is to be hoped that there will be repeated presentations of the facts themselves, until they sink deep into the popular mind. Such a summary, however, is not the function of this review. To the technical scientist the details of this study are of such importance that any condensation would do an injustice to the work and would lessen rather than enhance its value. The purpose of this review will be rather to indicate certain attitudes which are implicit in the theoretical approach of the authors which lead them to find erroneous implications in their data, which may in turn mislead the lay reader as well. Precisely because the work itself is continuing, and because the authors will bring out several further reports, it seems to the writer that the most useful function he can perform, and also the highest tribute he can pay to it, is to point out the imperfections of this first report, in the hope that they will be eliminated from those which are still to come.

The chapter on interviewing is a case in point. It can be commended to every young student of psychiatry for its human wisdom and its technical adroitness. Yet it will also be illuminating for its deficiencies: (1) its failure to consider the influence of the various types of transference situation which arise at once in any such intimate interview; (2) its failure to include any guide to the recognition of latent as well as overt trends; (3) the absence of any concern with the varied emotions which must have attended these revelations; and (4) the absence of any preoccupation with either therapeutic or noxious forces which such interviews always set in motion, whether or not the interviewer has any intentions of this kind.

I have already paid tribute to the striking success of the authors in securing sexual histories: yet it would be an over-simplification to think that an ability to win confidences is all that is necessary. Clinical experience shows that the willingness to cooperate can itself be a screen behind which rigid defences may hide. The cultural and personal forces which oppose our facing ourselves or revealing to others the truth about ourselves are very strong: and as a result many who have studied the results of interviews with medical and college students and with nurses as well as with patients, question the validity of data which is derived through the questionnaire type of interview. Some report errors on vital information running as high as 90 per cent. The personality structure of the interviewer and the interviewee and can introduce distortions into this technique of fact gathering. The interviewer's emotional blind-spots may obstruct his vision, and his own emotional needs may lead him to grind axes of which he is unaware: while in the subject all manner of rationalizations, conscious and unconscious guilt feelings, his compensatory needs, and his anxieties influence the data which he gives, no matter how consciously co-operative he may feel. It is for this reason that even in the more dependable non-directive psychiatric interview the information which is obtained at first has to be corrected many times before it can be accepted as factual. The type of interview which is used as the basis for this study must give rise to a fear lest we have here an example of accurate recording of inaccurate data.

With respect to the data itself, there can be no quarrel with the methods of tabulating it. There are, however, various uncertainties concerning its statistical treatment. There seem to be at least three possible sources of error which may tend to exaggerate the statistical summaries with respect to the incidence of deviant patterns:

> (a) The inclusion of all early exploratory experiences, as though these were identical in kind with the same behavior when it occurs later in life.
>
> (b) The use of mean deviation and cumulative incidence in drawing conclusions from skew distribution curves.
>
> (c) The neglect of screen memories.

The extent of the errors attributable to these ambiguities is hard to determine with precision; but the nature of each as a potential source of error will be discussed in the course of this review.

In a round-table discussion of Kinsey's book which was held at the School of Medicine at Yale University, Professor Frederick D. Sheffield pointed out that while the sampling methods seem adequate for Dr. Kinsey's purpose, his utilization of his statistical data gives the reader an exaggerated impression of the incidence of orgasm, and particularly of those forms of sexual behavior of which the general public most disapproves. This is seen in Kinsey's highlighting of the *mean* frequency and of the *cumulative* incidence curve. In statistical analysis it is well known that with skewed distributions, such as are uniformly found by Dr. Kinsey, the *mode* always will give the smallest value, the *median* the next, and the *mean* the highest value. This is because the mean is pulled up by the relatively few individuals who have very high scores. Therefore the mean does not represent accurately the central tendency of the majority of the group. Furthermore, Kinsey's use of cumulative incidence with age may cause many readers to confuse *current* with *past* experiences. Thus the *cumulative* incidence of one homosexual orgasm in a lifetime will be highest for the middle-aged; whereas the great majority of such isolated homosexual experiences actually occur in the pre-adolescent and adolescent periods, where its significance is fundamentally different.

Another important consideration concerns what we call "screen memories." These are late memories which in various ways may fuse with and obscure or distort the memory of earlier events; or dreams and fantasies which are recalled and reported in good faith as though they had really happened. This source of "false positives" is overlooked throughout this report. Because screen memories may be described unaltered in repeated interviews, the unchanged repetition of a story does not, as the authors assume, establish its validity.

The effects of the failure to take into consideration this source of error is evident throughout the book and gives rise to many inconsistencies. For instance, in the last two paragraphs on page 443 the comments on the extreme sensitivity of the three- and four-year-old to subtle hints of adult attitude towards all bodily and sexual matters might well have been written by a psychoanalyst. Yet the following paragraphs on page 444 describe "experiences" of children with a disregard of all the forces which can distort a child's recollections. Here the analyst would be on the watch for screen memories, for fantasies which had acquired the quality of reality, and for dreams which had become confused with actual occurrences. Therefore the analyst would record as psychic facts but not necessarily as historical facts many reports of early "experiences." This is a distinction which the authors do not make. They attribute to human memory a precision which unfortunately it does not possess. They recognize that we can "forget" but not that we can "misremember." It is impossible to guess at the extent of the error which this may introduce into their statistics, but since screen memories come to light in almost every analysis, the error may be not inconsiderable.

Before going any further, I would like to say that none of the criticisms which I will direct at this report will be aimed at the authors. Like their positive achievements in this work, their mistakes are quite obviously the predictable results of the background of training and experience which they brought to it. Every mistake is a result of their lack of experience with the phenomenology and psychology of illness. It would be wholly unfair to criticize the authors for what they could not be expected to know, but it is harder to excuse those who played an advisory role in the planning of the study for their failure to insist that it be a combined operation, in which all that is known from the study of sick individuals would constantly be used in the evaluation and interpretation of the statistical data on large groups. Avowedly I will use my own experience to point out omissions which have led these workers into avoidable error. Surely other specialists, from other allied fields, could make similar criticisms. It is our hope that such frank criticism will lead to a reorganization of the working team so as to avoid a continuation of past errors as this investigation goes forward.

The theoretical preconceptions which I will challenge concern (1) the concept of normality, (2) the significance of conscious and unconscious psychologic forces in the interpretation of all reported variations, and (3) the concept of sexuality. Furthermore I will plead repeatedly that the work of these investigators should be supplemented by an intensive psychiatric and social study of enough individuals to constitute a statistically adequate random sample of each of the various behavior groups which are recognized in this report. The importance of such an intensive study of individuals, to supplement the broad study of large groups, will be discussed in relation to each specific issue as we come to it.

Let us consider first the authors' concept of normality; and why it is incorrect and misleading to assume, as they do, that because something is widespread in human behavior it must therefore be regarded as "normal." In the first place on purely logical grounds this is demonstrably fallacious. In times of epidemic the common cold may afflict more than 50 per cent of the population. This, however, does not make colds normal. Secondly, and of greater importance, is another point: the fact that the normality or abnormality of any act depends, in its ultimate analysis, upon the relative roles of the conscious and unconscious purposes, of the attainable and unattainable goals which are sought through that act. It is this balance that determines whether any act should be regarded as sick or well.

This implies that a heterosexual act may be quite as neurotic as a homosexual act, and that masturbation or homosexual behavior or other deviations may be either normal or neurotic or (and more often) a mixture of both; and that in each case the normality or abnormality depends upon the nature of the purposes served by the act. This differentiating point between normality and neurosis is of practical as well as theoretical importance; and it will be referred to repeatedly in our discussions of heterosexuality and of homosexuality and all sexual deviations.

Obviously the relative overall incidence of neurotic and normal forces in any one form of deviant sexual behavior as compared to any other can be determined only by a study of many individuals who practice such deviation, and the comparison of their whole psychologic adjustment to life with the adjustment of a majority of those who practice either some other deviation or the biologically useful form of sexual activity. Thus every psychiatrist knows that among homosexuals, as among all other deviants as well, are many individuals who have been able to segregate their problems in their "perversions," just as many individuals with frank neuroses are able to segregate their conflicts in their neurotic symptoms, and are enabled thereby to live socially useful and effective lives. This is not true, however, for most sufferers from neurotic difficulties. In most instances such problems infiltrate subtly into every aspect of life, causing great distress and frustration. Therefore we are not misled into calling a neurotic symptom "normal" either because it may be prevalent, or because some of the individuals who have that particular symptom can live effective and productive lives, whether in spite of the neurotic symptoms or even because of them. Before we can evaluate any symptomatic act we must know first its meaning in terms of the purposes it serves for the individual, and then, from the social point of view, what its meaning is for the lives of the majority of those who exhibit it.

The evaluation of the "normality" of sexual deviations rests on a consideration of the same two questions; and such an evaluation can be made only after statistically adequate and representative samples of individuals who manifest each of the various deviations have been studied intensively for comparison with a statistically adequate sample of all other groups in the community. Certainly no such study has ever been reported, either by these authors or by anyone else. Therefore no generalizations are warranted by anybody. The present study does not include any information which illuminates this problem. Not even gross comparative data are presented as to the general life adjustments found among different types of sexual patterns; e.g., through such external manifestations as income levels for the economic group in which the individual was raised, educational level as compared to his background, social productivity, general community achievements, family adjustments, etc. Therefore as far as the material presented in this study goes, the implication that because homosexuality is prevalent we must accept it as "normal," or as a happy and a healthy way of life, is wholly unwarranted.

The same consideration applies to every other deviation which is described. This point is emphasized here, because the popular press has already given wide and uncritical currency to this misinterpretation of Kinsey's data.

For the education both of these workers and their backers and advisers, I will develop the contrasting viewpoint. Everywhere throughout the discussion of bisexuality and of homosexuality there is a failure to understand the essential core of the analyst's concern with this whole problem. A few preliminary theoretical discussions and clinical case presentations would have sufficed to lay a basis of agreement for this aspect of their task. They would have learned that the analyst recognizes that the total goal of human sexual activity is never the orgasm alone. This simple biologic aim is overlaid by many subtle goals of which the individual himself is usually unaware. Some of these are attainable; some are not. Where the majority are attainable, then the end result of sexual activity is an afterglow of peaceful completion and satiation. Where, however, the unconscious goals are unattainable, then whether orgasm has occurred or not there remains a post-coital state of unsated need, and sometimes of fear, rage, or depression. This may happen with any form of intercourse or of self-stimulation; and no sexual history which omits subjective data on this, gives an adequate basis for estimating the normality of the sexual adjustment. Furthermore there is some reason to believe that in a particularly large proportion of homosexuals the unconscious goals are unattainable, although this is by no means confined to them.

One consequence of this is a fact which Kinsey recognizes, namely, that the homosexual is always on the prowl, and that it is rarely possible for him to establish enduring relationships. He seems always to be seeking something that cannot be achieved in the simple physical experience with anyone, no matter how complete this may be; and this drives him on constantly to new excesses and to new relationships. Comparable unconscious forces contribute to the occurrence of heterosexual promiscuity and compulsive extramarital affairs. Here again statistical frequency is no evidence of social or psychologic normality.

The psychiatrist is far from believing that homosexuality is in and of itself an index of psychopathology (as Kinsey implies on page 660). It is rather that the psychiatrist recognizes that quite apart from social condemnation there is in the life of most homosexuals this haunting search for something unattainable; and while the psychiatrist recognizes something not dissimilar in all human living, including heterosexuality, this futile search seems to characterize the homosexual to a greater extent. Adequate statistics on this basic issue are lacking; but if the analyst's selected experience is in any way characteristic of the whole group, it would indicate that the role of unconscious and unattainable goals is greater in the homosexual than in the heterosexual adjustment.

I hope that in their future investigations and reports, Kinsey and his co-workers will have a more accurate picture than they have at present of the analytic view of this problem; because such mutual understanding would lead to cooperation in further studies of the same material.

As a further complication the analyst would also point out the fact that not infrequently a man who is living as a homosexual has unconscious heterosexual fantasies, as if his homosexual activity were intended to work a magical change on his own body which would make him capable of becoming heterosexual "like everybody else." This is one of the many paradoxical findings which emerge from any intimate study of the homosexual, and which make it impossible to dismiss homosexual activity casually or to accept it as "normal," merely because it is prevalent. Then we would add the parallel observation that homosexual fantasies may underlie heterosexual activity, as for instance when a man in coitus identifies with the woman and lives out a conscious or unconscious fantasy of being the woman. Obviously the latent content of behavior and experience should not be left out of consideration, in any rounded evaluation of the problem. It is important to determine what intrapsychic forces and what external social pressures determine which conscious and unconscious tendencies will achieve overt expression. This will require full data on latent or unconscious sexual orientation, to correlate with statistics on the incidence of overt forms of sexual activity. This again will require a detailed study of many individuals out of each of the various groups.

Of some interest in this connection is the observation which is recorded on page 630, that the incidence of homosexual activities is highest in that group of men who became adolescent at an early age and who showed the highest incidence of early masturbation and early heterosexual contact and indeed of all forms of sexual activity. This would seem to indicate that in youths whose sexual behavior is most free of restraints the pattern of sexual behavior changes frequently and lacks specific meaning; and that in this group homosexual episodes may be quite accidental, and may mean something quite different from the obligatory homosexuality of later life. In such cases the overflow of uncensored genital interests into homosexual activity may not mean that there is any specific homosexual inclination in the psychologic sense.

It is misleading to include the exploratory genital experiences of early adolescence in the over-all statistics on the incidence of homosexuality. At the turning point between puberty and adolescence, to the boy the genitals of girls are more taboo than are the genitals of other little boys. Another little boy "is just like me—there is no harm in looking at him or touching him." Indeed at that age touching himself seems to the child a far greater sin than to touch someone else. In the child's hierarchy of crime to touch a little girl is worst of all; next is to touch oneself; and least sinful and dangerous is to touch another little boy. During adolescence this series gradually is reversed, so that homosexual contacts gradually come under the heaviest taboos. It is only after this shift has occurred that a homosexual contact becomes evidence of an obligatory or dominant homosexual drive. Therefore to include in statistics on the incidence of homosexuality the mutual explorations which little boys make of one another's bodies is as misleading as it would be to include in statistics on the incidence of alcoholism every child who surreptitiously samples his father's bar. It is a further flaw in the report that the data do not make it possible to determine whether there is any statistical correlation between obligatory homosexual needs in adult years and the incidence of homosexual explorations at various earlier ages.

Similar considerations apply to the significance of sexual relationships with animals. The fact that such contacts are "part of the normal mammalian picture and that such contacts occur in as high a percentage of the population as we have already indicated," as Kinsey points out on page 677, is by no means all that need be said about the problem.

Surely it has a corrective value for Kinsey to challenge any idea that "deviant" or "perverse" sexual behavior is rare, or that any form of sexual activity which is not biologically useful is alien to the nature of the common man; but this does not justify the implication that there are no differences in the relative "normality" of different forms of sexual life, judging normality as we have already indicated in terms of (1) the relative roles of conscious or attainable and of unconscious or unattainable goals; and (2) of the total psychologic make-up and adjustment of the human being.

To emphasize this point it may be well to point to the fact that any experienced psychiatrist and certainly every analyst is aware that many inherently "normal" acts can serve neurotic purposes, as when hard work or handwashing or eating becomes a compulsion. Furthermore all neurotic symptoms, all heterosexual activity, and all perversions can occur in any of a wide variety of psychopathological settings. The patient with a "perversion" may come to a psychiatrist for the treatment not of his sexual pattern but for relief from other symptoms. During the course of any deep exploration of such cases, however, it soon becomes apparent that the neurotic symptoms are closely related to the sexual pattern. This is never, as Dr. Kinsey assumes the psychiatrist to believe, a simple cause-and-effect relationship, but something more intricate. It would represent the psychiatrist's viewpoint more accurately to say that he holds that any obligatory emphasis on any one mode of sexual expression to the exclusion of all others will usually indicate that some underlying neurotic forces are at work; and that the cure of those underlying neurotic forces will automatically and inevitably alter the pattern of sexual expression. Thus the psychiatrist would not consider a woman "normal" even if she is heterosexually and orgastically free, if this can occur only with men she does not love. In fact the analyst cannot accept any form of sexual activity as inherently and inevitably either normal or abnormal. He must always consider the total setting, the play of compulsive and phobic mechanisms, the role of conscious and unconscious guilt and fear, etc. To him the ultimate sign of health is always the degree of psychic freedom from the automatic operation of unconscious mechanisms.

My next major objection concerns Dr. Kinsey's interpretation of the meaning of variations in the amount of sexual activity. About this the analyst will find it impossible to accept the authors' repeated oversimplifications. Thus, as an example, the analyst finds nothing abnormal in eating or in liking to eat a great deal; but when a child is afflicted with an insatiable eating compulsion, which drives the child far beyond his physiologic requirements, the psychiatrist recognizes that a compulsive neurotic mechanism has taken hold of a biologic mechanism and is driving it overtime. He would not leap to the conclusion that such compulsive eating is a true measure of that individual's inherent caloric needs, not even if he continued to be a compulsive eater and to be obese throughout his entire life. The analyst would employ the same reasoning about the quantity of sexual activity. His concern is not with the quantity per se, but with the question of what makes it either great or small. Is it due to a compulsive overdrive or to a phobic inhibition? A man or woman who in spite of full and satisfactory orgasms remains unsatisfied is neurotically ill; just as the child who eats until he vomits is sick. This is not because there is anything either immoral or abnormal in multiple orgasms or in heavy eating; but because in each instance neurotic forces are distorting normal biologic mechanisms.

Because of the neglect of these basic considerations, the weakest section of the report is that which discusses the total sexual outlet. Here the authors make unwarranted deductions concerning the extent to which human beings vary in their inherent constitutional sexual endowments. No psychiatrist would take the position which the authors impute to him, namely that all men and all women are created equal in this respect; but we cannot shut our eyes to the clinical evidence that psychologic forces exercise a profound influence on the quantity of instinctual activity.

For instance, on page 325 the authors point out that those individuals who reach psychologic adolescence late usually delay the start of their sexual activities and maintain a low frequency of sexual activity not only in their early years but throughout the remainder of their lives. This is an important observation; but it does not justify their conclusion: "It is probable that most of these low rating individuals never were capable of higher rates and never could have increased their rates to match those of the more active segments of the population." This of course is an unwarranted assumption. What would these authors say about the patient who under the influence of analysis changes from a faltering rate of sexual intercourse of scarcely once a fortnight or once a month to an active and confident sexual life with intercourse several times a week? This is not an unusual experience in analytic therapy. No psychiatrist would be so rash as to claim on the basis of such experiences that there are no inherent constitutional differences in sexual vigor. But we do not know what percentage of men or women rate low because of constitutional deficiencies, and what percentage because of the inhibiting effects of their conscious and unconscious guilts and fears, or in what percentage both forces are operative. Nor do we know what percentage of those who rate high, do so because of a high constitutional endowment, and what percentage rate high because they are overdriven by compulsive forces which utilize the instinctual endowment for unconscious neurotic purposes.

This problem has much more than academic interest. It is important both as a scientific fact and in relation to our sexual mores. We should not be misled into thinking that our mores are wrong when they fail to meet the needs of those compulsion neuroses which manifest themselves through exaggerated and insatiable sexual activity, any more than we should be misled into thinking that our culture is excellent where it is dictated by neurotic phobias and neurotic guilt. Therefore, it is a matter of importance for human society to determine the range of actual physiologic variation around which the compulsive and phobic mechanisms operate. It does not clarify this point to assume, as this report tends to—not constantly but recurrently, that most of the variations which are encountered arise from physiologic differences,[1] when any experienced psychiatrist knows what tremendous variations in sexual activity can be manifested in any one individual under the influence of depressions and elations, hate and fear, compulsions and phobias, whether these be conscious or unconscious. Here again is where detailed investigation of individuals becomes an absolute necessity.

Even the age at which adolescence occurs is in itself not free from the influence of psychologic factors. Critical endocrinologists describe young women in whom the onset of menstruation is delayed until their neurotic difficulties are relieved, and obese little girls and boys whose sexual maturation is delayed by their compulsive overeating of fatty foods. Many of these would correspond to the type described on page 326; yet with the relief of their psychologic difficulties these youngsters change their food habits, slim down, and pass through a swift maturation, with rapid development of all secondary sexual characteristics. These clinical experiences must be kept in mind as correctives to some of the deductions which Kinsey draws from his statistics. They indicate again how valuable it would be for endocrinologists, internists, taxonomists, and psychiatrists to make a combined study of psychologic and physiologic variants in the processes of pubescence.

The next major blind spot in this study is towards psychiatrists and all clinical and psychologic considerations. Perhaps because these workers are experienced primarily in the biologic rather than the clinical sciences, as they approach this clinical field they attribute to the psychiatrist a degree of naivete which may once have been true of all of us, and which undoubtedly is still true for some of us, but which certainly is not true of the advancing frontiers of modern dynamic psychiatry. Without being unduly defensive, it seems fair to ask that the formal technical presentation of such a work as this should be in terms of the mature forefront of psychiatric thinking and not in terms of that part of the psychiatric column which lags in the rear. Nor, for that matter, are well-trained psychiatric social workers as naive in their theoretical concepts as these authors seem to feel.

I would repeat that my concern is not to defend psychiatrists or social workers; but to eliminate misunderstandings between disciplines which should work together. Many of Kinsey's criticisms are valid with respect to part of the psychiatric profession. They trouble me, however, when they are expressed as part of the authors' general attitude toward psychologic forces which should be given fuller consideration in the interpretation of their data.

At times it almost seems as though the authors are trying to caricature the psychiatrist by attributing to him ideas which are patently absurd;[2] as, for instance, when they refer to some hypothetical "older psychiatrist" (p. 374) who is supposed to have claimed that for the female to assume the dominant position in coitus will always lead to nervous disturbances and to divorce. It is difficult to believe that any psychiatrist who is representative of the profession holds such an opinion. It would of course be quite legitimate for a psychiatrist to argue that any rigid and obligatory ritual with respect to the position during coitus could indicate a neurotic maladjustment which would inevitably be linked to other neurotic troubles. This quite different interpretation of the same phenomenon is not considered by these authors.

This underestimation of psychologic considerations crops up repeatedly.

On page 523 the fact that adolescents may masturbate without conscious fantasy (or for a year or so before conscious fantasies are permitted to appear), is taken as a measure of the relative role "of the physical and the psychic in the sex life of the human animal." Here as usual the authors fail to appreciate the importance of the role of conscious and unconscious fear and guilt. It takes courage and at least some degree of freedom from incest taboos before a child can allow himself to indulge in conscious sexual fantasy, especially in association with masturbation. To the child the erotic fantasy often seems to be more sinful than the act. Many a child will have sexual fantasies without masturbation on one occasion, and will masturbate without fantasy on another. It may be some years before he will have the courage to synchronize the two, thereby defying the parental image which is embodied in his own conscience. There are important psychopathologic differences between the child in whom the act is more taboo than the fantasy, and the child in whom the fantasy is more taboo than the act. Without knowledge of the relative roles of act and fantasy, we have only one part of the picture of a child's psychosexual development, and not necessarily the more important part.

Again on page 580 is an example of a failure to include adequate consideration of psychologic forces in the interpretation of their data. Here it concerns premature ejaculations. The authors impute to clinical observers the notion that intense, vigorous, and rapid erotic responses are abnormal. This is patently absurd. Uncontrollability would be significant, however; and particularly if the uncontrollability is associated not with intensity of feeling or sensation but with its absence; and if the rapidity of orgasm has its roots either in profound hostility to women, or in such anxiety that the man has to have his orgasm in a hurry in order to get away as quickly as possible. Here again, the nature of the forces which determine the speed of ejaculation must be determined; and if evidence on this point is lacking one is in no position to judge the nature of the act. Whether there is anything comparable to this in the speedy ejaculation which is sometimes observed in lower animals is something that we have as yet no way of determining. Certainly, however, it is a misinterpretation of the psychiatric viewpoint to say, as the authors do here, that the clinician feels that a man should always be able to control his orgasm until the woman has come to orgasm, no matter how pathologically slow she may be. Such an attitude would be a masochistic distortion of control, which would in its own right invite investigation as to its neurotic determinants.

The chapters on extramarital intercourse and prostitution are marred by the same defects as those on homosexuality and total sexual outlet. They present useful statistical data, but lack adequate psychologic consideration. Here it is particularly important that the activity should be understood in terms both of the conscious and the unconscious goals and their subtle interweaving. It is not the fact of extramarital intercourse but the conscious and unconscious "why" of it which determines whether it is healthy or neurotic. Every analyst knows that monogamous fidelity can sometimes be the result of free, healthy, conscious choice, and at other times an escape from profound neurotic guilt and fear. Similarly extramarital sexual activity can be normally and freely determined, or it can be the product of blind, unconscious hostilities, of unconscious, repetitive needs to test out one's potency, or of unconscious homosexuality. Its prevalence is surely an important fact to establish, but warrants no deductions as to either its individual or social "normality." The authors seem to be oblivious to such considerations.

The discussion of sublimation (pp. 205 to 213 and elsewhere) brings to light several other fallacies in the authors' approach. In the first place a significant bias is revealed, which leads the authors to overlook completely both the existence and the effects of compulsive sexual overdrives, although they acknowledge eagerly the role of neurotic inhibitions in lessening the total amount of sexual outlet. They seem to take the position that while many people limit themselves to less sexual activity than they are capable of, no overactivity should ever be looked upon as in excess of physiologic needs. This bias influences the authors' reasoning in many matters, including the problem of sublimation. Furthermore, in this connection they concern themselves exclusively with the popular misuses of the concept, accepting these as though they were accurate. Indeed nowhere do they give any indication that they themselves understand its precise scientific meaning.

Thus it is obvious that the individuals who suffer from neurotic sexual inhibitions tend to rationalize these on pseudo-moralistic grounds. Similarly others who suffer from compulsive sexual overdrive often attempt to control their compulsions by will power alone. Such efforts can be no more effective than are any efforts to control compulsions by mere self-control. In each case these efforts and rationalizations are often miscalled "sublimation," which has nothing to do with either of these neurotic phenomena. Analysts, on the other hand, are quite aware of the fact that the concept of sublimation is not entirely clear. Its accurate differentiation from symptom-formation is uncertain. Therefore, the best that one can say for Kinsey's contribution to the clarification of this problem is that it may stimulate the analyst to clarify his own concepts and terms in this area. In the meantime, no matter how sceptical Kinsey and his co-workers may be about the basic value of the concept, no biologist will find it possible to dispense with it entirely. If biochemical forces are the source of our psychologic activities, then it is self-evident that these biological energies are translated into forms of behavior which are as many and as varied as is human conduct. This is the essence of the concept of sublimation; and the biologist who rejects this is rejecting the biochemical origins of human psychologic processes. Perhaps it will help the authors to clarify their thinking about sublimation in their future work, if they will keep this fact in mind, plus the further fact that sublimation is a name for a process which applies to all basic instinctual energies but *not* to their phobic or compulsive derivatives.

A similar failure to understand the psychiatric point of view is evident in many other places. For instance, the authors make much of the fact that auto-eroticism is severely condemned at lower cultural levels (p. 375). This certainly is no news to the psychiatrist. More than thirty years ago William Healy in *Mental Conflicts and Misconduct* pointed out the fact that among juvenile delinquents who were arrested for stealing were many who had been taught at the same time, and often by the same older boy, both to masturbate and to steal. When stirred by erotic impulses these lads would often steal rather than masturbate, because a genital "crime" usually seems far more serious to the child than does the social crime.

This brings up the next important obscurity in the theoretical concepts of these authors. The social crime in such a case carries much of the psychic "energy" of the pubescent sexual need. This raises an important question concerning concepts and terminology. Under such circumstances should the stealing be called a sexual outlet, since it discharges some part of the sexual need? Surely in such a study as this we ought to be clear how we are going to use this word. Should we name a wind by the direction from which it comes or towards which it blows? Which is more useful in dealing with human behavior? This is a question which these authors neither ask nor answer.

On page 498 the same semantic problem is raised concerning the meaning of the word "sexual." For instance, in the discussion of masturbation the authors state that "rubbing or scratching one's body, even one's genitalia, is not masturbation when it serves some other function than that of effecting erotic arousal. Throughout this volume the word has not been applied to anything except deliberate self-stimulation." Since all human activities serve both conscious and unconscious purposes, and since without careful investigation of the individual it is impossible to determine the balance between the two, it should be clear that we cannot draw so hard and fast a line. For instance, genital activity which culminates in orgasm can serve many purposes in addition to simple erotic needs; just as we may eat for many reasons other than the biologic need for food. The complexity of human behavior is such that no instinctual activity serves only its primitive biologic purpose. Therefore it is never easy to make so simple a distinction between sexual and nonsexual data.

This lack of conceptual and terminological clarity about the meaning of the word "sexual" leads the authors into many inconsistencies. They brush aside the analytic emphasis on the sexual nature of many apparently nonsexual activities in children; and then give evidence which conclusively supports the analytic position. For instance, on page 162 they speak of certain types of genital play as "purely exploratory, animated by curiosity, and as devoid of erotic content as boxing, or wrestling, or other non-sexual physical contacts." Later on the same page, when giving a list of the sources of erotic responses among pre-adolescents and younger adolescent boys, boxing and wrestling were specifically mentioned. Their difficulty seems to arise (1) from a failure to recognize the diffusion and overlap of instinctual impulses on the psychologic level, (2) from their failure to recognize the multiple symbolic significance of many such activities, and (3) from their lack of any awareness of how frequently aggressive activities can be used as a mask for subtly disguised erotic impulses, and vice versa. It is unfortunate that these authors who are so superb in their ability to divorce themselves from prejudiced condemnation of all frankly sexual activities are not equally free of bias in their evaluation of the latent sexual significance of many seemingly nonsexual actions.

As further example of this, we would point to the fact mentioned on page 164, that the pre-adolescent boy reacts without discrimination to a wide array of varied emotional situations, whether these seem to be sexual or nonsexual in nature; whereas his sexual response becomes more specific as the years go on. Here Kinsey's own observations give evidence of the early diffuseness of the sources of erotic arousal, and demonstrates the validity of certain fundamental psychoanalytic concepts. This makes all the more perplexing the statement on page 180 that his data "give no support to the Freudian concept of a pre-genital stage of generalized erotic response that precedes more specific genital activity." Here again is a problem which should be explored in detail. What happens to the boys in whom the sexual response does not become more discriminating? In what percentage is this true? What kinds of boys are these? What is the mechanism by which the more sharp discrimination is gradually established? Questions such as these could be answered only by detailed psychiatric and social studies of an adequate statistical sample of various types of individuals. Only out of such studies can come an increase in our knowledge of the genesis of sexual deviations, and of their correlation with normal and pathologic psychology.

There are many other important questions which can be answered only by intensive studies of individuals taken as samples of their various groups. For instance, it would be important to know how often there is an inverse relationship between the early occurrence of nocturnal emissions and early masturbation or early intercourse. In other words, do those individuals who early in life have a sexual outlet through masturbation or through intercourse therefore not need nocturnal emissions? And do those who are too inhibited to masturbate or to have intercourse have nocturnal emissions, simply because this is the only outlet which their unconscious guilts and fears can tolerate? Or do the two go hand in hand? The answer to this has many consequences. If there is such a negative correlation then early intercourse need not necessarily mean a higher charge of sexual energy (i.e., a more highly endowed sexual apparatus) as Kinsey assumes; but may mean merely a less powerful restraint by conscious and/or unconscious guilt and fear. In this connection it is of interest that the breakdown of the data by social and educational and economic levels offers a hint that where intercourse occurs early nocturnal emissions are more rare than where masturbation is the chief early outlet. If this is true, then masturbation would appear to be a less effective "protection" against nocturnal emission than is intercourse; which would indicate that the same psychologic forces which make a youth choose masturbation rather than intercourse leave him in the grip of a considerable conflict, with the result that some part of his sexual need can achieve expression only during sleep, when his psychologic defenses are down.

Because of these various deficiencies the discussion of each of nine different forms of sexual expression which is presented in Part III (Chapters 14 to 22) is the least satisfactory section of the book; precisely because the conscious and unconscious forces which determine the choice of sexual aim and object are never adequately considered. This does not mean that the chapters are devoid of factual material which is of value and interest. But the treatment of the material and the implied deductions as a whole are far less valuable than elsewhere in the book.

We must also point out certain important omissions; such as attitudes towards intercourse during menstruation, attitudes towards genital size, actual data on genital size (both male and female), attitudes towards the size of breasts (both male and female), attitudes towards erection of the nipples, the influence of early or late circumcision, etc.

Similarly there is a great deal of social data which is needed if we are to evaluate the phenomena which have been statistically recorded by Kinsey. We would like to know what is the ordinal position of the subject of the inquiry in his own family, whether he is the oldest, or the youngest, or in between, whether he is an only child; whether he has sisters, and whether these are older or younger; whether he was brought up in a matriarchal or patriarchal family; whether there had been early separation from father or mother; whether the initial experiences were through any process of seduction, etc. In pointing out such omissions, it is only fair to say that some of these data may already be in the possession of the investigators and may appear in later volumes. It is known that this is true about certain anatomical facts. Nevertheless, it is perhaps unfortunate that more of it has not been incorporated into this report where it is relevant.

The attention of psychiatrists will be drawn to the challenge on page 576 to the usually held ideas about vaginal orgasm, a matter which will surely be discussed more fully in the forthcoming reports on female sexuality.

In spite of all these defects, the data on sexual behavior at different social levels will be of great value to everyone who is concerned with the organization of our educational and disciplinary institutions. Especially interesting is the evidence that there has been little significant change in patterns of sexual behavior over the course of at least one generation, in spite of vigorous educational influences, both deliberate and accidental. A more detailed study of the subtle processes by which to such an extraordinary degree sexual patterns are stabilized in various occupational and cultural groups would add greatly to the scientific value of this section.

In addition to the psychologic studies of individual representatives of the various types and patterns of sexual behavior, certain neurophysiologic studies should also be made. It is extraordinary that we have no information on the existence of variations in the innervation of the sacral segments of individuals who manifest different types of overt sexual responsiveness. Thus it would be illuminating to know what differences there may be in the distribution of axonal reflexes throughout the perineum, in the degree of referral of prostatic stimulation to perianal or penile areas, in the precision with which sensations are localized in those areas, in the extent to which sharply defined epicritic or diffuse protopathic sensations dominate. If there is a significant degree of individual variation, such variations could contribute to the choice of patterns of sexual behavior. It is to be hoped that in forthcoming studies of the sexual patterns of women, such physiologic investigations will not be omitted. It would certainly be significant to know whether among women there are differences in vaginal sensitivity and in the supply and distribution of sensory end-organs within the vagina, which might contribute to variations in degree of responsiveness to vaginal stimulation.

Such studies will require a high degree of critique if they are to rule out the influence of psychogenic anesthesia and of conditioning. For instance, if in the sensory examination of an experienced anal pederast, anal and perianal stimulation caused specially intense penile sensations, it would not be safe to jump to the conclusion that this was evidence that there were special reflex pathways. Such a sensory link might equally well depend upon the conditioning effects of that man's experiences in passive anal intercourse. Therefore, although it is important to collect information on constitutional anatomic variations in the distribution of sensory nerves, since such variations might play a role in determining deviations in sexual behavior, nevertheless the interpretation of such neuroanatomic and neurophysiologic findings will have to be made with great care.

SUMMARY

If this report by Dr. Kinsey and his co-workers does no more than present us with incontrovertible statistics concerning the incidence of manifest infantile sexuality and of manifest adult polymorphous sexual tendencies, it will be a major contribution to our understanding of human development and of human culture. Psychiatry and psychology will always be in their debt for this. Nevertheless, two of the basic implications of their report must be rejected. One is that the overt manifestations of sexual patterns are all that we need to know about human sexuality. The other unacceptable implication is that where any behavior pattern is widespread among human beings, it is superfluous to attempt to explain it. The physiologist does not feel that he does not have to explain the mechanism of the heart beat merely because everybody's heart beats. Nor does the epidemiologist dismiss the problem of the common cold merely because everybody catches cold. Universality is not synonymous with normality; and our obligation to explain every variety of sexual activity, whether heterosexual, homosexual, or anything else, is not lessened in any way by the fact that every form of sexual behavior is widespread.

Nevertheless I want to restate my conviction that this report is a significant contribution and that in balance it will undoubtedly do more good than harm in spite of its errors and its exaggerations. Thus, almost all of the statistics on the incidence of various patterns of sexual behavior are probably somewhat excessive, because of errors in sampling, errors in interviewing, and errors in the treatment of the statistics. Furthermore the important role of chronic compulsive inflation of instinctual needs and of their phobic inhibition is scarcely recognized. This oversight is particularly serious in the case of compulsive sexual athleticism, because in the report one finds the implication that we should remake our culture and our laws to conform to "high scores," as though such compulsive exaggerations of sexual need constituted the ideal for all men. This is just as misleading as are the pseudo-moralistic restrictions which are placed on our sexual mores by unrecognized phobic inhibitions. My fear is that the overstatement of Kinsey's case will lessen the effectiveness of the report in freeing our sexual mores and our laws from the domination of neurotic anxiety and neurotic guilt.

Freud related the universality of deviant sexual trends to the development of the neurosis, indicating that it is neither the latent nor the overt trend which in itself produces the neurosis, but rather the conflict between these trends and the intrapsychic forces which oppose them. I believe that it would help to bring into harmony the observations of the biologist and of the psychoanalyst if we could agree that it is never the deviant drive as such which is abnormal, but (1) the conflict which arises around it and (2) the compulsive and obligatory quality which may attach itself to the drive. Thus an obsessional furor can manifest itself in heterosexual activity just as readily as in masturbation or in homosexuality or in any other deviant form of sexual conduct. It is this obsessional furor plus the phobic exclusion of alternative outlets which is the mark of abnormality, rather than the specific pattern of sexual behavior itself.

The failure of Kinsey and his co-authors to give full and consistent consideration to the powerful psychologic forces which influence the objects, the aims, and the quantity of sexual activity is a source of errors in many conclusions which they draw from their data. It would add immensely to the value of all of the observations made by Dr. Kinsey and his co-workers if we could know more about the physiologic and psychologic setting of the various forms of sexual behavior whose incidence they have determined. To this end it would be essential to make intensive individual physiologic, anatomic, psychiatric, and social studies of individuals who would constitute a statistically adequate random sample of each form of sexual behavior. This would give us vital additional information as to their general life adjustments and the ways in which they handle instinctual processes other than sex, particularly those having to do with food and fluid intake, with excretion, with exercise, and with sleep. The addition of such information as this would be of great importance for our understanding of human nature in general and of sexual nature in particular.

I hope that I have succeeded in making several points clear:

(1) We need a detailed study of enough individuals to constitute a statistically adequate sample of each of the many subgroups which are here described.

(2) Dr. Kinsey and his co-workers were wise not to allow themselves to characterize any individual as good or bad, as sick or well, as neurotic, psychotic, or psychopathic. Certainly from the point of view of establishing their contacts and gathering their material this was essential.

(3) On the other hand, from a social and scientific viewpoint the work must not stop at the gathering of this raw material. Not for the purpose of pigeonholing individuals, but in order to learn more about the significance in human life of all variations in patterns of sexual behavior, representative individuals should be studied in great detail so that we may learn more about their personality make-up and general life adjustment. We must know what variations there are in each sexual pattern and what different

kinds of people manifest the same or different types of sexual deviations, so as to establish what correlations there may be between such deviations and all other aspects of human nature.

(4) For this purpose it will be essential to bring to this work a mature understanding of fundamental principles of dynamic psychopathology, both conscious and unconscious, latent and overt. This will require the cooperative effort of teams of psychoanalysts, clinical psychologists, neurophysiologists, endocrinologists, cultural anthropologists, and psychiatric social workers, as well as biologic taxonomists. That such a study will present formidable difficulties is evident; but that it is essential is equally true.

NOTES

[1] The authors point out certain quantitative differences in total sexual activity among three educational levels. This indicates that the authors realize the importance of psychologic forces; but they do not always seem to keep this point clearly in mind.

[2] The only reference to the important problem of incestuous drives, whether overt or latent, is a statement on page 558. This is so fantastically untrue that I almost hesitate to quote it. However, it reads, "There are some psychoanalysts who contend that they never had a patient who has not had incestuous relations." There has never been and never will be any psychoanalyst who has made such a statement; it would be in the interest of scientific progress if the authors will correct this. We expect such distortions from occasional biased and irresponsible ignoramuses, but not from responsible fellow-scientists.

Abram Kardiner (essay date 1953)

SOURCE: "Behaviorism with a Vengeance," in *The American Scholar,* Vol. 23, No. 1, Winter, 1953-54, pp. 106-110.

[*In the following review of Kinsey's* Sexual Behavior in the Human Female, *Kardiner finds the work invaluable as a study in social trends, but faults several of his conclusions as too reliant on behaviorism.*]

Dr. Kinsey and his associates have by now, with their volume on ***Sexual Behavior in the Human Female,*** established themselves among the great sexologists of history. This book is a true product of our time, and it carries the popular authority of the opinion poll and the questionnaire method of tracking down social phenomena. It has, therefore, the timely authority of the statistical method that is so prominent in our American ethos, and it has introduced in our American ethos, and it has introduced into the study of sexology the technique of the assembly line. 'If Havelock Ellis was the naive describer and historian, Freud the researcher into psychodynamics, Kinsey *et al.* represent the invasion of the field by the behaviorist armed with a computing machine.

Like any assembly-line procedure, it is efficient and slick. It is a veritable encyclopedia of information; and its data are arranged in such a way that with very little trouble any woman can thumb through this book and come out with a chart of her own personal standing in the great norm that is herewith established. It is also a source for satisfying the most prurient in every possible detail of what other people are doing in their sexual lives.

Dr. Kinsey's method is one of many for studying sexual behavior, and it yields some information that cannot possibly be ascertained in any other way. For this part of his labors all students of sex will be indebted to him for a long time. Notwithstanding serious flaws in sampling, the undue weighting of the sample toward urban groups, educated groups and certain religious groups, this book gives a broad sweep of the distribution of certain forms of sexual activity. We doubt whether more accurate sampling would materially affect his results, though it might satisfy those who are now willing to penalize him by disqualifying all his findings. There is some information here that is invaluable to the student of contemporary social trends: the demonstration of the shift in the sexual behavior of the female toward greater sexual freedom in the past fifty years is decisive and startling; the consistent effect of deep religious conviction on sexual behavior is likewise dramatic and challenging. These and a score of other valuable correlations make this book indispensable to any student of contemporary culture. This is what makes it one of the great human source books of our time.

But Dr. Kinsey is not fully aware that his method of working is not only his tool, but also his tether. He is unwilling to remain within the confines that his method logically demands in the canons of scientific procedure. This failure to recognize the limitations of his procedure leads him to draw conclusions to which he is not entitled and to ignore others of high import because they cannot be fitted into the procedure. What else can be expected? He first divides sexual behavior into a fixed number of identifiable "parts," only one of which, the orgasm, can be qualified by "yes" or "no." This alone can be quantified and then correlated against certain fixed social conditions like age, marital status, profession, education, religion, et cetera. Motivations cannot be measured in the same way. Therefore, they are omitted. Not being in any position to evaluate the relative importance between the items he can and those he cannot include, he therefore does not hesitate to draw his conclusions from those data that his procedure has rendered relevant. Naturally he treats the findings of all other procedures in a very cavalier manner.

This is behaviorism with a vengeance! Moreover, his behaviorism is stretched to include mammalian sex behavior and the averages of sexual norms in other cultures. Trying to establish a norm for sexual behavior including mammals and primitive cultures is like setting out to take the mean temperature of all patients in a five-hundred-bed hospital on the principle that since they are all in a hospital, they must be sick. We can then get a mean temperature of 101.8. This figure is meaningless because it is taken out of the only meaningful context in which temperature would be significant, namely, what disease the patient has. So Dr. Kinsey ignores the fact that sex custom and sex behavior are always embedded in a social context without which they cannot be understood and in a motivational context without which they are meaningless. Therefore, Dr. Kinsey's assumptions lead him astray. He insists, for example, that human homosexuality is a biological variant because it occurs in lower forms of life. This is a misleading conclusion, because homosexuality means persistent choice to the exclusion of the opposite sex. Such a phenomenon is unknown in lower forms of life, notwithstanding transient phenomena that resemble it.

Dr. Kinsey, therefore, not only misleads us: he takes sexual behavior out of its motivational context, whereas man is distinguished by the fact that sexual behavior is integrative, cumulative, subject to discrimination and choice, and ultimately tied to the total emotional development. Moreover, although his data show a distinct change in sexual behavior in the past fifty years, Dr. Kinsey cannot tell us why this took place, but he insists he is describing the "human female." He is merely describing the American female, 1939-1950.

The limitations of his methods lead Dr. Kinsey into great difficulties in establishing the meaning of the orgasm which is central in his quantifying procedure. This is really the pivot of the entire work. The extent of female frigidity in Kinsey's sample proves to be, according to his method, very small—and for a very good reason. Whereas the male orgasm is unmistakable, the female orgasm is not. None but those who have had gradations of orgastic experience know what is meant when the question is put. In clinical practice many females answer this question "yes," when the fact is, as is ultimately discovered, any tickle or thrill is interpreted as orgasm. Moreover, by making the clitoral orgasm the basis for his standard and refusing to acknowledge the difference between this and the vaginal orgasm, many a woman in his sample is recorded orgastic on a technicality. Thus a woman who is capable of clitoral orgasm through masturbation but incapable of coital orgasm, clitoral or vaginal, unless manipulated by herself or her mate emerges as orgastic in the record. Besides, he ignores the fact that orgastic potency is the resultant of the total emotional relationship with the mate and is not merely a spinal reflex. This failure to standardize his central unit of study is therefore a high source of error.

What faith can we place in Dr. Kinsey's work? There is still a good deal. Since the same standards are used throughout, relative differences can be relied upon, and this still leaves a great store of valuable information.

However, when Dr. Kinsey steps out of his role as reporter and becomes both an interpreter and an advisor, we can no longer trust him. His advice is often misleading and in some issues perhaps harmful. Masturbation is not a training school for coital potency, nor is premarital intercourse a way of improving one's chances for successful marriage. It is advice of this kind, explicit or implied, that shows up the importance of the motivational factors that Dr. Kinsey could not include in his armamentarium. He inevitably winds up putting the statistical cart before the motivational horse, and it is upon this kind of upside-down reasoning, in which the role of cause and effect is reversed, that Kinsey comes by the advice he so freely offers. Furthermore, the entire work is conceived without regard for those ends that sex morality purports to bring about and without regard for the social evolution of which this sex morality is the end product. Sex custom is one of the main supports of the entire structure and functioning of society.

What is of value in this book could have been stated in one-tenth the space, and the high merit of what is of value is spoiled by the overconfidence the authors show in a method that is limited and pressed into the service of attempting problems it cannot solve. One cannot use arithmetic to solve problems in tensor physics. At a time when crucial issues in sex morality are being wrought in the toils of painful and costly social experimentation, misinformation is dangerous and can only have one outcome. It will add still more confusion to the sexual unrest of our time. And for this, not Dr. Kinsey, but the public will pay the price.

Joseph K. Folsom (essay date 1954)

SOURCE: "Kinsey's Challenge to Ethics and Religion," in *Sexual Behavior in American Society: An Appraisal of the First Two Kinsey Reports,* edited by Jerome Himelhoch and Sylvia Fleis Fava, W. W. Norton & Company, Inc., 1955, pp. 226-36.

[*In the following essay, Folsom considers Kinsey's work as a long overdue statistical examination of human sexuality and a harbinger of related works in ethics, philosophy, and religion.*]

"Maybe it's true, but it's not good policy to *broadcast* detailed truth without some consideration of how people are going to use it." Such is a common reaction to Kinsey. It is not peculiar to traditionalists nor to those lacking reverence for modern science. For example, Margaret Mead, in an eloquent Appendix on "The Ethics of Insight Giving" says: "When one writes in a way that is easily accessible to all interested citizens, I believe one should put oneself in those readers' place, and not force them either to accept or to reject [or to choose which to do?] interpretations the implications of which they would not have chosen to hear had they been fully aware of them." "The sudden removal of a previously guaranteed reticence has left many young people singularly defenseless in just those areas where their desire to conform was protected by a lack of knowledge of the extent of non-conformity."[1] The most important aspect of the Kinsey studies is their challenge to re-examine the relation of science to ethics and religion and this connected issue of intellectual paternalism versus complete intellectual democracy.

The medieval harmony of science, ethics, and religion, documented by St. Thomas Aquinas, became more and more disturbed by the rapid development of science. In 1790 Kant seemed to solve the problem in a novel and revolutionary way, by making a complete separation of science and ethics. However the ethics which actually operate in our society have never yet been reduced to any single principle, but are based on several different types of thinking. Wayne Leys has done a great service to social science by making explicit these ethical thoughtways.[2] He compares Kant's ethic of pursuing an ideal of social relations with the casuist ethic of following precedents, the Bentham utilitarian ethic of estimating the pleasant and painful consequences to all affected, the Hegelian ethic of loyalty to the larger whole, or destiny toward which history moves, and the Deweyan pragmatic ethic of solving the essential problem. The last seems like a kind of negative, objectivist, practical utilitarianism: doing what will most reduce complaints and conflicts.

The alarm over the Kinsey reports seems to be based on a fear that our fellow citizens are largely guided by an extremely realistic form of casuistry which says, "When in Rome do as the Romans *do*—read their laws—but also notice which laws are enforced." It is well known, of course, that many a person will thus appeal to custom when what the Romans do fits in with his felt needs, but when it does not, he may turn to an idealistic, utilitarian, or even a Hegelian argument. This is one of the commonest types of rationalization.

F. S. C. Northrop vigorously opposes this type of casuistry which would derive ethics from actual practice. With Robert Hutchins he opposes "legal realism" and agrees that legal thinkers need an "idea of the good." Furthermore, Northrop sees a similar error in Hegelian and Marxian thinking. Hegel on the level of nations, and Marx on the level of classes, assume that in some important sense the "ought" can be derived from the "is." Yet Northrop rejects also the Kantian solution of making ethics independent of science. He believes that ethics can and should be derived from science. Not, however, from "social science," by which he seems to mean descriptive cultural sciences, but rather from "natural science," in which he seems to include biology and psychology.[3] The Kinsey reports would belong mostly to Northrop's descriptive "social science." Biology, psychology, and studies such as Kardiner's[4] which attempt to apply universal criteria to several cultures would seem to belong mostly to Northrop's "human and natural science," which he regards as a proper basis for ethics. However, while Kinsey's titles "Human Male" and "Human Female" seem to the anthropologist like a bit of ethnocentric conceit, there are many things in the reports which contribute to omnihuman natural science in Northrop's sense. Such for example are the data on the tremendous age, sex, and individual differences.

There is a job to be done, and Northrop has suggested what it is. It is to translate our factual knowledge about human sexuality into ethics, legislation, social policy, and religious guidance. The time has now come to do it. Not because Kinsey has told us anything so very surprising, anything that was not known, in rough approximation, before. Rather, because he has told it so statistically to so many people that now there may be enough steam up to do what should have been done a long time ago.

This task should be done gradually through discussion. In this writer's view the discussion should be in no way secret, however benevolent and high-minded; but it should be *led* by men and women of unquestionable honesty, devotion to the general good, and free from any concealed personal motive or bias. Given the present organization of our intellectual life, these discussion leaders should be clearly distinguished from the factual researchers, although both groups require intellectual and moral integrity.

The kind of discussion we need is well represented by *Sex Ethics and the Kinsey Reports* by Dr. Seward Hiltner,[5] a clergyman and member of the University of Chicago theological faculty. Hiltner not only understands Kinsey's methods and results with uncommon acumen, but shows theoretical skill after the fashion of a Max Weber. He is interested in *patterns,* not of sex behavior and "outlets," but of sex attitudes and values. He constructs seven types, each logically consistent within itself, and most of them also well represented empirically. The first three are mass types correlated with Kinsey's three socio-educational levels: the "child-of-nature" attitude of the lower level, the "respectability-restraint" attitude of the middle level (especially before 1920), and the "romantic" attitude (romantic toward licit and illicit sex and not merely toward conventional courtship and choice of mate) of the upper level, now filtering down to other levels. Then there are three consistent patterns which Hiltner has observed among thoughtful individuals but which do not appear in the Kinsey data, either because Kinsey did not ask the necessary questions, or because the holders of these attitudes are too few. These are the "no harm" attitude, the "toleration" attitude, and the "personal-interpersonal" attitude. The last named is the one frankly admired by Hiltner. It is implied in the works of Erich Fromm.[6]

The person with this attitude "believes that the ordering of sex by society should be for the realization of personal and interpersonal values, not for the sake of control of such." It is neither legalistic nor libertarian, biologistic nor spiritistic, unreflectively conformist nor yet rebellious for the sake of proving non-conformity. "It does not consider naturalness or unnaturalness as adequate criteria."[7] Hiltner measures all these six types against a seventh type as a standard. This is the *Christian view*[8] of sex, which Hiltner derives, in an objective, scholarly manner, from the Bible and Christian history, but also "taking into account the modern knowledge." The Christian view turns out to be essentially the personal-interpersonal attitude with the addition of Christian theological support. It is summarized in five points, here condensed: (1) sex is good if it serves the fulfillment of man as a total being, i.e., God's will for man, (2) the aim of all human interrelationships is to foster love, (3) the aim of sex is toward a progressive integration of the several necessary levels of sexual function, (4) human sex requires both intensity and steadfastness with a proper relationship between them, (5) the good of any sex act always depends in some measure upon the inner meaning to the persons involved, but the sole ultimate standard is the judgment and love of God.[9]

How is this Christian view different from the traditional sex mores? For one thing, it is adequate and inspiring on the positive side, whereas the traditional code emphasizes the negative, and the concrete. Hiltner thinks that Kinsey has distorted the Judaeo-Christian view by reading it through the ideas of his subjects. He asserts that this Judaeo-Christian tradition assigns more positive value to the sex act itself, than is generally realized. He agrees in general with D. S. Bailey, an Anglican clergyman, who reads real flesh and not merely a symbol in the Biblical doctrine on "one flesh."[10] These scholars both seem to feel that although the sex act should be kept within marriage, yet it has a God-sanctioned value which is not dependent upon marriage as an institution nor upon the intention to procreate.

John J. Kane argues that the Catholic attitude toward sex has been seriously misunderstood by many Catholics as well as outsiders. Actually it is warmer, healthier, more positive than it seems. Catholic thought is not responsible for the identification of sex with the obscene or pornographic. But there is a certain caution in verbalizing it. "Since conjugal love is both a legitimate and beautiful kind of love, and since it is expressed in sexual union, the marital sex union should also be considered in that light."[11] If this approach differs significantly from the approach of the other branches of the Judaeo-Christian tradition, the difference, according to the present writer, involves a general tendency to leave many things publicly unsaid, to assume a benevolent, paternal control over the circulation of symbols and ideas. This may have had value in protecting the sex drive from fears and disgusts as well as guarding it against superfluous stimulation. This may account for a certain kind of healthy-mindedness in the Catholic attitude toward sex. The question is, can any such paternalistic control stand up indefinitely in the open ideological market of modern society, or must it be replaced by other controls?

The popular belief in a negative relation between sexuality and religion seems supported by Kinsey's findings that religiously active persons are on the average sexually less active—within marriage as well as illicitly! This difference occurs within all three faiths and is greater than any difference between the faiths as such. Such a correlation must be explained by factors other than the content of ancient Hebrew law or of the words of Jesus. From the very numerousness and detail of the sexual prohibitions in Leviticus, without any general, blanket prohibition of sex outside marriage, one can make certain inferences as to what was *not* forbidden. But also in the words of Jesus one can find no authority for the official modern Anglo-American respectable middleclass definition of sex morality as sex within marriage only and even there excluding certain "perversions" and "excesses." The moral theme of Jesus was loving kindness, humility, and forgiveness in interpersonal relations in general. He said little about marriage and sexual relations specifically. Apparently he accepted the sex and marriage mores of his culture, but opposed the drastic punishments prescribed by Mosaic law. When a woman was taken in the very act of adultery, he said: "He that is without sin among you, let him first cast a stone at her." This is also what the Kinsey Reports seem to say implicitly, between the lines, and this is perhaps the reason why some people fear them. In the biblical case, however, Jesus then added privately to the woman, "Go and sin no more." (John 8:1-11)

The Christian ethic exalts love and peace and therefore in general condemns giving offense. This policy necessarily implies the avoidance of sexual behavior which gives offense in the community and culture in which one lives. But it does not define for all cultures and for all eternity what shall be offensive and what shall not. It does not concretely define "lust," "purity," "adultery," and so on, but leaves these concepts free to change their concrete objective meaning, provided there is sufficient scientific support and democratic agreement on the changes, and no unfair advantage taken through deception, concealment, and hypocrisy. Mormon polygamy proved itself intolerable to the American culture and value system, even when it was segregated in Utah. But to show that it was *unchristian,* it would be necessary to show that it was more selfish, cruel, unfair, or deceitful than arrangements recognized as Christian.

Hiltner's Christian view, or in purely humanistic terms, his personal-interpersonal attitude, emphasizes "man as a total being." Two serious problems will arise: one has to do with the individual man as a total being, and the other with the total population of men as endowed with the same human needs and intrinsic worth.

In the total of needs, drives, and interests which make up the individual man, there is a class of *defensive* drives such as anger-and-aggression, and fear-and-escape. In a sense these are antagonistic to the rest of the personality; they are necessary evils, weapons held in reserve against emergencies, and they operate through a branch of the nervous system which is antagonistic to the branch concerned with hunger, sexual excitation, and the routine bodily processes. Anger does sometimes become linked with sexual desire, and the result may be sadism. Do we want more of that? Do we want to encourage the very natural linkage of sex with jealousy, a partly defensive emotion, because of the useful weapon this gives against sexual infidelity; or would we minimize jealousy as an evil and try to find adequate substitute weapons? We do wish to link sex more closely with tender love toward the mate, a linkage which seems to be deficient in some persons and cultures. Yet we sometimes seem to fear that tenderness toward other love-objects such as children, one's own sex, or the spouse of one's friend, might lead to erotic feeling.

Perhaps no group of drives plays so large a part in the higher development of man as do the *exploratory* drives of curiosity, acquisition, construction, aesthetic creation, and the like. The full story of man as a total being is not understood until we recognize that man strives to make new connections, craves new experiences, strives to enter all fields he can within the limits of time, energy, and empirically adequate safety. When George Mallory, who perished in the 1920s trying to climb Mt. Everest, was asked why it was so important to climb that dangerous and desolate mountain, he replied, "because it's there." No man seeks adventure in all fields, but given enough men, all possible fields will be invaded. This is not an approval of any particular adventure, but a human fact to be reckoned with. Denis de Rougemont seems to recognize that sexual adventure provides some positive values which cannot be dismissed merely by calling them bad names. His answer is that marital fidelity is also a value, a faith chosen for its own sake, and to choose it means to renounce the values both of "spontaneity" and "manifold experience."[12]

Kinsey's outstanding discovery about sex differences is that males are erotically stimulated by a much greater variety of objects and mental images than are females. He thinks this is due to some biological difference. Hiltner is inclined to question this interpretation. That there is such a *biological* difference, however, is suggested by Slater and Woodside. "If the race were so constituted that female orgasm occurred before male, she might very well thereupon terminate coitus before the chance of conception had occurred. A male constitution that provided for ejaculation at the earliest possible moment after intromission would be a selective advantage."[13] More generally, we may theorize, nature is wasteful, and reproduction may be best assured by having an excess of male *excitement* present all the time, at the same time that the female, for short periods, may seem almost insatiable. Clearly ethics cannot be derived simply from natural law any more than it can from existing custom. But, on the other hand, an ethic of human fulfillment would continually seek harmless ways to use rather than waste, to integrate rather than to keep separate, the various and abundant potentialities of man.

Kinsey's findings bid us define more carefully the "single standard of morals." The goal worth striving for is not an equalizing of the average behavior of the two sexes, but honesty and justice in the way that society evaluates and treats this behavior. A double standard of sex morality has existed in ancient Greece, in modern Japan and modern America. But the role of the Greek hetaira, the Japanese geisha, and the Japanese prostitute were more honest and just than the role of the American prostitute.

The other serious problem is the problem of humanity as a whole population. Does the Christian view of sex hold that persons, when they cannot achieve the ideal, should renounce sex altogether? Must sex be used only during some limited period of one's life time, depriving especially men in youth and women in older years, often at the very times they are strongest in biological drive? Strange to say, these absolute deprivations would be much easier to endure were it not for the existence of a rather elastic supply of surplus sexuality in the non-deprived people of the opposite sex. Conversely, the surplus sexuality of these latter would not bother them so much were it not for their knowledge of the absolute deprivations existing among potential partners. One might almost say that sex, like "nature," abhors a vacuum, and that this characteristic is likely to increase the more we rationalize (in Max Weber's sense) and civilize our sexuality.

The problem is not a simple choice between two alternates. At least four distinct values are involved: (1) sexual exclusiveness, (2) permanence of marriage or intimate relationships, (3) male initiative in courtship and economic production, (4) better intersexual balance and wider satisfaction of the biological sex need. Any three of these might be attained better by sacrificing, or honestly subordinating and risking, the fourth. The least discussed possibility, though not necessarily the most hopeful, is the subordination of value three. That is, if boys were to marry soon after sexual maturity, taking wives a few years older, expecting more economic responsibility and courtship initiative from the girls, much of the problem as Kinsey portrays it might be relieved, and there would also be less widowhood.

But perhaps there are weightier considerations than these. If so, they will endure the strain of public exposure and discussion. Sex may be a dangerous thing, but now that we have radioactive dust floating about, any alarm over the insidious consequences of the "Kinsey bomb" should seem to be somewhat amusing.

Indeed it is possible that more honest and humane sex mores would help to reduce interpersonal and international tensions and thereby decrease the chances for world destruction. Let no one imagine, however, that such an improvement could be achieved by complete "sex freedom." Without mores, sexual privileges, like land and gold, might become the object of unbridled competition and fighting, or else revert to some grossly undemocratic pattern of "haves" and "have-nots" such as we see among animals and undemocratic human societies. Sex anarchism may argue that sex is not like land and gold because the supply always equals the demand—in fact the supply is *ipso facto* the demand. But this argument ignores the universal human, and even animal, tendencies to pre-empt more than one's share, to perceive gradations of the object, and to struggle for the "better" grades. The way to better social arrangements lies not in scrapping what we have already achieved but in building upon it.

The mores are standards by which we judge behavior. The suggestion of this chapter is not to reverse the relation, not to judge the mores by our actual behavior, but to judge our sex mores by the standard of our more general, comprehensive mores. Let the standard of chastity be judged by the standard of charity, and not by the standard deviation!

We may find that the most basic question is whether we shall choose, or perhaps are irrevocably committed to what Wilhelm Reich calls a sex-affirming, or a sex-denying, culture.[14] The answer to this might not make much practical difference for the immediate future. A sex-denying culture may permit much sexual activity for the sake of reproduction, health, tender love, and other values. On the other hand a sex-affirming culture may regulate and restrain sex a great deal to prevent excesses of reproduction, of sexual competition or fighting, or to prevent disease, poverty, or other evils. Granted that sex with tenderness, aesthetic embellishment, and so on, is always better than the sex which is like a glass of water to a thirsty man, granted that sex like all other drives must be restrained where it hurts other persons or other interests, yet the crucial question still remains. Namely, does the sexual act in and of itself have any independent value, or only an instrumental, derivative value? If it has independent value, then the burden of proof lies upon those who would restrain it. If it has only instrumental value, the burden of proof is upon those who would permit it. This question is especially debatable because of a curious biological paradox: sex is one of the strongest impulses yet also the impulse which can be deprived with least harm! Consequently sex is, of all human drives, the one most susceptible to regulation by cultural values.

If one accepted Sorokin's great super-classification of value systems into the Sensate, the Idealistic, and the Ideational,[15] and believed that our present culture is too sensate, he might logically choose the sex-denying policy. But if so, he should also *logically* deny aesthetic satisfactions and creature comforts as independent values. This is approximately the position of early Puritanism and of Communism in its present phase. To produce fanatically, not in order to consume, but for the sake of production itself and of national strength, is fully as *ideational* as the value system of the Medieval world although the *ideas* are different.

But Sorokin's way is not the only way in which values can be classified. We might think of values as expressive versus receptive, or of giving versus getting. Our present sex morality seems to be tied up with a fundamental semantic assumption that the sex act, apart from procreation or marriage, is of the nature of getting: sensations for the male; sensations, economic rewards, or nothing at all for the female. But the act, whether licit or illicit, is also a giving of intense satisfaction to another human being, commonly with reciprocation, sometimes long-craved and long pleasantly remembered. This fact is verbally emphasized in some cultures which anthropologists regard as rather sex-affirming. It is soft-pedaled in our culture, except in very intimate or lately in clinical conversation, despite the fact that our religion exalts giving in general. Yet this is logical. If the thing given has no value apart from some approved context, then, apart from that context, it is not a gift. However, neither do we rhapsodize upon sexual pleasure given to the marital partner.

This analysis will not decide the question, it merely points up its essential nature.

NOTES

[1] Margaret Mead, *Male and Female,* New York: William Morrow and Co., 1949, p. 450.

[2] Wayne Leys, *Ethics for Policy Decisions,* New York: Prentice-Hall, Inc., 1953.

[3] F. S. C. Northrop, *The Meeting of East and West,* New York: The Macmillan Co., 1946, pp. 245, 256-258.

[4] Abram Kardiner, *et al., The Psychological Frontiers of Society,* New York: Columbia University Press, 1945.

[5] Seward Hiltner, *Sex Ethics and the Kinsey Reports,* New York: Association Press, 1953.

[6] Erich Fromm, *Man for Himself,* New York: Rinehart and Co., 1947; *Psychoanalysis and Religion,* New Haven: Yale University Press, 1951.

[7] Hiltner, *Sex Ethics and the Kinsey Reports,* p. 177.

[8] The Jewish view seems to be incorporated within this.

[9] Hiltner, *Sex Ethics and the Kinsey Reports,* pp. 179-180.

[10] D. S. Bailey, *The Mystery of Love and Marriage, A Study in the Theology of Sexual Relations,* New York: Harper and Brothers, 1952. See Genesis 2:24 and Ephesians 5:31.

[11] John J. Kane, *Marriage and the Family, A Catholic Approach,* New York: Dryden Press, 1952, p. 258.

[12] Denis de Rougemont, *Love in the Western World,* New York: Harcourt, Brace and Co., 1940, p. 290.

[13] Eliot Slater and Moya Woodside, *New Patterns in Marriage,* London: Cassell and Co., 1951, p. 175.

[14] Wilhelm Reich, *The Function of the Orgasm,* New York: Orgone Institute Press, 1942.

[15] Pitirim Sorokin, *Social and Cultural Dynamics,* New York: American Book Co., 1937.

Manford H. Kuhn (essay date 1954)

SOURCE: "Kinsey's View of Human Behavior," in *Sexual Behavior in American Society: An Appraisal of the First Two Kinsey Reports,* edited by Jerome Himelhoch and Sylvia Fleis Fava, W. W. Norton & Company, Inc., 1955, pp. 29-38.

[*In the following essay, originally published in 1954, Kuhn challenges Kinsey's conclusions as succumbing to reductionist fallacies.*]

One would expect a zoologist, when he addresses himself to the study of some aspect of human behavior, to elect from the current assortment of theoretical orientations toward human behavior—such as psychoanalytic theory, field theory, symbolic interaction theory and learning theory—that one which has the most in common with the zoological orientation toward organisms in general. It is therefore not surprising to find that Kinsey takes what is essentially the learning theorist's point of view, with its heavy reliance on physiological explanations for human (social) behavior. This much was evident in the first Kinsey report, but one had to infer it from his unit for analysis, his choice of language, his use of data from infra-human species and from his interpretive statements scattered here and there throughout the book. In the second Kinsey report he has in Chapter 16, "Psychologic Factors in Sexual Response," given a fairly explicit account of his view, one which corroborates the judgment that his is a learning theory position, at least insofar as he takes into account factors which are not patently physiological in the first place.

He makes it clear that he regards with misgivings the distinction between the physiologic and the psychologic.[1] He says, for example, "It might properly be contended that all functions of living matter are physiologic . . ." only regarding it as "customary" to regard "certain aspects of animal behavior as psychologic functions." (p. 642)[2] This "customary" distinction he evidently regards as treacherous, for he suggests that an end product of the distinction encourages "the opinion that the psychologic aspects of human sexual behavior are of a different order from, and perhaps more significant than, the anatomy or physiology of sexual response and orgasm. Such thinking easily becomes mystical, and quickly identifies any consideration of anatomic form and physiologic function as a scientific materialism which misses the 'basic,' the 'human,' and the 'real' problems in behavior. This, however, seems an unnecessary judgment. Whatever we may learn of the anatomy and physiology and of the basic chemistry of an animal's responses must contribute to our understanding of the totality which we call behavior. Those aspects of behavior which we identify as psychologic can be nothing but certain aspects of that same basic anatomy and physiology." (pp. 642-643)

REDUCTIONISM

In this statement he commits the reductionist fallacy which learning theorists persist in making.[3] The basic error in reductionism consists of failing to recognize that *all* levels of analysis are abstractions.[4] Different scientific disciplines exist because their concepts are deemed appropriate to the particular phenomena under analysis, not because they are maintaining, respectively, that the objects and events as they structure them are more "real" than those under analysis in other levels of scientific inquiry. One may properly insist on the unity of science, and indeed on the derivative principle that concepts, used at a given level of analysis, must be of such a nature that they be *reducible* to those at the level next below, without in any wise committing himself to the unparsimonious and misleading principle of the *necessity* for dealing with data at a given level only in terms of the concepts belonging to the level next below.

It is apparent from Kinsey's treatment of sex in these first two volumes that there is here a mysticism of an inverted sort from the one he warns against; that is, a mysticism of regarding the physiological as the "basic" reality of human behavior, and therefore "more real" than symbolic, attitudinal behavior. It is evident from his chapters on the physiology, neurology and endocrinology of sexual response that there is very little known about these matters that can inform us regarding the rather limited and gross matters Kinsey wants to know about human sexual behavior. Yet it is Kinsey's constant presumption that variables at these levels "cause" human sexual behavior and are in the main responsible for its variations as well. It is one thing to admit, what is eminently desirable, that we would know more if we could pair predictive statements at the social psychological level with predictive statements at the physiological level about the same raw events. It is quite another matter to attempt to construct predictive statements using variables drawn more or less indiscriminately from the two levels of analysis, or to assert that a statement at the physiological level is more "basic" than one at the social psychological level.

DERIVATIVE ASSUMPTIONS

Most of the other difficulties with Kinsey's view of human behavior are derivatives from the reductionist position, and indeed they are difficulties common to Hullian learning theory. These difficulties inhere in the following assumptions and points of view: 1. the extension to human behavior of a frame of reference and of generalizations made from observations of infra-human behavior; 2. the conception that influences from outside the organism are to be structured in terms of mechanical activation of nerve endings; 3. a view of sexual behavior as segmentalized with respect to other human behavior; 4. the arbitrary analytic definition of an act; 5. the general view of learning as something outside conscious control or symbolic manipulation; and 6. the peculiarity of position accorded the first act in a train of activity. I shall attempt to deal in brief compass with the difficulties which lie, in turn, in each, using as my frame of reference the general social psychological orientation, developed in the social sciences, known variously as the symbolic interaction, self-theory or reference-group theory orientation.

1. *Zoomorphism:* The application to man of a frame of reference developed in connection with the study of infra-human animals is justified by those who do this on the basis of the principle that there ought to be a *general* science of behavior rather than a special science of man. This seems plausible enough until one observes that under the aegis of this principle there is committed a direct inversion of the old practice of anthropomorphism—that is, *reverse* anthropomorphism or zoomorphism—in which those regularities of behavior which have been discovered in infra-human species are extended and imputed to man, ignoring the probably crucial differences in human learning and in human behavior which accrue to his use of symbolic language both in communication and in thoughtful organization, initiation, redirection and control of behavior.

2. *"Stimuli" vs. "objects":* The use of the concept "stimulus" to refer to that which impinges on the individual from the outside of his neural system is one which begs questions regarding thought, attention, giving oneself signals which initiate overt activity, and the effects of intention and goal on that which will be perceived—in short, all those matters now receiving special attention among those investigating "social perception." It parallels, but contrasts markedly with, the concept of "social object" in social psychology. The term "stimulus" refers to any simple physicalistic event capable of activating nerve-endings; it is a concept taken over directly from conditioning experiments on infra-human animals. The term "social object," on the other hand, refers to anything, large or small, simple or complex, which has been designated as an object by shared definition, and toward which there is a plan of action contained in the social norms. A stimulus has drive- and cue-value depending on its strength and distinctiveness. A social object, by contrast, has whatever meaning has been socio-culturally assigned to it.

3. *Sex as segmentalized:* The segmentalization of sexual behavior from other human behavior rests not on what would be the partially defensible ground that a scientist may arbitrarily abstract from total behavior that which he desires to inquire into, but rather on the notion that sex (stemming, as it is alleged to do by the learning theorist, from a distinct and disjunctive "primary drive") is *in nature* a segmentalized phenomenon. The learning theorist forgets that drives, as discrete motives, are his hypotheses and not demonstrably real and disjunctive entities in nature. He has, in short, reified them. Hull derived his drives from a logical consideration of what it would take to insure an organism's survival, and then went ahead to impute these to the organism as if they were built-in intentions developed genetically through the process of evolutionary selection. To the social scientist they bear a strong resemblance to the now-discredited instincts of a half century ago.

4. *The physiologic act* vs. *the social act:* It is permissible for the scientist to "slice up" ongoing events in any way which appears to be useful in his endeavor to arrive at predictive statements of the regularity of behavior. It is, in the final analysis, the empirical—"Which conceptual scheme gives the most predictive results?"—which determines which unit for analysis will continue to be used. Again it was the drive-reduction paradigm of the learning theorist which apparently prompted Kinsey to take the physiological act, beginning with arousal and tumescence and ending with orgasm, as the basic unit for analysis in his overall study of sexual behavior. If one is oriented, on the other hand, to look upon human beings as universally bringing their behavior under the control and direction of verbal plans of action, he would be inclined to take as his unit for analysis the acts as defined by the individual actors themselves, expecting this to yield more predictive results. I shall enlarge on this point later. It is sufficient here to note that Kinsey, having chosen his analytic unit, allows this unit to slip quietly over in his thinking to be a definition of what the actors themselves are in their own minds attempting to do.

5. *Learning = conditioning:* The development of preferences and avoidances may be construed to result from the vicissitudes of the drive during early experiences having to do with that drive. In short the preferences and avoidances may be construed as mere overtones of physiological and neurological events, or mere cortical reflections of what is essentially a subcortical series of events. But if one holds the view that man's behavior is under the control of social (symbolic) recipes, one would look to the reference groups of subjects for evidence that these prejudices and avoidances were verbal importations, defining events and indicating positive and negative social objects.

6. *Initial acts crucial in switchboard theory of neural system:* Finally, if one takes the view that words and thoughts are mere epiphenomena which, after the fact, rationalize behavior for man, and if one holds further, that learning consists of neural modifications which result when behavior is successful in reducing a drive, then it follows logically that the first successful behavior, in this sense, is peculiarly important in establishing the form of subsequent behavior. This is the learning theory view, and it is Kinsey's view, at least regarding female sexual behavior. (The evidence he found for males was complicated and contradictory.) If one holds the view, on the other hand, that behavior is organized and directed by means of shared symbols, then one proceeds to examine persistent behavior for evidence that it continues as associated shared norms persist, and changes when they change.

In sum, we may infer from these particulars that Professor Kinsey looks upon man's "true" nature as being his animal nature which would somehow find its most satisfying expression freed from the limiting and inhibiting norms imposed by culture. He treats culture implicitly, as Miller and Dollard do explicitly—that is, as a "maze." With this as a scientific orientation he goes beyond science (in the general tone which is apparent in the two volumes thus far published) to take what amounts to a moral position; an alignment, not just with the principle of a freer discussion and inquiry of sex, but with the principle of greater and freer sexuality, the superiority of quick responses, the desirability of 100% orgasm in the sexual activity of both sexes.

AN ALTERNATIVE VIEW

Before making such a sweeping and indiscriminate plea for change Professor Kinsey might better have considered how far the validity of his view of human nature, either in the broad or in the particulars with which he is dealing, has been demonstrated. We may agree with J. Robert Oppenheimer regarding the basic viewpoint of science that it is "a way of life in which the discovery of error is refined, in which almost all the ingenuity that goes into experimental, analytical, or mathematical techniques is devoted to refining, sharpening, making more effective the way of finding out that you are wrong: this is the element that creates discipline. The nature of the discipline of science is its devotion, its dedication to finding out when you are wrong, to the detection of error . . ."[5]

Let us consider an alternative structuring of sexual activity. A symbolic interaction view of sex would go something like this: Sex acts, sexual objects, sexual partners (human or otherwise) like all other objects toward which human beings behave are *social objects;* that is, they have meanings because meanings are assigned to them by the groups of which human beings are members, for there is nothing in the physiology of man which gives any dependable clue as to what pattern of activity will be followed toward them. The meanings of these social objects are mediated to the individual by means of language just as in the case of all other social objects. That the communications which involve these definitions are frequently—at least in our society—surreptitious and characterized by a high degree of innuendo does not in any wise diminish the truth of this assertion. In short the sexual motives which human beings have are derived from the social roles they play; like all other motives these would not be possible were not the actions physiologically possible, but the physiology does not supply the motives, designate the partners, invest the objects with preformed passion, nor even dictate the objectives to be achieved. Furthermore, since sexual activity in the many hundreds of existing human societies involves a wide variety of differences in the reciprocal roles of the sexual partners, it is even most likely that differences between male and female sexual activity in our own society are attributable to the *social* sex role differentiation rather than to anatomical or physiological differences between the sexes.[6] And finally one would expect to find that the attitudes toward sex, sexual partners, sexual rules and sexual roles are inextricably related to attitudes toward the protection and rearing of children, toward the desired configuration of family life, and in fact toward all of the vast range of situations involving differential role playing on the basis of sex (and this includes just about all human activity in almost all societies).

With this orientation let us see what we might hypothesize regarding the differences Kinsey found between the sexes.[7]

It would follow from our alternative orientation that a "lack of susceptibility to 'psychological stimulation'" would result from a lack of communication—or at least from ambiguous communication—which would leave the individual without social objects. Without communication we would have no words. Without words we would have no objects. Without objects our fantasies could not be informed. Is it not at least impressionistically apparent that, despite the much heralded emancipation of women, communication in the female world and for that matter between the sexes, about sex, is very different in our society from the communication which is so very explicit about sex in the male world? Then it would seem that the process of communication in the female subculture in our society needs to be investigated.[8]

It is also consistent with the hypothesis that the female world of communication about sex is different from that of the male world, that females are more variable in their sex lives, that their first experiences tend to define the activity for them in their subsequent behavior, and that they reach the height of their sexual "potential" later than do males. If there is a considerable lack of communication, then this whole area is, as we are in the habit of saying in social psychological circles, "relatively unstructured." Female behavior then would be somewhat analogous to the behavior of subjects in Sherif's well-known experiment on the autokinetic effect.[9] In the realm specifically of masturbation Kinsey's own data indicate that a much larger proportion of the male universe is involved in the activity, and a much larger proportion of the males who masturbate (75% of the males compared with only 43% of the females) *started as a result of communication from others about the activity.* (p. 173)

It is also consistent with our hypothesis regarding differential communication and its relation to the differences in the sexual behavior of the two sexes that males reach a peak of sexual activity in their late teens which is several times as high as the highest level reached by females. The communication about sex in the male subculture would be im-pressionistically judged to be at its height in the late teens.

As we previously noted, Kinsey chose as the unit for analysis what we called "the physiological act," ending with orgasm. As indicated earlier, any arbitrary unit for analysis by a scientist is defensible, for it will be tested in the final analysis by its utility in making empirical prediction. What Kinsey did which is not defensible was to let this definition of the objective of sexual activity slip quietly over to be *the* physiologically justified objective in sexual activity. By demonstrating that a significant minority of women regularly have orgasms in sexual activity he seems to have thought himself justified in assuming that all women ought regularly to "achieve"[10] orgasm. Our view of human behavior which we have contrasted with his indicates that men and women may very well have differing objectives in their sexual activity (even though most of the activity is conjoint) not because they are physiologically different but because their role definitions (and hence their conceptions of themselves) differ. It would seem reasonable to hypothesize that sexual activity is modally defined by and/or for women in our society as having a somewhat different relation to personal acceptance, love, marriage, offspring and many other activities than it has for men. It may also be noted that while sexual activity in the male much more regularly "ends" in orgasm, it would be a mistake to conclude without any further evidence that orgasm even for the male is *the* objective in all sexual activity.

If Kinsey had held this alternative symbolic interactionist view of human behavior he would not have left his attempted correlations of differentials in sexual activity of various kinds with social variables, particularly religion and educational level, where he did. For example, he made only the simple division of Protestant, Catholic and Jewish (with subdivisions for Protestants and Catholics of "devout," "moderate" and "inactive"). Surely there is a tremendous difference in the definitions put upon sexual activities among, say, Episcopalians, Mormons, Holiness sects, Quakers, Methodists and Jehovah's Witnesses—yet these are all presumably lumped together simply as "Protestants"!

A meticulous breakdown by reference groups rather than by gross imputed reference categories might have shed a great deal of light on say the problem of regret (or acceptance) regarding premarital coitus (pp. 316-321), or the many differences in so-called "psychological factors in sexual response" such as differences in arousal over observing the opposite sex (p. 651), observing genitalia (p. 655), exhibitionism (pp. 656-658), seeing movies (pp. 659-660), voyeurism (pp. 663-664), etc., which Kinsey found among females. Indeed with respect to all the differences, whether among males or females, or between males and females, with respect to sexual activity in all its manifestations, the only way to have demonstrated that sexual variations are attributable to physiological variations (at least at this stage of our knowledge of and techniques for inquiry in physiology) would have been to have made a truly exhaustive study of human attitudes in terms of their possible derivation from reference groups. Having sustained the null hypothesis he might then rightly have considered his view of human behavior validated. As it was he made attempts to test relations between sexual variations and only the most gross, superficial and conglomerate of social categories.

It is pertinent to wonder how Kinsey conceives the purpose of addressing his report to human beings. If we behave essentially as do infra-human animals, if we are conditioned rather than informed and reflective, if our attitudes are *ex post* rationalizations of physiologic activity—then how could he expect the publication of this knowledge to affect materially our ability to control and re-direct our actions? One can only say that there appears to be a disjunction imputed by him between the (physiologically directed) subjects he studied and the (attitudinally controlled) human beings to whom he addresses his books.

NOTES

[1] He makes it abundantly clear in the subheadings he uses in Chapter 16 that he includes the social psychological in the "psychologic."

[2] All otherwise unspecified page notations refer to Alfred C. Kinsey, *et al., Sexual Behavior in the Human Female,* Philadelphia. W. B. Saunders Co., 1953.

[3] Clark Hull at least attempted to avoid reducing his concepts to neurological concepts but failed.

[4] Furthermore, even if we were to grant the reductionists' assumptions, their argument if carried to its logical conclusion would insist on stating all phenomena in terms of electrical fields of force—hence there is no justification, even in their own assumptions, for leaving the reduction of social psychological phenomena at the physiological level of abstraction.

[5] Quoted in a pamphlet "Science and Conscience," by Henry J. Cadbury (no place, date or publisher given), from Oppenheimer's paper, "The Relation of Research to the Liberal University," in *Freedom and the University,* Ithaca, N. Y., 1950, p. 110.

[6] Cf. Kinsey's own findings, including his inability to find physiological or anatomical differences between men and women of the sort which would possibly account for the differences between the sexes in their respective sexual behaviors (chs. 14-15, 17-18); note also that he found wider differences in sexual patterns among women than among men, a point which may pertain to this argument.

[7] And for which he was able to posit only the unsupported hypothesis that the differences must lie in the cerebral cortex. (pp. 710-712)

[8] It might seem that this should have suggested itself to Kinsey from his having found many women who *are* psychologically stimulated and who do fantasize; had he not been looking for physiologic explanations he might have thought to see whether these females differed in their socio-experiential backgrounds from the majority.

[9] It might also be noticed in passing however that with respect to premarital intercourse our culture, in so far as it defines the matter, tends to suggest that the female loses all that she has to lose with the first act, a matter quite different from the definitions put upon male premarital sexual activity.

[10] "Achieve" used in this way would appear to be a loaded word.

Martin B. Loeb (essay date 1955)

SOURCE: A review of "Sexual Behavior in the Human Female," by Alfred Kinsey, in the *American Journal of Sociology*, Vol. LX, No. 4, January, 1955, pp. 409-10.

[*In the following review of Kinsey's* Sexual Behavior in the Human Female, *Loeb questions Kinsey's methodology and characterizes the interpretations of his findings as Victorian.*]

One can hardly review the latest Kinsey report [***Sexual Behavior in the Human Female***] unmindful of other summaries and critiques which have appeared in the last several months. Kinsey has been criticized, to list a few of the charges, for poor or inappropriate sampling, lacking a sense of humor, not being a woman, gathering lies as data, showing disrespect for love, and not being conscious of the unconscious. It is also frequently though not unanimously agreed that Kinsey and his associates have been and are carrying on important and perhaps monumental research.

With the publicity that Kinsey, his co-workers, and his books receive, anyone interested in sexual activity set to print has, in some way or another, confronted both volumes. Added interest is to be found in the second volume, with its comparisons of male and female behavior, and in the excellently written Part III, which summarizes recent physiological findings concerning sexual activity and response. However, in this section, Kinsey's notion of "the psychologic factors" is somewhat Victorian or Krafft-Ebingish.

Anyone involved in field research will recognize the great achievement in interviewing for an average of two hours nearly 16,000 men and women across the United States. This feat may not impress armchair philosophers or couch clinicians. For the first time, an attempt has been made to obtain information on sexual behavior from a large nonclinical sample. As the authors modestly say, "The sample is still, at many points, inadequate, but we have been able to secure a greater diversification of subjects than had been available in previous studies." They have collected and tabulated a lot of informative data. For this accomplishment social scientists ought to be grateful, in spite of the occasional and understandable enthusiasm which leads the authors to claim more for their data than can be sustained.

Nonetheless, one may question whether Kinsey knows quite what to do with his data. His sociological and psychological understanding is inadequate. For instance, he categorizes his subjects by age, education, occupation of parent or husband, rural or urban, religious background. These are only common-sense categories. Why, one may ask, are these more relevant than hair color, shoe size, or food habits? Even when one finds a juicy correlation, what does it mean? This question is deeper than, but similar to, some of the questions that have arisen about the sampling procedures. Sexual behavior is more socially controlled than other biological functions because the sex drive does not have to be satisfied to maintain life in the organism. This is not true of food or air, for instance. The social nature of man provides him with choice concerning sexual activity. There are sublimations and substitutes.

The values by which choices are made make sense of the variety of choices, and the social forces and institutions which give rise to the value systems are the relevant sociological variables. There is the question then as to whether sociologists have developed the concepts of social forces and institutions adequately to communicate with fellow scientists, even zoölogists, who are highly motivated to find out about them or whether Kinsey is sufficiently sensitized to sociological concepts to have tried to find them.

Secondly, when Kinsey interprets the meaning of his findings, he again reflects his nineteenth-century view of ethics which modern social science could dispel. Kinsey finds that "the law is an ass" because it is so far from being lived up to—it is not rational. But the law is only a guide and frequently only an ideal; it is more likely to be based on what people think they ought to do than on what they do. Similarly, it is only a minor aspect of legal punishment to consider the culprit and his reclamation. The major function is to reinforce the "oughts" of the value system. A study of the anthropology of law would make Kinsey's zeal for reform more realistic and realizable.

As much as I like to argue with Kinsey and his associates, I am grateful that they are around to argue with. Even now, through the smoke of heated argument, it can be recognized that Kinsey's studies of sexual behavior provide a solid groundwork for fruitful discussion and have opened up new vistas for much-needed further research.

Regina Markell Morantz (essay date 1977)

SOURCE: "The Scientist as Sex Crusader: Alfred C. Kinsey and American Culture," in *American Quarterly*, Vol. XXIX, No. 5, Winter, 1977, pp. 563-89.

[*In the following essay, Morantz presents a historical overview of the cultural shift aided by publication of Kinsey's work and provides detailed biographical analysis of Kinsey's motives for studying human sexuality.*]

In January 1948, Robert Latou Dickinson, noted gynecologist and sex researcher, dashed off a note to his friend and colleague Alfred Charles Kinsey. Dickinson's copy of the newly published ***Sexual Behavior in the Human Male,*** which he had awaited "with one of the keenest anticipations of a lifetime," had arrived. "I have my copy at last of SBHM!" he informed Kinsey. "Glory to God!"[1] In a lively correspondence throughout the 1940s the two men had shared enthusiasm for Kinsey's studies in human sexuality, their mutual respect enhanced by appreciation of the social significance of this work. Given the chance to see Kinsey's labors in print,

Dickinson's excitement grew: "Dear ACE:" he wrote Kinsey in February, "In sex education, and marriage counsel [*sic*] and v.d. and prostitution attacks . . . we would, in America, hereafter, speak of the Pre-Kinsey and the Post-Kinsey eras."[2]

The press, the public, and expert opinion subsequently confirmed Dickinson's assessment. Writers dubbed ***Sexual Behavior in the Human Male*** "the most talked about book of the twentieth century." Others ranked it with *Das Kapital, The Origin of Species,* and *Wealth of Nations.* Indeed, the reception accorded Kinsey's work was unprecedented. Although Kinsey's publishers authorized an inadequate first printing of 5,000 copies, less than two months after publication ***Sexual Behavior in the Human Male*** had sold 200,000 copies and stood in second place on the non-fiction best-seller list. George Gallup reported that one out of every five Americans had either read or heard about the book, while five out of six of those interviewed judged its publication "a good thing." Multiple reviews appeared in literary periodicals. Medical and lay organizations held symposia to assess its impact. Overnight "Kinsey" became a household word, his name forever embedded in popular culture.[3]

Response to the Kinsey report testified more than anything else to the revolution in sexual mores that its text, charts, and statistical tables so laboriously documented. No one would now dispute that a generation of Americans who had come of age in the first decades of the twentieth century had begun to lift the mantle of fear and shame from their sexual activities. Since 1913 American newspapers had been hailing what one headline writer called "sex o'clock in America." Even the scientific study of sex had gotten underway years before Kinsey: the Male Report cites 19 prior investigations of human sexuality. But journalists who wrote about America's sex obsession before World War I rarely elaborated on what factors underlay the new freedom in manners, while postwar professionals who had begun to analyze its components increasingly avoided sharing their findings with a popular audience. What made Kinsey different—indeed, what made him unique—was his confidence that Americans were ready for a confrontation with their own sexuality. In dispassionate prose he laid bare the facts.

Most of his contemporaries understood Kinsey's research to be a monumental achievement of twentieth-century science. He managed where others had failed to discuss sexual matters before a public still ignorant and uncomfortable with the subject. His own liberalism was grounded in the conviction that nothing human should be alien to the realm of science.

Of course Kinsey's detractors were vindictive. Some disputed his findings, questioning his evidence and doubting his methods; others condemned him for publicizing his facts. But though Kinsey may have underestimated the reaction of those ill-equipped to handle his candor, his faith in the American people was not misplaced. Accepting the legitimacy of his research with the respect they afforded all science, they rapidly made his work part of the conventional wisdom. After summarizing the origins of sex research in America, this essay will attempt to analyze this process of acceptance. It will focus on Kinsey the man, the content of his reports and the critical response they evoked, and the larger cultural meaning of Kinsey's work.

. . . . .

Victorian aversion to the investigation of sexual matters relegated sex to the backroom almost as effectively in 1900 as in the previous century. Scientists and physicians either shared their society's view of what was proper, or else kept quiet about it. Research into the socially taboo took courage; chastisement was often swift and forceful. When the distinguished Chicago physician, Denslow Lewis, proposed in 1899 to speak to the American Medical Association on the "Gynecologic Consideration of the Sexual Act," he was denounced by Howard A. Kelly of Johns Hopkins. "The discussion of the subject," Kelly asserted, "is attended with filth and we besmirch ourselves by discussing it in public." Characteristically, the Association refused to publish Lewis' paper.[4]

Nineteenth-century moralism gradually succumbed in the first decades of the twentieth century to the combined attack of purity advocates (including feminists, clergymen, and social reformers), idealistic physicians inspired by bacteriological discoveries facilitating the control of venereal disease, and the diverse but insistent proponents of the Freudian revolution. Social and economic factors also underlay the emergence of new sexual attitudes. As early as 1907 Simon Patten predicted the gradual economic shift away from austerity and production to a concern with consumption.[5] An interest in leisure and luxury fostered pleasure and personal fulfillment as positive goods, and undermined Victorian prescriptions of thrift, self-denial, and personal control. Urbanization eroded community and religious controls on behavior. In addition, the increasingly visible women joining the labor force were freed from some of the constraints of home and family.

Though sex was discussed in the Progressive era, sex research remained controversial. Not until 1921 did scientists and social reformers organize a two-day conference under the auspices of the National Research Council to examine the status of American sex research. Acknowledging the importance of such investigation, conference members decried the "enshrouding of sex relations in a fog of mystery, reticence and shame." Sensing the national faith in science, participants argued that scientists were best qualified to study sex because "their standing in the community would prevent fears that their findings would be put to propaganda purposes." The meetings resulted in the formation of a Committee for Research on Problems in Sex chaired by Yale psychologist Robert Yerkes and connected with the National Research Council.[6] Funded largely by the Rockefeller Foundation, and working closely with the Bureau of Social Hygiene, another Foundation project, the Committee directed most sex studies in the next two decades. Alfred Kinsey turned to this committee for financial support in 1939. Aid for his project opened the door to a new and controversial era in sex research.

While the Committee for the Study of Problems in Sex quietly encouraged research on sexuality in the 1920s and 1930s, Kinsey built his career as a leading expert on the gall wasp.[7] Twenty-six years old in 1920, Kinsey came to Indiana University as an assistant professor of zoology. For the next two decades he taught courses in entymology, general biology, and insect taxonomy, and by the mid-thirties he had published two specialized books, numerous articles, and an innovative high school biology text.

Few facts are available to explain Kinsey's subsequent interest in sex. His own sexual history, like those of the people he interviewed, will presumably remain locked forever in the confidential files at the Institute for Sex Research. Though he spoke little of his past, it is clear that his parents were strict and puritanical. The product of a deeply religious home, Kinsey suffered as a youngster because of his proficiency in the natural sciences and his fascination with Darwinian evolution. When Kinsey rebelled, science offered him a set of values which emotionally rivalled his juvenile commitment to religion. His sympathetic attitude toward the sexual dilemmas of the young may have grown out of memories of his own pain, frustration, and ignorance; science granted him the tools to make his sympathy more objective. But cloaked in the unbiased empiricism of the dispassionate scientist lay the emotional preferences of a moral crusader.

Kinsey's involvement with sex research began quietly in 1938 when he was chosen as the faculty coordinator of a newly established marriage course. The course consisted of interdisciplinary guest lecturers, with Kinsey lecturing on biology. His class notes reveal sophistication with published works on sex. Indeed, in a letter to Robert Latou Dickinson written in 1941, he admitted: "It was your own work which turned my attention to the purposes of research in this field some ten or twelve years ago although circumstances were not propitious for starting the work until three years ago." In a talk delivered in 1935 to a faculty discussion club he had proved himself familiar with previous sex studies by G. V. Hamilton and Katherine B. Davis. The lectures displayed his concern with both the influence of social institutions on sexual behavior and the "sexual conflicts of youth." Significantly, he reflected that such conflicts arose because of the "long frustration of the normal sexual activities."[8]

Kinsey emphasized the central importance of sexual adjustment to stable unions. "I know of no evidence," he stated flatly, "that this biological basis can be completely sidestepped and still lead to a successful home." He accused modern education "through its system of mores, laws, and ethics," of conditioning attitudes toward sex which were "wrong in the sense that they interfere with the successful consummation of the marriage . . . [and] develop the sexual maladjustments that appear most often after marriage. Our ignorance of copulatory techniques," he continued, "which is the direct outcome of the impressions that are imprinted on the young, our ignorance of satisfactory contraceptive devices above all, produce attitudes which make our concepts of sex wrong." By delaying sexual activity until marriage, he argued, young people only made the achievement of successful marriage more problematic. Responses repressed for ten or twelve years after an individual is first capable of sexual activity could hardly be changed by a marriage ceremony. Distorted attitudes formed in adolescence required years of adjustment after marriage. "Why offer a marriage course?" Kinsey asked his listeners. "Society," he answered, "has been responsible for interfering with what would have been normal biological development. . . . It behooves us to make amends to society by taking you as you approach the time of marriage and giving you the results of scholarly thinking on these several problems."[9] Repeatedly, Kinsey the scientist would side with biology when it conflicted with accepted social mores.

In the summer of 1938 Kinsey began taking the sex histories of his students and within a year had scheduled interviews outside the university to vary his sampling. Aware of their potential significance, he termed these histories "a scientific goldmine" and wondered to a colleague if they would not account "for the largest volume of research I will yet publish."[10] Under mounting pressure from conservative elements of the community, Kinsey terminated his connection with the marriage course in 1940. Soon afterward he received his first grant from the Committee for Research in Problems of Sex. Abandoning his interest in the gall wasp, he prepared to devote himself solely to the study of human sexual behavior.

. . . . .

While attempting to dispel his own ignorance, Kinsey learned much about the state of sex research in America. The introduction to ***Sexual Behavior in the Human Male*** best summarizes his beliefs and the purpose of his work. People of different persuasions, he explained, have come to desire scientific data on sex which could be "divorced from questions of moral value and social customs." His purpose would be to

> bring an educated intelligence into the consideration of such matters as sexual adjustments in marriage, the sexual guidance of children, the premarital sexual activities which are in conflict with the mores, and problems confronting persons who are interested in the social control of behavior through religion, custom, and the forces of the law.

Scientists knew more about the sexual behavior of animals than about human beings, he lamented. Before men could think scientifically about human sexuality, they needed facts about actual behavior. The link between behavior and the "biologic and social aspects" of people's sex lives demanded exploration. Lack of information resulting from the influence of "religious evaluation, social taboo, and formal legislation" imposed unwarranted restrictions on investigation. Kinsey's study attempted "to accumulate an objectively determined body of fact about sex which strictly avoids social or moral interpretations." Scientists, he cautioned, "have no special capacities for making such evaluations."[11]

Kinsey adapted the methods of modern taxonomy to his new research. Biologists, he observed had become increasingly aware of the uniqueness of individuals, "and of the wide range of variation which may occur in any population. . . . " A taxonomist measured the variation in series of individuals who stood as "representatives of the species in which he is interested."[12] Taxonomic faith led Kinsey to a position that his critics would label moral relativism. His gall wasp investigations had made him so sensitive to individual uniqueness and the endless possibility of variation as fundamental biological principles that it is a wonder he managed to generalize at all. Uncomfortable with dichotomous classifications, he preferred to speak of changes on an infinite continuum. The problem arose when he applied such premises to human behavior by arguing that "our conceptions of right and wrong, normal and abnormal, are seriously challenged by the variation studies."[13] Critics instantly accused Kinsey of maintaining that what is ought to be. Sexual behavior, they insisted, was culturally as well as biologically determined; in the face of such a conviction Kinsey's position seemed morally outrageous.

Undaunted, Kinsey united this taxonomic approach with interviewing techniques recently developed in public opinion research. It was a brilliant synthesis. Only a couple of earlier sex surveys had used the interview to gather data, and none with the skill and flexibility which was Kinsey's forte. He asked from 300 to 500 questions of each subject in a conference that took nearly two hours. Interviews were not standardized and questions varied in order and language according to the respondent's class, profession, or educational background. Despite critics' scepticism about the interview situation, there seems little reason to doubt that it was an extraordinarily successful invention. Kinsey proved a genius at establishing rapport with a variety of people.[14]

Both the Male Report (1948) and the Female Report (1953) measured sexual activity almost exclusively in terms of orgasm.[15] The incidence and frequencies of orgasm through six sexual outlets—masturbation, nocturnal emissions, heterosexual petting, sexual intercourse, homosexual activity, and animal contacts—were then discussed. The Reports analyzed behavior in terms of race, sex, age, marital status, age at puberty, educational level, occupational class, class of parents, rural-urban background, religious affiliation, frequency of church attendance, and geographic origin. Kinsey and his associates explored every level of American society: gay bars, back-country villages, schools, prisons, private clubs, city slums, YMCA groups, professional associations, hospitals, and medical clinics across the country. Though several critics found fault with this sample, the study was the most complete, detailed, and sophisticated of its kind. Much of what was reported had been suspected by professionals for decades but had never been verified. Never before had such a large sampling of sexual behavior been quantified. Sociologist Robert MacIver, in reviewing the criticism of statisticians in 1948, observed,

> Kinsey's 95 per cent may be only 91 per cent. He may not have equally good samples for all the groups he deals with. He may be criticized on this point or that. . . . But all such criticisms together, even were they all justified, would still leave practically unchanged the broader picture he presents, would still leave his major conclusions unchallenged.[16]

Indeed, most of Kinsey's statistical estimates have held true in subsequent studies, and those that have been corrected have not been far from the mark.[17]

Consistent with Kinsey's earlier writings, both volumes emphasized the behavioral range of sex activity. This prompted Kinsey to question formerly accepted norms. Perhaps the most significant finding of the Male volume was the discovery of distinctly different sexual patterns between males of different social and economic levels. Kinsey's data emphasized cultural determinants of sexual behavior by measuring the influence of class, religion, and decade of birth.[18]

Kinsey's books demonstrated a widespread violation of traditional socio-sexual mores. No longer could masturbation, premarital or extramarital intercourse, and homosexuality be viewed as occasional deviations. Questioning the arbitrary and unrealistic nature of contemporary sex laws, he estimated that 95 percent of American men had engaged in "illegal" sexual activity. His sympathy with the predicament of the young led him to examine youthful behavior carefully. He was the first to statistically verify Freud's theory of infantile sexuality. His data also emphasized the high incidence of male adolescent sexuality, demonstrating that 95 percent of men establish a regular sexual outlet by the age of fifteen. Noting the almost universal occurrence of male masturbation, Kinsey argued that men reached their peak activity in their late teens.

The Male Report introduced a heterosexual-homosexual rating scale which measured an individual along a continuum from complete homosexuality to complete heterosexuality by considering both overt behavior and psychic response. This scale represented Kinsey's discomfort with dichotomous classifications and his determination to investigate behavior independent of a preconceived notion of normality.[19] Using such a scale Kinsey computed that 37 percent of American men had at some point engaged in homosexual behavior involving orgasm. Other notable statistics in the Male volume included the high incidence of premarital intercourse (86 percent of the sample), extramarital intercourse (50 percent), and the almost universal occurrence of premarital petting, much of it to orgasm.

Kinsey's volume on women contributed decisively to the growing twentieth-century sophistication concerning female sexual response. His premises led him to a deep sympathy with women's sexual rights. Contradicting both popular and scientific lore, he found no basic physiological differences in the sexual response of men and women. Demonstrating the nearly identical nature of the anatomical structures most essential to orgasm, he argued that sexual climax was virtually the same for both sexes. Masturbatory data, he pointed out, contradicted the "widespread opinion that the female is slower than the male in her sexual responses." Women's allegedly slower reactions were due not to anatomical differences but "to the ineffectiveness of the usual coital techniques," which did not respect female anatomy.[20] Indeed, the only significant difference in male and female response that Kinsey noted was the lesser reaction of women to psychological stimuli.[21]

In retrospect perhaps Kinsey's most controversial finding was that the vaginal orgasm was a "biologic impossibility."[22] For years prior to publication Kinsey had corresponded with a handful of gynecologists who were trying to pinpoint the female sexual response. The tentativeness of existing professional knowledge about the female orgasm was striking.[23] Marriage counselors and psychiatrists, influenced by Freudian theory, had been advising patients to transfer immature "clitoral responses" into the only psychologically "satisfactory" culmination of sex activity for the "sexually mature female," the vaginal orgasm. Kinsey cited the absence of anatomical data to indicate that such a transformation had ever been possible: the lack of nerve endings in the interior vagina made it insensitive to touch. Mustering data from female masturbatory techniques and homosexual behavior, he accused therapists of causing unnecessary conflicts in their patients. "In most females," he observed,

> the walls of the vagina are devoid of end organs of touch and are quite insensitive when they are gently stroked or lightly pressed. For most individuals this insensitivity extends to every part of the vagina. . . .
>
> This insensitivity of the vagina has been recognized by gynecologists who regularly probe and do surface operations in this area without using anesthesia. . . .
>
> Many males . . . basing their concepts on their understanding of coitus and upon their conceit as to the importance of the male genitalia in coitus, imagine that all female masturbation must involve an insertion of fingers or of some other object into the depths of the vagina. . . .
>
> The relative unimportance of the vagina as a center of erotic stimulation is further attested by the fact that relatively few females masturbate by making deep vaginal insertions. (P. 161, Table 37) Fully 84 percent of the females in the sample who had masturbated had depended chiefly on labial and clitorial [*sic*] stimulation. . . . Some of the psychoanalysts and some other clinicians insist that only vaginal stimulation and a "vaginal orgasm" can provide a psychologically satisfactory culmination to the activity of a "sexually mature" female. It is difficult, however, in the light of our present understanding of the anatomy and physiology of sexual response to understand what can be meant by a "vaginal orgasm." . . . Freud . . . contended that psychosexual maturation involved a subordination of clitoral reactions and a development of sensitivity within the vagina itself; but there are no anatomic data to indicate that such a physical transformation has ever been observed. . . . [24]

Pointing out that most past investigators were men, Kinsey chided them for projecting their own copulatory needs onto women. He disliked the term "frigidity" so in vogue with psychiatrists, and he believed that most females were physiologically capable of response to the point of orgasm. Their failure to do so was mostly the fault of ignorance, guilt, or lack of sufficient physical stimulation.[25]

The lack of attention paid to this controversial aspect of Kinsey's research remains puzzling, in view of the intensity of our contemporary debate among sexologists, psychoanalysts, and feminists over the existence of the vaginal orgasm. A handful of psychiatrists denounced Kinsey for undermining a basic tenet of Freudian theory about women, but always in conjunction with more complex issues pertaining to Kinsey's cavalier treatment of psychosexual factors in general.[26] One suspects that although many marriage counselors and sex therapists grasped the implications of the new findings regarding female orgasm, few were prepared to discuss them in print.[27] Kinsey's evidence implied that intercourse was not the most efficient method for women to achieve pleasure. Indeed, his statistics on female homosexuality suggested that lesbians were more likely to achieve orgasm consistently. "The higher frequency of orgasms in the homosexual contacts," he observed,

> may have depended . . . on the fact that two individuals of the same sex are likely to understand the anatomy and the physiologic responses and psychology of their own sex better than they understand that of the opposite sex. Most males are likely to approach females as they, the males, would like to be approached by a sexual partner. They are likely to begin by providing immediate genital stimulation. They are inclined to utilize a variety of psychologic stimuli which may mean little to most females. . . . Females in their heterosexual relationships are actually more likely to prefer techniques which are closer to those which are commonly utilized in homosexual relationships. They would prefer a considerable amount of generalized emotional stimulation before there is any specific sexual contact. They usually want physical stimulation of the whole body before there is any specifically genital contact. They may especially want stimulation of the clitoris and the labia minora, and stimulation which, after it has once begun, is followed through to orgasm without the interruptions which males, depending to a greater degree than most females

> do upon psychologic stimuli, often introduce into their heterosexual relationships.[28]

In contrast, psychoanalysts predicated the theory of the vaginal orgasm on the assumption of certain irreconcilable psychological and biological differences between the sexes. Mature intercourse represented the one means by which these differences could be resolved, if only temporarily. As Erik Erikson eloquently put it: "The total fact of finding, via the climactic turmoil of the orgasm, a supreme experience of mutual regulation of two beings in some way takes the edge off the hostilities and potential rages caused by the oppositeness of male and female, of fact and fancy, of love and hate." By devaluing the role of the penis in stimulating female sexual response and by arguing that male and female orgasm were essentially alike, Kinsey inadvertently helped to undermine an almost universally accepted theory of sex differences. Furthermore, his findings hinted at the need for a redefinition of the concept of genital sexuality. Although some feminists in the 1960s would view their emancipation from the "tyranny of the vaginal orgasm" as a mark of liberation and the beginning of a new age of equality between the sexes,[29] the persistent influence of Freudian theory on definitions of female nature and the absence of an organized feminist movement in the early 1950s softened the impact of this most radical of Kinsey's findings. Only when Masters and Johnson reaffirmed his theories and published their conclusions in drastically altered social circumstances did Kinsey's early work receive attention.[30]

Another striking finding of Kinsey's statistics was their documentation of a liberalization of female behavior patterns in generations of women born after 1900. The accumulative incidence among women of masturbation (62 percent of the sample), premarital petting (90 percent), and premarital intercourse (50 percent) increased dramatically, especially after World War I. Although frequency figures for marital intercourse over four decades went down, Kinsey's data showed a steady rise in the numbers of women reaching orgasm in marital coitus. Closely paralleling this development was the fact that precoital petting techniques in marriage had become more varied and more prevalent. These findings led Kinsey to conclude that males of the younger generation were more inclined to respond favorably to female sexual rhythms, both in terms of desired frequency of intercourse and in recognizing the legitimacy of female pleasure.

. . . . .

The current permissiveness surrounding sex research should not obscure the fact that thirty years ago Kinsey's findings disturbed, shocked, and threatened not just ordinary men and women but professionals as well. A good deal of the hostile criticism directed at Kinsey's work had little to do with its scientific value. Princeton University president Harold Dodds likened the Male volume to "the work of small boys writing dirty words on fences." The Chicago *Tribune* termed Kinsey a "menace to society." The Reverend Henry Van Dusen, president of Union Theological Seminary and a member of the Rockefeller Foundation, called for a "spontaneous ethical revulsion from the premises of the study," and chided the Foundation for its sponsorship. Kinsey's work, he lamented, revealed "a prevailing degradation of American morality approximating the worst decadence of the Roman era."[31] Harvard sociologist Carle C. Zimmerman labelled the Male volume an "attack on the Western family," and accused Kinsey of irresponsibility in making it public. Millicent McIntosh, indomitable president of Barnard College and mother of five, worried in 1954 that Kinsey's books had already contributed "to the difficulties encountered by young people in establishing a good relationship between the sexes."[32]

Hysteria reached Congress when New York Representative Louis B. Heller called upon the Postmaster General to bar the Female Report from the mails until it could be investigated, charging Kinsey with "hurling the insult of the century against our mothers, wives, daughters and sisters." Soon rumors spread that the Special House Committee founded during the McCarthy era to inquire into the use of funds by tax-exempt foundations would ask Kinsey to testify regarding financial aid from the Rockefeller Foundation. Others accused Kinsey of aiding communism.[33] Shortly thereafter the Rockefeller Foundation informed Kinsey that his grant would not be renewed.

Much of the criticism of Kinsey's work, however, was not hysterical. Most commentators admired his research and welcomed its publication.[34] Yet serious critics also offered objections. The debate centered on two issues: the possibility of conducting a scientific investigation that was value-free (and whether Kinsey had done so); and the extent to which a behavioristic approach could solve fundamental questions of human existence.

Kinsey never admitted publicly that scientists based their investigations on cultural assumptions. He remained deaf to the charge that his work reflected his own biases. Yet his objectivity was itself polemical: his research subverted the status quo specifically because it examined individual deviance dispassionately. Many critics were repelled by the idea of studying sexual nonconformity objectively. By definition norms are not always rational. Kinsey's non-judgmental approach aligned him with the twentieth-century rebels against Victorian repression. Though many critics shared the Progressive faith that the truth would make men free, they resisted applying this conviction to sex research. In this instance the truth was dangerous and might help destroy the American value system. Reinhold Niebuhr passionately argued this point of view when he declared that Kinsey's assumptions represented "a therapy which implies a disease in our culture as grievous or more grievous than the sickness it pretends to cure."[35]

Soon after the publication of the Male volume, Lionel Trilling wrote of Kinsey and his co-authors that "nothing comes more easily to their pens than the criticism of the subjectivity of earlier writers on sex, yet their own subjectivity is sometimes extreme."[36] A retrospective reading of both volumes reveals why Kinsey was an easy mark for Trilling's pen. In neither book did he disguise either his admiration for the sexually active or his suspicion of the sexually repressed. His statistical interpretations fell invariably on the side of sexual liberalism. In a chapter on the onset of male puberty, for example, he recorded his approval of men who began their sexual activities early. On scant evidence he asserted that early-adolescent males were often "the more alert, energetic, vivacious, spontaneous, physically active, socially extrovert, and/or aggressive individuals in the population," while late-maturing males tended to be "slow, quiet, mild in manner, without force, reserved, timid, taciturn, introvert, and/or socially inept."[37] He revealed his own biases most clearly when he linked the aggressive, success-oriented personality type—an American paragon—to vigorous sexuality.

Equally controversial were Kinsey's interpretations of the data concerning the relationship between premarital intercourse and marital adjustment. Although he admitted that premarital petting contributed "definitely to the effectiveness of the sexual relations after marriage," he nevertheless remained contemptuous of the hypocrisy involved in adolescent petting behavior. "It is amazing," he wrote,

> to observe the mixtures of scientifically supported logic, and utter illogic, which shapes the petting behavior of most of these youths. That some of them are in some psychic conflict over their activities is evidenced by the curious rationalizations which they use to satisfy their consciences. They are particularly concerned with the avoidance of genital union. The fact that petting involves erotic contacts which are as effective as genital union, and that it may even involve contacts which have been more taboo than genital union, including some that have been considered perversions, does not disturb the youth so much as actual intercourse would. By petting, they preserve their virginities, even though they may achieve orgasm while doing so.[38]

Coupled with his disdain for this hypocrisy was his finding of a "marked, positive correlation between experience in orgasm obtained from premarital coitus [for women], and the capacity to reach orgasm after marriage." Over half the female sample who had experienced premarital coital orgasm had reached sexual climax in nearly all of their coitus during the first year of marriage. Only 29 percent of women without such premarital experience were able to achieve regular orgasm during the first year.[39]

Kinsey dismissed selective factors as accounting for the correlation, and emphasized that almost half of those women sampled who had premarital intercourse had it exclusively with their fiancés. This figure led some critics to question whether such behavior could properly be termed "premarital coitus" at all. Kinsey found that the overall number of women achieving orgasm *at least occasionally* within the first year of marriage was as high as 75 percent. Indeed, the percentage rose steadily according to the number of years married. What Kinsey's statistics seemed to indicate was that reaching orgasm for women was a *learned* skill that took time to develop. Kinsey's data, critics argued, could or could not be interpreted to justify premarital intercourse.[40]

Kinsey nevertheless used his findings to suggest that traditional mores regarding premarital intercourse were outmoded. In an impassioned paragraph, he made his sympathies clear. His carefully selected phrases, typical of numerous passages in the books, bristled with an aggressive undertone barely couched in the language of scientific neutrality: "The attempt," he wrote,

> to ignore and suppress the physiologic needs of the sexually most capable of the population, has led to more complications than most persons are willing to recognize. This is why so many of our American youth, both females and males, depend upon masturbation instead of coitus as a premarital outlet. Restraints on premarital heterosexual contacts appear to be primary factors in the development of homosexual activities among both females and males. (pp. 460, 465)
>
> The considerable development of petting, which many foreigners consider one of the unique aspects of the sexual pattern in this country, is similarly an outgrowth of this restraint on premarital coitus. (pp. 227-228)
>
> The law specifies the right of the married adult to have regular intercourse, but it makes no provision whatsoever for the approximately 40 per cent of the population which is sexually mature but unmarried. Many youths and older unmarried females and males are seriously disturbed because the only sources of sexual outlet are either legally or socially disapproved.[41]

Such statements challenged the 1950s social and sexual standards. Most marriage manuals still preached the virtues of premarital chastity, while only a few professionals had given serious thought to the problems of sexual adjustment for the unmarried.[42]

Kinsey's detractors feared that his premises implied an animalistic philosophy of sex devoid of emotional and social content. They accused him of a crude behaviorism that failed to place sexual activity within the larger context of human values. Thoughtful reviewers, many of them psychiatrists and psychologists, chided him for his recurrent neglect of the psycho-dynamics of sex. Denying that as a biologist Kinsey was equipped to examine complex psycho-social questions, analysts decried his measure of sex activity in terms of outlet and orgasm. By reducing sex to the mechanistic Kinsey ignored motivation. Should orgasm in and of itself, they asked, be the goal of human sexual behavior? Where was the place of love in Kinsey's universe? Speaking of sex solely in terms of outlet negated its relationship to the creative, integrative, and inspirational aspects of human life. Sexuality, though important, remained only one dimension of the human personality. "It was Freud's idea," wrote Karl Menninger, "that sexuality in the broad sense, the life instinct, was represented not nearly so much by orgasm as by human love, and that the goal of all sexual behavior was better integration, better inter-human concern, and thereby less mutual destructiveness."[43]

The psychoanalytic case against Kinsey extended beyond his failure to consider the emotional content of the sex act. Kinsey avoided placing sexuality within a developmental framework. Except for confirming infantile sexuality, he refused to see any substantiation for other central tenets of psychoanalytic theory. His animus toward psychoanalysts remained clear. He denied that "normal" psychosexual development preceded from narcissism through homosexual to heterosexual activities. In a final affront to Freudian theory, he questioned the significance to women of such concepts as penis envy, castration fear, defense against incestuous wishes, and fixation at the clitoral stage. "The psycho-sexual pattern in the human animal," he wrote, "originates in indiscriminate sexual responses which as a product of conditioning and social pressures, become increasingly restricted in the directions of traditional interpretations of what is normal or abnormal in sexual behavior. . . . It is simply a picture of physiologic response and psychologic conditioning in terms that are known to the biologist and psychologist."[44] Psychoanalysts found this approach simplistic. "Frigidity," argued Marie Robinson, "is in the vast majority of cases, essentially a psychological problem. No amount of mechanical manipulation can make a difference. Anybody who tells you differently," she cautioned her patients, "is . . . wrong." "Kinsey's credo," wrote Edmund Bergler and William S. Kroger, "amounts to naiveté of the first order. . . . It overlooks the complex mechanisms of inner-unconscious-conscious. . . . Sex, though biologically present in every human being, goes through complicated (not simple) transformations before maturity is reached."[45]

While psychoanalysts worried over Kinsey's behaviorism, theologians accused him of materialism. Kinsey's animal analogy represented a conscious tool in his revolt against Victorian sexual attitudes which for a century had exalted ecstasy of the spirit and devalued the pleasures of the flesh. In contrast, Kinsey embraced man's mammalian heritage. Admiring Freud for reasserting the primacy of physical drives, Kinsey believed that man's pretensions to uniqueness had accounted for untold sexual unhappiness. As a biologist he took for granted that, in the long run, physiological factors were more effective than man-made regulations in determining patterns of human behavior. Reinhold Niebuhr read him correctly when he charged Kinsey with referring consistently to analogies between man and the sex practices of infrahuman species "without once calling attention to uniquely human characteristics of man's sexual life."[46]

This alleged materialism led Kinsey to the controversial assumption that the prevalence of certain types of behavior indicated both their mammalian origins and their biological normality. The frequency of types of behavior socially labelled "deviant" testified to the persistence of biologic over cultural determinants. Such a view demanded a reevaluation of homosexuality. Regarding the "normality" of such behavior Kinsey wrote:

> In view of the data which we now have on the incidence and frequency of the homosexual, in particular on its coexistence with the heterosexual in the lives of a considerable portion of the male population, it is difficult to maintain the view that psychosexual reactions between individuals of the same sex are rare and therefore abnormal or unnatural, or that they constitute within themselves evidence of neuroses or even psychoses.[47]

Theologians and other humanists united in their revulsion against this view of sex. Man, they reminded their readers, was not just a little above the apes, but a little below the angels. The difference between human beings and animals lay in the capacity of men to control their instincts, to use language, and to develop creativity, imagination, and culture. In the end, critics maintained, sex was a social activity, culturally and psychologically influenced.[48]

Many of Kinsey's difficulties with the humanists may have arisen from his narrow philosophy of science. He often argued that as a scientist he reserved the right to limit his investigation in any way he saw fit. Though he never denied the significance of the social and psychologic components of human behavior, he insisted that science was "by its method limited to the consideration of material phenomena. The accumulation of scientific data depends upon the reduction of such material to quantifiable units which can be measured." He implied that any other order of facts or values than his could be explored only by non-scientific or ultra-scientific means. He accused psychiatrists studying Freudian stages in psycho-sexual development of investigating "mystic impulses." Theologians, and those "concerned with the moral values of sexual behavior" he considered to be antagonistic to science altogether.[49]

Kinsey's refusal to answer the criticism of the humanists also revealed his shortcomings as a sexual theorist. Kinsey's work is peculiarly joyless. "If someone," wrote Karl Stern in *Commonweal,* "attempted to set the stage for a dehumanized, de-personalized society, for the great beehive—he would start out with things like the Kinsey Report." Ironically, the Victorians themselves had been accused of joylessness, though for different reasons. Kinsey, it seemed to some, represented a new kind of puritan. "There is in all this," Stern remarked with considerable irony, "a subtle, hidden despising of nature."[50]

In the present period of sexual permissiveness, the arguments of the humanists loom more salient than they did thirty years ago. A general theory of sexuality cannot remain grounded in only one academic discipline, but must seek to integrate the methods and findings of many. Undoubtedly Kinsey would have renounced the role of sexual theorist. He died too soon for us to speculate on whether subsequent research would have led him beyond a crude empiricism. Yet in stubbornly labelling even thoughtful critics as Victorian moralists in disguise, perhaps Kinsey had a point. His findings may not have helped to cure the sexually neurotic, but, given the prevailing atmosphere surrounding the public discussion of sex, his behavioristic approach may have liberated sexually active men and women still haunted with Victorian prudery. *Look* magazine recognized this therapeutic effect: "What they [the authors] have learned and will learn may have a tremendous effect on the future social history of mankind. For they are presenting facts. They are revealing not what *should be,* but what *is.* For the first time data on human sex behavior is entirely separated from questions of philosophy, moral values, and social customs."[51]

The fact that Kinsey himself had been raised under the canons of sexual puritanism probably made him sensitive to the problems of ordinary men and women. Certainly his democratic tendencies convinced him that for most people questions concerning the ultimate significance of sexuality were not only unimportant, they were irrelevant. The first task was to unshackle a generation from its repressive past. Relieving guilt and reassuring readers that everyone had similar sexual impulses, Kinsey's books contributed to a changing sexual climate in which ordinary people lived and worked. They probably had the same emancipating effect on the unpsychoanalyzed masses that Freud's work achieved for generations of intellectuals.

. . . . .

Not long after the publication of the Female volume, Kinsey's health began to deteriorate. For over a decade he had maintained a schedule which left him little free time. The emotional criticism that accompanied the release of his second book hurt him deeply. Cessation of foundation backing left the future of his research in the balance; for three years he struggled to reestablish the Institute for Sex Research on a solid financial footing. In 1956, at the age of 64, he died of a heart attack.

In the years between the publication of the Male Report and his premature death, Kinsey grew petrified of yellow journalism and the danger of misinterpretation. The importance of his scientific approach in achieving acceptance for his work cannot be overstressed. Indeed, his insistence on the legitimacy of his research and his scientific credentials eventually made him a heroic figure, even in the eyes of his enemies. Nowhere was this fact more poignantly demonstrated than in the following obituary published in the *Catholic Record,* one of his most severe critics:

> The death of Dr. Kinsey, famous Indiana University zoologist, and compiler of the controversial studies on human sex life, removes a truly dedicated scholar from the Bloomington campus. Few could disagree more strongly than we with Dr. Kinsey's views or deplore more deeply the evil influence such views could have on individuals and society. Yet one cannot deny that Dr. Kinsey's unremitting efforts, his patient, endless search, his disregard for criticism and ridicule, and his disinterest in financial gain should merit him high marks as a devoted scholar. While we have hurled our share of brickbats at some of Dr. Kinsey's ideas when he was living, and still hold these ideas to be poisonously wrong, we must admit that we would welcome on our side many more scholars with something of Kinsey's devotion to knowledge and learning.[52]

Kinsey hoped that his work would be widely publicized and that its effect would be educational, not trivializing. Contemporary observers credited him with achieving his goal. Donald B. Hileman's study of magazine coverage of the Female volume in 1953 found that Kinsey had already forced a reorientation of attitudes toward sexual matters among journalists.[53] *Time* magazine agreed. Kinsey's biggest impact, they argued, was "conversational." Despite the increase in talk about sex after World War I, printed and public discussion remained taboo. "No single event," they concluded, "did more for open discussion of sex than the Kinsey Report, which got such matters as homosexuality, masturbation, coitus and orgasm into most papers and family magazines."[54]

Though some critics feared that the reports would have an immediate adverse effect on public behavior, there is little evidence that such fears were justified. On the other hand, studies undertaken soon after publication suggested that Kinsey's work did liberalize attitudes, especially among the young.[55] His findings publicized not only the sexual diversity but also the gap between ideals and reality in America. Such information about the prevalence of certain "questionable" practices tended to alter attitudes in the direction of tolerance. In this sense Kinsey's books probably were a catalyst. With consummate skill he dispelled ignorance about changes in sexual mores which had already taken place, *sub rosa,* since World War I. In presenting Americans with a *fait accompli,* his work demanded more realistic, more humane sex mores. He forced a public debate over the meaning of sex in modern life as no other author had except Freud.[56]

Marriage counselors and sex therapists hailed the reports' role in alleviating guilt and promoting understanding between the sexes. For over a generation liberal therapists had struggled with their own ignorance and the greater ignorance of their patients. Lack of sexual harmony was deemed the most frequent cause of family disruptions. Dr. Lena Levine, director of the Margaret Sanger Research Bureau, recalled the early period of marriage counseling "with no nostalgia whatever."

> We had no authorities to turn to, no reference books to give the women. We listened to the same story over and over again, and we counseled patients as best we could on technique. The worst job was to get the message across to the husbands, who were usually at fault, chiefly because they hadn't the slightest idea how a woman was put together and what she needed in the way of stimulation.[57]

Kinsey paved the way for modern approaches to sex therapy. Masters and Johnson built on the groundwork laid by their more controversial predecessor.

Ironically, Kinsey's friends as well as his enemies responded only to the obvious Kinsey: the broad-minded, democratic rebel, the sexual libertarian. While he was surely all of these things, there was another side to this complex and subtle man, more easily understood only in historical retrospect. In many ways Kinsey remained bound to his Victorian past. Despite his studied neutrality concerning the various forms of sexual outlet, his acceptance of homosexuality, and his tolerance of extramarital sexuality, Kinsey was not a social revolutionary. His revolt against his society's outmoded sexual mores did not lead him to question other aspects of the value structure. Like most of his contemporaries, he had an attachment to happy, stable marriages, and he expected his research to ease the majority of Americans into a permanent monogamy so satisfying that social stability would be guaranteed. His data suggesting that sexual liberation had *not* destroyed cherished social institutions should have reassured his detractors, had they been composed enough to pay careful attention. It was no accident that Kinsey admired other personality traits of sexually precocious youths—their aggressive energy, their drive and spontaneity. Here he is most candid and also most reactionary; sexual abandon is coupled with the time-honored assumptions of enterprising capitalistic society.

Kinsey's faith in this social order is evident in his lecture notes for the 1938 marriage course, and in his special relationship with the American Association of Marriage Counselors. For many years an associate member, Kinsey was made an affiliate in 1952. Many critics erroneously interpret the failure to treat reproductive issues in the two reports as evidence of Kinsey's lack of interest. Yet approximately ten percent of Kinsey's standard interview was devoted to this subject and his silence on these matters reflects anything but indifference. He withheld his statistics on pregnancy, contraception, and abortion because the AAMC had convinced him to devote an entire book to these questions.[58] Thus Masters and Johnson have only followed in the direction that Kinsey led. Like him they emerge as resolute foes of guilt and shame; like him they do not champion the cause of premarital chastity. But their ideal sexual order, like Kinsey's, leads to a retreat into privatism. They link greater sexual permissiveness with happier marriages, and they conceive of sexual life in terms of "enduring, heterosexual relationships of substantial affection."[59]

Thus the cultural and intellectual revolution that Kinsey touched off was archetypically American: its purpose was to keep basic institutions the same, especially at a time when, in the aftermath of world war, they might have been fundamentally altered.[60]

. . . . .

In the thirty years since Kinsey published his volumes, his data have become a rich potential source for measuring social change. Unfortunately, historians have yet to mine his findings with any persistence. Used primarily to verify the "sexual revolution" in the first decades of this century, Kinsey's work has been virtually ignored by students interested in broader social and cultural issues. Few commentators, for example, have explored the implications of Kinsey's discovery that men from different classes exhibit divergent sexual behavior. The report maintained that lower- and working-class males had a decidedly higher incidence of premarital intercourse than college-educated men, tended to frown on extended foreplay in intercourse as "unnatural," were less likely to make love in the nude, masturbated less frequently, and viewed sex more as an uncontrollable impulse, less as a question of right and wrong. Middle-class and college-educated youths were moralistic; they tended to be virgins at marriage, although they petted and masturbated more often. The upwardly or downwardly mobile male, moreover, tended to form such attitudinal and behavioral patterns *long before he moved into his destined class.*

Kinsey's findings raise questions about the relationship of sex behavior, character structure, social mobility, and class, some of which might be read back into the past. Indeed, his data suggest a connection between twentieth-century middle-class behavior patterns and the emergence of the "modern" temperament, a primary attribute of which seems to be, at least for the nineteenth century, the ability to defer present gratification for future rewards. Historians of the nineteenth century have been struggling to link Victorian sexual repression to the emergence of a personality type comfortable with industrial capitalism. Thrift in semen, they argue, mirrored the injunction to be frugal materially. The ability to control passion and the denigration of personal pleasure as a goal created men and women who fit the demands of the take-off period of industrialization, when production, economy, and austerity took precedence over consumption. Marx eloquently characterized this stage in capitalistic growth:

> Political economy, the science of wealth, is therefore, at the same time, the science of renunciation, of privation and of saving . . . The science of a marvelous industry is at the same time the science of asceticism. . . . The less you eat, drink, buy books, go to the theater or to balls, or to the public house, and the less you think, love, theorize, sing, paint, fence, etc. the more you will be able to save. . . . [61]

Historians have based their theories about nineteenth-century sexuality on evidence drawn from the prescriptive literature—advice books, political and social writings, medical treatises. Surely Kinsey's statistics give us some hard evidence that the repressive Victorian sexual theory was somehow linked to the behavior patterns of an upwardly mobile middle class.

Yet when we examine Kinsey's data more closely we must qualify Marx's contention that deferred gratification was always a prerequisite for capitalistic growth. By the 1920s, at least, it seems clear that middle-class youths were no longer deferring *gratification;* they were merely delaying *copulation.* The upwardly mobile petted and masturbated frequently despite guilt. Kinsey's figures for *total* sexual outlet (achieving orgasm by any means) showed only minor class differences. Presumably, the mature industrial economy no longer requires the full repression of sexual desires, it merely demands that those desires be gratified in particular ways. Thus, middle-class youths, in order to contribute to the system, deferred not necessarily sexual pleasure, but intercourse, marriage, children, and family obligations. Lower-class men, on the other hand, postponed neither early copulation, nor marriage, nor large families, all of which probably helped to insure their docility, if not contentedness, in the factory.

Recent sex surveys report that the behavioral gap between men of different classes has substantially narrowed since Kinsey. Probably because of the widespread dissemination of effective contraceptive devices, pre-marital intercourse has increased among college-educated males, while sex behavior among the lower classes has differentiated to include nudity, extended foreplay, and increasing oral-genital contacts.[62] Indeed, it appears that in an economy characterized by abundance and oriented toward the production of luxury items and consumer goods, sexual pleasure has become a means of recreation for all classes. Character structure and child rearing practices have shifted accordingly, away from an emphasis on autonomous self-control and toward the rational acceptance of pleasure, personal fulfillment, and happiness. Education, mass media, and the increase in leisure time among all social strata have tended to homogenize popular culture and narrow behavioral differences between social groups.

These developments suggest that we have entered a third phase of capitalistic growth. As yet we have proved incapable of dealing with problems of overproduction. The goal of the system remains consumption, and sexual liberation is encouraged primarily through advertising, as a means of orienting people toward new *things,* new ideas, new forms of luxury and pleasure. The encouragement of hedonism in all spheres seems essential for the affluent society. Thus sexual freedom has not been tied to social revolution. Championing privatism and the concern with individual adjustment, the new permissiveness has focused on self-fulfillment, not social change. Social historians interested in generational shifts in personality structure would do well to explore the implications of these changes in sexual behavior.

Kinsey's findings also indicate that knowledge of female sexuality has gradually become more sophisticated. If a sexual revolution has occurred, its base has been changes in female attitudes and behavior. While male trends shifted only minimally between generational cohorts in Kinsey's sample, women moved steadily toward the male standard. The evidence of the Female Report that women born after 1900 were more likely to reach orgasm in marriage, and that educated middle-class women achieved greater sexual satisfaction than their lower-class sisters deserves special attention. It would seem that sexual liberation, fostered by greater educational opportunities, presupposes and encourages the development of individuality and autonomy among women.

On the other hand, students of lower-class sexual patterns have found that among the less educated "both husbands and wives feel that sexual gratification for the wife is much less important than for the husband." Lower-class lovemaking tends to be less "technically versatile," lacking in the extended foreplay intended to facilitate the wife's satisfaction. Lower-class women, perhaps as a consequence, view sex primarily as a duty. Yet although they enjoy sex less they rarely refuse intercourse. Sociologist Lee Rainwater links these sexual patterns to a patriarchal family structure, a radical separation between male and female spheres, and a lack of meaningful communication between sexual partners, all characteristic of lower-class groups.[63] Recent work on nineteenth-century sex roles has pictured a similar family structure exhibiting the same well-defined differentiation between male and female culture.[64] One is tempted to use Kinsey's statistics to posit the prevalence among the middle class in the last century of contemporary lower-class patterns of love-making, oriented toward male satisfaction. For an age which barely accepted the legitimacy of female pleasure and still linked intercourse with reproduction, such a thesis appears plausible and is borne out by Kinsey's data revealing a gradual increase in female orgasm in the twentieth century.[65]

The evolution of consciousness over the last century has altered expectations concerning what is sexually natural and possible. Human needs diversify with changing social and cultural conditions, and things become desirable merely because they are suddenly possible. Kinsey's data offer us an insight into this transformation in the meaning of marriage and sexual relations. His findings suggest that this century has witnessed a merging of spiritual love and passion in a novel way. His evidence indicates that middle-class lovemaking techniques are a recent dimension of the popular imagination. The emergence of almost universal petting in the 1920s and 1930s represents a new psycho-sexual intimacy.[66] The increasing sexual responsiveness of middle-class women may be a function of this.

It has become fashionable to mourn the passing of the old sexual order in which the omnipresence of guilt, anxiety, and dread over the violation of taboos guaranteed at least that life would be interesting. "If . . . nothing is grave," a recent commentator has written, "satire cannot bite and tragedy gives way to the social illness of maladjustment. For many, human life under such conditions would lose its music."[67] Such an attitude offers further proof of the distance we have travelled from the sexual culture of Kinsey's generation. Privy to the tragic ways in which people's sexual lives were blighted by society, Kinsey welcomed a new order while he helped to bring it about. We are the richer for Kinsey's conviction that human beings should get more joy out of all sexual activity.

Yet Kinsey was no revolutionary. Though he wished that the world would be a better place because of his books, his vision required no fundamental social or economic changes.[68] He understood neither the revolutionary nor the disintegrative potentialities inherent in sexual liberation. In the end, Kinsey's hedonism has become a conservative force, and he himself the unwitting agent of an increasingly callous and wasteful society.*

NOTES

[1] Dickinson to Kinsey, Aug. 24, 1947, Jan. 7, 1948. Kinsey-Dickinson Correspondence, Institute for Sex Research, Bloomington (hereafter cited as ISR).

[2] Dickinson to Kinsey, Feb. 7, 1948, Kinsey-Dickinson Correspondence. Kinsey's *Sexual Behavior in the Human Male* (Philadelphia: W. B. Saunders Co., 1948) and *Sexual Behavior in the Human Female* (Philadelphia: W. B. Saunders Co., 1953) will hereafter be cited as *SBHM* and *SBHF*. Both books will be referred to collectively as the "Kinsey Report."

[3] Response to the Kinsey Report can be measured by a cursory reading of the several hundred books and articles listed in "The Kinsey Report: A Selected Bibliography," in Jerome Himmelhoch and Sylvia Fava, eds., *Sexual Behavior in American Society* (New York: W. W. Norton, 1955). ISR has collected over 38 volumes of newspaper and magazine articles. (Readers interested in more specific documentation should contact me at the University of Kansas.) See also Paul D. Brinkman, "Dr. Alfred C. Kinsey and the Press," Diss. Indiana University 1971.

[4] John Burham, "The Progressive Era Revolution in American Attitudes Toward Sex," *Journal of American History*, 59 (Mar. 1973).

[5] *The New Basis of Civilization* (New York: Macmillan, 1908), Ch. 1, 6, and p. 143.

[6] Sophie D. Aberle and George W. Corner, *Twenty-Five Years of Sex Research: A History of the National Research Council Committee for Research in Problems of Sex, 1922-1947* (Philadelphia: W. B. Saunders, 1953), 13-14. See also James H. Jones, "The Origins of the Institute for Sex Research: A History," Diss. Indiana University 1972.

[7] Biographical information on Kinsey was taken from Jones, ibid., and two biographies: Wardell Pomeroy, *Dr. Kinsey and the Institute for Sex Research* (New York: Thomas Nelson and Sons, 1972), and Cornelia V. Christenson, *Kinsey: A Biography* (Bloomington: Indiana Univ. Press, 1971).

[8] See Kinsey's lecture notes for the marriage course, ISR. Kinsey was probably referring to Dickinson's *One Thousand Marriages,* written with Lura Beam and published in 1931. See Kinsey to Dickinson, June 23, 1941, Kinsey-Dickinson Correspondence, ISR. For his faculty talk see Christenson, 97.

[9] Marriage course lecture notes, ISR.

[10] Christenson, 106.

[11] *SBHM,* 3-5.

[12] *SBHM,* 17.

[13] "Individuals," quoted in Christenson, 8.

[14] For an example of the objections raised to the interview see A. H. Maslow and J. M. Sakoda, "Volunteer-Error in the Kinsey Study," *Journal of Abnormal and Social Psychology,* 47 (Apr. 1952), 259-62. For favorable reports by subjects see George W. Corner, "The Origin, Methods, and Findings of the Kinsey Report," in *Problems of Sexual Behavior* (New York: American Social Hygiene Association, 1948) and Jo Caro, "The Kinsey Interview Experience," in Albert Ellis, ed., *Sex Life of the American Woman and the Kinsey Report* (New York: Greenburg, 1953).

[15] The one exception was heterosexual petting.

[16] For the purposes of this essay it is impossible to cover in detail the criticism of the statisticians. See William Cochran, Fred Mosteller, and John W. Tukey, "Statistical Problems of the Kinsey Report," *Journal of the American Statistical Association,* 48 (Dec. 1953), 673-716. For MacIver's comments see "Sex and Social Attitudes," in Donald Geddes, ed., *About the Kinsey Report* (New York: New American Library, 1948).

[17] See Pomeroy, 464.

[18] Social class proved less important in determining the sexual behavior of females than of men. Religious devotion and decade of birth more commonly had an impact on women's sex activity.

[19] See Paul Robinson's critique of this rating scale in *The Modernization of Sex* (New York: Harper and Row, 1976), 117.

[20] *SBHF,* 163-64, 374. Masters and Johnson have subsequently confirmed these findings.

[21] By "psychological stimuli" Kinsey meant erotic pictures, stories, mood music, movies, nudity, etc. Subsequent studies have questioned this finding. See Paul H. Gebhard, "Sex Differences in Sexual Response," *Archives of Sexual Behavior,* 2 (1973) 201-03, and Alice Rossi, "Maternalism, Sexuality and the New Feminism," in John Money and Joseph Zubin, eds., *Contemporary Sexual Behavior* (Baltimore: Johns Hopkins Univ. Press, 1973), 160-65.

[22] *SBHF,* 162, 574-84, 467.

[23] See for example Kinsey's correspondence with New York gynecologist Sophia Kleegman, ISR.

[24] *SBHF,* 580-82, 162.

[25] See, for example, Edmund Bergler and William S. Kroger, *Kinsey's Myth of Female Sexuality* (New York: Grune and Stratton, 1954), for an extreme psychoanalytic point of view.

[26] Ibid. See review by J. A. H. in *Stanford Medical Bulletin,* Nov. 1953 (Clipping in ISR files).

[27] The one exception was Albert Ellis. See "The Psychology and Physiology of Sex," in Ellis, *Sex Life of the American Woman.*

[28] *SBHF,* 468.

[29] See for example Anne Koedt, "The Myth of the Vaginal Orgasm," in Anne Koedt, Ellen Levine, and Anita Rapone, eds., *Radical Feminism* (New York: Quadrangle, 1973), and Susan Lydon, "The Politics of the Orgasm," in Robin Morgan, ed., *Sisterhood is Powerful* (New York: Vintage, 1970). For Erikson's comments see *Childhood and Society* (New York: W. W. Norton, 1963), 265. The psychoanalytic point of view is discussed in Mary Ryan, *Womanhood in America* (New York: New Viewpoints, 1975), 277-87.

[30] William Masters and Virginia Johnson, *Human Sexual Response* (Boston: Little, Brown, 1966).

[31] *Reader's Digest* (Sept. 1948), 130; *Tribune* editorial, Aug. 20, 1953; "The Moratorium on Moral Revulsion," *Christianity and Crisis,* 8 (June 21, 1948), 81.

[32] "A Sociologist Looks at the Report," in ASHA *Problems of Sexual Behavior;* "I Am Concerned," in Donald Geddes, ed., *An Analysis of the Kinsey Reports on Sexual Behavior in the Human Male and Female* (New York: Dutton, 1954).

[33] *Newsweek* (Sept. 7, 1953); John B. Chapple in the Ashland *Daily Press,* quoted in Brinkman, 82; Christenson, 166.

[34] Glenn V. Ramsey, "A Survey Evaluation of the Kinsey Report," *Journal of Clinical Psychology,* 6 (Apr. 1950), 133-43.

[35] *Christianity and Crisis* (May 24, 1948), 65. See also the cogent comments by Jessie Bernard in "A Note on Sociological Research as a Factor in Social Change: The Reception of the Kinsey Report,' *Social Forces,* 28 (Dec. 1949), 187-90.

[36] Lionel Trilling, *The Liberal Imagination* (New York: Viking Press, 1950), 223.

[37] *SBHM,* 325-26.

[38] Ibid. 543-44.

[39] *SBHF,* 329.

[40] See for example Dorothy Dunbar Bromley, "Dr. Kinsey's *Summum Bonum,*" in Geddes, ed., *An Analysis.*

[41] *SBHF,* 14-15.

[42] See ibid., for a long explanatory footnote on manuals. There were a number of articles published in response to Kinsey which defended premarital chastity. See for example Margaret Culkin Banning, "The Case For Chastity in 1949," *Cosmopolitan* (Oct. 1949), 36-37, 105-09; "Kinsey's Case for Virginity," *Pageant* (Apr. 1955), 47-51.

[43] The psychoanalytic literature on Kinsey is voluminous. Typical examples are the Roundtable cited in *Psychoanalytic Review,* 43 (Oct. 1955), 471-500; Lawrence Kubie, "Psychiatric Implications of the Kinsey Report," *Psychosomatic Medicine,* 10 (Mar.-Apr., 1948) 95-106; Karl Menninger, "What the Girls Told," *Saturday Review* (Sept. 26, 1953), 21, 30, 31; R. Wood, "The Psychological Reaction to the Kinsey Report," *Journal of Sex Education,* 3 (June-July, 1951), 241-46; Menninger statements at Psychoanalytic Roundtable published in *Psychoanalytic Review,* 489.

[44] Quoted in Manfred S. Guttmacher, "The Kinsey Report and Society," *Scientific Monthly,* 293; *Stanford Medical Bulletin,* op. cit.; Arthur J. Mandy, "Frigidity," in Ellis, ed., *Sex Life of the American Woman.*

[45] Marie Robinson, *The Power of Sexual Surrender* (Garden City, N. Y.: Doubleday, 1952), 22, 24; Bergler and Kroger, op. cit., 193.

[46] "Kinsey and the Moral Problem of Man's Sexual Life," in Geddes, ed., *An Analysis,* 64-65.

[47] *SBHM,* 659; Roundtable in *Psychoanalytic Review,* 500.

[48] Representative examples: Manford H. Kuhn, "Kinsey's View of Human Behavior," George Simpson, "Nonsense about Women," and Robert J. Havighurst, "Cultural Factors in Sex Expression," all in *Sexual Behavior in American Society.*

[49] Roundtable in *Psychoanalytic Review;* Manfred S. Guttmacher, "The Kinsey Report and Society," 293.

[50] Oct. 16, 1953, 33. See also Margaret Mead's comments at the ASHA Symposium, *Problems of Sexual Behavior,* 67.

[51] (Dec. 7, 1947), 106-07.

[52] "Kinsey the Scholar," Aug., 1956. Quoted in Brinkman, 203.

[53] "The Kinsey Report: A Study of Press Responsibility," *Journalism Quarterly,* 30 (Fall 1953), 434-35.

[54] (August 24, 1953). See also *People Today,* Apr. 7, 1954. A study of the *Reader's Guide to Periodical Literature* from 1922-1975 revealed that in certain significant subcategories listed under the heading "sex" the number of articles published since Kinsey's work first appeared in 1948 has sharply increased. For example, articles on "sex

behavior" and "sex relations" appeared 99 per cent more often in the period from 1948 to 1975.

[55] See Jessie Bernard, "A Note on Sociological Research as a Factor in Social Change"; Leo P. Crespi, "Youth Looks at the Kinsey Report," *Public Opinion Quarterly,* 12 (Winter 1948), 687-96; Harold F. Giedt, "Changes in Sexual Behavior and Attitudes Following Class Study of the Kinsey Report," *Journal of Social Psychology,* 33 (1951), 131-41; C. Kirkpatrick, Sheldon Stryker, and Philip Buell, "An Experimental Study of Attitudes Towards Male Sex Behavior with Reference to Kinsey's Findings," *American Sociological Review,* 17 (Oct. 1952), 580-87.

[56] Particularly noteworthy was the response of the liberal clergy who began to call for a reevaluation of traditional Judeo-Christian morality. See Seward Hiltner, *Sex Ethics and the Kinsey Reports* (New York: Association Press, 1953); Richard E. Lentz, "The Challenge of the Kinsey Report," *International Journal of Religious Education,* 30 (Jan. 1954), 19-20.

[57] See Abraham Stone, "The Kinsey Studies and Marriage Counseling," *Sexual Behavior in American Society;* Gladys Hoagland Groves, "Marital Sex Intercourse," in Ellis, ed., *Sex Life of the American Woman;* Emily Mudd, "Implications for Marriage and Sexual Adjustment," in Geddes, ed., *An Analysis.* Quote from Lena Levine in Jean Libman Block, "Are Those Marriage Manuals Any Good?" *Cosmopolitan* (Oct. 1948), 140. Many of the popular magazines emphasized Kinsey's potential impact on marriage and relations between the sexes. Kinsey also had a profound impact on the increasing tolerance of homosexuality; see Robinson, 42-119.

[58] See correspondence with Robert Laidlaw and other members of the AAMC in files at ISR. Information about *Pregnancy, Birth and Abortion* (published by the Institute after Kinsey's death in 1958) gained in a conversation with Jim Jones.

[59] See Paul Robinson's excellent essay about Masters and Johnson in *The Modernization of Sex,* 141, 169.

[60] About Kinsey's reaction to World War II Pomeroy has written: "I am aware that once more it may be difficult to understand how anyone could have lived through one of the cataclysmic events of human history without being affected by it. . . . His scientific dedication to the project and his overwhelming involvement with it simply placed a wall between him and the events that were shaking the world." Pomeroy, 225-26.

[61] See Peter Cominos, "Late Victorian Sexual Respectability and the Social System," *International Review of Social History,* 8 (1963); 18-48, 216-50; Steven Marcus, *The Other Victorians* (New York: Basic Books, 1966): Charles Rosenberg, "Sexuality, Class, and Role," *American Quarterly,* 25 (May 1973), 131-53; Robert V. Wells, "Family History and Demographic Transition," *Journal of Social History,* 9 (Fall 1975), 1-20. Marx quote from T. B. Bottomore, ed., *Early Writings.* 171. quoted in Cominos, 217.

[62] See Morton M. Hunt, *Sexual Behavior in the 1970s* (Chicago: Playboy Press, 1974).

[63] Lee Rainwater, *And the Poor Get Children* (New York: New Viewpoints, 1974), 94; "Some Aspects of Lower Class Sexual Behavior," in Ailon Shiloh, ed., *Studies in Human Sexual Behavior: The American Scene* (Springfield, Ill.: Thomas, 1970); and "Marital Sexuality in Four Cultures of Poverty," in John N. Edwards, ed., *Sex and Society* (Chicago: Markham, 1972).

[64] Carroll Smith-Rosenberg, "The Female World of Love and Ritual: Relations between Women in Nineteenth-Century America," *Signs,* I (Autumn 1975), 1-29.

[65] Kinsey's data seem to contradict Carl Degler's thesis in "What Ought to Be and What Was: Women's Sexuality in the 19th Century," *American Historical Review,* 79 (Dec. 1974), 1467-90 that many ordinary women managed to resist nineteenth-century prescriptive norms. Carroll Smith-Rosenberg has reminded us in a recent paper that the Mosher survey used by Degler must be interpreted with more caution. "A Gentle and a Richer Sex: Female Perspectives on Nineteenth Century Sexuality," paper delivered at Third Berkshire Conference on Women's History, Bryn Mawr, 1976. Rainwater's data suggest that the relationship between female sexuality and family structure is intricate and complex.

[66] Ira L. Reiss, "How and Why Sex Standards are Changing," in Shiloh, ed., *Studies in Human Sexual Behavior.* See also *Redbook* survey of contemporary female behavior, *Redbook* (Sept.-Oct., 1975).

[67] J. M. Cameron in *New York Review of Books* (May 13, 1976), 28.

[68] Kinsey revealed this wish to Nanette Kutner, who interviewed him shortly before his death. New York *Journal American* (Jan. 20, 1957), 14.

[*] The author would like to thank Bill Chafe, John Clark, James Jones, Eric Foner, James Reed, Martin Pernick, John Sweets, and Janet Sharistanian for their comments. Clifford Griffin and especially Ellen Chesler were particularly helpful, and many of my ideas were sharpened in the course of discussions with them.

FURTHER READING

Biography

Christenson, Cornelia V. *Kinsey: A Biography.* Bloomington: Indiana University Press, 1971, 241 p.

Biography drawn from the author's personal association with Kinsey as a researcher and subject, as well as more than one hundred questionnaires sent to colleagues who knew Kinsey at various stages of his life. Christenson also reprints several articles authored by Kinsey.

Jones, James H. *Alfred C. Kinsey: A Public/Private Life.* New York: W. W. Norton, 1997, 937 p.

Attempts to depict Kinsey as a man who detested Victorian morality, and who was determined to defuse sexual repression and guilt.

Pomeroy, Wardell B. *Dr. Kinsey and the Institute for Sex Research.* New York: Harper & Row, 1972, 479 p.

Account by a former researcher with Kinsey at the Institute for Sex Research.

Criticism

Allyn, David. "Private Acts/Public Policy: Alfred Kinsey, the American Law Institute and the Privatization of American Sexual Morality." *Journal of American Studies* 30, No. 3 (December 1986): 405-28.

Argues that Kinsey and his work contributed to the abandonment of the concept of public morality.

Cochran, William G., Frederick Mosteller, and John W. Tukey. *Statistical Problems of the Kinsey Report on Sexual Behavior in the Human Male: A Report of the American Statistical Committee to Advise the National Research Council Committee for Research in Problems of Sex.* Washington, D.C.: The American Statistical Association, 1954, 338 p.

Concludes that probability sampling might have provided more accurate results in the Kinsey Report.

Deutsch, Albert, ed. *Sex Habits of American Men: A Symposium on the Kinsey Report.* New York: Prentice-Hall, 1948, 244 p.

Presents papers on such topics as religion, sociology, psychiatry, legal issues, and Kinsey's methodology.

Robinson, Paul. *The Modernization of Sex: Havelock Ellis, Alfred Kinsey, William Masters and Virginia Johnson.* New York: Harper & Row, 1976, 200 p.

Argues that Havelock Ellis, Kinsey, Masters, and Johnson have been unfairly forgotten because they dealt exclusively in sexual topics, unlike Sigmund Freud, who researched and wrote on many different topics.

Weinberg, Martin S., ed. *Sex Research: Studies from the Kinsey Institute.* New York: Oxford University Press, 1976, 320 p.

Anthologizes key papers published by the Kinsey Institute, including works by Kinsey, Paul Gebhard, and Wardell B. Pomeroy.

Ivan Petrovich Pavlov

1849-1936

Russian physiologist.

INTRODUCTION

Pavlov was a Nobel Prize-winning physiologist, whose research into the process of the conditioned reflex is considered a landmark discovery in both modern physiology and behavioral psychology. Pavlov was recognized by the Nobel Committee for his work with mammalian digestion; however, later experiments with canine salivation led to his theorization of the learned or conditioned reflex—a physiological response to associated but otherwise unrelated stimuli. Pavlov observed that dogs presented with some additional stimulus that accompanied regular feedings, such as a flash of light, could be made to salivate when only the additional stimulation, and no food, was offered. From these and similar experiments, Pavlov established the physiological basis of certain types of learned behavior. In theory, Pavlov also applied his discovery of the conditioned reflex to human beings. In addition to his study of digestion and higher nervous activity, Pavlov is remembered for his work with the physiology of blood circulation and as an accomplished scientific administrator.

Biographical Information

Pavlov was born on 26 September 1849 in Ryazan, Russia. He was educated at Ryazan Ecclesiastical High School and later attended the Ryazan Ecclesiastical Seminary, where he exhibited considerable interest in the natural sciences. In 1870 Pavlov opted to leave the seminary and to continue his studies at St. Petersburg University. There Pavlov began working with the physiologist Elie de Zion and honing his surgical skills. After graduation in 1875, Pavlov entered medical school at the Military Medical Academy in St. Petersburg, and served as a laboratory assistant to Zion, who had recently been named chair of the academy's physiology department. Pavlov later transferred for two years to the Veterinary Institute following Zion's dismissal, and in 1877 traveled to Breslau, Germany (now Wroclaw, Poland) to study digestion under Rudolf Heidenhain. Pavlov was honored with a scholarship for postdoctoral study after earning his medical degree in 1879 and returned to Germany to further his research into circulation and digestion. In 1895 Pavlov was named chairman of physiology at the St. Petersburg Institute for Experimental Medicine and remained in this position for much of his subsequent career. For his continued studies into the process of mammalian digestion he was awarded the Nobel Prize for Medicine or Physiology in 1904. By this time, Pavlov had begun his experiments on conditioned reflexes in laboratory dogs. Following the Bolshevik Revolution in 1917, Pavlov occasionally spoke out against the Soviets, but was nevertheless given preferential treatment by the Communist Party, which hoped to use his experiments with the conditioned reflex for political ends. In 1935 the Soviet government built Pavlov an extensive, state-of-the-art laboratory where he could continue his work. He died of pneumonia shortly thereafter on 27 February 1936 in Leningrad (now St. Petersburg).

Major Works

Few of Pavlov's works are available in English translation and, in addition, critics discern that most of the writings attributed to him represent to some degree the combined efforts of Pavlov and his many laboratory assistants—though it is clear that Pavlov is the principal intellectual force behind all of the following texts. *The Work of the Digestive Glands* (1902) contains the culmination of Pavlov's experiments on the alimentary canal of dogs performed in the late 1880s and 1890s. Pavlov and his fellow researchers studied digestion by surgically altering laboratory dogs, principally by modifying canine stomachs to create a "Pavlov pouch," into which gastric juices could be separated for observation and testing. Pavlov's later and more well-known work on the conditioned reflex is available to English-speaking audiences in *Lectures on Conditioned Reflexes* (1923) and *Conditioned Reflexes: An Investigation of the Physiological Activity of the Cerebral Cortex* (1960). These texts record the results of Pavlov's further experimentation with dogs. Again using surgical procedures, Pavlov and his team studied the relationship between the higher nervous system and the action of the salivary glands. By associating certain unrelated stimuli—such as the presence of a lab assistant, the ring of a bell, or a flash of light—with the routine feeding of the dogs, Pavlov was able to demonstrate the performance of conditioned reflexes. This he succeeded in doing by stimulating salivation without actually offering food, through the simple recreation of those stimuli (bell, light, assistant's presence) that had been related to feeding. Drawing from these experiments, Pavlov theorized the existence of a physiological component to psychological processes, and differentiated between the mechanisms of innate and conditioned reflexes. Pavlov's collected works, including a significant number of scientific articles and research essays, appear in the five-volume Russian compilation *Polnoe sobranie trudov* (1940-49).

Critical Reception

Critics have observed that Pavlov's discovery of the conditioned reflex has been quite influential in the scientific community, particularly in Russia, where research into Pavlovian physiology has continued, uninterrupted, through the end of the Soviet regime and of the twentieth-century. Since Pavlov's death, however, many reassessments of Pavlovian theory have occurred. Contemporary scientists have uncovered a number of errors within the details of Pavlov's thought. Critics likewise have acknowledged that Pavlov's failure to satisfactorily explain the true mechanism of the conditioned reflex represents a serious limitation. Nevertheless, scholars have continued to see Pavlov as a pioneering figure in the study of physiology and have observed the tremendous influence his work with the conditioned reflex has exerted on the modern field of behavioral psychology.

PRINCIPAL WORKS

**Experimental Data Concerning the Accommodating Mechanism of the Blood Vessels* (physiology) 1877
Lektsii o rabote glavnykh pishchevaritelnykh (physiology) 1897 [*The Work of the Digestive Glands,* 1902]
***Lectures on Conditioned Reflexes* (physiology) 1923
"The Conditioned Reflex" (physiology) 1934 [published in the book *The Great Medical Encyclopedia*]
Dvadtsatiletnii opyt ob'ektivnogo izucheniia vysshei nervnoi deiatel'nosti zhivotnykh (physiology) 1938 [*Conditioned Reflexes: An Investigation of the Physiological Activity of the Cerebral Cortex,* 1960]
Polnoe sobranie trudov. Five vols. (physiology) 1940-49
Psikhopatologiia i psikhiatriia (physiology) 1949 [*Psychopathology and Psychiatry,* 1960]
Izbrannye trudy (physiology) 1951 [*Selected Works,* 1955]
***Experimental Psychology, and Other Essays* (essays) 1957

*Published in Russian.

**English edition of work originally published in Russian.

CRITICISM

Edwin R. Guthrie (essay date 1934)

SOURCE: "Pavlov's Theory of Conditioning," in the *Psychological Review,* Vol. 41, No. 2, March, 1934, pp. 199-206.

[*In the following essay, Guthrie offers a critique of Pavlov's theory of the conditioned reflex.*]

Pavlov's recent article, **'The Reply of a Physiologist to Psychologists,'**[1] deals with two items printed some time ago in the *Psychological Review,* one by Lashley on 'Basic neural mechanisms in behavior,' and one by the writer, 'Conditioning as a principle of learning.' The issues raised by Pavlov deserve some further discussion because they are fundamental. My own article would have been justified if its only effect had been to persuade Pavlov to additional writing on the conditioned reflex, since by his laboratory experience he is undoubtedly its most competent exponent. However, on a number of points I remain quite unconvinced after reading his **'Reply.'**

The first difference of opinion that he mentions concerns a very general issue. He says,

> The psychologist takes conditioning as a principle of learning, and accepting the principle as not subject to further analysis, not requiring ultimate investigation, he endeavors to apply it to everything and to explain all the individual features of learning as one and the same process. . . . The physiologist proceeds in quite the opposite way. At every phase of his investigation he endeavors to analyze the phenomena individually and in connection with facts, determining as much as is possible of the conditions for their existence, not trusting to mere deduction or to a single hypothesis.

This characterization is substantially correct. Pavlov has been reporting many detailed experiments with resulting generalizations as numerous as the varieties of experimental procedure. It was the writer's belief that the time had arrived when an hypothesis could be set up in order to direct experimental work. The hypothesis suggested was an old and familiar one, that the phenomena of learning, when described in terms of altered movement or secretion, may be described in terms of one principle, which was called the principle of conditioning. Its statement was this: *Stimuli acting at the time of a response tend on their recurrence to evoke that response.* In other words, it was suggested that the outstanding characteristics of learning, which have been expressed in terms of frequency, intensity, irradiation, temporary extinction, conditioned inhibition, forgetting, forward and backward conditioning, and so on, are all derivable from a more general law, the law of simultaneous conditioning or association by contiguity in time. To this end an analysis of these various phenomena was undertaken, an analysis that was, to the writer at least, very plausible.

Pavlov's second objection concerns this analysis in so far as it applies to backward conditioning. According to him the question is: What elementary properties of the brain-mass form the basis of conditioning? Backward conditioning, practice with the conditioned stimulus following the unconditioned, has a double effect, " . . . at first, temporarily, it assists in the formation of the conditioned reflex, and then destroys it,"—becoming eventually an inhibiting stimulus.

Pavlov's explanation of this is that

> . . . the cell excited by the conditioned stimulus is inhibited or comes to an inhibited state with repeated concentration on the part of the unconditioned stimulus—and the conditioned stimulus in this way meets in its cell a permanent state of inhibition.

To this there is an objection. An understanding of the phenomenon of backward conditioning can be had only by finding the conditions under which it occurs. No properties of the brain-mass have been observed; no technique for observing states of inhibition in cells has yet been suggested. An explanation in these terms is and will remain unverifiable and entirely useless for prediction. In place of this unverifiable and useless hypothesis the writer had suggested that experimental search might disclose overlapping stimuli whose presence or absence would mark the presence or absence of backward conditioning. This would be to explain backward conditioning in terms of simultaneous conditioning. No act is instantaneous, and in backward conditioning the belated cue may accompany the later part of a sustained mascular contraction. This may be the explanation for the lessening effect of backward conditioning as the interval between cue and original stimulus is increased. In the writer's experiments with backward association[2] with human subjects the cue could be practised before or after the original stimulus with like associative strength, and the writer is convinced that backward conditioning occurs only when, and in some measure to the degree that, there are overlapping stimuli.

Concerning remote forward conditioning, or "delayed and 'trace' reflexes," the writer had evidently not made himself clear. Pavlov says,

> . . . if we grant with the author that not the bell but the centripetal flow of impulses from the motor act of listening is the true stimulus for the conditioned effect, why does that effect, in the case of delayed reflexes, nevertheless come out, not at once, but after an interval—and (furthermore) in accordance with the length of the interval between the beginning of the stimulus and the beginning of the unconditioned reflex?

For this Pavlov's explanation is two-fold.[3]

> Many cyclic phenomena take place inside the animal's body. . . . The alimentary canal is periodically filled or emptied; and, in fact, changes in practically all the component tissues and organism are capable of influencing the cerebral hemispheres. This continuous cycle of direct and indirect influences upon the nervous activity constitutes the physiological basis for the estimation of the duration of time.

This is his first suggestion. The second is as follows:

> Although prolonged for a significant length of time, the conditioned stimulus remains one and the same; but for the central nervous system (and it is especially necessary to think of the cerebral hemispheres) it is distinctly different in different periods of its course. This comes out particularly clearly with olfactory stimuli, which we sense at first very keenly, and then quickly as weaker and weaker, even if they remain objectively constant. Obviously the state of the stimulated cortical cell under the influence of an external stimulus undergoes successive changes and in the case of delayed reflexes only the state of the cell near the time of the addition of the unconditioned reflex acts as a signal for the conditioned stimulus.

The writer had made his suggestion expressly to account for the fact that the delayed reflex was elicited not at once but after an interval. The 'clock' by which this timing occurred was taken to be regular changes in the movement-produced stimuli following the cue. Pavlov's first suggestion would be in entire agreement with the writer's views if he emphasized not cyclic visceral changes but skeletal muscle changes. The visceral cycles to which Pavlov refers are more or less independent of the training situation. The skeletal muscles are in much closer touch with the external world. In practice there is no guarantee that the salivary flow would be regularly accompanied by the same phase of any visceral cycle, whereas this would be possible in skeletal movements initiated by the bell. Listening, for instance, is not a sudden explosive act, but a series of acts, one movement leading to another, that to a third, and so on. Just as an orchestra player keeps time through an interval by counting or by 'beating time,' so it is possible that the timing of the delayed and trace reflexes may be accomplished by characteristic movement series. It is true that such movement series might not be regularly the same, but it is also true that this variation may account for the variations observable in the response. Pavlov cites another fact which the writer believes is aptly explained in terms of these movement-produced conditioners.

> If the conditioned reflex be formed first with the short interval of a few seconds between the beginning of the conditioned and of the unconditioned stimuli, and then suddenly that interval be increased to a few minutes—then the conditioned effect, hitherto quick to come forth, will promptly go on to gradual but utter disappearance. And then, on continuing the experiment, there appears for a considerable lapse of time a period of absence of all conditioned effects. Only then does the conditioned reflex appear anew, at first just the moment preceding the addition of the unconditioned stimulus. Thence it grows gradually and recedes somewhat from the time of appearance of the unconditioned stimulus.

The writer's suggestion is that it has been necessary to condition the reflex to a new point in the movement-produced series, and that it has been 'extinguished' as a response to the original point.

Of Pavlov's second suggestion, that a constant stimulus has diminishing effects on the central nervous system, Adrian has demonstrated instances of such sense-organ adaptation to mean the gradual cessation of afferent impulses. Changes in the cortical cells are not the occasion of sense-organ adaptation. Now the effect of cutting off afferent impulses from a sense organ is to diminish the contraction of muscles and so to change actively the movement-produced pattern of stimulation. Here is positive stimulation which may serve as a delayed conditioner and we are not forced to invoke cortical cell changes invented solely for the purpose of explaining delayed reaction. Furthermore, movement-produced stimuli are essentially observable, though with difficulty, and cortical cell changes of the sort invoked by Pavlov are not. To assert that delayed reflexes take place under certain unobservable conditions is to be safe but futile.

So much for remote conditioning. To the writer's analysis of temporary extinction in terms of simultaneous conditioning of inhibiting responses there are offered similar objections. From Pavlov's article,

> First of all the author takes a stand against us by saying that it is not the brevity of the interval between repetitions of the non-reinforced conditioned reflexes that contributes to extinction of these reflexes, but the number of repetitions. But this is absolutely untrue.

The writer's inference was made from the following table in Conditioned Reflexes, page 53.

> With an interval of 2 minutes, extinction was obtained in 15 minutes.
>
> With an interval of 4 minutes, extinction was obtained in 20 minutes.
>
> With an interval of 8 minutes, extinction was obtained in 54 minutes.
>
> With an interval of 16 minutes, extinction was incomplete in 2 hours.
>
> With an interval of 2 minutes, extinction occurred in 18 minutes.

The rate of extinction depends, according to Pavlov, on the nature of the dog, the extent to which the reflex is established, the intensity of the unconditioned reflex underlying the conditioned one which is undergoing experimental extinction, *the length of pause between successive repetitions of the stimulus without reinforcement,* and the number of times the given reflex has been subjected to extinction in the same animal. The writer would agree to all of these but the one in italics, for which he would substitute conditioned inhibition. From the table there seems to be a regular increase in the time required to extinguish with the increase of interval. But it will be noticed that application every two minutes for fifteen minutes, application every four minutes for twenty minutes, application every eight minutes for fifty-four minutes, and application every sixteen minutes for two hours (with incomplete extinction) involve respectively 7.5 applications, 5 applications, 6.75 applications, and 7.5 applications, which are certainly approximately equal. The reason why Pavlov calls the writer's suggestion 'absolutely untrue' is the new fact offered by Pavlov that one application *prolonged from three to six minutes* gives an uninterrupted extinction. To this the writer would suggest sense organ adaptation, or exhaustion of the receptor, or the emotional inhibition resulting from the withholding of food described by Winsor,[4] as the explanation, and plead that his version of Pavlov's table, while not absolutely true was approximately true and not 'absolutely untrue.'

The writer's contention is that temporary extinction differs only from conditioned inhibition in that it is inhibition conditioned on a temporary set, posture, or proprioceptive pattern. When this set is broken up by extraneous stimuli it no longer is present to act as an inhibitor. This is an hypothesis open to verification. Pavlov's objection to it is that

> . . . the most important part of these impulses (proprioceptive) proceed to the lower divisions of the brain, and . . . under usual circumstances absolutely do not make themselves known to the cerebral hemispheres but serve only for the self-regulation and greater precision of movements, such as, for example, the continuously occurring cardiac and respiratory movements.

To the writer this seems not only a rather broad statement, but a statement which would, since Pavlov believes conditioning to be the exclusive function of the hemispheres, deny the possibility of acquiring any motor skills based on the conditioning of one movement on the stimulus of another, and deny that serial motor habits conform to the law of the conditioned response.

Pavlov's own explanation of temporary extinction is that it is

> . . . the manifestation, according to law, of the most important properties of the cortical cells, as the most reactive of all cells of the organism, when they remain at work for a greater or less period of time—even if generally a short one—without a satisfying accompaniment for the fundamental innate reflexes; for, the chief physiological role of excitation of these cells is to serve as signals in place of the special stimuli of the latter reflexes. As the most reactive cells, they quickly become fatigued from work and go on not to an inactive state but to inhibition, which probably not only assists in their rest but also hastens their recovery. But when they are accompanied by unconditioned stimuli, then these stimuli . . . at once, and so to speak by way of protection, inhibit them and thus contribute to their recovery.

Since no observations have been made of states of these cells supposed to have gone 'on strike' and no observations are likely to be made, this hypothesis would appear to be not only unverifiable, but unassailable and at the same time of rather little value in the prediction of behavior.

Two more differences remain. Pavlov says,

> In regard to the fact of gradual, intensification of the conditioned effect during the process of its formation, it is necessary to state that in this case it is the gradual removal of extraneous stimuli which disturbs the formation of the reflex, and not the opposite, namely—the author's view which consists in attributing to these stimuli an

> ever-growing rôle in creating the conditions for the effect. During our first experiments often 50 to 100 or more repetitions of the procedure were required in order to develop a complete conditioned reflex, but now 10 to 20 times are sufficient, and often much fewer.

The writer had evidently failed to make his meaning here clear because there is on this point no difference of opinion. In fact he had suggested that perfect control of the experimental conditions, which would include the proprioceptive situation as well as the exteroceptive, might well result in a certain conditioned reflex with *one* repetition.

The final issue is this: The writer had suggested that the phenomenon of irradiation, involving the effectiveness of receptors which were near, but distinct from the practised conditioning receptors, could be explained by the fact that neighboring receptors, by virtue of their nearness, called out responses (avoidance of a touch, for instance) which were substantially identical, and that these approximately identical movements furnished the effective conditioners of the saliva flow. According to Pavlov this is an irradiation of stimulation spreading over a definite part of the cortex. Pavlov's objection to the writer's explanation is that in many cases the phenomenon is observed 'without any trace of orientation.' To this the writer suggests that in such cases it is possible that closer observation would find such a trace.

It is also possible that it would not. As was said at the beginning of this article the writer was putting forward an hypothesis which still has for him a certain plausibility. It is only observation and experiment that can say the last word. It remains his opinion that this hypothesis is at least not inconsistent with any of Pavlov's facts.

It is evident that the differences between us do not concern Pavlov's laboratory findings. These have been of immense service to psychology. Our differences concern a strong tendency found throughout Pavlov's reports to interpret the facts in terms of supposititious events and states in the cortex. These events and states are not the characteristics of nerve conduction described by such men as Adrian and directly demonstrable in the laboratory. They are, on the contrary, quite unlike any of the properties of nervous tissue that have been so directly demonstrated, and they are of such a nature that they can not be observed by any available technique. A proper and scientific theory of learning must describe the phenomena of learning, and also describe the conditions under which these phenomena appear. Both the phenomena and the conditions determining them must be clearly defined and observable. Pavlov's work has satisfied these requirements in so far as laboratory practice is concerned, but his excursions into interpretation and theory are not so fortunate.

If further experiment should establish the law of association by contiguity in time, it will not be the first occasion in the history of science that a variegated lot of experimental results have been found on analysis to be cared for by one descriptive generalization.

NOTES

[1] I. P. Pavlov, Psychol. Rev., 1932, 39, 91-126. All quotations will be from this article where not otherwise indicated.

[2] Association as a function of time interval, Psychol. Rev., 1933, 40, pp. 355-367.

[3] Conditioned reflexes, Oxford Univ. Press, 1927, p. 42.

[4] A. L. Windsor, Observations on the nature and mechanism of secretory inhibition, Psychol. Rev., 1930, 37, 399-411.

M. A. Wenger (essay date 1937)

SOURCE: "A Criticism of Pavlov's Concept of Internal Inhibition," in the *Psychological Review,* Vol. 44, No. 4, July, 1937, pp. 297-312.

[*In the following essay, Wenger points out a flaw in Pavlov's theory of conditioned response concerning the notion of "internal inhibition."*]

The concept of the conditioned response, with or without Pavlovian terminology, has become an important consideration in any contemporary theory of the learning process.[1,2] The major phenomena discovered in the laboratories of Pavlov (18) and Bekhterev (2) have been verified by many other workers. However, Pavlov's interpretations of some of these phenomena have not met with general acceptance. The specific concept bearing the brunt of attack has been that of 'internal inhibition.' About it Razran (19), Guthrie (11), Beritoff (3), Wendt (24), Winsor (28), Chappell (5), Lashley (17), and others have had something derogatory to say.

The term 'inhibition' has found general use in two different contexts. First, it has been used in a descriptive sense to designate a condition of an organism characterized by various degrees of response decrement. Decrement during a competing reaction or Pavlov's external inhibition illustrates this behavioral use of the term. A second connotation of 'inhibition' involves an assumed process or substance affecting the neurones with a resulting decrement in response. In this context, the term is not only descriptive, but explanatory, and it is here that Pavlovian 'internal inhibition' must be classified.

Pavlov regards it as some neural condition which at times irradiates over the entire cortex, and which at other times becomes concentrated in one limited cortical area. It holds an important place in his theories for he uses it to explain experimental extinction of a conditioned response, and to account for negative, differential, trace, and delayed conditioned reflexes. Furthermore, the phenomenon of disinhibition, or the reinstatement of an extinguished or partially extinguished response, is supposed to occur through a temporary removal of internal inhibition as a result of some distracting stimulation. Of still further interest is Pavlov's belief that sleep is the result of a general irradiation of internal inhibition.

The present paper is a criticism of this concept. It will attempt to show (1) that the behavior which probably led Pavlov to conceive of a gradually irradiating cortical inhibition may be explained more parsimoniously, and (2) that such behavior is not necessarily a phenomenon of learning but instead is an artifact due to certain experimental conditions.

The first suggestion of the tenability of such a point of view presented itself during an investigation of external inhibition and disinhibition of a conditioned galvanic skin response in human adults (25). The subjects reclined on a cot in a relatively dark environment, and a masking tone was applied through a set of head phones. The situation, therefore, was conducive to sleep. In the report of the study the following statement occurs:

> The subjects of this experiment reported somnolence during the extinction series. Although they had been instructed to remain as quiet as possible, their efforts to remain awake resulted in many slight movements and adjustments in posture and a tendency toward sporadic deep inspiration. Almost invariably, an increment in the conditioned responses followed. The proprioceptive sensations arising from these movements and inspirations are believed to have resulted in autonomous disinhibition, and their frequent occurrence to have been directly responsible for the prolonged extinction series. This interpretation suggests that at least part of what is usually termed extinctive inhibition may be explained in terms of a decreased level of tonicity.[3]

Observations made during a conditioning experiment with newborn human infants in the Iowa Infant Laboratory (26) have redirected attention to the problem. In work with infants the same general picture of sporadic activity described in the foregoing paragraph may be seen. Frequent periods of sleep alternate with irregular breathing and states of activity. Thus there existed conditions of tactual and proprioceptive stimulation comparable to those referred to in the above experiment.

In the first ten days of life, which is the time infants were available, it was found that conditioning did not reach 100 per cent response. Thus there was not opportunity to study extinction or disinhibition of conditioned responses as such. It was with some surprise, therefore, that behavior similar to these two phenomena was noted. Although it has been long known that infant responses are quite variable, it seemed unusual that a subject, when no sign of self-stimulation was apparent, should suddenly not respond after having given several successive responses to the conditioned stimulus. These states of no response seemed to occur when the subject was very quiet, and were frequently followed by sleep. Of equal interest was the observation that conditioned responses first seemed to appear when the infant was very slightly active, and also that it was under conditions of very slight activity that the conditioned response reappeared after having disappeared. The latter fact strongly suggested spontaneous or autonomous disinhibition by tactual or proprioceptive stimulation. Yet, it was occurring here in infants not only before conditioning was complete but before any specific attempt had been made to build up internal inhibition, *i.e.,* to extinguish the response. Two interpretations of these observations are possible. One, in terms of Pavlov's concept of irradiated internal inhibition, would hold that both response decrement and muscular relaxation are the result of a development of cortical inhibition, the dissipation of which would be accompanied by the termination of muscular relaxation and the reinstatement of the conditioned response. He states, " . . . in all cases of internal inhibition, . . . drowsiness and sleep are met with continually . . ." (18, p. 251), and further, "The development of inhibition with its ultimate expression in the form of sleep is due to functional fatigue of the cellular structures of the cortex" (18, p. 259).

The other interpretation has not been expressed so succinctly. It is peripheral rather than central in nature. According to it, the magnitude of response of an organism at any moment depends to a certain extent upon the state of tension of the skeletal musculature at that moment. This interpretation will be amplified throughout the paper. According to it, decrement of the conditioned responses in these infants occurred when other conditions had induced relaxation of the skeletal musculature, and when relaxation had been interrupted, the response reappeared.

There is abundant evidence to support such an interpretation. Within the past two decades a considerable amount of work has been done (1) on the effect of changes in muscular tension upon behavior, and (2) on the effect of changes in behavior upon muscular tension. Dodge (6) G. L. Freeman (9), Bills (4), and Jacobson (16) have figured prominently in these investigations. The results have been surprisingly consistent and have produced a body of fact which has been summarized by Freeman (10) in his recent text on physiological psychology. The main generalizations are:

> 1. Augmented tension, up to a certain limit, results in response increment; beyond that limit it results in response decrement.
>
> 2. Decreased tension results in response decrement.
>
> 3. Mental work results in tension increment.
>
> 4. Cessation of mental work results in tension decrement.

Freeman therefore has been led to make the statement that,

> . . . all response contains two aspects, the exteroceptive-phasic influence and the proprioceptive-

tonic influence. . . . Tonic contraction precedes and underlies all phasic contraction (10, 458-59). [It] . . . may be called the postural substrate—a general neuromuscular background which operates to facilitate, inhibit, or otherwise modify phasic responses (10, p. 451).

Illustrations of these generalizations are numerous, and have already been summarized by Bills (4) and Freeman (7). A few are cited here. Concerning response decrement, Dodge (6) has stated that during voluntary relaxation there is an inhibition of reflex processes. Jacobson and Carlson (15) have found that the amplitude of the knee jerk is decreased during conditions of relaxation. A familiar example of response decrement is the decreased speed and extent of movement under conditions of rest or relaxation. Recently, Bagchi (1) has experimentally demonstrated with the electromyographic technique that latency of voluntary movement during relaxation is two to four times greater than that during normal posture. Concerning response increment, Tuttle (23) has shown that the amplitude of the knee jerk is increased about ten times over the passive state when the subject is attending to mathematical symbols, and Freeman (8) has completed the picture by showing that increments in quadriceps tension occur during mental arithmetic. Therefore under a condition of hypertension the amplitude of the knee jerk is increased. A familiar example of response increment following tonus increment is the 'handgrip' technique, long used by neurologists in order to augment weak reflexes.

If this collation of experimental results pertained only to response decrement during muscular relaxation, there would be no basis upon which to contradict Pavlov's interpretation. Since, however, it also includes examples of response increment following experimentally induced tension increment, there is excellent ground for maintaining that the state of the peripheral musculature *per se* in some way affects the responses of an organism. Regardless of the causation of a given state of muscular tension, and regardless of how it serves to modify phasic responses, it becomes possible to proceed from a premise about peripheral conditions. Such a premise might be stated as follows:

(*a*) If, in an organism functioning at a level of maximum magnitude of response, there occurs a reduction in tension in the skeletal musculature, there will likewise occur a reduction in magnitude of response.

From this premise it may be predicted that

(*b*) Any condition or set of conditions inducing relaxation of the skeletal musculature in an organism functioning at an optimum level of response, will also induce a decrement in response.

Now we know from Pavlov that relaxation and sleep did occur in his experiments. To quote a passage already partially cited, " . . . in all cases of internal inhibition, . . . drowsiness and sleep were met with continually. In the case of extinction of a conditioned reflex some animals even at the first extinction showed not only a disappearance of the secretory and corresponding motor reaction, but also a great dullness as compared with the normal state of the animal before extinction" (18, p. 251). The conclusion may therefore be drawn that

(*c*) At least part of the decrement in response noted in Pavlov's experiments on extinction of conditioned responses may be attributed to relaxation of the skeletal musculature.

Here, then, is the logical exposition of the interpretation which was suggested but not analyzed during the experiment upon disinhibition (25).

Since the response decrement which occurs with general relaxation and drowsiness is not confined to any specific response or pattern of responses, the above deduction might be amplified.

(*d*) If there exists a generalized relaxation of the skeletal musculature there will exist a generalized decrement in response.

It is not surprising, then, to find Pavlov saying:

. . . experimental extinction of any single conditioned reflex results, not only in a weakening of that particular conditioned reflex which is directly subjected to the extinction (primary extinction), but also in a weakening of other conditioned reflexes which were not directly subjected to extinction (secondary extinction). . . . Sometimes secondary extinction reaches a profound degree, involving even the unconditioned reflexes (18, p. 54).

Nor is it surprising that he felt the need of an irradiating general inhibition to explain the phenomena he witnessed.

Now if this peripheral explanation of response decrement in some extinction experiments is accepted, certain questions arise:

1. How is muscular relaxation itself to be explained?

2. Does muscular relaxation account for all of the response decrement in experimental extinction?

The answer to the first question is considered to be without the scope of the present paper. Let it suffice to say that certain factors influencing muscular tension, as well as some of the nerve pathways over which they operate, are known. Since the latter are fairly well localized, there is small need to postulate a vague "internal inhibition' irradiating over the cortical hemispheres. The second question, however, is essential for the present discussion, and it has already been answered in the negative, for there are repeated examples in Pavlov's own work wherein the response decrement has become specific and is accompanied by no reduction in other responses. It must be concluded, therefore, that

(*e*) The construction of the original premise is correct, not only in form but in fact. Only part of

> the response decrement occuring in experimental extinction may be attributed to reduction in the postural substrate.

It follows then that:

> (*f*) Experimental extinction is a two-fold process when muscular relaxation is known to have occurred.

And further,

> (*g*) Experimental extinction of a conditioned response should be possible without the general decrement induced by muscular relaxation.

Since experimental extinction is involved in establishing delayed, trace, and differential conditioned responses in that in the first two the immediate response to the conditioned stimulus becomes extinguished and in the last the responses to all but a specific conditioned stimulus become extinguished, it becomes possible to predict that,

> (*h*) The development of delayed, trace and differential conditioned responses should be possible without the general decrement induced by muscular relaxation.

Data already exist supporting these predictions. Wendt (24), in a recent experiment, has presented evidence purporting to show that extinction of a conditioned response is an active process, explainable in terms of competition between reactions systems. His experiment, the subjects of which were monkeys, is briefly described in his own words:

> Each animal is trained to respond to the onset of a tone by opening a drawer to get a piece of food. The animal is confined in a cage with a barred aperture (grille) through which it can reach out to grasp the handle of the food drawer. The grille can be closed by a roller curtain attached just beneath the grille so that raising of the curtain closes the grille. . . . The situation confronting the animal is this: At approximately one minute intervals a ready signal is given and five seconds later the curtain is opened, giving the animal access to the drawer. It eventually learns to come to the grille when the curtain opens, waits there in a listening attitude until the tone occurs, then promptly opens the drawer and takes out a piece of food. The tone occurs either eight seconds or sixteen seconds after the curtain opens, the delay interval being changed in an unpredictable order. If the animal responds before the onset of tone, the drawer is empty. It therefore learns to inhibit response during the delay period (pp. 263-264).

It will be seen that the training involved learning to respond to the drawer for food, then learning to inhibit that response until the tone was heard. According to Pavlov this would involve both extinctive inhibition and the inhibition of delay, both of which are aspects of internal inhibition. Furthermore, we should expect an irradiation of internal inhibition during the period of delay which should result in observable muscular relaxation and a decrement in other responses. On the contrary, Wendt found that his subjects, if anything, exhibited greater activity during this period. *In no case did he find relaxation, sleep, or any general decrement in other responses.*[4] He did find a change in activity, which continued to vary during training, but the change always involved some more or less specific response appropriate to the situation and to the species involved. The important consideration is that the monkeys learned to inhibit immediate response to the drawer by *substituting* some other activity. He holds that this substitute activity must be regarded as a competing response which has become dominant over the anticipatory conditioned response, and thus that extinction and delay are explainable in terms of the principle of reciprocal innervation.

Now, how shall these disparate results be reconciled? Both Pavlov and Wendt worked under well-controlled conditions. There was, however, a major difference in their experimental techniques. Pavlov's animals were held stationary in harness while Wendt's were free in a cage. As Wendt has already pointed out, the characteristic behavior of a confined animal in a controlled environment is quiescence after a short period of adjustment, while the behavior of a monkey free in a cage results in continuous self-stimulation from proprioceptive and tactual end organs. Wendt has suggested that perhaps something in Pavlov's experiments facilitated the pattern of relaxation and sleep. He notes three factors (1) restraint of the animal, (2) absence of varied stimulation with its possibility of varied reactions, and (3) repetitive monotonous stimulation. Actually, the first factor is the important one for, in controlled experiments on extinction, stimuli with the exception of those of proprioceptive and tactual origin are eliminated and the presentation of the conditioned stimulus by design is repetitive and therefore monotonous since other stimuli are absent. The point is that in Wendt's experiment muscular relaxation never appeared because the stage was not set for it, while in Pavlov's experiments the stage was set for muscular quiescence, and therefore for relaxation.

It has been experimentally demonstrated, then, that experimental extinction, trace, and delayed responses can be established with little or no indications of irradiation of inhibition and the predictions may be regarded as substantiated. The question immediately arises, how are these phenomena to be explained if not by internal inhibition? Razran (19) has suggested an interpretation in terms of changes in dominance of certain neural patterns. Wendt's interpretation is not essentially different. He believes that his subjects succeeded in inhibiting the anticipatory response to the food drawer when some substitute response apparently had become dominant. Regardless of how that shift in dominance occurred, it offers an opportunity to explain tentatively the inhibition of a given response in terms of the principle of reciprocal innervation of a competing reaction system.

Wendt needlessly belabors his interpretation, however, when he claims that relaxation and sleep also are to be interpreted as competing reactions. It is not intended to suggest that this is never possible. There are many indications for believing that these patterns *may be* conditioned to certain stimuli and some of the instances described by Pavlov should probably be so interpreted. Nevertheless, there are at least three reasons for questioning any generalized conception of relaxation and sleep as competing reactions.

In the first place, when one thinks of a competing reaction, he thinks of a positive muscular reaction. Wendt indicated his realization of this implication when he cited McDougall's references to contracture of the eyelids and to certain postures favoring sleep, as possible muscular components of the competing reaction of sleep. Relaxation however is, to the best of our knowledge, the fundamental prerequisite of sleep, and it is a passive muscular reaction. So far as is known, it is not dependent upon peripheral innervation but instead upon reduction of that innervation. Even if there is a sleep center, its mechanism will probably be found to be a reduction of stimulation at the nuclei controlling muscular tension.

In the second place, even though it is admitted that sleep may become conditioned to normally distracting stimuli, in the usual analysis relaxation and sleep, except in the greatly fatigued or intoxicated organism, is rather a fragile process during its onset. Instead of it competing with other reactions, the latter typically compete successfully with it.[5]

In the third place, if we agree on the ground of passivity and fragility that the competitive potency of relaxation and sleep is questionable, it seems theoretically premature to cast these responses in the mold of other more dominant reaction patterns and speak of only one form of inhibition. Since we know that experimentally induced increments in muscular tension will facilitate response, and conversely that experimentally induced decrements in tension will inhibit response, we have both logical and parsimonious reasons for recognizing an *inhibition due to reduction of proprioceptive facilitation as well as an inhibition due to a competing reaction.*

Summarizing the foregoing discussion several established principles and one postulate appear.

> *Principle 1.*—Decrement in muscular tension usually will be accompanied by a general decrement in response.

> *Principle 2.*—Increment in muscular tension usually will be accompanied by a general increment in response.

> *Principle 3.*—The inhibition of a conditioned response may occur without the accompaniment of muscular relaxation and therefore without the phenomenon of general response decrement.

> *Principle 4.*—When muscular relaxation accompanies the inhibition of a conditioned response, decrement in response will be generalized, and the total process must be regarded as two-fold.

> *Postulate 1.*—There are at least two forms of inhibition: (*a*) Reduction of proprioceptive facilitation and (*b*) a shift in dominance to a competing reaction.

These premises may be utilized in a further analysis of behavior.

> *A.* (From 3 and 4.) Muscular relaxation and its accompanying generalized decrement in response is not necessarily related to the inhibition of a conditioned response and when it occurs it must be regarded as an experimental artifact as far as the conditioning process itself is concerned.

> *B.* (From 1 and 2.) During the development of inhibition of a conditioned response which is being accompanied by muscular relaxation, any extraneous stimulus producing an increment in muscular tension will be followed by an increment in the conditioned response.

This prediction has already been realized in the data which Pavlov refers to as 'disinhibition' (*cf.* footnote 5).

> *C.* (From Principle 4 and Deductions *A* and *B.*) Disinhibition is not necessarily a law of the conditioned response per se.

It is only known to operate upon that phase of inhibition which has been shown to be an experimental artifact. Disinhibition, therefore, is a law of response as influenced by muscular tension. Whether it also is a law of the pure conditioned response remains to be determined.

> *D.* (From Principles 1, 2, and 4.) After the extinction of a conditioned response which has been accompanied by muscular relaxation, a reinstatement of a more normal level of muscular tension will be accompanied by at least a partial reinstatement of the conditioned response.

This prediction also has been realized in the findings of Pavlov and others. It is referred to as 'spontaneous recovery' and is supposed to occur within a short time (varying according to the 'depth of inhibition') after the extinction process. In terms of the present interpretation the length of the time interval becomes unimportant. Importance attaches instead to the changes in tension of the skeletal musculature during the interval.

> *E.* (As in *C* above.) Spontaneous recovery is not necessarily a law of the conditioned response *per se.*

Like disinhibition, it is only known to operate upon that phase of inhibition relating to muscular relaxation. It also is a law of behavior as relating to muscular tension, and its operation in the pure conditioned response remains to be determined.[6]

Other deductions relate to the effect of drugs upon the conditioned response.

> *F.* (From Principle 1.) The extinction of a conditioned response should be facilitated by administration of a drug known to effect muscular relaxation.

> *G.* (From Principle 1.) The extinction of a conditioned response should be impaired by administration of a drug known to interfere with muscular relaxation.

Switzer's work (22) concerning the effect of caffeine on extinction already affords support of the latter deduction.

Another deduction takes the form of an explanation of the inhibition which is purported to adhere to the conditioning process itself. It has been reported by Platonov (*cf.* Razran's review, 20) and more recently by Hovland (12), that a conditioned response immediately after the conditioning process is occasionally lesser in magnitude than it is some time later. Since it seems that monotony of stimulation is one factor which effects muscular relaxation, and since there is a certain monotony in the conditioning process especially if the stimulations occur at short intervals, it is possible to assume that some relaxation of the skeletal musculature may occur during the conditioning process itself. The logical deduction follows:

> *H.* (From Principle 1.) If, during the conditioning process, there occurs a decrement in muscular tension there will occur a decrement in the conditioned response.

If this deduction is the proper explanation for the inhibition in question then the conditioned response so inhibited should be subject both to disinhibition and spontaneous recovery. Only the latter has yet been demonstrated.

A final inference would question the validity of a smooth curve of experimental extinction. It proceeds from the assumptions that (*a*) learning is not a smoothly progressive process but is interrupted by numerous plateaus and regressions, and that (*b*) muscular relaxation, if uninterrupted, is a smoothly progressive process. A slight degree of relaxation reduces the postural substrate. The facilitative effect upon higher nervous centers is thereby reduced and cortical and bulbar stimulation of the peripheral musculature are in turn decreased, again diminishing the proprioceptive bombardment upon the higher centers. The latter assumption would, of course, explain parsimoniously the smooth curve of extinction which Pavlov and others have reported, but leave the true nature of the curve unpredicted. If Wendt is right in maintaining that extinction of one response involves learning of another, the curve of pure extinction may be the inverse of the learning curve of the newly dominating response.

It is apparent that the picture of inhibition presented in this paper is radically different from that presented by Pavlov. If the present analysis is tenable, much of the work of Pavlov and his pupils is questionable, for their researches on inhibition were accompanied to such an extent by drowsiness and sleep that Pavlov, at least, regarded the whole as one process. Probably most of the data concerning inhibition present an erroneous picture *as far as the conditioning or learning process itself is concerned.* In short, the work on inhibition of conditioned responses must be repeated under conditions of known stable muscular tension before many laws of conditioned responses can be recognized and applied to the more complex processes of human behavior.

NOTES

[1] The writer is indebted to Drs. Orvis C. Irwin, Charles Van Riper, Eliot H. Rodnick, and Carl Iver Hovland, for their critical reading of the manuscript.

[2] The substance of this paper was reported at the summer meetings of the A.A.A.S. held in Minneapolis, Minnesota, May, 1935.

[3] Recently the data have been re-read and consistent though variable increases in skin resistance have been found during extinction in eighteen of the twenty subjects. In the light of a recent experiment by Wenger and Irwin (27) which demonstrated that increases in palmar skin resistance are related to muscular relaxation, these data confirm the report of the subjects that much relaxation occurred during extinction. In order to determine whether the same would be true of a seated subject one adult was conditioned and readings were taken of resistance during conditioning and extinction. During conditioning, resistance maintained a nearly constant level. During extinction it rose. Therefore relaxation also occurred in the seated subject.

[4] It should, perhaps, be stated that Hull (13) has reported some evidence of irradiation of inhibition to another conditioned response. Trace conditioned galvanic responses were established in human adult subjects and during the period of delay between the presentation of the conditioned stimulus and the onset of the conditioned response, the stimulus for a previously conditioned lid closure was given. According to Pavlovian theory, a decrement in amplitude of lid closure would have been expected. On the contrary, results from ten subjects showed little or no indication of a weakening of the conditioned lid reaction during the period of delay of the trace conditioned response. However, the mean latency of the lid responses was found to have increased 17%. Dr. Eliot H. Rodnick (21) informs the writer that he has repeated Hull's experiment under slightly different conditions and has attained a 19% decrement in amplitude and a 15% increment in latency.

Under the conditions of the experiments the response decrement and latency increment can hardly be explained in terms of muscular relaxation. However, it is not necessary to revert to 'irradiation of internal inhibition' for an explanation. One needs only to refer to Wendt's application of the principle of competition between reaction systems. If this explanation is valid, the 'set' to perform some other response should inhibit the interpolated lid response just as much as did the conditioned delay stimulus which Rodnick used.

[5] It is pertinent here to cite from Pavlov (18, p. 50): ". . . to obtain a smooth curve of extinction of a conditioned reflex it is necessary to maintain the unreinforced con-

ditioned stimulus rigidly constant in character and strength; the environing experimental conditions also must remain absolutely constant . . . the effect of an extra stimulus of even small intensity is a temporary weakening, not of the reflex, but of the progress of experimental extinction."

[6] Humphrey (14) has reported disinhibition (which he terms 'dehabituation') and spontaneous recovery in experiments on negative adaptation in controlled environments. If, as has been postulated, these phenomena are the result of tension increment, it should be possible to find that tension decrement had occurred previously. Unfortunately, Humphrey's data do not provide the necessary information. The literature was searched and paradoxically the only pertinent data were found in Pavlov (18) where the 'investigatory reflex' of a dog to a whistle was negatively adapted. Pavlov says (p. 255) "Special experiments . . . showed that the disappearance of the investigatory reflex is based on the development of inhibition, and is in all details analogous to the extinction of conditioned reflexes." Even more specifically (p. 256), "The inhibition of the investigatory reflex invariably leads to drowsiness and sleep (even more easily than the inhibition of conditioned reflexes)."

It is thus found that under certain conditions negative adaptation results in relaxation, which, among other observations, seems to have led Pavlov to state that it also is mediated through an irradiation of internal inhibition. It is known, however, in common experience, that adaptation of a response may occur in active and uncontrolled environments. Therefore it seems that negative adaptation, like extinction, must be considered as a twofold process when it occurs in a controlled environment, and that the relaxation which there is observed must likewise be regarded as essentially artificial to adaptation as such. Perhaps both 'dehabituation' and 'disinhibition' as well as 'spontaneous recovery' might more accurately be described as 'de-relaxation.'

REFERENCES

1. Bagchi, B. K., An electromyographic study with respect to speed of movement and latency, disparate and reciprocal innervation, attention and relaxation, *Psychol. Monog,* (to be published).

2. Bekhterev, V. M., General principles of human reflexology, New York: International Publishers, 1932, pp. 467.

3. Beritoff, J. S., On the fundamental nervous processes in the cortex of the cerebral hemispheres, *Brain,* 1924, 47, 109-148.

4. Bills, A. G., The influence of muscular tension on the efficiency of mental work, *Amer. J. Psychol.,* 1927, 38, 227-251.

5. Chappell, M. N., Inhibition, facilitation, learning, *Psychol. Rev.,* 1931, 38, 317-331.

6. Dodge, R., Conditions and consequences of human variability, New Haven, Conn.: Yale University Press, 1931, pp. xi, 162.

7. Freeman, G. L., Mental activity and the muscular processes, Psychol. Rev., 1931, 38, 428-449.

8.———, The spread of neuromuscular activity during mental work, *J. Gen. Psychol.,* 1931, 5, 479-494.

9.———, Studies in muscular tension [Collected papers], 1929-1933, pp. 182.

10.———, Physiological psychology, New York: Ronald Press, 1934, pp. 579 + xv.

11. Guthrie, E. R., The psychology of learning, New York: Harper & Bros., 1935, pp. viii, 258.

12. Hovland, C. I., The effects of varying amounts of reinforcement upon the generalization of conditioned responses, *Psychol. Bull.,* 1935, 32, 731-732.

13. Hull, C. L., The alleged inhibition of delay in trace conditioned reactions, *Psychol. Bull.,* 1934, 31, 716-717.

14. Humphrey, G., The nature of learning in its relation to the living system, New York: Harcourt Brace, 1933, pp. vii, 296.

15. Jacobson, E. and Carlson, A., The influence of relaxation on the knee jerk, *Amer. J. Psychol.,* 1925, 73, 324-328.

16. Jacobson, E., Progressive relaxation: a physiological and clinical investigation of muscular states and their significance in psychology and medical practice, Chicago: University of Chicago Press [C. 1929], pp. xiii, 428.

17. Lashley, K. S., Nervous mechanisms in learning, in 'The Foundations of Experimental Psychology' (Ed. by Carl Murchison), Worcester: Clark University Press, 1929, pp. 907.

18. Pavlov, I. P., Conditioned reflexes: an investigation of the physiological activity of the cerebral cortex, Oxford University Press: Humphrey Milford, 1927, pp. 430-xv.

19. Razran, H. S., Theory of conditioning and of related phenomena, *Psychol. Rev.,* 1930, 37, 25-43.

20.———, Conditioned withdrawal responses with shock as the conditioning stimulus in adult human subjects, *Psychol. Bull.,* 1934, 31, 111-143.

21. Rodnick, E. H., Characteristics of delayed and trace conditioned responses (to be published).

22. Switzer, St. Clair, The effect of caffeine on experimental extinction of conditioned reactions, *J. Gen. Psychol.,* 1935, 12, 78-94.

23. Tuttle, W. W., The effect of attention or mental activity on the patellar tendon reflex, *J. Exper. Psychol.*, 1924, 7, 401-419.

24. Wendt, G. R., An interpretation of inhibition of conditioned reflexes as competition between reaction systems, *Psychol. Rev.*, 1936, 43, 258-281.

25. Wenger, M. A., External inhibition and disinhibition produced by duplicate stimuli, *Amer. J. Psychol.*, 1936, 48, 446-456.

26.———, An investigation of conditioned responses in human infants, in 'Studies in Infant Behavior,' III, *Univ. Iowa Stud., Stud. in Child Welfare,* 1936, 12, No. 1, pp. 207 (pp. 7-90).

27.——— and Irwin, O. C., Fluctuations in skin resistance of infants and adults and their relation to muscular processes, in 'Studies in Infant Behavior,' III, *Univ. Iowa Stud., Stud. in Child Welfare,* 1936, 12, No. 1, pp. 207 (pp. 141-179).

28. Winsor, A. L., Observations on the nature and mechanism of secretory inhibition, *Psychol. Rev.*, 1930, 37, 399-411.

Orvis C. Irwin (essay date 1939)

SOURCE: "Toward A Theory of Conditioning," in the *Psychological Review,* Vol. 46, No. 5, September, 1939, pp. 425-44.

[*In the following essay, Irwin outlines Pavlov's general theory of conditioning, provides a critique, and presents an alternative interpretation of the subject.*]

The manner in which the title of this paper is worded—*toward* a theory—implies a conviction that aside from Pavlov there exists no fully-developed systematic theory of conditioning. There are, however, some experimental data which may be used for the beginnings of a new formulation. A great deal of incidental questioning, if not outright criticism, is current in the literature on the subject, although it has not resulted in a concerted attempt to restate the conventional viewpoint. This situation is probably due to the enormous prestige of Pavlov's name. One should not be unmindful, of course, of the possibility that whoever proposes to raise questions concerning the underlying assumptions of a great scientific enterprise is himself vulnerable. On the other hand, he may be fortified by the knowledge that in the free atmosphere of modern science there are no faultless and enduring Messiahs, so that the prestige of Pavlov's achievement need not deter him from entertaining a healthy scientific skepticism of a powerfully entrenched dogma.

After summarizing in a preliminary way the main results of some experiments on the conditioning process in infants, certain items of data which seem to be pertinent to the problems of interpretation will be emphasized. The article is organized into four parts: the first will deal with our own experimental results; the second will outline Pavlov's general position; the third will consist of a critical estimate of his fundamental assumptions; and the last will attempt a different interpretation, especially of the somewhat knotty problem of internal inhibition.[1]

THE EXPERIMENTAL RESULTS

Previous to Wenger's (30) study, the only really systematic investigation of conditioning in newborn infants in America was done by Dorothy Postle Marquis (21). Wenger's primary object was to make an exploratory study into the possibility of conditioning a variety of different stimuli. For conditioned stimuli he used a cutaneous vibrator, a tone, a light, and a buzzer. The unconditioned stimuli were a light, a shock, and food (milk). He paired these conditioned and unconditioned stimuli in various combinations. The first experiment involved the pairing of tactile vibrations and light in an attempt to condition eyelid responses to touch. In other experiments he investigated the conditioning to a tactile stimulus of a withdrawal response from electric shock, of a withdrawal response to a sound, and also to light. Infants were used from their second to their eighth day. In all these experiments the criterion of conditioning was a differential score between the responses of experimental and control groups.

Wenger (30) confirmed Marquis' (21) finding that conditioning may be set up during the first week of life, but he demonstrated that it is of an unstable nature. Only six of fourteen infants were conditioned, the remaining cases giving unsatisfactory results. Best results were secured when electric shock was used as the unconditioned stimulus. A very large number of pairings are required to condition newborns, varying from 120 to 280. Wenger (30) demonstrated the presence of a variety of conditioned phenomena such as anticipation, external inhibition, and disinhibition. Having a considerable bearing on the interpretation of the conditioning process is the observation that while the infant is in a state of complete muscular quiescence the vigor of the response decreases and finally drops out.

Kantrow's (14) study was done on sixteen infants between the ages of six weeks and four months. The conditioned stimulus was the sound of a buzzer; the unconditioned stimulus was milk. Kantrow was interested not only in the problem of conditioning the sucking reaction, but also in the much neglected problem of the effect of conditioning the sucking reaction upon other concomitant behaviors, such as body activity, crying, etc. From the theoretical standpoint, therefore, her study is more broadly based than the conventional conditioning experiment. Analyses of the rates of acquisition and of decrement of the responses were made. In all of her experiments, she adopted a method which insured the presence of controls, thereby obtaining differential scores as indices of conditioning. Another matter of theoretical importance is the fact that the experiment was set up with a view to obtaining data on the effect of the internal state of the infant, such as hunger and satiety.

Fifteen of the sixteen infants were successfully conditioned, a much larger proportion of the group than in the case of Wenger's subjects. Vincent curves were constructed to show the rate of acquisition. These curves reveal an initial acceleration and then flatten out into a plateau. An item of considerable interest is the fact that with continued reinforcement the curve shows a decrement, which in turn achieves a plateau at a lower level than the first plateau, but still significantly higher than the values for the controls. She also showed that during the state of satiation little progress in conditioning occurs.

PAVLOV'S WORK AND HIS THEORY OF CONDITIONING

The empirical results of Pavlov's work on conditioning, including those on the generalization and specificity of stimuli, have been amply confirmed in many experiments until they are as certainly established as any datum in modern physiology and psychology. Let us take a look at Pavlov's explanation of them. For Pavlov, as for most neurophysiologists, there are at least two processes in the central nervous system, the processes of excitation and inhibition. To elucidate their actual working, he has recourse to two phenomena which apply to both of them. These are irradiation and concentration of nervous impulses and he is confident that they have been established under firmly fixed quantitative laws. They have spatial and temporal characteristics. When in the experiment the point on the shoulder of the dog is stimulated, a corresponding spatial point in the dog's cortex is excited. In time this point of cortical excitation tends to spread to other spatial points on the brain. Irradiation of cortical excitation, therefore, according to Pavlov, accounts for the phenomenon of generalization. Later the irradiation recedes once more upon the originally excited point. This is concentration and is intended to explain specificity of salivation to the single shoulder point. In the same manner, he explains inhibition. While salivation to the point on the dog's rump is being extinguished by failure to reinforce with food, a nervous process at a corresponding cortical point is inhibited. Inhibition then irradiates to other points, and is followed by a recession or concentration upon the originally inhibited point. This is the explanation offered for his doctrine of internal inhibition, which for him is the crucial concept in his general theory.

These laws were arrived at on the basis of six different investigations on the nature of internal inhibition. To illustrate, let me describe a simplified typical experiment. Suppose we select four equidistant points on the dog's side, one upon the shoulder, one behind the shoulder, and one on the flank and the last one on the rump. Let us condition the first three points equally, so that upon stimulation they each yield, say, ten drops of saliva. Let us, on the other hand, extinguish the point on the rump so that it gives zero drops. We are now ready to perform the experiment crucial to the establishment of his laws of irradiation and concentration. In the experiment, the point on the rump is tested twice in order to verify the presence of extinction. Then at selected intervals the other three points are stimulated, and the resulting drops of saliva are counted in order to determine quantitatively the extent to which the irradiated inhibition from the rump has influenced them. Suppose the flank point now gives only five drops, the side eight, and the shoulder its original number of ten drops. We will then say that inhibition has irradiated to this amount. Continuing the testing we can determine when the shoulder point will yield zero drops. Moreover, we can test when recovery occurs at this point and the time it requires to occur at each of the other two points. The rump point will not show recovery. This reverse process is called concentration. Pavlov's (24) statement of the results of these experiments is included in his address on physiology and psychology, "Our explanation is purely physiological, purely objective, and purely spatial. It is obvious, that in our case the skin is a projection of the brain mass. The different points of the skin are a projection of the points of the brain. When at a certain point of the brain, through the corresponding skin area on the shoulder, I evoke a definite nervous process, then it does not remain there, but makes a considerable excursion. It first irradiates over the brain mass, and then returns, concentrating at its point of origin. Both these movements naturally require time" (p. 273).

CRITICAL ESTIMATE

There can be only occasional quarrel with Pavlov's data. This will become apparent as we proceed, but it is not the main issue. However, in my opinion, the assumptions underlying his interpretation of conditioning phenomena need reanalysis.

There are seven such assumptions. If we can raise a reasonable doubt about some or all of them, then presumably the theory will need revision. The direction which this revision should take and the fundamental thesis which I shall try to explicate is that in a typical experiment you do not condition only the single response, you condition an organism. From this thesis there arise several alternative principles to that of Pavlov. The following paragraphs consider Pavlov's assumptions.

1. In his Oxford volume Pavlov (23) devotes a whole chapter to the conditions under which the successful outcome of a conditioning experiment may be achieved. Foremost among these is the necessity for a temporal overlap of the conditioned and unconditioned stimuli. He emphasizes this overlap or contiguity in spite of the fact that it is not necessary in setting up his trace reflex. On the score of contiguity he left himself open and his critics have taken advantage of it. As a matter of fact, there are situations in which the process of conditioning fails even though contiguity is meticulously observed. If Kantrow did nothing else, she demonstrated that contiguity is not enough. She reports, "The curve for the frequency of sucking drops precipitously during the last part of the

experimental feeding period to a point below the level of the critical control period. This striking drop . . . is associated with a complete loss of the conditioned feeding response" (p. 52). In other words, besides the item of contiguity, the state of hunger or satiety of the organism is a decisive factor in the process. Now there are similar items in Pavlov's own data, which should have made him wary in his emphasis upon contiguity. The point here, not at all new by any means, is that conditioning is as much a matter of the organism as of either the stimulus or the response *per se*.

2. A second assumption, which underlies the work and the conceptualization of the whole Russian school, is that the organ of conditioning is the cerebral cortex. In fact, on Krasnogorski's last visit to America, he stated in his lectures that the term 'conditioned reflex' in Russia has been displaced by the term 'cortical reflex.' That the cortex is the organ of conditioning is an original motif of Pavlov's work. Without it, there is no rationale to his experimental efforts. But this proposition no longer is the dogma it once was. The evidence from a number of American laboratories, especially the work of Marquis (20) at Yale and Culler (6) at Illinois, convincingly indicates that subcortical levels of the nervous system may be conditioned. Correspondingly there is a widespread view held by neurophysiologists, that the cortex of the human infant at birth is nonfunctional, that the infant is a thalamic organism. Pavlov and especially Krasnogorski consequently held that newborns could not be conditioned. Dorothy Postle Marquis (21), however, did condition newborn infants. Since she also accepted the nonfunctional view of the cortex, she was driven by the results of her experiment to assume that conditioning in neonates is mediated by subcortical structures. Wenger (30) showed that, although conditioning may be established after much labor, the result is not very stable. Kantrow's (14) work makes it clear that by the end of the second month conditioning can be satisfactorily achieved. These results may mean that the cortex at birth is incipiently functional if not to a very great degree, and that this function during the first months has developed enormously. On the other hand they may mean that neonatal conditioning is a subcortical function, which by the third month has been taken over by the cortex, captured, so to speak, from lower centers. It is a nice question and difficult to answer. The problem has been introduced here because it raises a question about the validity of one of Pavlov's fundamental assumptions, namely that the cortex is exclusively the organ of conditioning.

3. Pavlov assumed that since conditioned responses are cortical reflexes they may be treated from the point of view of a reflexology. In fact, it was his explicit intention to extend the notion of the spinal reflex to the cortex, he himself considering this to be his greatest contribution to science. In his lecture on the higher nervous system, he said a little grandiloquently, "The time has come, gentlemen, to add something to this old notion of the reflexes, to admit that, parallel with this elementary function of the nervous system to repeat preformed reflexes, there exists another elementary function—the formation of new reflexes" (p. 224). He pointed out that there has not been heretofore "a general acceptance and systematic application of this formula in the study of the higher parts of the nervous system." Now the logical and practical implication of the conventional reflex theory is that complex behavior is the outcome of the association or integration of units; this view is very explicit throughout Pavlov's writings. Here it is evident that time has just outrun him. While we must undoubtedly find a place for integration in the course of development, it cannot at present be accepted as an exclusive principle. More and more evidence is accumulating against the view. Reflexes and much specific behavior are products of a process of differentiation rather than a sheer integration of units by a cortical process. One needs to remind himself only of the long series of researches, contemporary with those of Pavlov, by Coghill on the development of behavior of Amblystoma. Similar results to those of Coghill have been found in the behavioral development of the rat fetus by Swensen and by Angulo, on the cat fetus by Coronios, and by Tuge in the reptile and bird. That differentiation as well as integration of reflexes and other specific behavior is a principle operating in the development of the human fetus is suggested by the observations of Minkowski, of Baloffio and Artom, and quite recently has been substantiated in studies by Hooker. All this work quite unsettles the foundation upon which a rigid reflexology rests.

4. An assumption, which is not unequivocally supported by experimental evidence, is Pavlov's doctrine of spatial projection. In the experiments outlined earlier, it will be recalled, four points on the skin were conditioned. Pavlov stated in regard to his results: "Our explanation . . . [is] . . . purely spatial. . . . The different points of the skin are a projection of the points of the brain" (p. 273). This statement was made in an address delivered in 1916. Shortly before Pavlov made this statement T. Graham Brown, without rejecting in toto the doctrine of localization, had completed some related investigations on this same question of spatial projection. In essence, his experiments consisted in stimulating a series of cortical motor points at stated intervals and recording the peripheral responses. He then reversed his series; that is to say, he stimulated the series of points in an opposite direction. The second sequence of peripheral responses was not invariably the same as the first. He also varied the experiment by stimulating adjacent points and interpreted the results as indications of instability of cortical points. Had Pavlov known of these results on the instability of the cortex, his concept of spatial projection would not have been formulated quite as rigidly as it was, and his theory of inhibition very likely would have been set up differently.

5. Earlier in this paper, Pavlov's theory of irradiation and concentration of nervous impulses from and upon a cortical point was outlined. These laws are the keystone of the general concept of internal inhibition to which he

devotes a large portion of his ablest book, the Oxford volume (23). While the whole of his theoretical construction stands or falls upon the dubious assumption of rigid spatial projection, there is another demonstration of the inadequacy of these laws. It will be noted in all of Pavlov's theoretical discussions of conditioning that his explanations tacitly assume that only one response, the one in question, is conditioned. The laws of irradiation and concentration are always presented in this guise. This was perfectly natural, for during his professional career Pavlov conditioned few responses other than salivation in the dog. Now when one sets up a conditioning experiment, one selects a response to work with, which is simple, definite, and readily isolated. Then one constructs a recording device which will clearly register that particular response together with its peculiarities. When one has, by dint of whatever inventiveness he may possess, set up the device, one proceeds with the recording of his data. The salivary response is just such a response (and there can be no caviling that in recording it Pavlov meticulously isolated it from other responses). By the very conditions of his experiment, however, one has eliminated the recording of all other responses of the organism. For the purposes of any given experiment, this is a justifiable procedure, for the investigator has the privilege of selecting his own problem. But for the purpose of formulating an adequate theory, it is questionable. For in the experiment, one is conditioning not only the one little response item in which he is interested, but also concomitant or associated responses. In a word, one is conditioning an organism.

When Kantrow conditioned the sucking response in infants, we have seen that other responses were conditioned concomitantly. This makes it probable that whole congeries of responses were set up. What bearing, then, does this fact have upon the laws of irradiation and concentration? Perforce all of these simultaneous conditionings must be explained according to Pavlov's theory in terms of spatial projection and of irradiation and concentration. Inexorably one is driven by the logic of Pavlov's thesis to the view that many irradiations and concentrations are proceeding simultaneously to and fro over the brain mass during an experiment in which many responses are being conditioned. This places too great a burden on Pavlov's laws, *especially on the possibility of a concentration occurring upon a point.*

6. Pavlov's account of what happens in the nervous system when an impulse arrives there is hardly accurate. For he has repeated on a physiological level the old *tabula rasa* error of John Locke. Implicated in his view of the nervous system is the assumption that it is an inert physiological substance receiving at definite points certain impulses, which after the lapse of time irradiate to other definite points. The tacit assumption is, that when these points are not activated, the nervous system is a passive structure. The fact is, however, that there is nothing static or passive about it. It is continuously being bombarded by proprioceptive impulses from the muscles, joints and tendons, by interoceptive impulses from the sense organs located in membranes lining the body cavities, and by impulses arising in external peripheral sense organs. The sense organs vary on this central activity; sometimes, as in sleep, they are greatly reduced in volume and intensity; at other times, one or the other varies in the degree to which they influence the central nervous system, and still at other times, they may co-operate in an increased bombardment. At any given moment there probably is an organized pattern of central neural activity, which innervates the response system of the organism. Any single new impulse does not get through this central pattern as over an insulated pipeline to result in a certain definite response of a particular motor organ. The single impulse, conditioned or otherwise, may modify the central pattern, may distort it, facilitate or inhibit parts of it, but the resulting peripheral response is the outcome of this modification in the ongoing neural pattern, and not of the single stimulus directly influencing the particular response by means of a neat and simple scheme of irradiation and concentration. If this situation is true, then the laws of irradiation and concentration together with Pavlov's formulation of internal inhibition based upon them cannot be used as the explanation of the generalization and specificity of conditioned behavior.

There is good experimental evidence against his view. Travis (29) showed that impulses in the Achilles tendon reflex of the rat arrive not only at an appropriate level in the spinal cord, but that they also arrive at several places in the brain. He placed electrodes in several areas and upon stimulating the Achilles tendon, found that impulses were recorded with similar latencies at different points. Similar results have been reported by Leese and Einarson (16) and by Gasser and Graham (8). There are other experiments done by Bishop (1) and his students which further elucidate how impulses arrive at the cortex. If the brain of the cat is exposed, electrodes placed over the auditory and adjacent areas, and the ear stimulated, impulses are found to arrive in the auditory regions, but simultaneously voltages are picked by the electrodes in outlying regions. An interesting observation is that there is a gradation of voltages from a place within the auditory area tapering off to surrounding parts. Superficially this bears a resemblance to Pavlov's irradiation, but the time and spatial factors are handled differently, and the concentration phenomenon is not present in these experiments.

TOWARD A POSITIVE VIEW

So much for a critical estimate of Pavlov's assumptions. What can we say on the positive side? What view or views of conditioning are available as a substitute for the concept of irradiation and concentration?

Since the numerous conditioning experiments have yielded much data, it may be economical to select only a few but diverse samples. Moreover, in this way we can learn whether a general theory is at all possible or whether we must be content for the present with several special theories.

Three such diverse samples of data are available in the work with infants, one by Wenger (30), and two by Kantrow (14). Wenger reports that in the midst of a conditioning experiment after a series of successful trials, conditioning lapses and then spontaneously reappears. Kantrow reports that toward the end of a given experimental period when the infant is satiated, conditioning fails utterly. She reports also a very interesting finding regarding a decrement in the strength of conditioning which occurs with continued reinforcement. From the ninth to the fifteenth training unit the curve of acquisition becomes relatively horizontal. Subsequently, even with continued reinforcement, it descends from this plateau to attain a second plateau at a lower level. The second plateau nevertheless still indicates the presence of the conditioned state. The characteristics of each of these items of data are different. In the first instance apparently the same stimulus which is originally excitatory becomes inhibitory and then again excitatory. In the second, a complete decrement occurs with continued feeding, and in the third a partial decrement is superimposed upon an excitatory condition.

In order to find the best fitting explanation to these three diverse phenomena let us survey the present stock of theories, especially theories of inhibition. Such a list will be found to fall into two groups: (1) ultimate or technical theories, and (2) intermediate theories. The former are concerned with the bioelectrical, mechanical or chemical nature of inhibition. They include: Lucas' refractory phase theory; Lapique's heterochronic view; Howell, Sherrington, and Hoagland's chemical views; Ostwalt and Lillie's membrane theory; McDougall's drainage theory; and Max Meyer's deflection theory.

By intermediate or special theories I mean those which make no assumptions concerning the underlying chemical, mechanical, or bioelectric nature of inhibition, and which make no claims toward all-inclusiveness.

Such a theory of course is Pavlov's notion of irradiation and concentration, as is also the peripheral theory. Wenger has proposed a theory of proprioceptive inhibition which I prefer to designate, for reasons which will appear, as a tonus hypothesis. A final theory belonging to this group is the theory of competing reaction systems which we all use when our favorite hypotheses break down.

Let us begin with the refractory phase theory of Lucas (18) and apply it to the first of our three items of data. This view states that when the wave of electronegativity sweeps down a peripheral nerve or axone, it leaves behind it an area inexcitable to stimulation. This period of inexcitability, the refractory period, is found to be divided into an absolute and a relative refractory state. Just as the refractory condition sweeps along behind the wave of negativity, it in turn is followed by a supernormal state of excitability. So much for refractory decrement. But now let us look at Wenger's (30) datum. He found that during a conditioning experiment with babies a period of positive conditioning, for no apparent reason, would be followed by a lapse of the response. This of course looks like experimental extinction. But he also reports that a brief period of hypersensitivity ensues to both the conditioned and unconditioned stimuli. You will note that at first glance there seems to be a perfect parallel between this datum and the refractory phase theory. The resemblance however is only superficial for the following reasons: (1) the refractory phase decrement in axones is a matter of thousandths of a second. In Wenger's experiment it is many minutes. Thus the decrement in the conditioning situation endures for periods never contemplated by the theory. (2) Refractory phase phenomena were worked out experimentally upon the peripheral axone; they have not been experimentally established for central nervous tissue. On the contrary there is reason to question whether the electrical pattern in the brain tissue, which consists of a multitude of cell bodies and their intricately ramifying dendrites, is the same as in the axone. In fact Gasser and Graham have produced evidence to show that it is not. Now conditioning is not a matter of mere conduction across axones. Its neural basis is brain tissue, not only of the cortex, but, as Marquis has shown, the lower central nervous structures as well.

Thus not only are the time factors different, but there is danger in uncritically applying processes which hold for the peripheral nerve to the central nervous system.

Furthermore the objection on the basis of the time factor holds even more emphatically if we attempt to apply the refractory phase theory to Kantrow's phenomena of silent extinction and the decrement which occurs with continued pairing of the conditioned and unconditioned stimuli.

The next problem is to fit the heterochronic principle to these data. Lapicque discovered that in addition to the intensity factor there is a time factor in the excitability of nerve tissue. It is defined as the minimal time which it takes a stimulus current of arbitrary intensity to excite a nerve. There are different chronaxies for different nerves and different muscles. Impulses will pass from a given nerve to a given muscle if the two have the same chronaxie, or if their chronaxies have certain ratios. In this view isochronism is the condition for the excitation of a response and heterochronism accounts for inhibition. The theory could probably explain Wenger's datum with the supplementation of some factor which will account for a sudden change to heterochronism from a state of isochronism in all three of our experiments, if it were not for the fact that there are some fundamental physiological difficulties.

Chemical theories of inhibition are the most attractive of all, and they are buttressed by a history of excellent experimentation. The first were Ringer's (25) investigations on the perfusion of the heart muscle of the dog by potassium, calcium, and sodium chloride solutions, followed by Howell's (13) work. Sherrington (26) used it to explain reciprocal inhibition in the spinal animal. Recently Hoagland (11) has applied the principle to the explanation of sensory adaptation in cutaneous and muscle sense organs. He suggests that in spite of lack of evidence, it be applied to the central nervous system. The theory is founded upon his experiments on the effect of potassium upon adaptation of sense organs. There is a ratio of *K* ions between the inner and outer parts of these tissues—the *Ki/Ko* ratio. Normally the ratio is 10. *Ki/Ko* = 10. When the *Ko* factor is built up on the tissue, inhibition occurs. This view fits in nicely with the fact that in Ringer's solution the potassium salt is inhibitory to heart muscle.

If now this concept is applied to our three data, the lapse in each case is explained as a piling up of *K* ions on the surfaces of such brain tissues as are involved in the decrement in conditioning. The time factor here presents no difficulty but the view needs supplementation to account for the reversal from excitation to inhibition.

The membrane theory of Lillie (17), if rigidly carried to its conclusion, is reduced to a refractory phase theory. Usually it is applied in connection with the chemical theory as is the case with Hoagland.

Among the general theories then there remains to be considered McDougall's drainage hypothesis. Briefly this assumes the presence of a reservoir of free nervous energy in the nervous system. This energy gets directed by stimulation into various parts of the organism. On this view inhibition is the mechanical draining of neurin from one part of the system to another. It reminds one of Descartes' concept of the flow of 'animal spirits' and scarcely needs refutation. If a volume of energy really is drained, it could be verified in ten minutes in an experimental animal. The notion is squarely at variance with the nature of the nerve impulse. If there is a constant quantity of neurin it is difficult to explain why a generalized decrement in conditioning over a long or short period occurs.

So much for the technical interpretations. There are several secondary theories which make no assumptions concerning the biochemical mechanisms of excitation and inhibition. They are concerned rather with the two phenomena as they are found.

One such view is known as peripheral inhibition. It assumes that there are excitatory and inhibitory efferent peripheral fibers which innervate each muscle. Such an arrangement is known to exist in the large pincers of the crayfish and in the powerful adductor muscle of bivalve molluscs. They are definitely present in the autonomic nervous system, but are not present in the parts of the nervous system which controls striate or skeletal muscle. So we may summarily discard this view so far as conditioning is concerned.

Indeed it is precisely the condition of skeletal muscle which is involved in the process of conditioning since the responses of this type of muscle are used as criteria of conditioning. And this brings us directly to Wenger's proprioceptive facilitation theory. This is also a theory of inhibition. At this point we should re-examine his report. He says, "Although it has been long known that infant responses are quite variable, it seemed unusual that a subject, when no sign of self-stimulation was apparent, should suddenly not respond after having given several successive responses to the conditioned stimulus. These states of no response seemed to occur when the subject was very quiet, and were frequently followed by sleep. Of equal interest was the observation that conditioned responses first seemed to appear when the infant was very slightly active, and also that it was under conditions of very slight activity that the conditioned response re-appeared after having disappeared. The latter fact strongly suggested spontaneous or autonomous disinhibition by tactual or proprioceptive stimulation. Yet it was occurring here in infants not only before conditioning was complete, but before any specific attempt had been made to build up internal inhibition" (31, p. 299).

These observations suggest that so far as body activity is concerned, there is an optimum during which conditioning occurs. The optimum appears to be a situation of not too great general body activity. During quiescence, conditioning fails. Now in terms of the nervous system, this means that tonic impulses arising proprioceptively in the muscles during body activity are pouring into the central nervous system. Such proprioceptive stimulation is the basis of posture and Freeman (7) calls the process in the nervous system the postural substrate. On the basis of this approach Wenger has formulated two following principles of conditioning (31, p. 307). (1) "Decrement in muscular tension usually will be accompanied by a general decrement in response." (2) "Increment in muscular tension usually will be accompanied by a general increment in response." On the basis of these maxims, he makes an application to the process of conditioning by suggesting that an inhibition of the conditioned response is due to reduction of the proprioceptive substrate. In other words, the reduction or the increase of proprioceptive processes occurring in the central nervous system accounts for inhibition or facilitation of conditioning. It will be seen at once that this formulation is consistent with the experimental evidence in the studies of Leyton and Sherrington, Graham-Brown, Lashley, Travis, and Bishop. There is also the suggestive experiment by Harlow, who paralyzed the striate musculature of the ape and found that without proprioceptive stimulation from this musculature, conditioning failed. Moreover, Wenger's view avoids the *tabula rasa* error, which Pavlov repeated in his doctrine of spatial projection.

There are several qualifying comments to be made about this proprioceptive facilitating and inhibitory theory, one of which should not be overlooked; namely, that the source of the central neural pattern or substrate is not exclusively proprioceptive. The matter is well illustrated by the experimental work upon tonus involved in postural reactions. In these antigravity behavior patterns, innervation originates in a number of sense organs including proprioceptive, vestibular, cutaneous, labyrinthine and visual organs. The neural substrate pattern underlying this behavior pattern involves processes going on in the spinal cord, the cerebellum, Deiter's nucleus in the medulla, the red nucleus in the midbrain, and the cortex of the hemispheres. Thus the activating forces of the nervous system are not merely proprioceptive; they are also extero- and interoceptive. Moreover, and this is something all of us more or less forget, it is intimately and constantly influenced by the fluid matrix of the body, by what Claude Bernard called the *milieu interne*.

Now Wenger's proprioceptive view of inhibition was designed to account for the result of his own experiment. Even if my qualifications are neglected I think his view succeeds in its purpose, but it could not contemplate Kantrow's two subsequent findings. Take the instance of silent extinction. Here in addition to proprioceptive inhibition we probably must have recourse to another factor, namely the fluid matrix. For in a state of satiation there is a temporary shift of blood from the peripheral musculature to the gastrointestinal organs, and the consequent temporary state of relaxation is accompanied by a reduced bombardment of impulses from muscle sense organs. Quite decidedly the *milieu interne* is a factor to be considered here, but the immediate factor should be sought in the tonus condition of the muscles.

In Kantrow's second datum paired conditioning was continued over a much longer period and for more frequent training units than is usual. This period lasted for several days. After the fifteenth unit the strength of the conditioned response dropped from an initial level to a lower plateau. Now the tonus conditions of the infants as measured by amount of body activity remained at the same average level during both plateaus. The graphs show, however, that during the lower plateau body activity was much more variable than on the initial one. Apparently a *steady* tonus state is necessary for maintaining strong conditioning, whereas a variable condition of tonus weakens the response. Quite evidently this phenomenon can be considered as an instance of the tonus theory, provided that the optimal tonus condition varies only within rather narrow limits. This notion may be implicit in the concept of an optimum, but Kantrow's findings render it necessary to state it explicitly. Under the conditions of this experiment the factor making for variability cannot be hunger. Some other factor, possibly in the fluid matrix, must be responsible for the tonic variability. Interpreted neurally this may mean that under the influence of this matrix certain interoceptors bombard the central nervous system and compete with both conditioned and unconditioned stimuli. However, this is going beyond any direct evidence.

The formulation of the theoretical problem of infant conditioning as it has been presented here makes no attempt to include all of the data in this field of research. Its extension to them is, of course, desirable. The treatment here is merely an effort to select from an array of possible theories one which may be taken as 'the best fit' to a restricted group of data resulting from our work with infants. It assumes that in the conventional Pavlovian interpretation there are some limitations, and it takes a modest first step toward a different theory of conditioning.

NOTES

[1] The actual experimental work on which this discussion is based was performed by Drs. M. A. Wenger and Ruth Wildenberg Kantrow and to them goes the credit for originating any positive contributions toward a theory. My part is merely that of a catalyst and precipitating agent.

REFERENCES

1. Bartley, S. H., & Bishop, G. H. The cortical response to stimulation of the optic nerve in the rabbit. *Amer. J. Physiol.*, 1933, 103, 159-172.

2. Bolaffio, M., & Artom, G. Ricerche sulla fisiologia del sistema nervosa del feto umano. *Arch. di. Sci. biol.*, 1924, 5, 457-487.

3. Brown, T. G., & Sherrington, C. S. On the instability of a cortical point. *Proc. Roy. Soc. London*, 1912, 85B, 250-277.

4. Coghill, G. E. *Anatomy and the Problem of Behavior.* New York: Macmillan, 1929. Pp. xii, 113.

5. Coronios, J. D. Development of behavior in the fetal cat. *Genet. Psychol. Monogr.*, 1933, 14, 283-289.

6. Culler, E., & Mettler, F. A. Conditioned behavior in a decorticate dog. *J. Comp. Psychol.*, 1934, 18, 291-303.

7. Freeman, G. L. *Introduction to Physiological Psychology.* New York: Ronald Press [c. 1934]. Pp. xvii, 579.

8. Gasser, H. S., & Graham, H. T. Potentials produced in the spinal cord by stimulation of dorsal roots. *Amer. J. Physiol.*, 1933, 103, 303-320.

9. González Angulo Y, A. W. The prenatal development of behaviour in the albino rat. *J. Comp. Neurol.*, 1932, 55, 395-492.

10. Harlow, H. F., & Stanger, R. Effect of complete striate muscle paralysis upon the learning process. *J. Exper. Psychol.*, 1933, 16, 283-294.

11. Hoagland, H. *Pacemakers in Relation to Aspects of Behavior.* New York: Macmillan, 1935. Pp. x, 138.

12. Hooker, D. Early fetal activity in mammals. *Yale J. Biol. & Med.*, 1936, 8, 579-502.

13. Howell, W. H. *A Text-Book of Physiology for Medical Students and Physicians.* (11th ed. rev.) Philadelphia: W. B. Saunders, 1931. Pp. 1099.

14. Kantrow, R. W. Studies in infant behavior IV: An investigation of conditioned feeding responses and concomitant adaptive behavior in young infants. *Univ. Ia. Stud. Child Welf.*, 1937, 13, No. 3, Pp. 64.

15. Lapicque, L. M. *L'excitabilité en fonction du temps*. Paris: Les Presses Universitaires de France, 1926. Pp. 371.

16. Leese, C. E., & Einarson, L. Conduction time in the afferent tracts of the spinal cord in relation to the flexion reflex. *Amer. J. Physiol.*, 1934, 109, 296—302.

17. Lillie, R. S. *Protoplasmic Action and Nervous Action*. Chicago: University of Chicago Press [c. 1923]. Pp. xiii, 417.

18. Lucas, K. *The Conduction of the Nervous Impulse*. London: Longmans, Green, 1917. Pp. xi, 102.

19. McDougall, W. The nature of the inhibitory processes within the nervous system. *Brain*, 1903, 26, 153-191.

20. Marquis, D. G. Phylogenetic interpretation of the functions of the visual cortex. *Arch. Neurol. Psychiat.*, 1935, 33, 807-812.

21. Marquis, D. P. Can conditioned responses be established in the newborn infant? *Ped. Sem. & J. Genet. Psychol.*, 1931, 39, 479-492.

22. Minkowski, M. Über frühzeitige Bewegungen, Reflexe und muskuläre Reaktionen beim menschlichen Fötos und ihre Beziehungen zum fötalen Nerven und Muskelsystem. *Schweiz. med. Wschr.*, 1922, 3, 52; 721-724; 751-755.

23. Pavlov, I. P. *Conditioned Reflexes: An Investigation of the Physiological Activity of the Cerebral Cortex*. Trans. & edited by G. V. Anrep. Oxford: University Press, 1927. Pp. xv, 430.

24.———. *Lectures on Conditioned Reflexes: Twenty-Five Years of Objective Study of the Higher Nervous Activity (Behaviour) of Animals*. Trans. by W. Horsley Gantt. New York: International Publishers [c. 1928]. Pp. 414.

25. Ringer, S. Concerning the influence exerted by each of the constituents of the blood on the contraction of the ventricle. *J. Physiol.*, 1882,.3, 380-393.

26. Sherrington, C. S. *Integrative Action of the Nervous System*. New York: Scribner's, 1906. Pp. xvi, 411.

27. Swensen, E. A. Motion pictures of activities of living albino-rat fetuses. *Anat. Rec.*, 1928, 38, 63. (Abstract.)

28.———. The simple movements of the trunk of albino-rat fetus. *Anat. Rec.*, 1928, 38, 31. (Abstract.)

29. Travis, L. E., & Herren, R. Y. The relation of electrical changes in the brain to reflex activity. *J. Comp. Psychol.*, 1931, 12, 23-39.

30. Wenger, M. A. An investigation of conditioned responses in human infants. In Wenger, M. A., Smith, J., Hazard, C., & Irwin, O. C. Studies in Infant Behavior III. *Univ. Ia. Stud. Child Welf.*, 1936, 12, No. 1, Pp. 90.

31.———. A criticism of Pavlov's concept of internal inhibition. *Psychol. Rev.*, 1937, 44, 297-312.

Bernard Shaw (essay date 1944)

SOURCE: "The Man of Science," in *Everybody's Political What's What,* Constable and Company Limited, 1944, pp. 200-13.

[*In the following excerpt, Shaw considers the absurdity of Pavlov's experiments as they refelct modern scientific practice.*]

The department of science with which governments are most concerned is biology, the science of life. It includes physiology and psychology, and is the basis of public health legislation and private medical practice. It has gone far beyond the Churches in its violations of individual liberty and integrity. The Christian Church takes an infant from its mother's arms, sprinkles a few drops of water on it, and dedicates it as a soldier and servant of God: a ceremony that has never harmed any infant and has beneficially edified many godfathers and godmothers. The State, by the advice of the biologists, takes the infant from its mother's arms and poisons its blood to exercise its natural power of resisting and overcoming poison. It lays hands on soldiers, nurses, and other adult persons supposed to be specially liable to infection, and repeats the operation with various specific poisons guaranteed to produce specific immunities. A well-known soldier friend of mine told me he had undergone forty inoculations and been none the worse. His blood had been healthy enough to make short work of all the poisons.

Not everyone is so lucky. Every inoculation has effects which vary from a few hours malaise with perhaps a faint or two, or disablement for about a week, to temporary paralysis following inoculation against diphtheria, permanent ill health, and at worst death from the horribly disfiguring disease called generalized vaccinia following inoculation against smallpox.

Now we have here the danger of a tyranny which was not thought of by the authors of Magna Carta, of the Habeas Corpus Act, of the Petition of Rights, or the American Declaration of Independence and Constitution. I would make the Government a present of all my rights under these famous documents rather than be compelled, whether as infant or adult, to have my person violated and my blood poisoned on the advice of a trade union of doctors with a pecuniary interest in the operation, or an array of figures compiled by self-styled men of science with childish notions of statistics and critical evidence. Men have submitted to castration to secure lucrative employment as superintendents of seraglios or singers in opera houses and churches; and Chinese parents have had the feet of their female children painfully bound and lamed because it was the fashion under the Manchu dynasty; but compulsion of everybody willy-nilly to dangerous blood poisoning repeated for every virus discoverable by the new electron microscope, to sterilization, to extirpation of the uvula and tonsils, to birth delivery by the Caesarian operation, to excision of several folds of the bowel and of the entire appendix, to treatment of syphilis and malaria by doses of mercury and arsenic, iodine and quinine, all of which have been advocated by eminent physicians and surgeons, and some of them legally enforced today, and this without protest or even mention from the loudest champions of individual liberty of thought, speech, worship, and trade (especially trade), marks the rise of an abjectly credulous worship of everything calling itself Science which goes beyond any tyranny recorded of the religious creeds of Rome, Mexico, or Druidic Britain. I have often said that there is in nature a law of the Conservation of Human Credulity (like Joule's law of the Conservation of Energy) so inexorable that it is impossible to dispel one delusion without creating another equivalent one; but as I witness the atrocities and stupidities of professional science, and the extent to which its claim to be exempt from all moral obligation in its pursuit of knowledge is conceded by our statesmen, I am tempted to throw Joule over, and regard credulity and idolatry as plagues in which action and reaction are not equal, and to conclude that as the domain of genuine science is unlimited, so also is the domain of delusion. The omniscience, infallibility, and incorruptible truthfulness formerly reserved for an ideal variously called God, Allah, Brahma, etc., is transferred to every Tom, Dick, or Harriet who has cut up a dog or a guinea pig in a laboratory, and written a book or a paper describing how the unfortunate animal responded.

Let me describe a flagrant and famous example of this infatuation. For the moment the Pontifex Maximus in biological science is Ivan Petrovich Pavlov, lately deceased, in celebration of whom I have just heard a broadcast eulogy which would have been excessive if Pavlov had been all the greatest benefactors of mankind rolled into one, with all the gods and their prophets and all the philosophers and discoverers thrown in. He was in fact the prince of pseudoscientific simpletons. What did he do to impose on us so outrageously?

He devoted 25 years of his life to the study of Conditioned Reflexes, and gave the result to the world in 23 lectures translated into English by his colleague Dr Anrep and published here in 1927. The book is entitled ***Conditioned Reflexes: an Investigation of the Physiological Activity of the Cerebral Cortex.*** This is an imposing title; but all it means is Our Habits: How We Acquire Them and How Our Brains Operate Them. There have been some complaints of the style of the book as difficult. This is unjust: there is not an ambiguous sentence in it: both its sense and its nonsense are quite lucidly expressed in language which is, like Dr Johnson's, pretentious and unvernacular but never obscure. Its translator must not condescend to write that there are milestones on the Dover road; but an announcement that a communicatory channel between the metropolis and the seaport is indicated by a series of equidistant petrifacts is equally clear if you know the language; and it looks much more dignified and learned.

What, exactly, is a conditioned reflex? I became intellectually conscious of one some fifty years ago, when there was opened at Chelsea a Naval Exhibition. It contained facsimiles of Nelson's last flagship and of the first class passengers' quarters in a modern Peninsular and Oriental Liner. I gazed without discomposure on the cockpit in which Nelson kissed Hardy and died. But in the passage between the P. and O. cabins I suddenly felt seasick, and had to beat a hasty retreat into the gardens.

This was a perfect example of a conditioned reflex. I had often been made seasick by the rolling and pitching of a ship. The rolling and pitching had been accompanied by the sight of the passengers' quarters and the smell of paint and oakum. The connection between them had been so firmly established in me that even when I stood on the firm earth these sights and smells made me squeamish.

At first this experience of mine seems merely funny. But on further consideration it becomes not only scientifically interesting but appalling. If a reflex can persist when it has become completely detached from its original cause, it can itself produce a new reflex which can become similarly detached and produce yet another new reflex, and so on *ad infinitum.* What if all human activity be nothing but the operation of innumerable reflexes with all rational connection between them and the original facts hopelessly lost? May not this explain why the human race is at present (1944) concentrating all its energies on destroying itself? Is not such a possibility frightful enough to make a scientific investigation of conditioned reflexes a matter of the most urgent importance?

It is Pavlov's great merit that he must have had some sense of this importance; for he devoted his life to its investigation.

Unfortunately he was handicapped by two powerful conditioned reflexes in himself which he failed to recognize as such and allow for. One was the nineteenth century reaction against an old tribal idol called Jehovah, who demands blood sacrifices and dominates the Bible from Noah to Samuel, and then gives way to the more civilized gods of Koheleth (Ecclesiastes) and Micah, finally softened by Jesus into "Our Father which art in heaven." Unfortunately the disciples of Jesus went back on Micah by making the Crucifixion a blood sacrifice and thus reviving Jehovah as the final infallible authority on scientific questions (that is, on all questions), to be worshipped as such on pain of severe punishment on earth and eternal torment after death. The revolt of modern common sense against this atavistic idolatry is called Iconoclasm (an VIII century movement), scepticism, atheism, materialism, agnosticism, rationalism, secularism and many other names. It is now so strong that it denies not only the existence and authority of Jehovah but of any metaphysical factors in life whatsoever, including purpose, intuition, inspiration, and all the religious and artistic impulses. It boycotts volition, conscience, and even consciousness as unaccounted for by Science. In short, it seeks to abolish life and mind, substituting for them a conception of all motion and action, bodily and mental, as a senseless accidental turmoil of physical collisions. Such a divorce from the facts makes it not only useless to the statesman but extremely dangerous.

In Pavlov's case this reduction of Science to absurdity was arrived at not by reasoning but by an entirely unreasonable association of ideas: that is, by a series of "conditioned reflexes" of precisely the same nature as that which led my stomach to imagine that the firm earth of Chelsea Botanic Gardens was the Bay of Biscay in a gale. When reading him one must bear in mind that his use of the word "therefore," like most of his assertions of "obvious relations" between this and that, indicates, not a logical sequence, but only an association of ideas, or, as he would say, a conditioned reflex. But do not forget that a reflex may be a good guess, just as a perfect verbal syllogism may be only an absurd pun. You have to be careful with Pavlov. When he is thinking-out a theory of reflexes he is worth reading. When he is trying to fit his theory into his experiments he entangles himself in such nonsense that you may be tempted to pitch the book to the other side of the room and take up a detective story. He all but admits this in his final lecture whilst desperately defending the experiments, and urging his successors to continue them as the only genuinely scientific method of investigation.

For here you have come up against the second specific reflex which damns him as an investigator. Let us study its history for a moment.

Those who have studied the orientation of the monoliths of Stonehenge know that the first scientists were priests who impressed their congregations by their apparently prophetic knowledge of the solstices and the stars and the right times to sow and reap. But to impress people incapable of grasping scientific achievements priests had to propitiate their terrible gods by human sacrifices (Jephtha's daughter and Iphigenia for instance), and later on, with more profit to themselves, by the slaughter of birds and animals. For these dedicated butcheries they invented the altar; and to make the altar august and awful they invented the temple with its holy of holies. To give to their precepts and laws the authority of divine revelation they invented the oracle and the holy scriptures. As Augurs, they practised the crude magic of cutting birds open and reading the future in their entrails. Thus, being at the same time men of science, priests, magicians, astrologers, and political rulers, they at last got science so mixed up with religion, priestcraft, popular superstition, and politics in the same porridge that the task of extricating science from it still baffles our subtlest analytical powers.

The conditioned reflexes produced by the mixture are innumerable and untraceable. Many of them cancel one another out; for some are too cruel for civilized people to tolerate, and from being what Pavlov calls excitatory have become inhibitory. But some of the worst and some of the most ridiculous still flourish. They were at work in Pavlov's laboratory far more authoritatively than in the cabin of the peasant who on Holy Eve poured molten lead into cold water and played at divining the future by the fantastic shapes the crumbs of lead took as they solidified. The modern communion table, like the heathen altar, still commemorates a blood sacrifice; but instead of sacrificing human flesh and blood we symbolize them by bread and wine eaten and drunk by the celebrant or the worshippers or by both.

Thus the ancient god whom Noah bribed by a meal of roast meat got blended with the cannibals' god who was eaten by his worshippers to acquire his qualities, just as they are their vanquished enemies in war to acquire their strength and bravery and skill with weapons. Sir James Frazer, who has just died, devoted his life to tracing these crisscrossed rites and their reflexes in a monumental book called *The Golden Bough,* extending to many volumes. I read the first chapter or so forty years ago, when the first volume was new, but soon got oppressed by the sameness of its instances of human delusion, and have not opened it since. Lest I should make this book of my own unreadable I shall confine myself here to the reflexes which connect science with the sacrifice of living animals.

The most striking recent instance is the action of the British medical profession when it was shaken by the impact of American osteopathy. An American doctor named Still had discovered that certain ailments were connected with displacements in the spine, and that he could cure them by correcting these displacements. He called himself an osteopath, and founded a manipulative technique which, like Kellgren massage and other manipulative systems, needed about two years training to acquire. In England, where the highest surgical degrees can be obtained by postulants who have never performed a surgical operation, Still's addition to the things a doctor ought to know and be able to practise was very ill received, especially as the established period of training already occupied five years and cost much money. But the resistance to it was not only a trade union resistance: it was also undertaken as a scientific resistance. In spite of an overwhelming mass of clinical evidence in its favor it was held that it could not be scientifically demonstrated and proved unless a dog in a laboratory had its spine dislocated with the usual results, and then cured by correcting the displacement by Still's method. The osteopaths accordingly went solemnly through this ritual, whereupon it was reluctantly admitted that osteopathy had become so far scientific.

Obviously this senseless sacrifice of a dog on the laboratory altar had nothing to do with science: it was simply obedience to a conditioned reflex acquired before the Pyramids were built, and "reinforced" (Pavlov's word) again and again through so many centuries that it had become inveterate. There is no other explanation of Pavlov's choice of a ridiculous and revoltingly cruel routine of research when so many sensible and humane methods were open to him, and of his insistence on its continuation in the very pages in which he confesses its failures.

What he actually did was to devote twenty-five years of his life to experiments on dogs to find out, as data for his biological theory, whether their mouths watered, and if so how much (counted in drops of saliva) when they had certain sensations such as the sight or smell of food, the hearing of words or noises, the feeling of certain touches, or the sight of certain persons and objects. He set metronomes ticking at them, buzzers buzzing at them, musical tones sounding at them, heat glowing at them. He tickled marked places on their bodies, and then fed them, with the result that they came to associate these sensations so invariably with food that soon their mouths watered when without any offer of food they were simply buzzed at, ticked at, played at, glowed at, or tickled. The natural mouthwatering at the sight or smell of food he called an unconditioned reflex. The watering provoked by some sensation which had become connected in the dog's experience with food, like my nausea at the Chelsea Exhibition, he called a conditioned reflex.

All the experiments involved tapping the salivary ducts by boring holes in the dog's cheek and establishing a permanent fistula there, as the very delicate apparatus needed to measure the saliva could not be attached to the dog's tongue, its natural channel.

From these observations Pavlov drew inferences for which he claimed a thoroughly scientific character. He had committed himself to the condition that the sequences of salivation and insalivation observed by him must be consistent, inevitable, invariable, and necessary if they were to be accepted as scientific evidence. They failed to fulfil this condition. The sequences as often as not—indeed more often than not—contradicted his theory flatly. Sometimes their actual order exactly reversed the theoretical order. Far from being consistent, inevitable, invariable, necessary, they were often capricious and contradictory. Pavlov was honest enough to admit their failure in his final lecture, though his conclusion is that there must have been either something wrong with the laboratory apparatus or "temperamental" with the dogs; for he urges his successors to persevere with his method until they contrive better apparatus and discover a sort of dog with sufficient consideration for his theory to react in the desired manner.

As it may seem incredible that so clever a scientist could be so absurd, I hasten to add that his naturally keen intelligence did not reach imbecility in a single jump. He deceived himself step by step by a method which welcomed every failure as a new discovery and an addition to his theory. Thus when he stimulated the dog, and the dog did not salivate, he did not conclude that either his theory or his method must be wrong. He thought he had discovered that reflexes have negative phases as well as positive ones, and can be classed as Excitatory or Inhibitive. This, if not an original discovery, had some common facts to back it; for though the mention of jam may make a child's mouth water, and it will eat the jam greedily at first, yet if you give the child a whole pot of jam and a spoon, and invite it to eat it all up, it will presently leave the pot unfinished, refusing to swallow another mouthful. Its unconditioned reflex to jam has become negative and inhibitive. Pavlov could have learnt this from the nearest nursemaid without the expense and trouble of buying a dog and making a hole in its cheek; but his Druidic reflex forced him to reject the testimony of nursemaids unless consecrated by the ritual of dog sacrifice.

When the sequences occurred in the reverse order to the expected one, Pavlov announced the discovery of a new phenomenon: the Paradoxical Phase. And here also he was fortified by the fact that when a man wants to get up and work he puts on his clothes in their accustomed order, and when his work has tired him out and he wants to go to bed and sleep (the negative phase) he takes off his clothes in the reverse order (the paradoxical phase).

Pavlov then tried to make his dogs produce the paradoxical phase at his will. He failed. He immediately announced the failure as the discovery of an ultra-paradoxical phase.

Now it is clear that an experimenter who can interpret results either positively or negatively, logically or paradoxically, paradoxically or ultra-paradoxically, can make them prove anything he likes. Give me that much latitude and I can prove, by spectrum analysis, that the moon is made of green cheese. Perhaps I will some day, and be proclaimed by the British Broadcasting Corporation the greatest scientist of all time.

Pavlov did not confine his researches to the reflexes. He wanted also to discover and localize the different spots in the brain which operated the reflexes when the dog was stimulated in different ways or in different places on its skin.

To effect this the most obvious method was to cut out portions of the dog's brain and see how it got on without them. In the nineteenth century experimenters with the same object burnt out portions of monkeys' brains; but Pavlov preferred his salivation method as being more exactly measurable. It was exact enough as far as counting the drops of saliva went; but here again the results were not consistent, not invariable, not inevitable. But Pavlov's reasoning method was proof against this discouragement. When he traced the reflex to a particular spot in the brain, and presently found that some neighboring spot would do just as well, he announced a new discovery: Irradiation. He was no doubt familiar with the fact that if you let a drop of ink fall on a piece of blotting paper it does not concentrate itself on the spot on which it falls, but spreads all round. Evidently an impact on the brain did the same. The apparent failure of the experiment was therefore accounted for by the two words Concentration and Irradiation.

Sometimes, however, when he tested a connexion between a spot in the dog's brain and its front paw, he found that the same spot responded equally to the dog's hind paw, or, conversely, that the front paw set quite another spot going. Another failure? Not at all. He knew that a wire charged with electricity can induce a parallel current in a neighboring wire. Evidently the message from the dog's skin to its brain has the same property: there are induced messages as well as original ones. Not another failure: only another discovery.

Pavlov's conclusions were now impregnable. Every experimental observation fitted them like a glove. No control experiment could upset them: no contradiction could remain unreconciled: no house of cards or castle in the air could be better put together. It sounds so like genuine physical objective science that people who are no better reasoners than Pavlov, and want to believe in him, cannot see that the story of his dogs in his book is a crackle of blazing nonsense from beginning to end.

It imposed, and still imposes, on people of first-rate ability. When it appeared, my friend and fellow sage H. G. Wells was so impressed that he announced that if he saw Pavlov and myself drowning, and only one lifebuoy were within his reach, he would have to throw it to Pavlov and leave me to drown. He had met Pavlov in Russia and been charmed by him to the extent of maintaining that he was a tender humanitarian in his methods, loving his dogs and being loved by them, whereas I, never having met him, had gone so far on the evidence of his experiments as to call him a scoundrel, meaning a person who repudiates common morality in the pursuit of his personal or professional interests. As a matter of fact anyone except a professional scientist doing the things to his dogs (bought for the purpose) that Pavlov did would be not only prosecuted for cruelty to animals but held up in court as a monster. Here is Pavlov's own account of the matter in his nineteenth lecture (pp. 320-22).

> The only method so far available for such a study consists in observing the effects of partial destruction or complete extirpation of different parts of the cortex. This method naturally suffers from fundamental disadvantages, since it involves the roughest forms of mechanical interference and the crude dismembering of an organ of a most exquisite structure and function. Imagine that we have to penetrate into the activity of an incomparably simpler machine fashioned by human hands, and that for this purpose, not knowing its different parts, instead of carefully dismantling the machine we take a saw and cut away one or another fraction of it, hoping to obtain an exact knowledge of its mechanical working! The method usually applied to the study of the hemispheres or other parts of the central nervous system is essentially as primitive as this. Hammer and chisel, the saw and the drill; these are the instruments which must be used to open up the strong protective skull. Then we tear through the several layers of enveloping protective membranes, rupturing many blood vessels, and finally we injure or destroy whole lumps of the delicate nervous tissue in different mechanical ways—concussion, pressure and incision. But such is the marvellous functional resistance and the peculiar vitality of the living substance, that, in spite of all these gross manipulations, within the lapse of only a single day it is sometimes impossible without special and exact investigations to observe anything abnormal in animals submitted to cerebral operations. Accordingly, even by these primitive methods, some insight into the functions of the cortex can be gained. But the obvious usefulness of these crude methods should on no account satisfy the physiologist. He should strive to apply new advances of technical science and to seek ever new and more appropriate methods for the study of the exquisite mechanism of the hemispheres. Naturally the methods available for the investigation of the cortex at present, by means of extirpation of different parts, can but lead to entangled pathological states, and even the most guarded deductions with regard to the constitution of the cortex cannot therefore be ensured against a high probability of error. Indeed, since the special function of the cortex is to establish new nervous connections and so to ensure a perfect functional correlation between the organism and its environment, every disturbance of any part of it will be reflected upon the whole mechanism. Besides this direct influence of the operative procedure, which may reasonably be expected with time to diminish spontaneously, there is another very serious complication of the operation which appears later on—namely, the development of a scar at the place of cerebral lesion which now becomes a source of irritation and leads to further destruction of the surrounding parts. On the one hand the scar, owing to its mechanical irritation of the surrounding normal parts of the brain, sets up recurrent outbursts of nervous excitation; on the other hand, owing to pressure, distortion and rupture, it progressively disintegrates the hemispheres. I have been unfortunate in attempting to improve the operative technique, having made, as I now think, a big mistake. In order to obviate haemorrhage during the operation I used to remove in the dogs, long before the operation on the brain, the temporal muscles which cover the skull; this resulted in a partial atrophy of the bones of the skull, so that these could now be opened, often without the loss of a single drop of blood. But the dura mater in these cases also undergoes considerable atrophy, becomes dry and brittle, so that in most cases it is impossible to make use of it to close up the cerebral wound completely. As a result the wound was left after the operation in direct communication with the more external tissues, which led to the formation of a very hard scar ultimately penetrating and growing into the cerebral tissue. Almost every animal that was operated upon suffered from attacks of convulsions which on some occasions occurred so soon as five to six weeks after the operation. A few animals died during the first attack, but more usually the convulsions were not severe in the early stages and occurred at infrequent intervals. In the course of several months they recurred more frequently and increased in force, finally either proving fatal or else leading to a new and very profound disturbance of the cortical

> activity. Therapeutic measures in the form of repeated anaesthesia or extirpation of the scar were found to be unreliable, though sometimes they were unquestionably effective.

On page 353 we learn that "the dogs lived from one to six months after operation: death occurred in all cases on account of severe attacks of convulsions." On other pages we read of dogs living for three or four years with their brains mutilated. On page 284, "one and the same injurious influence causes severe and prolonged disorders in some dogs; in others the disorders are only slight and fleeting; while yet other dogs remain practically unaffected."

It must be agreed that the case against the experiments has here been stated with masterly clearness and extraordinary candor by Pavlov himself. He admits not only their crudity and their cruelty, but their uselessness. And yet the conditioned reflex which has associated science with blood sacrifice is so strong in him that his final appeal to his successors is not only to carry on his research but to persist in his futile and revolting method.

Note that Pavlov never mentions pity. He excludes it on the ground that it is psychological and therefore unknown to physiology; that it is subjective and not objective; that it is metaphysical and not material; and as he will not admit that psychology is science or that subjective or metaphysical considerations are scientific, such unconditioned reflexes (natural feelings) as pity, mercy, compassion, kindness, are out of the question and should be discarded by legislators as sentimental trash. But as the attempt to blind himself to this extent is contrary to his nature and beyond his powers as a human being, he has no sooner postulated it as a condition of his integrity as a physiologist than we find him describing certain reflexes as self-preservative, investigatory, freedom seeking ("it is clear that the freedom reflex is one of the most important," p. 12): that is, as psychological, subjective, and metaphysical. And he does not notice this. His whole attention is engaged elsewhere. He does not see that even the alimentary reflex, which is standard in all his experiments and observations, is a vital and not merely a mechanical reflex. Only once does he allow himself to be sentimental. He speaks of "the twenty-five years in which numerous fellow workers on whom I now look back with tender affection have united in this work their hearts and hands." Why should his unfortunate dogs have had no share in this surprising lapse from objective physiology into vulgar subjective emotion?

The political administrator cannot deal with Pavlov's faulty reasoning, his bogus correlations and corollaries, his counting the ratios of three or four observed facts as percentages, because there is no law penalizing these dangerous aberrations, nor against his pretension that laboratory-made science is the whole of science. It is nothing to the magistrate (officially) that the experimenter confesses that his laboratory methods are crude, ill-advised, futile, and in their intention impracticable. That does not make them illegal. But their cruelty does. The existing law is clear on the point that if you keep a dog you must not ill treat it; and as Pavlov not only ill treated his dogs horribly but assumed that as a scientist he could do so with impunity, he brought the police up against the very troublesome public question of how far they should tolerate, and even enforce, practices which both common law and common sense class as criminal and detestable. For the case of the Pavlovists is by no means unique. The slaughter of sentient creatures for food, the hunting of them for sport, the poisoning of them as vermin, the trapping and killing of them for fur, oil, hides and tallow, involve much cruelty which nevertheless nobody dreams of prosecuting. War and the punishment of criminals are atrociously cruel; but they are licensed as acts of justice and patriotism. The Pavlovian vivisectionist, when reproached for cruelty, always retorts that it does not become men of pleasure who cruelly hunt foxes and stags to death without anaesthetics, merely for the fun of it, to reproach men of science for cruelty to dogs in the pursuit of knowledge.

I am no sportsman; and if I had the power I should say to the stag hunter "Your cruelty is neither necessary nor unavoidable; and you must find some other way of amusing yourself." For there are obviously other ways. The vivisector, if I said the same to him, would plead that for him there are no other ways. I should reply "Then you must find some." If he asked how, I should say "Use your brains and shake off your Druidic superstitions. There are probably fifty lawful and decent ways discoverable by human thinkers. You are not a thinker: you are only a mentally lazy fathead doing what was done last time, like all fatheads." He would no doubt retort that he could not argue with a sentimental aesthete whose mind is hopelessly unscientific; and all the vivisectionists would agree with him; but the statesman must not let public questions be settled by epithets (he sometimes does, I am sorry to say), and must be as critical of the sect of scientists as of any other denomination.

The scientist may here remind me that this summary dismissal of cruel sports does not cover the cruelty of the criminal courts, the fear of which is a necessary factor in our civilization. It is true that governments have to restrain anti-social behavior by attaching deterrent consequences to it, and that these consequences will not deter unless they are unpleasant enough to be dreaded. But the vivisector's victim has not been guilty of anti-social behavior, nor can its torture deter other animals from such behavior.

The fear of government may be the beginning of civilization just as the fear of God is the beginning of wisdom. In practice both are fear of consequences; but we shall see later on that these consequences must not involve physical mutilation and torture. For the moment, however, my subject is the Man of Science; and I have not yet dealt with the practitioners of the art of healing, who are much more numerous than the laboratory researchers, and who enjoy extraordinary privileges and widespread faith in their knowledge as men of science. Vivisectors are not popular and never will be; but "the doctor" is everywhere regarded as the friend of man and foundation of Science.

Robert C. Tucker (essay date 1956)

SOURCE: "Stalin and the Uses of Psychology," in *World Politics*, Vol. VIII, No. 4, July, 1956, pp. 455-83.

[*In the following essay, Tucker explores Soviet attempts to use Pavlovian theory in the creation of a policy for the controlled transformation of humanity.*]

The influence of ideological conceptions upon the men who make Soviet policy has been frequently and rightly emphasized. Some observers are so deeply impressed by this influence that they tend to regard the Soviet system as a kind of ideocracy. It is undeniable that ideology has been one powerful factor in the shaping of Soviet policies and actions from the time of the October Revolution to the present. But one must not lose sight of the fact that, in Soviet Russia, the relationship between ideology and policy is one of mutual interaction. It is a two-way process in which theoretical conceptions affect the making of policy and practical considerations affect the content of the ideology. The ideological system is not a completely static thing. It has evolved over the years, and the realities of Soviet politics have been the driving force behind this evolution.

We may regard the Soviet ideology as consisting of two parts: a hard core of basic principles which has persisted more or less unchanged from the beginning of the Soviet period, and several surrounding layers of doctrine which have been subject to modification or accretion in accordance with the dictates of Soviet policy. There is no hard-and-fast line of demarcation between the two parts, yet the division between them is something which demonstrably exists.

The immediate purpose of this paper is to investigate certain Soviet ideological trends of recent years in their relation to the regime's policy in internal affairs. These trends center around the militant revival in Soviet psychology of Pavlov's teachings on the conditioned reflex. The Pavlovian revival, which began in 1949, will be examined in connection with various developments in biology, political economy, and other fields, and the entire ideological complex will be related to a central policy motivation to which I have given the name "transformism." The final part of the study will consider various indications of a post-Stalin retreat from "transformism" and from the ideology associated with it. The study can then serve as a basis for a tentative interpretation of some of the changes in Soviet internal policy since Stalin's death that have aroused interest and speculation in foreign circles.

I. The Will to Transform

A prominent tendency of Soviet thought during the last years of Stalin's reign was the quest for formulas by which reality could be transformed and remolded to the dictates of the Soviet regime. The idea of transforming things in accordance with a formula was not in itself new; the notion of a revolutionary transformation of capitalist society is as old as Marxism and is rooted particularly deeply in the ways of thought characteristic of Russian Bolshevism. But in recent years this "transformist" concept seemed to acquire an obsessive hold upon the regime, and along with it went a mania for bigness and a tendency to apply the various formulas with a dogmatic and indiscriminate rigidity.

During the postwar period, "transformism" became the regime's reaction whenever it was confronted with a genuinely difficult domestic situation which clearly called for remedial measures of some kind. Instead of using the materials at hand and adapting its conduct to the realities present in the situation, it habitually responded with a grandiose project of transformation. In 1949 it came out with the so-called "Stalin Plan for the Transformation of Nature," an immense and costly undertaking of irrigation and afforestation which was to convert rural Russia into a fertile, blooming garden. Closely linked with this was the scheme for transforming the industrial landscape of the country by a series of giant "construction projects of communism"—canals, dams, and hydroelectric power stations which, it was boasted, would eclipse the best and biggest accomplishments along this line in the United States or any other country. To cite a further example, the Soviet regime, faced with an acute shortage of housing and office space in Moscow, responded with a plan for "transforming the face of the capital." This was to be accomplished by the erection of an ensemble of skyscrapers which would rival those of New York, although, unlike New York, Moscow had abundant space for less ambitious structures which would have resolved the problem more quickly and economically.

This kind of transformist thinking was reflected in the "biological discussion" of 1948, at which the Michurin-Lysenko doctrines on heredity were accepted officially, with the full authority of the Central Committee of the Communist Party and of Stalin himself. "Michurinism," as these doctrines were called, was a perfect model of transformist thinking. Their founder, the Russian naturalist I. V. Michurin (the "Great Transformer of Nature"), had, it was said, taken a "gigantic step forward" in the further development of Darwinism. Darwin had merely explained the evolutionary process, while "I. V. Michurin made evolution."[1] Michurin, it was said, had discovered laws and methods by which it would be possible to "mold organic forms."

The Michurin-Lysenko teachings are commonly associated with the Lamarckian principle of the inheritance of acquired characteristics. This was the practical crux of the matter. However, the biological issue was only one aspect of an ideological problem. Underlying the controversy over the inheritance of acquired characteristics was a clash between two radically different conceptions of the relationship between the organism and its environment. The Soviet geneticists whose work was based upon the Mendelian school postulated "autogenesis"—evolution under the influence of certain hereditary forces inherent in the organism itself. In this view, the so-called "internal factors of development" assume primary importance, and the role of external environmental conditions in the evolutionary process is reduced to either a "starting mechanism" or a limiting factor. It was essentially this "autogenetic" conception of the organism that Lysenko and his followers, backed by the full authority of the Soviet state, denied and attempted to expunge from Soviet biological thought.

Lysenko was led to this standpoint not by the weight of carefully sifted scientific evidence but by the imperatives of transformist ideology. Transformist thinking is fundamentally opposed to any conception which endows the object which is to be transformed (in this case, the organism) with developmental autonomy; it must not have spontaneous internal forces for growth or change which the transformer has to reckon with and respect, because that would impose unwanted limits upon the extent to which the object could be transformed from without.

The Michurinist doctrine arose out of this need to conceive the active factor of evolutionary change as residing not in the organism but in controllable conditions of the environment. For Transformism, the role of these conditions must be decisive. Accordingly, Michurinism proclaims the "unity of the organism with the environment," a conception which holds that the organism has no separate existence apart from the particular configuration of environmental conditions which sustain it. In other words, the organism and its environment constitute an adaptational system in which the forces for change reside *exclusively* with the environment. Changing environmental conditions make the unity of the organism with the environment a "contradictory unity," and the organism then resolves the contradiction by successive adaptations which become hereditary. Or else it falls by the wayside: "Organisms which cannot change in accordance with the changed conditions of life do not survive, leave no progeny."[2] The Darwinian concept of a natural selection of chance variations of organisms engaged in a struggle for existence is thrown overboard. Michurinism rules out both chance variations and an intra-species struggle for existence. The struggle for existence takes place between the individual organism and its environment. Variations are the organism's strictly determined responses to environmental change. They are its weapons in the struggle to survive when the external conditions change. The law of evolution is: Change or die.

If, as this doctrine holds, environmental change is the sole active agent of the evolutionary process, then man's power of control over the environmental conditions of plants and animals enables him to direct their evolution according to his needs and purposes. He can then, as the participants of the 1948 session declared in their message to Stalin, "govern the nature of organisms by creating man-controlled conditions of life for plants, animals, micro-organisms." The relationship of this trend of thought to the transformist motivation of the Stalin regime becomes transparently clear. The Michurinist agrobiology, said the final resolution of the session, is "a powerful instrument for the active and planned transformation of living nature." The validity of this claim is more than debatable. The recent attacks on Lysenko in the controlled Soviet press suggest that the post-Stalin regime in Russia found his theory fallible. But, in the period from 1948 to 1953, Lysenko's theory was an integral component of Stalinism. It provided a rationalization in the biological sphere for Stalinism's effort to impose its dictates upon the world, to transform reality according to its wishes.

II. The Cult of Necessity

But while reality can be transformed, the "scientific" laws that govern the transformation are themselves fixed, necessary, and immutable. The will to transform reality was coupled with a vehement denial that there was anything arbitrary, subjective, or risky and unpredictable about the various schemes for transformation which the regime put forward. In this respect, Stalinism made a break with a deep-seated tradition of Bolshevism. The characteristic Bolshevist belief in determinism, its general "denial of accidents," had always previously co-existed with belief in an "indeterminist tendency" with respect to the details of the future with an allowance for the future's "partial unpredictability."[3] In 1948, this tempered view gave way to an absolutely rigid and all-embracing determinism. All the processes of nature and society began to be viewed as working themselves out with an iron necessity; they were seen as perfectly predictable provided one could grasp their "regularities." Nothing whatever was left to chance. Lysenko's oft-quoted slogan, "Chance is the enemy of science," formulated the new attitude. Mendelian genetics, resting as it does upon the concept of chance mutations, was derided by Lysenko for having to "resort to the theory of probability" and for reducing biological science in this way to "mere statistics."[4] Michurinism, on the other hand, not only posed the far-reaching goal of transforming organic nature, but guaranteed the attainment of the goal by absolutely predictable scientific means. It had worked out the "laws and methods" of obtaining directed variations and of perpetuating them in the species concerned. It was all based upon the discovery of "necessary relationships" in organic nature. And so, promised Lysenko, "We will expel fortuities from biological science."[5]

The mounting obsession with necessity, determinism, and the expulsion of chance from every area of Soviet policy came to a climax in Stalin's last work, *Economic Problems of Socialism in the U.S.S.R.*, published in October 1952. Until its appearance, it had been an accepted practice for Soviet theorists to maintain that the all-powerful Soviet state, owing to its control over every aspect of the economic life of the country, could repeal or transform the laws governing its economic operations and create new ones in their stead. But in 1952 Stalin protested vehemently against this idea of the transforming of laws. Those who had spoken in such terms were denounced as economic adventurists whose disdain of "objective regularities" was fraught with great danger.

For what would it lead to if the Soviet state should regard itself as competent to create or transform economic laws? It would lead, said Stalin, to "our falling into a realm of chaos and fortuities; we would find ourselves in slavish dependence upon these fortuities; we would deprive ourselves of the possibility not only of understanding but even of finding our way around in this chaos of fortuities." Therefore, he insisted, the Soviet state must base its economic policy upon "scientific laws." Scientific laws, in turn, were reflections of "objective processes in nature or society, taking place independently of the will of human beings."

But Stalin simultaneously protests against what he calls the "fetishizing" of laws: "It is said that economic laws bear an elemental character, that the effects of these laws are inexorable, that society is powerless before them. This is untrue. This is fetishizing of laws, the surrender of oneself into slavery to laws. It has been shown that society is not powerless in the face of laws, that society, by perceiving economic laws and relying upon them, can restrict their sphere of action, use them in the interests of society, and 'saddle' them, as happens with reference to the forces of nature and their laws."[6]

There is thus a contradiction present in Stalin's new doctrine about scientific laws. On the one hand, he insists that Soviet policy must conform with "objective processes taking place independently of the will of human beings." This would eliminate choice and spontaneity from Soviet economic development, which would now be subordinated completely to the dictates of economic necessity. On the other hand, he cannot endure the thought of slavery to laws. He must regard his regime (or himself) as somehow superior to them, able to "saddle" them, subdue them, or "attain mastery over them," as one saddles and subdues the elemental forces of nature. He endeavors to resolve this conflict through the medium of the knowing mind. The function of the mind, he says, is to discover, grasp, study, and apply scientific laws. This intervention of the knowing mind enables him to feel that subordination to objective regularities is different from slavery to them. To settle this point, he cites the statement of Engels (derived from Hegel) equating freedom with "apprehended necessity."

Why was it that Stalin, while dead set on saddling, subduing, or attaining mastery over the supposedly objective laws of social-economic development, found utterly intolerable the thought of creating, repealing, or transforming them? What explains the enormous importance which this quasi-verbal distinction evidently had for him? The answer, I suggest, can be discovered in the psychological concept of "externalization," a process by which a person may experience his own thoughts, drives, or standards as operative in the external environment. In Stalin's case this tendency eventually found expression in a legislative attitude toward reality. In other words, what he referred to as "objective scientific laws" were an externalization of his inner policy dictates; they were a projection upon future Soviet history of the formulas for social-economic development generated in his own mind. *His own ideas appeared to him as natural necessities governing the development of society.*

This process of externalization performed for Stalin a double psychological function. First, it stilled any gnawing uncertainty in his own mind about the validity of the formulas and directives which he evolved; there could be nothing arbitrary or capricious about formulas which represented "objective processes taking place independently of the will of human beings." Subjective considerations entered only in the sense that his mind was the first to discover them, as Newton had been the first to discover the law of gravity. Secondly, this mental operation shut off all possible argument. It is reasonable to question a proposition about Soviet policy, even if its author be Stalin, but to question a law of nature is pure impertinence. With this in mind, we can understand how irritated Stalin became at the idea of creating, repealing, or transforming the objective laws of nature and society; such an attitude toward laws was a potential threat to his infallibility, a challenge to his externalized policy dictates. His heavy-handed insistence on the objectivity of all scientific laws, on their independence of the will of human beings, was a means of backing up his own claim to legislate the future course of nature and society. On the other hand, he could easily admit the possibility of "saddling" or "subduing" the laws, because this did not in any way affect their validity but only the manner in which society reacted to the discovery of them. It was his role as Supreme Architect of Communism to discover the laws, and it was the business of Soviet society to study them and put them into effect, and thus to "attain mastery" over them.

These considerations make it plain that the frantic preoccupation with causality, objectivity, and scientific laws which emerged in Soviet theoretical writings and the popular press during 1952 did not signify a retreat into a more empirical and pragmatic temper. Far from implying adoption of a scientific outlook, in the proper sense of the term, this tendency was part and parcel of the drift of the regime (no doubt under the commanding influence of the dictator himself) into the realm of political fantasy and wish-fulfillment. The extreme and at times almost hysterical emphasis upon necessity, iron regularities, objective scientific laws, etc., apparently expressed an imperative need to cover up the arbitrary and willful character of the decisions to transform things to suit the dreams and dictates of the autocracy. The further Stalin went in his schemes for the transformation of nature and society, the more he needed the reassurance that everything was proceeding in accordance with objective laws. The appeal to mechanical causality was a rationalization of rampant adventurism in Stalinist policy.

We have noted Lysenko's expression of scorn for Mendelian genetics because it "resorts" to the theory of probability and relies on "mere statistics." In later years this attitude led to a conscious rejection of any concept of scientific method that ruled out the absolute character of scientific laws. The physicist Bohr, for example, was attacked in 1952 for attempting to transform the law of the preservation of energy from an absolute law of nature into a statistical law which only holds good on the average. The "indeterminacy principle" enunciated by Heisenberg in connection with the quantum theory proved highly bothersome to Soviet philosophers of science, who felt called upon to contend that beneath the superficial appearance of indeterminacy the micro-particles of quantum theory must fully conform to a law of "deeper causal determination" of the micro-processes.[7] Especially strongly did they react against the speculation of Western quantum theorists to the effect that the electrons "choose their path," as it were, and thus (metaphorically speaking) possess a certain amount of "free will"; in other words, that there are certain moments when "nature makes a choice." The emotional intensity with which such thoughts were flayed reflects the psycho-ideological motivation of the Stalinist position. To the Stalinist mind it was imperative that nature at all its levels, from the micro-processes to man, be governed by mechanical laws of causality. For only on that condition could it be regarded as infinitely manipulable. The behavior of every single object must be reducible to a rigid, hard-and-fast formula, discovery of which would make it possible to saddle or subdue the object, to gain complete mastery over it, to transform it at will. Therefore, autogenesis was unacceptable. Nothing can behave in spontaneous ways not completely reducible to its objective formula. Everything "subjective" becomes suspect. The endowing of electrons with spontaneity was similar to the endowing of living organisms with developmental and mutational tendencies inherent in their genes. In either case the ideal of total control and transformability would be jeopardized. Here was an outlook which might fairly be described as the projection of totalitarianism upon Nature.

III. The Formula for Man

Inevitably, the postulates of transformism and mechanical causality penetrated the areas of Soviet thought concerned with the behavior of man. There were also special reasons for this. The most difficult problem faced by the Stalin regime in the postwar years was the profound passivity of the Soviet populace, its failure to respond positively to the goals set before it. Throughout all classes of Soviet society, the hopeful moods which had prevailed widely during the war years evaporated as the regime's endeavors to mobilize them for fresh exertions in the postwar period got under way. The root of the matter was not the incapacity of people to endure another season of privation, but rather the meaninglessness of the sacrifices they were called upon to make, the pointlessness of Russia's being in eternal conflict with the rest of the world, the total lack of prospect for tranquility in their time. The result was widespread apathy, resignation, spiritual disengagement from the goals of the Stalin government.

Stalin evidently decided that the problem could be solved, or at least greatly alleviated, by a massive propaganda effort coupled with improved controls over an intermediate element—the artists and writers—whose work in the service of the goals of the state would in turn influence the public in the required ways. This was the impulse behind "Zhdanovism," the drive which started in the summer of 1946 to enlist and organize the creative intelligentsia of the Soviet Union as a corps of conscious instruments of state policy, as missionaries of patriotic enthusiasm among the dispirited multitude of the Russian people. This attempt to elicit popular enthusiasm by means of a propaganda campaign continued through the postwar years, but with little apparent success. The whole undertaking was an example of Stalinism's characteristic overevaluation of the potentialities of propaganda.

As indicated earlier, the stock reaction of the Stalin regime to a situation in which certain forces in the environment were proving recalcitrant to its goals was not to re-examine the goals, but to search for a formula by which it could transform or remold the forces and thereby overcome their recalcitrance. If the material at hand was showing itself perverse to the dictates of the regime, then some way had to be found to conquer its perversity. The dictates themselves were righteous and unalterable; their frustration only evoked redoubled insistence upon their realization. In the case in question, the regime was faced with persistent popular apathy and passive resistance to its control in various sections of Soviet society, especially the peasantry. People were not responding in the expected way to the techniques of political education and indoctrination. This led the Stalinist mind to find some magic formula for making people respond properly. If Russians were failing to respond to the goals set before them, then something was the matter with the Russians and with the means employed to elicit their response. Their minds had to be remolded to the point where inner acceptance of the Soviet ideology and all the behavior patterns it imposed would come as a matter of course. But for mind control to become a reality, it had to be based upon scientific bedrock. What was required was a *formula for man.*

By 1949, when the need for a new formula in terms of which human nature could be scientifically explained and "saddled" had become more or less obvious, the Soviet leadership found in the Michurin-Lysenko doctrines a theory of the transformation of organisms on the biological level. Could it not draw in some fashion upon these doctrines for the purpose of constructing a more perfect science of man? Stalin himself tended to employ the biological analogy in his sociological thinking. In his essay on "Dialectical and Historical Materialism" published in 1938 as a chapter of the new *Short Course,* he had written that the science of society "can become as precise a science as, let us say, biology, and capable of making use of the laws of development of society for practical purposes."[8] Lysenko, with Stalin's blessing, had become the reigning authority of a new biology which boasted of its ability to "expel fortuities" from this area of knowledge. If Michurinism could produce new species of plants and animals, might it not serve in the hands of the all-powerful Soviet state as a means of eventually creating a new species of "Soviet man"?

Actually, a "Michurinism for man" was germinating during the aftermath of the genetics controversy of 1948, but it did not come forth as a Soviet version of eugenics. It was a transference to man not of the specific biological concepts and techniques of Michurinism but of its basic underlying ways of thought, of its general theory of the relationship between the organism and the environment. In his search for a counterpart of Michurin in the field of psychology, for a Russian who could qualify as the "great transformer of human nature," Stalin rediscovered Pavlov. *The formula for man was the conditioned reflex.*

Stalin's rediscovery heralded a Pavlovian revolution in the Soviet behavioral sciences. The principle of the conditioned reflex was made the basis of a new Soviet concept of man. According to this concept, man is a reactive mechanism whose behavior, including all the higher mental processes, can be exhaustively understood through a knowledge of the laws of conditioning, and can be controlled through application of this knowledge. The new movement began in 1949, and continued with ever-increasing momentum during 1950, 1951, and 1952. From the fields of physiology and medicine where it took its rise, it radiated out into numerous adjacent areas of science, including psychiatry, pedagogy, and psychology.

It must be emphasized once again that the motivating springs of this movement were not scientific but political, not intellectual in the proper sense but psycho-ideological. That is, the neo-Pavlovian movement did not grow spontaneously out of the scientific investigations of Soviet physiologists, pathologists, and psychologists working independently at their respective problems. It was, on the contrary, imposed upon them from above by political authorities whose interest in the matter was non-scientific. According to Academician K. Bykov, who played a part in the Pavlovian revolution similar to that of Lysenko in genetics, the whole development took place "under the directing influence of the Party" and was inspired by Stalin personally: "The initiator of the events which have elevated the teachings of Pavlov in our country, the initiator of the creation of the most favorable conditions for the development of Soviet physiology for the benefit of the people is the brilliant architect of Soviet culture—Joseph Vissarionovich Stalin. We are indebted to Comrade Stalin for the victory of the Pavlovian cause in our country and for the creative upsurge which we now observe in the development of this most important field of contemporary natural science."[9] There appears to be no reason to doubt the testimony of Bykov on this crucial point.

IV. The Enthronement of Pavlov

The year 1949 was the turning point in the official Soviet attitude toward Pavlov. Prior to that time, Pavlov's memory had been venerated in Soviet writings. But in the new phase, which began in 1949, this gave way to a positive glorification of both the man and his teachings. As the potential practical use of these teachings dawned upon the Stalin regime, they began to receive official endorsement in a new spirit of dogmatic authority. A major development in Pavlov's rise was the nation-wide observance in September 1949 of the one-hundredth anniversary of his birth. Although the Pavlovian revolution was at that time still in its formative stages, some of the themes of the centenary materials were highly indicative of the direction in which the thought of the regime was moving. The mounting antipathy toward "subjectivism" was evident in the boast by Academician Bykov that Pavlov "drove the soul out forever from its last refuge—our minds."[10] The logic of facts, wrote Bykov, led Pavlov to the necessity of "putting an end forever to the conception of the soul." And *Pravda,* in its anniversary editorial, said that Pavlov had invaded the sphere of spiritual phenomena, established the material basis of higher nervous activity, and in this way had smashed for all time the "idealistic fables about the supernatural character of our minds." Moreover, this editorial revealed vividly the relationship of the new official interest in Pavlov to the transformist trend of thought: "To master nature, to subjugate her to the interests of man, to achieve unlimited power over the most intricate type of motion of matter—the work of the brain—such was Pavlov's ardent dream. Like another great Russian scientist, I. V. Michurin, Pavlov did not wish to await 'favors' from nature, but took the view that it is possible and feasible for man himself to take these 'favors,' actively to intervene in nature, to remake her."[11] The coupling of the names of Pavlov and Michurin was far more than a casual rhetorical flourish.

The tendencies toward an official enthronement of Pavlov came to fruition in June 1950, shortly after the publication of Stalin's papers on linguistics; this was an event, as we shall see presently, with which the Pavlovian revolution was closely connected. On June 22, 1950, *Pravda* announced that there was to be held a joint scientific session of the Academy of Science of the USSR and the Academy of Medical Sciences to discuss problems of the physiological theories of Pavlov. The session opened in Moscow on June 28. There were two keynote reports, given by Academician K. M. Bykov and Professor A. G. Ivanov-Smolensky. Seventy-five others followed. The theme of the occasion was struck by Vavilov, President of the Academy of Sciences, in the opening speech. The development of Soviet physiology since Pavlov's death, he said, had diverged from the "direct paths laid down by the great Russian scientist" into secondary bypaths. The center of gravity had shifted considerably from the "Pavlov line." The present session would be a turning point beyond which Soviet physiology would develop squarely in the Pavlovian heritage. This basic theme was developed by Bykov. It was a mistake, he stated, to think of Pavlov's teaching as a mere addition to physiology or a new chapter in its development. It would be more correct to divide all physiology, and all psychology as well, into two phases: the pre-Pavlov phase and the Pavlov phase.

Bykov and Ivanov-Smolensky attacked the leaders of all the "deviationist" tendencies in Soviet physiology and medicine. Academician Orbeli, who until 1948 had directed the main Pavlovian institutes in the USSR, and had been recognized as the principal custodian of the Pavlovian heritage, was the foremost target. He was criticized primarily for his view that the principles of the conditioned reflex can explain only the more elementary forms of behavior, and that the existence of a "subjective world" must be reckoned with at the human level. Orbeli had written in 1947 that "in those temporary connections which Ivan Petrovich [Pavlov] studied, we have only the most elementary process of higher nervous activity." And he had called attention to the phenomenon in man of *resistance* to the formation of conditioned reflexes. Both of these propositions were now totally unacceptable. The conditioned reflex was to be regarded as a universal formula for all higher nervous activity, and no exceptions could be allowed, even at the human level, to the principle of total determination by conditioning. "Also incomprehensible," added Ivanov-Smolensky, "is Academician L. A. Orbeli's assertion that a qualitative singularity of man is the rise in him of a 'subjective world.'"[12]

The relationship of the Pavlovian doctrine to the transformist goals of the Soviet regime and to the Michurinist ideology was made explicit by Bykov and Ivanov-Smolensky. Pavlov, declared the latter, had aspired not only to study but also to *master* the phenomena being studied, to direct them, command them, change them in the required directions. Through a knowledge of the laws of conditioning combined with control over the environment, behavior could be conditioned in whatever ways were considered desirable. In addition, the conditioned connections, repeated for a number of generations, could "by heredity turn into unconditioned ones." The organic relationship between Michurinism and Pavlovianism in the minds of the Soviet proponents of these doctrines was reflected in the later appearance in Soviet writings of a new hyphenate expression: the "Michurin-Pavlov biology." According to this conception, the common basic principle of the two doctrines was the "law of the unity of organism and environment." The difference between them related only to the spheres of application of the basic principle. Michurinism applied it to agriculture, while Pavlovianism applied it to physiology, psychology, and medicine.

A notable detail of the Pavlov session was the frequent reference to hypertension, or high blood pressure, as foremost among the diseases which would prove amenable to therapeutic methods derived from the Pavlovian arsenal. This is interesting in view of the fact that Stalin himself apparently suffered from hypertension in a chronic form; according to the official announcement of March 4, 1953, the brain stroke from which he died resulted from his condition of hypertension. Whether or not the clinical interests of Soviet medicine were guided in part by Stalin's personal medical needs, the fact remains that the participants in the Pavlov session of 1950 devoted a remarkable amount of attention to the problem of hypertension. Both of the leading speakers, in particular, laid special stress upon a Pavlovian approach to the cure of this complaint. The Pavlovian view, as they developed it, was that this, like other internal diseases such as ulcers, is ultimately caused by a disordered state of the cerebral cortex. In technical Pavlovian terms, employed by A. L. Myasnikov in his speech at the session, hypertension is based upon "disorders of the first and second signal systems," i.e., the non-linguistic and linguistic systems of conditioned reflexes. This being so, therapy should concentrate upon bringing influence to bear upon the patient via the central nervous system. Ivanov-Smolensky mentioned sleep treatment, hypnosis, and suggestion as three specific techniques for possible use in this connection. Bykov alluded to some sort of linguistic therapy, saying that "speech can cause deep changes in the whole organism." Can it be that Stalin was in effect mobilizing the Soviet medical profession to discover a Pavlovian miracle treatment for his high blood pressure? The answer to this question must remain for the time being one of the intriguing mysteries of Stalin's reign. However, in view of what is known about the sustained efforts of Soviet specialists to satisfy Stalin's interest in pushing back the frontiers of human longevity, an affirmative answer to the question must be regarded as entirely possible.

Although problems of physiology and medicine largely dominated the deliberations of the Pavlov session, its momentous implications for Soviet psychology did not escape the minds of those present. A "reconstruction of psychology on scientific principles" was one of the tasks which the session's decree laid down for the specialists in this department of knowledge. Among those who addressed the session were two of the most prominent Soviet psychologists, B. M. Teplov and S. L. Rubinstein. Teplov's speech was a piece of abject self-criticism on behalf of Soviet psychology as a whole. The task of constructing a system of psychology based upon the teachings of Pavlov had not, he said, been fulfilled.[13] All of the existing textbooks and treatises on psychology were "utterly unsatisfactory." Soviet psychologists had suffered from "a fear of the simplicity and clarity of the Pavlovian teaching," a fear which reflected in part the regrettable influence on Soviet psychologists of certain fashionable foreign schools in psychology. Now, however, Soviet psychology was entering upon a new stage of its development, the Pavlovian stage.[14]

There is abundant evidence to show that during the early postwar years the professional psychologists of the USSR were quite oblivious of the impending revolutionary reorientation of their science on the basis of the reflex principle. Reflexology in all its forms was viewed as an aberration of the 1920's, as a stage which had been traversed and transcended once and for all. Furthermore, there is nothing to suggest that the majority of psychologists regretted this. Reflexological concepts do not appear to be particularly congenial to their ways of thought. In any event, the irrelevance of the reflex concept to an understanding of the higher forms of human experience was taken more or less for granted. Teplov, for example, had written in 1947: "The explanation of all the phenomena of psychic life by the principle of the formation of associative or conditioned-reflex connections is, of course, utterly wrong. . . . By itself the theory of conditioned reflexes is not even adequate for understanding the physiological foundation of human behavior."[15] At the time it was made, this statement merely expressed a view which had come to be accepted with the force of dogma by all the leading figures of Soviet psychology.

That was how matters stood when the command was issued in 1950 for Soviet psychology to be radically reconstructed on the basis of the reflex principle. Implying as it did that this discipline had been on the wrong track for the past twenty years, the command came as a shock to those on the receiving end. It forced the psychologists to raise again the most fundamental problems concerning the concepts and methods of psychology. The pessimism and perplexity which this prospect aroused among the psychologists were reflected in an incident which occurred some time after the Pavlov session. A number of psychologists wrote a collective note to Ivanov-Smolensky, inquiring, "What is the subject of psychology and what are its tasks?" The note was signed: "Group of Psychologists Seeking the Subject of Their Science."[16] There is no record that they received a reply. According to a Soviet source, in the aftermath of the Pavlov session many of the psychologists were "at a loss" in the face of the necessity it had proclaimed for a reconstruction of their science. This found expression "either in liquidator attitudes toward the subject-matter of psychological science or else in efforts somehow to cut themselves off from the Pavlovian teaching, to stand aside and wait it out until the reconstruction had taken place."[17]

The next major development was a conference on psychology held in Moscow in July 1952 and attended by over 400 psychologists from all parts of the country. Its task was to take stock of the results already achieved in the Pavlovian revolution and to chart its future directions. The conference admitted in its final resolution that the reconstruction of psychology was proceeding at an "inadmissibly slow" pace, and urged that the task be approached more boldly and resolutely. Professor A. A. Smirnov, the main speaker, declared that the reconstruction had to be fundamental and decisive. It had to extend to "the entire content of psychology." The psychological concepts had to be radically recast, purged of "all elements of idealism, subjectivism, introspectionism."[18] However, this did not mean, according to Smirnov, the reduction of psychology to physiology, the dissolving of psychological concepts into physiological ones. The concept of consciousness, for example, was not to be discarded, as some psychologists had proposed in this aftermath of the Pavlov session. Instead, it was to be so reinterpreted that all the phenomena of conscious experience could be strictly correlated, on the basis of the reflex principle, with their environmental determinants. Far from facing liquidation, psychology was destined to occupy a position of crucial importance among the sciences. By employing the theory of Pavlov, it would open up the subjective world of man to objective study and *thereby to regulation.*

V. The Pavlovian Model of Personality

The leading Soviet psychologies of the 1920's were characterized by their exclusive interest in overt behavior and by their emphasis on environmental influence. But in the new model of personality which emerged in the 1930's, the center of gravity shifted to the subjective side. The individual recovered his psyche. His overt behavior was now seen as a product of processes taking place inside him as shaped by his previous experience and the educational efforts of the Soviet state. While the principle of causality was not abandoned, there was a significant shift away from exclusive stress on environment. Soviet man was accorded in psychological theory a capacity for self-determination, for consciously regulating his conduct by norms and ideals which, though assimilated from the "socialist environment," were a genuine part of him and hence, supposedly, commanded his sincere and spontaneous allegiance.[19] This was in essence an optimistic conception. It presupposed that people growing up in the Soviet social order and subject to the formative influences which the state could bring to bear upon them through the family, the school, the press, and all the other channels of control would, in the vast majority of instances, develop true "Soviet selves." Once formed in this manner, the personality system would become an autonomous force in the individual's life, ensuring his loyalty to the regime, his conformity to its doctrines, and his allegiance to its goals.

Seen in this perspective, the Pavlovian revolution of the early 1950's marks an event of historical significance: the breakdown of the optimistic conception of man with which the Stalin regime had officially been operating for nearly two decades. It was a reflection of the quiet resistance of the majority of Russians to the Sovietization of their real selves, a resistance which had proved relatively immune to the massive propaganda pressures of the postwar years. The fact was that Soviet society, with all its controls and its immense resources for indoctrination of the citizenry, was not producing a generation of New Men. The optimistic model of personality endowed the individual person with a capacity of spiritual self-determination, but the results did not bear out the confident prediction of the 1930's. And there was nothing in the working model which would point the way toward the attainment of better results. Naturally, these implications were not openly acknowledged in the writings of the early 1950's that centered around the teaching of Pavlov. But they were omnipresent below the surface of these writings, and occasionally showed through unmistakably.

The attempted reconstruction of Soviet psychology was far more, of course, than a confession of the bankruptcy of the optimistic model of personality. It was also an expression of Stalin's iron determination to elaborate a new model which would answer the needs of his regime, a truly workable model based upon a perfected technique of soul-forming which would leave nothing to chance and, if properly mastered, could not fail to achieve the goal. In his address to the psychological conference of 1952, Professor Smirnov formulated the goal rather candidly: "Soviet psychologists are confronted in all definiteness with the problem of the *formation of the personality of man,* the formation of it in the concrete social-historical conditions of people, in the conditions of our socialist reality, under the influence of the educational work of the school" (italics added).[20] Since the master-formula for the attainment of the goal was to be the conditioned reflex, the model of personality had to be revolutionized. *Man had to be understood as a being whose character and conduct are controlled at every step by the conditioning process, whose every psychic act is a reflex.* As Smirnov put it, "I. P. Pavlov's teaching on temporary connections is a firm basis for understanding *all* the conscious activity of man."[21] Thus the reflex mechanism was seen as an all-inclusive key to the workings of the mind. The basic premise of the new Pavlovian model of personality is that there is nothing in man that transcends in principle the conditioned salivary responses of Pavlov's dog.[22]

From this starting point, Soviet psychology inevitably moved back into a rigid environmental determinism. The leading spokesmen of the neo-Pavlovian movement never tired of pointing out that the Pavlovian model of personality is deterministic. The psyche's existence is not denied, but all causal determination is shifted to the external environment, natural and social. "The causes of psychological facts," says Smirnov in a typical formulation, "are influences emanating from without, primarily influences of a social character."[23] According to another authority, "Determinate agents of the external world are the cause, the impetus, of determinate activity of the organism."[24] In taking this position the Soviet psychologists saw themselves as applying to psychology the principle of the unity of organism and environment which the Michurinist doctrine had applied to biology. Just as Michurinism denied the existence of autogenetic forces in animals and plants, so neo-Pavlovianism denies the existence of psychogenetic forces in man. The result is to deprive the human being of all spontaneity, all inner sources of activity. He is jerked into motion, tugged this way and that, by "determinate agents of the external world" in which all causal efficacy resides. This is a view which might have been summed up in the slogan: Overboard with self-determination! It marked a clean break with the conception of the New Man. Employing the terminology of the American sociologist Riesman, the transition from the New Man to the Pavlovian model of personality can be described as a shift from an "inner-directed" type, whose character operates as an autonomous determining force in his life, to an "other-directed" type, whose behavior is guided by signals received from outside. In the Soviet version, however, the sole source of the signals to which the "other-directed" person responds is the State.

To the outsider who studies the materials of the neo-Pavlovian movement, nothing is more striking than its insistent endeavor to empty man of all inner springs of action, to visualize human nature as motivationally inert. Man is "hollow." He has no wishes, instincts, emotions, drives, or impulses, no reservoir of energies of his own. No motive is allowed to intervene between the stimulus emanating from the environment and the person's reflex response. Rubinstein, for example, protests vigorously against the notion that the individual has "inner impulses" (drives, instincts, tendencies, etc.) which underlie his reflexes and "guide the action of the reflex mechanisms in a direction desirable to the organism." His new view is as follows: "The Pavlovian conception of reflex action does not require and does not allow for any 'motive,' drive or impulse lodged behind the reflex, in the depths of the organism, which by some means unknown to us sets the reflex mechanism in motion."[25] True, a person's responses are seen as influenced to some extent by his habits, but these in turn are a crystallization of past conditioning and consequently an integral part of the system of reflex mechanisms.

The linguistic orientation which Stalin imparted to the neo-Pavlovian movement has already been touched upon above. In the reconstruction of Soviet psychology, the conception of the regulative function of language took on decisive importance. And it was at this point that Stalin's theoretical interests impinged most directly upon the new movement in psychology. In emphasizing the all-important role of language in conditioned-reflex behavior at the human level, the Soviet psychologists referred constantly to Stalin's *Marxism and Questions of Linguistics,* a series of papers which were published in the summer of 1950. The first and longest of these papers appeared in *Pravda* only two days prior to the announcement of the forthcoming Pavlov session, and this close coincidence in time is probably an indication of the intimate relationship in Stalin's mind between the linguistic doctrines which he enunciated and the revival of Pavlovianism in physiology and psychology. Such a relationship was, at any rate, taken for granted by the psychologists themselves.

The passages of Stalin's work on linguistics which are quoted most frequently by the psychologists are those in which he stresses the enormous significance of language in all departments of social activity, and the inseparability of language and thought. With reference to the first point, he writes that language is directly linked with every activity of man "in all areas of his work." It "embraces all the spheres of activity of man" and is "virtually unlimited."[26] Moreover, Stalin equates language with *word-language,* rejecting the notions about gesture-language and wordless thought which had been emphasized by the founder of Soviet linguistics, N. Ya. Marr. Thus, language to Stalin means word-language exclusively, it is inseparable from thought, and it penetrates and pervades every aspect of the social behavior of man. These propositions formed a starting point for constructing the new Pavlovian model of personality, which pictures man as a creature whose behavior is controlled and regulated by verbal signals.

The concept of the "second signal system" provided a connecting link between Stalin's generalities about language on the one hand and the theory of conditioning on the other. This concept is one which Pavlov casually developed in some of his later writings and in conversations with his students. The minor part which it played in his system can be judged from the fact that there are scarcely more than a dozen brief references to it in all his writings and recorded conversations. His idea seems to have been that word-language functions in the context of the individual human being's behavior as a system of verbal signals, higher-order conditioned stimuli which evoke indirectly the same responses as those conditioned to non-verbal stimuli. One of the most striking features of the neo-Pavlovian movement is the disproportionately heavy emphasis which it places upon this minor appendage of the original Pavlovian system. Until 1950, the concept of the second signal system had been generally ignored by Soviet psychologists. Among the physiologists, the only two who gave it much attention were—significantly enough—Ivanov-Smolensky and Bykov. Then, however, it was lifted out of obscurity and erected as the central pillar of the new Stalin-Pavlov system of psychology. According to Rubinstein, "all the specifically human characteristics of the psyche" are revealed in the functioning of the second signal system.

The Pavlovian revolution placed great emphasis upon the semantic side of Pavlov's theory of conditioned reflexes. In fact, the Soviet neo-Pavlovianism of the early 1950's is essentially a theory of semantics constructed on a physiological basis. The foundation upon which the whole structure rests is, in the words of Bykov, the "principle of signalization." The concomitant of a stimulus, such as the sound of the metronome in Pavlov's well-known experiment with the dog, becomes a "signal" of the presence of the stimulus (in this instance, food) and evokes the reflex action appropriate to it. The totality of concomitants which in the natural life conditions of the organism take over the stimulus function and serve as signals constitute, in Pavlov's terminology, a "first signal system of reality." The first signal system is common to man and animals. But at the human level an "extraordinary addition" emerges in the form of speech. Speech is a system of signals of the second order—"signals of signals," in Pavlov's phrase. It forms in its totality a "second signal system of reality" which is peculiar to man and which, according to Pavlov, operates on the same fundamental laws as those that govern the conditioning process at the lower level. Finally, the generalized verbal signals comprised in the second system are assigned a position of hegemony in the life of man; the second system takes precedence over the first in orienting the human being in his environment. This is the substance of Pavlov's "wonderful idea" of the second signal system, which, according to Bykov and others, had heretofore been mistakenly ignored by Soviet science.

In using the phrase "signals of signals," Pavlov apparently had in mind the view that the word is a generalized "substitute signal" of the object it denotes and, as such, evokes the behavioral reaction appropriate to the object in the same way that the sound of the metronome evokes in the experimental dog the behavioral reaction appropriate to the signalized food. Since this line of speculation was outside the direct purview of his scientific work, he did not pursue it further. However, his present-day Soviet followers accepted it as the literal truth and made it the cornerstone of the new psychological theory which they had been ordered to build on a Pavlovian basis. The theory rests squarely on Pavlov's surmise that verbal substitute signals evoke behavioral tendencies or reactions in the same way that ordinary conditioned stimuli do. One writer, for example, illustrated the thesis as follows: "By mastering the word, that is, by learning to pronounce the appropriate auditory complex and to relate this complex correctly to specific objects, the child masters the significance of the given word. After that the word can play the part of a signal of signals: the word 'apple' can signalize the very same stimuli as those evoked by a real apple."[27] If, in other words, the sight of an actual apple lying on the table will cause a hungry child's mouth to water, hearing the word "apple" will eventually, after the proper language training, evoke a similar reaction. The function of words is, then, to trigger behavioral responses appropriate to the objects with which people have been trained to associate the words.

We may note here that this Pavlovian concept of the function of language is appropriate to a hypothetical primitive condition of man in which speech was exclusively an instrument of social control and had not yet acquired an autonomous representative function. By treating words as second-order signals to action, it overlooks the acquired *symbolic* function of language. The distinction between words used as signals to action on the one hand and purely as symbols of their objects on the other is illustrated by an American semanticist in the following way: "A term which is used symbolically and not signally does *not* evoke action appropriate to the presence of its object. If I say: 'Napoleon,' you do not bow to the conqueror of Europe as though I had introduced him, but merely think of him. If I mention a Mr. Smith of our common acquaintance, you may be led to tell me something about him 'behind his back' which you would *not* do in his presence. . . . Symbols are not proxy for their objects, but are *vehicles for the conception of objects.*"[28]

The failure of the Soviet psychologists to recognize and take account of this crucial distinction is no mere accident. The practical importance which was discerned in the neo-Pavlovian movement, its electrifying educational implications to the Stalinist mind, depended entirely upon reducing language to its signal-function exclusively, upon regarding words as "proxy for their objects." The whole movement would have collapsed instantly had its initiator forced himself to consider the possibility that words can be employed purely symbolically as neutral vehicles for the conception of objects. The goal was to treat language as an instrument of social control. For this purpose it was imperative that words should always be signals which touch off responses appropriate to their meaning. Here was the needed link between semantics and politics. As Smirnov expressed it, the Pavlovian teaching reveals the conditions under which stimuli, including verbal stimuli, become signals *"and by virtue of this fact regulate the behavior of man"* (italics added).[29] On this view of the function of language, a person hearing the word "Napoleon" should indeed make at least a mental bow to the conqueror of Europe, or whatever other gesture his earlier conditioning had linked with this verbal signal. Or, to take a familiar example from the Soviet context, on hearing the signal "warmonger" a properly Pavlovianized Russian should respond with a shudder of fury. Granted the initial premise that the word is in every case primarily a call to action, linguistics logically takes its place at the head of the list of political sciences. Of all the monopolies enjoyed by the Soviet state, none would be so crucial as its monopoly on the definition of words. The ultimate weapon of political control would be the dictionary.[30]

At this point it may be useful to summarize briefly the argument of the foregoing pages. I have suggested that the movement initiated by Stalin to reconstruct Soviet psychology marked a decline of the optimistic conception of man which had officially prevailed in the USSR since the early 1930's. This in turn was an indirect reflection of the fact that millions of Russians, especially under the impact of their experiences during and after World War II, showed tendencies to deviate radically from the norm of Soviet selfhood which, according to the optimistic conception, they should have naturally assimilated as a result of their education and spontaneous personality development. In the face of this disturbing fact, Stalin resorted to the peculiar mode of coming to terms with perverse situations which we have termed "transformism." In the Pavlovian model of personality he found a formula which seemed to place human nature in the arbitrary power of a state-controlled educational environment. Emptied of all inner springs of character and conduct, man appeared in this model as a passive plaything of determining influences from without, particularly influences of a social character brought to bear through the medium of language. By mastering the "objective scientific laws" of the language-conditioning process, the state could—theoretically—bring about the "directed alteration of psychic processes," i.e., it could transform the minds of its citizens, mold them in the Soviet personality image. The crowning concept of this theoretical edifice was the second signal system. In the Stalin-Pavlov model of man, the second signal system is the mechanism of mentality. Consciousness is the distinctive capacity of human beings to respond to and regulate their behavior by verbal signals. Man is basically a signal-receiving animal. And since it is the state which calls the signals, an appropriate name for this theoretical new species of Soviet humanity would be "state-directed man."

VI. The Counter-trend Since Stalin's Death

The interpretation offered here of the neo-Pavlovian chapter of Soviet thought assigns a crucially important place to Stalin. The evidence for such a view converges from a number of directions. First, there is the direct public testimony of Bykov, Rubinstein, and others that Stalin initiated the back-to-Pavlov movement. Secondly, the neo-Pavlovian movement was in its way an outgrowth, an extension to man, of the Michurin-Lysenko line in biology, which enjoyed Stalin's personal patronage. Further, it was closely linked up with the ultra-deterministic conception of scientific law which he developed in his final work on political economy. Finally, in its medical aspect, the movement impinged upon an area in which Stalin had shown all along, and especially toward the end, a most intense personal interest. These various indications of Stalin's role as the instigator and guiding spirit of the Pavlov revival lend special interest to the course which the movement has taken since Stalin died.

The Stalin-Pavlov line was not altered immediately after Stalin's death. As late as August 1953, Bykov was quoted in a Soviet journal as saying: "We must preserve the purity of the Pavlov teaching, which has affected all major issues of contemporary natural science."[31] But then subtle signs of a counter-trend began to appear. One of these was the move to topple Lysenkoism from its monopolistic position in biology. This emerged into the open in early 1954. Later in that year, the counter-trend went further. A prominent physicist, S. L. Sobolev, was permitted to publish an article in *Pravda* stating that scientific progress "is always connected with the abandonment of preconceived points of view, with the bold breaking-down of old norms and conceptions." Sobolev attacked the previous disparagement of Einstein's physical theories by physicists of the Moscow University. He coupled this with a caustic reference to the unmerited claims of certain Soviet scientists to monopoly of the truth, mentioning three names in this connection: Lysenko, Bykov, and Ivanov-Smolensky.[32] To the psychologists, the inference could only be that the twin dictators of Stalin's neo-Pavlovian movement had fallen from the pedestal of official infallibility. The way was now opened for a reaction against this movement.

The reaction came shortly afterward in an editorial summation in *Problems of Philosophy* of the whole discussion of recent years on psychology.[33] The editorial did not attack Pavlov or question the importance of his teachings for psychology. But in various significant ways it undermined the Stalin-Pavlov line. It redefined psychology in pre-1950 terms as "the science of the psychic activity of man." Next, it announced—with something of an air of discovery—that psychic activity is both real and subjective in nature: "The subjective—man's psyche—really exists." (!) It reproached the 1952 conference on psychology for banning the introspective method. It told the psychologists not to be afraid of describing the rediscovered subjective world of man in terms of the traditional psychological categories: mind, feeling, will, imagination, etc. "This observation," it added, "we address to certain nihilistic tendencies in the matter of the so-called recasting or redefinition of the psychological terms and concepts on the basis of the Pavlovian physiology." The reader will recall that these "nihilistic tendencies" were part and parcel of the Stalin-Pavlov line. They expressed the very crux of what Stalin was directing the Soviet psychologists to do. Finally, the editorial referred in sharply negative terms to those who would "dogmatically apply to man" all the methods which Pavlov evolved in the study of animal behavior. The effect of all this was, of course, to revise the whole orientation imposed on Soviet psychology from high political spheres in 1950.

The counter-trend is still no more than a trend at the time of this writing. It could not be classed as a counter-revolution. There is no suggestion of a rejection of Pavlov or a denial of the relevance of his ideas to psychology. *What has apparently been discarded is, specifically, the Stalin idea of finding in Pavlov the scientific key to mind control.* The new admission that "the psyche really exists" reflects something quite crucial—the abandonment of total environmental determinism in the sense that was implied in the Stalin-Pavlov line. This was made explicit in early 1955 in the first issue of a new Soviet journal, *Problems of Psychology*. The programmatic leading article was contributed by Rubinstein. In it he rejects the idea of determinism "as the theory of a cause which operates as an external impetus and directly determines the terminal effect of the external stimulus." This, as we have seen, is precisely the kind of determinism implicit in the model of the state-directed man. The verbal signals called by the state are supposed to determine directly his attitudes and acts. No intervention of the psyche as an autonomous inner force in man is allowed; no self-determination, no spontaneity, no motives are to be presupposed by psychology. Having formulated the deterministic principle as implicit in this model, Rubinstein continues: "It is easy to understand the invalidity of such determinism. All the facts of science and everyday observation testify against it. We may convince ourselves at every step that one and the same stimulus can evoke various different reactions in various different people. One and the same stimulus evokes different reactions in one and the same individual under various different conditions of that person. . . . External causes operate through the medium of the internal conditions which represent the foundation of the development of phenomena."[34] Here the principle of "autogenesis," the idea that the personality is to some extent an autonomous determining force in the person's life and behavior, is restored. The core of the Stalin-Pavlov line is cut away. The model of the state-directed man presupposes a one-to-one correspondence between the verbal propaganda stimulus and the individual's reflex response. It implies "direct" determinism in the sense here denied. Such determinism, concludes Rubinstein, "would signify the *complete disintegration of personality* and would lead to a defective mechanistic conception holding that each influence on a person has its own 'separate' effect irrespective of the dynamic situation. . . . The central link here is the 'psychology of personality.' This is the point of departure and the point of arrival for an adequate theory of motivation" (italics added).[35] Not only does this statement slough off the model of the state-directed man on behalf of Soviet psychology. It admits by indirection that the Stalin-Pavlov line envisaged nothing less than the complete disintegration of human personality.

What are the policy implications of the counter-trend? The Stalin-Pavlov line, as shown earlier, was an expression of the Will to Transform which was operative in Stalin's postwar policies. It was a search for a sure formula of mind control which would yield techniques for the psychic transformation of human beings, rendering them plastically receptive to the official propaganda image of the world and of themselves and their tasks in Soviet society. Underlying it was the idea that "propaganda can do anything" if only the psychic conditions of receptivity to it could be scientifically set and controlled. This was a theory of environmentalism in which the state-operated organs of education and indoctrination were seen as the sole active sector of the environment, the determining environmental force. The remainder of the environment, including the material living conditions of Soviet people, would *not* have to be ameliorated in order to accomplish the transformist objective. The illusion of a happy life could be built up and maintained in Soviet minds no matter how miserable the actual living conditions might be.

If this aspect of transformism were subsiding in Soviet official thought, how might we recognize the shift? There would be some sign of recognition that propaganda, as it were, "cannot do everything," that actual living conditions would have to be improved in order to assure a better popular response to the regime and its goals. Policy, in other words, would be governed by a more pragmatic approach, one that combined continued heavy stress on indoctrination with some effort to ameliorate the real environment of the masses of Soviet citizens. The beginnings of such a shift in the policy orientation of the Soviet regime have, in fact, appeared. One of the most interesting manifestations of it is the recognition of the limitations of coercion and propaganda persuasion as means of controlling mass behavior. For example, the Central Committee's journal, *Party Life*, has recently written that private commercial "speculation" (classed as a "survival of capitalism") cannot be combated by legal regulation and propaganda alone. It is also necessary "to show concern for the all-round development of Soviet trade, the improvement of supplies for the population, and the creation of an abundance of consumer goods. Only on this condition will all ground for speculation disappear."[36] It is questionable whether "this condition" will soon or ever be realized under the Soviet economic system, but the statement itself is of real interest as an indication of the decline of transformism in the regime's official thinking. An even clearer indication comes in a direct criticism by the Soviet philosophical journal of the tendency to overvalue the potentialities of propaganda. Some, it states, have reasoned "as though the survivals of capitalism in the minds of people could be overcome *solely by means of propaganda*, by means of education, while neglecting the solution of economic tasks, the necessity of steadily developing social production, which creates objective conditions for improving the material position and cultural standard of the people" (italics added).[37] But such reasoning, it contends, is mistaken. A policy operating "solely by means of propaganda" will not do. The inference is that the new Soviet leadership recognizes direct mind control of the kind Stalin sought as, at the least, an impractical proposition. In other words, it recognizes the imperative need to combine indoctrination with improvement of "objective conditions" if Soviet popular attitudes and behavioral patterns are to be altered in its own favor.

No substantial shift of internal Soviet economic policy has resulted from such recognition, although the Malenkovist stress on the consumer and welfare goals seemed for a while to point in that direction. The new sixth five-year plan is founded squarely on the traditional primacy of heavy industry. But within this framework there is still evident a cautious, pragmatic orientation toward economic meliorism. This does not seem to have been basically affected by the various shifts in the top leadership during the post-Stalin years. For example, the policy of raising material incentives for the Soviet peasantry, initiated while Malenkov was premier, has continued since his demotion. The recent reaction against Stalinist architectural extravagance is accompanied by a new stress on utilitarian modes of construction and "conveniences for the population." As announced at the Twentieth Party Congress, reductions of the 48-hour working week are planned. Tuition fees for schooling are to be eliminated in a return to the system that prevailed before 1940. Some particularly onerous regulations, such as the ban on abortion, have been repealed. Wages for the lowest categories of industrial workers are to be increased somewhat in the impending general reorganization of the system of remuneration for industrial labor. In these and other ways, the post-Stalin regime is making clear its renunciation of the idea that propaganda "can do everything."

The other expressions of Stalin's transformism reviewed in the early part of this study have suffered more or less the same fate as the Stalin-Pavlov line. The accompanying cult of necessity has also shown a tendency to subside somewhat, and the open criticism of *Economic Problems of Socialism in the U.S.S.R.* from the rostrum of the Twentieth Party Congress may foreshadow a modification of Stalin's rigid view on "scientific laws." Michurin, like Pavlov, continues to hold a very high place of honor in Soviet official opinion. But Lysenko's dogmatic version of Michurin*ism,* with its flashy promises to "make evolution," is no longer being pressed in the previous spirit of militant intolerance. The plan to "transform the face of the capital" by erecting huge skyscrapers has not only been dropped but openly attacked in Soviet writings. The "Stalin Plan for the Transformation of Nature" has faded away as a policy slogan, although many of the individual projects comprised under it are being carried out—some, such as the reforestation scheme, on a much reduced scale.

A Soviet academician has contributed to the *Literary Gazette* an interesting epitaph on the Stalinist Will to Transform. Answering a reader's question, "Can the weather be controlled?" he notes various advances in this direction, but cautions against expecting too much. It is wrong, he says, to believe, as some do, that the weather changes of recent years in Soviet Russia are connected with "the newly constructed reservoirs, hydro-electric power stations, canals and other such circumstances" (i.e., the "Stalin Plan for the Transformation of Nature"). "It must be borne in mind that fluctuations of this kind have taken place previously in the historical past. Thus, for example, temperatures which we experienced this summer [1954] in the central zone were also experienced in these parts in 1891, 1892, 1920, 1936, and 1938."[38] In other words, despite the colossal expenditure of effort to "transform nature" in Soviet Russia, the weather there is basically no different now from what it was in the reign of Czar Alexander III. The effect of the academician's remarks is to explode the presumption upon which the Stalin scheme was based. His message is that the scheme was faulty in its underlying preconception that the climate is at the present stage of science controllable by man. In a deeper sense, he seems to be saying that, if unlimited control is not now an attainable objective, the drive to attain it is irrational.

To paraphrase an epigram, politics as practiced by Stalin in the final years of his reign was an art of the impossible. Under the regime of his successors, Soviet policy appears to be executing a strategic retreat into the realm of possibility.

NOTES

[1] *The Situation in Biological Science,* Moscow, 1948, p. 274.

[2] *Ibid.,* p. 37.

[3] Nathan Leites, *A Study of Bolshevism,* Glencoe, Ill., 1953, pp. 67, 84.

[4] *The Situation in Biological Science,* pp. 614-15.

[5] *Ibid.,* p. 615.

[6] J. V. Stalin, "Ekonomicheskie Problemy Sotsializma v SSSR" ("Economic Problems of Socialism in the USSR"), *Voprosy filosofii* (*Problems of Philosophy*), No. 5 (1952), pp. 6, 8, 47.

[7] B. M. Kedrov, "O materialisticheskom ponimanii zakonov prirody" ("On the Materialist Conception of Laws of Nature"), *Voprosy filosofii,* No. 6 (1952), pp. 69, 71.

[8] *History of the Communist Party of the Soviet Union (Bolshevik): Short Course,* Moscow, 1945, pp. 114-15.

[9] *Pravda,* April 19, 1952.

[10] *Ibid.*, September 23, 1949.

[11] *Ibid.*, September 27, 1949.

[12] *Ibid.*, July 1, 1950.

[13] For understandable reasons, Teplov failed to add that this task had also not previously been set.

[14] *Pravda*, July 2, 1950.

[15] B. M. Teplov, *Sovetskaya Psikhologicheskaya Nauka za 30 Let (Thirty Years of Soviet Psychological Science)*, Moscow, 1947, p. 14.

[16] N. P. Antonov, "Dialekticheskii materialism-teoreticheskaya osnova psikhologii" ("Dialectical Materialism—The Theoretical Foundation of Psychology"), *Voprosy filosofii*, No. 1 (1953), p. 195.

[17] A. V. Petrovsky, "K itogam soveshchaniya po psikhologii" ("On the Results of the Psychological Conference"), *Voprosy filosofii*, No. 5 (1953), p. 261.

[18] A. A. Smirnov, "Sostoyanie psikhologii i ee perestroika na osnove ucheniya I. P. Pavlova" ("The State of Psychology and Its Reconstruction on the Basis of the Teaching of I. P. Pavlov"), *Sovetskaya Pedagogika (Soviet Pedagogy)*, No. 8 (1952), p. 76.

[19] In this brief summary of earlier trends, I have followed the interpretation set forth by Raymond A. Bauer in his important study, *The New Man in Soviet Psychology*, Cambridge, Mass., 1952.

[20] Smirnov, *op.cit.*, p. 78.

[21] *Ibid.*, p. 76.

[22] For the sake of historical accuracy, it should be recorded that one N. P. Antonov, a psychologist from the town of Ivanovo, raised a lone and ineffectual voice of protest against this basic premise. In an article contributed to *Voprosy filosofii* (No. 1 [1953], p. 197), he wrote: "By attempting to reduce the whole psyche to reflexes, to temporary connections, we are thereby equating the salivation of a dog at the sound of a metronome with the most intricate phenomena of the spiritual life of man, with the conscious activity of people, with the brilliant creations of human intelligence in poetry, art, science, social and political life." Antonov's article immediately became the object of severe and concerted attack on the part of the other psychologists. But the quoted statement is valuable as an acknowledgment from a Soviet source of the full implications of the neo-Pavlovian trend.

[23] Smirnov, *op.cit.*, p. 67.

[24] V. P. Yagunkova, "Ob osnovnykh printsipakh reflektornoi teorii Akademika I. P. Pavlova" ("On the Fundamental Principles of the Reflex Theory of Academician I. P. Pavlov"), *Voprosy filosofii*, No. 3 (1953), p. 110.

[25] S. L. Rubinstein, "Uchenie I. P. Pavlova i nekotorye voprosy perestroiki psikhologiii ("The Teaching of I. P. Pavlov and Certain Questions of the Reconstruction of Psychology"), *Voprosy filosofii*, No. 3 (1952), p. 203.

[26] J. V. Stalin, *Marksizm i Voprosy Yazykoznanii (Marxism and Questions of Linguistics)*, Moscow, 1950, p. 39.

[27] D. P. Gorsky, "O roli yazyka v poznanii ("On the Role of Language in Cognition"), *Voprosy filosofii*, No. 2 (1953), p. 82.

[28] Suzanne K. Langer, *Philosophy in a New Key*, New York, 1948, pp. 48-49.

[29] Smirnov, *op.cit.*, p. 68.

[30] It is of interest in this connection to note the extraordinarily intense activity, after 1950, in the writing and rewriting of dictionaries in the Soviet Union.

[31] *Sovetskaya Kniga (Soviet Book)*, No. 8 (1953), p. 33.

[32] *Pravda*, July 2, 1954.

[33] "O filosofskikh voprosakh psikhologii" ("On Philosophical Questions of Psychology"), *Voprosy filosofii*, No. 4 (1954).

[34] S. L. Rubinstein, "Voprosy psikhologicheskoi teorii" ("Questions of Psychological Theory"), *Voprosy psikhologii*, No. 1 (1955), pp. 14-15.

[35] *Ibid.*, p. 17.

[36] *Partiinaya zhizn*, No. 11 (June 1955), pp. 39-40.

[37] *Voprosy filosofii*, No. 2 (1955), p. 85.

[38] *Literaturnaya Gazeta*, August 14, 1954.

H. E. Hoff (essay date 1959)

SOURCE: A review of *Experimental Psychology, and Other Essays*, in *Isis*, Vol. 50, No. 162, December, 1959, pp. 514-16.

[*In the following review, Hoff investigates the limitations and likely abuses of Pavlovian theory.*]

The esteem in which the world of science, and physiologists in particular, hold Ivan P. Pavlov is equalled only by that exhibited by the public at large. Indeed, he is one of the few physiologists of any age or country whose views have captured the public fancy and entered its everyday thinking; probably Freud alone in this century has had as great an influence. These considerations alone should insure for this volume of the selected works of Pavlov [***Experimental Psychology and Other Essays***] a large, interested, and favorably oriented audience. Beyond this, however, the western world has become aware that in the Soviet Union the works of Pavlov are accorded an even greater status as the foundation of Soviet psychiatry, as a fundamental guide to education, and presumably as the operating principle of "brainwashing." For these reasons this volume must, and very likely will, be read very carefully indeed. The reader will be disappointed and fail to find the clue to such weighty problems in these academic exercises so redolent of the nineteenth century, when, as Sherrington wrote, scientists knew far less and spread themselves out more than today.

The publisher tells us little about the auspices of the present volume, but the subtler details of expression indicate that the translator was probably Russian, while the designation of two paintings of Pavlov, one showing a visit by Maxim Gorky as "rare pictorial material," and the repeated references to Pavlov as "Academician Pavlov" or as "the eminent physiologist Pavlov" suggests that primarily the volume may well have been intended for a public less acquainted with Pavlov than is to be found in the English-speaking world.

The reader will expect to find a reasoned, and reasonable, account of the connection between the work of Pavlov and modern Russian psychiatry in the Introduction, which purports to deal with the significance of Pavlov's work; in this he will also be disappointed. Rather, the chapter begins by forwarding the argument that the main channels of Russian physiological thought, and in particular those determining the contributions of Sechenov and Pavlov, were indigenous. It then presents the developments that led to the concept of the conditioned reflex, and concludes with the statement that the last fifteen years of Pavlov's life (i.e., during the Soviet regime) were the best and most fruitful years of his school. During this period, and thereafter, "the theory of conditioned reflexes has been theoretically advanced by Pavlov's followers; it has found wide practical application in analyzing the various disturbances of the nervous activity and in elaborating ways and means of restoring it to normal."

Whatever the original audience for which this volume may have been intended, it is amply clear from the particular selections included, from the Introduction and from other recent publications, that this presentation is official, and represents present-day physiological orthodoxy in Russia. Nor are clues lacking to indicate why the Soviet hierarchy has been so attracted to Pavlov's doctrines: (a) Pavlov's injunction that physiologists must "control" physiological phenomena, (b) that the conditioning stimuli for the conditioned reflex are "indifferent," and (c) that conditioned reflexes may be transferred genetically to subsequent generations, where they become part of the unconditioned reflex apparatus. Here are the germs of thought control or manipulation of the human mind, of the cynical view that human beings can be conditioned to absolutely anything, and the wishful thinking that once a population is conditioned in this way, future generations will be born with ready-made replicas of their parents' painfully acquired conditioning. We learn from Jones's biography of Freud that he too believed in the inheritance of acquired characteristics; indeed, this belief was common throughout the nineteenth century. Few scientists clung to the belief as long as did Pavlov, and no one else found a powerful state to sponsor it as an article of faith.

The earlier papers of the volume do much to indicate the physiological climate from which Pavlov's contributions sprang, and which formed the matrix of his development of the conditioned reflex. Fundamentally, Pavlov thought in terms of the primitive reflexology of the pre-Sherringtonian period, when the explanation for much of the normal and even pathological behavior was being sought in the reflex. In Pavlov's paper concerning "Trophic Innervation" published in 1922, we see the persistence of this all-pervading, non-specific "nervism" in a discussion that has little to add to Whytt's essay on the sympathy between parts or to the Brounonian doctrine of hyperirritability and hypoirritability as the cause of disease—indeed throughout the volume Pavlov makes it clear that to him the major etiological factor in many if not most diseases of the nervous system is the "weakness" of one system or another, and, like Brown, Pavlov prescribes appropriate stimulants or sedatives.

But the main concern of this book—and the main concern of the reader—centers around what the Russians term "the higher nervous activity" and the explicit claim by his followers that Pavlov's work constitutes an essential break-through on the age-old problem of the relation between psychical and physical phenomena. Pavlov himself may not have been quite so certain of this, for as late as 1932 he declared at the International Congress of Physiology at Rome, "I am convinced that an important stage in the development of human thought is approaching—a stage when the physiological and the psychological, the objective and the subjective, will really merge, when the painful contradiction between our mind and our body and their contraposition will either actually be solved or disappear in a natural way." With this hope, no one could take exception; that it has already been accomplished, either by Pavlov or by anyone else, is quite another matter and the very bone of the contention.

With Pavlov's intention, no physiologist can quarrel; to express the action of the whole in the terms of its parts, to explain organismal behavior by unit behavior is indeed the function of the physiologist. It is then his task to explain those phenomena that center in the brain in the vocabulary of the nerve impulse, the reflex, the synapse and whatever concepts describe the behavior of the single units of nervous activity and their mutual interrelations. This approach presupposes, of course, a complete understanding of neurophysiology on the one hand, and of psychology and psychiatry on the other. It will be abundantly clear to the unprejudiced reader that neither requirement has been fulfilled, and that terms like excitation, inhibition, and facilitation, fail more and more to explain the phenomenon of the simplest reflex, much less the behavior of the whole organism, for one very good reason at least that *place* and *time* must be integrated with *process* before a really satisfactory account of the function of the nervous system can be given.

Here is probably the reason that Freud and Sherrington are listed as the greatest enemies of Pavlov's teachings, and why such a sharply defined dichotomy is established between the "idealistic" Western neurophysiology and psychiatry and the "materialism" attributed to Pavlov. To Sherrington, who knew not a little about the workings of the cortex, the reflex was simply an inadequate basis for a full explanation of the operation of the brain; to Freud, the mind was too complicated to be anchored to the reflex. The least pleasant parts of this book are, indeed, pages devoted to intemperate attacks on Sherrington, attributed to Pavlov. Some light might be thrown on their authenticity by quoting from an address by an "official" Soviet Pavlovian disciple, A. G. Ivanov-Smolensky, referred to below: "His attempt to prove the incorrectness of my views regarding the relation between the subjective and the objective by quoting *The Pavlov Wednesdays* is unconvincing. The notes of one of Pavlov's disciples and the stenographic reports which make up the three volumes of *The Pavlov Wednesdays* were never read, checked, or initialled by Pavlov. They contain many errors, inaccuracies, and distortions of what Pavlov actually said, and this is true of the passage which Professor Gushuni quoted."

This volume, a monograph by Ivanov-Smolensky entitled "Essays on the Patho-Physiology of the Higher Nervous Activity," published in 1954 by the Foreign Languages Publishing House of Moscow, an earlier report of a "Scientific Session on the Physiological Teaching of Academician I. P. Pavlov" of the Academy of Sciences of the U.S.S.R., published by the same bureau, and Wortis' account of "Soviet Psychiatry" (Baltimore: Williams and Wilkins, 1950), indicate unmistakably that we are witnessing the creation of a new dogma in neurophysiology, and the canonization of its ostensible creator, Pavlov. We will probably have to go back to Galen to find a phenomenon quite to equal it. In both cases we see that it entails the rejection of the main attributes of the protagonists; the unfettered utilization of the experimental method, and the broadest possible integration of the work and ideas of other people. It is well known how Galen's views were sharpened, crystallized and solidified by later commentators; his actual views on the circulation were by no means as rigid as the conventional "Galenical" dogma, of Arabic origin. So, too, there is an essential difference between Pavlov's statement at Rome in 1932, previously quoted, and the claim that the stage where "physiological and the psychical, the objective and the subjective will really merge" is now here, or past, and that Pavlov's work provides the detailed blueprint of the unification.

Looking back over the centuries to the long period when a Galenical dogma was slavishly adhered to, and then to the revolution against it and the renaissance of science in Europe, one is struck by the thought that the renaissance was in reality a return to the essence of real Galenism—the experimental method in medicine—and that Galen's real contributions have since been lost sight of and largely neglected. We can thus predict that the present trend in Russia may well stultify the very qualities that made Pavlov one of the great physiologists, and lessen the recognition that is his due.

W. Horsley Gantt (essay date 1960)

SOURCE: "Pavlov and Darwin," in *Evolution after Darwin,* edited by Sol Tax, University of Chicago Press, 1960, pp. 219-38.

[*In the following essay, Gantt equates the importance of the scientific discoveries of Pavlov with those of Charles Darwin and surveys Pavlovian and post-Pavlovian research.*]

The lives of Pavlov and Darwin overlapped. When Darwin was producing the great work which we now celebrate, Pavlov was a stripling lad of ten years, romping and scuffling with the urchins on the streets of Ryazan in central Russia. They both lived in the great age of the adolescence of science, in the century when science, like a rambunctious youth, felt the cocksureness of the teen-ager.

Darwin's theory of evolution liberated thinking among the masses. He gave to science a freedom from authority; he justified its right to stand in a new field upon facts. Pavlov was perhaps a more militant and conscientious champion of science than Darwin. The liberalization of science for which Darwin was responsible arose more from the impact of the theory of evolution than from any missionary zeal on Darwin's part. But Pavlov had the ardor of the reformer. He felt very much the prevalence of subjective thinking, the vague, confused arguments that permeated the psychology of that period. And it was against this kind of reasoning and false explanations that Pavlov struggled rather than against the existence and the importance of our subjective living.

Although Darwin and Pavlov were unlike in personality and in methods of working, in one major way they resembled each other. Darwin's concepts were compounded from numerous detailed observations—observations made under many conditions, in many organisms, in many environments. Pavlov, too, was a keen observer. Over the portals of the new building for research in Koltushi, erected for him a few years before his death in 1936, he had inscribed the words "Observation and Observation." Not only did Pavlov rely on this attribute in his own experiments, but in epitomizing the characteristics of the scientist, he emphasized the strict collection of facts, the method which Darwin used as the basis for his theory of evolution (Pavlov, 1941, p. 189).

Darwin's theory of evolution, although perhaps less firmly established as a law than are some of the Pavlovian principles, has nevertheless had a more profound effect upon popular thinking than have the discoveries of Pavlov. This is because Darwin's facts seemingly conflicted with the teachings of "orthodox" religion. Darwin has had the effect not so much of confuting the basis for religious beliefs as of defining the proper domains of religion and science.

Pavlov accomplished what was of equal importance for our mental life. He no more settled the age-old riddles of the fundamental nature of mind and of our spiritual life than Darwin solved the fundamentals of religion. But he did show that mental phenomena—the elements of our psychical life—have a physiological component and that in many of their aspects they should be studied by strictly scientific methods, the same methods that had been successfully used in the study of the digestive juices—for which Pavlov received the Nobel Prize in 1903.

This discovery was new in its field, but it was not new in principle for the function of the living organism. The study of the laws of nervous activity by physiological methods involved no principles that had not been employed, e.g., for the study of muscular activity: when we move our arm it can be explained as a voluntary action or as a system of levers and fulcrums according to Archimedes or as a utilization of chemical energy. For the thinking of the general public, this was nothing revolutionary.

But whenever science deals with the most complex functions of the nervous system and its contact with the subjective life and mental life, whether this be in psychology, psychophysiology, or psychiatry, Pavlov's discoveries have a profound influence, an influence which at present is barely realized. The "battle for the mind"[1] initiated by Pavlov is only in its infancy; it is still enshrouded in a good deal of obscurity or even confusion.

Despite the general photographic resemblances between Darwin and Pavlov, their marked differences in personality led to the equally marked differences in their methods. Though both were accurate observers, Darwin's observations were as a naturalist, Pavlov's as an experimenter. Darwin laboriously accumulated facts over a long period and methodically assembled them until they convincingly supported the theory of evolution, which had been known beforehand. Pavlov's observations of laboratory facts were collected with equal care, but he then elaborated them into novel and original theories of brain action, often hypothetical. Also, in theorizing, Pavlov occasionally allowed himself great latitude of generalization, as when he spoke of the "reflex of freedom" and the "reflex of purpose."

Pavlov on Inheritance of Acquired Characteristics

Both Darwin and Pavlov considered the question of the inheritance of acquired characteristics. Before Darwin, Lamarck had given a dogmatic formulation for the mechanism, and Darwin felt that new traits were passed on to the progeny through the mixing of blood of the parents. Darwin's view, of course, was later superseded by the work of Mendel and subsequently by the principles of the gene theory (Weissmann, Morgan, *et al.*).

This belief of Darwin's is perhaps one reason why he is so popular currently in Russia. As his views on inheritance are generally known, I shall quote him only briefly:

> It seems probable that some actions, which were at first performed consciously, have become through habit and association converted into reflex actions, and are now so firmly fixed and inherited, that they are performed, even when not of the least use (Darwin, 1872, p. 39).

Chauncy Leake quotes a Russian physiologist as follows:

> Darwin means to us, perhaps, something a little different from what he means to Western Europeans or Americans. You think mostly of Darwin, I believe, or Darwinism as the ruthless struggle of nature, in which the strong conquer and eliminate the weak; in which nature rends, tooth and claw, and so on. We do not think that is Darwinism. That is Nietzsche and Huxley. But, to us, the important aspects of Darwinism is his principle of the survival of living things on the basis of their adaptations to a changing environment (Leake, 1959, p. 155).

The position of Pavlov in supporting Lamarckianism is surrounded by confusion, chiefly from two sources. First, although Pavlov often asserted in the 1920's that some of the educational efforts of the Bolsheviki were misdirected—because they considered as conditional reflexes what were really unconditional reflexes and therefore unmodifiable through education—he has been used as a champion of environment versus heredity by the dominating Lysenko school in the U.S.S.R. in its emphasis on modification by environment and in its struggle against the geneticists.

Second, this seeming contradiction in Pavlov's beliefs stems from a paper he read in 1923 concluding that conditional reflexes established experimentally in mice could be inherited—a position that Kleitman and Razran emphasize he did not refute (Razran, 1958). In the speech, delivered to the Eleventh International Physiological Congress meeting in Edinburgh, Pavlov said, apropos of inheritance:

> The latest experiments (which are not yet finished) show that the conditioned reflexes, i.e., the highest nervous activity, are inherited. At present some experiments on white mice have been completed. Conditioned reflexes to electric bells are formed, so that the animals are trained to run to their feeding place on the ringing of the bell. The following results have been obtained:
>
> The first generation of white mice required 300 lessons. Three hundred times was it necessary to combine the feeding of the mice with the ringing

> of the bell in order to accustom them to run to the feeding place on hearing the bell ring. The second generation required, for the same result, only 100 lessons. The third generation learned after 30 lessons, the fourth generation required only 10. The last generation which I saw before leaving Petrograd learned after 5 repetitions. The sixth generation will be tested after my return. I think it very probable that after some time a new generation of mice will run to the feeding place on hearing the bell with no previous training.
>
> It is well known that a chicken when it just comes from the egg immediately begins to pick up any black spot on the floor trying to find some grain, thus showing that it was an inborn reflex from the eye to the food. Why should we not build up the same reaction, not from the eye but from the ear as indicated in the case of the white mice? (quoted in Razran, 1958).

Razran points out in his paper, "Pavlov and Lamarck," that the theme of this address was not primarily inheritance of acquired characteristics, that this was "really only a small, but striking, aside." Previously, as Razran mentions, Pavlov had inclined to the view that it was possible for some habits to become fixed by heredity, viz., the unconditioned reflexes. For example, Pavlov said in 1913: "One may suppose that some of the conditional temporary connections may be later transformed into unconditional reflexes by heredity" (1928, p. 236). Again, in 1914, he said, "It is highly probable (and there are to this effect some factual indications) that, when the same conditions of life are maintained in series of successive generations, newly formed conditional reflexes uninterruptedly become constant unconditioned reflexes" (1928, p. 242).

Razran says, "No mention whatsoever was made of the problem in any of Pavlov's subsequent writings before 1923."

Much attention has been devoted to the postwar conflict in the U.S.S.R. between Lysenko and Michurin, on the one hand—the champions of environmental influence—and the geneticists represented by Vavilov and I believe earlier by the views of Kozlov. There has been so much written in this country concerning Lysenko and his claims that it is unnecessary to give details. Although the question of environment and heredity still has its different advocates, the opinions of competent authorities such as H. J. Muller, who spent eighteen months in Russia and knew both sides of the Vavilov-Lysenko controversy, indicate that Lysenko's claims are political rather than scientific (Zirkle, 1950).

The question of Lysenko's false claims is not so much of interest to us as is his effect in Russia on the views attributed to Pavlov there. Pavlov has been set up twenty years after his death as in violent opposition to Morgan and the Western geneticists, whereas Morgan's statement in regard to the 1923 address is by no means the virulent, anti-Pavlovian attack which the Russians have attributed to him. Morgan said, "There was some consternation in 1923 when the great Russian physiologist, Pawlow, reported the results of experiments that go far beyond what most Lamarckians have dared hope. Pawlow's conclusions—and as yet we have only his conclusions—are very surprising" (1925, p. 157).

I was in Pavlov's laboratory at the time that the experiments in question were being conducted by Studentsov; the purpose was to determine whether successive generations of mice would form conditional reflexes more quickly then their forebears. There was an ingenious apparatus, designed by Professor Hanike, by means of which laboratory mice were given all their feedings preceded by a conditional stimulus. At this signal the mice went from one cage into another, where they received food, and the number of times before they learned to go when the bell rang was recorded. Studentsov reported the facts of the lesser number of trials required for successive generations of mice to learn, as mentioned in Pavlov's Edinburgh address.

Studentsov died before the end of the experiments, I believe after they had been carried through 11 generations. When, with Pavlov's emphasis on thorough control of experiments and his habit of giving the same theme to at least two, sometimes three, collaborators working in different institutions, this problem was assigned to another investigator, the results did not show that successive generations formed the conditional reflex of going into the food cage at the signal any more quickly than did their forebears. The repetition of these experiments was done, as I recall, about 1924-26.

Since the later experiments turned out negatively, i.e., did not support inheritance of conditional reflexes, and since Pavlov had never read a paper the main theme of which was the inheritance of acquired characteristics, no significance is to be attached to the fact that he did not write a special article retracting these views. In fact, in the bibliography of his ***Lectures on Conditioned Reflexes,*** there is no record of any article by Studentsov or on the subject of inheritance.

I have described Pavlov's revised experiments as follows:

> The apparatus for forming conditioned reflexes in mice is very ingenious; it was perfected by Professor Hanike in 1925. When a given bell sounds, the mice run to a certain place to get food, and in going there they have to cross a platform attached to springs. When they step on this platform the act is registered on a revolving drum. A revision of the former work on inheritance of conditioned reflexes is being carried out with an entirely new apparatus. The mice now receive all their food (twenty times during each night) preceded by the bell. It is all done mechanically, so that the presence of the operator is not required. A clock arrangement makes twenty electrical contacts during the night (the natural time for the feeding of mice), rings the bell, and a few moments later opens a valve which allows grain to drop into a certain compartment of each cage. When the bell

rings there is a general migration of the mice into the "dining room." The mice never get food without the bell. Males and females are kept in separate cages, so that the number of oncoming generations can be carefully regulated. When an experiment is made the mice are removed to a special cage where the results can be registered automatically (Gantt, 1928).

In a discussion which I had in 1926 with Pavlov about this work, he told me that his conclusions about the inheritance of acquired characteristics was one of the biggest errors of his scientific career. He attributed the mistake to the fact that he accepted—contrary to his usual custom—the results of Studentsov without personally supervising the experiments. He told me then that he had given the problem to another collaborator, whose results did not confirm those of Studentsov.

Neither in this case nor in any other is there evidence that Pavlov tended to cling to his theories or his concepts when further facts did not support them. Like other scientists, he made errors. One of these was his statement that the regulation of the pancreatic secretion was effected solely through the nerves. The discovery by Bayliss and Starling of the hormone secretion overthrew Pavlov's theory of nerve control as the *sole* regulator. To give up this conviction was difficult, but Pavlov stated to his collaborators after he had confirmed the experiments of Bayliss and Starling: "Of course they are right. We cannot claim to a monopoly on all scientific truth."

Pavlov and Types

Darwin's teachings emphasize the almost imperceptible gradations occurring in nature between different organisms in the process of evolution. Ernst Mayr (1959) emphasizes how the Darwinian cannot be a typologist:

> Darwin introduced into the scientific literature a new way of thinking, "population thinking." What is this population thinking and how does it differ from typological thinking, the then prevailing mode of thinking? Typological thinking no doubt had its roots in the earliest efforts of primitive man to classify the bewildering diversity of nature into categories. The eidos of Plato is the formal philosophical condification of this form of thinking. According to it there are a limited number of fixed, unchangeable "ideas" underlying the observed variability, with the eidos (idea) being the only thing that is fixed and real while the observed variability has no more reality than the shadows of an object on a cave wall, as it is stated in Plato's allegory. The discontinuities between these natural "ideas" (types), it was believed, account for the frequency of gaps in nature. Most of the great philosophers of the 17th, 18th and 19th centuries were influenced by the idealistic philosophy of Plato, and the thinking of this school dominated the thinking of the period. Since there is no gradation between types, gradual evolution is basically a logical impossibility for the typologist.
>
> The ultimate conclusions of the population thinker and of the typologist are precisely the opposite. For the typologist, the type (eidos) is real and the variation an illusion, while for the populationist the type (average) is an abstraction and only the variation is real. No two ways of looking at nature could be more different.

Pavlov said that the great difference between the human and the subhuman animals was in the language function, which he called the "second signaling system." He recognized that language represents a new function, present only in the human, upon which is based the quality responsible for the superior advances of *Homo sapiens*, viz., the capacity for symbolization and abstraction. Pavlov considered words not only as secondary signals—the signals of signals—but as a distinct and new function of the brain.

> Here is introduced a new principle of higher activity (abstraction—and at the same time the generalisation of the multitude of signals of the former system, in its turn again with the analysis and synthesis of these new generalised signals), the principle of the conditioning limitless orientation in the surrounding world and of creating the highest adaptation of the human—science both in the form of a humanitarian empiricism as well as in its specialised form (1941, p. 114).

Pavlov divided the human being (perhaps without sufficient justification) into two main types according to the extent of the development of the second signaling system: In the first group were those who used mainly the first signaling system (e.g., artists), and in the second group were those with a more highly developed second signaling system—the scientist, mathematicians, etc., who depend chiefly upon abstractions. That Pavlov considered this function a definite human one is attested to by his statement (1941, p. 162):

> Until the time when *Homo sapiens* appeared animals were connected with environment so that the direct impressions fell upon the different receptors and were conducted to the corresponding cells of the central nervous system. These impressions were the several signals of the external object. However there arises in the developing human an extraordinary perfection, the signals of the second order, the signals of the primary signals in the form of words—the spoken, the heard, the seen word. Finally it came about that through these new signals everything was designated that the human being perceived both from the environment and from his inner world, and these signals commenced to serve him not only in communicating with other men, but also when he was alone.

The theory of natural selection rests upon the breaking-down of types. Pavlov, on the other hand, found definite variations among his dogs which led him to put them into four categories based upon the Hippocratic division into four temperaments—the extremes of choleric and melancholic, and the middle types of sanguine and phlegmatic (1928, p. 370).

Although the division into four rigid types on the basis of the predominance of excitatory and inhibitory conditional reflexes, as well as on the general behavior, may not be entirely satisfactory, there does seem to be some division possible, derived from the circumscribed conditional reflex studies in the dogs. In my own studies, although I have not been able to substantiate the strict conformity to the four Hippocratic temperaments, I do find it profitable to divide the dogs into groups according to their susceptibility to stress (Gantt, 1943).

Recent work from Russia on the typology of dogs, as well as of the human, is even more promising. Thus the work of Krasusky on the reaction of dogs to certain drugs (e.g., caffeine) is claimed to give a more rational basis for a classification of types. Krasusky makes the important revision in describing the behavior that external behavior is not to be taken as an adequate criterion, since this depends to a great extent upon what the individual is accustomed to, such as the presence of the human being, its early training, and environment. This work depends upon concepts that seem to be opposed to those of Lysenko. Though heredity is emphasized in Krasusky's research, there is no definite mention made of its relation to Lysenkoism.

A biochemical basis for a study of types in the human being has been laid by the Protopopov School of Psychiatry in Kiev. Their results support the view that manic psychotic attacks can be predicted by biochemical and metabolic studies some months before they occur and can be prevented by appropriate therapy.

Validity of Darwin's Observations in the Light of Modern Research

In his book *The Expression of the Emotions in Man and Animals* (1872) Darwin made profound deductions from careful observations, but his formulations have been neglected in the century since publication. I must admit that I was also unaware of Darwin's concepts on these subjects until this year. However, his formulations, made without benefit of laboratory or equipment, are so close in many cases to what I have found over the past thirty years by the conditional reflex methods that I must insert a digest of his observations, gathered from various statements throughout his book and placed here under the headings by which we now express the topics.

SCHIZOKINESIS

As I have defined this principle, it involves (1) specifically, a lack of parallel between the general autonomic (respiratory, cardiac) patterns and the more voluntary motor ones and (2) the extension of this principle to a persistance of useless reactions to the environment, representing maladaptations. There are at least twelve separate references in Darwin's book to differences between cardiac and muscular responses, similar to those I have seen in the laboratory and which I call "schizokinesis." Thus on page 28 Darwin says, "Some actions ordinarily associated through habit with certain states of the mind may be partially repressed through the will, and in such cases the muscles which are least under the separate control of the will, [the cardio-respiratory] are the most liable to act, causing movements which we recognize as expressive."

He goes further and states: "In all cases there seems to exist a profound antagonism between the same movements, as directed by the will and by a reflex stimulant, in the force with which they are performed and in the facility with which they are excited." Darwin also invokes the support of Claude Bernard: "L'influence du cerveau tend donc à entraver les movements réflexes, a limiter leur force et leur étendue."

In regard to the principle of schizokinesis (maladaptation) in disease Darwin quotes Maudsley as saying that "reflex movements which commonly effect a useful end may, under the changed circumstances of disease, do great mischief, becoming even the occasion of violent suffering and of a most painful death." According to Darwin, many of these responses that he states become purposeless or even harmful do so through a relationship between another emotional state and the original one, so that the secondary emotional state may produce an entirely inappropriate response. Many examples are given, such as cats shaking their feet at the mere sound of flowing water, as if they were actually standing in it, and the pounding of kittens with their extended claws against numerous objects, a movement appropriate only for the mother's mammae.

In regard to the self-destructiveness of the cardiac reaction, he says, "The heart beats quickly, wildly, and violently; but whether it pumps the blood more efficiently through the body may be doubted, for the surface seems bloodless and the strength of the muscles soon fails." Darwin repeatedly emphasizes the maladaptability of certain habits (conditional reflexes): "My object is to show that certain movements were originally performed for a definite end, and that, under nearly the same circumstances, they are still pertinaciously performed through habit when *not of the least use*" (italics mine).

CARDIAC CONDITIONAL REFLEX

Although the existence of a cardiac component of the conditional reflex has not yet been recognized in physiology in this centenary year, Darwin repeatedly cites well-known instances of what could be called a *cardiac component of the conditional reflex:* "When a man or horse starts, his heart beats wildly against his ribs, and here it may be truly said we have an organ which has never been under the control of the will, partaking in the general reflex movements of the body." The relationship is clearly expressed by him on page 73: "When the heart is affected it reacts on the brain; and the state of the brain again reacts through the pneumogastric nerve on the heart; so that under any excitement there will be much mutual action and reaction between these, the two most important organs of the body. . . . We must not overlook the indirect effects of habit on the heart."

Again he points out that this is so even though the heart is not "under the control of the will." A clear statement of cardiac conditioning follows indicating that muscular exertion is not the cause of the increase in cardiac activity: "On the principle of association, of which so many instances have been given, we may feel nearly sure that any sensation or emotion, as great as pain or rage, which has habitually led to much muscular action, will immediately influence the flow of nerve-force to the heart, although there may not be at the time any muscular exertion."

He states further that when the cerebrospinal system is highly excited "violent movements follow," and he points out that "voluntary muscular exertion relieves pain. . . . The anticipation of a pleasure leads to purposeless and extravagant movement. . . . Persons suffering from grief seek relief from violent frantic movements" (p. 176). In infants, too, he observes that "screaming brings relief."

All these observations by Darwin are strikingly parallel to what we have observed in the laboratory—that a quiescent state follows intense activity (Cruet and Gantt, *The Bulletin of the Johns Hopkins Hospital,* December, 1959).

EFFECT OF "PERSON"

We have devoted considerable attention at our Laboratory to the marked influence on dogs of the presence of other dogs and of human beings. We have seen an especially strong effect during tactile stimulation, such as rubbing behind the ears; in some animals the heart rate is reduced from 160 to 40 or less.

Darwin notes the wide prevalence of the effect of tactile stimulation in nature, plus a "strong desire to touch the beloved person. . . . Dogs and cats manifestly take pleasure in rubbing against their master and in being rubbed. . . . Monkeys delight in fondling and in being fondled" (1872, p. 233). He mentions kissing, rubbing noses, patting of the arms, etc. as human expressions, regarding kissing as innate "insofar as it depends on the pleasure derived from contact with the beloved person" (p. 352). He also describes a patient with heart disease and an extremely irregular pulse which "invariably became regular as soon as my Father entered the room" (p. 339).

While not agreed as to whether this desire for social contact is innate and constitutes a homeostatic drive, psychologists are well aware of its importance to mental health; much clinical data is accumulating on the effects of personal isolation and the implications of family environment for subsequent intellectual and personality growth.

EARLY LEARNING

In recent years the sterile environment-heredity issue has been succeeded by studies of a number of more specific factors that determine learning. There is an awareness of "critical periods," at which the individual reaches a state of maturation that facilitates learning of a particular skill or where he "suddenly" begins to respond to a certain set of environmental stimuli.

The phenomenon of "imprinting," introduced by Heinroth in 1911 and since studied in many species using various behavioral items, occurs at an exceptionally early age and involves sudden learning of a very tenacious sort. Perhaps the best-known example is that of Konrad Lorenz' greylag geese who were hatched in isolation by him and thereafter, as their behavior clearly indicated, regarded him as their mother.

If the young individual at a readiness point is not given opportunity in the form of the necessary equipment or a reasonable substitute or if he is denied the freedom to act, the normal behavior involved may fail to appear. Young mammals at Liddell's "Animal Behavior Farm" at Cornell, separated from their mothers soon after birth, failed to develop skill in sucking. Such was probably the case leading to observations by Hippocrates and by Harvey and later quoted by Darwin in *The Expressions of the Emotions,* namely, that "a young animal [removed from its mother] forgets in the course of a few days the art of sucking, and cannot without some difficulty again acquire it." An interesting corollary is the oft-observed refusal by the mother to accept the return of the offspring which has been snatched away.

There is certainly an element of timing here, too. Soon after birth, or later at "weaning-time," the young animal readily adapts to substitutes for mammae. However, being separated at a point in-between from that to which he has become accustomed, may result in abnormal and even fatal behavior.

Another learned item, eating habits, play a prominent and often pernicious role. Darwin (1872) refers to various caterpillars that, having regularly fed on the leaves of a particular tree, refused to eat the leaves of another kind of tree, although it could have supplied all their nutritional needs. We have observed similar food habits in dogs, and Stefansson has told me that arctic dogs refuse meat, which is not customarily part of their diet.

POST-PAVLOVIAN RESEARCH

The main concepts of Pavlov have stood firm against assaults, as have the principles he derived. Many of his statements which he regarded as working theories are still in the realm of theory: difficult differentiation as the source of experimental neuroses; the nature, perhaps even the existence, of the processes of induction; concentration and irradiation, as he conjectured them; the explanation of sleep as the spreading of internal inhibition. On the other hand, many of his theories have later been supported by facts; thus, long before the discovery of chemical transmitters such as acetylcholine and sympathin, Pavlov postulated that excitation and inhibition in the brain depend upon definite chemical substances.

EVOLUTION OF CONDITIONAL REFLEX FUNCTION

Using two criteria for the extension of the conditional reflex, (1) formation of the positive reflex and (2) its differentiation, Pickenhain (1959) concludes that in Hydra, Infusoria, and other organisms up to the echinoderms, there is a summation of excitation rather than new formation of the conditional reflex.

A central nervous system is necessary for the conditional reflex. Boycott and Young formed food and defense, excitatory and inhibitory, conditional reflexes in goldfish. Through extirpation of the phylogenetically most recent formations, viz., the cerebral ganglia, the conditional reflex formation was impaired or destroyed. Voronin formed conditional reflexes to light and to defense in crabs; these could be extinguished but were spontaneously restored the next day. In many insects conditional reflexes have been elaborated. Nikitina produced secretory fibers based on temperature in silk worms after 10-15 reinforcements, using change in light as stimulus. In bees Von Frisch has formed many diverse conditional reflexes reinforced by sugar syrup. Voskresenskaya determined that the head ganglion in the bee was required for the conditional reflex. Fankhauser and Vernon showed in salamandors that the number of ganglion cells is related to the conditional reflex formation. Simple formation of conditional reflexes, as well as differentiation, occurs after virtually the same number of reinforcements throughout the animal kingdom. Thus Angyan of Budapest states that he was able to form conditional reflexes in worms after 7 reinforcements. But how the experiments are performed is also important, as shown by the work of Voronin; he obtained formation in crabs after 25-50 reinforcements; in fish, after 30-45; in birds, after 40-120; in rabbits, after 47-107; in dogs, after 3-36; in chimpanzees, after 4-6 reinforcements.

For optimal formation of the conditional reflex in the various genera, it is necessary to observe the natural living conditions and not to base conclusions too strictly on the artificial laboratory environment, e.g., fish are grossly disturbed by an environment in which birds, rabbits, and higher animals are undisturbed. Also fish can form conditional reflexes to such complex stimuli as light plus tone better than to these separately. Nor can fish form trace reflexes where the interval is longer than 5-10 seconds. Trace reflexes are difficult in fowls, rabbits, and dogs, and unstable, while in apes inhibition is elaborated after 3 reinforcements and can be retained, as shown by Voronin, for 8 years.

The development of a centralized nervous system is expressed (1) in the ganglionic chain of the insects and (2) in the central nervous system of the chordates, with its opportunity for plasticity. There is added another mechanism, that of language, Pavlov's second signaling system, in the human being. A primitive form of abstraction is present in subhuman species, some of which can differentiate 7 different kinds of optical stimuli, e.g., in some birds 2 and in others 7. These abstractions seem to be limited in various analyzers to 7 possibilities, and even in the human being with tachistoscopic stimuli it is said that there can be only 7 good differentiations (Pickenhain, 1959).

It is interesting to emphasize that the simple formation of the conditional reflex occurs with nearly the same speed in all animals, viz., after a few combinations of the environmental situation and the unconditional stimulus. But the conditional reflex, though formed, may not be overtly expressed, as I have demonstrated with the cardiac conditional reflex.

The cardiac conditional reflex may be formed in the dog after 1 reinforcement, while the motor conditional is not seen until after 30 or 40 reinforcements, a phenomenon which I call *schizokinesis*.

The difference among the species of animals is not in the speed of the formation of the simple conditional reflex, but in the complexity, elaborations, and extension of the symbolizations that are possible. In the area where there can be formation, however, there is comparable plasticity in adaptation, which means that the lower animals can adapt to those situations within their limitations with the same readiness as can those animals higher on the zoological ladder.

The comparable speed of formation of the conditional reflex throughout the animal scale may rest upon a basic property of nervous tissue. This finds a parallel in the statement of von Muralt that everywhere in nature the passage of the nerve impulse is mediated through acetylcholine or nor-adrenalin, and everywhere the conversion of energy into movement occurs by one mechanism, viz., the chemical change involving adenosine triphosphate (ATP).

EXTENSION OF PAVLOVIAN CONCEPTS

Many other responses and reactions in the organism have been brought within the CR methodology since Pavlov. Bykov (1957) in Russia has done more than anyone else in this field. He has shown that renal secretion of urine, metabolic exchanges, thermal regulation of the body, hormonal secretions, ovulation, electrophysical components, and many others can be readily elaborated as CR's. In the Pavlovian Laboratory of the Johns Hopkins Medical School, we have also extended this field to include vestibular reactions of equilibration (Gantt, Löwenbach, and Brown, 1953), respiratory and cardiovascular responses, including heart rate and blood pressure (Dykman and Gantt, 1958; Gantt and Dykman, 1957), as well as responses to stimuli placed within the central nervous system (interoceptors) (Bykov, 1957). In the human being we have added to these the psychogalvanic response (Reese, Doss, and Gantt, 1953).

The cardiovascular conditional reflex.—Our chief interest since 1939 has been a study of the cardiac responses.

I began this with Dr. W. C. Hoffmann, who came from Norway as a Rockefeller Fellow to work in my laboratory in September, 1939. The cardiovascular responses have both advantages and disadvantages for this type of work. The disadvantage lies in the widespread connections of this system with nearly all events occurring within and outside the organism and the consequent difficulty of controls and isolation of the individual. The advantage of including the cardiovascular system is that, on the theoretical side, it reveals mechanisms, to be pointed out subsequently, which we could never discover from the conventional secretory or motor components. Moreover, the cardiac response, unlike the motor and secretory, can give a measure below zero, as it were, viz., by a decrease in heart rate (HR) or blood pressure below the control, whereas with movement or with secretion, we cannot get such a negative measure, since the absence of secretion or movement is as far as we can go at present without complicated procedures, e.g., muscle potentials.

The first question that concerned us was whether there really existed a cardiovascular conditional reflex—which, for the sake of brevity, I will call the "HR-CR." The majority of physiologists and cardiologists whose opinions we sought were inclined to the view that the cardiovascular system would not participate to a measurable extent in the CR. There is, of course, another aspect of the question, and that is whether there is a cardiac CR to an adequate stimulus to the heart, as well as whether the cardiac system participates as a component in responses that are not primarily specific to the heart, viz., food and slight faradic stimulation. This has not been investigated so thoroughly, although there is sufficient evidence of a specific cardiovascular response to adequate stimuli.

To epitomize two decades of work from my laboratory on the cardiac reactions: the cardiac component of the CR's are, in general, parallel to the secretory and motor; there is a quantitative relationship with the intensity of the excitatory CR, a marked difference between the cardiac component of the excitatory and inhibitory CR's, a precise cardiac time reflex, etc. The inhibitory CR is characterized by a slight rise in HR, with a marked subsequent decrease below normal. Here we have in the cardiac response a measure of inhibition which gives an explanation to the quiescent phase and sleep, which Pavlov found resulting from inhibitions.

More important, however, than the resemblances between the specific CR movements and secretions and the cardiac rate (HR) component of the CR are the differences. First, the cardiac response is often the more sensitive of the measures we have employed. Second, contrary to our expectation, the HR-CR appears more quickly than either the motor or the secretory component. Thus it is often necessary to give 50-100 reinforcements before we see the elaboration of the CR to the motor or to secretory stimuli. But with the cardiac measure, we often see that a CR is formed after one reinforcement with the unconditional stimulus (food or pain) (Pinto, Newton, and Gantt, 1957). This quick formation of the CR explains much that was not evident previously; thus from laboratory studies it appeared that many repetitions were necessary to produce the CR, while the experiences of life showed that a CR was frequently formed after one coincidence of a physiological stimulus and its symbol, e.g., a single coincidence of a strong emotional experience often resulted in, at a later time in life, the same feelings being reproduced, although the original and real physiological unconditional stimulus was subsequently, as at first, lacking (Gantt, 1957).

Schizokinesis.—Now another unexpected event appeared to us. If the heart was sensitive enough to respond so quickly, would these earliest-formed CR's also disappear more quickly? Ask yourself the same question, and see whether you do not predict, as we did, that the cardiac CR's would be unstable and disappear more quickly than other components. In many, though not all, individuals, however, the HR-CR's are extremely stable; once formed, they outlast the more specific components, such as secretion and movement. In many dogs, even after repeated attempts to extinguish, the cardiac CR persisted as strong as ever and for as long as one to four years without practice, while the secretory and motor components remained extinguished!

This marked difference—the early formation and the extreme durability, in contrast to the greater plasticity of the specific secretory or motor responses—is what we have called *schizokinesis* (Gantt, 1953). In this term I intend to include not only in a narrow sense a difference between the general emotional components of the acquired responses and the specific ones, but in a broader way the lack of perfect adaptation that exists in our biological systems. The heart is doing one thing, out of adaptation to present reality; superficially, the individual may be in repose and undisturbed, but beneath, in the autonomic components of the response, there may be violent turbulence. Here may lie the explanation for the persistence of psychogenic hypertension to past experiences long forgotten (Gantt, 1957).

The tremendous advantage of the conditional reflex is the adaptability of the individual dependent upon experience. This adaptability consists in a readiness to act to the signals of an event and a certain plasticity added to the more stereotyped inborn reactions inherent in structure. But the increasing complexity of the conditional reflex function, seen especially in the human being, carries with it a great liability. First, on account of the complexity, there is a greater possibility for malfunction, just as there is a greater probability of a complex machine going wrong. Second, as we amass conditional reflexes, in order to preserve adaptability, there are of necessity more and more inhibitions with their consequent stresses. Third, as pointed out in connection with schizokinesis, these inhibitions are frequently only partial and imperfect adaptations. Thus, through an accumulation of only partially adaptive conditional reflexes, the individual becomes increasingly a museum of antiquities.

Autokinesis.—In several decades of studying neurotic as well as normal dogs, I have been struck by the changes occurring over a long period, based on past experiences but developing in the absence of the repetition of the original experience. Thus in "Nick" appeared a whole train of neurotic symptoms related to the original stress, but developing and becoming worse during 3 years when the animal was removed from this environment. Even more severe symptoms developed in "V3." These are examples of negative *autokinesis*, but there is also evidence of a positive autokinesis, e.g., when a single therapeutic conference or some single experience in the life of an individual has a profound and lasting effect for good. In the normal animal, autokinesis can be seen in the elaboration of new relationships among the original excitatory foci, modifying or completely changing the relationship between the conditional reflexes.

This is a circumscribed view of autokinesis, but one may conclude that there is a normally occurring basic principle of inner development—that this is a basic physiological law. Besides the examples from my laboratory, which provide striking contrasts because we have quantitative measurements for comparison and precise stimuli, there are a host of other examples from the laboratories of other workers, as well as from ordinary life. Embryology itself is an example of development determined from within, changes depending upon the internal structure more than on the external environment.

Although the peripheral impulses go into the cortex in specific patterns according to the receptor with definite mosaic arrangements, as shown by Vernon Mountcastle (personal communication), beyond that point is the possibility for integration, combination, and change. The neurological basis for such changes is described by Eccles (1958) in regard to synapses: "The initial activation of the synapses brings about a lasting improvement in the efficacy of these functions. . . . One explanation is that the synaptic knobs grow in size, another that the synaptic transmitter substance is increased." When he says that "usage enhances synaptic efficacy for days or months," here is evidence of central, internal change. Pavlov's action of induction over periods far beyond the action of the stimulus, his interaction of cortex and subcortex, are reinforced by the more recent "reverberating circuits" of the electrophysiologists. The effects of cerebral trauma on memory of events within 20 minutes of the trauma indicate that demonstrable changes are proceeding in the brain for at least this length of time after the stimulation has ceased.

These facts constitute the sketchy outlines of a shifting inner structure, with remodeling and rebuilding going on within. This function and capacity to change from within is what I mean by *autokinesis*.

This is something new for the organism. It apparently involves a changed relationship between centers in the central nervous system, and it occurs as the result primarily of *new relationships within* the organism. Since the organism is a little universe of its own, why should there not be possible changes occurring between the units of this organism on the basis of internal stimulation? Besides these facts, is there anything more impossible for reciprocal relations to be changed internally, among the inner centers of excitation, than for the organism to be capable of changing in respect to the external environment?

There is too much evidence to refute this idea. Its recognition will open up an entirely new field for exploration, a field which requires special emphasis for its future scientific development. This is an endeavor in which psychiatrists as well as physiologists should join.

The principle of homeostasis, so well developed by the genius of Claude Bernard and amplified by Cannon, now needs to be joined by the principle of schizokinesis and autokinesis, equally cogent for the understanding of normal behavior and psychopathology.

Conclusions

The conditional reflex function—at the apex of the evolutionary process—is itself not only an asset but a liability. Even more so is the supreme development of this function as represented by the second signaling system of the human. Not only do our great successes in science, mathematics, and literature rest on this quality but also our tragic failures—prejudices—and often our cataclysms of destruction—individual, national, international. Not only can the individual be categorized, branded, and persecuted through the function of such words as "capitalist," "Nazi," "Communist," and racial designations, but wars, with their annihilation of millions of lives, can be waged on the same basis.

Darwin's observations reveal the plasticity inherent in living organisms, the ability to cope with the environment, and the marvelous function for adaptations throughout the ages, while Pavlov's work on the conditional reflexes emphasizes the ability of the individual to adapt during its life.

To criticize Darwin and Pavlov because they did not discover what could not be discovered until their original contributions had been made and understood is not justifiable. Such criticism cannot be made by those who understand the history of science. Because Darwin did not enunciate the principles of Mendelism and of the later geneticists and because Pavlov did not demonstrate the rolе of acetylcholine or reveal the exact mechanism of inhibition or arrive at a final classification of types—these do not constitute scientific errors. Science has to take one definite step before it can attempt the next, and the next step will often give a point of view which will reveal the previous one in a perspective which was not possible before. Voltaire, in discussing Descartes, pointed out that he should no more be expected to make all the necessary elaborations of his theories which were made later than could Columbus be expected to describe in detail all the mountains and rivers of America.

Though Darwin and Pavlov differed in their methods, temperaments, and personalities, they were alike in their qualities of thoroughness, consistency, and patience in collecting facts on which to base their principles. Their ability to listen to the voice of nature, whether expressed in life or through the planned laboratory experiment, their capacity for laborious accumulation of data, their scientific zeal, their insight, their establishment of scientific laws by the facts—these are reasons why they both are foremost pioneers in the long procession of scientific explorers throughout the ages.

NOTES

[1] The phrase "battle for the mind," though dramatizing the struggle for a scientific and objective point of view, perhaps gives the wrong slant. It is more properly a battle for the right of scientific investigation of what is available to "scientific methods," even if these are phenomena usually dealt with exclusively by subjective and vague formulations.

REFERENCES

Bykov, K. M. 1957. *The Cerebral Cortex and the Internal Organs.* Edited and translated by W. H. Gantt. New York: The Chemical Publishing Co.

Darwin, Charles. 1872. *The Expression of the Emotions in Man and Animals.* London. (Reprinted New York: Philosophical Library, 1955).

Dykman, R. A., and W. H. Gantt. 1958. "Cardiovascular Conditioning in Dogs and in Humans," in *Physiological Bases of Psychiatry,* ed. W. H. Gantt. Springfield, Ill.: Charles C Thomas.

Eccles, J. C. 1958. "Physiology of Imagination," *Scientific American* (September, 1958) pp. 135-46. (Also data from lecture at the Johns Hopkins University, October, 1958.)

Gantt, W. H. 1928. *Medical Review of Soviet Russia.* London: British Medical Association. 112 pp.

———. 1943. "Measures of Susceptibility in Nervous Breakdown," *Amer. Jour. Psychiat.,* XCIX, No. 5.

Gantt, W. H. 1952. "Pavlovian Methods in Psychiatry," in *Progress in Psychiatry.* Edited by J. L. Moreno and J. Masserman. New York: Grune & Stratton.

———. 1953. "Principles of Nervous Breakdown—Schizokinesis and Autokinesis," *Ann. New York Acad. Sci.,* LVI, 143-63.

———. 1956. "What the Laboratory Can Teach Us about Nervous Breakdown," in *Medicine in a Changing Society.* Edited by I. Galdston. New York: International Universities Press.

Gantt, W. H., and R. A. Dykham. 1957. "Experimental Psychogenic Tachycardia," pp. 12-19 in *Experimental Psychopathology.* Edited by P. H. Hoch and J. Zubin. New York: Grune & Stratton.

Gantt, W. H., H. Lowenbach, and C. N. Brown. 1953. "Acquired Vestibular Balancing Responses," *Trans. Amer. Neurol. Assoc.,* pp. 212-15.

Leake, Chauncey. 1959. *Central Nervous System and Behavior.* New York: Macy Foundation.

Mayr, Ernst. 1959. In *Evolution and Anthropology: A Centennial Appraisal,* p. 2. Washington, D.C.: Anthropological Society of Washington.

Morgan, T. H. 1925. *Evolution and Genetics.* Princeton, N.J.: Princeton University Press.

Pavlov, Ivan. 1928. *Lectures on Conditioned Reflexes, Vol. 1.* Edited and translated by W. H. Gantt. New York: International Publishers.

———. 1941. *Lectures on Conditioned Reflexes, Vol. 2.* Edited and translated by W. H. Gantt. New York: International Publishers.

Pickenhain, Lothar. 1959. *Grundries der Physiologie der hoheren Nerventatigkeit,* pp. 109-16. Berlin.

Pinto, Teresa, J. W. Newton, and W. H. Gantt. 1957. "Comparative Speed Formation: Cardiovascular and Motor Conditioning," *Fed. Amer. Soc. Exper. Biol.* (April, 1957), pp. 15-19.

Razran, Gregory. 1958. "Pavlov and Lamarck," *Science,* CXXVIII, 758-60.

Reese, W. G., Richard Doss, and W. H. Gantt. 1953. "Autonomic Responses in Differential Diagnosis of Organic and Psychogenic Psychoses," *Arch. Neurol. and Psychiat.,* LXX, 778-93.

Zirkle, Conway. 1950. *Death of a Science in Russia.* Philadelphia: University of Pennsylvania Press.

Francis H. Bartlett (essay date 1961)

SOURCE: "Pavlov and Freud," in *Science & Society,* Vol. XXV, No. 2, Spring, 1961, pp. 129-38.

[*In the following review of* Pavlov and Freud *by Harry K. Wells, Bartlett cites Wells's failure to produce a satisfying materialist critique of Freud using Pavlovian theory.*]

Wells' *Pavlovian Critique of Freud* [*Sigmund Freud: A Pavlovian Critique,* by Harry K. Wells. (Volume II of *Pavlov and Freud.*) New York: International Publishers, 1960, 252 p.] is based upon a one-sided but commonly-held view of what constitutes philosophic materialism in the field of mental disorder. Thus, it requires an attention out of proportion to its actual merits, for, in my opinion, this book makes little or no contribution to a critique of Freud and tends to harden and dogmatize certain limitations of Pavlov. At bottom, it is an attack upon any and every psychological approach to mental disorder.

On the surface we are confronted with what appears to be a puzzling insistence on a comparison of incomparables—a forcing into opposition of concepts which deal with related but quite different phenomena. The keynote of the book, carried through for a full chapter, is an almost bizarre comparison of Pavlov's use of the "salivary fistula" with Freud's use of the "dream fistula." Pavlov, says Wells, "had to find or construct a fistula or window which would allow him to observe the functioning of the unconscious activity of the nervous system, and particularly of its apex, the brain" (p. 40). Freud "had to find a fistula or window, through which he could observe the functioning of unconscious mental activity" (p. 40). Only if the two concepts, "unconscious mental activity" and "unconscious cerebral activity" are equivalent, does it make sense to bring them into opposition; only if, as Wells states, the former is Freud's unscientific substitute for Pavlov's physiological concept (p. 177). But the identification is a completely false one.

The Freudian and Pavlovian concepts attempt to grasp two quite divergent areas which Wells himself delineates very clearly. First there is the physiological. This consists broadly of physico-chemical processes involved in cerebral functioning, the formation of conditioned reflexes and the development of functional cortical systems in their inter-relation. The second related area of investigation is the psychological which includes the *content* of mental life. Now these two related areas of investigation are not identical. Wells says: "While there can be no mental life apart from higher nervous activity, this does not mean the reduction of the mental to the physiological." And Wells spells out the essential distinction plainly. "The *content* of thought, feeling and action," he says, "is *not* a product of cerebral functioning. It is a product of society. The kind of society in which a person lives and the individual manner in which he participates in this society will ultimately determine the character of his thinking, feeling and acting" (p. 237).

Pavlov did not deal with the content of thought, feeling and action. In the case of mental illness, he specifically excluded this realm. Freud, on the other hand, however idealistic and frequently fantastic in his formulations, was primarily concerned with the development of and impairments in the content of the thinking, feeling and acting of individuals. If we were to identify the subject matter of his concept, "unconscious mental activity," it would be with those aspects of the content of consciousness which are irrational, with ideas, perceptions and responses which violate the essential features of reality. Freud's concept, however unscientific, is not at all an equivalent of "unconscious cerebral activity." Why then does Wells continue to force into incongruous opposition these two necessary and intimately related aspects of human functioning, the physiological and the psychological? It is because Wells actually believes that, in mental disorders, the psychological development is largely irrelevant. He believes that while the content of consciousness is *normally* a product of society, distorted forms of consciousness are determined by "anatomical and physiological disturbances of the higher part of the brain" (p. 209 *et passim*). ". . . what is thought and expressed in behavioral action," he says, "does not depend on, is not determined by physiological functioning . . . except in the case of mental illness" (p. 237).

Before taking up the fundamental question of whether Wells is or is not right about mental disorder, it is desirable to illustrate briefly that from his point of view it is virtually impossible to conduct any significant critique of Freudian psychology. If Pavlov's physiological solutions to the problems in question are essentially right and Freud's investigations are not only unscientific but totally irrelevant, then beyond dismissing Freud, there is no way to take issue with him. Actually this turns out to be Wells' position, but in the beginning of the book we do not realize this and therefore it is puzzling and disappointing to discover the emptiness, the missing of contact in the lengthy "confrontations."

Pavlov's concept of "instinct" for instance is certainly modest enough and helps to throw into contrast the admittedly speculative "instincts" of Freud. But the two concepts are formulations of entirely different phenomena. Pavlov's concept does not pretend to embrace the phenomena of human purpose, emotion and irrationality which are contained in Freud's. All that Wells' confrontation allows us to conclude is that, with regard to inborn reactions, Pavlov is on solid ground and that, by comparison, Freud is fantastic. But there is nothing in Pavlov's concept of a "chain of reflexes" which allows us to approach the very real questions which Freud solves so badly with his concept of instincts.

The same barrenness occurs on the question of dreams. According to Pavlov's analysis of sleep, the spreading cortical inhibition tends to affect the speech-signalling system first and therefore tends to "liberate" the two lower systems, especially the sensory-signalling system. From this, Wells concludes that dreams are merely "transitory physiological phenomena characteristic of falling asleep and awakening." And, he adds, "This view too is fully in accord with the popular notion that dreams do not really mean anything and are therefore better ignored" (p. 109). From such a viewpoint there is nothing to say about Freud's dream theory except that it and every other effort to understand the content of dreams is nonsense. There is no basis in this position for an extended critique of Freud's particular theory. Actually of course, it does not by any means follow from Pavlov that the emergence of the sensory signalling system into relative dominance results in nonsense. That dreams are dependent upon certain physiological processes does not exclude their having a meaningful content. It seems to me that any scientific conclusion in this respect would depend upon an examination and study of the actual content of dreams in relation to the dreamer's life-process.

A particularly puzzling chapter is the one on "repression." Here, if anywhere, one would think that a really significant critique of Freud might be made. A Pavlovian might be in a position to counterpose the idealist concept of "repression" with rather extensive experimentation on mental conflict, including human conflict. Of this, Wells says not a word. Nor does he mention the attempts to identify the concept of repression with various physiological processes. (See: *Personality and Psychotherapy*, by John Dollard and Neal Miller, pp. 198 ff.) Disappointingly, after an extended exposition of the concept of repression in which its central importance in Freud's system is emphasized, Wells confronts it only with the most elementary form of the conditioned reflex theory of "forgetting" and "recalling" in animals.

The lack in these and other instances of a direct and fruitful analysis of Freud is complemented by page after page of ridicule. In the absence of a more comparable basis of comparison, Wells is constrained to present Freud's theories in a vulgarized and ridiculous form. No doubt Freud lends himself to such treatment, but it does not take a Pavlovian to do it, much less a Marxist. It is much more difficult to deal with Freud at his best, to contend with his concepts when they really represent in some fashion what actually happens in the lives of neurotic people. It is more difficult still to salvage from Freud the mass of empirical data for formulation in more scientific concepts. Such tasks Wells never even approaches. Instead of criticism, we get a comparison, a kind of "look upon this picture and on this," in which Pavlov is above criticism and Freud turns out to be an advocate of medieval demonism. Wells becomes increasingly vitriolic and what emerges is a caricature of Freud which is virtually unrecognizable to clinicians who are familiar with his work. It is very unconvincing especially since his violent dismissal of Freud includes in one grand sweep all others who approach mental disorder as involving a pathological process in the development of personality (see p. 218).

We now come to the fundamental issue of mental disorder which, to avoid any misunderstanding, includes neuroses as well as functional psychoses (p. 208). When Pavlov at an advanced age began to study mental disease in human beings, he approached this new problem with the effort to be as objective as he had been in his studies of animals, i.e., without reference to anything subjective. In observing the case of a catatonic schizophrenic or an obsessional neurotic, he was not particularly concerned with the life history, the ideas, feelings, purposes, values or mode of living of the patient. He went directly to what he called the "mechanism of the symptom," that is, the physiological reaction most immediately accounting for the main symptom. These "protective inhibitions" of various degrees and kinds occurred, he believed, to prevent organic damage to the cortical cells in a state of "exhaustion." Pavlov knew that these states of nervous exhaustion were related to various circumstances of life or even to the ideas and values of the patient, but these were regarded as "remote" causes not involved in the mechanism itself. The symptoms, he thought, were the direct result of a particular patho-physiological state of the brain. The therapeutic approach was necessarily a medical one, to help the cells recover from exhaustion, thereby making the protective inhibition unnecessary and thus doing away with the symptom.

This conception of human mental disorder appears to Wells to be the quintessence of philosophical materialism in psychiatry. Here at last we seem to have a theory which fits the "cornerstone of scientific psychiatry the world over," namely that "in mental illness it is the brain that is ill, while the mind manifests symptoms in the form of disturbances of emotional and thought processes . . ." (p. 179). Here at last, apparently, we have an objective theory developed "without recourse to probing human consciousness," without inquiring into those elusive subjective aspects, those ideas, feelings, purposes and conceptions of a patient which get so in the way of rigid experimental science.

So obvious and certain does this theory appear to Wells that any other position is inconceivable to him. He is even convinced that Freud too knew from the beginning that the answers to his questions were to be found in brain physiology, but that for practical if not mercenary reasons, he repudiated science. "Under the pressure of his private practice," says Wells, "Freud turned his back on science and sought out the by-ways and back alleys, the forbidden and the sensational, the discarded and the repudiated, the offal of human intellectual history, as source material. 'Let down' by science, he turned to pseudoscience. It is as though an astronomer, frustrated in the solution of a great astro-problem, were to 'take it out' on the science that 'failed' him by turning to astrology where the 'answers' can be found. Freud turned from physiology and neurology to dream-symbol reading, perverted sexology, and a spurious social psychology and anthropology" (p. 234).

Many readers of this book who believe that Freud's theories are an albatross around the neck of psychiatry and who are also impressed with Pavlov's contributions may find themselves inadvertently siding with Freud in this context, not only because of the grotesqueness of the picture of Freud but all the more because Wells is really including in his attack anyone who insists that mental disorders cannot be understood apart from an understanding of the patient's *consciousness* in its development. For Pavlov to have been able to make a significant contribution to human psychiatry without going into questions of consciousness is all to the good. But to insist, as Wells does, that in psychiatry the consciousness of the patient and his actual life process as a conscious human being are irrelevant, is to harden a contribution into a dogma.

Pavlov himself stressed that "cerebral functioning consists in the nervous work of establishing, maintaining and perfecting a most delicate correlation between the organism and the environing world" (p. 167). In human beings, this "most delicate correlation" is maintained through the functioning of the higher nervous processes on a human level, that is, as human consciousness developing in complex and ever changing situations. Wells is fond of saying that "mental life *is* higher nervous activity." Right! Therefore the higher nervous activity of human beings *is* human consciousness. The reactions of a person to the surrounding world, his whole activity is guided by his perception of the reality. In turn, his consciousness develops through his current interaction with the surrounding world. To try to understand disturbances in this delicate interplay without inquiring into the particular ideas, feelings and purposes involved in the living process of the patient is clearly impossible. One can, for example, study the physiological mechanisms involved in the symptom of anxiety which might include impairments in the ability to think or drowsiness or tension. But it would be absurd to insist that an objective and scientific psychiatry precludes our inquiring into the conditions which make a particular person anxious in particular situations. One patient may perceive as dangerous situations which to others do not ordinarily seem so, and we have to inquire into what particular ideas and feelings may be involved in such inappropriate reactions. There may even be a generalized anxiety based on the fact that there is a systematic and deeply rooted discrepancy between the reality of situations and the particular person's perception of the reality. It is of the utmost importance to the person concerned to come to understand what this discrepancy may be in order that something can be done about it.

What Pavlov did not fully appreciate is that neurotic and psychotic symptoms cannot be taken as isolated entities. An exclusive emphasis upon the physiological "mechanism" of a particular symptom means to study it in isolation from other relevant considerations. This can be briefly illustrated by one of Pavlov's own cases cited by Wells (Vol. I, p. 170). A young woman apparently reacted to being sexually attracted to a man by developing the obsession that lechery so blatantly showed on her face that consequently she could not go out of her house. Pavlov concentrated exclusively on the physiological state involved in an obsessive symptom. But it is no wild speculation to suspect that, long before the appearance of this symptom, there must have been a developmental process at work to produce the kind of a person who could, in a certain complex situation, develop such a symptom and ultimately become psychotic. We can be reasonably sure that her whole grasp on reality must have been much more tenuous and her whole mode of living more elusive, evasive and unsubstantial than appeared on the surface.

To focus on the isolated symptom means not being able to recognize the development of a mental disorder until certain selected gross and chronic physiological reactions appear. It means taking mental disorder as a purely internal problem, reduced to the relation between the chemical state of the cortical cells and the functional reaction to this state. It means conceiving of the person in isolation from his actual relations to the world. The recognition that external causes of various sorts lead to the "nervous exhaustion" does not mean that these causes get any serious consideration. On the contrary, the strictly physiological position prevents any serious examination of the person's actual social practice. The social relations in which these disorders develop are then seen only as external to the person, not as his own social practice. Thus we get from Wells as well as Pavlov only the most casual references to the social relations such as the "stresses and strains of life" (p. 212), "the impact of life's difficulties and problems" (p. 124). In this category of "remote causes" we find an indifferent lumping together of such things as "overwork," "emotional or intellectual stresses, strains or conflicts" (p. 211), "worries and problems," and even "unrequited love" (p. 239). From such a point of view there can be no appreciation of the profound causal connection between an impaired mode of life and the development of mental disorder. There can be no appreciation of the inner connection between mental disorder and the underlying social relations in which the person is involved.

It is very distressing but entirely consistent to see Wells ending his book with an optimistic heralding of the prospects of a mass test of drug therapy to check the "fantastically high incidence of functional mental disorder in its host nation, the United States" (p. 217). "Psychoanalysis," he says, "together with its limitless number of therapeutical variations has by and large dismally failed in its practical mass test in the United States as an effective cure of mental illness" (p. 218). And he adds, "medically oriented psychiatry appears to be on the verge of gaining a decisive victory over the 'psychical forces' theory, Freud's as well as the many variations of it" (p. 218).

But if the "high incidence" in this "host country" has something to do with the way people lead their lives, then all the "miracle drugs" in the world are not going to stem the tide any more than all the psychotherapy in the world—a fact which should not lead us to dispense with either. But one would think that a Marxist, instead of putting all his hopes in drugs, would have more to say about the pathology of the social relations.

To be a consistent materialist, it is not enough to treat consciousness as the mode of functioning of the brain and disturbed consciousness as the impaired functioning of the brain. As Wells himself puts it, "the content of thought, feeling and action is not a product of cerebral functioning. It is a product of society" (p. 237). And now we may add, a distortion in consciousness may be the product of distorted social relations! Wells knows this and even devotes more than half a page of his long book to mentioning that "life experience often produces distorted conceptions and disordered emotional reactions" (p. 228). But he makes no connection, in fact he prohibits a connection, between such psychological developments and true "mental disorder" in which physiological derangements manifest themselves in mental derangements. In spite of his Marxism, Wells does not free us from Pavlov's philosophical limitations; he ends by consolidating and petrifying Pavlov's one-sided position. There is no criticism of Pavlov. In fact, by a verbal sally, Wells manages to smuggle Marx into the intellectual heritage of Pavlov (p. 130). But Pavlov was not a Marxist and did not understand the relation of mental disease to the social relations.

The limited kind of philosophical materialism which is at issue here assumes that if consciousness becomes increasingly distorted and irrational, this can only mean that something has gone wrong with the brain. But this is not true. Gross and increasing distortions in consciousness can and do develop which are not determined by impairments in physiological functioning. In fact it was Marx who first showed how consciousness could develop a completely fantastic reflection of reality if the social reality itself was distorted and if the people in question were involved in distorted forms of social practice. His whole concept of commodity fetishism explains a multitude of fantastic, even magical ideas as being generated by the deceptive form of capitalist relations. Marx did not treat those irrationalities as the product of disturbed brains, but of disturbed social relations. Naturally he handled such questions only on the broadest level but in doing so he solved a problem, as a materialist, which has been an insuperable stumbling block for investigators of individual irrationality. Wells, as a Marxist, should, it seems clear, have questioned Pavlov's limited materialism and counterposed other possibilities raised by Marx.

The problem for a materialist is this: if human consciousness develops as an approximate reflection of reality, how can a person's experience of life lead to greater distortions in his consciousness? Freud started out by trying to understand how various experiences of life might lead to disturbances in rationality, that is, to account for distortions within the process of the development of consciousness. At first he thought he had discovered what experience of life is responsible for irrationality, namely, sexual seductions in childhood. When he discovered that these experiences had not usually in actual fact taken place, he had two alternatives. He could have extended his efforts to understand what kinds of experience then *do* lead to irrationality, to probe more deeply into the individual's conditions of life and try to see how his participation in them might lead to the development of a precarious grip on reality. Instead, he abandoned the search for relevant life experiences and began to assume that the irrationality which he had set out to explain must already be in existence as an inborn system. He began to assert in effect that disturbances in rationality stem from instinct, from a source outside the sphere of development of consciousness itself. Now Pavlov too, in an entirely different way, also provides us with the answer that distortions in consciousness must come from outside the development of consciousness, must come from physiological disturbances. In neither case is there the conception that distortions in consciousness can arise out of distorted life practices.

But there can be and are the most profound distortions in consciousness of the most basic and elementary features of reality which do not depend on any physiological impairment. And these distortions are deeply rooted in the practice of the person and govern his immediate perceptions and his most spontaneous responses. The "delicate correlation between the organism and the environing world" can be completely and continually upset by the grossest falsification in consciousness of the actual relation between one's self and the world. One common distortion for instance which may pervade every area of a person's life is that his own consciousness is independent of material circumstances. The manifestations of such a concept range all the way from anxiety, say, at the prospect of having to do something involving another person to extreme assumptions of grandiosity and contempt for everything human to a point where other people count for nothing, the very materiality of the world is thrown into question and the power of one's own thought appears dominant.

Such twisted modes of thought do not depend upon twisted molecules or upon physiological disfunctions. They depend upon a twisted relation to the world. The individual process of becoming a rational being is not automatic; it depends upon personal participation in productive and cooperative human living. Whatever impairs a person's direct and intelligible relation to other human beings leads to the development of individual modes of life which are inherently irrational and cannot but foster irrational consciousness. If from an early age a person begins to develop, as his own, forms of social practice such as sponging or using others or any other means of freeing himself from responsibility, work and constructive participation in human life, then the illusion is generated that he is independent of the material conditions of existence. His very form of practice maintains a distorted prism between him and reality. His very experiences of life give rise to and confirm ideas which violate the elements of reality. The constant clash between the way things are and the way he perceives them may by no means be resolved in favor of greater truth, but rather in favor of maintaining some vested interest in a twisted relation to life and, consequently, further distortions in thought.

The strange thing is that Wells, as a Marxist, has to admit that distortions do arise in this way (p. 228), but his whole book is based from beginning to end upon the denial that these processes have any essential connection with "mental disease." But it is only because there *is* such a connection that the conditions of life in the United States can make this a "host nation" to such a "fantastically high incidence of mental disease." This connection, which is the essence of the matter, can never be understood so long as we remain on a purely physiological level.

There is no dispute here over the value of Wells' purpose, which is to contend against the tremendous growth of obscurantist theories of human behavior which depend so heavily upon Freudianism. One might attribute the ineffectiveness of his attack to Wells' not having any professional experience in this field since he writes as a philosopher.

But the chief criticism of this book is that Wells' philosophy is at fault. In spite of his reiterated denials that he means any reduction of mental life to physiology, the fact is that the theme of the whole book is the reduction of mental disorder to physiological disorder. By an "objective science" of psychiatry he means one which develops "without recourse to probing human consciousness." He easily dismisses explanations which are "purely mental" or rely on "psychical forces," but he does not indicate at any point how it would be possible to include ideas and feelings in an objective psychiatry. But these subjective aspects of human functioning must be included. This can be done if they are understood as aspects of the material life process of the person. But the material life process is not equivalent to the physiology of the brain. The material life process of the person includes his consciousness as it functions and develops in his actual social practice. How, to what extent, and how quickly such processes are to be brought within the grasp of an objective science is an important question. But it is not a valid shortcut to solve psychiatric problems by simply leaving out human consciousness.

Raymond E. Fancher (essay date 1979)

SOURCE: "Psychology as the Science of Behavior: Ivan Pavlov and John B. Watson," in *Pioneers of Psychology,* W. W. Norton & Company, 1979, pp. 295-338.

[*In the following excerpt, Fancher surveys Pavlov's life, experiments, theories, and influence.*]

At the turn of the present century, the Russian physiologist Ivan Petrovitch Pavlov (1849-1936) was on the horns of a dilemma. He had just completed a monumental series of studies on the physiology of digestion that would win him a Nobel Prize, and he was looking for new scientific challenges. Some incidental observations he had made in the course of those studies seemed to point to a new and promising area, but Pavlov was uncertain about its scientific propriety.

The new idea was to study a class of responses that Pavlov initially called "psychic secretions." His earlier research had concerned itself only with *innate* digestive responses that occurred in response to clear-cut and measurable *physical* stimuli, such as the salivation of a dog whenever food powder or dilute acid was placed in its mouth. He could not help but notice, however, that many digestive responses were *learned,* and occurred in the presence of *psychological* stimuli. The watering of a dog's mouth at the sight of its keeper as its customary mealtime approached was the clearest example. Pavlov knew that he had already developed a series of procedures and apparatuses that could enable him to study and measure these psychic secretions with the same precision he had achieved on the innate responses. But he was worried by the nature of the scientific company he might have to keep if he plunged into this new venture. The study of psychic secretions seemed bound to have connections with psychology, and Pavlov was disdainful of the introspection-based theories of academic psychology. He thought of himself as a hard-headed, completely scientific *physiologist,* and was reluctant to contaminate his work by associating it with questionable doctrines about unverifiable subjective states. "It is still open to question," he wrote, "whether psychology is a natural science, or whether it can be regarded as a science at all."[1]

Finally, in 1902, Pavlov saw his way to a solution. His compatriot Ivan M. Sechenov (1829-1905) had years before written a book entitled *Reflexes of the Brain* which argued that all behavior could be accounted for in terms of an expanded reflex concept. Acquired reflex processes in the cortex of the brain could presumably become superimposed on innate reflexes lower in the nervous system, thus exerting control over them. The cortical reflexes were hypothesized to be the neurological underpinnings of such psychological phenomena as thinking, willing, or deciding. After pondering Sechenov, Pavlov realized that psychic secretions could be interpreted as the result of new, cortical reflexes becoming attached to the innately given neural circuitry of the basic digestive reflexes.

From this new point of view, everything could be described in proper physiological terms, and embarrassing references to subjective psychological states could be dropped altogether. Psychic secretions could be renamed *conditioned* (or *conditional*) *reflexes* to emphasize their acquired and variable character; by contrast, the innate digestive responses could be called *unconditioned reflexes.* Observed relationships between conditioned and unconditioned reflexes could form the basis of inferences—not about vague psychological states, but about potentially observable physiological processes in the brain.

Pavlov formally banned all psychological terminology from his laboratory, threatening to fire anyone who discussed findings in subjective terms, and spent the rest of his long life studying conditioned reflexes. To his dying day he maintained that he was not a psychologist, but a physiologist studying the brain.

Inevitably, however, psychologists began to take an interest in Pavlov's work. Prime among them was the young American professor John Broadus Watson (1879-1958) who, like Pavlov, had grown suspicious of the unverifiable nature of introspective psychology. In 1913 Watson electrified his colleagues by asserting that the proper subject matter for psychology was not the abstract concept of the "mind," but objective, observable *behavior* instead. Shortly thereafter, he realized that Pavlov's conditioned reflex concept could be applied to responses other than digestive ones, and could be an ideal tool for the objective analysis of learned behavior in general. Armed with this new conceptual weapon, Watson created the school of *behaviorism* that was to dominate American psychology for many years, and that remains a major force today.

The present [essay] deals with the biographies of Pavlov and Watson. Though different from one another in many respects, both were effective advocates of their behavioristic visions who pursued their ideas with single-minded energy and zeal. Each was a powerful personality who swept others along with his enthusiasm, and who exerted a lasting influence on the intellectual life of his country.

IVAN PAVLOV: EARLY LIFE AND EDUCATION

Ivan Pavlov was born on September 27, 1849, in the central Russian farming village of Ryazan. His father was the village priest and his mother the daughter of a priest, but the family's life differed little in its external respects from that of the other peasant families in the town. At the age of ten, Pavlov suffered a serious fall, which led to a prolonged period of ill health. Since his family had to work the fields, he was placed under the care of his godfather, the abbot of a nearby monastery. Here, Ivan was encouraged to read, and at first he always rushed to tell his godfather about any book he had just finished. Instead of giving the boy an immediate audience, the godfather always insisted that he write down his observations on the book so they could be examined and commented on at leisure. This strategem not only bought the abbot time free from interruption, but also provided excellent training in systematic observation and reporting for the young Pavlov.

In his formal education, Pavlov benefitted from the educational reforms of Czar Alexander II, which guaranteed that gifted but poor students could receive proper educations. Pavlov received complete primary and secondary educations in ecclesiastical schools, and in 1870 he was permitted to enroll in the University of St. Petersburg as a student in the natural sciences. His choice of subject had been partly determined by his reading a translation of G. H. Lewes's *The Physiology of Common Life.* This standard physiological text fascinated Pavlov, particularly by its treatment of the digestive tract. "How does such a complicated system work,"[2] he asked himself, and he was embarked on the scientific quest that would eventually win him the Nobel Prize.

Pavlov's most influential professor at St. Petersburg was a mercurial young physiologist named Ilya Cyon (1843-1912). Cyon had been trained in Leipzig, where he was assistant to Carl Ludwig, one of the leaders of the mechanist movement in physiology. Cyon imbued Pavlov with a firm belief in physiological mechanism, as well as an appreciation for the importance of precise experiments. Pavlov was an excellent student, and was asked to become Cyon's assistant. The plan fell through, however, when Cyon was dismissed from the university for his political activities. Pavlov was offered the job as assistant to Cyon's successor, but he refused it because he did not respect the new man's scientific integrity.

After completing his undergraduate work, Pavlov went on for a degree in medicine. He supported himself (and after 1881, his wife as well) through several poorly paying assistantships. He also found time to conduct several independent experimental studies, which were so impressive that he was asked in 1878 to become director of a new experimental laboratory attached to a clinic in internal medicine. This was extraordinary, since Pavlov had not yet completed his own doctoral thesis. Nevertheless, his organizational and experimental abilities were already apparent, and he guided many fellow students through experiments on the effects of different drugs on the heart and vascular system. Finally in 1883, after five years at the laboratory, Pavlov finished his own thesis on the nerves of the heart. He then studied and travelled abroad for two years, spending some time in Leipzig with Carl Ludwig.

Even though Pavlov had outstanding credentials, jobs were scarce for young Russian scientists when he returned home. For several years he had to conduct his research from subordinate and ill-paid positions. Not until he was past the age of 40 did he obtain a post which provided him with the scientific independence he needed. In 1890 he was appointed professor at St. Petersburg's Military Medical Academy, where he was to remain for most of the rest of his life and win worldwide fame.

PAVLOV'S LABORATORY

Ivan Pavlov showed two distinctly different faces to the world, depending on whether he was inside or outside his physiological laboratory. Outside, he was an impractical, absent-minded, and often sentimental man whose misadventures sometimes aroused the wonder of his friends. Inside, he was a vigilant, implacable, and superbly efficient administrator who aroused not only wonder, but also respect and fear in those who worked under him.

In private life Pavlov was notoriously careless about money even though he often lived just above the poverty line. Many months he simply forgot to pick up his salary. Once, after he had just won an academic promotion which brought with it a badly needed cash bonus, Pavlov lent an unscrupulous acquaintance most of the sum before he even got home. The money was never seen again. After this, all family financial affairs were conducted by Pavlov's wife, and he was seldom allowed to carry more than loose change. One of the few times he did carry much money was on a visit to the United States, made without his wife. All of his money—more than $800 in small bills—was jammed into a bulky wallet that protruded visibly from his jacket pocket. When

Pavlov ventured onto the crowded New York subway, the predictable felony occurred. Fortunately for him, he was already world famous and the guest of the Rockefeller Institute, which replaced his funds.

Sometimes Pavlov's impracticality took a sentimental turn. When he was engaged, he spent almost all of his available money on luxuries for his financée—candy, flowers, theater tickets, and such. The only practical gift he bought her was a new pair of shoes, which she badly needed for a trip she was planning. She arrived at her destination and opened her trunk, to find only one shoe! Upon writing to Pavlov about the mystery, she received this answer: "Don't look for your shoe. I took it as a remembrance of you and have put it on my desk."[3]

If negligence, sentimentality, and impracticality characterized Pavlov's personal life, they were absolutely banned from his laboratories. In his pursuit of science he overlooked no detail. Though he often lived uncomplainingly in poverty, he spared no effort to ensure that his laboratory was always equipped and his experimental animals well fed. He was punctual in his arrival at the laboratory, perfectionistic in his experimentation, tyrannical in his control, and unhesitating in docking or firing workers who failed to meet his standards.

One of the most famous Pavlov stories concerns a worker who was late to the laboratory one day during the Russian Revolution, because he had to dodge skirmishes in the streets. Believing that devotion to science should supersede all other values, Pavlov did not regard that as a proper excuse. According to some versions of the story he fired the worker, though it is more probable he simply issued a reprimand. Less extreme manifestations of this same attitude occurred almost every month, as Pavlov would become irritated when his workers had to take time off to collect their pay.

In spite of his often unreasonable demands, Pavlov did inspire great loyalty among those workers who remained in his laboratory. Whatever else might be said, he was always honest in his reactions. So long as his workers were conscientious and careful, there were no long-term recriminations. Perhaps most important of all, his assistants realized that Pavlov never demanded more of others than of himself, and that his quirks were the result of a single-minded devotion to his science.

Unquestionably the most remarkable aspect of Pavlov's laboratory was its organization. Despite his troubles in looking after the necessities of private life, Pavlov ran a large and efficient laboratory that would be the envy of any administrator. Experiments were performed systematically by the thousand, according to a simple but ingenious scheme. Each time a new worker came into the laboratory, he would not be given a new or independent project to work on, but instead be assigned to replicate a series of experiments that had already been performed by Pavlov's other workers. In a single stroke, the new person learned first-hand about the work already in progress, and provided Pavlov with a check on the reliability of results already in. If the replication were successful, all was well and good and the new workers was ready to move on to something new. If it were not, a new replication by a third party would be done to clarify the situation. Because of this system, workers tended to know exactly what their co-workers were doing and could fill in for one another if necessary.

Pavlov's role in the laboratory was that of general planner and administrator. He designed the experiments, and assigned them to specific workers. He also liked to work on the experiments himself, and since he was familiar with all of their details he frequently took over for his workers when they took lunch breaks.

When he was an old and famous man, Pavlov wrote an article for the Soviet youth movement in which he described the secret of his own scientific success: "This is the message I would like to give the youth of my country. First of all, be systematic. I repeat, be systematic. Train yourself to be strictly systematic in the acquisition of knowledge. First study the rudiments of science before attempting to reach its heights. Never pass on to the next stage until you have thoroughly mastered the one on hand."[4] Someone who knew Pavlov only non-professionally might understandably have been incredulous of such advice from him. Those who worked with him in the laboratory, however, knew that he had accurately described the secret of his own success.

The Physiology of Digestion. During his first decade in the St. Petersburg laboratory, Pavlov set out to solve the mystery that had intrigued him since secondary school: the complicated workings of the digestive system. In many respects, his success in this venture was like Pierre Flourens's success in investigating the brain. Both men devised or perfected techniques for studying physiological functions in living and nearly normal organisms, which were effective because of their great surgical virtuosity. Originally, most physiological research had been performed simply by operating on an experimental animal to expose the organ under study. Often the animal was already dead, as in Helmholtz's studies of the nerves in frogs' legs, and in other cases the organ was simply observed in the still-living animal. While these procedures revealed some important information, they also had obvious limitations. Newly operated upon animals with their organ systems exposed were in a highly traumatized state, and there was no guarantee that their physiological functions were the same as in normal animals. Digestive functions, which are notoriously susceptible to the effects of stress, were especially difficult to study this way. Pavlov's problem, then, was to replace these *acute preparations,* in which organs were investigated immediately after being surgically exposed, with *chronic preparations,* in which the organs could be made permanently observable and be studied after the animals had recovered from surgical trauma. In the case of the normally well-concealed digestive organs, this was no mean feat.

Pavlov knew, however, that at least one spectacular chronic preparation of the digestive system had already been achieved, as the result of an almost incredible accident. In 1822, a young French-Canadian trapper named Alexis St. Martin suffered a terrible gunshot wound to his stomach. He was tended by the physician William Beaumont (1785-1853), who assumed the wound was fatal but patched him up as best he could. Surprisingly, St. Martin recovered and went on to live an almost normal existence. The only unusual thing about him was that the hole in the wall of his stomach never closed up, but remained for the rest of his life as a "window" through which the inside of his stomach could be seen. In gratitude for Beaumont's surgical skill, St. Martin agreed to serve as an experimental subject. He allowed the physician to observe his digestive processes, and even to insert instruments for collecting and measuring the digestive substances. Until Pavlov, Beaumont's observations of St. Martin remained the single greatest source of knowledge about the normal digestive processes.

In the 1890s Pavlov sought to replicate Beaumont's studies on a more controlled basis, through chronic preparations of different parts of the digestive tracts of dogs. Others had tried this before, without notable success. Pavlov succeeded, for two major reasons. First, Pavlov was among the first to recognize the importance of preventing post-operative infection through the use of aspectic surgical techniques. At a time when many humans were still dying from infections contracted in unsanitary surgical wards, Pavlov went to extreme lengths to assure the antiseptic cleanliness of his operations. Operations on the digestive tract were especially dangerous sources of possible infection, but Pavlov's methods ensured that most of his animals lived, whereas most of his predecessors' animals had died.

The second factor in Pavlov's success was his technical virtuosity as a surgeon. He was made uncomfortable by the sight of blood, and so always tried to perform his operations with the absolute minimum of physical trauma to the structures involved. Sure-handed and precise, he perfected a particularly delicate surgical preparation known as the *gastric fistula,* a channel leading from the inside of a digestive organ to the outside of the body through which various digestive products could be collected.

Using fistulas, Pavlov was able to study the functions of virtually every part of the digestive system. In his systematic way, he conducted hundreds of experiments in which the stimuli impinging on the different parts of the system were varied, and the resulting secretions were collected, measured, analyzed—and sometimes even bottled and sold as medicines to provide extra revenue for the laboratory. These were the studies that won him the Nobel Prize for physiology in 1904, and they are still cited as authoritative in modern textbooks of physiology.

CONDITIONED REFLEXES

By the time Pavlov became a Nobel laureate, his primary interest had already shifted from digestion per se to conditioned reflexes; in fact, his first public mention of that term occurred in his Nobel address. He soon put his familiar research strategy to use in this new field, devoting the rest of his life to thousands of studies which systematically varied the four basic components of the conditioned reflex.

The four components were labelled by Pavlov the *unconditioned stimulus,* the *unconditioned response,* the *conditioned stimulus,* and the *conditioned response.* Before any conditioning occurred, the unconditioned stimulus and response were united in the innate unconditioned reflex. For example, food or acid in the mouth was an unconditioned stimulus which automatically elicited the unconditioned response of salivation. The conditioned stimulus—say the sight of the animal keeper, or the sound of a tone in an experiment—originally failed to elicit any salivary response, but after it had been paired with the unconditioned stimulus a number of times, it elicited salivation even in the absence of the unconditioned stimulus. In mentalistic terms, one could say that the conditioned stimulus had been "associated" with the unconditioned stimulus, and so came to elicit a response similar to the unconditioned response. In Pavlov's laboratory, of course, such terms had been banished. But Pavlov could express the relationships among the concepts objectively, in terms of the magnitudes of the unconditioned stimuli and responses, the numbers of pairings between the conditioned and unconditioned stimuli, the conditions under which the pairings took place, and so on.

Consider a simple Pavlovian experiment. The unconditioned stimulus was a certain amount of dilute acid on a dog's tongue, which had been shown by repeated trials to elicit a certain average number of drops of saliva as an unconditioned response. The conditioned stimulus was a tone of a certain pitch and loudness, which was sounded a certain number of times and immediately followed each time by the acid. Then, in the crucial test trial, the tone was sounded but not followed by the acid. The dog salivated, and the number of drops was taken as a measure of the strength of its new conditioned reflex.

Within this simple design there was room for the systematic variation of many factors, and the precise calculation of many laws of conditioning. For example, the numbers of pairings of conditioned with unconditioned stimuli prior to the test trial were varied, and as expected, few pairings produced weaker responses than many. The interval between the conditioned and unconditioned stimuli was varied, and it was found that the strongest and quickest conditioned responses occurred when the interval was very short. If the conditioned stimulus *followed* the unconditioned stimulus, however—even by a very short interval—no conditioned reflex at all could be produced.

Generalization and Differentiation. In one series of experiments Pavlov investigated the effect of a test stimulus that was somewhat different from the original conditioned stimulus. He discovered that if an animal were tested with a stimulus that was similar to the conditioned stimulus—say a tone of a slightly higher or lower frequency than that which had been paired with food during the conditioning—a response occurred, but it was weaker than it would have been in response to the original conditioned stimulus. The more dissimilar the test stimulus was, the weaker the response. This phenomenon is known as *generalization,* since the subject generalizes its conditioned response from one stimulus to other, similar ones.

Repeated generalization tests led to further developments. For example, a dog was repeatedly fed following the sounding of a certain musical tone. On the first generalization trial a tone one-half an octave lower was sounded, and a substantial salivary response occurred. Thereafter, the two tones were randomly sounded on different trials, with the original tone always being "reinforced" by the immediate presentation of food, and the lower tone never being reinforced. Gradually, the generalized response to the lower tone decreased, until it finally disappeared altogether. In Pavlov's terminology, the conditioning procedures had led to a *differentiation* [Most English-speaking psychologists today use the term *discrimination* instead of differentiation, but the concept is identical to Pavlov's.] between the two stimuli. That is, the animal had learned not only to respond positively to one stimulus, but also to inhibit the generalization of the response to a similar stimulus.

Experimental Neurosis. Some of Pavlov's most intriguing findings occurred when he attempted to test the limits of his animals' ability to differentiate. He discovered that while it often required many trials to establish the first differentiation, it was easy to sharpen it after it had been established. Thus, in one study, a differentiation was established in a dog between the flashed image of a circle on a screen, which was always followed by reinforcement, and a flashed ellipse, which was never followed by reinforcement. The ellipse was quite oblong. Then, after the differentiation was strongly established, the ratio between the ellipse's axes was gradually reduced, making it more and more circle-like. The animal quickly learned to discriminate these new stimuli from the circle—up until a dramatic breaking point. When the ratio was so reduced that the ellipse was almost circular, the dog became extremely agitated. Whereas it had previously been placid and had submitted to the restraining harnesses of the experimental apparatus with no difficulty, it now made frantic efforts to escape and became very difficult to handle. The experimenter tried returning to some of the earlier differentiation trials that the animal had previously mastered easily, but there was no alleviation of the symptoms. All of the earlier differentiation conditioning had disappeared completely, and the dog remained highly agitated. Only after it was given a long rest and treated with much patience was the original, easy differentiation re-learned. The breakdown in the dog's behavior became known—perhaps misleadingly—as an *experimental neurosis.*

Other experiments demonstrated other conditions under which experimental neuroses could be produced. In one, a dog had been conditioned with great difficulty to salivate when an electric shock to one of its rear feet was the conditioned stimulus. Originally, the dog had responded to the shock by struggling in its harness and trying to escape the situation. After many reinforcements with food, however, it began to accept the shock calmly, and immediately began salivating when it was administered. On the crucial trial, the shock was applied to a different part of its leg from that to which it had become accustomed. This stimulus elicited a much stronger avoidance response than the animal had ever shown before, even to the earliest shocks before the conditioning had become established. All of the earlier conditioning disappeared, and the animal required several months to recover from its experimental neurosis. In sum, Pavlov showed that experimental neuroses were likely to occur whenever an animal was subjected to an unavoidable conflict between two strong but incompatible response tendencies, like salivating or suppressing salivation at the ellipse, or tolerating or pulling away from the shock to the new part of the leg.

PAVLOV'S THEORY OF THE BRAIN

Pavlov attempted to account for all of his findings in a speculative and rather complex theory of the brain and its functions. Following Sechenov, he argued that *un*conditioned reflexes are mediated by connections between sensory and motor nerves at the spinal and lower brain centers of the nervous system. Conditioned reflexes supposedly occurred when neural pathways in the *cortex* became part of the circuitry, establishing connections between certain stimuli and responses that had not been interconnected before. Crude evidence for the importance of the cortex was provided by animals whose cortexes were completely removed after they had already acquired a number of conditioned reflexes. These animals, who were kept alive by attentive keepers for up to four and a half years, retained their unconditioned reflexes. Their conditioned reflexes disappeared with their cortexes, however, and no amount of training could make them return.

Pavlov's belief that the cortex was the site of conditioned reflexes naturally involved him in the localization of function question, for it became only logical to ask if different kinds of conditioned reflexes were localized in different specific regions of the cortex. In deciding the question, he became briefly embroiled in one of the most spectacular controversies of his career. His antagonist was a colleague at the Military Medical Academy, named Vladimir Bechterev (1857-1927).

The trouble began when Bechterev's students ablated the portion of a dog's cerebral cortex which, when electrically stimulated, had produced a salivary response (just as stimulation of the motor strip produced a motoric response). They reported that all previously acquired conditioned salivary responses were lost following removal of this "salivary center," and that no new ones could be produced. Pavlov was initially pleased to learn of this experiment, since it was consistent with his own view of the importance of the cortex in conditioned reflexes. But when Pavlov tried to replicate the study, he found that the dog regained a full capacity for conditioned salivary reflexes if given a few days to recover from the operation. The Bechterev experiments had apparently not allowed the dog sufficient recovery time before testing. Pavlov concluded that the salivary center, however efficacious it might be in producing salivation upon electrical stimulation, was *not* a necessary component of conditioned reflexes involving salivation.

Pavlov began attacking Bechterev vigorously in print, until finally a public test was arranged between the two sides. The salivary centers were removed from two dogs in Bechterev's laboratory, and after a few days the animals were presented in a public demonstration—placed in front of a rotating glass drum with meat inside. The sight of the meat elicited not a drop of saliva, so the Bechterev forces claimed that conditioned salivary reflexes had been removed. However, Pavlov immediately saw that meat inside a glass drum was a very weak conditioned stimulus for these dogs. One of his assistants has described what happened next:

> Pavlov rose from his seat and firmly demanded a weak solution of hydrochloric acid. He had a resolute appearance, with his lips set and his brows knitted. When he was given the acid, . . . he poured [it] into the dogs' mouths several times. This produced an abundant salivary secretion. After the secretion had stopped, the mere sight, smell, or splash of the acid in a test tube caused the secretion of saliva, that is, a conditioned salivary reflex to the acid was formed . . . notwithstanding the absence of the cortical salivary centers. After this, Pavlov did not pay much attention to the proceedings and soon left.[5]

The dramatic Bechterev episode indicated that there was not a single cortical location necessary for all conditioned salivary reflexes, but it did not completely deter Pavlov from adopting the localizationist position. While there was clearly no cortical *salivary* center required for the reflexes, there just as clearly *were* necessary *sensory* centers for different kinds of conditioned reflexes. For example, all reflexes involving visual conditioned stimuli were entirely absent following complete removal of the visual center of the occipital cortex; auditory reflexes similarly disappeared following removal of the auditory areas of the temporal lobes. Thus, Pavlov could and did argue that different conditioned *stimuli* result in the arousal of different specific centers in the sensory cortex, even though the conditioned *response* did not have to originate from a single specific location.

Excitatory and Inhibitory Processes. Pavlov believed that there were two separate kinds of processes occurring in the various sensory areas of the cortex to produce conditioning. The one process was *excitatory,* and occurred in the acquisition and generalization of conditioned responses. The other was *inhibitory,* and occurred when a conditioned response was suppressed, as in differentiation training. Excitatory processes were aroused and strengthened by the repeated reinforcement of a conditioned stimulus through the presentation of the unconditioned stimulus; inhibitory processes were aroused by repeated non-reinforcement.

To account for the phenomena of generalization, differentiation, and experimental neuroses, Pavlov made two further assumptions about the structure and function of the brain. First, he assumed that the specific sensory locations representing similar stimuli are close to one another on the cortex. Second, he assumed that whenever excitation or inhibition is aroused in a particular location, it spreads out in a "wave" over nearby centers. Like a wave in water or air, its strength dissipates as it gets farther from the center. Pavlov called this hypothetical cortical phenomenon, which has never been actually observed, *irradiation.*

The irradiation of excitation and inhibition presumably caused the generalization and differentiation of conditioned reflexes. In generalization, a stimulus similar to the conditioned stimulus arouses excitation in a cortical center close to that for the conditioned stimulus. The excitation irradiates until, in a somewhat weakened state, it arouses the center for the conditioned stimulus, which in turn triggers a somewhat weakened response. If the similar stimuli are not reinforced, however, their centers begin to irradiate surrounding areas with waves of inhibition instead of excitation. As differentiation increases, the portion of the cortex surrounding the center for the true conditioned stimulus becomes increasingly irradiated with inhibitory potential. The final state has been almost poetically described as follows: "When a [differentiation] is firmly established, only a small region of the brain corresponding to the conditional stimulus will produce a response. Inhibition lies over the rest of the brain like winter over the empty plains of central Russia, limiting all activity to the lonely stockades."[6]

It would be wrong to think, as the winter image above might suggest, that the inhibition-irradiated areas are inert. Pavlov thought of them as fields of potentially highly active forces, which under the conditions of the experimental neurosis can have a disruptive effect on learning and behavior. An experimental neurosis occurs when a stimulus which cannot be avoided arouses strong excitation and inhibition at the same time; that is, its cortical position lies on a "boundary" between two nearby and very powerful centers of excitation and inhibition. Pavlov envisaged the resulting neurophysiological events as a *rupture* of the boundary, so that the entire surrounding area becomes inundated with an indiscriminate mixture of both excitation and inhibition. Instead of being confined within their boundaries, and thus producing the precise and regular effects of generalization and differentiation, the two forces conflict with one another in the same area and produce disorganized behavior whenever their centers are stimulated.

Human Psychiatric Disorders. In the course of his work on experimental neuroses in dogs, Pavlov made an observation that determined his major interest for the last few years of his life. He noted that there were striking individual differences among dogs in the specific symptoms of their experimental neuroses. Some dogs—especially those who had been naturally very active before the experiments—became hyperexcited in their neuroses, snapping, chewing, howling, and clawing in an indiscriminate manner. Other dogs—mainly those whose normal dispositions had been relatively placid—developed neuroses whose major symptoms were excessive lethargy and apathy. Pavlov concluded that these two "types" resulted from innate differences in the balance between excitatory and inhibitory processes in their brains. In one type, excitation naturally predominated, and the rupture led to a relatively indiscriminate dominance of excitation. In the other type, the opposite occurred.

In 1929, though past the age of eighty, Pavlov began to consider the implications of this work for the understanding of psychiatric disorders in humans. He familiarized himself with the varieties of psychiatric illness, and then attempted to account for them in terms of excesses and deficiencies in excitation and inhibition, the weakening of cortical cells, and the other variables he had found to be related to experimental neuroses. The therapies he prescribed for these conditions were strictly physical in nature, consisting mainly of regimens intended to rest or exercise the brain cells presumably at fault. Pavlov was also intrigued by the therapeutic potential of certain chemical substances, especially bromides, which he thought could rejuvenate injured or exhausted neurons. This work was influential in the development of several organically-based therapeutic programs in the Soviet Union.

Pavlov continued to be active in this work until February 21, 1936 when he fell ill following a full day at work. As his symptoms worsened and developed into pneumonia, he made systematic observations about his mental functions even with a high fever and a racing pulse. On the afternoon of February 27, he remarked to a consulting neuropathologist, "My brain is not working well, obsessive feelings and involuntary movements appear; mortification may be setting in."[7] One hour after making this final scientific observation, Pavlov died.

PAVLOV'S REPUTATION AND INFLUENCE

By the time of his death Pavlov was a national hero in the Soviet Union; with even a town named in his honor. His final attitude toward his government was correspondingly grateful, though this had not always been the case. Just after the Revolution, when times were hard for scientists and Pavlov's Nobel Prize money had been confiscated by the State Bank, he did not hesitate to speak out against the Bolsheviks. Characteristically, he complained much more bitterly about his scientific hardships than about his personal loss of wealth. In the following years, he was investigated by the secret police, and lampooned in a state-sanctioned play. The government gradually recognized his value, however, both as a prestigious representative of Soviet science and as the promulgator of a new and properly materialistic theory that could become the foundation of a Marxist psychology. Pavlov was provided with increasingly generous research funds, and his attitude toward the government warmed correspondingly. By the 1930s, he was an avid supporter of the government, and conditioned-reflex theory was the official psychological doctrine of the Soviet Union. His theories had by now also been appreciatively noted in the United States, where they were an integral part of J. B. Watson's behaviorism.

It is perhaps ironic that Pavlov's greatest impact was on Soviet and American *psychology,* since he maintained to the end of his life that he was a physiologist, and that his work was of no interest to psychologists. The psychologists he had in mind, however, were those who studied the subjective states of consciousness. Little did he imagine a breed of psychologists who would cast all subjective phenomena to the winds, and concern themselves exclusively with the observable relationships between measurable stimuli and behavioral responses. These new psychologists did not feel constrained to speculate about the cortical underpinnings of their observed data, as Pavlov did, but recognized that objective techniques like his could be used to establish *behavioral* laws that would stand by themselves. This viewpoint, as championed by John B. Watson, was the foundation of the behaviorist movement that was to dominate American psychology for many years.

NOTES

[1] Ivan P. Pavlov, *Conditioned Reflexes: An Investigation of the Physiological Activity of the Cerebral Cortex* (New York: Dover, 1960), p. 3.

[2] Quoted in B. P. Babkin, *Pavlov: A Biography* (Chicago: University of Chicago Press, 1949), p. 214.

[3] Ibid., p. 37.

[4] Ibid., p. 110.

[5] Ibid., p. 94.

[6] George A. Miller and Robert Buckhout, *Psychology: The Science of Mental Life,* 2nd Edition (New York: Harper & Row, 1973), p. 231.

[7] W. Horsley Gantt, Introduction to I. P. Pavlov, *Conditioned Reflexes and Psychiatry* (New York: International Publishers, 1941), p. 35.

George Windholz (essay date 1986)

SOURCE: "Pavlov's Religious Orientation," in *Journal for the Scientific Study of Religion,* Vol. 25, Summer, 1986, pp. 320-27.

[*In the following essay, Windholz demonstrates that Pavlov, although a professed atheist, advocated the tolerance of religion as part of his theory of higher nervous activity.*]

> "Religion is the most basic and predictable human instinct" I. P. Pavlov.

In the post World War II era, Soviet anti-religious propaganda supported its position by describing Ivan P. Pavlov as a convinced atheist. As we shall see, in his personal belief, Pavlov was an atheist. But the propagandistic campaign distorted Pavlov's more complex stand on religion by ignoring his position on the tolerance of religious practices. Moreover, the Soviet anti-religious policy disregarded Pavlov's views on the function of religion in his theory of higher nervous activity.

A number of Soviet books have stressed Pavlov's atheism. In particular, J. W. Schorochowa (1956) contrasts Pavlov's materialistic theory of higher nervous activity with idealistic conceptions of human nature. According to A. N. Studitskii (1964), Pavlov both privately and professionally was a materialist and atheist. B. V. Andreev (1964) maintains that privately Pavlov was an atheist, but that he was tolerant of religious practices, and that his theory of higher nervous activity considered religion from the naturalistic point of view. However, Andreev failed to draw the logical conclusion from Pavlov's theory that anti-religious suppression was counter-productive and intensified the need for religion for some individuals.

Pavlov's attitude toward traditional religions became more important than the issue of his own beliefs. From the Soviet State's inception, its rulers engaged in an open struggle against religion. One argument they used against religion involved the ascendancy of science in the progress of humankind (Curtiss, 1953). During the 1920s and 1930s, Pavlov was the country's most renowned scientist and also the only Nobel Prize laureate living at that time in the Soviet Union. Since he had immense prestige and was known for his brilliance and personal integrity, Pavlov's religious views were of considerable interest to the Soviets and they used a biased view of his religious beliefs to further the government's policy to stamp out religion.

The works of Andreev, Schorochowa, and Studitskii go deeper than just the presentation of Pavlov's position toward religion. They point out the utility to the materialistic orientation of his views for opposing religious expression. Andreev first draws a parallel between Engels' and Lenin's writings on religion and Pavlov's theory of higher nervous activity. He concludes:

> . . . the entire outlook of I. P. Pavlov, his entire devotion to science, his opposition to idealistic teachings, his personal atheism, cannot fail to play a gigantic role in the struggle against religious superstitions and prejudices (1964: 97).

Andreev's conclusions about the importance of Pavlov's beliefs are correct as far as they go. But Pavlov's position on religion was not wholly supportive of the Soviet government's policy struggle with religion. It was antagonistic as well.

The present article focuses on three topics: First, it considers whether Pavlov personally was or was not religious; Second, it considers Pavlov's position on the free exercise of religion; and, third, it considers the elements of religion in Pavlov's theory of higher nervous activity.

PAVLOV ON HIS OWN RELIGIOSITY

Some disagreement exists on the issue whether Pavlov was or was not personally religious. He was brought up in a religious background, but later he seemed to be an atheist. Andreev, Schorochowa and Studitskii are convinced that Pavlov was an atheist. Other voices claimed that Pavlov was a religious believer. Pavlov's disciple E. M. Kreps (1967: 129), referring to contemporary Soviet public opinion, reports:

> . . . opinions widely held by the public maintain that Pavlov was a religious believer, even a fervent believer, who attended church services, and contributed funds toward the restoration of church buildings, especially in the village of Koltushi where his Physiological Laboratory was located.

A similar thesis is sometimes expressed in the West. In particular, G. L. Kline (1968: 155) writes that "the academician Pavlov . . . remained a devout Russian Orthodox believer to the end of his days."

The issue can be decided by Pavlov's own words. In the early 1920s, Kreps (1967) asked Pavlov whether or not he was religious. Kreps wrote that Pavlov smiled and replied:

> Listen, good fellow, in regard to [claims of] my religiosity, my belief in God, my church attendance, there is no truth in it; it is sheer fantasy. I was a seminarian, and like the majority of seminarians, I became an unbeliever, an atheist in my school years (1967: 131).

A decade later, during the October 9, 1935 *Clinical Wednesday,* Pavlov, at the age of 86, made the following statement in regard to his own religious belief:

> I am a son of a priest; I was reared in a religious environment; however, when I was 15 to 16 years, I was reading all kinds of books and I changed my position (Bykov, 1957: 360).

Indeed, I. P. Pavlov grew up in a religious environment. His father, Petr D. Pavlov, a Russian Orthodox priest, was married to the daughter of a priest, Varvara I. Uspenskaia. Traditionally, sons of priestly families followed in their fathers' footsteps. From 1860 to 1870, I. P. Pavlov attended church schools, including the Riazan Ecclesiastical Seminary. In view of Pavlov's statement that he abandoned his religious belief at the age of 15 or 16, the change must have occurred in the mid-1860s, during a decade of profound upheaval in Russia's political and social life. In 1861 the relatively liberal Tsar Alexander II abolished serfdom. The public debate on Russia's future was widespread and intense. Western ideas proliferated.

In his brief autobiography, Pavlov (1952) reported that his thoughts were profoundly influenced by the writings of D. I. Pisarev. Pisarev was a popularizer of scholarly works. Although Pisarev's published writings did not directly challenge the existing political and social conditions, they were, nevertheless, unsettling. In 1864, five years after the publication of Charles Darwin's *The Origin of Species,* Pisarev (1894) described its theses for the general public. Considering that Pavlov's formal education during his adolescence was mainly in theology and the humanities (Gureeva & Chebysheva, 1969: 13), Pisarev's essays dealing with biological sciences made a powerful impression on him (Babkin, 1949).

According to Pavlov's son, V. I. Pavlov (1967: 351), in 1931 the writer Maxim Gorkii asked I. P. Pavlov whether he was religious. Pavlov replied:

> Of course, I have lost the faith of my childhood. How this has happened? This is difficult to explain. I became fascinated with Vogt, Moleschott and later with natural sciences; I worked my whole life in this field: I worked with matter.

Pisarev's writings lauded the achievements of scientists and offered a new scientific perspective to the youthful Pavlov. Later, the mature Pavlov's orientation was positivistic and humanistic: he believed that science would improve the human condition. Pavlov described to Kreps (1967: 131) his beliefs as follows:

> My belief is that the progress in science will bring happiness to humans. I believe that human intellect and the higher manifestation thereof—science—will free the human species of disease, hunger, hostility, and will reduce human suffering. This belief has given and continues to give me strength and helps me to continue my work.

Note that Pavlov believed science would free humankind from hostility and suffering. In view of his statement about his own religiosity, we may conclude that Pavlov was an atheist and this part of Soviet anti-religious propaganda was based on fact.

PAVLOV'S POSITION TOWARD THE FREE EXERCISE OF RELIGION

As atheistic as he was, Pavlov was also tolerant toward the free exercise of religion. He explained his position on religious tolerance in his discussion with Kreps (1967: 131):

> Why do many [people] think that I am a believer, a religious believer? It is because I speak out against the persecution of the Church and religion. I do not think that it is proper to take away from people a religion without substituting for it another religion. A Bolshevik does not need to believe in God because he has another religion—Communism.

In his personal life, Pavlov was ready to oppose those who disrespected other people's religious conviction. This was noted, for example, by his disciple E. A. Asratian (1967). In 1931 Asratian, under Pavlov's direction, worked at the Physiological Institute of the Academy of Sciences U.S.S.R. One day Pavlov asked Asratian to his office. Politely, yet with thinly disguised anger in his voice, Pavlov asked Asratian whether he—against the rules made by Pavlov—worked on Sundays, on religious holidays. Pavlov became mollified only after Asratian explained that his experimental design demanded experiments to be performed on Sundays and holidays.

It is worth considering some reasons for Pavlov's tolerant attitude toward religious belief and practice. It is unlikely that Pavlov was taught the spirit of tolerance during his adolescence; the Russian Orthodox Church of the Tsarist period was intolerant toward other religions. It is also unlikely that Pavlov's father advocated tolerance of other religions since a small town priest could not oppose the official policies of the ecclesiastic powers and retain his position.

A possible explanation for Pavlov's position on religious practices may be found in the following events. Pavlov became an unbeliever at the age of 15 or 16. Yet a letter of reference, required for admission to the University of St. Petersburg and written by the Inspector at the Riazan Ecclesiastical Seminary, Petr Losev, failed to reveal any opposition to the "Christian religion" on the part of the 21 year old seminarian (Gureeva & Chebysheva, 1969: 13). This was all the more notable in view of the inquisitorial responsibilities of the Inspector. Through these five years, Pavlov must have kept his doubts to himself, which, considering his excitable temperament (Babkin, 1949), was not a trifling matter. It is possible that this inner struggle between the desire for self-expression and the threat of societal sanction taught Pavlov the importance of tolerance.

A second reason for tolerance may have been brought about by a tragic incident. Pavlov told Kreps (1967) that a close friend of his, N. P. Bogoiavlenskii, asked him whether there is life after death. When Pavlov denied this possibility, Bogoiavlenskii committed suicide the next day. Pavlov then explained:

> I took away the faith that he had. Another faith he did not have . . . I am his murderer (Krops, 1967: 132).

Pavlov's reaction to Bogoiavlenskii's suicide went beyond the feeling of guilt; his reaction brought him to recognize the need for the toleration of others' religious beliefs. Pavlov's assumption that Bogoiavlenskii's suicide was related to a loss of faith suggests that he considered religion an important naturalistic phenomenon. Religion, regardless of whether it is Orthodox Christianity or Communism, is a characteristic of the human species.

Pavlov's view that religion is a naturalistic phenomenon may stem from his reading of Wilhelm Wundt's work.

Pavlov read a Russian translation of Wundt's *The Soul of Humans and Animals* (Orbeli, 1949: 344). Wundt was the founder of experimental psychology, and wrote on religion in 1863:

> . . . it can be said with considerable certainty that the religious feeling is a common characteristic of the human species. . . . The worship of the forces of nature is a basic characteristic of all religions and the genesis of their development (Vundt, 1866: 280).

Like Wundt, Pavlov approached religion naturalistically. His belief that religion was a natural phenomenon can be gleaned from the following exchange with Gorkii:

> [Gorkii:] "I understand you, Ivan Petrovich! You do not believe, but you respect other people's belief." [Pavlov:] "That's that! You put it neatly. Respect, that's where the dog is buried. . . . But belief is something that can be subjected to scholarly investigation. In the final analysis, belief develops in the working brain" (V. I. Pavlov, 1967: 352).

The last sentence is significant because Pavlov devoted three decades of his life to the study of the functions of the brain. One function of the brain is the organism's higher nervous activity, that is, the activity that interacts with the environment. Religion is one aspect of higher nervous activity. Since the functioning brain is a naturalistic phenomenon, religion can be investigated by the scientific method.

PAVLOV'S THEORY OF HIGHER NERVOUS ACTIVITY AND RELIGION

Pavlov's interest in the functions of the brain developed gradually. Without graduating from the Riazan Ecclesiastic Seminary, Pavlov matriculated at the Faculty of Science of the University of St. Petersburg in 1870. In 1883 he received an M.D. degree and in subsequent years had a successful career in the physiological research dealing with circulatory and digestive systems. From 1901 until his death in 1936, he was developing his theory of higher nervous activity. Under the influence of Darwin's concept of the struggle for existence, he was concerned with the function of the brain in the adaptation of the organism to its environment.

Pavlov held that higher organisms are biologically endowed with unconditioned reflexes, or instincts. The crucial characteristics of unconditioned reflexes, or instincts, was their permanence (Pavlov, 1949) and innateness:

> Reflexes—constitute innate reactions, functional from the moment the animal is born (Pavlov, 1951: 356).

For Pavlov, unconditioned reflexes (a product of evolution) promote the organism's survival by directing it toward life sustaining conditions and by helping it to avoid harmful situations. Thus, the alimentary reflex allows the organism to obtain life sustaining substances in the environment. The defensive reflex protects the organism from harmful environmental factors.

The organism's survival is, however, enhanced by the conditioned, or acquired (temporary) reflexes. Conditions that accompany the life sustaining substances evoke a behavior response similar to that produced by the substances themselves. Thus, the sight of a dish from which a dog once ate, evokes movements toward the dish. Conditions that accompany harmful events evoke behavior similar to that brought about by the harmful events themselves. For example, physical discomfort experienced by an animal in a specific location leads to the avoidance of that location. Hence, signals, which enhance the organism's survival, are generated by the environment. The psychological experience is the formation of conditioned reflexes at the neural level of the cortex.

In addition to the acquisition of life sustaining substances and the avoidance of harmful agents, there exists in higher organisms the tendency to seek out knowledge. As an example, Pavlov noticed that chimpanzees are very curious (Windholz, 1984). According to Pavlov, the "exploratory reflex" prompts the organism to seek out knowledge by engaging in a trial and error behavior. The accumulation of knowledge by humans through scientific methods is a refined form of trial and error behavior (Pavlov, 1975).

Human reactions to trying environmental conditions differ among individuals. According to Pavlov, biological or constitutional factors determine the nature of an individual's nervous system as either "strong" or "weak." People endowed with a "strong" nervous system can handle the taxing environmental conditions; individuals endowed with a "weak" nervous system cannot. In Pavlov's view, religion (an instinct) is manifest when the individual's ability to deal with difficult environmental conditions falters. He explained the emergence of religion as an instinct in Darwinian evolutionary terms:

> When human beings first surpassed the animal and became aware of their own existence, then their position was extremely precarious. Their understanding of the environment was minimal, the natural events terrified them. Humans saved themselves by creating religion, which enabled them to maintain themselves somehow, to survive in the midst of an uncompromising, all-powerful nature. It is a very basic instinct that is thoroughly rooted in human nature (Bykov, 1957:360).

Pavlov asserts that the religious experiences of contemporary humans has been acquired phylogenetically, that is, it developed through the Darwinian process of struggle for existence. Early humans developed a religious tendency, and passed it genetically to the next generation. This thesis suggests that Pavlov accepted the concept of inheritance of acquired characteristics. This should not be surprising since Darwin himself considered the inheritance of acquired characteristics as "probable" (1902: 54).

Pavlov also explained under which conditions the religious instinct manifests itself:

> There are many people who cannot live without religion. There are weak people over whom religion has power. The strong ones—yes, the strong ones—can become thorough rationalists, relying only upon knowledge, but the weak ones are unable to do this (Bykov, 1957: 360).

Consequently, Pavlov, in his theory of higher nervous activity, considered religion in purely naturalistic terms. This position has many implications for the attempt to eradicate religion.

IMPLICATION FOR THE ERADICATION OF RELIGION

In view of Pavlov's immense prestige, his own atheism may be considered as a useful argument for the Soviets in their struggle against religion. The question arises, within the framework of Pavlov's theory of higher nervous activity, whether the practices of religion can be eradicated. Pavlov was explicit in regard to the nature of religion: One has to realize that religion is the most basic and predictable human instinct (Bykov, 1957: 360). He believed that the religiosity of a human being is determined biologically: Whether [a person] is a rationalist or a believer—is a matter of natural selection (Bykov, 1957: 360).

However, Pavlov described to Gorkii a person who was an outstanding intellect yet was religious:

> Long time ago, at a meeting in England, we, the participant scholars, were led before the opening [of the meeting] into a church, in some abbey to hear the mass. The bishop held a beautiful speech on the relation of science and religion—we all heard it with pleasure. During the mass, I became interested in the architecture of the church, in the decorations. Beside me stood Ramsay, you know, the chemist. I asked him what is that? He answered. Then I became interested in something else; I asked him again, but he answered with some displeasure. When I asked him the third time, he remained silent. So I asked the other neighbor why is Ramsay so proud and he does not answer. He smiled and said: "You Russians are strange. Ramsay is praying; he is deep in prayer, and you are disturbing him." Well, here you have a world famous scientist, also a materialist and a chemist, believing in his own way; he finds in it rest . . . (V. I. Pavlov, 1967: 351-2).

According to Pavlov's theory of higher nervous activity, religion is a species-specific instinct, whereby the individual's rationalistic or religious orientation is determined biologically. Phylogenetically, religion is the outcome of the human species' struggle for existence. Ontogenetically, religion develops more acutely among individuals biologically endowed with a "weak" nervous system, and manifests itself in times of environmental crises.

On the basis of his humanistic values, Pavlov's advocacy of tolerance of religious practices is consonant with his theory of higher nervous activity. The theory predicts that intolerance would *strengthen* the religious behavior of individuals prone to religiosity. Since religion is a basic instinct, deeply rooted during the phylogenetic development of the human species, its complete eradication is impossible as long as the biological structure of the human species remains unchanged. This is the part of Pavlov's position on religion left out by Soviet propaganda. Within every society, individual members with "strong" constitutions will overcome religion in favor of a rationalistic worldview and will remain free of religious expression even under trying environmental circumstances. In contrast, individual members endowed with a "weak" constitution will need religion. As a corollary, forceful struggle against religion will subject such "weak" individuals to more trying environmental conditions and thus *strengthen* their religiosity; the ultimate form of threatened religiosity may express itself in martydom.

REFERENCES

Andreev, B. V. 1964, *Ivan Petrovich Pavlov i Religiia.* Moscow, Leningrad: Izdatel'stvo "Nauka."

Asratian, E. A. 1967, "Stranitsy vospominanii ob I. P. Pavlove." Pp. 41-51 in E. M. Kreps (Ed.), *I. P. Pavlov v Vospominaniiakh Sovremennikov.* Lenningrad: Izdatel'stvo "Nauka."

Babkin, B. P. 1949, *Pavlov, a Biography.* Chicago: University of Chicago Press.

Bykov, K. M. (Ed.) 1957, *Pavlovskie Klinicheskie Sredy; Stenogrammy Zasedanii v Nervnoi i Psikhiatricheskoi Klinikakh,* Vol. 3. Moscow, Leningrad: Izdatel'stvo Akademii Nauk SSSR.

Curtiss, John S. 1953, *The Russian Church and the Soviet State.* Boston: Little Brown and Company.

Darwin, Charles 1902, *The Descent of Man* (2nd ed.), Vol. 1. New York: P. F. Collier & Son.

Gureeva, N. M. and N. A. Chebysheva 1969, *Letopis' Zhizni i Deiatelnosti Akademika I. P. Pavlova.* Leningrad: Izdatel'stvo "Nauka."

Kline, George L. 1968, *Religious and Anti-religious Thought in Russia.* Chicago: University of Chicago Press.

Kreps, E. M. 1967, "Ivan Petrovich Pavlov i religiia." Pp. 129-33 in E. M. Kreps (Ed.), *I. P. Pavlov v Vospominaniiakh Sovremennikov.* Leningrad: Izdatel'stvo "Nauka."

Orbeli, L. A. (Ed.) 1949, *Pavlovskie Sredy: Protokoly i Stenogrammy Fiziologicheskikh Besed,* Vol. 1. Moscow, Leningrad: Izdatel'stvo Akademii Nauk SSSR.

Pavlov, I. P. 1949, "Uslovnyi refleks." Pp. 223-46 in Kh. S. Koshtoiants (Ed.), *I. P. Pavlov, Izbrannye Proizvedeniia.* Leningrad: Gosudarstvennoe Izdatel'stvo Politicheskoi Literatury.

———. 1951, "Strogo ob" ektivnoe izuchenie vsekh vysshikh proiavlenii zhizni zhivotnykh." Pp. 355-8 in I. P.

Pavlov, *Polnoe Sobranie Sochinenii,* Vol. 3: Book 1. Moscow, Leningrad: Izdatel'stvo Akademii Nauk SSSR.

———. 1952, "Ivan Petrovich Pavlov, avtobiografiia." Pp. 441-4 in I. P. Pavlov, *Polnoe Sobranie Sochinenii,* Vol. 6. Moscow, Leningrad: Izdatel'stvo Akademii Nauk SSSR.

———. 1975, "Psikhologiia kak nauka." Pp. 99-103 in E. M. Kreps (Ed.), *Neopublikovannye i Maloizvestnye Materialy I. P. Pavlova.* Leningrad: Izdatel'stvo Nauka.

Pavlov, V. I. 1967, "Vstrecha Gorkogo s Pavlovym." Pp. 347-53 in E. M. Kreps (Ed.), *I. P. Pavlov v Vospominaniakh Sovremennikov.* Leningrad: Izdatel'stvo "Nauka."

Pisarev, D. I. 1894, "Progress v mire zhivotnykh i rastenii." Pp. 327-496 in F. Pavlenkov (Ed.), *Sochineniia D. I. Pisareva,* Vol. 3. St. Petersburg: Tipografiia P. P. Soikina.

Schorochowa, J. W. 1956, *Die Bedeutung der Lehre Pawlows für die Atheistische Weltanschauung.* Berlin: Dietz Verlag.

Studitskii, A. N. 1964, *O Velikom Uchenom i Ateiste.* Moscow: Izdatel'stvo "Znanie."

Vundt, V. 1866, *Dusha Cheloveka i Zhivotnykh,* Vol. 2. St. Petersburg: Tipografiia I. Tiblena i Komp.

Windholz, George 1984, "Pavlov vs. Köhler; Pavlov's little-known primate research." *Pavlovian Journal of Biological Science* 19: 23-31.

Daniel P. Todes (essay date 1997)

SOURCE: "Pavlov's Physiology Factory," in *Isis,* Vol. 88, No. 2, June, 1997, pp. 205-46.

[*In the following essay, Todes details the work produced in Pavlov's laboratory at the Imperial Institute of Experimental Medicine, analyzing Pavlov's scientific and managerial vision, as well as the forces and relations of production in the lab.*]

> What is a scientific laboratory? It is a small world, a small corner of reality. And in this small corner man labors with his mind at the task of . . . knowing this reality in order correctly to predict what will happen, . . . to even direct this reality according to his discretion, to command it, if this is within our technical means.
>
> —Ivan Pavlov (1918)

In four successive years Ivan Pavlov was nominated for the Nobel Prize, and each time the committee confronted the same question: To what extent were the products of Pavlov's laboratory truly Pavlov's? The nominee had himself pronounced his most substantial work, ***Lectures on the Work of the Main Digestive Glands*** (1897), "the deed of the entire laboratory" and credited his coworkers by name for conducting the relevant experiments. Moreover, he referred those readers seeking detailed experimental evidence for his most important arguments to the publications of his coworkers, where many of these arguments first appeared. Did Pavlov's major works, then, represent his own, original contributions to science, or were they merely "a type of compilation of the experimental dissertations upon which they are based"?[1]

Guided by an image of the heroic lone investigator, the Nobel Prize Committee here confronted a different form of scientific production.[2] Just as the workshop was yielding pride of place to the factory in goods production, so, as the nineteenth century wore on, were leading laboratory scientists increasingly likely to be the managers of large-scale enterprises. Justus von Liebig and Felix Hoppe-Seyler in chemistry, Karl Ludwig and Michael Foster in physiology, Robert Koch and Louis Pasteur in bacteriology, and Paul Ehrlich in immunology all presided over distinctively social enterprises involving substantial capital investment, a relatively large workforce, a division of labor, and a productive process that involved managerial decisions. Clearly, their achievements owed something not only to their scientific (and rhetorical) skills but also to their qualities as masters of large-scale production.[3]

In this essay I explore the forces and relations of production in Pavlov's laboratory at the Imperial Institute of Experimental Medicine during the first phase of its operation (1891-1904). As in St. Petersburg's massive Putilov ironworks, the forces of production in Pavlov's laboratory included its physical site and technologies, its workforce (with its skills), and management's ideas about what constituted good products and how best to produce them. In my discussion of Pavlov's laboratory, I refer to the first set of ideas—consisting of his notions about good science and good physiology—as his "scientific vision." I refer to the second set of ideas—concerning how best to produce good physiology with the resources at his disposal—as his "managerial vision." Like analogous visions in the Putilov factory, Pavlov's scientific and managerial visions suffused all aspects of the production process, shaping (along with the obvious "objective factors") the construction of the laboratory's physical site; the development and use of its technologies; the choice, training, and deployment of its workforce; and the processing, form, and marketing of its final products.

BERNARD AND PAVLOV: ONE SCIENTIFIC VISION, TWO FORMS OF PRODUCTION

When Ivan Pavlov (1849-1936) embarked in the early 1870s upon a career in physiology he may well, in his headier moments, have dreamed of becoming the Russian Claude Bernard. A much-revered figure among Russian intellectuals, Bernard appealed both to the radical theorists who inspired Pavlov to abandon his seminary studies in Ryazan and to the generation of physiologists that greeted him in St. Petersburg. For radicals, Bernard was an apostle of modern life science and an ally in the battle against tsarist metaphysics; for Russian physiologists, he was the leading prophet of their professionalizing discipline. Pavlov once identified Bernard as "the original inspiration of my physiological activity" and claimed to have read the master in the original French.[4] He certainly read Bernard's work closely while studying physiology at St. Petersburg University, where he apprenticed himself to Bernard's former student and collaborator Ilya Tsion. Tsion set his protégé to work on two topics dear to his own French mentor, and Pavlov's first two scientific reports—on the nervous regulation of the heart (1874) and on the innervation of the pancreatic gland (1875)—bore the distinct marks of their Bernardian paternity.[5]

Throughout his career, Pavlov's scientific vision was unwaveringly Bernardian and his rhetoric bore a striking similarity to that in Bernard's *Introduction to the Study of Experimental Medicine* (1865).[6] For both physiologists, the organism was a purposeful, complex, specifically biological machine governed by deterministic relations. The physiologist's task was to uncover these unvarying relations, to control experimentally or otherwise account for the "numberless factors" that concealed them behind a veil of apparent spontaneity. Physiology would thus attain mastery over the organism and give birth to an experimental pathology and therapeutics that would revolutionize medicine. In this spirit, Pavlov always insisted upon results that were *pravil'nye*—a word that means both "regular" and "correct," capturing his view that, in physiological experiments, the two meanings were one and the same. Pavlov also shared Bernard's commitment to organ physiology, which addressed a level "high" enough to encompass the vital, purposeful activity of complex organic machines but "low" enough to discover the unvarying laws without which physiology would not qualify as a science.[7]

There were, to be sure, some differences between the French visionary and his Russian admirer. Pavlov's holism was, if anything, more developed than Bernard's—as we shall see, this was reflected in his distrust of vivisection—and Pavlov directed his attention less toward the complexities of the organism's *milieu interieur* and more toward the relationship between the organism and external circumstances. Moreover, beginning in the 1890s Pavlov addressed a qualitatively different type of scientific question than had Bernard; and his determination to uncover unvarying patterns for the complex phenomena he encountered led him quietly to modify one of the Frenchman's epistemological positions.[8] For our purposes here, though, another difference is more important: that between a workshop physiologist and a factory physiologist.

Bernard held that, as William Coleman has put it, "because access to the living workshop-organism is so difficult, we must create another workshop that is specially devoted to this task." Bernard's discussions of experimental work highlighted both its visionary and craft dimensions and emphasized the physiologist's need for an appropriately equipped place in which to conduct it. Bernard was also a "workshop physiologist" in another sense: he worked either alone, with a single assistant, or with an occasional collaborator, pursuing a single line of investigation at a time in a relatively small space.[9]

As the product of Bernard's reflections upon his own practice, *An Introduction to the Study of Experimental Medicine* addressed the epistemological, craft, and, one might say, psychological challenges that confronted the individual investigator. For Bernard, the same individual devised, conducted, and interpreted an experiment, and so had to adopt the fundamentally different "qualities of mind" required at each juncture. Thus when devising an experiment, one must have a preconceived idea; when observing its results, one must become a passive "photographer of phenomena"; when ascribing meaning to these results, "reasoning intervenes, and the experimenter steps forward to interpret the phenomenon." The fluid dynamics of experimental trials made these stages "impossible to disassociate" in practice, but they remained conceptually distinct. So, "in the experimenter we might also differentiate and separate the man who preconceives and devises an experiment from the man who carries it out or notes its results. In the former, it is the scientific investigator's mind that acts; in the latter, it is the senses that observe and note." Thus, even the blind naturalist François Huber had "left us admirable experiments which he conceived and afterward had carried out by his serving man, who, for his part, had not a single scientific idea. So Huber was the directing mind that devised the experiment; but he was forced to borrow another's senses. The serving man stood for the passive senses, obedient to the mind in carrying out an experiment devised in the light of a preconceived idea."[10]

Pavlov began his career in a workshop, but two sets of circumstances—and his response to them—transformed him in the early 1890s into Russia's first factory physiologist. The first of these concerned the founding of the Imperial Institute of Experimental Medicine by Prince A. P. Ol'denburgskii, a member of the extended tsarist family and heir to a tradition of medically oriented philanthropy. A series of events and contingencies—the timely announcements of Pasteur's rabies vaccine and Koch's tuberculin, the politics of the prince's enterprise and his tactics in securing a place for it on the state payroll, and Pavlov's connection to Russia's most eminent physician, Sergei Botkin—led Ol'denburgskii to appoint Pavlov chief of the institute's Physiology Division in 1891. Two years after failing in competitions for assistant professorships at two different Russian universities, Pavlov thereby became master of the country's largest and best-equipped physiological laboratory.[11]

Yet that laboratory would have remained a roomy workshop were it not for the appearance of a new labor force. Immediately upon opening its doors, the institute was transformed by an "unexpected influx of scientific forces wishing to use [its] facilities." Originally, the institute's six scientific divisions were housed within a single building; laboratory facilities for each were designed to accommodate the division head and an assistant or two. This unanticipated flood of "scientific forces," however, precipitated a radical expansion, and several divisions acquired separate buildings designed to accommodate a large contingent of laboratory workers.[12]

This new labor force was created by a medical bureaucracy that sought to modernize Russian medicine by encouraging physicians to make a "detour through the lab." Convinced of the military and economic importance of medicine, and persuaded that the progress of Western European medicine rested upon the triumph of "scientific positivism," the Ministry of Internal Affairs launched a grant program to encourage physicians "to improve themselves scientifically." Participating physicians were granted a service leave lasting from six months to two years for studies at the Military-Medical Academy, a university medical school, a university clinic, or a hospital close to a university. By the 1890s, the state offered substantial incentives for using this study leave to earn a doctorate in medicine: these included a higher salary and survivor benefits, elevation on the Table of Ranks, preferential hiring to desirable posts in the medical establishment, and, for Jewish physicians, exemption from a number of discriminatory laws.[13] There was, however, one "catch": largely unlettered in the sciences, these physicians had a maximum of two years to define, research, complete, and defend a doctoral thesis.

The flood of these temporary investigators at the institute—where they were termed *praktikanty* (the singular is *praktikant*)—offered its division chiefs the opportunity to establish a large-scale laboratory enterprise. Some, like S. N. Vinogradskii in the Microbiology Division, preferred workshop science and demurred. Others accepted large numbers of *praktikanty* and then, depending on their motives and their scientific-managerial vision, incorporated them into laboratory work in various ways. For his part, Pavlov immediately put his *praktikanty* to work within a tightly managed, unified productive unit guided by his own scientific vision.[14]

The managerial vision animating this operation involved the transformation of Bernard's "qualities of mind" into a highly rationalized division of labor. Pavlov himself (in principle) assumed control over the qualities that Bernard had credited to Huber's "directing mind," while using his coworkers—like Huber's servant—as extensions of his own senses, as largely "passive photographer[s] of phenomena."[15]

The obvious challenges inherent to this transformation of an epistemological issue into a managerial policy underscore the close relationship between scientific and managerial visions. Our story, in fact, involves not one factory but two. Pavlov referred to the digestive system itself alternately as a "chemical factory" and a "laboratory." He ascribed to it the very same qualities that he did to successful human endeavors: both were "precise, regular, and purposeful."[16] In laboratory investigations, the factory metaphor expressed and guided the search for *pravil'nye* results—for precise, repeated (or "stereotypical"), and purposeful patterns in the glandular responses of dogs to varying quantities of different foods. Pavlov never referred to his laboratory as a "factory"—to do so would have demystified the ethos that helped make it hum—but his management style and rhetoric clearly expressed his belief that "the marvelous mechanism" of the digestive system would reveal its secrets only to a laboratory endeavor that matched its most essential qualities.

FORCES OF PRODUCTION

> Everything is in the method, in the chances of attaining a steadfast, lasting truth . . .
>
> —Ivan Pavlov

The Factory Site

When the institute formally opened in 1891, Pavlov's Physiology Division occupied five rooms in the single wooden building that housed all the institute's scientific divisions. Pavlov used the smallest room for surgical operations and the four larger ones to house animals and conduct experiments. In addition to a laboratory budget more than five times greater than that of any other Russian physiologist, he had the use of two attendants, one paid assistant, and a growing number of *praktikanty*.[17]

However lavish by Russian standards, these facilities quickly came to seem cramped and inadequate. Designed as a workshop for a handful of men, they were soon swarming with *praktikanty*—twelve in 1892, seventeen in 1893—and the animals for their experiments.[18] Furthermore, Pavlov's experiences with the Ekk fistula (which linked the portal vein with the inferior vena cava) soon convinced him that it was difficult or impossible to maintain the aseptic standards necessary for successful surgical operations in the single room available for that purpose.

The influx of *praktikanty* that caused these problems also cemented Pavlov's previously shaky loyalty to the institute. As an assistant in Botkin's clinical laboratory in the 1880s, Pavlov had supervised the doctoral research of many physicians but had been frustrated by Botkin's scientific-managerial style. Physician-investigators in that laboratory addressed a wide variety of topics—ranging from the pharmacological action of various substances to the mechanism of the coating of the tongue—complicating immeasurably Pavlov's task of seeing their research to a successful conclusion. Even before the institute formally opened, Pavlov had begun to work there with *praktikanty* who addressed topics of his own design. A friend recalled his response to the flood of *praktikanty* that soon followed: "When Pavlov became convinced that one could acquire here all the means for scientific work and that the physicians collaborating with him would be able to work without spending their own resources for experiments, that everything would be provided to him—dogs, feed, and, mainly, that he would have many coworkers—this bound him entirely to the institute."[19]

The space problem was resolved in 1893-1894, when an unexpected contribution from Alfred Nobel enabled the Physiology Division to become the institute's third scientific division to acquire a separate building. Perhaps motivated by the institute's efforts against the cholera epidemic that swept through his Baku oilfields in 1893, Nobel asked his nephew Emmanuel—one of several Nobels who built an oil-based industrial empire in Russia—to relay his intention to donate 10,000 rubles to the institute. This was an unconditional gift, but the ailing sixty-year-old philanthropist did express the hope that the beneficiary would address two questions that he found particularly pressing: Would transfusions of blood from a young, healthy animal (Nobel suggested a giraffe) revivify an ailing animal of the same, or another, species? Could the stomach of a healthy animal be transplanted to an ailing one with salutary effect? Emmanuel added a short cover note (mentioning Alfred's "interest in physiology") and forwarded his uncle's letter to Prince Ol'denburgskii, who, after receiving the tsar's permission, accepted the gift in August 1893.[20] Some months later Pavlov, who was temporarily filling in as institute director, formally thanked Nobel and informed him that his gift would be applied to the general needs of the institute. The money was, in fact, already being used to finance a two-story stone addition to Pavlov's laboratory.[21]

The new quarters, constructed under Pavlov's close supervision and completed in 1894, more than doubled the laboratory's space, allowing Pavlov more fully to implement his vision of the physiological enterprise. The basement became a full-service kennel with individual cells for experimental animals, the first floor provided three more rooms for experiments, and the second floor housed a surgical and recovery complex that embodied Pavlov's commitment to investigating the normal functioning of organs through what he termed "physiological surgery" and the "chronic experiment." This expression of Pavlov's holism was central to laboratory production, so we must address it briefly here.

For Pavlov, the "chronic experiment" allowed the physiologist to investigate normal physiological processes that, he claimed, were often distorted during an "acute experiment" (a term he used synonymously with "vivisection"). In contrast to acute experiments—which were conducted upon animals immediately after an operation from which they were soon to die—chronic experiments began only after the animal had recovered from surgery and regained its "normal" physiological state. Acute experiments had their uses—and Pavlov employed them himself—but they yielded only "analytic" knowledge, not a "synthetic" understanding of the organism at work. Shortly after the completion of his new building, Pavlov explained that acute experiments conducted on a freshly operated-upon and bleeding animal that was either writhing in pain or heavily narcotized so distorted physiological processes that they led inevitably to "crude errors." It was impossible for the experimenter reliably to untangle the results of the operation itself from normal physiological functions. In chronic experiments, on the other hand, "the physiologist counts on the animal living after the removal of parts of organs, after the disturbance of connections between them, the establishment of a new connection, and so forth"—in other words, after a surgical procedure that afforded permanent access to the physiological processes of an animal that had been purposefully altered but remained essentially normal.[22] The surgical and recovery complex, then, embodied Pavlov's view that it was necessary and possible to explore normal physiological processes—specifically, the responses of the digestive glands to various stimuli (for example, to teasing with food, the act of eating, or the passage of various foods through the digestive system).

The "normalcy" (*normal'nost'*) of the experimental animals undergoing chronic experiments was, then, central to laboratory work and a source of authority for Pavlov's arguments *vis-à-vis* both physicians and other scientists. Physicians who drew upon clinical experience to dispute the laboratory's results were often reminded, in the sympathetic tones of a fellow medical man, that they encountered an impossibly complex mass of interconnected phenomena in their daily practice and that these could not be disentangled outside the laboratory.[23] Similarly, when the experimental results of other scientists conflicted with Pavlov's own, these could be explained (and either reconciled or dismissed) by reference to the physiological abnormalities that resulted from their crude acute experiments.

The notion of "normalcy" inevitably entailed a series of "interpretive moments." Pavlov acknowledged, as we have just seen, that physiological surgery and chronic experiments involved some departure from normal physiological relations ("removal of parts of organs, . . . disturbance of connections between them, the establishment of a new connection, and so forth"). Since the laboratory setting itself, to say nothing of the surgical operations performed there, always had *some* effect on the dog's behavior and reactions—how was one to determine whether the dog remained acceptably "normal"? For example, were a dog's digestive processes functioning normally if, after an operation, its appetite diminished, it accepted only one kind of food, or it lost weight? It fell, then, to the experimenter, the *praktikant*—within, as we shall see, a matrix of social relations in the laboratory—to answer such questions and to affirm the "normalcy" of an experimental dog.

Or to affirm its *lack* of normalcy. Pavlov and his coworkers were, after all, dealing with a large, complex organism; and *pravil'nye* results were inevitably difficult to obtain. Feeding two different dogs the identical quantity of the same food *always* produced somewhat different secretory results and sometimes radically different ones. Even the results of identical experiments on a single dog varied. For Pavlov (following Bernard), these variations reflected the "numberless factors" that concealed determined regularities behind a veil of apparent spontaneity. So, when two dogs yielded strikingly different results, one animal was pronounced relatively "normal" and the other relatively "abnormal." Divergent results with a single dog were handled similarly.[24]

I shall discuss briefly the social-cognitive dynamics of this interpretive moment later in this essay; for now, we need only note that the notion of "normalcy" was simultaneously a laboratory goal, a reservoir of interpretive flexibility, and a source of authority for the laboratory's knowledge claims. To the outside world, Pavlov's laboratory consistently represented its experimental dogs as "normal"—as happy, energetic, and long lived. Within the laboratory, however, Pavlov and his coworkers struggled constantly to create and define "normalcy," while also exploiting fully the interpretive flexibility afforded by such judgments.

Since chronic experiments depended upon the animal surviving surgery, Pavlov conceded no essential difference between physiological surgery and clinical surgery upon humans. In his speech to the Society of Russian Physicians on "the surgical method of investigation of the secretory phenomena of the stomach" (1894), and more extensively in ***Lectures on the Work of the Main Digestive Glands*** (1897), he proudly presented the plan of his surgical ward—"the first case of a special operative division in a physiological laboratory." Dogs were washed and dried in one room, narcotized and prepared for surgery in a second, and operated upon in a third. A separate room was devoted to the sterilization of instruments, the surgeon, and his assistants. Separated from the surgical ward by a partition were individual recovery rooms for dogs. These were well lit and ventilated, heated with hot air, and washed by means of a water pipe with minute apertures—enabling rooms to be "copiously syringed from the corridor without [anyone] entering the room."[25] Figure 3, a posed photograph, communicates this essential identity between physiological and clinical surgery; looking at the photo, one realizes with a slight start that the patient is a dog.

For the physiologist to master nature's most complex phenomena, Bernard had argued, his workshop must be "the most complicated of all laboratories." In this spirit, Pavlov explained to the Society of Russian Physicians in 1894 that the demands of chronic experimentation—of this qualitative extension of the physiologist's grasp on the organic whole—required a radical expansion of the laboratory's physical plant. "In the final analysis the very type and character of physiological institutes should be changed; they should definitely include a surgical section answering the demands of surgical rooms in general." For physicians in his audience, this was yet another of Pavlov's constant injunctions that they use their social connections to secure greater financial support for physiology; for Russian physiologists, it was a reminder that only Pavlov possessed the resources to practice what he preached.[26]

The Workforce

In the years 1891-1904 about a hundred people worked in Pavlov's laboratory. A small minority—about ten—were permanent or semipermanent staff: the chief (*zaveduiushchii*), the assistants (*pomoshchniki*), and the attendants (*sluzhashchie*). The great majority were temporary investigators (*praktikanty*).

As chief, Pavlov provided the laboratory's scientific-managerial vision and ruled in firm patriarchal fashion. He hired coworkers, assigned research topics, performed complex operations on dogs, participated in the *praktikanty*'s experiments as he saw fit, edited and approved completed work, rewarded success and punished failure. His were the governing ideas in the laboratory, and he tolerated no alternatives. He was also the spokesman for the laboratory's achievements, defending his coworkers and explaining the broader significance of their work when they delivered papers or defended dissertations to outside audiences. Pavlov himself wrote articles on a wide range of specialized subjects—including the nature of pepsin, the effect of hunger on the stomach, and the effects of a double vagotomy—but most important were his periodic publications synthesizing laboratory results and explaining their significance for physiology and medicine. In the years 1891-1904 these included **"Vivisection"** (1893), **"On the Surgical Method of Investigation of the Secretory Phenomena of the Stomach"** (1894), **"On the Mutual Relations of Physiology and Medicine in Questions of Digestion"** (1894-1895), ***Lectures on the Work of the Main Digestive Glands*** (1897), **"The Contemporary Unification in Experiment of the Main Aspects of Medicine, as Exemplified by Digestion"** (1899), **"Physiological Surgery of the Digestive Canal"** (1902), and, during the laboratory's transition to research on conditional reflexes, **"The Psychical Secretion of the Salivary Glands (Complex Nervous Phenomena in the Work of the Salivary Glands)"** (1904).

The great majority of the workforce were temporary investigators, *praktikanty,* drawn to the Physiology Division by the state medical policies I have described. Most came to Pavlov's laboratory between the ages of twenty-five and thirty-five, during their first decade of work as practical physicians, and lacked training in physiology beyond that provided in a single medical school course. Many were military physicians, and all but one were male. They entered the laboratory from a wide range of medical settings: of the 75 percent for whom information is available, twenty-eight were physicians in St. Petersburg's hospitals and clinics (twelve of these in the clinics of the Military-Medical Academy), thirteen served in hospitals and clinics outside of the capital, ten came from the empire's academic institutions (universities and institutes), ten were rural physicians, and nine worked for the Medical Department of the Ministry of Internal Affairs. The *praktikanty* were drawn almost entirely from the diverse middling social stratum known in Russia as the *raznochintsy.* Their nationality is often difficult to determine, but clearly the great majority were Russian and a disproportionate number were Jewish. *Praktikanty* usually spent one to two years in the laboratory, during which time about 75 percent wrote dissertations, defended them at the Military-Medical Academy, and received their doctorates in medicine.[27]

The nature of this workforce—young and transient, largely untrained in physiology, and intent on gaining a quick doctoral degree—facilitated Pavlov's use of its members as extensions of his own eyes and hands. Consider longtime coworker Boris Babkin's perspicacious description of the most numerous contingent among the laboratory's *praktikanty*, military physicians pursuing their doctorates at the Military-Medical Academy:

> About sixty or seventy of them were enrolled [in the academy] yearly, remaining for two years. During the first year they had to pass their examinations for the degree of doctor of medicine—a repetition of the state examinations—and during the second year they had to work in one of the academic clinics or laboratories, presenting the results of their clinical or experimental investigations in their M.D. [doctoral] thesis. The majority of the doctors attached to the academy were regimental doctors who had had no opportunity to work in the hospitals and to refresh their knowledge and perfect their medical skill. The greater part of the Russian army was stationed on different strategic borders, far from any cultural center, even of the most modest kind. Because of this, many of the military doctors, especially those who had been stationed for a long time in some dreary little town, were very backward in medicine and even more in science.

"Very backward in medicine and even more in science," these physicians provided the basic human "material," as another observer put it, for the production process.[28]

The *praktikanty* were not, of course, an undifferentiated mass; and at special junctures in laboratory production—when the chief was engaged in "retooling"—he sometimes employed coworkers for their special expertise. For example, Pavel Khizhin's surgical skills and training played a critical role in the creation of a key dog-technology; and Pavlov's later transition to research on conditional reflexes owed much to perspectives he imported by recruiting the *praktikanty* Anton Snarskii and Ivan Tolochinov. These exceptions, however important, also illustrate the rule: when the physiology factory was operating normally, the *praktikanty* served as skilled hands.[29]

The *praktikanty* conducted thousands of experiments in Pavlov's laboratory, painstakingly collecting, recording, measuring, and analyzing the dogs' secretory reactions to various excitants during experimental trials that often continued for eight or ten hours at a time. The strains of this work are clearly, and poignantly, evident in an obituary for Iulian Iablonskii, Pavlov's *praktikant* and assistant in 1891-1894, who died in 1898 after a protracted mental illness: "Increasingly fascinated by physiology, he soon decisively abandoned the clinic for the laboratory. For entire days he sat, collecting digestive juices, making calculations, and later, as an assistant to the professor, making necessary preparations for experiments and complex operations. In his third year . . . there appeared the first signs of overexhaustion, and then a sinister mental illness. Undoubtedly already ill, the deceased defended his dissertation and was sent to the provinces."[30] Iablonskii's fate was unique, but the rigorous work process he endured was not.

Pavlov also had at his disposal each year two paid assistants and one unpaid "member-coworker," who provided a relatively stable supervisory stratum amidst the transitory *praktikanty*. Although they conducted scientific research, their principal task was to incorporate *praktikanty* into the laboratory's productive process—to inculcate the laboratory's procedures and culture, facilitate the smooth progress of their work, and keep the chief informed of their abilities, progress, and problems.[31] All but one of these assistants were physicians with a developing specialty of some use to the laboratory. V. N. Massen, a gynecologist, established the laboratory's initial aseptic and antiseptic procedures; N. I. Damaskin and E. A. Ganike were biochemists, and A. P. Sokolov brought a background in histology. Damaskin and G. A. Smirnov came to the laboratory with doctorates already in hand, while Massen, Iablonskii, and Sokolov acquired their doctorates for these researched there. None possessed a broad physiological education beyond that acquired at Pavlov's side. As long-standing members of the laboratory, Ganike, Sokolov, and Smirnov became bearers of its institutional memory.

This was especially true of Ganike. Arriving at the Physiology Division in 1894 from the collapsed Syphilology Division, he remained Pavlov's close collaborator until the chief's death in 1936. Ganike's background in chemistry and his "unusual technical inventiveness" made him the laboratory's resident technician and problem solver. He was also Pavlov's all-purpose right-hand man and chief supervisor. Ganike handled the laboratory budget, supervised its chief moneymaking enterprise, and drafted the annual reports for the chief's approval. He also enjoyed a close personal relationship with Prince Ol'denburgskii. When Pavlov was absent or busy, it was Ganike, whom the prince addressed with the familiar *"ty,"* who represented the Physiology Division at meetings of the institute's governing council. Self-effacing, intensely private, and devoted to Pavlov, Ganike left only the skimpiest of memoirs, but Babkin, who worked with him closely, has provided the following portrait:

> Ganike was an exceptional person. He was extremely original and at the same time one of the most modest, cultured, well-bred and honorable of men. He was a bachelor and lived in the Institute of Experimental Medicine. He worked at night and slept most of the day, arriving at the laboratory about 3 or even 5 in the afternoon. He was very musical and played the violon-cello in the laboratory at night to an accompaniment provided by a mechanical device. For his accompaniment he cut out notes in paper tape and inserted this in a special mechanical piano, which was set in motion by an electric motor, while he himself played the solo part on his violoncello.[32]

That Pavlov, who demanded punctuality and regularity from his coworkers, accepted Ganike's nocturnal ways speaks volumes about the taciturn assistant's value to the laboratory. The other long-term workers in the laboratory were the attendants charged with caring for the dogs and preparing them for experiments, assisting during surgical procedures, troubleshooting at the bench, keeping the laboratory in order, and other miscellaneous tasks. Several attendants worked in the laboratory for many years, accumulating important craft knowledge. One *praktikant* recalled that two attendants, Nikolai Kharitonov and a certain Timofei, thus became "indispensable participants in each experiment, and such active participants that they were not so much helpers as, rather, almost the directors." Another *praktikant* wrote of Kharitonov and a younger attendant, Ivan Shuvalov, that their accumulated experience with the sometimes puzzling behavior of dogs and fistulas enabled them to provide in many cases absolutely invaluable assistance." They also became the chief's valued assistants during surgical operations. Pavlov's wife, Serafima, later recalled that when Kharitonov was absent "it was as if Ivan Petrovich [Pavlov] had lost his hands." When Kharitonov grew too old, Shuvalov assumed this task, which required some knowledge of the irascible chief as well:

> It was not easy to assist Pavlov when he was operating. He did not like to call out the name of the instrument he wanted at a given moment or to say what he would do next, and at the same-time he was extremely impatient. The instruments were handed to him by the very able young laboratory attendant, Vania [Ivan] Shuvalov, who knew the operational procedures perfectly and handed Pavlov the required instrument at the right moment. But [in Shuvalov's absence] the assistants, especially the newcomers, often failed to give Pavlov the help he wanted or did so at the wrong time. Then he would push the assistant's hand away and say: "I speak with my hands—you must get used to that," or he would begin to mutter irritably: "Well, hold this, hold this," or some such words. He had no patience with new assistants . . . and they would feel altogether at a loss during an operation and would give him even less help than they were capable of.[33]

. . . The laboratory workforce, then, consisted of the chief, the assistants, the attendants, and the *praktikanty*—all with their prescribed roles. Before we can explore their interaction in the laboratory's productive process, however, we must introduce its last and by no means least, participant.

The Laboratory Dog as Technology and Organism

At the center of the productive process were laboratory dogs modified by ingenious surgical procedures to Pavlov's investigative ends. In the physiology factory, these dogs were simultaneously technologies, physiological objects of study, and products.[34] I shall defer discussion of dogs-as-products and explore here their dual character in the production process itself.

Laboratory dogs were technologies (or "intermediate products") created in the laboratory to produce something else—as in a factory that assembles machines for the manufacture of another product. As Bruno Latour puts it, "you cannot make the facts if you do not have the machines, any more than you can make iron without the big furnaces and the big hammers." Laboratory dogs were particular kinds of "machines" designed and produced in the laboratory to generate particular kinds of facts. As with any technology, their existence and design influenced the organization and nature of the work process. As intermediate products, these dogs also created "local knowledge" and rendered problematic the replication of laboratory results by others. Physiologists incapable of creating, say, a dog with an isolated stomach could reproduce the laboratory's experiments only by acquiring a dog from Pavlov or journeying to St. Petersburg. These dogs were also pedagogical technologies, serving as "wonderful material in all regards for teaching," and so were "no less indispensable for university laboratories than the most important physiological apparatuses."[35]

I distinguish between the laboratory dog as "technology" and as "physiological object of study" to emphasize that it remained a living, functioning, and infinitely complex organism. Designed to perform "normally" in laboratory experiments, the laboratory dog possessed biological attributes that often complicated its use as a technology for the production of *pravil'nye* facts. This tension between dog-as-technology and dog-as-organism was rooted both in the laboratory dog's "lifestyle" and in the confrontation between its biological complexity and Pavlov's scientific vision. We shall be prepared to explore this tension after a closer look at the principles and practices of physiological surgery.

The varied operations performed in Pavlov's surgical ward to produce a laboratory dog for chronic experiments were developed to satisfy three basic criteria: the animal must recover to full health and its digestive system must return to normal functioning; the product of the digestive gland must be rendered accessible to the experimenter at any time for measurement and analysis; and the reagent in that glandular product must be obtainable in pure form, undiluted by food or the secretions of other glands. For Pavlov, a convinced "nervist," the digestive system could function normally only if surgical operations left intact the basic nervous relations that controlled physiological processes.[36]

The simplest and most common operation was implantation of a fistula to draw a portion of salivary, gastric, or pancreatic secretions to the surface of the dog's body, where it could be collected and analyzed. Fistulas were not original to Pavlov's laboratory; for each digestive gland, however, he and his coworkers refined the operation to meet the three criteria I have enumerated.[37] This proved relatively simple with the gastric and salivary glands. Gastric and salivary fistulas diverted only a small portion of glandular secretions to the surface, so any disturbance to normal digestive processes was presumably minimal; both could be opened or closed at the experimenter's discretion, and neither resulted in any visible pathological symptoms.

The creation of a "normal" dog with a pancreatic fistula, however, posed great difficulties. Pavlov himself had devised one procedure in 1880 and assigned several *praktikanty* to improve it in the 1890s; but he conceded even in 1902 that, despite "much labor and attention," the pancreatic fistula left much to be desired. The problem resided in the complex "physiological connections of this gland" and in the constant leakage of pancreatic juice from the fistulized dog. Escaping pancreatic ferments macerated the abdominal wall, causing ulceration and bleeding; and the chronic loss of pancreatic fluid undermined the dog's health in dramatic and mysterious ways. Animals often suddenly fell ill a few weeks or even months after the operation, losing their appetites and developing various nervous disturbances; sometimes "acute general weakness" was followed by fibrillations and death.[37] Conceding that the pancreatic fistula was "not ideal," Pavlov insisted that its usefulness was nevertheless clear in "the numerous, clear, indubitable, and decisive results of investigations." The "normalcy" of these dog-technologies always remained problematic.[38]

A second standard operation was the esophagotomy, which Pavlov and his collaborator E. O. Shumova-Simanovskaia had used in combination with the gastric fistula in 1889-1890 to obtain pure gastric juice from an intact and functioning dog. The esophagotomy involved dividing the gullet in the neck and causing its divided ends to heal separately into an angle of the skin incision. This accomplished "the complete anatomical separation of the cavities of the mouth and stomach," allowing the experimenter to analyze the reaction of the gastric glands to the act of eating. Food swallowed by an esophagotomized dog fell out of the opening from the mouth cavity to the neck rather than proceeding down the digestive tract. Since the dog chewed and swallowed, but the food never reached its stomach, this procedure was termed "sham feeding." Sham feeding an esophagotomized dog equipped with a gastric fistula gave the experimenter access to the gastric secretions produced during the act of eating. The experimenter then collected these secretions through the fistula at five-minute intervals, later measuring them and analyzing their contents. This dog-technology allowed the experimenter to collect virtually unlimited quantities of gastric juice and to analyze the secretory results of the act of eating. Since ingested food never reached the stomach, however, it did not permit investigation of gastric secretion during the second phase of normal digestion, when food was present in the stomach.

This task was addressed by the complex dog-technology that soon became both a symbol of Pavlov's surgical virtuosity and the source of the laboratory's cardinal theoretical achievements. In 1894, after a series of frustrating failures, Khizhin and Pavlov created "the remarkable Druzhok" with an "isolated stomach" (or "Pavlov sac"). The dog's name, which means "Little Friend," reflected the exhilaration, relief, and gratitude with which Pavlov and his collaborators greeted the dog's survival after surgery. The isolated stomach operation was difficult and complex, but the principle behind it was simple. The goal was surgically to create an isolated pocket in part of a dog's stomach—and to do so in such a way that, after the dog's recovery, the entire stomach continued to work normally while this "small stomach" could be studied separately. As Pavlov explained to the Society of Russian Physicians:

> The stomach is divided into two parts; a large part, which remains in place and serves as the normal continuation of the digestive canal; and another, smaller part, completely fenced off from the rest of the stomach and having an opening to the surface, through the abdominal wall. The essential thing in this operation is that in one part of this small stomach the fence [separating it from the large stomach] is formed only of mucous membrane while the muscle and serous layers are preserved, because through them passes the vague nerve, which is the main secretory nerve of the gastric glands. In this manner we acquire in an isolated part of the stomach a completely normal innervation, which gives us the right to take the secretory activity of this part as a true representation of the work of the entire stomach.[39]

Food, then, came into direct contact only with the large stomach, but it would excite presumably normal gastric secretion in both this large stomach and the isolated sac. Since the isolated stomach remained uncontaminated by food and the products of other glands, the experimenter could extract pure glandular secretions through a glass tube and analyze the secretory responses to various foods during the "normal" digestive process.

Pavlov was not the first to create an isolated stomach, but his substantial variation upon that developed by Rudolf Klemensiewicz (1875) and Rudolf Heidenhain (1879) reflected his nervism. Heidenhain doubted that central nervous mechanisms played an important role in gastric secretion, and so the "Heidenhain stomach" involved transection of the vagus nerves. For Pavlov, however, this transection rendered the "Heidenhain stomach" abnormal. He therefore modified Heidenhain's operation, making it "more difficult" but preserving vagal innervation. Two related assumptions were built into the "Pavlov stomach": that exciters of the gastric glands did not act locally (in just one part of the stomach) but, rather, generally (distributing any excitation to the small sac as well); and that mechanical stimulation of the stomach wall played no role in gastric secretion (since such stimulation was exerted by food upon the large stomach, but not upon the isolated sac). These assumptions contradicted a loose consensus among physiologists and a firm one among physicians, yet they were central to Pavlov's claim that what took place in the isolated sac mirrored normal digestive processes.[40]

Pavlov cultivated the image of laboratory dogs that, after recovering from these surgical operations, led normal, "happy" lives. The reality was somewhat different. For one thing, many dogs died as Pavlov and his coworker developed new surgical procedures. About twenty perished before Khizhin and Pavlov successfully created an isolated stomach, and an untold number were sacrificed during attempts over more than a decade to perfect the pancreatic fistula. Survivors usually developed fatal conditions long before their natural lifespan had expired: the isolated stomach would slip or become infected, the pancreatic fistula would lead to various illnesses, spasms, softening of the bones, and a terrible death. In 1897 Pavlov referred proudly in his ***Lectures on the Work of the Main Digestive Glands*** to the fact that one dog (Druzhok) had lived for two and a half years with an isolated sac. He assured his readers that the operation did not bring in its wake "any sensory unpleasantness, to say nothing of danger to the life of the animal operated upon."[41] By this time, however, it was obvious to Andrei Volkovich, the *praktikant* then working with Druzhok, that this assertion was—at least in spirit—untrue. The severe deterioration of Druzhok's isolated stomach had rendered the dog useless for experimentation. Furthermore, the erratic functioning of Druzhok's gastric glands led Volkovich to speculate that the abnormal manner in which the dog had been fed for years (through a fistula) had caused the glands to "gradually atrophy." Pavlov himself observed in 1898 that, after acquiring an isolated sac, dogs tended "to lie on their backs with their legs up," apparently because they experienced "unpleasant or painful sensations when in a normal position."[42] Thus the relative "normalcy" of these dogs, like that of the dogs with pancreatic fistulas, remained a matter of interpretation.

Whether or not they were happy and normal, the dog-technologies used in chronic experiments lived much longer than those consumed in acute experiments; and this facilitated a relationship with experimenters that sometimes resembled that between pet and master.[43] Each dog received a name and manifested an identifiable personality (*lichnost'*). This simultaneously rendered the dogs both more and less "normal." On the one hand, what better testimony to a dog's "normalcy" than a recognizable personality? On the other, personalities varied, and that of any single dog inevitably influenced the results of experimental trials—making the results, if not "abnormal," at least somewhat idiosyncratic and subject to interpretation.

Had laboratory dogs been simple, ideal mechanical technologies, the *praktikant*'s task would have been relatively straightforward: turn them on under conditions prescribed by the chief, then measure and analyze the secretory results. The contradictory nature of these laboratory animals, however, and the drive to gain from them *pravil'nye* results, inevitably entailed a series of interpretive moments.[44] The "numberless factors" presumed to conceal *pravil'nye* results were frequently identified with a dog's psyche and individual personality.

Pavlov characterized the psyche as a "dangerous" "source of error" in experiments on digestive secretion. The dog's "thoughts about food" threatened constantly to introduce the "arbitrary rule of chance" to experiments and so to produce "completely distorted results." Only through the "complete exclusion of psychic influence" could experimenters uncover the otherwise factory-like regularity of the digestive machine. So, *praktikanty* conducting chronic experiments came to work in separate, isolated rooms and were enjoined to "carefully avoid everything that could elicit in the dog thoughts about food." Such procedures, however, could not, even in principle, exclude the psyche from chronic experiments, since a dog's personality and food tastes shaped the "psychic secretion" that constituted the first phase of its response to a meal. In chronic experiments, then, the idiosyncratic psyche acquired "flesh and blood," and its results were incorporated into descriptions of the *pravil'nye* processes of the digestive machine.[45]

So familiar were the secretory consequences of a dog's psyche and personality that, as one *praktikant* wrote in 1896, "it is taken as a rule in the laboratory to study the tastes of the dogs under investigation." Some dogs had pronounced food preferences; others refused the horse meat offered in the laboratory or ate it without enthusiasm. "In such picky dogs sham feeding with an unpleasant or even undistinguished food produces an extremely weak [secretory] effect." Inattention to the individual "character" (*kharakter*) of dogs, he continued, explained the inability of some Western European scientists to elicit gastric secretion by teasing a dog with food:

> Dogs exhibit a great variety of characters, which it is well to observe in their relation to food and manner of eating. There are passionate dogs, especially young ones, who are easily excited by the sight of food and are easily subject to teasing; others, to the contrary, have great self-possession and respond with great restraint to teasing with food. Finally, with certain dogs it is as if they understand the deceit being perpetrated upon them and turn their back on the proferred food, apparently from a sense of insult. These dogs only react to food when it falls into their mouth. . . . Certain dogs are distinguished by a very suspicious or fearful character and only gradually adapt to the laboratory setting and the procedures performed upon them; it stands to reason that the depressed state of these dogs does not facilitate the success of experiments. The age of dogs is also important in determining their character: the older the dog the more restrained and peaceful it is, and vice versa.[46]

The acknowledged importance of the dog's psyche and individual character made these not only the "main enemy" of the experimenter seeking *pravil'nye* results, but also his "best friend" when attempting to reconcile conflicting data with laboratory doctrine. As we shall see, judgments about the individual particularities of one's experimental animal invariably played a part in the interpretation of data.

By their very nature, then, laboratory dogs constantly generated not "clean" quantitative data but, rather, complexities engendering interpretive flexibility. This was fully recognized in the laboratory, raising a question about the work process there: How could the *praktikant*—a mass of "borrowed senses" fit only for simple observation—render the interpretive judgments appropriate only for the chief's "directing mind"?

RELATIONS OF PRODUCTION

With a good method, even a rather untalented person can accomplish much.

—Ivan Pavlov

We, the Laboratory

The workforce in Pavlov's physiology factory was bound together by an authoritarian structure and cooperative ethos. The chief's administrative authority was absolute: he hired and fired, assigned research tasks, decided when a task had been satisfactorily completed, and determined whether a *praktikant* would receive his doctorate. His intellectual authority was also, of course, considerable—by virtue of his knowledge, experience, and administrative power. The atmosphere of free, cooperative inquiry in the laboratory permitted coworkers to disagree openly with Pavlov on scientific questions, although the chief's legendary temper could make this extremely unpleasant. Laboratory *glasnost* both suited the spirit of scientific inquiry and socialized the laboratory's cognitive process, serving as one of several means by which the chief's "directing mind" presided over the interpretive moments inherent to experimental trials. Institutional realities and the career trajectory of the *praktikanty*—who lacked physiological education and were chiefly interested in quick doctoral degrees—shaped the results of this mixture of authority and cooperation. *Praktikanty* came and went, but "we, the laboratory" remained.[47]

The laboratory's cooperative ethos was embodied in Pavlov's addition to the institute's statues of one rule specific to the Physiology Division: "Every *praktikant* is required to participate in the work of his comrades, specifically when there is being conducted a complex experiment or operation demanding a large number of assistants, greater than the constant paid contingent in the laboratory." *Praktikanty* frequently paid tribute to this ethos in memoirs and acknowledgments, of which the following, written in 1894, is typical: "My fervent thanks to the profoundly esteemed professor Ivan Petrovich Pavlov, according to whose thought and guidance this work was conducted; and whose active participation and precious help greeted its every step. . . . [My thanks also] . . . to all the laboratory comrades, who always came to my aid enthusiastically as a result of both their personal goodwill and the principle of broad mutual aid that reigns in Professor Pavlov's laboratory."[48]

Laboratory *glasnost* meant that scientific issues were openly discussed among *praktikanty* in general meetings and in one-to-one sessions with Pavlov. As one *praktikant* recalled, "everybody felt himself a member of one common family and learned much, studied much, knowing the course of the work of his comrades. No secrets were permitted."[49] The interaction of these two dimensions of laboratory life—*glasnost* and Pavlov's immense authority—was central to the productive process, allowing Pavlov to direct, monitor, and process the research of the fifteen or so *praktikanty* who worked for him at any one time and to incorporate the observations of their "borrowed senses" into ongoing laboratory traditions.

Pavlov always openly and proudly acknowledged that the data for his own general works were obtained almost entirely by his *praktikanty*, whom he credited by name for specific results and technical innovations. He himself, however, took credit for the laboratory's methodologies, thus implicitly assuming much credit for his *praktikanty*'s achievements. "With a good method," he once remarked in a lecture, "even a rather untalented person can accomplish much." Furthermore, the concepts that gave these results meaning belonged to "the laboratory." As Pavlov put it in the preface to ***Lectures on the Work of the Main Digestive Glands:***

> In the text of the lectures . . . I use the word "we," that is, I speak in the person of the entire laboratory. Citing constantly the authors of specific experiments, I discuss jointly the experiment's purpose, sense, and place among other experiments, without citing the authors of opinions and views. I think it is useful for the reader to have before him the unfolding of a single idea increasingly embodied in tenable and harmoniously linked experiments. This basic view that permeates everything is, of course, the view of the laboratory, encompassing its every fact, constantly tested, frequently corrected, and, consequently, the most correct. This view is also, of course, the deed of my coworkers, but it is a general deed, the deed of the entire laboratory atmosphere in which everybody gives something of himself and breathes it all in.
>
> Looking upon everything the laboratory has accomplished in our field, I value especially the participation of each separate worker and therefore feel the need on this occasion to send to all my dear coworkers, scattered throughout the broad expanses of our motherland, heartiest greetings from the laboratory which they, I hope, remember as it does them.[50]

This citation goes to the heart of the division of labor and intellectual property. For Pavlov, "we, the laboratory" involved the collective work of all its personnel over the years, but he himself provided its stable personal and interpretive identity (the others were soon "scattered throughout the broad expanses of our motherland"). The experiments belonged to the *praktikant,* but the "basic view" or "single idea" that united them and gave them meaning belonged to "the laboratory," that is, to Pavlov himself. At the same time, his constant references to "the laboratory's view" and to the experiments of various *praktikanty* gave Pavlov's conclusions greater authority, portraying them as the results of collective thinking and independent experimentation by numerous individuals on countless dogs.

These values were embodied in the highly standardized structure and language of laboratory dissertations. These invariably began with a review of previous literature that developed into a rationale for "Professor Pavlov's proposal" that the *praktikant* investigate a particular issue in a particular manner.[51] The impression created is captured nicely by the words with which one of Pavlov's favorite *praktikanty* concluded this section of his thesis: "To the author of the present work fell the happiness of participating in the elaboration of a small part of this great task: Professor Ivan Petrovich Pavlov proposed that . . ." In the body of the dissertations, the word *I* appears almost exclusively with reference to specific observations or to the actual process of conducting experiments; either the passive voice, the word *we*, or the name of the chief himself is attached to conclusions and ideas. So, for example, A. S. Sanotskii (1892) writes that "I tested the influence of teasing with meat" and refers to "my observations," "my experiments," and so forth; but "we have a right to conclude," "we come to the conclusion," and so on.[52] Pavlov's central role in the interpretive moments arising during the *praktikant*'s work was acknowledged in standard phrases: "suggestion of the theme," "constant guidance and aid in word and deed," "constant participation and warm attention." The chief no doubt expected such phrases, yet this was not the empty rhetoric of obeisance. It reflected, rather, Pavlov's extraordinary energy and engagement and a production system that made him an active participant at critical junctures in the *praktikant*'s work.

Lines of Investigation

Pavlov's scientific-managerial vision meshed with the workforce at his disposal in a system of production that gave both the chief and most *praktikanty* what they most wanted. For Pavlov, the *praktikanty* were set to work on his own scientific vision, multiplying his sensory reach manyfold while enabling him constantly to monitor the work process and its results, to incorporate these into his developing ideas, and to convert them efficiently into marketable products. For the *praktikant*, this system provided a sometimes exciting investigatory experience and justified the confident expectation "that after one year in Pavlov's laboratory the thesis would be written and the degree of doctor of medicine would be received."[53] This doctoral thesis originated in Pavlov's scientific-managerial vision, by which he generated an endless series of topics that, within his laboratory system, could be quickly and successfully completed by a *praktikant* with no prior physiological training.

A fundamental, unalterable principle was that Pavlov assigned all research topics. One *praktikant* later recalled that Pavlov appreciated initiative among his coworkers, but "he could not give it a wide range, since this would interfere with the development of his scientific idea, which proceeded according to a set plan." A coworker could express a desire or intention, and this might be sanctioned temporarily if it corresponded with Pavlov's plans. Otherwise, should the *praktikant* contest the point, "there arose an argument that rarely ended with the victory of the coworker." Another coworker recalled that "when a young scientist had matured and was able to formulate his own ideas and plans for research, work with Pavlov became difficult. Subjects that had no direct relation to the work of the laboratory did not interest him, and often he would even refuse to discuss them."[54]

By what rationale did Pavlov assign topics? Wandering into his laboratory in any year, one would find *praktikanty* engaged in a wide variety of subjects. If we look at the chronological development of research topics, however, Pavlov's "set plan," and the reason for his insistence on assigning research topics, is readily apparent. In the years 1891-1904 the topics assigned to *praktikanty* reflected a standardized approach to the main digestive organs (the gastric glands, the pancreatic gland, and, somewhat less and somewhat later, the salivary and intestinal glands). Research on each organ followed a general sequence: establish nervous control over the gland, develop an appropriate dog-technology, identify the specific exciters of glandular secretion, establish quantitatively the *pravil'nye* patterns of glandular activity, and verify the "stereotypicity" of these secretory responses. Research on the different glands proceeded in parallel, each providing models for research on the others. Alongside these principal lines of investigation, *praktikanty* were often assigned topics designed to fortify the Physiology Division's institutional position, explore possible new research paths, respond to critics of laboratory doctrine, or examine puzzling results that lay off the main investigative paths.

When these lines of investigation developed normally, Pavlov never assigned two different *praktikanty* to the same topic simultaneously. This made good sense, since one *praktikant*'s results were a necessary prelude to the research of the next along the standardized route of investigation. This practice also required the chief to interpret only a single set of experimental results at a time. Pavlov departed from it only three times: in assignments for work on the pathology of the digestive system in 1898-1900; on the psychic secretions of the salivary gland, beginning in 1903; and on the influence of nerves and humors upon pancreatic secretion in 1902. In the first two cases, he was considering a major shift in the focus of laboratory work and quickly generalized initial results in a public speech hailing the dawn of a new era not just for his laboratory but for physiology itself. In the third case, Pavlov was responding to the discovery of secretin—a major blow to the nervist views underlying laboratory work.

This scientific-managerial strategy can be illustrated by a brief look at work assignments concerning the pancreas. Before acquiring his laboratory at the institute, Pavlov had traversed the first part of his standard investigatory path, demonstrating to his own satisfaction that the vagus and sympathetic nerves controlled pancreatic secretion. Animals with a pancreatic fistula, however, died unexpectedly and were still considered insufficiently "normal" for chronic experiments. The main task, then, was to improve this dog-technology. In the Physiology Division's first year (1891), Pavlov assigned two *praktikanty* to this objective—one to develop a better fistula, the other to explore various dietary means to keep animals with pancreatic fistulas alive. In 1894 and 1895, armed with the results of this research, Pavlov assigned new *praktikanty* to test likely exciters of pancreatic secretion. By this time, experiments with Druzhok had convinced Pavlov that the gastric glands responded to specific foods with specific secretory patterns; in 1896 he assigned an especially promising *praktikant*, A. A. Val'ter, to find similar patterns in the pancreatic gland. When Val'ter succeeded in doing so, Pavlov assigned A. R. Krever to confirm his results. Two other *praktikanty* elucidated mechanisms of nervous control.[55]

Two interesting observations about Pavlov's scientific-managerial style emerge here. First, Pavlov assigned Krever to verify Val'ter's results in 1898—a year *after* Pavlov had showcased those results in his own ***Lectures on the Work of the Main Digestive Glands.*** Indeed, Pavlov declared Val'ter's results "stereotypical" even before Val'ter had managed to complete his thesis, let alone before Krever's (as it turned out, tortured) confirmation of them. This raises an obvious question about the process and meaning of such verification. Second, since Pavlov was satisfied by 1897 that research on the pancreas had confirmed that, like the gastric glands, it produced precise, purposive secretory reactions to various foods, laboratory research on this gland was slowing by the end of the century. New *praktikanty* were assigned instead to other topics (for example, to the study of intestinal secretions and to the interaction of the glands). This changed suddenly in 1902, with William Bayliss and Ernest Starling's announcement of a humoral mechanism for pancreatic secretion. Pavlov immediately assigned several *praktikanty* (P. Borisov, A. A. Val'ter, V. V. Savich, and Ia. A. Bukhshtab in 1902) to investigate this challenge to his nervism and to repair Val'ter's earlier findings in light of this and other new developments.[56]

This great productive capacity and flexibility was an important advantage of factory production. Pavlov was able to develop concurrently his standardized line of investigation for each gland while also using incoming *praktikanty* to respond quickly to critics, new developments, and simply curious phenomena. No workshop physiologist could do so. Furthermore, the chief's position in the factory afforded him a "panoramic view." Moving at will from one *praktikant*'s work to another's, he could concentrate his own efforts on the key task of the moment while keeping his eye on synthetic possibilities. He confided to his son some years later that "I have turned this into a system. If I did not move simultaneously from one work to another I would never have been able to conduct one work as successfully as I now conduct tens of them."[57] We now look more closely at the managerial system by which Pavlov "conducted" the research of his *praktikanty*.

Working for Pavlov

Upon entering the physiology factory, the *praktikant* was incorporated into a highly structured production system that harnessed his "borrowed senses" to Pavlov's "directing mind." Little was left to chance. An attendant cared for the *praktikant*'s dog and provided the craft skills necessary at the bench; an assistant socialized him into laboratory culture, familiarized him with necessary procedures and interpretive models, and supervised his work; and, when experimental results proved baffling, "all physiological difficulties were solved by Pavlov or his assistant."[58]

Typically, a physician desiring to work in the laboratory made his application directly to Pavlov, who interviewed and quickly accepted him. Sometimes the laboratory was filled to capacity and a strong letter of recommendation was necessary for an applicant to gain admission.[59] Pavlov was chiefly concerned in the interview to begin sizing up the applicant's ability and to establish that the *praktikant* would be completely at his disposal.

Once accepted, the *praktikant* was assigned to an assistant, under whose watchful eye he spent several weeks or even months familiarizing himself with laboratory procedures. This lengthy period both facilitated his socialization into laboratory life and gave Pavlov and his assistant an opportunity to determine an appropriate work assignment. As Babkin observed:

> This lengthy ordeal to which the worker had to submit was partly due to the fact that, according to Pavlov, one of the most difficult tasks which devolved on him as laboratory chief was the choice of problems for his co-workers. He gave most careful thought to each question that he was planning to investigate with a new collaborator and worked out a preliminary plan in his mind, but all this required time.[60]

Babkin's choice of words here—his reference to problems that Pavlov "was planning to investigate with a new collaborator"—is most appropriate.

The *praktikant*'s socialization involved all aspects of laboratory culture. During his first few weeks in the laboratory, he observed the experiments of other coworkers and imbibed general laboratory values. For example, upon arriving thirty minutes late to the laboratory one day, the new *praktikant* I. S. Tsitovich found his assistant, A. P. Sokolov, waiting for him: "With his very first words Sokolov criticized my half-hour tardiness. I was a little insulted by such captiousness, which I ascribed to hostility on his part. Later I became convinced that his criticism was fully deserved, since Ivan Petrovich and the entire laboratory worked like the mechanism of a watch. With the laboratory's strict discipline my lateness really could not be justified."[61] Tsitovich also learned, to his surprise, that a mere *praktikant* had the right to disagree with the chief, and he cheerfully engaged in his first exchanges with Pavlov regarding scientific developments.

After a few weeks the *praktikant* received his own dog, either that of a departing investigator or, if a new animal was required, one prepared surgically by Pavlov or an assistant. The choice of dog reflected Pavlov's decision about which line of investigation the *praktikant* would pursue. Under the assistant's eye, the *praktikant* now familiarized himself thoroughly with the appropriate techniques. He also read the "relevant literature"—which consisted almost exclusively of reports of previous work in Pavlov's laboratory—thus further familiarizing himself with the chief's expectations. Pavlov sometimes stopped by his bench for a moment or two and conferred with the assistant about the *praktikant*'s progress.

When both assistant and chief judged the *praktikant* ready for work and had sized up his abilities, Pavlov assigned him a specific task. Work began under careful supervision. Tsitovich's recollection is typical: "The assistant related to me in great detail how and what I must observe, how to take notes on the experiment, how to avoid extraneous influences [on the dog]." Chronic experiments demanded a great deal of patience and self-discipline, often compelling the *praktikant* to sit virtually motionless for hours. (Pavlov later liked to recount an anecdote about walking into an experimental room to find both dog and *praktikant* asleep at the job.) The ability to endure these lengthy periods of observation and collection was the chief obstacle between the *praktikant* and his doctoral degree. Possessing a surgically prepared dog and an expertly defined topic, and guided by attendants, assistants, and the chief himself, "all that was necessary for a doctor's success was that he should perform his work carefully, bringing to it all his concentration and understanding."[62]

The relationship between observation and interpretation, however, is rarely that simple, especially within a context that locates the two in different personages. In Pavlov's physiology factory, this relationship was shaped by two interactions: that between Pavlov and the *praktikant*, and that between the *praktikant* and his laboratory dog(s).

Pavlov and the Praktikant

Pavlov's presence permeated the laboratory daily. Unless he was lecturing at the Military-Medical Academy, he arrived at the laboratory between 9:30 and 10:00 A.M., immediately checking the coatrack in the entrance hallway to ascertain who was present and who was not. "He never missed a day at the laboratory and did not like anybody to be absent or late."

> When in the mornings he entered, or, more correctly, ran into the laboratory, there streamed in with him force and energy; the laboratory literally enlivened, and this heightened businesslike tone and work tempo was maintained until his . . . departure; but even then, at the door, he would sometimes rapidly deliver instructions regarding what remained to do immediately and how to begin the following day. He brought to the laboratory his entire personality, both his ideas and his moods. He discussed with all his coworkers everything that came into his mind. He loved arguments, he loved arguers and would egg them on.[63]

Pavlov spent his mornings and afternoons attending to the work of one or more *praktikanty*—observing, commenting, and participating in experiments if moved to do so. About fifteen *praktikanty* were working in the laboratory simultaneously, but Pavlov managed to make himself a presence in the work of each, although he singled out one or two whose work interested him especially at any given time. At the very least, the chief dropped by occasionally to check the protocols; if the experiments proved exceptionally interesting he often worked alongside.

> From the moment that a problem was assigned to a worker, Pavlov took a most active interest in it and inquired about its progress almost daily. Often he would sit for an hour or more in the worker's room observing an experiment. He would examine the protocols and often remembered the figures previously obtained better than did the worker himself. Finally, if he was especially interested in the work, he would participate in the experiments himself.[64]

The memoir literature makes clear that Pavlov used his sessions with *praktikanty* to exercise a steady influence upon both the course of experiments and the interpretation of their results. L. A. Orbeli recalled that

> in regard to the correctness of the [experimental] protocols, Ivan Petrovich was very demanding. He did not limit himself to asking how things were going. He would take the notebook with the protocols and begin to look through it. He might ask one of the workers how much juice he had acquired over a quarter of an hour. He would then take the notebook and check. If the verbal answer conflicted with the notes in the protocols, even by several tenths [of a cubic centimeter], the session would end with a dressing down. He knew how to retain in his memory for several days or weeks the most minor details of a work, and sometimes would recall that "at such and such a time an experiment yielded such and such figures." This extraordinary demandingness, perspicacity, and attention to the protocols; this extraordinary memory for all the details of the work conducted in his laboratory, was Ivan Petrovich's unique quality.[65]

Aside from these one-to-one sessions, there were frequent laboratory-wide discussions, which Pavlov would initiate sometimes in the division's common room and sometimes by drawing others into his discussion with a single *praktikant*. V. P. Kashkadamov, who worked in the laboratory from 1895 to 1897, recalled:

> Not less than once a week he would confer with each of us and attempt to draw all the workers into these discussions. Thanks to this we were always aware of all the work being conducted in the laboratory. All facts were subjected to an all-sided discussion and to the strictest criticism. If the slightest carelessness, inattentive relationship to work, or hurried conclusion was revealed Ivan Petrovich would hurl himself upon the guilty party and criticize him sharply. Such sharpness, especially at first, offended me, and I reacted to it very painfully. Then, when I became convinced

> that Ivan Petrovich's rage cooled in fifteen minutes and he forgot about it entirely, relating to the guilty party as he had previously, I came to regard it much more calmly.

Orbeli recalled similarly that, excited about a new fact or observation gathered at a *praktikant*'s side, Pavlov would wander from room to room, informing all the coworkers about the event and its significance. "Having established an important proposition or having noticed a new fact, he would call everybody together and begin a public discussion on the spot. This habit (thinking publicly) facilitated the precision of his ideas and thoughts, and also attracted the coworkers to the work."[66]

These discussions also helped the chief direct the work of his subordinates and unite the laboratory behind a single perspective: "each scientific fact, achievement or error was heatedly discussed at our daily general meetings. . . . Everybody knew what others were working on, what interpretation to ascribe to new facts, how one could interpret them otherwise, what perspectives were revealing what results."[67] In the great majority of cases, Pavlov's guidance was exercised smoothly, as his greater authority, knowledge, and commitment allowed him to dominate free-ranging discussions and shape the interpretation of data.

Sometimes, however, the *praktikant* proved less pliable, eliciting the chief's intolerant, even belligerent, reaction to results and interpretations that contradicted his own views. For example, in 1901 a self-confident *praktikant,* V. N. Boldyrev, showed Pavlov the protocols of some experiments that apparently contradicted the laboratory's doctrine of purposefulness. Boldyrev had not fed his dog for an entire day but observed that, nevertheless, the pancreatic gland secreted periodically. This seemed to contradict Pavlov's view of the factory-like response of the digestive glands to specific excitants. The result was an "extraordinarily stormy scene." Pavlov hollered that Boldyrev was obviously a sloppy observer, that he must have had food in his pockets, or smelled of food, or made some inadvertent movement that excited the dog. The scene ended with Pavlov literally chasing Boldyrev out of the laboratory. Yet the stubborn *praktikant* returned and repeated the experiment with another dog. The result was identical, as was Pavlov's response. Boldyrev then sat with the dog for twenty-four straight hours, with the same result. Finally, Pavlov joined Boldyrev and confirmed his observation—which was soon incorporated into laboratory doctrine.[68]

The memoir literature contains several such examples, always with Pavlov exploding and then finally surrendering to the force of scientific facts. In any case—as this literature also makes clear—it was a rare *praktikant* who stood up to Pavlov's authority and legendary temper, and who was as committed as the chief to a particular interpretation of laboratory results. Furthermore, it was the chief who decided which data and perspectives revealed by a *praktikant*'s research would be pursued—and which would not.[69]

Pavlov's most direct intervention in the work of the *praktikant* was his editing of all reports, articles, and dissertations. This allowed him to shape the interpretation of data, to incorporate the *praktikant*'s work into the laboratory's institutional memory, and to project a unified laboratory voice into the broader scientific and medical communities. Upon drafting one of these "literary products," the *praktikant* was invited to Pavlov's office in the laboratory, where he was treated to sweet tea, black bread, and Ukrainian bacon while he read his draft aloud to the chief. (In the case of a dissertation, this continued for two hours a day over about two weeks.) Pavlov sat with his head back and his eyes closed, frequently interrupting with questions or corrections, and "sometimes revising all through, most attentively, before publication. He even wrote some of them himself."[70]

Each literary product was edited to a particular style. Reports to the Society of Russian Physicians, for example, were no more than ten minutes long, with a simple presentation of data and conclusions. When one *praktikant* submitted a draft in which he polemicized with other scientific traditions and elaborated future research perspectives, Pavlov reacted negatively: "'What is this? What have you scribbled about here? Let me see this!' With a highly skeptical look he took my notebook and leafed through it. 'Well, what have we here!' and tore out about one-half of it. 'Words, little brother, are just words—empty sounds. Just give the facts, *this* will be valuable material.'"[71]

Pavlov's editing lent a highly standardized structure and content to laboratory publications. By the mid 1890s, discussions of previous research and issues in digestive physiology—even the language itself—were almost identical from one literary product to the next. (The exceptions were written by the few people who came to Pavlov's laboratory with well-developed scientific interests and inclinations.)

This editing reached deeply into the content of the *praktikant*'s product. Babkin later recalled one revealing detail about Pavlov's editorial preferences:

> One of [Pavlov's] favorite expressions was "quite definite." An experiment had to show "quite definite" results, and if the results were indefinite then the worker had to ascertain the reasons for this. Pavlov was never satisfied with half measures. Either some wrong technique had been employed or the phenomenon was more complex than the experimenter had imagined. In the latter case it was necessary to change the plan of attack, taking the new factors into consideration. In both his own and his students' publications Pavlov tried as far as possible to avoid such expressions as "it would seem" and "probably." In other words, he avoided "suggestive results." He was a determinist by conviction and believed that every phenomenon had its cause.[72]

As editor, then, Pavlov "processed" results—pressing the *praktikant* to offer "quite definite" conclusions and offering helpful interpretations to this end. The *praktikant* himself, with little physiological training, needed to explain quite complex phenomena in a short period of time and knew that he would not receive his doctorate until he had done so to Pavlov's satisfaction. The chief's suggestions, then, seldom fell upon deaf ears.

So, "all scientific works were filtered" through Pavlov, who took this final opportunity to relate the *praktikant*'s data to laboratory doctrine. A common recollection about this filtering process is worth pondering: "He loved not to read, but to hear the work, immediately elucidating inexactnesses, demanding explanation and confirmation of the material through experiments. There frequently arose heated discussions, during which Ivan Petrovich, using his brilliant memory, would refute the figures and propositions offered by the writer of the dissertation." This curious point—that Pavlov remembered the data better than the *praktikant* himself—arises repeatedly in the memoir literature.[73] It appears suspicious, even absurd, on the face of it—however prodigious Pavlov's memory—when we consider that he was usually supervising the work of some fifteen *praktikanty* conducting hundreds of experiments, each generating columns of data.

I am inclined, however, to accept the recollection as essentially accurate—and as an important reflection of Pavlov's scientific style. He could not, of course, remember *all* the experimental data, but neither was he equally interested in it all. Just as he considered the research of some *praktikanty* more important than that of others, so he considered some experiments more telling than others. Contrary to his carefully cultivated image, Pavlov was a deeply intuitive thinker. Like Bernard's, his notion of experimental reason left ample room for the "preconceived idea"; and, like Gerald Geison's Pasteur, he confidently identified the "signal" amid the "noise."[74] Pavlov carried with him an ideal "template" of what good experimental results along his main lines of investigation should look like. When he observed results that fit this template, he remembered them well and so was quite capable of citing such data to refute or amend interpretations of other experiments that fit his preconception less snugly.

This highlights a critical point for reading the *praktikanty*'s literary products: Pavlov was the coauthor of each. Throughout the *praktikant*'s tenure in the laboratory—during his initial socialization, the meetings with assistant and chief at the bench, the give-and-take of general laboratory discussions, and his editorial sessions with Pavlov—his "borrowed senses" constantly confronted the chief's "directing mind." In the dissertations, this confrontation was often reflected in detailed physiological explanations downplaying results that threatened long-standing laboratory doctrines and emphasizing those that affirmed them. Reading these dissertations, one sometimes notices that their argumentation "changes direction"—that data and prose that run counter to, say, the notion of a purposeful pattern in pancreatic secretions suddenly shift and take the opposite direction; or, more commonly, that tentative suggestions become "quite definite" conclusions. This, I think, testifies to Pavlov's hand, and to the deeper significance of Babkin's observation that "all physiological difficulties were solved by Pavlov or his assistant."[75]

Appreciation of Pavlov's role brings us back to the interpretive moments inherent to the chronic experiment. We now turn, then, to the second critical interaction in the laboratory.

The Men and Their Dogs at Work

We have seen that the tension between laboratory dogs as technologies and as intact organisms created a series of interpretive moments in chronic experiments. As technologies, the dogs were expected to yield *pravil'nye* results. For example, the gastric glands in one dog were expected to produce the same pattern of secretions in response to 200 grams of meat from one meal to the next, and this "secretory curve" was expected to be "essentially" the same as that produced by another dog. Pavlov and his *praktikanty* also recognized, however, that, as an intact organism, each dog possessed a psyche and a distinctive personality and that these influenced experimental results. The *praktikant*'s task, then, went far beyond collecting, measuring, and analyzing digestive fluids; he had also to assess the normality and personality of his dog(s) and interpret his results accordingly—with Pavlov's help and until gaining Pavlov's approval. Reviewing the doctoral dissertations produced in the laboratory reveals several features of this interpretive process.

In keeping with Pavlov's scientific vision, a *praktikant* necessarily assessed the "normalcy" of his dog. This assessment rested in part on such objective indicators as the animal's maintenance of a stable weight and temperature, but it was not limited to these. The word *happy* (*veselyi*) occurs regularly in attestations of normalcy. For example, Sanotskii (1892) assured his readers that, having recovered from their operations, "the dogs were happy and energetic, possessed a marvelous appetite, and gave at a glance the general impression of completely normal animals." Attesting to the full recovery of his dogs from the implantation of the troublesome pancreatic fistula, Val'ter (1897) noted that they "create the impression of entirely normal, well-fed, happy animals." The dog upon whom most of his conclusions were based, Zhuchka, "ate its food enthusiastically," ran a normal temperature, and "produced the impression of a healthy animal enjoying its life." Sometimes, as in a dog with a pancreatic fistula, the *praktikant* knew that the operation had fundamentally disrupted the dog's digestive system and would eventually lead to its death. He then needed to attest that the dog was "sufficiently normal" to generate trustworthy data. To this end, Bukhshtab (1904) described the medical ups and downs of his Lada, who suffered from both a pancreatic fistula and the transection of the nerves between its stomach and intestines. Bukhstab related that Lada actually gained weight and "felt good" but had lost some of its "former stamina": "It would become exhausted from standing in the stand, and ate unenthusiastically after the end of the experiment; therefore, the next day its weight declined. Therefore, we began to conduct experiments, not every day, but with breaks of a day or two, to allow the dog to recover and preserve its health and weight longer." Despite these efforts, Lada's "ability to withstand various external influences was lessened." The animal developed mouth ulcers, refused food, and lost weight, finally dying three months after its nerves were transected. Bukhshtab insisted, however, upon the validity of his data, since experiments with Lada were conducted only when the dog was "in complete health."[76]

The *praktikant* also needed to identify the dog's personality (*lichnost'*), character (*kharakter*), or individuality (*individual'nost'*) and to interpret experimental results accordingly. "Professor Pavlov has many times told those working in his laboratory that knowledge of the individual qualities of the experimental dog has important significance for a correct understanding of many phenomena elicited by the experiment," wrote one coworker in 1901. "During the conduct of our experiments we always kept this in view."[77] Here the *praktikant* drew upon observations concerning the dog's ease in adapting to the laboratory settings, its reaction to teasing with food, its preference for certain foods, the relative quantity of its secretory reactions, the consistency of these reactions from day to day, and so forth.

This assessment of the dog's personality was often invoked in interpreting experimental data. For example, V. N. Vasil'ev (1893) noted that his two dogs produced markedly different secretory reactions, perhaps owing to their differing ways of life before entering the laboratory: one was a "simple street dog" and so ate any food readily; the other was "obviously a hunting dog, judging by the breed and by its nervous temperament." A. R. Krever's dog Sokol (1899) was "distinguished by the great sensitivity of its digestive canal" and was so easily disturbed that it had to be taken for calming walks between experiments. Even the possible effect of these walks themselves played a role in the interpretation of experimental results. Ia. Kh. Zavriev's Volchok (1900) was "very cowardly, reacting to every manipulation with panicky terror." N. P. Kazanskii's Laska (1901) was "peaceful, happy, and affectionate" and "very greedy for food. It trembled at the sight of the food bowl and burst off the stand, almost tipping it over." Kazanskii's other dog, Pestryi, was entirely different:

> As for particularities in Pestryi's nature, we can note that he was not distinguished by greed for food. He never threw himself upon the food being brought to him; he always ate calmly, unhurriedly, but with visible appetite. During the initial experiments he did not eat raw meat enthusiastically, as a consequence of which the quantity of juice in the first hour sometimes was less than during the second (a little); but then having become accustomed to meat he began to eat it enthusiastically. He was happy and always obedient during the experiments; but was also distinctively nervous and easily offended. It was enough to raise one's hand at him for him to begin to squeal, bark and grumble. . . . Pestryi initially leaned toward the pieces of meat and sausage offered him [in teasing experiments]; but then, as if he had been offended or had understood the deception, he would turn away from the food offered him in that way.[78]

Here Kazanskii invoked Pestryi's personality and relative apathy toward food in order to reconcile experimental data with laboratory doctrine. According to the "stereotypical secretory curves" (constructed earlier through interpretation of experiments with Druzhok), the rapidity of gastric secretion elicited by a meal of raw meat should peak in the first hour, not the second (as was sometimes the case with Pestryi). This rapid secretion during the first hour, however, owed much to "psychic secretion," which, according to Kazanskii's argument, was muted by Pestryi's particular character. Similarly, Pestryi's changing disposition explained the different results in presumably identical experimental trials (sometimes secretion peaked in the first hour, sometimes in the second). Finally, laboratory doctrine held that appetite itself—rather than the actual mechanical effects of food upon the nerves of the mouth—generated the initial "psychic" phase of gastric secretion. This could usually be demonstrated by teasing animals with food and observing the secretory results. Pestryi, however, often failed to produce this secretory response, instead turning away from the food "as if he had been offended or had understood the deception." Kazanskii's voracious Laska would of course respond both to feeding and to teasing with a more copious "psychic secretion" than would the restrained Pestryi, and their differing "psychological profiles" were necessarily borne in mind when constructing a single, "stereotypical" curve from the differing data produced by the two animals.

Such interpretive moments constituted an "industrial secret" well known to those who worked on the factory floor but largely unappreciated by consumers familiar only with its finished products.[79]

LABORATORY PRODUCTS AND THEIR MARKETS

Pavlov's physiology factory efficiently produced a large number of diversified products that appealed to various markets. The product line included knowledge claims of varying character and scope; literary products (dissertations, reports, articles, generalizing statements); methodologies, techniques, and dog-technologies; pure digestive juices; and alumni. Each product had an independent history beyond the laboratory, contributing to a "composite"—Pavlov's reputation and authority—that was greater than the sum of its parts. The fate of these products in their different markets is the subject for another essay. Here I will offer only a few general observations.

The knowledge claims produced in the laboratory ranged from relatively simple facts (e.g., the pepsin content of gastric secretions) to larger claims about the functioning of the glands (e.g., the important role of the vagus and the psyche) to unifying metaphorical statements (e.g., that the digestive system is a purposeful, precise, and efficient factory). As is generally true with complex knowledge claims, these existed both as a package and as separable components. Just as some naturalists accepted Darwin's argument for evolution (or his description of island finches) and rejected his emphasis on natural selection, so did physicians and scientists pick and choose among the knowledge claims generated by the Pavlov laboratory.

These knowledge claims were formulated and communicated in a constant output of various literary products, which were processed differently for various markets. The raw material for literary products—the experimental protocols—was the private property of the laboratory, where it remained in the form of laboratory notebooks arranged by dog. These provided an immense reservoir of data that was often drawn upon years after the trials that they recorded. The least-processed public product was the dissertation, which was edited by the chief for a few readers. Dissertations often contained contradictory data and interpretations, confessions about experimental difficulties, and other impurities absent in more refined products. Next came the *praktikanty*'s public reports and published articles. These were tightly edited, highly focused, self-consciously public products that projected the laboratory's confident voice to scientific and medical audiences. Here many of the contradictions and complexities contained in the dissertation were omitted (although they sometimes re-emerged in public discussions). The most highly processed form—in which vision and data meshed most grandly and smoothly—were the publications of the chief himself. These (and selected articles by *praktikanty*) were the only literary products readily available to the laboratory's foreign consumers.

The laboratory also produced methodologies, techniques, and dog-technologies whose usefulness to other investigators was somewhat independent of the laboratory's knowledge claims. These products ranged from the Mett method for measuring the proteolytic power of glandular secretions to the Pavlov sac, and they attracted a number of Western scientists to St. Petersburg. Enhancing production in other laboratories and fortifying the scientific status of physiology in general, these products provided a stable source of Pavlov's authority even when his specific knowledge claims were called into question.[80]

Perhaps the most important of these technical products were the dog-technologies, which were impressive embodiments of the laboratory's surgical and doctrinal achievements. Pavlov displayed several of these dogs at the All-Russian Hygiene Exhibit in 1893 to impress the general public with the power of experimental physiology. They served in public lectures not only for scientific-pedagogical purposes but, more broadly, as Pavlov put it, for "convincing the usually so stubborn public of the correctness and obvious usefulness of experiments on animals." Exhibited proudly to the laboratory's visitors and in a 1904 photo album celebrating Pavlov's achievements, laboratory dogs also made an impressive gift to a valued colleague.[81]

These dog-technologies also enabled Pavlov's laboratory efficiently to produce large quantities of pure digestive juices, which themselves proved an especially successful product among both scientists and clinicians. A number of Russian and Western European investigators requested samples of gastric and pancreatic secretions in order to pursue their own studies of digestive fluids. Even after the publication of Pavlov's ***Lectures on the Work of the Main Digestive Glands,*** one Russian physiologist could write that "I. P. Pavlov's great significance consists in his introduction and perfection of a method to obtain various digestive juices in pure form."[82]

Pure gastric juice created a sensation in the international medical market. Pavlov's "small gastric juice factory," which swung into production in 1898, bottled the gastric juice drawn from esophagotomized dogs by sham feeding and sold it as a remedy for dyspepsia. By 1904 this enterprise was selling over three thousand flagons a year, increasing the laboratory budget by over 65 percent. Perhaps more importantly, Pavlov's "natural gastric juice of a dog" provided a dramatic demonstration of the clinical value of experimental physiology, considerably enhancing the chief's reputation among physicians and physiologists both in Russia and abroad. Indeed, Pavlov's status as a hero of Russian science was bolstered considerably by several articles in the country's medical press accusing a Frenchman of unscrupulously pirating this treatment for dyspepsia and marketing it under the sanitized label "gastérine."[83]

The laboratory also produced alumni. Just as they had as *praktikanty*, alumni qualitatively extended Pavlov's reach. Armed with doctoral degrees, they often rose to influential positions in Russia's medical establishment. About half acquired professorial positions in clinical medicine (often combining these with a clinical position in a hospital); others assumed posts in the state medical bureaucracy and in a wide range of military and civilian institutions throughout the empire. Few became physiologists, although this began to change at the turn of the century.[84] Even alumni who attained only modest professional heights enhanced Pavlov's reputation simply by making their way, in the course of their everyday lives, into innumerable milieus that were inaccessible to the chief for many reasons, including the sheer limitations upon the time of any single person. Former *praktikanty* lived throughout the empire, treating and chatting with patients, attending meetings, delivering and commenting upon papers, recommending the laboratory's home remedy for dyspepsia, and, apparently quite often, regaling acquaintances with tales of their investigative experience in St. Petersburg. Like alumni of other academic institutions, many preserved some connection with the laboratory long after graduation: corresponding with the chief, visiting him when in the capital, requesting letters of recommendation, and so forth. Favored alumni continued to perform important tasks: several traveled abroad on study leaves, teaching Pavlovian techniques and otherwise extending the chief's European contacts. One alumnus, A. A. Val'ter, qualitatively enhanced Pavlov's European reputation by translating ***Lectures on the Work of the Main Digestive Glands*** into German (1898). These foreign contacts were especially important to Pavlov given the rarity of his own forays beyond Russia's borders, and they generated significant return traffic to St. Petersburg.

These considerations highlight an important advantage of factory production: the efficient generation of *sheer numbers* of products. The enormous quantity of experiments and data—over which only Pavlov had total access and control—allowed him to mobilize them selectively for his purposes. The sheer quantity of *praktikanty* and lines of investigation afforded him great flexibility and a "panoramic view," allowing him to move among related projects at will, to note interesting similarities and differences among them, and to initiate new ones as seemed fit. The sheer quantity of alumni amplified his voice and extended his reach both in Russia and abroad.

The impact of sheer quantity of literary products can be illustrated through Pavlov's participation in the St. Petersburg branch of the Society of Russian Physicians. Founded in the 1880s as a leading organ of the medical profession, the society provided a principal market for the laboratory's reports and articles. Its membership included about 150 of St. Petersburg's most eminent physicians, professors of clinical medicine, and medical administrators, a number of whom gathered twice a month to hear and discuss brief reports. Society proceedings were widely published, both in *Trudy Obshchestva Russkikh Vrachei (Works of the Society of Russian Physicians)* and in other Russian medical journals (which sent their own reporters to meetings). Rarely did any investigator take the podium more than once a year, but between 1891 and 1904 representatives of Pavlov's laboratory presented about ninety reports. Delivered by physicians and buttressed by impressive experimental data, these reports conveyed the range, methodologies, fundamental conclusions, and therapeutic promise of the laboratory's research. At the conclusion of a *praktikant*'s report, the chief usually rose to summarize its significance and, almost always, to handle any questions or objections. The sheer number of these occasions created a role for Pavlov: he became, as he once put it, "the voice of contemporary times"—the experimental physiologist explaining to practicing physicians the nature and value of scientific medicine.[85] Elected to society membership only in 1892, Pavlov became its vice president the following year and held that post until he assumed the presidency in 1907.

This brings us to the laboratory's final product: Pavlov himself. The talented but undisciplined procrastinator who labored erratically during the 1870s and 1880s himself became part of the purposeful, precise, and regular operation of his physiology factory. No longer did he work by inspiration or stroll along the Neva River during weekdays dreaming of future accomplishments. Every moment was accounted for, and those who sought unscheduled counsel could usually obtain it only—literally—on the run. Placed upon the public stage by his laboratory's products, Pavlov used the spotlight skillfully. As the nation's most visible experimenter on animals, he became physiologists' spokesman against antivivisectionists; as the Russian physiologist whose works were most familiar in the West, he became the Russian medical establishment's candidate for a Nobel Prize; as the source of numerous technical innovations, a laboratory-based therapy for dyspepsia, and a precise portrayal of subtle physiological mechanisms, he became a spokesman for—and, later, a symbol of—the unlimited possibilities of experimental biology.

The role of factory production in creating this new Pavlov is evident throughout the Nobel Prize Committee's deliberations. Pavlov was first nominated in 1901 both by a collective letter from the professors of the Military-Medical Academy—who apparently saw him as Russia's best hope for a prize in physiology or medicine—and by the Johns Hopkins University physiologist W. H. Howell, who had read ***Lectures on the Work of the Main Digestive Glands*** in Val'ter's German translation. Pavlov's candidacy rested on a wide range of laboratory products and so weathered doubts about some of his specific knowledge claims (including his doctrine of purposefulness, his discovery of "stereotypical" patterns of gastric and pancreatic secretion, and his nervist account of pancreatic secretion). The nominee succeeded in neutralizing some of these criticisms in the eyes of the Nobel judges by the timely deployment of *praktikanty* and the rapid publication of responses to objections. When informed that several judges would attend the Conference of Northern Physiologists in Helsinki in 1902, Pavlov mobilized his laboratory to impress them with seven separate reports. The committee that finally awarded him the prize in 1904 included two members who, for either therapeutic or investigative purposes, had obtained from the nominee some "natural gastric juice of a dog."[86]

As for the "downside" of factory production—the questions it raised about intellectual credit and originality—the committee ultimately agreed with two of Pavlov's supporters. Their visit to the laboratory had convinced them that "all the works issued from it, whether or not they carry prof. Pawlow's name, to a substantial degree constitute his intellectual property, as he has not only carried out all the operations on the animals used in the experiments but has also been the leader and organizer [*ordnaren*] with regard to the planning, development, and implementation of the special investigations." As another committee member expressed it, Pavlov remained "the soul and the leader even in the research that his workers and students in the laboratory carry out."[87]

Even as Pavlov accepted the Nobel Prize, he was turning laboratory investigations toward the ghost in the digestive machine—toward the psyche itself. By 1904 he was well on his way toward a redefinition of "psychic secretion" that rendered it accessible to his laboratory system. The physiology factory of 1891-1904 proved only a small prototype for the immense enterprise that he would build and direct in subsequent years. The challenges of a new, seemingly very different scientific subject, and the passage from tsarism to bolshevism (and from Lenin to Stalin), changed the system of production in Pavlov's laboratory very little. His "small world" proved remarkably successful in—even preadapted to—the larger world of twentieth-century science.

NOTES

[1] This was the physiologist Robert Tigerstedt's characterization of the "totally incorrect" opinion of other members of the Nobel Prize Committee. This view appears in his memo of 8 Sept. 1901, entitled "P. M. angaende prof. J. P. Pawlowa arbeten," in *P. M. Forsandelser och Betankanden 1901,* Nobel Archives, Karolinska Institutet, Stockholm, Sweden. My thanks to Johan Ledin for this and other translations of the Swedish texts. For a discussion of Pavlov's candidacy for the Nobel Prize see George Windholz and James R. Kuppers, "Pavlov and the Nobel Prize Award," *Pavlovian Journal of Behavioral Science,* 1990, *25:*155-162. For the epigraph see Ivan Pavlov, "Ob ume voobshche" (1918), Arkhiv Rossiiskoi Akademii Nauk, Peterburgskii filial (Archive of the Russian Academy of Sciences, St. Petersburg branch), *fond 259 opis'* 1a *delo* 3, *list* 12. Hereafter references of this sort will be cited as ARAN 259.1a.3:12.

[2] Among the many works that treat science as social production are Bruno Latour and Steve Woolgar, *Laboratory Life: The Social Construction of Scientific Facts* (Beverly Hills, Calif.: Sage, 1979); Karin Knorr-Cetina, *The Manufacture of Knowledge: An Essay on the Constructivist and Contextual Nature of Science* (Oxford: Pergamon, 1981); Steven Shapin and Simon Schaffer, *Leviathan and the Air-Pump: Hobbes, Boyle, and the Experimental Life* (Princeton, N.J.: Princeton Univ. Press, 1985); Adele Clarke and Joan Fujimura, eds., *The Right Tools for the Job: At Work in Twentieth-Century Life Sciences* (Princeton, N.J.: Princeton Univ. Press, 1992); and Robert E. Kohler, *Lords of the Fly:* Drosophila *Genetics and the Experimental Life* (Chicago/London: Univ. Chicago Press, 1994). I read Kohler's splendid book closely while thinking about Pavlov's laboratory and acknowledge the benefit of his many insights.

[3] For the differing scientific-managerial styles in six large chemistry laboratories see Joseph Fruton, *Contrasts in Scientific Style: Research Groups in the Chemical and Biochemical Sciences* (Philadelphia: American Philosophical Society, 1990). There exists no similar work for large physiological laboratories, but reminiscences and the observations of historians point to important differences among them. See, e.g., Gerald L. Geison, *Michael Foster and the Cambridge School of Physiology: The Scientific Enterprise in Late Victorian Society* (Princeton, N.J.: Princeton Univ. Press, 1978), pp. 162-190; Simon Flexner and James Thomas Flexner, *William Henry Welch and the Heroic Age of American Medicine* (Baltimore/London: Johns Hopkins Univ. Press, 1941), pp. 84-86; Robert Frank, Jr., "American Physiologists in German Laboratories, 1865-1914," in *Physiology in the American Context, 1850-1940,* ed. Geison (Bethesda, Md.: American Physiological Society, 1987), pp. 11-46, esp. pp. 27-38; Merriley Borell, "Instruments and an Independent Physiology: The Harvard Physiological Laboratory, 1871-1906," *ibid.,* pp. 293-321; and E. M. Tansey, "The Wellcome Physiological Research Laboratories, 1894-1904: The Home Office, Pharmaceutical Firms, and Animal Experiments," *Medical History,* 1989, *33:*1-41. On Pavlov's and V. M. Bekhterev's contrasting styles see Boris Babkin, *Pavlov: A Biography* (Chicago/London: Univ. Chicago Press, 1949), pp. 67-76, 80-82, 115-129. Babkin described these laboratories more fully in his original manuscript, which is held by the McGill University Archive, Montreal; hereafter this version of the text will be cited as Babkin, *Pavlov* (manuscript).

The comparison of laboratory and factory has a long history. For two quite different reflections see Max Weber, "Science as a Vocation" (1919), in *From Max Weber: Essays in Sociology,* trans. and ed. H. H. Gerth and C. Wright Mills (New York: Oxford Univ. Press, 1946), pp. 129-156, on p. 135; and Bruno Latour, "The Costly Ghastly Kitchen," in *The Laboratory Revolution in Medicine,* ed. Andrew Cunningham and Perry Williams (Cambridge: Cambridge Univ. Press, 1992), pp. 295-303, on p. 299. My thanks to Keith Barbera for bringing Weber's comments to my attention.

For an overview of Pavlov's laboratory from 1891 to 1936 see George Windholz, "Pavlov and the Pavlovians in the Laboratory," *Journal of the History of the Behavioral Sciences,* 1990, *26:*64-74; and D. G. Kvasov's prefatory essay, in Kvasov and A. K. Fedorova-Grot, *Fiziologicheskaia Shkola I. P. Pavlova* (Leningrad: Nauka, 1967), pp. 3-18. For a characterization of "Pavlov's school" at work on conditional reflexes see David Joravsky, *Russian Psychology: A Critical History* (Oxford/Cambridge, Mass.: Basil Blackwell, 1989), pp. 389-400.

[4] Pavlov made this revelation to a Parisian audience likely to appreciate it, but his high regard for Bernard is evident throughout his corpus. For this comment see his remarks upon accepting an honorary doctorate from the University of Paris in 1925, in *Neopublikovannye i maloizvestnye materialy I. P. Pavlova* (Leningrad: Nauka, 1975), p. 77. In 1897 Pavlov compiled a reading list on physiology for laypeople and recommended that they begin their specialized reading with three works by this "brilliant mind." See N. M. Gureeva, "Uchastie I. P. Pavlova v deiatel'nosti pedagogicheskogo muzeia voennykh uchebnykh zavedenii," *Fiziologicheskii Zhurnal SSSR,* 1959, *45*(9):1157-1162, on p. 1159. Proponents of radical scientism embraced Bernard's determinism and opposition to metaphysics in science; liberal and conservative opponents of radical scientism used Bernard's antimetaphysical stance to separate the materialist metaphysics of radical thinkers from the authority of science. Three successive professors of physiology at St. Petersburg University—I. M. Sechenov, I. F. Tsion, and I. R. Tarkhanov—assumed that post after some experience in Bernard's laboratory.

[5] The first, a joint work with another of Tsion's students, was delivered to the St. Petersburg Society of Naturalists.

The abstract is republished in I. P. Pavlov, *Polnoe Sobranie Sochinenii*, 6 vols. (Moscow/Leningrad: Akademiia Nauk SSSR, 1951-1952) (hereafter cited as Pavlov, *Polnoe Sobranie Sochinenii*), Vol. 1, p. 27. The second, written in collaboration with yet another of Tsion's students, was awarded a gold medal from St. Petersburg University and was subsequently republished in *Pflüger's Archiv;* see *ibid.*, Vol. 2, Pt. 1, pp. 49-87.

[6] To give one of many examples: In *An Introduction to the Study of Experimental Medicine,* Bernard writes: "Ideas, given form by facts, embody science." See Claude Bernard, *Introduction to the Study of Experimental Medicine*, trans. Henry Copley Greene (New York: Dover, 1957), p. 26. In *Lectures on the Work of the Main Digestive Glands,* Pavlov offers his readers "the unfolding of a single idea increasingly embodied in tenable and harmoniously linked experiments." Ivan Pavlov, *Lektsii o rabote glavnykh pishchevaritel'nykh zhelez* [*Lectures on the work of the main digestive glands*] (1897), preface to the first edition, in Pavlov, *Polnoe Sobranie Sochinenii,* Vol. 2, Pt. 2, p. 11. In the authorized English translation by W. H. Thompson, *The Work of the Digestive Glands* (London: Charles Griffin, 1902), this phrase is found in the first page of the unpaginated "Preface to the Russian Edition." Unless otherwise noted, the translations that appear here are mine. Hereafter I will refer to the Russian edition as Pavlov, *Lektsii* and to the English as Pavlov, *Lectures.*

[7] Bernard, *Introduction to the Study of Experimental Medicine,* pp. 59-86; William Coleman, "The Cognitive Basis of the Discipline: Claude Bernard on Physiology," *Isis,* 1985, *76:*49-70; and Latour, "Costly Ghastly Kitchen" (cit. n. 3), pp. 295-303.

[8] Bernard denied the usefulness of mathematical averages or means to characterize physiological phenomena. These, he argued, were inappropriate to the search for unvarying, deterministic laws. In *An Introduction to the Study of Experimental Medicine* he made this point by describing his own relentless search to reconcile (rather than average) conflicting results. These examples all concerned questions that could finally be answered with a simple "yes" or "no." See, for example, the description of his path to the discovery that an animal could be made diabetic by puncturing its fourth ventricle (pp. 173-178). Pavlov, on the other hand, used chronic experiments to analyze secretory *patterns* that he could never describe with a simple "yes" or "no." His construction of "stereotypical" patterns involved comparisons of varying data and, ultimately, reliance upon a flexible, homegrown statistical logic.

[9] Coleman, "Cognitive Basis of the Discipline" (cit. n. 7), p. 56. For Bernard's scientific style see F. L. Holmes, *Claude Bernard and Animal Chemistry: The Emergence of a Scientist* (Cambridge, Mass.: Harvard Univ. Press, 1974).

[10] Bernard, *Introduction to the Study of Experimental Medicine* (cit. n. 6), pp. 21-23, 23-24.

[11] On the early history of the Imperial Institute of Experimental Medicine see A. P. Salomon, "Imperatorskii Institut Eksperimental'noi Meditsiny v S.-Peterburge," *Arkhiv Biologicheskikh Nauk,* 1892, *1:*3-22; and Iu P. Golikov and K. A. Lange, "Stanovlenie pervogo v Rossii issledovatel'skogo uchrezhdeniia v oblasti biologii i meditsiny," in *Pervyi v Rossii issledovatel'skii tsentr v oblasti biologii i meditsiny* (Leningrad: Nauka, 1990), pp. 7-75.

[12] The citation is from Ol'denburgskii's report to Tsar Alexander III in 1893, in Tsentral'nyi Gosudarstvennyi Istoricheskii Arkhiv Peterburga (hereafter TsGIAP) 2282.1.56:80.

[13] The phrase "detour through the lab" is Latour's, in "Costly Ghastly Kitchen" (cit. n. 3), p. 297. Geison argues convincingly that a similar "detour"—in the form of a requirement that medical students attend "a practical course of general anatomy and physiology" involving "experiments; manipulations, & c."—transformed Foster's laboratory and "may have been the most important factor in the transformation of late Victorian physiology." See Geison, *Foster and the Cambridge School of Physiology* (cit. n. 3), pp. 150-151, 174-179. On the widespread perception that "scientific positivism" was the key to improving medical practice see V. I. Pashutin, *Kratkii ocherk Imperatorskoi Voenno-Meditsinskoi Akademii za 100 let eia sushchestvovaniia* (St. Petersburg, 1898), p. 19. The statutes describing the advantages of a doctorate in medicine are collected in *Svod uzakonenii i rasporiazhenii pravitel'stva po vrachebnoi i sanitarnoi chasti v Imperii* (St. Petersburg, 1895-1896), pp. 129-130.

[14] Pavlov probably came to appreciate the advantages of large laboratory groups while working in Karl Ludwig's and Rudolf Heidenhain's laboratories in 1884-1886. His managerial style, however, differed markedly from theirs. The authoritative dictionary of the Russian language defined the root word, *"praktik,"* as "a man of deeds, applying his understanding to a task, fulfilling it in experience," and offered the antonyms "theoretician, speculator, philosopher." See Vladimir Dal', *Tolkovyi slovar' zhivogo velikorusskogo iazyka,* Vol. 3, "P" (1882; Moscow: Russkii Iazyk, 1990), p. 381.

[15] As David Joravsky has noted, many years later Pavlov's friend and colleague Nikolai Kol'tsov observed of the coworkers who explored conditional reflexes that "these ephemeral scholars were often only hands, for which their teacher provided the head." For Joravsky, "the important question is whether or to what degree Pavlov turned his assistants into factory hands, made them do science in the regimented way that stifles creativity regardless of voice level or other peculiarities of command and execution. He was a pioneer of the twentieth century's 'big science,' which raises that troubling question everywhere." See N. K. Kol'tsov, "Trud zhizni velikogo biologa," *Biologicheskii Zhurnal,* 1936, 5(3): 387-402, on p. 401; and Joravsky, *Russian Psychology* (cit. n. 3), p. 390.

[16] Pavlov first publicly referred to the digestive system as a factory in a speech of 1894: "Rech' tovarishcha predsedatelia obshchestva russkikh vrachei," *Trudy Obshchestva Russkikh Vrachei,* Dec. 1895, pp. 151-165, on p. 155; also in Pavlov *Polnoe Sobranie Sochinenii,* Vol. 2, Pt. 1, pp. 245-274, on p. 250. His use of this metaphor corresponds in a number of interesting details to an article about factories published just prior to this speech by his acquaintance, the chemist Dmitrii Mendeleev: "Zavody," in *Entsiklopedicheskii slovar' Brokgauza i Efrona,* Vol. 12 (St. Petersburg, 1894), pp. 100-104. For Pavlov's elaboration of this guiding metaphor in *Lectures on the Work of the Main Digestive Glands* see Pavlov, *Lektsii,* p. 20. The English translation (Pavlov, *Lectures,* p. 2) muffles this passage. Where Pavlov writes that the digestive canal "is, obviously, a chemical factory," the English version reads "It may be compared to a chemical factory." In the Russian edition, Pavlov develops this metaphor by reference to a specific Russian productive relationship, *kustarnyi lad.* This is omitted in the English translation. For a reference to the digestive system as a "chemical laboratory" see Pavlov's lectures of 1911-1912 in Pavlov, *Polnoe Sobranie Sochinenii,* Vol. 5, p. 17. In the mid-nineteenth century, the Russian word *"laboratoriia"* was still defined univocally as "an institution for chemical or metallurgical works, for filling explosive shells, for the preparation of fireworks": Dal', *Tolkovyi slovar'* (cit. n. 14), Vol. 2, "I-O" (1881), p. 231. Dal's dictionary was compiled decades prior to its publication, so this definition does not reflect common usage by the time of its publication. My thanks to Nikolai Krementsov for pointing this out.

[17] Pavlov's laboratory budget for 1891 was 3,200 rubles: TsGIAP 2282.1.396:164. His nearest competitor was I. R. Tarkhanov at the Military-Medical Academy, whose annual budget was 600 rubles. See Lev Popel'skii, *Istoricheskii ocherk kafedry fiziologii v Imperatorskoi Voenno-Meditsinskoi Akademii za 100 let (1798-1898)* (St. Petersburg, 1899), p. 118. For the epigraph to this section see Ivan Pavlov, "Experimental Psychology and Psycho-pathology in Animals" (1903), in Pavlov, *Lectures on Conditioned Reflexes: Twenty-five Years of Objective Study of the Higher Nervous Activity (Behavior) of Animals,* trans. W. Horsley Gantt (New York: International Publishers, 1928), pp. 47-60, on p. 60.

[18] I have identified *praktikanty* from Pavlov's yearly reports to Ol'denburgskii in TsGIAP 2282.1; Kvasov and Fedorova-Grot, *Fiziologicheskaia Shkola I. P. Pavlova* (cit. n. 3); and N. M. Gureeva, N. A. Chebysheva, and V. A. Merkulov, *Letopis' zhizni i deiatel'nosti akademika I. P. Pavlova* (Leningrad: Nauka, 1969).

[19] D. A. Kamenskii, "Moe znakomstvo s Ivanom Petrovichem," in *Pavlov v vospominaniiakh sovremennikov,* ed. E. M. Kreps (Leningrad: Nauka, 1967), pp. 103-105.

[20] For the questions see Alfred Nobel to Emmanuel Nobel, 21 June 1893, TsGIAP 2282.1.47:1-3. Some of the relevant archival material has been published recently in V. S. Meshkunov and A. M. Blokh, "Al'fred Nobel' i Imperatorskii Institut Eksperimental'noi Meditsiny v Sankt-Peterburge," *Voprosy Istorii Estestvoznaiia i Tekhniki,* 1994, *1*:121-128. On the Nobels in Russia see Robert W. Tolf, *The Russian Rockefellers: The Saga of the Nobel Family and the Russian Oil Industry* (Stanford, Calif.: Hoover Institution Press, 1976). The new chemistry building was completed in 1892, the new pathological anatomy building in 1893.

[21] Ivan Pavlov to Emmanuel Nobel, 18 May 1894, TsGIAP 2282.1.47:19. In his official report to the tsar for 1894 Prince Ol'denburgskii referred to this as Nobel's original intention. Whether seeking to justify his use of Nobel's money or genuinely excited by Nobel's ideas, Pavlov assigned one *praktikant,* V. N. Geinats, to develop a surgical procedure for uniting the circulatory systems of two different dogs. Pavlov expressed great hopes for this project and, in one enthusiastic moment, announced that he would soon turn the entire lab to such "sewing." The operation, however, failed repeatedly and was reluctantly abandoned. E. A. Ganike, "Vospominaniia ob Ivane Petroviche Pavlove," in *Pavlov v vospominaniiakh,* ed. Kreps (cit. n. 19), pp. 76-78, on p. 77.

[22] Ivan Pavlov, "K khirurgicheskoi metodike issledovaniia sekretornykh iavlenii zheludka" (1894), in Pavlov, *Polnoe Sobranie Sochinenii,* Vol. 2, Pt. 1, pp. 275-281, on pp. 275-276.

[23] In much the same way, Latour's Pasteur insisted that the simplifying precision of laboratory microbiology could reveal secrets of infectious disease that would always remain invisible to hygienists encountering the multifactorial complexities of illness outside the lab. See Bruno Latour, *The Pasteurization of France* (Cambridge, Mass.: Harvard Univ. Press, 1988).

[24] See note 79. The classic treatise on the problem of "normalcy" is Georges Canguilhem's brilliant work *The Normal and the Pathological* (1943; New York: Zone, 1991).

[25] Pavlov, *Lektsii,* p. 37 (*Lectures,* p. 18).

[26] Bernard, *Introduction to the Study of Experimental Medicine* (cit. n. 6), p. 141; and "Pavlov, "K khirurgicheskoi metodike" (cit. n. 22), p. 275. The envy of another leading Russian physiologist is clear in his assessment of Pavlov's scientific contributions: "The arena for Pavlov's scholarly activity is not only the Military-Medical Academy, but also the Institute of Experimental Medicine, in which he heads the wealthy physiological division. Thanks to the wealthy scientific setting of the physiological laboratory of this Institute and the lavish sums available to produce scientific investigations, the majority of Pavlov's works, and those of his students, are produced within the walls of this Institute, to which science is already indebted for many valuable and important investigations." I. R. Tarkhanov, "Fiziologiia," in *Rossiia: Entsiklopedicheskii Slovar',* ed. F. A. Brokgauz and I. A. Efron (1898; Leningrad: Lenizdat, 1991), p. 768.

[27] The sources for these data are given in note 18, above. The one woman, E. O. Shumova-Simanovskaia, was Pavlov's collaborator, friend, and benefactor from his preinstitute days. Her scientific credentials and relationship with Pavlov were unusual for a *praktikant.* The number of women in Pavlov's laboratory increased substantially after 1905. A minority of coworkers—fourteen in the years 1890-1904—came to the laboratory with a doctorate already in hand. Of these, seven were either assistants or enjoyed a special personal relationship with the chief; another was recruited specifically for work on his own area of expertise. Twenty *praktikanty* worked in the lab for less than one year; the great majority of these did not complete their doctoral theses. Information about this group would much enhance our understanding of laboratory dynamics but is unfortunately unavailable.

[28] Babkin, *Pavlov* (manuscript), p. 139; and Kamenskii, "Moe znakomstov" (cit. n. 19), p. 105. Babkin's manuscript is not paginated consecutively, so page numbers are my own.

[29] On Khizhin's contribution see the discussion of the "isolated sac" in the section "The Laboratory Dog as Technology and Organism." At the turn of the century, having decided to confront the phenomenon of "psychic secretion," which he regarded as psychological and so beyond his expertise, Pavlov recruited Snarskii (1900) and Tolochinov (1901). They brought with them perspectives developed in psychology and psychiatry and in the laboratory of Pavlov's subsequent rival, V. M. Bekhterev. For a brief discussion see Daniel P. Todes, "From the Machine to the Ghost Within: Pavlov's Transition from Digestive Physiology to Conditional Reflexes," *American Psychologist* (forthcoming, 1997).

[30] S. A. Ostrogorskii, *Vrach,* 1898, *7:*212.

[31] These assistants, with their years of service, were V. N. Massen (1891-1893), Iu. M. Iablonskii (1893-1894), E. A. Ganike (1894-1936), E. A. Kotliar (1895), N. I. Damaskin (1895-1898), and A. P. Sokolov (1899-1909); the "member-coworker" was G. A. Smirnov (1893-1934). Smirnov's duties were the same as those of the assistants, but he chose his research topics independently. In 1916 Ganike became head of the newly formed Physico-Physiological Division at the institute, but this served largely as a workshop attached to Pavlov's factory.

[32] D. A. Sokolov, *25 let bor'by: Vospominaniia vracha* (St. Petersburg, 1910), p. 77; and Babkin, *Pavlov* (manuscript), pp. 273-274.

[33] Sokolov, *25 let bor'by,* p. 31; Babkin, *Pavlov* (manuscript), p. 138; Serafima Vasil'evna Pavlova, *Vospominaniia,* ARAN 259.1.170:505; and Babkin, *Pavlov* (manuscript), p. 265 (I have corrected minor spelling errors in the typescript.

[34] In *Lords of the Fly* (cit. n. 2), Robert Kohler approaches laboratory *Drosophila* as both biological entities and technologies (see his general discussion on pp. 6-11). For analysis of another organism-technology see Bonnie Cause. "The Wistar Rat as a Right Choice: Establishing Mammalian Standards and the Ideal of a Standardized Mammal," *Journal of the History of Biology,* 1993, *26:*329-349. My approach to this duality is somewhat different, no doubt in part because of the differences between fly, rat, and dog, the various laboratories, and the premise experimental uses to which these organism-technologies were put.

[35] Latour, "Costly Ghastly Kitchen" (cit. n. 3), p. 299; and Ivan Pavlov, "Fiziologicheskaia khirurgiia pishchevaritel'nogo kanala" (1902), in Pavlov, *Polnoe Sobranie Sochinenii,* Vol. 6, pp. 285-334, on p. 286. This article was first published in German and figured prominently in the Nobel Committee's evaluation of Pavlov's candidacies. On "local knowledge" see Susan Leigh Star, "Scientific Work and Uncertainty," *Social Studies of Science,* 1985, *15:*391-428; and Harry M. Marks, "Local Knowledge: Experimental Communities and Experimental Practices, 1918-1950" (unpublished manuscript, 1988).

[36] Pavlov, *Lektsii,* p. 22 (*Lectures,* p. 4). See also Pavlov, "Fiziologicheskaia khirurgiia," p. 289. In his doctoral dissertation, Pavlov explicitly embraced "nervism," which he termed Botkin's "great service" to physiology and defined as "the physiological theory that attempts to extend the influence of the nervous system to the greatest possible number of the organism's activities." Ivan Pavlov, *Tsentrobezhnye nervy serdtsa* (1883), in Pavlov, *Polnoe Sobranie Sochinenii,* Vol. 1, p. 197. For a later expression of this sentiment as it applied to physiological surgery see Pavlov, "Fiziologicheskaia khirurgiia," p. 290.

[37] On the history of the gastric fistula and the isolated sac see Horace W. Davenport, *A History of Gastric Secretion and Digestion* (New York/Oxford: Oxford Univ. Press, 1992), esp. pp. 138-143.

[38] Pavlov, "Fiziologicheskaia khirurgiia" (cit. n. 35), pp. 290, 309, 312, 313. Pavlov noted that one dog in five possessed a "favorable individual predisposition" that enabled it to survive the operation with relative ease. For the concession that the pancreatic fistula was "not ideal" see Pavlov, *Lektsii,* pp. 27-28 (*Lectures,* p. 8).

[39] Ivan Pavlov, "O vzaimnom otnoshenii fiziologii i meditsiny" (1894), in Pavlov, *Polnoe Sobranie Sochinenii,* Vol. 2, Pt. 1, pp. 245-274, on p. 251. For the trials and tribulations leading to the success with Druzhok see P. P. Khizhin, *Otdelitel'naia rabota zheludka sobaki* (Military-Medical Academy Doctoral Dissertation Series) (St. Petersburg, 1894), pp. 12-33.

[40] On the "Heidenhain stomach" see Davenport, *History of Gastric Secretion and Digestion* (cit. n. 37), pp. 14, 140. Heidenhain did, however, concede that if emotions affected gastric secretion, as was sometimes reported, this would be evidence for the importance of central nervous mechanisms. On Pavlov's modifications see Pavlov, "K khirurgicheskoi metodike" (cit. n. 22), p. 279.

The isolated sac was sometimes referred to as the "Heidenhain-Pavlov sac." The difficulty of convincing Russian clinicians that the isolated sac reflected normal gastric secretion is evident in the published protocols of the discussion at the Society of Russian Physicians in 1894. See *Trudy Obsh, Russk, Vrach.*, Sept. 1894, *64:*38-46; an abridged version of this discussion is published in Pavlov, *Polnoe Sobranie Sochinenii,* Vol. 6, pp. 40-45.

[41] Pavlov, *Lektsii,* pp. 33, 147 (*Lectures,* pp. 13, 108). On the pathological effects of the pancreatic fistula see, e.g., Iu. M. Iablonskii, *Spetsificheskoe zabolevanie sobak, teriaiushchikh khronicheski sok podzheludochnoi zhelezy i vliianie molochno-khlebnogo rezhima na deiatel'nost' podzheludochnoi zhelezy* (Military-Medical Academy Doctoral Dissertation Series) (St. Petersburg, 1894).

[42] Pavlov made this remark while invoking his experience with the disorders among his laboratory dogs as a source of authority in discussions of pathology. See Ivan Pavlov, "Laboratornye nabliudeniia nad patologicheskimi refleksami s briushnoi polosti" (1898), in Pavlov, *Polnoe Sobranie Sochinenii.* Vol. 1, pp. 550-563, on pp. 553-554. On the deterioration of Druzhok's isolated sac see A. N. Volkovich, *Fiziologiia i patologiia zheludochnykh zhelez* (Military-Medical Academy Doctoral Dissertation Series) (Kronstadt, 1898), pp. 41-42. The laboratory seems never to have explored the potentially subversive implications of Pavlov's and Volkovich's observations for conclusions based upon Druzhok's "normalcy." Rather, Druzhok's illness, and that of Sultan, the second dog to receive an isolated sac, was used to launch a new line of investigation: the experimental pathology and therapeutics of digestion.

[43] Susan Abrams discusses this aspect of the laboratory dog in "A Dog's Life: Conflict and Contradiction in Horsley Gantt's Pavlovian Laboratories" (unpublished manuscript, 1994). See also Michael Lynch, "Sacrifice and Transformation of the Animal Body into a Scientific Object: Laboratory Culture and Ritual Practice in the Neurosciences," *Soc. Stud. Sci.,* 1988, *18:*265-289.

[44] The acknowledged importance of the psyche was the most important source of these interpretive moments, but hardly the only one. As experience with various surgical operations increased, even dogs-as-technologies acquired a "personality" of sorts. For example, the size of the isolated stomach varied from dog to dog, requiring some mathematical recalculations to compare the secretory responses in two animals. Similarly, in later years, with a growing appreciation of the differences between the fundal and pyloric regions of the stomach, the location of the isolated sac acquired significance. See, e.g., Ia. Kh. Zavriev (Abo-Zavaridze), *Fiziologiia i patologiia zheludochnykh zhelez sobaki* (Military-Medical Academy Doctoral Dissertation Series) (St. Petersburg, 1900), p. 155.

[45] Pavlov, *Lektsii,* pp. 102, 104 (*Lectures,* p. 73, 75); and Pavlov, "Fiziologicheskaia khirurgiia" (cit. n. 35), pp. 304-305.

[46] I. O. Lobasov, *Otdelitel'naia rabota zheludka sobaki* (Military-Medical Academy Doctoral Dissertation Series) (St. Petersburg, 1896), pp. 30-31, 32-33.

[47] For the epigraph to this section see Ivan Pavlov, *Lektsii po fiziologii* (1911-1913), in Pavlov, *Polnoe Sobranie Sochinenii,* Vol. 5, p. 26.

[48] TsGIAP 2282.56.1 (1894):98; and Khizhin, *Otdelitel'naia rabota* (cit. n. 39), p. 153.

[49] V. G. Ushakov, "Laboratoriia Pavlova v Institute eksperimental'noi meditsiny," in *Pavlov v vospominaniiakh,* ed. Kreps, (cit. n. 19), pp. 246-250, on p. 248.

[50] Pavlov, *Lektsii,* pp. 11-12 (*Lectures,* p. ix).

[51] The literature review almost invariably obeyed the following sequence: first, a statement about the fundamental importance of methodology; second, summaries of earlier research conducted in various laboratories; third, a statement about the cardinal methodological achievements of the Pavlov lab; and fourth, summaries of recent research, almost exclusively produced in the Pavlov lab.

[52] A. A. Val'ter, *Otdelitel'naia rabota podzheludochnoi zhelezy* (Military-Medical Academy Doctoral Dissertation Series) (St. Petersburg, 1897), p. 35; and A. S. Sanotskii, *Vazbuditeli otdeleniia zheludochnogo soka* (Military-Medical Academy Doctoral Dissertation Series) (St. Petersburg, 1892), pp. 19, 16, 11, 51, 39. I have discovered only two exceptions to this pattern: both Popel'skii and Tolochinov refer in their work to "my" decisions and conclusions. Each subsequently clashed with the chief. See L. B. Popel'skii, *O sekretorno-zaderzhivaiushchikh nervakh podzheludochoi zhelezy* (Military-Medical Academy Doctoral Dissertation Series) (St. Petersburg, 1896); and I. Tolotschinoff, "Contribution à l'étude de la physiologie et de la psychologie des glandes salivaires," in *Comptes Rendus du Congrès des Naturalistes et Médecins du Nord* (Helsinki, 1903), pp. 42-46.

[53] Babkin, *Pavlov* (manuscript), p. 137.

[54] I. S. Tsitovich, "Kak ia uchilsia i rabotal u Pavlova," in *Pavlov v vospominaniiakh,* ed. Kreps (cit. n. 19), pp. 251-264, on p. 260; and Babkin, *Pavlov* (cit. n. 3), pp. 116-117. Babkin adds: "Pavlov was not greatly interested in the general education in physiology even of his most earnest pupils. Once, at the very beginning of my work in his laboratory, I asked his advice on how best to learn physiology. He quickly replied: 'Read the *Ergebnisse [der Physiologie]* and so approach the subject gradually' and at once turned the conversation to laboratory matters."

[55] For the work to improve the dog-technology see V. N. Vasil'ev, *O vliianii raznogo roda edy na deiatel'nost' podzheludochnoi zhelezy* (Military-Medical Academy Doctoral Dissertation Series) (St. Petersburg, 1893); and Iablonskii, *Spetsificheskoe zabolevanie* (cit. n. 41). For the work on exciters of pancreatic secretion see I. L.

Dolinskii, *O vlianii kislot na otdelenie soka podzheludochnoi zhelezy* (Military-Medical Academy Doctoral Dissertation Series) (St. Petersburg, 1894); I. O. Shirokikh, "Spetsificheskaia vozbudimost' slizistoi obolochki pishchevaritel'nago kanala," *Arkh, Biolog. Nauk*, 1895, *3*:5; and N. I. Damaskin, "Deistvie zhira na otdelenie podzheludochnogo soka," *Trudy Obsh. Russk. Vrach.*, Feb. 1896, pp. 7-14. For further work on the pancreas see Val'ter, *Otdelitel'naia rabota* (cit. n. 52); Popel'skii, *O sekretornozaderzhivaiushchikh* (cit. n. 52); A. R. Krever, *K analizu otdelitel'noi raboty podzheludochnoi zhelezy* (Military-Medical Academy Doctoral Dissertation Series) (St. Petersburg, 1899); and W. Sawitsch [V. V. Savich], "Die Wirkung des Wagus auf Pancreas," in *Comptes Rendus du Congrès des Naturalistes et Médecins du Nord* (cit. n. 52), pp. 41-42.

[56] See note 79. P. Borissow [P. Borisov] and A. Walther [A. A. Val'ter], "Zur analyse der Saurewirkung auf die Pancreas secretion," in *Comptes Rendus du Cong es des Naturalistes et Médecins du Nord*, p. 42; V. V. Savich, "Mekhanizm otdeleniia podzheludochnago soka," *Trudy Obsh. Russk. Vrach.*, Nov.-Dec. 1904, pp. 99-103; and Ia. A. Bukhshtab, "O rabote podzheludochnoi zhelezy posle pererezki vnutrennostnykh i bluzhdaiushchikh nervov," *ibid.*, Mar.-May 1904, pp. 72-78.

[57] Ivan Pavlov to Vladimir Pavlov, 23 May [1912], in *Perepiska Pavlova*, ed. E. M. Kreps (Leningrd: Nauka, 1970), p. 427. One way of reading Gerald Geison's account of the competition between Louis Pasteur and Jean-Joseph Touissant is as a mismatch between a factory and a workshop. Touissant, in his workshop, was able to pursue only one line of investigation at a time, while Pasteur, in his factory, pursued several (including Touissant's). See Gerald L. Geison, *The Private Science of Louis Pasteur* (Princeton, N.J.: Princeton Univ. Press, 1996), pp. 145-176.

[58] Babkin, *Pavlov* (manuscript), p. 138.

[59] See, e.g., N. D. Strazhesko, "Vospominaniia o vremeni, provedennom v laboratorii Ivana Petrovicha Pavlova," in *Pavlov v vospominaniiakh*, ed. Kreps (cit. n. 19), pp. 225-229, on p. 225.

[60] Babkin, *Pavlov* (manuscript), pp. 227-228.

[61] Tsitovich, "Kak ia uchilsia" (cit. n. 54), p. 255.

[62] *Ibid.;* and Babkin, *Pavlov* (manuscript), pp. 255 (sleepers), 138.

[63] Babkin, *Pavlov* (manuscript), p. 269; and A. F. Samoilov, "Obschaia kharakteristika issledovatel' skogo oblika I. P. Pavlova" (1925), in *Pavlov v vospominaniiakh*, ed. Kreps (cit. n. 19), pp. 203-218, on pp. 203-204.

[64] Babkin, *Pavlov* (cit. n. 3), p. 112. On Pavlov's singling out of work that interested him see, e.g., V. V. Savich, "Ivan Petrovich Pavlov: Biograficheskii ocherk," in *Sbornik posviashchennyi 75-letiiu akademika I. P. Pavlova* (Leningrad, 1924), pp. 3-31, esp. p. 24.

[65] L. A. Orbeli, "Pamiati Ivana Petrovicha Pavlova," in *Pavlov v vospominaniiakh*, ed. Kreps (cit. n. 19), pp. 162-175, on pp. 163-164.

[66] V. P. Kashkadamov, "Iz vospominanii o rabote v Institute eksperimental'noi meditsiny (1894-1897 gg.)," in *Pavlov v vospominaniiakh*, ed. Kreps, pp. 106-110, on p. 109; and Orbeli, "Pamiati," p. 164.

[67] Tsitovich, "Kak ia uchilsia" (cit. n. 54), p. 256.

[68] Orbeli, "Pamiati" (cit. n. 65), p. 171. See V. N. Boldyrev, *Periodicheskaia rabota pishchevaritèl'nago apparata pri pustom zheludke* (Military-Medical Academy Doctoral Dissertation Series) (St. Petersburg, 1904). This episode also demonstrates how the acknowledged importance of the psyche could be used to explain away discordant results.

[69] E.g., frequent indications of possible humoral mechanisms in gastric secretion were systematically ignored or explained away. On Pavlov's temper see, e.g., Tsitovich, "Kak ia uchilsia" (cit. n. 54), where the former *praktikant* recalls that, when dissatisfied, Pavlov frequently screamed at coworkers and at himself: "Those surrounding him at such times girded themselves tightly, since at such a moment it was easy to fall victim to his hot hand" (p. 259).

[70] W. N. Boldyreff [V. N. Boldyrev], "I. P. Pavlov as a Scientist," *Bulletin of the Battle Creek Sanitarium*, 1929, *24*:212-229, on p. 224. My thanks to Gerald Geison for suggesting the term "literary products" in his very helpful response to an earlier version of the present manuscript. He employs it in his essay "Organization, Products, and Marketing in Pasteur's Scientific Enterprise" (unpublished manuscript, 1996).

[71] Tsitovich, "Kak ia uchilsia" (cit. n. 54), p. 263.

[72] Babkin, *Pavlov* (manuscript), p. 229.

[73] Tsitovich, "Kak ia uchilsia" (cit. n. 54), p. 263. We have already encountered it twice, in the quotations from Babkin and Orbeli cited in notes 64 and 65, above.

[74] Geison, *Private Science of Pasteur* (cit. n. 57), p. 237.

[75] Babkin, *Pavlov* (manuscript), p. 229. For an especially dramatic change in direction see Krever, *K analizu* (cit. n. 55). See also Khizhin, *Otdelitel'naia rabota* (cit. n. 39), pp. 104 (for a tentative suggestion), 117 (where, in a summary, it becomes a "quite definite conclusion"); similarly, compare Lobasov, *Otdelitel'naia rabota* (cit. n. 46), pp. 89, 98.

[76] Sanotskii, *Vozbuditeli otdeleniia* (cit. n. 52), p. 9; Val'ter, *Otdelitel'naia rabota* (cit. n. 52), pp. 23, 38; and

Ia. A. Bukhshtab, *Rabota podzheludochnoi zhelezy posle pererezki bluzhdaiushchikh i vnutrennostnykh nervov* (Military-Medical Academy Doctoral Dissertation Series) (St. Petersburg, 1904), pp. 45-46, 46.

[77] N. P. Kazanskii, *Materialy k eksperimental'noi patologii i eksperimental'noi terapii zheludochnykh zhelez sobaki* (Military-Medical Academy Doctoral Dissertation Series) (St. Petersburg, 1901), p. 22.

[78] Vasil'ev, *O vliianii raznogo roda edy* (cit. n. 55), p. 23; Krever, *K analizu* (cit. n. 55), p. 20; Zavriev, *Fiziologiia i patologiia* (cit. n. 44), p. 92; and Kazanskii, *Materialy,* pp. 27, 23-24.

[79] In my forthcoming book I explore in detail the processing of data and the relationship between knowledge claims, the literary products in which they were embedded, and the market for which they were intended. This processing involved the choice of a single "template dog" for each gland—Druzhok for the gastric glands and Zhuchka for the pancreas; the identification of "good" and "bad" experiments (and relatively "normal" and "abnormal" experimental animals) based on an assessment of "numberless factors," and a flexible, homegrown mathematical logic of "mean and instantiation." An important conceptual and rhetorical tool was the construction of "stereotypical curves" (rather than data charts). Constructed on the basis of mean data obtained from "good" experiments on the template dogs, these curves provided the background against which other experiments on other dogs were interpreted and presented publicly.

[80] An especially interesting case in point is the Pavlov sac. I have identified only one laboratory in which scientists claimed, by 1904, to have created their own dog with a Pavlov sac. Investigators there used this dog-technology not to verify or elaborate Pavlov's claims but, rather, to pursue their own clinical interests (one studied the effect of sugar upon gastric secretion; the other investigated the action of various medicines). See W. N. Clemm, "Uber die Beeinflussung der Magensaftabscheidung durch Zucker," *Therapeutische Monatshefte,* Aug. 1901, *15:*403-411; and F. Riegel, "Uber medicamentose Beeinflussung der Magensaftsecretion," *Zeitschrift fur Klinische Medicin,* 1899, *37:*381-402. In subsequent years, the "stereotypical secretory curves" that Pavlov constructed through use of this sac fell into obscurity. The Pavlov sac itself, however, remained (and remains) useful to physiologists and so continued to be a source of his authority. Among Western scientists who had, by 1904, requested permission to come to St. Petersburg to study laboratory technologies were Walther Straub (ARAN 254.9.1286), Waldemar Koch (ARAN 254.9.1116), Hermann Munk (ARAN 254.9.1208), Johann Orth (ARAN 254.9.1216), G. Stewart (ARAN 254.9.1250), Ernest Stadler (ARAN 254.9.1284), F. A. Steeksma (ARAN 254.9.1285), and Alois Velich (ARAN 254.9.1119).

[81] Pavlov, "Fiziologicheskaia khirurgiia" (cit. n. 35), p. 286. Pavlov offered a dog with esophagotomy and fistula to Robert Tigerstedt during the physiologist's visit to St. Petersburg in 1901 on behalf of the Nobel Prize Committee. See Robert Tigerstedt to Ivan Pavlov, 5 Sept., 17 Dec. 1901, ARAN 259.2.1117:2, 13-14; Russian translations of these letters are published in *Perepiska Pavlova,* ed. Kreps (cit. n. 57), pp. 193-194. Pavlov also presented the physiologist I. R. Tarkhanov with a dog-technology for use in his lectures at St. Petersburg University. See Babkin, *Pavlov* (manuscript), p. 24.

[82] Tarkhanov, "Fiziologiia" (cit. n. 26), p. 768. Among the Western physiologists who asked Pavlov for samples of the gastric juice produced in his lab were H. J. Hamburger (ARAN 254.9.182), Carl Lewin (ARAN 254.9.1188), F. Rollin (ARAN 254.9.1232), Paul Mayer (ARAN 254.9.1375), and Nobel Prize Committee members Robert Tigerstedt and Karl Morner.

[83] I address this history in a chapter of my forthcoming book entitled "Gastric Juice for Sale: The Laboratory's Gift to the Clinic." On the development of this treatment see I. P. Pavlov and E. O. Shumova-Simanovskaia, "Innervatsiia zheludochnykh zhelez u sobak" (1890), in Pavlov, *Polnoe Sobranie Sochinenii,* Vol. 2, Pt. 1, pp. 175-199, on p. 180; and P. N. Konovalov, *Prodazhnye pepsiny v sravnenii s normal'nym zheludochnym sokom* (Military-Medical Academy Doctoral Dissertation Series) (St. Petersburg, 1893). On clinical results in Russia see A. A. Troianov, "O gastroenterostomii," *Trudy Obsh. Russk. Vrach.,* Nov. 1893, p. 28; and A. A. Finkel'shtein, "Lechenie estestvennym zheludochnym sokom," *Vrach,* 1900, *32:*963-965. For Pavlov's insistence upon his priority see his "Istoricheskaia zametka ob otdelitel'noi rabote zheludka" (1896), in Pavlov, *Polnoe Sobranie Sochinenii,* Vol. 2, Pt. 1, pp. 320-322; and Pavlov, *Lektsii,* p. 30 (*Lectures,* p. 10). For an example of patriotic Russian reactions to the vogue of gastric juice treatment in France at the turn of the century see *Vrach,* 1900, *6:*179.

[84] These future physiologists (with their dates in the lab) were A. F. Samoilov (1892-1895), L. B. Popel'skii (1896-1897), A. A. Val'ter (1896-1902), V. V. Savich (1900-1904, 1907, 1915), V. N. Boldyrev (1900-1911), B. P. Babkin (1902-1904, 1912), L. A. Orbeli (1901-1915), and I. S. Tsitovich (1901-1903, 1911). Val'ter, Savich, Boldyrev, Orbeli, and Babkin developed long-term working relations with the laboratory atypical for *praktikanty;* the chief clearly perceived them as the beginnings of a "Pavlov school." His favorite, Val'ter, died in a train accident in 1902. Boldyrev and Babkin emigrated after the Bolsheviks took power in 1917 and built successful careers as physiologists in the United States and Canada. With Pavlov's help, Savich became a professor of pharmacology (a discipline that Pavlov viewed as properly the province of physiology); and Orbeli became a renowned physiologist and powerful scientific entrepreneur, inheriting his mentor's empire upon Pavlov's death.

[85] I. P. Pavlov, "Sovremennoe ob'edinenie v eksperimente glavneishikh storon meditsiny na primere pishchevareniia,"

(1899), in Pavlov, *Polnoe Sobranie Sochinenii*, Vol. 2, Pt. 1, pp. 247-284, on p. 270. This pattern is clear from the protocols of the society's discussions, an edited version of which is republished *ibid.*, Vol. 6. These edited versions often omit critical comments by other discussants, leaving the misleading impression that Pavlov always had the final word.

[86] The ups and downs of Pavlov's candidacy are evident in the reports of 1901-1904 in *P. M. Forsandelser och Betankanden* in the Nobel Archives. Some of these are discussed in Windholz and Kuppers, "Pavlov and the Nobel Prize Award" (cit. n. 1). For Pavlov's mobilization of the laboratory to impress the Nobel judges see Babkin, *Pavlov* (cit. n. 3), p. 82. One Nobel judge, Robert Tigerstedt, requested in a letter of 17 Dec. 1901 that Pavlov send him "a little natural gastric juice." Six years later, when Tigerstedt embarked on a study of animal fluids, he requested "gastric juice and, if possible, other digestive juices." See ARAN 259.2.1117:2, 13-14; and *Perepiska Pavlova*, ed. Kreps (cit. n. 57), pp. 194, 197-198. In 1902, after attempting unsuccessfully to create an esophagotomized dog according to Pavlov's instructions, another Nobel judge, Karl Morner, received a shipment of gastric juice from the nominee. See ARAN 259.9.1206. My thanks to Sander Gliboff for deciphering Morner's German script.

[87] The view of Pavlov's "intellectual property" comes from J. H. Johansson and Robert Tigerstedt's assessment of July 1901, after their trip to Pavlov's lab: "Rapport afgifven till den Medicinska Nobelkomiteens fran J. E. Johansson och Robert Tigerstedt Juli 1901," in *P. M. Forsandelser och Betankanden, 1901*, p. 9, Nobel Archives. The second quotation presents Karl Morner's sympathetic summary of Johansson and Tigerstedt's position in "Betankande ar 1903 angaende J. P. Pawlow," in P. M. Forsandelser och Betankanden, 1903, p. 3.

FURTHER READING

Biography

Asratian, Ezras Asratovich. *I. P. Pavlov: His Life and Work*. Moscow: Foreign Languages Publishing House, 1953, 163 p.

Critical biography of Pavlov.

Babkin, B. P. *Pavlov: A Biography*. Chicago: University of Chicago Press, 1949, 365 p.

Early account of Pavlov's life and scientific achievements. Babkin, a former pupil of Pavlov, considers this volume "only as material for a future more comprehensive biography."

Cuny, Hilaire. *Ivan Pavlov: The Man and His Theories*, translated by Patrick Evans. New York: P. S. Eriksson, 1965, 174 p.

Introductory study of Pavlov and his thought.

Gray, Jeffrey A. *Ivan Pavlov*. New York: Penguin Books, 1981, 153 p.

Assesses Pavlov's research, theories of conditioning and the brain, and influence in the fields of physiology and psychology.

Criticism

Lashley, K. S., and Marjorie Wade. "The Pavlovian Theory of Generalization." *Psychological Review* 53, No. 2 (March 1946): 72-87.

Offers experimental evidence that contradicts the Pavlovian theories of stimulus irradiation and generalization.

Wells, Harry Kohlsaat. *Pavlov and Freud*, 2 volumes. New York: International Publishers, 1956-60, 476 p.

Studies "the Pavlovian science of higher nervous activity," and presents a critical comparison of the psychological themes of Pavlov with those of Sigmund Freud.

Georges Sorel

1847-1922

French social and political theorist

INTRODUCTION

While adhering to no organized philosophical or political schools of thought, Sorel's theories are credited with influencing such major twentieth-century movements as Russian Bolshevism and Italian Fascism, as well as inspiring many left-wing radical agitators of the 1960s. Sorel's theories combined socio-economic elements from the writings of Karl Marx with the philosophical writings of Arthur Schopenhauer, Henri Bergson, Benedetto Croce, and Friedrich Nietzsche. Believing that rational and empirical methods of thought failed to include humanity's nature beyond the logical, Sorel developed a system of belief that recognized human sexuality, religion, and nationality as integral factors in human social and political interaction. Sorel believed these basic human instincts form a timeless mythology governed by the desire for freedom of thought and action. This desire recognizes no systematic philosophical pattern, and is often and justifiably pursued through violent means as Sorel expressed in his most popular work, *Reflexions sur la violence.*

Biographical Information

Sorel was born in Cherbourg, France, to a middle-class Roman Catholic family. Despite the revolutionary nature of much of his writings, he remained devoutly Catholic and firmly middle-class throughout his life. His father was a struggling businessman who attained only moderate success, and his mother was the daughter of the mayor of Barfleur. During his childhood, Sorel vacationed at the seashore with his family, which included his cousin, Albert Sorel, the future historian and president of France's Third Republic Senate. Sorel graduated with distinction from the College de Cherbourg in 1864; attended the prestigious Ecole Polytechnique in Paris; and graduated from the Ecole des Ponts et Chaussees in 1870, before embarking on a career as an engineer with the French Bureau of Bridges and Highways. Sorel worked mainly in the provincial areas of France, a factor that many critics believe encouraged him to develop his theories independent from Paris's prevailing schools of thought. Another source of Sorel's theories is his relationship with Marie-Euphrasie David. Nearly illiterate and two years older than Sorel, David became his common-law wife. Her impoverished background caused Sorel's parents to refuse their consent for the pair to marry, wishes that were honored even after his parents's deaths. David's working-class status and staunch Catholicism raised Sorel's awareness of society's downtrodden. After her death in 1897, Sorel credited his intellectual life to his meeting David, and wrote that he "worked to raise a philosophical monument worthy of her memory." The inheritance he received upon the death of his mother in 1887 enabled Sorel to dedicate himself to a full-time intellectual life. He retired with the Legion of Honor and moved to Paris at the age of forty-five. In Paris, Sorel conducted impromptu lectures at the offices of Charles Peguy's *Cahiers de la Quinzaine*, an intellectual journal.

Major Works

Sorel's theories eschewed dogma, and were in a constant state of flux. At various stages of his life he championed Marxism, Socialism, monarchism, nationalism, Pragmatism, Fascism, and Bolshevism. His initial works are categorized as Marxist, and challenge the writings of Ernest Renan and Emile Durkheim, who claimed that the ideal society adheres to rational empiricism. In *Le Proces de Socrate,* Sorel wrote that intellectualism as epitomized by Socrates ultimately results in an effete, ineffectual, and decadent society, and disregards the true, physical desires of humankind. He believed that humanity's instinct to survive is the source of all human thought, and that all reality is a subjective experience dependent upon imagination and creativity. He disparaged what he called the era's *esprit de systeme, le petit science*, which he blamed for stifling the *elan vital* and inspiring mediocrity. In *Les Illusions de progres* Sorel decried the increasing mechanization of society, believing that machines exacerbated the sterility of modern life. He also attacked capitalism as an exploiter of the working class. *Reflexions sur la violence* reflects Sorel's view that labor unions would unite France's working class against the oppression of the capitalist bourgeoise, using violence as necessary to attain their goals. He argued that the capitalist State kept the working class submissive through the threat of police or militia violence, and this legitimization of violence justified the use of counter-violence by the labor unions. Sorel encouraged the unions to view the class war in mythological terms, and to employ "heroic violence" against the State's potential for violent protection of its capitalist principles.

PRINCIPAL WORKS

Insegnamenti sociale della economica contmporanea (political theory) 1906
Les Illusions de progres (political theory) 1908
Reflexions sur la violence (political theory) 1908
Le Decomposition du marxisme (political theory) 1908
La Revolution dreyfusienee (political theory) 1909
From Georges Sorel: Essays in Socialism and Philosophy (essays) 1976

CRITICISM

A. O. Lovejoy (essay date 1916)

SOURCE: A review of "Reflections on Violence", by Georges Sorel, in *The American Political Science Review*, Vol. X, No. 1, February, 1916, pp. 193-95.

[*In the following excerpted review of Sorel's* Reflections on Violence, *Lovejoy identifies key differentiators between Sorel's socialist concepts and traditional socialist theories.*]

Whatever the future of revolutionary syndicalism in Europe, the movement will at least continue to have interest for the historian as a type of social agitation, based upon novel and distinctive theories, which had attained somewhat formidable proportions at the moment when *"le régime bourgeois"* eventuated in an outbreak of "violence" more atrocious and more widespread than any of which the syndicalist had dreamed. An English version of [***Reflections on Violence***] the principal book of the chief philosopher of the movement is therefore to be welcomed. The translation, it may be said at once, is clear and idiomatic, and for the most part accurate. There are occasional errors, such as the rendering of *moeurs* by "customs" (29, 44, 57), and of *cléricaux* by "clergy" (249). This last makes nonsense of the passage in which it occurs. "Worthy progressives" is an over-translation of *braves gens.*

To be rightly understood the book needs to be read backwards. For it is concerned with two questions, that of the ends to be accomplished by the social revolution, and that of the means by which it can be effectually brought about. The latter question is discussed first and at much greater length; but the spirit of this discussion, and the main premises of it, are sure to be missed by readers who do not bear in mind the ethical ideal of the syndicalist revolution, as set forth in the concluding chapter on *la morale des producteurs.* It is primarily, though not solely, Sorel's conception of the ends to be accomplished, that prescribes the choice of those means to which he gives the sensational and partially misleading name of "violence."

The moral ideals which inspire Sorel are highly dissimilar to those which have animated most of the older Socialism. His hostility to the existing *régime* is not chiefly due to a demand for justice in the distribution of the produce of industry, nor to a humanitarian sympathy with the victims of capitalistic 'exploitation,' nor to a sense of the waste and disorder involved in the competitive system. The *morale des producteurs* is a sort of 'gospel of work.' Its ideal will be realized only when productive industry is freely and joyously carried on by every man for its own sake, with no desire for compensatory sugar-plums, in the form either of material rewards or the praise of others. The new social order is to be one in which men have become capable of finding their chief satisfaction in the activity that is inevitably their destiny, and in which life is lived simply, unaffectedly, and with a certain austerity. "The striving towards perfection which manifests itself in spite of the absence of any personal, immediate and proportional reward, constitutes the secret virtue that assures the continued progress of the world." The syndicalist millennium is to give this virtue constant play in the daily business of every man.

In order to bring about this consummation two things are chiefly necessary. The first is that the working class shall be kept undebauched by the ideals and ambitions of the existing *bourgeois* society. Among the workers, and among them alone, is to be found the germ of that "virtue which has power to save civilization—a virtue which middle-class intellectuals are incapable of understanding" (267). Hence the necessity for avoiding the methods of parliamentary socialism—which merely have the effect of robbing the proletariat of its leaders, by exposing them to the corrupting influence of middle-class associations. Hence also the necessity for "violence" i.e., for frequent strikes, undertaken not for the sake of gaining specific concessions, but to prevent the *rapprochement* of the two classes and the consequent infection of the workers with the base and vulgar standards dominant among the *bourgeoisie.* But a second requisite, for syndicalism, as for every great popular movement, is that it shall be animated by a "myth"—by a vivid and stirring image of some single, near-by, divine, event, in which every participant in the movement can picture himself as having a part. The "myth" which thus functions in syndicalism is that of the general strike. "Strikes have engendered in the proletariat the noblest, deepest and most moving sentiments that they possess; the general strike groups them all into a coördinated picture, and by bringing them together, gives to each its maximum of intensity" (137). It is not the practicability of the general strike that Sorel assets, but only the efficacy of the "idea" of it. A "myth must be judged as a means of acting on the present; any attempt to discuss how far it can be taken literally, as future history, is devoid of sense" (135).

The most crushing comment upon the book has been, unwittingly, uttered by Sorel himself, when he remarks that "the revolution has no place for intellectuals who have embraced the profession of thinking for the proletariat." His own (former) profession is there defined with precision. He is an intellectual of the intellectuals—all the more so in that he is, after the present Bergsonian fashion, an "anti-intellectualist"—who seeks to save the unlettered classes from the depraving influence of middle class culture by offering them a large and learned volume of social philosophy, heavily buttressed with footnotes. He is an avowed "pessimist" who sets out to inflame the popular mind with unconquerable hopes, by preaching a "myth" concerning which his own scepticism is unconcealed. The lofty, austere, and almost ascetic, moral ideals which he looks to the revolutionary proletariat to realize, are not such as the proletariat, left to itself, has ever shown much disposition to pursue. The very glamor which the working-class soul possesses in his eyes is a typical *bourgeois* illusion. One may well doubt whether Sorel has ever genuinely expressed the real temper of the movement which he has sought to interpret and to promote. And it is not at all surprising that he has of late looked rather towards royalism and Catholicism and a return to the ancient traditions of French culture, for a more congenial expression of that distaste for the vulgarity of middle-class ideals, and that contempt for the pedestrian methods of the mere 'intellect,' which first inspired his syndicalist philosophy.

Bernard Bosanquet (essay date 1917)

SOURCE: A review of "Reflections on Violence", by Georges Sorel, in *Social and International Ideas,* Macmillan and Co., Ltd., 1917, pp. 183-88.

[*In the following excerpt, political philosopher Bosanquet admires Sorel's thesis in* Reflections on Violence, *but takes exception to translator and philosopher T. E. Hulme's interpretation.*]

I may say at once that M. Sorel appears to me to have worked out for himself a fine philosophy of life and social forces. Whether or no he has seen to the end of it, either as a gospel of humanity or as a motive in social process, at all events his attitude is one which commands respect.

In his preface of seven pages, the translator applies himself to explain the general misconception of Sorel's work. His point is, in a word, that Sorel, while at the very heart of the working-class movement, is absolutely hostile to "democratic" theory. But in saying this, he proceeds, we must know what we mean. "Democratic" ideology here stands for "Liberal" doctrine, the pacific, rationalist, and hedonist temper of social democracy; and is inseparably bound up with the conception of man's natural goodness,[2] his perfectibility, and the necessary progress of the species. Against all this, in Mr. Hulme's view, Sorel stands for "classical pessimism," which is to mean, not the mere disillusionment of the shallow optimist, but the belief that man's nature has in it a radical evil, and can only come to good by heroism and the sublime, in short, by war.

It is not necessary here to enter upon the doubtful speculations with which Mr. Hulme has interwoven his exposition. The reader must not accept his dicta either about Rousseau or about Hegel—his reference to Condorcet seems more justifiable. And I hope it will not be believed that because some progress-of-the-species humanism has been shallow, therefore we are to look for the higher faith in an anti-humanistic ethics.

For a first introduction to Sorel it is enough to note the thesis that "the transformation of society is not likely to be achieved as a result of peaceful and intelligent readjustment on the part of literary men and politicians." The whole region of liberal and democratic politics, it may be added, Sorel regards as a mere hotbed of corrupt compromise, where the true Socialist temper cannot live, and the virility of the middle class itself is bound to die.

At the close of the introductory letter to Halévy, an excellent résumé of his position in some fifty pages, he accepts a simile thrown out by the latter in which the legend of the Wandering Jew is taken as the symbol of man's highest aspirations, fated as he is to wander for ever without repose. And his social gospel frames itself consistently with this attitude. The true position of the working class, at once their hope and their destiny, is the "marche vers la délivrance"; the "délivrance," the great catastrophic liberation by the general strike, being to them what Christ's Second Coming was to the early Christians, what the final restoration is to the Jews,[2] or the unity of Italy was to the Mazzinians. This is what M. Sorel describes as a true myth—a conception absolute, single, unanalysable, not proposed for discussion, but one thing with the class-gospel which expresses and inspires the class's soul.

The myth, it is to be carefully observed, is not to be confused with a Utopia. A Utopia is a thing of shreds and patches, an intellectual imagination botched together out of old material, and intended for piecemeal fulfilment. (M. Bergson's idea of intelligence has had an influence here.) The myth is essentially a faith in a total transformation, not intended for piecemeal fulfilment, nor for analysis nor discussion. It is like the hope of victory over the world entertained by the Catholic Church. It cannot be refuted, and conveys undying inspiration. A Utopist, on the contrary, is *ipso facto* a reactionary. When Professor Beesly, in 1869, wrote an article on the future of the working class, Karl Marx (the story comes through Brentano) wrote to him that he had hitherto regarded him as the only revolutionary Englishman, but henceforward he should hold him a reactionary, "for any one who composes a programme for the future is a reactionary."

Thus when the critic, whether parliamentary Socialist or wholly anti-Socialist, objects that Sorel tells one nothing of the future social organisation, Sorel, I imagine, admits and defends his silence. What we gather comes to this, I think. The faith in the general strike is a faith in the future of free men, capable of taking up the highest organisation of the workshop at the point at which they will force the capitalist employer to lay it down. Art at its best is but an anticipation of the spirit in which they will live, produce, and invent.

But it is not prediction, but the necessary present condition of a better future, on which his mind is bent. The essence of this necessary condition is the avoidance of the gospel of social peace, which means degeneration of the middle class, enfeeblement of the wage-earner's spirit, and a corrupt compromise between the two, constructed by the politician as broker, who does nothing for nothing. A masterful, virile, and competent middle class over against a strong, improving, and industrially very capable working class, fanatically inspired by its gospel of the great deliverance—this is the class war which is the condition of social health, and will, by the victory of the workers, one day regenerate the world.

And the "violence"—what about that? The poison of violence—the horror which attends the revolutionary memories—all came from the presence of the idea of the State first on one side and then on the other. The very red flag of the revolutionist was—so we are told—the symbol of martial law under the *ancien régime;* and its adoption by the revolutionist meant that the State was now to be on his side, and his opponents were to be traitors who merited extermination. With the rejection of the idea of the State all this poison vanishes. A degree of roughness will survive in the self-defence of the workmen by means of strikes; and it will be desirable to mishandle the emissaries of the corrupt politicians who will try to mislead the wage-earners into the primrose path of the *quid pro quo.* The ingenuity with which this parallel is drawn out—the parallel between the actual bribing—the *pot-de-vin* by which the contractor buys advantages from the politician, and the transaction by which the democratic politician, with his hand on the throttle-valve of labour agitation, sells peace and protection to a cowardly middle class—this ingenuity backed by a bitter confidence in the fidelity of the loathsome picture, makes the argument very painful reading. "I assume," he writes, "that no one is ignorant that no considerable transaction takes place without a *pot-de-vin.*"

But to return to violence. It is better than ruse, than corruption and the furthering of private interests by this skilful handling of "politico-criminal" associations which systematically terrorise the middle class at the politicians' instigation. Parnellism is cited as a type. The working class, left to themselves and to their gospel, will use roughness to protect their strikes; but they will not enter upon these calculated terrorisms, nor cherish the envenomed malice which is associated with the idea of revolution, and which springs from rival claims to the control of the State.

The modern history of the Catholic Church in France is a demonstration that politics and compromise do not even pay. It is characteristic of Sorel's whole position that the relation of the Church to the democratic State is analogous for him to that of the workers. Concessions invite further pressure; an aggressive policy is the only one that is safe.

It is natural that from such a standpoint English Collectivism and the whole English temper, both in internal and in external politics, are very severely judged; and the English attitude to international arbitration is attributed to want of sensitiveness on the point of honour rather than to the motives which we should claim for it. On all this, of course, as on the general question of English democracy, and the alleged essential corruptness of the democratic régime, I am at the opposite pole to M. Sorel. It would be interesting to know whether on this and analogous questions—*e.g.* the anti-patriotic bias of Syndicalism—the war has affected the author's views. So lately as on the publication of the third French edition he expressly observed that he had seen no reason to modify them. But it may be noted that even should those who think with him have followed the whole of France in its rush to the country's defence, this would not necessarily be a serious inconsistency in their position. They might well maintain that while aiming at the abolition of national exclusiveness they were justified in championing their country against a worse exclusiveness than any she ever symbolised.

To the present writer the true thing in M. Sorel's speculations is his insistence on the necessity of suffering and conflict; although the solution by a future event, about which we have seen that M. Sorel himself speaks uncertainly, seems inadequate and indeed self-contradictory, and a deeper explanation is demanded.

And the practical thing in M. Sorel's attitude is his concentration on the actual conditions of present social health and virility, as opposed to dreaming of the future. Give us, we are inclined to cry, in every class or functioning organ of the community, such a faith and inspiration as he claims for the workers and their gospel, and we could have confidence in the future, not because we could predict the detail of what must come, but because whatever comes, under the influence of such inspiration, and to a people so prepared to suffer and be strong, could not be other than good.

NOTES

[1] *Reflections on Violence.* By Georges Sorel. Translated by T. E. Hulme.

[2] Cf. a similar characterisation of certain movements for social reconstruction, p. 179 above.

[2] One can almost hear M. Sorel quoting:

> "Thy face took never so deep a shade,
> But we fought them in it, God our aid."

A. L. Orage (essay date 1935)

SOURCE: "Sorel, Marx, and the Drama," in *Selected Essays and Critical Writings,* edited by Herbert Read and Denis Saurat, Stanley Nott, 1935, pp. 110-13.

[*In the following review of* Reflections on Violence, *economist and philosopher Orage credits Sorel with providing a necessary mythology to socialist philosophy, and declares Sorel a worthy disciple of Karl Marx.*]

Sorel's ***Reflections on Violence*** is one of the few works upon Socialism that can be, and deserves to be, read by the non-professional student. Socialist authors for the most part are for Socialist readers exclusively. They are usually economic dissenting parsons addressing a conventicle of the already saved in language of a sectarian circumscription. Occasionally, however, one of them breaks loose from the sect and the language of the sect, and addresses the world in the language of the world. And Sorel is one of these. Regarding his thesis that a 'myth' is necessary to the creation of a revolutionary movement, and that in particular the 'myth' of the General Strike is indispensable to the modern proletarian movement, I am not convinced, nor is it necessary that any man should be. It is rather poetry than a political idea, and belongs to the same order of thought as the Republicanism of Plato. But there is no doubt in my mind that the idea is of value on that very account. What has been lacking in Socialism—with the exception of Marx's *Capital,* in which the tremendous historical tragedy of capitalism is recorded—is sublimity, the sense of the grand. Sorel's contribution of a 'myth' to the movement is therefore of the nature of art; it lifts the commonplace into the ideal world by deepening its significance. 'Socialists', he says, 'must be convinced that the work to which they are devoting themselves is a serious, formidable, and sublime work; it is only on this condition that they will be able to bear the innumerable sacrifices imposed on them by a propaganda that can procure them neither honours, profits, nor even immediate intellectual satisfaction.' Even if the only result of the idea of the General Strike is to make the Socialist conception more heroic, it should on that account alone be looked upon as having an incalculable value.

Over against this view of Socialism as something tremendous, sublime, heroic, and hence worthy of the unrewarded devotion of a lifetime, may be set the views of the merely political Socialists who look for results, both to their own advantage and to the advantage of the movement, here and now. Sorel is properly critical of the character of such men. Of the leaders, for example, he says that they have preserved the Marxist vocabulary while allowing themselves to become completely estranged from the thought of Marx. They talk of revolution when all the time they mean evolution. And seldom without some personal object either. 'The leaders who foster this sweet illusion (that of immediate reform by political action) see the situation from quite another point of view than that of their followers; the present social organization revolts them just in so far as it creates obstacles to their ambition; they are less shocked by the existence of the classes than by their own inability to attain to the positions already reached by older men; and when they have penetrated far enough into the sanctuaries of the State, into drawing-rooms and places of amusement, they cease, as a rule, to be revolutionary and speak learnedly of "evolution".' The violence of a proletarian movement, when it is spontaneous, is incalculable: there is no telling to what lengths it might go. But not only calculability is necessary, but control of the movement as well, if the leaders are to be able to dispose of it to their own advantage. For this reason, not only is violence denounced, but measures to nip it, even before it is in the bud, are taken by working class leaders who themselves aspire to belong to the middle classes. The organization of the proletariat in political Trade Unions under a centralized political control, and their diversion from economic to political methods, are plainly dictated by the nature of the problem; and these, as we know, are carried out so effectively that in England the Trade Union leaders, by the power they exercise, are the greatest obstacles to Socialism that exist. From this it may come about that the social revolution of which these leaders have a political vision may end in nothing better than the Servile State. It is hard, indeed, to foresee any other consequence from it. 'It is even possible', says Sorel, 'that, since the transmission of authority operates nowadays almost mechanically, thanks to the new resources at the disposal of the Parliamentary system, and since the proletariat would be thoroughly well organized under the official Trade Unions, we should see the social revolution culminate in a wonderful system of slavery.'

Sorel claims to be the true disciple of Marx, but much to the amusement, it appears, of present-day Marxists. The latter, however, are certainly wrong, for the relation between Marx and Sorel is that of the draughtsman of the plot of the Capitalist tragedy to the artist who concentrates upon the dénouement. Marx unfolded the series of Acts commencing with the birth of the wage-slave, and concluding with the death of the villain of the piece, namely, Capitalism, at the hands of its victim. Sorel, on the other hand, chose for his lesser drama the tragical moment of the climax in the General Strike. Both, however, had the same conception of the secular tragedy; but Marx supplied the whole framework, while Sorel worked out the conclusion only. Marx, it is certain, would no more have repudiated Sorel than Sorel has repudiated Marx. The difficulty with modern Marxists is, as Sorel has said, that they have lost their Master's grand conception of the real nature of the Capitalist tragedy. They employ his terms, but whittled down to the size of a paltry movement of a few years. It is as if Milton's epic of the Loss and Regaining of Paradise should become the textbook of earnest Plymouth brethren who might continue to employ Milton's phraseology, but with their mind upon their parish pump, or, as Ben Jonson said, hearing of Helen of Troy, but thinking all the time of Elinor Rumming. To such minds the very notion of the rise and fall of Capitalism, as representing a tragedy in the history of Mankind, is romantic and ridiculous. Nothing spiritual do they observe in it; nor do they climb to the vision of the Proletariat and the Capitalist as grandiose protagonists in a play lasting over many centuries. The impatient little creatures want something done at once: they want, in fact, a cinema for an evening rather than a tragedy for a thousand years.

James Burnham (essay date 1943)

SOURCE: "The Function of Myth," and "The Function of Violence," in *The Machiavellians: Defenders of Freedom*, The John Day Company, Inc., 1943, pp. 119-32.

[*In the following excerpt, Burnham examines what he perceives as Sorel's contempt for political science.*]

1. THE FUNCTION OF MYTH

Georges Sorel cannot be considered in all respects a Machiavellian. For one thing, he was a political extremist. Though Machiavellian principles are not committed to any single political program, they do not seem to accord naturally with extremism. Further, Sorel partly repudiates, or seems to repudiate, scientific method, and to grant, in certain connections, the legitimacy of intuition and of a metaphysics derived from the French philosopher, Henri Bergson. To the extent that he rejects science, Sorel is certainly outside the Machiavellian tradition.

However, Sorel's repudiation of scientific method is largely appearance. In reality, he attacks not science, but academic pseudo-science, which he calls the "little science," that pretends to tell us about the nature of society and politics, but in truth is merely seeking to justify this or that group of power-seekers. Sorel does indeed contend that genuine scientific doctrines are not enough to motivate mass political action; but this conclusion, far from being anti-scientific, is reached by a careful scientific analysis. Moreover, Sorel shares fully what I have called the "anti-formalism" of the Machiavellians, their refusal to take at face value the words and beliefs and ideals of men. In common with other Machiavellians he defines the subject-matter of politics as the struggle for social power; and he makes the same general analysis of the behavior of "political man," of men, that is to say, as they act in relation to the struggle for power.

Sorel also requires mention because of his influence on the other Machiavellian writers, Robert Michels and Vilfredo Pareto, with whom we shall be concerned. Pareto more than once gives tribute to Sorel. He writes, for example: "It was the surpassing merit of Georges Sorel that in ***Réflexions sur la violence*** he threw all such fatuities overboard to ascend to the altitudes of science. He was not adequately understood by people who went looking for derivations and were given logico-experimental reasonings instead. As for certain university professors who habitually mistake pedantry for science, and, given a theory, focus their microscopes on insignificant errors and other trifles, they are completely destitute of the intellectual capacities required for understanding the work of a scientist of Sorel's stature."[1] Sorel, both through his writings and through personal acquaintance, played a considerable part in the transformation of Michels into a Machiavellian, which occurred when Michels took up residence in Switzerland after an earlier career at a German university.

I propose to deal only with two points discussed by Sorel in his most famous work, ***Reflections on Violence.***[2] However, to understand the treatment of these points, it is necessary to summarize briefly the context in which the book was written.

Sorel was at that time active, chiefly as a journalist and theoretician, in the French and to some extent the international revolutionary labor movement. The greater part of the politically organized labor movement adhered in those days to the various social-democratic parties of the Second International. The activities of these parties were reformist. The parties were large in size and institutional strength, and devoted themselves to winning economic concessions (higher wages, social insurance, and so on) for the workers, and parliamentary or governmental posts for the party leaders. Ostensibly, however, the party programs still professed the goals of revolutionary socialism: the overthrow of capitalism and the institution of a free, classless society.

Sorel spoke for the dissident revolutionary *syndicalist* wing of the labor movement. The syndicalists were opposed both to the state—not only to the existing state but to all states and governments—and to all political parties, including the professedly labor parties. They advocated the economic "self-organization" of the workers, in revolutionary syndicates (that is, unions), with no professional officials and absolute independence from the state and all political parties. The state, whether the existing state or any other, they considered to be merely a political instrument for the oppression of the masses. Political parties, socialist as well as all the rest, have as their object the attainment of state power. Consequently, political parties are part of the machinery of oppression. If the socialist party took over governmental power, this would not at all mean the introduction of socialism, of a free and classless society, but simply the substitution of a new élite as ruler over the masses.

This analysis, we may remark, coincides exactly with that made by the other Machiavellians. In the later discussion of Robert Michels, we shall see in detail how it applies to the parties of socialism.

In contradistinction to the allegedly "scientific socialism" of the official parties, to their elaborate programs of "immediate demands" and desired reforms, to their lengthy treatises on how socialism will be brought about and what it will be like and how it will work, Sorel insists that the entire revolutionary program must be expressed integrally as a single catastrophic *myth:* the myth, he maintains, of the "general strike." The myth of the general strike is formulated in absolute terms: the entire body of workers, of proletarians, ceases work; society is divided into two irrevocably marked camps—the strikers on one side, and all the rest of society on the other; all production wholly ceases; the entire structure of the existing society, and all its institutions, collapse; the workers march back to begin production again, no longer as proletarians, but as free and un-ruled producers; a completely new era of history begins.

Only such an all-embracing myth, Sorel believes, can arouse the masses to uncompromising revolutionary action. No detailed rationalistic program, no careful calculation of pros and cons, no estimate of results and consequences, can possibly be efficacious. Indeed, the effect of such programs is to paralyze the independent action of the workers and to place power in the hands of the leaders who devise and manipulate the programs.

It is not the specific myth of the general strike, as treated by Sorel, that particularly concerns us, but rather the more general problem of the positive role of myth in political action. What kind of construction is such a political myth? If we interpret it as a scientific hypothesis, as a prediction about the future, it must be regarded as absurd, fantastic, false. But this interpretation, Sorel thinks, would be irrelevant. Nor is the myth in the least like a Utopia, though at first there might seem to be a close resemblance. Like a scientific hypothesis, a Utopia is an "intellectual product; it is the work of theorists who, after observing and discussing the known facts, seek to establish a model to which they can compare existing society in order to estimate the amount of good and evil it contains. It is a combination of imaginary institutions having sufficient analogies to real institutions for the jurist to be able to reason about them. . . . Whilst contemporary myths lead men to prepare themselves for a combat which will destroy the existing state of things, the effect of Utopias has always been to direct men's minds towards reforms which can be brought about by patching up the existing system . . . " (***Reflections on Violence,*** pp. 32-3.)

A myth, in contrast to hypotheses or utopias, is not either true or false. The facts can never prove it wrong. "A myth cannot be refuted, since it is, at bottom, identical with the convictions of a group, being the expression of these convictions in the language of movement; and it is, in consequence, unanalyzable into parts which could be placed on the plane of historical descriptions." (P. 33.) "In the course of this study one thing has always been present in my mind, which seemed to me so evident that I did not think it worth while to lay much stress on it—that men who are participating in a great social movement always picture their coming action as a battle in which their cause is certain to triumph. These constructions, knowledge of which is so important for historians, I propose to call myths; the syndicalist 'general strike' and Marx's catastrophic revolution are such myths. As remarkable examples of such myths, I have given those which were constructed by primitive Christianity, by the Reformation, by the [French] Revolution and by the followers of Mazzini. I now wish to show that we should not attempt to analyze such groups of images in the way that we analyze a thing into its elements, but that they must be taken as a whole, as historical forces, and that we should be especially careful not to make any comparison between accomplished fact and the picture people had formed for themselves before action." (P. 22.)

"The myths," summing up, "are not descriptions of things, but expressions of a determination to act." (P. 32.)

"People who are living in this world of 'myths,' are secure from all refutation. . . . No failure proves anything against Socialism since the latter has become a work of preparation (for revolution); if they are checked, it merely proves that the apprenticeship has been insufficient; they must set to work again with more courage, persistence, and confidence than before . . . " (Pp. 35, 36.)

Though the myth is not a scientific theory and is therefore not required to conform to the facts, it is nevertheless not at all arbitrary. Not just any myth will do. A myth that serves to weld together a social group—nation, people, or class—must be capable of arousing their most profound sentiments and must at the same time direct energies toward the solution of the real problems which the group faces in its actual environment. "Use must be made of a body of images which, *by intuition alone,* and before any considered analyses are made, is capable of evoking as an undivided whole the mass of sentiments which corresponds to the different manifestations of the war undertaken by Socialism against modern society." (Pp. 130-1.) "It is a question of knowing what are the ideas which most powerfully move [active revolutionists] and their comrades, which most appeal to them as being identical with their socialistic conceptions, and thanks to which their reason, their hopes, and their way of looking at particular facts seem to make but one indivisible unity." (P. 137.)

The myth, though it is not fundamentally a utopia—that is, the picture of an ideal world to come in the future—does ordinarily contain utopian elements which suggest such an ideal world. Is there any probability that the ideal will be achieved? "The myth," Sorel replies, "must be judged as a means of acting on the present; any attempt to discuss how far it can be taken literally as future history is devoid of sense." (Pp. 135-6.) If we should nevertheless put the question, it is plain that the ideal will in truth never be achieved or even approximated. This in no way detracts from the power of the myth, nor does it alter the fact that only these myths can inspire social groups to actions which, though they never gain the formal ideal, yet do bring about great social transformations. "Without leaving the present, without reasoning about this future, which seems for ever condemned to escape our reason, we should be unable to act at all. . . . The first Christians expected the return of Christ and the total ruin of the pagan world, with the inauguration of the kingdom of the saints, at the end of the first generation. The catastrophe did not come to pass, but the Christian thought profited so greatly from the apocalyptic myth that certain contemporary scholars maintain that the whole preaching of Christ referred solely to this one point. The hopes which Luther and Calvin had formed of the religious exaltation of Europe were by no means realized. . . . Must we for that reason deny the immense result which came from the dreams of Christian renovation? It must be admitted that the real developments of the [French] Revolution did not in any way resemble the enchanting pictures which created the enthusiasm of its first adepts; but without those pictures would the Revolution have been victorious? . . . These Utopias came to nothing; but it may be asked whether the Revolution was not a much more profound transformation than those dreamed of by the people who in the eighteenth century had invented social Utopias." (Pp. 133-5.)

2. THE FUNCTION OF VIOLENCE

A great myth makes a social movement serious, formidable, and heroic. But this it would not do unless the myth inspired, and was in turn sustained by, violence. In his analysis of violence—the most notorious and attacked part of Sorel's work—Sorel begins, as in the case of myth, with the narrowed problem of violence as related to the proletarian revolutionary movement. He is, however, seeking conclusions that will hold generally for all great social movements.

Sorel was writing, some years prior to the first World War, at a time when humanitarian and pacifist ideas were almost universally professed by the leaders of official opinion. International war was going to be stopped by treaties and arbitration; class war, by reforms and the internal policy of "social peace"; violence was a relic of barbarism, soon to disappear altogether. Ironically enough, in spite of the two world wars, these notions retain their hold in many quarters, and are always prominent in the dreams of what the world is going to be like after the current war. In the face of these official opinions, Sorel presents a defense of violence. However, we must exercise care in determining just what he is defending, and why.

Sorel does not take the ideas of humanitarianism and pacifism at face value. As in the case of any other ideas, he relates them to the historical environment in which they function. Their prominence does not mean that force has been eliminated from social relations: force is always a main factor regulating society. But, under advanced capitalism, much of the force is exercised as it were automatically and impersonally. The whole weight of the capitalist mode of production bears down upon the workers, keeping them in economic, political, and social subjection. From one point of view, the humanitarian chatter serves to obscure the social realities. Still more important, the moral denunciation of violence helps to keep the workers quiet and to prevent them from using their own violent methods in strikes and for the revolution.

It is true that overt acts of violence have become less frequent than in many former ages. Is this in all respects an improvement? It is, to the extent that "brutality"—such as used by robbers and brigands in earlier times, or by the state in the punishment of criminals—has become rarer. Sorel is careful to explain that by "violence" he does not mean brutality of this sort. From another point of view, the lessening of overt acts of violence in social relations is merely the correlative of an increase in fraud and corruption. Fraud, rather than violence, has become the more usual road to success and privilege. Naturally, therefore, those who are more adept at fraud than at force take kindly to humanitarian ideals. Crimes of fraud excite no such moral horror as acts of violence: "We have finally come to believe that it would be extremely unjust to condemn bankrupt merchants and lawyers who retire ruined after moderate catastrophes, while the princes of financial swindling continue to lead gay lives. Gradually the new industrial system has created a new and extraordinary indulgence for all crimes of fraud in the great capitalist countries." (P. 222.)

Similarly in the case of the modern working class when under the control of reformists and politicians. The frank acceptance of the method of proletarian violence would threaten all the existing institutions of society. Consequently, violence is deplored by all those who have a stake in existing society. Cunning, in the form of doctrines of "social peace," "co-operation," and "arbitration," is in favor. An occasional act of violence by the workers is comfortably overlooked, because it can be used by the labor bureaucrats—or a government allied with the bureaucrats—to scare the employers, to win concessions for themselves, and to prove their indispensable role in controlling proletarian violence. "In order that this system may work properly, a certain moderation in the conduct of the workmen is necessary. . . . If financiers are almost always obliged to have recourse to the services of specialists, there is all the more reason why the workmen, who are quite unaccustomed to the customs of this world, must need intermediaries to fix the sum which they can exact from their employers without exceeding reasonable limits.

"We are thus led to consider arbitration in an entirely new light and to understand it in a really scientific manner. . . . It would be evidently absurd to go into a pork butcher's shop, order him to sell us a ham at less than the marked price, and then ask him to submit the question to arbitration; but it is not absurd to promise to a group of employers the advantages to be derived from the fixity of wages for several years, and to ask the *specialists* what remuneration this guarantee is worth; this remuneration may be considerable if business is expected to be good during that time. Instead of bribing some influential person, the employers raise their workmen's wages; from their point of view there is no difference. As for the Government, it becomes the benefactor of the people, and hopes that it will do well in the elections . . . " (Pp. 235-6.)

"In the opinion of many well-informed people, the transition from violence to cunning which shows itself in contemporary strikes in England cannot be too much admired. The great object of the Trades Unions is to obtain a recognition of the right to employ threats disguised in diplomatic formulas; they desire that their delegates should not be interfered with when going the round of the workshops charged with the mission of bringing those workmen who wish to work to understand that it would be to their interests to follow the *directions* of the Trades Unions." (Pp. 247-8.)

Furthermore, the growth of the humanitarian and pacifist ideologies, this effort to hide the force that nevertheless continues operating in vicious and distorted ways, to place reliance for rule upon cunning and fraud and bribery and corruption, rather than frankly used violence, is the mark of a social degeneration. It is not only the masses who are lulled and degraded. The rulers, too, decay. The rulers rule hypocritically, by cheating, without facing the meaning of rule, and a general economic and cultural decline, a social softening, is indicated. "When the governing classes, no longer daring to govern, are ashamed of their privileged situation, are eager to make advances to their enemies, and proclaim their horror of all cleavage in society" (p. 213), they are acting like cowards and humbugs, not saints. "Let us therefore do more and more every day for the disinherited, say these [worthy liberals]; let us show ourselves more Christian, more philanthropic, or more democratic (according to the temperament of each); let us unite for the accomplishment of *social duty*. We shall thus get the better of these dreadful Socialists, who think it possible to destroy the prestige of the Intellectuals now that the Intellectuals have destroyed that of the Church. As a matter of fact, these cunning moral combinations have failed; it is not difficult to see why. The specious reasoning of these gentlemen—the pontiffs of 'social duty'—supposes that violence cannot increase, and may even diminish in proportion as the Intellectuals unbend to the masses and make platitudes and grimaces in honor of the union of the classes. Unfortunately for these great thinkers, things do not happen in this way; violence does not diminish in the proportion that it should diminish according to the principles of advanced sociology." (Pp. 213-4.)

An open recognition of the necessity of violence can reverse the social degeneration. Violence, however, can serve this function, can be kept free from brutality and from mere vengeful force, only if it is linked to a great myth. Myth and violence, reciprocally acting on each other, produce not senseless cruelty and suffering, but sacrifice and heroism.[3]

But, by what is only superficially a paradox, the open acceptance of violence, when linked with a great myth, in practice decreases the total amount of actual violence in society. As in the case of the early Christian martyrdoms, which research has shown to have been surprisingly few and minor, the absolute quality of the myth gives a heightened significance to what violence does take place, and at the same time guards against an endless repetition of vulgar brutalities. "It is possible, therefore, to conceive Socialism as being perfectly revolutionary, although there may only be a few short conflicts, provided that these have strength enough to evoke the idea of the general strike: all the events of the conflict will then appear under a magnified form, and the idea of catastrophe being maintained, the cleavage will be perfect. Thus one objection often urged against revolutionary Socialism may be set aside—there is no danger of civilization succumbing under the consequences of a development of brutality, since the idea of the general strike may foster the notion of the class war by means of incidents which would appear to middle-class historians as of small importance." (Pp. 212-3.)

This seeming paradox, that the frank recognition of the function of violence in social conflicts may have as a consequence a reduction in the actual amount of violence, is a great mystery to all those whose approach to society is formalistic. If men believe and say that they are against violence, if they express humanitarian and pacifist ideals, it must follow, so formalists think, that there will be less violence in the world than when men openly admit the necessity of violence. Historical experience does not, however, bear out this hope, as all the Machiavellians understand. The humanitarian ideals of much of the French aristocracy in the 18th century did not in the least mitigate the enormous bloodshed of the Revolution and may indeed have greatly contributed to its excess. It cannot be shown that humanitarian conceptions of criminal punishment, such as have flourished during the past century or more, have decreased crimes of violence. Pacifist, "anti-war" movements are a prominent feature of modern life. They have not at all served to stop the most gigantic wars of history. They have, rather, in those countries where they were most influential, brought about a situation in which many more men have been killed than would have been if political policy had based itself on the fact that wars are a natural phase of the historical process. Countless experiences have proved that a firm blow now may forestall a thousand given and suffered tomorrow. A doctor who denied the reality of germs would not thereby lessen the destructive effect of germs on the human body. In politics those magical attitudes which medicine has left behind still prevail. It is still firmly believed that by denying the social role of violence, violence is thus somehow overcome.

Sorel's attitude toward violence is part of a more general social attitude which he does not hesitate to call "pessimism." He is quite prepared to defend the ethics of pessimism. "The optimist in politics," he writes, "is an inconstant and even dangerous man, because he takes no account of the great difficulties presented by his projects. . . . If he possesses an exalted temperament, and if unhappily he finds himself armed with great power, permitting him to realize the ideal he has fashioned, the optimist may lead his country into the worst disasters. He is not long in finding out that social transformations are not brought about with the ease that he had counted; he then supposes that this is the fault of his contemporaries, instead of explaining what actually happens by historical necessities; he is tempted to get rid of people whose obstinacy seems to him to be so dangerous to the happiness of all. During the Terror, the men who spilt most blood were precisely those who had the greatest desire to let their equals enjoy the golden age they had dreamt of, and who had the most sympathy with human wretchedness: optimists, idealists, and sensitive men, the greater desire they had for universal happiness the more inexorable they showed themselves.

"Pessimism . . . considers the *march towards deliverance* as narrowly conditioned, on the one hand, by the experimental knowledge that we have acquired from the obstacles which oppose themselves to the satisfcation of our imaginations (or, if we like, by the feeling of social determinism), and, on the other, by a profound conviction of our natural weakness. . . . If this theory is admitted, it then becomes absurd to make certain wicked men responsible for the evils from which society suffers; the pessimist is not subject to the sanguinary follies of the optimist, infatuated by the unexpected obstacles that his projects meet with; he does not dream of bringing about the happiness of future generations by slaughtering existing egoists." (Pp. 9-11.)

[1] *Mind and Society*, footnote 2 to 2193, p. 1535, Vol. IV.

[2] The English translation, by T. E. Hulme, of *Réflexions sur la violence*. Originally issued in New York by B. W. Huebsch, this was re-published by Peter Smith, in 1941. The French text first appeared in 1906. Georges Sorel lived from 1847-1922.

[3] By the romantic moral overtone of this view, Sorel steps abruptly away from Machiavellism—though he is probably quite conscious of what he is doing.

Max Nomad (essay date 1948)

SOURCE: "The Evolution of Anarchism and Syndicalism: A Critical Review," in *European Ideologies: A Survey of 20th Century Political Ideas*, edited by Feliks Gross, Philosophical Library, Inc., 1948, pp. 328-342.

[*In the following excerpt, Nomad examines Sorel's philosophical history, identifying Sorel's links with Marxism, democratic socialism and Bolshevism as key to understanding his body of work.*]

It is a truism that in all political movements a distinction must be made between what their participants profess and believe, on the one hand, and what subconsciously they are actually striving for, on the other.

This distinction is rendered somewhat complicated with regard to anarchism. For there are various schools of anarchism differing from each other on many essential points. Some of them accept the principle of private property, (the "mutualist" and the "individualist" anarchists), while others reject it. Among the latter there are those who believe in renumeration according to performance (the "collectivist" anarchists), and those who advocate the right of unrestricted enjoyment of all good things without compulsion to work (the "communist" anarchists). The latter believe in the essential goodness of man, while their "collectivist" predecessors took a more realistic view. And there are also differences of opinion as to the methods to be used for the attainment of the goal: the believers in peaceful persuasion were opposed by the advocates of violent revolution; and even among the latter there were those who, like the followers of Bakunin, believed in methods of conspiracy, and those who saw, or see, in the revolution a spontaneous process. And last but not least, there were and are those who believe in the class struggle, and those who reject it.

They all agree on one point only: the negation of the state, i.e., the rejection of all forms of government. But even on this point there is no uniformity in the concepts of the various anarchist thinkers. Proudhon's "anarchist" rejection of the state was at bottom merely an advocacy of a "federalist", or decentralized form of state administration; his concept of an "anarchist" France did not go beyond the idea of breaking up his country into twelve small administrative entities. Bakunin's "collectivist anarchism" was compatible with the idea of a revolutionary dictatorship by his own group, which apparently was to constitute the first phase of his classless and stateless ideal. On the other hand, there is no such dictatorial or governmental transition period in the "communist-anarchist" concept of Kropotkin. The realization of his ideal consequently recedes into the mists of a distant future. In a still later variant of anarchism, known as anarcho-syndicalism, the various local and regional federations of trade unions are to assume the tasks entrusted to the state under the systems of democratic collectivism.

At the time of their vogue each of these variants of anarchism represented the current interests or aspirations of certain social groups. Proudhon's "mutualist anarchism", with its panacea of a "People's Bank" granting free credit to all in need of it, championed the cause of the small producers and skilled workers anxious to attain economic independence at a period when modern large scale industrialism was still in its infant stage. His "anarchism" or "anti-statism" was at bottom only an Utopian or paradoxical formulation of the small producer's hostility to a voracious, ubiquitous and all-powerful bureaucracy swallowing up a substantial part of the national income. It was also in line with Proudhon's championship of this social group that he was opposed to labor unions and to the class struggle. For these had no meaning to a group of aspiring independent producers. With the growth of large-scale industrialism which demonstrated the futility of the skilled workers' hopes for economic independence, the followers of Proudhon gradually turned either to Bakuninism, or to Marxism or to plain trade-unionism. (The individualist anarchism of Max Stirner, the fame of his *Ego and His Own,* notwithstanding, never gave rise to a movement properly speaking. His complete rejection of all ethical obligations, coupled with a few sympathetic remarks about the underdogs' violent resistance to their masters, occasionally served as a theoretical justification to stray groups of marauders who had chosen a life of outlaw parasitism and banditism.)

BAKUNIN—A PRECURSOR OF LENIN

It was different with the anarchism of Bakunin. His collectivism—at that time the panacea of nearly all radical schools—coupled with the conspiratorial and insurrectionist tactics of Blanqui and invigorated and embellished by the class struggle concept of Marx and the "anti-statist" verbiage of Proudhon, expressed the aspirations of a stratum then very numerous in all economically and politically backward countries. These were the declassed professionals, intellectuals and semi-intellectuals, the then proverbial lawyers without clients, physicians without patients, newspapermen without jobs and college students without a future. At that time these elements were anxious for an immediate revolution leading to the seizure of all power by their own respective group. Unconsciously, their profession of anarchism served both as a blind for concealing their ambitions and for outdoing in revolutionary radicalism their competitors on the Left: the Blanquists whose open championship of a revolutionary dictatorship had discredited them, as mere office-seekers, in the eyes of many radical workers and the Marxists whose "proletarian" radicalism was drifting towards parliamentary and trade-unionist gradualism, particularly in the economically more advanced countries.

Bakuninism which, for almost a decade, from the late sixties to the late seventies of the past century, was attracting the same elements which Leninist communism attracts at present, eventually receded. Its decline was due to the economic upswing which during the last two decades of the past century gradually began to bring industrialism even to the backward countries. It is as a result of this upswing that those educated malcontents, who usually assume the leadership of the labor movement, eventually deserted Bakunin's insurrectionary anarchism for the gradualist socialism of Marx whose revolutionary professions had in time become a mere lip-service. It is only in Spain that anarchism (though not in its undiluted original Bakuninist version) has retained its hold upon a large section of the labor movement. This is due largely to the fact that in that country the followers of Bakunin had laid the foundations of the labor movement, thus securing for the anarchists a lasting reputation as champions of the workers' cause. It may be added that the anarchists of that country, whether they were conscious of it or not, to a certain extent represented the extreme left wing of the democratic-liberal opposition to clerical semi-absolutism.

Bakuninism, for all its anarchist verbiage, had been at bottom merely a sort of ultra-leftist variant of Marxism. (It must not be forgotten that Marx, too, accepted the idea of a stateless society, i.e. of anarchism, in a higher phase of socialism). A well-known Bolshevik historian, Y. Steklov, in a monumental four-volume biography of Bakunin, written during the early period of the Soviet regime, established beyond any doubt, on the basis of Bakunin's less known writings, particularly his correspondence, that the founder of revolutionary anarchism was in reality a forerunner of Lenin, and that his concept of revolutionary activity and post-revolutionary reconstruction really did not differ much from those of the Communist International and of the Soviet system, as established immediately after the November Revolution of 1917.

COMMUNIST ANARCHISM

The failure of Bakuninism to give rise to a successful revolutionary mass movement resulted in the conversion of many of its followers into a sect of millennial, if sometimes violent, dreamers. The outstanding theorist of this school, Peter Kropotkin, postulated the pure ideal of "communist anarchism" based on the principle of "to each according to his needs", as against Bakunin's collectivist anarchism based on the idea of "to each according to his works." For a certain period the outstanding feature of the Kropotkin school was its advocacy of terrorist acts of protest ("propaganda by the deed") which were intended to arouse the masses against existing injustices. Some outstanding representatives of this movement, such as the Italian Errico Malatesta, visualized the role of the anarchists in the revolutionary process as that of a sort of extreme-left wing of the anti-capitalist army, helping the Socialists in the task of overthrowing the capitalist system and, once democratic socialism was established, engaging in the task of winning over the majority by means of propaganda and experimentation. This was a recognition of the impossibility of establishing the anarchist ideal by the methods of revolution. The anarchists of that period can therefore be characterized as a group of intransigeant "nay-sayers" among the intellectual and self-educated manual workers who were dissatisfied with the slow progress of the anti-capitalist struggle and wanted to hasten the coming clash between democratic socialism and capitalism. They did not foresee that the violent clash they hoped for would lead to the victory of a totalitarian form of collectivism which would give the anarchists no chance to win over the majority through "propaganda and experimentation".

ANARCHO-SYNDICALISM AND REVOLUTIONARY SYNDICALISM, PURE AND SIMPLE

The futility of their propaganda, by "deed" and otherwise, caused many followers of the Kropotkin school of anarchism to revert to some of the concepts of Bakuninism and to seek a closer contact with the labor movement. The result was the emergence of what is known as "anarcho-syndicalism" with its emphasis upon such methods of the class struggle as direct action, sabotage and the general strike, and its substitution of the trade union to the "free group" as the basis of a free, state-less society. The class basis of this new departure was the antagonism of many French trade union militants to the influence exerted by socialist politicians over the labor movement. During a certain period the undeveloped rudimentary state of the French trade unions, coupled with the discredit into which socialist political leadership had fallen among many workers, enabled the anarcho-syndicalists and the syndicalists without the anarchist prefix, to achieve ascendancy over the French trade unions and to inspire the emergence of similar movements in other countries as well. However, the very growth of the French trade union movement in which the anarcho-syndicalists held the upper hand, spelled the eventual decline of anarcho-syndicalism. For that growth brought in its wake the formation of a self-satisfied trade union bureaucracy which eventually went the way of all trade-unionist flesh. The anarcho-syndicalist revolutionists became gradually trade-union bureaucrats, dabbling at the same time in politics, either of the gradualist socialist or of the radical "communist" brand. The French General Confederation of Labor (CGT), once the stronghold of anarcho-syndicalism, was until 1947 entirely under the control of the Communist Party. In those countries in which syndicalism was a minority group within the trade union movement, the revolutionary slogans and promises of Bolshevism easily won over many of the more temperamental anarchist and anarcho-syndicalist elements, both among the leaders and the following.

In this connection it may be also mentioned that the theory of revolutionary syndicalism, pure and simple, of those syndicalists who prefer not to attach the label of anarchism to their syndicalism, though otherwise they differed very little from the anarcho-syndicalists, has undergone a certain modification since the Bolshevik revolution. Previously they completely ignored the question of power, assigning in their concept, to the local and regional trade union federations, the function of production and distribution. After 1917 they coined the slogan of "(Political) Power to the Trade Union" *(Au syndicat le pouvoir.)*[1] Which implies the acceptance of state power—rejected by the original syndicalist theory—provided that power is wielded by syndicalist trade-union leaders, and not by Communist politicians.

THE SOREL INTERLUDE

The vogue enjoyed for a long time by Georges Sorel's ***Reflections on Violence*** has had the effect that, to the uninitiated, the idea of syndicalism has become inextricably connected with his name. As a result many of his personal inconsistencies and theoretical vagaries have often been erroneously attributed to the movement of which he had become the self-appointed philosophical champion.

Now, in justice to Sorel it must be said that he himself never claimed to be the originator of revolutionary syndicalism. He frankly admitted his indebtedness to Fernand Pelloutier, an erstwhile while Marxist who later became an anarchist, and who, still later, formulated the basic concept of revolutionary syndicalism. A concept which can be condensed in two simple propositions: 1. The general strike is the method of the working class uprising that will overthrow the capitalist system. 2. The labor union (in French, *syndicat*) with its local and national federations, is the basis for building up a cooperative, non-exploitative commonwealth.

Sorel himself made no essential contributions to syndicalist theory. The "violence" which he glorified, was at bottom merely a sensational synonym for the "direct action" advocated and practiced during a certain period by the French syndicalist militant who ignored Sorel and his writings. And as for the general strike to which Sorel devoted so many pages, that idea had been in vogue in the French labor movement since the early nineties of the past century. And it is one of those curious twists of history that one of its first and most glamorous propagandists at that time was a man who in time was to become the embodiment of that democratic opportunism which Sorel so hated: it was a rising young socialist politician by the name of Aristide Briand who had borrowed the idea from Pelloutier, used it as a stepping stone in his career, and eventually, as Prime Minister, crushed the first general strike attempted by the French labor unions.

However, both concepts—that of violence and that of the general strike—assume under Sorel's pen a significance which they did not have in the minds of the militants and of the rank and file of the syndicalist movement. Sorel was at bottom a moralist. He saw in working class violence a means of disturbing the "social peace" which in his opinion was a corrupting influence both upon the workers and their capitalist masters; an influence which was bound to lead the world to decadence and barbarism. Application of violence would, in his view, reduce and discredit the influence of the parliamentary socialists who were trying to reconcile the working masses with the existing social order. It would also arouse the enthusiasm of the masses and thus lift the individual worker above the level of a purely animal existence. It would bring the element of beauty and heroism into his life. And, last but not least, it would serve as a healthy stimulus for the bourgeoisie. Under the impact of proletarian violence the employers themselves would become "class-conscious", they would abandon philanthropy and resort to an aggressive attitude both in repelling the attacks of the workers and in attempting to do their utmost in developing their own productive and organizational potentialities. The purely economic, or bread-and-butter, aspect of directaction violence, aiming at immediate results in terms of wages and hours, was in the eyes of Sorel not particularly important. Moral uplift of both workers and employers thus becomes the chief purpose of revolutionary violence as Sorel sees it.

The general strike became the victim of a similar distortion under the pen of the revolutionary moralist. To him the *grève générale* is not the hoped-for reality of the future, envisioned by the dissatisfied workers eager for security, a fuller dinner-pail, shorter hours and more liberty. It is merely a social "myth" whose function it is to inspire the workers in their struggles. This concept was in keeping with Sorel's pessimistic disbelief in what is called the final emancipation of the working class, and with his approval of violence for the sake of moral uplift, so to speak. Critics were not slow in pointing out that nothing short of religious fanaticism could induce the masses to risk life or limb if no prospects of immediate benefits were beckoning to them.[2] Sorel was, no doubt, cognizant of this fact; and it was out of this realization that he advocated the "myth" of the general strike as a substitute for traditional religious fervor which no longer animated the modern industrial worker of France. Sorel's critics have very pertinently pointed out the fact that once the general strike was openly declared to be a "myth", the myth itself would lose all its religious, stimulating force; for mass enthusiasm could be aroused only by actual faith in the possibility of achieving their salvation by a practical method.

Sorel's later pro-medievalist and finally pro-Bolshevist enthusiasms can be explained by the basic psychological attitude on which his original pro-syndicalist position was based. It was his disgust with the corruption of bourgeois political democracy or democratic politics of France—as manifested in the orgy of profiteering indulged in by the victorious liberal "Dreyfusards"—which had turned his sympathies from democratic socialism to the revolutionary "a-political" labor movement, as expressed by syndicalism. In that movement Sorel saw a force openly at war with bourgeois democracy. In due time, however, he discovered that this movement was not measuring up to his expectations. The labor union militants were not exactly like the romantic heroes who, he felt, should be worthy of the name of a "proletarian elite". They were thinking in terms of material results; and they also believed in birth control and sex freedom. All these things were abominations to Sorel who, to quote a friendly Catholic critic, the Jesuit Father Victor Sartre, was "a tormented moralist, a non-believer in search of God". Yes, a moralist in the most vulgar sense of the word; for he could actually write that "there will be no justice until the world becomes more chaste" (in Sorel's volume entitled ***Matériaux d'une·Théorie du Prolétariat,*** p. 199).

As a result, Sorel turned to another group of men who, he felt, were fighting with real fervor against the corruption and the decadence of the bourgeois democratic republic. These men happened to be the pro-monarchist nationalists of the *Action Française* movement, who were the closest approach to what a decade later was to appear as Fascism.[3]

But they too failed to come up to his expectations, for they proved quite ineffectual in eliminating the corrupt politicians of the bourgeois republic. So in the end, a few years before his death, he turned to Lenin, though in the past he had nothing but scorn for those French revolutionists—they were called Blanquists during the Second Empire—who, in the name of socialism, advocated dictatorial rule by their party. For in Bolshevism he saw, at last, a force heroically and successfully opposing bourgeois democracy, and he gave vent to his new enthusiasm in his since famous "Plea for Lenin," a chapter added to a later edition of his ***Reflections on Violence.***

Paradoxical as it may seem, Sorel's adherence to Bolshevism was not a mere whim of a wayward philosopher of violence. For at about the same time that he hailed Lenin as the embodiment of the proletarian revolution, most of the prominent old-time revolutionary syndicalist militants, such as Pierre Monatte, Robert Louzon and others, joined the French Communist Party whose appeal to the radical section of the French working class was proving irresistible in the early twenties—just as in the later forties, for that matter. Apparently both Sorel and the syndicalist militants who ignored him, saw in Communism the potentialities for a triumph of what they called the "proletarian elite", composed largely, if not exclusively, of ex-horny handed trade union leaders. They were all headed for a bitter disappointment; for, after a short honeymoon—Sorel had died in the meantime—the syndicalists realized that they were slated to play second fiddle to political adventurers in tow or in the pay of the Moscow oligarchy. Those who were not satisfied to play that role struck out for themselves by elaborating a sort of combination of syndicalism and communism, claiming, as mentioned before, all power for the syndicalist trade union leadership.

A curious feature of both "Sorelism" and plain revolutionary syndicalism (without the anarchist prefix or adjective) was a mild—and not always very mild—sort of anti-Semitism pervading the utterances of some of their outstanding representatives, such as Sorel and his friends and followers Berth and Delesalle, as well as the top leader of the electrical workers' union, Pataud, and the editor and "angel" of the theoretical magazine, *Revolution Proletarienne,* Robert Louzon. It was a sort of throwback to the middle of the past century, when men like Marx, Proudhon and Bakunin—and the syndicalists as a rule were inspired by all three of them—found it possible to identify Jewry with capitalism and to indulge in generalizing, sweeping statements which made their followers of a few decades later blush with shame. That attitude of Sorel and of other syndicalists—not all of them to be sure—could be attributed to the fact that *French* Jewry was largely an upper middle class group with many financiers among them, and that French radicals, like many other Frenchmen, were, as a rule, altogether ignorant of political and social conditions outside their own country.

"ANARCHO-BOLSHEVISM"

For a while, during the early twenties, those among the "bolshevizing" anarchists in Russia who were either unable or unwilling to throw overboard all their anarchist past at one stroke, found a sort of ideological refuge in a theory called "anarcho-bolshevism" which openly advocated a revolutionary dictatorship by anarchists during the transitional period from capitalism to anarchist communism. It was a frank reversion to that aspect of Bakuninism which as a rule was ignored or denied by the later anarchists. In most cases, however, "anarcho-bolshevism" proved merely a short "transitional period" between anarchism and complete acceptance of official Russian "Communism."

In Spain both the Russian Bolshevik revolution of 1917 and the Spanish revolution and civil war of 1931-1939, had a marked effect upon the anarchist movement. The bloodless revolution of 1931 which ushered in an era of political democracy, resulted in the breaking away of a powerful wing of anarcho-syndicalist trade-unionists who decided to abandon the old revolutionary tradition and to pursue gradualist tactics of typical trade-unionism while retaining the old slogans of syndicalism, very much as the gradualist socialists retained the old slogans of revolutionary Marxism. On the other hand, the same event, and the example of the Bolsheviks of 1917 led to the formation of a strong organization of insurrectionist anarchists called FAI (*Federacion Anarquista Iberica*) which was frankly out for an immediate anticapitalist revolution headed by anarchists, with a thinly veiled program of anarchist dictatorship, Bakunin style. These were the younger, more impulsive elements among the self-educated manual and "white collar" workers who were just as hungry for power as the corresponding elements which in other countries embrace the Communist "line". The subsequent events in Spain (1936-1938) led to the further abandonment by the Spanish anarchists of some of the traditional concepts of anarchist tactics: they voted for the democratic parties during the elections of 1936 (hitherto, voting was taboo with all anarchists); and, after the Falangist military uprising, they actively participated as cabinet members in the Loyalist Government. Anarchists in theory, the Spanish followers of the "anti-state" gospel became hardly distinguishable from democratic socialists.

WACLAW MACHAJSKI OR THE REBEL'S DILEMMA

In conclusion, it may not be amiss to mention the curious story of a Russian revolutionary group which was usually classfied as "anarchist" even though it did not use that label. That group made its appearance about the turn of the century, at a time when Leninism as a distinctive theory was as yet non-existent. It centered around the person of the Polish-Russian revolutionist Waclaw Machajski (Makhaysky) who became known by his criticism of nineteenth century socialism as the ideology of the impecunious, malcontent, lower middle class intellectual workers. These, according to Machajski, were out to remove the capitalists, not for the purpose of emancipating the working class, but with a view to establishing a new system of exploitation: a system of government ownership under which well-paid office-holders, managers and technicians would take the place of the private owners. In short, he predicted what is now called the "managerial revolution" more than forty years before the appearance of the book of that title.

Writing in the peaceful days of capitalism's upward trend, Machajski saw this change coming as a result of the gradualist policy of the Social-Democratic (Socialist) parties whose leadership in the Western democratic countries had become quite a respectable group of Leftist politicians averse to any revolutionary adventures. At that time the rebellious, declassed professional (or "intellectual") of the decades preceding and following 1848 was no longer a mass phenomenon outside of such politically backward countries as Russia (including Russian-Poland) and Spain. That phenomenon was to recur in the wake of the first world war when the hordes of unemployed or underpaid professional or white collar workers began to embrace, en masse, the Bolshevist gospel of immediate anti-capitalist revolution. Long before Lenin, Machajski, a conspirator by temperament, hoped to initiate an international, anti-capitalist revolution with the help of those then not very numerous, déclassés who, in Russia, were not satisfied with a mere democratic, bourgeois revolution, and who, in the democratic West, wasted their anti-capitalist intransigency in the Utopian protest of various post-Bakuninist anarchist sects. His criticism of the intellectual workers, as a growing middle class stratum whose more active members were heading the gradualist socialist movements, was the theoretical drawing card with which he was trying to attract those radical elements who were dissatisfied with the tempo of the anti-capitalist struggle.

Machajski's criticism of socialist leadership as the champions of a new rising middle class of would-be organizers and managers of a collectivist form of economic inequality, might have been inspired by a remark made by Bakunin in his *Statism and Anarchy* (in Russian) in which he accused the Marxists of aiming at such a new form of exploitation. The similarity of Machajski's views to those of Bakunin shows up in another respect as well. Bakunin operated with two contradictory theories, as it were: one, for the general public, which advocated the complete destruction of the state immediately after the victorious revolution, and another which was expressed in letters to members of his inner circle (and in other documents as well), in which he favored a revolutionary dictatorship by his own leading elite. Machajski, who may or may not have been aware of this dualism of Bakunin's, likewise had two theories: one was somewhat related to syndicalism, in which he advocated an exclusively non-political mass struggle for higher wages and for jobs for the unemployed—a sort of direct action movement against private employers and against the state; a struggle which in its further development would lead to the expropriation of the capitalists and to the complete equalization of incomes of manual and intellectual workers—thus bringing about the liquidation of the state by the process of the disappearance of economic inequalities. The other theory postulated the seizure of power in the form of a "revolutionary dictatorship." It was hidden away in some passages of his earlier writings; in the opinion of most of his followers it was considered abandoned by the teacher himself. But Machajski never explicitly repudiated that "outdated" view of his. And, thus, his non-political, direct-action, equalitarian semi-syndicalism, as it were,[4] was allowed to exist side by side with a pre-Leninist form of Bolshevism, i.e. advocating a "world conspiracy and dictatorship of the proletariat," and seizure of power by his own group. This view was in contradiction to his basic sociological thesis about the exploitative, unequalitarian tendencies animating the owners of higher education with regard to the manual workers. For it implied that those members of the new middle class of intellectual workers who were to constitute the bureaucratic setup of a Machajski-controlled revolutionary government would be exempt from those tendencies. Thus the thinker's logic and consistency—because of their pessimistic, non-revolutionary implications—were sacrificed on the altar of the revolutionist's will to power.

———

The post-war period has seen the revival of traditional anarchism of the Kropotkin school, and of anarcho-syndicalism in some of the countries in which they had been in vogue before, such as France and Italy. But they seem doomed to remain small groups of "irreconcilables" unable, so far, to break the spell which the revolutionary anti-capitalist halo of official Russian Communism is still exerting upon most malcontent elements among white collar and manual workers.

[1] The anarcho-syndicalists too changed their attitude towards government power. During the period following World War I, the French anarcho-syndicalists in their organ, *Le Combat Syndicaliste,* carried on the front page the motto *Toute l'Economic aux Syndicats! Toute Administration Sociale aux Communes!* (All economic activity to the trade unions! All social administration to the municipalities) which actually implies the acceptance of a decentralized form of state administration.

[2] Race riots—also one of the forms of "proletarian violence"—have always an un vowed, subconscious economic motive, directed as they are against those who, rightly or wrongly, are hated as exploiters or job competitors.

[3] It was this short phase of his spiritual wanderings, coupled with his "myth" theory and his glorification of violence, which gave the Italian Fascists—many of whom had come from the syndicalist camp—the pretext for claiming Sorel as one of the teachers of Mussolini.

[4] Machajski himself did not apply any label to his views. His group which aspired to become an international secret organization of professional revolutionists was called the "Workers Conspiracy." The idea of seizure of power in the wake of a revolutionary mass struggle for the workers' bread-and-butter demands was a carefully guarded "top secret"—lest the group lose its appeal as a genuinely working class organization.

James H. Meisel (essay date 1950)

SOURCE: "Disciples and Dissenters," in the *South Atlantic Quarterly,* Vol. XLIX, No. 2, April, 1950, pp. 159-74.

[*In the following excerpt, Meisel examines how Sorel's contemporaries reacted positively and negatively to his theories.*]

There are the honorable titans of the spirit, the good masters who hold our admiration, whose every word we endorse and file away for reference because it is the truth. But, as the years go by, we find that something has been happening to us. Our esteem of the masters has not changed; we would not dream of casting doubt upon their findings; only, we no longer care. Our integral assent has come embarrassingly close to boredom, whereas lesser figures who are neither sound nor honorable and in no way titans prove to be a lasting source of inspiration. They irritate us, they infuriate us, but they keep us interested. Their premises are unconvincing, their logical transactions dubious, their conclusions impossible. And yet what was at first merely entertaining, keeping us indignantly amused, finally becomes a challenge, serious business. We have a sense of shame, of having sinned because a second-rate mind has gained such a strong hold on us. But there it is; and the inferior and objectionable may yet prove to be the inspiration for a major truth.

Such is perhaps the case of the French thinker, Georges Sorel. The case is complicated further by the fact that he seems to fall between the solid-but-dull thinkers on the one hand and the intellectual gypsies on the other. Both as a person and as a thinker, Sorel is at once intensely honorable and deceptive, elusive and candid, pedestrian and fanciful. If, however, his stature be measured exclusively by the amount of antagonism he aroused in his lifetime and afterwards, Georges Sorel merits the title of greatness.

This is not to say that he lacked ardent friends: if the number of loving disciples that rallied around the "hermit of Boulogne sur Seine" never amounted to more than a small clique, their quality was truly remarkable. Men of the first order such as Benedetto Croce, Vilfredo Pareto, and Henri Bergson treated Sorel as their intellectual equal; and the contemporaries who, calling him their master, were yet distinctly figures in their own right make an impressive list. Although history will likely never rank Sorel among the Prime Movers, he nevertheless belongs to that select circle of provocative thinkers who do not themselves create a system but assemble the materials for one or even for more than one philosophy. Such men are the indefatigable explorers of the area which is both the meeting place of all the intellectual currents of the time and their Great Divide. No wonder that Sorel, who disliked Socrates, played in his disputations a Socratic role, evoking either love or hatred, but never indifference.

But the study of "reactions to Sorel" is not merely a study in extremes, violent adulation or vitriolic abhorrence; rather it is a study in ambivalence. The enthusiasm of some has an almost hysterical pitch, revealing symptoms of overcompensation or of resentment overcome by a successful effort to love; the opposition to Sorel is often suggestive of a suppressed, frustrated affection that would have preferred to worship but was not quite strong enough to follow the master on his endless and uncertain quest. This intriguing blend of love-hate or hate-love is merely characteristic of the past and current estimation of Sorel's work and reveals something in Sorel's own make-up: a contradiction at work in his mental processes. Not that his failure to co-ordinate his thought into a comprehensive system needs to be ascribed to a lack of integrating power. It may be that his refusal to sum up his work was a deliberate act of self-limitation, an abstention reflecting integrity of mind and the modesty of a scholar content to be a sensitive recorder of historic trends. Sorel's questions may be of greater help toward the clarification of contemporary issues than all the answers given by the systematic thinkers. The Sorelian whirlpool of ideas in which idealistic and materialistic currents mingle curiously, in which the diversity of forces obstructs any unity and yet implies it, seems at least well worth exploring.

No one has done more for Sorel's reputation than his disciple, Edouard Berth, though Berth's voice had a tendency to magnify the master's virtues as well as his shortcomings with all the force of a good amplifier. But to call this most authentic of all the Sorelians a mere epigonus would not be fair. He was not Sorel's equal, but neither was he insignificant. If he did not succeed and supersede his tutor as Enfantin eclipsed Henri de St. Simon, he nevertheless had one major advantage over his spiritual father: he was the better, or, at any rate, the more eloquent writer. His work is one long peroration, exhortation, *plaidoyer*. Berth's supercharged style tells all about Berth and not a little about his master; there was at work behind Sorel's jolly countenance a palpitating passion, which showed only in his conversation and his correspondence. When he wrote for publication, his style, as is often the case with people who speak well, became self-conscious, cramped. Berth is Sorel relaxed and often dangerously uninhibited. Where Sorel hesitates and ponders, Berth declaims and lectures with a high, shrill voice. While Sorel for a brief period toyed with the idea of National Syndicalism, only to retract soon after and to reject firmly the amalgam later known as Fascism, Berth fell for it hook, line, and sinker, and by vociferously synthesizing Sorel and Maurras did more to incriminate his old friend as a "premature Mussolini" than all the enemies of Sorel put together.

The record shows that Berth was leading Sorel on rather than following his lead in the embarrassing episode during which Sorel permitted himself to become the darling of French monarchists, actively contributing to their journals though not giving up the essence of his earlier convictions. The active role was played by Berth, but he could play it only because Sorel wanted to be led. There is in all creative natures the yearning to be understood without so many words. It is a hide-and-seek game which remains a pleasure as long as the junior partner understands his duty: he must not incriminate the leader. He is expected to be an interpreter and nothing more. But all interpreters have an urge to overstep that line, to emerge from the anonymity of service and *to rule the master*.

Berth was not small enough to submerge his own personality in that of the greater man nor independent enough to break with him as other disciples did; he remained instead transfixed in an intermediate position. He sacrificed his intellectual autonomy, but for a consideration: he attempted to be another Sorel, the true Sorel, a better Sorel. He did not do this consciously. His assertions of indebtedness, of humble gratitude, abound in dedications, introduction to, and innumerable quotations from Sorel's work; but the impression remains that the temptation of stepping into the shoes of "Papa Sorel" was too strong to be resisted. The right of the interpreter seems to include the duty of *succession*, of fulfilling the unfinished task in Sorel's name. Always in his name. Yet devotion cannot help becoming arrogation; self-effacement turns into substitution of Berth for Sorel. It is the human tragedy of the second prophet following the initiator: Elisha coming after Elijah, the titanic trailblazer for God, the worker of unprecedented miracles. After him, even the most magnificent magic feat cannot be anything but repetitious.

Sorel knew how fortunate he was in having at his side a friend of Berth's unflinching loyalty. Had he ever found him unbearable, he would have told him so, for the old man was as rigorous with his friends as he could be kind and considerate, and eventually he quarreled and broke with most of them. We may wonder at the tolerance with which Sorel watched the process of mimicry in Berth's work; we may ask whether the old man ever felt any uneasiness about the streamlined, monotonously high-strung Sorel as he appears in the writings of Edouard Berth, whether he was not at times a whit nervous about that terrifying loyalty of the disciple who knew him better than he knew himself. It is perhaps no accident that the controversial figure of the Paris Socrates never quite comes to life in Berth's work of possessive devotion. Perhaps we can learn more of Georges Sorel from his detractors.

There is a type of writer who loathes and despises Georges Sorel and yet lives from him. The only question in his mind is whether he ought merely to write Sorel off as scurrilous or expose his viciousness. In most instances he decides that the author of the ***Reflections on Violence*** is a dangerous character, but also harmless, since the fallacies of his argument are blatantly evident. There is thus no reason to get excited about Sorel; in fact, the reasons why Sorel is wrong will easily fill a book.

Wyndham Lewis, no mean author, wrote such a book. It purports to deal with the predicament of society between the two great wars. Our system is on trial, and a great number of intellectual representatives are called upon to testify. The lines between prosecution and defense are so fluid that the same figures may find themselves both on the witness stand and in the dock. From Plato to Shaw, from Swift to Joyce and Bertrand Russell, Rousseau, Proudhon, and, of course, Marx, the panel is illustrious. Sorel is mentioned only twice in the table of contents, but he appears for the first time on page 1 and remains the hero-villain throughout the entire book of 434 pages. Sorel, it seems, is a good man to call upon for definitions. For instance, he "defines so happily the true nature of revolution that I cannot do better than quote him rather fully." Mr. Lewis proceeds to quote almost two pages from ***The Dreyfus Revolution.*** Soon afterwards, the problem of progress presents itself, and the author finds the "ideology of progress . . . so admirably exposed by Georges Sorel" that he cites from his ***Illusions of Progress*** twice and at considerable length. He even uses Sorel instead of consulting the original when he wants to quote somebody else. This is not simply the case of an author pleased to find his views corroborated—Mr. Lewis does not merely end up, he starts with Sorel and, be it added, with Edouard Berth. The whole "intellectual topography" of *The Art of Being Ruled* is extremely familiar to anyone acquainted with the Sorelian and Berthian preoccupation with Marx and, especially, with Proudhon.

Wyndham Lewis, then, may be put down as one who knows his Sorel well and not merely from hearsay—something that cannot be said of many Anglo-Saxon writers in the 1920's. Nor does he fail to acknowledge his debt. Not even Edouard Berth dared to claim, as Mr. Lewis does, that "Georges Sorel is the key to all contemporary political thought." To be exact, he qualifies this judgment by saying that "Sorel is, or was, a highly unstable and equivocal figure," and he defines the Sorelian puzzle with great acuteness: "He seems composed of a crowd of warring personalities, sometimes one being in the ascendant, sometimes another, and which in any case he has not been able, *or has not cared,* to control." The blend of detachment and passion in conjunction with his unquestionable sincerity makes Sorel "a sensitive plate for the confused ideology of his time."

It does not take long, however, to discover that Wyndham Lewis is not only using Georges Sorel for his own ends, which is his good right; he also puts Sorel on a high pedestal merely to tear him down again with great ferocity. Sorel, we learn, appeals to the worst instincts of the mob, the poor (the same Sorel who actually said that he was interested, not in the perennial, futile rebellion of the slaves against their masters, but in the struggle of the producers against the parasitism of the intelligentsia and the ruling bourgeoisie). Sorel, Mr. Lewis announces, longs for a new caste system (caste is a "bad" word!), and not, as we thought, for a free and self-sufficient proletariat minding its own business and letting the capitalists manage capitalism. Mr. Lewis is occasionally conscious of what he is doing, as when he remarks: "This [the notion of a caste system] is not explicit in the syndicalist doctrine: nor is, I had better add, much of the interpretation I am about to provide." But then he goes on to attribute to the theorist of syndicalism the notion that "the bootmaker must have only bootmaking thoughts. No godlike, éclairé, gentlemanly thoughts must interfere with his pure, sutorial onesidedness." One who has not read Sorel could never guess from that sentence that Sorel wanted the proletariat to develop its own institutions and disregard everything else for the very purpose of living down the curse of modern specialization. Out of their work—Sorel hoped not quite unnobly—would rise not only the particular morality of the producers but also one which would enclose the broader beliefs of a true community which our civilization has destroyed. If this hope proved to be an illusion, it was at any rate the precise opposite of what Wyndham Lewis made it to appear.

Why all this legerdemain? One of the two chapters of *The Art of Being Ruled,* officially dedicated to Sorel, provides the clue. In this chapter the author strikes terror into the heart of the law-abiding citizen by exposing in blood-curdling words Sorel's philosophy of violence. It is not, as the reader of the ***Reflections*** is asked to believe, the only effective weapon that enables the proletariat to save its class identity from being swallowed up by Leviathan. Sorel's violence is that thing most contemptible in the opinion of a writer; it is literature: "All the emotional and 'heroic' section of Sorel is deeply romantic, . . . and by that I understand untrue." Sorel, who called himself the "disinterested servant of the proletariat," is in truth the very prototype of the demagogue, whom he fought all his life: "This crowd-master . . . takes his revolutionary blessings to them 'whip in hand,' with a girding pedagogic intolerance. Coriolanus could not be more contemptuous asking for their 'voices.' . . . He approaches his proletariat with the airs of a missionary among 'natives.'" A quotation from Sorel is used to prove that he actually despised the proletariat. But that passage obviously is a critique, not of the working class, but of its Marxist leaders, who failed to realize the historic fact that "our nature always tries to escape into decadence" and that mankind will surmount the "law of regression" only under energetic pressure. The point is that Sorel has no faith in a leadership coming from without, from the intellectual class; he set his hopes in a proletarian élite that would be "masterless."

If Wyndham Lewis has no use for such rectifications, it is not because he is separated from Sorel by an abyss. On the contrary, he does not want it to be known, or does not want to admit to himself, how much he owes to the authentic Georges Sorel. Because he wants to use Sorel's pro-labor argument for something else, he has to discredit Sorel as a proletarian thinker; because he wants to impress us with the superiority of his own esoteric creed, he has to depict Sorel as a "vulgarizer of aristocracy," who took his cue from that other vulgarizer, the "vociferous showman," Nietzsche. It is, however, a vulgarized Nietzsche and a vulgarized Sorel who provide the materials for Wyndham Lewis's brand of gentleman authoritarianism. Hence his fury against the original Sorel and the original Nietzsche. We resent nothing so much as to owe the thing we wish to own. Rather than to return a property to the rightful owner, we will turn it upside down and change the paint, hoping prayerfully that we may not be found out.

The situation that confronts us in *The Art of Being Ruled* is (to paraphrase the famous witticism about the Hapsburg monarchy) desperate, but not serious. It is not the Wyndham Lewises that Sorel has to fear, for they share most of his likes and dislikes, rejecting merely his particular conclusions. Their resentment is more that of a competitor than of a genuine opponent. Sharing Sorel's antidemocratic bias, they are unable to dislodge him from his main position. It is quite another thing when a man of the convictions and abilities of Guido de Ruggiero joins the camp of Sorel's critics. His attack, the counterattack of a liberal, commands not only the attention due to the prestige of the author but respect for a feat of great moral courage, since Professor de Ruggiero published his remarks under circumstances which made discretion absolutely imperative.

Another interesting aspect is the place of publication: the essay's appearance in Benedetto Croce's own review. The great historian and philosopher had been linked to Georges Sorel by a friendship lasting more than twenty years. Croce had been instrumental in making the French autodidact well known in Italy. His sponsorship of what must be considered one of the severest judgments ever passed on Sorel's work is awkward, but it should not be misinterpreted as a change of mind on the part of the editor toward his late friend. It is more likely that there had always been room for ambivalence in Croce's mind, a last reserve at least against some of Sorel's more extravagant speculations. Even if this were not so, if de Ruggiero's article came to him as a shock, Benedetto Croce must have been pleased with it, nevertheless, for a reason which will become evident in a moment.

In taking as his text and pretext Pierre Lasserre's important study of Sorel's significance, de Ruggiero tones down moderately the angry, bitter tension that pervades that book, while at the same time going far beyond his source in the intransigence of his conclusions. Both the Italian and the Frenchmen are agreed on the historic importance of Sorel as a sincere moralist incapable of any Machiavellian "double-talk." Because he was a fundamentally honest thinker, his final nationalism must have been based on something more than intellectual curiosity; it must have been a genuine sympathy.

It seems that this particular assertion is to remain a fixture of what may be called "the myth of Sorel," and since a myth, in Sorel's own definition, is the vision of a goal that cannot be refuted by rational argument, the attempt to set Sorel's ideological record straight might well be given up as hopeless. The tradition which has Sorel end his life as a "premature Fascist," and at the same time become a convert to Bolshevism, seems firmly established. We read, in an article written for the centennial of Sorel's birth: "Characteristically, he turned at the end to Charles Maurras and the *Action Francaise*." The fact is, that for the last ten years of his life Georges Sorel, having repudiated all relations to that group, firmly reasserted his old faith in the proletariat and died as a leftist, convinced that his syndicalist hopes had come true in Lenin's Russia.

And what are we to think of M. Lasserre, who, reputable scholar that he is, informs us in all seriousness that Sorel preached the *lévee en masse* to the workers, who, once victoriously installed in the strong points of the old ruling class, would "impose their will in imperial fashion." Out of that conquest of power were to issue all the juridical and legal institutions of the working class. "It has been said that our epoch is the epoch of imperialism. Sorel has invented proletarian imperialism." Sorel did nothing of the sort. He wrote many hundreds of pages precisely to combat the Marxist thesis of the proletarian dictatorship. Sorel rejected the idea of the "workers' state" even as a transitory necessity. Neither did he believe that the pattern of a new morality and its institutional framework would be set by a victorious revolution; on the contrary, the new morality was, in Sorel's view, the indispensable prerequisite of ultimate "deliverance." Institutions are not the creation of a revolutionary "fiat" (which he called "arbitrary") but the result of the "struggle for rights," the road posts marking the advance toward the "possession of morality." The revolution, if any, only "recognizes" what is an accomplished ethical and social fact.

Lasserre knew all that, of course. Why, then, did he falsify the record? Merely in order to coin a fetching phrase that would provide him with a forceful title for his book? Or was he simply baffled by the almost perverse reticence of a theorist who advocated violence while simultaneously pronouncing a *Gran Rifiuto* of the Will to Power? Lasserre and de Ruggiero decide to reconcile the "nationalist" with the socialist Sorel as well as the man of violence with the man of reflection by discovering Sorel the theorist of the conservative revolution. Thus understood, the use of warlike methods by the working class was to bring about the regeneration of a decadent mankind. This conceptual achievement, the critics say, imposed a heavy strain on Sorel's critical faculty. To build up the proletariat into an "aristocratic élite" which would preserve by violent means the "ancient heroisms" was not possible without romanticizing and falsifying the character of a movement which, the historian de Ruggiero insists, was bound up with its democratic and egalitarian origins. Sorel's antirationalism, his distaste for democracy are the denial of what is, to de Ruggiero, the essence of true socialism. No wonder "the philistine reality of the strike" had to undergo, in Sorel's laboratory, "a fantastic deformation" in order to become the myth of moral rebirth; no wonder the proletarians and their leaders refused to act out the sublime precept of the philosopher and continued to wallow in their democratic swamp. That would have been disastrous for Sorel had he started out from socialism; but since, according to Ruggiero, he had been a revolutionary first and was as much influenced by Nietzschean notions as by Marx, his conversion to nationalism was no self-betrayal.

We are here confronted with another "myth about Sorel." The intellectual fatherhood of Nietzsche is taken for granted by most students, but it is not borne out by the evidence. In questions involving intellectual paternity the well-known injunction of the Code Napoléon ought to be heeded. Nor is de Ruggiero on safer ground when he speaks of the revolutionary origins of Sorel's thought. It took the author of the ***Reflections*** many years to overcome his initial leanings toward reformism, the democratic socialism of the Eduard Bernstein variety. The evidence in Sorel's correspondence with Croce, if not in Sorel's published early works, should have forewarned de Ruggiero. At least he does not hold Sorel responsible for fascism. His death came at a moment when the application of his doctrine to counterrevolutionary purposes was still in the experimental stage. Yet the conversion of Sorel's leftist, proletarian myth into the myth of the Italian nation must be called legitimate: "the revolutionary leaders of both right and left," Lenin as well as Mussolini, were "fighting Sorel's battle" against parliamentary liberalism.

But de Ruggiero is not yet through with his subject. What was it that transformed that kind and cautious scholar, Georges Sorel, into the raving enemy of the "intellectual"? Lasserre called Sorel "a revolutionary of the brain, not of the heart"; he compared him to Rousseau: both men were rebels against the dominant rationalist spirit of their time, both rose against the cold, arid conventionalism of the enlightenment. Rousseau's tempestuous protest was an isolated phenomenon, while Sorel's impatience with the "Illusions of Progress" not only betrayed its "pale, bookish" origin but also lacked originality. Sorel's voice was only one in a loud chorus of anti-intellectualism led by Henri Bergson and William James, who both influenced Sorel. The growing complexity of our civilization explains their yearning for a new innocence, which is to be found in "pure intuition": the growing depersonalization instils the sentiment for the decisive action, which will break the chain of logical, determined evolution and restore freedom.

At this point Professor de Ruggiero puts in a demurrer: the Bergsonian protest, even as interpreted by Sorel (and that means very freely), was not intended to provide a charter for barbaric instincts. Sorel never intended to go so far as that. His "violence" was the primitivism of a sophisticated mind suffering from intellectual indigestion: the denial of reason was the product of "rationalistic exasperation." But the best reasons and the best intentions of the world cannot prevent that words, once uttered, are misunderstood because they may mean more than they were meant to. Sorel himself knew that only too well. And so, if one is to believe Professor de Ruggiero, the gentle old man *was* in a way responsible for the return of the barbarians: "Sorel thought to evoke the sublime and unleashed the beast."

Fortunately, the doctrine of Sorel is neither derived from practice nor meant for it, but is a hothouse flower like Bergson's intuition. To be sure, it is possible to endow such aspects of experience as strikes, acts of violence, dictatorships with Sorelian significance, but the varnish dissolves in the fire of reality. "Contrary to all appearance, Sorelianism, Nietzscheanism, D'Annuncionism . . . are ideas of the past, ideas dated and depleted, and whatever seems to be enacted in their name, has quite another meaning and releases forces and ideals of a very different order." This enigmatic sentence everyone familiar with the crypto-language used by writers subject to totalitarian censorship will ponder with closest attention. It was impossible for de Ruggiero to list Fascism together with Sorelianism, Nietzscheanism, and D'Annuncionism, having attacked all three. On the other hand, he did not have to dot his i's; the Duce had publicly acknowledged his debt to both the Frenchman and the German, if not to the Duce of Fiume.

But even the Italian reader who preferred to take his de Ruggiero straight could still marvel at those unidentified forces of a "very different order" which had been released in Sorel's name. If it was the Fascist order of the day, Mussolini's censor could be pleased, since Fascism setting wrong Sorelianism right would appear justified. Or perhaps Fascism was merely Sorel's disastrous pipedream come true, bound to be defeated by the forces of outraged humanity. There is room for the suspicion that the target was not Sorel, but the dictator himself, by way of Sorel. His argument against Sorel should not be dismissed on that ground, however; it remains a formidable criticism. But it is still far from complete.

"At first sight, religion and rationalism seem to be contradictory. Still, a mind that has intelligence but no religion, is offensive to us, it will strike us as dry, harsh, opaque. In turn, a religious mind which does not endure well the yoke of rational discipline, will repel us as feeble. Both lack something, something human." M. Lasserre, continuing, has no doubt that the mark of a fully human intellect is the faculty of "reconciling the demands of reason and the religious sentiment." This reasonably sentimental man is the democratic liberal. Sorel's equation of democracy and abstract intellect leads him astray. As Professor Georges Guy-Grand puts it: "The hatred of abstraction, logic, intellectualism, translates itself for Sorel into hatred of democracy." Still worse, in Sorel's view, "democracy always seeks unity." It always tends "toward equality, toward assimilation, toward the fusion of all classes into a regime of abstract egalitarianism." Because he was convinced that the main reason for the degradation of the modern world was its penchant for unity, Sorel opposed to it his principle of *"scission,"* severance; to the "general will" of mass democracy he opposed the "precise will," or, as Rousseau would call it, the "corporate will" of one class, the proletariat, the only class not yet dissolved in the great democratic melting pot.

The comparison between Sorel and Rousseau breaks down at a crucial point. Yet Professor Guy-Grand remains undisturbed. Rousseau's sovereign community was not meant to obliterate individuality but, on the contrary, to free it from the intervening, petty tyrants of the feudal past. What Sorel confused was the democratic reconciliation of "the wills of all" with their nivellation and destruction. If there is in the present day some evidence of "democratic absolutism," this merely means that "the democratic mechanism is not fully functioning; it only proves that the idea of democracy has not yet become a fact." Democracy, therefore, is not, as Sorel believed, a monistic creed; rather, "the democratic rule of law, a law determined by all, is much less unitarian than are such regimes as absolute monarchies or unilateral dictatorships," which subordinate everything "to the will of one man or one class." Afraid that this allusion to Sorel's pro-Lenin stand might be lost on the reader, Guy-Grand proceeds: "What could be more absolute than Bolshevism, what more abstract than Internationalism, what more opposed to the spirit of Empiricism than a violent revolution?"

Considering Guy-Grand with Lasserre and de Ruggiero, the accusations against Georges Sorel narrow down to two contentions mutually exclusive: (1) that he severed what belongs together, arraigning the forces of instinct, intuition, class, diversity against intellect, democracy, and unity; and (2) that he is himself a rationalist, absolutist, doctrinarian, paying lip service to multiformity but actually meaning unity. But is it possible that one and the same man could be "a foe of progress through reform, and believe in progress through violence; be a foe of the democratic intellectual and exalt the revolutionary intellectual; be the enemy of superannuated notions about the State of Nature and praise the spontaneous virtue of the proletarian; a firebrand against aristocracy who was himself essentially aristocratic, one who denied the absolute but believed in the absolute of the myth. . . . "

The concept of the myth, first sketched in a work belonging to Sorel's prerevolutionary period, has likewise been subjected to a severe scrutiny by Guy-Grand. Sorel distinguishes between a social utopia, which is the description of a rational scheme of economic or political organization, and a social *will,* imaginative in origin and expressed in religious or poetical terms—a myth. The particular proletarian, or rather Sorelian myth of the general strike, symbolizes the faith in ultimate liberation, which was in Sorel's view the core of the Marxian doctrine, although Marx had done his best to bury it under an abstract structure far too heavy for the working class to carry. What keeps the proletarian movement alive, then, is the myth; not a blueprint of the socialist future, but an "activating image" readying the proletarian class for battle. The ultimate "napoleonic" finale may never come, and yet the myth will have fulfilled its purpose: to keep morale alive.

But, observes Guy-Grand, if the workers really go into battle without any concrete design, without a program, it is difficult to see why they should want to fight at all. "The movement is everything, the goal nothing"—there is, of course, some truth in Eduard Bernstein's saying, but like all generalizations, this one too exaggerates, for "if the goal were really of no account, the movement would not exist, or it would be mere stupid energy and savagery." What redeems the proletarian dream and makes it, to use Sorel's favorite expression, sublime, is precisely the aim pursued, the ardent vision of a better social order that makes the greatest sacrifices possible and understandable. An intelligent and intelligible plan of social change, blurred as it may be, must and will exist. A myth is, therefore, a utopia that has caught on, that has fired the passionate imagination of the mass mind into action. This sounds like common sense, and once again Sorel seems to be guilty of gross exaggeration. Instead of being content to point out the fallacious overestimation of the rational factor, he went into the opposite extreme of proclaiming irrational will as the sole creative force.

There remains the possibility that Georges Sorel knew what he was doing and that the extremism of his views was deliberate. He may reply to Guy-Grand that his myth concept alone explains why movements survive even when results are not forthcoming, that it helps to understand the heroic persistence of persistent losers. As an example of a myth sustaining a movement toward a receding goal, Sorel cites the early Christian faith in Christ's second coming. The rationalization of the ends is not the cause but merely a by-product of faith. We may, on the other hand, reject Sorel's notion of the myth altogether on the ground that it forces him to talk intelligently about the unintelligible. But if we do so, Sorel might answer us with Bernard Shaw: "You could not have Æsop's fables unless the animals talked." How are we to identify the manifestations of the irrational unless we apply to them the categories of rational description? Not able to explain the unexplainable, we may still interpret our awareness of it. In defining the symptoms of the instinct we should be conscious of our limitations, of our duty as intellectuals not to interfere but to remain, in all humility, observers or servants at best of the vital process.

While paying attention to all nonutilitarian drives, Sorel did not try to minimize the role of the material factor. He put Marx's methodology to good use without making a fetish out of historic materialism. "There is a force which always leads the mind toward idealism; one would do well to study the nature of that force and try to find out whether idealism has not a legitimate place in the intellectual process, but outside of economics and law. . . . " There are "three great aspects of human activity. . . . " One is that of "free spontaneity disregarding all material obstacles and replacing reality by the creations of its own imagination. . . . " This is the realm of mythology, of legend and, on a higher plane, all imaginary abstraction: "man retires into himself and saturates his conscience in the contemplation of the ideal." Another aspect is "of a social and political nature; it includes everything that pertains to association and protection"—here appears "the State, imposing peace by means of penal law." Sorel, it is plain, was no loyal Marxist, since he did not derive social morality from economics, which is something else again, "the world of distribution of exchange, amendable to external, abstract manipulation." It must be distinguished from production proper, the material realization of our creative urge. A society in which distribution ("abstract" intellectualism) dictates to production (Bergson's "intuition") will be a frustrated society.

Sorel has been called a relativist. But he said: "First of all, one ought to distinguish a very small and narrow portion of the human mind in which thought touches on the absolute; we may call it the domain of science . . . which reaches its perfection in physical mathematics. At the opposite pole of conscience, there is to be found another very small but equally important sector where we also reach the absolute. This is the corner in which we conceive ideas freely; we may call it the corner of morals and religion. Between these two narrow regions, there extends the immense domain which occupies almost the entire reach of our consciousness: here the operations of our daily life take place. Here, logic operates very poorly." Sorel's relativism was thus not absolute.

Sorel has been called a pluralist. But in his view diversity and unity were not exclusive:

> Depending on the position we assume, we will have the right of conceiving society as a whole or as a multiplicity of antagonistic forces. There exists in many cases an approximation to economic and juridical uniformity. . . . On the other hand, there are many highly important questions which will not make sense unless we take the view that the activity of class war institutions is the preponderant influence. . . . A great number of organizations are more or less intimately integrated into the social ensemble, so whatever unity is required will follow automatically; other organizations, less numerous and sifted out by a severe selective process, conduct the class struggle; it is they who create the ideological unity necessary for the proletariat to accomplish its revolutionary task. . . .

If we want to sort out the confused mass of experience, we can do so only at the risk of breaking it up into segments and assigning to the detail full autonomy: "Social philosophy, in order to trace the most important happenings of history, is obliged to practice the method of disruption, to examine certain parts without regard for their connection with the whole, and to determine somehow the nature of their activity by pushing them toward independence. Once our understanding has reached an optimal point, it is no longer capable of restoring the disrupted unity." The part has become a whole; unjustly so, but the whole from which we broke it loose is not a constant either; it is history in motion. We can never know it until it has become the past, and likewise the philosophic observer "has no right to believe that he can give orders to the future."

This means that what at one time or another looks like unity exists only in the mind of the onlooker who takes his partial truth to be the whole. In reality, there is no such thing as a synthesis unless it be, for a fleeting second of history, the equilibrium resulting from the many pulls and hauls of all the social groups each trying to drag all the rest in their direction. What Sorel did was to bring the different group wills into sharper relief, even if that meant patent exaggeration. Not until we clear the ground and fight for our bourgeois or proletarian truths as absolutes, can "the" new truth emerge, and then it will contain whatever valor and validity these absolutes possess, no more, no less. The composite picture of our social world, as Sorel saw it, is at all times the product of a collective workshop in which everyone must exert himself as if he were the only artist. Finally:

> It has been pointed out to me that I wrote without the least concern for any didactic order whatsoever. . . . Yet, I am convinced that the educational merit of these studies—and that is the only merit they have—would be greater if their primitive form remained unaltered: I am carrying on an intimate conversation with the reader; I submit to him ideas, and I force him to do his own thinking in turn, so that he may correct me and complete my work.

E. H. Carr (essay date 1950)

SOURCE: "Sorel: Philosopher of Syndicalism," in *Studies in Revolution,* Grosset & Dunlap, 1964, pp. 152-65.

[*In the following excerpt, Carr identifies the intellectual sources of Sorel's most important writings.*]

Born at Cherbourg on November 2, 1847, Georges Sorel was, from the early twenties to the age of forty-five, a blameless *ingénieur des ponts-etchaussées.* Then in 1892 he abandoned his profession to devote himself to his newly found hobby of writing about socialism. He helped to found two reviews and contributed to many more, wrote several books (of which one, ***Reflections on Violence***—the only one of his works to be translated into English—enjoyed a *succès de scandale*) and became the recognized philosopher of the French trade-union or "syndicalist" movement. He died in August 1922 at Boulogne-sur-Seine, where he had spent the last twenty-five years of his uneventful life.

Sorel wrote—or at any rate published—nothing till he was in the forties; his masterpiece was written at fifty-nine, and he wrote with undiminished vigour till well on in his sixties. His late maturity gives a peculiar shape to his career. His formative years covered two intellectual generations; he wrote primarily for a third. He stands, a solitary and daring pioneer, at the most important cross-roads of modern social and political thought. Born a few weeks before the *Communist Manifesto* and living on till the eve of the "march on Rome", he looks back to Marx and Nietzsche (of the great thinkers who, more than anyone, undermined the foundations of bourgeois society and bourgeois morality—Marx, Nietzsche and Dostoevsky—Sorel missed only the third) and forward to Lenin, to the neo-Catholicism of Bloy and Péguy, and to Mussolini. There is no conceivable parallel in any other country to Sorel, except perhaps Bernard Shaw, ten years his junior in age, his contemporary in literary apprenticeship. But this parallel breaks down in at least one respect: Sorel was no artist and not even a very good writer.

Marx was Sorel's first master. He states in his ***Confessions*** that he was an orthodox Marxist till 1897; and this is as nearly true as it could be of one who was temperamentally incapable of bowing the knee to any orthodoxy. His starting-point, according to his own statement, was to discover "how the essential of the Marxist doctrines could be realized". He drew largely from Nietzsche, in part directly, in part through Bergson, the philosopher of *L'Evolution créatrice* and the *élan vital.* The other, though less important, literary influence was Renan. Sorel wittily describes Renan as one of those French writers—he also counts Molière and Racine among them—who have eschewed profundity for fear of being excluded from the *salons* of their female admirers. But it was from Renan's belief in religious dogma as "a necessary imposture" that he derived his famous conception of the socialist "myth".

The study of Sorel reveals unexpectedly numerous points of contact between Marx and Nietzsche. It is often puzzling whether Sorel's thought should be described as Marx reflected through a Nietzschean prism, or vice versa. But the dual influence, blended with an extreme subtlety, is always there, and colours all Sorel's fundamental beliefs.

The first article in Sorel's corrosive creed is derived equally from both his masters—his conviction of the decadence of bourgeois society. Sorel, one of his commentators has said, was literally haunted with the idea of decadence. ***La Ruine du monde antique*** was his first major work. The persistent attraction of Christianity for him is its dogma of original sin. The "princes of secular thought", from Diderot onwards, are "philistines"; they bear (like Marx's "vulgar economists") the hallmark of bourgeois culture—the belief in progress. ***Les Illusions du progrès,*** published in the same year as ***Réflexions sur la violence,*** is the most clearly and closely reasoned of his books.

Secondly, the rejection of the bourgeoisie and of bourgeois philosophy carries with it a revolt against the intellect. Sorel's earliest literary essay, ***Le Procès de Socrate,*** denounces Socrates for having corrupted civilization through the false doctrine that history moves forward through a process of intellectual inquiry and persuasion. This is the essence of the bourgeois heresy: "Est bourgeois", in Alain's well-known aphorism, "tout ce qui vit de persuader." Like Marx, Sorel believes in Nietzsche's (or rather, Pindar's) "eternal strife, father of all things". Struggle and pain are the realities of life. Violence is the only cure for the evils of bourgeois civilization.

Thirdly, Sorel shares the common contempt of Nietzsche and Marx for bourgeois pacifism. In his specific glorification of war he harks back to Proudhon rather than to Marx (though Marx, in preaching class war, did not condemn national wars provided they were the right ones). Never, he remarks in ***La Ruine du monde antique,*** was there a great State so averse from war as the Roman Empire in its decadence. "In England the pacifist movement is closely connected with the chronic intellectual decadence which has overtaken that country." The surest symptom of the decay of the English bourgeoisie is its inability to take war seriously; English officers in South Africa (the date is 1900-01) "go to war like gentlemen to a football match". The only alternative to a proletarian revolution as the creator of a new and healthy society would be a great European war; and this seemed to Sorel in the early 1900s a solution scarcely to be hoped for.

The fourth target of Sorel's animosity is bourgeois democracy. The case against bourgeois democracy has been so amply developed by others from the original Marxist premises that Sorel's contributions, though copious, are no longer specially significant:

> Government by the mass of the citizens has never yet been anything but a fiction: yet this fiction was the last word of democratic science. No attempt has ever been made to justify this singular paradox by which the vote of a chaotic majority is supposed to produce what Rousseau calls the "general will" which is infalliable.

Sorel's bitterness against democratic politics and democratic politicians was further sharpened by the *affaire Dreyfus,* when what had started as a noble campaign to vindicate justice was exploited for the mean ends of party or personal ambition. It was an error to look for noble aims in the masses. The majority, he had already declared in ***Le Procès de Socrate,*** "cannot in general accept great upheavals"; they "cling to their traditions". The audacious minority is always the instrument of change.

Sorel does not, however, remain merely destructive. His pessimism, he insists, is not the barren pessimism of the disillusioned optimist but the pessimism which, by accepting the decadence of the existing order, already constitutes "a step towards deliverance". Yet while the goal is the goal of Marx, the voice is the voice of Nietzsche:

> Socialism is a moral question in the sense that it brings into the world a new way of judging all human actions or, following a famous expression of Nietzsche, a transvaluation of all values. . . . The middle classes cannot find in their conditions of life any source of ideas which stand in direct opposition to bourgeois ideas; the notion of catastrophe [Nietzsche called it "tragedy"] escapes them entirely. The proletariat, on the contrary, finds in its conditions of life something to nourish sentiments of solidarity and revolt; it is in daily warfare with hierarchy and with property; it can thus conceive moral values opposed to those consecrated by tradition. In this transvaluation of all values by the militant proletariat lies the high originality of contemporary socialism.

The two moralities of Marx (proletarian morality and bourgeois morality) have oddly blended with the two moralities ("master" and "slave" morality) of Nietzsche. Sorel preached a "morality of producers" (among whom intellectuals were apparently not included); and in a further echo of the German philosopher he branded Christian morality as a "morality of mendicants". Curiously enough it was Jaurès, a favourite target of Sorel's ridicule, who made the apt remark that the proletarian was the contemporary superman.

Such is the basis of Sorel's cult of "revolutionary syndicalism". Syndicalism is, in Sorel's eyes, the true heir of Marxism. It is anti-political in two senses, both of them Marxist. In the first place it rejects the State, as Marx did and as most contemporary Marxists did not; it seeks not to capture the machinery of the State—much less to find places for socialist ministers in bourgeois governments—but to destroy it. Secondly, it asserts, as Marx did, the essential primacy of economics over politics. Political action is not class action: only economic action can be truly revolutionary. The *syndicats,* the trade unions, being not political parties but organizations of the workers, are alone capable of such action.

Revolutionary syndicalism, the economic action of the workers, can take the form only of the strike, and of the most absolute form of strike, the general strike, which had been a central point in the French syndicalist programme since 1892. A sworn enemy of all Utopias, Sorel refuses to draw any picture at all of the social order which will follow this health-giving outburst of proletarian violence. He borrows a phrase from Bernstein, the German "revisionist" who, from a different point of view, also laboured to purge Marxism of its Utopian ingredients: "The end is nothing, the movement is all". And if critics drew attention to the motivelessness of the general strike so conceived, Sorel boldly rejected this excursion into rationalism. The general strike was not a rational construction, but the "myth" of socialism, necessary like the dogmas of the Christian Church and, like them, above rational criticism.

This famous Sorelian concept of the myth involves two significant consequences. The first is a purely relativist and pragmatic view of truth which in his earlier writings he had vigorously rejected. The myth is not something which is true in any abstract sense, but something in which it is useful to believe: this is indeed the meaning of truth. From the implied pragmatism of Bergson Sorel went on to the avowed pragmatism of William James and the American school. The last of all his writings was ***De l'utilité du pragmatisme,*** published in 1921.

The other consequence, which Sorel faced less clearly, was an "aristocratic" view of the movement which was asked to accept this philosophy. The syndicalist movement was to be based on a myth devised and propagated by an *élite* of leaders and enthusiastically accepted by the rank and file. Such a view accorded well with Sorel's long-standing rejection of democracy and belief in "audacious minorities". But it was not an easy view to fit into the principles and programmes of the CGT. The rift between the syndicalist movement in France and syndicalist philosophy elaborated for it by Sorel and his disciples was never really bridged.

It was perhaps some dim consciousness of the unreality of his position which brought Sorel to an intellectual crisis in 1910. It was a lean year in the history of socialism. It marked the nadir of the fortunes of Bolshevism; and even Lenin fell a prey to some discouragement. What is more to the present point, it was in this year that Benedetto Croce, who had hailed syndicalism as "a new form of Marx's great dream, dreamed a second time by Georges Sorel", declared that socialism, whether in its old Marxist or its new Sorelian form, was "dead". Sorel, in his sixty-third year but still at the height of his powers, was too restless a spirit to resign himself to defeat. His main work had been done. But the turn which he now took is of immense significance in assessing his ultimate influence. Of the three paths which led forward from the crossroads at which Sorel stood—Neo-Catholicism, Bolshevism and Fascism—all were tentatively explored by Sorel himself. But he followed none of them to the end.

One of the more baffling by-products of the *affaire Dreyfus* had been the formation of a tiny group of which the moving spirit was a young Dreyfusard, the self-taught son of a peasant, Charles Péguy. It centred round a modest periodical, *Les Cahiers de la Quinzaine,* edited, and for the most part written, by Péguy himself. Contrary to all the traditions of the *affaire,* Péguy was strongly nationalist, pro-Catholic, anti-democratic and a hater of the bourgeoisie. Since 1902 Sorel had written occasional papers for the *Cahiers,* had attended the weekly Thursdays of the group, and had been accepted as its "elder statesman" and mentor. Through this group Sorel elaborated the idea of a reconciliation between French syndicalism and French nationalism. His first contribution to the *Cahiers* had borne the significant title, "Socialismes nationaux": its theme was that "there are at least as many socialisms as there are great nations".

French nationalism was at this time scarcely thinkable outside the framework of Catholicism, and it was therefore logical, though surprising, that Sorel and his syndicalist disciple Berth should in 1910 have formed, in alliance with three members of the *Action Française*, a group which they called *La Cité Française*, to publish a periodical under the title *L'Indépendance Française;* and in the same year Sorel wrote in *Action Française* (his sole contribution to the journal) an appreciation of Péguy's *Mystère de la charité de Feanne d'Arc*. The whole enterprise, the form of which changed in 1912 to a "Cercle Proudhon", was short lived; the cohabitation was never easy. But the break came in 1913, not from Sorel but from Péguy.

The causes of the rupture are obscure, and Péguy may have suffered from persecution mania. But it seems clear that Peguy, young, devout and austere, could not in the long run accommodate himself to a philosophy which enthusiastically hailed the dogmas of the Church as necessary myths. Nevertheless, when Péguy died on the Marne in September 1914, it was in that firm faith in war as the means of salvation for a decadent French society which Sorel had held from the outset of his career. No study either of the movement represented by the *Cahiers de la Quinzaine* or of the revival of French nationalism in general in the decade before 1914 can ignore the author of ***Réflexions sur la violence.*** It is these years which have led Sorel's able German biographer, Michael Freund, to give his book the inept subtitle, "Revolutionary Conservatism".

The story of Sorel's affinities with Bolshevism is less complex and probably less important. The documents are at least unequivocal. Lenin was a sworn enemy of syndicalism, which he regarded as tantamount to anarchism. He had no faith in the all-sufficiency of the general strike. He believed firmly in political as well as economic action; and, though he was more deeply committed before 1917 than after to the ultimate denial of the State, he was convinced that a political dictatorship of the proletariat was the immediate goal of revolution. He seems to have mentioned Sorel only once in his published works, dismissing him curtly as "muddleheaded" and his writings as "senseless". Nobody familiar with the clear logic of Lenin's own thought will find the verdict surprising.

Sorel, on the other hand, welcomed the October revolution with open arms. For five years he had written scarcely anything. The war, begun as a war for the French nation, which he loved, was being more and more widely hailed as a war for democracy, which he loathed. Here was a long-awaited breath of fresh air—a revolution which preached and practised a salutary violence, spat on bourgeois democracy, exalted the "morality of the producer", *alias* the proletariat, and installed Soviets as autonomous organs of self-government. Moreover, the Bolshevik Party—had Sorel cared to note the fact—was built up precisely on the Sorelian premises of an "audacious minority" leading the instinctive proletarian mass.

Sorel made no formal declaration of adhesion to the new cause and creed. But he wrote several articles for the French *Revue Communiste;* and in 1920, when Bolshevism was at the height of its unpopularity in France, he added to the fourth edition of ***Réflexions sur la violence*** a "plaidoyer pour Lénine" in which he hailed the Russian revolution as "the red dawn of a new epoch".

> Before descending into the tomb [concluded the "plaidoyer"] may I see the humiliation of the arrogant bourgeois democracies, to-day so cynically triumphant.

Bolshevism was not yet prosperous enough to ignore its few distinguished friends, even if they were not wholly orthodox. After Sorel died the *Communist International*, the official journal of Comintern, opened its columns to a lengthy, if critical, appreciation of this "reactionary petty-bourgeois Proudhonist and anarcho-syndicalist" who had rallied to the defence of the proletarian revolution.

> Sorel [concluded the article] for all his mistakes has helped, and will continue to help, the development of the will to revolution, rightly understood, and of proletarian activity in the struggle for Communism.

The facts of Sorel's relations with Fascism are also beyond dispute. Italy always held a special place in his affections; in no other foreign country were his works so widely read, admired and translated. The shabby treatment of Italy by the peacemakers at Versailles had deepened his resentment at the triumph of bourgeois democracy. His writings teem with anticipations of Fascist doctrine. "What I am", said Mussolini himself, "I owe neither to Nietzsche nor to William James, but to Georges Sorel." Georges Valois, one of the *Action Française* group which collaborated with Sorel in 1910, called him admiringly the "intellectual father of Fascism"; and his first biographer was Lanzillo, the Italian Fascist. He praised the first achievements of Fascism. But when the Fascist revolution brought Mussolini to Rome, Sorel was already dead.

What Sorel would have thought of the Fascist regime in power is an unprofitable, though inevitable, speculation. When he praised the first Fascists in a letter to Croce it was because "their violence is an advantageous substitute for the might of the State"—a modern equivalent of the Mafia and the Camorra, whose extra-legal activities and organization had always fascinated him. He saw in Fascism a realization of the syndicalist dream of an administrative power independent of the State. The question which Sorel died without having to answer was that of his attitude to the totalitarian State. All his life he had been a strong, almost violent, individualist; all his life he had fought, not for the concentration of power but for its dispersal and decentralization to the very limit of anarchism. At the very end of his life he argued against any absolute religious belief on the ground that it could not be successfully propagated without restoring the Inquisition. It would have been disconcerting—to say the least—to find Sorel as a prophet of totalitarianism. But his thought contains too many inconsistencies, his career too many unexpected turns, for anyone to pronounce with assurance on this hypothetical question.

But the most interesting point raised by Sorel's career is that of the resemblances and differences between Bolshevism and Fascism. If Sorel stands on the common ground where Marx and Nietzsche meet, this is also the common ground from which Bloshevism and Fascism diverge. Marx and Nietzsche, Bolshevism and Fascism, both deny bourgeois democracy with its bourgeois interpretations of liberty and equality; both reject the bourgeois doctrines of persuasion and compromise; both (though this is where Sorel held aloof from both) proclaim absolutes which command the obedience of the individual at the cost of all else.

There was, however, an essential difference. The absolute of Nietzsche and of Fascism ends with the super-man or the super-nation or simply with power as a good in itself and for its own sake. Marx and Bolshevism propound a universal end in the form of the good of the proletariat of all countries, in which the whole of mankind is ultimately merged; and the ideal stands, whatever shortcomings may be encountered in the pursuit of it. Sorel, while clear enough about what he rejected, never committed himself on the positive side. That, among other reasons, is why he has left no school or party, even among the syndicalists whom he sought to serve and teach. He cannot be assigned either to Bolshevism or to Fascism (and still less to the Catholics). Sorel's thought is not a beacon—or even a candle—throwing a steady beam within a defined radius; it is rather a prism reflecting, fitfully but brilliantly, the most penetrating political insights of his day and of our own.

John Bowle (essay date 1954)

SOURCE: "Georges Sorel: Myth and Anarchy," in *Politics and Opinion in the Nineteenth Century*, Oxford University Press, 1954, pp. 398-413.

[*In the following excerpt, Bowle attempts to discredit Sorels by tracing an unflattering connection between Sorel's absorption of the theories of Marx and Nietzsche with the rise of Fascism.*]

When Pope Leo XIII restated Catholic political principles and Acton developed the idea of commonwealth as the expression of conscience, both were adapting traditional ideas to a new mass society. By the closing decades of the nineteenth century great urban industry and world-wide expansion had altered the scale of Western civilization and brought the mass of the people to the threshold of political and economic power. Only political ideas which took account of these facts remained relevant. Revolutionary theories, insignificant hitherto, now achieved greater influence. Ruling circles had either to come to terms with them or promote counter-revolution on a popular scale.

In the wealthier Western states, prospects of compromise were better than in the mid-century. In England liberal legislation had been influenced by T. H. Green and Bosanquet, Tory democracy had been devised by Disraeli, and growing prosperity had diminished discontent. The Fabian socialists began to extend the moralization of politics into the field of economics within the constitution, ultimately to absorb Liberalism into social democracy. In Germany, prosperity and nationalism distracted the masses from extremist programmes, and Bernstein revised Marx. In France, social democracy found expression in the writings and oratory of Jaurès. Though German social democrats were to be trampled under the heel of militarism, and the murder of Jaurès long crippled socialist leadership in France, the dominant trend of socialism in the West remained constitutional.

But this development had brutal enemies. Apart from the basic inadequacy of European institutions, still organized in competing sovereign states, the tide of class war and nihilism had been rising since the turn of the nineteenth century. Ideas taken from Marx and Nietzsche were to be combined by Sorel, a forerunner of Fascism. Before the main development of social democracy and its reinforcement by a new environmental and psychological sociology is examined, account must be taken of his ideas. Where the Fabians were to make their selection from Marxism, and Bernstein and Jaurès their revision of it, Georges Sorel gave a new twist to the Marxist revelation. He declared that the revisionists were traitors and blended the Marxist class war with a new Nietzschean Myth. He differs from Marx in being pessimistic, with a sombre view of life, akin sometimes to de Maistre's. Hence his contribution to Fascism. He preached anarchy because he held, with Bergson, that the tide of events is not susceptible to control; that the future could not, as Marxists held, be foreseen. History proceeds in a series of creative improvisations, each age being characterized by the Myth which reflects the interest of its dominant class. His thought derives from ideas which descend from Vico, Marxist determinism, Nietzsche and Bergson. The scepticism of this misguided moralist made his attitude ambivalent. He wavers between the improvisations of the Right and the Left. His principal effect on the twentieth century was upon Italian Fascism. He made a destructive perversion of a new psychological approach to politics, here discoloured, like the thought of Nietzsche, by moral and religious disillusion.

To the irrationalism of Nietzsche and Bergson and the class hatred of Marx, he added anarchist ideas taken from Proudhon. While he was devoid of immediate political judgment, his criticisms are striking. He is a gadfly of political philosophy. His ideas, if often pernicious, are astringent to humbug. He understood that what counted in politics were myths for which men would die. Like Nietzsche, Sorel was primarily a moralist. Along with a Bergsonian cult of will, he believed in the assertion of human dignity by *Homo Faber,* by a proletarian elite. Like his forerunner, Proudhon, he was a Puritan, compensating himself for the spectacle of ordinary human nature. A man whose lost faith made him observe life with sceptical gloom, who brought strange gleams of insight to deep problems, and the vulgarization of whose ideas affected the gutter-elites of whom Mussolini and Goebbels are representative. But all his work shows strong individuality. Like Pareto, he was an engineer, and his thought reflects the technician's desire for results.

Sorel's numerous writings are contradictory and confused. 'A self taught man,' he writes, 'exhibiting to other people the notebooks which have served for my own instruction . . . That is why the rules of the art of writing have never interested me very much.' But certain ideas are dominant. First, the assumption, common to Marx and Nietzsche, that liberal democratic society is doomed, and what he terms 'bourgeois' thought 'decadent'. It is doomed, not for the abstract considerations described by Nietzsche, but because modern industry demands a civilization of self governing producers, free from the interference of the state. Traditional culture has hitherto been parasitic. Sorel is determined to make all things new. 'For twenty years', he writes, 'I worked to deliver myself from what I retained of my education.' Next, he declares, the decisive events of history are influenced not by the leadership which liberal historians describe, but by myths created by the people independently of the surface rationalizations of intellectuals. These two ideas lead to a double attack on 'intellectuals' as such, and to the repudiation of any reformist constitutional programme. The workers, he believes, must keep themselves uncontaminated from bourgeois leadership and exploitation. The whole intellectual capital of civilization, the range of professional knowledge, the achievements of the arts, are labelled 'bourgeois culture' and repudiated.

But the most sinister creation of the old order is the state. As against Bernstein and Jaurès, Sorel thinks it superlatively corrupt. Far from the means of the gradual transmission and broadening down of civilization, the state is something that must be smashed. Hence a detestation of the Fabians and of Jaurès. They would merely substitute one set of corrupt politicians for another. To take over the machinery of the bourgeois state is not enough; it must be destroyed. Hence the error even of the Marxist conception of proletarian dictatorship.

The only way out is Anarcho-Syndicalist class war. This conflict must be inspired by the supreme myth of the age, the General Strike. Paradoxically, the destructive myth was to herald an age of untrammelled production. The 'Syndicat', which has more in common with the Soviet than with the Trade Union, is the 'cell' whereby the proletarian masses will be inspired to wreck bourgeois society and repudiate its leadership. Even, perhaps, to galvanize decadent capitalism into its old vitality, so that the Marxist scriptures may be fulfilled and the proletariat inherit a world in the full vigour of production. Out of the Syndicates will come not only a society of self-governing producers, but, Sorel's fourth master idea, a moral revolution. For Sorel, like Proudhon, was an idealist. He romanticized the elite technician—the pioneer of a cleaner world. Puritan in sexual morality, atheist in religious belief, here is another cult of man.

So the first two assumptions, the decadence of bourgeois culture and importance of myth, lead to total revolution and the discarding of the state. The Anarcho-Syndicalists must create their own future. It will be mysterious. Sorel, with his cult of will, cannot foretell the manifestations of the Life-Force, in themselves their own end. Influenced by Schopenhauer and Nietzsche, by Bergsonian Creative Evolution, he saw in the destruction of the state an immediate and all-embracing goal. Yet he regards himself not so much as a prophet, as an observer of the doings of the Life Force through the proletariat. *'Gesta Vitae',* as it were, *'per Populos'.*

So from Sorel's works these major ideas emerge. The decadence of bourgeois civilization; the importance of myth; the need to destroy the state by Syndicalist class war inspired by the General Strike, and economic and moral redemption by the released creativeness of proletarian producers.

This gospel of destruction, akin sometimes to the ideas of Nietzsche, was wildly unsuited to the elaborate and precarious structure of modern civilization. Sorel is in fact careless of the actual interests of the proletariat. For this engineer of roads and bridges, the bogus mythology of the General Strike was the supreme tactic. He appears, too, singularly blind to the appalling evils of modern war and to the urgent necessity for international order. Impatient of all existing institutions, he looked first to Lenin (who regarded him with contempt) as the founder of the 'Rome of the proletariat'; then to Mussolini, of all people. An obsession with French politics—in particular with the dreary Dreyfus case and with the part subsequently played by Jaurès—gives him scope for a poisonous irony.

As an observer of society and a critic of thought, Sorel is more interesting. In the first of his main contributions, the attack on bourgeois civilization and leadership, his criticisms are trenchant. No one has better put the case against all the values in which liberal democrats have believed. To understand the twentieth century one must take account of Sorel. Like Nietzsche's, his criticisms can be answered: they cannot be ignored.

In the wide range of his works the early ***La Ruine du Monde Antique, Conception matérialiste de l'Histoire,*** compares the alleged dissolution of democratic society with the collapse of Graeco-Roman Antiquity. Sorel admired the hard pagan virtues, but he relates early

Christianity to Sorelian socialism. The intellectuals of Antiquity, Sorel believes, undermined the civic and imperial myths which were its strength.

Yet the decline of Antiquity was different from the break up of the eighteenth-century order. The former marked a dead end—'véritable culbute idéologique'—one of the 'ricorsi' which Vico had seen in history. This social and economic decadence was only painfully restored by the barbarians, in spite of the handicap imposed on them by Christianity. The French Revolution, on the other hand, occurred in an expanding society. Far from marking a collapse, it was a great 'mutation of property'. It was due not to intellectual convictions but to a massive change in habits of life. Here the promise of a mass civilization of producers first appeared. Irrelevant liberal ideologists, who attempt, like the Christians, to impose their intolerance and misunderstanding on this vast social and economic change, must be brushed aside. They will interfere with production and rob it of its fruits. For these modern slaves to abstraction, these despicable secular clerics, are as incapable of directing great scale production as were the barbarians of using the broken-down institutions of the Graeco-Roman world. The Christian 'economy of asceticism' was parasitic: useless to the kind of progress (command of environment) in which Sorel believed. 'It contains no element which assures the passage to superior forms.' As for Christian literature, there was nothing original in that, either, except for the 'drama' of the religious life, which was confined to a few and 'unconstructive'. Christianity had merely taken over the pagan concept of the 'good life' for an idle minority and developed it in selfish and ascetic terms. 'In a society of idlers, of rich parasitic patricians, . . . what was there better than such wisdom?' 'Although, of course,' he adds characteristically, 'most will prefer debauchery.' Christian education, also, had nothing to contribute. It merely took over a pernicious system of literary culture and conserved it. This 'parasitism of literary talent' still deeply infects civilization. Sorel idealized the cult of manual work. This destructive intellectual set little store by the more strenuous enterprises of the mind.

Socrates, regarded by John Stuart Mill as a hero of intellectual liberty, has for Sorel, says Perrin, but one title to fame: he was the precursor of Dr. Pangloss. This attack already shows implacable hostility to the assumptions of liberal thought.

The onslaught is further worked out in the ***Les Illusions du Progrès,*** Sorel's most interesting work, where the influences of Marx and Bergson are equally apparent. Here he again insists on the need to penetrate to the roots of society. For its laws are mysterious. The obscurities of Marx more deeply reflect life and history than the artificial and shapely simplifications of liberal thought. The ideas or myths of an epoch are those of its dominant class, and since the most characteristic ideology of the middle class is the idea of progress, it should be carefully examined. For the historian must concentrate upon the outlook of the 'winners' in a given epoch.

Another typical bourgeois myth is the idea of the general Will. Inheriting the admiration of the old régime for strong government, social democrats have always demanded centralization. Hence the cult of popular Will, a new myth to justify the old state. Naturally, the idea is fantastic. With the social grades on such different levels of development, so that the leaders may be living intellectually several centuries before the majority, who trail in varying stages of political consciousness behind them, it is ridiculous even to imagine a general Will. Yet the myth has worked. Popular opinion is always subordinated in each epoch to the ideas of elites. Behind these ideas—'which nobody has and in which every one is supposed to participate'—are concealed the fundamental causes of human action. Just as the historian reconsiders historical persons, so myths and slogans should be reassessed. 'It is in democratic times, especially, that one can say that mankind is governed by the magic power of great words rather than by ideas, by formulae rather than by reason, by dogmas of which no one knows the origin, rather than by doctrines founded on observation.'

There is no better example of such dogma than the myth of progress. It should be historically analysed, in terms of class. Following the Marxists, Sorel regards 'bourgeois' ideology as repellent. It owes much, he thinks, to the 'neo-fetishism' of Comte, though his Religion of Humanity was little regarded, and his hierarchy of 'bourgeois saints laïques' is ridiculous. Middle-class thinkers, indeed, have never escaped from the assumptions of the eighteenth century. To destroy this outlook is not only 'a question of conscience but of immediate practical interest'. French 'Enlightenment', which set the tone for all Europe, was profoundly artificial, conditioned by the mentality of class. The great French tradition of clarity and elegance was regarded by this ruthless iconoclast as dangerous and misleading. Its very elegance masks the truth. Writers become good craftsmen, 'clever advocates', who establish an artificial orthodoxy. Here, he says, are to be found the origins of the doctrine of progress. It reflects the outlook of a class. 'In formulating his famous principle of methodical doubt', for example, Descartes was only 'applying to thought the habits of an aristocrat'. Such writers have little respect for tradition, and while Pascal yearned for the constant presence of God, Descartes, intoxicated with the prospects of new knowledge was, in effect, content with His absence.

Naturally this bold scepticism was attractive to people of quality, to the *gens du monde.* It justified their desire 'to talk with assurance on subjects imperfectly understood', relying on native wit, and reckless of middle-class caution. When the practical middle class came to predominance, this aristocratic desire for clarity was reinforced by the demand for a total explanation, by a confidence in reason, which reaches its climax in Herbert Spencer. 'Hence', says Sorel, 'the insensate confidence in the decisions of enlightened people which has remained the ideological basis of the superstition of the modern state. Hence, also, the illusions of liberal rationalism, with its view of history as the education of the human race. In that originally eighteenth-century outlook, the mysterious, complex and irrational process of history is reduced, with deceptive lucidity, to an intelligible and elegant compass. Such simplification was natural to writers who catered for a beau monde 'which turned everything into conversation'. If French literature lacks the depth of a Shakespeare or a Goethe—*cherchez la femme.* Reason, tolerance, humanity—they are the values of the salon. Modern democrats have never escaped from this stuffy, artificial, inheritance.

'There is no reason', either, 'to think opinion made by the Press any better than that made in salons.' All attempts to assimilate the masses into bourgeois culture should be resisted. 'An education which aims to make the people participate in middle-class culture is useless to the proletariat.' The Welfare State is brushed aside. In English terms, W.E.A. activities, extra-mural studies—all are pernicious. Sorel turns to a vitriolic attack on both secular and classical education in France—the latter, he says, has descended to 'the level of fetishes'. Intellectuals, indeed, show for their abstractions the respect of savages for their hieroglyphs. Could there be a worse or more cruel government than that of 'mandarins'? The pretended century of enlightenment was the supreme age of humbug, of the 'bric-à-brac of the *Encyclopedia*'. Even Saint-Simon is tarred with this brush. As for the religion of Comte, 'one might as well worship the Bibliothéque Nationale'. Like de Maistre, Sorel holds that the healthy gloom of medieval Catholicism, the sombre dignity of Calvin's beliefs, more nearly reflect the realities of life. They were perverted into fatuous and delusive hope through the shallow optimism of ideologists. This rationalist nonsense reflects the class bias of parasitic minds. Actually it is emotion, not reason, that dominates mankind. All political life is an improvisation before fate.

The French, of course, will always accept anything sufficiently theoretical. Rousseau's sophistries are a notable example. His own countrymen knew better. The *Contrat Social* was regarded in Geneva as a seditious libel and burnt. But Rousseau was a supreme popularizer; he condensed ideas, largely taken from Locke, into a 'masterpiece of style which is wonderfully obscure'. He thus proved himself a master of myth, and altered the development of history. The power of this myth was extraordinary. It did not matter in the least that Rousseau was unintelligible. 'Enlightened people dare not admit that they cannot understand arguments that are presented in very sophisticated language by an illustrious writer.' The idea of the General Will and the Marxist theory of Value—notable and perennial torments for students of political thought—both prove, says Sorel, 'how important obscurity can be in giving force to a doctrine'. Of course it is quite beside the point to try to understand either.' But when, later, Rousseau's book came into the hands of the small bourgeoisie, it became a programme of immediate action. 'Everyone found in it what he wished.'[10]

Of course the idea of government by all is a fiction; yet it is the last word of democratic political thought. But the theory of the bourgeois state merely reflects a class myth. It is outdated. The whole ideology must be superseded by the proletariat, by the Syndicats, a 'powerful means of moralization'.[11] The objective is not to capture the bourgeois machine, but to deprive it of life.

Further, he again emphasizes, the whole middle-class outlook is vitiated by the cult of concentrated state power. It was inherited from the ancien régime; it is now unchecked by the Church, and backed by the myth of the General Will. What future can it have but tyranny? The danger of the omnipotent state was ever in Sorel's, as in Proudhon's, mind. Eight years before, he had written, in a society in which state, church and property exist, 'there is some chance of finding chinks without being completely crushed'[12] . . . But what can one do when the state will be 'alone, absolute in temporal and spiritual affairs, and more absolute than the Pope, because it will be represented by the expert—the man of science'? Here is the danger even of Saint-Simonean planning: the opportunity for demagogues to capture power and stultify the Revolution. Of this 'political clerisy', the intellectuals, the parasites who sell ideas, Jaurès—that Sorelian bugbear—is the representative. He has the mentality of a successful cattle merchant.

Along with the attack on democratic politicians, here is another denunciation of middle-class culture. This omnivorous reader, this self-taught beneficiary of organized knowledge, again had to undermine the intellectual capital of civilized society. History, as interpreted by liberals in terms of the leadership of individuals of genius and elites of talent, is unreal. He denies the creativeness, the decisive influence, of individuals. So-called great men are only the 'carriers of symbols' which the creative and irrational imagination of the masses have made. This is a process intellectuals cannot understand. He quotes Anatole France—'c'est toujours à l'insu des lettrés que les foules ignorantes créent des dieux'. The moving power of history is the proletariat; the 'individualist and aristocratic doctrine of talents' is false.[13] Here Sorel's sceptical view of elites and masses reinforces his political programme.

In his most notorious, though not his most able, book he worked this programme out. In the ***Reflections on Violence*** anarcho-syndicalism is interpreted in terms of the synthetic myth of the General Strike. Reiterating ideas previously formulated, it is primarily a call to misguided action. The introductory 'Letter to Halévy' contains some of Sorel's most striking phrases. 'But philosophy', he says, 'is perhaps, after all, only the recognition of the abysses which lie on each side of the footpath that the vulgar follow with the serenity of somnambulists—Profound understanding of life, he argues darkly, produces pessimism, for conventional philosophy and industrial civilization have created false hopes. The prosperous urban Greeks of Antiquity were shallow, regarding the world with a trader's mentality as 'an immense shop full of excellent things'. The concept of Natural Law is equally empty, a mere projection of the mind. He quotes Pascal: 'three degrees of latitude nearer the Pole reverse all jurisprudence, a meridian decides what is truth'.[15] It is impossible, he says, to reason about justice, a relative term. International arbitration, with its appeal to abstract right—that decrepit Rosinante—merely evokes a secularized mythology. There can be no justice in politics.

With the rise of Calvinism, the shallow and vulgar optimism of the Renaissance gave place to a juster estimate of life. But Protestantism soon became 'soft' and degenerated into 'mere lax Christianity'. Then 'the immense success of industrial civilization . . . created the belief that, in the near future, happiness would be produced automatically for everybody'. All this reformist optimism is nonsense. The syndicalists will have a tougher outlook, both in theory and politics. With the destruction of bourgeois ideology, 'the partiamentary régime, so dear to intellectuals, will be finished with—it is the abomination of desolation'! The kind of social democracy which says 'do what you like, but don't kill the goose', [the bourgeois state] must give place to a militant, destructive creed. For in a crisis the fanatics, the extremists, win. The early Christians, as he had said in the ***Illusions of Progress,*** who really counted were the Tertullians—the men who refused compromise. Bruno, who was burnt for his *'convictions',* is more important than Galileo, who was merely 'certain—with that particular kind of *certitude* about the accepted theories of science which instruction ultimately produces'. The idea of a dynamic myth, of a Holy Army, is the contribution to political theory which we draw from Bergson. He was concerned with the inner self, constantly creative in Duration, not Time. This creative consciousness, whereby we invent our world, must be applied to the eternal improvisations of politics. It must be expressed in a mythology accepted by the masses, not as description 'of things', but as means of action. For action is what counts.

And myth is a redoubtable weapon. 'People who are living in this world of "myths" are secure from all refutation'. It was a queer gospel for the increasingly precarious, interdependent, world of the twentieth century. Sorel glories in this dark thinking with the blood. He repudiates a constructive programme. 'We on the contrary have invented nothing at all, and even assert that nothing can be invented.' He has merely asserted that 'a new culture might spring from the struggle of the revolutionary trade unions against the employers and the State'. He is original, he declares again, only in repudiating the leadership of intellectuals. He has no wish at all to direct the great surge of proletarian vitality; only to put the workers on guard against 'bourgeois' thought. 'The proletariat must be preserved from the experience of the Germans who conquered the Roman Empire: the latter were ashamed of being barbarians, and put themselves to school with the rhetoricians of the Latin decadence; they had no reason to congratulate themselves upon having wished to be civilized.'[19] 'I do not believe . . . that I am labouring in vain,' he continues, 'for in this way I help to ruin the prestige of middle-class culture, a prestige which up till now has been opposed to the complete development of the principle of the "class war".' The heady vintage of Bergsonian intuition is mixed with the muddy brew of Marxist determinism.

From this theoretical background emerges the full myth of the General Strike. Sorel apparently believed that it was already 'established in the minds of the workers'. The myth was to spread through the Syndicalist cells; the infecting of the syndicates by anarchism is one of the outstanding events of the early twentieth century.

The great surge of proletarian violence, even if unsuccessful, creates a revolutionary state of mind. In pursuit of his new proletarian culture, cut off from the past, he denounces all attempts to avoid class war. 'Social duty', he writes, 'no more exists than international duty.' Sorel pours vitriolic contempt on the 'cowardice' of the middle class, who 'continue to pursue the chimera of the social peace'.[22] The natural bellicosity of the French, which subdued most of the continent under Napoleon, must be turned inwards.

It is essential, he insists, to keep the bourgeois on the run. A watered-down Capitalism would merge into a dreary sub-bourgeois state. So the class war must be kept going; the capitalists driven to fight. Proletarian violence is 'the only means by which the European nations, at present stupefied by humanitarianism, can recover their former energy'. Sorel need not have worried on that score.

He recurs to the contrast between the creative French Revolution, coming in a time of prosperity, and the Christian revolution which took over a bankrupt and decadent world. He proceeds to a glorification of Napoleon, to quotations from de Tocqueville on the dangers of democratic centralization, and to the assertion that the General Strike is not illegal since it ranks as an operation of war. But he pays the English a fine compliment. They 'are distinguished', he says, 'by an extraordinary lack of understanding of the class war'. Sidney Webb he finds peculiarly contemptible. He 'enjoys a reputation for competence that is very much exaggerated: all that can be put to his credit is that he has waded through uninteresting blue books and has had the patience to compose an extremely indigestible compilation on the history of trade unionism; he has a mind of the narrowest description'. Sorel, as one might expect, underestimates that formidable political influence.

This miscalculation was due in part to his insularity. To his obsession with French political intrigue, to the constant harping on the Dreyfus case and its consequences, to the dreary feud with Jaurès which runs with a certain gross humour, a kind of bass accompaniment, throughout the books. He labours the comparison between the corrupt demagogues of social democracy, blackmailing the rich, imposing their own will on the masses in the guise of constitutional government, and the clean Proudhonian enterprise of the Syndicalist elite.

To keep the myth alive there must be unremitting agitation. 'Consider', he says, 'the ethics of violence'.

Consider how few were the Christian martyrs, yet what a resounding legend they made! One need not necessarily achieve violence on a scale so large as to wreck society: 'there is no danger of civilization succumbing under the consequences of the development of brutality'. The myth of the General Strike—the widespread revolutionary state of mind—may indeed, foster the class war 'by means of incidents which would appear to middle-class historians of small importance, as the execution of a few Christians seemed insignificant to established opinion in Rome'.[24] There is even a 'good chance' of a Syndicalist revolution succeeding without resort to the centralized terror of bourgeois intellectual fanatics.[25] Good clean violence in factory and shipyard, railroad and power station—that Sorel admires. When this violence is sidetracked into 'cunning', into bargaining, as in the English trade unions, then there is spiritual death. Blows, on the contrary, beget heroism. Here, already, is part of the mythology of Fascism.

He becomes more interesting when he leaves his programme of action. Discussing the 'Ethics of Producers', he resumes a fruitful theme. What, he asks, with Renan, will replace the old myths? ' "On what will those who come after us live?" '[26] This is the great problem. We need, he insists, a new morality of producers, broadbased on the creative impulse of the people. He quotes, with approval, the notorious remarks of Nietzsche about the blond beast, and asserts that this kind of master type still exists in the United States. Had Nietzsche lived to see the gathering tide of American prosperity, 'he would have been struck by the singular analogies which exist between the Yankee . . . and the ancient Greek sailor, . . . sometimes a pirate'.[27] After this unexpected compliment to capitalists in their wild state, he turns to rend Aristotle and the Catholics, with their 'consumer mentality', their contemptible ideas of stability and order. But for the 'free producers of tomorrow, working in factories, there are no masters'. They must show an heroic, an Homeric, élan. The incredible victories of the revolution were due to French individualism, 'to intelligent bayonets'. 'The same spirit is found in the working-class groups . . . eager for the general strike', that 'manifestation of individualistic force in the revolted masses'.[28] Ingenious artisans, working like creative artists, are inspired by Syndicalist cells. They will develop their missionary, and spontaneous, idea. What a prospect for all-out production! Here is no 'Welfare' State, ridden by conservative bureaucrats, exploited by a clerisy, infested with the corruption of politicians. Here is a new, a healthy society, driven by its proper myth, fulfilling its own phase of a Vicoesque 'course' of history. The Holy Army is restored. This time it is not Satan who is the enemy: it is the bourgeoisie.

These ideas are further elaborated in the later ***Materials for a Theory of the Proletariat,*** a collection of early essays which was Sorel's penultimate work. Here, again, the intellectuals are attacked. Sorel denounces their superstititious respect for the expert, the parasitism of 'democrats' and 'Mandarins', the glorification of the 'pontiffs of science'. The world of dreary abstractions, of tedious and artificial classification, in which this clerisy has its being, he finds most suitable for the mentality of women, such 'research fitting the female mind'. But the shrewder bourgeois realize that once women are let in, the prestige and rewards of their calling will be diminished. Hence their anxiety to exclude them from such suitable occupations. As science progresses, the workers can actually do without the so-called experts, who will dwindle into an intellectual proletariat. Sorel remarks, foolishly enough, that in medicine 'the progress of science and the better organization of assistance has already diminished the numbers of doctors used'. Further, the managerial class is superfluous. Executive capacity is not rare.' The workers can soon provide their own self-governing institutions. 'The socialization of the means of production will translate itself into a prodigious lockout of intellectuals.' Their natural and meretricious role as exploiting politicians will no longer have any scope. 'Mort aux intellectuels!' cries this renegade of the École Polytechnique. For the collective soul is profoundly mysterious, and the tides of history are determined not by the puny laws of man's mind but by the purpose, or Bergsonian lack of it, of creative Life.

The habits of this new proletarian age will be chaste. There is 'a psycho-erotic "law" ' which demands the conservation of energy. Fourier's 'penchant for perverse debauchery' is quite out of order. Sorel, indeed, makes a cult of the family. But the proletarian family will extend to 'free unions'. As in so many French writers, the ideal of the 'femme forte' is glorified. The proletarian woman is to be a 'compagnon sévère et intelligente'.

Within their self-governing factories, meanwhile, the workers will develop their creative tasks. The cult of the General Strike will pass into the cult of work. Like 'skilled vine dressers', absorbed in their art, they will feel like a gardener about his dahlias. Accustomed to exploits of sabotage, habituated to violence and destruction, the Syndicalist elites, Sorel assumes, will quickly revert to the routine and responsibility of modern industry. For here is 'an economic epic'. 'Rejuvenated by the feelings roused by proletarian violence', they will be inspired by Sorelian myth to an 'entirely epic state of mind'. Here is the answer to the supreme question of the age—by what shall we live? An ideology for the new civilization of the people. 'It is to violence,' Sorel concludes, 'that socialism owes the high ethical values by means of which it brings salvation to the modern world.'

And why, the reader may ask, is Sorel held to be important? He had, indeed, little influence in his own country in his own time. He was destructive, immediately irresponsible. His ideas were part of the wave of irrationalism promoted by Bergson. But he is a writer, like de Maistre, who raises profound problems. He was in tune with two most formidable facts of his age. The growing political and economic power of the masses, and the new psychological interpretation of politics. He combines Marx's belief in the class war with a Nietzschean understanding of myth, and a new understanding of the subconscious mind. Above all, he brings a profound pessimism to bear on politics. His view of life was sombre, and his morality puritan. In history he saw no plan and little progress: in politics only improvisation: in ideas only myth. This dark revolutionary sceptic was to provide Fascism with a much needed political philosophy. He was to make a major contribution to the disasters of the twentieth century.

NOTES

[1] *Reflections on Violence,* translated by T. E. Hulme. Allen & Unwin, 1915 (Letter to Halèvy), p. 3.

[2] *La Ruine,* p. 311.

[3] p. 320.

[4] p. 105.

[5] p. 67.

[6] *Illusions,* p. 45.

[7] p. 50.

[8] p. 59.

[9] p. 107.

[10] ibidem.

[11] p. 332.

[12] *La Ruine,* p. 319.

[13] p. 235.

[14] *Reflections* (Letter), p. 12.

[15] p. 17 (Fragment 294, Braunschweig Edition quoted).

[16] p. 19.

[17] p. 26.

[18] p. 32.

[19] p. 38.

[20] p. 39.

[21] p. 35.

[22] *Reflections,* p. 71.

[23] p. 132.

[24] p. 213.

[25] *La Ruine,* p. 315.

[26] p. 269.

[27] p. 272.

[28] pp. 284-5.

[29] *Matériaux,* p. 91.

S. P. Rouanet (essay date 1964)

SOURCE: "Irrationalism and Myth in Georges Sorel," in *The Review of Politics,* Vol. XXVI, 1964, pp. 45-69.

[*In the following excerpt, Rouanet examines the European political and cultural landscape in which Sorel wrote and thought.*]

I

The First World War is sometimes credited with the dissolution of the well-ordered universe of the nineteenth century. In fact, by 1914 there was very little left to destroy, for most of the essential work had already been accomplished. The aftermath of the war merely helped to make the collapse of order and stability more visible. But the post-1918 atmosphere of gloom, later crystallized in the "Lost Generation" and in the escapist movements of the twenties, gave the impression that the war had been responsible for the moral and intellectual *Zusammenbruch* of the period. The feeling of decay was everywhere; the old values, the former certainties and criteria had vanished, leaving an impression of emptiness behind. The old order had crumbled, without dignity, "not with a bang but with a whimper," as T. S. Eliot put it. And the war-to-end wars, as it was believed, was responsible for this complete "transvaluation of values," to use Nietzsche's terminology. Actually, of course, this is very remote from the truth. The years of crisis that changed the intellectual physiognomy of Europe had their pivot around 1900. In ten or fifteen years the work of destruction was completed, and nothing remained of the proud structure of European certainties. The demolition was systematic, and covered almost every field of culture.

In the sphere of science, the proudest achievement and most cherished possession of nineteenth-century civilization, a nondeterministic physics gradually began to take shape. As early as 1874, Emile Boutroux, in a famous book, *De la Contingence des Lois Physiques,* placed reason in a wider context that he designated as "une raison plus générale," although he did so without formally departing from rationalist premises. This meant the implicit recognition that everyday reason was incapable of coping with certain phenomena of the physical world. Poincaré, in his essays on the philosophy of science, confirmed this thesis, and conclusively demonstrated that many fields of nature are irreducible to pure intelligence. By 1900 Max Planck had challenged one of the most fundamental assumptions of nineteenth-century science, the principle of continuity, and had revolutionized physics with the quantum theory. Only five years later, Albert Einstein laid the essential groundwork of the relativity theory, and exposed as false the absolute space and absolute time of classical physics.

In the sphere of philosophy, positivism and evolutionism began to lose their dominant position. Bergson's *Essai sur les Données Immédiates de la Conscience* (1889) argued reason's incapacity for apprehending life and charged that intelligence succeeds at most in dissecting and analyzing reality. Reason operates through concepts, which can function only in the world of space. It is completely unable to apprehend subjective experiences and to capture duration which, in contrast to objectified time, cannot be measured and can only be grasped through intuition. This critique of rationalism was followed by a critique of mechanist philosophy, *Matière et Mémoire* (1896). In this work Bergson showed that living reality transcends the purely physico-chemical mechanisms and that the brain is not the source of thought but merely its instrument. Finally, Bergson in *L'Evolution Créatrice* (1907) contended that all matter is permeated by a current of energy, the source of all life, which increases in power and intensity as it multiplies its ramifications. The impact of Bergson's theories on the new world views that were gradually taking shape can scarcely be overemphasized. If reason was unable to exhaust all reality, there was a secret world to be discovered, inaccessible to reason but accessible to intuition. The world that the nineteenth century considered definitely explored and susceptible of exact measurement proved to be filled with unrevealed possibilities. Life was much more creative than reason, and it was argued that men should yield to vital impulses rather than submit their emotions to the control of a desiccated intelligence.

A "Copernican revolution" in the sphere of psychology took place with the the publication, in 1900, of Freud's *Science of Dreams*. With the discovery of the unconscious, the existence of a subterranean world of instincts and obscure drives was brought to light. The traditional assumption of Christian ethics that man could guide his behavior by the light of reason, and could control his passions by a conscious act of will was challenged by the discovery that sexual instincts are more powerful than reason and that repression is a source of neurosis. With the advent of psycho-analysis, it was shown that most of the time man lived under the effect of demonic forces, and that his conscious life was only a small part of his total psychical life.

As a consequence of the emphasis on life and vital values, the morals of quiet rationality that had been an integral part of bourgeois civilization since its origins was blown to pieces and replaced by a morals of energy. In order to be fully alive, man had to scorn the anti-vital values of peaceful mediocrity and to "live dangerously," giving full vent to his urges and instincts. An assertive voluntarism emerged, superseding the traditional ethics of reasonableness. The aristocratic morals of "the blond beast" and of heroic life had a tremendous diffusion, and were manifested by such writers as D'Annunzio and Barrès. Bergson himself was not exempt from the cult of the exceptional personality. His mystics and saints uncomfortably resemble Nietzsche's Superman: "The great mystic is to be conceived as an individual being, capable of transcending the limitations imposed on the species by its material nature, thus continuing and extending the divine action."[1]

In short, the general atmosphere is the exact reverse of the rationalistic climate that had prevailed in Europe in the middle of the nineteenth century. Everywhere science is downgraded, and intuition and instinct are idolized. In every sphere of culture and society there is a movement towards spontaneous life, away from the closed world of concepts and categories. Andre Gide noted that he had come to mistrust the science which at first had been his pride. Such studies, he continued, which originally were his very life, appeared to have no other bearing on himself than an accidental and conventional one.[2] It was nothing less than the crumbling of intellect, and the rejection of the principles that had governed civilization since Antiquity. As Yeats put it, with apocalyptic overtones,

> Things fall apart, the center cannot hold,
> Mere anarchy is loosed upon the world.

The breakdown of the "center" is undoubtedly the most revolutionary development of modern times. For the first time mankind abdicated from reason and, as the complete triumph of the Dionysian principle, put complete reliance on the instincts. It seemed that Zarathustra was entirely justified in proclaiming to the world not only the death of God but the death of Reason.

II

In the midst of all this irrationalist turmoil, politics and political ideas at first remained uncontaminated. Liberalism still survived with the same assumptions and underlying principles. At a time when belief in immutable laws was fast disappearing, liberalism still believed in the natural laws of competition and in the automatic adjustment of interests; at a time when the future was an individual creation and as unpredictable as human spontaneity, liberalism still involved the belief that human history was governed by the principle of indefinite material and moral progress, pushing mankind towards a future of abundance and harmony; finally, at a time when the emphasis was on quick action and apocalyptic renovation, liberalism still relied on parliamentary techniques and on an evolutionary approach. Socialism was possibly even more vitiated by the rationalist assumptions of the preceding century. In the first place, socialism was characterized by an implicit faith in science, derived from the intellectualist environment in which it evolved. The very pretense of being scientific placed Marxism somewhat out of tune with the new mentality. Its rigid historical determinism left very little room for human initiative and creativity. Instead of relying on human action, Marxism tended to give priority to impersonal economic forces. The creative role of the leader and of an active minority are excessively underplayed in Marxist thinking. If socialism seemed out of date in its doctrine, it was even more incongruous in its practice. For the parliamentary socialists, like Jaurès, socialism had become a mere instrument for winning elections, and, at least in the opinion of Jaurès' adversaries, a trick for gaining the support of both the bourgeoisie and the proletariat. In practice, even more than in theory, socialism had become stereotyped, lifeless, and strangely out of fashion in the new irrationalist atmosphere. Thus, an effort to rejuvenate socialism seemed imperative, in order to adjust its premises and methods to the new intellectual conditions. Georges Sorel was one of the first to undertake this effort of adaptation, and his most representative book, ***Réflexions sur la Violence*** exerted an influence probably out of all proportion to its merits. With this work, political theory was brought in line with other cultural fields and became saturated with the prevailing irrationalist atmosphere.

It might be argued that an irrationalist theory of politics had already been evolved in conservative thought. In fact, since the end of the eighteenth century, a very important movement of opinion took shape in order to combat the rationalist ideas of the Enlightenment. Conservatism, generally professing distrust of abstract schemes and untried proposals, believes in "the slow work of generations," in the "silently working forces" (Savigny), in the divine tactic of history (Burke). For the conservatives, it is impossible to create new institutions *ex nihilo,* by a decree of pure reason. "The science of constructing a commonwealth or renovating it or reforming it is, like every other experimental science, not to be taught a priori."[3] The attention of the conservative mind is always focused on the irrational realm of politics, on the mysterious area irreducible to rational formulation, on the historically crystallized institutions that defy human manipulation. This conservative irrationalism, however, is very different from the revolutionary irrationalism of the twentieth century. In the perspective of conservatism, everything that exists, by the simple fact of existing, is endowed with a religious and almost intangible character. The dualism of *Sein* and *Sollen* is practically abolished, since the mere circumstance of having endured entitles an institution to automatic reverence: "It is a presumption in favor of any settled scheme against any untried project that a nation has long existed and flourished under it."[4]

In contrast, the new irrationality of the early nineteen-hundreds is radically revolutionary and tends to engage in revolutionary action for its own sake, losing sight, momentarily at least, of the goals to be achieved. The new irrationalism does not come in the name of tradition, but in the name of renovation, and opposes reason not because it is destructive but because it has become a conservative force on the side of the *status quo.* In the nineteenth century, rationalism had an unlimited revolutionary vigor, being identified with an ascending social stratum. By applying to existing reality the standards of pure reason, the bourgeoisie was led unavoidably to attempt to remold society in accordance with an abstract model. With the triumph and consolidation of the bourgeoisie, rationalism lost its revolutionary implications and became a defensive instead of an offensive ideological weapon. Similarly, irrationalism in the eighteenth century was a counter-ideology, evolved in response to the onslaughts of bourgeois liberalism. In the twentieth century it became an attacking force. Both forms of irrationalism, however, have one point in common: the enemy is the same. For conservatives and syndicalists alike, the bourgeoisie represents the adversary to be crushed: for the former because it is too aggressive, and for the latter because it is not aggressive enough.

This is the main point to be kept in mind: the basic reason why Sorel scorned the middle class was because it was complacent, unheroic, and steeped in the values of decadence. The bourgeoisie had become the symbol of everything that the new irrationalist atmosphere held most despicable, and to that extent Sorel attacked it. He, however, always had a deep admiration for the bourgeoisie in its heroic times, when it was not demoralized by compromise and humanitarianism. As will be seen later, he spoke respectfully of the American robber-barons and the ruthless capitalists engaged in a war-to-death to arrive at the top. He compared this unspoilt bourgeoisie with warriors and pirates, and paid enthusiastic tribute to its warlike virtues of aggressiveness, self-denial, and endurance.

Thus, Sorel's ideological position and his membership in the syndicalist movement were basically motivated by his revulsion from the class that embodied the corrupt values of intellectualism and by his affinity with a class that was supposed to represent the values of revolution. It was a temperamental and psychological rather than a consciously ideological commitment. This can be demonstrated by the liberties he took with Marxist thinking, even in his syndicalist phase. It can be demonstrated even more conclusively by his subsequent apostasy. In fact, Sorel had no qualms in switching to the right, after announcing his disillusionment with syndicalism in 1910. He joined groups of the extreme right, composed of former syndicalists like himself, monarchists, nationalists, militarists, and antidemocrats of all persuasions. Shortly after eschewing syndicalism, he became a coeditor of the authoritarian magazine *L'Indépendence,* which included Paul Bourget and Maurice Barrès, two notorious extremists, in its editorial board. Later he reverted to the left, after the Bolshevist *coup d'état* of 1917, which he considered as the forerunner of the great apocalyptic revolution that would regenerate mankind.[5]

Throughout all these episodes, Sorel never had the feeling of changing sides. He felt absolutely consistent all the time, since for him the enemy was always the same: abstract rationalism and abstract morality, both of which were responsible for compromise, for reformism, and for the rejection of heroic virtues. At one moment he believed that his natural allies against this adversary were the syndicalists, at another time he thought he should be associated with monarchical and ultra-rightist groups, and at still another time he found the anti-intellectualist feeling embodied in Bolshevism. He never wavered, however, in his basic personal loyalties, which did not always coincide with official ideologies but did coincide with the general climate of his age.

Réflexions sur la Violence is unmistakably permeated with the anti-intellectualist atmosphere of the beginning of the century and with the basic themes of this irrationalist climate. These themes were, as was remarked, the theme of the revolt against reason, the theme of action at any cost, and the theme of heroism. The three are very much present in Sorel's work, especially in ***Réflexions sur la Violence,*** although irrationalist elements are not conspicuous in some of his previous works, for example, ***Le Procès de Socrate*** (1889) and ***L'Introduction à l'Economie Moderne*** (1903). In examining Sorel's irrationalist outlook the three themes will provide a general framework.

Sorel's revolt against reason is manifested, first of all, in his open contempt for intellectuals. He identified professors and intellectuals with the worst vices of pusillanimity, watered-down humanitarianism, and moral cowardice. This is one of the basic reasons for his quarrel with the parliamentary socialists, who, according to him, were hoping to "dilute revolutionary syndicalism in the spittle of the professors."[6] In a later passage, Sorel indignantly observed that the policies of parliamentary socialism would take the country to the brink of disaster, in the event of a political victory: "but what does the future of the country matter, provided that the regime gives a good time to a few professors, who imagine that they have invented socialism, and to a few Dreyfusard financiers?"[7]

For Sorel the original vice of the intellectuals is the attempt to civilize socialism, depriving it of its vitality and of its aggressiveness. "The *civilized* socialism of our professors has many times been presented as a safeguard of civilization: I believe that it would produce the same effect as was produced by the classical education given by the Church to the barbarian kings. The proletariat would be corrupted. . . . "[8] He is convinced that as soon as socialism is freed from the emasculating influence of the intellectuals, class struggle will regain its savagery, thus precipitating the catastrophic revolution: "The more Syndicalism develops, by abandoning the old superstitions which come to it from the Old Regime and the Church—through the men of letters, professors of philosophy, and historians of the Revolution—the more will social conflicts assume the character of a simple struggle, similar to those of armies on campaign."[9] With the advent of the socialist millenium, no place will be offered to the intellectuals, and society will be forever liberated from this parasitical group: "the revolution appears as a revolt, pure and simple, and no place is reserved for sociologists, for fashionable people who are in favour of social reforms, and for the Intellectuals who have embraced *the profession of thinking for the proletariat.*"[10]

Later he came back to the same idea, in a much more forceful way. After the victory of instinct and life over abstract reason, represented by the triumph of the revolutionary proletariat over the bourgeoisie, "our Intellectuals, who hope to obtain the highest places from democracy, would be sent back to their literature; the Parliamentary Socialists, who find in the organizations created by the middle classes means of exercising a certain amount of power, would become useless."[11] He often labelled the intellectuals as "idéologues," employing the word exactly in the same sense in which Napoleon used it, designating an individual given to abstractions and always formulating impractical schemes to save mankind. Only two or three times did he use the word ideology in the Marxist sense of a set of ideas corresponding to a given network of economic relationships. Thus, he said that capitalism itself will destroy the traditional order, "against which the critics of the idealists (idéologues) had proved themselves to be so deplorably incompetent."[12] Then, making the point that revolution should occur in a period of prosperity and not of economic decay he sadly noted that "the ideologists hardly trouble themselves at all with this question."[13] The triumph of the French Revolution was quite unexpected; "this was because reasons drawn from theory could not explain this paradoxical success."[14] The most bitter criticism he managed to level at Kautsky was that he was "more an ideologue than a disciple of Marx."[15]

For Sorel ideology was an abstract system of ideas, without any correspondence with social reality and quite incapable of apprehending the facts of social and political life. In this sense, it is similar to the word utopia, used in the special Sorelian sense. As to the "idéologues," they are the bourgeois intellectuals, more concerned with the construction of rational systems than with living human beings and with the realities of a revolutionary movement. Sorel regarded them as the embodiment of compromise and attributed to them an almost exclusive responsibility for the shift of socialism from revolutionary to parliamentary techniques, and for the adulteration of the original apocalyptic vision, banalized into a tawdry sentimentalism. Thanks to the intellectuals, what should have been the regeneration of mankind had become a vehicle for the electoral ambitions of a few politicians. Still worse, they had transformed socialism from a spontaneous mass movement into a conceptual scheme, thereby depriving it of its revolutionary possibilities.

It might be argued, of course, that this anti-intellectualist feeling of Sorel is common in the socialist movement. In fact, bourgeois intellectuals in the socialist parties have inevitably been regarded with suspicion by party members of a pure proletarian origin and of no intellectual ambitions.

> In Germany, as in Italy, France and some of the Balkan states, the gravest accusations have been launched against the intellectuals. There have been times in the history of German socialism in which the educated members of the party have been exposed to universal contempt. It suffices to recall the Dresden congress, during which the whole

> complicated question of tactics seemed to be reduced to the problem of the intellectuals. Even today they are often treated as suspects.[16]

Some, as Sorel did, regarded the intellectuals as reformists, while others, on the contrary, charged them with being excessively revolutionary, an accusation that Sorel in disgust would have brushed aside.

At any rate, whether they were too violent or not violent enough, the fact is that anti-intellectualism seemed to be a common feature of all socialistic movements. Paul Lafargue, for instance, in *Socialism and the Intellectuals* (1900), was particularly virulent. "We should have to put off the triumph of socialism not to the year 2000 but to the end of the world if we had to wait upon the delicate, shrinking and impressionable hesitancy of the intellectuals," he wrote. And then:

> It is not in the circle of intellectuals, degraded by centuries of capitalist oppression, that we must seek examples of civic courage and moral dignity. . . . The intellectuals who on all occasions display their transcendental ethics, have still a long road to travel before they reach the moral plane of the working class and of the socialist party.[17]

There is, however, an important difference between Sorel's attacks on the intellectuals and those made by other socialists. The latter, in spite of everything, were as firmly convinced of the validity and omnipotence of science as Flaubert's Monsieur Homais. They debunked the intellectuals but not the intellect, and still thought that socialism was invulnerable precisely because of its scientific foundations. With Sorel, the attacks against the intellectuals are part of a much larger picture. What he criticized is science itself, and as a result he challenged not only the right of the intellectuals to interfere in the working-class movement but the very legitimacy of the scientific principles that they represent. His irritation at the declamations of the "professors" and at the schemes of the "sociologists" arose more from a basic disbelief in their science and in their sociology than from a suspicion of the soundness of their proletarian convictions, as was often the case with other socialists. His intent was "to escape the influence of that intellectualist philosophy, which seems to me a great hindrance to the historian who allows himself to be dominated by it."[18]

As a consequence of this anti-intellectualistic profession of faith, he avoided clear-cut definitions and affirmed that socialism, like everything of value, is necessarily obscure, "since it deals with production, i.e., with the most mysterious part of human activity, and since it proposes to bring about a radical transformation of that region which it is impossible to describe with the clearness that is to be found in more superficial regions."[19]

Like all irrationalists, Sorel felt the attraction of the abyss and was concerned mainly with the dark sides of social and psychological phenomena. He had only contempt for what he called "la petite science," which is characterized by the complete reliance on reason and by the half assumption that every form of reality is reducible to a rational explanation. This incredible provincialism, according to him, was based on the belief that the methods of physical science could be applied to the study of society, and that because it had been possible to calculate the tables of the moon, it was possible to forecast with accuracy the behavior of human beings.

According to Sorel, the "little science" had failed successively in all spheres of culture. In philosophy the once dominant positivism had been replaced by Bergsonism, demonstrating the illusion of so-called scientific solutions and delighting in exploring the obscure areas that the "little science" abhorred. Religion, too, was regaining lost ground, despite the prophets of doom who prognosticated its quick disappearance. In fact, as Sorel pointedly noted, Catholicism in his day was very fashionable in cultivated circles. In art more and more attention was being paid to nonfigurative painting, and clarity of design was being replaced by intensity and depth of expression as an artistic ideal. Every sphere of human activity and every compartment of thought had its unclear areas, which were generally the most important.

Thus, in ethics the easiest part to render in reasoned exposition refers to equitable relationships among men, while the part having to do with sexual relationships, the basic part of morality, had been systematically ignored, because it is not easily translatable into conceptual language. Without it, the alleged clarity and self-evidence of moral principles are only an illusion. In the field of legislation, much attention had been paid to the law regulating contracts and debts, for this law can be reduced to half a dozen principles of general application. The obscure part of law, the family, had been virtually ignored, precisely because of its lack of clarity. The same was true in economics: questions relating to exchange could easily be expounded in impeccably clear language, by means of a few elegant logical principles; but production was generally ignored by "la petite science," because of the inextricable complexity of its principles. In short, a science concerned with visible manifestations rather than inner realities, and with its scope limited to abstract relationships susceptible of logical formulation, is shallow, superficial, and inadequate.

This, of course, is the very denial of Cartesianism and of the traditional concern with "clear and distinct ideas" that had haunted European science for the last three centuries, in spite of some occasional empiricist intrusions. Straightaway Sorel applied this anti-Cartesian approach to social affairs.

> The Utopists excelled in the art of exposition in accordance with these prejudices; the more their exposition satisfied the requirements of a school book, the more convincing they thought their inventions were. I believe that the contrary of this belief is the truth, and that we should distrust proposals for social reform all the more, when every difficulty seems solved in an apparently satisfactory manner.[20]

The second theme of irrationalism appearing prominently in Sorel's work is activism. Programs are considered less important than action. Elaborate blueprints mapping the future should be left for the utopians: the revolutionary syndicalist, in Sorel's opinion, should act first and theorize later. *"On s'engage, puis on voit,"* might be the phrase summarizing Sorel's position. For Sorel, there is an intrinsic opposition between action and thought, since the latter exerts a crippling influence on the former. In order to act, a man "must have in himself some source of conviction which must dominate his whole consciousness, and act before the calculations of reflection have time to enter his mind."[21] This was a major ground for his opposition to the intellectuals, who were responsible for the decrease in action characteristic of recent socialist trends:

> The professors of the *little science* are really difficult to satisfy. They assert very loudly that they will only admit into thought abstractions analogous to those used in the deductive sciences: as a matter of fact, this is a rule which is insufficient for purposes of action, for we do nothing great without the help of warmly-coloured and clearly defended images, which absorb the whole of our attention. . . . [22]

Images instead of ideas: this is the principle of action. This opposition of theory to practice is entirely alien to Marxist thinking, to which Sorel paid lip service. For Marx, theory and action are inextricably interwoven, and it is as impossible to act without theory as to think *in abstracto,* independently of action. There is a dialectical relationship between theory and practice, whereby theory, arising out of a definite pattern of social relationships, clarifies the situation and the situation itself is changed in the process of becoming. The changed situation, in turn, gives rise to another theory.

> When the proletariat by means of the class struggle changes its position in society and thereby the whole social structure, in taking cognizance of the changed social situation, i.e., of itself, it finds itself face to face not merely with a new object of understanding, but also changes its position as a knowing subject. The theory serves to bring the proletariat to a consciousness of its social position, i.e., it enables it to envisage itself—simultaneously both as an object and a subject in the social progress.[23]

For Sorel, however, theory is only a hindrance to action and is incompatible with a political belief in spontaneity and in the collective emotions of the masses, directed by a responsible minority.

The third and last component of Sorel's irrationalist outlook is the theme of heroism. Sorel was obsessed with the motif of "sublimity" and of Homeric virtues, and this obsession provides a key to most of his social philosophy. His antagonism to the bourgeoisie is largely associated with the scorn he felt for the transformation of the middle class from a highly active group into a static social class, entrenched behind a lifeless humanitarianism. In its heyday, the bourgeoisie was full of warlike virtues, and was concerned with nothing but power. By yielding to the schemes of the "idéologues," however, this class of supermen became emasculated, lost its aggressiveness and instead of opposing its natural enemy, the proletariat, on the battlefield, tried to secure proletarian leniency by purchase and to placate the workers with higher wages and high-sounding humanitarian phrases: "the race of bold captains who made the greatness of modern industry disappear to make way for an ultracivilized aristocracy which asks to be allowed to live in peace."[24]

The old race, however, was not entirely extinguished, for its descendants survived in the United States. In a very revealing chapter in which Sorel summarized Nietzsche's contrast between the morality of masters and the morality of slaves, he compared the ethics of the old European bourgeoisie with the aristocratic ethics described by Nietzsche. After exploring the disappearance of the European bourgeoisie's will-to-power, Sorel affirmed that the ancient Homeric virtues were preserved by American businessmen. There are striking analogies, he said, "between the Yankee, ready for any kind of enterprise, and the ancient Greek sailor, sometimes a pirate, sometimes a colonist or merchant. . . . "[25] Despite these sporadic survivals, however, the warlike spirit had nearly disappeared and had been replaced by a diluted and complacent conformity.

This was the necessary outcome of all attempts to mitigate primitive vitality, as he believed that history demonstrated. Thus, when the Merovingian barbarians became civilized by ecclesiastical influence, they automatically lost their willingness to fight and the Merovingian dynasty entered a phase of rapid decadence. Another illustration is provided by the transformation of the Church from a militantly antiliberal organization into an allegedly "progressive" institution. When science was condemned as heretical, and heliocentrism and evolution were attacked as demoniacal theories, the Church kept its vitality. The issues were clear, the two fields were sharply marked, and the task to be accomplished was the destruction of the spirit of Evil. While it maintained this single-mindedness and this heroic simplicity, remaining free from crippling intellectualisms, the Church commanded the loyalty and blind obedience of the faithful. When the Church decided to yield to the liberal spirit and to tolerate evolutionism and democracy, its vitality was lost. The issues lost their clearness, the border line between the two opposing fields was blurred, and a general climate of compromise replaced the old aggressiveness. The former values of warfare and of martyrdom were replaced by a prosaic belief in peaceful coexistence.

The attenuation of conflict had particularly disastrous effects in social affairs. The bourgeoisie, in the name of social peace, abdicated from its militant position *vis-à-vis* the proletariat, and made concession after concession, encouraged by the good offices of the so-called socialist intellectuals and by the parliamentary socialists. In turn, the proletariat forgot its apocalyptic outlook and betrayed its revolutionary mission in the petty squabbles of trade unions and in the prosaic, bread-and-butter efforts to obtain higher pay and better working conditions. A practice more consistent with the ideals of the proletarian movement is difficult to imagine. "It has never been thought that discussions about prices could possibly exercise any ethical influence on men. . . . "[26] Instead of revolution, humanitarianism and the ideal of social peace succeeded to the idea of the class struggle.

Proletarian violence, then, should be used as a technique of socialist action. Let the parliamentary socialists discuss schemes to improve mankind; the revolutionary syndicalists will ignore intellectualist arguments and resort to direct action. Violence will have a surprisingly salutary effect. It will awaken the proletariat to the consciousness of its historical mission and it will shake the bourgeoisie from its humanitarian torpor, forcing it to revert to its former attitude of militancy and to the open defense of its own interests. Social tensions will be sharpened, the fields will again be more clearly defined, and class struggle will become aggressive. These developments will thus create conditions favorable to the triumph of revolution. With proletarian violence, the values of heroism will finally prevail, for violence is equivalent to open warfare. War excludes pettiness, revenge, and deliberate cruelty, and is based on spontaneous action, on a single-minded devotion to unselfish goals, and on generosity. Thus, proletarian *violence* is in marked contrast with bourgeois *force,* which is practiced with repressive purposes when the bourgeoisie takes power. This repressive action, aimed at perpetuating the rule of the bourgeoisie and the preservation of bourgeois authority, is defensive, not aggressive, and arises from legal codes and abstract principles rather than from the spontaneous unleashing of human emotions.

Being defensive and legalistic, bourgeois force is generally brutal; being aggressive and practiced in the spirit of loyal warfare, proletarian violence is devoid of pettiness. "Everything in war is carried on without hatred and without the spirit of revenge . . . force is then displayed according to its own nature, without ever professing to borrow anything from the judicial proceedings. . . . "[27] The same idea is more fully developed in a later passage:

> The Syndicalist general strike presents a very great number of analogies with the first conception of war [that waged for the sake of glory] . . . the proletariat . . . is very clearly conscious of the glory which will be attached to its historical role and of the heroism of its militant attitude; it longs for the final contest in which it will give proof of the whole measure of its valor.[28]

In addition, proletarian violence, practiced through the vehicle of the general strike, gives to each worker the feeling of participating in a great collective action, without sacrificing his individuality and his spontaneous drives by subordinating himself to a purely abstract and intellectualist strategic plan. Every man acts on his own, with the certainty that he is cooperating in a common objective. He acts as the French soldier acted during the Revolutionary wars: for the first time in history the soldiers behaved as free agents and not as robots. In that way, they were wholeheartedly devoted to the cause of freedom without in any way sacrificing their own individuality. Through violence, it will thus be possible to restore the ethics of heroism, and the morality of the "élan vital."

III

The diffuse atmosphere of irrationalism that permeates Sorel's work finds its complete crystallization in the concept of myth. This is extremely appropriate, for since pre-Socratic times myth has been associated with irrationality and mystery. In the Homeric period, *mythos* or *word,* was used in opposition to *ergon* or action. Subsequently, *mythos* began to be used in opposition to *logos* or discursive thinking. Myth meant word in the sense of a religious narrative, a cosmogonic revelation on the origin of man and the world, while *logos* meant word in the sense of human narrative, to describe actual historical events, or events supposed to be historic, and to express abstract relations between ideas. From the very beginning, myth was associated with religion, with mysticism, with mysterious events transcending human understanding. Precisely because of this irrational character, myth has always intrigued mankind. Many attempts have been made to come to grips with this obscure product of the human mind. For our purposes, we shall try to classify these attempts, distinguishing three basic approaches: the methodological, the etiological and the functional. The classification, while admittedly arbitrary, may yield some fruitful results for the study of the Sorelian conception of myth.

According to the first approach, myth is regarded as a technique for investigating certain areas of reality or for explaining phenomena that cannot be satisfactorily clarified by discursive language. In this sense, myth is only a scientific instrument, a didactic method, and is never confused with reality. The typical example is the Platonic myth. In order to facilitate exposition and teaching, Plato sometimes used a deliberately figurative and poetical language, as an allegorical device, to transmit ideas that only with much difficulty could have been transmitted by normal logical procedures. It is a poetical narrative, expressing relationships of images, in order to symbolize relationships of ideas. In this sense, myth resembles some contemporary scientific hypotheses, which have no intrinsic validity, but are useful from a methodological point of view. Such is the case of Poincaré's image of a hypothetical planet covered with perpetual clouds, or the image of the universe free from the law of inertia, or with an orbit devoid of eccentricity and of inclinations, or the image of infinitely flat animals. Such myths are rational constructions, established to explore certain phenomena of nature, and to facilitate the understanding of some theories.[29] Toynbee's use of myth in *A Study of History* may be included in the same category:

> It is necessary for us to be on our guard against the . . . error of applying to historical thought . . . a scientific method devised for the study of inanimate nature. . . . Let us follow Plato's lead and try the alternative course. Let us shut our eyes, for the moment, to the formulas of science, in order to open our eyes to the language of mythology.[30]

Finally, the "methodological approach" has also been used by many contemporary writers and poets, as a technique for expressing some philosophical situations and for illustrating systems and ideas that seemed incompatible with analytical language. Thus, Camus used the myth of Sisyphus to symbolize the ethics of absurdity. Sartre used the myth of Orestes in "Les Mouches" and Cocteau used the myth of Orpheus. In all these instances, myth is not sought for itself, but as an instrument of expression regarded as more direct than normal language.

The second approach to the problem of myth is a causal and analytical approach, rather than a merely instrumental one. There is a deliberate attempt to dissect myth, to investigate its nature, to discover its underlying laws, to find out the origin and functioning of the myth-making process. In varying degrees, all the theories belonging to the etiological approach are essentially rationalistic, that is, myth is considered as a product of the mind similar to its other products, and as such is regarded as an appropriate subject matter for scientific investigation. The etiological theories are extremely varied and need not concern us here in a detailed form.[31] It will be enough to list very briefly the main theories. Thus, there is the euhemerist school, which maintains that all mythical figures are idealizations of historical human beings and not imaginary characters; there is the allegorical theory, which maintains that mythological beings are symbolic representations of natural processes, like the winds, or of abstract vices and virtues, like avarice or prudence; there is the naturalistic school, asserting that myths are symbolic expressions of celestial bodies (solar or lunar mythology) or of the vegetative processes of the earth (Frazer's ritualist theory); there is the philological school, for which myths result from a misinterpretation of forgotten metaphors; there is the psychoanalytic school, for which myths, like dreams, spring from repressed emotional impulses, and are the crystallization of unfulfilled wishes, and so on. The list could be prolonged indefinitely, but the mere enumeration of theories would serve no useful purpose. The important thing is that all these schools, however divergent they may be, are joined together by a common characteristic: they try to assign specific causes to the mythical phenomenon, and to explain it exhaustively in the best rationalist tradition. In all of them, there is an emphasis on efficient causes and a total disregard of teleological considerations.

The third approach, on the contrary, is concerned exclusively with final causes. No attention is paid to the forces responsible for the myth-making process. All interest is shifted to the role of myth in the community after it is fully formed, whatever its original cause might have been. The functional approach is used mainly by contemporary anthropological schools. From this point of view, myth is regarded as an agent of tribal cohesion, as an underlying atmosphere of habits and beliefs that give meaning to life, justify human acts, and provide guidance in complex situations.

> Myth fulfills in primitive culture an indispensable function: it expresses, enhances, and codifies belief; it safeguards and enforces morality; it vouches for the efficiency of ritual and contains practical rules for the guidance of man. Myth is thus a vital ingredient of human civilization; it is not an idle tale, but a hard-worked active force; it is not an intellectual explanation of an artistic imagery, but a pragmatic charter of primitive faith and moral wisdom.[32]

In effect, all three approaches may be found in Sorel, in a rather diffuse form. Sorel dealt with the problem of myth in three different places: in ***Le Procès de Socrate,*** in ***Introduction à l'Economie Moderne,*** and in ***Réflexions sur la Violence.*** In the first, Sorel described the Platonic use of myth as a didactic technique. In the second, he suggested that a method somewhat akin to that of Plato might be more appropriate than conceptual techniques for the study of certain phenomena. In addition, he discussed what he called "fiction" and warned sociologists against the dangers these fictions present to exact knowledge. Finally, in ***Réflexions sur la Violence*** Sorel discussed the theory of the social myth. After a careful analysis of these several discussions of myth, it is possible to systematize Sorel's thoughts on the matter, by using the intellectualist techniques that he despised so much. Thus, we can isolate at least three different senses in which he used the word myth, and which fit fairly well within the general framework of methodological, etiological, and functional approaches.

The first meaning originates from Bergson's critique of conceptual tools when applied to a reality in process of becoming. Such tools are adequate to the study of static reality, that may be measured and described in terms in space, but are quite inappropriate to the study of social life, which is essentially changeable and is in a state of perpetual flow. In order to deal with this dynamic universe Sorel suggested the use of myths, or, as he put it, "stylized images arranged with sufficient art so that they give the impression of being auxiliary realities, each possessing its own principle of life, order, and development."[33] Those stylized images are merely techniques for apprehending social phenomena, and need have no authentic existence of their own. Like Plato's myths or the modern scientific myths mentioned in the beginning of this section, those images are rigorously scientific devices, without any affinity to mysticism or metaphysics: "These systems of images allow no escape for any characteristic which in being known proves useful to the research pursued."[34]

The etiological or causal meaning of myth is found in the theory of "ideological dissociations," by which Sorel meant the autonomy achieved by certain spheres of the superstructure with regard to the infra-structure. Orthodox Marxism, of course, admits, in certain circumstances, the autonomy of the ideological sphere. But the strongly critical and evaluative undertones of his theory marks Sorel's departure from the Marxist tradition. For him, such dissociations or "fictions" are a source of sophisms, of wishful thinking, and of obstacles to critical thinking.

The ideal situation, for him, is the exact correspondence of the ideological superstructure with the underlying economic basis. Whenever a dissociation occurs, some undesirable effects may result. Thus, in the case of complete parallelism of super- and infrastructure, no worker would ask for a reward according to his skills, since this is an extra-economic criterion, but according to his needs, which is a strictly economic and biological concept. Besides stimulating selfshness, such "fictions" or myths interfere with scientific thinking, and encourage lies and illusions. While he recognized that such myths are necessary "As long as men have no other means of reasoning about the scientific relationships of the economy,"[35] they should be replaced by analytical techniques as soon as feasible. This conception of myth may be called etiological because a definite origin is attributed to the fictions, namely the productive infra-structure of society. Besides, the critical attitude towards these fictions closely corresponds to the rationalist views of myth held by some nineteenth-century anthropologists, who thought, for instance, that the myth maker was a primitive philosopher and that myths represented abortive attempts at philosophical speculation. As such, they constituted very inadequate substitutes for experimental science.

The preceding conceptions of myth are very untypical of Sorel's mature thinking, as may readily be perceived. The irrationalist outlook that permeated his later work is inconsistent with such intellectualist views of myth. It is in ***Réflexions sur la Violence,*** therefore, that his final formulation of the problem of myth must be sought. And, not surprisingly, this formulation coincides with the functional approach of modern anthropology. This approach, as was seen, ignores the problem of causes and places myth in a suprarational perspective. Instead of being an attempt to interpret the universe, as the rationalists conceived it, myth is an allpervading atmosphere, irreducible to reason, responsible for the vitality of the group, and motivating all human behavior. For Sorel, myth is a social force, a system of images, whose function is to galvanize the masses, to justify all sacrifices, to prevent compromises, and to facilitate action by simplifying the problems at stake. Like Malinowski, Sorel was not interested in the content of myth, but in its social function. He emphatically stated that myths cannot be defined and cannot be decomposed into their constituent elements:

> I now wish to show that we should not attempt to analyse such groups of images in the way that we analyse a thing into its elements, but that they must be taken as a whole, as historical forces, and that we should be especially careful not to make any comparison between accomplished fact and the picture people had formed for themselves before action.[36]

At the origin of this conception of myth we find Bergson's theory of the free act. In Bergson's view there are two different selves, one of which is the external projection of the other, its spatial representation, as it were. The inner self is reached by introspection, through a conscious psychological effort. It is when we grasp possession of our inner self, according to Bergson, that we are really free. In commenting on Bergson, Sorel added that at such moments, when the mind is entirely free from outward pressures, we create imaginary worlds, placed ahead of the present and composed of movements that depend only on our inner self. To be free is to act creatively, and to act is to generate artificial worlds. Generally, these worlds disappear from our minds without leaving any trace: "but when the masses are deeply moved it then becomes possible to trace the outlines of the kind of representation which constitutes a social myth."[37] Thus, social myths are projections of artificial worlds, constructed freely by a few individuals, and shared, with passionate conviction, by the masses, thereby acquiring a considerable measure of permanence. These images may be legends concerning the past, or anticipations regarding the future, regardless of their content and independent of their historical validity. The nature of myth will appear more clearly in a comparison with utopias.

In the first place, myths are supra-intellectual, that is, they originate in modes of thought substantially distinct from discursive thinking. By contrast, utopias are intellectualist and proceed essentially from abstract thought. Thus, the revolutionary utopia of the eighteenth century was based on the assumption that all men are exactly alike in every climate and in every latitude, are subject to the same appetites and are governed by immutable principles of reason and self-interest. Secondly, myths have to be absorbed "en bloc," and may not be taken apart for study. Utopias are composite constructions, resulting from the juxtaposition of several clear and distinct ideas. A utopia is "an intellectual product; it is the work of theorists who, observing and discussing the known facts, seek to establish a model to which they can compare" existing societies.[38] Thirdly, utopias may be discussed like every rational construction, while myths have a religious character and cannot be refuted. Fourthly, utopias are external to the individual, like all products of pure reason, while myth becomes incorporated in man's personality and is made a part of his psychic life. "The believer in a myth will live the myth with all his being; the myth dominates him, obsesses him, becomes his reason for being and the principle of all his important actions."[39] Finally, utopias are barren and myths are creative.

Sorel, thus, believed that concepts are completely inadequate as a motivating force for action and that history reveals the tremendous fecundity of myths. Such, for instance, are: the eschatological myths concerning the end of history and the establishment of the kingdom of the Saints, which helped to maintain the fervor of mediaeval Christendom; the myth of Italian unity, that permitted the realization of Mazzini's dream; and the myth of Christian renovation cherished by Luther and Calvin, that was responsible for the Reformation.

Myth and utopias seldom appear in a pure state. As an almost pure example of utopia, however, Sorel cited classical political economy's ideal of perfect competition. This ideal is extremely logical and coherent as a conceptual scheme but could never work satisfactorily in practice. As an illustration of myths combined with utopias, Sorel mentioned the ideals of political liberalism. Rousseauist theory, for instance, is utopian insofar as it corresponds to a rationalist construction, but it has a strong mythical basis represented by the concrete aspirations and world view of the rising bourgeoisie. Finally, as a perfect example of pure myth, free from any utopian contamination, he proposed the myth of the general strike. For Sorel, this myth was extremely effective as a revolutionary instrument and summed up and contained all socialist thinking. It crystallized the division of society in two antagonistic groups, thus facilitating revolutionary action and simplifying the task to be accomplished. In the second place, it maintained the feeling of revolt in the masses. Thirdly, it avoided compromise and sharpened social tensions and class struggle, effectively blocking reformist schemes. Finally, it rallied the proletariat to a relentless, passionate, and organized resistance against the *status-quo.*

Regardless of the validity of Sorel's claim that the general strike was a complete summing up of socialism, there is no doubt that the theory of myth contains a complete summing-up of Sorel's irrationalist *Weltanschauung.* This irrationalist atmosphere, as was remarked, contained three basic motifs: the themes of anti-intellectualism, activism, and heroism. The idea of myth embodies all three elements.

Its anti-intellectualist nature is predicated by its very definition, and is of the very essence of myth. If myth could be analyzed and reduced to concepts, it would automatically cease to exist as such.

> The intellectualist philosophy finds itself unable to explain phenomena like the following—the sacrifice of his life which the soldier of Napoleon made in order to have had the honour of taking part in "immortal deeds" and of living in the glory of France, knowing all the time that "he would always be a poor man"; . . . the extraordinary virtues shown by the Romans . . . ; "the belief in glory (which was) a value without equal," created by Greece. . . . [40]

The theme of action is also inseparable from the concept of myth. Actually, the only reason for which myths are created is to induce action. The system of images contained in the myth is of an essentially motor character (*images motrices*), for action is its very *raison d'être.*

> As long as there are not myths accepted by the masses, one may go on talking of revolts indefinitely, without ever provoking any revolutionary movement. . . . By means of myths it is possible to understand the activity, the feelings and ideas of the masses preparing themselves to enter on a decisive struggle; the myths are not descriptions of things, but expressions of a determination to act.[41]

Finally, myths are the keys to the concept of heroic life. The morals of heroism are based on a blind belief in the superior ethical worth of a cause and in the almost religious loyalty elicited by the latter. When reason intervenes, heroism becomes a calculation of alternatives rather than an unqualified devotion to a transcending reality.

> These facts show us the way to a right understanding of the nature of lofty moral convictions; these never depend on reasoning or on any education of the individual will, but on a state of war in which men voluntarily participate and which finds expression in well-defined myths.[42]

In concluding it may be observed that there are glaring inconsistencies in Sorel's work and a few unacceptable oversimplifications. But Sorel shares the peculiar immunity that protects all irrationalist writers: since their position is irrationalist to begin with, there is very little point in going into their logical flaws, because inconsistency is of the essence of an irrationalist philosophy. As Sorel himself asserted: "People who are living in this world of myths, are secure from all refutation. . . . "[43]

On the positive side, his work is certainly a breath of fresh air, and a welcome departure from the closed intellectualist atmosphere that characterized most works on political theory since Locke and Rousseau. With Sorel, and almost for the first time in political theory, man is conceived as a bundle of emotions rather than as a living theorem. There is no doubt that one extreme is as regrettable as the other; but again, as Sorel affirmed, the great virtue of irrationalism is precisely that it makes it impossible to accept "le juste milieu": "as long as socialism remains a *doctrine expressed only in words,* it is very easy to deflect it towards this doctrine of the golden mean; but this transformation is manifestly impossible when the myth of the 'general strike' is introduced. . . . "[44] The worst that can be said of Sorel is that his doctrine became one of the sources of the Fascist movement. But it is not fair to judge a political doctrine solely by its effects and in the perspective that fifty years distance give to us. Sorel foresaw the criticisms of posterity, and gave a very satisfactory excuse for his intellectual shortcomings: "We are perfectly aware that the historians of the future are bound to discover that we laboured under many illusions, because they will see behind them a finished world."[45]

NOTES

[1] Henri Bergson, *The Two Sources of Morality and Religion,* translated by R. Ashley Audra and Cloudesley Brereton (Garden City, n.d.), pp. 220-221.

[2] André Gide, *L'Immoraliste* (Paris, 1939), p. 61.

[3] Edmund Burke, *Burke's Politics,* ed. by Ross J. S. Hoffman and Paul Levack (New York, 1949), p. 304.

[4] *Ibid.,* p. 227.

[5] Edward A. Shils, "Georges Sorel," Introduction of the American Edition of *Reflections on Violence,* trans. by T. E. Hulme and J. Roth (Glencoe, 1950), p. 25.

[6] Georges Sorel, *Réflexions sur la Violence* (Paris, 1946), p. 65. The English translation, used for subsequent passages, has for this passage "overturn . . . by the breath of the professors." See Sorel, *Reflections on Violence,* trans. Hulme and Roth, int. by Shils (Glencoe, 1950), p. 70. Later references will cite the French edition as *Sorel* and the English edition as *Reflections.*

[7] *Sorel,* pp. 110-111; *Reflections,* p. 100.

[8] *Sorel,* p. 130; *Reflections,* p. 113.

[9] *Sorel,* p. 161; *Reflections,* p. 132.

[10] *Sorel,* p. 200; *Reflections,* p. 157.

[11] *Sorel,* p. 434; *Reflections,* p. 301.

[12] *Sorel,* pp. 112-113; *Reflections,* p. 102.

[13] *Sorel,* p. 122; *Reflections,* p. 108.

[14] *Sorel,* p. 126; *Reflections,* p. 110.

[15] *Sorel,* pp. 368-369.

[16] Robert Michels, *Political Parties,* trans. by Eden and Cedar Paul (New York, 1959), p. 325.

[17] Paul Lafargue, "Socialism and the Intellectuals" in *The Intellectuals,* ed. George B. de Huszar (Glencoe, 1960), pp. 323-324.

[18] *Sorel,* p. 35; *Reflections,* p. 50.

[19] *Sorel,* p. 217; *Reflections,* p. 167.

[20] *Sorel,* p. 207; *Reflections,* p. 161.

[21] *Sorel,* pp. 316-317; *Reflections,* p. 232.

[22] *Sorel,* p. 218; *Reflections,* p. 168.

[23] Georg Lukacs, quoted by Karl Mannheim, *Ideology and Utopia,* trans. Louis Wirth and Edward Shils (New York, 1936), p. 127.

[24] *Sorel,* p. 109; *Reflections,* p. 99.

[25] *Sorel,* p. 358; *Reflections,* p. 258.

[26] *Sorel,* p. 324; *Reflections,* p. 237.

[27] *Sorel,* p. 161; *Reflections,* p. 132.

[28] *Sorel,* p. 249; *Reflections,* p. 189.

[29] See Paul Kahn, "Mythe et Réalité Sociale Chez Sorel," *Cahiers Internacionaux de Sociologie,* VI (1951), 131-132.

[30] Arnold J. Toynbee, *A Study of History,* Abridgement by D. C. Somervell, Vol. I (Oxford University Press, 1954), 60.

[31] For a complete account of these theories, see, among other works, *Myth and Mythmaking,* edited by Henry A. Murray (New York, 1960); Georges Gusdorf, *Mythe et Métaphysique* (Paris, 1953); Richard Chase, *Quest for Myth* (Baton Rouge, 1949).

[32] Bronislaw Malinowski, *Magic, Science and Religion* (Garden City, 1948), p. 101.

[33] Paul Kahn, *op. cit.,* p. 133.

[34] Georges Sorel, *Introduction a l'Economie Moderne,* quoted by Paul Kahn, *op. cit.,* p. 133.

[35] *Ibid.,* p. 137.

[36] *Sorel,* pp. 32-33; *Reflections,* p. 49.

[37] *Sorel,* p. 44; *Reflections,* p. 56.

[38] *Sorel,* p. 46; *Reflections,* p. 57.

[39] Rossignol, *Pour Connaitre la Pensée de Sorel,* quoted by Paul Kahn, *op. cit.,* p. 142.

[40] *Sorel,* pp. 35-36; *Reflections,* pp. 50-51.

[41] *Sorel,* pp. 45-46; *Reflections,* p. 56.

[42] *Sorel,* p. 319; *Reflections,* p. 234.

[43] *Sorel,* p. 49; *Reflections,* p. 59.

[44] *Sorel,* p. 39; *Reflections,* p. 53.

[45] *Sorel,* p. 219; *Reflections,* p. 169.

Neal Wood (essay date 1968)

SOURCE: "Some Reflections on Sorel and Machiavelli," in *Political Science Quarterly*, Vol. LXXXIII, No. 1, March, 1968, pp. 76-91.

[*In the following excerpt originally written in 1965, Wood expands on James Burnham's (excerpted above) thesis that Sorel was a Maciavellian thinker.*]

The comparison of Georges Sorel and Niccolò Machiavelli is not without precedent. Some twenty years ago James Burnham maintained that Sorel (along with Mosca, Michels, and Pareto) shared in a tradition of thinking called Machiavellism.[1] The principal tenets of the tradition consist of a faith in an empirical science of politics, and a conception of politics as a struggle for power involving force and fraud, in which the role of a ruling elite and non-rational action arising from an ideology are central. Burnham's approach tends to distort rather than illuminate the ideas of Sorel and Machiavelli, although I have no intention of taking issue directly with his position. Instead I shall argue that grounds for the comparison of the two thinkers are to be sought in their common devotion to a regenerative morality born out of strife and conflict, for which they find a source of inspiration in the ancient classical world. Despite the four centuries separating the two thinkers, both view politics as a kind of warfare and describe it in military terms. Oddly enough, a strikingly similar outlook is reflected in much of contemporary American thinking on the political process, a fact to which little if any attention has been directed.

I

Like many of his Socialist predecessors, Sorel turns to classical antiquity. His first book, ***Le procès de Socrate,*** is evidence of his fascination with ancient Greece and its formative influence upon his thought.[2] In this work he discusses the Athenian polis prior to what he considers its period of corruption and decline, from the beginning of the fifth century B.C. onward. These ancient Athenians were far superior to the ignorant and avaricious bourgeosie of his own age.[3] Their society was one of industrious and thrifty equals. In comparison with the modern bourgeoisie, the Athenian citizens were not merchants clamoring for guarantees of trade, for protection of their industry, or for governmental favors; they were soldiers whose very reason for being was the grandeur of their polis, whose slightest weakness endangered the common good. According to Sorel the significance of the life of ancient Greece and Rome cannot be grasped unless heed is given to their military arrangements.[4] Ancient constitutions were shaped by the necessities of war; the education of youth was fundamentally preparation for war. The polis was indeed a warriors guild. Classical thinkers, among them Aristotle, were fully aware of the basic military nature of the polis. So, for example, the Stagirite attempted to imitate the ancient Athenian military order in his preliminary outline of the ideal constitution contained in the last two books of the *Politics*.[5]

A life of military preparedness, of constant war and the threat of war, were for Sorel not the only interesting characteristics of classical times. He was greatly attracted to what he understood of the ancient economy, predominantly rural and agrarian, as opposed to the urbanism and commercialism of the later decadent years.[6] Agrarian life in itself, however, was not so much the attraction as the fact that the citizen-soldiers were landed proprietors who formed a fraternity of producers. Instead of living a parasitic life of indolence and luxury, the warrior-farmers actually planned the labor, did much of it themselves, and closely supervised their workers. Their unusual understanding of the productive process is manifest in the careful records kept by the ancient Roman agriculturalists.

Two articulate representatives of the hardy, traditional spirit survived the increasing decay of commercial Athens: Aristophanes and Xenophon.[7] As have few commentators, Sorel succeeds in penetrating to the heart of Xenophon's thought in a brief evaluation of the *Oeconomicus,* which he judges one of the most remarkable works of antiquity. The *Oeconomicus,* the first extant treatise on estate management, is by the famous soldier-farmer and founder of Western military science, whose exploits are largely known through his account of the trek of the Ten Thousand in the *Anabasis*. Xenophon is a kind of archaic survival of Greek military and agrarian life. Sorel notes that he approaches the problem of estate-management from the standpoint of a man of war. Military imagery and comparisons are employed to explain the performance of various tasks and the duties of the different workers. The ideal farm, in fact, is organized and managed like an efficient army.[8] Xenophon, comments Sorel, carries on in the *Oeconomicus* the ancient tradition of a great national poetry, without resorting to the overly polished exposition or the fine dialectical hair-splitting of his master Socrates. Much later, in the ***Reflexions sur la violence*** (1906), Sorel, referring to the *Memorabilia* as well as the *Oeconomicus,* affirms that Xenophon represents an older Greek tradition than Plato.[9] The soldier-farmer understands the nature of production; the philosopher does not. Speaking in the guise of Socrates in the *Memorabilia,* Xenophon advises a destitute citizen, who must provide for a large family, to establish a workshop in his home manned by the members of his family. Sorel's implication is that a recommendation of this kind represents a tradition older than Plato, because the ancient Greeks did not shun labor if by it they could free themselves from subjection by others and become self-sufficient.

What, then, are the reasons for Sorel's fixation upon the military and productive characteristics of the ancient polis? Obviously, he is not urging the revival of the polis as a form of social organization for his own industrial Europe. He does believe, however, that something of its élan and social solidarity can be recaptured at a new and higher level by the creation of revolutionary syndicates of workers. An indication of his ideal is found in a concluding statement of ***La ruine du monde antique*** (1902): "Socialism returns to ancient thought; but the warrior of the polis has become the worker of large industry; his weapons have been replaced by machines."[10] The vigorous, patriotic, almost ascetic soldier-farmer is replaced in Sorel's mind by the proletarian artisan, exercising control over the means of production in the small workshop, experiencing the joy of genuine creation, and becoming the master rather than the slave of the works fashioned by his art.[11] United in syndicates, the proletarian warriors will be locked in constant struggle with the bourgeois enemy. Out of the new warfare and the new production a new morality will emerge, completely transforming human relations and revolutionizing society.

Excited as he is by the ancient polis, Sorel never views its life of war and production as an end, only as a means to the fruition of a heroic morality. Ancient strife between cities was responsible for a virtue hardly equaled since. The industrial workers' revolutionary action against capitalism, in preparation for the ultimate clash of the general strike, is the latter-day substitute for the warfare of antiquity: "The revolutionary Syndicates argue about socialist action in the same manner as military writers argue about war."[12] Much of Sorel's outlook is clarified in an article on Proudhon.[13] The Proudhonian community is analogous to the polis, which "had always been a congregation of soldiers." War for Proudhon "reveals our ideal to us . . . creates the great epics . . . reinvigorates nations gone soft." In the course of battle "man discovers his own best qualities: courage, patience, disregard of death, devotion to glory and the good of his fellows, in one word: his virtue." Repeatedly in the ***Reflections on Violence*** Sorel refers to the ancient heroic morality dependent upon the pursuit of honor and glory in military ventures.[14] Nietzsche's eulogy of the Homeric heroes is quoted with obvious relish: "that audacity of noble races, that mad, absurd, and spontaneous audacity, their influence and contempt for all security of the body, for life, for comfort."[15]

But, according to Sorel, the ancient Athenian heroism had practically disappeared by the time of the Peloponnesian War, once the city had become the emporium of a vast commercial empire with a consumer's economy characterized by avarice, luxury, and indolence. The emergence of oligarchical government catering to the masses and encouraging mediocrity in all walks of life suggests modern bourgeois democracy to Sorel. A morality of the golden mean, of moderation, based upon reason instead of conflict and war, replaced the morality of soldier-producers. The rationalism of the Sophists and of Socrates and his disciples was responsible for an intellectual orgy of introspection and self-consciousness, the ideological manifestation of a dying culture. Sorel's observations concerning the decline of Athens in ***Le procès de Socrate*** are his first efforts to formulate a general theory of decadence, elaborated in subsequent writings.[16] By adopting Vico's conception of *ricorso,* he conceives of each organized society passing through successive ascending and descending phases of grandeur and decadence. Western civilization has experienced at least three phases of decadence: the breakup of the Hellenic polis, the disintegration of the Roman empire, and the corruption of nineteenth-century bourgeois Europe. Decadent periods of history display political disunity, economic stagnation, military weakness, disrespect for tradition, creative decline, and the leveling of all social classes to the lowest common denominator. A prime causal factor seems to be the disappearance of conflict. When a people no longer are compelled to struggle for survival, when internal contention is reduced to a minimum, their original vigor, hardiness, and decisiveness decline and disappear. Self-seeking and the loss of a sense of civic duty destroy the social fabric. Disintegration is accelerated by the questioning of rationalism; a malady of reflection and self-analysis paralyzes the will to action. Sorel's lifelong quest is for a solution to the decadence of his own epoch, and for the foundation of a heroic morality in a new dimension.

II

Machiavelli also looks to the ancient world for moral inspiration. His political theory, reconstructed from the four major works, *The Prince, the Discourses, The Art of War,* and the *History of Florence,* is informed by the notion of an ideal man and the kind of society necessary to produce his hero.[17] The model is the sturdy citizen-soldier of the Roman republic prior to the first Punic War. He is the patriot dedicated to the common good, a man of action exhibiting foresight, constancy, boldness, self-discipline, fortitude, determination, and bravery—qualities often summarized by Machiavelli's use of the single term *virtù.* The Machiavellian hero of *virtù* is *homo militans,* the very opposite of *homo oeconomicus,* the self-seeking, acquisitive individual who aims at economic aggrandizement through a life of commerce, the model for the concept of human nature found in many of the early liberal thinkers and in the classical economists. *Homo militans* is the glory-seeker desirous of immortality, that is, some permanence in a cosmos of perpetual flux, through a personal triumph remembered and cherished by his contemporaries, and, more importantly, by posterity. Glory of the highest variety can be achieved by founding a new order of things, a new religion or a new state, by giving an existing state a new code of laws, and by great political or military leadership.[18] True glory can never be won simply by the acquisition of wealth and power,[19] but the glory-seeker may win fame even in failure, as defeat brought posthumous renown to a Leonidas or Cato Minor. While Machiavelli stresses the military virtues of the Romans, and gives scant attention to their economy, he does refer to the simple agrarian life of his hero, who in times of peril may be called by his city to the highest office, only to return like Cincinnatus, after the fulfillment of his civic obligation, to the ploughing of his humble acres.

The Romans, as presented by the Florentine, were a frugal, disciplined people, devoted to a life of arms. A single, steadfast attachment to the common good accounted in great measure for their glorious exploits. Moreover, Roman glory resulted from an ardent and deep-rooted republicanism. Citizen-soldiers of Rome won the greatest glory in their continuous struggle for existence in a hostile environment of ferocious enemies, by fighting, as it were, for themselves, not for the sake of a commander or ruler. Roman glory was the citizen's glory, and the citizen's achievements redounded to the credit of the whole military brotherhood. The liberty provided by the republican form of government proved to be the ideal condition for the pursuit of glory.

Rome, for Machiavelli, is the model of the best government because it secured most adequately the ends of good government in general. The foundation of good government is an adequate military establishment for protection against the external foe. Internally, security must be provided for a citizen's life, family, property, and honor. Although general economic prosperity is important, individual acquisition and conspicuous consumption are to be strictly regulated. Merit is to be rewarded generously, and the pursuit of honor and glory in the service of the state is to be encouraged. The mixed constitution of the Roman republic, with institutions such as dictatorship, censorship, public accusations, popular assemblies, sumptuary laws, and a citizens' army, are fundamental means to these ends. In addition, Machiavelli emphasizes the significance of the rule of law as a guarantee of the citizen's liberty and security. Machiavelli's ideal, therefore, was a republic of citizen-soldiers, designed to provide peace and security in a hazardous world and to offer opportunities for heroic actions.

Machiavelli also offers a theory of civic degeneration similar to Sorel's. Commonwealths can be virtuous only under conditions of necessity, when, in order to survive, a people must display a spirit of cooperation and of dedication to the common good and act with industry, determination, and courage. The necessity that unites a people and generates such spirit may be a hostile physical environment, the constant threat of an external power, or the actual aggression of an enemy. Once a commonwealth succeeds in securing and maintaining its existence, degeneration begins. Although well-devised laws can serve as a substitute for an external foe by forcing a people to be virtuous, those responsible for executing the law and adjusting it to new conditions will grow lax in any prolonged period of peace and prosperity. Of course, class conflict, providing it takes place within the limits of a patriotic devotion to the common good and a willingness to abide by the rules of the game, will invigorate the body politic. Once corruption sets in, however, healthy class conflict deteriorates into factional strife and civil war. Long periods of peace and plenty result in a general relaxation and indolence, a decline of the old spirit and vigor, a propensity to acquire personal wealth, power, and luxury at the expense of the common good. Respect for authority and the sense of civic duty are weakened; questioning of traditional values begins; the original social solidarity is transformed into a collection of individuals, each for himself. Religious belief ceases to be a vital social bond; extremes of wealth and poverty develop. From the political standpoint, conspiracy, assassination, and governmental instability become commonplace. From the military standpoint, the degenerate commonwealth may at any time be a victim of foreign aggression. Every commonwealth is doomed to such eventual corruption. Inspired leadership and rational social organization may delay, but cannot indefinitely prevent the spread of decay. Even the most virtuous of all peoples, the Romans, could maintain their liberties for only four hundred years. Machiavelli summarizes his views in his case-history of civic decadence, the *History of Florence:*

> It may be observed that commonwealths amid the vicissitudes to which they are subject, pass from order into disorder, and afterward return from disorder to order. Since the nature of the world does not allow things to continue in an even course, when they have arrived at their greatest perfection, they soon begin to decline. Similarly, having been reduced by disorder to their worst condition and, unable to descend lower, they, of necessity, reascend. Thus from good they gradually decline to evil, and from evil again return to good. The reason is that *virtù* produces peace; peace, indolence; indolence, disorder; disorder, ruin; so from disorder order springs; from order *virtù,* and from this, glory and good fortune. Hence, wise men have observed that the age of literary excellence follows that of distinction in arms, and that in commonwealths and cities, great commanders are produced before philosophers. Arms having secured victory, and victory peace, the spirited vigor of the martial mind cannot be corrupted by a more excusable indolence than that of letters. Nor can indolence with any greater or more dangerous deceit, enter a well established commonwealth. Cato was aware of this when the philosophers, Diogenes and Carneades, were sent as ambassadors to the Senate by the Athenians. Perceiving with what earnest admiration the Roman youth began to follow them, and knowing the evils that might result to his country from this excusable indolence, he enacted that no philosopher should be allowed to enter Rome.[20]

III

Sorel and Machiavelli were moralists in the sense that both were profoundly disturbed by the behavior of their contemporaries and wished to change it for the better. They were not moralists as, for example, Plato and Kant were, for they did not arrive at universal moral principles from an elaborately conceived and intricately developed philosophic system. Sorel and Machiavelli begin directly with a more or less vague notion of a good society, not from a cosmology or metaphysic. Their moralizing consists of recommendations for a mutually sustaining individual behavior and social organization. Each rejects the commercial, exploitative life of his own age, analyzes its nature, determines its causes, and suggests how a new era of grandeur and heroic morality could be introduced. Each emphasizes the value of social conflict for the new morality and conceives of politics as a kind of warfare.

This emphasis upon conflict represents a radical break with the classical-medieval tradition of political thought, and is distinctively modern. Machiavelli must be credited for first assigning a positive social and political value to domestic conflict. While traditional thinkers like Plato and Aristotle had clearly recognized the existence of conflict within the polis, they thought of it as an unnatural condition arising from the domination of the human soul by the baser appetites. Since the nature of the soul was thought to be a harmony of parts under the rule of reason, social conflict represented a defection of the psyche from nature. Consequently, a social organization was recommended in which a harmony, if not a unison of parts, would replace all antagonisms, and in which civic education would mold healthy, harmonious human souls. This social-psychology of harmony has a parallel in the ancient physical concept that matter at rest is more natural than matter in motion. During the Cinquecento both theories were challenged by two Italian thinkers. Machiavelli argued that social disorder and decadence cannot be solved by the elimination of conflict. Conflict, so natural to man, the slave of contending desires, will always be present in human society. Any attempt to eliminate conflict will eventuate in the destruction of man. The solution to social and governmental instability must lie in conflict itself. Through proper regulation conflict can be a strengthening, vitalizing, creative, and integrating social factor, a way of freeing man from the domination of man. Galileo performed much the same service for physics that Machiavelli earlier had rendered politics by arguing that the natural state of matter is motion instead of rest.

Unlike Sorel, Machiavelli does not give class-struggle an economic basis. Class-warfare is considered largely in psychological terms. The major cause for intermural and intramural conflict stems from an individual lust for power and domination. In all societies a few wish to dominate the many, while the majority wish to be free and secure from the domination of this minority. Economic aggrandizement is simply a manifestation of the lust for power in all men, what St. Augustine calls the *libido dominandi.*[21] The power-seeking elite may be a rich and powerful commercial class, such as that of Renaissance Florence, or a relatively poor warrior class, like the patricians of early republican Rome. The difference between the struggle of the plebes with the patricians in the well-ordered Roman commonwealth and the contention of the *ciompi* and oligarchs in decadent Florence is that the former occurred within specific limits while the latter did not. In republican Rome, patriotism, a sense of civic duty, and a respect for law and authority prevented class conflict from erupting into civil war. Moreover, Roman constitutional arrangements had been modified by experience to embody a balance of powers between the Senate, representative of the patricians, and the plebeian assemblies with their tribunes, thus institutionalizing and regulating conflict.

Sorel's view of society as a battlefield for the economic class-struggle is much more extreme than Machiavelli's outlook. Yet, after Machiavelli, theorists of limited conflict as a social good and of the state as the umpire of contending interests, including the British empiricists, the classical economists, and Montesquieu and his great disciple Tocqueville, broke ground for the later and more radical Socialist position on class-warfare in bourgeois society. Machiavelli, however, tends to be much closer to Sorel than most intervening non-Socialist thinkers, because out of his military interests and experience he conceived of domestic politics as a kind of warfare between groups and individuals struggling for power. Indeed, his model for leadership is military, and his political recommendations are often little more than the translation of the stratagems of classical military thinkers into maxims of statecraft.

To a marked extent much of the vocabulary of politics used today by American politicians, journalists, and political scientists is a military vocabulary. Whether one reads a description and assessment of an election in the newspaper or the erudite evaluation of practical politics in textbook, dissertation, or monograph, the language is often that applied traditionally to accounts of military operations, never to the quest for the good society. Our use of military metaphor and simile is so habitual that we are rarely conscious of it and of its historical novelty. The very use of the words struggle, contest, conflict, warfare, battle, enemy, arena, campaign, soldier, troops, recruits, and deserters is highly significant. The political enemy is attacked or defeated; he advances or retreats; from a defensive position, he assumes the offensive. A political party is a camp to be stormed or besieged, an army to be conquered. At the head of the political army is the commander who plans his campaign in his headquarters and marshals his forces with the aid of a staff and a chief-of-staff. Communities favoring one party over another become strongholds, bastions, fortresses, and citadels. Military organization provides columnist and scholar with terms like ally, auxiliary, echelon, cadre, column, rank and file, wing, flank, rear guard, vanguard, base, battalion, and division. The words strategy and tactics never could have been applied by the ancients to domestic politics; they could be applied only to the foe in military operations, because all citizens of the polis were considered to be friends. In the second half of the twentieth century, what American politician, pundit, or political scientist is not perpetually indebted to them! Tactical terms particularly are savored: mobilize, maneuver, disposition, deployment, flanking, foray, sortie, thrust and counter-thrust, confrontation, infiltration, penetration. And when the battle is over we even talk of an armistice, or if a mutually arranged lull in hostilities occurs, we often refer to a cease-fire, a parley, or a truce.

If early modern thinkers, with their emphasis upon the value of limited social conflict and the state as umpire of competing interests, contributed to this contemporary American way of conceptualizing domestic politics, they, of course, cannot be held wholly responsible for it. Certainly the recent concept—a particular favorite among some American students of politics—that politics is purely a struggle for power, and the decline of the idea that politics is a moral science, may have contributed to the new image. Suggestive also is the group theory of politics. Perhaps the polarization of international politics into the maneuvering of two super-powers in a "cold war" to eliminate or neutralize each other has been unconsciously projected upon the domestic scene. Nor should we forget that Freud, whose thought has so shaped directly and indirectly the attitudes of the present American generation, offers a psychology of conflict in which men are in a virtual state of war and the psyche itself is a battlefield.

Certain practical developments may well have been more important. The organization of centralized, disciplined parties in the nineteenth century to achieve the social and economic demands of the masses is quite possibly a decisive reason. Socialist theory and practice have always been especially concerned with the formation of militant, fighting parties. *The Communist Manifesto* of 1848 was an open declaration of war in the name of the worker against the bourgeoisie. Its portrayal of past and present is in terms of extreme conflict: "The history of all hitherto existing society is the history of class struggles," and within society there rages a "more or less veiled civil war," in which the "bourgeoisie finds itself involved in constant battle" with the proletariat.

It is not a coincidence that one of Sorel's foremost disciples, Roberto Michels, devoted a chapter of his very influential book, *La Sociologia del Partito nella Democrazia Moderna* (1912), to "The Modern Democratic Party as a Fighting Party, Dominated by Militarist Ideas and Methods."[22] Michels writes that rules essential to the conduct of military affairs are equally applicable to modern political life, which is uniquely characterized by a "perpetual condition of latent warfare."[23] Modern fighting parties must conform to the laws of tactics, and the similarity between such parties and military organization is reflected by the Socialist vocabulary, which especially in Germany comes from military science. Scarcely one expression of military tactics and strategy, he writes, hardly a phrase of barracks slang, does not occur again and again in the Socialist press. Even early anti-militarist French Socialists referred to their leader, Gustave Hervé, as "our General." Interesting, although not mentioned by Michels, is the fact that a small group of British middle-class moderates who banded together in the eighties for social reform through education and piecemeal action should call themselves Fabians. Michels continues that a number of Socialist leaders, including Engels, Bebel, and Jaurès, wrote extensively on military affairs. Since Michels, the Russian disciples of Marx and Engels did transform their party into a military organization in an almost literal sense, and increasingly employed military imagery in discussing the struggle between proletarians and bourgeoisie. In his *Foundations of Leninism*, Stalin allots a chapter to "Strategy and Tactics," which he terms "the science of proletarian leadership," and then proceeds as if he were writing a military handbook for proletarian generals. For each different political situation he enumerates the appropriate "main blow," "reserves," and "disposition of forces."[24]

That many American scholars and European Socialists should employ a military vocabulary to describe and assess domestic politics is one of the minor ironies of history. Precisely the justification of the Socialists in using a military model is their central doctrine of class struggle, the insistent denial of which appears to be the stock-in-trade of most American analyses of the political scene. If Socialists were pitted against the bourgeoisie in America, the use of a military vocabulary by non-Socialist students of politics would be appropriate. But the very nature of American political parties, the similar class composition, the minimal ideological differences, the obeisance to some kind of sacred consensus—all these traits would seem to reflect an almost obsessive dread of social conflict, even a denial of its very existence. The use of military metaphor to describe the relatively mild and gentlemanly rivalry among singularly like-minded men so characteristic of American politics today is, to say the least, somewhat incongruous. The much vaunted end of ideological politics in America appears to be accompanied by the emergence of a new ideology, an ideology arising from the presumed absence of conflict but expressed nevertheless in the idiom of conflict and military struggle.

IV

Notwithstanding the many parallels between the ideas of Sorel and Machiavelli, a fundamental difference in their styles of political thinking cannot be overlooked. This difference, most apparent in their accounts of the ideal man, gives to each a unique role in the history of political ideas. Machiavelli's classical hero, supremely rational and calculating, is engaged in a rational enterprise of fighting a war, ruling a people, or organizing a viable civil society. The statesman like the general is a master manipulator of men. He may assume a charismatic role for the sake of more effective control and management, but he is undone if he neglects the rational calculation of self-interest, his own and those he seeks to manipulate. On the basis of his perception of the inherent order and form of things social and political, he can meticulously plan his course of action in terms of the most efficient means to achieve the public utility, and then act in a vigorous, decisive, and flexible manner. The organization and leadership of an army or a commonwealth is always a highly rational enterprise in the eyes of the Florentine. His faith in the molding of a civic-minded, sturdy, and courageous people by the rational construction of society makes him a true forerunner of the eighteenth-century Enlightenment.

By contrast, Sorel is deeply distrustful of what he calls the utopianism and the rationalism of the Enlightenment. His proletarian hero is a truly charismatic figure, a man of spontaneity, feeling, and virility, not the objective, calculating type.[25] His philosophical inspiration is the *élan vital* of Henri Bergson rather than the *phron sis* and *s phrosyn* of Aristotle. At the heart of his theory of action is the notion of action for the sake of action. Admittedly, acting in a prescribed manner will produce a new heroism; but this new heroism seems to be for its own sake, in large part to satisfy Sorel's own esthetic sensibility. Although Machiavelli places a premium upon heroic action, he is clear that it is a means of achieving a society of peace and security and a happy people. In addition, Machiavelli's rationalism is suggested by his faith in law as an instrument of social control. Whether he discusses an army or a commonwealth he has in mind the elimination of uncertainty and insecurity in human relations by the institution and maintenance of a rational legal order. In these various senses, therefore, Machiavelli is a political thinker, while Sorel is fundamentally apolitical. His society of proletarian-warriors would be characterized by constant novelty, excitement, and upheaval. He possesses no vision beyond the anarchy of the class struggle, beyond the heroic brotherhood forged in battle with the bourgeoisie, and the joy of creation in the workshop. Sorel may possibly be the spirit of the Erinyes reincarnate, but Machiavelli never forsakes the shrine of Athena.

NOTES

[1] James Burnham, *The Machiavellians, Defenders of Freedom* (New York, 1943).

[2] Georges Sorel, *Le procès de Socrate* (Paris, 1889).

[3] *Ibid.*, 170-72.

[4] *Ibid.*, 167.

[5] *Ibid.*, 170-71; also Sorel, *Matériaux d'une théorie du prolétariat* (Paris, 3d ed., 1929), 388.

[6] *Le procès,* 375 ff.; *Matériaux,* 387-89.

[7] *Le procès,* 375 ff.; *Matériaux,* 387.

[8] For a full discussion of this perspective, see my article, "Xenophon's Theory of Leadership," in *Classica et Mediaevalia* XXV (1964), 33-66. On this score my view of Xenophon is in agreement with Sorel's, although I did not discover his interpretation until after my article had gone to press.

[9] Sorel, *Reflections on Violence,* trans. T. E. Hulme and J. Roth, Introduction by Edward Shils (Glencoe, 1950), 263, n. 50.

[10] Sorel, *La ruine du monde antique: conception matérialiste de l'histoire,* Introduction by Édouard Berth (Paris, 3d. ed., 1933), 311.

[11] Sorel believed that a true art would develop only on the basis of syndicates of workers. Such an art would be one of utility. See Pierre Angel, *Essais sur Georges Sorel* (Paris, 1937), 229-30.

[12] *Reflections,* 137.

[13] "Essai sur la philosophie de Proudhon," *Revue Philosophique,* XXXIII (1892), XXXIV (1892). The following quotations are from page 44, as found in James H. Meisel, *The Genesis of Georges Sorel, An Account of His Formative Period Followed by a Study of His Influence* (Ann Arbor, 1951), 96. Also see Sorel, *Le procès,* 170, n. 3; *Matériaux,* 389, n. 2.

[14] *Reflections,* 50-57, 187-88, 257-60, 268-69, 276.

[15] *Ibid.,* 257.

[16] A very useful analytic summary of Sorel's concept of decadence drawn from his various works is Jean Wanner, *Georges Sorel et la Décadence: Essai sur l'idée de décadence dans la pensée de Georges Sorel* (Lausanne, 1943). Also see especially Sorel, *Les illusions du progrès* (Paris, 4th ed., 1927), 287-336; *Reflections, passim.*

[17] Unless otherwise indicated, what follows on Machiavelli summarizes certain of my views in my Introduction to Machiavelli, *The Art of War,* a revised edition of the Ellis Farneworth translation (Indianapolis, New York, and Kansas City, 1965).

[18] Machiavelli, *Discourses,* I, x.

[19] For the distinction between true and false glory, see Machiavelli, *Prince,* VIII, XIX; *Discourses,* I, ix-x.

[20] Machiavelli, *History of Florence,* V, i. The translation is a modification of that of the Harper Torchbook edition, Introduction by Felix Gilbert (New York, Evanston, and London, 1960), 204.

[21] See Herbert A. Deane, *The Political and Social Ideas of St. Augustine* (New York and London, 1963), 48-53.

[22] Roberto Michels, *Political Parties: A Sociological Study of the Oligarchical Tendencies of Modern Democracy,* trans. Eden and Cedar Paul (Glencoe, 1949), 41-44.

[23] *Ibid.,* 41.

[24] Joseph Stalin, *Foundations of Leninism* (New York, 1939), 88-106. The chapter on "The Party" begins by proclaiming that it "must be, first of all, the *vanguard* of the working class" (p. 109).

[25] Note the excellent appraisal in Irving L. Horowitz, *Radicalism and the Revolt Against Reason: the Social Theories of Georges Sorel with a Translation of his Essay on "The Decomposition of Marxism"* (New York, 1961), 156-58.

Robert A. Nisbet and John Stanley (essay date 1969)

SOURCE: An introduction to "The Illusions of Progress", by Georges Sorel, translated by John and Charlotte Stanley, University of California Press, 1969, pp. ix-xxxix.

[*In the following excerpted foreward and introduction to Sorel's* The Illusions of Progress, *Nisbet and Stanley, respectively, examine Sorel's view of virtue as action, and attempt to put his work in perspective.*]

TRANSLATOR'S INTRODUCTION

I

Georges Sorel is known to English and American readers mainly through his ***Reflections on Violence*** which, aside from one small work,[1] is until now the only one of his dozen books to have been translated. It is not difficult to understand why this is so; the ***Reflections*** appeared at a time when there was intense interest in the treatment of socialism, and the work's militant stand against rationalism conformed to the temper of the times. Today, the idea of the creative role of violence in social movements is of great interest to students of contemporary events. Even the title of Sorel's work is a bit sensational.

As a consequence of this rather one-sided exposure, English-language readers regard Sorel primarily as an exponent of anarchosyndicalism and the now famous (or infamous) myth of the general strike. It is true that some of the narrow impressions have been corrected in the course of several recent American works[2] but, however competent, these treatments correct the misunderstandings or superficial impressions of Sorel only with the greatest difficulty. Even in France, many of Sorel's own lesser-known works are relatively unread, and a considerable amount of oversimplified thinking about him remains. Jean-Paul Sartre, for example, recently dismissed Sorel's writings as "fascist utterances,"[3] a statement that, despite any particle of truth it may contain, is equivalent to condemning the *Communist Manifesto* as Bolshevik propaganda. Sorel's writings, however offensive they may be to us, must be studied on their own merits.

Interpreting Sorel is not an easy thing to do. He is a poor writer. His organization is bad; one idea is thrown on top of another helter-skelter, and Sorel thought it desirable to keep his writings difficult; the reader has to work in order to understand him. But the translators believe that the presentation in English of another of his important works is an excellent way to facilitate study of this important thinker. This particular work, published originally in 1908 as ***Les Illusions du progrès,*** was selected for a number of reasons. The idea of progress is of great interest to contemporary scholars and it is partly for this reason that the ***Illusions of Progress*** along with the ***Reflections*** is considered Sorel's most interesting and influential work.[4] This is why it is the one work that should be read by students and scholars of the history of the idea of progress, as well as of Sorel's ideas.

The work, however, is more than academic. Because of almost two hundred years of expansion, continuous westward migration, and an almost exclusively liberal rationalist tradition of political thought, the idea of progress has a particular magic for Americans. Rare indeed is the politician who does not invoke the great "progress" we have made and even rarer the State of the Union address or convention keynote speech that does not invoke progress as one of the great purposes in American life. America in fact might be said to be one of the few industrialized nations in the Occident whose citizens are still ardent believers in the idea that the use of human reason produces human betterment or that every new discovery improves the lot of mankind: though the splitting of the atom may end the human race, it will still provide abundant sources of cheap electric power.[5]

Far from American shores, Sorel wrote ***The Illusions of Progress*** at a time in European history when there was not only a general disenchantment with the ideas that led Gustave Eiffel to build the tallest monument in Europe, but with the very concept of rationality itself. The new studies in psychology, plus a sense that fantastic opulence was devoid of any taste or refinement, produced an awareness of decadence and immorality. Reason and science had not emancipated man; they had enslaved and debased him. In Sorel's own case this awareness was confirmed by his observations of the very forces that he at first regarded as being the saviors of European civilization. The liberals and socialists had disillusioned him by their disgraceful behavior during the Dreyfus affair, and it was this disaffection that led to Sorel's opposition to the mainstream of French radicalism. To Sorel, the Dreyfusards were not really interested in socialist reconstruction. He observed[6] that many of them had motives of personal ambition in supporting the beleaguered French officer. Sorel thought that the radicals, far from being interested in reforming the order of things, merely wanted a portion of that same order for themselves. They wanted power, not a more virtuous society; or at least they confused personal success with the success of the social revolution, when in fact their achievements consisted primarily in strengthening the existing order.

Consequently, Sorel spent a good portion of his intellectual career waging a two-front war against the agents of European capitalism and those of parliamentary socialism. Part of the difficulty, as Sorel saw it, was that both capitalism and reform socialism shared the same liberal rationalist assumptions that many of the European intellectuals began to question at the turn of the century. At the base of these assumptions, according to Sorel, lay the idea of progress.

It is particularly interesting that someone with Sorel's background should call the idea of progress into question. Born into a middle-class French family in 1847, Sorel was educated at France's prestigious *Ecole Polytechnique* and later he went to work as a government engineer. Engineering was not his first love, however, and he retired early in 1892. It was only after his retirement that he did most of his writing. To whatever degree his personal experience led him to a disenchantment with existing institutions, Sorel certainly did not allow a genuine respect for scientific progress to obscure his skepticism of an idea that went far beyond technical sophistication. Sorel knew that the idea of progress arose and flourished in a technological age, but he was aware that the idea spread far beyond the more efficient construction of highways or the multiplication of more efficient means of production. For he rightly thought that the idea of progress was a kind of guiding ideology or myth (in the pejorative sense) of the age—an ideology that had far-reaching political consequences.

II

In order to explain Sorel's view of the idea of progress, we should compare the idea of simple improvement or technological sophistication with the idea of progress in modern times. In order to do this it might be fruitful to leave Sorel and to discuss briefly three works that maintain that Sorel's understanding of the idea of progress—the modern understanding—actually was held in antiquity. Following this discussion, an analysis of what is meant by "ideology" will be attempted so that we can discuss how Sorel views the "ideology of progress."

The late Professor Ludwig Edelstein contended that the Greeks and Romans had an idea of progress which Edelstein defined with Arthur O. Lovejoy as "a tendency inherent in nature or in man to pass through a regular sequence of stages of development in past, present, and future, the later stages being—with perhaps occasional retardation—superior to the earlier."[7]

If this general definition of progress is what one might call "developmental improvement," it is easy to establish that some of the ancients did believe in progress. It is certainly not true, as one scholar has asserted, that the "ancients looked upon change with dread because it was identified with calamity."[8] To take one note-worthy example, Aristotle regarded the development of the polis as change, and this change was regarded as natural and good; that is, that the polis was both better and in one sense more "natural" than earlier and more primitive forms of political organization. If this kind of thinking is what Mr. Edelstein regards as progress, then the Greeks most certainly believed in it.

But it is fair to say that the modern idea of progress is more than the natural tendency toward developmental improvement (which is the essence of the Lovejoy-Edelstein definition). For in Sorel's time, and even today, the idea of progress was both a law of historical development, a philosophy of history, and as a consequence also a political philosophy. It combined a descriptive analysis of history with a philosophical position that this development was right and good, and this position was used, as we shall see, for political purposes.

Now, the Lovejoy definition is vague enough to entail the possibility of the modern formulation being included in it. It is broad enough to include historical, philosophical, and political analysis. But Edelstein makes it quite clear at the beginning of the work that "the definition of progress with which the historian begins cannot be that of the philosopher."[9] Thus any example of recognizing piece-meal improvement in any one field is taken by Edelstein to mean a concept of progress. To be sure, he implies that the criterion for improvement can be either piecemeal or total: "The criterion of improvement can be physical survival, the increase in material riches, or even novelty itself, moral advance, intellectual improvement, or greater happiness. Improvement can be looked for in all sectors of life or in a few alone."[10] But it is quite clear from all of his examples that piecemeal progress was the only kind of improvement that the ancients regarded as possible; it virtually excluded the all-encompassing total view of improvement characteristic of the modern view of progress.

In order to understand the modern viewpoint more completely, it is profitable to examine briefly the view of another author who asserts that the ancients went beyond a piecemeal view of progress and approached the modern view. In *The Open Society and Its Enemies,* Professor Karl Popper says that Aristotle's teleological view constituted part of the roots of the Hegelian school of modern progressivism. By this Popper means that Aristotle's "progressivism" was based on the Stagirite's notion of ends or final causes. The cause of anything is also the end toward which the movement aims, and this aim is good. The essence of anything that develops is identical with the purpose or end toward which it develops.[11] Aristotle uses biological analogies: the teleology of the boy is manhood; if we switch and extend this biological analysis to the political arena, we can say that the end toward which the village develops is the most natural and the highest form of organization: the polis.

Popper says that the doctrine of ends or final causes leads to the "historicist" idea of a historical fate or inescapable destiny which can be used to justify all kinds of horrible institutions such as slavery[12] because they are inevitable. It is true that this "historicist" view that events are inevitable (and to a limited extent predictable) is essential to the modern view of progress. But it is doubtful that Aristotle's doctrine of final causes was as deterministic as Popper implies. Determinism is historical, and even Popper is constrained to admit that Aristotle was not interested in historical trends and made no *direct* contribution to historicism.[13] Determinism aside, Aristotle did not see the growth of the city as being synonymous with either moral or technological growth. Technology had reached perfection in some areas and stood in need of further coordination in others.[14] Furthermore, the growth of the political institutions of the city did not *necessarily* entail a corresponding improvement in morality. Thus Aristotle took care to draw the distinction between the "good man" on the one hand and the "good citizen" on the other; that is, that the good man and the good citizen were identical only in the best city.[15] Theorists of progress, on the other hand, tend to regard moral, technical, and political development as an interrelated whole.

Indeed, the separation of morality from what we call "history" today is one of the distinguishing characteristics of ancient times, assuming that the ancients had a theory of history at all. It is left to Eric A. Havelock in his *The Liberal Temper in Greek Politics*[16] to put forth the view that the Sophistic idea that virtue can be taught possessed the essential qualities of the modern identification of history and virtue. Havelock starts his thesis with the example of the myth of Prometheus, in which fire was stolen from the hearth of Zeus for the benefit of man.[17] But there is no evidence that this theory is like the modern one. For one thing, as has been pointed out, Prometheus' myth reveals no infinite progress, which is more characteristic of modernity. Prometheus' punishment turns progress into a great illusion, a false hope which is ultimately destroyed. More important, the Sophistic viewpoint that virtue can be taught does not itself prove progress in the modern sense. Havelock maintains that Protagoreanism rationalizes an age of social progress.[18] And it does this in rather the same way that Pericles extols Athens in the Funeral Oration.[19] But again, little indeed can be said about progress in antiquity beyond a vague sense of technical improvement; it lacks a sense of history. As Leo Strauss persuasively argues, "Liberalism implies a philosophy of history. 'History' does not mean in this context a kind of inquiry or the outcome of an inquiry but rather the object of an inquiry or a 'dimension of reality.' Since the Greek word from which 'history' is derived does not have the latter meaning, philological discipline would prevent one from ascribing to any Greek thinker a philosophy of history at least before one has laid the proper foundation for such an ascription."[20] As he points out, there is no evidence from the Greek sources that the Sophists or any other school possessed what we would call a philosophy of history—a philosophy that is peculiar to the modern idea of progress. And the Platonic dialogues, it may be assumed, would have gone out of their way to record such views if they had occurred, since progress is so easily attacked and is so antithetical to the Platonic view of ultimate reality as unchanging.

Finally, even if it can be said that ancient historians themselves had a philosophy of history, that philosophy if it was at all progressive was so only in the larger context of a cyclical view of history such as is found in Polybius. It remains to ask, however, just what the modern philosophy of history is. In order to do this let us say what it is not. We can do this if we return to Professor Edelstein's book to help us to enumerate the half dozen characteristics that clearly differentiate modern progress from the notions of improvement or "development" which occur in antiquity.

Instead of focusing on the Sophists, Edelstein turns his attention to Seneca, who is singled out as giving a clearer and more comprehensive view of progress than any other ancient thinker and one that, as a consequence, is closest to the view of progress held in the nineteenth century. In Seneca, the door to the future is opened. Mental acumen and study will bring forth new and presently unknown discoveries. Progress has not only led to the present but will be extended into the future. According to Edelstein, this will be so not only in the field of science but in all fields of human activity.[21]

Edelstein asserts that by linking all branches of human activity together, Seneca came closer to the modern theory of progress than anyone else.[22] Now, it is true that for modern progressives, progress is not, as we have repeatedly said, a piecemeal process but takes place in all fields, intellectual, moral, political, technical; it extends to liberty of thought as well as to the development of virtue; to science as well as to the eradication of superstition and prejudice. In this way Seneca embodies the first two principles of modern progress.

1. Progress today is multifaceted; each field of human endeavor is looked upon as a member of a team of horses; each animal is held in harness with the others and all advance in the same direction, down the same road. To Edelstein, though not as much to Bury,[23] Seneca fulfilled this view.

2. Most of the thinkers of the past did not speculate on the future as much as comment on the development of the present, but Seneca looked to future development, which is definitely characteristic of the modern view.[24]

There are four other qualities that neither Seneca nor other ancients mentioned in their idea on development.

3. Despite his forward-looking perspective, Seneca and most of the other ancients (including Lucretius and the atomists) were reconciled to the annihilation of the world.[25] Though annihilation was viewed by them as virtually certain, in modern progressive thinking annihilation is open to question. Optimism pervades modern progressivism, not only about the future but about all things human.

4. Not only are modern progressives open to doubt on annihilation, but as a consequence they are open to the idea of "indefinite perfectibility,"[26] an optimism that is shared by no known ancient.

5. Though Seneca views annihilation as an eventual certainty and holds that all the great accomplishments of man will be abolished, a new civilization will arise on the ashes of the old one. In this respect, insofar as he has any historical theory at all, Seneca's view is cyclical: civilizations rise and fall, and this viewpoint is almost universal in ancient thought. All advances in civilization are preludes to a subsequent decline or ultimate end. What little independent identity the idea of "history" had at all, it had in the form of a wheel that, in one or another respect, returned to the same place in the order of things. Modern progressivism is a different approach. The latter depicts history as a line—occasionally broken to be sure—destined to rise in an upward direction of indefinite perfectibility. This linear rather than cyclical concept of history is perhaps the most important single attribute of the contemporary view of progress.

6. In addition to all the above characteristics, modern progressivism has an aura of religious certainty about it. In ancient times history meant the possibility of chaos or tragedy, and this was accompanied by a feeling of resignation against the idea of *Moira*, roughly translated as "fate," which possessed a certain mysterious, unknown

quality.[27] The modern view of progressive history, on the other hand, sees future progress as not only inevitable but, to a limited extent, predictable on the basis of rational calculation of existing data. It is this character of inevitability which contributes most strongly to the modern views of historical determinism and sees social science as a science of prediction.[28] Events had always been characterized by some form of necessity, but only modernity has made this necessity into a virtue.

The idea of progress had its origin in the seventeenth century and matured in the age of Enlightenment. Perhaps no better summaries of the idea of progress are found than in the concluding paragraphs of the *Outline of the Historical View of the Progress of the Human Mind* by the archetypal proponent of the modern idea of progress, the Marquis de Condorcet. In this work, Condorcet puts forth all six of the concepts that make it a new idea in the eighteenth century (though not originating with Condorcet) and an idea that characterizes the following age. (1) Progress occurs in all fields; (2) is projected into the future; (3) rejects inevitable annihilation and the pessimism that goes with it; (4) renders civilization indefinitely perfectible; (5) has a linear view of history; (6) regards the future as having certain inevitable patterns which are calculable.

Condorcet sloughs off the prospect of an apocalyptic end of the world as:

> . . . impossible to pronounce on either side [and] which can only be realized in an epoch when the human species will *necessarily* have a degree of knowledge of which our shortsighted understanding can scarcely form an idea . . . By supposing it actually to take place there would result from it nothing alarming either to the happiness of the human race or of its *indefinite perfectibility* if we consider that prior to this period the progress of reason will have walked hand in hand with that of the sciences; that the absurd prejudices of superstition will have ceased to infuse into morality a harshness that corrupts and degrades instead of purifying and exalting it.[29]

Now, this statement does more than describe what we would call "development." It means more than the sophistication of the arts and sciences. By joining a vast number of human activities together and asserting that moral improvement will result from this union, Condorcet depicts the attitude of nearly perfect optimism without which the modern theory of progress would not have arisen. Since progress now means improvement in all fields, the history of all human activity—of mankind itself—is the history of progress. At this point "history" and "progress" become virtually synonymous; so Condorcet opens the future to a definite improvement in all fields, and this improvement is associated with knowledge or "enlightenment." This ever-expanding enlightenment becomes part of the historical process itself; further, this enlightenment not only should take place but, because history is linear, it *will* take place. Progress is both a pattern of development perceived through historical observation and a law of human inevitability. It is this law of inevitable progress which produces the most extraordinary optimism. Here is Condorcet's concluding paragraph, written shortly before he was driven to suicide by the Terror:

> How admirably calculated is this view of the human race, emancipated from chains, *released alike from the dominion of chance,* as well as from the enemies of progress, and advancing with firm and *inevitable* step in the paths of truth, to console the philosopher lamenting his errors, the flagrant acts of injustice, the crimes with which the earth is still polluted! It is the contemplation of this prospect that rewards him for all his effort to assist the progress of reason and the establishment of liberty. He dares to regard these efforts as part of the eternal chain of the destiny of mankind; and in this persuasion he finds true delight of virtue, the pleasure of having performed a durable service which no vicissitude will ever destroy. This sentiment is the *asylum* into which he *retires,* and to which the memory of his prosecutors cannot follow him: he unites himself in imagination with man restored to his rights, delivered from oppression, and proceeding with rapid strides in the paths of happiness; he forgets his own misfortunes while his thoughts are thus employed; he lives no longer to adversity, calumny, and malice, but becomes the associate of those wiser and more fortunate beings whose enviable condition he so earnestly contributed to produce.[30]

It is this attribution of an independent character and dignity to history which converted it from a method of inquiry to an object that had such revolutionary consequences. Despite Sorel's contention that the Enlightenment ignored historical necessity, the idea of linear development and advancement in all fields gave "history" a power and coherence it had never attained before. By coming together in all fields progress meant the history of humanity; by becoming linear this advancement was made infinitely good. By becoming infinitely good it strengthened history itself and thereby enabled "history" to become a source of political legitimacy. As long as history was cyclical in nature it could not be used to legitimize a regime. Cycles meant not only improvement but a subsequent decline and fall. Therefore one could not use "history" to justify a regime if the history of that regime would result in ultimate disaster. That is why the ancients found it impossible to justify their best regimes as historical products. Plato's *Republic* as well as Aristotle's ideal state in *The Politics* are not historical products; they are in fact specifically anti-historical because history means imperfection and tragedy. The etymology of the word "Utopia" as a "city of nowhere" underscores the character of the *Republic* whose discussion of "history" ensues only before and after the *Republic* itself is discussed.[31] It is "reason" or at least "reasonableness" which justifies the best regime, and this reason never becomes identified with "history." Condorcet and the *philosophes,* by identifying history with the progress of enlightenment, make reason itself into a historical product.

As a consequence of the idea of progress, then, it was no longer merely reason that served to justify regimes, but "history" itself. In order more fully to understand the concept of legitimacy, we should note that it is that quality or qualities which lend credibility to and secure obedience for a government or regime and its institutions. This concept depends of course on our criteria of legitimacy and morality. Utilitarians, for example, view a regime as "legitimate" if it strives for the maximum of social pleasures. Whatever the school of thought, however, theories of political legitimacy are usually accompanied by what one writer has called the quality of "beneficence";[32] of producing certain benefits which other regimes do not do as well, whether it be order, security, pleasures, reason, or what not. But the quality of beneficence could not be attributed to "history" until "history" became an object as well as a method of study, and until this object became devoid of any concept of ultimate decline and fall—that is, of a cyclical nature. When this cyclical aspect of history was removed, and when modernity viewed history as a universally progressive phenomenon, "history" as such assumed the character of an independent object and became possessed of a quality of infinite beneficence for the first time. It was at this point that the idea of history came increasingly to dominate political discourse: if a government is an actual entity, it is viewed as a historical event and as such the "product" of historical development; if "history," is beneficient, then so is the regime. As a product of "history," it becomes the best possible regime, while the best regime (as opposed to the best possible regime) becomes the *end* of the historical process. But the difference between the best possible regime and the best regime (e.g., Plato's Cretan city of the *Laws* versus the *Republic*) is obscured, with the virtual disappearance of the latter. The best regime, in ancient times, assumed the qualities of definition. Plato admitted that the Republic might never be attained in the world of becoming (i.e., history), which is why the most brilliant of the theorists on progress, Karl Marx, could proclaim himself an anti-Utopian.[33] As long as a regime could distinguish between the good man and the good citizen, as long as history was viewed at most as a story, a story of disaster and tragedy, a certain plurality in human affairs was axiomatic. History meant chaos and this meant a complicated clash of motives and events. But when the idea of "history" became linear and was coupled with indefinite improvement, tragedy was replaced by a series of minor setbacks on the path to perfection. Heroes were replaced by "reason" or "world historical individuals"[34] who became great, not through great deeds but by their ability to grasp historical necessity. Fate, which had the character of great mystery, was replaced by "history," a history in which everything is either explained or explainable. Tragedy could be explained as a reasonable (necessary) part of the greater plan of historical fulfillment.[35]

In the world in which tragedy becomes rational and in which everything can be explained, truth assumes a broad unitary character. By becoming historical it becomes part of a broad continuum which obscures the difference between what is and what ought to be, by making both part of the same line extending between past and future. If perfection is possible in this world, events can attain the same unity which had heretofore been characteristic only of Utopias that had in ancient times been explicitly ahistorical. Now, instead of Plato's unitary city, history itself provides man with a sense of oneness with other men and with events themselves.

III

The unitary advance which the linear notion of progress was to make so important in the century following the French Revolution was to extend far beyond society and morality and reach into the province of thought itself. If history was viewed as an extension of all fields of human activity, not the least of which was the "progress of the human mind" itself, the exalted place that "enlightenment" originally had in Condorcet's theory of progress was to give way to the notion that knowledge itself is just another factor in historical progress. For what is "thought" but another human activity that can be "explained" historically? At this point philosophy, which had always meant love of wisdom, began to be simply another pattern of human behavior. The use of prudence which was the way political philosophy confronted corporeal reality gave way to a science of historical prediction; and political philosophy, which had heretofore been a method of inquiry about why we should obey, was transformed into a study of the historical origins and background of ideas. This development is credited to Condorcet's near-contemporary Destutt de Tracy, who in his *Eléments d'Idéologie* (1801-1815) calls for a "science of ideas."

The importance of this development should be noted primarily for those who do not understand the fundamental character of the change of thinking which converted philosophy into what is called "ideology": the significance of explaining all thought in terms of its historical background had the effect of minimizing the importance of philosophy altogether; that is, of denuding it of any intrinsic value and replacing it with explanations of its place in "history." Thus the liberal idea of, say, limited government was not discussed on the basis of the merits of limiting sovereignty, but was viewed instead as a rationalization or justification of certain social interests—in this case of a dominant capitalist class preventing factory legislation, etc. This tendency is found most prominently in the thought of Karl Marx, who asserted even before he wrote the *Communist Manifesto* that ideas were the products of material relations.[36]

It is easy to see, under these circumstances, that the idea of history itself becomes the only viable basis of political legitimacy. If, as in the writings of Marx, all ideas except one's own are placed on the same plane as social classes or conventions, they become as ephemeral as any social phenomena; they pass into nonexistence, just as so much social data changes with those historical preconditions that are proclaimed to have brought them into being.

Thus an idea is "true" only if it is close to actual "historical conditions." If it is not proximate to the historical conditions, it is "false consciousness." For this reason Marx was quite consistent in maintaining the truth of capitalism as compared to feudalism insofar as the former represented a more "advanced" stage of historical development; but that the idea of capitalism in a sense became "false consciousness" when confronted with socialism, while the latter would become false after giving way to communism. Under this approach to ideas, thought loses any permanent quality which distinguishes it from society itself.[37]

But the notion of ideology, particularly that which is found in Marxism, is further complicated by the appreciation of competing ideas within the same historical periods. Thus capitalism is the ideology of the dominant class, whereas the proletariat whose ideology should be socialism manifests "false consciousness" if it accepts the capitalist argument. Even the temporary efficacy of ideas is weakened when the progress of history is not only used to explain ideas, but is turned against them. For if ideas are only excuses for interests and conscious rationalizations for exploitation, then the idea is not only made temporary but is thrust aside; the idea becomes a mask to be ripped off, if the true face of the proponents is to be discovered.[38] Ideas are changed from being temporary explanations to false consciousness and from false consciousness into unconscious falsehood.[39]

The profound misunderstanding that has arisen with the contemporary use of the term "ideology" should be viewed in this context. An "ideology" is not simply a political idea such as "capitalism" or "Socialism," but is rather a justification or rationalization for a particular group in society. In this respect Marx could not have viewed an ideology as merely a political idea. Rather it is a *product* of history; as such, only the idea (socialism) which is closest to historical reality is legitimate, and since history progresses, each succeeding idea is more legitimate. Under these conditions, only the progress of history itself can become the ultimate legitimizing idea and the study of ideas becomes historical. But if ideas are studied historically, then the study of ideology is really not a study but a method. Here then *ideology* as such must be differentiated from the ideological *method* which is the actual process of unmasking or explaining the "real" or historical basis of political philosophy and all other thought.[40]

IV

Since the imprimatur of historical progress is the one legitimizing concept that the proponents of the concept of ideology can accept (at least if they are consistent), it was only a matter of time before the idea of progress itself would be brought under the microscope of the *ideological method.* The rather interesting quality of Georges Sorel's ***The Illusions of Progress*** is that the ideological method, a consequence of the idea of progress, is itself used against the idea of progress and with it the whole idea of historical inevitability.

As Sorel pictures it, however, progress is an ideology which is not part of Marxism, but a bourgeois creation. His purpose in writing the book is to oppose the bourgeoisie by demolishing "this super-structure of conventional lies and to destroy the prestige still accorded to the 'metaphysics' of the men who vulgarize the vulgarization of the eighteenth century."[41]

Methodologically, the concept of ideology has many difficulties. Not the least of these is determining the exact relationship that ideas have to the material conditions out of which they (allegedly) arise. For example, do these conditions "cause" ideas to arise purely and simply; or do ideas arise independently and then become taken over and "used" by particular interests or institutions?[42] Sorel seems to opt for the latter explanation. This is an important part of Sorel's thinking, for it allows him to attribute to ideas themselves a causative influence—an independence—which might raise eyebrows in more orthodox Marxian circles. Thus Sorel is able to say that the concept of progress could be traced back, not to material conditions but to a purely literary conflict between ancient and modern writers; or that the Voltairian spirit also disappeared as the result of a literary revolution and not on the day that the bourgeoisie somehow "decided" that its interests necessitated a return to the church. The latter explanation Sorel rejects as an "ideological and highly superficial explanation."[43]

Furthermore, Sorel maintains that the creator of an idea is as free as an artist working with new materials, but that ideas, once formed, establish links with other current ideas and thereby become part of the predominant doctrine of a given period. This period will find in that doctrine certain meanings and interpretations that may be quite different from the initial intention of the author. Similarly, other classes in other periods may take yet another meaning from the idea. Primary importance is granted to what others see as only secondary; where some see only literature, others see philosophy. Thus, the same idea is upheld in radically varying ways according to the social position (class) of the people upholding it. This is as true for the doctrine of progress (which changes form as it is adopted by different periods: it becomes more deterministic in the nineteenth century) as it is for Marxism, which is looked upon by parliamentary socialists with far less seriousness than by the founders of the doctrine.

There is a definite importance to Sorel's attributing a certain independence to moral ideas. Sorel was a moralist; this is the single most outstanding trait of the man, and no explication of his ideas is possible until it is emphasized that the fundamental and underlying principle behind most of his writing was a genuine despair at the moral decadence of modern Europe. Moral rebirth is possible only under conditions that lie outside the idea of progress and the social institutions that foster the idea.

Thus it is imperative that Sorel not regard morality as simply the product of historical forces but rather grant it some autonomy. He maintains, therefore, that the lowering of the moral level of Europe was not due to the persecution of the Jansenists but that it was the other way around.[44]

Sorel's use of the Marxian theory of ideology recalls to mind his notion of *diremptions:* "to examine certain parts of a condition or event without taking into account all of the ties which connect them to the whole, to determine in some manner the character of their activity by isolating them."[45] The difference between Sorel's use of ideology and Marx's is that Marx views ideas as necessarily part of a social whole, much as a physician regards parts of the body, while Sorel views ideology as a method without necessarily relating it either to the whole movement in human society—the totality out of which it arises. The difference between Sorel's diremptive method and Marx's theories is that for the latter the theory of ideology (as well as his other ideas) is viewed as part of a total system, a world view (*weltanschauung*). Ideology must be viewed in the context of this total system. For Sorel, it was desirable to extract certain parts of the system and merely "use" them for the purposes of greater understanding of phenomena. It was therefore not necessary to accept the total system, and obviously Sorel does not accept all aspects of Marxism.

But Sorel still takes care to dissociate Marx from his more simplistic followers and to assert that Marxist ideological methods are devoid of simplified notions and vulgar determinism. In this way, Sorel avoids the pitfalls of ideology and the ideological method. By dissociating Marx from vulgar historicism, he can employ constructively one of the aspects of the total theory without having to accept the total theory itself.

Sorel sees Marx's followers as putting forth a far more unitary system than Marx himself,[46] though he says later that Marxism does indeed share many of the characteristics of the unitary progressive view of the world, which the bourgeoisie first put forth in the notion of progress. The idea of progress has fostered a false sense of social unity in society, and this unity has gone a long way in contributing to social decadence. Sorel's purpose is therefore to use the ideological *method* (unmasking) to break down an ideology (progress). Sorel rarely faces the fact that the ideological method sprang forth from the very ideology he is trying to destroy. He admits it only covertly by playing down Marx's progressivism. Anyway, by using the diremptive method, the concept of ideology can be separated from the idea of progress; the ideological method is independent (diremptive) from the total system that he is trying to destroy.

In fact the whole purpose in Sorel's writing on progress is to separate the idea from other ideas and to break the idea itself down into its component parts rather than to build up a unified structure or system. As T. E. Hulme wrote some years ago in the introduction to his translation of ***Reflections on Violence,*** Sorel saw modern democracy as inheriting most of the ideas of progress which were originally put forth in the seventeenth and eighteenth centuries. As Hulme notes, modern democracy, in seeing itself as the product of undifferentiated progress in society, fails to distinguish between democracy and progress. Similarly, Sorel's fight against the "radicals" of parliamentary socialism was that they were part of the same movement: they too saw no difference between democracy, socialism, and the working-class movement.[47] The idea of progress, in welding all these notions into an interrelated totality, has sapped them of their vitality and moral efficacy. This totality regards itself as possessing moral force; it is actually devoid of morality. It produces only smugness and helps to obscure the truth that contemporary society is not part of the natural order of things.

Sorel's purpose in the ***Illusions of Progress,*** and in much of his other writings, is to show that moral superiority has long ago been separated from political progressivism (assuming they were ever joined) and has attached itself to the socialism of independent producers.[48] In order to keep this superiority intact, the new men of virtue must retain full independence from all the ideas and institutions which are associated with the idea of progress—an idea whose very purpose is to obscure these distinctions and the social conflict which would result from their being made. This is another reason why Sorel does not regard Marx, a theorist of class conflict and strife, as a progressive thinker.

Sorel tries to demonstrate that progress embraces the various institutions of bourgeois society, and it enables these institutions to encompass and thereby to dominate all of the various disparate elements of society into an apparent unity. Rather than representing the natural order of things, progress is in reality part of the ideology of the modern institutions of domination.

The first aspect of this domination has been the quality of *continuity*. Sorel accepts Tocqueville's version of the French Revolution as having, in reality, strengthened rather than weakened the institutions that grew up in the ancien régime. The ancien régime, bourgeois liberal democracy, and the modern "welfare state" of parliamentary socialism are all different manifestations of the growing power of the institutions of the modern state. Both liberal democracy and parliamentary socialism strengthen the state.

The continuity leads to the second aspect of domination: the elite of one era has survived and strengthened itself in another. Being the ideology of the "victors" of an epoch, the idea of progress serves to mask the interests of the dominant class which inherits power. Democracy itself masks its opposite for, as Sorel says, "nothing is more aristocratic than democracy." Thus parliamentary socialists are compared to officials whom Napoleon made into a nobility and who labored to strengthen the state bequeathed by the ancien régime.[49] Parliamentary socialism strengthens the state machinery and the economic powers of the state through an elite of intellectual and political professionals, civil servants, hangers on, etc.

In Sorel, the two concepts of elitism and the power of the state go hand in hand. As long as the workers accept the idea of unity in the progressive state, the latter is legitimized, and true moral rebirth is impossible because the domination of the old elite is preserved. Furthermore, the ruling oligarchy by flattery and progressive rhetoric encourages mediocrity in the masses and saps them of their virtue—the simple fighting vigor characteristic of the early Greeks and Romans.[50]

Associated with the idea of continuity in the elite domination of the state is Sorel's third concept of domination; that is, that the idea of progress is essentially a conservative force in society. Instead of emphasizing its revolutionary implications, Sorel depicts the idea of progress as legitimizing each strengthening of the state. But since the state keeps the same characteristics throughout these changes, progress really legitimizes the status quo. *Plus ça change, plus c'est la même chose.* Sorel's case might have been bolstered if he had further examined the lives of the proponents of progress. Often they are quite as conservatives as Turgot whose "boldness" is responsible for the rise of the third estate but who could remain a loyal servant of the French monarchy—that enlightened despotism which Tocqueville viewed as the real origin of the French Revolution—and who could approve of the hanging of a number of rioters. Condorect, Turgot's less able successor, could proclaim, "I am a Royalist" only shortly before his more evangelical wife urged him into becoming a moderate liberal (Girondin). The postrevolutionary progressives, St. Simon and Comte (and indirectly Hegel), were even more conservative, being sometime supporters of their respective contemporary regimes.[51]

But Sorel is aware that the idea of progress can produce not only conservatism but a certain political "quietism." Why act at all if progress makes change somehow "inevitable" anyway? Thus Sorel criticizes Marx for the excessiveness of his Hegelian biases, which produce a kind of passivity in the socialist movement itself. Marx's materialist revision of Hegelian dialectics constitutes the Marxian version of progress. Thus American socialists have greeted the success of trusts with enthusiasm because, according to these socialists, trusts represent the final stages of capitalism before its deliverance to socialism. This rationalist construction of history was, to Sorel, a falsehood. (It is interesting to note that a decade after Sorel's death the German Marxists could proclaim *Nach Hitler uns!*—after Hitler, us—in which German Marxists actually lent support to the Nazi movement in expectation that it too was a "stage of development.")[52]

The kind of passive mentality produced by the idea of progress is one of the bases of Sorel's criticism of the radical movement. Progress is a total "law" of human development as well as an ideology; as such it is a rationalistic construction of the human mind which imposes a false sense of unity in society itself. The reason for this is that it is usually rationalistic and positivistic in its base of formulation, and both rationalism and positivism confine themselves to what is at hand. What is shown to the observer is what is true and what is true is what is shown. This circular unity of thought prevents action because the latter depends on breaking out of what is already given; on striking out in new directions. Action is possible only if a judgment is made that is adverse to the system. However, if all judgments are made on the level of historical analysis and all events legitimized as historically necessary, everything is permissible, including conservatism. Here, as one modern philosopher has said, all action and thought become "one-dimensional."[53] No distinction is made between what is and what ought to be.

Sorel's criticism of modern social scientists can be seen in this light. Rationalist progressives want to see logical development patterns in everything. As such, "development" is often seen as part of a total scheme of things. All of society is looked upon as being swept along in the progress of events. Modern social scientists, regarded by Sorel as handmaidens of the bourgeoisie, earn their living by placing very different things on the same plane from the love of logical simplicity; sexual morality, for example, is reduced to the equitable relations between contracting parties and the family code to the regulation of debts.[54] Thus, throughout his works, Sorel directs barbs at the esteemed professors of social science or the "learned sociologists," the "little science," etc.

But whereas the social scientists see primarily a progressive unity, Sorel says that reality is manifested more in chaotic struggle. Rather than viewing the entire world as representing some stage of what is today called "development,"[55] Sorel sees history as a sea of decline *(décadence)* punctuated by occasional moments of historical greatness. Only at exceptional periods of human history have manifestations of greatness *(grandeur)* occurred, and it is quite obvious that Sorel does not regard his contemporary Europe as manifesting any characteristic of "greatness." Greatness occurs only at those rare times when, through heroic acts of human will, men have "forced" history. Sorel's syndicalism, as well as his occasional flirtations with Leninism and fascism, must be regarded as an attempt to find some movement or individual which would personify the new elements of greatness. For example, Lenin is able like Marx himself to combine action with thought. But it should be noted that, unlike Lenin, Sorel from a distance attached great importance to the Soviet workers' councils, which possessed many of the same characteristics that Sorel saw in the French syndicates.[56] These institutions Sorel saw as alternatives to the harbinger of modern decadence, the modern state. They represented a total revolution or a sweeping aside of the state itself, and they represented the embodiment of a new vitality—Bergson's *élan vital*—a life force which sustained itself through incessant struggle.[57]

The reason for this is that these institutions placed themselves outside of the old order. They have effectively destroyed the false principle of unity and replaced it with a principle of struggle. The same principle of struggle Sorel saw as embodied in the moral fiber of great regimes: of ancient pre-Socratic Greece, of the early Roman Republic, of early Christianity, and of the Napoleonic armies. These periods were not corrupted by the sophistry of false philosophy. Rather their virtue was brought forth by the necessity of action and it is through action itself more than any other activity that "man discovers his own best qualities: courage, patience, disregard of death, devotion to glory, and the good of his fellows, in one word: his virtue."[58]

It follows, ironically enough, then, that Sorel juxtaposes the false unity of the modern progressives, which legitimizes the parasitic life of the ruling classes by obscuring all struggle, to the Homeric virtues of the early ancients whose unity was solidified by the action of constant struggle with enemy cities. The closest equivalent of the latter is the modern class war.

The ideology of progress and democracy, once free of Hegelian idealism, leads to the separation of thought from action. In order to reunite action with human thought, a radically different type of thinking is necessary. The unity of thought and action is brought about, not through a new rational ideology, but through myth. It is characteristic of myth—as opposed to other types of thinking—that it obscures distinctions; that is because it is similar to a tale told to children and is incapable of separation of fact from fantasy. In his revolutionary myth of the general strike, then, Sorel sees a modern version which has some of the heroic qualities of Homeric myths. But he emphasizes both the vagueness and the psychological nature of the myth which he defines as a group of images, which by intuition alone and before any considered analysis has been made, is "capable of evoking, as an undivided whole, the mass of sentiments which correspond to different manifestations of war taken by socialism against modern society." All logicality and rationality have been set aside and replaced by what we would likely call "impulses." "It is the myth in its entirety which is alone important."[59]

To Sorel, myths cannot be interpreted as being similar to ideology. Ideology is essentially a pejorative term. Sorel views it as a defense mechanism which, once exposed, is destined to fall by being revealed as false consciousness when it becomes surpassed by historical events. But Sorel's myth is the answer to the problem of ideology. The myth is indestructible because by virtue of its own vagueness and its own nonrational composition it can change and refine itself in accordance with practical experience. Ideologies are most likely to be surpassed, precisely because their rational characteristics give them a fixed quality which myths do not possess. It is for this reason that Sorel shares Marx's hostility to Utopias and cites Marx in saying that he who draws a blueprint for the future is a reactionary.

But we may raise the interesting question here of whether Sorel, despite his departures from the Marxian notion of ideology, is not contributing further to the denigration of philosophy. Instead of speaking of a rebirth of philosophy and of reason apart from "history," he offers us myths which become further integrated into practical experience and which constitute not "true reason" but impulse. It is Sorel's view of mythology that stands at the core of the accusations leveled against him as a "fascist." As I have stated at the outset of this introduction, such accusations are fruitless: both fascism and Sorel must stand on their own merits, and little can be accomplished by associating one with the other.

The kind of regime actually envisioned by Sorel at the time in which he wrote the ***Illusions of Progress*** (1908) is a regime of producers bound together in their place of work. In the context of their place of work, Sorel respects the idea of a purely technical and economic progress. It is during periods of economic progress, not times of stagnation and decline, that transformations to the new order of things should occur. It is during these times that people best appreciate the artistic basis of technology on the factory floor. Then the productive arts would become infused with the same qualities of mystery and myth which political and religious movements possessed in earlier times. In this same vein, Sorel calls production "the most mysterious form of human activity."[60]

Sorel has an extremely pragmatic view of the world. He insists that by accepting the idea of the general strike, although we know it is a myth, we are proceeding exactly as a physicist does who has complete confidence in his science, although the future will look upon it as antiquated. "It is we who really possess the scientific spirit, while our critics have lost touch with modern science."[61]

Sorel's equation of science and art—the "social poetry" of the general strike—is justified by the idea that both dislike reproducing accepted types and being dominated by the external standards artificially imposed by liberal rationalists. The progressives of liberal rationalism are not really progressives. Constant dynamic improvement in a workshop or in society is only possible if the models of production or of society imposed from above by bureaucratic or scientific "experts" in the social and managerial sciences are thrown aside in favor of the new mythology. "Constant improvement in quality and quantity will be thus assured in a workshop of this kind."[62] It is interesting that a thinker who sets out to debunk the modern idea of progress should conclude the main sections of his two most important works with an affirmation of the material progress of production. It is this constant innovation in the field of production or in everyday experience, carried on *within* the regime of producers, that constitutes Sorel's version of progress. In this sense, Sorel's idea of true progress is almost as necessary to his perspective as the general idea of progress was necessary to the *philosophes.* In one way, Sorel represents the idea of progress run amuck. Much of his work—even after the syndicalist period of his writings—consists in the anguished protests of a progressive who has been betrayed and who places the blame on the men of his time rather than on "history," on the lack of sufficient will to control one's environment and not on "unfavorable social conditions." Sorel's desire to control this environment is certainly an idea he shares with modern liberalism. The trouble with the latter, according to Sorel, is that it has lost its will to do so. Sorel would give the social movement a revived moral basis by showing that the liberal idea of progress is really not identical with virtue; virtue belongs only to those who act.

NOTES

[1] I refer to Irving Louis Horowitz' translation of *La Décomposition du Marxisme* contained in the former's *Radicalism and the Revolt Against Reason* (New York: Humanities Press, 1961). *Reflections on Violence* was published in 1950 by the Free Press with an introduction by Edward Shils. It was translated from *Réflexions sur la violence* in 1920 by T. E. Hulme with three appendixes by J. Roth. Hulme's introduction is available in his *Speculations* (New York: Harvest Books, n.d.), pp. 249 ff.

[2] Most of the works on Sorel in English were written after 1950. The best of the lot, Horowitz, *op. cit.*, was published in 1961. See also Richard Humphrey, *Georges Sorel, Prophet Without Honor, A Study in Anti-Intellectualism* (Cambridge: Harvard, 1951); James Meisel, *The Genesis of Georges Sorel* (Ann Arbor, Michigan, 1953); C. Michael Curtis, *Three Against the Republic* (Princeton University Press, 1959); H. Stuart Hughes, *Consciousness and Society* (New York: Vintage ed., 1961), chaps. 3, 5; Scott Harrison Lyttle, "Georges Sorel: Apostle of Fanaticism," in *Modern France: Problems of the Third and Fourth Republics* (Princeton, N.J., 1951), pp. 264-290. See also the introductory essays by Shils to the *Reflections.* Neal Wood, "Some Reflections on Sorel and Machiavelli," in *Political Science Quarterly*, LXXXIII, March 1968, pp. 76-91, is a correction of James Burnham, *The Machiavellians, Defenders of Freedom* (Chicago: Regnery ed., 1963; first published in 1943).

[3] In his introduction to *The Wretched of the Earth* by Franz Fannon (New York, 1968), p. 14. More important is Sartre's admission that Fannon's writings owe a great deal to Sorel's notion of the creative role of violence. I find it hard to understand why Sartre finds Sorel more "fascist" than Fannon who emphasizes hatred and race more than Sorel does.

[4] Sorel had a profound influence on Camus. See *The Rebel* (New York: Vintage ed., 1956), p. 194. Camus speaks only of the *Illusions of Progress.* See also John Bowle, *Politics and Opinion in the Nineteenth Century* (New York: Oxford, 1967 ed.), p. 403, and H. Stuart Hughes, *Consciousness and Society*, p. 162. Among Sorel's other works are *Contribution à l'étude profane de la Bible* (1889); *Le Procès de Socrate* (1889); *La Ruine du monde antique* (1898); *Introduction à l'économie moderne* (1903); *Le Système historique de Renan* (1906); *La Décomposition du Marxisme, Réflexions sur la Violence,* and this work, *Les Illusions du Progrès,* all of which were published in 1908 at the height of Sorel's syndicalist period and are the only works translated into English; *La Révolution dreyfusienne* (1909); *Matériaux d'une théorie du prolétariat* (1919); *De l'utilité du pragmatisme* (1921); *D'Aristote à Marx* (1935).

[5] For a good example of the modern American view of progress, see George Gallup, *The Miracle Ahead* (New York: Harper, 1965).

[6] Sorel, *La Révolution dreyfusienne* (1909).

[7] Edelstein, *The Idea of Progress in Classical Antiquity* (Baltimore: Johns Hopkins, 1968), p. xi, cites the definition of Arthur O. Lovejoy and George Boas, *Primitivism and Related Ideas in Antiquity, A Documentary History of Primitivism and Related Ideas* (Baltimore, 1935), I, 6. For other works on the idea of progress, see J. B. Bury, *The Idea of Progress* (New York: Dover ed., 1955); Charles Frankel, *The Faith of Reason: The Idea of Progress in the French Enlightenment* (New York, 1948); John Baillie, *The Belief in Progress: A Reevaluation* (London, 1953); Frederick J. Teggart, *Theory and Processes of History* (Berkeley and Los Angeles, 1962) and *The Idea of Progress: A Collection of Readings* (Berkeley, 1949); Ernest Lee Tuveson, *Millennium and Utopia* (New York: Harper, 1964); R. V. Sampson, *Progress in the Age of Reason* (London, 1956). Robert A. Nisbet, *Social Change and History: Aspects of the Western Theory of Development* (New York: Oxford University Press, 1969).

[8] J. Salwyn Schapiro, *Condorcet and the Rise of Liberalism* (New York).

[9] Edelstein, *The Idea of Progress in Antiquity*, pp. xxix-xxx.

[10] *Ibid.*, p. xxix.

[11] Karl Popper, *The Open Society and Its Enemies* (New York: Harper paper ed., 1962), II, 5.

[12] *Ibid.*, pp. 7-8.

[13] *Ibid.*, p. 7.

[14] Edelstein claims that the "perfection" envisaged by Aristotle is perfection in all fields (p. 127), but earlier on he says that Aristotle recognizes that some arts have reached a stage of excellence not to be surpassed, whereas the art of money-making is limitless since acquisition knows no limits. But Edelstein seems to ignore an important matter here. Aristotle distinguishes between sound and unsound forms of acquisition, i.e., acquisition based on selfish desire for gain and the sound type of acquisition which is concerned with *economics,* the art of household management, which is limited by the natural needs of the household. The importance of this distinction with regard to modern progress will become apparent. Modern progress prefers limitless acquisition and

indefinite improvement, whereas Aristotle prefers natural limits. Also, the very notion of the kind of natural end in Aristotle differs from the eschatological visions of Marxist progressives. (For the modern view of limitless acquisition, see Locke's *Second Treatise an Civil, Government*, 31, 37, 50; cf. *Politics*, 1258.)

[15] *Politics*, 1276*b*.

[16] Yale University Press, New Haven, 1957, chap. 3.

[17] *Ibid.*, pp. 52 f.

[18] *Ibid.*, p. 176.

[19] *Peloponnesian War*, II, 43.

[20] Leo Strauss, "The Liberalism of Classical Political Philosophy," in *The Review of Metaphysics*, XII (1959), p. 400.

[21] Edelstein, *Progress in Antiquity*, pp. 175-176.

[22] *Ibid.*, pp. 180, 175.

[23] J. B. Bury, *The Idea of Progress* (Dover ed., 1955), pp. 13-15. For Bury the value of natural science in Seneca was confined to a few chosen individuals and not mankind at large. The latter constitutes the modern view.

[24] *Ibid.*, p. 15. Cf. Edelstein, p. 170. Bury and Edelstein agree. (Seneca, *Naturales Quaestiones*, VII, 25, 4-5). Edelstein would have us believe that even Plato flirted with indefinite future progress. Thus he says (p. 108) that in the *Laws* Plato asserts that "not everything can have been debased at the end of the previous civilization." But Edelstein concentrates here on the various arts, whereas the central import of the passage cited is that morally speaking men were "manlier, simpler and by consequence more self-controlled and more righteous generally" before the deluge (*Laws*, 679*b*).

[25] *Naturales Quaestiones*, III, 30, 1. Edelstein, p. 173. Bury, *op. cit.*, p. 15, says that Seneca's belief in the "corruption of the race is uncompromising."

[26] The expression is Condorcet's in *Outlines of an Historical View of the Progress of the Human Mind*, 10th epoch. The anonymous translation is from the London edition of 1795, p. 346.

[27] "*Moira*, it is true, was a moral power; but no one had to pretend that she was exclusively benevolent, or that she had any respect for the parochial interests of mankind. Further—and this is the most important point—she was not credited with foresight, purpose, design; these belong to man and to the humanized Gods. *Moira* is the blind, automatic force which leaves their subordinate purposes and wills free play within their own legitimate spheres . . . " (F. M. Cornford, *From Religion to Philosophy* [New York: Harper ed., 1957] pp. 20-21). Moira is antithetical to progress because it leads to a sense of resignation about a fixed order in the universe (Bury, p. 19). See also William Chase Greene, *Moira: Fate, Good and Evil in Greek Thought* (New York: Harper ed. 1963). Recent scholarship has tried to show that the idea of progress dates back to the millenarian and chiliastic thinkers of the Middle Ages. Certainly Augustine and the church fathers, with their severely pessimistic view of earthly human nature, were not progressive thinkers. In placing the good city in heaven, St. Augustine and the church fathers stand in marked contrast to the millenarian sects who placed the good city on earth. Literature on modern revolution makes frequent reference to the apocalyptic battle between good and evil in chiliastic literature, the result being the establishment of the heavenly city on earth. (See Ernest Lee Tuveson, *Millennium and Utopia* [New York: Harper ed., 1964] and Norman Cohn, *The Pursuit of the Millennium* [New York: Harper ed., 1961]. The view according to these writers is that the medieval chiliasts, inheriting many of the concepts found in the *Book of Revelation* and in Jewish apocalyptic ideas, regarded the world as moving toward a final battle which would result in a New Jerusalem.) Yet even Tuveson admits that these sects fell into disfavor for a thousand years after the death of Constantine (p. 14), while Hanna Arendt notes that hysteria should not be confused with a theory of history, that no revolution is made in the name of Christian teachings until the modern age (*On Revolution* [New York: Viking, 1963] p. 19). Sorel notes the number of Jewish members of Marxist movements; he notes, however, that they are not members of these movements for ethnic reasons but because of their station in life as independent intellectuals. Those who view Marx as "the last of the Hebrew prophets" must contend with the secular and rationalist element which permeates the modern view of history and stands in marked contrast with religious revelation. (Cf. Edmund Wilson, *To the Finland Station* [New York: Anchor ed., 1940], chap. 5.)

[28] Democritus could explain prerecognition of the future through a radically materialist view of the universe, but this universe had no design (F. M. Cornford, *Principium Sapientiae* [Harper ed., 1965], p. 130). Democritus had little influence (Bury, p. 15).

[29] Condorcet, *Progress of the Human Mind*, 10th epoch, London ed., 1795, p. 346 (italics added). Charles Frankel, in defending Condorcet's view of progress, asserts that the notion of indefinite perfectibility merely implies that man can never assume that we have reached the limit of human hopes. "The principle of the indefinite perfectibility of man is simply the denial that there are any absolutes which the human mind can safely affirm. It is not a prediction about the future; it is a statement of a policy . . . " (*The Case for Modern Man* [Boston: Beacon, 1959], p. 104). But Frankel ignores Condorcet's assertion that "the human species will *necessarily* have a clearer knowledge" and that this in turn will result in releasing man "from the dominion of chance." (See the final statement from Condorcet below and n. 30.)

[30] *Ibid.*, pp. 371-372 (*italics added*).

[31] By "history" is meant here the affairs of men placed in a sequential order, not the modern view. Cf. *Republic*, 367*e*-374*e* in which the rise of the luxurious state is described; 543*a*-575. Despite Sorel's oft-repeated contention that the men of the Enlightenment were "ahistorical" and had no appreciation of necessity, it is probably true in this case that it took an ahistorical man to produce a historicist. If Condorcet was not historicist, the failure of the French Revolution was the event which sparked a reliance on historical determinism as a thing far greater than the wills of individual men but whose apparent thoughts worked to a higher unity and realization. It was this resolution of opposites which led Marx as well as Hegel to the camp of the progressives.

[32] Bertrand de Jouvenel, *On Power* (Boston: Beacon), p. 25. The author separates beneficence from force and legitimacy as the common elements in stable power. But he says they cannot be isolated except analytically.

[33] *Communist Manifesto*, III, 3: "The significance of Critical Utopian Socialism and Communism bears an inverse relation to historical development. In proportion as the modern class struggle develops and takes definite shape, this fantastic standing apart from the contest, these fantastic attacks on it, lose all practical value and all theoretical justification. Therefore, although the originators of these systems were, in many respects, revolutionary, their disciples have, in every case, formed mere reactionary sects. They hold fast by the original views of their masters, in opposition to the progressive historical development of the proletariat." For a defense of Utopianism, see Andrew Hacker, "In Defense of Utopia," in *Ethics*, 65 (Jan. 1955), pp. 135-138.

[34] The expression is Hegel's in *The Philosophy of History*, trans. J. Sibree (New York: Dover, 1956), p. 29.

[35] There are numerous critiques of what is known as historicism. See Karl Popper, *The Poverty of Historicism* (New York: Harper ed., 1964). For a natural law analysis, see Leo Strauss, *Natural Right and History* (Chicago, 1953), Chap. I. For an existentialist view, see Albert Camus, *The Rebel*, trans. Anthony Bower (New York: Vintage ed., 1957), Pt. III. See also Karl Jaspers, *The Origin and Goal of History* (New Haven: Yale, 1953); Sir Isaiah Berlin, *Historical Inevitability* (London and New York: Oxford University Press, 1954).

[36] See *The German Ideology* (New York: International Publishers, 1947). "The production of ideas, of conceptions, of consciousness, is at first directly interwoven with the material activity and the material intercourse of men . . . the *direct* efflux of their material behavior" (pp. 13-14; *italics added*). The importance of the word "direct" is not to be underestimated.

[37] "We set out from real, active men, and on the basis of their real life processes we demonstrate the development of ideological reflexes and echoes of this life process. The *phantoms* formed in the human brain are also, *necessarily*, sublimates of their material life process, which is empirically verifiable and bound to material premises. Morality, religion, metaphysics, all the rest of ideology and their corresponding forms of consciousness, thus no longer retain the semblance of independence. They have no history, no development . . . " (*ibid.*, p. 14). By "no longer" Marx does not mean that they did once possess independence, but rather that in contradistinction to German idealist philosophy, ideas in his materialist view "no longer" retain independence. In short "Life is not determined by consciousness but consciousness by life" (p. 15).

[38] Hanna Arendt says that even during the French Revolution, the elevation of hypocrisy from a minor sin to a major crime had the effect of doing away with the classical distinction of one's *persona* or legal mask, a word originally developed from theatrical masks into the concept of a "legal personality" or a "right and duty bearing person." "Without his *persona* there would be an individual without rights and duties." See *On Revolution* (New York: Viking, 1965 ed.), pp. 102-103.

[39] George Lichtheim says that Marx's vision was that in a rational order, thought determines action. "Men will be free when they are able to produce their own circumstances. Historical materialism is valid only until it has brought about its dialectical negation. . . . " The "mature consciousness which comprehends the necessity of 'prehistory' will not be an ideological one" (*The Concept of Ideology and Other Essays* [New York: Vintage, 1967], p. 21). As a consequence Marx believed that there were some permanent truths which rise above changing social circumstances. "The concept of ideology illumines the historical circumstance that men are not in possession of the true consciousness which—if they had it—would enable them to understand the totality of the world and their own place in it" (*ibid.*, p. 22). It is true that Marx regarded his own ideas as having some measure of transcendent truth; but Lichtheim admits that Marx refused to recognize the dilemma of asserting all thought as determined on the one hand and some ideas rising above being determined on the other. Lichtheim cites Engels' letter to Mehring of July 14, 1893, in which the former says, "Ideology is a process accomplished by the so-called thinker consciously, it is true, but with a false consciousness. The real motive forces impelling him remain unknown to him; else it simply would not be an ideological process" (Marx, Engels, *Selected Correspondence* [Moscow, 1953], p. 541; Lichtheim, p. 15). Thus Marx, according to Lichtheim, held that the difference between "objective" and "ideological" thinking is in the ability "to comprehend the particular determinations which condition each successive phase of human activity" (Lichtheim, p. 20). But the young Marx would not have gone along with this Engels formulation. (See nn. 36 and 37 above.) Lichtheim recognizes Marx's own ambiguity on the question of ideology, i.e., that he retained enough Hegelian idealism and Enlightenment rationalism to take ideas seriously. The consequence of the theory of ideology as being the end of all independent thought was

a possibility never squarely faced by Marx; even Engels says that we will be subject to necessity even when we do understand its laws, and it is reasonable to include thought in this process of necessity. "Freedom does not consist in the dream of independence from natural laws, but in the knowledge of those laws, and in the possibility of making them work towards definite ends. This holds good in relation both to the laws of external nature and to those which govern the bodily and mental existence of men themselves—two classes of laws which we can separate from each other at most only in thought but not in reality. Freedom of the will therefore means nothing but the capacity to make decisions with knowledge of the subject. Therefore the *freer* a man's judgment is in relation to a definite question, the greater is the *necessity* with which the content of this judgment will be determined" (*Anti-Düring: Herr Eugen Düring's Revolution in Science* [Moscow: Foreign Languages Publishing House, 1959], p. 157; italics are Engels'). This was written prior to Marx's death. (See the following note.)

[40] For the logical conclusion of Marx's historical materialist analysis of ideas, see Karl Mannheim, *Ideology and Utopia.* Mannheim faces the consequences of Marx's theory of ideas, which sees its culmination in what Mannheim calls the sociology of knowledge. Like Marx, Mannheim sees the perfected ideological method—the sociology of knowledge—as gradually transforming "the Utopian element" in man's thinking into thought which is more and more coterminous with historical reality and thus losing its function of opposition. "But the complete elimination of reality-transcending elements from our world would lead us to a 'matter of factness' which ultimately would lead to the decay of the human will. . . . The disappearance of utopia brings about a static state of affairs in which man himself becomes no more than a mere thing. We would be faced then with the greatest paradox imaginable, namely, that man, who has achieved the highest degree of rational mastery of existence, left without any ideals, becomes a mere creature of impulses. Thus, after a long, tortuous, but heroic, development, just at the highest stage of awareness, when history is ceasing to be blind fate, and is becoming more and more man's own creation, with the relinquishment of utopias, man would lose his will to shape history and therewith his ability to understand it" (*Ideology and Utopia, An Introduction to the Sociology of Knowledge,* trans. Louis Wirth and Edward Shils [New York: Harvest Books ed., n.d., originally published in 1936], p. 262).

[41] See below, p. 152.

[42] For an elaboration of the problems which the ideological method poses, and the ramifications which this has for a science of knowledge, see Robert Merton, *Social Theory and Social Structure* (Glencoe: Free Press, 1957 ed.), pp. 460 f.

[43] See below, p. 9.

[44] See below, p. 10.

[45] *Reflections on Violence* (New York: Collier ed., 1961), p. 259. The editor of this volume, Edward Shils, thinks that Sorel may have coined the word "diremption" as no English equivalent can be found.

[46] Lichtheim agrees with this judgment but for different reasons than Sorel. He sees Marx as retaining enough Hegelian idealism that a certain dualism remains in his system between Marx's ideas—pure knowledge—and ideology. (See n. 39 above.) However, he also recognizes that this theory looks to the unity of mankind, an attribute of progressivism. (See *The Concept of Ideology,* p. 22.) But it was left to the positivists to bring the concept of unity to its logical conclusion. It was no longer an ideal but actually existed. Thus Marx was right in asserting that the utopian successors of St. Simon such as Auguste Comte were reactionary. This was true, however, because of their positivism, as much as their utopianism.

[47] T. E. Hulme *Speculations* (Harvest Books ed., n.d.), pp. 249 ff.

[48] This is the basic theme of the *Reflections on Violence.*

[49] *Ibid.,* pp. 275-276; see also p. 94 where he discusses Tocqueville's view of the conservatism of the French Revolution.

[50] What is called "consensus" in American political science and politics is anticipated by Sorel in his discussion of parliamentary socialists who must have working-class, middle-class, and upper-class constituents. Only in this way can they obtain influence (*Reflections,* p. 120). See also *La Ruine du Monde Antique: Conception matérialiste de l'histoire* (Paris, 3d ed., 1933) for the classic concept of virtue as seen by Sorel.

[51] For a lively and sympathetic portrait of the great progressive thinkers, see Frank E. Manuel, *The Prophets of Paris* (New York: Harper ed., 1965). See especially pp. 15, 45, 58, and 111 for the moderation and even conservatism of Turgot, Condorcet, and St. Simon. For Comte's emphasis on order, see pp. 274-286. For Hegel's practiced conservatism, see his attack on the "English Reform Bill" in Carl Frederich, ed., *The Philosophy of Hegel* (New York: Modern Library, p. 540).

[52] For an excellent portrait of the actual conservatism not to say quietism of the German Social Democracy, see J. P. Nettl, *Rosa Luxemburg* (London: Oxford University Press, 1966), Vol. II passim. (See also n. 40 above.) Rosa Luxemburg's quarrel with Kautsky, the great theorist of Marxism who proved conservative in actual practice, is detailed.

[53] The expression is Herbert Marcuse's, *One Dimensional Man* (Boston: Beacon, 1964). Marcuse's Hegelianism obscures his appreciation of the connection between progress and the one-dimensionality of existence, but he seems to suspect it. See especially, pp. 188-189.

[54] *Reflections,* p. 147.

[55] The literature of modern political science, particularly in the fields of comparative government and sociology, seems to inherit many of the progressive conceptions. The "functional" theorists seem particularly interesting in this respect. See, for example, Gabrial A. Almond and G. Bingham Powell, Jr., *Comparative Politics: A Developmental Approach* (Boston: Little Brown, 1966). "The independent nation has become a nearly universal phenomenon. The past several decades have seen a national explosion on the continents of Asia and Africa. This has produced an extraordinary confusion of cultures, and mixtures of archaic and modern institutional forms. In some way this confusion must be brought to order, and the capacity to explain and predict must be reaffirmed" (pp. 214-215). The authors claim that they "will not repeat the naiveté of Enlightenment theorists regarding the evolutionary progression in political systems" (215). But the authors' concluding paragraph poses "the ultimate question of the Enlightenment. Can man employ reason to understand, shape, and develop his own institutions. . . . ? The modern political scientist can no longer afford to be the disillusioned child of the Enlightenment, but must become its sober trustee" (pp. 331-332). The authors agree that ethical judgments on the system are important although they ignore them. However Seymour Martin Lipset, *Political Man* (Garden City: Doubleday, 1959) reveals a great concern for democracy.

[56] See the appendix to the *Reflections* entitled "In Defense of Lenin."

[57] See Irving Louis Horowitz, *Radicalism and the Revolt Against Reason,* for an analysis of Bergson's influence on Sorel.

[58] Georges Sorel, "Essai sur la philosophie de Proudhon," in *Revue Philosophique,* XXXIII (1892), XXXIV (1892), cited in James H. Meisel, *The Genests of Georges Sorel* (Ann Arbor, 1951), p. 96. See also Neal Wood, "Some Reflections on Sorel and Machiavelli," in *Political Science Quarterly,* LXXXIII, no. 1, March 1968, pp. 79-80.

[59] *Reflections,* pp. 126-127.

[60] *Ibid.,* p. 148, and *Illusions* below, p. 156.

[61] *Ibid.,* p. 150.

[62] *Ibid.,* p. 242, and *Illusions* below, p. 156.

J. L. Talmon (essay date 1970)

SOURCE: "The Legacy of Georges Sorel: Marxism, Violence, Fascism," in *Encounter,* Vol. XXXIV, No. 2, February, 1970, pp. 47-60.

[*In the following excerpt, Talmon examines Sorel's legacy on such European contemporaries as Hulme, Lenin, Wyndham Lewis, Ramon Fernandes, and Benedetto Croce.*]

At a time when words like violence, "direct action," "confrontation," "the bourgeois world," "cleansing," "total destruction," etc. are shouted into our ears with obsessive persistence, there is every justification for (and there may even be some intellectual profit in) taking another look at the most famous European apologist of violence—Georges Sorel. The more so, if one wishes to examine the view (which seems to be implied, for instance, in the title, "The Age of Violence," given to the last chapter of the concluding volume of the New Cambridge Modern History) that the terrorist totalitarian régimes of both Left and Right so characteristic of this century, should not be seen as two primary, self-sufficient, and all-embracing alternatives pitted against each other, but as two different versions of the same phenomenon, the urge for violence. And it is surely legitimate to go on asking whether the present wave of defiant and intransigent extremism should not also be classified as the latest variety thereof?

Georges Sorel lived long enough to see and to hail the Bolshevik Revolution as a great fulfilment, and long enough if not to congratulate Mussolini on the accomplished march on Rome, at least to express his fascinated interest in and keen admiration for rising Fascism. There is the story that in the same week, in the late 1920s, the Director of the *Bibliothèque Nationale* in Paris was approached by the Ambassadors of Soviet Russia and Fascist Italy, on behalf of their respective governments, with offers of sums of money for the repair of the tombstone on Georges Sorel's grave. True or apocryphal as the story may be, Sorel did utter shortly before his death the prayer to which adherents of either ideology could have responded with a fervent amen—"to be allowed, before descending into the grave, to see the humbling of the proud bourgeois democracies, today so cynically triumphant. . . . "[1]

If Benedetto Croce spoke of Georges Sorel as one of "the two sole original thinkers thrown up by socialism" (the other was Karl Marx), Wyndham Lewis, the grim hater of philistinism and ferocious kill-joy, and one of the first intellectuals in the West to hail Hitler with a special book, saw in Sorel "the key to all contemporary political thinking." Mussolini repeatedly acknowledged Sorel as his master: "What I am, I owe to Sorel."

And Sorel, in turn, called Mussolini "a man no less extraordinary than Lenin . . . of a greater reach than all the statesmen of the day . . . not a socialist *à la source bourgeoise;* he has never believed in parliamentary socialism."

Notwithstanding Lenin's dismissal of him as a muddlehead and a mischief-maker, Sorel described Lenin as the greatest theorist that socialism had had since Marx and a head of state whose genius recalls that of Peter the Great—in the effort of "orienting Russia towards the constitution of a republic of producers, capable of encompassing an economy as progressive as that of our capitalist democracies." Although he modestly stated that he "had no reason to suppose that Lenin may have accepted my ideas," Sorel was proudly sure that his "syndicalism was a slope inclining toward Bolshevism."[2]

In the light of these statements, one need not be startled by the opinion of the French Fascist, Ramon Fernandes, expressed in 1937, that *"Georges Sorel fut un inspirateur direct des régimes totalitaires."* Recent scholarship has been increasingly more inclined to focus attention on that strange encounter just before 1914 between the ageing Sorel and some of his Syndicalist disciples on the one hand, and, on the other, a few youthful ultra-Rightist nationalists in France and Italy, as a kind of curtain raiser to post-1918 Fascism. And it is impossible not to be struck by similarities of thought and speech between the young New Left radicals of today and the author of the ***Réflexions sur la violence*** seventy years ago.

THE HEROIC LEAP

Sorel was a seeker. His restless and easily discouraged quest, his tentative enthusiasms and bitter disillusionments epitomise the spiritual biography of his age, the pathetic pilgrimage of modern man who had lost the certainties and fixities of the early days. Sorel was fascinated by the legend of the Wandering Jew—"the symbol of the highest aspirations of mankind condemned to be forever marching, without knowing any repose." In his vehement rejection of the 18th century's facile and optimistic substitute for the religious Theodicea and in his revulsion from Bourgeois civilisation based on it, Sorel joins the ranks of the 19th century's great prophets of wrath—de Maistre, Carlyle, Schopenhauer, Burckhardt, Nietzsche, Dostoevsky, Ibsen, among others.

Born in 1847 into a royalist bourgeois family in Normandy (he was a cousin of the historian Albert Sorel, author of the monumental work, *L'Europe et la Révolution Française*), Georges Sorel was destined to take his first bearings in the world just as France was going through the ordeal of national defeat and civil war—the Commune—in 1870-71, and then to follow the anguished post-mortem to which such conservative thinkers as Taine, Renan, Le Play and others had submitted the history of France, making the Revolution of 1789 responsible for that zig-zag course of revolution, anarchy, terror, Bonapartist dictatorship and restoration, vast conquest and terrible defeat, the triumph of liberty and its demise. The arrival of the masses filled these writers with dread. As for the universal suffrage which the Third Republic—a pathetic caricature of the great Revolution—seemed to have enthroned forever, had it not in 1848 swept Louis Napoleon Bonaparte into power, and enabled him, as both the elect of the masses and the defender of bourgeois property against the Red Revolution, to strangle liberty? The vagaries of the blind multitude and its associated demagoguery could no longer be held in check by any of the proposed dams—a restored monarchy, religion, *"les autorités sociales."*

Nothing shows better the impact that this national self-questioning had on Sorel than his frequent reference to Ernest Renan's anguished question—"On what will the future generations live?" after the inherited Christian habits of thought and conservative inhibitions will have lost their grip completely (as they clearly were losing it all the time).

It was in order to sort out to himself these bewildering things that the civil engineer (roads and bridges) left government service at the age of 45 and retired on a small pension with the ribbon of *Légion d'honneur*, into a Paris banlieue, to study, meditate and write. He frequented intellectual circles composed of very young men, mostly disciples on the Left Bank, attended regularly the lectures of Henri Bergson at the College de France, and worshipped the memory of his deceased (apparently illiterate) wife, who died childless in 1897. Sorel, incidentally, never tired of extolling chastity as the virtue of virtues, as the sign of moral health and social cohesion, and of stigmatising the lack of it as proof of sickness and degeneracy.

The very titles of his earliest books—***Contribution à l'étude profane de la Bible*** (1889), ***Le proces de Socrate*** (1889), and ***La fin du monde antique*** (1898)—betray Sorel's preoccupation with the phenomena of integration and disintegration, decadence and rebirth. While the tract on the Bible is an attempt to bring into relief the naïvely heroic tone of the Biblical life stories, and their educational value as antidotes to utilitarianism and revolutionary ideology, ***Procès de Socrate*** is an essay on the free-wheeling intellectual who, by questioning and criticising the ways of men from an abstract stand, undermines the instinctive certainties, the massive traditions, the life-sustaining prejudices and the inherited institutional framework of the nation. Socrates stands condemned for arrogantly trying to replace the earthly, concrete, "social" reality of family by the abstract ideal of the "fictitious moral family," the organically and historically structured state with an essentially "ecclesiastic" conception of society, based on pure reason and spiritual values, and for inspiring moods of ecstatic and orgiastic intoxication that invite the imposition of both revolutionary and tyrannical solutions.[3]

La fin du monde antique is a study in disintegration and decline. The late Roman Empire has its strength, its very life, all the values and institutions which had made it great sapped by too much self-consciousness and by other-worldly spirituality. The victory of Christianity had been prepared by the spread of Oriental cults and introspective philosophies which "sowed everywhere the seeds of despair and death," by putting personal salvation above country, family and social ties, holiness above law, poverty above the productive effort, renunciation above responsibility, contemplation above virile struggle, the heavenly fatherland above the city. *"Le moyen âge peut commencer; il n'y a plus de cité, plus de droit."* At a later date Sorel will portray early Christianity as the most powerful impulse towards spiritual and social rebirth in the midst of total decay. A naïve, narrow, but heroic message, it enabled its believers to lift themselves into the highlands of a strenuous, new beginning—the *ricorsi* of Vico. This juxtaposition of decomposition and reintegration, decadence and rebirth expresses Sorel's deepest and most abiding sentiments: his aggressive and overwhelming pessimism and his yearning for deliverance. "This pessimism is a metaphysic of ethics (*moeurs*) rather than a theory of the world." It stems from "the experimental knowledge which we have acquired of the obstacles which oppose the satisfaction of our imaginations" and from "the profound conviction of our natural weakness." The pessimist regards the prevailing social conditions as "constituting a system held together by an iron law (*loi d'airain*)," which must either be supported *en bloc* as something inevitable, or made to disappear "through a catastrophe carrying all with it." Do not therefore blame any particular persons for the evils that be, and do not engage in partial reforms.

In language very reminiscent of de Maistre, Schopenhauer, Burckhardt and Nietzsche, Sorel pours scorn upon all those who promised easy solutions and rapid improvement, and who proclaimed happiness as our right and pleasure as man's legitimate aim. Pain and suffering riveted us to life; its reality, dignity and depth; pleasure-seeking marked an escape from it, a gliding away from its inexorable determinations. Decadence fascinated Sorel, as, incidentally, it did so many philosophers of history and culture, from whom the extreme Right derived much of its inspiration. The natural tendency towards dissolution and decay was to him a universal law. Civilisation was a most precarious possession, and was being maintained by the skin of its teeth. Any sign of relenting was soon followed by rot, collapse and ruin. Barbarism was always creeping into the weak ramparts built against it. What gave meaning and grandeur to our life was the state of tension and unyielding struggle to ward off the forces of decay and destruction, and above all the yearning and striving for deliverance. This "deliverance" Sorel did not see in the ease of *détente* and the repose of relaxed muscles, or in Schopenhauer's loving communion with art in an all-dissolving Nirvana; or in Burckhardt's vision of a secular neo-monasticism as a refuge for the chosen few; he saw it rather in the spirit of Nietzsche, in the elation which came from tearing oneself out of the maze of snares and the miasma of feebleness; the heroic leap into a new and immensely strenuous discipline which had been resolutely chosen, without ever looking back or sideways—a monastic order, the early Puritan communities, the *Grande Armée.*

This faith—pessimism linked to a vision of deliverance—was a doctrine "without which nothing truly great has ever been accomplished in this world." This is clearly a religious frame of mind. Sorel was never a believer; he never used the word God; but he never ceased to be fascinated by religion and to write on religious problems. Sin and purification, guilt and redemption, self-willed arrogance and objective certainty, right and force, legitimacy and revolution—these speculations are at the source of his quest.[4]

THE REVOLT AGAINST POLITICS

By 1893-1894 Georges Sorel became a full-fledged Marxist. As he writes,

> I hold the theory of Marx for the greatest innovation introduced into philosophy for centuries. . . . All our ideas are bound today to congregate around the new principles posed by scientific socialism. . . . The human spirit refuses to be content with old economic scepticism . . . with registering of facts, with reasoning about the balance of profits, with comparing the increase of prosperity in the various countries.[5]

The accent is clearly not upon the evils of capitalism or the sufferings of the poor, but upon objective certainty and impersonal necessity, in contrast to the "subjective personal and crude notions of a philosophy delivered to accident," emotional preferences or speculative conjecture. The Archimedean point of Marxist philosophy was according to Sorel the conception of man as *"tout entier comme travailleur,"* never separated "from the instruments with which he earns his living," in other words the constant and intimate relationship betwen men and the machine; between the free and creative freedom of the worker as tool-maker, *homo faber,* manipulator of inert matter on the one hand and the inexorable determinations thrown back by the medium and the tools on the other. In comparison with this, the abstract ideologism of intellectuals and the would-be metaphysical external moral principles of philosophers represented vague conjectures, imaginings or emotional states. Sorel goes so far as to maintain that the great theoretical advances in science had in most cases been nothing but generalisations of technological inventions. This quest for certainty and abhorrence of arbitrariness and vagueness caused Sorel, from the first, to envisage integral Trade Unionism as the expression of all authentic values, and to view Socialist party politics as a sign and a danger of corruption. Sorel expected the *syndicats* to become a separate and self-sufficient kingdom of God, bearers of a new morality and a new civilisation. The idea of secession, of total separation from the surrounding world, was not yet worked out at this stage by Sorel, but the tutelage exercised by professional politicians at the head of the political labour parties was already bitterly assailed by him.[6]

Before Sorel had an opportunity to develop those ideas, he became deeply involved in the tremendous experience that at the turn of the century shook France to its foundations.

In becoming a *Dreyfusard* Sorel was not really concerned with destroying the power of the Church, the Army, or militant chauvinism as an end in itself. He gave himself soul and body to a mystique pitted against another mystique: the fight for abstract justice and the pure truth against the supposedly life-giving and powersustaining forces of national myth, prejudice and tradition, represented by *"les autorités sociales"* of bygone days. In a sense Sorel took the side of the Socratics whom he had earlier so bitterly condemned. Sorel's hopes for a purifying *ricorsi* soon gave way to disillusionment. In the words of another significant figure who went through a somewhat similar experience, Charles Péguy, the Dreyfus "*mystique* degenerated into *politique*. . . . " The Dreyfus affair and its aftermath, says Sorel,

> produced an extraordinary accumulation of accidents, very much like those which sometimes enable the physicist in his laboratory to see suddenly in a wholly unexpected manner, and under an almost transparent veil, laws which had escaped long methodological investigation.[7]

The consequences of the affair revealed "the inadequacy of the Socialist teachings of the day." In joining the non-proletarian forces in a struggle for not distinctly proletarian aims, the workers lost their own identity and the clarity of their proletarian purpose. Anti-clericalism proved to be, in fact, only a springboard for power-thirsty demagogues of both varieties, the bourgeois radical and the socialist politicians. The Marxist principle of class war was "definitely submerged in the democratic ocean of the unity of the people."

Sorel goes on to draw a momentous lesson from this failure: "The parliamentary socialists lost a great deal of their prestige, men of violence covered themselves with glory." The affair revealed the vital importance of sustained direct action "with its very frequent accompaniment of acts of violence," as a method distinct from sporadic acts of violence, which were no more than "simple accidents which come to trouble the normal advance" of a movement. This discovery called for a revision of Marxism or, rather, a return to its authentic tradition. Sorel's reappraisal of Socialist teachings was carried out not only under the impression of the *Affaire*, but not less importantly also under the impact of and in direct reference to the great "Revisionist" controversy, begun by Eduard Bernstein at the turn of the century.

Sorel's reaction to the Revisionist heresy should be considered alongside the violent responses of Lenin, Mussolini (the first Communist in Europe in that he forced the Reformists out of the Party), Rosa Luxemburg and Parvus-Helphand. Theirs was a passionate reassertion of revolutionary voluntarism and élitism, and of the early revolutionary and universalist Messianism of Marx, in opposition to Bernstein's tendency to turn the Socialist parties into a Left-wing of parliamentary democracy and an integral part of the national body politic. The revulsion from the Revisionist renunciation of Revolution propelled others into a quite different direction. One of the Italian theoreticians of Syndicalism (he later became a prophet of the corporate state and a close collaborator of *il Duce*), Sergio Pannunzio, traces the beginning of his evolution from Socialism to Fascism to the shock administered to him by the "Revisionist heresy." Unlike the above-mentioned anti-Revisionists, Sorel accepted the whole of Bernstein's social-economic critique of Orthodox Marxism, but drew diametrically opposite political conclusions from those of Bernstein.

In his ***Décomposition du Marxisme*** (1908)[8] Sorel agrees with the thesis (indeed states it more emphatically than Bernstein himself) that Capitalism had not failed at all. More than that, the progress of capitalist production and of its inevitable concomitant, trade unionism, had not only raised the workers' standard of life but also blunted the edge of Class War, since collective bargaining had turned the workers into partners of management rather than enemies thereof. In the early days of the Industrial Revolution it was the financiers and usurers, totally ignorant of the problems of technology, who laid down the law for industrialists and engineers; while at the same time the workers, stupid brutes, snatched away from the plough or artisan workshop, had to be kept in line with the help of brutal methods. But in the meantime technologically-trained employers had come into their own, and workers had learned to handle the machine and even to like it. Capitalism had evolved sufficient powers of adjustment to cope with passing crises. There were, thus, no technological or social-economic reasons for interfering with the workings of capitalism. Not even in the sphere of salaries and wages, since a rough kind of justice of reward proportionate to contribution was being realised by capitalism. Socialism was not going to change that, because in this respect, Marxism, Sorel claims, was closer to the Manchester School than to the "justice"-obsessed Utopians of the earlier days (who thought in terms of fool-proof blue-prints and perfect egalitarian justice, consciously and artificially contrived, and not of the workings of the mechanism of production).

If this be so, then why Revolution at all? The question is especially insistent as Sorel has no sympathy at all with what he regards as the modern version of a *Jacquerie*—the envious desire of the poor to redistribute property for the sake of equality? And if the Revolution is an absolute imperative, for moral or other reasons, are we not thrown back upon the idea of a *putschist* seizure of political power for the purpose of imposing the socialist order by violence and ukase—in a word, "Blanquism"? Sorel will not give up the Revolution, but he will reject Blanquism, and this on quite original (though mistaken) grounds. Blanquism—he claims—did not really envisage the uprising of a class, but the arrogation of the revolutionary mission by a political party, in fact by bourgeois intellectuals, who shared neither the needs and the way of life nor the real aspirations of the genuine workers. We reach here the nodal point already foreshadowed in Sorel's theory of revolutionary syndicalism based on the idea of violence. Sorel sees the proletariat—organised in *syndicats*—not as paupers fighting for "a larger share of the cake" but as the force predestined by history to enthrone a new civilisation and a heroic morality on the ruins of the decaying bourgeois world. The authenticity of this force and singleness of its purpose were—as said before—vitiated and distorted by professional politicians, intellectuals, and by the corrupting effects of parliamentary party politics. Sorel believes he is fighting for a return to "the true Marx." He tries to depict Marx as a prophet of the embattled class and the enemy of party politics. He fails to mention the relevant passages in the *Communist Manifesto* as well as the famous article 7a of the general Rules of the International—"the proletariat can act as a class only by constituting itself as a distinct political party." But he quotes with fervent approval the concluding passage in *The Poverty of Philosophy,* Marx's famous tract against Proudhon,

> The antagonism between the proletariat and the bourgeoisie is a struggle of a class against class, a struggle which carried to its highest expression is a total revolution . . . the clash of body with body, as its final denouement . . . combat or death: bloody struggle or extinction. . . . It is in this form that the question is inexorably put.

Sorel then makes much of the International's Circular (in which Marx's share is rather uncertain) against Bakunin's "Alliance of Socialist Democracy and the International Working Men's Association." This ridicules the idea of putting a "vanguard" of men recruited from the privileged classes above the masses ("cannon fodder"), to act "as intermediaries between the revolutionary idea and the popular instincts," in order to bring to the fore "advocates without a cause, doctors without treatments and without science, students of billiards, shopkeepers and others employed in commerce, and especially journalists of the petty press . . . *déclassé* . . . who retrieved, in the International, a career and an issue."

Sorel quotes with glee Engels' description of the political struggle in the modern (bourgeois) state in *The Origins of the Family:* "a body of intellectuals invested with privileges and possessing so-called political means for defending itself against the attacks of other groups of intellectuals and to acquire the profits of public offices. Parties are organised for the acquisition of these public posts." Sorel not only refuses to draw any distinction between bourgeois politicians and socialist politicians; all his scorn is directed against the latter—because of their greater hypocrisy.

These were two entirely different things: the revolutionary élan of a class acting from instinct and in full simplicity, also a class that had accomplished its apprenticeship, evolved a system of ideas and values, a juridical framework of its own, and had reached full awareness of its historic mission to enthrone a new civilisation and a new moral order; and the connivance of professional party politicians, banking on the revolution to deliver to them "the object of their cupidity," the state. Sorel refers also with approval to Bernstein's exposure of the cant which under the guise of formal popular sovereignty makes civil servants, professional politicians, and newspaper owners run the show, and to his definition of the dictatorship of the proletariat as "the dictatorship of club orators and literati."

At bottom, we are faced here with the problem which had never ceased to perplex mankind—the question of the very legitimacy of politics. Its utter vagueness and elusive character, the mixture of abstract principle and crass ambition, of objective goals and sheer histrionics, of rational argument and squalid bamboozling; its seeming remoteness from the concrete, measurable, and truly necessary things—all this leads to the despairing conclusion that whatever the politicians, men of no particular training, ultimately dilettanti, say or do is but a mask and pretence for the will to power, power for its own sake. "Politics!" exclaims Paul Valéry, "at the word I am overcome with silence. . . . I regard the political necessity of exploiting all that is lowest in man's psyche as the greatest danger of the present time." Sorel would add *bourgeois* politics, but he means democratic politics: the competition for power or rather for the favour of the people who held the prize of power. Politics of this type emerged—Sorel claims—in Europe, more precisely in France, only at the end of the 18th century, as a function of an all-embracing new *Weltanschauung.* This leads him to undertake a fundamental reckoning with the 18th-century tradition. He rejects it root and branch as a colossal derangement, an alienation, and thus it justifies his prophecy of its imminent demise at the hands of the victorious proletariat.

> All our efforts [Sorel writes] should aim at preventing bourgeois ideas from poisoning the class which is arriving; that is why we can never do enough to break every link between the people and the literature of the 18th century . . . to demolish this whole scaffolding of conventional falsehoods and to ruin the prestige still enjoyed by those who vulgarise the vulgarisation of the 18th century.[9]

One is reminded of Mussolini's boast made in 1926 for which many parallels could be found in statements by Fascist and Nazi spokesmen: "We represent a new principle in the world; we represent the exact, categorical, definitive antithesis of the whole world of democracy, plutocracy, freemasonry, in short the whole world of the immortal principles of 1789."

In this utter repudiation of 18th-century values and the conscious endeavour to replace them by different, indeed contrasting principles, Sorel parts company not merely with the liberal-democratic tradition of the modern era, but in the last analysis also with every shade of socialism known hitherto.

FORCE, TERROR, & RENEWAL

"Les illusions du progrès" is the central issue on which Sorel takes up his fight against the 18th-century tradition: that belief in some final salvationist station of the historic process, the preordained dénouement of all contradictions and conflict into a state of concord, harmony, resulting from the final victory of the basic rationality and social nature of man over all the disturbing and corrupting influences of bygone ages—ignorance and selfishness, oppression and evil teachings. The essential features of this religion of progress were its abstract universalism and its humanitarian optimism. Sorel proclaims his bitter enmity for this religion of peace and concord, in the name of a religion of struggle and war. The opposition between the two approaches was to him fundamental and all-embracing. Sorel's most faithful disciple, Edouard Berth, put his finger on it, invoking Nietzsche's uncompromising challenge ("are you pacific, or are you warrior-like?") and Proudhon's famous disquisition on the place of war in the scheme of civilisation (its role as the lever of all the great values). It was either the one or the other. Each of the two basic attitudes determined a system of values, a morality, a pattern of behaviour quite irreconcilable with the ones shaped by the other; in brief, of concord on one side, and violence on the other, of universal reconciliation or the victory of the best. Sorel entirely ignores the 18th-century humanist and universalist ingredients in both the original impulse and the ultimate vision of Socialism.[10]

The facile optimism of the rationalists rouses Sorel to a fury of contempt. He takes a malignant pleasure in the resistance, recalcitrance, and intractableness of things; he is hypnotised by insoluble contradictions and conflict. Sorel despises Descartes, the philosopher of clarity and harmony, and adores Pascal, the tormented prophet, weighed down by the mystery of evil and consumed by a yearning for salvation. The former epitomises the "small science" of smug positivism and automatic mechanism, the latter represents the "great science"—true vision suspended over unfathomable abysses. To take a characteristic instance, Sorel is scathing about the social catholicism of the Modernist movement in the Church of Leo XIII, and its endeavour to explain away the mysteries, "absurdities" and irrationalities of revealed religion as parables and symbols of rational truths and liberal social ethics. Needless to say, he prefers a "tough," wholly "indigestible" religion.

Humanitarian rationalism appears to Sorel a colossal lie which had a most stultifying and corrupting effect, breeding an arrogant and capricious wish to obtain full gratification quickly and cheaply, to make a cowardly escape from the realities of life and the lessons of history. It was a dishonest simplicism that reduces the mysteries of nature and complexities of existence into encyclopaedias and digests, glib rhetoric and castles in the air, and fosters an unprincipled readiness to compromise and bargain. Conflict and War were the fathers of all true morality and manly responsibility.

We need not be detained by Sorel's critique, at times acute, at times quite fanciful, of the roots of the 18th-century philosophy. More important for us are Sorel's connection with the farreaching and lasting course of the rationalist ideology.

For the French Revolution produced the strange type of the fanatical would-be saviour in a hurry who sees himself justified in forcing everybody to be free. A unanimous happiness would follow the extermination of all evil recalcitrants, in any case deviants who were doomed by History. The more common breed of "the religion of progress," however, has been the professional politician or intellectual in politics who banded together in political parties ostensibly to serve and guide the people in the direction of the desired state of social happiness, but in fact to cajole the people with promises, blandishments, and tricks into giving them power. The progressive ideology had little real relevance. Rhetors, sophists, adventurers, speculators, clowns all rolled into one, neither coping with real problems, nor rooted in any ancient group loyalties, nor part of historic institutions; they were ultimately parasites. They gambled on the frustrations and envious dissatisfactions of men. They encouraged indolent craving for easy gratification. Their weapons were ruse and cunning.

As against "bourgeois deceit and decadence" (of which Socialist politicians had become an integral part), the arrival of the proletariat presages a purifying *ricorsi.* The proletariat comes to bring war and not peace; to add burdens, not to alleviate them; to heighten tension, and not to offer a *détente.* It struggles on in the full consciousness of its destiny to inherit the earth: not to come to an accommodation with the existing establishment, but to eradicate it entirely. Its heroes are warriors, and not politicians, diplomats, or negotiators.

A new, revolutionary, and all-transforming principle associated with the modern industrial effort—the communion with the machine—is a lever of creative freedom, a warrant of integrity, an educational discipline, a vantage point for seeing things in their full concreteness and interaction, in contrast to the vagueness, the abstractness, and indeterminacy as well as the moral laxity and selfish arbitrariness of liberal-democratic and socialist politics, indeed of bourgeois society in general.

Sorel's terms of reference, metaphors and simili are all taken from religious movements and war. The abounding words are honour and glory, sublimity, heroism, virility and loftiness. The comparison is between the *syndicats* and their impending general strike and the early Christians or the extreme Protestant sects waiting for a Second Coming or the monastic orders which arose to purify the Church. Sorel says again and again that the fact that these historic expectations were never fulfilled did not matter. All that mattered was that in each case the myth had enough vitality to sustain the believers' resolve and to turn them into little kingdoms of God, with an ethos, a high morality, indeed a culture of their own, in strenuous opposition to the rotten world around them. The proud self-awareness of representing a higher civilisation and morality was bound to inspire the workers with puritan virtues: love of the job for its own sake, precision and loyalty, care for the heritage of the future heirs of the earth. The redeemed proletariat would be marked above all by the heroic selflessness and disinterestedness peculiar to crusaders and soldiers of liberty.

To keep themselves pure and resolute it was absolutely essential for the workers to cut themselves off entirely from the unregenerate world. This meant in the first place shaking off the tutelage of politicians and intellectuals, with all their machinations and corrupt practices. In the second place, it meant class war *à l'outrance:* no truck with the employers. The more isolated the *syndicats* were, the more they would have to fall back upon their own resources: the more intensely would they become aware of their own identity and high calling: the richer and deeper and more authentic would their own values become. In the form of direct action and sporadic strikes (in preparation for the break-through of the great General Strike) the struggle would also gradually shape a new and wholly autonomous juridical system, which would be based on the morality of a confraternity at war. War—as in the Proudhonian vision—would be the begetter of the virtues of heroism, total devotion, sense of solidarity, right, and honour. The strikes were sure to engender and sustain new conceptions and new patterns of relationship between the leaders and the led (the former embodying the true general will, and not the mystical general will of Rousseauist democracy). Occupation of factories would accustom the workers to see themselves as the legitimate owners and managers of social wealth. The physical clash with employers, state authorities, and strike breakers would educate the strikers in the use of violence. Sustained by the spirit of a Revolutionary Army, the workers would not be moved by envy, by a craving for revenge or a vision of spoils, let alone self-pity. They wanted a clean fight—a judgment of God—in the heroic tradition of medieval chivalry. But their campaign was also conceived in the spirit of a Napoleonic resolve utterly to annihilate the enemy.

It was the vision of the General Strike that was to inspire and sustain the proletariat in their heroic struggle.[11] The General Strike was the great myth, but it was most emphatically not a vision of Utopia. The Utopia was, according to Sorel, an intellectual proposition, a description of a desirable state of affairs which would be an improvement upon the existing one, thus a contrivance and concoction of intellectuals. Myth, however, was not a truth to be analysed and taken to pieces, but a power that stirs the soul, an ensemble of images that satisfy and propel all our faculties. Upon it are focused all our urges and drives, dreams and hopes. It was a vision of life turned drama, a spasm of final fulfilment, like the revolutionary breakthrough, or the Second Coming, the arrival of the Messiah, or the last war of liberation.

The myth presupposes man to be not a creature of reason, but a suggestible being, whose intuitive grasp of and reaction to an uplifting heroic vision would raise him out of himself into that *élan vital* which opens to him the domain of creative freedom. He then ceases to be a link in the chain of natural causality, and (in the spirit of Henri Bergson) makes a new beginning towards a unique destiny.

The General Strike signified the triumph of violence at the end of a series of turbulent clashes. Sorel's eloquent pages on the general strike read like a poetic evocation, a prophecy rather than a prognosis or a blueprint. We are left in the dark as to how the great drama of violence would really unfold. We are told that its essence would not be in much bloodshed or acts of brutality, in a large number of victims or untold destruction. These would be few; they would bear rather the character of a warning. What Sorel seems to have had in mind is the overwhelming will to win, the supreme confidence of conquerors, the iron determination to go to the bitter end, in the face of all which the adversary flinches, reels back, because he lacks the conviction and the self-assurance of those who embody manifest destiny and know it.

> A social policy founded on middle-class cowardice, which consists in always surrendering before the threat of violence, cannot fail to engender the idea that the middle class is condemned to death, and that its disappearance is only a matter of time. Thus every conflict which gives rise to violence becomes a vanguard fight, and nobody can foresee what will arise from such engagements. . . . Each time they come to blows the strikers hope that it is the beginning of the great *Napoleonic* battle. . . . In this way the practice of strikes engenders the notion of a catastrophic revolution.[12]

At a later date Sorel defined violence as

> an intellectual doctrine, the will of the powerful minds which know where they are going, the implacable resolve to attain the final goals of Marxism by means of syndicalism. Lenin has furnished us a striking example of that psychological violence.[13]

The determination of the assailants and the faltering of the attacked mutually condition each other.

The capacity and readiness to resort to violence become the test of faith and of belonging to the elect. " . . . *en se regardant comme le grand moteur de l'histoire . . . il a le sentiment très net de la gloire . . . son rôle historique et de l'héroisme. . . . La mesure de sa valeur.*" Sorel resorts in this connection to nomenclature of stern determinism. The final act of violence in the victorious strike would be "no more than the necessary effort to make the old withered branches fall to the ground." The fall would be like the final crush of the glacier tearing itself away from its old base, "after having been attacked by the sun for many centuries."

An apologia for "violence"? Sorel devotes quite a few pages to the distinction between force and violence, and it is a distinction which later would become a commonplace among ideologists of violence of all kinds, Force was an instrument for maintaining existing power (what would nowadays be called "the establishment").

> The object of force is to impose a certain social order in which the minority governs, while violence tends to the destruction of that order. The middle class have used force since the beginning of modern times, while the proletariat now reacts against the middle class and against the State by violence.

It was hidden and camouflaged, operating not so much with weapons of direct coercion as by manipulating the levers of power, blocking insidiously all attempts at change or cunningly denuding them of any real effectiveness, while making much of form and ritual.

> Thus we see that economic forces are closely bound up with political power, and capitalism finally perfects itself to the point of being able to dispense with any direct appeal to the public force, except in very exceptional cases. . . .

Sorel gives an interesting slant to the Marxist description of the bourgeois State as the executive of the exploiting classes (and to Engels' denunciation of parliamentary "cretinism") by substituting intellectuals and politicians for capitalists and their stooges:

> There is a great resemblance between the electoral democracy and the Stock Exchange; in one case as in the other it is necessary to work upon the simplicity of the masses, to buy the co-operation of the most important papers, and to assist chance by an infinite of trickery. There is not a great deal of difference between a financier who puts big-sounding concerns on the market which come to grief in a few years, and the politician who promises an infinity of reforms to the citizens which he does not know how to bring about, and which resolve themselves simply into an accumulation of Parliamentary papers. . . . Democrats and businessmen have quite a special science for making the deliberative assemblies approve of their swindling; the Parliaments are as packed as shareholders' meetings . . . profound psychological affinities resulting from these methods of operation; democracy is the paradise of which unscrupulous financiers dream.

In brief, the régime of bourgeois liberalism rested on force: on ruse, cunning, and make-believe. Sorel proclaims the violence preached by him to be noble and chivalrous because it was open and direct and constituted a full and unequivocal commitment, without subterfuge, reservations, and convenient avenues of retreat.

As for terror, it is not always to Sorel only a question of inspiring fear or self-confidence by demonstration. Andreu calls "extraordinary" the sentence in which Sorel asks himself "whether in liquidating so large a number of literati and *férus d'idéologie* the Terror had not rendered a service to France. Perhaps Napoleon would not have so easily consolidated his administration had his régime not been preceded by a great purge. . . . "[14]

Violence in effect is the token of authenticity. The revulsion from hypocrisy (which is just another way of putting the quest of "authenticity") leads to the glorification of instinct and force, and to a contempt for devious men, especially intellectuals. The greater the contempt for conventional "falsehood," the greater the glory of violence. Sorel ponders over the difference between the severity with which old heroic societies punished deceit and fraud (while being lenient towards crimes of violence) and the heavy punishments meted out to crimes of violence (coupled with the indulgent treatment of crooks) in modern commercial society. He upbraids the rude justice meted out to offenders by primitive societies in accordance with their ancient notions of honour. Surely a thrust of the knife by an *"homme honnête en ses moeurs, mais violent"* will have less serious moral consequences than thievery and deceit, or *"les débordements de la luxure."* For "old ferocity," Sorel complains, "tends to be replaced by ruse."

On the eve of World War I we find Sorel speculating on the two possible ways of arresting bourgeois decadence and Socialist demoralisation that accompanies it. At the end of the *Insegnamenti sociali della economica contemporanea,* he writes that "a great international war [which he regards as not very likely] may have as its effect the suppression of the causes which tend today to favour the taste for moderation and the desire for social peace." It would certainly bring to power "men with the will to govern." Sorel's other hope is

> a great extension of proletarian violence, which would make the bourgeoisie see the revolutionary reality and fill it with disgust for the humanitarian platitudes with which Jaurès has been lulling them to sleep.

Indeed, Sorel wants the capitalists to fight, to believe in themselves and in their class interests, to be like the early captains of industry or American robber barons. Let them mind their own business, and not act as philanthropists with a social conscience, always ready to conciliate, to give in. This softness was a sign of effeminacy, and it demoralised the workers. By being what history has meant them to be—harsh and ruthless taskmakers—the employers would deploy their potentialities to the full, and keep their workers on their tiptoes as fighters, and thus hasten the Day of Confrontation.

> When the governing classes, no longer daring to govern, are ashamed of their privileged situation, are eager to make advances to their enemies, and proclaim their horror of all cleavage in society, it becomes much more difficult to maintain in the minds of the proletariat this idea of cleavage without which Socialism cannot fulfil its historical role.

Reformist socialists who wish to act as conciliating go-betweens, who work for "social peace" and national unity were traitors to the working class, and destroyers of morality. "Finally . . . anti-patriotism becomes an essential element in the Syndicalist programme . . . an inseparable part of socialism."

In words reminiscent of Lenin's élitism, Sorel says that the *syndicats* must search less for the greatest number of adherents than for the organisation of the vigorous elements; revolutionary strikes are excellent for effecting a solution by weeding out the pacifists who would spoil the best troops, "dedicated to the absolute."

BETWEEN MARX & MUSSOLINI

What will be the state of affairs on the morrow of the victorious General Strike? What kind of society was desirable or likely to emerge? On this Sorel is maddeningly vague, and he has many excuses. He had rejected

Utopianism from the start. He believes in the unpredictable Bergsonian creativeness of the *élan vital.* He was prepared to endorse Mussolini's famous slogan: "Every system is an error, every theory is a prison." But what Sorel does say on the subject reminds one very much of Lenin's Old Left conceptions in *State and Revolution* and of contemporary New Left notions. Sorel rejects the idea of any guidance, supervision, or control from outside and from above, even if those supervisors are democratically elected (since the supervisors would always be thinking of the next election). And he would not conceive of tribunals or penalties or prisons to coerce the victorious proletarians. There would be no need for anything of that kind. Steeled in revolutionary ideology and having gone through the fire of strikes, the workers would, in the manner of true Soldiers of Liberty (or, perhaps, warriors of God) have developed a superb blend of dignity, pride, individualistic self-reliance, and an enthusiastic readiness and capacity to engage in cooperative effort. They would thus be totally free in their utter unanimity. The key phrases here are "heroic exploits . . . extraordinary enthusiasm . . . ardour takes the place of discipline . . . the greatest possible zeal . . . ," etc.

A few lines later, Sorel drops the very revealing remark that as a result of his farouche individualism on the one hand and his keen sense of responsibility on the other, the soldier of the Revolutionary armies

> felt no pity for the generals or officers whom he saw guillotined after a defeat on the charge of dereliction of duty. . . . In his eyes failure could only be explained by some grave error on the part of his leaders . . . made him approve of rigorous measures against men who . . . caused it to lose the fruit of so much heroism.

Obviously, where absolute perfection is postulated as predetermined, any failing is found to appear as the result of ill-will, perversion, and treason. Where unanimity—*"l'unanimité qui va se former incessamment"*—is expected as inevitable, any dissent must seem an arbitrary and selfish deviation. Unanimity must be made manifest by all means. The road from perfectionist anarchy to democratic centralism (perhaps better called totalitarian democracy) is not a very long one.

And yet, numerous and close as are the points of contact between Sorel and Bolshevism, the spirit and temper that pervade his writings are utterly uncongenial to proletarian mentality, and alien to Marxist philosophy and Socialist values. It was not for nothing that on being asked whether he had been influenced by Sorel's work one Syndicalist leader replied, with a shrug of the shoulders, that he had "read only Alexandre Dumas"! Reality was different. The real workers could hardly have been expected to lend an ear to appeals to heroic self-abnegation in order to enthrone someone else's lofty morality, or to entertain the idea that they should make superhuman efforts on behalf of a proffered mythology.

In spite of Sorel's insistent claim to be remembered as "the faithful servant of the proletariat," he decisively parts company with Socialism and comes close to Fascism. It is true that Lenin, like Marx before him, struck many élitist notes; he belaboured the bourgeoisie (and the Mensheviks and Social Revolutionaries) for their philistinism, flabbiness, and hypocrisy, and extolled the resoluteness and determination of his own revolutionary fighters. Yet the heroic qualities to him were never an end in themselves, but only a means of arriving speedily at a terminal régime of social justice; at most, they were tokens of devotion. The display of vitality or the achievement of glory are not values in themselves. The Socialist Revolution is not made to create a superior breed of man. The institutions of the Socialist system are sure to beget better men: better for being, above all, less rapaciously selfish and more cooperative, more rational and more civilised; but certainly not for being inspired by a combative urge for self-expression as members of some superior élite or master race. Nothing is more alien to Socialism than Nietzscheanism. One could thus hardly call the teachings of Sorel "socialism." What they are in fact is a Nietzschean repudiation of bourgeois mediocrity and deceit and a Nietzschean philosophy of élitism applied to the proletariat. Sorel turned the tables on Nietzsche. While the prophet of "the Will to Power" denounced socialist ideology as slave ethics, Sorel expects a revaluation of all values and the enthronement of a heroic civilisation to come from the proletariat. Its *syndicats* are called upon to play the part of *"les autorités sociales"* fulfilled in the past by the ruling families of an aristocracy or patriciate. The impulse of both thinkers was (to say it again) the same: revulsion from the shabbiness, the hypocrisy, the meanness and mediocrity of bourgeois society in the 19th century. A resurgence of heroic virtues was an end in itself to both prophets. It is scarcely true to say that Sorel's aim was to replace the political authoritarian state of the bourgeois intellectuals by "a network of the free *syndicats.*" This new type of social organisation had, in his eyes, no value in itself except as a lever for the new heroic morality. In spite of Sorel's preoccupation with juridical concepts and institutions, his concern was really with a "new heart" and not with an new institutional order. Sorel's glorification of the sense of manifest destiny, of the will to conquer and the joy of struggle as the begetters of all heroic virtues, transforms these from means into ends in themselves. Heroic for what? It does not, in the last analysis, much matter for what purpose. After all, Sorel speaks with deep admiration of the heroic qualities of the bourgeoisie in its prime, and he enjoins the proletarians to be fierce and uncompromising so that even their effeminate philanthropic employers might recover the kind of militant virtues which characterised the early captains of industry.

Sorel opts for the heroic proletariat and not for the reborn bourgeoisie—as he might well have, and as indeed some of his followers did—because, it appears, he has the Hegelian sense that the next phase of history belongs to the proletariat. It is not because he wants to redeem the proletariat as an oppressed class. He speaks with the same admiration of the heroism of the Spartans, the early Christians, the apocalyptic Protestant sects, the monastic orders, the soldiers of the *Grande Armée,* and the Mazzinians.

> In the total ruin of institutions and of morals there remains something which is powerful, new, and intact, and it is that which constitutes, properly speaking, the soul of the revolutionary proletariat. Nor will this be swept away in the general decadence of moral values, if the workers have enough energy to bar the road to the middle-class corrupters, answering their advances with the plainest brutality. . . . The bond which I pointed out in the beginning between Socialism and proletarian violence appears to us now in all its strength. It is to violence that Socialism owes those high ethical values by means of which it brings *salvation* to the modern world.

> Proletarian violence . . . appears as a very beautiful and heroic thing . . . in the service of the primordial interests of our civilisation. . . . [It] may save the world from barbarism. . . . Let us salute the revolutionaries just as the Greeks saluted the Spartan heroes who defended Thermopylae and thus contributed to maintaining light in the ancient world.

The turn soon came for Syndicalism to be rejected by Sorel as "hyper-demagoguery"—as Socialism had been before, also for its "demagoguery" and "stupidity." Sorel stumbled upon (or rather was lured into) a new view of historic opportunity: the extreme nationalist Royalist Right as candidates for a revival of virility and heroism. He gave his blessing to a bizarre flirtation between a handful of young enthusiasts of the Syndicalist Left and of the extreme Right. It was not really, as far as Sorel himself was concerned, a joyous espousal of the Royalist-nationalist cause, rather a half-hearted, uneasy relationship, hampered by a certain sense of incongruity. But the young disciples, who came from syndicalism as well as those who came from integral nationalism, and who had as yet no past to live down, were able to enjoy the *affaire* with undisturbed relish.

A signal event in Sorel's *rapprochement* with the Right was his article on Charles Péguy under the title **"Le Réveil de l'âme francaise, le Mystère de la Charité de Ieanne d'Arc"** (1910). In it he hailed the proud and defiant resurgence of traditionalist Catholic French patriotism and militarism as a *revanche* of the anti-Dreyfusards upon the "dregs of the humanitarianism" of the Sorbonne (and democracy in general). Sorel prophesied that these old-new ideas were destined to "direct contemporary thought."

The programmatic Declaration of the *"Cité Française,"* the still-born organ of the Syndicalist-Nationalist alliance, was signed by Sorel (who drafted it), his two disciples Georges Valois and Edouard Berth, and the two royalists Pierre Gilbert and Jean Variot (author of the *"Propos de Georges Sorel"*). The aim of the editors was to "liberate French intelligence from all those ideologies . . . which dominated Europe in the last century." Whatever the differences dividing them, they were perfectly united in the opinion that

> for any solution of the problems of the modern world . . . it is absolutely necessary to destroy the democratic institutions . . . as the greatest social peril to all classes of the community, in the first place the working classes. Democracy mixes up the classes, in order to enable a few bands of politicians, associated with financiers or dominated by them, to exploit the producers.

The editors pledge themselves to foster the self-awareness of every social class by weaning it away from the stultifying teachings of democracy, and to restore to it its original virility and sense of mission.

For some years Sorel became a regular contributor to the nationalist *L'Indépendance;* he also emerges as the somewhat reluctant patron saint of the *"Cercle Proudhon,"* where his disciples and the young Rightist enthusiasts (Henri Lagrange, Gilbert Maire, René de Maranes, André Vincent) were trying with the blessing of Maurras, Barrès, and other nationalist luminaries, to evolve a type of French national socialism—Proudhon against Marx—which would fight democracy, "the stupidest of dreams . . . the mortal error." Capitalism was also the enemy: "the capitalist régime which destroys in the community what the democratic ideas destroy in the domain of the spirit, that is the nation, the family, the *moeurs,* substituting the law of gold for the law of the blood."[15]

NIHILISM: FROM SOREL TO VALOIS

The man who used Sorel as a foundation stone for a genuine and full-blooded Fascist philosophy was Georges Valois. Valois has been called the French Mussolini *manqué,*[16] who in 1925 tried to emulate the Duce's triumphant march on Rome (but failed to reach Paris). He started out as one of the wildest young Leftists on the Left Bank, and then wandered for years across the globe to South-east Asia, Russia, and other distant places. On his return to Paris Valois was smitten by a revelation—the idea of élitist authority. He writes a book entitled *L'Homme qui vient: Philosophie de l'Autorité,* and dedicates it to the "young, energetic men, whose intelligence has been stultified and whose muscles had been rendered flabby by voluptuousness," as a result of a philosophy of "moral anarchy" which for generations now had been teaching "the abolition of all restraints." Valois defines his new ideal as "work, and its condition: authority and the State." He intends to confound the *"horde juive triomphante"* in the Dreyfus affair. Valois proclaims war on the three prophets who

> wrought ruin upon the modern world . . . three great criminals, three great impostors, Fathers of the lie . . . J. J. Rousseau, the false man of nature, Immanuel Kant, the false man of duty, and Karl Marx, the false man of necessity.

Valois identifies his own prophets: in the first placel, Sorel; then Charles Maurras, Carlyle, Kipling, H. G. Wells; the now-forgotten scientist René Quinton; the old masters (de Maistre, Bonald, Auguste Comte and Taine), but above all Nietzsche.

> I owe to Nietzsche my liberation. At a time when we stuck in the democratic humanitarian swamp . . . wasting our energies in an effort to solve inept problems . . . Nietzsche . . . *coup de fouet* . . . forced to us consider with true sincerity the real problems . . . to see ourselves without pity . . . the liberator of our energy.[17]

In fact, Valois' whole theory is nothing but a smudged, coarse-grained, and petulant variation on Nietzsche and Sorel.

Sorel's élitist conception of the proletarian *syndicats* and their revivalist mission is transformed by Valois into a vision of the rule of born masters, "holders of the whip" over the slavish, indolent, swinish multitude. The masters are no longer á hereditary social class like ancient aristocracy—something quite impossible in the 20th century—or an élite of brains, but men endowed with the undefinable gifts of leadership who prove themselves in a Darwinian struggle and rivalry. You recognised them when you saw them coming, these men at the top, the successors to the medieval barons, the famous *condottieri* and the great capitalists. Their success is their title to legitimacy. The "strongest will reveal himself incontestably . . . no one will doubt his qualification, once he has defeated all the others." Never mind the means. Without ruthless, uninhibited urge for power and leadership, those *"enthousiastes, des hommes pleins d'appétits, avides de jouissances du commandement et des cruautés"* would never get there. It was the impotent but envious and cunning demagogues of democracy who spoke of "rights" and "justice" and flattered the masses.

Sorel's earliest concern was with authenticity, certainty, and social cohesion. He sought them first in the realities of organic historic tradition, then successively in Marxist teaching, in the inexorable determinations of productive effort, in the existential situation of the proletariats, finally in the life-giving collective myth. He never ceased to fear and hate self-willed arbitrariness and intellectual vagrancy. Georges Valois goes far beyond his master when he raises the instinctive will-to-power of the individual and the visceral ties of the community of blood—*"la vérité charnelle"*—to the dignity of absolutes.

It was the instincts that mattered most, and not the intellect. Man's mission was not to "know the world" or to learn to "know himself," but to fight.

> The means which you wish to employ for knowing yourself—intelligence—put it into second place, and do not use it for tasks for which it was not made. . . . It is a gift which was given to you not that you may know yourself, nor that you may know our *raison d'être,* but to enable you to understand, with the aid of experience and instinct, in what way the things surrounding you may serve and contribute to your growth. Apart from that, there is for you nothing but doubt, confusion, trouble, and death. . . .

We are faced here with a fear of thought and analysis, a dread of choosing between alternatives, and a craving to be propelled mindlessly by powerful instincts or, for that matter, the force of habit.

"False sages and liars!" exclaims Valois, "to say that one is led by his intelligence is an error or a lie. Man is guided by his instincts. . . . What is the brain? An organ like his foot, his hand, his eye, utilised by his instinct. . . . Who commands in living nature? It is the instinct of life." The power to act was superior to the ability to think. "Intellectuals!" calls Valois, "if you are true *hommes de commandement,* speak in the name of your energy, do not ask for power, take it. If you are strong, the people will recognise you as leaders." All creative force came from instinct, and this is why *"le maître de la vie,* the Aristocrat, will never be an intellectual but an Energetic, the one whose life instinct had the greatest strength." The supreme fact of life—of men as well as of nations—was war.

> All the things that we call the pacific blessings of civilisation are the creations of war; civilisation itself is the fruit of war. . . . The nations . . . working today to develop a civilisation of peace, had themselves been formed by war and maintain their work of peace, of solidarity and of brotherhood thanks to nothing but war. War is the primary law of life, and it is for the species the only way of achieving the highest elevation of its life instinct. . . .

This situation did not have to express itself in actual fighting. War-like rivalry was also present in an accumulation of so much power that all dangers from within and from without would be staved off without going to war. War is "a happy necessity for civilisation." It was also an instrument for realising social justice among the nations, "by wresting lands and resources which indolent and incompetent nations knew not how to utilise," and thus "abuse their sovereign rights over them."

The democratic politicians—a breed that emerged in the French Revolution—represented a kind of anti-élite of the *déclassé* of all classes. "The democratic régime is in the full sense an organised, systematic disorganisation of the nation, and carries with it its own ruin. . . . " As for Socialism, it was only a new form of parliamentary exploitation which has simply changed the electoral formulae, but it pursues the same aim as the other parties—"the conquest of power in order to obtain the wealth which that conquest provides. . . . "[18]

Behind the anti-élite of democratic and socialist politicians, a loose congerie of adventurers who come and go, there stood an anti-élite acting from behind the scenes, but of the most distinct identity, cohesion, and continuity—the Jews. The politicians were no more than the puppets or agents of that Jewish power. The Jews were an anti-élite *par excellence:* few and physically weak, with no aristocratic tradition or martial qualities, intellectuals and reasoners, they could succeed and obtain the power that they so craved not by imposing themselves in an elemental irresistible sort of way, but through manipulation and scheming. They represented and embodied everything that was not instinctive and concrete, but was abstract and universal. Cut off from the land and its pursuits for so long, with no country of their own, with no share in the hard productive effort, they had developed two weapons which had no particular home or race: ideas and money. These became the instruments with the help of which those aliens could worm their way into French society and overcome the natural resistance and healthy egoism of a deeply rooted, idiosyncratic nation. Against French instinctive certainties, traditions and customs, the French conception of justice, they proclaimed and fostered an abstract universal natural law, the idea of Man *per se,* eternal ideal justice. Their *"patrie 'idéelle'"* was pitted against authentic soil-bound French patriotism: the French were seduced into adopting the abstract ideology of Revolution as their national ideology. The alien Jews could thus appear as most excellent Frenchmen, while remaining themselves a closely knit entity apart. Finance capitalism, *laissez-faire,* liberalism, rationalism as such, finally socialism founded on class war—all were Jewish devices to sap the self-assurance, the cohesion, the unity, and the authenticity of the French nation.

Parliamentary democracy became the convenient façade for the wire-pullers. Apparently an expression and guarantee of popular sovereignty, it was but a camouflage for the occult but real powers. Sorel had already drawn attention to the close similarity, and indeed the link, between speculators who gambled on the stock exchange and parasitic democratic politicians who gambled for power. He did that without specifically mentioning the Jews. However, the Dreyfusard eventually developed into a bitter anti-Semite, calling upon Europe to defend itself against "the Jewish peril" in the same way as the U.S. fought "the Yellow peril"; he blamed the Chekist terror upon the Jewish members of the Bolshevik Party. The Jews (Valois claims) had their agents in all parties, but they had lately concentrated their attention on the Socialists: for the sake of a better disguise, and in order to make sure that they became the heirs of the expropriated French bourgeoisie on the morrow of the Revolution which they were plotting. Once the revolutionary General Strike succeeded in paralysing all production, the ensuing chaos could be overcome only with the help of ready cash—gold. The Jewish financiers will have kept it in their safes; they will then appear as saviours, offer help, but extort a heavy price, namely complete domination over the economic and political life of the French nation. "It is probable that a terrible anti-Semitic movement will then develop and it will manifest itself through the most beautiful massacre of Jews in history." The Jews would then call in foreign troops to rescue them, in order that Jews and foreigners together share the spoils. Some of the participants in the debate on "The Monarchy and the Working Class" initiated and analysed by Valois see the Jews as working for the enemies of France—for England, Germany, and Italy. Others depict the Jew as the enemy of every authentic nation, and call for an international alliance against the common Jewish danger. Georges Valois himself coined the slogan *"L'or juif contre le sang français."*

The Jew thus appears as the lynch-pin of the whole theory, solving the contradiction between socialism and nationalism.[19]

A CAUTIONARY TALE

The evolution of syndicalist Sorelism towards pro-fascism is a cautionary tale which our younger as well as our older contemporaries might well take to heart. The revulsion from "hypocrisy" and the resulting quest for "authenticity" very easily evolve into a glorification of instinct and direct action. The condemnation of arbitrariness and the craving for certainty can so rapidly take the form of an apologia for an élite and its cult of violence. The emphasis upon the existential situation or collective myth has as its corollary the denial of individual judgment and personal decision, for it raises abstract sentiments to the level of absolutes. A downward slope leads from a populist apotheosis of primary and all-embracing experience—in contrast to analytical reasoning—to "gut thinking" and *Blut und Boden* racism. Finally, the idea of a Manichean confrontation between the forces of darkness and of light—both taken to be indivisible totalities and never just human admixtures of good and evil—easily becomes a warrant for violence without end.

[1] Georges Sorel, *Réflexions sur la Violence* (4th edition, Paris, 1919), Appendix X 3, *"Plaidoyer pour Lenine,"* p. 454; *Reflections on Violence* (tr. Hulme & Roth, introduction by Edward Shils, 1950), "In Defense of Lenin," p. 311.

[2] *Réflexions,* pp. 442, 451. See also G. Sorel, *Lettres à Paul Delesalle, 1914-1921* (Paris, 1947), p. 234; Jean Variot, *Propos de G. Sorel* (Paris, 1935), p. 57; Gaëtan Piron, *Georges Sorel* (Paris, 1927), pp. 53, 55-6; James H. Meisel, *The Genesis of Georges Sorel* (1951), pp. 219, 226, 230.

[3] Michael Freund, *Georges Sorel: der revolutionäre Konservatismus* (Frankfurt-am-Main, 1932), pp. 17, 34, 69; Georges Goriely, *Le pluralisme dramatique de Georges Sorel,* (Paris, 1962).

[4] Richard D. Humphrey, *Georges Sorel, a Prophet without Honor: a study in anti-intellectualism* (1951).

[5] Georges Sorel, *"Science et socialisme,"* in *Revue Philosophique* (1893), pp. 509-11.

[6] G. Sorel: *Avenir Socialiste des Syndicats* (1898); *Mes raisons du syndicalisme* (1910); both reprinted in *Matériaux d'une théorie du prolétariat* (Paris, 1919); also Sorel: *D'Aristote à Marx* (Paris, 1935), pp. 263 ff.

[7] *Matériaux,* pp. 283-4.

[8] Translated into English by Irving L. Horowitz as an Appendix to his *Radicalism and Revolt against Reason: the Social Theories of Georges Sorel* (1961), pp. 207-54.

[9] G. Sorel, *Les Illusions du progrès* (5th ed.; Paris, 1947), pp. 275-86.

[10] Edouard Berth: *Les Méfaits des intellectuels* (1926), pp. 95 ff.; also under the pen-name of Jean Darville, in *La Monarchie et la Classe Ouvrière: une Enquète* (ed. Georges Valois, 1914), pp. cxxx ff.

[11] The great wave of proletarian militancy of the first decade of the 20th century was accompanied by much violence and bloodshed. It produced the first general strike in history, in Italy in 1904; it saw the revolutionary upheaval in Russia carried by a vast strike movement a year later; it sent hundreds of thousands of workers on to the streets of Paris on the First of May in 1906; it witnessed the bloody clashes between strikers and security forces all over Europe, coming in France to a climax in the terrible battles at Villeneuve-Saint-Georges and Darveil with numerous casualties on both sides; the Belgium Socialist Party resorted successfully to mass strike to obtain universal suffrage. Those were the days of the grand debate on the general strike as the instrument of the "revolutionary breakthrough" and as a means of stopping an international war. It is enough to recall Rosa Luxemburg's pamphlets on the subject.

[12] *Reflections,* pp. 90-1.

[13] J. Variot, *Propos de G. Sorel,* p. 55.

[14] Pierre Andreu, *Notre maître, M. Sorel* (1953), p. 192.

[15] *Cahiers du Cercle Proudhon* (*I er cahier,* Jan.-Feb. 1912); Meisel, *op. cit.,* pp. 183 ff. Edouard Berth will say in years to come that "in forming, together with Georges Valois, the *Cercle Proudhon,* with the aim of fighting democracy from the dual standpoint, the Nationalist and the Syndicalist, we came close to creating Fascism *avant la lettre. . . .* " This statement is re-echoed by Valois himself in his post-war book on Fascism, when he says that the *Cercle* "laid in 1912 the foundations for the Fascist synthesis." Georges Valois, *Le Fascisme,* p. 29; Freund, p. 231; for parallel developments in Italy see John A. Thayer: *Italy and the Great War, Politics and Culture* (1904); Enzo Santarelli: "Le Socialisme nationale en Italie: Précédents et origines," *Le Mouvement Social* (Jan.-Mar. 1965. Nr. 50); Jack J. Roth: "The Roots of Italian Fascism: Sorel and Sorelismo," *Journal of Modern History* (Vol. 39, 1967).

[16] Ernest Nolte: *Three Faces of Fascism* (1966), p. 473; Eugen Weber, "Nationalism, Socialism and National-Socialism in France," *French Historical Studies,* Vol. II. N. 3 (Spring, 1962); Yves Guchet: "Georges Valois ou l'Illusion Fasciste," *Revue Française de Science Politique* (Vol. XV, 1965).

[17] Georges Valois: *L'Homme qui vient: Philosophie de l'Autorité* (1909), Introduction.

[18] G. Valois: *La Monarchie et la classe ouvrière* (1914), p. 18.

[19] To cap it all, Georges Valois died in the Nazi concentration camp of Bergen-Belsen in 1944, having successively fallen out with the *Action Française,* given up Fascism, renounced anti-Semitism, embraced technocratic planning, invented the term *"Libéralisme communautaire,"* and returned to simple French patriotism. . . . What a comment on the spiritual torment of our century!

Isaiah Berlin (essay date 1971)

SOURCE: "Georges Sorel," in *Against the Current: Essays in the History of Ideas,* edited by Henry Hardy, The Hogarth Press, 1979, pp. 296-332.

[*In the following excerpt, Berlin assesses Sorel's work as incendiary and disorganized, while declaring him one of the century's foremost political thinkers.*]

Sorel remains an anomalous figure. The other ideologists and prophets of the nineteenth century have been safely docketed and classified. The doctrines, influence, personalities of Mill, Carlyle, Comte, Darwin, Dostoevsky, Wagner, Nietzsche, even Marx, have been safely placed on their respective shelves in the museum of the history of ideas. Sorel remains, as he was in his lifetime, unclassified; claimed and repudiated both by the right and by the left. Was he a bold and brilliant innovator of devastating genius as his handful of disciples declare? Or a mere romantic journalist, as George Lichtheim calls him? A pessimist 'moaning for blood',[1] in G. D. H. Cole's contemptuous phrase? Or, with Marx, the only original thinker (according to Croce) socialism has ever had? Or a notorious muddle-head, as Lenin unkindly described him? I do not volunteer an answer: I only wish to say something about his principal ideas, and also—to employ that much-abused word—the relevance of these ideas to our time.

I

Georges Sorel was born in 1847 in Cherbourg. His father was an unsuccessful businessman, and the family was forced to practise extreme austerity. According to his cousin, the historian Albert Sorel, Georges Sorel early showed exceptional mathematical gifts. In 1865 he became a student at the École Polytechnique in Paris, and five years later entered the Department of Public Works (Ponts et Chaussées) as an engineer. During the next twenty years he was posted to various provincial towns. During the débâcle of 1870 and 1871 he was in Corsica. In 1875 he fell ill in an hotel in Lyon, and was nursed by a servant called Marie David, a devoutly religious, semi-literate peasant from the borders of Savoy, with whom he set up a household. In his letters he refers to her as his wife, but in fact he appears never to have married her, probably out of deference to the wishes of his family, which was evidently shocked by this *mésalliance.* It appears to have been an entirely happy relationship. He taught her, and learnt from her, and, after her death in 1898, wore a sacred image that she had given him and worshipped her memory for the rest of his days.

Until the age of forty, his life had been that of a typical minor French government official, peaceful, provincial and obscure. In 1889 his first book was published. In 1892, being then forty-five years old, having attained the rank of Chief Engineer and been rewarded with the rank of Chevalier of the Légion d'Honneur, he suddenly resigned. From this moment his public life began. His mother had left him a small legacy, and this enabled him to move to Paris. He settled in a quiet suburb, Boulogne-sur-Seine, where he lived until his death, thirty years later, in 1922. In 1895 he started to contribute to left-wing journals, and from then on became one of the most controversial political writers in France.

He appeared to have no fixed position. His critics often accused him of pursuing an erratic course: a legitimist in his youth, and still a traditionalist in 1889, he was by 1894 a Marxist. In 1896 he wrote with admiration about Vico. By 1898, influenced by Croce, and also by Eduard Bernstein, he began to criticise Marxism and at about the same time fell deeply under the spell of Henri Bergson. He was a Dreyfusard in 1899, a revolutionary syndicalist during the following decade. By 1909 he was a sworn enemy of the Dreyfusards, and, in the following two or three years, an ally of the royalists who edited the *Action française* and a supporter of the mystical nationalism of Barrès. He wrote with admiration about Mussolini's militant socialism in 1912, and in 1919 with still greater admiration about Lenin, ending with whole-hearted support for Bolshevism and, in the last years of his life, an unconcealed admiration for the Duce.

What credence could be placed in the thought of a man whose political views veered so violently and unpredictably? He did not claim to be consistent. 'I write from day to day', he wrote in 1903 to his faithful correspondent, the Italian philosopher Benedetto Croce, 'following the need of the moment.'[2] Sorel's writings have no shape or system, and he was not impressed by it in those of others. He was a compulsive and passionate talker, and, as is at times the case with famous talkers—Diderot, Coleridge, Herzen, Bakunin—his writings remained episodic, unorganised, unfinished, fragmentary, at best sharp, polemical essays or pamphlets provoked by some immediate occasion, not intended to be fitted into a body of coherent, developed doctrine, and not capable of it. Nevertheless, there is a central thread that connects everything that Sorel wrote and said, if not a doctrine, then an attitude, a position, the expression of a singular temperament, of an unaltering view of life. His ideas, which beat like hailstones against all accepted doctrines and institutions, fascinated both his friends and his opponents, and do so still not only because of their intrinsic quality and power, but because what in his day was confined to small coteries of intellectuals has now grown to world-wide proportions. In his lifetime Sorel was looked on as, at best, a polemical journalist, an autodidact with a powerful pen and occasional flashes of extraordinary insight, too wayward and perverse to claim for long the attention of serious and busy men. In the event, he has proved more formidable than many of the respected social thinkers of his day, most of whom he ignored or else regarded with unconcealed disdain.

II

The ideas of every philosopher concerned with human affairs in the end rest on his conception of what man is and can be. To understand such thinkers, it is more important to grasp this central notion or image (which may be implicit, but determines their picture of the world) than even the most forceful arguments with which they defend their views and refute actual and possible objections. Sorel was dominated by one *idée maîtresse:* that man is a creator, fulfilled only when he creates, and not when he passively receives or drifts unresisting with the current. His mind is not a mechanism or organism responsive to stimuli, analysable, describable and predictable by the sciences of man. He is, for Sorel, in the first place, a producer who expresses himself in and through his work, an innovator whose activity alters the material provided by nature, material that he seeks to mould in accordance with an inwardly conceived, spontaneously generated, image or pattern. The productive activity itself brings this pattern to birth and alters it—as it fulfils itself freely, obedient to no law, being conceived as a kind of natural spring of creative energy which can be grasped by inner feeling and not by scientific observation or logical analysis. All other views of what men are, or could be, are fallacious. History shows that men are essentially seekers not of happiness or peace or knowledge or power over others, or salvation in another life—at least these are not men's primary purposes; where they are so, it is because men have degenerated from their true humanity, because education or environment or circumstances have distorted their ideas or character or rendered them impotent or vicious.

Man, at his best, that is, at his most human, seeks in the first place to fulfil himself, individually and with those close to him, in spontaneous, unhindered creative activity, in work that consists of the imposition of his personality on a recalcitrant environment. Sorel quotes his political enemy Clemenceau as saying: 'Everything that lives, resists.'[3] He believed in this proposition as strongly as he believed in anything in his life. To act and not be acted upon, to choose and not be chosen for, to impose form on the chaos that we find in the world of nature and the world of thought—that is the end of both art and science and belongs to the essence of man as such. He resists every force that seeks to reduce his energy, to rob him of his independence and his dignity, to kill the will, to crush everything in him that struggles for unique self-expression and reduce it to uniformity, impersonality, monotony, and, ultimately, extinction. Man lives fully only in and by his works, not by passive enjoyment or the peace and security that he might find by surrender to external pressures, or habit, or convention, by failure to use for his own freely conceived goals the mechanism of the laws of nature to which he is inevitably subject.

This is, of course, not a new idea. It lies at the heart of the great revolt against rationalism and the Enlightenment, identified particularly with French civilisation, that animated the more extreme German Protestant sects after the Reformation, and which, towards the end of the eighteenth century, took the form of celebrating the primacy of the human will against material forces and calm, rational knowledge alike. This is not the place in which to discuss the origins of romanticism. But one cannot understand Sorel, or the impact of his views, unless one realises that what caused the ferment in his mind was a passionate conviction which he shares with some of the early romantic writers, that the pursuit of peace or happiness or profit, and concern with power or possessions or social status or a quiet life, is a contemptible betrayal of what any man, if he takes thought, knows to be the true end of human life: the attempt to make something worthy of the maker, the effort to be and do something, and to respect such effort in others. The notion of the dignity of labour, of the right to work as opposed to the mere Pauline duty to engage in it, which is at the heart of much modern socialism, springs from this romantic conception, which German thinkers, notably Herder and Fichte, brought up in earnest Lutheran pietism, impressed upon the European consciousness.

Sorel's violent and lifelong disgust with the life of the Parisian bourgeoisie of his time, in its own way as ferocious as that of Flaubert, with whom temperamentally he has something in common, is bound up with a Jansenist hatred of the twin evils of hedonism and materialism. The opportunism and corruption of French political life in the early years of the Third Republic, together with the sense of national humiliation after 1870, may have been a traumatic experience for him, as for many Frenchmen. But it seems unlikely that he would have felt differently in the greedy and competitive Paris of Louis-Philippe or the plutocratic and pleasure-seeking Paris of the Second Empire. An agonised sense of suffocation in the commercialised, jaunty, insolent, dishonourable, easy-going, cowardly, mindless, bourgeois society of the nineteenth century fills the writings of the age: the works of Proudhon, Carlyle, Ibsen, Marx, Baudelaire, Nietzsche, almost the whole of the best known Russian literature of the time, are one vast indictment of it. This is the tradition to which Sorel belongs from the beginning to the end of his life as a writer. The corruption of public life appears to him to have gone deeper than during the decadence of classical Greece, or the end of the Roman Empire. Parliamentary democracy, with its fraudulence and hypocrisy, appeared to him to be an odious insult to human dignity, a mockery of the proper ends of men. Democratic politics resembled a huge stock exchange in which votes were bought and sold without shame or fear, men were bamboozled or betrayed by scheming politicians, ruthless bankers, crooked businessmen, *avocasserie et écrivasserie*—lawyers, journalists, professors, all scrambling for money, recognition, power, in a world of contemptible fools and cunning knaves, deceivers and deceived, living off the exploited workers 'in a democratic bog' in a Europe 'stupefied by humanitarianism'.[4]

III

The western tradition of social thought has been sustained by two central doctrines. The first taught that the ultimate causes of human misery, folly and vice were ignorance and mental laziness. Reality, it was held by rationalists from Plato to Comte, is a single, intelligible structure: to understand it and explain it, and to understand one's own nature and place in this structure—this alone can reveal what, in a specific situation, can, and what cannot, be realised. Once the facts and the laws that govern them are known to him, no man, desiring as he does happiness or harmony or wisdom or virtue, can pursue any but the sole correct path to his goal that his knowledge reveals to him. To be a rational, even a normal, human being, is to seek one, or several, of the limited number of the natural ends of human life. Only ignorance of what they are, or of what are the correct means for their attainment, can lead to misery or vice or failure. The scientific or naturalistic version of this doctrine animated the Enlightenment and the forms which it took in the two centuries that followed—until, indeed, our own day.

Sorel rejected this entire approach. He saw no reason for believing that the world was a rational harmony, or that man's true perfection depended on understanding of the proper place assigned to him in it by his creator—a personal deity or an impersonal nature. Influenced by both Marx and the half-forgotten Italian thinker, Vico, of whom he was one of the few perceptive readers in the nineteenth century, Sorel believed that all that man possessed he owed to his own unflagging labour. Certainly natural science was a triumph of human effort; but it was not a transcription or map of nature, as the positivists had claimed in the eighteenth century; they, and their modern disciples, were mistaken about this. There were two natures: artificial nature, the nature of science—a system of idealised entities: atoms, electric charges, mass, energy and the like—fictions compounded out of observed uniformities, particularly in regions relatively remote from man's daily concerns, like the contents of the world of astronomy, deliberately adapted to mathematical treatment that enabled men to identify some of the furniture of the universe, and to predict and, indeed, control parts of it. The concepts and categories in terms of which this nature had been constructed were conditioned by human aims: they abstracted from the universe those aspects that were of interest to men and possessed sufficient regularity to make them capable of generalisation. This, of course, was a stupendous achievement, but an achievement of the creative imagination, not an accurate reproduction of the structure of reality, not a map, still less a picture, of what there was. Outside this set of formulas, of imaginary entities and mathematical relationships in terms of which the system was constructed, there was 'natural' nature—the real thing—chaotic, terrifying, compounded of ungovernable forces, against which man had to struggle, which, if he was to survive and create, he had at least in part to subdue; with the help, indeed, of his sciences; but the symmetry, the coherence, were attributes of the first, or artificial nature, the construction of his intellect, something that was not found but made. The assumption that reality was a harmonious whole, a rational structure whose logical necessity is revealed to reason, a marvellously coherent system which a rational being cannot think or wish to be otherwise and still remain rational, and in which, therefore, it must feel happy and fulfilled—all this is an enormous fallacy. Nature is not a perfect machine, nor an exquisite organism, nor a rational system; it is a savage jungle: science is the art of dealing with it as best we can. When we extend such manipulation to men as well, we degrade and dehumanise them, for men are not objects but subjects of action. If Christianity has taught us anything, it has made us realise that the only thing of absolute value in the universe is the human soul, the only thing that acts, that imagines, that creates, that resists the impersonal forces which work against it and, unless they are resisted, enslave us and ultimately grind us into dust. This is the menace that perpetually hangs over us. Consequently life is a perpetual battle.

To deny this truth is shallow optimism, characteristic of the shallow eighteenth century for which Sorel, like Carlyle, felt a lifelong contempt. The laws of nature are not descriptions, they are, as he came to learn from William James (and perhaps also from Marx), strategic weapons. Croce had taught him that our categories are categories of action, that they alter what we call reality as the purposes of our active selves alter: they do not establish timeless truths as the positivists maintained. 'We consider as matter, or as the base, that which escapes, less or more completely, from our will. The form is rather what corresponds to our freedom.[5] Systems, theories, unrelated to action, attempting to transcend experience, that which professors and intellectuals are so good at, are only abstractions into which men escape to avoid facing the chaos of reality; scientific (and political) Utopias are compounded out of them; the pseudo-scientific predictions about our future by which such Utopias are bolstered are nothing but modern forms of astrology. When such schemes are applied to human beings they can do dreadful damage. To confuse our own constructions and inventions with eternal laws or divine decrees is one of the most fatal delusions of men: this is what had happened in the French Revolution. The confusion of the two natures, the real and the artificial, is bad enough. But the *philosophes* were not, by and large, even genuine scientists: only social and political theorists who talked about science without practising it; the *Encyclopédie* had not improved one's real knowledge or skill. Ideological patter, optimistic journalism about the uses of science, were not science. They only lead to positivism and bureaucracy, *la petite science;* and when theory is ruthlessly applied to human affairs, its result is a fearful despotism. Sorel speaks almost the language of William Blake. The Tree of Knowledge has killed the Tree of Life. Robespierre and the Jacobins were fanatical pedants who tried to reduce human life to rules that seemed to them based on objective truths; the institutions they created crushed spontaneity and invention, enslaved and maimed the creative will of man.

Men, whose essence, for Sorel, is to be active beings, are perpetually menaced by two equally fatal dangers: a Scylla and a Charybdis. Scylla is weariness, the loss of nerve, decadence, when men relax from effort, return to the fleshpots, or else fall into quietism and become the victims of the trickery of the clever operators who destroy all honour, energy, integrity, independence, and substitute the rule of cunning and fraud, the dead hand of bureaucracy, laws that can be turned to their advantage by unscrupulous operators, aided and abetted by an army of experts—prostitutes and lackeys of those in power, or idle entertainers and sycophantic parasites, like Voltaire and Diderot, the 'buffoons of a degenerate aristocracy',[6] bourgeois who aspire to ape the tastes of an idle and pleasure-loving nobility. Charybdis is the despotism of fanatical theorists—'the bloodthirsty frenzy of an optimist maddened by sudden resistance to his plans',[7] who is ready to butcher the present to create the happiness of the future on its bones. These alternations mark the unhappy eighteenth century.

How are men to be rescued from the horns of this dilemma? Only by moral strength: by the development of new men, fully-formed human beings not obsessed by fear and greed, men who have not had their imagination and emotion fettered by doctrinaires or rotted by intellectuals. Sorel's vision resembled that of Tolstoy and Nietzsche when they were young—of the fullness of life, as it was once lived by the Homeric Greeks, free from the corrosive effect of civilised scepticism and critical questioning. It is not the possession of common ideas, convictions bred by reasoning, that creates true human bonds, but common life and common effort. The true basis of all association is the family, the tribe, the *polis,* in which cooperation is instinctive and spontaneous and does not depend on rules or contracts or invented arrangements. Associations for the sake of profit or utility, resting on some artificial agreement, as the political and economic institutions of the capitalist system plainly do, stifle the sense of common humanity and destroy human dignity by generating a spirit of competitive opportunism. Athens created immortal masterpieces until Socrates came, and spun theories, and played a nefarious part in the disintegration of that closely knit, once heroic, community by sowing doubt and undermining established values which spring from the profoundest and most life-enhancing instincts of men.

Sorel began to write in this fashion when he was still a municipal engineer in Perpignan; his friend Daniel Halévy assures us that he had not then read a line of Nietzsche, whom he later came to admire. But their charge against Socrates is identical: both Nietzsche and Sorel take the side of his accusers: it was Socrates, and his disciple Plato, arch-intellectuals, who planted the life-destroying seeds that led to the glorification of abstractions, academies, contemplative or critical philosophies, Utopian schemes, and so to the decline of Greek vitality and Greek genius.

Can decadence be averted? Where is permanent salvation to be sought? There is another ancient doctrine in which men have traditionally sought reassurance: teleology. History, it was thought, would be meaningless—merely a causal sequence, or a chaos of unrelated episodes—if it lacked some ultimate purpose. This was considered unthinkable: reason rejects the notion of a mere collocation of 'brute' facts; there must be advance or growth towards the fulfilment of some goal or pattern; the mind demands some guarantee that, despite all accidents and collapses, the story will have a happy ending; either Providence is leading us towards it in its own inscrutable fashion; or else history is conceived as the self-realisation from stage to stage of the great cosmic spirit of which all men and all their institutions, and perhaps all nature, is the changing and progressive expression. Or, perhaps, it is human reason itself that cannot and will not for ever be frustrated, and must, late or soon, triumph over all obstacles, both external and self-generated, and build a world in which men have become everything that, as rational creatures, they consciously or unconsciously seek to be. In its metaphysical or mystical or secular forms this amalgam of Hebraic faith and Aristotelian metaphysics dominated the ideas of the last three centuries and gave confidence to many who might otherwise have despaired.

These central intellectual traditions to which men have pinned their hopes—the Greek doctrine of salvation by knowledge and the Judaeo-Christian doctrine of history as theodicy—were all but rejected by Sorel. All his life he believed in two absolutes: that of science, and that of morality. Science, even though, or perhaps because, it is a human artifice, enables us to classify, predict, control certain events. The concepts and categories in terms of which science puts its questions may vary with cultural change: the objectivity and reliability of the answers do not. But it is a weapon, not an ontology, not an analysis of reality. The great machine of science does not yield answers to problems of metaphysics or morality: to reduce the central problems of human life to problems of means, that is, of technology, is not to understand what they are. To regard technical progress as being identical with, or even as a guarantee of, cultural progress, is moral blindness. Sorel devoted a series of essays to demonstrating the absurdity of the idea of general human progress which springs from confusion of technology with life, or of the preposterous claim, first advanced by men of letters in the late seventeenth century, of their inevitable superiority to the ancients. As for theological or metaphysical beliefs in human perfectibility, they are only a pathetic clutching at straws, a refuge of the weak. Neither science nor history offer comfort: Turgot and Condorcet and their nineteenth-century disciples are poor, deluded optimists who believe that history is on our side; so it will be, but only if we make it so, if we fight the good fight against the oppressors and exploiters, the dreary, life-destroying levellers, the masters and the slaves, and protect the sublime and the heroic against democrats and plutocrats, pedants and philistines.

Sorel has no doubt about what is health, and what is disease, whether in individuals or in societies. The Homeric Greeks lived in the light of values without which a society could not be creative or possess a sense of grandeur. They admired courage, strength, justice, loyalty, sacrifice, above all the struggle itself; freedom for them was not an ideal but a reality: the feeling of successful effort. Then (and this probably comes from Vico) came scepticism, sophistry, ease of life, democracy, individualism, decadence. Greek society disintegrated and was conquered. Rome, too, was once heroic, but it had given in to legalism and the bureaucratisation of life; the late Empire was a cage in which human beings felt stifled.

It was the early church that had once held high the flag of man. What the early Christians believed is less important than the intensity of a faith that did not allow the corrosive intellect to penetrate it. Above all, these men refused to compromise. The early Christians could have saved themselves from persecution by coming to terms with the Roman bureaucrats. They preferred faith, integrity and sacrifice. Concessions, Sorel repeats, always, in the end, lead to self-destruction. The only hope lies in ceaseless resistance to forces that seek to weaken what one instinctively knows that one lives by. When the church triumphed and made its peace with the world, it became infected by it and therefore degenerated: the barbarians were converted to Christianity, but to a worldly Christianity, and so fell into decay.

The heroic Christianity of the martyrs is a defence against the decadent state, but it is itself intrinsically socially destructive. Christians (and Stoics too) are not producers: the Gospels, unlike the Old Testament or Greek literature, are addressed to paupers and anchorites. A society indifferent to riches, content with its daily bread, allows no room for vigorous, creative life. Christianity, like every ideology, like its secular imitation—the Utopian socialism of a later day—'cut the links between social life and the spirit, sowing everywhere germs of quietism, despair, death'.[8] Too little was accorded to Caesar, too much to the church—an organisation of consumers, not (in Sorel's sense) of producers. Sorel wishes to return to the firm values of the hardy Judaean peasants or the Greek *polis,* where merely to question them was considered subversive. He is concerned neither with happiness nor salvation: only with the quality of life itself, with what used to be called virtue (which in his case much resembles Renaissance *virtù*). Like the Jansenists, like Kant and the romantics, he values motive and character, not consequences and success.

The accumulation of public wealth in the hands of priests and monks played its part in the exhaustion and fall of the Roman west. But after decay there is always hope of a revival: does not Vico speak of a *ricorso*—when one cycle of history has ended in moral weakness and decadence, a new one, barbarian, fresh and simple and pious and strong, begins the story again? Sorel dwells on this with the enthusiasm of Nietzsche. He is fascinated by every example of resolute moral resistance to decay, and consequently by the story of the church under persecution and of the church militant; he takes little interest in the church triumphant. It is in connection with movements of resistance and renewal that he develops (increasingly after falling under the influence of Bergson) the theories of which he became the most famous upholder: of the social myth, of permanent class war, of violence, of the general strike.

Even in the darkest moments of decadence, the social organism develops antibodies to resist the disease—men who will not give in, who will stand up and save the honour of the human race. The dedicated monastic orders, the saints and martyrs who preserved mankind from total contamination by late Roman society—what men today embody such qualities, possess the *virtù* of the great *condottieri* and artists of the Renaissance? There may be something of it in the American men of business, bold, enterprising, creative captains of industry who make their will prevail over nature and other men; but they are tainted by the general corruption of capitalism of which they are the leaders. There was, it seemed to Sorel, only one true body of this kind: those who are saved by work—the workers, the only genuinely creative class of our day. The proletarians, who are not morally caught in the toils of bourgeois life, appear to Sorel heroic, endowed with a natural sense of justice and humanity, morally impregnable, proof against the sophistries and casuistries of the intellectuals.

In the last years of the century, during the united front of the left created by the Dreyfus Affair, and perhaps influenced by the reformist socialism of Bernstein in Germany which seemed to him to be at any rate based on economic realities, Sorel supported the idea of a political party of the working class. But soon he accepted the position of the syndicalist journalist, Lagardelle, in whose journal, *Le Mouvement socialiste,* a good many of his articles appeared, that it is not opinions that truly unite men, for beliefs are a superficial possession, blown about by ideologists who play with words and ideas, and can be shared by men of different social formation who have basically nothing in common with each other. Men are truly made one only by real ties, by the family—the unchanging unit of the moral life, as Proudhon and Le Play had insisted—by martyrdom in a common cause, but above all by working together, by common creation, united resistance to the pressures both of inanimate nature, which provides the workers with their materials, and of their masters, who seek to rob them of the fruits of their toil. The workers are not a party held together by lust for power or even for material goods. They are a social formation, a class. It was the genius of Marx that discovered the true nature of classes defined in terms of their relationship to the productive processes of a society torn, but also driven forward, by conflict between capitalist and proletarian. Sorel never abandoned his belief in Marx, but he used his doctrines selectively.

Sorel derives from Marx (reinforced by his own interpretation of Vico) his conception of man as an active being, born to work and create; from this follows his right to his tools, for they are an extension of his nature. The working tools of our day are machines. Machinery is a social cement more effective, he believes, than even language. All creation is in essence artistic, and the factory should become the vehicle of the social poetry of modern producers. Human history is more than the impersonal story of the evolution of technology. Inventions, discoveries, techniques, the productive process, are activities of human beings endowed with minds but, above all, wills. Men's values, their practice, their work, are one dynamic, seamless whole. Sorel follows Vico in insisting that we are not mere victims or spectators of events, but actors and originators. Marx, too, is appealed to, but he is, at times, too determinist for Sorel, especially in the versions of his more positivist interpreters—Engels, Kautsky, Plekhanov, men inclined to *la petite science,* like bourgeois economists and sociologists. Social and economic laws are not chains, not a constricting framework, but guidelines to possible action, generated and developed by, and in, action. The future is open. Sorel rejects such determinist phraseology as 'tendencies working with iron necessity towards inevitable results' and the like, of which *Das Kapital* is full. Marxism 'is a doctrine of life good for strong peoples; it reduces ideology to the role of a mere instrument'.[9] History for Sorel is what it was for Hegel, a drama in which men are authors and actors; above all it is a struggle between the forces of vitality and those of decay, activity and passivity, dynamic energy versus cowardice and surrender.

Marx's deepest single insight, for Sorel, is his notion of the class war as the matrix of all social change. Creation is always a struggle: Greek civilisation for Sorel is symbolised by the sculptor who cuts the marble—the resistance of the stone, resistance as such, is essential to the process of creation. In modern factories the struggle is not merely between men—workers—and nature, which provides raw material, but between workers and employers, who seek to extract surplus value by exploiting other men's labour power. In this struggle men, like steel, are refined. Their courage, their self-respect, their solidarity with each other, grow. Their sense of justice develops too, for justice, according to Proudhon (to whom Sorel's debt is greater than even to Marx), is something that springs from the feeling of indignation aroused by the humiliation inflicted on others. What is insulted is what is common to all men—their humanity which is ours; the insult to human dignity is felt by the offender, by the injured man, and by the third party; this common protest which they all feel within them is the sense of justice and injustice. It is this that united some among the socialists with the liberal bourgeoisie against the chicanery of the army and the church during the Dreyfus case, and created Sorel's bond with Charles Péguy, who was never a Marxist but was prepared to work with anyone who did not wish to see France dishonoured by a cynical miscarriage of justice. In 1899 he speaks of the 'admirable ardour' with which the Allemanist workers are marching for 'truth, justice, morality'[10] by the side of Jaurès whom he was soon to attack so violently for lacking these very qualities.

Justice in particular is for Sorel an absolute value, proof against historical change. His conception of it may, as in the case of Kant and Proudhon, be rooted in a severe upbringing. Sorel dreaded sentimental humanitarianism; when people cease to feel horror at human crimes this will, he thinks, mean a collapse of their sense of justice. Better wild retribution than indifference or a sentimental tendency to forgiveness characteristic of humanitarian democracy. It is his indignation with what he saw as the dilution in the public life of France in his day of the sense of justice—to him a kind of intuitive sense of absolute moral pitch—that drove him from one extreme remedy to another and caused him to reject anything that he suspected of inclining towards compromise with stupidity or wickedness. It is the absence of the sense of absolute moral values, and of the decisive part played in human life by the moral will, that, for Sorel, is Marx's greatest single weakness: he is too historicist, too determinist, too relativist. Sorel's uncompromising voluntarism is at the heart of his entire outlook; there is in Marx too much emphasis on economics, not enough ethical doctrine.

The carrier of true moral values today is the proletariat. Only workers have true respect for work, for family, for sacrifice, for love. They are frugal, dignified, honest. For him, as for Fernand Pelloutier, the true founder of French syndicalism, they are beings touched by grace. For Sorel they were what peasants were for Herzen, what 'the folk' was for Herder and the populists, what 'the nation' was for Barrès. It is this traditionalism, which he shared with a certain type of conservative, and the quality of his domestic life with the simple and religious Marie David, that may have deepened his sense of the gulf between the moral dignity of the workers and the character and values of the pliable and the clever who rose to success in democracies. He found, or thought he found, this farouche integrity in Proudhon, in Péguy, in Pelloutier and other uncompromising fighters for justice or independence at whatever cost; he looked for it in the royalist *littérateurs,* in ultra-nationalists, in all resistance to time-serving supporters of the Republic and its demagogues. Hence his lack of sympathy for the populist nationalism of Déroulède, as for the entire Boulangist front. He might have approved of the *Croix de Feu,* but never of Poujadism.

Sorel's relationship to Marx is harder to define: classes and the class war as the central factor in social change; universal, timeless ideals as disguises for temporary class interests; man as a self-transforming, creative, tool-inventing being; the proletariat—the producers—as the bearer of the highest human values; these ideas he never abandoned. But he rejected the entire Hegelian-Marxist teleology which fuses facts and values. Sorel believed in absolute moral values: the historicism of the Hegelian-Marxist tradition was never acceptable to him, still less the view that issues of basic moral or political principle can be solved by social scientists, psychologists, sociologists, anthropologists; or that techniques based on imitation of the methods of natural science can explain and explain away ideas or values, to the permanence and power of which all history and art, all religion and morality, testify; or can, indeed, explain human conduct in mechanistic or biological terms, as the positivists, the blinkered adherents of *la petite science,* believe.

Sorel regards values, both moral and aesthetic, though their forms and applications may alter, as being independent of the march of events. Hence he regards sociological analysis of works of art, whether by Diderot or Marxist critics, as evidence of their profound lack of aesthetic sense, blindness to the mystery of the act of creation, and to the part that art plays in the life of mankind. Yet he shows little consistency when engaged on exposing the motives of the enemy; then he is more than ready to use all the tools of psychological or sociological analysis provided by those who probe for true springs of action by 'unmasking' interests disguised as unalterable laws or disinterested ideals. Thus he fully accepts the Marxist view that economic laws are not laws of nature, but human arrangements, created, whether consciously or not, in the interests of a given class. To look upon them as objective necessities, as bourgeois economists do, is to reify them, an illusion that plays into the hands of that class to whose advantage it is to represent them as being eternal and unchangeable. But then he draws the un-Marxist, voluntarist corollary that freely chosen effort and struggle can change a great deal; and parts company with the orthodox who insist on a rigorous and predictable causal correlation between productive forces and the superstructure of institutions and ideas. The moral absolutes must not be touched: they do not alter with changes in the forces or relations of production.

History for Sorel is more of a wild flux than Marx supposed: society is a creation, a work of art, not (as, perhaps, the state is) a mere product of economic forces. Marx's economism he regards as overstated; this may have been necessary (as Engels, in effect, admitted) in order to counter idealistic or liberal-individualist theories of history. But in the end such theories may, he thinks, lead to a belief in the possibility of predicting the social arrangements of the future. This is dangerous and delusive Utopianism. Such fantasies may stimulate the workers, but they can arm despotisms too. Even if the workers win their fight against the bourgeoisie, yet, unless they are educated to be creative, they too may generate an oppressive élite of doctrinaire intellectuals from within their own class. He accuses Marx of relying altogether too much on that Hegelian maid-of-all-work, the world spirit, although Marx is credited with understanding that science (and especially economic science) is not a 'mill' into which you can drop any problem facing you, and which yields solutions.[11] Methods of application are everything. Did not Marx himself once declare, 'Whoever composes a programme for the future is a reactionary'?[12] Nor, according to Sorel, did Marx believe in a political party of the working class; for a party, once in the saddle, may well become tyrannical and self-perpetuating, no matter what its manifestos state. Marx, after all, Sorel tells us, believed in the reality of classes alone.

This is a greatly Sorelified Marx: Sorel rejects everything in Marx that seems to him political—his notion of the workers' party, his theory of, and practical measures for, the organisation of the revolution, his determinism, above all the doctrine of the dictatorship of the proletariat which Sorel regards as a sinister recrudescence of the worst elements of repressive Jacobinism. Even the anarchist classless society with which true human history is to begin is virtually ignored by Sorel: evidently it is too much of a conceptual, ideological construction. 'Socialism is not a doctrine,' he declared, 'not a sect, not a political system; it is the emancipation of the working classes who organise themselves, instruct themselves and create new institutions.'[13] The proletariat is for him a body of producers at once disciplined and inspired by the nature of the labour they perform. It is this that makes them a class and not a party. The proletarians are not simply the discontented masses; the proletarian revolution is not merely a revolt of poor against rich, of the *popolo minuto* of the Italian communes, organised and led by a self-appointed general staff, the kind of rising advocated by Babeuf or Blanqui; for this can happen anywhere and at any time. The true social revolution of our day must be the revolt of a heroic class of producers and makers against exploiters and their agents and parasites, something that cannot happen unless—this was Marx's crucial discovery—a society has reached a certain stage of technological development, and the truly creative class has developed a moral personality of its own. (It is this emphasis on the intrinsic value and revolutionary character of the culture of the producers—the proletariat—that appealed to Gramsci and caused him to defend Sorel against his detractors.) Sorel does not seem to have contemplated a society so mechanised as to generate a technocratic bureaucracy involving both managers and workers, in which social dynamism is stifled by the organisation required by the sheer size of the industrial system. According to Daniel Halévy, France at the turn of the century, and in particular Paris and its environs, were relatively unindustrialised compared with England or Germany. Sorel is closer to Proudhon's world than to that of General Motors or I.C.I.

Only conflict purifies and strengthens. It creates durable unity and solidarity; whereas political parties, which anyone, of whatever social formation, can enter, are remashackle structures, liable to opportunist coalitions and alliances. This is the vice of democracy. Not only is it the sham denounced by Marxists, a mere front for capitalist control; but the very ideal of democracy—national unity, reconciliation of differences, social harmony, devotion to the common good, Rousseau's General Will raised above the battle of the factions—all this destroys the conditions in which alone men can grow to their full stature—the struggle, the social conflict. The most fatal of all democratic institutions are parliaments, since they depend on compromise, concessions, conciliation; even if we forget about the ruses, equivocation, hypocrisy of which the syndicalists speak, political combinations are the death of all heroism, indeed of morality itself. The member of parliament, no matter how militant his past, is inevitably driven into peaceful association, even cooperation, with the class enemy, in committees, in lobbies, in the chamber itself. The representative of the working classes, Sorel observed, becomes an excellent bourgeois very easily. The hideous examples are before our eyes—Millerand, Briand, Viviani, the spellbinding demagogue Jean Jaurès with his easily acquired popularity. Sorel had once hoped for much from these men, but was disillusioned. They all turned out to be squalid earthworms, rhetoricians, grafters and intriguers like the rest.

Sorel goes even farther. Creative vitality cannot exist where everything gives, where it is too soft to resist. Unless the enemy—not the parasitic intellectuals and theorists, but the leaders of the capitalist forces—are themselves energetic and fight back like men, the workers will not find enemies worthy of their steel, and will themselves tend to degenerate. Only against a strong and vigorous opponent can truly heroic qualities be developed. Hence Sorel's characteristic wish that the bourgeoisie might develop stronger sinews. No serious Marxist could begin to accept this thesis, not even the mildest reformist, not even those who, like Bernstein, denied the validity of the Marxist historical libretto and declared in language worthy of Sorel himself: 'The goal is nothing: the movement is everything.'[14] Sorel averts his gaze from the aftermath of the ultimate victory of the working class. He is concerned only with rises and falls, creative societies and classes and decadent ones. No perfection, no final victory, is possible in social existence; only in art, in pure creation, can this be achieved. Rembrandt, Ruysdael, Vermeer, Mozart, Beethoven, Schumann, Berlioz, Liszt, Wagner, Debussy, Delacroix, the impressionist painters of his own day—these were capable of reaching an unsurpassable summit in their art. Hence his attack on those who sell their genius for fame or money. Meyerbeer can be despised but not blamed: he was a true child of his age and milieu: his gift was as vulgar as the audience which he knew how to please; not so Massenet, who prostituted his more genuine talent to please the bourgeois public. Something of this kind, he seems to think, is true of Anatole France too.

The total fulfilment that is possible in art, in science, in the case of individual men of genius, cannot occur in the life of society. Hence Sorel's distrust of the entire Marxist scenario: the expropriation of the expropriators, the dictatorship of the proletariat, the reign of plenty, the withering away of the state. He ignores practical problems; he is not interested in the way in which production, distribution, exchange, will be regulated in the new order, nor in whether there is any possibility of abolishing scarcity without performing at least some tasks that can hardly be described as creative. Marxists can scarcely be blamed if they did not regard as their own a man who wished to preserve the enemy in being lest the swords of his own side rusted in their scabbards, who had nothing to say about the ideal of a free society of associated producers combining to fight inanimate nature, but, on the contrary, declared, 'Everything may be saved if the proletariat, by its use of violence . . . restores to the middle class something of its former energy',[15] a man who did not seem to care about the problems of poverty and misery as such, and protested against sabotage of factories, because this was wilful destruction of the fruits of someone's creative labour. No man could claim to be a Marxist if he condemned revolutionary terror as a political act and damned Jacobins as tyrants and fanatics—man on whom Marx, to some degree, and even more Lenin, looked as their legitimate ancestors. Sorel denounces activity that springs from morally impure feelings, from motives infected by bourgeois poisons: 'The fierce envy of the impoverished intellectual,' he declares, 'who would like to see the rich merchant guillotined, is a vicious feeling that is not in the least socialist.'[16] He cares only for the preservation of heroic vitality and courage and strength which may decline if total victory leaves the victor no enemy.

Sorel was aware of the oddity of his position, and took perverse and somewhat malicious pleasure in exposing the weakness or confusions of his allies. He pronounced socialism to be dead in the early years of our century. He made no effort to influence any active social or political group. He remained true to his professions: isolated, independent, a man on his own. If he has any parallel within the socialist movement, it is with the equally independent and unpredictable Viennese critic and journalist Karl Kraus, also concerned with morality, and the preservation of style in life and literature.[17] Even Bernard Shaw, who admired vitality, style, Napoleonic qualities, the 'life force', had a greater affinity with him than learned theorists like Kautsky, Plekhanov, Guesde, Max Adler, Sidney Webb, and the other pillars of European socialism. To him they were everything that he despised most deeply—arid, cerebral, latter-day sophists, clerks and glossators who turned every vital impulse into abstract formulas, Utopian blueprints, learned dust. He poured the vials of his scorn upon them. They repaid him by ignoring him completely.

Jaurès called Sorel the metaphysician of syndicalism. And, indeed, Sorel believed that in every human soul there lay hidden a metaphysical ember glowing beneath the cinders. If one could blow this into a flame, it would kindle a conflagration that would destroy mediocrity, routine, cowardice, opportunism, corrupt bargains with the class enemy. Society can be saved only by the liberation of the producers, that is, the workers, particularly those who work with their hands. The founders of syndicalism were right: the workers must be protected against domination by experts and ideologists and professors—the intellectual élite of Plato's hideous dream—what Bakunin (with Marx in mind) had called 'pedantocracy'. 'Can you conceive', asked Sorel, 'of anything more horrible than government by professors?'[18] In these days such men, he observes, tend to be, as often as not, *déraciné* intellectuals, or Jews without a country—men who have no home, no hearth of their own, 'no ancestral tombs to protect, no relics to defend against the barbarians'.[19]

This is, of course, the violent rhetoric of the extreme right—of de Maistre, of Carlyle, of German nationalists, of French anti-Dreyfusards, of anti-Semitic chauvinists—of Maurras and Barrès, Drumont and Déroulède. But it is also, at times, the language of Fourier and Cobbett, Proudhon and Bakunin, and would later be spoken by Fascists and National Socialists and their literary allies in many countries, as well as those who thunder against critical intellectuals and rootless cosmopolitans in the Soviet Union and other countries of eastern Europe. No one was closer to this style of thought and expression than the so called left-wing Nazis—Gregor Strasser and his followers in the early days of Hitler, and in France men like Déat and Drieu la Rochelle.

There is an anti-intellectual and anti-Enlightenment stream in the European radical tradition, at times allied with populism, or nationalism, or neo-medievalism, that goes back to Rousseau and Herder and Fichte, and enters agrarian, anarchist, anti-Semitic and other anti-liberal movements, creating anomalous combinations, sometimes in open opposition to, sometimes in an uneasy alliance with, the various currents of socialist and revolutionary thought. Sorel, whose hatred of democracy, the bourgeois republic, and above all the rational outlook and liberal values of the intelligentsia, was obsessive, fed this stream, indirectly at first, but towards the end of the first decade of our century more violently and openly until, by 1910, this caused a breach between him and his left-wing allies.

Doubtless his devout upbringing, his deep roots in traditional, old-fashioned French provincial life, his unspoken but profoundly felt patriotism, played their part: what seemed to him the demoralisation and disintegration of traditional French society plainly preoccupied him throughout his life and intensified his basic xenophobia and hostility to those who seemed to him to wander beyond the confines of the traditional culture of the west. His anti-intellectualism and anti-Semitism sprang from the same roots as those of Proudhon and Barrès. But there was also the decisive influence of the philosophy of Henri Bergson. With his friend Péguy, Sorel attended Bergson's lectures, and, like Péguy, was deeply and permanently affected.

It was from Bergson that he derived the notion, which he could equally well have found in the francophobe German romantics a century earlier, that reason was a feeble instrument compared with the power of the irrational and the unconscious in the life both of individuals and societies. He was profoundly impressed by Bergson's doctrine of the unanalysable *élan vital,* the inner force that cannot be rationally grasped or articulated, which thrusts its way into the empty and unknowable future, and moulds both biological growth and human activity. Not theoretical knowledge but action, and only action, gives understanding of reality. Action is not a means to preconceived ends, it is its own policy-maker and pathfinder. Prediction, even if it were possible, would kill it. We have an inner sense of what we are at, very different from, and incompatible with, the outside view, that is, calm contemplation that classifies, dissects, establishes clear structures. The intellect freezes and distorts. One cannot render movement by rest, nor time by space, nor the creative process by mechanical models, nor something living by something still and dead—this is an old romantic doctrine that Bergson revivified and developed. Reality must be grasped intuitively, by means of images, as artists conceive it, not with concepts or arguments or Cartesian reasoning. This is the soil which gave birth to Sorel's celebrated doctrine of the social myth which alone gives life to social movements.

There is another source, too, whence the theory of myth may have sprung—the teachings of the founder of modern sociology, Émile Durkheim, who stood at the opposite extreme from Bergson. Rational and sternly positivist, he believed, like Comte, that science alone could answer our questions; what science could not do, no other method could achieve; he was implacably opposed to Bergson's deep irrationalism. Durkheim, who became the leading ideologist of the Third Republic, taught that no society could remain stable without a high degree of social solidarity between its members; this in its turn depended on the prevalence in it of dominant social myths bound up with appropriate ritual and ceremonial; religion had in the past been by far the most powerful of the forms in which this sense of solidarity found natural expression. Myths are not for Durkheim false beliefs about reality. They are not beliefs about anything, but beliefs *in* something—in descent from a common ancestor, in transforming events in a common past, in common traditions, in shared symbols enshrined in a common language, above all in symbols sanctified by religion and history. The function of myths is to bind a society, create a structure governed by rules and habits, without which the individual may suffer from a sense of isolation and solitude, may experience anxiety, feel lost; and this in its turn leads to lawlessness and social chaos. For Durkheim myths are ultimately a utilitarian, if uncontrived, spontaneous and natural, response to a quasi-biological need; his account of their function is treated by him as an empirical discovery of a Burkean kind, of a necessary condition for social stability. Sorel abhorred utilitarianism, and in particular the quest for social peace and cohesion by cautious republican academics, as an attempt to muffle the class war in the interests of the bourgeois republic.

For Sorel, the function of myths is not to stabilise, but to direct energies and inspire action. They do this by embodying a dynamic vision of the movement of life, the more potent because not rational, and therefore not subject to criticism and refutation by university wiseacres. A myth is compounded of images that are 'warmly coloured',[20] and affect men not as reason does, nor education of the will, nor the command of a superior, but as ferment of the soul which creates enthusiasm and incites to action, and, if need be, turbulence. Myths need have no historical reality; they direct our emotions, mobilise our will, give purpose to all that we are and do and make; they are, above all, not Utopias, which from Plato onward are descriptions of impossible states of affairs, fantasies in the heads of intellectuals remote from reality, evasion of concrete problems, escape into theory and abstraction. Sorel's myths are ways of transforming relationships between real facts by providing men with a new vision of the world and themselves: as when those who are converted to a new faith see the world and its furniture with new eyes. A Utopia is 'the product of intellectual labour; it is the work of theorists who, after observing and discussing the facts, seek to build a model against which to measure existing societies . . . it is a construction which can be taken to pieces',[21] its parts can be detached and fitted into other structures—bourgeois political economy is just such an artificial entity. But myths are wholes perceived instantaneously by the imagination. They are, in effect, political aspirations presented in the form of images 'made warm' by strong feeling. They reveal, as mere words cannot, hitherto invisible potentialities in the past and present, and so drive men to concerted efforts to bring about their realisation. The effort itself breeds new vitality, new effort and militancy in an endless dynamic process, spiralling upwards, which he called 'giving an aspect of reality to hopes of immediate action'.[22]

The Christian vision of the Second Coming that is at hand is, for Sorel, a myth of this kind—in its light men accepted martyrdom. The Calvinist belief in the renovation of Christianity was a vision of a new order that was not of this world, but fired by it the believers successfully resisted the advance of secular humanism. The idea of the French Revolution, referred to with fervour at civic gatherings in French provincial towns, lives on as a vague but ardent image that commands loyalty and stimulates action of a particular kind, but a myth that cannot, any more than a hymn, or a flag, be translated into a specific programme, a set of clear objectives. 'When masses of men become aroused, then an image is formed which constitutes a social myth.'[23] This is how the Italian Risorgimento presented itself to the followers of Mazzini. It is by means of myths that socialism can be converted into a kind of social poetry, can be expressed in action but not in prose, not in treatises intended merely to be understood. The French revolutionary armies in 1792 were inspired by an ardent myth, and won; the royalist forces lacked it, and were defeated. The Greeks lived and flourished in a world filled with myths until they were subverted by the sophists, and after them by rootless oriental cosmopolitans who flooded into Greece and ruined her. The analogy with the present is all too patent.

Sorel's myth is not a Marxist idea. It has a greater affinity with the modernist psychologism of Loisy or Tyrrell, William James's doctrine of the will, Vaihinger's 'philosophy of "as if"', than with Marx's rationalist conception of the unity of theory and practice. The notion of 'the people', 'the folk'—good, simple and true, but unawakened, as it is conceived by populists, both radical and reactionary, of the eternal 'real nation' in the thought of nationalists, as opposed to its corrupt or craven representatives—Barrès's 'la terre et les morts'—these are Sorel's, not Durkheim's myths. Unsympathetic critics might say the same of most Marxists' use of the concept of the true, dialectically grasped interests of the proletariat, as opposed to its actual 'empirical' wishes, perhaps even of the notion of classless society itself, provided that its outlines remain blurred. The function of a myth is to create 'an epic state of mind'. Sorel's insistence on its irrationality is, perhaps, what caused Lenin to dismiss him so curtly and contemptuously.

What is to be the myth of the workers? What is to raise them to the state of heroic grandeur, above the grey routine of their humdrum lives? Something which, Sorel believes, already inspires those activists in the French *syndicats* who have found their leader in the admirable Fernand Pelloutier, who has rightly kept them from contamination by democratic politics—the myth of the general strike. The syndicalist general strike must not be confused with the ordinary industrial or 'political' strike which is a mere effort to extort better conditions or higher wages from the masters, and presupposes acquiescence in a social and economic structure common to owner and wage slave. This is mere haggling and is the very opposite of the true class war. The myth of the syndicalist general strike is a call for the total overthrow of the entire abominable world of calculation, profit and loss, the treatment of human beings and their powers as commodities, as material for bureacratic manipulation, the world of illusory consensus and social harmony, of economic or sociological experts no matter what master they serve, who treat men as subjects of statistical calculations, malleable 'human material', forgetting that behind such statistics there are living human beings, not so much with normal human needs—to Sorel that does not appear to matter much—but free moral agents able collectively to resist and create and mould the world to their will.

The enemy for Sorel is not always the same: during the Dreyfus affair it was the nationalist demagogues with their paranoiac, Jacobin cries of treason, their fanatical search for scapegoats and wicked incitement of the mob against the Jews,[24] who play this role. After their defeat, it is the victors—the 'counter-church' of the intellectuals, the intolerant, dehumanising, republican 'politico-scholastic' party, led by academic despots, bred in the École Normale—who increasingly become the principal targets of his fury. The general strike is the climax of mounting militancy and 'violence', when, in an act of concentrated collective will, the workers, in one concerted move, leave their factories and workshops, secede to the Aventine, and then arise as one man and inflict a total, crushing, permanent, 'Napoleonic' defeat upon the accursed system that shuffles them into Durkheim's or Comte's compartments and hierarchies, and thereby all but robs them of their human essence. This is the great human uprising of the children of light against the children of darkness, of fighters for freedom against merchants, intellectuals, politicians—the miserable crew of the masters of the capitalist world with their mercenaries, men promoted from the ranks, bought off and absorbed into the hierarchy, careerists and social planners, right-wing and left-wing power- or status-seekers, promoters of societies based on greed and competition, or else on the stifling oppression of remorselessly tidy rational organisation.

Did Sorel believe, did he expect the workers to believe, that this final act of liberation would, or could, in fact, occur as a historical event? It is difficult to tell. He had nothing favourable to say of the general strikes, designed to secure specific concessions, that broke out (during his most syndicalist phase) in Belgium in 1904, above all in the abortive Russian revolution of 1905. This, for him, was Péguy's *mystique* reduced to mere *politique*. Moreover, if he believed, as he appeared to, that if the enemy weakened so would the class of producers, would not total victory lead to the elimination of the tension without which there is no effort, no creation? Yet without a myth it is impossible to create an energetic proletarian movement. Empirical arguments against the possibility or desirability of the general strike are not relevant. It is, one suspects, not intended as a theory of action, still less as a plan to be realised in the real world.

The weapon of the workers is violence. Although it gives its name to Sorel's best-known work ('my standard work',[25] as he ironically referred to it), its nature is never made clear. Class conflict is the normal condition of society, and force is continuously exerted against the producers, that is, the workers, by the exploiters. Force does not necessarily consist in open coercion, but in control and repression by means of institutions which, whether by design or not, have the effect, as Marx and his disciples have made clear, of promoting the power of the possessing class. This pressure must be resisted. To resist force by force is likely to result, as in the case of the Jacobin revolution, in the replacing of one yoke by another, the substitution of new masters for old. A Blanquist *putsch* could lead to mere coercion by the state—the dictatorship of the proletariat, perhaps even of its own representatives, as the successor to the dictatorship of capitalists. Dogmatic revolutionaries easily become oppressive tyrants: this theme is common to Sorel and the anarchists. Camus revived it in his polemic with Sartre. Force, by definition, represses; violence, directed against it, liberates. Only by installing fear in the capitalists can the workers break their power, the force exerted against them.

This, indeed, is the function of proletarian violence: not aggression, but resistance. Violence is the striking off of chains, the prelude to regeneration. It may be possible to secure a more rational existence, better material conditions, a higher standard of living, security, even justice for the workers, the poor, the oppressed, without violence. But the renewal of life, rejuvenation, the liberation of creative powers, return to Homeric simplicity, to the sublimity of the Old Testament, to the spirit of the early

Christian martyrs, of Corneille's heroes, of Cromwell's Ironsides, of the French revolutionary armies—this cannot be attained by persuasion, without violence as the weapon of liberty.

How the use of violence can in practice be distinguished from the use of force is never made clear. It is merely postulated as the only alternative to peaceful negotiation which, by presupposing a common good, common to workers and employers alike, denies the reality of class war. Marx, too, talked about the need for revolution to purify the proletariat from the filth of the old world and render it fit for the new. Herzen spoke of the cleansing storm of the revolution. Proudhon and Bakunin spoke in similarly apocalyptic terms. Even Kautsky declared that revolution raises men from degradation to a more exalted view of life. Sorel is obsessed by the idea of revolution. For him, faith in revolutionary violence and hatred of force entails, in the first place, the stern self-insulation of the workers. Sorel fervently agrees with the syndicalist organisers of the *bourses de travail* (a peculiar combination of labour exchanges, trades councils, and social and educational centres of militant workers) that proletarians who allow themselves any degree of cooperation with the class enemy are lost to their own side. All talk of responsible and humane employers, reasonable and peace-loving workers, nauseates him. Profit-sharing, factory councils that include both masters and men, democracy which recognises all men as equal, are fatal to the cause. In total war there can be no fraternisation.

Does violence mean more than this? Does it mean occupation of factories, the seizing of power, physical clashes with police or other agents of the possessing class, the shedding of blood? Sorel remains unclear. The conduct of the Allemanist workers who marched with Jaurès (then still well thought of) at a certain moment of the Dreyfus affair, is one of his very few allusions to the correct use of proletarian violence. Anything that increases militancy, but does not lead to the formation of power structures among the workers themselves, is approved. The distinction between force and violence appears to depend entirely on the character of its function and motive. Force imposes chains, violence breaks them. Force, open or concealed, enslaves; violence, always open, makes free. These are moral and metaphysical, not empirical, concepts. Sorel is a moralist and his values are rooted in one of the oldest of human traditions. That is why Péguy listened to him, and why his theses do not belong only to their own times but retain their freshness. Rousseau, Fichte, Proudhon, Flaubert, are Sorel's truest modern ancestors; as well as Marx the destroyer of rationalisations, the preacher of class war and of the proletarian revolution; not Marx the social scientist, the historical determinist, the author of programmes for a political movement, the practical conspirator.

IV

The doctrine of myths and its corollary, the emphasis on the power of the irrational in human thought and action, is a consequence of the modern scientific movement, and the application of scientific categories and methods to the behaviour of men. The relatively simple models of human nature which underlay the central ideas of social and political philosophers until quite far into the nineteenth century were gradually being superseded by an increasingly complicated and unstable picture as new and disturbing hypotheses about the springs of action were advanced by psychologists and anthropologists. The rise of doctrines, according to which men were determined by non-rational factors, some of them refracted in highly misleading ways in men's consciousness, directed attention to actual social and political practice and its true causes and conditions, which only scientific investigation could uncover, and which severely limited the area of free will or even made it vanish altogether. This naturalistic approach had the effect of playing down the role of conscious reasons by which the actors mistakenly supposed themselves, and appeared to others, to be motivated. These may well have been among the most decisive causes of the decline of classical political theory, which assumes that men who are, to some degree, free to choose between possibilities, do so for motives intelligible to themselves and others, and are, *pro tanto,* open to conviction by rational argument in reaching their decisions. The penetration of the 'disguises', of concealed factors—psychological, economic, anthropological—in individual and social life by examination of their actual role, transformed the simpler model of human nature with which political theorists from Hobbes to J. S. Mill had operated, and shifted emphasis from political argument to the less or more deterministic descriptive disciplines that began with Tocqueville and Taine and Marx, and were carried on by Weber and Durkheim, Le Bon and Tarde, Pareto and Freud, and their disciples in our time.

Sorel rejected determinism, but his theory of myths belongs to this development. His social psychology is an odd amalgam of Marxism, Bergsonian intuitionism, and Jamesian psychology, in which men, once they realise that they are, whether they know it or not, shaped by the class conflict (which he treats as a historical datum), can, by an effort of the will reinforced by the inspiration of the appropriate myth, freely develop the creative sides of their nature, provided they do not attempt to do so as mere individuals but collectively, as a class. Even this is not entirely true of individual men of genius—especially of artists, who are capable of creation in adverse social conditions by the strength of their own indomitable spirit. Of this dark process James and Croce and Renan seemed to him to show a deeper understanding than the blinkered sociological environmentalists. But Sorel is not a consistent thinker. His desperate lifelong search for a class, or group, which can redeem humanity, or at least France, from mediocrity and decay, is itself rooted in a quasi-Marxist sociology of history as a drama in which the protagonists are classes generated by the growth of productive forces, a doctrine for which he claims objective validity.

V

The effect of Sorel's doctrine upon the revolutionary syndicalist movement was minimal. He wrote articles in journals, collaborated with Lagardelle, Delesalle and Péguy, offered homage to Fernand Pelloutier, and talked and lectured to groups of admirers in Paris. But when Griffuelhes, the strongest personality since Pelloutier among the syndicalists, was asked whether he read Sorel, he replied, 'I read Dumas.'[26] Sorel was himself what he most despised in others—too intellectual, too sophisticated, too remote from the reality of the workers' lives. He looked for biblical or Homeric heroes capable of the epic spirit and was constantly disappointed. During the Dreyfus case, he denounced the anti-Dreyfusards who seemed to him to stand for lies, injustice, and unscrupulous demagoguery. But after the Dreyfusards had won, he was in turn disgusted by the ignoble political manoeuvring, cynicism and dissimulation of the friends of the people. Jaurès's humanity and eloquence seemed to him mere self-interested demagoguery, democratic claptrap, dust in the workers' eyes, no better than Zola's rodomontades, or the silver periods of Anatole France, or betrayals by false friends of the workers, the worst of whom was Aristide Briand, once the fervent champion of the general strike.

He continued to live quietly in Boulogne-sur-Seine. For ten years, until 1912, he took the tram to attend Bergson's lectures, and on Thursdays came to the gatherings in the offices of Péguy's *Cahiers de la Quinzaine,* which he dominated. There he delivered those vast monologues about politics and economics, classical and Christian culture, art and literature, which dazzled his disciples. He drew on a large store of unsystematic reading; but what lingered in his listeners' memories were his mordant paradoxes. Péguy listened reverently to *le père Sorel,* but in the end, when Sorel, disillusioned with the syndicalists who had gone the way of all workers into the morass of social democracy, began to look for new paladins against political impurity, and denounced the radical intellectuals, especially the Jews among them, too violently, even he became uncomfortable. When Sorel's anti-Semitism became more open and more virulent, and he did an unfriendly turn to Julien Benda (a ferocious critic of Bergson and of every form of nationalism, whom Péguy nevertheless greatly admired), and finally entered into an alliance with the militant royalists and chauvinists led by Maurras and the mystical Catholic nationalists grouped round Barrès, men who alone seemed to him independent, militant, and not tainted by the republican blight, this proved too much for Péguy, and he requested Sorel not to return. Sorel was deeply wounded. He preferred talk to writing. The audience of gifted writers and intellectuals was necessary to him. He began to frequent the bookshop of a humbler follower, and went on talking as before.

The flirtation with the reactionaries in the so-called Cercle Proudhon did not last long. In 1912 Sorel acclaimed Mussolini, then a flamboyant socialist militant, as a *condottiere* who, one day, 'will salute the Italian flag with his sword'.[27] By 1914 he was once again on his own. When war broke out he felt abandoned; Bergson, Péguy, Maurras, even Hervé, all rallied to the defence of the Republic. During the war he was depressed and silent. He corresponded with Croce, who seemed to him critical and detached, and told his friend Daniel Halévy that the war was nothing but a fight between Anglo-American finance and the German General Staff. He did not seem to care greatly which gang emerged victorious.

After the war, in his letters to Croce, he criticised the beginnings of Fascism, but, perhaps under the influence of Pareto, and Croce's initial pro-Fascist moment, pronounced Mussolini a 'political genius'.[28] Lenin excited him far more. He saw him as a bold and realistic rejuvenator of socialism, the greatest socialist thinker since Marx, who had roused the Russian masses to an epic plane of revolutionary feeling. Lenin was Peter the Great or Robespierre, Trotsky was Saint-Just; their concept of the Soviets seemed to him pure syndicalism: he took it at its face value, as he did, perhaps, Mussolini's denunciation in 1920 of 'the state in all its forms and incarnations; the state of yesterday, of today and of tomorrow'.[29] He applauded the Bolsheviks' contempt for democracy, and, still more, their ferocious attitude to intellectuals. He declared that the mounting terror of the Bolshevik Party was less harmful than the force which it was designed to repress; in any case it was probably the fault of its Jewish members. He averted his eyes from the strengthening of the party apparatus, and would not speak of Russia as a socialist state, since this concept seemed to him, as it had seemed to Marx, a blatant contradiction in terms.

To use the state as a weapon against the bourgeoisie was, he declared, like 'Gribouille who threw himself into the water to avoid getting wet in the rain'.[30] He still thought well of Mussolini, but he thought better of Lenin, to whom he wrote a passionate paean. By this time few listened to him; he was living in solitude and poverty—he had invested too much of his property in tsarist and Austrian bonds. His death, a few weeks before Mussolini's march on Rome, passed unnoticed. His last uttered word is said to have been 'Napoleon . . . '.

Of the two heroes of his declining years, Lenin ignored him; Mussolini, in search of distinguished intellectual ancestry, claimed him as a spiritual father. Fascist propaganda found useful ammunition in Sorel's writings: the mockery of liberal democracy, the violent anti-intellectualism, the appeal to the power of irrational forces, the calls to activism, violence, conflict as such, all this fed Fascist streams.[31] Sorel was no more a Fascist than Proudhon, but his glorification of action, honour, defiance, his deep hatred of democracy and equality, his contempt for liberals and Jews, are, like Proudhon's brand of socialism, not unrelated to the language and thought of Fascism and National Socialism; nor did his closest followers fail to note (and some among them to be duly influenced by) this fact. The ideological link of his views with what is common to romantic Bolshevism and left-wing strains in Fascism is painfully plain. 'The cry "Death to the Intellectuals",' he wrote hopefully in his last published collection of articles, 'so often attributed to the Bolsheviks, may yet become the battle-cry of the entire world proletariat.'[32]

At this point, one might be tempted to bid Sorel goodbye as an eccentric visionary, a penetrating and cruel critic of the vices of parliamentary democracy and bourgeois humanitarianism—of what Trotsky once called 'Kantian-Quaker-liberal-vegetarian nonsense'—a writer chiefly read in Italy, both in leftist and nationalist circles, duly superseded by Pareto, Mosca and Michels, a friend of Croce, a minor influence on Mussolini, the inspirer of a handful of radicals both of the right and the left, a half-forgotten extremist safely buried in the pages of the more capacious histories of socialist doctrines. Yet his ghost, half a century later, is by no means laid.

VI

Sorel, like Nietzsche, preached the need for a new civilisation of makers and doers, what is now called a counter-culture or an alternative society. The progressive left in the nineteenth century believed in science and rational control of nature and of social and individual life, and on this based their attacks upon tradition, prejudice, aestheticism, clericalism, conservative or nationalist mystiques, whatever could not be defended by rational argument—these men have, to some extent, won. The technocratic, post-industrial society in which we are said to be living is governed by men who make use of skilled, scientific experts, rational planners, technocrats. The theory of convergence used to inform us, in its heyday, now evidently past, that societies on both sides of the Iron Curtain are conditioned by similar forces in all essential respects, whatever the differences in kind or degree of individual liberty enjoyed by their members.

This is the kind of order—democracy both real and sham—based on respect for blueprints and specialists, that Sorel most deeply feared and detested. A society of consumers without authentic moral values of their own, sunk in vulgarity and boredom in the midst of mounting affluence, blind to sublimity and moral grandeur, bureaucratic organisation of human lives in the light of what he called *la petite science,* positivist application of quasi-scientific rules to society—all this he despised and hated. Who would revolt against it? The workers had not fulfilled his expectations. They failed to respond to his trumpet calls; they continued to be preoccupied with their material needs; their mode of life remained hopelessly similar to that of the *petite bourgeoisie,* one day to be the main recruiting-ground of Fascism, a class which Sorel regarded as the greatest source of moral contamination. He died a disappointed man.

Yet, if he were alive today, the wave of radical unrest could scarcely have failed to excite him. Like Fanon and the Black Panthers, and some dissenting Marxist groups, he believed that the insulted and the oppressed can find themselves and acquire self-identity and human dignity in acts of revolutionary violence. To intimidate the cowardly bourgeoisie (or, in Fanon's case, imperialist masters) by audacious acts of defiance, though Sorel did not favour terrorism or sabotage, is in tune with his feeling and his rhetoric. Che Guevara's or Fanon's concern about poverty, suffering and inequality was not at the centre of Sorel's moral vision; but they would have fulfilled his ideal of revolutionary pride, of a will moved by absolute moral values.

The idea of repressive tolerance, the belief that toleration of an order that inhibits 'epic' states of mind is itself a form of repression, is an echo of his own view. The neo-Marxist dialectic according to which all institutions and even doctrines are frozen forms of, and therefore obstacles to, the ever-flowing, ever-creative, human praxis, a kind of permanent revolution, might have seemed to him, even if he had understood the dark words of Hegelian neo-Marxism, mere incitement to anarchy. The metaphysics of the School of Frankfurt, and of Lukács (who was in his youth affected by Sorel's views), would surely have been roundly condemned by him as the latest Utopian and teleological nostrums of academic pedants, visionaries or charlatans.

In England anti-liberal critics—Wyndham Lewis and T.E. Hulme—took an interest in his ideas. Hulme translated the ***Reflexions.*** They found his emphasis on self-restraint and self-discipline sympathetic. Like them he hated disorder, bohemianism, the lack of self-imposed barriers, as symptoms of self-indulgence and decadence. But the revolt of those whom a German writer has recently described as the anabaptists of affluence, the preachers of an alternative society uncontaminated by the vices of the past, might well have made an appeal to him. He would have been disturbed by their sexual permissiveness; chastity was for him the highest of virtues; their slovenly habits, their exhibitionism, their addiction to drugs, their formless lives would have enraged him; and he would have denounced their neo-primitivism, the Rousseauian belief that poverty and roughness are closer to nature than austerity and civilised habits, and therefore more authentic and morally pure. He regarded this as false and stupid and attacked it all his life. But the present state of western society would have seemed to him a confirmation of Vico's prophecy of social disintegration as a prelude to a second barbarism, followed by a new, more virile civilisation, a new beginning in which men would again be simple, pious and severe. Barbarism did not frighten him.

He might have found reasons for acclaiming the Cultural Revolution in China. 'If socialism comes to grief,' he once observed, 'it will evidently be in the same way [as Protestantism], because it will be alarmed at its own barbarity,'[33] with the implication that it must not stop but plunge on—barbarism is, after all, an antidote to decay. This is instinctively believed by all those today who have opted out of a wicked society, as Sorel, who admired the early Christians and Puritans for their renunciation, so ardently wished the workers to do. Sparta rather than Athens. This alone created an unbridgeable gulf between Sorel and the easy-going, generous, humane Jaurès. It is this very quality that appeals to the grimmer dynamiters of the present.

But the strongest single link with the revolutionary movements of our day is his unyielding emphasis on the will. He believed in absolute moral ends that are independent of any dialectical or other historical pattern, and in the possibility, in conditions which men can themselves create, of realising these ends by the concerted power of the free and deliberate collective will. This, rather than a sense of the unalterable timetable of historical determinism, is the mood of the majority of the rebels, political and cultural, of the past two decades. Those who join revolutionary organisations, and those who abandon them, are more often moved by moral indignation with the hypocrisy or inhumanity of the regime under which they live (or alternatively with similar vices in the revolutionary party which, disillusioned, they leave), than by a metaphysical theory of the stages of history—of social change by which they do not wish to be left behind. The reaction is moral more than intellectual, of will rather than reason; such men are against the prevailing system because it is unjust or bestial rather than irrational or obsolescent. More than seventy years ago Eduard Bernstein became convinced that Marxism failed to provide an acceptable view of the ends of life, and preached the universal values of the neo-Kantians. So did Karl Liebknecht, who could not be accused of lack of revolutionary passion. This is far closer to Sorel's position, and connects him with modern revolutionary protest.

Yet, of course, this anti-rationalism was, to some degree, self-refuting. He knew that if faith in reason is delusive, it is only by the use of rational methods, by knowledge and self-knowledge and rational interpretation of the facts of history or psychology or social behaviour, that this could be discovered and established. He did not wish to stop invention and technology; he was no Luddite, he knew that to break machines is to perpetuate ignorance, scarcity and poverty. He might have admitted that the remedies offered by the modern insurgents are delusions; but this would not have troubled him. He proposed no specific economic or social policies. Like Hegel's opponents in post-Napoleonic Germany he appealed to love, solidarity, community; this, in due course, offered sustenance to 'extra-parliamentary' oppositions both of the right and of the left. If Fanon, or the militants of the Third World, or the revolutionary students, were not healders, he might have recognised them as the disease itself. This is what Herzen said about himself and the nihilists of his own generation. His lifelong effort to identify and distinguish the pure from the impure, the physicians from the patients, the heroic few who should be the saviours of society—workers, or radical nationalists, or Fascists, or Bolsheviks—ended in failure. Would he have tried to find them in colonial peoples, or black Americans or students who have mysteriously escaped contamination by the false values of their society? We cannot tell. At any rate, the dangers of which he spoke were, and are, real. Recent events have shown that his diagnosis of the malaise is anything but obsolete.

He was almost everything that he so vehemently denounced, an alienated intellectual, a solitary thinker isolated from men of action who achieved no relationship with the workers and never became a member of any vigorous, cooperative group of producers. He, whose symbol of creation was the cut stone, the chiselled marble, was productive only of words. He believed implicitly in family life and for twenty-five years had none. The apostle of action felt at home only in bookshops, among purveyors of words, talkers cut off, as he had always been, from the life of workers and artists. He remained eccentric, egocentric, an outsider of outsiders. This is an irony that, one may be sure, could scarcely have escaped him.

No monument to him exists. Ten years after his death, so Daniel Halévy tells us, Rolland Marcel, the director of the Bibliothèque Nationale in Paris, came to Halévy with an odd story. He had recently met the Ambassador of Fascist Italy who informed him that his Government had learnt that Sorel's grave was in a state of disrepair: the Fascist Government offered to put up a monument to the eminent thinker. Soon after this, the Ambassador of the U.S.S.R. approached him with an identical proposal on behalf of the Soviet Government. Halévy promised to get in touch with Sorel's family. After a long delay he received a communication which said that the family regarded the grave as its own private affair, and that of no one else. Halévy was delighted. The message was dry, brusque and final. It might have come from Sorel himself.

The prophet of concerted collective action, of pragmatic approaches, prized only absolute values, total independence. He was to be the modern Diogenes bent on exploding the most sacred dogmas and respected beliefs of all the establishments of his enlightened age. Sorel is still worth reading. The world about and against which he was writing might be our own. Whether he is, as he wished to be, 'serious, formidable and sublime',[34] or, as often as not, perverse, dogmatic and obsessed, with all the moral fury of perpetual youth (and this fiery, not wholly adult, outraged feeling may in part account for his affinity with the young revolutionaries of our time), his ideas come at us from every quarter. They mark a revolt against the rationalist ideal of frictionless contentment in a harmonioussocial system in which all ultimate questions are reduced to technical problems, soluble by appropriate techniques. It is the vision of this closed world that morally repels the young today. The first to formulate this in clear language was Sorel. His words still have power to upset.

NOTES

[1] G. D. H. Cole, *The Second International* [*A History of Socialist Thought,* vol. 3], part 1 (London, 1956), p. 387.

[2] Letter of 28 April 1903, *La critica* 25 (1927), 372.

[3] *Réflexions sur la violence* (Paris, 1972) (hereafter *R.V.*), p. 80.

[4] *R.V.*, p. 101.

[5] 'Osservazione intorno alla concezione materialista della storia', in *Saggi di critica del marxismo* (Palermo, 1902), p. 44.

[6] *Les Illusions du progrès,* 5th ed. (Paris, 1947), p. 133.

[7] *R.V.*, p. 14.

[8] *La Ruine du monde antique,* 3rd ed. (Paris, 1933), p. 44.

[9] loc. cit. (p. 306, note 1 above).

[10] 'L'Éthique du socialisme', *Revue de metaphysique et de morale* 7 (1899), 301.

[11] *R.V.*, p. 173.

[12] *R.V.*, p. 168. This letter, by Marx, which Professor L. J. Brentano reported as having been sent to Marx's English friend, Professor Beesly, in 1869, has never, so far as I know, been found. Nor does the sentiment sound very Marxian, although Eduard Bernstein is reported to have said that it seemed to him to be so. See *Mouvement socialiste,* 1 September 1899, p. 270.

[13] 'La Crise du socialisme', *Revue politique et parlementaire* 18 (1898), 612.

[14] Quoted by Sorel, op. cit. (p. 309, note 1 above), p. 296.

[15] *R.V.*, p. 110.

[16] *Matériaux d'une théorie du prolétariat,* 2nd ed. (Paris, 1921), p. 98, note 1.

[17] Marxism is in danger of becoming 'a mythology founded on the maladies of language', he wrote in a letter to Croce of 27 December 1897 (*La critica* 25 (1927), 50-2).

[18] *Le Procès de Socrate* (Paris, 1889), p. 183.

[19] op. cit. (p. 315, note 3 above), p. 158.

[20] *R.V.*, p. 184.

[21] *R.V.*, p. 38.

[22] *R.V.*, p. 149.

[23] *R.V.*, p. 36.

[24] Destined, Sorel declared in 1901, to become a formidable weapon. See *De l'église et de l'état* (Paris, 1901), pp. 54-5.

[25] Letter to Croce of 25 March 1921, *La critica* 28 (1930), 194.

[26] Quoted by Michael Curtis, *Three Against the Third Republic: Sorel, Barrès, and Maurras* (Princeton, 1959), p. 53.

[27] In a conversation with Jean Variot reported by Variot in *L'Éclair,* 11 September 1922. Quoted by Gaetan Pirou, *Georges Sorel* (Paris, 1927), p. 53.

[28] J. Variot, *Propos de Georges Sorel* (Paris, 1935), p. 55.

[29] Quoted by Gaudens Megaro, *Mussolini in the Making* (London, 1938), p. 319.

[30] *R.V.*, p. 144.

[31] A romantic, bitterly anti-democratic nineteenth-century Russian reactionary once declared that when he thought of the bourgeois in their hideous clothes scurrying along the streets of Paris, he asked himself whether it was for this that Alexander the Great, in his plumed helmet, had ridden down the Persian hosts at Abela. Sorel would not have repudiated this sentiment.

[32] op. cit. (p. 315, note 1 above), p. 53.

[33] *R.V.*, p. 19, note I.

[34] *R.V.*, p. 170.

Richard Vernon (essay date 1973)

SOURCE: "Rationalism and Commitment in Sorel," in *Journal of the History of Ideas,* Vol. XXXIV, July-September, 1973, pp. 405-20.

[*In the following excerpt, Vernon draws distinctions between traditional interpretations of Marxism and Sorel's interpretation.*]

In this essay I shall explore Georges Sorel's thought in the light of two contrasting conceptions; the idea that history forms an intelligible whole, knowledge of which provides criteria for political action, and the idea that no valid criteria exist for evaluating our actions, which rest on nothing more than a personal decision. The former idea is what Sorel thought of as "rationalism"; it is not what is thought of as rationalism today; in fact, later theorists have rejected that notion as an irrational one.[1] The latter idea is what is now described as "commitment"—though this term is not always used with a sense of its real implications—and is the theory which has usually been attributed to Sorel. Whereas the former idea is regarded as irrational because it involves a fallacious extension of reason, an attempt to reduce history to a rational scheme, the latter is held to be irrational because it represents an outright rejection of reason for action; thus Sorel's theory of the myth, for example, supposedly asserted that ideas have a merely instrumental value in provoking action, and should not be judged as true or false.

This interpretation of Sorel is a long-standing one; much of it was implicit in Julien Benda's condemnation of him as one of a generation of intellectuals who inverted the traditional values of philosophy.[2] But a closer examination of Sorel's conception of history suggests that his irrationalism should be interpreted in terms of the former idea rather than the latter; for while his thought contains hints of the theory of commitment which was to become so influential in the twentieth century, the context of its development was supplied by the philosophies of history of the nineteenth, the influence of which he was never able to escape.

I. Part of Sorel's criticism of rationalist philosophies of history, such as the neo-Comtean doctrines current in Third Republic France, was directed against their content, that is, against the vision of the emergence of a rational order from the archaic remnants of the past, a vision which he held to be illusory and frivolous.[3] But he was also critical of the possibility of representing history as an orderly development towards *any* single goal; from this standpoint, he was as severe a critic of Marx, with whom he sympathized, as he was of the Comteans, whom he despised. His fundamental objection to rationalism in this sense—to the view that history corresponds to an intelligible plan—was that it mistook what was only an "interesting" or "illuminating" interpretation of events, a factitious construction imposed by the observer, for a kind of force inhering in the events themselves. It is characteristic of what Sorel meant by rationalism to treat what is only an explanatory device as reality itself; to substitute "machines," following logical rules, for "historical complexities"; to confuse the rational and the real, by abstracting a coherent pattern from a mass of events, rejecting whatever has no place in it as "accidental."[4]

Sorel never in fact held that reality was incomprehensible, but only that it was not conclusively comprehensible as a whole. He thought of reality as an immensely intricate mass of interlocking events, related by a complex logic; in attempting to understand it, one was confronted by a choice between establishing the details of a certain limited situation from the inside, as it were, examining the motives of those involved and the inter-relationships between their actions, and standing outside the events in order to impose a bold and "frankly subjective" interpretation of their meaning.

The most explicit source for this dualism of Sorel's is ***Le système historique de Renan,*** one of his most apolitical works, written in 1900, and intended, according to the Preface, for a readership of "enlightened priests."[5] A long introduction to the book is devoted to the problem of the compatibility of theology and historical science; Sorel's argument is that the Church's hostile reaction to Renan's *Life of Jesus* was misplaced, for the historical examination of phases in the development of Christianity is on a plane quite distinct from that of Christian belief or disbelief. In support of this position he develops a distinction between two conceptions of history, each of which, he suggests, has a sphere sharply delimited from the other's. Usually, historians concern themselves with "the emergence of the future" from the initial situation, explaining the genesis of events by means of "exact knowledge of the men who occupied the scene at this moment." But one can adopt a quite different technique, "considering the past as a congealed mass, the general appearance of which is susceptible to schematic outline." One can explain the course of events causally, in other words, or else one can retrospectively assemble the accomplished facts into a general pattern. "The first system takes its stand on a process generated by certain determinate men; the second regards men as bearers of symbols rather than creators. . . . The first claims, thanks to psychology, to penetrate to the roots of living reality, explaining it completely; the second aims at no more than an illumination of the past."

The first conception of history—the causal and psychological conception—is the one which "corresponds to the instincts"; it has the advantage that, being narrative, it is close to the documents, and that its plausibility can be established by common sense, for it is concerned primarily with establishing human motivations. But the second conception is at once more ambitious in its scope and more modest in its explanatory claims. This second, retrospective historical method—which Sorel calls "scientific"—can make sense of the historical process at a high level of generality, by tracing the relationships between institutions and ideas, and interpreting change in teleological terms, as the "birth" of future achievements; Renan's theory of the historical missions of successive civilizations is offered as an example. However, scientific history can achieve this generality only by forfeiting any claim to providing a causal explanation; from this point of view, all the material of history must be regarded as "chance," and the task is to reduce the infinity of chance events to a comprehensible order. Because it is inherently retrospective, this type of history is perfectly compatible with a theological explanation of any specific set of events; since it says nothing about the causes of things, it cannot contradict any causal hypothesis. Hence Renan's very wordly historiography was quite compatible with the Christian view of the nature of Christ.

Though he is primarily concerned with defending Renan from his clerical critics, Sorel also takes the opportunity to attack the neo-Comtean philosophy of progress. The Republican ideologues, he objects, interpret post-revolutionary history in terms of such "occult forces" as "progress," "democratic evolution," "the tendency to equality," and so on; but this sort of theory rests on a confusion of the two historical methods, since it involves attributing causal force to essentially *ex post facto* generalizations. This confusion, Sorel suggests, owes something to the profound influence of the historical novel on historical thought; presumably he means that the novelist can shape his material towards a conclusion with a freedom that the historian does not have, and that in modeling his method on that of the novelist the historian imagines that his own ideas "control" the course of events in the way that the novelist controls the events he narrates.[6]

Sorel's comments on the philosophers of progress are typical of his criticism of the nineteenth-century philosophers of history, who all, in his view, neglected the distinction between causal and retrospective history. He seized, for example, on Plekhanov's use of Saint-Simon's maxim, "One may easily deduce the future from sound observation of the past,"[7] for this implied that the patterns constructed by historians were forces whose future direction could be deduced by extrapolation. He took Proudhon to task for supposing that the "general tendency" of civilization could be deduced from the balance of forces among "the various interests" in society. "When the historian speaks of a general tendency," he objected, "he does not deduce it from its constitutent elements, but constructs it by means of the results revealed in the course of history." The "synthesis" of conflicts in society takes place historically, not logically; it is "outside the realm of reasoned thought."[8] In short, the philosophers of history had thought that their schematic representations explained the course of events, whereas in reality such representations can only be formed after the events have run their course, in accordance with a complex logic which cannot be schematically reduced.

Sorel's criticism of Marx was much more elaborate and requires detailed treatment. Initially, however, it is worth noting that Sorel's dualism, applied to Marxism, corresponds to what has since been recognized as a major problem of interpretation. In his distinction between the history of "the men of this moment" and the history of schematic representation, there is an echo of the young Marx's rejection of the abstract, hypostatized history of Hegel in favor of a materialist history of "sensuous human activity"; in fact, Sorel's use of the term "bearer" (*porteur*) to express the instrumental role attributed to the actor in retrospective histories recalls precisely Marx's use of *Träger* in the course of criticizing Hegel in *The Holy Family*.[9] However, those of Marx's contemporary interpreters who regard the later economic writings as a better guide to Marx's thought contend that he *did* think of the historical actors as "bearers" (of "objective structures," that is), and argue that the study of the activities and perceptions of "the men" is irrelevant to true Marxian analysis.[10] Thus Sorel's dualism foreshadows to some extent the debate between those who, appealing to the young Marx, regard history as human action, mediated by its own products, and those who advise us to read *Capital* and interpret historical development in terms of an underlying structure beyond the consciousness of the actors.[11] In this sense, Sorel's categories of psychological and scientific history anticipate those of phenomenological and structuralist sociology.

Sorel's interpreters have not often placed him in the context of the development of French Marxism, not least because his "fascist utterances" (the phrase is Sartre's[12]) have commanded no respect among his Marxist successors. But Sorel had rather more sophistication than he has been given credit for, and the problem of the relationships between "structural" and "phenomenal" reality in Marx's thought was familiar to him, even though the terms are those of a later generation. In 1910 he published a Preface to the French translation of Labriola's *Karl Marx;* Labriola's thesis, essentially, turned the young Marx against the later Marx, applying the categories developed in *The Holy Family* to the later economic writings. Labriola pointed out that Marx himself had criticized Hegel for introducing a speculative or "esoteric" history into the empirical or "exoteric" course of events, but that he too had introduced an esoteric history to the extent that he had interpreted development in terms of economic categories which were not necessarily visible to the historical actors.[13] While Sorel never offered so cogent a formulation as this, his discussion of historiography in ***Le système historique de Renan*** involves a precisely similar problem, one can write an exoteric history in terms of the men and their consciousness, or one can write an esoteric history which imposes an overall pattern by means of a retrospective ordering of the events. If Marxism is a theory which attempts to combine these radically opposed methods, one which treats the retrospective schemas as explanations of the events in a causal sense, then it would seem to involve the same fatal ambiguity as Comtean positivism. Sorel's attempt to rescue Marxism from this trap occupied him for some twenty years.

II. Sorel's problem was to develop a variety of Marxism which respected the complexity of the historical process, and did not misread it in some rationalistic manner of attributing to the course of events the qualities of a logical process. During the 1890's, when he devoted an energetic flurry of articles and prefaces to the task of "revising" Marxism, his solution took the form of attempting to rescue an empirical Marx from a rationalistic Engels. His principal target was Engels' dialectical materialism; those who owed more to Engels than to Marx "replaced real history with a succession of forms engendered by causes independent of human action; they reverted to Idealism; they substituted for class struggle antagonisms between abstractions and the resolution of antinomies." They think that "history is ordered by the immanent logic of concepts"; for them, "it is words that regulate things, signs which provide the motive power of history"; having constructed an ideal conception of the historical process, they imagine that this imposes necessity on the course of events itself. In reality, concepts such as "capitalism" or "the proletariat" are only abstractions, and to imagine that history is reducible to such concepts is to invest what is only "a product of the intelligence" with objective reality.[14]

Sorel presents Marx himself as an empirical sociologist; in fact, Marx's technique is distinguished so sharply from Engels' "historicism" that at times Marx emerges as something of a "methodological individualist" in the manner of Professor Popper. Marx, according to Sorel, did not mistake models for reality; when he used abstractions such as "productive forces," he did so only "symbolically," for beneath such references there was always an empirical appraisal of the concrete "producers."[15] Marx saw history as human action mediated by the "logic of the situation," or, in Sorel's term, by the "social mechanism."[16] If Marx sometimes used deterministic language, regarding socialist revolution as a necessary event, it was not because he deduced it from metahistorical categories, as Engels did, but because his empirical study of the social mechanism of the industrial society of his day convinced him that revolution was imminent; "since he believed revolution to be imminent, he did not warn his disciples of the contingent historical basis of the mechanism observed by him."[17] As it happened, Marx's social observation was mistaken, for the revolution did not take place; but instead of blindly continuing to insist on the imminence of revolution, erecting Marx's empirical error into a necessary truth, socialists should continue Marx's empirical work, examining the logic of contemporary society in order to determine the potential of the workers' movement.

It was considerations of this kind that lay behind Sorel's distinction between the two types of history in ***Le système historique de Renan.*** If one wants to make predictions and examine possibilities, then the relevant technique is that of causal analysis, and this should be conducted in terms of the projects of the actors themselves and the ways in which they interrelate. The concepts which Engels employed really belong to a more abstract order of reflection; they are essentially categories for organizing masses of accomplished facts in a meaningful way, and tell us nothing about the motive forces which brought the facts into being. Thus the distinction which Sorel was to make between the standpoint of the agent and the standpoint of the observer is foreshadowed, in 1899, by a distinction between the concrete groups within which people act and the descriptive abstractions employed in speculation. "To remain on the realistic ground of Marxism," he wrote, "it is necessary to speak not of 'society' and 'the proletariat,' but of economic and political organizations the functioning of which is known and about which one can reason. 'Society' and 'the proletariat' are passive aggregates; the state, local government, cooperatives, trade unions, and friendly societies are active bodies, which follow considered projects."[18]

However, Sorel found this distinction between the speculative and the concrete increasingly hard to sustain, for it imposed an unacceptable division between the sphere of empirical research and the sphere of meanings. Quite obviously, one cannot examine the potential of socialism unless one has some conception of what socialism is. Although he attempted, with Bernstein, to define socialism simply in terms of the workers' movement, he found it impossible to avoid considering the end to which it should develop. Although he attempted to dissimulate this end—"it is useless to discuss it at length," he wrote[19]—it was inescapably there, for he was prepared to identify socialism with the workers' movement only if it fulfilled certain strict conditions. It had to "struggle against bourgeois traditions" and acquire a sense of its "historic mission."[20] Such conceptions clearly belong to the eschatology which Sorel attributes to Engels rather than the empiricism which he considers Marxist, for they imply that the working class is something more than an empirical aggregate of men, "moved by the influence of observable sentiments"; they imply that the class has an essential nature, derived from its place in historical development, which empirical men must struggle to fulfill.

Similarly, Sorel was obliged to recognize that the "speculative" elements in the thought of Marx himself could not be so lightly dismissed; although the cruder elements of dialectical materialism could plausibly be attributed to Engels, Marx himself had quite obviously had some historical schema in mind. His conception of the transition from capitalism to communism, Sorel suggests, was a transposition of Hegel's vision of a process from the individual to the universal[21]; and while he would like to free the essential, sociological Marx from such metaphysical trimmings, for "it is impossible to show that such logical arrangements can govern the course of history," he has to admit, in other contexts, that Marxism cannot be understood in isolation from its Hegelian foundations. Sorel's objection to other revisionists of the period is that their evolutionary conception of socialism fails to do justice to "the Hegelian manner" of Marx, who saw history as a succession of epochs marked by "sharp oppositions."[22]

By the turn of the century, Sorel was in fact prepared to abandon his distinction between the empirical and the speculative, admitting that the categories of empirical analysis could only be supplied non-empirically. In 1899, he admitted that Marx was "an impassioned man," who found it difficult to separate the scientific and persuasive parts of his thought, and had failed to distinguish between speculative constructions and real entities[23]; by 1901, he was arguing that no such separation could be made, for all understanding of social events depended on "a personal conception" of a "process" held to be under way, "for example, the theory of class struggle in Marx depends on the idea which Marx held of the historical process by which the proletariat had to emancipate itself. If one suppresses the idea of the future of the world conceived by the author, the class struggle becomes no more than a vague notion of an antagonism between groups of interests. Everything in his system is bound together and depends on a preconceived idea of revolution."[24]

III. Thus from arguing that true Marxism was a strictly empirical affair founded on patient, detailed research, Sorel developed a very different opinion of the nature of the doctrine, according to which it was to be seen as essentially speculative; the Marxist had to interpret the present in terms of an imagined process of development. In terms of Sorel's historical dualism, this involved abandoning the agent's standpoint for the observer's; just as the retrospective, speculative historian ignores the conceptions of the men of the past and locates their actions in the framework of the process which he has constructed, so the Marxist cannot rely simply on observation of the ideas and behavior current in the workers' movement, but must think of the present in terms of "the future of the world."

It was this logic that led Sorel to conclude that Marx's philosophy of history could rest only on a myth. For whereas the historian constructs a "process" with the advantage of hindsight, relating actions to later events of which the actors were unaware, the present cannot be understood retrospectively. Just as the history retrospectively constructed by present historians differs from history as it was experienced by the men of the past, so the historians of the future will not see the present as we see it. "The historians of the future," Sorel wrote, "are bound to discover that we labored under many illusions,"[25] for the meaning that we attach to events will not be the meaning that emerges after the event, when the general outlines of the "congealed mass" of accomplished facts will have become discernible.

This objection applied very forcibly to Marx, whose interpretation of the present, Sorel had realized, depended completely on a conception of the future by means of which contemporary development could be assessed. Marx had indulged in prospective speculation, whereas only retrospective speculation was possible; in short, he had neglected Hegel's dictum on the Owl of Minerva. He had applied to history as a whole conceptions such as "evolution" or "development" which could in fact be applied only to past history. "The term 'evolution' has a really precise sense only when it is applied to a definitively closed past in an attempt to explain this past by the present"[26]; applying it to the present, therefore, involved a sort of pretense that the present state of things has no future, that its potential is exhausted, and that it can therefore be regarded as "finished," since no decisively new events will emerge to alter the relevant standpoint of interpretation. Marx's conception of history is therefore defensible only if one agrees from the outset that capitalism is exhausted, and that society is on the eve of a great catastrophe[27]; Marxism itself obviously cannot afford such a prediction, for it rests on the assumption that the prediction is true.

Sorel is most Bergsonian here, for Bergson, too, argued that what is often regarded as prediction of the future is really only a stretching forward of the present, a mental act which is appropriate to static physical systems but inappropriate to vital phenomena.[28] Vital development is characterized by the emergence of genuine novelty which cannot be deduced from the patterns abstracted from past behavior; similarly, Sorel held that historical development involved genuine novelty and that the future could never be assumed away—Marx's conception of the imminent exhaustion of capitalism, for example, failed to take account of modifications ("mutations") such as finance capitalism which secured its continued survival.[29] Furthermore, Sorel agreed that while deterministic conceptions could to some extent be applied to past events, even though this misrepresented the quality of the *durée* which had produced them, they could have no place in the consideration of future events; thus Marx's error—Sorel makes explicit use of Bergsonian categories—was that he confused the *se-faisant* and the *tout-fait*, presenting the future, which would be the work of free creation, in mistakenly finished terms, appropriate only to the past.[30]

The principal effect of this critique of Marx was to remove from Marxism its privileged status. Since the future is open there is no presently available standpoint from which to judge the historical meaning of the present; therefore, although prospective interpretations of contemporary development have the appearance of reflective speculation, since they locate events in terms of their long-term meaning, they have the status of actor's conceptions, not observer's conceptions; they are comparable to the ideas through which the men of the past interpreted their world, not to the privileged knowledge of observers, for the observers are, by definition, of the future.

Hence Marxism itself, as a philosophy of contemporary history, belongs to the realm of "exoteric" history, of consciousness and action, not to the "esoteric" realm of reflective knowledge; it is a contribution towards contemporary development, not a summary of historical evolution. Sorel's doctrine of the myth was the formal statement of this perception; the conceptions which Marx had regarded as elements of a philosophy of history are transferred to the consciousness of the "militant." The revolutionary syndicalist is to engage in a kind of simulated retrospection; he is to imagine that "he has been transported into a very distant future, so that he can consider actual events as elements of a long and completed development."[31] The interpretation afforded by the myth is explicitly compared to the retrospective notion of "development" constructed by the historian; just as the historian traces a "theoretical axis" through a host of detail, so the myth imposes an idea of finality on the complex mass of situations which comprises present reality.[32] The militant's right to disregard the complexity of the present in order to impose a unitary interpretation upon it is the same as the historian's right to impose a selective "schema" upon the events of the past.

Whereas the historian makes his selection in the light of subsequent events which he knows to have taken place, the selective vision of the syndicalist can rest only on hypothesis; he can only imagine that he is looking at the present from the standpoint of the future, he cannot know what will be known about the course of present events in the real future. It has usually been thought that Sorel welcomed this situation, rejoicing in the vital unpredictability of history and applauding the myth of the general strike as a romantic "gesture" with unpredictable consequences. But nothing could be further from the truth. Sorel was in fact a stern opponent of romantic gestures; when he quoted, from Marx, George Sand's "Combat or death! Bloody struggle or nothing!" it was only in order to reject this notion as irresponsible and immature.[33] He approved of the myth of the general strike because he approved of its probable consequences, and thought it valuable as a revolutionary strategy; his estimate of its likely effects is presented in ***Reflections on Violence*** in almost obsessive detail.

Alternative strategies, notably the electoral politics of the socialist reformers, he regarded as "irrational" because "they leave the future completely indeterminate."[34] In addition to the syndicalist militants, Sorel proposed that there should be a "social science" of revolution, formulating "rules of prudence" and speculating shrewdly on the probable consequences of the militant's action[35]; in addition to violence, in other words, there should be "reflection on violence," although this reflection, being prospective, could not provide the certainty which Marx had assumed.

Thus Sorel's myth was a kind of make-believe rationalism; the highly intellectualized speculation of Marx, in condensed form, was transferred from the theorists to the militants, who were to continue believing it to be true; while the more sophisticated theorists, knowing that such speculation was beyond the scope of demonstration, would attempt to supply by prudential calculation that certainty which Marx had wrongly assumed. What Sorel was attempting to recover, in a patched-up form, was the conviction that contemporary development made sense as a stage in the evolution of an objective, knowable, and total historical process, and that, consequently, action could be taken in the secure knowledge that it contributed to the ultimate ends of history. As such, it had more in common with Hegel than with Bergson; for the myth, in Sorel's view, was not like the *elan* which contributes to an unforeseeable evolution, but like the "passion" which is essential to history, but is of value only as an instrument of a process of development.[36] Sorel believed, with Hegel, that history was "ruseful," but he did not regard it as "rational"; one, therefore, had to connive with it, projecting as accurately as possible the consequences of current convictions. Thus any socialist theory had to contain not only a conception of the meaning of history but also consideration of the impact of this conception on the "mechanisms" of contemporary history; otherwise the tactics of the socialists would not generate "a process appropriate to their nature,"[37] for the historical process cannot be relied upon to conform to the intentions and meanings of those who contribute to it.

IV. By means of this proposed division of labor between militant and theorist, Sorel believed that he had rescued the essentials of Marxism and "recomposed" the doctrine.[38] The myth of the general strike would, he calculated, bring into operation a process which would lead to socialist revolution. It would intensify conflict between workers and employers, ruin the politicians' plans for social peace, and in general return the historical actors to the roles which Marx had written for them. But though the doctrine's essentials may have been preserved, there would no longer seem to be any reason for regarding it as true; its validity, in its revised syndicalist form, would seem to rest simply on the decision that it was worth preserving; it would only be made true by a well-conceived revolutionary strategy. In the last resort, therefore, the myth would seem to have become a theory of "commitment." However, there are hints in Sorel's theory of an attempt to claim more than this for it; for the syndicalists, in his view, were the bearers of a universal value.

Sorel found it necessary to distinguish between the consciousness of the historical actors and the reflective knowledge of the historian because he saw history as a complex and devious process which did not correspond to the intentions of those who made it. The results of actions are modified to such an extent by the "mechanisms" of the historical environment that their meaning can only be understood after the event. History is therefore an alien process, a "weight" on human action, following a blind logic of its own which is incommensurable with our intelligence.[39] Such a conception of the alien nature of history may be connected with a vision of human unity which, by suppressing conflict, will eliminate the impersonal mechanisms which distort human effort, and thus render history "transparent" to the participants whose common will it would reflect. There is such a component, for example, in Sartre's desire to suppress the "polyvalency" of the world and dissolve history into "the men who make it in common"[40]; and Sartre's conception is anticipated in significant respects by a suggestion made by Cournot, whose writings Sorel knew and admired. Cournot's view of history in general, as a set of intersecting causal chains which can be organized into broad tendencies by the historian, was very like Sorel's. But within this general process, Cournot singled out for special consideration the development of science; as science becomes more organized, and as communications between practitioners improve, it will tend to leave its "historical phase," that is, its development will no longer be composed of a succession of causes and effects, but will reflect the working out of the collective purpose of the scientific community; its evolution, in other words, will become rational as distinct from causal.[41] What is especially significant is that Cournot contrasted scientific history with political history, which is, he said, of all the aspects of history, that in which, "the fortuitous, the accidental and the unforeseen" exercise the most powerful influence, and which, therefore, can be understood only as a series of causes and effects.

Sorel put forward a precisely similar conception, though in his case, it was technological rather than scientific history that was contrasted with political history. As far as technology was concerned, Sorel held what amounted to a full-fledged theory of progress. Those who contribute towards the development of technology are united by a purpose which is immanent in the apparatus of advanced industrial production; as a producer, each of us has "a modest place in a society urged on by an irresistible current of productive scientific research."[42] The direction of this current is indeed unpredictable, for in Sorel's view scientific theories could only follow concrete advances in technology; nevertheless the development of science and technology is progressive because its ultimate goal, the subjection of nature to human control, is a universally accepted value, and therefore the unpredictable inventions contribute towards a wider purpose.

Hannah Arendt has suggested that Vico, today, would have been far more likely to turn to technology as an example of the self-made pattern which man collectively imposes on himself than to the history of civilization in general.[43] Like Dr. Arendt's hypothetical modern Vico, Sorel accepted the view of technology as a human, and hence intelligible creation, but looked more skeptically on the history of civilization as a whole. For outside the technological sphere, there was no common purpose to render change intelligible. Political history, in particular, reflected only the random clash of ideologies and personal ambition. In fact it was quite possible—and Sorel believed this to be ,true of early twentieth-century France—that politics could actually impede the development of production[44]; in their hungry quest for votes, politicians propagated plans for social peace, distracting the capitalists from their true role of ruthless profiteering, and sponsored pacific wage increases in order to settle strikes, turning the workers into money-conscious *petit bourgeois* and thus distracting their attention from the factory. In general, democratic politics turned people into citizens, and degraded ideas of *m tier;* but as citizens, men contributed nothing to the single valuable task of increasing the productive power of man.

Thus Sorel allotted a special status to technological history. On the whole, he held a relativist view of historical reconstructions; the patterns discerned by historians are only "theoretical axes" with a largely subjective basis. However, technological history was to be exempted from this judgment, for Sorel held—in opposition to certain pragmatists—that scientific theories were true, and hence the development of scientific knowledge was to be regarded as an absolute, an axis of development derived not from a "subjective" point of view but from the standpoint of a permanent human value. The products of technology, therefore, unlike social and political institutions, are "commensurable with our intelligence"; hence technological history has the progressive character ascribed by rationalists to the historical process as a whole, for it is the history of an "artificial milieu" constructed by the collective intelligence of the productive groups.[45] The scope of this artificial milieu—or "artificial nature," as he calls it in his last book, to distinguish it from "natural nature"—is identical with the scope of the rational and of the human; for this is the sphere which man wrests from nature, and which alone is comprehensible to him. Nature cannot really be understood; it can only be interpreted metaphorically in various ways, but the artificial nature can be understood rationally and objectively, since technology can demonstrate in practice the truth of scientific laws.

Sorel thought that the syndicalists, as the community of industrial workers, were the group which embodied this mission against nature. He regarded them as men who were totally devoted to the factory, and whose victory would inaugurate a civilization in which industrial work would absorb the individual completely—as industry advanced, Sorel predicted and hoped, the hours of work would become longer and longer, and the nature of work increasingly technical and difficult.[46] In other words, syndicalist man would inhabit the artificial nature, constructed by technology, to the exclusion of the irrational natural nature; hence the history of technology, hitherto a sacred thread in an otherwise profane history, would become the whole of history. The function of the syndicalists' violence was to protect the factory from the malign influences of politics; for in Sorel's view—Saint-Simonian rather than Marxist, insofar as it presented politics as a parasitic growth rather than as a functional superstructure—political life had rather the same qualities as the despised natural nature; it involved insidious emotions and appetities, it was devious, unpredictable, treacherous, and destructive.

The function of violence, therefore, was not at all creative; it was strictly instrumental. Sorel approved of the syndicalists' violence because, by rebuffing the pacific politicians, it established a strict demarcation between the artificial nature of the industrial world and the indeterminacy of politics. Violence, in short, was to refine history down to its only rational element, the history of technology; and as history was purged of its irrational elements, becoming the history of the collective technological endeavor, the dualism of experienced history and retrospective history would vanish, for experience would become collective, and the course of events would reflect the collective will of mankind.

V. Thus it is misleading to regard Sorel as a theorist of commitment and to ignore his profound debt to the rationalism which he criticized. For in the first place, he shrank from the conclusion to which his criticism of Marx had led him, his demonstration that Marx had confused retrospective and prospective reflection; he continued to attempt a "philosophy of modern history,"[47] even though he had discovered that such an attempt rested on a rationalistic illusion, since only past history could be the object of speculation. In the second place, he did not see his attachment to syndicalism as an arbitrary decision, or as a commitment adopted for the sake of sheer vitality or excitement; on the contrary, he saw it as an attempt to remove arbitrariness and emotion from history altogether, by expunging the irrational elements from history. Sorel's technological Utopia, of course, lacks the rationalist content of Marx's "realm of freedom"; furthermore, one should not overlook Sorel's personal irrationality and the romanticized primitivism characteristic of much of his later thought. But I believe that in the limited context in which I have been considering him here, there is a case for regarding Sorel as a rationalist *manqué,* who tried to retain the substantive ambitions of nineteenth-century philosophy of history while skeptically narrowing the scope of reason.

NOTES

[1] For criticism in three very different styles: K. R. Popper, *The Open Society and Its Enemies* (London, 1945); E. Voegelin, *The New Science of Politics* (Chicago, 1952), Ch. IV; A. Camus, *L'Homme Révolté* (Paris, 1951).

[2] J. Benda, *La trahison des clercs* (Paris, 1928), 183.

[3] *Les illusions du progrès* (Paris, 1908).

[4] *D'Aristote à Marx* (Paris, 1935), 131ff.; *Matériaux d'une théorie du prolétariat* (Paris, 1919), 35, 184.

[5] *Le système historique de Renan* (Paris, 1905), 3.

[6] Sorel's comment (*ibid.*, 25) that Scott was "prudent" not to make real historical heroes the central characters of his novels anticipates a theme of Georg Lukàcs' study, *The Historical Novel,* Eng. trans. (London, 1969), 35ff.

[7] Letter to Croce, 23 April 1898, *Critica,* 25 (1927), 169.

[8] *Les illusions du progrès,* 7-8.

[9] L. D. Easton and K. H. Guddat, *Writings of the young Marx on Philosophy and Society* (New York, 1967), 375.

[10] For a particularly clear example: N. Poulantzas, "The Problem of the Capitalist State," *New Left Review,* 58 (Nov.-Dec. 1969), 70.

[11] Compare Sartre's rejection of the view that men are "les simples véhicules de forces inhumaines qui régiraient à travers eux le monde social," in *Critique de la raison dialectique* (Paris, 1960), 61, with Althusser's conception of history as "l'inaudible et illisible notation des effets d'une structure des structures," in *Lire le Capital* (Paris, 1970), 14.

[12] Preface to F. Fanon, *The Wretched of the Earth,* Eng. trans. (London, 1967), 12.

[13] A. Labriola, *Karl Marx,* French trans. (Paris, 1910), 110ff.

[14] "Y a-t-il de l'utopie dans le marxisme?," *Revue de métaphysique et de morale* (1899), 165ff.

[15] *Ibid.,* 167.

[16] Preface for S. Merlino, *Formes et essence du socialisme* (Paris, 1898), V.

[17] "Y a-t-il de l'utopie dans le marxisme?," 158.

[18] *Ibid.,* 159.

[19] Merlino, *op cit.,* XXVII

[20] "L'éthique du socialisme," G. Belot *et al., Morale sociale* (Paris, 1899), 150-51.

[21] "Y a-t-il de l'utopie dans le marxisme?," 173.

[22] Merlino, *op. cit.,* XL-XLI.

[23] *Matériaux d'une théorie du prolétariat,* 182-92.

[24] Preface to F. Pelloutier, *Histoire des bourses du travail* (Paris, 1902), 2-3.

[25] *Reflections on Violence,* trans. T. E. Hulme (New York, 1961), 149; *Réflexions sur la violence* (Paris, 1908).

[26] *Introduction à l'économie moderne* (Paris, 1903; 2nd ed., 1922), 2.

[27] "La marche au socialisme," *Les Illusions du progrès,* 4th ed., 374-75.

[28] A major theme of *Les données immédiates de la conscience* (Paris, 1889), and of *L'évolution créatrice* (Paris, 1907); also R. Aron, "Note sur Bergson et l'histoire," *Les études bergsoniennes,* IV (1956), 41ff.

[29] "La marche au socialisme," 373ff.

[30] *L'indépendance,* II (1911), 30. Sartre makes a very similar criticism of orthodox Marxism, which, he says, confuses "teleological" and "finalist" explanations: *Critique de la raison dialectique,* 40.

[31] *Reflections on Violence,* 58; in Sorel's idea of simulated retrospection there is perhaps an echo of Proudhon's fear that only posterity could learn the lessons of history; cf. *De la capacité politique des classes ouvrières* (Paris, 1864), *Nouvelle édition,* 1924, 73-74.

[32] *Matériaux d'une théorie du prolétariat,* 11-12.

[33] *Introduction à l'économie moderne,* vi, xi.

[34] *Reflections on violence,* 89-90.

[35] Preface for Pelloutier, *op. cit.,* 3.

[36] G. W. F. Hegel, *The Philosophy of History,* trans. J. Sibree (New York, 1956), 32-33.

[37] *Matériaux d'une théorie du prolétariat. loc. cit.*

[38] The theme of *La décomposition du marxisme* (Paris, 1908).

[39] *Matériaux d'une théorie du prolétariat,* 7.

[40] *Critique de la raison dialectique,* 63.

[41] A. A. Cournot, *Considérations sur la marche des idées et des évènements dans les temps modernes* (Paris, 1872), 8-9.

[42] *De l'utilité du pragmatisme* (Paris, 1921), 28.

[43] H. Arendt, *Between Past and Future* (New York, 1954), 57-58.

[44] *Reflections on Violence,* 137.

[45] *D'Aristote à Marx,* Chaps. XIII, XIV; *De l'utilité du pragmatisme,* 83-85, 413-27. Unlike Bergson, who regarded the truths of physics as only predictive abstractions, and looked to the "intuition" of the biologist, Sorel retained a positivistic attachment to physics, and regarded biology as no more scientific than sociology.

[46] *De l'utilité du pragmatisme,* 426-27.

[47] *Reflections on Violence,* 57.

D. C. Band (essay date 1977)

SOURCE: "The Question of Sorel," in *Journal of European Studies,* Vol. 7, No. 27, September, 1977, pp. 204-13.

[*In the following excerpt, Band declares that Sorel is more important as a populizer of ideas rather than as an original thinker.*]

The publication of Professor John L. Stanley's splendid collection (*From Georges Sorel: Essays in Socialism and Philosophy*) affords students of Sorel and, indeed, of modern European social thought an opportunity to address themselves to the question of Sorel's "place"—the question, that is, of the sources and importance of his system. Tracing intellectual influences is an exercise of about the same degree of difficulty as hunting the snark, and this may be the reason why, in the case of Georges Sorel, attempts to carry out the exercise have been characterized by massive and undefended assumptions, false trails and no little amount of confusion. Nevertheless, volumes such as Professor Stanley's testify to the need for this problem to be faced assiduously and, if necessary, at length, not least because practically all serious scholarship on Sorel is, in effect, addressed to this question of his place.

Perhaps one useful way to commence this undertaking would be for scholars of Sorel to acknowledge that a very great deal of their subject's thought was simply unoriginal. This is certainly an impression which is often reinforced as the reader is carried along on the waves of Sorel's polemics in Professor Stanley's collection. Many purportedly "Sorelian" notions have passed into the history of ideas under that label because Sorel was their popularizer, not because he was their author (and no less worthy or important for that). To take but one example for the moment, as one reads his most famous (or notorious) work, ***Reflections on Violence*** (1908), with its central theme of the rottenness of society, and of the urgent need for its spiritual revitalization if it is not to decompose altogether, one is struck by its similarity to many of the concerns of Max Stirner, not least the latter's claim that society is not ill but aged, palsied, in need not of salvaging measures designed to extend its miserable life by a few more hours, but of a new life altogether. Indeed, this particular likeness has recently been noted by one critic, who observes that Stirner "takes the position that Georges Sorel was to popularize . . . , arguing that society, if it is not to decay, must be revitalized. With no presentiment of the reality of twentieth-century fascism he can enthusiastically argue that new sources of passion must be tapped."[1] (As will be seen, the same sorts of links have often been drawn between Sorel and various twentieth-century fascisms.) But, even were one to concentrate on the specifics of Sorel's political thought, one would still be forced to acknowledge that a great many of them were, to a large extent, products of "the times".

Syndicalists and syndicalism were important political phenomena in Sorel's day: he did not invent them. Syndicalism's basic political tactic was to engage in ceaseless struggle against the forces of capitalism in the factories of Europe and at the same time to await and prepare for an apocalyptic general strike. This would reduce the bourgeois political system to impotence and thus to its doom. Now, of course, twentieth-century Europe has witnessed not a single example of the general strike as the thin edge of a proletarian state, but the "myth" of the general strike was a by-no-means unimportant factor in revolutionary politics during the middle period of Sorel's intellectual career. The question of the general strike was the subject of long and heated argument among socialists, both internationally and within their own parties, at this time. The myth of the general strike already had a long proletarian pedigree, but rarely before had it been an issue of such contention, and that contention was at least one of the factors which allowed Sorel to make such assertions as: "The bond . . . between Socialism and proletarian violence appears to us now in all its strength. It is to violence that Socialism owes these high ethical values by mans of which it brings *salvation* to the modern world."[2] The general strike, says Sorel, is the "powerful construction which the proletarian mind has conceived in the course of social conflicts"

> It must never be forgotten that the perfection of this method of representation would vanish in a moment if any attempt were made to resolve the general strike into a sum of historical details; *the general strike must be taken as a whole and undivided, and the passage from capitalism to Socialism conceived as a catastrophe, the development of which baffles description.*[3]

The concept of the general strike involved, by extension, that of working-class consciousness as well, and together they assisted in clarifying the growing estrangement of the radical and violent socialism emerging in Russia from the socialism practised—although, as Eduard Bernstein had complained,[4] not always preached—by the hitherto organizational and theoretical leader of European 'Marxist' parties, the SPD in Germany. Yet Sorel's aspirations and Bernstein's trepidations were both signs of the collapse of the standard interpretation of Marx's predictions—namely, that the socialist society would appear according to certain canons of economic development and that it would realize all the hopes of the Enlightenment in producing stability and benevolence in relations between citizens and between states. Such a hopeful faith in the power of reason is absent from both Bernstein and Sorel. Bernstein rejects what he takes to be the mechanicism of Marx's historical canons and avers that "Social conditions have not developed to such an acute opposition of things and classes as is depicted in the *Manifesto*".[5] Sorel is just as unequivocal in his rejection of what he perceives as Marx's views, but comes to very distinct inferences to those of Bernstein. For Sorel, two prerequisites for the socialist society are the rejection of rationalism and the taking of a determined position against the idea of development in terms of goods and wealth: " . . . use must be made of a body of images which, *by intuition alone,* and before any considerable analyses are made, is capable of evoking as an undivided whole the mass of sentiments which corresponds to the different manifestations of the war undertaken by Socialism against modern society."[6]

It is sentiments such as these which have led many commentators to assert that the answer to our "question" is that Sorel is a "reactionary". This claim typically assumes one or both of two forms: a view that his thought is literally reactionary, inasmuch as he is an advocate of prerationalist modes of political thinking and behaviour; and a view that these sorts of prescriptions logically and predictably were picked up by many extreme right-wing elements in European politics in the years after his death. The descriptive element of this latter view has a certain validity, and I shall leave it aside for the moment. The first view, however, needs to be dealt with at once. A social theorist's rejection of what he takes to be fashionable modes of thought and behaviour does not necessarily render his views reactionary. We need to ask *why* a Sorel advocates alternative modes of political thought and action: *what purpose* does he believe that they will serve? The answer, surely, is that they will help to create *myths.*[7] If Sorel is interested in what are essentially premodern modes of thought and action, it is because he sees in them the capacity to beget myths. Ruskin, Kropotkin, Proudhon and others are surely not reactionaries by virtue of their being students of mediaeval society; Engels is surely not a reactionary because he is interested in the organization and life-style of American Indians. As with Sorel, such theorists as these are attempting to see what assistance their fields of study can provide in the corroboration of their particular prescriptions for political endeavour. As one recent writer puts it: "Our judgment as to whether a thinker is reactionary or progressive must be based on the content of [his] model, not on the mere fact that a model from the past, even from a particular epoch of the past, exists."[8]

Thus, Sorel's supposedly "reactionary" irrationalism is, in fact, pursued with a view to creating myths, which will in turn lead to the appropriate forms of political action being taken. Myths are, in other words, central to his system and, for that reason, central also to our question. Typically and regrettably, however, the tendency in scholarly treatments of that system has been to glide rather furtively over this crucial Sorelian concept—although this is not an accusation that can be levelled against Professor Stanley.[9] Inasmuch as the largest part of our question is concerned with Sorel's "place", it is instructive to make a comparison of Sorelian myths with some of the ideas of his near-contemporary, Vilfredo Pareto,[10] for, whereas avowed followers of Marx think in terms of ideology and Sorel thinks in terms of myth, Pareto is concerned with what he terms 'derivations'. But Sorel's and Pareto's concepts have a great deal in common. Marx holds that, in bourgeois society, the concerns of social classes find expression in ideologies and that the proletariat, through the development of class consciousness, will become singularly free of ideological blinkers. Neither Sorel nor Pareto holds either of these views as far as his respective alternative to ideology is concerned.

Indeed, Sorel's and Pareto's attempts to distance themselves from Marx reveal certain scholarly fashions—fashions that are still with us—in the discussion of political beliefs. Both myths and derivations can be defined as groups of opinions or tenets which act as vindication of and, partly, as guide to the behaviour of political associations. Pareto holds that this behaviour has as its source instincts which accord with 'residues'. Residues are that which is shared by ideas, the particulars of which vary but the purposes of which do not, allowing for the debt of each to environmental and contextual considerations. Similarly, Sorel claims that this behaviour's source can be found in what he calls 'impulses'. I have not the space to pursue the subtleties of meaning of terms such as instincts, impulses and residues, let alone the question of whether or not, as employed by their respective authors, they enjoy subtleties of meaning. I shall content myself with operating upon the basis of my judgement that, for the sake of the argument of this paper, the meaning and role of Sorel's impulses and Pareto's instincts are virtually identical. Pareto holds that instincts can be discovered in all persons *sempre,* but that they will be of different force in different individals. The behaviour issuing out of them, and thus the derivations which are that behaviour's vindication and guide, varies as required by each particular case, since the way in which behaviour is the expression of instincts hinges very largely on the circumstances of those whom they provoke into that behaviour.

Now, all this is very similar to the role that Sorel claims for impulses. Yet another similarity is to be found in the fact that each thinker assumes that the behaviour arising out of impulses or instincts is irrational.[11] Here, of course, we come across a major problem in Sorel, for this assumption is hard to defend. It is true that individuals more than occasionally do behave irrationally, in the sense of behaving in accordance with their passions and not stopping to reflect upon the situation. Yet their passions, their unreflective sources of behaviour, may in addition produce felt wants and thus objectives. To the extent that these objectives are not contradictory or irreconcilable and that behaviour is aimed sensibly at reaching them, that behaviour is reasonable. This holds even when the individual so conducting himself is ignorant of the passions which are the origins of his felt wants and objectives. It seems that Sorel never acknowledged this. He, like Pareto, in addressing himself to behaviour buttressed by myths, does not conceive of the individuals involved as men who hold achievable and congruous objectives and who join forces in an attempt to realize them. Instead, he holds that they converge because of the necessity to express impulses that they do not know are within them. Such impulses have these men's behaviour as their *débouché,* but for Sorel the hypotheses that they employ to vindicate their actions are no more than pretexts for behaviour the secret impulses of which they do not know.

Sorel is a revolutionary like no other. He romanticizes the radical disposition and is Marxist at least to the extent that he believes the proletariat to be the unrivalled vanguard of the revolution, and to the extent that he is primarily interested in the myths and the deeds of the workers. He rejects, however, Marx's notion of the proletariat's seeking the fulfilment of its concerns *qua* class. Sorel's view is that social upheaval does not take place for the benefit of a single social group. It simply expresses radical *impulses,* that is, the impulse to progress, to go forward without the burdens imposed by history: the impulse to smash whatever seem to be corrupt impediments of man's development. The role of the myth, then, is to validate the deeds that spring from the impulses. "The myth is accepted, not because it has been critically examined and found to be true, nor because it justifies the pursuit of common interests, but because it justifies what those who accept it are impelled to do."[12] In yet another sense, of course, Sorel is a true descendant of Marx, since the latter's prophecies concerning the higher phase of communist society[13] are similarly pieces of revelation and not of political theory.[14] Socialism has been provided with its aura precisely because of the predictive trappings with which Marx embellishes his system.

It is Sorel's view that all creeds, all groups that seek to win over the people must have their myths, which can grasp the people's mind and fire it to revolutionary deeds. Society will be overturned by the very credence that is placed in the fact of an 'impending event'. "What that event is and how it will come to pass is never clearly defined, for if it could be it would lose its potency; but there is always something praiseworthy or glorious in contributing to its consummation."[15] And yet loss of potency can also occur as a result of this very lack of clarity and definition. Pre-war European socialism—of whatever stripe—had no systematic theoretical response to offer to the phenomenon of nationalism. The Italian syndicalists were advocates of their country's Mediterranean adventures, even the Libyan War of 1911-12; British naval and colonial policy had no more consistent supporter than Hyndman; few luminaries of the SPD were unconcerned with the bolstering of Germany's international position;[16] and the French syndicalists publicly conceded the people's nationalist prejudices and bellicosity very early in the new century. It was in this atmosphere that Sorel was to achieve what he took to be an intellectual accommodation with Gallic chauvinism, a *rapprochement* that ran counter to the spirit, but not the letter, of his writings, since those writings were so often imprecise in their formulation.

But this fact does not minimize Sorel's importance. Indeed, to return to a previous point, one of his genuinely original achievements was the extension of the activities of Bernstein and other revisionists. Bernstein claims to have corrected Marx in asserting that in no social system is the bourgeois social and economic structure faced with certain extinction by means of a revolutionary holocaust. That with which the Marxian argument should rather concern itself is a particular sort of associational behaviour: that of groups who form for the purpose of creating new political forms and practices. Now, of course, Bernstein is especially interested in Marxist groups, formed to try to overturn the forms and practices of capitalist society. Sorel, however, extends Bernstein's point to include every kind of group seeking political change. In this way, Sorel is rendering Marxism into an attack on the classifications employed by economics, sociology, political science and their kin: after Sorel, Marxism is never again merely an attack on bourgeois economics, although he probably would not have thought of his activity in those terms, for he works, as mentioned, in the name of French syndicalism, and the adjective is important. French syndicalism does not address itself to many of the issues which the scientific Marx felt compelled to confront. It is unconcerned with the nature of socialist society, the dictatorship of the proletariat, or how the passage to classlessness will be effected. It has no theory of the state.

It is a product both of the French proletariat's *souvenirs* and of the actual circumstances of society and politics in France at the time. Its intellectual origins are to be found with Blanquism and with Proudhon's *Système des Contradictions economiques* (1850) and *De la Justice, dans la Revolution et dans l'Eglise* (1858). French syndicalism's alienation from the totality of bourgeois society can be seen in two ways. It rejects the notion that the proletariat is becoming richer in, and therefore happier with, the capitalist system—a notion reflected in some of the "bread-and-butter" attempts to revise Marx; and it believes in the existence of a working-class essence, a fundamental fellowship, which it seeks to arouse. Sorel, as in his treatment of Marxism, takes syndicalism one step further. He disavows the entire liberal, reasoned ethos that the revisionists attempt to claim for socialism. Sorel takes an irrational pleasure in the imminent destruction of all the perfidious mores of bourgeois society. He has moved beyond the point of merely seeking protection from the capitalist economic system and its bourgeois class structure. "Sorel and Bernstein stand at the point of highest interdependence between socialist theory (and especially Marxism) and the Continental working-class movement."[17]

Let us finally and very briefly consider just one more of the many aspects of the question of Sorel's place that are stimulated by Professor Stanley's original collection—the problem of the affinities between Sorel's thought and fascism. Indeed, since this has been a problem of considerable moment in Sorelian scholarship, Professor Stanley might well have concentrated more of his energies upon it in his Introduction.

A great deal of this scholarship has been concentrated on the impact of Sorel's ideas upon Mussolini, especially the young Mussolini. It is apparent that, in the early years of the century, Mussolini—at that stage a revolutionary follower of Marx—had started to imbibe of the "irrational" or "sentimental" views of Sorel and Pareto, among others, and thus to qualify the particular variety of socialism to which he had previously been attached. In 1908, the student of Pareto and Sorel wrote "The Philosophy of Violence" for his local newspaper. It was the work, not just of a devotee of violent methods, but of a nationalist, and the Italian nationalists of the time were as fervent in their proclaimed adherence to the thought of Sorel as were their syndicalist compatriots. (This, indeed, is a large part of the explanation of Italian fascism's split personality. It was always characterized by both radical and anti-radical elements, a legacy of its having absorbed so many diverse persuasions.) At any rate, there seems to be no other way of viewing Sorel's intellectual effect on Mussolini as other than a "clear case of influence", a "known fact of direct influence".[19] But may we also say that "It was not entirely illogical *from his point of view* that he should have become a philosophical progenitor of Italian fascism"?[20]

One thing, at least, is clear: by the time that the Great War erupted, the Italian followers of the chauvinists, Alfredo Rocco, Enrico Corradini[21] and Scipio Sighele; the political economists and socialists, Pareto, Roberto Michels and Gaetano Mosca; the social psychologist Gustave Le Bon; and Sorel, with his elements of both Marxism and syndicalism, felt unconstrained in biting from each of these cherries and assuming that they came from the one basket.[22] Unlike Mosca and Pareto, however, Sorel neither had his origins in democratic progressivism nor ever fell under its sway. He perceived the emergence and strengthening of Marx's "indefinite, disintegrated mass" of "parasites and self-indulgent drones", the *lumpenproletariat,*[23] and he sought to combat this growth with a Marxist/syndicalist proletariat. This is the sense in which Freund was able to describe Sorel as a revolutionary conservative: the one term refers to his means, the other to his ends. Charles Maurras's royalist movement, the Action Française, hailed him as "notre maître Sorel" and he was, indeed, involved in its activities from 1910 to 1914. Yet he rejected the notion of party, placing his faith in the *proletariat's* taking actions which would culminate in the general strike. But, he says, the situation of each national proletariat is unique, and the particular actions of each proletariat will vary accordingly.

In this way the repudiator of party felt able to hail both the March on Rome and the October Revolution. (Consistency, *pace* Professor Stanley, is not his subject's long suit—indeed, it seems to me not a claim that Sorel would *wish* to be made on his behalf.) The proletarian activists and supporters of both revolutions had realized their myths. There was no little raw material, in other words, for an Ernst Jünger[24] to get hold of, accurately call it 'Sorelianism', and provide a new yet harmonious ingredient to the blend of inter-war German nationalist philosophy. In Italy some of Sorel's views were translated more directly into action. The creed of the *squadristi* resulted from their seizing his *leimotiv* of violence and giving expression to it in the language of Marinetti. The claim that all Italians were "working-class" was the *chiodo del mozzo* of a body of thought which Mussolini's adherents dubbed 'national syndicalism'. Italian Fascism, in settling to its own satisfaction the question of working-class sentiments versus nationalist sentiments, achieved a fusion foreseen by Pareto, Michels, Corradini[25]—and Georges Sorel.

This is but a sample of the evidence for the prosecution. Taken in its entirety—and surely no single individual has ever seen it thus—it would represent a very persuasive case. Yet the case for the defence, if unable to draw on as great a quantity of documentation, can make its points no less tellingly, and it has found the perfect advocate in Professor Stanley:

> The last thing that Sorel desires is what he calls "creative hatred" of the kind used by demagogues—a hatred that creates . . . brutality.[26]
>
> Sorel defines *violence* specifically as a rebellion against the existing order, while *force* is the might of the state used to maintain the existing order.[27]
>
> . . . confusing Sorelianism with Fascism is to make the same mistake as to single out war as the most characteristic trait of Fascism rather than internal state terror, which Sorel abhorred.[28]

Sorel is best regarded, says Professor Stanley, "as a highly suggestive social theorist, in the grand manner",[29] which might well be even an underestimation of his worth, for this grand social theorist is richly suggestive in so many different ways. The Sorelian paradox lingers, tantalizingly: our question remains unanswered.

NOTES

[1] John Carroll, *Break-Out from the Crystal Palace. The Anarcho-Psychological Critique: Stirner, Nietzsche, Dostoevsky* (London, 1974), 52.

[2] Georges Sorel, *Reflections on Violence,* trans. by J. Roth and T. E. Hulme (New York, 1961), 249; italics in original. (I shall refer to the Roth and Hulme edition, rather than the Stanley translation, for the latter provides only excepts from the *Reflections* in the work under review. This is a curious editorial decision on Professor Stanley's part, for there is surely no intellectually satisfying way in which to decide which sections of the *Reflections* constitute the more notable contributions to "Socialism and Philosophy".)

[3] *Ibid.*, 148 (italics in original).

[4] In his *Evolutionary Socialism: A Criticism and Affirmation* (1898).

[5] *Ibid.*, p. x.

[6] Sorel, *op. cit.*, 130.

[7] See *ibid.*, 50.

[8] Philip Rosenberg, *The Seventh Hero: Thomas Carlyle and the Theory of Radical Activism* (Cambridge, Mass., 1974), 151. I am indebted to Mr Rosenberg's splendid analysis of this problem and to his provision of the examples of Kropotkin, Proudhon and Engels.

[9] See especially pp. 39-47 of his Introduction.

[10] Sorel's dates are 1847-1922, Pareto's 1848-1923. The points raised about Pareto can be illustrated by referring to his *Sociological Writings*, ed. S. E. Finer (London, 1966), especially Part II.

[11] Pareto's term is 'non-logical'.

[12] John Plamenatz, *Ideology* (London, 1970), 126.

[13] See especially the "Critique of the Gotha Programme", *Selected Works*, ii (New York, 1950), 23.

[14] The same might be said of the predictive passages of Engels's *Condition of the Working Class in England in 1844*.

[15] R. N. Carew Hunt, *The Theory and Practice of Communism: An Introduction* (Harmondsworth, 1963), 106.

[16] *Cf.* H. B. Davis, *Nationalism and Socialism* (New York, 1967), chs 4 and 5.

[17] Adam B. Ulam, *The Unfinished Revolution: An Essay on the Sources of Influence of Marxism and Communism* (New York, 1964), 158.

[18] Pareto's view of 'sentiment' and 'solidarity' is outlined in his "Applicazione di teoria sociologiche" (1901).

[19] The terms employed by Leonard Schapiro, *Totalitarianism* (London, 1972), 73.

[20] R. N. Berki, *Socialism* (London, 1975), 169 n.52; italics added.

[21] See his *La Vita nazionale* (Florence, 1907); *La unità e la potenza della nazioni* (Florence, 1912); and *Discorsi politici* (*1902-1923*) (Florence, 1923).

[22] This point is elaborated in A. James Gregor, *The Ideology of Fascism* (New York, 1969), ch. 2.

[23] Marx, *The Eighteenth Brumaire of Louis Bonaparte* (New York, 1963), 75; also *Theorien ueber den Mehrwert,* quoted in Ronald L. Meek (ed.), *Marx and Engels on the Population Bomb* (Berkeley, 1971), 176.

[24] See, for example, his *Der Arbeiter, Herrschaft und Gestalt* (1932).

[25] The case of Corradini is an interesting one. In 1900 Sorel pointed to him as a "remarkably intelligent" person who had grasped "very well the value" of Sorel's philosophy. Quoted in James Meisel, *The Genesis of Georges Sorel* (Ann Arbor, 1953), 219.

[26] Stanley, "Editor's Introduction", 44.

[27] *Ibid.*, 43 (italics in original).

[28] *Ibid.*, 4.

[29] *Ibid.*, 5.

Jack J. Roth (essay date 1978)

SOURCE: "Georges Sorel: On Lenin and Mussolini," in *Contemporary French Civilization,* Vol. II, No. 2, Winter, 1978, pp. 231-52.

[*In the following excerpt, Roth examines the influence of the writings of Marx, Prudhomme, Vico, and Bergson on Sorel's system of beliefs.*]

The noted *littérateur* Daniel Halévy, for some years a close associate of Georges Sorel, tells a story about Sorel that is too good to be true.[1] In the early 1930s, about a decade after Sorel's death; the ambassadors of Soviet Russia and fascist Italy in Paris, upon hearing that Sorel's grave was in disrepair, independently and almost simultaneously informed the director of the Bibliothèque Nationale of the desire of their respective governments to erect a monument to him. Rolland Marcel, the director of the library who had himself known Sorel, asked Halévy for guidance in this delicate matter. Halévy, somewhat nonplused and not without embarrassment, made inquiries with Sorel's friends and relatives. After some time, he returned to Marcel with the response that Sorel's tomb was a family matter which concerned no one else. And Halévy speculated, "Sorel l'aurait ainsi donné." For Sorel, in truth, there probably was no inconsistency in his common admiration for Lenin and Mussolini while at the same time he would have insisted on a certain detachment with respect to both. The reason is clear enough: the development of his thought is a problem in apocalyptic political conceptions. Since 1886, he had been preoccupied with the problem of decadence. Almost from the start, Sorel's search was for a politico-spiritual conquest which by the 1930s (if not before) had become a quest of considerable relevance to young Frenchmen who came of age during the interwar years.

Sorel had turned initially to a Proudhonian moralism.[2] It may be that the disasters of 1870-71 which took place in his youth led him to Proudhon, though he rejected the specifics of anarchism. As Proudhon before him, however, he was convinced that France had lost her morals, her sense of the "heroic" and the "sublime." France, in short, was threatened with decadence. By decadence he meant the growth of a utilitarian and materialistic democracy and the predominance of rationalistic intellectuals. They corrupted bourgeois and proletarian alike. From the start, he wanted a moral transformation, a revival of "pessimistic values essential to Christian morals" and a "society based on work."

With the socialist parliamentary success of 1893, he announced his conversion to Marxism—it was the bourgeoisie who were decadent.[3] Though Sorel initially pronounced himself orthodox, he turned shortly to Bernstein's revision of Marx. Then, after his discovery of Bergson, he went radically beyond Bernstein. In the meantime, Sorel had been drawn to the Italian political and intellectual scene. He was attracted by the tradition of political realism and emphasis on the psychology of politics and was soon publishing in Italian as well as French Marxist reviews. He discovered Bergson and Vico almost simultaneously. From an amalgam that also included Proudhon and Marx emerged a unique conception of socialism. There was no determinism in history. But there were periodic *"ricorsi"* or renewals which arose spontaneously in the masses. Only a *ricorso,* a return to a primitive state of mind, could create new moral values and restore *élan* to the historical process. In syndicalism he saw the authentic manifestation of the proletarian movement Marx had written about—Marxism he called "social poetry." He urged French and Italian workers to isolate themselves from the corrupt world of politicians and intellectuals. The trade unions were to work silently at the creation of a proletarian order of the future.

Sorel, however, was among the first to join the Dreyfusards with the opening of the *affaire* in 1898.[4] The moral issue, for him, was overriding. The proletariat had to emancipate all who suffered injustice. In an abrupt reversal, he urged the workers to join with the enlightened bourgeoisie in rallying to the defense of Dreyfus and the republic. But after the great Dreyfusard electoral victory of 1899, he had grave misgivings. Once in power the defenders of Dreyfus displayed the same selfish immorality as their opponents. He was repelled by what he thought a vulgar anticlericalism and antimilitarism. He had nothing but contempt for socialist politicians who used proletarian support to win power and once installed became indistinguishable from other politicians. Parliamentary democracy, he was finally convinced, corrupted everything it touched.

By 1903, fortified by studies of such epic themes as the decline of Rome and the rise of Christianity, Sorel had become convinced that only a catastrophic revolution could bring a *ricorso.* In the decade that followed he reached the height of his career.[5] He had become a regular Thursday afternoon visitor of the bookshop of the young poet, Charles Péguy, on the rue de la Sorbonne. With a standing-room-only audience firing questions at him, mostly friendly young students, but also French and visiting Italian political and literary figures, he discussed any and all subjects. The "Socrates of the Latin Quarter," he was called. What must have intrigued his audience as well as his readers during these years was his extraordinary political and intellectual transformation.

Sorel turned first to revolutionary syndicalism in France and Italy. The turn of the century was the "heroic" period of syndicalism with the formation of the Confédération générale du travail (CGT) in 1903 and the Confederazione generale del lavoro (CGL) in 1906. These were years of violent strikes, sabotage, and repeated clashes with the police and army. In 1906 the first version of the ***Reflections on violence*** appeared.[6] Here, and in other books and articles, Sorel attempted to explain, primarily to French militants, the historical potential of their movement.[7] What Sorel saw in syndicalism was something comparable to primitive Christianity. It was impelled by a revolutionary myth—all great movements were impelled by myths. A myth was an expression of the strongest beliefs of a group, born of daily struggle and nourished by the loves, fears, and hatreds of the group. Its adherents felt themselves to be an army of truth fighting an army of evil. The myth of the proletariat was that of the general strike, an apocalyptic vision of the day the rotten and detested bourgeois regime would be destroyed. Moreover, he viewed syndicalists as an elite. The unions did not include all workers, only the most militant. They deliberately isolated themselves from the corrupt world about them. The technique of the movement was violence. Violence was the refusal to compromise in word and deed. Proletarian violence would culminate (he refused to speculate when) with a catastrophic revolution, but he did not rule out the possibility that proletarian violence might restore in the bourgeoisie something of its former vigor. As for the post-revolutionary regime, Sorel saw it impelled by a *morale.* A new value system would emerge from the revolution. It would inspire the perfection of machinery and the advance of production. Syndicalist society would be a society of producers. There was no need for the apparatus of the state. Politics he likened to friction in a machine. The new order would be dedicated to the creation of a society of heroes, heroes of production.

By 1908 Sorel began to doubt the future of syndicalism in France.[8] The CGT, he observed, had been compromised by turning to the Socialist party for support and protection. Except for a handful of close associates, he appeared to have no serious following. Two years later Sorel broke with Italian syndicalism (where his following was considerably greater) for substantially the same reasons. But by 1910 Sorel was already deeply involved with the monarchist Action française (AF), the exponent of "integral nationalism."[9] In France a group of young monarchists had seized upon Sorel's notion of a bourgeois revival, declared themselves disciples of both Sorel and the monarchist leader Charles Maurras, and from 1906 to the war attempted a doctrinal and organizational merger of monarchism and syndicalism. In Italy roughly parallel efforts were underway in the nationalist movement. Sorel was obviously flattered by the attention he now received. He noted, moreover, that the Action française with its para-military units, the *camelots du roi,* was beginning to look like a formidable movement. In 1909 he announced in the monarchist newspaper that he was not in principle opposed to a restoration. In 1910, after a monarchist playwright had produced a play on bourgeois cowardice (based on the ***Reflections***) and Péguy had published his widely acclaimed *Jeanne d'Arc,* Sorel announced that a patriotic and Catholic renaissance was underway—he had found another *ricorso.*

From 1910 to 1913 Sorel devoted himself to the cause of integral nationalism. He now inspired or participated in attempts to launch reviews that brought together antidemocrats of left and right.[10] One may be tempted to dismiss what he now wrote as opportunist, but in fact, the basis for his reversal of 1910 was at least partly inherent in the widely quoted passage in the ***Reflections*** on bourgeois revival. He saw nationalism, in any case, impelled by a myth compounded of the patriotic and the religious. The myth was rooted in the widespread fear that France was in peril. For France, he argued, there was a way of life whose validity had been established by history: the complex of institutions and values, classical and Catholic, of the Seventeenth century. The myth of nationalism was that of a revitalized nation purged of alien elements (Jews, Protestants, Freemasons) and aberrant institutions (notably, parliamentary democracy). The AF he thought a bourgeois elite, though sorely lacking in revolutionary leadership. The violence of the *camelots* (which he greatly admired) could lead to a successful *coup.* As for the order to be established, its *morale* would be classical and Catholic. A king or dictator would restore the state as the foremost institution, though syndicalist ideas could be incorporated in its structure. The regime would foster a cult of the nation, the perfection of national institutions at home, and the pursuit of *"grandeur"* abroad. Whatever enthusiasm Sorel may have had for the AF (and it was never without reservation) had vanished, however, by 1913.[11] Sorel was excluded from Péguy's shop when Péguy could no longer tolerate Sorel's new anti-Semitism. Provincial monarchist circles would have nothing to do with anything that smacked of proletarian revolutionism. Even Maurras was eventually horrified by Sorel's lack of intellectual discipline. Moreover, Sorel himself had detected flaws in the AF. It was led by intellectuals who seemed interested only in writing about revolution and it ignored the proletariat. By 1914 Sorel was convinced that both the proletariat and the bourgeoisie were, especially in France, "under the direction of Mammon."

When war came in August 1914 Sorel was in despair.[12] He was contemptuous of the "plutocratic Entente." If anything, he wanted a German victory. He wrote to Benedetto Croce, with whom he had corresponded since 1896, that the war would, nevertheless, shake Europe to its foundations. But when he scanned the horizon for a *ricorso,* he saw nothing: "Whoever believes in the doctrines of Vico looks everywhere in vain . . . for the direction from which rejuvenation may come. . . . [And he added, significantly,] . . . the Slavs are alien to the ideas which have directed our civilization; by succumbing to decadence we become Slavs; we are ripe for Russian domination."[13] What the world needed, he asserted in 1916, was a "catastrophe" capable of plunging it into a "new Middle Ages"—a "severe medieval penitence."[14] But at no time in 1917 did he exhibit any great interest in Russian events.

The first act of the Bolshevik Revolution to command Sorel's attention was Lenin's dissolution of the Constituent Assembly on January 19, 1918, an act, he thought, of "powerful originality."[15] By degrees, Sorel mobilized his energies. He had meanwhile found another bookshop on the Left Bank where he held court, that of Paul Delesalle, an associate of his syndicalist days. To his death in 1922 it was primarily to Lenin and the Bolshevik Revolution that he gave his allegiance.

During the first months of 1918, however, he feared that the regime would not survive: "Everything," he wrote to Delesalle in February, "may end in an immense disaster."[16] From the start he had at least one reservation about the revolution—too many Jews. Trotsky, he speculated, must resemble the Russian Jewish revolutionaries he had encountered in Paris, "talkative, braggarts, half-hallucinated." Trotsky might be in the pay of the Entente. In any case, he noted, events in Russia indicated that European socialism "will go down before Bolshevism." It was not yet clear what bolshevism was or how it could be adapted in the West. But by June he was ready to set aside his faint hopes in syndicalism by publicly supporting the bolsheviks.

Still preoccupied with the nature of bolshevism, in the latter half of 1918 Sorel grew increasingly bitter at efforts of the Entente to stifle the new regime.[17] Plekhanov who had sided with Kerensky and against Lenin, he speculated, must be a "British agent." Entente diplomacy was behind the Social Revolutionary uprising in July. The entire bourgeoisie, he was convinced, European and American alike, saw in bolshevism the gravest danger yet to the established order. It was "because of . . . [their] . . . hatred," he wrote, "that I have so much sympathy for Lenin and his companions." He was still uncertain, he told Delesalle, of the meaning of the revolution—what could have been said of the French Revolution if it had ended with the Convention? But when he read that the Fifth Congress of Soviets had reserved political rights exclusively to producers, he was elated. And when he heard that the Red Guard shouted "Death to the intellectuals," he was convinced—a society of producers was in the offing. If only the regime could hold on long enough, a socialist renaissance would follow. In a note appended to a collection of prewar articles on syndicalism he asserted that the victory of the Entente in November had been the triumph of a demagogic plutocracy that had now turned on the bolsheviks. "But," he asserted, "what will the plutocracies gain by the extermination of the Russian revolutionaries? Will not the blood of the martyrs once again be fertile . . . ? One must be blind not to see that the Russian Revolution is the dawn of a new era."[18]

In 1919 Sorel began to publish regularly once again, notwithstanding his illness. Lenin, he wrote to Croce, had shown himself to be "a really practical man."[19] American journalists had observed a constant improvement in conditions in Russia. He now became a regular contributor to the *Resto del Carlino* of Bologna and the *Tempo* of Rome, as well as the *Ronda,* the Roman literary review. Most of some 60 articles that he was now to publish in Italy were addressed to the new Russian regime. But his most important article of 1919, the "Pour Lénine," was published in France.[20] The essay was a response to an article in the *Journal de Genève* in which the well-known Swiss professor and journalist Paul Seippel had asserted that Lenin and Trotsky must have read Sorel's ***Reflections*** during their exile in Switzerland, that the Bolshevik Revolution was a "terrifyingly logical" application of Sorel's doctrine of violence, and that the Bolshevik Revolution was a mere prelude to a great revolutionary wave about to engulf all Europe. Sorel replied to these charges in an essay appended to the fourth edition of the ***Reflections,*** though later published in the French and Italian press. He had no reason to believe, Sorel asserted, that Lenin had employed his ideas. But if that were true, he would be uncommonly proud to have contributed to the intellectual formation of a man who seemed to be simultaneously "the greatest theoretician that Socialism has produced since Marx" and "the head of a state whose genius recalls that of Peter the Great." He explained that the ***Reflections*** contained no apology for terrorism. He expressly regretted the brutality of the bolsheviks but the number of people shot was considerably smaller than the victims of the Entente blockade. The excesses of the revolution he attributed to its "Muscovite character" and the large number of Jews attracted to the movement. What was transpiring, in any event, transcended these considerations: Russia was "Rome" bringing to the world a new civilization. He concluded on an ecstatic note: "May the plutocratic democracies who are starving Russia be cursed! I am only an old man whose life is at the mercy of trifling accidents; but may I, before descending into the tomb, see the humiliation of the arrogant democracies, today so shamelessly triumphant."[21]

Throughout 1920 Sorel scanned the horizon for a socialist renaissance. He avidly followed the great wave of strikes in France and Italy.[22] But when the Quai d'Orsay recognized the Wrangel regime, he charged France with becoming the citadel of reaction. When the strikes came to nothing, he was convinced that European socialist leaders would betray Lenin at the next congress of the Third International. "In a word," he wrote to Croce in August, "everything is rotten in Europe." That year he began to contribute to the new *Revue communiste,* dedicated to Integral Communism and to the support of the Third International. He had, in fact, been asked to join the staff of *Humanité* but that, he complained, would have been too arduous. By 1921 Sorel was once again bedridden and was only occasionally able to visit old friends and haunts. In March he met Jean Variot on a Paris street.[23] Variot was a monarchist who had assiduously recorded Sorel's talks since 1908 when he met Sorel at Péguy's. Variot informed him that it was widely bruited about that both Lenin's regime and Mussolini's fascist movement were inspired by his doctrines. Sorel replied that he had heard the same thing and was greatly flattered. He doubted, however, that one individual could be that influential. Besides, he had not invented anything new. His doctrines were "in the air." With regard to Lenin, it was hardly necessary for a man of Lenin's genius to have read his books. Lenin too had taken part in the attempt to restore Marxism to its pure form. Lenin had also become a proponent of violence, that is, of Marxism "to the hilt." That year Sorel's illness reduced the volume of his correspondence dramatically, while he published no more than a half-dozen articles. But among these was "Lénine d'après Gorki," of which he was inordinately proud.[24] It appeared in both the *Revue communiste* and Antonio Gramsci's *Ordine Nuovo,* organ of the Turinese communists. Sorel took Maxim Gorki's brief study of Lenin as confirmation of views he himself had expressed in "Pour Lénine" on the role of bolshevik myths. He boasted to friends that Bergson had read the article and had commented, "You give the pragmatic criterion a precision and a universality that it has not yet received."[25] Briefly, Sorel revived a prewar correspondence with the historian of Rome, Guglielmo Ferrero.[26] Ferrero had recently compared the coming of bolshevism with the disasters that shook the Roman Empire in the Third century. At the beginning of 1922 Sorel prepared the second edition of a prewar study of the fall of Rome, adding a forward in which he continued the quarrel with Ferrero.

News that Sorel was gravely ill early in 1922 prompted the editor of *Humanité,* the official organ of the French Communist Party since the Congress of Tours in December 1920, to interview Sorel.[27] Sorel turned repeatedly to the subject of Russia: "We must go forward! That is the sole objective! We must save her!" On March 22 Roberto Michels, a prewar enthusiast of Sorelian syndicalism now at the University of Basel, met Sorel at Delesalle's bookshop. He recorded that Sorel expressed confidence in the vital energies of the Russian, Italian, and perhaps, the German people. Sorel asked Michels to send as many writings of Lenin and Trotsky as he could obtain in Switzerland. Michels, whose politics had changed, expressed the belief that these might "set the world aflame." When the conversation threatened to become difficult, Michels left the bookshop and never saw him again. The summer of 1922 was Sorel's last. On his deathbed, not surprisingly, he received visits from old friends in the Action française and on the staff of *Humanité.*[28] In a voice that was barely audible he was heard to gasp: *"Il faut aider la Russie!"*

What clearly emerged from Sorel's work on Lenin and the Bolshevik Revolution were the outlines of what Sorel took to be still another *ricorso*.[29] To be sure, as in the case of French revolutionary syndicalism and integral nationalism, Sorel saw in the Bolshevik Revolution a national phenomenon. But the war and postwar era had also given to the revolution a significance of far greater magnitude.

The revolution was impelled, Sorel argued, by bolshevik myths. Though explosive in character, these had a distant and obscure origin in the Russian past. Their rapid appearance had been favored by Russia's conflict with the Entente and her isolation from the bourgeois world. Both the social and national discontents of the masses had shaped these myths: the hatred of the workers for their masters (which had merged with the working class myths of Europe) and the protest of the "real Russia" against ideas and institutions imported from the West. What sustained bolshevism, therefore, was the hatred of the masses for the "rich foreigners" who had succeeded in infiltrating what Gorki called the "Republic of the Poor." The revolution was also sustained, however, by the vision of a new world in formation. The desire was ambivalent and incoherent but Gorki had given brilliant expression to it in "visions worthy of the Hebrew prophets." He quoted Gorki: "It is the Russians who are going into battle for the triumph of Justice, the vanguard of the peoples of the world, . . . Only yesterday the world considered them half-savage and yet today, almost dying of hunger, they are marching to victory or death, ardent and brave like old warriors."[30] Gorki's vision, he asserted, was no rhetorical device. It was an expression of "the noblest sentiments . . . in the soul of an oppressed people." Lenin, moreover, knew how to use the desire of the masses for a cataclysmic transformation.

Sorel gave primary attention to the role of charismatic leadership in matters concerning organization. The emphasis on leadership now went far beyond anything developed in his previous work. That Russia patiently endured the revolution was because she felt herself ruled once again by a "true Muscovite." But Lenin, though hard, was a "genius in politics," a "doctrine in action." He possessed, according to Gorki, something of the saint about him. His temperate, almost ascetic life set him apart from the masses. He had already become, according to Gorki, a saint in India—Asia, Sorel noted, was a good judge in matters of sainthood. He served as *"l'homme-exemple"* of the revolution, providing the masses with "a *mystique* that gave them the strength to suffer for the sake of a goal." Sorel quoted Gorki on Lenin: "Respect for the ascetic life, disinterested devotion to the cause of the poor, a sincere pity for human misery, . . . the world still wants these heroes to lead the way to liberation."[31] The elite that served Lenin was to be found in the soviets. The soviets, by assuming the role of educating and disciplining the masses, were not unlike the syndicates to whom he had previously assigned this role. The soviets were, in any event, prepared to accept all the hard and implacable realities of the revolution.

The technique of bolshevism, Sorel argued, was violence, a pragmatic Marxism prepared to "go the limit." The employment of violence could not be determined in advance in accordance with scholastic formulas, as Kautsky had asserted. A revolution is "a storm in which the unforeseen triumphs." The bolsheviks, therefore, could not recoil from the most terrifying severities. He conceded that the design of history which obliged Lenin to kill some for the good of others might "torment the soul." But he quoted Gorki: "One cannot demand of someone who has not known justice that he be just." It was pointless, therefore, to compare bolshevik police and tribunals with European institutions that bore the same names. The Red Army struck Sorel as a unique institution in this regard. It was a revolutionary army to be compared with Cromwell's "Ironsides." The class struggle and the war of liberation had been brilliantly joined in the idea of the worker-soldier. This was a far cry from the bourgeois nation-in-arms that still maintained the military traditions of the old monarchies. The essential purpose of revolutionary violence, in any case, was to maintain the idea of *"scission"* in the masses. He recalled his writings on primitive Christianity: violence maintained the vision of an army of good facing an army of evil.

Bolshevism, though fighting for its life, was also a functioning revolutionary order. The transformation, he maintained, had already gone well beyond anything achieved by the French Revolution. The bolsheviks had brought about the "greatest revolution that has taken place in two thousand years."

What impelled the new regime was a revolutionary *morale,* what Sorel called *"mass-force"*—the tsarist regime, so hard and violent, had none. It was the overnight release of moral energies in the masses that had saved the regime and more than once. The apparatus of constraint did not maintain the regime. Neither were its military and economic achievements to be credited to the exercise of Lenin's absolute authority. What the masses saw in socialism was the hope of a great technological and industrial advance, the first revolution of its kind in history. They knew that the difficulties to be faced were far greater than revolutionaries had ever confronted. They were obliged to destroy and reconstruct in a fashion that eliminated dependence on foreign or domestic capital. The revolutionary *morale* of the masses, however, would prevent their becoming bourgeois, that is "hallucinated by the mirage of becoming wealthy by a stroke of fortune." This was the "aim of old and decrepit people." The regime's most important "orders of the day" to workers and peasants were: " . . . be honest in money matters, be economical, do not be lazy, do not steal, observe the strictest discipline in work."[32] This might appear to be bourgeois advice but these rules, Sorel asserted, were always valid.

Sorel saw in Lenin's dictatorship of the proletariat the emergence of a society of producers. Jacobin methods would not in the long run provide a durable foundation for the regime, nor would the withering away of the state be an easy matter. That Lenin played a preponderant role in the interim disturbed him not at all. He was, after all, to be compared "with tsars and not with presidents of the United States." For Sorel the organization of soviets was ideally suited to facilitate the genesis of law. The juridical development of a society of producers bore the closest relation to the process of production. The soviets could readily determine on the basis of experience which practices were beneficial and which harmful to production. The legal system might center on the basic concept of the right to work, the equivalent to the bourgeois right to property: "The Soviet dictatorship . . . will no longer have any reason for being when the working masses of Russia realize their . . . rights are based on their merits as producers."[33] Though Sorel had initially greeted workers' control as a vindication of prewar syndicalism, he was quick to recognize the superiority of managerial control in largescale industry. He noted that Bertrand Russell, who had visited Russia, had recognized in Lenin a talent for engaging as managers "men of the American type." Such men were far more interested in the satisfactions which derive from power and achievement than they were in the accumulation of personal wealth. Marx, moreover, had clearly indicated that Russia was not obliged to follow in the wake of the more advanced capitalist countries—the manager made this possible. What prevented capitalism from exploiting the full potential of modern industry was its usurious and commercial origins. The removal of the capitalist removed from the economy the element that threatened to limit its progress. By means of managers Russia could skip a full-blown capitalism, avoid its tortures and appropriate its fruits, while developing her own institutions.

What Sorel saw as the technique of the regime was to be found in Lenin's idea of the "general line," that is, a "pragmatic Marxism, exactly informed and free from prejudice," that aimed at conquest at home and abroad. The key to technological and industrial conquest was invention. He noted that the Taylor system, reward and punishment, piece work, and even the payment of capitalist wages to specialists and technicians had been introduced to increase or improve production both in industry and agriculture. That Lenin employed certain bourgeois ideas was all to his credit. The new regime must take over from capitalism its capacity for making constant inroads on the unknown. The worker-inventor, he thought, was on the same level as the artist. Artists and workers in Russia already understood that they were both victims of the bourgeoisie and had come to regard each other as brothers. Conquest of another kind was also foreseen by Sorel—imperialism was fundamental to the Russian spirit. For centuries Russia had looked on Europe as a prey that would someday be hers. The revolution had only reinforced these sentiments. Lenin and his followers in their bitter polemics with Western social democrats had long made clear their hatred of the West. Moreover, the bolsheviks would never forgive the attempt to dismember Russia. Once internal difficulties were overcome, Russia would once again menace Europe. But Europe, Sorel thought, seemed unaware of the danger. The extraordinary longevity of Byzantium had given Europe no reason to despair. The capitalists hoped that they could continue to produce goods in great abundance and thereby last indefinitely. A bolshevik conquest would, in any event, be violent. It would suppress all the conventional lies. Everywhere the Russians would introduce either institutions similar to their own or integral Bolshevism itself. But Russian imperialism would not be limited to Europe. The entire would, under the influence of an effete and decadent West, deserved to be destroyed. The revolution, consequently, was as anti-Western as it was anti-bourgeois. Patriots everywhere already looked to Russia for assistance. The isolation imposed by the Entente only drove Russia closer to them. Bolshevism alone would profit from anti-Western sentiments in Asia and in the Near East. He urged Lenin to seize the opportunity: "If we are grateful to Roman soldiers for having replaced abortive, stray, or impotent civilizations by a civilization whose pupils we are still in law, literature, and monuments, how grateful will the future have to be to Russian soldiers of Socialism! How lightly will historians take the criticism of the orators hired by the democracies to denounce the excesses of the Bolsheviks. New Carthages must not triumph over what is now the Rome of the proletariat."[34]

Sorel's career appeared to reach its climax with Lenin and the Bolshevik Revolution. But there is a complication. After 1919 Sorel became increasingly aware of another revolutionary and another revolution in postwar Europe—Mussolini and the nascent fascist movement.

For at least a decade before the March on Rome, if not earlier, Sorel had followed the career of Mussolini. When Mussolini, who had been an intense admirer of Sorel, was appointed editor of the *Avanti!* in 1912, becoming virtual head of the Italian Socialist party, Sorel had asserted: "Our Mussolini is no ordinary socialist. Believe me: you will see him one day, perhaps, at the head of a sacred battalion saluting the Italian flag with his sword. He is an Italian of the fifteenth century, a *condottiere!*"[35]

During the latter stages of the war and the immediate postwar years Sorel, now completely in despair of France, seemed to be on the lookout for some kind of *ricorso* in Italy.[36] But when the great wave of strikes came in the north in 1919-20, he was mystified by the failure of the socialists to seize power. With Mussolini's revival of the Fasci in 1919 and the beginning of Blackshirt punitive raids, he identified fascism with bourgeois reaction. For some months he genuinely feared that the Blackshirts might become masters of the street. By 1921, however, he was prepared to admit that Mussolini was a "political genius no less extraordinary than Lenin." When Variot had suggested that not only Lenin but Mussolini too was Sorel's disciple, Sorel did not deny the possibility in the latter case. But Mussolini, he said, was the inventor of something that was not in his books, "the union of the national and the social, which I studied but never fathomed."

In his correspondence of 1921 Sorel's alarm gave way to admiration and then conviction that fascism would triumph. "All Europe," he was convinced in April, was "destined to experience" a Thermidorian reaction.[37] Moreover, the fascists were "not entirely wrong" by invoking his name—their action demonstrated clearly "the value of triumphant violence." Fascism, he wrote in August, was "the most original social phenomenon in Italy." In September he asserted that the fascists were defending the Italian national heritage. The Italian state had not only failed to protect the bourgeoisie, but had also failed to receive Italy's just demands at the Peace Conference. "We are at the beginning of a movement," he asserted, "that will completely destroy the parliamentary edifice."

Though he had not quite called the fascist movement a *ricorso,* it is likely that by 1922 Sorel was close to it. Michels recalled that when on March 22 Sorel spoke highly of Lenin at Delesalle's bookshop, he also exhibited great sympathy for Mussolini.[38] Variot noted that at Delesalle's Sorel had said: " . . . the two capital facts of the postwar era are: the action of Lenin, which I believe lasting, and that of Mussolini, who will certainly triumph in Italy, notwithstanding the coalition of the left and the revolutionaries."[39] Within two months after Sorel's death on August 29, Mussolini was named prime minister after armed Blackshirts staged the March on Rome.

One must resist the temptation to dismiss Sorel's career as politically irresponsible or opportunist. Moreover, no part of it may be viewed in isolation. The essentials in apocalyptic politics are not political but religious and his views on Lenin and Mussolini assume meaningful perspective only against the entire sweep of his career.

Sorel's search was always for a *ricorso* for which primitive Christianity was the prototype. A *ricorso* was a movement impelled by a charismatic excitement. Though it arose out of decadence, it strove for a sublime end. His search led him always, therefore, to the political extremes, among those who seemed most eager for drastic and total renovation. But Sorel was no mere observer. He was also a believer. So deeply did he believe that he frequently saw in a movement what in reality was not there. His career, therefore, was almost necessarily a succession of hopes and deceptions. What facilitated his movement among the extremes was his essential pragmatism. To be sure, he most desired a *ricorso* on the "left." The break would be more dramatic, the transformation more complete. But he found in the extremes alternatives which, apparently, were personally acceptable. The extremes were for him aspects of a single system of thought, a single mood of revolt. Though the basic pattern of his ideas was apparently repeated for each of the movements to which he was attracted, his views nonetheless underwent important evolution. The movements were impelled by revolutionary myths, led by elites, and dedicated to violence. They were capable of creating a new order, each with its own *morale,* its own organization, its own technique. But they were all "totalist," that is, permeated by the myth that brought them to power and a revolutionary *morale* that sustained their purity of purpose once in power. They all aimed at the establishment of a society of heroes. The *ricorsi* he anticipated, nevertheless, changed progressively in character. Until the war he was thinking largely in terms of a French or possibly, an Italian national revival. But the Bolshevik Revolution had for him a "civilizational" significance and so too the Italian fascist movement, though less clearly so. Sorel's conception of revolutionary syndicalism appeared to be dominated by the idea of class. But the class idea was obscured in his later work. Though he saw in the AF a bourgeois elite, what he described seemed more like a self-constituted national elite. Neither bolshevism nor fascism, in any case, was exclusively a class movement but compounded of both the social and the national. And finally, Sorel's *ricorsi* changed in quality. The apocalyptic idea was always in evidence in his work, but it tended to deteriorate. Though never vulgarized, it nevertheless lost much of its initial subtlety. The *ricorso* became less an essay in Christian pessimism and more a problem in social engineering.

Sorel's argument in support of Lennin's revolution was unique. It was not a Marxist argument. Indeed, there is some question if Sorel ever was a Marxist except for a brief period during his formative years. Quite apart from the overall development of his thought, which can hardly be called Marxist, was the centrality of his notion of myth. Sorel saw movements impelled by a variety of myths throughout history. To be sure, in describing contemporary movements he used such terms as "proletarian" and "bourgeois" and rather freely. But these were not so much class designations as states of mind. For Sorel what impelled the historical process was the struggle of a revolutionary sect animated by a value system containing expectations of apocalyptic success. But nothing required the myth to be based on class grievances or class grievances alone. Sorel's argument was designed to fit pre-existing notions regarding *ricorsi* in general and revolutionary syndicalism in particular. Lenin's revolution had come as the vindication of a frustrated old man who had given up all hope of a *ricorso.* It is significant that Sorel appended the "Pour Lènine" to the ***Reflections,*** written on behalf of revolutionary syndicalism. But in doing so, Sorel did not become a bolshevik. Lenin was made out to be a Sorelian. Indeed, what one sees in Sorel's conception of the soviets was his prewar idea of a self-governing elite of producers but with Lenin as their chief. So great was his aversion to politicos and intellectuals that Sorel did not see or refused to see the Bolshevik party, the reality behind the soviets. His interpretation of bolshevism, therefore, was not only in conflict with Marxism but also with Leninism. The argument Sorel presented was his own. It assumed implicitly, if not explicitly, a complex of postwar revolutionary possibilities that included both bolshevism and fascism. Some such complex had been implied in his prewar move from revolutionary syndicalism to the AF. Sorel was drawn to bolshevism and fascism (and almost concurrently) not so much because he thought them similar but because he saw them as alternatives. To posit, as he did, the "decline of the West" was to raise the possibility of at least two revolutionary choices: one could be on the side of the barbarians and start all over again, or on the side of an equally barbaric reaction that would initiate the rejuvenation of an aging civilization. One could, conceivably, be enthusiastic about either *ricorso* or even both. It was unfortunate that Sorel's comments on fascism were fragmentary, that he never explicitly endorsed it, and that he never quite clarified its "European" significance. But others were to fill these gaps. During the 1920s and '30s Sorel's vision, that the choice for Europe lay between communism and fascism, became a commonplace in many revolutionary quarters.

This was especially the case in France among the young "non-conformists" of the 1930s described by Loubet del Bayle.[40] Many sought inspiration in Sorel's work, though some were perceptive enough to sense the dangers in the quest for renewal and the heroic. Sorel's search for the Apocalypse and those who continued the pursuit during the interwar years come close to revealing the character of the crisis among intellectuals in the Twentieth century. Their work was symptomatic of a profound intellectual and moral disturbance—the desertion by intellectuals of the democratic idea. And their story was something of a tragedy. They sought to evoke the sublime, but helped, rather, to unleash the beast.

NOTES

[1] Daniel Halévy, "Préface," in Pierre Andreu, *Notre maitre: M. Sorel* (Paris, 1953), pp. 19-20; Andreu is possibly the best single source on the biographical aspects of Sorel's career.

[2] See especially, *Contribution à l'étude profane de la Bible* (Paris, 1889); *Le procès de Socrate* (Paris, 1889); and "Essai sur la philosophie de Proudhon," *Revue philosophique,* XXXIII-XXXIV (June-July 1892), 622-638 and 41-68.

[3] "Science et socialisme," *Revue philosophique,* XXXV (1893), 509-511; "Lettere de Georges Sorel a Benedetto Croce" (hereafter cited Sorel to Croce), June 2, 1897, *Critica,* XXV (1927), 45; "Préface pour Colajanni," *Matériaux d'une théorie du prolétariat* (hereafter cited *Matériaux*)(3d ed.; Paris, 1929), pp. 175-200; "Études sur Vico," *Devenir social,* II (October-December 1896), 786, 796-809, 934-935, and 1046. The argument concerning a syndicalist *ricorso* was best presented during these years in *L'Avenir socialiste des syndicats* (Paris, 1898).

[4] "Lettere di Giorgio Sorel a Uberto Lagardelle" (hereafter cited Sorel to Lagardelle), August 10 and 15, 1898 and August 21 and September 14, 1901, *Educazione fascista,* XI (March-November 1933), 239-242, 242-243, and 328-330. See also "De l'église et de l'état," *Cahiers de la quinzaine,* III (1901), 55-58 and 61-64; and "Préface pour Gatti," *Matériaux,* pp. 201-237.

[5] Sorel's interest in these themes were in evidence from the beginning of his career but especially in an extended series of articles on "La fin du paganisme" which appeared in the Marxist periodical *Ere nouvelle* in 1894 and revised several years later as *La ruine du monde antique* (Paris, 1901). Five years later came *Le système historique de Renan* (hereafter cited *Le système*) (Paris, 1905-06) where he developed the idea of the rise of Christianity as the classic example of a *ricorso.* For "Thursday afternoon's" at Péguy's see Halévy, *Péguy and les Cahiers de la quinzaine* (New York, 1947), pp. 71-74.

[6] The *Réflexions sur la violence* (hereafter cited *Réflexions*) first appeared in article form in the *Mouvement socialiste* and the *Divenire sociale* (Rome) in 1906 and in book form (with the editorial aid of Halévy) in 1908 published by the Librairie Pages Libres.

[7] For matters cited in the text, see especially: *Introduction à l'économie moderne* (2d ed.; Paris, 1922), pp. 131 and 137; *Le système,* pp. 198-208 and 377; *Insegnamenti sociali della economia contemporanea* (Milan, 1907), pp. 38, 53-55, 172-173, 278n, and 389-398; "Préface de 1905," *Matériaux,* p. 70; *Réflexions* (10th ed.; Paris, 1946), pp. 35-36, 44, 50, 110, and 434; *Les illusions du progrès* (hereafter cited *Illusions*) (4th ed.; Paris, 1927), pp. 12, 136, and 385; and *La décomposition du Marxisme* (Paris, 1908), p. 50. To these may be added articles published in the *Mouvement socialiste* and the *Divenire sociale.*

[8] See especially Sorel's letters to Croce and Lagardelle in 1908-09; also *Lettres à Paul Delesalle* (hereafter cited Sorel to Delesalle) (Paris, 1947), November 2, 1908, p. 108. On Sorel's break with Italian syndicalism see: A. Pezzotti, "Une partie syndicaliste en Italie," *Mouvement socialiste,* XIII (March 1911), 184-185.

[9] "Socialistes antiparlementaires," *Action Française,* August 22, 1909; also "Giorgio Sorel e i monarchici francesi," *Giornale d'Italia,* November 20, 1910. On Péguy's *Jeanne d'Arc,* see especially Sorel's "Le réveil de l'âme française," *Action Française,* April 14, 1910, published on the same day in the Florentine review the *Voce.* For Sorel and the AF generally during this period see Eugen Weber, *Action française: royalism and reaction in twentieth-century France* (Stanford, 1962), pp. 73-85; for Sorel and Italian nationalism see Gian Biagio Furiozzi, *Sorel e l'Italia* (Florence, 1975), pp. 237-264.

[10] The reviews were the *Cité française, Indépendance,* and the *Cahiers du Cercle Proudhon.* The ideas developed below are to be found largely in the *Indépendance* which Sorel directed from 1911 to 1913; the *Cité française* (except for a brochure announcing its publication) never saw the light of day and the *Cahiers* was the work of monarchist disciples to which Sorel did not contribute. Other sources include: *Propos de Georges Sorel* (hereafter cited *Propos*), ed. Jean Variot (Paris, 1935), "Grandeur et décadence," appended to the *Illusions,* and several articles which appeared in the *Resto del Carlino* of Bologna in 1910.

[11] On the break with Péguy, see Marcel Péguy, *La rupture de Charles Péguy et de Georges Sorel, d'après des documents inédits* (Paris, 1930), pp. 14, 19, 38, and 58; see also

Sorel's letters to Croce from September to November 1912. As for Sorel and his relations with the AF, see Sorel to Croce, November 20, 1912, January 12 and June 22, 1913, and March 20, 1914, XXVI, 438-439, 440 and 442. On Sorel's views on the eve of the war see, "Préface," to Édouard Berth, *Les méfaits des intellectuels* (Paris, 1914), p. xxix.

[12] See Sorel's letters to Croce from September 1914 to May 1915.

[13] Sorel to Croce, December 5, 1915, XXVII, 295-296.

[14] Jean Labadie (ed.), *L'Allemagne a-t-elle le secret de l'organisation?* (Paris, 1916), pp. 11-19. See brief references to Lenin in *Lettere a un amico d'Italia* (hereafter cited Sorel to Missiroli), ed. Mario Missiroli (San Casciano, 1963), May 15 and 28, 1917, pp. 220-221.

[15] Sorel to Delesalle, February 6, 1918, pp. 127-128; Halévy, *Péguy and les Cahiers de la quinzaine,* pp. 222-223.

[16] See Sorel to Delesalle, February 6, March 14, and June 23, 1918 and Sorel to Croce, March 15, 1918, XXVIII, p. 45.

[17] Sorel to Delesalle, July 10, August 1, 18 and 26, 1918, pp. 155, 165-167, and 168-170.

[18] "Post-scriptum," *Matériaux,* p. 53.

[19] Sorel to Croce, February 1, 1919, XXVIII, p. 50; Sorel to Delesalle, February 20, 1919, p. 177.

[20] "Pour Lénine," *Réflexions,* pp. 437-454; see Paul Seippel, "L'autre danger," *Journal de Genève,* February 4, 1918. Lenin, incidentally, expressed his opinion of Sorel in a brief passage in his *Materialism and emperio-criticism,* a vigorous polemic against revisionism written in 1909. Addressing himself to the mathematician Henri Poincaré, Lenin wrote, "Your works prove that there are people who can give thought to absurdity. To that category belongs the notorious muddlehead, Georges Sorel." This is the only reference to Sorel in N. Lenin, *Collected works,* XVIII (New York, 1930), p. 58.

[21] *Ibid.,* pp. 453-454.

[22] See Sorel's letters to Delesalle in 1920, pp. 189-193; and Sorel to Croce, August 13, 1920, XXVIII, p. 193.

[23] *Propos,* March n.d., 1921, pp. 53-55.

[24] "Lénine d'après Gorki," *Revue communiste,* II (January 1921), 401-413; and "Lenin secondo Gorki," *Ordine Nuovo,* February 27, 1921. Gorki's brochure on Lenin was published by *Humanité.*

[25] Quoted in Édouard Dolléans, *Proudhon* (3d ed.; Paris, 1948), p. 507.

[26] M. Simonetti, "Georges Sorel e Guglielmo Ferrero fra `cesarismo' borghese e socialismo (con 27 lettere di Sorel a Ferrero, 1896-1921)," *Pensiero politico,* V (1972), pp. 102-151; see especially, letters dated February 24, March 5 and 13, and June 26, 1921, pp. 147-151.

[27] Bernard Lecache, "Chez Georges Sorel, apôtre du syndicalisme révolutionnaire, ami de la Russie des Soviets," *Humanité,* March 9, 1922; "Lettere di Georges Sorel a Roberto Michels" (hereafter cited Sorel to Michels), *Nuovi studi di diritto, economia e politica,* II (September-October 1929), 293n (from a note in Michels' diary dated March 22, 1922).

[28] René Johannet, "Un précurseur de la Révolution nationale: Georges Sorel," *Candide,* XVII (July 16, 1940), p. 5.

[29] The presentation which follows is based largely on Sorel's articles in the *Resto del Carlino, Tempo, Ronda, Revue communiste,* his comments in the *Propos,* and the work previously cited in the text written in support of the new regime in Russia. Many of the articles in the *Resto del Carlino* and the *Tempo* are included in the following collections edited by Mario Missiroli: *L'Europe sotto la tormenta* (Milan, 1932) and *Da Proudhon a Lenin* (Florence, 1949).

[30] "Lénine d'après Gorki," p. 408.

[31] *Ibid.,* pp. 412-413.

[32] "Chiarimenti su Lenin," *Resto del Carlino,* July 23, 1919.

[33] "Le travail dans la Grèce ancienne," *Revue communiste,* II (November 1920), pp. 221-222.

[34] "Pour Lénine," p. 453. The "Roman model" was sometimes reversed as in the following: "Just as ancient Rome merited its fall, so the crimes of the contemporary world justify the necessity of its destruction" ("Lénine d'après Gorki," p. 409).

[35] Jean Variot, "Quelques souvenirs: le père Sorel," *Éclair,* September 11, 1922.

[36] Sorel to Delesalle, September 6, 1919 and March 19, 1921, pp. 186 and 215; Sorel to Croce, July 30, 1920, XXVIII, p. 192; and *Propos,* March n.d., 1921, pp. 53-56.

[37] Sorel to Delesalle, April 9, 1921, p. 219; Sorel to Missiroli, April 16, 1921, pp. 306-307; Sorel to Croce, August 26, 1921, XXVIII, p. 195; and especially, Sorel to Missiroli, September n.d., 1921, quoted in Missiroli, "Prefazione," *L'Europa sotto la tormenta,* pp. xxxii-xxxiii (for unexplained reasons Missiroli did not include this letter in the collection of 1963).

[38] Sorel to Michels, March 22, 1922, 293 n.

[39] *Propos,* n.d., 1922, p. 66.

[40] Jean-Louis Loubet del Bayle, *Les non-conformistes des années 30* (Paris, 1969). See also Jean Touchard, "L'esprit des années 1930," *Tendances politiques*, ed. Guy Michaud (Paris, 1960), pp. 89-138. Both studies make much of the period 1930-34 as a "tentative de renouvellement" in French political thought and emphasize the role of the February 1934 riots in re-establishing a deadly polarization.

David Gross (essay date 1982)

SOURCE: "Myth and Symbol in Georges Sorel," in *Political Symbolism in Modern Europe: Essays in Honor of George L. Mosse*, edited by Seymour Drescher, David Sabean, and Allan Sharlin, Transaction Books, 1982, pp. 100-17.

[*In the following excerpt, Gross traces the treatment of myth and symbolic images in Sorel's body of work.*]

Every student of modern political symbolism must sooner or later confront the work of Georges Sorel (1847-1922). As one of the more engaging minds of his generation, Sorel made a number of original and important observations about the nature of symbolic images and their relationship to political action. These observations are not always easy to uncover, since they are scattered throughout an enormous range of work, some of it dealing with topics as seemingly remote from the subject as the history of Christianity, modern economics, the methodology of the sciences, or the trial of Socrates.[1] Often Sorel's most interesting ideas are mentioned only in passing, or else developed in a fragmentary and unsatisfactory manner. At other times he disdains to follow step-by-step the logic of his own thought, saying that what he writes is entirely "personal and individual," and consequently there is no need to be concerned with the transitions between things "because they nearly always come under the heading of commonplaces."[2]

Despite these many difficulties Sorel's work easily repays careful study. This is especially true with regard to what may well be the most innovative aspect of his *oeuvre:* his study of the psychology of political motivation, including the numerous irrational, spontaneous elements that affect all human behavior. Sorel was one of the first to explore this area with any degree of sophistication, and his conclusions had notable consequences.

In the following pages the focus of attention will be on one part of Sorel's "psychology of political motivation": the place that myths and symbols must occupy in modern political movements and in modern life in general. Three aspects of this topic need to be investigated in some detail: first, how it came about that myths and symbols moved into a central, pivotal position in Sorel's thought; second, what he meant by these terms and what he expected to achieve by utilizing them; and third, what significant differences, if any, exist between the concepts of mythology and symbolism as found in Sorel, and these same concepts found later in fascism and national socialism. To pursue each of these issues, it is important to grasp the cultural and intellectual context out of which Sorel emerged. This will help explain why he felt compelled to enter into the study of myths and symbols in the first place.

The more one looks at the period in Europe roughly between 1870 and 1914, the more this age seems to represent a decisive turning point in Western consciousness. It was at this time that a "crisis of certainty" gripped many of Europe's leading intellectuals, artists, and writers. The aftereffects of this crisis have remained with us. What began to be asserted during this period was the following, put here in the most condensed terms. (1) There is no objective, verifiable structure to existence. (2) There is no *telos* operating in the universe, including inevitable progress. (3) There is no essence behind appearance, but rather only appearances referring to other appearances ad infinitum. With only appearances, and nothing solid behind or within them, everything becomes arbitrary—hence a collapse of signification itself. (4) On the social and scientific level there are no facts, only interpretations. (5) On the personal level there are nothing but masks hiding other masks which lie still deeper inside a fiction called the "self." (6) In all areas of life there is no ultimate eternal truth. In earlier times, truth usually meant the identity of an idea or concept with reality, but since reality itself was now being called into question, there was no way to measure the truth of anything. This line of reasoning represented a profound development in modern thought which had become fairly widespread by the end of the nineteenth century. Before this time most thinkers assumed there was a truth: they simply disagreed about the best methods of reaching it (by reason, feeling, intuition, etc.). By 1900 many influential thinkers had come to doubt whether the word *truth* had any meaning at all. Moreover, if there were no truths, perhaps there were no values either.

In this context the whole "appearance vs. reality" problem emerged strongly in all areas of European culture: in literature (Hofmannsthal, Musil, Strindberg, Gide, Huysmans, D'Annunzio), in art (impressionism, expressionism, futurism), and in philosophy (Nietzsche, Bergson, Husserl). Oscar Wilde put it this way: "Try as we may, we cannot get behind the appearance of things to reality. And the terrible reality may be, that there is no reality in things apart from their experiences."[3] Nietzsche pushed matters still further by suggesting the even more frightening prospect of no anchorage whatever: "We have abolished the true world [reality]: what has remained? The world of appearances perhaps? . . . Oh, no! With the true world we have also abolished the apparent one!"[4] These concerns led to one of the central dilemmas of the period: if there are no fixed truths or values, how then should one live? Some, like the fin de siècle dandies, answered this question by saying that one should live wholly in appearances, since this is all there is. Others urged hedonism, or the life of pure sensation, where as many pulsations as possible are crammed into every moment. Still others argued that one should live "as if" there were ascertainable truths, even though there were none, since this was the only way to give life meaning.

Sorel was aware of these and other solutions to the dilemma of his age—and rejected most of them. Each seemed built upon the assumption that truth was undiscernible; and each was an alternative to this state of affairs, a way of being-in-the-world without any grounding in an ultimate reality. Sorel denied the premise of this argument. The truth of an idea or value could be determined, though not by the usual methods of studying its "inherent worth" or measuring it against some putative "objective reality," which Sorel admitted did not exist.[5] Rather, the truth of something was discovered solely by looking at its effects. A thing is true if, subjectively speaking, it has true or useful consequences, and a thing has value if its results are valuable for the individual.[6]

An idea can be judged good or bad exclusively in terms of the results it produces in those who hold it and believe in it. He seemed to have three criteria to determine whether an idea was true, i.e. beneficial: if it made the individual who embraced it more creative; if it increased an individual's character or moral consciousness; and above all if it led to action—a combative, engaged orientation toward life. For Sorel life is action, and ideas must be valued by the degree to which they lead to praxis, or produce lifeenhancing qualities. In all this there is some amount of determinable truth from Sorel's point of view, but it lies entirely in its efficacy and advantageous consequences. Sorel very adroitly managed to shift the whole question of truth to a new level and thereby overcome the pervasive appearance/reality dualism that obsessed so many of his contemporaries. The point was not to distinguish, as Yeats put it, the "dancer" (reality) from the "dance" (appearance), but to investigate the completely different area of how the dance is received by those observing it. If it increases an individual viewer's creative energy, if it drives him toward more intense participation in life, then the dance possesses "truth" regardless of the supposedly objective qualities of the performance. All that is important about anything resides in its consequences.

Once Sorel hit upon this instrumental notion of truth, he felt that he had solved a problem that continued to transfix many other thinkers of his generation. He no longer had to remain incapacitated by the crisis of certainty, but could transcend it and move on to more important matters. One of these was what he considered the deplorable moral and spiritual condition of his age. It was sunk in a miasma of decadence, mediocrity, and corruption. No one was shriller in condemning the general tone of European civilization around 1900 than Sorel. Everywhere he saw attitudes which revolted him. The leading ideas of his age appeared to encourage selfindulgence, resignation, degeneration. Since he judged the consequences of these ideas to be uniformly pernicious—the decadence he saw around him seemed incontrovertible, for its effects were everywhere[7]—the ideas that produced them had also to be judged pernicious.

The major blame for this condition was placed at the feet of the bourgeoisie. To Sorel the dominant class in Europe had become desiccated by too much rationality, or what he called, following Vico, the "barbarism of reflection."[8] Furthermore, it generally lived "without morals," and had gradually given up certain important "habits of liberty" with which it was once acquainted.[9] The result was a total loss of virtue and honor, a drastic decline in the "heroic" qualities which Sorel believed the bourgeoisie once possessed. But something more was involved. Since this class also controlled the dominant political, economic, and cultural institutions of the period, the corruption unavoidably spread out beyond the class itself and became firmly embedded in the very fabric of modern society. When the middle class became decadent, so did the whole world of institutionalized values it created. There was therefore the added danger that other classes would be dragged down with the bourgeoisie unless something drastic were done to remedy the situation.

What was needed, Sorel thought, was the infusion of a new sense of morality into modern life. As a French moralist of the type extending back to Pascal and Rousseau, Sorel defined the central problems of the age in ethical terms. Therefore the principal solutions also had to be ethical. According to Sorel, the bourgeoisie lost its morality because it ceased to have convictions or believe in anything "indemonstrable." This took the mystery and elevation out of life, and the bourgeoisie lost contact with the energizing ideals that any group must have to be great or ethical. Without ideals or strong beliefs, there can be no inward force capable of stimulating creativity, morality, or the impetus to act—the three qualities Sorel identified with his instrumental view of truth. This loss of belief had happened before in history, in ancient Greece around the time of Socrates,[10] and in Christian Europe after the "age of the martyrs."[11] In the face of this kind of spiritual enervation the only hope lay in a revitalization or restoration of heroic ideals. Only in this way could a dynamic quality be restored to daily life. Even more important, only such energizing ideals could animate the inner state of the soul, out of which might come a more vigorous social ethic. It was a matter of indifference to Sorel what the ideals might happen to be. All that mattered was that they produce vigorous moral sentiments. "It is not a question of knowing what is the best morality, but only of determining if there exists a *mechanism capable of guaranteeing the development of morality*."[12] Much of Sorel's thought was taken up with precisely these two questions: how to reconstruct morality now that it had broken down, and what "agent" to rely on in order to bring this about.

Sorel's reasoning unfolded in the following sequence: The only way out of decadence was to support some group which is in society but not of it—a group able to believe in something again—for only such a group could find its way to a new ethic. Sorel was resolute in his claim to defend any social element that could accomplish this. The working class seemed the most likely group in contemporary life with the potential to remoralize society.

But, Sorel added, this was true only if the proletariat was rescued from the bourgeoisie, which was trying to make it decadent, and from parliamentary socialists like Jaurès who wanted to lure the proletariat into a dependence upon the state. Only by forming independent syndicates or *bourses du travail* could workers acquire the initiative and autonomy from bourgeois values that would be necessary to reinstate virtue. Still, even determining that the proletariat offered the greatest possibility for a revaluation of values, Sorel felt that it could not originate action toward this end without outside help.[13] The workers needed to be spurred into action, since only by doing, rather than talking or theorizing (another middle-class fault!), does a new morality get embodied in practice. Consequently, the way to motivate the workers was through myths or "mobilizing ideas" which would decisively move them into action. Even if it could be shown that these myths were objectively untrue, they might still be effectively true if they had significant consequences—if they set the working class in motion and helped it bring about a transforming ethic. These myths had to be embodied in symbols and images of great power. Otherwise the impact of a myth was not successfully communicated. The pivot of Sorel's theory turned on these last points: the effective use of both myths and symbols vis à vis the working class. We shall now take a closer look at what he intended to achieve by means of each of these.

What is a myth? For Sorel a myth is an emotionally charged artificial construct or interpretation which, though perhaps inaccurate or absurd, reaches people at a deeply unconscious level and inspires them to action. Being an "imaginary picture" rooted in and inseparable from the sentiments it evokes, a myth is always mysterious. It can never be cognitively understood because it operates in some prereflexive area of the mind where intuition and beliefs are also stimulated. Even more mysteriously, a myth is frequently the objectification of the convictions of a group, that is, an expression, in the form of images, of the goals and aspirations of an entire collectivity.[14] For these reasons it is too amorphous and volatile, too filled with "indeterminate nuances" ever to be accessible to scientific investigation. A myth cannot be broken down into its component parts, or subjected to face-value statements as to whether it is true or false, valid or invalid, since only its consequences can ultimately reveal that. It follows that a myth, because it is not a description but only an action-image, cannot be criticized. It is for all practical purposes irrefutable, just as a belief (as opposed to a fact) is irrefutable, since the power of a myth rests on faith, which does not lend itself to rational analysis.[15]

Myths are composed of a "body of images" which elicit a "mass of sentiments" that are then "grasped by intuition alone, before any considered analyses are made."[16] By their very nature they are indemonstrable, standing outside the realm of verification. But, Sorel insisted, this is why they are tremendously forceful constructions. People want and need to believe in things that are beyond confirmation.[17] Because myths "seize the imagination with an extraordinary tenacity," they provoke emotions and qualities of sacrifice and struggle without which nothing great or heroic has ever been achieved. Even if they are exaggerations or misrepresentations, myths are, precisely for this reason, more true than exact descriptions because they tap a vital part of the psyche which would otherwise never be activated.[18]

Yet for Sorel myths are not the same as lies. Nor do they carry connotations which would link them with propaganda or ideology as these terms are usually understood today. It is essential to Sorel that these are not cynically manufactured and imposed upon the masses but that they are already present, in latent form, within the mass itself, and need only be drawn out to become real forces in people's lives. Well before Jung's discussion of archetypes, there is some hint here of myths being anchored to predispositions within a collective unconscious. When myths work effectively they stir up, in Sorel's words, the "quickening fire . . . hidden under the ashes," making "the flames leap up."[19] Myths actuate sentiments never touched by ratiocination. The more successfully they hit responsive chords inside individuals, the more people are likely to become aware of their deepest needs and desires. And, Sorel conjectured, the more this awareness grows, the more they will be willing to struggle against decadence and *for* a new morality. This is why myths became so essential to Sorel's social philosophy. Without them there would be no movement and hence no moral change.

Just as for Sorel the value of a thing lay in its consequences, the same was true with myths. A myth was pronounced good (effective) if it yielded some or all of the following results. First, it had to arouse qualities of enthusiasm and inspriation, intensity and passion, since these were in danger of disappearing in periods of decline. Sorel thought that decadent ages like his own were more inclined to encourage utopias than myths. Utopias, in his view, always lacked the fire, the emotion, and the energizing power of myths since they were merely intellectual constructs, rationally formulated for some distant future, and therefore generally conducive to passivity rather than activism in the present.

Second, a myth had to engender an inclination toward action. Sorel was convinced that if people did not project an entirely "artificial world" out in front of them, and then let it affect their motivation, they would never act to "attain durable results."[20] According to Sorel there would probably have been no French Revolution if "enchanting pictures" of what might occur had not been prompted in people's minds beforehand. Sorel remained certain that the greatest value myths can have is to trigger action in those who adhere to them. "We do nothing great without warmly coloured and clearly defined images, which absorb the whole of our attention."[21]

Third, to be beneficial a myth had to produce freedom. By Sorel's reasoning, freedom developed in an individual when he acquired a more holistic or inclusive sense of himself, thereby making it possible to act from within and freely, since freedom was equated with self-direction. Sorel cited Bergson in this respect: "To act freely is to recover possession of oneself."[22] But myths help recover the fuller, unconscious, irrational side of the self. Consequently they necessarily lead toward freedom—and freedom means more than simply wanting something, it also implies training the will to pursue what one wants. An individual is most free when he wills. If he ceases to will, all his efforts begin to "fade away into rhapsodies" and he sinks into lethargy and mediocrity.[23] Myths can prevent this by focusing emotions and mobilizing will. They can keep people agitated and constantly attuned to an inner drive for the ideal. Even more, they can awaken in the depths of the soul a "sentiment of the sublime."[24] To cultivate such a sentiment under the guidance of a firm inward motivation would be the essence of freedom.

Fourth, a myth had to simplify the world, make it clear and transparent again, so that equivocation would be impossible and nothing could be left in a state of indecision.[25] It was especially important for myths to identify enemies so that an unbridgeable gulf could be established between two sides, as happened between Christians and pagans in the late Roman era. Sorel insisted on the necessity of this cleavage. Not only did it set up battle lines and promote the martial spirit so crucial for an unconditional war against the status quo; it also permitted one's own side to be portrayed as oppressed or unjustly abused, thereby provoking an active mood of resistance which always brings out the noblest elements of character. Like Proudhon, Sorel believed that only by resisting something, by fighting and struggling against it, were extraordinary accomplishments possible. Even the artist needed the physical resistance of his material in order to give it form. It was the same with myths. They distinctly point out who or what is to be opposed, so that monumental energies can be generated to fight against them.

Finally, a myth had to stimulate creativity, either in an individual or in whole groups. Because it so sharply cuts through the veneer of civilization and stirs up primitive residues within the mind, a myth can elicit an entire range of perceptions and feelings that would otherwise never be tapped. In Sorel's view, myths heighten the imaginary and even mystical quality of experience which appeared to be eroding under the impact of rational, bourgeois values. A myth, in contrast to the normal habits of mind, releases internal energies which are more "barbaric" (in Vico's sense), but also more creative, poetic, and revitalizing. However, a myth has not done enough when it merely arouses an "inner turmoil" no matter how creative; it fulfills its function only when it turns this inner turmoil in the direction of action bent on moral and spiritual liberation.[26]

In these five positive results of myths, all the qualities mentioned earlier which made something "true" for Sorel were present: morality, action, and creativity. To the extent that a myth encouraged each of these, it was a valid myth. To the extent that it did not, it was invalid. This latter type Sorel called "illusions." An illusion could have different origins. It could, for example, be an "artifice for dissimulating" purposely devised by a ruling group to manipulate other elements of society.[27] Illusions here became, in Sorel's words, "multiple fantasies" or "conventional falsehoods" which might roughly correspond with Marx's notion of false consciousness. Or an illusion could simply be an outdated myth which had become unserviceable because, with its loss of ability to evoke moral responses, it had assumed a co-optive and "morbid" influence on the population. Whatever its origin, an illusion performed a function almost exactly opposite that of a myth. When it had a "stranglehold on men's minds," as Sorel believed it did for most people during his own age, it produced passivity, immorality, and a stultifying frame of mind. This side of Sorel's work has never been closely studied, but it provides an interesting and important counterpoint to his more familiar ideas about myth.

If one accepts Sorel's definition of what a myth is and what it should achieve, there is still the question of how a myth is embodied or made manifest. Sorel's answer: by means of symbols. A myth cannot be conveyed except by being depicted in some striking form which appeals to the imagination and emotions. Thus, Sorel's discussion of mythology led him directly into a discussion of symbolism as well. Though Sorel nowhere specifically defined a symbol, it is obvious that his meaning was the traditional one. A symbol is, as Mosse has summarized it, a "visible, concrete objectification" of a myth, a myth made operative.[28] Symbolism occurs when one word or thing, perhaps not meaningful in itself, represents something else (or a whole line of emotional associations and wider meanings), and is therefore more dynamically charged because of these emotional associations.[29] When Sorel talked about symbols in relation to myths, he usually implied that symbols were forms which expressed a mythical content; in this sense they were treated as outward signs representing an inward message. At other times he implied that the symbols were themselves the content, or the form and content compressed into one, so that myths and symbols were intimately fused and analytically inseparable. In either case, a symbol was always understood to be an image, but an image with a double existence. It was present both in the mind of the believer and in an external manifestation which captured an awareness already in the psyche. This is why Sorel could speak of symbols that exalted deep-seated "psychological qualities," or enkindled latent awarenesses which were then drawn out of the unconscious, not implanted there.[30]

But by linking symbols with images Sorel did not always have artistic metaphors in mind. More often he seemed to think that not art but the spoken word was most effective in arousing "warmly coloured images" which incite people to act. The written word was played down. Except for Marx's *Das Kapital,* which Sorel found full of "social poetry" and moving apocalyptic images,[31] written language seemed to be associated with linear thinking, rationality, logic, and calculated expression. Writing was by nature "cunning" and analytical, the natural medium of intellectuals. Speaking was seen as evocative and inspiring, the appropriate medium for those who want action rather than thought. Sorel considered direct verbal communication the most conducive means for stirring others to movement because it "act[s] on the feelings in a mysterious way and easily establish[es] a current of sympathy between people."[32] The fact that the spoken word, not art forms or texts, was singled out as the primary agency for conveying or inducing symbols is important. It underscores how much Sorel thought symbols ultimately reside in the believer's psyche. He discussed no fixed embodiments of symbolic awareness in signs, emblems, or posters beyond the fleeting words of an inspiring speaker.

For Sorel, history supplied important examples of successful myths and symbols. The ancient Greek mind, for instance, was moved by Homeric myths and images mystically in tune with the Greek character and therefore eliciting its best qualities to epic achievements. Christianity had a myth of the Second Coming, beautifully captured in the symbolic evocation of the Apocalypse. Even though this image of the future was untrue, since the Second Coming never came, it was nevertheless effectively true because it aroused great courage and conviction in those who believed, and in the long run led to significant moral progress.[33] The French Revolution also evoked a number of highly effective myths and symbols. According to Sorel, the armies of the revolution fought with a ferocity unknown in the *ancien régime* because the symbols they responded to prompted a fervent "will-to-victory."

The age in which Sorel wrote was the early twentieth century. All the old myths and symbols seemed to have lost their efficacy. Precisely because, in Sorel's opinion, so much of Europe had stopped believing in anything, it had fallen into decadence and mediocrity. It was living by illusions rather than myths. However, there appeared to be one sector of the population that still revealed qualities of will, drive, idealism, and morality however buried or hidden they might be. If this sector could be set in motion to actualize its values, Europe would perhaps experience the moral revitalization which Sorel so greatly desired. The group Sorel had in mind was the proletariat. To perform its proper role, it had to be aroused to action by suitable myths. According to Sorel, the myth which most corresponded to the "working-class mind," and had the potential for "dominating [it] in an absolute manner," was the myth of the general strike.[34]

Since this is the concept for which Sorel is best known, there is no need to repeat what has been analyzed elsewhere.[35] It is sufficient to touch briefly on those aspects of the general strike which relate to the above discussion of myth and symbol. The myth of the general strike was for Sorel a kind of updated version of the Apocalypse. It was a vision of an approaching Dies Irae in which the whole bourgeois world would collapse under the impact of a mass proletarian strike. As a vision the myth acquired a compelling force because it was the projection of the collective "will to deliverance" of the entire proletariat, and not because it was the creation of a handful of syndicalist intellectuals.

To be effective as a myth, the general strike had to be pictured in vivid, catastrophic images. This meant that its inevitably violent nature had to be accented. Yet for Sorel the violence did not necessarily have to be carried out in practice. He appears to have been repelled by certain forms of violence such as terrorism, which one might be engaged in for impure motives, or sabotage, which he viewed as a blow against the objectification of some unknown worker's labor—labor that needed to be respected rather than destroyed.[36] When Sorel spoke of violence he usually meant the state of "battle readiness" which talk of violence usually brings. Being prepared to use violence, he believed, was often more effective than actual use of it, and the effectiveness or utility of an idea was always Sorel's primary concern. If violence were resorted to, Sorel set several conditions for its proper use. For instance, it would have to be done gratuitously, "without hatred and without the spirit of revenge."[37] It could not be exercised for material gain or the "profits of conquest," since this would reflect the value system of the bourgeoisie which violence was to overcome.[38] It had to be implemented with reserve, and in light of the high moral aspirations of the proletariat, violence only becomes "purified" when fused with the most exalted ethical intentions. Sorel seemed to think that proletarian violence would not get out of hand and become brutality because of the intensity and spiritual beauty of the workers who perpetrated it. They would always be responsible people, basically in possession of themselves, proud, confident, and disciplined due to the sense of rigor and self-control they learned as producers in their workplaces. From them, violence was always very beautiful and heroic, and it always produced the right effects of inspiring fear in the enemy. It simultaneously promoted class solidarity, determination to act, and primordial creative energies, which Sorel lyrically associated with that "torment of the infinite" which the timorous middle class had long since lost.[39]

For Sorel the general strike, embellished with frightful images of violence, did not have to be achieved in order to bring about the results he intended. Its efficacy as a myth rested solely on the action-inducing qualities it engendered among those who merely *believed* it would come about. This was the whole purpose of myth as opposed to illusion. It set people in motion to accomplish the moral revolution Sorel wanted to see in modern society. The general strike appeared to be the last viable myth that could successfully mobilize people to reappraise values. It alone could provide the motivation and "epic state of mind" out of which the proletariat could forge a new moral order.

This was Sorel's most pressing concern. It even appears at times that he availed himself of the proletariat not so much because he valued it as a class, but because of what he thought it could do for the renovation of morals. When, around 1908-13, Sorel became disillusioned with the syndicates and doubted that they would be "instruments of moralization" as he had once hoped,[40] he momentarily abandoned the working class as an agent of revolution and searched for other groups which might perform the same role. By the end of his life, he returned with somewhat less enthusiasm to the proletariat as the only sector of society still able to ethically refashion a decadent world.

Though Sorel must certainly be treated as a man of the Left, it is undeniable that he had some influence on extremist elements within the European Right. For a time the Camelots du Roi, a youth group tied to Maurras's Action Française, were attracted to him, and a curious association called the Cercle Proudhon was formed (1912) to bring together radical syndicalist and royalist elements on the basis of some of Sorel's ideas. Mussolini, too, was reputed to have been influenced by Sorel's views on myth and violence, though here the ties seem somewhat more dubious.[41] It is no wonder, then, that in the 1930s some of Sorel's remaining syndicalist followers often found themselves in the embarrassing position of defending their mentor from charges of being one of the progenitors of fascism.

Since a connection between Sorel and the far Right has consistently been made, it would be useful to investigate this link in more detail. Here there is space to do this only in the realm of myth and symbols. What follows is a brief comparison of Sorel's treatment of both these concepts with their treatment in fascism and national socialism. No effort at establishing a causal link between Sorel's ideas and the radical Right can be attempted here, nor is there any pretense at systematic analysis. Taking note of similarities and significant differences between Sorel's mythology and imagery and that found in fascism and national socialism, one may get a better sense of the dividing line that separates this theorist of proletarian violence from the theorists and practitioners of fascist violence.

First, some similarities. Sorel, fascism, and national socialism all attacked the status quo for its venality and decadence, and called for moral regeneration. All were antiparliamentarian, since they wanted to create a mood of solidarity outside bourgeois institutions. At the same time they were antiliberal, since liberalism seemed cowardly, weak-minded, "feminine." Sorel and the extreme Right were also repulsed by the alleged hedonism and materialism of modern life, and wanted to see a return to a more austere, rigorous, and self-disciplined lifestyle. Consequently each defended old middle-class, as opposed to modern bourgeois, values. Despite much talk about heroism, vitality, and the epic state of mind, one often finds underneath such rhetoric an emphasis on simple domestic virtues: family closeness, chastity, honesty, industry. In Sorel as well as in fascism and national socialism there was a strong idealization of some group as the embodiment of virtue. For Sorel it was the proletariat, which he characterized as pure in heart, rich in sentiment, resolute, noble, decisive, hostile to shallow rationality, and in possession of a superior "moral culture."[42] In national socialism the *Volk* was idealized, usually in terms very similar to Sorel's working class. Similarly, Sorel and the Right placed tremendous importance on the power of ideas to affect life, agreeing, as Sorel expressed it, that "ethics springs from aspiration." Both also believed, perhaps contradictorily, that the value of ideas lies in their effects, and that "truth" must be judged by results. Even myths and symbols were dealt with pragmatically, their operational function always foremost.

Both for Sorel and the far Right there was a fascination with the psychology of motivation. It seemed imperative to understand what makes people act, so that the masses or the proletariat could be set in motion. This meant exploring the subjective and nonlogical side of human behavior (which the Left at the time usually failed to do), since it was thought that emotion and sentiment held the key to the secrets of motivation. Once Sorel and the fascists grasped the role that instincts and subconscious drives play in collective psychology, both went on to utilize myths and symbols to stimulate purposive behavior. They sought to activate archaic residues by means of forceful images which often centered on suggestions that combat, struggle, the glory of war, and "barbaric simplicity" would restore vigor and vitality to life. Finally, both Sorel and the Right implied that ultimately just being in movement may be more important than arriving at a goal. The ferment of movement provides everything that is needed: action, morality, energy, creative turmoil. If the goal was reduced to the process, the process in turn was frequently reduced to a psychological disposition or a state of mind. The fascists often described their movements, not in terms of ideologies but of "attitudes" ("Our movement," said Primo de Rivera, "is not a manner of thinking; it is a manner of being.)"[43] The same was true of Sorel. In a revealing article on the ethics of socialism he wrote: "Little does it matter whether communism is realized sooner or later. . . . The essential thing is our ability to render account of our own conduct. What is called the final goal exists only for our *internal* life."[44]

These are the considerable similarities between Sorel and the radical Right; but they are offset by notable differences. Sorel always called for a *real* social revolution, not simply a "spiritual" one as the fascist ideologues did. At least in theory, he wanted bourgeois institutions (including capitalism) abolished and power turned over to the proletariat. Also unlike the extreme Right, Sorel was not hostile to modernity. He accepted the configurations of modern industrial society and leveled no attack on urbanization, the machine, or the technological depersonalization of man. Similarly, there was no *Führerprinzip* in Sorel. "Anonymous heroes" might be needed to evoke mythological thinking in the proletariat, but their role would fade as the myths took hold and became self-generating.[45] With fascism and national socialism it was different. The myths were intended to create a mystical symbiosis between leader and led, so that the leader was not to disappear but remain to guide and discipline the masses by manipulating symbols. Hitler never relinquished his role as leader, unless it was to tie the masses to symbolic rituals rather than to himself, since these would perpetuate the political system after he was gone.[46] Mussolini also learned how to direct popular energies to himself as leader, and then through this role to attach them to the state. Sorel was opposed on principle to leader figures and states. In this case, the radical Right learned more from Gustave LeBon than from Sorel, for it was LeBon who spoke of a leader mystique, the mobilization of crowds, and the manipulation of mass contagion.[47] All of this was foreign to Sorel's thought.

The attitude toward symbolism was markedly different in Sorel and the extreme Right. For Sorel symbols were internal psychic images (or external signs used to activate these images) which he had no interest in institutionalizing. In Sorel there was no focus on emblems, cultic rites, processions, holy flames, Thing convocations, and the like, so central to national socialism. There was also no nature mysticism, no concern with cosmic forces to be tapped, no blood and soil imagery. Neither was there any visual stereotyping of the Jew, since anti-Semitism was never a major issue for Sorel. (There was a streak of anti-Semitism in him, but it derived from Proudhon and Renan rather than Drumont; not the Jews as such, but the decadent nouveaux riches and their retainers, were defined as the real enemies of the working class.)

Like the fascist and nazi Right, Sorel placed great importance on the function of speech in symbol formation. He strongly believed that it was primarily through the spoken word that myths become activated. Hitler understood this well, and so did Mussolini, with his ritual balcony dialogues recalling the liturgy of the Christian Responsa.[48] But Sorel viewed the relationship between words and symbols very differently than either of them. In his opinion language always had to be ethical; even when an orator spoke before large crowds he was obliged to remain within the constraints of his moral attitude toward the world. It was otherwise with someone like Hitler. In *Mein Kampf* he unabashedly described how a speaker needs to manipulate his audience with propaganda and highly charged "verbal images" which appeal to the susceptibilities of the "narrow-minded" masses whose "powers of assimilation . . . are extremely restricted."[49] This kind of cynicism would have been wholly unacceptable to Sorel. But even more than this, the effect of a Hitler speech was not so much in what was said, ethical or not, as in *how* it was said. As Mosse has described it, there was an undulating rhythm and cadence to Hitler's speeches: the rhetorical question, followed by an unambiguous statement, with plenty of room for people to join in with exclamations at the right places.[50] The liturgical context in which words were spoken was also essential to Hitler—as for example at the Nuremberg rallies where the total impact was made by the visual and acoustical power of the setting, not the specific and easily forgotten message of Hitler's speech. This was a far cry from Sorel's stress on ethical words or his "body of images" which were supposed to strike a chord in the workers' hearts without manipulation.

Finally, there was a significant difference between Sorel and the far Right on the question of myth. Though myths performed the same function for both—they mobilized people—in practice they operated in divergent ways and were designed to achieve opposite results. For Sorel and the nazis, for example, one of the points of a myth was to simplify the world into opposing camps by encouraging a Manichean perception of reality. But to Sorel the approaching battle of virtue against vice would be waged between the proletariat and the bourgeoisie, not between Aryans and Jews. The intent of a myth like the general strike was to arouse "ardent sentiments of revolt" leading to a catastrophic class was and victory for the proletariat. In nazi mythology the effect was altogether different since myths were calculated to elicit at least three kinds of responses, none of which Sorel could approve. The first was self-abandonment, or the loss of one's individuality to the group (while Sorel, by contrast, wanted myths to spark autonomy, independence, and self-activity). The second was patriotism. Most nazi myths celebrated the joys of conformity and the excitement of belonging to a superior racial group. Consequently, tribal symbolism prevailed wherein the *Volk* worshipped itself—hence the stress on national festivals, monuments, and racial and traditional imagery drawn from the German past. Sorel's myths were antipatriotic; he was not interested in consolidating national identities but in demolishing them.[51] The third response was hatred of an enemy. In Nazi ideology the enemy was defined in racial terms. It was always the Jews, or the dark-haired *Tschandalas,* or the "dwarfed Sodomites," or the ape-like "creatures of darkness" who had to be overcome by the blond, Nordic "god-men."[52] Though Sorel had his enemy, the venal middle class, he never stereotyped it in this way, but rather treated it as a somewhat impotent adversary. The real issue for him was not the nature of an external enemy, but the more pressing internal task of creating proletarian self-consciousness.

In retrospect, Sorel's concept of myth may seem inherently dangerous, even if it was not identical with the mythology of fascism or national socialism. There are legitimate grounds for this position. But it should also be remembered that historical events since Sorel's time have made one think that any interest in myth or its psychological underpinnings must necessarily have fascist overtones. This has closed off discussion of areas which need further exploration from different points of view. There are many features of Sorel's thought which are wholly unattractive. Some of these might be mentioned in passing: his pronounced antidemocratic strain, his overzealous attack on reason, his rigid Huguenot puritanism, his excessive fascination (like Péguy's) with *mystique* over *politique,* his contempt for peace and humanitarianism, his moral absolutism bordering on dogmatism, his often mindless defense of violence without regard for the perils of collective mythology, and his simplistic division of the world into two hostile camps, with no sensitivity for nuances. Without justifying these numerous misjudgments and dubious positions, Sorel still deserves credit for being one of the first on the Left to try and grasp the psychological mainsprings of action without having recourse to the crude economism and positivism of Second International Marxism. It is this side of his thought which has been given most attention in this essay.

During his own lifetime Sorel's influence was minimal on orthodox syndicalist and socialist circles of Western Europe. Victor Griffuelhes, the anarcho-syndicalist secretary of the French Confédération Générale du Travail, was once asked if he read Sorel and he replied: "I read Dumas."[53] The Italian Marxist Arturo Labriola also spoke for many socialists when he voiced the following criticism of Sorel: "Myths, fables, and revelations are precisely the opposite of socialism, which proposes to teach individuals as such to fashion for themselves their own lives, and in thus constructing their lives, to see within themselves as in clear, transparent water."[54] In the work of some contemporary Marxists of the younger generation—Georg Lukács, Antonio Gramsci, Walter Benjamin, among others—the traces of Sorel are much in evidence in certain aspects of their thought. This topic has yet to be thoroughly investigated. Despite various differences, one thing this younger generation could agree on was that a comprehensive understanding of human behavior could not be attained without understanding the role that myths, symbols, and emotions play in motivating people to act. This was what Sorel grasped at the turn of the century.

NOTES

[1] See, for example, the following works by Sorel: *La Ruine du monde antique* (Paris, 1902); *Introduction à l'économie moderne* (Paris, 1903); *Le Procès de Socrate* (Paris, 1889).

[2] Georges Sorel, *Reflections on Violence,* trans. T.E. Hulme (New York, 1961), p. 28.

[3] Oscar Wilde, cited in Thomas Mann, *Last Essays,* trans. Richard Winston and Clara Winston (London, 1959), p. 157.

[4] Friedrich Nietzsche, *Götzen-Dammerung.* In *Werke in zwei Bänden,* vol. 2, ed. Karl Schlechta (Munich, 1967), p. 341.

[5] Sorel frequently spoke of reality being "fluid," "inexplicable," or merely "a hypothesis." In *Les Illusions du progrès* (Paris, 1908), for example, he claimed that reality is a "fundamental mystery" which is "protected by obscurity" (p. 2).

[6] This notion resembles the pragmatism of William James, but Sorel developed this approach to truth before his discovery of the American philosopher. For Sorel's later views on pragmatism, see his *De l'utilité du pragmatisme* (Paris, 1921).

[7] See Jean Wanner, *Georges Sorel et la décadence* (Lausanne, 1943), pp. 39-55.

[8] Sorel, *Reflections on Violence,* p. 88; id., *Matériaux d'une théorie du prolétariat* (Paris, 1919), pp. 145-51, passim.

[9] See Sorel, *Reflections on Violence,* pp. 80-98, 249.

[10] For Sorel's critique of Socrates (which in many respects resembled Nietzsche's, whose work Sorel did not then know), see his *Procès de Socrate,* esp. pp. 170-72, 375 ff. Sorel attacked Socrates for being an urban middle class intellectual whose strict rationalism destroyed the religious, heroic, and rural-warrior orientation which once made Greece thrive. Since pure rationalism cannot inspire either morality or faith, post-Socratic Greece fell into decadence.

[11] Sorel, *Ruine du monde antique,* pp. 1-28.

[12] Sorel, *Matériaux d'une théorie du prolétariat,* p. 127 (Sorel's italics).

[13] Sorel never adequately explained why he believed this. Perhaps it was his deepseated pessimism about most aspects of human nature. But ironically he was optimistic as well, since he did have confidence in the working class once they were *in movement.* The key problem of much of Sorel's most interesting work was how to set them in movement to begin with.

[14] Sorel, *Reflections on Violence,* p. 50.

[15] Sorel, *Matériaux d'une théorie du prolétariat,* pp. 61-68.

[16] Sorel, *Reflections on Violence,* p. 122.

[17] "According to a law embedded in our nature, we want to have something indemonstrable to believe in." Georges Sorel, *Procès de Socrate,* pp. 145-46.

[18] Sorel, *Reflections on Violence,* pp. 183-84, 240.

[19] Ibid., p. 30.

[20] Sorel, *Matériaux d'une théorie du prolétariat,* p. 138; id., "Critical Essays in Marxism." In *From Georges Sorel: Essays in Socialism and Philosophy,* ed. John L. Stanley (New York, 1976), p. 117.

[21] Sorel, *Reflections on Violence,* p. 148.

[22] Ibid., pp. 47-48.

[23] Ibid., p. 45.

[24] Georges Sorel, cited in Irving Louis Horowitz, *Radicalism and the Revolt against Reason: The Social Theories of Georges Sorel* (Carbondale, Ill., 1961), p. 82.

[25] Sorel, *Reflections on Violence,* p. 122.

[26] Horowitz, *Radicalism and the Revolt against Reason,* p. 49.

[27] Georges Sorel, "Vues sur les problèmes de la philosophie," *Revue de la Métaphysique et du Monde* (September 1910),

p. 616; see Richard Humphrey, *Georges Sorel: Prophet without Honor* (Cambridge, Mass., 1951), p. 122.

[28] George L. Mosse, *The Nationalization of the Masses* (New York, 1975), p. 7.

[29] Edward Sapir, "Symbolism." In *Encyclopedia of the Social Sciences,* vol. 14 (New York, 1934), p. 495.

[30] Sorel, *Matériaux d'une théorie du prolétariat,* pp. 7, 188-89.

[31] Ibid., p. 189.

[32] Sorel, *Reflections on Violence,* p. 28.

[33] Ibid., pp. 35, 182 ff.

[34] Ibid., p. 129.

[35] The best short discussion of the general strike can be found in the following works: Horowitz, *Radicalism and the Revolt against Reason,* pp. 78-89, 127-40; Humphrey, *Georges Sorel,* pp. 186-203; Jacques Rennes, *Georges Sorel et le syndicalisme révolutionnaire* (Paris, 1936), pp. 156-79; Helmut Berding, *Rationalismus und Mythos: Geschichtsauffassung und politische Theorie bei Georges Sorel* (Munich, 1969), pp. 102-17.

[36] See Isiah Berlin, "Georges Sorel." In *Against the Current: Essays in the History of Ideas* (New York, 1980), p. 314. Sorel also strongly attacked: (1) *brutality,* which he defined as an unnecessary excess of violence, or rather as a form of violence that had lost touch with the moral ends it was supposed to serve; and (2) *force,* which he invariably associated with the state, which used it as an instrument of control and domination. Force was always exercised by a ruling class to stabilize a status quo, whereas violence was a proletarian tool for destabilization.

[37] Sorel, *Reflections on Violence,* p. 115.

[38] Ibid., pp. 164-65, 167, 275.

[39] Ibid., p. 46.

[40] Sorel *Matériaux d'une théorie du prolétariat,* p. 129.

[41] In an inteview given in 1932, he claimed that Sorel was his intellectual "master," though for a long time before this he rarely referred to him and in fact called Marx "the magnificent philosopher of working-class violence." See James H. Meisel, *The Genesis of Georges Sorel* (Ann Arbor, 1951), p. 219; Ernst Nolte, *Three Faces of Fascism,* trans. Leila Vennewitz (New York, 1966), p. 153.

[42] Sorel, *Reflections on Violence,* pp. 122, 127, 129; id., *Matériaux d'une théorie du prolétariat,* p. 125.

[43] José Antonio Primo de Rivera, "What the Falange Wants." In *Varieties of Fascism,* ed. Eugen Weber (Princeton, 1964), p. 177.

[44] Sorel, cited in Meisel, *The Genesis of Georges Sorel,* p. 120. See Sorel's "The Ethics of Socialism." In *From Georges Sorel,* ed. Stanley, pp. 94-110.

[45] Only when Sorel temporarily gave up on syndicalism (ca. 1908-13) did he begin to toy with the notion of charismatic leadership. This was not typical, but it was in this context that he hailed (in 1912) the young Mussolini as a modernday condottiere, "the only energetic man capable of redressing the weaknesses of government." See Scott H. Lytle, "Georges Sorel: Apostle of Fanaticism." In *Modern France: Problems of the Third and Fourth Republics,* ed. Edward Mead Earle (Princeton, 1951), p. 288.

[46] Mosse, *Nationalization of the Masses,* p. 200.

[47] See Gustave LeBon, *The Crowd* (New York, 1966), pp. 1-71.

[48] George L. Mosse, *Nazism: A Historical and Comparative Analysis of National Socialism* (New Brunswick, 1978), pp. 34, 37. Marxism, by contrast, remained highly textual, building on a corpus of works that had to be interpreted.

[49] Hitler, cited in Werner Betz, "The National Socialist Vocabulary." In *The Third Reich,* ed. by the International Council for Philosophy and Humanistic Studies (New York, 1975), p. 784. See also Jean Pierre Faye, *Langages totalitaires* (Paris, 1972).

[50] Mosse, *Nationalization of the Masses,* p. 201.

[51] Sorel, *Reflections on Violence,* p. 117.

[52] For an excellent short discussion of this aspect of nazi mythology see Jost Hermand, "The Distorted Vision: Pre-Fascist Mythology at the Turn of the Century." In *Myth and Reason: A Symposium,* ed. Walter D. Wetzels (Austin, 1973), pp. 101-26.

[53] Edouard Dolléans, *Histoire du mouvement ouvrier,* vol. 2 (Paris, 1948), pp. 126-27.

[54] Arturo Labriola, cited in David Roberts, *The Syndicalist Tradition and Italian Fascism* (Chapel Hill, N.C., 1979), p. 78.

Wilfried Röhrich (essay date 1982)

SOURCE: "Georges Sorel and the Myth of Violence: From Syndicalism to Fascism," in *Social Protest, Violence and Terror in Nineteenth- and Twentieth-century Europe,* edited by Wolfgang J. Mommsen and Gerhard Hirschfeld, Berg Publishers, Ltd., 1982, pp. 246-56.

[*In the following excerpt, Rohrich examines French historical events during Sorel's lifetime that influenced his conservative political thinking.*]

Wyndham Lewis believed himself to be justified in saying: 'Georges Sorel is the key to all contemporary political thought'.[1] This dictum appears extreme and yet it contains a grain of truth. After all, Sorel did provide very disparate movements of his day with stirring slogans—albeit frequently unintentionally. And it was no accident that prominent leaders of these movements referred to him time and again. What they most often resorted to was his myth of violence. Two historic movements, in particular, made use of this idea, and Sorel's interpreters have dubbed him more than once the metaphysician of revolutionary Syndicalism and the pioneer of Fascism. Yet, possibly the most important trait of his intellectual attitude—his revolutionary conservatism—was brought out only rarely.

What argues for the hypothesis that Sorel's stance was essentially one of revolutionary conservatism is his deep-rooted hostility towards the French Republic and the ideology it was founded on, one which Sorel fought against alternately from the Left and the Right. Himself a member of the bourgeoisie, he detested his class, above all because he found it lacked the political energy and moral seriousness which it had once possessed. Sorel's criticism was directed against Liberalism and parliamentary democracy and he was never tired of reproaching the liberal enlightenment for having initiated the process of decay at the end of which there would be nothing but a void, unless some new faith replaced the old. One may see in this the true meaning of Sorel's attempt to secure for the myth of violence its due role in the dawn of a new age. And it was the latter which was the true concern of Georges Sorel, the 'revolutionary conservative'.

While this French thinker thus remained faithful to his cause, his public statements about the issues of his day changed with confusing speed. Let us here retrace some of these issues and Sorel's comments on them: Sorel was born in 1847 and reached the age of 45 before he gave up his profession as a civil engineer in order to devote himself to his private studies. He therefore experienced at first hand the period leading up to the Paris Commune and this no doubt helped to shape his hostility towards liberalism and parliamentary democracy. The June revolution of 1848 and the defeat of the proletariat were followed in 1851 by Bonapartism which, according to Marx's definition, represented 'the only possible form of government at a time, when the bourgeoisie had already lost its capacity to rule the nation, while the working class had not yet acquired that capacity'.[2] Thus, the bourgeoisie, which Sorel later described as lacking energy, had even at that time relinquished its political role in order to safeguard its social existence. Increasingly, the bourgeoisie longed for a period 'when it could rule without being responsible for its rule; when a bogus power, standing between it and the people, would have to act and at the same time serve as hiding place for it; when it would have a crowned scapegoat, whom the proletariat could hit at whenever it wanted to attack the bourgeoisie, and against whom it might make common cause with the proletariat, whenever the scapegoat became a nuisance or showed signs of establishing itself as a power in its own right'.[3]

This early observation by Marx characterises the situation of 1850/51 very accurately and at the same time reveals the indecisive attitude of the workers, who, as Marx noted in his 'Eighteenth Brumaire', denied themselves the honour 'of being a conquered force', but instead bowed to their fate and proved 'that the defeat of June 1848 had made them incapable of fighting for years to come'.[4] Even then that moral decline of the ruling classes, which Sorel later never ceased to deplore, revealed itself. But equally the French labour movement, which Sorel later turned to, was still far from assuming a historically significant role.

It is superfluous here to dwell on the details surrounding the rise of the Paris Commune, which was to weaken the labour movement very much further. As we know, after a siege of almost two months and an eight-day battle on the barricades, the Paris Commune was defeated. In the executions during the 'bloody week' that followed, the labour movement again, as in 1848, lost its most active members and its ablest leaders, not only in Paris, but also in Lyon, St Etienne, Marseilles, Toulouse, Narbonne, Limoges and all other places where the communard movement had awakened proletarian impulses.

The French labour movement was to recover only slowly from the defeat of the Paris Commune. Accompanied by heated internal controversies, it began to gain strength again in the period from 1880 to 1900.[5] Within the organised parties of the labour movement the greatest differences of opinion were provoked by the question as to the wisdom of a policy of electoral alliances with bourgeois democrats and gradual participation in the rule of government. In the somewhat overstated partisan terms of a prominent historian of Anarcho-Syndicalism, which could equally have come from Georges Sorel: 'Everything turned on a few, mostly illusory mandates to the Chamber of Deputies, on municipal mandates, rather agreeable to the incumbents, and on coveted jobs on daily papers, *Citoyen-Bataille*, etc.'. Only the Anarchists were dedicated to the 'economic struggle' and thus gained the sympathy of many workers; 'slowly there developed that absolute contempt for politicking, which was later, in the heyday of Syndicalism, to break through for a time with such elemental force'.[6]

Increasingly, this tendency was to find its expression in the new Syndicalist movement, which grew much more rapidly than the party organisations. In 1884 there followed the final abolition of the ban on coalitions with the passing of a new law on associations. Two years later, under the aegis of the *Parti Ouvrier Français* (Guesdists), the *Féderation Nationale des Syndicats* was formed. This, however, in contrast to the *Bourses du Travail* established soon thereafter, was to gain no lasting importance.

The *Bourses du Travail*—the first was created in Paris in 1887 as combined employment agency, assembly point and training centre—were the seat of the local branch offices established by the trade unions, and provided a variety of new impulses. Certainly the most important of these was the suggestion made in 1887 by the Paris labour exchange to create a federation of labour exchanges, a plan that was to be realised that very year at St Etienne. Three years later, the *Féderation Nationale des Bourses du Travail* was to find in Fernand Pelloutier the organiser and secretary who probably exerted the greatest influence on revolutionary Syndicalism. With him originated the idea of the general strike, which Sorel later adopted. In revolutionary Syndicalism embodying this specific idea, both the democratic and reformist Socialism of Jean Jaurès and the 'orthodox' Marxism of Jules Guesde had acquired a rival that could not be matched by the 'putschism' of a Blanqui or the mere anarchism of a Bakunin.

Especially hostile towards parliamentary Socialism, Pelloutier's main concern—just as very soon thereafter Sorel's—was to disabuse Anarchism of its faith in the persuasive power of dynamite, and the trade-union movement of the hope it vested in social reforms. The trade-union movement of revolutionary-syndicalist persuasion would have to rethink the direction of its economic-revolutionary thrust. This new thinking was to be provided by the *Bourses du Travail,* as study centres where, as Pelloutier's brother Maurice noted, 'the proletariat could reflect on its situation and investigate the individual elements of the economic problem, in order to become capable of its own liberation, which is theirs by right'.[7] Intent on the 'anarchist education of man', the trade-union movement had to aim at transforming society. Revolutionary Syndicalism had to become the practical training ground for the class war, as Fernand Pelloutier reiterated more than once in his programmatic article 'L'anarchisme et les syndicats ouvriers'.[8]

In the context of this paper it is neither possible nor necessary to trace the phenomenon of revolutionary Syndicalism in France in great detail, since this is in any case the subject of another contribution.[9] Only certain phases and basic ideas will be briefly sketched in here, so as to bring out Sorel's attitude towards Syndicalism more clearly:

After the organisational accord reached at Montpellier in 1902 (a year after Pelloutier's death), an agreement of views was achieved at the Congress of Amiens (1906), which provided an essential precondition for the strengthening of the Syndicalist movement. The Congress of Amiens confirmed the separation of revolutionary Syndicalism from the Socialist parties and determined that every member of the CGT (*Confédération Générale du Travail*) was free to 'participate outside his trade organisation in such forms of struggle as correspond to his philosophical and political views', but it also laid down that these views were not to be carried into the trade unions. According to the *Charte d'Amiens,* the CGT comprised all workers 'who are conscious of the need to fight in order to abolish wage slavery and private enterprise'. It demanded the 'recognition of the class struggle, which on the economic level brings the worker into revolt against all forms of material and moral exploitation and oppression deployed by the capitalist class'.[10]

The *Charte* brought out the concept of the general strike as the syndicalists' guiding principle very clearly indeed: 'Il (le syndicalisme) préconise comme moyen d'action la grève générale'.[11] Proletarian solidarity had to develop on the basis of its strongest, i.e. the economic, bond. According to the Congress' resolution already referred to, the class war had to be conducted on the economic plane. It had to stress direct action, as opposed to parliamentary or indirect actions. This implied what was probably the most significant syndicalist demand, namely that the emancipation of the proletariat would have to be the work of the proletariat itself. In the explanatory words of Victor Griffuelhes, 'direct action means action by the workers themselves, an action carried out directly by the participant himself. It is the worker himself who makes the effort, carrying it out personally against the powers which rule him, in order to gain from them the advantages he claims. By this direct action the worker takes up the fight himself; it is he who carries it out, determined not to leave the concern for his emancipation to anyone but himself.'[12] This direct action, in the form of street demonstrations, sabotage, boycott, union label or strike, implied also an appeal to moral exertion by the individual.

Thus, the means for the overthrow of the capitalist social order was the general strike. It implied the rejection of the private annexation of any surplus in nationalised production and therefore represented for the revolutionary Syndicalist movement the means of action par excellence. 'The refusal to continue production within the framework of capitalism', declared Emile Pouget,

> will not be wholly negative. It will go hand in hand with the seizure of the means of production and reorganisation on a communist basis, originating from the trade unions as the social cells. The trade unions, having thus become the focal points of the new life, will supplant and destroy the focal points of the old order—the State and the municipalities.[13]

The CGT thus declared itself a revolutionary organisation, whose aim it was to seize economic and political power by direct action, culminating in a general strike.

The period during which revolutionary Syndicalism developed into *unité ouvriere* had come to a close—an end which very soon was to be accompanied by a loss of *élan.* The general strike in particular, which revolutionary Syndicalism had propagated as the signal for revolution, became less an aspect of revolutionary technique and instead increasingly a social myth mobilising the creative forces of the proletariat and implying an irrational ideal of 'perfection'. It gained a more symbolic significance, not least thanks to Sorel's attempt, in his 'Réflexions sur la violence', to provide the Syndicalist movement with a theoretical base. Increasingly out of temper with the bourgeoisie, Georges Sorel had turned to revolutionary Socialism and Syndicalism, prompted not by direct experience of proletarian misery, but by the spectacle of the ruling classes' moral decline. It is important to bear this in mind, since Sorel's stance bespeaks that of a revolutionary conservative who came to Marx by way of Vico.

It is not least this genesis which helps to explain the objectives contained in his ***Réflexions sur la violence.*** They embody the philosophy of Sorel the Syndicalist and we must therefore now turn to them in greater detail. The ***Réflexions,*** a compilation of several articles previously published in *Mouvement Socialiste* contain the demand for a creative proletarian élite to grow out of the workers' movement, which would then be able to rise against parliamentary rule and at the same time, in order not to become weakened itself, stir a hostile bourgeoisie into militancy. The determining factor in this was the recognition that the proletariat's revolutionary energy would have to be mobilised by opposition from the bourgeoisie and that the movement could only be driven forward by *ricorso* to proletarian violence, in the sense of Giambattista Vico's theory of *corsie ricorsi.* The 'diplomatic alliance' between State and party-socialists would have to be fought. Their amorphousness was to be defeated by the passionate nature of the action. This constituted an appeal to the heroism of the proletariat, combined with an absolute rejection of the 'optimistic school' of reformism which, as the elitist theoretician Vilfredo Pareto once expressed it, was under the illusion 'that the ruling class, inspired by pure charity', would exert itself 'for the benefit of the oppressed class'.[14]

Sorel, then, with the weapon of the general strike sought to counter party-socialism with bellicose proletarian solidarity. 'The syndicalist general strike', he wrote, 'is most closely related to the system of war: the proletariat organises itself for battle . . . by regarding itself as the great driving force of history and by subordinating every social concern to that of the struggle.'[15] For Sorel it was the great battle images which were to fire this struggle, it was the mythos of the *grève générale,* as the spontaneous expression of group beliefs, representing an intellectually irrefutable 'unity'. Socialist action was to be understood as an inner, spiritual imperative, as a philosophy of action akin to Henri Bergson's.[16] Sorel, who stressed the importance of the *élan vital,* took up this philosophy of creative evolution, which to him meant proletarian evolution. Socialism, 'une vertu qui naît', had to grow out of the working classes' dynamic impulses of will.

More than by Bergson, however, Sorel was influenced by Proudhon,[17] particularly with regard to the proletarian ethic, and the concept of justice connected with it. To be sure, many ideas of this 'first truly proletarian-socialist theoretician' (Edouard Berth) went unheeded by Sorel. Then, more than in Proudhon's day, the future of Socialism depended on the *scala del capitalismo*—and from this recognition flowed Sorel's demand, already referred to, to arouse the proletariat to engage as equals in the battle with a strong bourgeoisie.

Sorel, the anti-parliamentarian, sought to fuse Proudhon's work with that of Marx. Already in his essay ***Le procès de Socrate*** (1889) he had begun to think in Proudhonist terms and even in his revolutionary Syndicalist phase he remained faithful to Proudhon's thinking. The idea of justice, just as the idea of the *bataille napoléonienne,* was an interpretation of Socialism based on Proudhon's concepts—a socialism conceived as a manifestation of the proletarian conscience, in the sense of a rugged, masculine moralism. Both men addressed themselves to the *homme révolté,* urging him to rise against the authoritarian forces; both emphasised the existential dialectic, in the sense of the *anima appassionata.* Sorel argued that the revolutionary energy of the proletariat alone 'could demonstrate the revolutionary reality to the bourgeoisie and spoil its pleasure in humanitarian platitudes'.[18] This French theoretician, who claimed to have 'moralised Marx a little',[19] interpreted Socialism as an inner tension, producing a combative spirit. Marx appeared not to have considered 'that there might occur a revolution whose ideal would be regression or at least the preservation of the social status quo'.[20] Marx was not able to conceive of such a 'revolution'. However, just such a revolution was now being sought, when the proletariat, originally perceived as a class on its own, began to develop, or rather its party organisation began to develop, into a vague community of interests. And in view of this phenomenon alone, the ***Reflections on Violence*** would be heard on the other side of the barricades as well, in their intention to rekindle social antagonism. Not least for this reason, violence, in spontaneous action, was to arouse proletarian impulses of will, conscious that the struggle to come would be the 'most profound and sublime phenomenon of moral existence'.[21]

Violence, growing out of a revolutionary spirit and aiming at a napoleonic battle, was thus sanctioned. The proletarial appeared as the hero of the drama; the *grève générale* would become an 'accumulation d'exploits héroiques' (Sorel), corresponding to that freedom of will which Proudhon had stressed, providing the 'sentiments of the beautiful and sublime' that went with it.[22] In the place of 'force', as the bourgeoisie's instrument of power, 'violence', as the manifestation of the class struggle, indicated the method of the proletarian general strike. This violence, incomprehensible to a bourgeois society, aimed at the real possibility of a struggle, oriented on those great creative elements from which, according to Carlyle, 'truth' springs.

With the myth of the general strike it was intended to separate the classes; yet if it were only to make Syndicalism more heroic, that would already be an achievement of incalculable value. It was here that the significance of the myth of violence lay, and here also that of which Sorel said: 'One must invoke total images, capable in their entirety and by intuition alone . . . of evoking attitudes corresponding to the various manifestations of the war, which Socialism has begun against modern society'.[23]

With this I have outlined Georges Sorel's main ideas with regard to revolutionary Syndicalism. This conservative revolutionary entertained them only for a few years before he gradually came to hold the view—expressed on the publication of Croce's essay 'La morte del Socialismo'—that Socialism was dead.[24] By 1909, when Mussolini the socialist, in his comprehensive review of ***Réflexions sur la violence,*** stressed how much 'contemporary Socialism in Latin countries' owed to Sorel,[25] the latter had already completed his turn towards nationalism, which up to 1914 was to become increasingly emphatic. In this he was in harmony with the ideas of his time. The Syndicalist movement, too, had capitulated before the more powerful nationalist impulses. Everywhere, the idea of the nation superseded other hitherto dominant notions of solidarity. Several syndicalists in France turned to the *Action française,* while in Italy revolutionary socialists and syndicalists had come together with irredentists and nationalists already during the founding congress of the 'Associazione Nazionalista' in Florence (1910). And no less a man than Georges Sorel reached out 'his hand to the *Action française,* while his work proclaimed . . . the return of the fatherland'.[26] Together with Edouard Berth he became editor of *Cité Française,* a publication founded in 1910, and with the aid of the *Cercle Proudhon,* inspired by Sorel, the alliance between Sorelians and the Valoi-Group was to become even closer. A synthesis between nationalist and syndicalist ideas came about and it was possible to refer to Sorel, if for no other reason than that his general ideas were sufficiently vague to serve nationalist movements equally well.

Decisive above all was the myth of violence, now no longer implying a general strike, but a nationalist act of supreme solidarity. In the search, then, for revolutionary energy and spontaneous activity, one looked for a new combination of ideas, bearing in mind that, according to Sorel, the idea of the struggle would have to be preserved, if *élan* and existential impulses were not to be lost. In Italy he was remembered not least in terms of his 'exploits heroiques'. Here if was among the nationalists, as represented by Enrico Corradini, where 'the man of the national struggle . . . could hold out his hand to the man of the class struggle, as Sorel had done'.[27] Corradini, whom Mussolini was later to describe as 'the Fascist of the very first hour',[28] proclaimed, like Sorel, the myth of the nation. And if one takes a look in isolation at the ideology of big business at that time, close to both nationalism and Fascism, one realises that a considerable step in the direction of Fascism had already been taken.

Here again it would be beyond the scope of this paper to retrace the genesis of Fascism in detail. Without wishing to pre-empt the following contribution, it should nevertheless be borne in mind that Fascism could only acquire political power, because prominent factions within the economically dominant class and their political and ideological representatives desired this. Max Horkheimer's famous remark that those who don't want to talk about capitalism should also keep quiet about Fascism,[29] indicates the perhaps most relevant link between the two phenomena, namely of capitalist production and reproduction and the form of rule that goes with it. If one adds to this socio-economic function of Fascism the anti-communist ideology fostered by the revolutionary threat posed by the Italian maximalists, as well as the mass support provided by social groups of middle-class mentality[30] even before the Fascist seizure of power, it is possible to make out the historically significant contours of the epochal phenomenon of Fascism. These brief indications must suffice before we return once more to our more restricted subject: Sorel's relation to Fascism.

If Georges Sorel's relation to emergent Fascism—he died shortly before the march on Rome-is to be assessed correctly, it will be necessary to remember not only how dominant for his thinking were his anti-parliamentarian and anti-democratic views, but also his myths—the mythos of violence, of the general strike, of the nationa. In this Sorel comes very close to Vilfredo Pareto's anti-democratic theory of the élite. Long before Sorel turned to politics, Pareto had recognised that parliamentary democracy, or at least the form it took at that time in Italy, was doomed. Already in his *Trattato di sociologia generale* (1916) Pareto had advocated the energetic rule of the élite and condemned as demagogy any form of democratic government. Thus, in his later writings, we find the close intellectual relationship to Sorel emphasised; just like the latter, Pareto stressed the 'futility of parliamentary and democratic dogmas',[31] pointed to the 'absurd idea of one half plus one'.[32] As Mussolini had jibed: 'Oh, precious naïvety of an era that believes in the *metà piú uno*'.[33] Both thinkers, in their advocacy of the elitist idea, aimed at a *trasformazione della democrazia,* according to the slogan with which Pareto headed his collection of articles, published in the *Rivista di Milano* in the historic year of 1920.

In the case of Sorel, his antidemocratic, elitist theory was combined with the element of myth. The characteristic features of this myth have already been referred to in connection with revolutionary Syndicalism and need now only be extended from the proletariat to the entire nation, in order to comprehend their impact. The social myth, directed at the creative proletarian energies and implying, as we have seen, an irrational idea of 'perfection', encapsulated the Socialist movement in images which—*en bloc et par la seule intuition*—were to stimulate individual acts in the proletarian struggle. The appeal to the heroic spirit of the proletariat needed only to be replaced by an appeal to the power instincts of national élites. These, as history has taught us, were equally able to spur fanaticised masses to unbridled violence by means of a mythos. This interpretation may sound a little harsh, but it pinpoints the constant ambivalence attaching to the mythos of violence, which after all, according to Sorel, could have a positive as well as a negative connotation—it could have revolutionary or reactionary application.

After all that has been said so far, it is hardly surprising that Italian Fascism invoked Sorel, and that he in turn did not hide his sympathy for Mussolini. The fact that Sorel had meanwhile written his ***Pour Lénine*** (1918/19) and praised the 'heroic efforts' of the Russian proletariat[34] may appear to contradict this. But above all Sorel emphasised that he saw in Russia's national myth 'the heroic rise of a modern nation'; and since Sorel at the same time wished to see Mussolini kindling the national energies, and had become an advocate of Italian interests, he saw the kind of 'heroism' that creates nations equally in the rise of Fascism; in a letter to Benedetto Croce, he called it 'perhaps the most original social phenomenon of contemporary Italy'.[35]

Thus it was possible to come to Fascism by way of Sorel and even to quote him, if one wished to extend the myth, as the spontaneous expression of group beliefs, to the nation as a whole.

Mussolini himself, who, once he became *duce,* was to confess that even when still a socialist, touched by the tragic quality of violence, he had been a fascist at heart, never ceased to stress the myth of the nation and to underline the significance of concepts such as *azione* and *sentimento,* the latter indicating the dominance of the myth.[36] In this no doubt the tactical consideration of a need to nourish idealised hopes predominated, just as his vague programmatic statements were intended to appeal to extremely diverse groups. But independent of such tactical questions, the 'heroic epics' of the author of ***Réflexions sur la violence*** remained vivid for Mussolini, and it was no accident that even in his *dottrina del fascismo* he was to stress the currents in Fascism that had flowed from Sorel: 'Nel grande flume del fascismo troverete i filoni che si dipartirono dal Sorel . . . '.[37]

The dialectic tension between Mussolini's theory and practice is seen perhaps most clearly in his answer to a question posed by an editor of the Madrid publication ABC, about influences he considered to have been decisive in his life: 'Sorel's. The main thing for me was to act. But I repeat, it is to Sorel that I owe most.'[38] There can be no doubt that it was Sorel's myth of violence aimed at arousing national energies, to which Mussolini referred. However careful one ought to be in designating certain thinkers as 'intellectual fathers of Fascism',[39] it would nevertheless be impossible to deny that Sorel had opted for Fascism. In several of his post-war articles he welcomed the reawakening of a national conscience in Italy; and when Sorel's friend Robert Michels met him in March 1922 for the last time, he was able to convince himself, as he noted in his diary, of Sorel's 'faith' in the new movement. 'Of Benito Mussolini he spoke with great sympathy. "Do we know", he said, "where he will go? At any rate, he will go far." '[40] Sorel's remark characterises the hopes he vested in Mussolini. It shows also what he had recognised in Fascism: the will to act which, as Sorel clearly stressed, in contrast to the maximalist's revolutionary experiment, aimed at arousing national energies. Neither in the *red signorie* nor in the traditional *classe dirigente* could he, who still hoped to witness the 'humiliation of democracy', detect an awareness of the 'historic hour'. It was no accident that his statement 'le gouvernement par l'ensemble des citoyens n'a jamais été qu'une fiction; mais cette fiction était le dernier mot de la science démocratique'[42] was time and again used by Fascism as an argument against the 'corrupt parliamentary democracy'.[43]

NOTES

[1] *The Art of Being Ruled* (London, 1926) p. 128.

[2] K. Marx, 'Der Bürgerkrieg in Frankreich', *Marx-Engels-Werke* (MEW), vol. 17 (East Berlin, 1973) p. 338.

[3] K. Marx, 'Die Pariser 'Réforme' über die französischen *Zustände*', *MEW,* vol. 5 (1973) p. 449.

[4] K. Marx, 'Der achtzehnte Brumaire des Louis Bonaparte', *MEW,* vol. 8 (1973) p. 157.

[5] This period was characterised by a remarkable development in French industrial production. Increased growth in basic industries and a rapid development of heavy industry determined the economic background. Typical for France remained the large share of agriculture in the overall economic development: it was that branch of the national economy which even at the turn of the century still employed a million more workers than factories, crafts, transport and mining taken together. It was a feature of French economic structure that there existed relatively few monopolies, very little horizontal or vertical concentration and initially also little modernisation, as a result of concentration on the domestic market and of protectionism, providing a shield against foreign competition. Small and medium businesses remained the dominant feature; as late as 1906 60 per cent of all workers were employed by enterprises with less than 10 employees.

[6] M. Nettlau, 'Fernand Pelloutiers Platz in der Entwicklung des Syndikalismus', *Internationale* (a publication of revolutionary Syndicalism in Berlin, which appeared for a short time), 1 (1927/28) p. 50.

[7] M. Pelloutier, *Fernand Pelloutier: Sa vie, son oeuvre (1867-1901)* (Paris, 1911) p. 62.

[8] Fernand Pelloutier's programmatic article appeared in: *Les Temps Nouveaux,* 1 (1895) pp. 2-4; quoted here from the German translation by Ursula Lange, in: E. Oberländer (ed.), *Der Anarchismus* (Olten, 1972) pp. 316-25.

[9] See the contribution by F. F. Ridley in this volume; for a detailed description see also W. Röhrich, *Revolutionärer Syndikalismus: Ein Beitrag zur Sozialgeschichte der Arbeiterbewegung* (Darmstadt, 1977).

[10] Congrès National des Syndicats de France, *Comte rendu des travaux du congrès* (Amiens, 1906).

[11] Ibid.

[12] V. Griffuelhes, *L'action syndicaliste* (Paris, 1908) p. 23.

[13] E. Pouget, *La C. G. T.* (Paris, 1907) p. 47f.

[14] V. Pareto, *Les systèmes socialistes (1902-03)* (Paris, 1926) p. 421.

[15] G. Sorel, *Über die Gewalt (Réflexions sur la violence)* (Innsbruck, 1928) p. 198.

[16] Cf. H. Bergson, 'Sur les données immédiates de la conscience' in *Oeuvre* (Paris, 1959) p. 151.

[17] 'Si l'on veut indiquer les inspirateurs véritables de Sorel, c'est Proudhon et Marx qu'il faut citer. Et, des deux, il me paraît incontestable que c'est Proudhon qui a été son plus authentique maître', G. Pirou, *Georges Sorel* (Paris, 1925) p. 56f.

[18] Sorel, *Über die Gewalt,* p. 87.

[19] Georges Sorel's letter to Benedetto Croce, dated 27/5/1899, *La Critica,* 25 (1927) p. 304.

[20] Sorel, *Über die Gewalt,* p. 96.

[21] P.-J. Proudhon, 'La guerre et la paix', in: *Oeuvres complètes,* vol. 13 (Paris, 1869) p. 38.

[22] Ibid., 'De la justice dans la révolution et dans l' lise', *Oeuvres complètes.*

[23] Sorel, *Über die Gewalt,* pp. 136-7.

[24] 'J'ai grand peur que vous n'ayez trop raison dans ce que vous avez dit sur la mort du socialisme', was what Sorel wrote about Croce's essay, in a letter to him, dated 19/2/1911, in *La Critica* 26 (1928) p. 347.

[25] B. Mussolini, 'Lo sciopero generale e la violenza' (review), *Opera Omnia,* vol. 2 p. 167. Typical of Sorel's influence on Mussolini, the Socialist, were also remarks such as: 'We have to accomplish a work of great magnitude—the creation of a new world! As Sorel has emphasised, our mission is awesome, serious and sublime!'—B. Mussolini, 'Ai compagni', in: *Opera Omnia,* vol. 2 (1951) p. 255.

[26] M. Freund, *Georges Sorel: Der revolutionäre Konservativismus* (Frankfurt/M, 1932) p. 220.

[27] Ibid., p. 256.

[28] B. Mussolini, 'Enrico Corradini', in: *Opera Omnia,* vol. 25 (1958) p. 69f.

[29] M. Horkheimer, 'Die Juden und Europa', *Zeitschrift für Sozialforschung* 8 (1939) p. 115.

[30] These social groups of middle-class mentality consisted of small property owners (artisans, small traders and peasants) and groups conscious of upward mobility (office employees, civil servants), who were determined to defend their 'middle-class' position against the lower social classes.

[31] V. Pareto, 'Georges Sorel', *La Ronda* 4 (1922) p. 542.

[32] Ibid., p. 546f.

[33] B. Mussolini, 'Quando il mito tramonta', in: *Opera Omnia,* vol. 17 (1955) p. 323.

[34] G. Sorel, 'Pour Lénine' in *Über die Gewalt,* p. 349-*361.*

[35] Sorel's letter to Benedetto Croce, dated 26/8/1921, *La Critica,* 28 (1930) p. 195.

[36] B. Mussolini, 'discorso a Trieste (20/10/1920)', *Opera Omnia,* vol. 15 (1954) p. 218.

[37] B. Mussolini, 'La Dottrina del Fascismo (1932)', *Opera Omnia,* vol. 34 (1961) p. 122.

[38] According to Pirou, *Georges Sorel,* p. 53.

[39] Such an interpretation, with Sorel in mind, was made by Georges Valois: 'Le père intellectuel du fascisme, c'est Georges Sorel.' G. Valois, *Le Fascisme* (Paris, 1927) p. 5.

[40] Entry in Robert Michels' diary on 22/3/1922, in: 'Lettere di Georges Sorel a Roberto Michels', *Nuovi Studi di Diritto, Economia e Politica,* 2 (1969) p. 293.

[41] Thus the closing words in Sorel's 'Pour Lénine,' *Über die Gewalt,* p. 361.

[42] Georges Sorel, 'Avenir socialiste des syndicats et annexes (1914)' in *Matériaux d' une théorie du prolétariat (1919)* (Paris, 1921) p. 118.

[43] B. Mussolini, 'Ne fasto! (10/6/1920)', *Opera Omnia,* vol. 15 (1954) p. 26.

John L. Stanley (essay date 1984)

SOURCE: An introduction to "Social Foundations of Contemporary Economics", by Georges Sorel, translated by John L. Stanley, Transaction Books, 1984, pp. 1-34.

[*In the following excerpt, Stanley examines the influence of the writings of Henri Bergson, William James, and Pierre-Joseph Proudhon on the writings of Sorel.*]

Perhaps the most interesting aspect of Georges Sorel's political and social thought is the difficulty one has in attempting to classify it. Just when we think we have Sorel conveniently pigeonholed into some tidy little category (protofascist being a recent favorite), he fools us by putting forth ideas which at first seem to be in complete contradition to all our preconceptions.

This elusiveness is partly responsible for the allegations of "shocking inconsistency" and negativism leveled against Sorel. These allegations have some truth. Anyone like Sorel born in France in the middle of the nineteenth century had numerous political traditions from which to choose, and it appears that he sampled a good many of them. As a young engineering student at the prestigious Ecole Polytechnique, Sorel expressed a sympathy with royalism and was a partisan of the Comte de Chambord in 1867. After his early retirement from the Department of Highways in 1892, he moved toward social democracy, but this attachment to a revised Marxism soon changed into a sympathy for antistatist syndicalism from about 1902 until about 1908. This was the period in which the present volume as well as ***Reflections on Violence*** and the ***Illusions of Progress***[1] were written. After 1908, Sorel regarded the snydicalist movement as a failure and flirted once more with royalism. After 1917, he embraced Lenin's Bolshevism and even occasionally made favorable remarks about Mussolini.

This seemingly bizarre series of changes is better understood if we keep in mind the historical backdrop of Sorel's youth: France's defeat in the Franco-Prussian war in 1870 profoundly demoralized French society. The political thought of the next decade and the parliamentary immobilism of the Third Republic reflected this malaise. The inertia of liberal institutions after 1871 had provoked a challenge from the Right in which Royalists and Bonapartists formed a coalition in support of Minister of War Boulanger in his demand for a reformed constitution and a more spirited foreign policy—an attempt which came to naught. Its failure helped to solidify the multiple stalemate between the forces of radicalism and conservatism. "France is dying," proclaimed Ernest Renan in 1882, and these words from the great religious scholar come close to summing up Sorel's own feeling about the period. Renan was moved by the French defeat to call for a reform of the educational system to teach the heroism of classical times and to synthesize French and German virtues. These sentiments were found in Sorel's first important work, ***Le Procès de Socrate*** (1889).[2] There Sorel drew an implicit analogy between the decline of heroic Athens at the hand of philosophers and the decline of France under Louis Napoleon and under the Third Republic. In its pages Sorel appears much more reactionary than the liberal Renan. We find a deeply pessimistic Sorel, hostile to the Enlightenment, a bitter critic of "the illusions of progress."

But appearances here are deceiving. Sorel was not a reactionary in any vulgar sense, but was espousing a new moral order that was sometimes profoundly hostile to the prevailing system of values. To Sorel, the malaise of contemporary European civilization was a moral one. But unlike Renan, he was not content to preach morality or to put forth small palliatives. He sought a genealogy of morals or what I have called a "sociology of virtue,"[3] which attempted to examine the historical and psychological roots of the moral basis of a social order and its decomposition. It was the search for the historical genesis of morals that Sorel said was "the great concern of my entire life."[4]

Le Procès de Socrate was a general indictment of philosophical teachers in ancient Athens, not merely an attack on Socrates. To Sorel, Athenian philosophers, with Socrates at their head, had replaced the preachments of intellectuals for the heroic teachings of the Greek mythic poets. In Sorel's view, such new teachings were largely ineffectual except in a negative sense, serving only to undermine the moral strength of the old institutions. (1) Philosophy had preached an abstract brotherhood of man instead of solid family institutions and Platonic instead of erotic love. The family life on which all other stable social institutions are based was thus undermined. (2) Philosophers preached the rule of experts instead of the rule of warriors and fighters. The military virtues on which Greek citizenship was based were weakened. (3) Philosophers emphasized the leisure necessary for philosophical and political activity; the ethic of productivity and energy was replaced by a morality of the weak based on consumption. It is the last two themes, the morality of struggle and of productivity, which stand as the major inspiration of the present work, *Insegnamenti sociali della economia contemporanea.*

Sorel derived this sociology of morals mainly from the work of Pierre-Joseph Proudhon, who had criticized his own social milieu on roughly these same bases. On the other hand, it was Proudhon who had emphasized the futility of war in modern society and who, instead of calling for battle, assimilated the heroism of war to the day-to-day struggles of the worker in production. The modern proletariat had replaced the Greco-Roman citizen farmer.

After publication of ***Le Procès de Socrate*** Sorel discovered the writings of Vico and Marx. To Sorel, Vico revealed the recurrent nature of the heroic virtues he had longed for. Vico argued that the natural cycles of history, of greatness and decline among peoples, always contained periods characterized by the heroic barbarism expressed in Homeric poetry or the medieval epics. Such recurrences, or *ricorsi,* the beginnings of new civilizations, are accompanied by a transvaluation of values, an upheaval that annihilates the old, decadent civilization with a moral catastrophe far greater than any material one; in such times, "the logic of imagination replaces the logic of philosophy."[5] The *ricorsi* embody new dynamisms, new vitalities and energies.

From Marx, Sorel discovered how he could apply the heroism of the Homeric epics to new conditions, through the class struggle. Marx's notion of absolute class separation, of the proletariat isolating itself from the mentality of bourgeois civilization, proved the key to Sorel's search for new beginnings. He embraced Marx as the one philosopher outside Proudhon who revealed a way in which a true Vicoian *ricorso* would occur in modern times. A combination of Proudhonian heroism and Marxian class struggle would pave the way for a rebirth of contemporary civilization.

Two more theorists contributed to Sorel's philosophy. From Henri Bergson, Sorel derived a psychology which revealed the nature of the heroic leaps of imagination that invariably accompany a *ricorso*. Bergson explained how such leaps could go beyond the scientific universe, whose routines threatened the vital life force, the very expression of which was necessary for moral renaissance.

In William James, Sorel found a philosophical expression of what he had always viewed as axiomatic: that the "success" of a doctrine is more important than its inner coherence. Once we keep in mind the instrumental nature of political and economic doctrines espoused by James, Sorel's continuing change of allegiances becomes more explicable. For Sorel embraced a doctrine only insofar as it revealed a potential for a *ricorso* and he rejected it if it was shown to be ineffectual. For example, he explained his most notorious switch, from syndicalism to royalism in 1909-10, when he said: "I do not know if Maurras will bring back the king of France and that is not what interests me in his thought; what I am concerned with is that he confront the dull and reactionary bourgeoisie in making it ashamed of being defeated."[6] As he later stated it, he had always been a traditionalist in a sense: "One can call me a traditionalist as one can call me a pragmatist, because in the critique of knowledge I attach a major importance to historical development. When I sided with Vico . . . I was in a certain sense a traditionalist."[7] Sorel's "monarchism" is a means by which he can envision a sharpened social struggle that makes possible the unfolding of virtue—that he defines in terms of the warrior ethos of courage and self-sacrifice. Each ideology is viewed in terms of its potential to uphold the *élan* of such a struggle. When it does not live up to these hopes, it is abandoned even more quickly than it was adopted.

The pragmatic nature of Sorel's use of Vico is further emphasized when we keep in mind Sorel's view that, in the realm of ideas as well as in social action, there is a "heterogeneity between the ends realized and the ends given."[8] For Sorel reality differs greatly from the ideas that we had of it before acting. Sorel's distinction between the psychological basis of the royalist actors themselves and the psychology of the observers of the royalists is similar to William James's distinction between the "religious propensities" of believers and the "philosophical significance" of those beliefs.[9] In modern sociological terms, beliefs have "latent functions," the most important of which is the role they play in struggle and economic productivity.

The pluralism between intention and result in pragmatic thought extends to historical pluralism as well. Despite Sorel's attraction to Vico, he was critical of his simplistic account of the relationships between psychological states and society.[10] Vico looked upon history almost as an organic growth in which thought and activity are brought together in an indissoluble whole: he treated phenomena *en bloc*. But to Sorel, if history developed in this fashion, there would be few chances for a durable renaissance. *Ricorsi* are produced when a body within society declares itself separate from the prevailing civilization; Vico's holistic approach to change obscures the importance of this separation; it hides the need for ideologies to coexist and compete with one another for supremacy. It is this competition which makes movements struggle in order to triumph, and it is the struggle itself, more than the outcome, which produces virtue in the hearts of the participants.

This doctrine of struggle stands at the basis of Sorel's treatment of various ideologies. One of the best illustrations of Sorel's position is found here in the *Insegnamenti* where he deals with the ideologies of liberal capitalism and socialism. In reading this work, we come to understand that Sorel admired each of these ideologies most insofar as it stood in resistance to (or at least in isolation from) the opposing ideology. The more an ideology represents struggle and the overcoming of resistance, the more it possesses dynamic elements, elements of creativity and mastery in which it represents the fight against decadence. The less an ideology embodies the ethos of struggle, the more it embodies degeneration and laxity. Each ideology contains both regenerative and degenerative components.

This striking parallelism between liberal and socialist degeneration and regeneration stands at the core of the ***Insegnamenti sociali della economia contemporanea.*** This work was completed in 1903-05 when Sorel had written off liberalism in France as a lost cause and had become fully disillusioned with the "official socialism" of the German and French Marxist parties. By then Sorel had turned to antipolitical syndicalism, and the ***Insegnamenti*** is especially interesting when viewed as a sort of *Grundrisse* or draft for his most renowned work (written the following year), ***Reflections on Violence.***

While ***Reflections*** is Sorel's clearest statement of syndicalist action and the social myths which sustain it, in the ***Insegnamenti*** we find the clearest theory of the idea of class separation as a function of the rise of syndicalism. In the ***Insegnamenti*** we also find the most detailed analysis of the role class separation had performed in the great periods of liberalism and socialism; and it is here that we find the most profound condemnation of what Sorel calls "social solidarity" (or social unity) and the role it has played in the degeneration of the two great European ideologies.

The work is doubly interesting because not only does Sorel discuss these ideologies, but he actually uses them as tools for analyzing these very ideologies. As Sorel expresses it: "The true method to follow to know the defects, inadequacies, and errors of a powerful philosophy is to criticize it by means of its own principles."[11] Thus he announces at the beginning of the ***Insegnamenti*** that he will use, as much as possible, the principles of historical materialism.

In this work Sorel is not only analyzing socialism according to its own system of historical materialism; he is also examining the ideologies of liberal capitalism. Yet there is no explicit reference here to a theory corresponding to capitalism that Sorel found useful as a means of analysis, though such a theory did exist at the time and was implicit in Sorel's analytical approach. That theory is pragmatism, one of the main philosophical progeny of liberalism. Since it is through pragmatic as much as Marxist criteria that Sorel evaluates the various European ideologies, and since it is more through pragmatic criteria that he pledges allegiance to so many of them at various times, not only does Sorel view Marxism using Marxian categories and liberalism in terms of its own pragmatic norms, but each of these ideologies is (here or in later writings) examined with the other's philosophical weaponry as well.

In the present volume Sorel is explicit about using historical materialism and says nothing about pragmatism because, at the time of writing (1904-05), Sorel had gravitated to pragmatism only by instinct. It was not until four or five years later in 1909 that Sorel would discover the writing of William James, and only long after 1909 would he extoll "the utility of pragmatism." Yet this still unarticulated pragmatic thought is at least as important as Marxism in Sorel's thinking; perhaps more so. Marxism was important to Sorel chiefly because of the role it played in analyzing the historical and economic roots of social phenomena. Sorel's pragmatism is important because it provided him with an expression of the plural nature of reality and of the necessarily partial and tentative nature of all explanatory theories. Marxism is important because it emphasizes man's interchange with nature as the basis of knowledge. Pragmatism will be imporatnt to Sorel because it, more than Marxism, emphasizes that nature cannot be viewed successfully as a totality.

Liberal capitalism and socialism, as dealt with in the ***Insegnamenti,*** are, among other things, also philosophies of man's relationship to nature, and Sorel's own pragmatic theory of nature is important in understanding the present work. Sorel developed this natural theory quite early, long before his formal discovery of pragmatism, and it informs his entire philosophy as few other aspects of his thought do. In no small measure, this philosophy is the basis of Sorel's method of looking at all social as well as scientific phenomena. Thus, before turning to an analysis of the ***Insegnamenti,*** this pragmatic methodology should be discussed in detail. It is the implicit method he employs (coupled with Marxism) throughout this work.

In Sorel's eyes, the examination of ideological phenomena, like the experimental controls involved in scientific questions, is necessarily limited to partial views of phenomena. The ideology of liberalism, for example, can be seen most effectively if we look at it from a single angle, say its period of decline. We can look at other stages of the ideology at other discrete moments. This method results in a series of representations roughly analogous to single frames of a motion picture which might give a closer and more detailed view of an otherwise confused action. On the other hand, this "still frame" cannot help but distort the full portrayal of the movement by virtue of its partial nature.

Sorel asserts that knowledge of the full social or ideological "newsreel" is impossible. Methodologically, Sorel attempts to deal with the problem of totality by using what in his early writings he called an "expressive support" and later called *diremption.* The term *diremption* is defined as "a forcible separation or severance."[12] As Sorel stated it: "In order to study the most important philosophy of history, social philosophy is obliged to proceed to a *diremption,* to examine certain parts without taking into consideration all their connections with the whole; to determine, in some way, the nature of their activity by isolating them. When it has attained the most perfect knowledge in this way, social philosophy can no longer try to reconstruct the broken unity."[13]

We can elaborate on the concept of diremption in a number of ways, and there is an anticipation here of Max Weber's "ideal types." It is a method of analysis which abstracts a phenomenon from social reality for the purpose of clarification. We know, however, that the process of abstraction, by its very isolation, distorts or blurs the totality from which it is derived, and that the diremptions themselves have been changed in the process of being isolated.

Sorel is aware that, to some extent, every social philosophy or political theory must use diremption, and he seems to argue that these theories are themselves diremptions. Yet to Sorel, most social and political theorists are only half conscious of the consequences of making these abstractions. Sorel insists that we shall gain insights from diremption, that is, from abstract social theories, but we must never forget what a diremption is; although diremptions must be used, we must be careful not to abuse them. According to Sorel, most of the errors of social philosophy stem from such abuses.

At the root of the problem of social analysis is the displacement of an empirically based theory with rationalist theories. This hostility to the rationalist tradition is partly responsible for Sorel's attack on the rule of philosophers and social scientists. Rationalism places the objecs of diremption in an extreme degree of isolation from the total milieu; it produces conclusions giving an appearance of logic, reasonableness, and necessity, but which are at complete odds with other diremptions derived partly from the same milieu which seem equally logical, reasonable, and necessary. When diremptions have been "pushed far enough along the path of such antinomies, it is easy to forget the historical and economic roots from which they derive." When diremption becomes rationalized, it undergoes a process of reification; diremption becomes, in Sorel's words, "without an object," that is, it floats free and "comes into conditions that are irreconcilable with the nature of their formation";[14] then we obtain distortions that are even further removed from reality than the original diremption. The insights and clarification derived from the original procedure have given way to sophistry, arbitrariness, and vagueness. In other words, by forgetting the historical and theoretical genesis of a diremption, a theorist makes the error or thinking that he can bring it back to social totality without causing further distortions. The reimmersion into the totality both results from, and in turn causes, an illusion of wholeness, a false consciousness of universality. Social diremption, like social philosophy itself, is a phenomenon that must be treated "diremptively."

Perhaps the best example of a misused diremption, in Sorel's view, is one that recurs throughout this work: the concept of economic man perfected by British political economy in the nineteenth century. For Sorel, the analytical utility of the concept of a calculating market bargainer is undeniable, but it is a great misuse of diremption to extend that concept to cover areas for which it was not intended. Nonetheless "subtle writers even worked to create a science which considered the relations of buyer-seller, capitalist-employee, lender-debtor in a market that no government penetrated." Hence a useful symbolic device was transformed into a utopia governed by the "natural harmony of mutual interests." Such utopias are wholly misguided because the "petty concerns of *homo economicus*" in no way can represent the totality of social relations. The adherents of the utopia "did not seriously examine the legitimacy of the diremption."[15]

But at what point do we know that such a diremption has been abused? Sorel's method of diremption is a pragmatic, trial-and-error method that makes each diremption a hypothesis to be tested against social reality. In this testing process Sorel comes close to replicating in social theory the philosophy of science he had developed in the early 1890s. The analogies Sorel had observed between the practices of science and those of laboring not only inspired his theory of diremption, but also affected his thoroughly pragmatic revision of Marxism.

To Sorel, as to Vico and Marx, man's knowledge of the world is derived from the act of making or manufacturing—either in the realm of ideas or in man's interaction with nature. Similarly, construction of laboratory models, in Sorel's view, effects an isolation—a diremption—from the world in the very process of our getting to understand the world through changing it. On these grounds, Sorel argues that the milieux of the scientist and of the worker become increasingly similar as science and productivity become more intense; and the more intense they become, the more they separate themselves from the realm of nature. The laboratory is "a small workshop where instruments are used that are more precise than those in manufacturing, but there is no essential difference between the two types of establishments."[16]

In other writings, Sorel calls this separation or diremption from nature "artificial nature," which he juxtaposes to "natural nature" or nature in its undisturbed or "pure" state.[17] The ***Insegnamenti*** does not contain specific discussion of these two natures, but the argument presumes this distinction as we shall see. Sorel argues that there is always plurality in these two realms in the industrial world. Thus the two natures represent a plural—hence pragmatic—view of understanding reality. On the one hand, the more a phenomenon is removed from nature, that is, the more nature is "artificial," the more precisely we can predict the results of our experiments. On the other hand, most natural nature, still immersed in the totality, remains comparatively vague. The physicist is thus dealing with a more "artificial" realm than the meteorologist. The result is a dilemma regarding the apprehension of totality: in natural nature the scope of our investigation is much wider, but the precision of our knowledge and the accuracy of our predictions is blurred, while in artificial nature, the scope of our understanding is more limited as our precision increases. Our knowledge of nature will thus never become total in the sense of an equally precise knowledge of all its parts. There is an uncertainty principle here which cannot be overcome. The unity of science and nature that had for Marx been alienated under capitalism, Sorel regarded as being shattered by the very process of manufacturing. Whereas Marx, and especially Engels, would overcome alienation through the establishment of an all-encompassing socialist laboratory-workshop and a unified science, Sorel insisted that, whatever the economic system, scientific and industrial production in the modern world cannot avoid being alienated from the rest of nature either through the actions of *homo faber* or through those of the laboratory scientist in the creation of experiments and controls. Knowledge of that nature cannot help but become alienated. Scientific knowledge is diremption, the analytic counterpart of artificial nature.

This alienated condition of modern industry is presented in another way by Sorel. The world of "artificial nature," the world in which nature is transformed through science and industry, is determined and predictable. But Sorel insists that this predictability and precision are insufficient to perpetuate a world of artificial nature. Left to itself, artificial nature reverts all too easily back to the world of natural nature. It "coasts" by sinking from the empirical world into the abstractions of rationalism. A perfectly predictable world is not sufficient to produce new science but invites stagnation in science as well as in society; it returns to the passive terrain of natural nature, because, in Bergson's terms, we become "enclosed in the circle of the given." Insofar as it is purely intellectual, "scientific knowledge presents itself as something alien to our person. . . . We attribute to it a dominant force on our will and we submit weakly to its tyranny."[18] Thus scientific determinism is self-negating; it becomes an adversary to continued scientific research because it affirms the "powerlessness of our creative forces; *we then have science only to the extent that we have the force to govern the world.*"[19]

To continue our practices in the realm of artificial nature, some motive force must make us "interfere" in nature; something must make us come to this nature, as it were, "from the outside"; intention must break this circle of determinism. This break comes only by bringing in a poetic dimension to the productive or scientific process. "Poetic fictions are stronger than scientific ones," Sorel says. They represent "the ability to substitute an imaginary world for scientific truths which we populate with plastic creations and which we perceive with much greater clarity than the material world. It is these idols that permeate our will and are the sisters of our soul."[20] The vision that inspires the syndicalist myth of the general strike, or assures the Marxist that his cause is certain to triumph, exists outside of science; it lives in the world of intuition, of instinct, of imagination, in a word, of creativity. It is these poetic visions that convince the inventor or producer of the moral certitude of his task. "If man loses something of his confidence in scientific certitude, he loses much of his moral certitude at the same time."[21] It is not science that gives men certitude; it is moral certitude that gives man the inner strength to wage constant war against the passive terrain of natural nature. Artificial nature, once established, requires constant struggle merely to keep even with natural nature. Artificial nature, sustained by poetic myths, means a twofold battle against the material on which we work as well as our own "natural nature"—the tendency to relaxation, sloth, and leisure. Because they are the very embodiment of such a struggle, Sorel can assimilate science and labor and assert that their successes constitute a rough measure of the virtue of a given culture. Artificial nature represents the triumph of self-overcoming as well as the triumph over external nature; natural nature represents the failure of self-overcoming; it is the terrain of surrender to our own worst inclinations and passions; natural nature is the realm of unity while artificial nature destroys that unity.

We can now see more fully why Sorel's pragmatic break with Marx alters so radically the conclusions of humanist Marxists. By dint of the necessity for continued struggle with natural nature, neither laboring man nor scientific man will ever triumph fully, never bridge the gap between man and the world around him. "We will never be able completely to subject phenomena to mathematical laws. . . . Nature never ceases working with crafty slowness for the ruination of all our works. We buy the power of commanding artificial nature by incessant labor." This command does not come easily. Marx was mistaken insofar as he believed that a utopia of abundance and leisure would ever be achieved: "The more scientific our production becomes, the better we understand that our destiny is to labor without a truce and thus to annihilate the dreams of paradisiacal happiness that the old socialists had taken as legitimate anticipation."[22]

Readers of the ***Insegnamenti*** will be struck by the importance the work ethic plays in Sorel's analysis of economic ideologies. Artificial nature, as the struggle against natural nature, means a world of production. In natural nature we are no longer in the realm of production and invention, but are instead in the realm of consumption and leisure. Sorel's judgments about the "success" of a given civilization are based on this overcoming process sustained by work, and the same criteria are applied to the economic ideologies which emerge from these civilizations. In the ***Insegnamenti*** Sorel favors Marxism when it represents the struggle of the laborer or scientist, the triumph of *animal laborans* and the overcoming of Feuerbachian naturalism; he scorns Marxism when it becomes ossified into the platforms of "official" political parties which promise that a "land of milk and honey" will be delivered on the silver platter of progress.

Sorel can be for liberalism when it embodies these same "Protestant" virtues of enterprise, productivity, and the conquest of new frontiers. He scorns liberalism when it becomes "democratic," that is, when "petty philosophers devoured by ambition to become great men" transform the productive aspects of liberalism into rationalist utopias in which parasitic politicians and financiers devour the natural wealth through usury and the chicanery of legislative logrolling. In the ***Insegnamenti*** Sorel evaluates socialism and liberal capitalism in this manner. Each of the two views has its dynamic side in which it represents a partial *ricorso;* each has fallen into decay. The twofold nature of these ideologies constitutes the theme of this book whose contents we shall now analyze in detail.

Sorel divides the ***Insegnamenti*** into four parts (an introduction and three parts). While many themes in each part overlap with those in other sections, the attentive reader can discern a basic theme in each part as well as a general theme for the whole book. The introductory segment announces the overall theme of the work, and it is interesting to note that a book on economic doctrine should have an especially political thesis. The ***Insegnamenti*** is, first and foremost, an attack on the time-honored notion of community solidarity whose Platonic and Aristotelian versions are expressed in the formulations of natural sociability and social obligation and which found its most enduring historical example in the church, "the most perfect example" of a completely duty-bound society "whose mission is to preach to the ruling classes their obligations toward the poor."[23]

Sorel stresses the great similarities found in the justifications for social unity in both the old and new political theories. Despite vast differences among various theories of sociability, the classical political theories resemble the modern Fourierian and Saint-Simonian utopias as well as Kantian ideas in regard to the permanence of the laws of nature. In much the same way as Plato attempted to apply to society the Greek philosophy of science—a science based on the need to rationalize everything by replacing the changing phenomenal world with the immutable laws of mathematics—so the nineteenth-century utopian socialists attempted to eliminate chance from human affairs. In Sorel's view, Kant too based his theories of social duty on the absolute harmony between the exigencies of reason and the methods of Newtonian physics. The Fourierian and positivist utopias were constructed in the same way as were philosophical explanations of matter. Fourier even aspired to the planetary regularity of Laplacean astronomy.[24]

The failure to recognize the difference between physical and social science, and more importantly, between natural and artificial nature within the physical sciences, meant, in Sorel's view, that naturalistic social theories would establish a social unity that would correspond to the one that supposedly existed in the physical world. Despite the great differences between physical and social sciences, Sorel regarded theories of social unity and community as corresponding to "natural nature" in the physical world.

For Sorel, this meant that utopian socialism was little different from the other social theories used to justify decadent societies. Most political and ethical theories, as Sorel later made clear, "take as their starting point . . . books written for declining societies; when Aristotle wrote the *Nichomachean Ethics,* Greece had already lost her own reasons for morality." The moral principles set forth in this work and in classical political philosophy, generally reflected "the habits which a young Greek had to take up by frequenting cultivated society. Here we are in the realm of consumer morality. . . . War and production had ceased to concern the most distinguished people in the towns."[25]

What is true for classical political philosophy, in Sorel's view, is even more true in the modern setting. Despite their pretensions to philosophical precision and abstraction, modern ethical and political utopias are characterized by the ease with which their utopian elements are carried over into programs for improving the existing order. The Saint-Simonian ideas on administration corresponded to the Napoleonic ideas of bureaucracy and social hierarchy; duty is expressed in the Prussian land law of 1794. Ninety years later, Bismarck proclaimed to the Reichstag that he intended to imbue his social legislation with the principles found in that law and stated that "it is a state concern to care for the maintenance of the citizenry who are unable to procure those same means of subsistence."[26] To Sorel, such proposals, and similar ones contained in socialist programs, demonstrated an almost uncanny continuity between the ancient and medieval philosophies of charity and social duty and the modern notions of welfare and economic right; between the paternalism of the lord of the manor who justified his social position on the basis of "natural law" and the *dirigisme* of the modern welfare state bureaucrat who justifies his power on the "right" of citizens to subsistence. The modern social welfare state, whose development Sorel foresees in this work, will be, in his view, deeply reactionary.

Not only is there a certain continuity in social policy in the old and new regimes as well as in the declining cities of antiquity, but the elite of the old regime shares many characteristics with those of the new ruling classes. Not only is the authoritarianism of the old court bureaucrats reproduced in the new society, but both elites are in decline, separated from war and productivity and become fundamentally urban in both their social attraction to the *beau monde* of salons or wealthy artistic patrons and in the consumer habits fostered by the urban environment.

Sorel concludes the introduction with a fascinating discussion of the effects of urbanism on moral decadence—its resistance to productivity in virtually all branches of industry save those devoted to luxury items consumed by tourists and courtesans.

The extraordinary pessimism shown by Sorel regarding moral theories and utopias does not extend to all philosophers and theories. In part I of the ***Insegnamenti*** Sorel deals with the economic, social, and psychological conditions which give rise to social theories which avoid the decadent quality of the ancient viewpoints. Since decadent theories embodied the spirit and the letter of social solidarity, Sorel argues that theories take on dynamic qualities when they partake of what he variously calls the "spirit of separation" or "the organization of revolt," clearly manifested in the Marxian view of the class struggle and in revolutionary syndicalism.[27] Here we find Sorel arguing that socialist ideas, like those of liberalism, have achieved their highest degree of vitality when they have attained the highest degree of independence from the notion of social totality; that is, when they have attained their most refined diremption. At this point a theory's explanatory power is most complete.

Sorel regarded ideas as being far more important than the epiphenomena depicted by vulgar Marxists. As he states it in the first chapter of this section, ideas rely more on antecedent theoretical formations, historical knowledge, and (especially) memories of past conflicts than on economic phenomena. Thus the socialist idea cannot be explained by economic factors alone because "the attitudes that man takes in the presence of reality are highly variable according to circumstances."[28]

From Vico, Sorel derived the idea of the importance of the psychological aspects of social movements. Vico suggested that memories of past struggles were expressed in "psychological concatenations" which members of a society experienced in the passage from one regime to another.[29] The difficulty with these notions, which Sorel saw very early in his writing career, was that Vico's concept of psychological upheaval did not always square with another notion Sorel derived from Vico, the idea that "man knows what he makes," which found its way into the Marxian theory of knowledge and, in a somewhat different form, into Sorel's theory of artificial nature. In Sorel's thought psychological upheavals were connected more directly than in Marxism to moral upheavals. There was in Sorel an autonomy of moral thought absent from conventional Marxism. How was Sorel to picture a psychological state without reverting to the very intellectualism he had condemned in rationalist utopias?

Sorel found a solution to this dilemma in an interpretation of these psychological states as "myths" which he depicts as states of mind roughly analogous to those accompanying religious conversion. Myths are highly subjective, and thus inevitably partial rather than societal. Thus in anticipating, subjectively, a total moral catastrophe, as for example in the Christian vision of the second coming of Christ, the very totality of the vision forced its adherents to isolate themselves from the larger society. The more total the vision, the higher the degree of psychological upheaval, and the more partial, the more isolated was the movement carried on in its name. For Sorel, psychological concatenations or myths are self-limiting and as such they inevitably produce only partial *ricorsi.* In a word, myths "dirempted" themselves from the totality.

Added to the paradox of a total vision becoming self-limiting was the notion that the more self-limiting the social boundaries of the new movement whose members had experienced psychological upheavals, the more effective their teaching became. What started as a total vision of catastrophe ended in transforming the world precisely by dint of the isolation the visionaries had imposed on themselves. Sorel responded to the difficulty of severing psychological upheavals from the productive process by separating mythical and scientific thought. Sorel does this largely by accepting what William James was later to call a distinction between the religious and the philosophical points of view. Religious or mythical points of view see the world subjectively, or, as Sorel expresses it here, they are like "optical devices turned around before our eyes and which mute the relative value of things." They obscure objectivity and are thus the opposite of scientific thought.

But to argue for the separation, for analytical purposes, of mythical from scientific thought is not to say that there are no relations between the mythical and scientific realms—especially if the science in question is economics. The relationship between mythical and economic thought is one of the most interesting questions that arises in the course of reading Sorel's works. The most explicit treatment of this relationship is in ***Reflections on Violence,*** where Sorel treats the myth of the general strike in syndicalist theory. This myth allows the subject to anticipate the future in which he feels certain his cause is to triumph. The subject does this without recourse to the historical "dialectics" of Marxian "science"—a rationalistic diremption having lost sight of its own limits and presuppositions.

Yet the myth too is a diremption because it is severed from its scientific offspring. It performs in economic life what the poetic spirit of invention performs in scientific life. It allows us to break out of the circle of the given. The myth of the general strike reinforces the feelings of heroic struggle against the enemies of the working class and the forces of natural nature. Even if there is nothing intrinsically scientific in the images of conflict engendered by the myth, the myth still has a scientific function in that such a struggle is a spur to creativity and hence to productivity. The myth is not an economic product; it is not as much acted upon by the economy as *it* acts upon the economy. It performs a role analogous to that which Sorel, in the present volume, assigns to heroic Norse and Homeric tales of historic legends of searches for lost treasure. These legends and tales produced a sort of intoxication in the minds of Medieval German metallurgists; they thereby encouraged the industry which was so important to the prosperity and independence of the old German cities.[30]

Sorel only touches on the role of his theory of myth in the ***Insegnamenti,*** but he does provide helpful explanatory analogies to his conception of myth in his discussions of religion. He suggests that the development of mythical or religious thought can be viewed over time in the form of a bell-shaped curve in which the peak of vitality in the history of a religious belief is found at the mid-point between, on the one hand, an utterly primitive superstition which takes the form of magic, the pseudoscience which attempts to "explain" spiritual and physical totality, and on the other hand, a highly sophisticated liberal religion such as Enlightenment pantheism or Renan's relaxed Christianity, which attempted to justify itself on the terrain of the sciences by giving "rational" explanations of Biblical miracles.

In both extremes we find doctrine enmeshed in the totality of nature—in a sort of theological natural nature. The mythical or heroic period of religion, its highest point of vitality, is the point at which mystical or mythical components predominate over pantheistic naturalistic or pseudoscientific magical aspects. Exponents of this heroic religion are neither unitarians, pantheists, nor witch doctors. Nourished by holy legends and great efforts of resistance, the mystic insists on an "absolute cleavage"[31] between his own beliefs and those of others. At this point, at which "science" has been rejected, religion, ironically, most closely approximates the diremptive efforts of the laboratory scientist or the inventor. Religion comes closest to science when it has most firmly excluded science from its realm, just as science attains its most dynamic point when it excludes religion, theology, and holistic philosophy from its realm. At this point religion (like science) attains its greatest meaning for its professors, its highest explanatory power for the believer, in no small part because of its centrality in the life of the believer who must devote much effort to preserving the integrity of the faith by severing it from other ideas.[32]

In Sorel's view, like mystical religion, myth is separated from social totality and, like religion, solidifies certain ties with the world in the very process of reaffirming itself. In the case of certain religions and certain myths, these ties are with the economic world. The Nordic myths that were so important to the German miners' search for treasure have a counterpart in the faith of the early Protestant sectarians in England and America, whose beliefs strongly encouraged economic virtues even though there was no overt economic dogma in the early stages of the development of these beliefs.[33] Belief intersects with the material world at the point of economic productivity, and its vitality is measured in terms of its economic efficacy. (This is one of the themes of Sorel's ***La ruine du monde antique.)***[34]

Sorel makes approximately the same claims for economic beliefs, only in reverse. Just as religion takes on a pecurliarly decadent quality when it attempts to ape scientific thinking and explain everything rationally, economic doctrine becomes moribund when it takes on the allure of a general belief system—when its diremptions have lost their empirical (hence limited) moorings and float free in a rationalistic totality. The particular example of the decay of economic dogma Sorel gives us in this section is the development of the labor theory of value and its particular Marxian applications. Sorel suggests that the labor theory of value had a useful application in early British political economy inspired by observations made in the operations of the British cotton industry. Soon this idea became transformed into a total system and deductions were made from these early observations in much the same way "as ancient physics was derived from the heavens."[35] In Marx's hands, labor is treated as a universal entity which is fairly nearly the same in all times, places, and circumstances. For instance, Marx said that there was little difference between skilled and unskilled labor and that any differences among workers were largely a matter of quantitative determination. To Sorel this universality was unfortunate. By assuming that all industries are equivalent and all workers reduced to a uniform type, the labor theory of value leads us to a homogeneous capitalism in which identical values of labor are exchanged. The result is that labor, which should be the basis of productive virtues, is now reduced to the process of exchange of equivalent values.[36] In Sorel's view, as long as socialism remains beguiled by this circular theory of value exchange, it will never be revolutionary. Instead, Marxism has remained steadfast to what is essentially a bourgeois law of Ricardo; it has merely replaced the fetishism of commodities with that of labor. "Isn't it odd," asks Sorel, "that socialism comes to regularize the order that, according to Marx, would be stabilized spontaneously and in large part in the manner of capitalist production?"[37]

What is worse, in Sorel's eyes, is that if such movements of the economy can be reduced to such simplistic calculations, Marxists are thereby encouraged to calculate other social movements through the same reductions. Marx and Engels "believed that they could (like the physicist) uncover laws as inevitable as that of gravitation."[38] As Marx himself puts it in *Capital,* "capitalistic production begets its own negation with the inevitability that presides over the metamorphosis of nature."[39] Such "scientific" predictions, if taken literally, lead to the utopian expectations of the social democrats who expect the progress of history to deliver the revolution to them. Such expectations not only discourage socialist action, but the vitality of the socialist movement becomes sapped, and the productive virtues which stem from the psychological tension that arises in the course of socialist action are replaced by a rationalistic pseudosocialist science of nature, a social "natural nature."

Elsewhere,[40] Sorel gives a perfect example of the scholasticism of the Marxian theory of value. If labor value can be calculated with certainty, the corollary theory of surplus value wherein the proprietor "steals" labor time from the worker can also be calculated precisely. By the abolition of capitalism, the precise and just compensation for the worker can supposedly be deduced. Authoritarian laws will be passed legislating the "just price" of labor in a harkening back to medieval concepts. Such concepts only lead to idyllic welfare utopias of a socialist land of milk and honey, of a consumers' paradise. In any case, they are not revolutionary, but based on a "medieval nostalgia," of which Marx was guilty at times in Sorel's view.[41] Such a nostalgia was part of the basis of Sorel's critique of the French and German social democratic parties whose scholasticism was in harmony with the current order because of their emphasis on consumption rather than production. The bell-shaped curve which Sorel observed in religious thought has now been replicated in the economic "science" of socialism. The more Marxism emphasizes the importance of the labor theory of value and like formulas, the more similar it becomes to the primitive socialism it professes to criticize. Holistic religious magic, which found its parallel in Fourier's magical visions, has now come full circle to the universalistic science of the human economy.

The question remains as to what is left in the labor theory of value that has a valid place in economic explanation. Is it possible to make a diremption from the labor theory which rejuvenates its scientific vitality and in which it intersects with the heroic myths? Sorel analyzes the positive aspects of the theory of the labor contract which "abolishes all bonds between the employer and the employee: after the presentation of his labor merchandise . . . the worker is in the same position vis-à-vis the master as a grocer is in regard to the customer who comes to buy coffee."[42] A strictly business relationship abolishes all social solidarity; employer and employee are mere buyers and sellers. Objectively, they can pursue entirely opposite political goals and organize for the struggle against one another, and this is all to the good in Sorel's view.

What is interesting about this diremption is that it relies on legal as well as economic thought. Such a market arrangement can come about only when it is accompanied by a transformation in legal arrangements. At this point Sorel sees economic theory dovetailing with "outside" (or mythical) influences that give a theory the same vitality that "outside" (poetic) inspiration gives the process of science. Sorel concludes the first part of this book by stating that the only things the proletarians can know are "the principles of juridical rules that the victorious class will impose on society after its victory."[43] In such considerations, Marxism makes an economico-juridical diremption: "It knows only the worker and takes him as he has been conditioned by the historical conditions of capitalism."[44] This is the least metaphysical and most scientific aspect of labor theory.

But by itself, this theory is no more able to produce working-class action than scientific theory can of itself generate further scientific advancement. Neither the spirit of class struggle nor the struggle against nature can be derived solely from science because, in themselves, neither of these struggles is purley scientific. Both must be inspired by a poetry. Socialism, as the organization of revolt, must be guided by a myth which "expresses with perfect clarity the principle of the separation of classes, a principle which is the whole of socialism."[45] Sorel's readers, as we have noted, were to await an elaboration of the content of the myth in ***Reflections on Violence.*** In the ***Insegnamenti*** Sorel is content to argue that both mythical and economic (as well as scientific) thought become most efficacious when they embody the spirit of separation. Myth and science—especially economic science—are inverse bell-curves of each other and achieve their highest dynamism when their peaks intersect.

But how, we might ask, can Sorel criticize the labor theory of value for its conservative implications at the hands of orthodox Marxism, when his own theory of the labor contract is quintessentially bourgeois, a bedrock of economic liberalism? It would appear that, in Sorel's eyes, liberalism and socialism have a good deal in common, and it is precisely this issue that is addressed in the second part of the ***Insegnamenti.***

In Part II, Sorel deals with the parallels between socialism and liberal capitalsim, pointing out that they have as much in common as they have differences, and that it is this very commonality which, ironically, sustains their separation from each other, both morally and intellectually when expressed in their dynamic forms. But commonality is also found in the degenerative forms of the two ideologies.

This section starts off with a comparison of two types of degenerative social thought, socialist utopias—especially Fourier's—and "bourgeois" democratic theories—Rousseau's in particular. Sorel maintains that there are strong resemblances between these two categories of thought which, if taken in certain ways, have particularly onerous social consequences. In Sorel's view, both sets of theories rely heavily on the notion of mathematical averages which, sometimes against the will of the inventors of these theories, bolsters state authoritarianism and arbitrary power. This authoritarianism in turn runs contrary to the productive virtues.

Sorel takes the thought of Charles Fourier as his archetypal utopian socialist. Fourier, relying on probability theory, allows passions and instincts free rein, regulating his utopian communities (or phalanxes) in such a way "as to obtain average results which translate precisely into natural laws. . . . A result will be obtained that will become independent of circumstances, and the entire society will have only to reproduce what was once produced on a small scale."[46] The uniformity of the world arises from "passional equilibriums" roughly analogous to those produced in free market theory.

In Sorel's opinion, Rousseau too was convinced by the importance of mathematical averages, which gave his theory of the general will a market orientation. In Rousseau the fatality of market relationships is transposed into the assembly in which the average opinion represents truth. Generalizing on the model of the almost completely mobile Swiss craftsman who, without roots, is able to move from job to job, Rousseau idealized *homo economicus* in such a way that "social atoms" would be obtained. The result would be a democratic government in which citizens, having had "no communication among themselves, the general will shall always result from the greater number of little differences, and their deliberations will always be good." Here, in Sorel's words, "the assembly produces reason as a prairie produces hay."[47]

In the case of both Fourier and Rousseau, we have instances of a breakdown of diremptions whose historico-empirical origins have been obscured. As a consequence of this obscuring process, economic theories (diremptions) are inappropriately applied to political phenomena. The result is that what starts out as a random multiplicity of wills and passions terminates in a passion for unity that can only be satisfied by state authoritarianism.[48] In Fourier we find a false analogy between passions and commodities. Fourier has blotted out the fact that his notion of mathematical averaging has its origins in the market, and has thus taken his passional equilibriums as an absolute mathematical truth. More importantly, he has ignored the fact that the inspiration for his own laxist moral system is found in the loose morality of the Napoleonic era and translates politically into the Napoleonic desire for a universal monarchy.

In Rousseau's case we find a political doctrine which cannot be directly translated from economic theory without grave dislocations. Assemblies are not markets; they possess political powers. The mathematical averages of the general will are not used by Rousseau as justifications for free, individual market choices, but rather for the suppression of the particular will by the city. Sorel argues that no general will is possible. In his view, no assembly can live up to Rousseau's maxim that, in expressing the general will, members of the assembly can have no communication among themselves. Rousseau has forgotten that the market orientation of *homo economicus* demands bargaining, and this form of communication is lacking in his ideal assembly. Bargaining on votes would result in the will of all, i.e., the sum of particular wills, and not the general will.

Sorel goes further than merely rejecting Rousseau's democratic theory, for he thinks that even if we reject the adequacy of Rousseau's argument and admit bargaining into the legislative process, in the manner of the *Federalist* or of American liberal pluralist theories, the transposition of market theory to the legislature fails. Not only do "pure" markets ignore legislation, but legislators all too readily ignore market conditions when power is connected to their own interests. Bargaining in assemblies means logrolling and influence peddling; tariff legislation and other restrictions come all too readily into being; the "free market" of legislative bargaining is thus a self-negating process. In Sorel's view, most legislators regard the prosperity of a group as depending on compromises with other groups to obtain a parliamentary majority. But when this majority is obtained, it can ruin any group which stands in its way and "annihilate a cumbersome competitor who is too weak to make the hungry wolves in parliament listen to reason."[49] Such a result, Sorel realized, was utterly contrary to Rousseau's idea, especially if it takes place in the representative assemblies that Rousseau scorned. Sorel's critique of legislative bargaining as an activity in which "both the revolutionary and the juridical spirit are extinguished at the same time" is covertly imitative of Rousseau. In any case, Sorel's critique of Rousseau and Fourier ranges far beyond the two thinkers and extends implicitly to a critique of Madison and of most liberal and democratic theory.

It would be a mistake to assume that Sorel is content with a criticism of the decadent moments of liberal democratic and socialist theories. Perhaps the most interesting aspects of part II consist in the parallels he draws between the two theories in their moments of greatest vitality. Here Sorel presents the dynamic aspects of socialism and liberalism not only as mirror images of their decadent counterparts, but as having strong similarities with each other.

The first similarity between the two schools is that they both attain their highest and most powerful moment when they do not extend their economic theories beyond their proper limits, that is, when their diremptions maintain their historical functions. Liberal theory was at its most triumphant stage when the idea of the free market was limited to the market and did not extend to analogies found in the political realm. "Commerce became quite powerful and capable when, and only when, nobody could see any longer what interest the state had in intervening to control it."[50] The idea of unity that had so transfixed Rousseau was now replaced by a division between economics and what Sorel scornfully called the magical power of the state. The state's old function as the great protector of industry was abandoned.[51]

Sorel interprets Marxism as possessing a general antistatist view similar to that of liberal, laissez-faire capitalism (or Manchesterism). This antistatist component of Marxism makes it, in contradistinction to socialist utopianism, the most virile socialist theory. In support of this view, Sorel points to Engels's assertion of the ultimate powerlessness of the state in the face of economic forces. If the state attempted to resist autonomous economic forces, in Engels's view, it would be destroyed; the state could only accelerate or retard development. Sorel was aware that Marx and Engels were not anarchists. But he insists that the idea of economic fatality was a far more important element in Marx's theory than was state action. For both Marxism and Manchesterism, "the combination of many events produces fatality of movement." Under such conditions, "it is possible to assign any cause to the same fact, and it is really a chance phenomenon; instead, the totality is so well determined that if anybody pretended to oppose the movement he would invariably be defeated."[52] In sum, the power of the economic theories of both capitalism and socialism lay in self-foreclosing their extension beyond economics, a self-imposed diremption.

A major consequence of the idea of economic inevitability in both capitalism and socialism is that both liberal capitalism and Marxism possess a view of historical development that foresees great sacrifice from their respective client classes. This sacrifice requires an ethic of struggle which is highly productive in the long run. Regarding liberal capitalism, Sorel argues that proprietors of most establishments had to change machinery or even abandon old enterprises altogether. Laissez-faire economics had the effect of imposing large fines on recalcitrant industries. Timidity was punished; boldness and innovation in the wrong direction could be equally disastrous. In regard to socialism, Marxist thought excuses the cruelest oppression in both past and present societies: slavery exploitation and despotism are necessary historical prerequisites to the development of capital, and capitalism is progressive.

The philosophy of struggle in both capitalism and Marxism is coupled with the view that events will develop "progressively." Free traders believe that their system will have the effect of satisfying every interest as products improve and prices become more reasonable. Similarly, for Marxists, the belief that the degradation of the working class under capitalism lays the ground for its future elevation is, Sorel argues, virtually identical to Manchesterism. To be sure, "the theoreticians of capitalism do not justify their judgments on the basis of the emancipation of the future proletariat, but this is the only difference."[53] In every other way, both theories are optimistic; both are certain that their cause will triumph. In Sorel's eyes, when this progressivism strayed from the economic realm into politics and other areas, this "certainty" degenerated into the "illusions of progress." But in its proper diremption, such a certainty has powerful psychological effects for economic practitioners—whether they be capitalists or socialists in their workshops.

Finally, both Marxism and Manchesterism regard political and historical developments as being "only a series of developments in the form of labor."[54] We have already mentioned that the idea of the labor contract is a juridical device accepted by both schools. Here we need only note Sorel's stress on the freedom the worker gains under such a system, in which the worker who has no ties to the master once his work has been performed thereby gains free labor time; conversely, the capitalist master is absolved of any paternalistic social duties to fulfill. Here we have the "perfect separation of classes through the encouragement of free labor time."

True to his own philosophy of science, Sorel insists that the self-limitation of diremption requires more than institutions, more than social "laboratory controls." For workers or capitalists to continue to rely only on the market without demanding state assistance requires extraordinary virtues not normally found among subject populations. Without the right character in the population, the free and fatalistic institutions of liberal capitalism as well as the factories run by free labor are doomed to failure.

Sorel is also aware that there are certain historical preconditions for the operation of these institutions. Free labor and free capital have, by virtue of their diremptive status, distorted the historical totality from which they have emerged. Certainly the development of the working classes is not produced as automatically as Marx believed it would; conversely, capitalist free markets and the advent of prosperity might coincide only accidently. Sorel maintains that government may play a more positive role in the development of the economy than allowed for by the Manchester school or even by Marxists. The presence of social legislation and government interference reveals the highly selective evidence cited by adherents of market fatality in support of their objections to government intervention. Just as liberal capitalism can have good and bad consequences depending on the uses to which it is put and the discipline to which its adherents subject themselves, so government interference in the economy has varying moral consequences according to its applications.

Sorel judges government intervention pragmatically, using the criteria of its effect on character and on the historical conditions under which the character develops. The historical possibilities of virtue constitute the main litmus test for the acceptability of government intervention in the economy, and to demonstrate this point Sorel takes two examples for discussion: tariffs and government legislation restricting the hours of labor (promotion of free labor time). In Sorel's view, protective tariffs can have various effects on a people, depending on their character. There are two types of protectionism: one is suitable for strong peoples, like Americans, who are growing in population and in wealth; the other is suitable for disheartened and lazy peoples with a stable population.

Sorel's other example is legislation that promotes free labor time so that the workers may develop their own autonomous institutions. It still leaves to the capitalists "the burden and profit of directing production for their own self-interest under certain legal conditions; let them leave socialism free to act on the working class, to educate it, and don't presume to 'civilize' it in the bourgeois way!"[55] On the other hand, Sorel observes that English workers use this free time in consumer and leisure activities, especially in sports and betting. Only a small and virile minority of English entrepreneurs has resisted the trend toward "laziness." This trend has increasingly gained sway among the British masses who, dominated by the desire for rest, "lack the power to think in a virile way."[56]

In both examples Sorel bases his evaluation of a people's character on the degree to which they are still willing to undertake struggles against nature and also against other classes, irrespective of the degree of government intervention in the economy. In the concluding portions of this section, Sorel renews his assertions that the index of that willingness is reflected in the degree to which a social group exhibits hostility toward the notion of social solidarity. There is a species of "symbiosis" among the three factors of social vitality, class antagonism, and productivity. As Sorel states it, "everything capitalism does to urge the workers on is a gain for socialism, whatever the opinions of ethical theorists or of the politicians always ready to encourage sloth."[57] Revolutionary socialism cannot have as its purpose the moderation of the progress of capitalism. Further on Sorel quotes Marx as saying: "The evolution of the conditions of existence for a large, strong, concentrated and intelligent class of proletarians comes about at the same rate as the development of the conditions of existence of a middle class correspondingly numerous, rich, concentrated and powerful."[58] In this quote from Marx, Sorel implies that the idea of increasing misery and especially the idea of the ever-diminishing productivity of capitalism contradicts Marx's suggestion that "there are never sufficient productive forces and . . . the capitalist class is never rich or powerful enough."[59]

We are left with the question of how these two opposing classes organize for the struggle. In ***Reflections on Violence*** Sorel deals with the organization of the working classes, but in the present work he concentrates on the organization of the capitalist class rather than on labor unions, for one obvious and urgent reason: "Capitalists have organized themselves in a methodical way; many people, moreover, estimate that the organization of the capitalists is progressing much more quickly than the organization of workers."[60] One type of organization in particular reflects this organizational superiority above all others: the cartel.

In the third and concluding section of the ***Insegnamenti,*** entitled "Cartels and Their Ideological Consequences," Sorel raises the same questions about cartels that he had raised about liberalism and socialism. While the first section of the work is devoted to the morally degenerative and regenerative side of socialism, and the second section concentrates on the similarities between socialism and liberalism in their various stages of moral development, the final part focuses on the regenerative and degenerative sides of capitalism and its corresponding ideologies and organizations, especially cartels.

In Sorel's view the cartel typifies a degenerative aspect of capitalist organization which finds a counterpart in the corruption of liberal political institutions. We will recall that in previous sections Sorel had criticized the liberal theory of legislative bargaining. In his view, capitalism, both in its corrupt beginnings and in its degenerative mature stages, is different from virile laissez-faire capitalism. Capitalism has its beginnings in a flaccid, feudal-style "collective seigneury" and it comes round full circle to conclude with an intimacy between cartels and state action. In both extremes of the continuum the power of government is harnessed to crush competitors. In both cases the virtues of laissez-faire capitalism, especially as represented in American and even German business, are being extinguished.

Sorel begins this section by discussing the institutions of the *ancien régime,* whose seigneuries resemble modern cartels in that both have had a species of eminent domain over the economic powers of their subjects, and this domain includes police and taxing powers. Both domains choose representatives to establish internal rules and defend their interests against outside forces. Just as the ancien régime's various estates were in large part cartels which deliberated and bargained on financial interests, so the cartels of modern times resolve their difficulties by sending delegates to mixed commissions, often including representatives of workers' organizations.

On the basis of this comparison between cartels and the ancien régime, Sorel comes out squarely against what we would call "functional representation." This feudalism, replicated in the industrial world, would entail the establishment of "little states": one for coal mines, one for mills, and so forth.[61] In previous sections Sorel objected to extending the diremption of *homo economicus* to the political arena. Now he reverses the argument: any extension of political analogies to the industrial regime will only succeed in corrupting both areas. Thus any form of what would later be called "corporativism" is utterly alien to Sorel's viewpoint—whether in the form of guild socialism, codetermination, or fascism. All these notions seem to share one familiar trait. They resemble modern democratic parliaments which are "not so much political bodies that legislate to realize a national ideal as they are medieval-style diets in which one undertakes diplomatic discussions among plenipotentiaries and which come to establish compromises among various interests."[62] In parliaments, corporate societies, and cartels we find the same blurring of economics and politics which Sorel had described as endemic to representative bodies where log-rolling leads to systematic annihilation of uncooperative competitors. In both cases a protectionism is solidified which transforms the state into a "benefactor of all those with no confidence in their personal strength." This system has the effect of producing renewed tendencies toward "social peace, moderation of desires, and respect for weakness" which ultimately regard consensus as the highest social duty.[63]

The emphasis on the need for consensus and for bargaining in parliamentary bodies brings Sorel to an interesting comparison between cartels and political parties. In Sorel's view cartels and political parties are not only functionally dependent on consensus and solidarity, but are invariably based on systems of representation with a hierarchical structure. Here the "admiration of the electors for the elected" arises from a superstitious veneration for the representative. The representative, in turn, legitimizes his position by virtue of his increased familiarity with the "official world." This veneration is a buttress for the ideal of community solidarity.

Not only does Sorel replicate Rousseau's antagonism to representation here, but he anticipates what Roberto Michels would later call "the iron law of oligarchy," which states that even professedly democratic organizations produce leadership cadres that are self-perpetuating and nonresponsible to their constituents.[64] Like Michels, Sorel argues that both cartels and parties coopt the potential leaders of workers' movements. For Sorel these leaders were potential forces for social tension, and the "negation" necessary for social vitality. Once this vitality is sapped by cooptation, according to Sorel, social life degenerates into what Herbert Marcuse would later call "one dimensionality."[65]

Worse still, oligarchic corporativism discourages men of real talent and replaces them with men who possess "political skills." This perverse value system helps to undermine the ideal of production, which gives way to the consumers' ideal of just distribution. Hand in hand with the idea of just distribution is the erroneous notion that the spare time resulting from decreased labor time should be spent in politics. "There is no popular instinct more powerful than that which pushes man into laziness: democracy especially regards man as obliged to occupy his time in politics and has never understood the law of labor."[66]

Implicitly, Sorel appears to be endorsing Aristotle's idea of the best possible democratic regime in which the best material for citizenship is found in the agricultural population. "Being poor, citizens have no leisure and therefore do not attend the assembly, and, not having the necessities of life, they are always at work and do not covet the property of others. Indeed they find their employment pleasanter than the cares of government or office."[67] According to Sorel, the opposite view of citizenship prevails in modern democracies, where the triumph of Kantian ideals is complete and men are no longer seen as means (of production or anything else). Instead we have an "ideology of supreme ends."[68]

Sorel's strong indictment of cartels and corporativism is qualified in much the same way as was his condemnation of protectionism and social legislation in the previous section. With cartels, as with protectionism and social laws, one must take account of the character of the people with whom we are dealing. The spirit of enterprise found in the practices of the great American financiers who organized American trusts has a completely different character from the European outlook. The German cartel is not like the American trust because, unlike the German cartel, the trust is "the result of a life and death struggle."[69] In America, unlike modern Germany, "we are in the presence of a population that has preserved to the highest degree the rural, combative, and dominant characteristics which gave them a certain resemblance to feudal knights."[70] As Sorel noted elsewhere, this feudal warrior type "was pushed to its extreme in the American cowboy . . . admirable in the face of danger, insouciant, intemperate, improvident, and animated with the spirit of liberty."[71] This independent spirit made Americans "the most daring people in existence," who defend their intellectual, moral, and civic independence as surely as they defend their property. Behind the facade of democratic political institutions in America there is an aristocracy, not of birth, but of ability and energy, personified in

Carnegie and Roosevelt, warrior types who look upon life as a struggle instead of a pleasure. Here is an "aristocracy of power," not the European "aristocracy of weakness."[72] The character of this aristocracy means in practical terms that even the most "reactionary" and unproductive form of capitalism, usury capitalism, has a unique character when practiced by the great American financiers whose spirit of enterprise is so strong. Sorel does not praise the trusts; he is simply stating that the historical conditions in America are such that trusts do not become a serious impediment to productivity.

The American spirit of enterprise has allowed the trusts to operate independently of the state. The few connections the trusts do have with political forces in the United States are of little consequence because American politicians "are universally regarded as rascals but have the ability not to interfere too much with the progress of business."[73] Economic and political power have sustained a separation in the United States, and this division between economic and political life makes the American economy the most dynamic and vital force in the otherwise decaying, bourgeois world. As Sorel stated in the previous section, this divorce of politics and economics is the greatest contribution of liberal thought. He has "dirempted" the positive aspects of liberalism which emphasize divided or checked power from those involving representative democracy.

The separation of politics from economics also means that liberalism can implicitly sustain a distinction between corruption and decadence.[74] Degeneration signifies the laxity of an entire culture—or a good part of it—while corruption can be confined to a small group of politicians and even, in the American case, function as a device to prevent degeneration of the larger society: corrupt politicians in America limit the extent to which the state can effectively intervene in the larger economy. In this case, the self-restraint of the state does not become a virtue; Sorel has reversed the argument of classical liberalism. Rather than private vices becoming public virtues—the standard moral justification for the free market—in Sorel's view public vices now enhance private virtues.

For Sorel the American experience also helps to confound traditional Marxian theory. The latter distinguishes three types of capitalism: primitive usury, commercial capitalism, and industrial capitalism. While accepting this typology as useful, Sorel points out that they do not succeed one another in serial fashion as some Marxists have argued. He insists that in most modern times there has been a mixture of the three. As his example, Sorel cites American trusts which, despite the advanced nature of the American economy, closely resemble usury capitalism. On the other hand, German cartels are largely marketing agreements and therefore resemble commercial capitalism.

One further element of Sorel's critique of cartels deserves mention. The social democrats of his day often cited cartels as an advanced form of capitalism because they were close in form and substance to state socialism and therefore constituted, in their eyes, a sort of final stage of the capitalist era. In Sorel's view no such interpretation is justified. Here Sorel appears to have reversed the social democratic argument. Rather than linking cartels and the state as forward-looking and progressive, he regards them as backward and unproductive. Once again the union of economics and politics, between state authority and production, can only result in the decadence of both capitalism and socialism. In misconstruing the role of the state, socialism decays, and "the degradation of socialism is everywhere accompanied by moral decadence, at least in our democratic countries."

What is the proper role of the state? There is some irony in Sorel's rejection of politics as an activity. In his complete embrace of *animal laborans,* it would appear that Sorel is totally opposed to the thesis of people like Hannah Arendt who insist on the autonomy of politics as a realm of self-revelation and fulfillment.[75] Yet in insisting that politics remain separate from the economic realm, Sorel appears to be arguing that each realm should reassume the dignity that had been denied it. For Sorel, politics would be an arena for the discussion of "a national ideal" or of "general principles," while economics would emphasize productivity without invading the political realm and transforming it into "national housekeeping," to use Arendt's term.

In other places Sorel, while not an anarchist, seems to scorn political life as such, and this scorn leaves Sorel's political thought shadowy. He argues that the pluralism of political centers of power is a good thing. But since he argues that a diremption such as market pluralism cannot be carried over into the legislative arena without disastrous consequences, the balanced equation that existed in liberalism between the pluralistic view of economics and its corresponding view of politics as bargaining is now abolished in Sorel's hands. So too is Marx's assumption that the state is little more than a handmaiden of ruling-class interests. But then what is left of government? The rather vague notion that politics should be an activity that concerns the discussion of "general principles" or "the national ideal" was not given much refinement by Sorel either in this work or in ***Reflections on Violence.*** It was not until 1913 and especially 1919 and the publication of ***De l'Utilité du pragmatisme*** that Sorel elaborated on the role of politics. Before that time, Sorel's implacable hostility to politics is inspired in large part by the traditions of French statism and centralization. In 1913, however, he juxtaposes the reality of sovereign authority in modern Europe to the memory of medieval Germanic kingships in which royalty did not execute tasks directly but remained mere "proprietors" of the crown. Surrounding the monarchies were networks of "true republics, the church, universities, religious orders, and corporations of all kinds."[76]

The authority structure of these "true republics" was based less on persuasion or force than on symbols, myths, and the ordering of groups of activities belonging incontestably to the same type and whose participants followed the opinions of men of experience and possessing "incontestable dignity." Political authority does not exist here as much as "social authority" or rather a complex array of social authorities. Such authorities Sorel calls *cités,* but they are not so much cities as institutions that are themselves highly authoritative and devoid of political power of the state. We find such authorities in science (*cité savante*), art (*cité esthétique*), society (the American business aristocracy which he calls the *cité morale*), and in socialism (the syndicalist carriers of the general strike myth). It is the authority rather than the politics of the cities that Sorel admires, because they scorn the bargaining, the persuasion, or the force of the state and limit their scope to their respective arenas of experience.[77]

That is why it is not only bargaining in the political realm that is unsatisfactory to Sorel, but even in the present volume he goes so far as to criticize it in the realm to which it is properly suited, the economic realm itself. Here as in ***Reflections on Violence,*** Sorel appears to condemn bargaining even between unions and management, and instead argues for a union movement that remains implacably hostile to having anything to do with the bourgeoisie. Yet Sorel's decentralized vision of socialist labor unions in the new society gave way to the reality of a labor movement with the same oligarchic tendencies and the same proclivity for bargaining he had condemned in political parties. These tendencies were already apparent to Sorel and are discussed in the last section of this work. Sorel's pragmatic myth of the general strike was already in the process of giving way to an even more pragmatic strategy of striking for more improved "consumer" benefits. In any case, Sorel's adherence to a labor movement as the motive force for a secular second-coming can only bring smiles today.

How valid is Sorel's critique of social unity in regard to its supposed undermining of productive virtues? Sorel's attack on social unity, whether of democracy, guild socialism, or (in the final section) any corporate state notions should give the lie to those who see in his thought a prelude to "fascist notions." Sorel's view of corporatism and of the state, and of social cohesion and community is generally the antithesis of fascism and owes much to liberalism. But there is no denying the powerful productive forces that social unity, in some form or another, has unleashed, especially in the modified corporatism of Japan or the profit-sharing and codetermination plans of West Germany and Sweden. The relatively unsolidaristic liberalism of the United States is appearing increasingly unproductive in comparison with these highly cohesive societies.

On the other hand, social insolidarity represents a stage in the development of a group whose conscious revolt against the existing order sustained by revolutionary myths has positive moral consequences for its adherents as is evidenced by the early stages of the Black Muslim sect in the United States. Sorel is useful to us today in the examination of sects such as the Muslims in seeing how their activities correspond to his sociology of virtue, the social and ideological bases that produce great transformations in a people or civilization. Sorel's concern with the subject of virtue has not been a prominent interest of academicians over the years, except perhaps in Nietzsche studies, and only recently have we seen a revival of interest in it on the part of philosophers with social science concerns.[78]

There is still another reason for an interest in Sorel, and that lies in the realm of social science methods. Sorel's method of diremption is a forceful supplement to Weber's ideal types, and as such provides a helpful guide to the evaluation of both social beliefs and movements.

NOTES

[1] Both *Réflexions sur la violence* and *Les Illusions du progrès* were originally published in the syndicalist journal *Mouvement Socialiste* in 1906 and in book form in 1908 by the publisher Marcel Rivirère. Excerpts from both works are translated in John L. Stanley (ed.), *From Georges Sorel* (New York: Oxford University Press, 1976).

[2] Georges Sorel, *Le Procès de Socrate* (Paris: Alcan, 1889).

[3] See John L. Stanley, *The Sociology of Virtue: The Political and Social Theories of Georges Sorel* (Berkeley, Los Angeles, and London: University of California Press, 1981).

[4] Letter to Benedetto Croce, 6 May 1907, *Critica,* 26 (20 March 1928): 100.

[5] Georges Sorel, "Etude sur Vico," *Devenir Social* (December 1896): 1020.

[6] Jean Variot (ed.), *Propos de Georges Sorel* (Paris: Gallimard, 1935). Statement of 14 November 1908.

[7] Edouard Dolléans, "Le Visage de Georges Sorel," *Revue d'Histoire Economique et Sociale* 26 (no. 2, 1947): 106-107. Citing letter of 13 October 1912.

[8] *From Georges Sorel,* p. 210.

[9] William James, *Varieties of Religious Experience* (New York: Mentor, 1958), pp. 22-23.

[10] Sorel, "Etude sur Vico" (October 1896): 794-95 (November): 916, 919.

[11] Georges Sorel, *De l'Utilité du pragmatisme* (Paris: Rivière, 1919), p. 4 and note.

[12] *Oxford English Dictionary,* Vol. 3, p. 394. The verb *dirempt,* first used in English in 1561, was derived from the Latin *diremere,* to separate or divide.

[13] *From Georges Sorel,* p. 228, citing *Reflections on Violence,* p. 259.

[14] *From Georges Sorel,* pp. 235, 231.

[15] Ibid, pp. 239, 344, n. 52.

[16] *Social Foundations of Contemporary Economics,* p. 81.

[17] Sorel deals with this question in "La préoccupation métaphysique des physiciens modernes," *Cahiers de Quinzaine* (16th *Cahier,* 8th series, 1901). This work was largely incorporated into chapter 4 of *De l'Utilité du pragmatisme* under the title "L'expérience dans la physique moderne."

[18] "La science et la morale," in *Questions de Morale* (Paris: Alcan, 1900), p. 7.

[19] Ibid., p. 15 (Sorel's italics).

[20] Ibid., p. 7.

[21] Ibid., p. 2.

[22] *From Georges Sorel,* p. 369, n. 33.

[23] *Social Foundations,* pp. 53, 56.

[24] Georges Sorel, "Vues sur les problèmes de la philosophie," *Revue de Métaphysique et de Morale* 18 (December 1910):609.

[25] Georges Sorel, review of Fouillée, *Eléments sociologiques de la morale* in *Revue générale de bibliographie* (December 1905):489; *From Georges Sorel,* p. 216.

[26] *Social Foundations,* p. 54.

[27] Ibid., p. 169.

[28] Ibid., p. 108.

[29] Ibid., p. 107.

[30] Ibid., pp. 106, 313.

[31] See Sorel, *Reflections on Violence,* p. 184; idem, *Le Système historique de Renan,* passim.

[32] See Georges Sorel, *La ruine du monde antique* (Paris: Rivière, 3rd ed., 1933), for an analysis of early Christianity in this regard.

[33] *Reflections,* p. 125n; *From Georges Sorel,* p. 335, n. 7.

[34] Sorel, *La ruine du monde antique,* pp. 16-17.

[35] *Social Foundations,* p. 150.

[36] Ibid., pp. 151-55.

[37] Ibid., p. 155.

[38] Ibid., p. 166.

[39] Ibid., p. 168. Cf. Marx, *Capital* (New York: Modern Library, n.d.), p. 837.

[40] See *From Georges Sorel,* pp. 152-53; Sorel, "Sur la Théorie marxiste de la valeur," *Journal des Economistes* (May 1897):215.

[41] Georges Sorel, *Lettres à Paul Delesalle,* ed. André Prudhommeaux (Paris: Grasset, 1947). Letter of 9 May 1918, p. 139.

[42] Sorel presents this view of the labor contract in *Social Foundations,* pt. II, ch. 8, p. 234.

[43] *Social Foundations,* p. 167.

[44] Ibid., p. 168.

[45] Ibid., pp. 170-71.

[46] Ibid., p. 186.

[47] Ibid., p. 70.

[48] Ibid., p. 184.

[49] Ibid., p. 214.

[50] Ibid., p. 205.

[51] Ibid.

[52] Ibid., pp. 199-200.

[53] Ibid., p. 201.

[54] Ibid., p. 200.

[55] Ibid., p. 216.

[56] Ibid., p. 217.

[57] Ibid., p. 237.

[58] Ibid., p. 289. Cf. Karl Marx, *Revolution and Counter-Revolution of Germany in 1848* (Chicago: Charles Kerr, n.d.), p. 22.

[59] *Social Foundations,* p. 289.

[60] Ibid., p. 281.

[61] Ibid., p. 265.

[62] Ibid., p. 267.

[63] Ibid., p. 297.

[64] Roberto Michels, *Political Parties,* trans. Eden and Cedar Paul (Glencoe: Free Press, 1958).

[65] Herbert Marcuse, *One Dimensional Man* (Boston: Beacon, 1964).

[66] *Social Foundations,* p. 292.

[67] Aristotle, *Politics,* 1318 a 38—b 20.

[68] *Social Foundations,* pp. 293, 296.

[69] Ibid., p. 310, citing De Rousiers, *Les Syndicats industriels,* p. 125.

[70] Ibid.

[71] Georges Sorel, review of Paul de Rousiers, *La Vie américaine: ranches, ferms, et usines, Revue Internationale de Sociologie* (October 1899): 744-45.

[72] *From Georges Sorel,* pp. 213-14; *Social Foundations,* pp. 311-12.

[73] *Social Foundations,* p. 289.

[74] I am indebted to Richard Vernon for this observation.

[75] See Hannah Arendt, *The Human Condition* (Chicago: University of Chicago Press, 1958).

[76] Georges Sorel, "Germanismo e storicismo di Ernesto Renan," *Critica* 29 (March-November 1931), citing Renan, *Questions Contemporaines* (Paris: Levy, 1868), p. 15.

[77] Sorel, *De l'Utilité du pragmatisme,* ch. 2; *From Georges Sorel,* pp. 257-83.

[78] Alasdair MacIntyre, *After Virtue* (Notre Dame, Ind.: University of Notre Dame Press, 1979).

Michael Tager (essay date 1986)

SOURCE: "Myth and Politics in the Works of Sorel and Barthes," in *Journal of the History of Ideas,* Vol. 47, No. 4, October-December, 1986, pp. 625-39.

[*In the following excerpt, Tager compares the theses of Roland Barthes and Sorel.*]

I. Roland Barthes once argued that in France the bourgeoisie lost its cultural voice during the Dreyfus Affair, when its writers and intellectuals released it.[1] In the eighteenth century intellectuals had championed the cause of the bourgeois individual against aristocratic privilege, but grew increasingly ambivalent about the triumphant bourgeoisie during the nineteenth century, and finally at the end of the nineteenth century were decisively detached from their native class by the aftershocks of the Dreyfus Affair. With the opening of the twentieth century landowners, employers, senior civil servants, and executives no longer had congenial access to intellectual culture because it called their very existence as a class into question. That the antibourgeois impulse of the French "clerks" has remained quite strong through the twentieth century is suggested by the similarity between the statement of Georges Sorel in the introduction to his most famous work that even if none of his ideas bore fruit, "I do not believe I am laboring in vain—for in this way I help to ruin the prestige of middle-class culture,"[2] and Barthes's claim that "the intellectual's (or the writer's) historical function, today, is to maintain and emphasize the decomposition of bourgeois consciousness."[3]

Barthes realized that this historical shift placed intellectuals in a tenuous position. Detached from the bourgeoisie, many sought to represent the proletariat. Yet the spread of bourgeois (now "mass") culture to the proletariat largely cut off that way of rapprochement. Indeed, the attack on bourgeois culture, settled in the universities so long, itself became an orthodoxy and integrated into the functioning of society. The search for an agent capable of transforming society led Sorel successively toward Marxism, syndicalism, nationalism, and Bolshevism, and perhaps on to other stages, had he lived beyond 1922. Barthes, too, worked successively under the aegis of various systems as ways of dismantling bourgeois ideals. Through their intellectual peregrinations both authors developed theories of myth, in Sorel's case to explain how the transformation of society did and would occur, and in Barthes's case to explain the continued hegemony of bourgeois norms. I shall examine those theories of myth, particularly for their political implications. Starting with a similar revulsion against contemporary society and a desire for radical change, Sorel and Barthes ironically created two very different dichotomies of myth and politics that reflected their own temperaments, changed historical conditions, and created two divergent perspectives on the persistence of capitalism.

II. Sorel's interest in myth arose from his belief that "intellectualist philosophy" could not explain why a man would willingly sacrifice his life for an ideal. How could one account for revolutions or empires without positing some superior motive force acting within people? In a more general sense the passage from principles to action always contained the presence of myth, which Sorel considered to be a group of images intuitively or viscerally apprehended. Myth led to action through the formation of an "imaginary world"[4] that people placed ahead of the present world. While most human activity proceeded from the calculation of self-interest or evolved from daily routines, myths gripped the mind with a much greater tenacity than self-interest or habit and enabled people to act in radically new ways. Myths produced their effects spontaneously without leading to reflection or a search for precedents. Historical myths surrounding the nation or the resurrection of Jesus provoked heroic individual actions and underlay great social transformations. Sorel hoped that a contemporary myth like that of a general strike might bridge the growing gulf he perceived between thought and action in European socialism.

A pragmatic rather than an analytical attitude characterized Sorel's study of myth. What concerned him was not whether an event like the resurrection actually occurred but only its capacity to evoke sacrifice and heroism among its believers. Social scientific standards happily did not apply to myth. Sorel wrote that "in employing the term myth I believed that I had made a happy choice, because I thus put myself in a position to refuse any discussion whatever with the people who wish to submit the idea of a general strike to a detailed criticism, and who accumulate objections against its practical possibility."[5] Sorel defended Marxism from its critics on this basis. Even if its "laws" like the increasing concentration of capital, the decreasing of wages to subsistence levels, or the worsening of periodic crises proved false as scientific propositions, they still remained indispensable for enlightening people about the nature of their exploitation and as a guide for action. Sorel moved toward considering *Capital,* with its archetypes of "Monsieur Capital" and the "Collective Worker," and Marxism more generally, a myth. He eventually concluded that "writers who criticized Marx often reproached him with having spoken in symbolic language which they did not consider suitable for scientific investigation. On the contrary, it is these symbolic portions which were formerly regarded of dubious worth that constitute the definitive value of his work."[6] Sorel came to regard the myth of the general strike as embodying the essence of Marx's doctrines of class conflict and revolution in their most explosive form. In his revision of Marx, motive power took precedence over predictive accuracy. Rather than examining the psychological or sociological aspects of myth, Sorel insistently asked a more immediate question: can it provoke a reformation of man and society? His descriptions of the myths associated with various movements therefore rarely contained any extended theoretical treatment because praxis interested him more than etiology. Even the myth of the general strike, the most fully elaborated of any of the myths he studied, remained a somewhat mysterious creature.

And so he intended it to be. Sorel's interest in the intuitive, nonrational comprehension of images paralleled developments occurring in the psychological study of personality. He wrote that "it is possible to distinguish in every complex body of knowledge a clear and obscure region and to say the latter is perhaps more important."[7] Myth operated in this obscure, mysterious region that held man's strongest impulses. In a sense Sorel hoped that myth would tap some of the unconscious energy of society and channel it into revolutionary movements.[8] These dynamic, myth-charged movements would reverse the decline of France into mediocrity by overturning the enervated bourgeoisie. This class of rational calculators were completely incapable of sustaining any mythic beliefs, and they squashed the vital drives underlying society. They had no higher ideal than the peaceful making of money and would compromise with the proletariat endlessly to maintain it. This produced a state that Sorel, borrowing from Proudhon, called "the most atrocious period in the existence of societies."[9] The only escape lay in myths that enclosed "the strongest inclinations of a class, inclinations which recur to the mind with the insistence of instincts . . . and which give an aspect of complete reality to the hopes of immediate action. . . . "[10]

Sorel contrasted myth with a more commonly used category in political theory, viz., utopia. Myths arose throughout history imperceptibly through concentrations of chance[11] that defied analysis. Only the effects, not the origins of myth, could be studied. Even though he wrote at length about the myth of the general strike in ***Réflexions sur la violence,*** he claimed that he created nothing and that myths did not arise from works of social criticism. Utopia, however, was clearly an intellectual product, representing the work of a theorist who developed an ideal model of society in order to criticize existing society; and it generally sprang from a self-interested motive to gain followers and ultimately some kind of state office. Usually utopias offered visions of a superrational order that neglected customs and historical traditions and relied on psychological reductionism to fit all people into an eternal ideal. As an intellectual product, utopias lacked the motive force of myth; they merely described possibilities, whereas myths were "expressions of a determination to act."[12]

In addition, since myth kept people's attention centered on the present moment and the impending revolutionary cataclysm, it can only be judged as a means of present action. It did not offer an abstract utopian picture of the future. Myth directed men to destroy the existing state of affairs, whereas "the effect of utopia has always been to direct men's minds towards reforms which can be brought about by patching up the existing system" (*ibid.,* 50). Utopia compared the present to an imaginary, though attainable, future and thereby encouraged relatively passive attitudes and behavior among its believers. Like Marx, Sorel attacked the trend toward utopianism (related to reformism in Sorel's mind) in the socialist movement.

An emphasis on myth implies a concomitant devaluation of language and politics. Aristotle had noted the connection between the latter two concepts when he wrote that only man could use language and settle disputes through dialogue. All other animals lived either through instinct or fighting. Language made man the only "political animal" because politics implied communication or a process of persuasion between people seeking to resolve common problems. Sorel, however, viewed language as a weapon of domination in the hands of those who had a facility with it. Parliamentary politics essentially ensured the subjugation of workers, who lacked this facility, no matter which party governed. He considered language the instrument of professors and politicans, and as long as socialism remained "a doctrine expressed only in words" (*ibid.,* 46), workers would eventually lose control of the revolution made in their name. Myth had the pragmatic function of forestalling the machinations of ambitious socialist leaders and functionaries. The sudden success of parliamentary socialism in France (forty socialist representatives were elected to the Chamber of Deputies in 1893) worried Sorel greatly. In 1896 the socialist deputy

Alexandre Millerand called for the nationalization of several large industries, and in 1897 the socialist leader Jean Jaurès toured France promoting his vision of a socialist society given unity and direction by the state. Sorel believed these socialist proposals reflected a misreading of Marx's original texts and derided their vision of the socialist future as "a gigantic factory managed by technical personnel enjoying unchallenged authority."[13] The performance of socialist politicans confirmed Sorel's fears about Marxism's encounter with parliamentary politics: it did not transform the conduct of politics but instead altered its own purpose and character. Sorel moved gradually toward advocating the direct action strategy of radical syndicalism.[14] The myth of the general strike was no mere syndicalist propaganda tactic but the most powerful means for the syndicates to resist cooption. It carried the "picture of complete catastrophe,"[15] which made gains achieved through reform and compromise seem inconsequential. He argued that the myth of the general strike "drags into the revolutionary track everything it touches. . . . [T]his idea is so effective as a motive force that once it has entered into the minds of the people they can no longer be controlled by leaders, and . . . thus the power of the deputies would be reduced to nothing" (*ibid.*, 134, 125).

Yet Sorel's antipathy toward language and politics went deeper still. He used the adjectives "noisy, garrulous, and lying" (*ibid.*, 122) to characterize parliamentary socialism and, rather than representing the worst excesses of language, he felt that language inherently possessed those attributes. He wrote that "it is not necessary to be a very profound philosopher to perceive that language deceives us constantly as to the true nature of the relationships between things" (*ibid.*, 251). Partially due to its innate deceptiveness, the use of language inhibited action. Only myths could move men across the threshold between speech and action by transcending politics based on rational calculation. Without myths one could talk indefinitely of revolts without ever provoking one. Revolution would not erupt through the use of ordinary language but through "a body of images capable of evoking as an undivided whole the mass of sentiments which corresponds to the different manifestations of the war undertaken by Socialism against modern society" (*ibid.*, 123). Sorel based his philosophy of action on the violent revolt of oppressed classes made possible by myths that united and incited individuals. The myth of the general strike suffused workers with a conception of socialism, "which language cannot give us with perfect clearness" (*ibid.*, 128), and also created feelings of military solidarity. Under these circumstances workers acted without speech, argument, or rational calculation. Myth could impel revolution even during a period of pervasive mediocrity.

Sorel's emphasis on the centrality of violence in social transformation reflected his preference for myth over political discourse. If politics involves people persuading each other about alternative courses of action, then violence rejects such techniques. As Hannah Arendt noted in *The Human Condition,* violence is "mute" because it destroys the efficacy of political discourse. Clearly Sorel hoped that the violence inspired by the myth of the general strike would render parliamentary politics insignificant. Violence perhaps constituted the discourse of the proletariat, beyond the control of intellectual discourse. It reflected the clearest manifestation of action motivated by myth. Violence emphasized the present moment and militated against gradual reforms. Sorel compared the violent syndicalist strikes to the early Christian martyrdoms in their positive effect on their respective movements. He envisioned a kind of pure violence without hatred or revenge, almost a spiritual weapon in the hands of the proletariat.

Like myth, violence had a pragmatic function in maintaining the integrity of the socialist revolution. It would rebuff the strategy of liberals and parliamentary socialists by reestablishing the hostility between the bourgeoisie and the proletariat. Sorel wrote that the syndicates must "repay with black ingratitude the benevolence of those who would protect the workers, to meet with insults the homilies of the defenders of human fraternity, and reply by blows to the propagators of social peace" (*ibid.*, 91). At the same time syndicalist violence would revitalize the bourgeoisie by reawakening its class interest. The French bourgeoisie had lost the conquering spirit that still animated American capitalism (which Sorel much admired), and through concessions they enervated the proletariat as well. Violence would energize both classes and create a revolutionary situation (an idea practiced by the Red Brigades without much success).

Sorel's animus against language and politics reflected his hope that myth could change the world in a way that the words and elections of the Third Republic never would. Norman Jacobson claims that political theory begins precisely "at the moment when things become, so to speak, unglued,"[16] and certainly Sorel had a strong sense of things coming unglued. To make things whole again required nothing less than the scrapping of politics, actually a not uncommon impulse in political theory beginning with Plato's *Republic.* Socialism, the creation of bourgeois intellectuals, needed a firmer foundation in myth to prevent it from succumbing to the twin dangers of utopianism and reformism.

Yet where did the emphasis on myth leave Sorel himself? He implicitly condemned his own work, the linguistic construction of complex and highly discursive arguments, to irrelevance (he perhaps carried the practical mentality of his first career as a civil engineer into his subsequent career as a social critic). This paradox appeared even more starkly in Luigi Pirandello's statement after he signed a fascist manifesto in 1925: "I have always fought against words."[17] And although Sorel generally stayed on the left and certainly considered himself a socialist when he elaborated the myth of the general strike, it seems that the anti-political, anti-rational doctrines he expressed were resolved historically by moving to the right, exemplified by Mussolini's fascism. In a speech made shortly before his march on Rome, Mussolini said "we have created a myth. This myth is a faith, a noble enthusiasm. It does not have to be a reality, it is an impulse and a hope, belief, courage. Our myth is the nation. . . . "[18] Myths of the nation, and in Germany of race, short-circuited reasoned discourse with disastrous effects, particularly from the perspective of someone who hoped for a socialist revolution led and controlled by workers themselves.

III. Barthes launched his literary career after World War II in a period that marked the beginnings of French consumer culture. In what was nominally a time of economic rationality, Barthes detected a plethora of new myths emerging that legitimated the existing order. By exposing these myths he continued in the spirit, if not the letter of Sorel's work. The new locus of myth in the bourgeoisie instead of the proletariat gave Barthes's work an indirect, rearguard quality: he attempted to pick holes in the ruling class's legitimacy rather than to advocate a frontal assault against its position. An impulse toward demystification underlay Barthes's study of myth which he thought prerequisite to the political advance of socialism. He exhibited a more aesthetic, less pragmatic sensibility than Sorel.

Barthes found myth consisted of groups of images and ideas emanating from a wide variety of sources including the press, advertising, movies, consumer goods, cultural or athletic events, and indeed almost anything capable of conveying meanings to people. Myths occurred in fragments, not in long fixed narratives. Wherever myth appeared, it substituted a connoted system of meanings for the denoted system already present. Myth emptied phenomena of their literal meaning and added its own meanings. Barthes conceptualized myth as "language robbery."[19] He used the example of a *Paris Match* cover that showed a young black officer crisply saluting the French flag in the foreground. At least this constituted the denoted system of meanings. But a connoted system of meanings slipped in that put the black man's biography in very small parenthesis. The photograph presented the myth that "France is a great empire, that all her sons, without any colour discrimination, faithfully serve under her flag, and that there is no better answer to the detractors of an alleged colonialism than the zeal shown by this Negro in serving his so-called oppressors" (*ibid.*, 116). Myth had an imperative, button-holing character according to Barthes, and in this case the myth of French imperialism condemned "the saluting Negro to be nothing more than an instrumental signifier" (*ibid.*, 125).

The significance of myth stemmed from its capacity to convert historically determined outcomes into natural phenomena. Things produced by class hierarchy and its moral, cultural, and aesthetic consequences became a matter of course, or what Barthes liked to call the "doxa" (when demystifying he looked for "paradoxa," things that went beyond the received wisdom). Through myth the subordination of colonials, women, and workers appeared eternally sanctioned—one could not argue with nature. Myth obliterated the memory that peoples were once conquered, hierarchies once imposed, and objects once made. With its anonymous universal representations, myths helped shape the forms and norms that sustained everyday life.

Not surprisingly, Barthes called myth "depoliticized speech" (*ibid.*, 143). Politics implies that alternatives exist and that people make their own world by choosing between them, but myth embodied a "defaulting" on any such process. It denied the fabricated, and therefore changeable, quality of reality. Barthes wrote that myth "abolishes the complexity of human acts, it gives them the simplicity of essences" (*ibid.*). Since 1789 myth had operated to erase the name of the bourgeoisie from culture and politics and instead substituted more universal concepts like the 'nation." In this way France became awash in an anonymous, disingenuous mythology that implicitly posited class rule. Barthes wrote:

> The bourgeoisie pervades France: practised on a national scale, bourgeois norms are experienced as the evident laws of a natural order—the further the bourgeois class propagates its representations, the more naturalized they become. The fact of the bourgeoisie becomes absorbed into an amorphous universe, whose sole inhabitant is Eternal Man, who is neither proletarian nor bourgeois. (*ibid.*, 140)

Ironically, capitalist wealth and power relied on constant technological progress, yet its mythology produced images of unchangeable solidity.

Thus Barthes reversed Sorel's categories. Myth prevented rather than stimulated action. The dominant class purified its history and motives through myth, which also taught subordinate people to obey and to accept even if only vicariously) the status quo. Statistically, Barthes saw myth on the right rather than on the left. Not only did the bourgeoisie need to appropriate myth to justify its dominance, but the proletariat existed in the realm of production, so that its language remained essentially political. In direct contrast to Sorel, Barthes argued that revolutionary language could not be mythical. Revolution, more than anything else, demonstrated the historically contingent character of human institutions and practices. It revealed "the political load of the world" (*ibid.*, 146) by remaking that world. Only when revolution changed into "the Left," or an established order seeking to distort itself into nature, did socialist myths emerge. However, Barthes restricted his attention to France and its bourgeois myths.

Other reversals of Sorelian categories included Barthes's attitudes toward language and violence. He openly declared his intellectual identity, and indeed defined himself by writing in the third person about himself, that "his place (his milieu) is language: that is where he accepts or rejects, that is where his body can or cannot."[20] He tended to interpret all behavior linguistically or aesthetically. Any attack on academic or specialized language he considered part of a broader attack on intellectuals. He wrote that "public opinion does not like the language of intellectuals. Hence he has felt himself to be the object of a kind of racism: they excluded his language" (*ibid.,* 103). His analysis of the rhetoric of Pierre Poujade, leader of a reactionary petty bourgeois movement in the 1950s, showed that he frequently used tautologies like "business is business," thereby negating the communicative value of language and, by extension, intellectuals. Like "helicopters," intellectuals had their heads in the clouds, not standing on firm ground like the "little people." Implicit in Poujadism Barthes found physical and racial claims to superiority, symptoms of an anti-intellectual movement tending toward fascism.

As one who lived for and through language, Barthes recognized that violence threatened to render him superfluous. He admitted he disliked the subject and therefore did not give it extended treatment like Sorel. He stressed the latent violence of Poujade and his followers, who presented themselves as strong and virile men of "common sense." Poujade's campaign rhetoric emphasized his rugged past, and he titled his autobiography "J'ai choisi le combat." Barthes wrote that in the myths surrounding Poujade, "physical plentitude establishes a kind of moral clarity"[21] that by implication intellectuals, without the aura of violence, lacked. Although Sorel and Barthes shared an understanding of the implications of violence, their respective dichotomies of myths and politics led them to evaluate its effects differently.

Barthes's approach to myth resembled Sorel's in that he chose not to delve into the historical genesis or development of myth. The mechanics of making an advertisement or the class imperatives behind the production of mass consumer goods did not interest him. He instead focused only on immediate, connoted meanings, not because, as Sorel had it, myths contained an impenetrable element of mystery, but rather because the implications of a statement or appearance of an object constituted its essential reality.[22] So that even though Barthes recognized that myths arose instrumentally because men "depoliticize according to their needs,"[23] this insight had little effect on his work. In the main text under study here, *Mythologies* (published in English under two titles, *Mythologies* and *The Eiffel Tower*), Barthes aimed only at exposure and demystification, without seeking to place myth in its larger historical context.

Several myths recurred through the work. One justified the subordination of Africans to Frenchmen. In "Bichon and the Blacks" Barthes analyzed a *Paris Match* story about a young professional couple who, accompanied by their baby Bichon, traveled to paint "cannibal country." The article stressed the heroism of the family and described their trip with the language of conquest. The reader received a vision of the original explorers in a setting "where the code of feelings and values is completely detached from concrete problems of solidarity or progress."[24] In addition, the piece perpetuated racial sterotypes, opposing "primitive" and "civilized" cultures in a way that encouraged the colonial relationship. It drained all the complexity from African life and transformed the native into an exotic totem that reflected the Frenchman's contrasting virtues. The article, which Barthes referred to as "Operation Bichon," succeeded in presenting the black world through a white child's eyes, thus negating the demystification of primitive cultures undertaken by ethnologists and anthropologists.

The rise of African liberation movements threatened these myths by abruptly converting natural relations into undeniably contingent ones. In his essay "African Grammar" Barthes analyzed popular descriptions of the Algerian crisis reminiscent of Orwell's examples in "Politics and the English Language." To bridge the rift between French norm and African fact required that words diverge from their usual meanings. War and peace underwent strange changes, "god" became a sublimated form of the French government, and rebels struck in "bands" representing "elements" of the native "population." Words like "dishonor," "destiny," and "mission" became prominent in the phraseology of French leaders. Barthes wrote:

> Destiny exists only in a linked form. It is not military conquest which has subjected Algeria to France, it is a conjunction performed by Providence which has united two destinies. The link is declared indissoluble in the very period when it is dissolving with an explosiveness which cannot be concealed." (*ibid.,* 104-05)

A vast effort at naturalization combatted the tide of current events.

Another myth justified the subordination of women to men by promoting the naturalness of domestic obligations. In "Conjugations" Barthes explored the reasons why the media so intently covered Sylviane Carpentier's (Miss Europe '53) marriage to an electrician. Rather than modeling or acting, which her title surely allowed her to do, she renounced it all for the anonymity of a bourgeois household. She was a modern bourgeois heroine, as the media implicitly recognized. He wrote:

> here love-stronger-than-glory sustains the morale of the social status quo: it is not sensible to leave one's condition, it is glorious to return to it. . . . Happiness, in this universe, is to play at a kind of domestic enclosure: "psychological" questionnaires, gadgets, puttering, household appliances, schedules, the whole of this utensil paradise of *Elle* or *l'Express* glorifies the closing of the hearth. . . . (*ibid.,* 24-25)

Even women novelists, who presumably established independent careers, did not escape mythological reduction. In his essay "Novels and Children" Barthes noted that an article in *Elle* introduced its female subjects by the quantity of their children and novels. While admiring their literary accomplishments, the article implied that women must always define themselves in terms of their family. Barthes outlined the myth involved—"Women are on earth to give children to men; let them write as much as they want, let them decorate their condition, but above all, let them not depart from it. . . . Women, compensate for your books by your children."[24] Men did not appear in the article, but their presence and authority clearly loomed large.

A third myth justified the subordination of workers to owners. As one example Barthes pointed to the movie "On the Waterfront," which depicted workers as a feeble group exploited by corrupt union leaders, while the state represented absolute justice and the workers' only recourse against exploitation. At the end a beaten Marlon Brando presented himself to the boss, signaling the restoration of order with the worker giving himself willingly into the hands of his employer. This relationship assumed the aura of naturalness because the audience identified powerfully with the Brando character. Another example concerned the exhibition of photographs called "The Family of Man," which tried to show the universalities in the daily lives of different peoples. The photographs appeared under abstract categories like birth, play, work, death, love, etc. accompanied by Old Testament proverbs. This myth of the "human condition" attempted to submerge relevant differences into a larger human community. Barthes asked rhetorically how the parents of Emmet Till or the North African workers in the slums of Paris might feel about `the great family of man." By making the gestures of man look eternal he exhibit emptied them of political content and thereby defused them.

One final recurring myth involved consumption. Consuming goods not only had intrinsic value but it embodied an entire experience or state of mind as well. Thus Barthes compared the new Citroen models to Gothic cathedrals in that they represented the supreme creation of the era done by unknown artists. The car signified more than a mere instrument of transportation. Similarly, the consumption of wine went beyond reasons of taste or alcoholic content because it embodied an essence of the French character mythologically. Of course these myths were not innocent—behind them lay the exploitation of workers that made their production possible. But myths kept that hidden and instead flooded the consumer with images of eternal states of mind unlocked by consumption.

However, Barthes eventually chafed at the limitations of his own theory of myth. Although he believed that demystification carried political implications for the freeing of public discourse, he still felt distant from political reality. Besides, the myth-making apparatus seemed to have an unlimited productive capacity. Barthes unveiled only a fraction of the myths to a fraction of their potential audience. The focus on myth led to an undue pessimism and an inability to imagine a better future. Barthes wrote that "we constantly drift between the object and its demystification powerless to render its wholeness" (*ibid.*, 159). Undoubtedly this stemmed from Barthes's ahistorical method of analysis—without probing beneath the surface, it is not surprising that he could not envision how to go beyond demystification.[26]

In addition, the study of myths increased Barthes's sense of alienation. Rather than discussing objects themselves, he always discussed their implications. Also, he excluded himself from the society of $$Word$$ By conceiving of an event like the Tour de France as a complex mythological event, Barthes felt removed from the people entertained by the event. He wrote that "the mythologist is condemned to live in a theoretical sociality; for him, to be in society is, at best, to be truthful: his utmost sociality dwells in his utmost morality. His connection with the world is of the order of sarcasm."[27] And although in the introduction Barthes suggested that in a consumer culture sarcasm may well be "the condition of truth" (*ibid.*, 12), in his conclusion he clearly saw its limitations.

This became more evident in a later essay titled "Change the Object Itself.." In it Barthes reviewed his earlier theory of myth and concluded that nothing about French society had fundamentally changed, so that "the mythical still abounds, just as anonymous and slippery, fragmented and garrulous, available both for ideological criticism and semiological dismantling."[28] Yet in the intervening years he perceived that demystification itself had become a "common sense" orthodoxy and indeed had developed its own mythology. The decipherment of myths no longer represented an adequate strategy. Instead he suggested that the object itself must be transformed, although he provided no clue as to how this might be done. He explained that "the problem is not to reveal the (latent) meaning of an utterance, of a trait, of a narrative, but to fissure the very representation of meaning."[29] Here Barthes's eloquence hardly disguised his inability to visualize how to progress from demystification to a more positive program for the nonmythological reconstruction of culture.

IV. Sorel and Barthes lived uneasy careers as intellectuals. Both sons of the bourgeoisie, they vigorously attacked the bourgeoisie throughout their work. Sorel presented the case of an anti-intellectual intellectual fascinated with myth and violence as a means of overcoming the stranglehold intellectuals exercised on politics and culture. Barthes did not exhibit this powerful double alienation (from society and from himself), but he did recognize what the estrangement resulting from his emphasis on myth cost him in terms of his ability to enjoy the world. Both Sorel and Barthes ultimately arrived at an impasse, one over finding a truly revolutionary myth, the other over dismantling bourgeois myth. By 1908 or 1909 Sorel realized the myth of the general strike did not have the effect he once attributed to it, nor did the syndicates maintain a purely apolitical orientation. His subsequent search for myth carried him to the far right and left ends of the European ideological spectrum, first with an ambivalent association with integral nationalism and the Action Française before World War I, and then as an ardent defender of Bolshevism, which he misinterpreted as a movement establishing soviets, or self-governing groups of producers, under the charismatic leadership of Lenin. Barthes, too, realized by the 1970s that his earlier study of myth no longer bore the weight of his original anti-bourgeois impulse, and in his last decade he concentrated on more literary and aesthetic subjects.

To some extent the contradiction between Sorel's and Barthes's formulations of myth rested in the semantic use of the terms "ideology" and "myth."[30] Sorel used "ideology" to refer to the justification for the activities of a particular group or class. An ideology articulated these justifications into a reasonably coherent system of thought that had an appearance of universality. The appearance of universality, as opposed to arguments from pure self-interest, helped legitimate the group's activities and also reflected the level of self-confidence of the group. Sorel followed Marx's argument that the ideology of the dominant class functioned as the society's ideology. His book ***Les Illusions du Progrès*** examined the ideology of progress that accompanied the emergence of the bourgeoisie in the seventeenth and eighteenth centuries. Though Barthes found the projection of universality not in an ideology of progress but in more fragmentary messages that erased the history of objects and relationships, one can see the parallels between Sorel's concept of ideology and Barthes's concept of myth. Barthes implied that myths helped solidify bourgeois ideology and gave it the appearance of uncontestability. In Sorel's work, however, ideology simply lacked the motive force of more intuitively apprehended myths. This more than anything else differentiated their theories of myth.

Sorel's fascination with, and Barthes's antipathy toward, myth also reflected the different intellectual climates of the late nineteenth and mid-twentieth centuries. Sorel reacted against the extreme version of positivism that dominated French intellectual life for much of the nineteenth century. Other thinkers throughout Europe revolted against the idea that an exact science of society could account for all human actions and began to reevaluate the importance of irrational motivations and practices heretofore ignored. Thus historians have placed Sorel in the broader "revolt against reason" afoot in the late nineteenth century.[31] Barthes, however, could not ignore the glorification of the irrational, of violence, and of myth by the European fascist movements. Ernst Cassirer reflected the shift in attitudes toward myth in a book published just after World War II in which he described myth as a primitive anachronism, banished but always waiting for a opportunity to subvert the rational organization of society.[32] Barthes saw Poujade as a lightening rod for contemporary myth and the potential leader of a revivified fascist movement. While Barthes considered contemporary myth a very sophisticated rather than primitive phenomenon and not at all an anachronism, he too perceived it negatively.

Barthes's preoccupation with demystification placed him closer than Sorel to the concerns of current American political science, which generally uses the term "myth" to refer to a widely held illusion. A popular introductory college textbook on American politics begins by listing several myths such as "the American way is the only democratic way" or "a ruling few dictate policy in America." The authors claim that these myths distort reality and hinder people's understanding of politics. They conclude their brief survey of political myths by writing, "by the time we have examined the actual conduct of American government, we hope the reader will be able to replace a misconception with an understanding more rooted in reality."[33] The textbook implies that if every citizen received a proper introduction to politics, then myths would lose their force, and gradually disappear. Political activity would become more rational and more susceptible to further logical analysis by political scientists. This study has attempted to show that myths are a more complex and significant entity than sometimes assumed; and, they are also, as Barthes might advise the political scientists, much more intractable.

NOTES

[1] Roland Barthes, "Languages at War in a Culture at Peace," *Times Literary Supplement* (October 8, 1971), 1204.

[2] Georges Sorel, *Réflexions sur la violence* (Paris, 1908); *Reflections on Violence,* trans. T. E. Hulme and J. Roth (New York, 1961), 54.

[3] Roland Barthes, *Roland Barthes,* trans. Richard Howard (New York, 177), 63.

[4] *Reflections,* 48.

[5] *Ibid.,* 43. Cf. Philip Wiener, "Pragmatism," *The Dictionary of the History of Ideas,* III, 564.

[6] Georges Sorel, "The Decomposition of Marxism" (Paris, 1907), in Irving Horowitz, *Radicalism and the Revolt Against Reason* (Carbondale, Ill., 1968), 251.

[7] *Reflections,* 144.

[8] See Jules Monnerot, "Georges Sorel ou l'introduction aux mythes modernes," in Jean Claude Casanova, *Science et Conscience de la Société* (Paris, 1971), 379-412, and Monnerot, *Sociology and Psychology of Communism* (Boston, 1953), 148.

[9] Georges Sorel, "The Advance Toward Socialism" (Paris, 1920), *The Illusions of Progress,* trans. John and Edith Stanley (Berkeley, 1969), 211.

[10] *Reflections,* 125.

[11] Georges Sorel, *Le Système historique de Renan* (Paris, 1905), 73.

[12] *Reflections,* 50.

[13] Georges Sorel, "Préface to *Formes et essence du socialism* by Saverio Merlino (1898)," in Richard Vernon, *Commitment and Change: Georges Sorel and the Idea of Revolution* (Toronto, 1978), 91.

[14] Georges Sorel, "The Socialist Future of the Syndicates" (1898), in John Stanley (ed.), *From Georges Sorel: Essays in Socialism and Philosophy* (New York, 1976), 71-93.

[15] *Reflections,* 135.

[16] Norman Jacobson, *Pride and Solace* (Berkeley, 1978), 10.

[17] Thomas Sheenan, "Myth and Violence: The Fascism of Julius Evola and Alain de Benoist," *Social Research,* 48 (Spring 1981), 53.

[18] Karl Mannheim, *Ideology and Utopia* (New York, 1968), 122-23.

[19] Roland Barthes, *Mythologies,* trans. Annette Lavers (New York, 1972), 131.

[20] *Roland Barthes,* 53.

[21] Roland Barthes, *The Eiffel Tower and Other Mythologies* (New York, 1979), 131.

[22] For a comparison of Barthes with two more historically and theoretically inclined authors, see David Gross, "Lowenthal, Adorno, Barthes: Three Perspectives on Popular Culture," *Telos,* 45 (Fall 1980), 122-40.

[23] *Mythologies,* 144.

[24] *The Eiffel Tower,* 35.

[25] *Mythologies,* 50.

[26] For a critique of Barthes along these lines see Eugene Goodheart, "The Myths of Roland," *Partisan Review,* 47 (1980), 199-212.

[27] *Mythologies,* 157.

[28] Roland Barthes, *Image-Music-Text,* trans. Stephen Heath (New York, 1977), 166.

[29] *Ibid.,* 167.

[30] Ben Halpern, "Myth and Ideology in Modern Usage," *History and Theory,* 2 (1961), 129-49.

[31] H. Stuart Hughes, *Consciousness and Society* (New York, 1958); Horowitz; S. P. Rouanet, "Irrationalism and Myths in Georges Sorel," *Review of Politics,* 26 (1964), 45-69.

[32] Ernst Cassirer, *The Myth of the State* (New Haven, 1946), 279-80.

[33] Marian Irish, James Prothro, Richard Richardson, *The Politics of American Democracy* (Englewood Cliffs, N.J. 1977), 8.

K. Steven Vincent (essay date 1990)

SOURCE: "Interpreting Georges Sorel: Defender of Virtue or Apostle of Violence?" in *History of European Ideas,* Vol. 12, No. 2, 1990, pp. 239-57.

[In the following excerpt, Vincent examines previous critical interpretations of Sorel's work, and categorizes him as a cautious pessimist.]

Georges Sorel has never failed to evoke strong reactions. From Sartre's dismissal of Sorel's ***Réflexions sur la violence*** as 'fascist prattle',[1] from G.D.H. Cole's contemptuous characterisation of him as a pessimist 'moaning for blood',[2] to Croce's recommendation that Marx and Sorel were the only original thinkers socialism ever had,[3] and to a recent estimation that he 'produced the most profound and extensive body of marxist analysis to appear in France until the post World War Two era',[4] assessments have covered the spectrum from prattler to *savant.* And, as these citations also indicate, Sorel has been interpreted as presenting a large variety of different social visions. Hailed by one recent author as the latter-day prophet of Vicoian *ricorso* and 'the cult of violence',[5] he is characterised by another as a 'Jansenist Marxist'.[6] Sorel has remained, as Isaiah Berlin pointed out several years ago, 'unclassified; claimed and repudiated both by the right and left'.[7]

The purpose of this paper is first, to point out the major interpretive approaches to Sorel's work and how they diverge, and second, to advance a hypothesis concerning his proper historical placement.

I

A few biographical details are necessary to introduce this curiosity of late-nineteenth century French thought. Sorel was born in Normandy in 1847. He was a pious and studious youth, got his higher education at the Ecole Polytechnique, and worked for the next 25 years as a government civil engineer (Ponts et Chaussées), spending time in such places as Corsica (1870-71) and Algeria (1876-79), and passing his last 13 years of government service in Perpignan (1879-92). His first works were not published until he was forty-two (in 1889), and it was not until he was 45 that he stepped down from his government post and began devoting his full energies to writing and publishing. Upon retirement, he returned to Paris, settling in a quiet suburb, Boulogne-sur-Seine, where he lived until his death in 1922. Several days each week he would travel into Paris to listen to lectures at the Collège de France, such as those of Henri Bergson, to read at the Bibliothèque Nationale, or to chat with his colleagues and disciples in the editorial offices of the journals for which he wrote, the best known probably being Charles Péguy's *Cahiers de la Quinzaine.*

Sorel was, as this path suggests, a special type of French intellectual, selftaught and prolific, and he remained, not unlike other largely autodidact French men of letters, an outsider, never quite accepted or taken seriously by the established intellectuals of the Ecole Normale, and translating the pain of this neglect into vicious attacks and acid criticisms. He remained throughout his life the discontented outsider, and his politics remained largely counter-politics.

During his thirty years in Paris (1892-1922) he was involved with a number of different groups on the political Left, as well as being, during the same years, engaged by methodological discussions concerning science and the newly-emerging field of sociology. A brief chronology of his intellectual interests and sociopolitical associations gives an indication of the variety of contexts within which he moved.

In the first years, roughly 1886-1892, Sorel was interested in classical and biblical studies, Renan and Proudhon, and attempted to lay the groundwork for his sociology of morals. I consider this period to be particularly important, and will discuss it at length further on.

In the next few years, roughly 1893-1897, Sorel became interested in marxism generally, and more specifically in the scientific assumptions presupposed by such social philosophies. Sorel's growing interest in socialism coincided with the emergence of French socialism as a serious political force in the municipal elections of 1892 and the national elections of 1893. During these same years, Sorel was interested in separating the scientific methodologies appropriate to the different branches of human knowledge, and he came to embrace a stance that may be termed, following Leszek Kolakowski,[8] 'conventionalism'.

From 1897/98 to 1902, Sorel continued to be interested in the theoretical discussions of marxism and socialism. But, increasingly he favored a 'revisionist' position *vis-à-vis* Kautsky and the so-called French marxists and advocated parliamentary socialism. Again, Sorel's trajectory corresponded with larger trends: this was the period of the so-called 'crisis of marxism' (the phrase was coined by Thomas Masaryk in 1898[9]) that elicited various redefinitions, from Rosa Luxemburg's 'spontaneism' to Eduard Bernstein's 'revisionism'. Sorel was also a Dreyfusard and supported Alexandre Millerand's entry into the cabinet of Waldeck-Rousseau.

After the Dreyfus Affair, from 1902 to 1908, Sorel became disenchanted with political socialism and with parliamentary politics generally, and entered into his so-called syndicalist phase, for which he is perhaps best known. He embraced the non-parliamentary workers' movement connected with the *bourses du travail,* believing that only such a movement, animated by the 'myth' of the general strike, could lead to social renewal. This was Sorel's most productive period: five of his 13 books were written and published during these years (including all of the books that have been translated into English).

After 1908, Sorel became disenchanted with organised syndicalism. This corresponded with the end of the 'heroic' period of the CGT, marked by the bloody repression of the strike at Villeneuve-Saint-Georges in 1908 and by the adoption of cautious stances by syndicalist leaders like Victor Griffuelhes and Alphonse Merrheim. Sorel turned his attention to a variety of other political movements, such as Maurras's 'integral' nationalism, and after the Russian Revolution of 1917, Leninism. This was accompanied by a new intellectual interest in philosophical pragmatism, especially with the thought of William James.

II

Given such wide-ranging associations and interests, it is not surprising that interpreters have differed considerably. Sorel always has enjoyed a certain notoriety, and he has received, especially since the early 1950, considerable scholarly attention.[10] Some issues have been clarified, but as the quotes cited earlier in this paper indicate, nothing close to a consensus concerning the meaning of his work has emerged. Of the wide range of conflicting—albeit overlapping—interpretations, there are four main categories: (1) Sorel the revolutionary syndicalist and revisionist marxist; (2) Sorel the apostle of violence; (3) Sorel the moralist; and (4) Sorel the methodological pluralist and political chameleon. My own preference is for the moralist Sorel, and I shall argue that it was Sorel's distinctive redefinition of certain moral-political ideas—like virtue—that provides the unifying element in his writings. However, since all four interpretive positions continue to find their defenders, a brief discussion of each is necessary.

The argument that Sorel was a pluralist and political chameleon takes the disunity of Sorel's writings as a stance consciously embraced by Sorel himself. There is, according to this view, no single purpose in Sorel's works. It is necessary to accept the variety of approaches that Sorel's writings illustrate, and, indeed, to view these as indicative of Sorel's vision of the complexity of the world. To assume that there exists one 'scientific' view that reflects the mutiplicity of reality is an illusion, and one is better served recognising the exclusive nature of different varieties of knowledge. H. Stuart Hughes has suggested that such a revolt against 'positivism' was a central component of Sorel's thought.[11] And, more recently, the English scholar J.R. Jennings has suggested that the journalistic quality of much of Sorel's writing and his tendency to write critiques of the works of others, rather than to produce any systematic treatise of his own, are related to Sorel's opinion that things present an impossible complexity which the intellect is unable to analyse and describe without producing insoluble contradictions.[12] In sum, the 'variations' in Sorel's writings reflect Sorel's view that reality is complex and fundamentally mysterious.

This view has considerable merit in that it avoids the obvious dangers that arise from attempting to force Sorel into a narrow interpretive straight-jacket. And it takes seriously Sorel's 'conventionalist' view of science. But it suffers by having prematurely given up the attempt to find unity. Perhaps there are discernible patterns in the midst of this multiplicity. And perhaps the task for contemporary historians, enjoying as we do a retrospective overview, is to search these patterns out.

The other interpretive groups have no such reluctance to find a unifying theme, nor to deciding which of the writings are central. For example, the group which argues that Sorel was essentially a neo-marxist or a revolutionary syndicalist (or both) characteristically focuses on Sorel's writings of the 1890s and early-1900s, when most of the famous (or infamous) books like ***Réflexions sur la violence*** were published. During this prolific period, as previously mentioned, Sorel was interested in marxism, in the social scientific assumptions which underlay marxism and sociology, and in syndicalism and the *bourse* movement. Neil McInnis, for example, in an extended article of 1960, pointed to the importance of Sorel in the development of serious marxism in France during the 1890s.[13] And Jacques Julliard, in a study of Fernand Pelloutier, has argued similarly that Sorel was a central figure in the renaissance of French marxism during the 1890s.[14] More recently, Daniel Lindenberg and Larry Portis have pointed to Sorel as a notable exception in the 'French desert' of late-19th century theoretical marxism.[15] Portis in particular has insisted that Sorel be viewed in the forefront of those on the political Left who broke away from the reductionist scientism which passed for marxism during the early Third Republic. Unlike his contemporaries, according to Portis, Sorel was a 'true revolutionary intellectual' who understood the complexities of the issues of proletarian organisation and proletarian culture, and of their relationships to revolutionary class consciousness. In particular, Sorel was sensitive to the ways that bourgeois culture could dull the revolutionary consciousness of the proletariat and thereby enjoy 'intellectual hegemony'. Sorel was, in essence, Gramscian before Gramsci, Marcusian before Marcuse. And, according to Portis, he was in all of this faithful to Marx.[16]

Certainly, Marx was important in the development of Sorel's thought; and there is little question that the polemic against deterministic marxists like Jules Guesde, Paul Lafargue, and Gabrielle Deville was an important motif of his thought in the 1890s and early 1900s. There are problems, however, with an interpretive strategy that suggests, as Portis' does, that this encompasses the entire context or thrust of Sorel's thought. Even other scholars who insist on the marxist basis of Sorel's thought have suggested that Portis has failed to sufficiently appreciate the degree to which Sorel diverged from the theory of the master, ultimately reducing marxism to the stature of a potent myth that could animate the proletariat in the coming revolution.[17]

The advocates of the other interpretations—the views of Sorel as an apostle of violence, or as an advocate of virtue—raise an even more fundamental objection to the stance of Portis in particular and the orientation of marxist interpretations of Sorel in general. They argue that the marxist approach tends to neglect the early writings of Sorel, as well as the volatile period after 1909 when Sorel's political allegiances began to fluctuate wildly.

The group which maintains that Sorel was an apostle of violence generally argues, for example, that in addition to the books of the marxist or syndicalist phase, it is also necessary to emphasise the writings of the following years: the post-syndicalist Sorel; the sympathetic observer of Maurrasian 'integral' nationalism, bolshevism and fascism. J.L. Talmon argued in a 1970 article that Sorel was 'the most famous European apologist of violence', one 'of the 19th century's great prophets of wrath' who rejected progress 'in the name of a religion of struggle and war'.[18]

A number of others have followed Talmon's lead, though they tend to provide more nuanced analyses. Jack Roth is probably the best-known English-language scholar to present such an interpretation, publishing a book in 1980 called *The Cult of Violence: Sorel and the Sorelians.*[19] The most prominent current advocate of this interpretation, however, is the Israeli scholar, Zeev Sternhell. In a controversial book about French fascist ideology, published in 1983, Sternhell attempted to demonstrate that the essentials of French fascism grew out of the intellectual struggles of Sorel and his ilk during the late-19th century.[20] Sternhell claims that French fascism emerged from a potent mix of the ideals of the nationalist, anti-liberal, anti-bourgeois right with those of the anti-marxist, anti-liberal, anti-bourgeois left. Both groups were disenchanted with the established liberal democratic order of the Third Republic, both were its outspoken critics, and therefore together ideologically undermined the Republic and 'prepared the fall of democracy' in the summer of 1940.[21] Sternhell is particularly interested in pointing to what he calls the *'fascisation'* of certain currents of French thought, and even more specifically in the slide toward fascism of schools of thought traditionally associated with the Left.

Sternhell's thesis created an uproar in French intellectual circles,[22] particularly his unfortunate tendency to lump together as fascist or proto-fascist many thinkers of the late-19th century.[23] One of the thinkers who fares particularly badly is Sorel. He is depicted as a critical transition figure, instrumental in catalysing the fascist synthesis. Indeed, Sternhell claims that by 1911 Sorel's 'writings were already openly fascist'.[24]

The legend of Sorel's fascist sympathies is a tenacious one, but rests on pitifully slender evidence. Sorel, we must remember, died in August 1922, two months before the 'March on Rome', so clearly there is no question of collaboration. And the latest analysts of Sorel's editorial production for the years 1919-1922 find no indication that he welcomed the fascist agitation in Italy or its chief, Mussolini.[25] Most accounts that insist on Sorel's fascist sympathies rely on the book published by Jean Variot in 1935,[26] 13 years after Sorel's death, at a time when the radical right (for which Variot had considerable sympathy) was in power in both Italy and Germany. Often cited, in addition, is the report by Roberto Michels that Sorel indicated that Mussolini would go far.[27] Thinking that someone will 'go far', however, is a tenuous basis for claiming sympathetic association.

This is not to claim, however, that Sorel had no right-wing associations. For the few years after 1909, when Sorel despaired of the proletariat and ceased to consider himself a syndicalist theoretician, he worked with Georges Valois (later to organise France's first fascist party) and other right-wing journalists. There was, during these same years, the emergence of a virulent antisemitism in his writings.[28] But, distasteful as all of this is, I nonetheless believe that it is a mistake to claim that Sorel converted to 'integral' monarchism, or to some form of protofascism.[29] The evidence suggests that Sorel was attracted to the 'integral' nationalists of the Right because they, like himself, had little patience with the parliamentary politics of these years. Sorel had come to believe that party politics in France was based on insincere chatter and on irresponsible grasping for personal prestige and material advancement, rather than on any concern for social or moral regeneration.

The less inflammatory suggestion of Sternhell and the others who embrace his interpretation is that Sorel contributed to the general ideological milieu that allowed a virulent nationalism to flourish in the post-Dreyfus years, and that he prepared the ground for the slide from the left to the right that Sternhell believes (as he put it in another article) is 'the classic gearing-in to fascism' in France.[30] At this level, the argument is not all that different from blaming Rousseau for creating the cultural milieu which produced the French Revolution, or blaming Nietzsche for the rise of the Nazis. Sternhell himself unconsciously seems to recognise the difficulty of finding 'fascist' quotes from Sorel, for in the pages of his books and articles that deal specifically with Sorel's 'fascism', there are exclusively quotes from Michels, Lagardelle, and others; Sorel himself is noticeably absent. What is troubling about this general approach is that it defines Sorel in terms of the movements that claim him as a precursor, rather than in terms of his own intentions.[31]

Having said this, however, it remains the case that Sorel did point in an ominous direction when he flirted with right-wing 'integral' nationalism. After 1909, he became radically disenchanted, truly depressed concerning the prospects of any syndical or moral renewal. At this time, he slipped into employing metaphors of pathology and decadence that were common in the discourse of late-19th century French writers.[32] It is difficult, when Sorel adopts such a stance, not to see him as another victim of the fin-de-siècle collapse of hope which, coming on the heels of frustrated radical expectations, all too often left reservoirs of unused turbulent energies searching for restorative outlets. Finding himself facing lassitude and the vacuity of mediocrity, Sorel fell victim to *ennui* and to the extremism of anarchic compulsion. He experienced what George Steiner has called 'the itch for chaos'.[33] But he never became an advocate of violence for its own sake; he did not allow the 'itch for chaos' to become a program for violence.

The final general category in the existing interpretive literature views Sorel as a moralist. Isaiah Berlin, for example, in a 1971 article, argued that what unified all of Sorel's productions was: (1) his view of man as a creator who is fulfilled only when he creates; and (2) his view of life as a constant struggle to avoid idleness, hedonism, and materialism.[34] Sorel viewed human nature as naturally tending to such idleness and pleasure-seeking, and he resolutely believed that man must do all in his power to avoid being overcome by sloth, greed, and fear. This was to be done, not by scepticism and critical reasoning, but by a common life of labor within the natural associations of humanity—the family, the tribe, the *polis*. Everything great in man's history, according to Sorel, was the result of unflagging labor against a chaotic and terrifying world, and mankind would grow and prosper only through continuing effort. Indeed, without such an effort, the natural human tendencies toward idleness and fanaticism would prevail.

It was this moral vision, according to Berlin, that led Sorel to look to the working class, for in the modern world he felt the workers were the only ones sufficiently endowed with the requisite strength and morality to resist decadence. It was this insight that led Sorel to Marx and then to revolutionary syndicalism, which shared the class perspective of Marx but which did not share his dedication to political action as the means of bringing about social regeneration. Here, quite clearly, Berlin's moralist Sorel merges with the neo-marxist-syndicalist Sorel of other interpretations.

Like such syndicalists as Fernand Pelloutier, Sorel was a moralist with little patience for politically oriented scientific socialists who had never dirtied their hands in the workshop. Nor was he enamored of political intellectuals who devised pseudo-scientific utopian scenarios for reaching the desired goal. Theirs was an intellectualised, desiccated, abstract, positivistic socialism which could neither chart the path of change nor stimulate men to action. Socialism, for Sorel and the syndicalists, would emerge from the workplace—this was the modern 'space' from which a truly vital society of makers and doers could emerge.

III

The appropriate intellectual placement of Sorel is this last interpretation: Sorel the 'moralist'. But Berlin and his followers (a category which would include scholars such as John Stanley[25] and Arthur Greil[36]) have not gone far enough in specifying what sort of moral position Sorel embraced.

One aspect, for example, that has been insufficiently emphasised is that Sorel drew from a French tradition of republican socialism which focused on the weakness of individuals, the decadence of modern society, the value of patriarchal family, and the importance of citizenship. This tradition was strongly influenced by ideals of 'virtue' and 'civil religion' which, though of ancient lineage, had become prominent again in French discourse with the writings of Montesquieu and Rousseau. These writers and their nineteenth-century descendants focused not only on institutions, but also on what Montesquieu termed the 'spirit' which animates the entire populace. They were particularly concerned with the sociopolitical consequences of weak, self-centered individuals who escaped from isolation only fitfully and who found society, at best, problematic. And they were especially critical of how this weakness of individuals was catered to in the context of modern societies, where decadence prevailed and selfishness was economically rewarded. Morality, in short, was a part of politics; and politics—republican politics—would succeed only if it became public, and only if an altruistic concern for the public interest prevailed over private self-interest.

The importance of this republican tradition in Sorel's thought is evident from his two earliest books, ***Contribution à l'étude profane de la Bible*** (1889) and ***Le Procès de Socrate*** (also 1889). In the first book, Sorel attempted to extract from the Bible moral teachings which, he believed, needed to be revived if France was to avoid further moral decline; in the second, he examined the trial of Socrates with the same end in mind. In both books, the moral model that Sorel extracted was the heroic virtue of the Athenian *polis,* which was based, according to his idealisation, on a strong family structure, a vital military life, and the absence of a leisure class devoted to consumption and professional politics. Heroism and ingrained dedication to personal sacrifice for community interests held these societies together, according to Sorel, and it was these virtues which recommended these societies over his own.

> The Athenians of olden times were quite superior to our envious, ignorant and gluttonous bourgeoisie. . . . Citizens [in early Athens] were not merchants, demanding a guarantee for their trade, protection of their industry and soliciting government favours. They were soldiers whose existence was tied to the greatness of the city.[37]

Sorel's criticism of Socrates was based on his belief that Socrates' teachings spread mysticism and fostered a new spirit of individualism which proved destructive of the moral foundations of society, particularly by undermining paternal authority, citizenship, and patriotism. 'Socrates', Sorel tells us in the opening pages, 'worked hard to break the chains that enclosed the citizen in the city of antiquity'.[38] In so acting, Socrates was at one with the Sophists, for whom Sorel reserved some of his harshest criticism. The Sophists were guilty of overlooking public moral ends in favor of their own selfish advancement and success. As Sorel himself put it: 'To succeed by demagogic flattery in a democratic society, by the most refined flattery in the court of a tyrant—such was the aim of the students of the Sophists'.[39]

This is not the place to discuss the subtleties of Sorel's arguments, nor their historical accuracy. What needs to be emphasised here is how central in this work are moral-republican themes. The fundamental polemical point of the book is to demonstrate that Socrates contributed to the general ideological subversion of the Athenian ethical system. Sorel argued that Socrates favored philosophy over poetry and government by privileged intellectuals over the farmer-soldiers who embodied heroic virtue, and that therefore he, Socrates, must be lined up with the Orators, the Sophists, who for different reasons also favored an oligarchy of politicians. Both Socrates and the Sophists are to be chastised for abstracting, through rhetoric and philosophy, politics from reality and, even more ruinously, for providing the intellectual foundation for a movement that ended by tearing politics from its social and moral roots. Such intellectual abstractions, Sorel charged, could only lead to a corruption of politics, which to remain sound must retain its roots in an economy of producers. Virtue, according to Sorel, is to be found in a system run by the producers themselves, and Socrates and the Sophists represent the ideological orientation of social rationalism that leads to the disintegration of this vital union.

What is so striking, then, about this work is the resonance of classical republican themes. As Neil McInnis has pointed out apropos this book, Sorel's argument leads him to perform 'some uncritical glorification of the old Athenian morality'.[40] Sorel does not offer a simple restatement of reified republican ideals. But the concern for social morality—for civic virtue—does have strong similarities with *polis* virtue as defined in Greek philosophy and reintroduced into French discourse in the mid-eighteenth century by such thinkers as Montesquieu and Rousseau. And the concern for a strong tie between military life and political and legal institutions also is similar to classical concerns for citizen-soldiers, and to early-modern European idealisations of the yeoman farmer.[41] Finally, Sorel's support for monogamous union and patriarchy, his concern to restrict action in the public sphere to independent autonomous men, and his relegation of women to the *foyer* are also prominent motifs in the republican tradition in France from the late-18th century.[42]

Not all of Sorel's concerns, of course, have such filiations. His commitment, for example, to an ethic of productivity is not a classical republican theme; indeed, labor replaces landed property as the basis for autonomy and independence. The background for this is probably the French socialism of people such as Proudhon who, like Sorel, was anxious that an ethic of productivity not be replaced by an ethic devoted to consumption and leisure, and whose thought also registered the influence of republicanism.[43] Sorel's classicism was filtered through Proudhonian socialism.

This remained the case in Sorel's subsequent works. In 1894, for example, Sorel returned to 'republican' themes in his book ***La Ruine du monde antique,*** which is concerned with assessing the role played by Christianity in the decline of the Roman Empire. It is important to point out that this was published contemporaneously with the first important book of his so-called 'marxist' phase ***L'Ancienne et la nouvelle métaphysique.***

The general message of ***La Ruine du monde antique*** is that Christianity is hostile to republican values. Christian ideology, Sorel wrote, 'cut the bonds that existed between the social spirit and the social life; it sowed everywhere the germs of quietism, of despair and of death'.[44]

Concerning the historical question of Christianity's role in the decline of Roman society and its civic morality, however, the book gives a more nuanced account than such blanket condemnations of Christian ideology might lead one to expect. In a section of the work added to the 1922 edition, entitled 'Hypothèses sur la conquête chrétien', Sorel suggested that during the initial phase of Christianity, when it was a persecuted sect, Christians possessed some of the aspects of the warrior mentality that he favored. Christians, Sorel charged in these pages, often exaggerated the actual extent of these persecutions, but this was probably beneficial, for it impelled the early Christians into being concerned above all with the preservation of their community, and this concern necessarily entailed the cultivation of the ideal of the spartan warrior to assist in the triumph of the Christian city over its persecutors. Christianity was a vital force, Sorel suggested, as long as it was dominated by this ideal—by this 'myth'—of being a world apart.

Sorel seems to suggest that during this heroic phase, Christianity was therapeutic for Roman society, which was already in decline and already ruled by an oligarchy of philosophers and politicians. Christianity accentuated the gulf between the social ideal of the republic and the reality of Roman society; in Sorel's own words, Christianity gave a 'clear consciousness of the incoherence which existed between reality and the traditional juridical edifice'.[45]

Unfortunately, Christianity did little to strengthen the general forces in Roman society which might have slowed this decline. It 'did not greatly change the morals of Roman society'.[46] Indeed, the influence worked, if it worked at all, in the opposite direction, for as Christianity was absorbed by certain segments of Roman society, it was transformed from a heroic myth-bound social movement to an organisation sustained by ideology and individual piety. As the social integration of Christians into Roman society took place, there was a 'dissociation between the metaphysical principles of religious morality and the rules of the practical life'.[47] Christianity became a cult preeminently interested in the relationship between individuals and God. The life of contemplation and idleness became the ideal, replacing the active virtuous life recommended by Cicero. Christianity, in short, became 'hostile to the ancient concept of the heroic city'.[48]

The mores that were cultivated in the clergy worked to undermine the life of industry and of social activity. There was a new emphasis on monastic retreat and the cultivation of metaphysical knowledge and dialectical talents. There was little interest in science; instead the Church wished to educate men of talent able to argue subtle metaphysical questions. Clerics were trained not to work or to make a positive productive contribution to society, but to carry to society 'homilies, hymns and theological dissertations'.[49] From the Romans (opposed to the Greeks) the Church learned to take assets from productive agriculture in order to build 'edifices of luxury . . . in order to amuse and to nourish a populace of loiterers'.[50] Instead of endorsing a view of property which recognised the collective interest and placed civic obligations on those who possess, Christianity 'gave to its adherents the clear conscience that property was not held, by its own nature, to such [civic] encumbrances; one is able to say that, in a certain sense, it brought about the final *coup* that emancipated property [from its social obligations]'.[51] By emphasising the contemplation of God, retreat, consumption, and 'mystical social relationships', Christianity undermined what remained of vigorous production-oriented mores in Roman society. It reinforced selfish inwardness.

> In a society of idlers, of rich patrician parasites nourished by manna from Heaven, what could be better than to search for a life of the mind (*vie sage*)?[52]

Perhaps the most destructive long-term effect of the new Christian morality, in Sorel's eyes, was its assault on pride and respectability, and on the civic and military virtues with which these were associated. The symbol of this change was the cult of the Eucharist, which taught the Christian soldier to be humble in the face of the Almighty. Rather than the prideful human relationships characteristic of participatory republican citizens, with their respect for civic duties and fighting virtues, the doctrine of the Eucharist recommended a quietistic morality. Given this perspective, Sorel found the Augustinian strain of piety, with its emphasis on the helpnessness of the human condition and the need for the Christian to rid himself of pride and to cultivate humility and a prayerful heart, a lamentable development. 'The ancient idea [of civic virtue] is completely obliterated by Saint Augustine'.[53]

Christianity, in sum, fostered what nineteenth century French writers usually termed 'individualism'. By showing the emptiness of worldly social obligations and civic ties, Christianity cultivated spiritual inwardness—what Sorel in one place termed 'Christian egotism'.[54] Indeed, for Sorel, Christian individualism was worse than liberal individualism. Both ruined all social solidarity, but Christian individualism was more insidious because, in addition, it undermined liberal conceptions of tolerance. Though the Christian is isolated before God, he enjoys no true *'liberté de conscience'*.

> The believer ceases to regard himself as uniquely tied by civic obligations and gets accustomed to this idea that it is better to obey God than men. This conception would lead to anarchy, if truly the Christian was absolutely alone; but the Church is near him, which is why this pretended independence turns into an absolute servitude.[55]

In a section added to the 1901 edition of ***La Ruine du monde antique,*** Sorel made explicit the message his historical discussion was to bring to his contemporaries: Modern socialists should emulate the civil religion of the Greek *polis,* and not the individualistic religion of Christianity. It was by living the classical ideal of Aristotle, for whom morality was a part of politics, and not the ideal of Christian love that modern workers could hope to find a fulfilling social existence. Sorel did credit Christianity with teaching three important new principles: the dignity of innocence; the infinite values of man; and sacrifice founded on love.[56] But such New Testament *agape* was insensitive to social obligations. The Gospel, therefore, 'is not able to teach us anything about what is necessary in modern civil society'.[57] Sorel's recommendation is for modern men to combine aspects of classical civic morality with the virtues of modern productivity.

> Socialism returns to ancient thought, but the warrior of the city-state has become the worker in large industry; arms have been replaced by machines. Socialism is a philosophy of producers.[58]

Sorel frequently returned to this theme. The final chapter of ***Réflexions sur la violence,*** for example, is about 'the ethic of producers'. Looking back in 1920, he was struck by how his preoccupations were the same as what he understood to be those of Proudhon: the connection between the genesis of new rights and the class struggle.

The point to be emphasised is that these moral concerns remained constant for Sorel throughout his productive years. He consistently stressed the values of work, the family, heroism, virtuous self-denial. It was an austere and pessimistic morality that partially drew its strength from the failures of modern French society to measure up. Sorel had the conviction that the contemporary world was suffering moral decline; he set himself the task of finding the means of virtuous regeneration.

IV

Sorel's focus on classical ideals, and on their relation to religion, to social mores, to moral decadence, etc., was not unique, of course. Such issues were common currency for nineteenth century French writers, as they had been for Western intellectuals for centuries. What merits some emphasis, given today's more secular outlook and the interpretive strategies of previous scholars, is that these debates were still so important to intellectual self-definition in fin-de-siècle France.

It is instructive, in this regard, to compare Sorel's thought with that of notable predecessors and contemporaries. It was common in early-nineteenth century European thought to identify the advent of Christianity with the emergence of the idea of what Hegel called subjective freedom (*'Subjektive Freiheit'*), and it was perhaps even more common to associate this interior subjective dimension with Luther specifically and with the Reformation more generally. Mme de Staël, Benjamin Constant, and Edgar Quinet, for example, saw the Reformation as the root of the modern ideal of freedom of conscience. And, whether embraced or rejected, this emergence of *liberté de conscience* and subjective freedom was commonly traced from the Reformation, via philosophical expressions of individual freedom in the writings of Voltaire, Kant, etc., to the ideals of liberty and equality of the French Revolution. Here, many believed, was the root not only of modern liberty, but also of modern egotism and individualism.

Not everyone, of course, looked solely at this particular legacy of Christianity, even when consideration was confined to its broad socio-cultural impact. Auguste Comte and Christian socialists like Philippe Buchez, for example, suggested that Christianity had played a positive historical role in promoting feeling over intellect and action, and that the Church had promoted harmony over atomism and had therefore assisted in the progress of Humanity. Perhaps more common, however, was an evaluation of Christianity that associated it with individualism, and that judged it as promoting not social solidarity, but an obsession with human suffering and personal piety that undermined social cohesion.

This latter position, clearly, was the one taken by Sorel. Like Comte, he was opposed to individualism, but Sorel took the position that Christianity played a negative role by promoting egoistic concern with personal spiritual salvation over social morality. He could agree with Comte that Catholicism had promoted feeling, but the closest the Church got to a social morality was to support almsgiving to help the poor. Any notion of 'introducing into the relations of production the idea of greater equity escapes the Church; a more exact justice of equal exchange is not able to emerge from its law of love'.[59] Here again, we hear echoes of Proudhon's attacks on the Church and its transcendent morality in favour of an immanent and social morality.

Such concerns were not confined to the Left, of course. Michael Sutton has pointed out that Charles Murras also believed that modern man's obsession with his conscience and his individual welfare was rooted in a barbaric individualism that was synonymous with the 'Christian spirit'.[60] There was an important difference in their respective positions concerning the role of Catholicism in this unfortunate historical development, however, a difference that entailed opposing political positions. Sorel made little distinction between Catholicism and Protestantism in regard to their social morality; Maurras, to the contrary, reserved his strictures for Protestantism. In fact, Maurras argued that Catholicism was quite different because the Church had carefully circumscribed egoistic concerns with a judicious use of dogma and discipline within the hierarchial structure of the Church. Catholicism was therefore to be recommended; indeed, the Church was one of the important collective groupings above the individual (the other was *la patrie*) that would counter the rebellious and destructive individualism emanating from the Reformation and the Revolution of 1789. The attack on individualism was therefore a common theme in the thought of Sorel and Maurras, but what this implied concerning their positions *vis-à-vis* the Catholic Church was diametrically opposed.

Another interesting similarity in the thought of these two men, related to their shared anti-individualism and to their assessment of the social role played by the Church, is their judgment of classical ideals. Both had a great admiration for classical Greek views of the *polis,* and both wished to see the 'classical spirit' again animate modern French society. Maurras's Hellenism, in this respect, was very similar to Sorel's. The divergence was again in their perceptions of the role of the Catholic Church in the historical fortunes of classical ideals. Maurras argued that they reciprocally supported each other and that Catholicism (unlike the rest of Christianity) was imbued with the spirit of classical antiquity. Sorel, as we have seen, took the exact opposite position.

Sorel's reference to the values of the classical city-state, and his rejection of the Church, had more in common with the Hellenism of French thinkers on the Left. The 'cult of antiquity' among prominent revolutionaries like Saint-Just and Robespierre is widely recognised,[61] and there has been a renewed interest in the classical themes of the *fêtes* of the Revolutionary period.[62] Given the prominence of this revolutionary identification of ancient institutions with the Terror, it is not surprising to find early-nineteenth century liberals responding with a variety of critical stances, from condemning outright Greek and Roman institutions (in the thought of Ideologues like Volney[63]), to measuring the distance separating 'ancient' from 'modern' (in, say, the thought of Constant[64]), to reconstructing athenian models that praise private property, civil liberties, and commerce (in, for example, the *'athènes bourgeoises'* of Pierre-Charles Lévesque and Victor Duruy[65]). Sorel and other writers on the Left, on the other hand, were generally more sympathetic to classical republican themes.

Sorel's moral politics are similar to the republican politics of Rousseau and Proudhon, two of the most influential of his left-wing French republican predecessors. Like Rousseau and Proudhon, Sorel condemned high society and social decadence, emphasized the importance of patriotic 'virtue', recommended the superiority of small republican societies, and supported a strong patriarchal family structure. Like Proudhon, Sorel was critical of Rousseau's conception of the 'general will', denounced the Jacobin tradition,[66] preferred classicism to romanticism, focused on workers' associations, insisted on the importance of an ethos devoted to productivity, not consumption, and distrusted centralised political power. Sorel, in short, sits squarely within a tradition of left-wing French republicanism.

V

Situating Sorel within a French republican tradition helps illuminate the general concern Sorel had with the corruption of French society and, more specifically, how he defined the scope of this issue. As Richard Vernon has perceptively pointed out, the contrary of virtue is corruption, not alienation.[67] The modern concern for the latter is rooted in Hegelian philosophy and has received a great deal of attention since the rediscovery of Marx's early writings. But what concerned Frenchmen like Sorel was not alienation, but corruption. And what they had in mind was the corruption of virtue which, according to the republican tradition in France, was brought on by a decline of public-spiritedness. Corruption meant a loss of public life, a turning inward, a transition from public concerns to selfish private considerations. That this tradition had a long history in modern French political thought is obvious: Rousseau, Robespierre, Tocqueville—to name just a few from across the political spectrum—were all concerned with corruption and the loss of republican 'virtue'. This seemed the constant problem of French society and, therefore, of its politics.

If Sorel was part of this tradition of pessimism about decadence, he also narrowed the focus. For Sorel, the politicans and many others in French society were hopelessly mired in egoistic pursuits. He wished to convince the only class that he felt demonstrated sufficient moral strength—the workers—that they should not become infatuated with such forms of selfish pride (*amour propre*). But he also wished to keep them from withdrawing from society and seeking salvation in a life of stoic virtue in solitary retreat. It was better for them to seek a life of republican virtue within industrial society; and indeed, for Sorel, the regeneration of French society required exactly this working-class commitment. To put it another way, Sorel set out to convince workers that the workshop, and only the workshop, could provide the creative locus for the moral identity and virtuous activity which the *polis* had provided for the citizens of ancient Greece and Rome.

Sorel's response to the moral crisis that he perceived as facing French society was therefore different from that of many of his republican predecessors. He did not, as did Robespierre, call for quasi-religious *fêtes* to rekindle republican enthusiasm; nor did he call for widespread associational activity, as did Tocqueville. Sorel looked specifically to workers' associations as the source for defeating corruption, having given up hope on the other social classes in France.

This is closely related to another point: the transformation (ultimately a dangerous transformation) of an essentially political tradition into an antiparliamentary social discussion. Following Sorel's disenchantment with the Dreyfusards, and with the reformist policy that they represented, he turned against the demagoguery of democratic politics and searched for an 'antipolitical' seat for true civic politics. 'Citizenship' lost its traditional moorings for him and was transposed onto industrially based institutions. Sorel was here following in the footsteps of writers like Saint-Simon and Proudhon, who also attacked parliamentary politics as hopeless, and who relocated their hopes in *industrie.*[68] For both Proudhon and Sorel, the 'politicization' of workers' associations would corrupt them and was therefore to be avoided. True regeneration would be achieved through social, not parliamentary action. To use Sheldon Wolin's suggestive terminology, politics is sublimated: organisation replaces politics.[69]

But what of Sorel's calls for rejuvenation through 'violence'?[70] And what of his flirtations with the 'integral' nationalism of the Right? Is it not difficult to reconcile the search for public-spiritedness and the morality of producers with calls for social 'violence'? It is indeed, and it is exactly here that Sorel's radicalism—and his modernism—pass beyond the republican tradition into something quite different. This occurred when Sorel became disenchanted with all social classes, and depressed about the prospects of moral revival. Employing metaphors of pathology and decadence, he came close to embracing a stance where meaning seemed to be reduced to action *qua* action. As suggested earlier, Sorel pulled back from this radical stance; he never became so frustrated that he allowed his pessimism to become a passion for destructive vitality.

But he came close. Sorel's pessimism—generally a source of pride to him—led him to embrace a critical and dangerous anti-politics which was primarily compounded of his refusals. He was always sensitive to and critical of the delusions of optimists, who he argued were dangerous because they took no account of the great difficulties which are always entailed in bringing a project to fruition.

> The optimist may lead his country to the worst disasters. He is not long in finding out that social transformations are not brought about with the ease that he had counted on; he then supposes that this is the fault of his contemporaries, instead of explaining what actually happens by historical necessities; he is tempted to get rid of people whose obstinacy seems to him to be so dangerous to the happiness of all. During the Terror, the men who spilt most blood were precisely those who had the greatest desire to let their equals enjoy the golden age they had dreamed of, and who had the most sympathy with human wretchedness: optimists, idealists, and sensitive men, the greater desire they had for universal happiness the more inexorable they showed themselves.[71]

Sorel reasonably recommended cautious pessimism, rather than the inflated hopes and frustrated ambitions of disillusioned optimists.

But, if Sorel was careful not to err on the side of optimism, he was less able to avoid the dangers of the other extreme—an all-consuming pessimism. Confronted with the dismal prospect of mankind's apparent powerlessness in the face of a seemingly inevitable historical slide into corruption—that is, confronted with the prospect of servility to objective forces—Sorel nearly made the mistake of going to the other extreme: the madness of refusing to recognise necessity. He himself, in short, came *via* pessimism dangerously close to embracing the position of the disillusioned optimist that he had warned against.

Sorel did however draw back. Many of his followers, unfortunately, have had more difficulty traversing the difficult path between servility and madness, and the consequences for modern politics have been disastrous. Too many have channeled their pessimism and frustration into a dangerous and destructive vitality. They, unlike Sorel, echo Gautier's frightening lament: 'plutôt la barbarie que l'ennui'.

NOTES

[1] Jean-Paul Sartre, 'preface' to Franz Fanon's *Les damnés de la terre* (Paris: Maspero, 1961), where Sartre refers to 'les bavardages fascistes de Sorel' (p. 14). For an analysis of the larger significance of this phrase, see Alice Kaplan, *Reproduction of Banality: Fascism, Literature, and French Intellectual Life* (Minneapolis: University of Minnesota Press, 1986).

[2] G.D.H. Cole, *The Second International;* vol. 3, part 1, *A History of Socialist Thought* (London: Macmillan, 1956), p. 387.

[3] Benedetto Croce, . . . *Pagine Sparse* (Napoli: R. Ricciardi, 1920), II S. 227; cited by Georges Goriely, *Le Pluralisme dramatique de Georges Sorel* (Paris: Rivière, 1962), p. 126, note 4.

[4] Larry Portis, *Georges Sorel* (London: Pluto Press, 1980), pp. 1-2.

[5] Jack J. Roth, *The Cult of Violence: Sorel and the Sorelians* (Berkeley: University of California Press, 1980).

[6] Leszek Kolakowski, 'Georges Sorel: Jansenist Marxist', *Dissent* (Winter 1975), pp. 63-80. And, Kolakowski, *Main Currents of Marxism,* vol. 2 (Oxford: Oxford University Press, 1978), pp. 149-174. Kolakowski is echoing Gramsci, who referred to Sorel's 'jansenist fury'. A. Gramsci, *Selections from the Prison Notebooks,* trans. Hoare and Smith (London: 1976), p. 395.

[7] Isaiah Berlin, 'Georges Sorel', *The Times Literary Supplement* (December 31, 1971); reprinted in *Against the Current* (New York: Viking, 1980), this quote, p. 296.

[8] Leszek Kolakowski, *The Alienation of Reason: A History of Positivist Thought,* trans. Norbert Guterman (New York: Doubleday, 1968), pp. 134-153.

[9] Thomas Masaryk, 'La crise scientifique et philosophique du marxisme contemporaine', *Revue internationale de sociologie* 6 (1898), pp. 511-28.

[10] One indication of the continuing interest in Sorel is the recent re-issue of Pierre Andreu's sympathetic and very readable book on Sorel, originally published as *Notre maitre Georges Sorel* (Paris: Grasset, 1953). Reissued, with a new preface, as *Georges Sorel entre le noir et le rouge* (Paris: Maspero, 1982).

There was, in addition, a conference on Sorel in 1982 at the Ecole Normale Superieure in Paris. The proceedings have been published as *Georges Sorel en son temps* (Paris: Seuil, 1985). This conference also founded the *Société d'études soréliennes* which since 1983 has published annually the *Cahiers Georges Sorel.*

[11] H. Stuart Hughes, *Consciousness and Society: Reorientation of European Social Thought 1890-1930* (New York: Random House, 1958).

[12] J.R. Jennings, *Georges Sorel: The Character and Development of His Thought* (New York: St. Martins Press, 1985).

[13] Neil McInnis, 'Les Débuts du marxisme théorique en France et en Italie (1880-1897)', *Cahiers de l'Institut de Science Economique Appliquée,* no. 102 (juin 1960), serie S, no. 3 (Paris), pp. 5-51.

[14] Jacques Julliard, *Fernand Pelloutier et les origines du syndicalisme d'action directe* (Paris: Seuil, 1971).

[15] Daniel Lindenberg, *Le Marxisme introuvable* (Paris: Calmann-Lévy, 1975). Larry Portis, *Georges Sorel: présentation et textes choisis* (Paris: Maspero, 1982). Larry Portis, *Georges Sorel, op. cit.*

[16] More successful is the approach adopted by Ernesto Laclau and Chantal Mouffe, who situate Sorel within a discussion of the genealogy of the concept of hegemony. [See their *Hegemony and Socialist Strategy: Toward a Radical Democratic Politics,* trans. Moore and Cammack (London: Verso, 1985).] Such a strategy, however, does not tell us very much about Sorel.

[17] The most extensive treatment of Sorel's confrontation with marxism is Shlomo Sand, *L'Illusion du politique: Georges Sorel et le débat intellectuel 1900* (Paris: La Découverte, 1985). Also see Maximilien Rubel, 'Georges Sorel et l'achèvement de l'oeuvre de Karl Marx', *Cahiers Georges Sorel* 1 (1983), pp. 9-36; and Yves Guchet, 'Georges Sorel, marxiste?', *Cahiers Georges Sorel* 2 (1984), pp. 37-56.

[18] J.L. Talmon, 'The Legacy of Georges Sorel', *Encounter* (February 1970), pp. 47-60.

[19] Jack J. Roth, *The Cult of Violence: Sorel and the Sorelians, op. cit.*

[20] Zeev Sternhell, *Ni droite ni gauche: l'idéologie fasciste en France* (Paris: Seuil, 1983). Also see Sternhell's *La Droite révolutionnaire, 1885-1914: les origines françaises du fascisme* (Paris: Seuil, 1978).

[21] Sternhell, *Ni droite ni gauche,* p. 40.

[22] Bertrand de Jouvenel, labeled a fascist by Sternhell, even brought a lawsuit against Sternhell. Raymond Aron, who testified on Jouvenel's behalf, died immediately following his appearance at the trial.

[23] For a longer analysis of the flaws in Sternhell's method, see my review of *Ni droite ni gauche* in *Substance* 15, 1 (1986), pp. 86-90.

[24] *Ni droite ni gauche,* p. 35.

[25] See Michel Charzat, 'Georges Sorel et le fascisme. Eléments d'explication d'une légende tenace', *Cahiers Georges Sorel* 1 (1983), pp. 37-51; and Maria Malatesta, 'Georges Sorel devant la guerre et le bolchevisme', *Georges Sorel en son temps* (Paris: Seuil, 1985), pp. 101-22.

[26] *Propos de Georges Sorel* (Paris: Gallimard, 1935).

[27] Roberto Michels, in *Nuovi studi di diritto, economica e politica,* II (septembre-octobre 1929), p. 295; cited by Charzat, *op. cit.,* p. 43.

[28] See Shlomo Sand, 'Sorel, les Juifs et l'antisémitisme', *Cahiers Georges Sorel* 2 (1984), pp. 7-36.

[29] The most thorough analysis of Sorel's association with the monarchist right is Lawrence Wilde, 'Sorel and the French Right', *History of Political Thought,* vol. 7, no. 2 (1986), pp. 361-74. Wilde concludes that Sorel's association with the extreme right was 'of an entirely different form from the gushing and overoptimistic support which he had given to revolutionary syndicalism. It is more tentative, more reserved, and never wholehearted.', p. 362.

Also see Paul Mazgaj, *The Action Française and Revolutionary Syndicalism* (Chapel Hill: University of North Carolina Press, 1979).

[30] Zeev Sternhell, 'Fascist Ideology', in Walter Laqueur, ed., *Fascism: A Reader's Guide* (Berkeley: University of California Press, 1976), p. 327.

[31] Gramsci made a similar point: 'Sorel is in no way responsible for the intellectual pettiness and crudity of his Italian admirers, just as Karl Marx is not responsible for the absurd ideological pretentions of 'Marxists'.' *Selections from Political Writings 1910-1920),* ed. Quentin Hoare, trans. John Mathews (New York: International Publishers, 1977), p. 330.

[32] In addition to the standard works of A.E. Carter, *The Idea of Decadence in French Literature, 1830-1900* (Toronto: University of Toronto Press, 1958) and Koenraad W. Swart, *The Sense of Decadence in Nineteenth Century France* (The Hague: Nijhoff, 1964), see the recent discussions in *Journal of Contemporary History,* vol. 17, no. 1 (January 1982) [this is a special issue on decadence], and Robert A. Nye, *Crime, Madness, and Politics in Modern France: The Medical Concept of National Decline* (Princeton: Princeton University Press, 1984).

[33] Georges Steiner, *In Bluebeard's Castle: Some Notes Towards the Redefinition of Culture* (New Haven: Yale University Press, 1971), p. 11.

[34] Isaiah Berlin, 'Georges Sorel', *op. cit.*

[35] John L. Stanley, *The Sociology of Virtue: The Political and Social Theories of Georges Sorel* (Berkeley: University of California Press, 1981).

Stanley has done more to make Sorel accessible to the English-reading public than any other person, past or present. In addition to this general interpretive book, he has also edited *From Georges Sorel: Essays in Socialism and Philosophy* (New York: Oxford University Press, 1976), and translated *Les Illusions du progrès* [*The Illusions of Progress* (Berkeley: University of California Press, 1969)] and *Insegnamenti sociale della economia contemporanea [Social Foundations of Contemporary Economics* (New Brunswick: Transaction Books, 1984)].

[36] Arthur L. Greil, *Georges Sorel and the Sociology of Virtue* (Washington, D.C.; University Press of America, 1981).

[37] *Le Procès de Socrate* (Paris: Alcan, 1889), p. 172.

[38] *Ibid.*, p. 6.

[39] *Ibid.*, pp. 177-78.

[40] Neil McInnis, 'Georges Sorel on the Trial of Socrates', *Politics*, vol. 10 (May 1975), pp. 37-43; this quote, p. 37.

[41] J.G.A. Pocock is perhaps the best known analyst of the importance of classical republican themes in the Italian Renaissance and in early-modern Anglo-American thought. For France, see Claude Nicolet, *L'Idée républicaine en France: essai d'histoire critique* (Paris: Gallimard, 1982).

[42] See Françoise Blum, 'Images de "la femme" chez Georges Sorel', *Cahiers Georges Sorel* 4 (1986), pp. 5-25.

More generally, see Siân Reynolds, 'Marianne's Citizens? Women, the Republic and Universal Suffrage in France', in Siân Reynolds, ed., *Women, State, and Revolution: Essays on Power and Gender in Europe Since 1789* (Amherst: The University of Massachusetts Press, 1987), pp. 102-22; and Joan B. Landes, *Women and the Public Sphere in the Age of the French Revolution* (Ithaca: Cornell University Press, 1988).

[43] See my *Pierre-Joseph Proudhon and the Rise of French Republican Socialism* (New York: Oxford University Press, 1984).

[44] Citations are from the third edition (Paris: Marcel Rivière, 1933), p. 44.

[45] *Ibid.*, p. 45.

[46] *Ibid.*, p. 57.

[47] *Ibid.*, p. 63.

[48] *Ibid.*, p. 132.

[49] *Ibid.*, p. 89.

[50] *Ibid.*, p. 94.

[51] *Ibid.*, p. 102.

[52] *Ibid.*, p. 67.

[53] *Ibid.*, p. 135.

[54] *Ibid.*, p. 143.

[55] *Ibid.*, pp. 155-56.

[56] *Ibid.*, pp. 288, 310.

[57] *Ibid.*, p. 311.

[58] *Ibid.*

[59] *Ibid.*, p. 297.

[60] Michael Sutton, *Nationalism, Positivism and Catholicism: The Politics of Charles Maurras and French Catholics, 1890-1914* (Cambridge: Cambridge University Press, 1982), pp. 11-75.

[61] The classic modern account of this is Harold T. Parker, *The Cult of Antiquity and the French Revolutionaries* (Chicago: University of Chicago Press, 1937). Also see the essay by Pierre Vidal-Naquet, 'Tradition de la démocratie grecque', which precedes the text of Moses I. Finley, *Démocratie antique et démocratie moderne* (Paris: Payot, 1976), see esp. pp. 15-39.

[62] See Mona Ozouf, *La Fête révolutionnaire, 1789-1799* (Paris: Gallimard, 1976).

[63] See Mouza Raskolnikoff, 'Volney et les Idéologues: le refus de Rome', *Revue historique*, 542 (avril-juin 1982), pp. 357-73.

[64] This contrast between ancient and modern liberty is a familiar theme in Constant's writings. It is extensively analysed by Stephen Holmes, *Benjamin Constant and the Making of Modern Liberalism* (New Haven: Yale University Press, 1984).

[65] See Nicole Loraux and Pierre Vidal-Naquet, 'La formation de l'athènes bourgeoise: essai d'historiographie 1750-1850', in R.R. Bolgar, ed., *Classical Influences on Western Thought A.D. 1650-1870* (Cambridge: Cambridge University Press, 1979), pp. 169-222.

[66] See Renzo Ragghianti, 'Critique du modèle jacobin chez Georges Sorel', *Cahiers Georges Sorel* 4 (1986), pp. 26-38; and Jacques Julliard, 'Sorel, Rousseau, et la Révolution française', *Cahiers Georges Sorel* 3 (1985), pp. 5-15. Unfortunately, I have been unable to consult the unpublished thèse de 3e cycle of Jean-Claude Despax, *Georges Sorel, Historien de la Révolution* (Université

de Montpellier III, 1984). See the review by Pierre Andreu, *Cahiers Georges Sorel* 4 (1986), pp. 161-65.

[67] See Vernon's review of John L. Stanley's *The Sociology of Virtue,* in *Political Theory* 10 (1982), pp. 623-26; and Vernon's *Citizenship and Order: Studies in French Political Thought* (Toronto: University of Toronto Press, 1986).

[68] For the earlier history of this concept, see Michael James, 'Pierre-Louis Roederer, Jean-Baptiste Say, and the concept of *industrie*', *History of Political Economy* 9:4 (1977), pp. 455-475; and Thomas E. Kaiser, 'Politics and political economy in the thought of the Ideologies', *History of Political Economy* 12:2 (1980), pp. 141-60.

[69] Sheldon Wolin, *Politics and Vision* (Boston: Little, Brown, 1960).

[70] The distinction between 'force' and 'violence' is central to the argument in *Réflexions sur la violence.* See pp. 39, 171-77, 186-90 of the English translation of this work, *Reflections on Violence,* trans. T.E. Hulme and J. Roth (New York: Collier Books, 1950). Also see the discussion of Richard Vernon, *Commitment and Change: Georges Sorel and the Idea of Revolution* (Toronto: University of Toronto Press, 1978).

[71] *Reflections on Violence,* pp. 32-33.

David Ohana (essay date 1991)

SOURCE: "Georges Sorel and the Rise of Political Myth," in *History of European Ideas,* Vol. 13, No. 6, 1991, pp. 733-46.

[*In the following excerpt, Ohana identifies apparent inconsistencies in Sorel's philosophy, which he attributes to the rapidly changing cultural mileau within his lifetime.*]

I

Georges Sorel (1847-1922) continues to be a problem for many researchers and ideologues of the Right and the Left. He has become a litmus paper by which thinkers, researchers, and political activists shape their own beliefs and try to formulate their own ideas. An international colloquium on Sorel which was held in 1982 at the Ecole Normale Supérieure resulted in the publication of *Georges Sorel en son temps* (1985);[1] and the Société d'Études Soréliennes which was founded in 1983 published the *Cahiers G. Sorel*[2] and plans to republish Sorel's complete works in fifteen volumes. It is not surprising that this 'nouveau discours',[3] this renewed interest, arose among the French Left when the Socialists came to power in France in this decade. This 'revision of Sorel' tries to achieve three main purposes: the Gallicisation of European socialism through Sorel; the reclaiming of Sorel by the Left; the rehabilitation of Sorel from the charge of contributing to the rise of Fascism, or to put it another way, the attempt to banish the memory of what Sartre called the 'Fascist speeches'[4] of Sorel.

Sorel was a thinker who called himself a true Marxist, but viewed young Mussolini and Lenin as the two greatest politicians ever produced by socialism. He was a Dreyfusard and an anti-Dreyfusard in the same decade. He waited for a cultural rejuvenation of decadent Europe, but kept silent during World War One. He was anti-Semitic but admired ancient Hebrew civilisation. A revolutionary who discovered the modern instruments of power of the twentieth century, at the same time he looked at ancient heroic cultures as an inspiring model for the France of the fin de siècle. He supported the C.G.T. and 'Action Française', Revolutionary Syndicalism and Marxism, the Soviets and the great American capitalists, Proudhon and Bernstein. In the very same year that Sergio Panunzio glorified Sorel as the father of Fascist syndicalism, Sorel looked at the Soviets as true revolutionary syndicates.[5] Two members of the 'Cercle Proudhon'—which brought together Monarchists and syndicalists, Nationalists and Socialists—sought to have a monopoly on Sorel as the father of their contradictory thoughts. These were Georges Valois, founder of the 'Faisceau', and the communist Edouard Berth.[6]

Sorel has influenced, in one way or another, French communist militants such as M. Michael, M. Fourrier, Barbusse, Delesalle, Louzon, Legardelle, and G. Bernier, as well as such French Fascists as Bourget, Variot and Johannet. He wrote in various French political journals including *Effort, Cahiers du Cercle Proudhon, Cité Française, Avant-garde, Action directe, Indépendence,* and *Mouvement Socialiste.* Daniel Halévy's well-known apocryphal story of the Bolshevik Russian and Fascist Italian ambassadors to France who proposed erecting a monument above Sorel's grave, once again emphasised the ambiguity that has surrounded Sorel's memory. Two days after Sorel died, Delesalle wrote in *Humanité:* 'Proletarians, exploited everywhere, believe me, one of your most lucid and greatest defenders has passed away.'[7] Three days later, Valois wrote in *Action Française:* 'I bow and pray before the tomb of the man to whom I owe so much.'[8]

Of course, Sorel himself is responsible for that 'baffling accumulation of paradoxes and contradictions',[9] as pointed out by H. Stuart Hughes. Tracing the paths of the historiography on Sorel teaches us more about the ideological discussions and political debates which took place during the 20th century than about Sorel himself. More than a thousand articles, reviews, and books have been written on Sorel since he published his first book on Socrates in 1889.[10] This literature points to the conclusion that the creator of the myth of the general strike and the sociologist of the myth himself became a myth used by different political activists and by various beliefs and ideologies. Just as every political camp has its own Sorel, so every generation also has its Sorel. It seems there is no other political theoretician in the twentieth century whose fame arose from a search for new myths and for cultural rejuvenation (ricorso). No wonder that Benedetto Croce called Sorel the 'Vico of the 20th century'.[11] Sorel broke ideological boundaries and felt himself both an insider and an outsider in various political camps. This is perhaps why everyone can find his own Sorel.

Was Sorel a barometer, a kind of seismograph of his time, or did he contribute to the emergence of 20th-century cults of violence? Of course he was both. Like the economist Marx, the sociologist Pareto, and the psychologist Le Bon, his analysis influenced his times. Sorel has to be considered as a thinker who thought in terms of civilisation, not just politics. That is why Sorel regarded myth as the subject-matter of renewal, rather than reason as the subject-matter of progress. From Marx, Sorel learned that the proletariat should be the center of civilisation and its modern agent of renewal. But unlike Marx, Sorel thought in moral concepts rather than economic terms, in terms of psychological phenomena such as myth rather than in a materialistic language. Sorel transformed Marxism from a model of social science to a myth of social poetry. Marxist ideology analyses reality; Sorel's myth mobilises masses. For Sorel, sociology exposes reality while myth tries to change it. True, Sorel was a sociologist, but he also built a modern political mythology.

II

The first formulations of Sorel's world-view, which placed myth at the center of his philosophy of history, can be found in his early writings.[12] In ***Contribution à l'etude profane de la bible*** (1889), Sorel gives prominence to the symbolic-mythical aspect of Hebrew culture rather than to its rational-intellectual dimension. In ***Le Procès de Socrate*** (1889), Sorel analysed the transition from an agrarian and mythical society to an urban and rationalistic one. He condemned the Socratic ethics which replaced the Homeric aesthetics. In ***La Ruine du monde antique*** (1901) Sorel described how the myth of the Roman Empire as a great power had become bureaucratised and how yesterday's conquerors had become today's policemen. In ***Le Système historique de Renan*** (1902), he described the politicisation of mysticism by the Church and its elevation of theology and philosophy above myth.

These books are especially important because they contain the foundations of the basic Sorelian view: myth stands at the center of his philosophy of history.[13] In his later political development and his fluctuations between the Left and Right, Sorel remained faithful to the attitudes expressed in his early writings. In his approach to ancient civilisations, Sorel was less interested in objective investigation of the Hebrew, Greek, Roman and Early Christian cultures than in finding a model of aesthetic heroism. Sorel was in search of virtue. Sorelian virtue concentrates on 'how' rather than focusses on 'what': Sorel's ethos emphasises values of struggle, suffering, solitude, determination and creativity—values which come into their own in a world of conflict. On the other hand, a harmonious world allows for false values of justice, the search for happiness and rational order.

Heroic vitality is the common denominator of civilisations before they become 'establishments', according to Sorel. He was only interested in the pragmatic component of the past, in the 'mythical past' which continues to operate and not in the 'historical past' as a passing interest. These early reflections on the vitality of the state of conflict of ancient civilisations led Sorel to attack the illusion of harmony in decadent modern culture which sprang, in his view, from the philosophy of the Enlightenment.

III

According to Sorel, the 'utopian' philosophers of the 18th century renewed to the concept of 'nature' which for them symbolised perfection and total adjustment.[14] This vision of harmony as a long-awaited goal, he said, was the common denominator of religious and secular messianism. The philosophy of the Enlightenment, he claimed, exchanged the religious concept of 'God' for the modern concepts of 'nature' and 'reason'. Sorel decried all forms of messianism. One of the basic perceptions guiding the messianic idea is that the end of mankind will be as its beginning: in the beginning, man lived in a harmony which became distorted over time, for whatever reasons, but in the future, man's historic destiny is reconciliation and a return to Paradise, where all the paradoxes will dissolve and the contradictions be resolved finally and unequivocably. At the gates of Eden lies eternal peace. In this respect, Sorel is the anti-Messiah: the harmony, he said, is false. Paradise, whether religious or secular, is the refuge of cowards fleeing for their lives.[15]

Sorel ridiculed the attempts of the rational philosophers to borrow the Church's ideas on the power of education to build utopian messianic societies: Turgot suggested to the king a clerical model of public education as a state project;[16] Condursa believed in a rapid secular conversion of the non-European nations, since the oriental religions were in decline. Secular missionarism likened Paraguayan villages to monasteries. Sorel replaced harmony with the idea of conflict; he replaced paralysing determinism with a lively voluntarism; he replaced linear development with cyclic development and in place of optimism, he preferred a pessimism divested of illusions.

Harmony as an initial or final vision of the world was for Sorel an artificial construction which has no place in reality.[17] The attempts of 18th century thinkers to construct a free society out of the everyday world of conflict was utopian in the full sense of the word: it could never be realised. The messianic utopias of the Enlightenment envisaged an ideal man to fit their ideal world. This abstract man divested of history was a fiction, an artificial model, which had no place in reality. He was an expression of a desire for eternal peace—a peaceful life of sweet illusions. The illusions of harmony, of man resolving all his contradictions were merely tranquilisers at the same time as weapons in the hands of the bourgeoisie trying to preserve the status quo. The bourgeoisie was the conquering class and the philosophy of progress of the Enlightenment was its ideology. Progress, as Nisbet and

Stanley explained in their introduction to the English edition of ***Les illusions du prògres*** (1908), legitimised the political power of the bourgeoisie.[18] But progress was only the tip of the iceberg of the Enlightenment. The Enlightenment, according to Sorel, was not only the ideology of a class, but also an expression of a state of consciousness: i.e. harmony as against conflict.

The purpose of Sorel's radical analysis was to reveal the dangers of the bourgeois state of mind: the search for harmony, illusions of progress, democracy, rationalism and optimism were a cover for class interest, attempts to temper conflict, appease strife, suppress vitality and harmonise the reality of conflict. The political rule of the bourgeoisie imposed a bourgeois mentality, the sanctification of the prevailing order. Thus, exposure was not just a method but also the principle of Sorel's political outlook: namely, a continual undermining of the status quo and the destruction of everything that was 'established'. Whereas Marx thought 'ideological exposure' was a means of understanding socio-economic reality as he saw it, the destructive awareness and Sorel's principle of negation are an essential part of his political philosophy.

For Sorel, there was no dialectic and there was no progress. Instead of progress, Sorel looked for a ricorso (renewal) of myths in history. Sorel took the concept of 'ricorso' from Vico,[19] who claimed that in order to understand human history, one must also investigate the hidden layers of human culture, especially the myths. While the development of reason was the essence of progress. Sorel saw myth as the essence of cultural renewal, of a ricorso. A civilisation needs a myth in order to flourish. Sorel set himself a double role: to invent such a modern myth for a decadent European civilisation and to distinguish between myth and anti-myth, or, to state it differently, between myth and utopia or ideology.

The French revolution was for Sorel a historical prism through which to examine the results of the philosophy of the Enlightenment: the increase in state power, bureaucratisation and centralisation, the establishment of new elites, the danger of abstract theories translated into the language of radical politics, and the domination of the physiocrats, the Jacobins and the Blanquists. Sorel warned that if the social-democrats gained power, they would be worse than the Inquisition of the 'ancien régime' and of Robespierre. The Jacobins were exposed to the theories of the Enlightenment and to the praxis of the revolution; Jacobinism was revealed as a theory of vigour.[20]

Sorel saw the Jacobin terror and social democracy as linked by a single Leitmotif: the strengthening of the state's power of suppression. When the time comes, said Sorel, the theorist of revolutionary syndicalism, 'the syndicalists do not intend to reform the state, like the people of the 18th century; they want to destroy it'.[21] Sorel saw the French Revolution as the modern political realisation of the ideas of the Enlightenment. Jacobin terror was evidence of the refutation of the 'natural order', and Sorel concluded that the need for terror to suppress deviation in a revolutionary era proved that the vision of harmony of the Enlightenment philosophers was totally false.

IV

In Sorel's political philosophy, one can see the sum total of the 'Fin de siècle' climate of opinion: Bergson's vitality, Croce's categories of action, Le Bon's psychology of the masses, James' pragmatism, Hartman's unconscious, and the discovery of Vico's ricorsi. The importance of Sorel is that he provided a political home for a wide range of contemporary opinions.

The growth of the new social sciences was also reflected in Sorel: the new psychological trends (Ribot, Poincaré and the 'Ecole de Paris') gave a sort of academic legitimacy to a preoccupation with the emotions of individuals and of the masses. In the same way, they legitimised the revolt against positivism, progress and Durkheims' sociology. Sorel, Le Bon, Mosca, Pareto and Michels are examples of the connection which developed between an interest in mass psychology and élitist political conclusions.

From 1901, Sorel and Charles Péguy participated in Bergson's lectures at the Collège de France.[22] In order to understand Sorel, it is necessary to understand the 'Bergsonian' Sorel. The ultimate cause, in Bergson's pantheist view, is creative evolution: the flow of life means that construction and destruction are a single continuum.[23] Bergson renewed the discussion of 'ex nihilo nihil fit': rejection of what now exists obviously involves the creation of something new. Bergsonian concepts, each one of which derives from the preceding one (e.g. durée, intuition, freedom, movement, the flow of life and élan vital), taken out of their broad philosophical context by Sorel and partially transposed, were therefore misleading in Sorel's theories. Bergson himself maintained that Sorel had too original and independant a personality to carry the banners of others and that 'there is no connection between his (Sorel's) daring innovations and my ideas'.[24]

Nietzsche's *Beyond Good and Evil* fascinated Sorel. Sorel wrote: 'In my view, the best way to understand any idea in the history of thought is to sharpen the contradictions as much as possible. I will adopt this method and take as my starting point Nietzche's contrast between two opposing sets of moral values. Much has been written of this contrast but it has never been seriously investigated.'[25] The Sorelian hero is typified not by his morality but by the heroic ethos. Sorel did not distinguish between the values of the proletarian and the capitalist fighters. Both had the same personality structure and mode of action. He was interested in their essential vitality, not in their moral content. Sorel's dichotomy of ethics and the heroic ethos cleared the state for the rise of an amoral aesthetics.

The morality of producers and the morality of consumers, Sorel's new categories, were beyond the old criteria of good and evil. These new categories were taken from the teachngs of Proudhon and not from Marxist terminology.[26] The criteria had passed from the ethical dimension to the dimension of struggle and production. The morality of producers was a mark of authenticity and the expression of a new heroic culture, whereas the morality of consumers was characteristic of decadence and an expression of the Enlightenment culture. Authenticity and decadence were the litmus paper of this new morality, which became a starting-point for the reorientation of European political culture at the beginning of the twentieth century.

For Sorel Lofty moral views are no longer dependent in any way on the individual's considerations, education or wishes; they are dependent on the state of war in which the people agree to participate and which is translated into exact myths. His abandonment of traditional ethics brought Sorel to the aesthetic language of the workshops.[27] In his view, the field of industrial production was similar to the field of art. There was an analogy between art, industry and war. The workers' tools were like the painter's brush or the sculptor's chisel, in that they became part of his very being. Sorel sang a hymn of praise to the ethos of the machine. 'If there is anything which is especially social in the activity of man, it is the machine. It is more social than language itself.'[28] The aesthetisation of the machine did not make a fetish of the worker or personalise the machine but challenged the Marxist concept of alienation; the machine did not alienate man: it made him free.

Sorel translated into political terms the Nietzschean transition from the Judeo-christian ethic to the aesthetics of the will-to-power. This is where the aesthetic politicisation of Nietzsche occurred: the general strike was discerned as a poetic myth and revolutionary syndicalism was a 'social poem'. Sorel changed the area of political discussion from science to myth, from ethics to aesthetics.

V

If we look carefully at Sorel's intellectual development, we see that he began to revise Marxism in terms of the Nietzschean, Proudhonnist and Bergsonian concepts which had already shaped his own thought-processes. Bernstein was right when he defined Sorel as a new Marxism in Nietzschean form. Sorel revolted against the rational tradition from Socrates to the Enlightenment and transformed reason by means of an aesthetic view of the world. Historicism, romanticism, historical determinism and the theory of progress all described man as an historical concept. By contrst, at the center of the Nietzschean energy existentialist approach, man shaped his own world through myth. The dimension of guidance from past experience was abandoned in favor of an open future invading the present through the medium of myth. It was the power of myth to achieve the unity of man and his world through an immediate aesthetic—existentialist—political experience such as the myth of the general strike.

The revision of Marxism by Sorel in the 1890's must be considered together with the revisions by Bernstein and Lenin. But whereas both the latter accepted Marx's ultimate aims with respect to a classless society and equality, one supporting the method of social-democracy and the other a revolutionary élite, Sorel's revision was centred on the concept of class warfare. In the years 1895-1898, Marxism split into two opposing camps, each of which claimed legitimacy. Those who wished to attain Marxism 'through the ballot box' focussed on the rational, and those who preferred a combative Marxism, who idolised the concept of class warfare and saw in struggle a way to preserve the energy of the proletariat, focussed on the irrational, vital, psychological and combative elements of Marxism. While the Bernstein and Lenin revisions claimed to be the heirs of the Enlightenment, Sorel's revision revolted against it and wanted to free Marx from Marxism.[29]

Marx gave to Sorel a coherent perception of the philosophy of history: history was class-struggle. The historical method and the ability to unite various elements within a single framework: this was the greatness of Marx, and this was what Sorel needed at the period when he assimilated different theories and thinkers such as Nietzsche, Bergson and Proudhon. When Sorel based Marxism on class struggle, he did not refer only to historical necessity and technological improvement, but gave priority to the subject of the class's responsibility to itself. The proletariat did not only swim against the stream, but created the stream; the concepts of 'war' and 'classes' not only represented historical forces but also an expression of self-consciousness and self-determination. The key-question for Sorel was motivation, and he concluded that exploitation was not an economic or social category, but a psychological one: Man was not an *Homo Economicus*, but was motivated by emotions, symbols and myths.

Sorel was never a Marxist in the true meaning of the term.[30] From the very beginning, he accepted only partially the basic principles of Marxism: he never espoused Marx's conclusions on the nationalisation of the means of production, on historical determinism socio-economic forces, the dictatorship of the proletariat, or the concepts of alienation, property, the fetishism of goods or the division of labour. Sorel had an a priori view of what Marxism ought to be: Marxism should be an ethical message and a test of authenticity. Sorel's revision of Marxism was not just the adding of another layer or a mere afterthought: from the first, his acceptance of Marxism was dependent on the revision he had made. Instead of economic mechanisms he wanted moral renewal, in place of Hegelian dialectics he returned to Proudhon, progress was to be exchanged for a perpetual struggle, voluntarism replaced the determinism of economic forces, and permanent violence took the place of the revolution.

The pace-setters in French politics were also examined according to the principle Sorel set himself in order to establish who was carrying the banner of these combative, vital, ethical values of Marxism. Sorel rejected the 'Parti Socialiste Révolutionnaire' because of its Blanquist tendency. At first he supported the 'Fédération des Travailleurs Socialistes' (the 'Possibilists'), founded in 1882 and led by Paul Brousse. However, closest of all to his heart was the 'Parti Ouvrier Socialiste Révolutionnaire', founded in 1890 by Jean Allemane, who opposed the trade-unionism of the 'possibilists' and supported the Proudhon view of direct proletarian action. The establishment of the National confederation of the 'Bourses du Travail' by Fernand Pelloutier in 1892 and the C.G.T. in 1895, which supported the general strike, direct action, the decentralisation of the syndicates and workers' unions, finally brought Sorel to abandon the political parties.[31] Sorel's final disillusionment with the socialist political parties as carriers of the flag of action occurred with the creation of the united socialist block in October 1898. Despairing of party politics, Sorel began to support direct political cults.

La Décomposition du Marxisme (1908), which was published in the same year as ***Réflextions sur la violence*** and ***Les illusions du progrès,*** is thought to be the summary of the Sorelian revision of Marxism. The aim of the booklet, based on a lecture given to the international conference of socialist syndicates in Paris on 3 April 1907, is 'to examine the significance of Marx's thought'.[32] Long before the ***Decomposition,*** Sorel had examined the meaning of Marx's ideas in the trilogy: ***L'avenir socialiste des syndicats*** which was published in *Humanité Nouvelle* in 1898 (and reprinted as ***Materiaux d'une théorie du prolétariat*** in 1919), ***Saggi di Critica del Marxismo*** (1902) and ***Introduction à l'Economie Moderne*** (1903). This Sorelian trilogy on Marxism proved that Sorel had always been critical of the orthodox Marxist assumptions as formulated, for example, by Engles, Kautsky and Gil Ged, and the social democratic assumptions as formulated by Bernstein and Jaùres.

Das Kapital was translated into French only in 1875, and as Daniel Halévi pointed out in 1880: 'Paris did not know anything about Marxism.'[33] Proudhon dominated the workers' political consciousness in France during the 19th century. By means of Proudhon, Sorel hoped to retrieve Marx from the rationalistic-harmonious-philosophical context of Marx's early writings, the inheritance of the Enlightenment, and to turn him into the militant Marx of class warfare. The Marx who attacked Proudhon was, in Sorel's opinion, a very Hegelian Marx: within Marx there was a clash between two contradictory trends, Hegel and Proudhon.[34] Whatever was historical for Hegel—that is, whatever was a temporary thesis or antithesis, swallowed up in the dialectical process—was immanent for Proudhon and Sorel. For them, contradictions existed side by side and balanced each other out: movement was everything and synthesis was a philosophical fiction. Sorel hung on to Proudhonism because he preferred Marx's class warfare (contradictions) to the Marxian classless society (synthesis).

In 1895, the interaction between Sorel and the Italian Marxist Circle became decisive. Sorel, in association with Lefargelle and Deville edited the *Devenir Social* which, together with the Italian *Critica Sociale,* founded by Turati in 1891, was the organ for promoting the revision of Marxism. The foremost Italian representatives were Fillipo Turati, leader of the socialist party, Severio Merlino, editor of *Rivista critical del socialismo,* the young Benedetto Croce and Antonio Labriola, professor of moral philosophy at Rome University and leader of the group.[35] Sorel accepted from their critique of Marxism those principles which suited him. He was particularly impressed by their critical and professional analysis. Marxism, henceforth, was regarded as a conception which extolled political struggle—both class and ethical—and thus forged the figure of a proletarian-militant who saw his work as creative rather than alienating: it was not the economic content which was important but rather the form of militancy.

Sorel's revision of Marxism gave birth to revolutionary syndicalism: syndicalism represented for Sorel the value of self-consciousness and the expression of the daily voluntary struggle of the proletariat for freedom and at the same time for the deliverance of civilisation. He saw the syndicate as a militant group of the proletarian masses and the microcosm of the free ideal producers' society. Syndicates were the avant-garde which had to be isolated from the bourgeois order to avoid being assimilated within it. This 'New School' revolted against the priority of theory over practice which, according to Sorel, typified the ideologists, politicians and social-democrats, and emphasised the primacy of the workers. It was the Syndicates and not the party which represented socialism.[36] This primacy of 'ouvrierism' brought Sorel to an unsolved dilemma and drove him away from Marxism. The role of violence was to 'rediscover energy . . . Thus', concluded Sorel, 'violence has become an indispensable factor in Marxism'.[37] Sorel clarified his meaning in the preface to ***Réflexions,*** 'We are ready to complete Marx's doctrines rather than simply interpreting his texts'.[38] It was the militancy of the conflicting classes that captured his heart. Violence was the proving-ground of the class war: only if it was violent was it an authentic class war. If violence ceased, then the class war became a distorted contest between two camps striving for class harmony.

Every ideology has its own philosophy of history: violence, which expressed itself in the general strike, revolutionary syndicalism and the cult of violence was the Sorelian philosophy of history. Sorel, who declared himself a true Marxist who wanted to complete his master's work through violence, turned Marxism upside-down. The result was absolutely different from the original: in order to arouse and stir up the working class, Sorel developed a theory of history that put violence in the centre. This creative violence as the energic factor of history was transformed into a new political content, and when, at this juncture, the theory of the myth and direct action were added, nothing remained of the original Marxist model.

VI

Violence was the Sorelian philosophy of history which was anchored, first and foremost, in his revision of Marx and class-warfare was for Sorel the cornerstone of the Marxist thought.[39] The decadent bourgeoisie and the proletariat as devotees of social peace were signs, for Sorel, of a dual process of degeneration. He concluded that violence 'tries to rebuild the class structure', and 'aspires to restore to capitalism the belligerence it once had'.[40] History, according to Sorel, was the history of violence; it is impossible, he believed, to understand history without understanding the rôle of violence: the positive value of violence, which was characterised by such terms as 'pure', 'idealistic', 'just' and 'purified',[41] lies in its vitalisation of history. Violence was not just the key to the philosophy of history: it was a moral testing-ground. Sorel not only analysed violence as an immanent historical tool but endorsed it as a permanent aesthetic value.

Myth was a central concept in Sorel's philosophy of history: the fuel that powered vitality in history was not to be found in ideologies, but in myths. The role of ideology, according to Sorel, was to perpetuate the existing system of interests or to replace it with another. On the other hand, the role of myth was to stage revolutionary actions and to undermine the existing order. Sorel used the study of history as a tool for a reorientation of political philosophy: he believed that an understanding of the inner logic of the rise and fall of ancient civilisations could give an impetus to present-day history. Sorel did not regard myths as historical legends which were elaborated over the years and finally interpreted retroactively as myths. He believed that just the opposite was true: namely, that the crystallisation of myth, from the beginning, encouraged those who believed in it to effect changes in a particular historical reality.[42] It is not the rationalisation of myth which was respected by Sorel, but rather its political effectiveness. Sorel diagnosed myth as acting in the service of politics.

Sorel differentiated between utopia and myth. Utopia was the image of reality, an imitation, a reflection. Utopia was not revolutionary vis-à-vis the existing order, but aimed, rather, 'to direct the powers-that-be towards reform'.[43] A corroboration of this view may be found in Sorel's attacks on Renan: 'He (Renan) sees in socialism a utopia: that is, something which may be compared to reality'.[44] Sorelian myth, unlike a utopia, was nihilistic with regard to the given historical reality: 'Our myths lead people to prepare for battle to defeat the existing order'.[45] Myth was not part of the harmonious order of things. It was an alternative order, a real substitute for the existing order, albeit artificial: in this way myth negated concrete historical existence and tried to eliminate whatever exists. Historical myths tried to negate the existing historical reality: examples are the myth of early Christianity, the myth of Roman power, the myth of the conquering barbarians, the myth of the Reformation, the myth of the Italian 'Risorgimento', the myth of the French Revolution and the myth of Napoleon.

Following Le Bon's social psychology, Sorel created a political philosophy according to which the future producers' society would understand socialism through the intuitive and spontaneous drama of the general strike. Sorel, who accused other intellectuals of inventing utopias, did the same; or, to put the matter in Frank E. Manuel's words, 'Sorel . . . was committed to a utopia of absolute principles internalized by a heroic proletariat . . . there was, of course, no final conquest because the utopia lay in the conflict itself'.[46] Sorel's myth of the general strike, the central concept of his political philosophy, was in fact a utopia.

The Sorelian distinction between power and violence parallelled his distinction between utopia and myth: bourgeois power rested on utopia while proletarian violence rested on myth. We saw how Sorel analysed bourgeois power and found its origins in the harmonious philosophy of the Enlightenment and the French Revolution. This philosophy represented an abstract construction, a Platonic state-of-mind, and for its realisation power was needed. Only the myth of violence could destroy this arbitrary compulsion or static power, and the 'general strike' was the crystallisation of this myth. Sorel chose the concept of the strike, as applied to the proletariat, to recreate the concept of the warrior, the producer, as the human basis for a new civilisation of creative men. The destruction of the bourgeoisie was at the same time the building-up of the creative proletariat through violence. In this respect, violence became creative at the very moment when it destroyed power. Power preserved order, while violence destroyed it; power was compulsion, while violence was freedom; power was decadent, while violence was authentic. No other thinker went as far as Sorel in glorifying the historical value of violence: movement, for him, was everything, and violence supplied the necessary energy.[47]

In Sorel's political philosophy one could find a new moral scale in the same way as in Nietzsche's thought: authenticity, creativity and vitality were regarded as good, and compromise, weakness and decadence as bad. Sorel examined Socialism according to these new criteria, and when he looked for a new lexicon for the modern world, he found it in religious terminology, as when he said: 'I owe to socialism all the highest ethical values, because it brings salvation to the modern world'.[48] Violence as the energising force of history passed beyond descriptive analysis and attained a metaphysical significance. At the beginning of the twentieth century, the political myth became the hallmark of a European political style and was formulated in terms of this creative violence.

VII

Sorel made his revision of Marxism in 1895, because the revolution did not take place as Marxist theory predicted. As a result, he turned from orthodox Marxism to revolutionary syndicalism in its French or Italian variants. But the 'new school' disappointed him also, and in 1910 Sorel broke away from syndicalism. It became clear to Sorel that the proletariat in France and Italy wished to integrate itself into the liberal state through political parties, trade unions, education and the army.

The syndicate, according to Sorel, did not carry out its function of liberating the proletariat and hence civilisation, and Sorel turned away from it and looked for renewal in the myth of the nation.[49] Sorel left the 'Mouvement Socialiste' in 1908, and declared that 'Action Français' was the only serious national movement. When he published the ***Révolution Dreyfusienne*** in 1909, Sorel condemned the pro-Dreyfus movement. In 1910 he expressed his disappointment with the Syndicalist movement, and in a letter to Agostino Lanzillo he claimed that his socialist writings had never been considered the most important part of his work.[50] In the same year, 1910, he participated in the planning of *La Cité française,* a national-socialist review he intended to found. In 1911 he joined the national group 'L'Independance' and together with Variot was the co-editor of the review which carried this name. Later, he was the spiritual father of the well-known 'Cercle Proudhon' although he never joined it formally.

The essence of Sorel's preoccupations arising from the past, concerning the ancient heroic civilisations and the syndicalist revision of Marxism, did not change at all: Sorel kept searching for a myth which would bring renewal. Sorel's move into nationalist circles in France and Italy did not conflict with the principles of his political theory, but served only to emphasise the more sharply that he attached greater importance to a myth (the revolution) than to its agents (the proletariat or the nation). In place of content (either left or right), which was the product of past tradition, there was an identification of the present reality with man as the essence of the existentialist idea. Since modern reality was dynamic, modern man was bound to identify with the rhythm of reality. Hence, Sorel introduced a concept which affirmed man's aesthetic (non-rational) view of (non-rational) reality. This view departed from the accepted rational and ethical criteria of good and evil, replacing them with new definitions of authenticity and decadence, of producers and consumers. Sorel transformed an aesthetic view of the world into concepts of political action.

The combination of the revolt against reason, the negation of progress, the affirmation of modernity and the theory of myths proved to be the point of collapse of the identification, hitherto regarded as essential, between the idea of reason and modern development. Man, for Sorel, created his modern world not by means of rational progress but through myth. The 'new man' did not receive his world from inherited culture or from history, but identified with his modern world which he himself created, thereby becoming authentic. The modern myth stripped the political avant-garde of its ideological clothing by using modern, radical political concepts such as energy, activism, and violence in place of history, determinism, and progress. To be authentic, one had to identify with the modern world, and if this reality was dynamic and non-rational, then a dynamic political style and aesthetic language had to be invented to suit it. This political style became the heart of a new *dynamic political culture* which emerged at the beginning of the 20th century.

In the above-mentioned modern phenomenon, aesthetics were no longer perceived in classical 18th-century terms, but as an active force embodying 'social poetry' as an existential life-style which stimulates heroic action. The new criteria transcended categories of left and right. The aesthetic of dynamics, which found expression in the affirmation of violence (even a 'symbolic' or 'metaphoric' violence) was transformed into a romantic protest against the frozen and static bourgeois order. This revolt of the fin de siècle period and afterwards became a political style which created the 'generation of 1914'.

NOTES

[1] Jacques Juliard and Shlomo Sand, ed., *Georges Sorel en son temps* (Seuil, 1985).

[2] *Cahiers Georges Sorel,* 1-5, Société d'Etudes Soréliennes (Paris, 1983-88).

[3] Michel Charzat, *G. Sorel et la Révolution au XXe siècle* (Paris: Hachette, 1977). Shlomo Sand, *L'Illusion du Politique, Sorel et le débat intellectuel 1990* (Paris: La Découverte, 1985).

[4] Jean-Paul Sartre, 'Preface', in Frantz Fanon, *Le damnés de la terre* (Paris, 1961).

[5] The best monographs on Sorel are: James H. Meisel, *The Genesis of Georges Sorel* (Ann Harbor, 1951). Richard Humphrey, *Georges Sorel: Prophet without Honour* (Cambridge, Mass, 1951). Irving L. Horowitz, *Radicalism and the Revolt against reason* (Carbondale, 1968). Jeremy R. Jennings, *Georges Sorel, The Character and Development of his Thought,* Forward by T. Zeldin (London: Macmillan, 1985).

[6] Jules Levey, *The Sorelian Syndicalists: Edouard Berth, Georges Valois, and Hubert Lagandelle* (Columbia University, 1967).

[7] Paul Delesalle, 'Georges Sorel', *Humanité* (1 September 1922).

[8] Georges Valois, 'Georges Sorel', *Action Française* (4 September 1922).

[9] H. Stuart Hughes, 'Georges Sorel's Search for reality', *Consciousness and Society: The Reorientation of European Social Thought 1890-1930* (New York, 1958), p. 162.

[10] Paul Delesalle, 'Bibliographie Sorélienne', *International Review for Social History,* IV (1939), pp. 463-487. 'Bibliographie des études sur Sorel', *Cahiers G. Sorel* I-V (Société d'Etudes Soréliennes, 1983-88).

[11] Benedeto Croce, *La philosophie de Jean-Baptiste Vico,* trans, H. Buriot-Darsiles and G. Bourgian (Paris, 1913), pp. 263-64, 266, 312.

[12] Georges Sorel, *Contribution à l'étude profane de la Bible* (Paris, 1889). Sorel, *Le Procès de Socrate* (Paris, 1889). Sorel, *La Ruine du monde antique* (Paris, 1901). Sorel, *Le Système historique de Renan* (Paris, 1905).

[13] David Ohana, 'The Role of Myth in History: Nietzsche and Sorel', *Religion, Ideology and Nationalism in Europe and America, Essays presented in honor of Y. Arieli* (Jerusalem, 1986), pp. 119-140.

[14] Sorel, *Réflexions sur la violence* (Paris, 1908), p. 24.

[15] David Ohana, 'Anti-Messiah: Sorel and the Critique of Enlightenment and the French Revolution and its Impact', *The French Revolution,* ed. Richard Cohen (Jerusalem, 1991), pp. 401-408.

[16] *Réflexion,* p. 194.

[17] Sorel, *Les Illusions du progrès* (Paris, 1908).

[18] Robert Nisbet, 'Preface, *The Illusions of Progress,* trans. by John and Charlotte Stanley (University of California Press, 1969), p. V-VIII.

[19] Sorel, 'Etude sur Vico', *Le Devenir Social* (1986).

[20] *Les Illusions,* p. 108.

[21] *Réflexions,* p. 163.

[22] Pierre Andrew, *Notre Maître, M. Sorel* (Paris, 1953), p. 239-68.

[23] Henri Bergson, *L'Evolution Créatrice* (Paris: P.U.F., 1962). Another point of view, see: Shlomo Sand, 'Quelques remarques sur Sorel critique de L'Evolution Créatrice', *Cahiers G. Sorel,* I (1983), pp. 109-24.

[24] In a letter to G. Maire from 1912, see: Bergson, Ecrites et Paroles, II (1959), p. 370. G. Maire, *Bergson mon maître* (Paris: Grasset, 1935), p. 216.

[25] *Réflexions,* p. 355.

[26] Sorel, 'Essai sur la philosophie de Proudhon', *Revue Philosophique* (1892).

[27] *Réflexion,* pp. 54, 360, 371.

[28] Sorel, 'L'Ancienne et la nouvelle métaphysique', *Ere Nouvelle* (1894), p. 72.

[29] Zeev Sternhell, Mario Sznajder, Maia Asheri, *Naissance de l'idéologie fasciste* (Paris: Fayard, 1989).

[30] Among other interpretations, see: M. Rubel, 'Georges Sorel et l'achèvement le l'œuvre de Karl Marx', *Cahiers G. Sorel,* I (1983), pp. 9-37.

[31] In 1902 Sorel wrote the introduction to: Fernand Pelloutier, *Histoire des bourses du travail* (Paris, Schleicher), pp. 27-67. See also: Jack Julliard, *Fernand Pelloutier et les origines du Syndicalisme d'action directe* (Paris, 1971).

[32] Sorel, *La Décomposition du Marxisme* (Paris: Rivièr, 1908), p. 5.

[33] See for example: C. Willard, *Le Mouvement socialiste en France (1893-1905). Les guesdistes* (Paris, Editions sociales, 1965).

[34] John L. Stanley, *The Sociology of Virtue, The Social and Political Theories of Georges Sorel* (University of California Press, 1981), pp. 105-6.

[35] Serge Hughes, 'Labriola and the Deviationist Marxism of Croce and Sorel', *The Fall and Rise of Modern Italy* (N.Y., Macmillan, 1967), pp. 37-59.

[36] See also: D.D. Roberts, *The Syndicalist Tradition and Italian Fascism* (University of North Carolina Press, 1979); E.E. Jacobitti, 'Labriola, Croce and Italian Marxism', *Journal of the History of Ideas,* 36, No. 2 (1975).

[37] *Réflexions,* p. 120.

[38] *Ibid.,* p. 48.

[39] *Ibid.,* p. 118.

[40] *Ibid.,* p. 120.

[41] *Ibid.,* p. 161.

[42] *Ibid.,* pp. 45-50, 176-182.

[43] *Ibid.,* p. 47.

[44] *Ibid.,* p. 50.

[45] *Ibid.,* p. 46.

[46] Frank E. Manuel and Fritzie P. Manuel, *Utopian Thought in the Western World* (Harvard University Press, 1973), p. 755.

[47] Jack J. Roth, *The Cult of Violence, Sorel and the Sorelians* (California University Press, 1980), p. 266.

[48] *Réflexions,* p. 388.

[49] A. Pezzotti, 'Un parti syndicaliste en Italie', *Mouvement socialiste* (13 March 1911), p. 185.

[50] Agostino Lanzillo, *Giornale d'Italia* (20 November 1910).

Michael Tratner (essay date 1995)

SOURCE: "Mass Minds and Modernist Forms: Political, Aesthetic, and Psychological Theories," in *Modernism and Mass Politics: Joyce, Woolf, Eliot, Yeats,* Stanford University Press, 1995, pp. 21-47.

[*In the following, Tratner links Sorel with Gustave Le Bon, author of* The Crowd, *to examine the modernist works of Ezra Pound, James Joyce, Virginia Woolf, T. S. Eliot, and W. B. Yeats.*]

Two French political theorists set the terms for most analyses of the mass mind in the early twentieth century: Gustave Le Bon, in *The Crowd* (1895), and Georges Sorel, who extended Le Bon's ideas into a method for inciting mass movements in ***Reflections on Violence*** (1906). Sorel's theory became the basis of syndicalism, which powerfully influenced such diverse movements as the International Workers of the World in the United States and the Fascists in Italy. (Mussolini began his career as a syndicalist.)

Much of the power of Le Bon's and Sorel's theories came from their usefulness to both the Left and the Right. Le Bon's influence on twentieth-century politics was somewhat paradoxical, since he declared in 1896 that the coming "Era of the Crowd" marked the end of all civilization. Previously in history, he claimed, the crowd had gained power only in brief "barbarian phases" between periods of "elevated . . . culture." The crowd always had slipped back into passivity when a new "intellectual aristocracy" arose. But in the twentieth century, Le Bon feared, there would be no new aristocracy because the masses were not only destroying leadership, they were taking it over: "The destinies of nations are elaborated at present in the heart of the masses, and no longer in the councils of princes" (p. xv). What Le Bon did not predict was that politicians and social analysts would study "the heart of the masses" and would use his analysis of the unusual mentality found there as the basis of new kinds of political appeals. And modernist writers were as attracted as any contemporary intellectuals by those appeals, the sociopolitical analyses that lay behind them, and the techniques of representation and address those analyses made possible.

At first, such appeals seemed to involve abandoning reason and culture, placing a "heart of darkness" at the center of the social order. But gradually, new political philosophies gained power that inverted Le Bon's evaluation of the rise of the crowd: arguing that rationality is not the basis of civilization but only of the capitalist system, a system that had destroyed culture, such theorists concluded that empowering the masses was a way of restoring civilization.

We might expect such arguments to have come largely from the Left. Le Bon himself equated the rising power of the masses and the remarkable rise of socialist or communist politics:

> Today the claims of the masses are becoming more and more sharply defined, and amount to nothing less than a determination to utterly destroy society as it now exists, with a view to making it hark back to that primitive communism which was the normal condition of all human groups before the dawn of civilisation. Limitations of the hours of labour, the nationalisation of mines, railways, factories and the soil, the equal distribution of all products, the elimination of the upper classes for the benefit of the popular classes, etc., such are these claims. (p. xvi)

But Le Bon went on to suggest that leaders could draw on the nature of the crowd to counter this communist trend: Crowds are "powerless . . . to hold any opinions other than those which are imposed upon them, and it is not with rules based on theories of pure equity that they are to be led, but by seeking what produces an impression on them and what seduces them. . . . In practice the most unjust may be the best for the masses" (p. xx). In other words, there was nothing inherent in the crowd's fascination with communism: rather, communism was simply what was being "imposed" on the workers in 1895, and they could be seduced to some other philosophy that would restore civilization.

Le Bon had little hope of using the crowd mind to develop civilization because, he argued, "civilizations as yet have only been created and directed by a small intellectual aristocracy, never by crowds. . . . A civilization involves fixed rules, discipline, a passing from the instinctive to the rational state, forethought for the future, an elevated degree of culture—all of them conditions that crowds, left to themselves, have invariably shown themselves incapable of realising" (p. xviii). The crowd at best would clear the ground for a new civilization, but if such a new order were to arise, according to Le Bon, it would owe nothing to the crowd mind, but would be merely a new aristocracy imposing itself. The conservatives who followed Le Bon, however, developed a different idea of the relation between the aristocracy that builds culture and the masses. The new conservatives, such as Georges Sorel, Charles Maurras, and Giovanni Gentile—social theorists that Yeats and Eliot followed—argued that the aristocracy is the part of society best able to express and make conscious what is in the crowd mind. Such conservatives argued for a culture based on instinct and irrationality, a culture growing out of the crowd, and hence a culture opposed to the old middle-class leaders. Le Bon noted some of this already going on in the 1880's: for example, he commented that many middle-class leaders, in response to the rise of the crowd, were turning to Catholicism, but he argued that it was a futile effort because "the masses repudiate to-day the gods which [the middle class] repudiated yesterday and helped to destroy. There is no power, Divine or human, that can oblige a stream to flow back to its source" (p. xvii). Eliot clearly disagreed, hoping for a Catholic revival. And Eliot could draw on Le Bon for support in this belief: though Le Bon believed that entirely new gods must emerge to restore civilization, he also said that the crowd always responded most powerfully to the oldest traditions, to the "soul of the race" (p. 67). Le Bon's contradictions made his theory useful to both the Left and the Right.

HOW TO THINK LIKE A CROWD

The key to Le Bon's influence did not lie in his predictions of which beliefs the crowd would continue to hold, but in his analysis of how the crowd functions. This analysis begins with his description of the moment of transformation of a collection of people into a crowd: "The sentiments and ideas of all the persons in the gathering take one and the same direction, and their conscious personality vanishes. A collective mind is formed, doubtless transitory, but presenting very clearly defined characteristics. The gathering has thus become what, in the absence of a better expression, I will call an organised crowd, or . . . a psychological crowd. It forms a single being" (p. 2). Such a transformation does not always occur with gatherings of people, but only under certain conditions. A few may become a crowd in the midst of hundreds who do not join together, or "an entire nation, though there may be no visible agglomeration, may become a crowd under the action of certain influences" (p. 3). Le Bon argued that the collective mind that emerges is not at all composed of the sum of the minds of the individuals who participate in it—"exactly as the cells which constitute a living body form by their reunion a new being which displays characteristics very different from those possessed by each of the cells singly" (p. 6). A single individual can be transformed in many different ways by different crowds, and hence Le Bon concluded that the kind of consistent character that had been glorified by literature is largely a fraud: "It is only in novels that individuals are found to traverse their whole life with an unvarying character. It is only the apparent uniformity of the environment that creates the apparent uniformity of character. . . . Among the most savage members of the French Convention were to be found inoffensive citizens who, under ordinary circumstances, would have been peaceful notaries" (pp. 4-5).

Le Bon's call for a literature that would show how character changes as environment changes is closely related to the attitudes that led to modernism. One of the basic differences between Victorian and modernist literature is a change in the relationship between environment or setting and character. In Victorian novels, the setting remains fairly constant while the characters move across it and eventually develop personalities that in some sense fit the environment. In *The Way of the World,* Franco Moretti describes the nineteenth-century *Bildungsroman* in such terms: the "individual's formation and socialization . . . is conceivable only if . . . social norms, for their part, enjoy a substantial stability." Moretti goes on to say that the nineteenth-century novel cannot really portray social and political change because the novel "revolves around individual destinies, while politics moves to collective rhythms." Moretti ends with the comment that the *Bildungsroman* disappeared when "in ideology after ideology, the individual figured simply as part of the whole"—in other words, when the movement of the collective appeared to be more fundamental than the movement of the individual.[1]

But the *Bildungsroman* did not disappear; it just changed form: writers developed methods of building novels around "collective rhythms" rather than around "individual destinies." Most of Woolf's major novels are *Bildungsromanen* in which the social setting changes, and those changes form the basic structure of the book. As Rachel Blau DuPlessis has argued, Woolf's later works are based on "a collective *Bildung* and communal affect" and so "suggest the structures of social change in the structures of narrative."[2] The individual is presented precisely as a "part of the whole" and as such changes along with the setting. The most striking example is *Orlando,* where a young person grows through four hundred years of English history, changing personality and even sex with each shift of period. Instead of suggesting that Orlando's inherent character is developed or hindered by these social influences, Woolf simply shows him/her having different traits in different eras—and all these traits end up layered on top of each other at the end. The book creates no sense of finality; it simply reaches the present, after which one expects that the next social shift will simply produce another layer of character to add to Orlando.

In modernist novels, setting is no longer a constant background against which individual character is defined but the main agent moving the "plot" along and determining what characters think and do. When we are following a character, we often lose track of the supposedly major issues of his life as his thoughts and actions get taken over by the concerns of the groups or the places he wanders through. How this differs from Victorian novels can be made clear by contrasting a dinner scene in Dickens and one in Joyce or Woolf. If people go to dinner in Dickens, we may read about the food they eat and the random conversation, but we are waiting for the clues to the destiny of the hero that are scattered throughout the scene. We are willing to enjoy the dinner, but expect the tale to pick up speed again as clues to the plot proliferate. In *Ulysses* and *To The Lighthouse,* in contrast, when people gather to eat, they talk and think about food, the house they are in, or each other, and major issues in individuals' lives fade into the background. A group of people coming together in these novels ends up defining the topics of conversation and even the thoughts that occur in the minds of the people in that group; each person is transformed. Woolf provides a metaphor for this process in *The Years*: she says that when two people join in conversation, weights underneath the skin of each of them shift to new positions, so that the two people do not even look the same as they did before they started talking. They have different bodies, different faces, different minds in the conversation than they would have had in other ones.[3] The mind is not an internal substance that can be molded to conform to a stable set of moral or intellectual principles; it is rather a space through which pass numerous streams of contradictory words, images, and feelings, most of which never even become conscious.

In *Ulysses,* changes of social setting are marked by changes of style so complete that we often lose track of which characters we are following. Most of the styles used in the text are, as Karen Lawrence has described them, "anonymous, collective discourse," so that sentences seem to derive from institutions that shape characters and author alike rather than from any individual mind.[4] In *The Waves,* Woolf shows six people all changing their thoughts together, not as they wander about the city, but as they age. Woolf emphasizes that setting is what is causing these changes, and not individual actions, by presenting before each chapter a setting that slowly changes throughout the book, tracing the cycle of a day, the sun rising and sinking. These "interludes" reveal the collective rhythm of the life of the group, and indeed of all of England, which rises to a moment of group glory in the triumphant group enterprise of imperialism and then falls with the sinking of the imperial sun.

Eliot and Yeats, in their later poems, also reverse the relationship of background and figure: instead of creating social worlds to define what the poet escapes in moments of lyrical reverie, they make us focus on the setting and suggest that the setting is the only agent in the poem. Yeats's poems often directly proclaim that the images in his brain are products of the surrounding social order and of the past, not of his own "genius." He is constantly trying to decide whether his images have truly emerged from a deep social tide, from the "blood" of the people, or from mere passing "winds" blowing about. In Eliot's poem "The Hollow Men," similarly, the images the writer uses do not emerge from his head (which is hollow), but from the surroundings. These later Yeats and Eliot poems are all epics that, in Pound's phrase, "contain history," poems structured around the collective rhythms of vast and shifting social landscapes. They present characters as minor, fleeting images that blend into the background. The poets present themselves not as individuals, but as parts of eras, of currents of history, of traditions.

Part of the reason that modernism involved such a change in the form of literature was that, according to contemporary theories of crowd psychology, the new mind that a person acquires by joining a crowd is not simply "another" personality: it is a different kind of mentality. Le Bon described the crowd mind in terms that are quite close to Freud's view of the id—pure desires running rampant and constantly shifting due to external stimulation:

> Isolated, he may be a cultivated individual; in a crowd, he is a barbarian—that is, he is a creature acting by instinct. He possesses the spontaneity, the violence, the ferocity, and also the enthusiasm and heroism of primitive beings, whom he further tends to resemble by the facility with which he allows himself to be impressed by words and images . . . and to be induced to commit acts contrary to his most obvious interests and his best-known habits. An individual in a crowd is a grain of sand amid other grains of sand, which the wind stirs up at will. (pp. 12-13).

Le Bon was clearly ambivalent about the crowd: it is violent, ferocious, primitive, but also spontaneous, heroic, and enthusiastic. The crowd becomes the ideal mobilizer of revolution, the vehicle of social change. As Le Bon notes, "It is crowds that have furnished the torrents of blood requisite for the triumph of every belief" (p. 18). Collectivists on the Left and the Right (anarcho-syndicalists, Fascists) drew on the power of the crowd and glorified violence, myths, and irrational images for their ability to produce enthusiasm and spontaneity and overcome the dull bourgeois life, effects that pacifists like Joyce and Woolf sought as well.

Modernist literary techniques, like the techniques of modern political rhetoric and its parent, advertising, developed at least in part in order to speak to and from this crowd mind, to extinguish "conscious personality" in audience and writer alike and appeal instead to the mass unconscious supposed to take its place. It is often presented as a prima facie commonplace of modernist criticism that stream of consciousness and Imagism are aesthetic devices that mark a rejection of social concerns and identify "high-brow" literature as the extreme opposite of "mass" literature. The obscurity and contradictoriness of modernism are said to prove that such literature cannot have been seeking to influence the masses. Mass art supposedly consists of clear, simple stories and straightforward images. Yet the forms taken by advertising and political campaigning in recent years contradict this view. Advertising has shown that the mass mind is influenced by utterly bizarre images and words. Politicians have borrowed such tactics, moving more and more toward the Imagist poetry of "sound bites" as modern media have become more and more mass media. Modernist literature itself contradicts the critical commonplace as well. If we extract "sound bites" from modernist works, we can find moments quite as propagandistic, pandering, randomly violent, titillating, and banal as anything in any ad. Modernist works are full of short passages that would be at home in horror movies, pornography, or late-night TV, just as advertising juxtaposes images from Shakespeare, Wagner, Marx, the Bible, and T. S. Eliot as freely as did Eliot himself.

Many modernists believed that they were gaining contact with the mass mind by using their strange forms; they also believed that if they wrote in clear, easily comprehensible, realistic forms, they would be disconnected from the masses, thus merely serving the nineteenth-century capitalist system. Yeats expressed this idea very strongly throughout his career; he even developed two different kinds of obscurity—Romantic and modernist—in opposition to what he perceived as capitalist realism. His early position can be seen in his essay "What Is Popular Poetry?"

> what we call 'popular poetry' never came from the people at all. . . . There is only one kind of

> good poetry, for the poetry of the coteries, which presupposes the written tradition, does not differ in kind from the true poetry of the people, which presupposes the unwritten tradition. Both are alike strange and obscure, and unreal to all who have not understanding, and both, instead of that manifest logic, that clear rhetoric of the 'popular poetry,' glimmer with thoughts and images.[5]

Yeats says that the manifest logic and clear rhetoric of what passes for "popular poetry" was created by "the counting-house" as part of its creation of a "new class." Before "the counting-house" had "set this art and this class between the hut and the castle, and between the hut and the cloister, the art of the people was . . . closely mingled with the art of the coteries."[6] Yeats's early poetry used Romantic strangeness to break out of the middle-class "clear rhetoric" and once again unite the masses and the coteries.

Later, Yeats defined the defects of clear and realistic forms of literature in somewhat different terms. In "Fighting the Waves," in 1934, he describes realism as part of the industrialism that brutalizes people into mechanical objects. Modernism, in all its obscurity, is part of the movement to escape this alienation:

> When Stendahl described a masterpiece as a 'mirror dawdling down a lane,' he expressed the mechanical philosophy of the French eighteenth century. Gradually literature conformed to his ideal . . . till, by the end of the nineteenth century . . . characters . . . had been brutalized into the likeness of mechanical objects. But Europe is changing its philosophy. . . . Certain typical books—*Ulysses,* Virginia Woolf's *The Waves,* Mr. Ezra Pound's *Draft of XXX Cantos*—suggest a philosophy like that of the *Samkara* school of ancient India, mental and physical objects alike material, a deluge of experience breaking over and within us, melting limits whether of line or tine; man no hard bright mirror dawdling by the dry sticks of a hedge, but a swimmer, or rather the waves themselves. In this literature . . . man in himself is nothing.[7]

The unrealistic modernist literature of flow, of tides, of waves, is thus part of a social movement to end the domination of mechanical, middle-class capitalism. Man in himself—the conscious personality of the individual—becomes nothing, extinguished in the greater social waves. In contrast, the popular realism of writers such as H. G. Wells, Yeats says, is "the opium of the suburbs."[8]

The moves away from realism in the later works of all the authors I am studying here, similarly, were efforts to escape "the suburbs," to break out of the clean, clear shapes of private life. Modernist efforts to eliminate "man in himself" were efforts to write of the underlying social medium. Both novelists and poets moved in their more radical works toward producing streams of images that were overtly identified as the flow of images of a crowd or, perhaps, a culture. *The Waste Land* is a stream of images in the consciousness of "the land," perhaps England, perhaps Europe, perhaps all of Western civilization. *Ulysses* repeatedly shows individuals being engulfed by flows of images that cross all the minds in a given social institution.

Most stream-of-consciousness novels entwine a whole collection of individual streams and trace the group movement that is not controlled by any one person. (Think of *As I Lay Dying* or *To the Lighthouse.*) The streams entwine different people together in a portrayal of a social unit, a crowd. The process of creating a united social body involves not merely finding some common history, but becoming part of intertwined streams of conscious and unconscious thought. Early in Yeats's life, he thought that all he needed was to find the central image of Irish history to accomplish this goal; later, he found that the mind of the nation is "multiform." When he describes this multiform mind, he sounds very much as if he is describing a modernist multiple stream-of-consciousness novel:

> Is there a nationwide multiform reverie, every mind passing through a stream of suggestion, and all streams acting and reacting upon one another no matter how distant the minds, how dumb the lips? A man walked, as it were, casting a shadow, and yet one could never say which was man and which was shadow, or how many the shadows he cast. Was not a nation, as distinguished from a crowd of chance comers, bound together by this interchange among streams or shadows; that Unity of Image, which I sought in national literature, being but an originating symbol? . . . How could I judge any scheme of education or of social reform, when I could not measure what the different classes and occupations contributed to that invisible commerce of reverie and of sleep: and what is luxury and what necessity when a fragment of gold braid, or a flower in the wallpaper, may be an originating impulse to revolution or to philosophy?[9]

Yeats summarized his anxiety in a phrase that could characterize all of modernism: "Was modern civilization a conspiracy of the subconscious?"[10]

Woolf's novels frequently focus on tiny fragments, such as a flower in the wallpaper, and suggest that such elements have great power. When Mrs. Dalloway asks if her roses are as important as her husband's political causes, she is not just being self-centered; it is a legitimate question of the sort that tormented both Yeats and Woolf in their efforts to discover the springs of social revolution. Yeats's description of the complexity of the "invisible commerce" that passes between "different classes and occupations" is quite similar to Woolf's description of the "invisible presences . . . immense forces that society brings to bear upon us," forces that cross classes and even decades of history.[11] Like Yeats, she believed that she needed to examine vast nets of unconscious influence that crisscross society if she was to make sense of her world.

Yeats went so far as to investigate supernatural phenomena. These investigations are considered by most readers as absurd and irrelevant to any real political effects his poetry may have. However, Le Bon gives strong credence to a belief in a certain kind of magic and supernaturalism. He says that the images that move crowds

> do not always lie ready to hand, but it is possible to evoke them by the judicious employment of words and formulas. Handled with art, they possess in sober truth the mysterious power formerly attributed to them by the adepts of magic. They cause the birth in the minds of crowds of the most formidable tempests, which in turn they are capable of stilling. . . . Reason and arguments are incapable of combatting certain words and formulas. . . . By many they are considered as natural forces, as supernatural powers. (pp. 95-96)

Le Bon's comments suggest that Yeats's investigations of supernatural phenomena ought not to be seen as disconnected from his politics. Yeats writes at one point that when he passes an Irish cottage, he has stepped outside of Europe into the realm of the supernatural, the realm of the "most violent force in history."[12]

These writers believed that in the twentieth century, political battles were not going to be waged by logical arguments read by individuals in private rooms: the battles were going to be waged between competing streams of images in the crowd mind. Logic has little to do with such streams: "These imagelike ideas are not connected by any logical bond of analogy or succession, and may take each other's place like the slides of a magic-lantern which the operator withdraws from the groove in which they were placed one above the other. This explains how it is that the most contradictory ideas may be seen to be simultaneously current in crowds" (p. 47). Many of the most distinctive modernist effects seem to be described here: the juxtaposing, overlapping, and rapid shifting of disparate images, the overlay of one image on top of another, the rapid shifting of images. Conversely, it is not an accident that the most famous Imagist poem, "In a Station of the Metro," is about a crowd:

> The apparition of these faces in the crowd
> Petals on a wet, black bough.[13]

From the title to the end of this poem, we pass from the mechanical, realistic world of subway stations, through the faces of individuals, into the collective world of a single organic unit, a bough. This transformation also involves moving from dry to wet and from light to dark—dissolving the visible world into the dark unconscious wave that carries everyone along.

Pound's poem sets up an opposition between the almost weightless individual faces, flitting apparitions or petals, and the deep solidity of the social branch that holds them together. The poem could be referring to all the short Imagist poems themselves, which exist each as a small petal in a large book and are held together only by the dark spine that is not visible in any single poem. The passage beyond realism is the passage into the unconscious basis of social unity. The realistic world is merely an ephemeral surface, flickering over something deeper. Le Bon similarly sees it as useful to divide the ideas that inspire the images in the crowd mind into two categories:

> In one we shall place accidental and passing ideas created by the influences of the moment; infatuation for an individual or a doctrine, for instance. In the other will be classed the fundamental ideas, to which the environment, the laws of heredity, and public opinion give a very great stability; such ideas are the religious beliefs of the past and the social and democratic ideas of to-day.
>
> These fundamental ideas resemble the volume of the water of a stream slowly pursuing its course; the transitory ideas are like the small waves, for ever changing, which agitate the surface, and are more visible than the progress of the stream itself although without real importance.
>
> At the present day the great fundamental ideas which were the mainstay of our fathers are tottering more and more. They have lost all solidity, and at the same time the institutions resting upon them are severely shaken. Every day there are formed a great many of those transitory minor ideas of which I have just been speaking; but very few of them to all appearance seem endowed with vitality and destined to acquire a preponderating influence. (pp. 46-47)

Le Bon's vision here is very similar to Pound's, Eliot's, and Yeats's: they all defined the goal of social change and of their art as the producing of a deep wave—a restored cultural center, a wet, black bough—that will hold together the chaotic small waves agitating society now. If the bough is in place, the leaves can randomly wave about all they want; if it is not, the leaves will blow apart in chaos. Modernist writers all recognized that it is very difficult to gain access to the invisible depths where deep waves are generated. In their poems, they constantly show their uncertainty—at times confidently presenting images of a new, deep order emerging, and at other times describing the impossibility of finding anything but dry, sterile words. The voice of thunder that brings water to the dry waste land, the beast that replaces the chaotic circling tides with a slow but unified motion of a giant social body, are presented as images of a new, unified social order—and both disappear in endings that express the doubts of the poets about their power to penetrate the current agitation of chaotic small waves.

Eliot and Yeats also shared Le Bon's belief that heredity and environment are the sources of the deep waves. Yeats went so far as to advocate eugenics as a way of altering the stream of images. Eliot also suggested racial and environmental criteria for producing the culture he would like, as I discuss in some detail in Chapter 4. Le Bon implied strongly that one needs some kind of hereditary unity to have a deep wave at all. He writes that people in the modern world often seem to have multiple and contradictory personalities because they are exposed to so many different influences and cultures. But "these contradictions are more apparent than real, for it is only hereditary ideas that have sufficient influence over the isolated individual to become the motives of conduct. It is only when, as the result of the intermingling of different races, a man is placed between different hereditary tendencies that his acts from one moment to another may be really entirely contradictory" (p. 48). Le Bon concludes that the "inferior characteristics of crowds are less accentuated in proportion as the spirit of the race is strong. . . . It is by the acquisition of a solidly constituted collective spirit that the race frees itself to a greater and greater extent from the unreflecting power of crowds" (p. 161).

Eliot's and Yeats's ideas of cultural unity are well known; what Le Bon provides is a way of linking those ideas to the wildly fragmented and contradictory flows of images that we find in their poems. Instead of trying to write out clearly the fundamental ideas that underlie deep waves (which would leave their writing in the conscious, surface mind), these poets were trying to operate in the medium of the unconscious crowd mind itself. Le Bon says that "ideas," especially "somewhat lofty philosophic or scientific ideas," must "undergo the most thoroughgoing transformations to become popular" (p. 48). This is a very unusual kind of popularizing, not via simple books that make complex ideas clear to the poorly educated, but via images that operate on the unconscious. The books that we would consider popularizing versions of great ideas engage only the conscious mind or the shallowest waves. Joyce, Woolf, Eliot, and Yeats were not seeking to do that at all: they did not wish to speak comprehensibly to average men because doing so was irrelevant to the job of creating deep waves.

Le Bon's distinction between deep and surface waves thus suggests an answer to the problem of how obscure poems and novels, to be read only by a few, might be written with the intent of influencing the masses and even popularizing lofty ideas. The surface of these works engages only the intellectuals, but the depths supposedly touch on the waves carrying the whole society along. Moreover, the whole problem with the threatening anarchy of the early twentieth century was not truly a problem with the masses because most theorists regarded them as carrying the tide of the future. It was the intellectuals who were thought to be weak and out of touch with these tides. As Yeats put it, the way to "deepen the political passion of the nation" is to make "current among the educated classes" the stories and images found among the "uneducated classes."[14]

The novels of Joyce and Woolf are similarly directed at the cultured few, trying to bring them to join with the masses—but in a subtly different way. Joyce and Woolf were seeking to bring high culture to serve socialist mass movements, and in particular were seeking to break with the whole idea of leadership, of ruling classes or individuals. Furthermore, Joyce and Woolf wanted to bring about the kind of hereditary mixture that Le Bon says produces contradictory personalities: Joyce and Woolf advocated such contradictoriness as a way out of the oppression that results from one race trying to hold itself separate and pure from others. We might even say that Joyce and Woolf inverted Le Bon's description of deep and shallow waves: the deep waves, in their view, are multiple and contradictory, and the appearance of a unified wave is a surface illusion produced by oppressive politics. Civilization can be made to appear orderly and disciplined by suppressing into the depths the waves that pass through the minds of, say, women, lower classes, and marginalized ethnic groups.

Le Bon joined in the debate between contrasting versions of an ideal collectivist state when he analyzed the factors that shape the deep waves that are fundamental to the shape of civilization. He describes two as essential: race and traditions. He says, "crowds are the most obstinate maintainers of traditional ideas," reaching the remarkable conclusion that the crowd is the most conservative part of society. We can see why conservatives embraced his theory even though he had at other points in his book equated the crowd with socialism. He also says that "political and social institutions" and "education" are very weak influences, almost negligible: "they are effects, not causes. Nations are not capable of choosing what appear to them the best institutions" (p. 66). Hence the emphasis in so much early-twentieth-century politics on ignoring overt political institutions and education, the cornerstones of liberal politics.

Collectivism was a politics that took place outside the political arena. This explains much of what appears to be the antipolitical attitude of modernists. Samuel Beer and Charles Maier both argue that the new mass politics involved a shift in the center of power to extraparliamentary institutions.[15] As Joyce wrote his brother Stanislaus in 1906 about the Italian syndicalists: "Their weapons are unions and strikes. They decline to interfere in politics or religion or legal questions" because "public powers" always end up supporting "the middle-class government."[16] In *Ulysses,* as I will show, Joyce developed a form of literary syndicalism: he attempted to change Ireland by acting on the collective consciousnesses, the "mental unions," we might say, that underlie institutions throughout the social order. He did not seek, however, to replace the government leaders or alter the religions or laws from within. Rather, so strongly did he believe in the need to alter those institutions that he could not work from within them: he thought they remained too completely tied to middle-class capitalism.

In order to make use of traditions and the "soul of the race" to move the crowd to join into unions, mass movements, or cultural wholes, the basic tools are the "magical power of words and formulas" and "the social illusion [that] reigns to-day upon all the heaped-up ruins of the past, and to it belongs the future" (p. 105). The most important illusions are those of legendary, marvelous events, especially those involving heroes. Le Bon therefore concludes that

> works of history must be considered as works of pure imagination. They are fanciful accounts of ill-observed facts, accompanied by explanations. . . . To write such books is the most absolute waste of time. Had not the past left us its literary, artistic, and monumental works, we should know absolutely nothing in reality in regard to bygone times. . . . Our interest is to know what our great men were as they are presented by popular legend. It is legendary heroes, and not for a moment real heroes, who have impressed the minds of crowds. (p. 31)

The importance of legends and heroes derives from Le Bon's belief in the "instinctive need of all beings forming a crowd to obey a leader" (p. 112). Le Bon concluded that all crowds, even those forming socialist movements, are essentially religious, with a deep need for gods and priests.

It is easy to see how Yeats, Eliot, and other conservatives found such analyses congenial: Le Bon seemed to argue that the crowd will maintain religion, leadership, and a belief in great men. Joyce, Woolf, and the socialists who sought to free the masses from religion and ruling classes struggled against Le Bon's conclusion that crowds inevitably view their leaders as gods. The debate between Left and Right was finally in many ways a debate about whether or not crowds require images of superhuman leaders to hold them together.

MYTHS AND VIOLENCE

Debates about the masses' desire for leaders did not focus as much on images as on another literary form: myth. The importance of myth in early-twentieth-century theory of the mass mind derived from Georges Sorel, who modified Le Bon in ways that were influential on both the Left and the Right. Sorel sought to understand how to turn a crowd into a movement, and he decided that the essential trick was to find a "group of images" that functioned as a "myth":

> men who are participating in a great social movement always picture their coming action as a battle in which their cause is certain to triumph. These constructions, knowledge of which is so important for historians, I propose to call myths; the syndicalist "general strike" and Marx's catastrophic revolution are such myths . . . [as are] those which were constructed by primitive Christianity, by the Reformation, by the Revolution and by the followers of Mazzini. . . . We should not attempt to analyse such groups of images in the way that we analyse a thing into its elements, but . . . they must be taken as a whole, as historical forces. (pp. 48-49)

Sorel's "myths" in this description are not what we usually think of as myths: he is speaking about what could be called histories of the future—theories of the social forces and currents moving the world that predict that a certain movement is going to triumph. During the early twentieth century, theories of history that described the present as on the cusp of some major change proliferated and were highly influential on the modernists. Yeats's cycles and Eliot's theory of the dissociation of sensibility dating from the seventeenth century are overt historical presentations; Woolf's later novels repeatedly trace history up to the present. Sorel suggested that the central point in any theory of the currents of history passing through the present is how such a theory motivates groups of people to act now.

Sorel dismissed the traditional forms of history and literature, saying the business of the true historian "is to *understand what is least individual* in the course of events; the questions which interest the chroniclers and excite novelists are those which he most willingly leaves on one side" (p. 70). We can being to see why Sorel's theories would imply a change in the nineteenth-century novel and in Romantic poetry. For one thing, Sorel's project was opposed to individualist theories of psychology: "I want to find out how the feelings by which the masses are moved form themselves into groups; all the discussion of the moralists about the motives for the actions of prominent men, and all psychological analyses of character, are, then, quite secondary in importance and even altogether negligible" (p. 68). Sorel objected to character for an unusual reason: because it is in his view a restriction on individual freedom. Character is formed of habits that keep people doing the same thing over and over again. So Sorel looked for moments when people "break the bonds of habit which enclose us"—and he concluded that the key to breaking habits is bringing people to be swept up in the enthusiasm of a mass movement (p. 55). Sorel was similarly opposed to liberal individualism because he viewed it as restricting people to thinking about their small, private lives. Sorel could thus regard the loss of conscious personality and individual psychology that occurs when people join the crowd as a liberation of the self, an improvement of the individual. By defining the crowd mind as the superior and deeper mind and the conscious personality as a dull complex of habits, Sorel inverted Le Bon's evaluations.

Sorel also separated what he was interested in from politics. He said that socialists became discouraged when it seemed "trades union organization was . . . becoming a kind of politics, a means of getting on" (p. 82). Sorel labeled as "politics," as means of getting on, such things as elections, governmental policies, and redistribution of income. Sorel, then, was as apolitical as he was anti-economic, even though he was seeking to cause a socialist (and hence an economic) revolution. Sorel sought to break free of all concerns about "getting on," all thoughts about goods, economic interests, or status. He asks, "Is there an economic epic capable of stimulating the enthusiasm of the workers?" (p. 276). He notes that "economic progress goes far beyond the individual life . . . but does it give glory?" (p. 276). Sorel disliked politics and economics precisely because they do not inspire enthusiasm, and such inspiration was his entire goal. Indeed, the myth that Sorel believed would bring about a socialist revolution was the myth of the general strike, a myth of stopping the economic system, a myth of an anti-economics, a refusal to care about goods entirely, no matter how distributed.

Sorel argued that the general strike could develop as a myth as a result of one particular tactic: violence. Violence and the general strike are quite similar as methods: they both are in essence disruptions that cause an intense need for something to happen with no sense of what that something will be. For Sorel, the moment of complete disruption, the general strike, is the best state of all, and an end in itself. The myth of the general strike "gives to socialism such high moral value and such great sincerity" because this myth has the "character of infinity" in its complete undefinability and its complete resistance to "argument" (p. 53). Modernists themselves have at times seemed also to valorize complete disruption. In a very Sorelian line, Yeats writes in "Under Ben Bulben" that "war completes the partial mind"—in the instant of action one becomes whole. Stephen Dedalus's desire to eliminate all space and time in a stroke of a Wagnerian sword named *Nothung* is an image of this general strike: Stephen strikes out at the whole world, seeking to free himself from space and time. And critics have valorized modernism for its embrace of these disruptions. Colin MacCabe sees *Ulysses* as enacting the "revolution of the word."[17] Lucio Ruotolo has argued that "interrupted moments" in Woolf's works provide access to a world beyond ordinary reality—and has suggested that Woolf was an anarchist.[18] Frank Kermode provides a subtly different vision of the importance of complete disruption in modernism: he sees modernists as dreaming of "apocalypse" and hence leading to totalitarianism (particularly Fascism).[19]

As part of my methodology of considering literary texts as participating in political debates, I regard modernist visions of ultimate revolutions of consciousness or of society—anarchistic, mystical, or apocalyptic moves beyond everyday reality—as ways of advocating or rejecting particular social changes. Modernist works themselves suggest that apocalyptic imagery may function as a transitional device. In many modernist works, the apocalyptic images appear in the middle, and show the world passing through complete or nearly complete annihilation. Both *To the Lighthouse* and Dangerfield's history use the apocalyptic imagery of a general strike to indicate such a moment of transition, a moment of political change. Similarly, *The Waste Land* passes through "death by water" to present an image of something beyond the sea change produced by social tides swamping the old capitalist system.

We can even apply this methodological principle to Sorel himself, treating his "theory of myth" as a political tactic, a narrative that functions to bring about a particular historical change. Sorel does much to make his theory of myth ahistorical: his use of many previous historical myths and the revolutions they produced imply that he is examining some eternally repeatable phenomenon, not something particular to his era. But as his own theory says, histories such as his own always serve simply to create a sense of inevitability about some future change. His history of myths adds a feeling of inevitability to the particular myth he is promoting: the general strike takes its place in the sequence of successful revolutionary myths that he presents. There is an even stronger way in which Sorel's entire theory and history of myths served one particular political goal of his era, that of breaking the rule of middle-class capitalism. He presents all earlier revolutions as precursors of the break with capitalist individualism. In each of these earlier revolutions, Sorel claims, myths disrupted the desire to "get on" and also disrupted "rational argument." Rational argument and the desire to get on may have always operated to keep people from joining revolutionary movements, and so may have always been the obstacle that myths overcome, but these two things are practically defining features of middle-class capitalism, according to Sorel. So Sorel can define the goal of his whole theory (including his accounts of ancient history) as helping "to ruin the prestige of middle-class culture" (p. 62). Sorel's history shows the decline of the Western world from the "mythic" life of the Greeks, especially the Spartans, into bourgeois individualism.

In his account of this decline, "myth" changes from referring to any collection of images that creates a sense of inevitability to referring to the collection of stories that have been labeled "myths," particularly the Greek ones. Sorel claims that in every revolution, the participants have felt they participated in *"truly Homeric conflicts,"* so Homeric epics provide the model for all other myths (p. 268). He blurs these two different senses of myth so that he can then say that the emergence of *any* myth will transform the people of any country into essentially Greek heroes and heroines.

These two different senses of "myth"—as the history of the future and as elements taken from ancient tales that will revive ancient values lost in capitalist society—appear in modernist works extensively. Yeats's *Vision* is a theory of history that produces a sense of the inevitability of certain changes about to occur, but Yeats supplements this extremely abstract history with powerful images drawn from what we would more easily recognize as mythic sources (particularly Greek and Irish tales) to add another kind of power to his history. The "scientific" history and the images together were supposed to produce a mass movement, and frequently Yeats describes his goal in terms that sound very much as if he were seeking a general strike—a complete disruption of current production (especially cultural production)—in order to allow a radical change in the social order that is inevitable. Eliot says that myths, as Joyce used them in *Ulysses,* function as "a way of controlling, of ordering, of giving a shape and a significance to the immense panorama of futility and anarchy which is contemporary history."[20] Eliot thus blurs together the use of ancient texts and the provision of direction for current mass movements—"shaping anarchy."

Eliot also treated Joyce as seeking to restore the kind of hierarchical order characteristic of Greek society. Joyce was strongly influenced by syndicalism and by Sorel's formulations, but I will show later that the novel's relation to history and to social change has been seriously misrepresented by Eliot. Eliot's essay is an effort to take a work that was written to serve left-wing anarcho-syndicalism and turn it to the right-wing corporatism of Eliot himself. Such an effort to transform works was not at all unusual in the early twentieth century—politicians switched sides constantly, and they frequently reinterpreted their own works written while aligned on one side as arguments for the other side. Eliot treated Sorel's text in precisely the same way, praising ***Reflections on Violence*** as one of the five central texts in the movement for a return to a royalist Europe.[21] That Sorel's book was written with clearly socialist goals did not disturb Eliot in the least, possibly because Sorel himself slid back and forth between right-wing and left-wing movements.

To understand the relationship of Sorel's theories to modernism, then, it is important to examine how they served opposed political movements. The two completely opposed directions syndicalism took are epitomized by pluralism and nationalism: the earliest syndicalists, at least in Italy, were, as the historian A. James Gregor puts it, "radically antistate, antinationalist, anticlerical, and antimilitant," and this form of syndicalism evolved into the nonviolent British pluralism of figures such as Harold Laski.[22] Another branch of syndicalism developed into a powerful part of nationalist (and racialist) movements in Italy (Benito Mussolini) and in Ireland (James Connolly), and in these movements syndicalism became synonymous with violence.

One way to understand the opposed developments is to see them as deriving from two opposed interpretations of a single clause in ***Reflections on Violence.*** Sorel says that syndicalism is based on "corporate exclusiveness, which resembles the local or racial spirit" (p. 80). The pluralists emphasized the importance of the word "local," while the nationalists emphasized "racial": the pluralists argued that only in very small groups can there be the feeling of corporate unity, while the nationalists believed that size isn't the issue, but rather "common blood"—and hence that racial and national groups are not only possible, but preferable to small units.

Socialist syndicalists moved toward nationalism in Italy and Ireland because they became convinced that the nation embodied the myth that most unified people.[23] Part of this conviction was due to their belief that their countries were too poorly developed to have a coherent proletariat that could respond to the image of the general strike. Socialists thus adopted nationalist and developmental goals—building up the industrial base of the country—as a step toward the socialist revolution. Le Bon's analysis of the crowd also supported switching from a class to a national or racial basis: he argued that the crowd is best formed by drawing on "the soul of the race."

In Sorel's works, there are also strong hints that he was particularly interested in a *French* general strike, not an international one. For example, he describes as the ideal revolutionary the "soldier of Napoleon . . . [who] felt that the epic in which he was taking part would be eternal, that he would live in the glory of France." Sorel then asks, "do there exist among the workmen forces capable of producing enthusiasm equivalent to those?" (p. 276). Sorel often seems to equate the "glory of France" with the results of the socialist revolution he advocates. Similarly, the Italian syndicalists who formed the core of Fascism (Roberto Michels, Paolo Orano, etc.) merged together the restoration of Italy as a glorious empire and the ending of the economic troubles of Italian workers.

The particular form of nationalist syndicalism that evolved in Europe required one more element: the theory of elites. This is a central feature of the particular visions of ideal cultures in Eliot and Yeats and a central element opposed by Joyce and Woolf. Arguments for elites derived from many sources, but for modernists Sorel provided two justifications for an elite that were especially important: an elite is necessary to produce the myths to which the masses will respond, and images of an elite, of an aristocracy, are always part of the mythic imagery that motivates the masses. Italian philosophers and social psychologists developed these two halves of the theory of elites and were highly influential on the modernists I am discussing. Vilfredo Pareto and Gaetano de Mosca argued that myths are always the product of an elite. Roberto Michels states the second point in its strongest form: "among the masses there is a profound impulse to venerate those who are their superiors. In their primitive idealism, they have a need for a secular 'divinity.' . . . This need is accompanied by a genuine cult for the leaders, who are regarded as heroes."[24]

As such theories suggest, syndicalism became intertwined with aristocratic and right-wing movements in many countries. In France, Charles Maurras developed a theory of "socialist monarchy" that relied on the monarch to provide the intense veneration that would hold together the nation and replace the capitalist leadership that was, in his view, destroying the underlying cultural unity. The solidarity of socialism, he argued, is in its essence identical to the unity provided by a king. Eliot, in his 1916 lectures on French literature and on Sorel, developed similar ideas, arguing that socialism and royalism were actually relatively similar alternatives to capitalism in that both led to "centralization in government."[25] Yeats put together the necessity of violence and of an elite in the thoroughly Sorelian poems praising the Irish syndicalist James Connolly written in reaction to the events in Ireland from 1916 until independence. His later poems anxiously consider the impossibility of restoring the Irish aristocracy and the consequent necessity of some further violence (Fascism or war) to develop some new form of leadership.

Though Sorel himself followed the nationalist trajectory of syndicalism, there is another part of the analysis in Sorel's ***Reflections on Violence*** that radically opposes the forms that syndicalist nationalism became. This part of syndicalist theory served as inspiration for the anti-elitism, anti-Fascism, and antimilitarism of Joyce and Woolf. Sorel argued that his myths do not produce the kind of enthusiasm that leads people to obey leaders. In fact, Sorel saw myths as serving the "transformation of the men of to-day into the free producers of to-morrow working in manufactories where there are no masters" (p. 264). These workers without masters, he claimed, would be similar to the peasants fighting for Napoleon; their labors would be "collections of heroic exploits accomplished by individuals under the influence of an extraordinary enthusiasm" (p. 267). The syndicalist revolution, in turn, would then be

> an immense uprising which yet may be called individualistic; each working with the greatest possible zeal, each acting on his own account, and not troubling himself much to subordinate his conduct to a great and scientifically combined plan. This character of the proletarian general strike has often been pointed out, and it has the effect of frightening the greedy politicians, who understand perfectly well that a Revolution conducted in this way would do away with their chances of seizing the Government. (p. 269)

We must distinguish this kind of "individualistic" life from liberal individualism: this is the individual as so completely a part of the group that he is devoted entirely as an individual to group goals. Sorel argued intriguingly that the individual who feels an epic enthusiasm does not lose himself, does not submit to domination by others, but becomes freer: "It might at first be supposed that it would be sufficient to say that, at such moments, we are dominated by an overwhelming emotion; but everybody now recognises that movement is the essence of emotional life, and it is, then, in terms of movement that we must speak of creative consciousness" (p. 55). Sorel's replacing of the phrase "dominated by an overwhelming emotion" with the term "creative consciousness" marks his denial of the common image of collectivism as an authoritarian system. Sorel defined the ideal revolutionary movement as one that eliminates authority, freeing each person from domination and to "creative consciousness." In a mass movement, every person becomes an artist.[26]

British pluralists drew a different conclusion than nationalists did from Sorel's argument that syndicates needed the "corporate exclusiveness that resembled local or racial spirit." Sorel overtly denied that mass movements turn people into "passive instruments who do not need to think." Such passivity is a *"morality of the weak"* promoted by those who would turn revolutionary syndicalism into the bourgeois fraud of "State Socialism" (p. 264). Sorel argued that his myths would eliminate large government and the division of society into rulers and followers. Labour theorists also spoke frequently about empowering the masses directly and eliminating any "ruling elite": in effect, they were against leadership. The organization of the British Labour Party thus reflected the theory of anarcho-syndicalism. The party conference dictated policy, and elected officials were delegates of this conference, not leaders of the party. The party had a strongly unified ideology, but that was not inherent in the structure: indeed, the party was set up to allow trade unions autonomy and to disperse control among multiple party bodies. Harold Laski wrote an influential book called *The Foundations of Sovereignty* in which he argued that there should be no sovereign power at all, no central leadership of the state. He and G. D. H. Cole developed pluralist theories that suggested government be divided into separate bodies for every social organization. These writers emphasized that the corporate unity of feeling could exist only in small groups. It is to maintain the enthusiasm and dissolution of self in the social body, they believed, that government should be broken up and leaders eliminated.

Woolf's "Outsiders' Society" was very much an image of revolutionary syndicalism in this sense of people sharing an enthusiasm without leadership. Woolf of course knew Laski and Cole well through Leonard Woolf and her own involvement with the Labour Party. Joyce reached much the same ideas through his fascination with early syndicalism in Italy and through his rejection of later syndicalism, with its nationalism and epic militarism.

Much of the debate in modernism thus consisted of efforts to separate the contradictory parts of Sorel's theory: Joyce and Woolf tried to show that one can have enthusiasm, the joys of group unity, and even myths, without elites, without "common blood," and without violence. Eliot and Yeats tried to show that one needs elites and blood ties to have the enthusiasm of group unity, and Yeats defended the necessity of violence.

Critics have frequently criticized Yeats for his advocacy of violence; in contrast, Joyce and Woolf are often praised for their seeming pacifism.[27] I want to question such distinctions, because Sorel's claim that violence is essential to liberation, to the release of what lies buried in the unconscious, haunts and undermines Joyce's and Woolf's supposedly nonviolent works. In their novels, though violence is condemned, it still serves a necessary function. In both *To the Lighthouse* and *Ulysses,* the authors use overt acts of violence connected in odd, indirect ways to war in order to bring about a transition from one dominant form of consciousness to another: a soldier knocks out Stephen Dedalus; Mrs. Ramsay dies in the midst of World War I—and these acts seem necessary to allow Leopold Bloom and Lily Briscoe to take charge and become in some sense images of the authors' new, modernist selves.

Throughout Woolf's novels, uncanny acts of violence liberate characters from oppressive relationships. Because they feel mistreated, her characters' minds are full of murderous wishes: these wishes are never carried out, but other violent acts occur that seem to accidentally and indirectly accomplish the same purpose. In the beginning of *To the Lighthouse,* nearly everyone is full of violent anger at Mr. Ramsay, yet it is Mrs. Ramsay who dies suddenly and whose death seems to alleviate much of the oppressiveness of the Ramsay household. In *The Voyage Out,* Rachel's father and Mr. Dalloway seem to abuse her and cause her to have monstrous dreams of cutting men's heads off, yet she is the one who dies, and her death just before her marriage has been taken by critics as a symbolic act of escaping abusive male sexuality in general (see Chapter 3). In *The Waves,* the six characters are full of angry desires to destroy each other, yet it is the seventh who never speaks, the leader, Percival, who dies and seems to release them from their competitiveness. Woolf created novels about the need for violent release from oppression, but did not allow anyone's anger to be directly expressed in action. She disconnected her characters from the mechanisms that bring about the violent liberations that fulfill their dreams. Her novels embody a problem that runs throughout her essays: she analyzes brilliantly the violence of the social system but refuses to countenance aggressive reactions to it. In *A Room of One's Own,* Woolf shows the violence surrounding the women's movement as a male reaction; she ignores or minimizes the violence performed by the movement itself. We have to be careful if we want to valorize Woolf's nonviolence: is she condemning methods of liberation of which she takes advantage?

Joyce also creates in his novels worlds of such oppression that characters dream of violent responses; he even shows them at times becoming violent, but such violent acts are presented as futile, generally a result of drunkenness, and always misdirected: Stephen, dreaming of using a Wagnerian sword to free himself from everything, slashes a prostitute's lamp shade with a stick; the poor man in "Counterparts," in anger at his boss's unfairness, hits his own son; the citizen, fulminating against the British, throws a tin at the Jew, Bloom; in *Finnegans Wake,* such absurd violence becomes a repeated motif, particularly in the tale of a military figure being shot in the bottom while relieving himself.

Joyce's works also include numerous allusions to historical violent acts that have only an indirect relationship to the everyday lives being presented, e.g., lengthy discussions of murders and allusions to the violence of figures such as "skin-the-cat" in *Ulysses* and accounts of Napoleonic battles in *Finnegans Wake.* The role of these allusions is similar to the role of allusions to World War I in *To the Lighthouse* and *The Waste Land:* they create a sense that violent forces are at work somewhere else, in a hazy but quite real political world that we cannot help but feel has a close relationship to the unconscious, violent impulses revealed inside everyone.

Joyce and Woolf thus recognized the power of violence to express and satisfy the unconscious desires for liberation created by social oppression, but they struggled to find some other method of change. While my sympathies lie with Joyce and Woolf in their projects to break up what seems an inherent connection linking radical change, violence, and militarism, I cannot dismiss Yeats's position that violence must be advocated at certain times, particularly in the effort to escape colonial rule. Modernism has a particularly strong relationship to postcolonial writers, who have never had any trouble seeing the sociopolitical underpinnings of this art form. Edward Said says that Yeats has been accepted as a great national poet of the postcolonial world; Yeats's advocacy of violence has been a source of that acceptance.[28] At the same time, Feroza Jussawalla and Reed Way Dasenbrock claim that "Joyce remains a central figure for many of the postcolonial writers in English."[29] We might, then, consider how postcolonial theories illuminate the debates within modernism. Frantz Fanon has argued that only a violent national movement can bring about the demise of a colonial government, a version of Yeats's position.[30] If Fanon is correct, the political agendas in Joyce's and Woolf's works may not only be unrealistic, they may even serve to support certain oppressive systems that Yeats's visions would help overthrow. By advocating "outsiders' societies" with no treasurers, no leadership, and no unity, and by refusing to be part of movements that are arranged hierarchically and act militantly, Joyce's and Woolf's works may in effect support oppressive regimes by undermining the only possible oppositional movement.

On the other hand, theorists of the subaltern such as Partha Chatterjee have argued that nationalist liberation movements, in their insistence on unity, too often end up recreating hierarchical and oppressive states after colonial rule has ended. Chatterjee advocates instead a form of social organization that sounds modernist, composed of what he calls "fragments."[31] Such a theory helps us see the political value of the fragmentary pluralism practiced by writers such as Joyce and Woolf, particularly as an antidote to the cultural homogeneity advocated by Eliot and Yeats.

PSYCHOLOGICAL THEORIES

During the modernist era, psychologists developed competing theories of the unconscious that played significant roles in the debates growing out of Sorel's work. Though Freud should be labeled a classical liberal in the scheme I have been employing, in which both socialism and conservatism stand at odds with liberalism, his own theories of the unconscious mostly supported the new conservatives because he argued that groups are held together by images of great male leaders, which merge with the unconscious mental formation that in English is called the super-ego. In a book on mass psychology (*Massenpsychologie und Ich-Analyse,* mistranslated as *Group Psychology and Analysis of the Ego*), Freud declared that a group such as an army, church, or nation is unified by an "I-ideal," or what Freud later called the "super-I," an image of the perfect self that everyone in the group admires and tries to emulate, and by whom everyone feels criticized and judged. The individual becomes a docile group member because joining the group allows the individual to identify with the super-I and thereby become a greater person. The ego, accepting the limitations of society and reality, recognizes that it cannot satisfy all desires. But by identifying with a leader or an image of a leader who functions as an ideal, "a man, when he cannot be satisfied with his ego itself, may nevertheless be able to find satisfaction in the ego-ideal." Joining such a group allows a return to primal feelings of unlimitedness and allows an "exaltation or intensification of emotion," especially feelings of love, or, as Freud puts it, libidinal ties. Humans, then, form mass movements not because of a natural need to be in herds, a kind of docility and unwillingness to stand alone, as Wilfred Trotter had argued, but because of a need to identify with and love a "primal father." Freud says he must "correct Trotter's pronouncement that man is a herd animal and assert that he is rather a horde animal, an individual creature in a horde led by a chief."[32]

Freud's theory of the super-ego was not so much a source of the modern politics of the leader as a part of the developing collectivist notions emerging all over Europe. He mirrored the attitudes of Le Bon and Sorel in declaring that the old ties that held social groups together, based on the religious worship of a "father god," were weakening: he celebrated this, arguing that the "weakening of religious feelings and the libidinal ties which depend on them" have reduced the "intolerance" in the world, or at least made it "less violent and cruel as in former centuries." But Freud warned that "if another group tie takes the place of the religious one—and the socialistic tie seems to be succeeding in doing so—there will be the same intolerance toward outsiders as in the age of the Wars of Religion."[33] Freud saw the socialist parties as following out his theories. Theodor Adorno says that Freud got it wrong, that Freud's essay actually serves much better to describe the power of Fascism;[34] but in the 1930's, theories of crowd and group psychology moved with strange ease from one end of the political spectrum to the other. Indeed, the reason that Freud's theories seem similar to Fascist practices is that Fascist propaganda was developed by people who originally sought to develop a syndicalist, socialist psychology—Roberto Michels and Paolo Orano. But even the fairly moderate Conservative Party in England believed in the natural deference of the masses and so sought to appeal to the masses by glorifying leaders and producing images of mythic national figures that formed a tradition in which to place current leaders.

The Labour Party in England and the anarcho-syndicalists who opposed the Fascists found support for their rejection of leadership in other theories of psychology. Harold Laski defended a pluralist political system as a way of adapting government to fit British theories of social psychology. Unified, sovereign governments with single leaders were based, he claimed, on outdated psychological theories that presumed individuals (both citizens and leaders) are unified wholes. Social psychologists had instead shown that "personality is a complex thing and the institutions—religious, industrial, political—in which it clothes itself are as a consequence manifold. The pluralistic state is an endeavor to express in terms of structure the facts we thus encounter."[35]

Laski was following up a peculiarly British vision of social psychology, one that modified Freudian theory. As the historian Greta Jones notes, Freud's belief in one central instinct, sexuality, that could transform itself into every human motive, struck the British as "anarchistic" because it would deny the basis for the multiplicity of institutions in society.[36] Laski's vision of the complexity of personality derived from the dominant psychology text in England in the early twentieth century, William McDougall's *Social Psychology,* which was organized around a long list of different instincts and purported to show how various social institutions were connected to these various instincts.[37] The debate between conservative focus on leadership and Laski's attack on sovereignty was then in part a mirror of the debate between Freud's theory of the necessity of a single object for the single dominant instinct in humans and McDougall's theory of multiple objects that appeal to multiple instincts.

Joyce and Woolf were influenced by the McDougall side of this debate about human psychology. The multiple-instinct schools of psychology appear in Woolf's writing about "contrary instincts" bred into women by society, about "severances and oppositions in the mind," about two sexes in the brain.[38] In the chart Joyce prepared to explain *Ulysses,* Joyce also developed a model of personality similar to the multiple-instinct schools. He presents the mind as influenced quite separately by different organs of the body and connects the influence of these organs to the influence of different social institutions. The alimentary system is connected to restaurants, the lungs to newspapers. We may read these connections as merely metaphorical, but Joyce was certainly presenting a person's mind as functioning differently at different times of the day and in different locations. He was showing, as was Woolf, that people's bodies are filled and shaped by social institutions in ways they cannot control, ways that also shape their consciousnesses. As Bloom says, "Never know whose thoughts you're chewing."[39]

Joyce referred directly to a psychologist Morton Prince, who carried the theory of multiple instincts further than McDougall, to a belief that every person has multiple personalities. Joyce indicated his affinity for Prince's psychology by basing Issy in *Finnegans Wake* on Prince's 1908 description of Christine Beauchamp, a woman with multiple personalities. Prince described the individual in terms similar to Le Bon's, as formed of multiple "systems" so that character is constantly changing: "this switching out and switching in, suppression and repression and resuscitation of enduring systems result in the ephemeral normal alterations of character in everyday life." He suggested we think of a person "as if he were a magic lantern with many colored slides passing in sequence before his eyes, and through which he looked; and as the world would be colored by those slides, so he felt and thought about it."[40] Prince argued, as did Le Bon, that this view of character ought to change literature. In an essay in 1924 entitled "The Problem of Personality: How Many Selves Have We?" Prince wrote out what could be a program for the novels of Joyce and Woolf:

> nearly all writers of fiction and even biographers have failed to recognize—what in these modern days the most advanced criminologists and penologists have recognized—that man is a many-sided creature. . . . No one is wholly good or wholly

> bad; or wholly hard, or wholly sentimental. . . . In the realm of fiction the dramatist is forced by the conventional canons of his art, if not by lack of wisdom, and for the purposes of dramatic effect, to depict but one side of the personalities of his characters. Consequently there is probably not a character of the drama, excepting Dr. Jekyll and Mr. Hyde, of which the whole personality has been portrayed. Iago, devil that he was, probably at home with his children, if he had a home and children, might have been the picture of an angel father. Melancholy Jacques, if he had had a couple of cocktails before dinner, might have forgotten his pessimism and shown *in vino veritas,* another side of his personality and entertained his company as a hilarious jester. Even Hamlet, though a good subject for a psychopathic hospital, if he had returned to his University at Wittenberg would have probably forgotten for one night, at least, all about his philosophies of life and his lamented father and exhibited himself in that other joyous, rollicking mood. . . . The world still awaits the great dramatist who will draw, if it be possible, a complete picture of a human personality, true to nature and under the confining canons of art.[41]

Joyce read Prince, but clearly Prince did not read Joyce, for *Ulysses* does just what Prince wanted—portrays all the sides of its main characters. Stephen is a Hamlet who does relax into jolly humor in the newspaper office, and into general pleasant talk in Bloom's living room; Bloom is a coward who hides from Blazes Boylan and then becomes a hero standing alone against the anti-Semitism of his friends and neighbors.

The break-up of character in *Ulysses,* as in other novels by Joyce and Woolf, was designed to reduce domination, to free the varieties of individual consciousness within society. In both psychological theories and modernist texts, domination has been figured often in relation to the sexuality of father figures. Prince developed his theory of multiple personalities partly out of a case in which an adult male tutor became frightening to a young woman; this is the case that Joyce refers to in *Finnegans Wake.* In Prince's case history and in Joyce's novel, there is a sense that the great power of father figures leads them to be implicated in sadistic or incestuous relations to their followers/family. Freud similarly commented on the "sadistic/masochistic" character of the relationship of masses and leaders who become "I-ideals." Woolf also equated Fascism and the sexual jealousies that cause fathers to mistreat their daughters.[42] Believing that people are inherently multiple, Joyce and Woolf presented all efforts to produce a single, all-encompassing relationship or identity—in a family, a social group, or a nation—as versions of dominating sexuality. They advocated instead multiple, partial, incomplete sexual relations and group identities.

In contrast, Eliot and Yeats frequently used images of restored passion and complete surrender to represent restored cultural wholeness. Incomplete and partial sexuality is, in their views, the result of alienation. They advocated a unified flood of emotion in the entire nation—the restored power of blood—while Joyce and Woolf feared such unified emotions. Joyce and Woolf were not seeking individual isolation, but rather the syndicalist local unities, local passions—a turbulent mix of passions that keeps any from dominating.

Both sides thus argued that they sought to release the passions of group involvement that capitalism had suppressed. Using Freudian terms, we can specify the difference in an intriguing way: both sides wanted to release the power of the id from the control of the "realist" ego. Both believed that domination by the ego is the result of capitalism, which empowers the calculating, rational part of the mind, the part that seeks the means of "getting on." Thus, all four of the modernists I am examining disagreed with Freud, who based his therapeutic practice on expanding the ego. His famous edict, "where id was, there ego shall be," could be interpreted as a method of maintaining a liberal order in the age of the masses, which is why, Adorno to the contrary, I have put him in that category. The ego, that is, rational, middle-class science, claims to be able to go where the id is buried, to speak for it, and to harness its power. In contrast to Freud, for conservatives such as Eliot and Yeats, the way to make use of the power of the id was by providing a real super-ego figure, a male leader: in a crowd with a powerful leader, everyone is released into passionate love of the leader, a return to the primal affections. Joyce and Woolf represented a third, socialist, possibility, that letting go of all super-ego figures and of rational, private selfhood are both necessary to experience the pleasure of communal unity, the pleasure of being part of the mass. In short, the modernism of both the Left and the Right sought to replace the politics of the ego with a politics of the id, to replace rational discourse based on the reality principle with unconscious discourse based on the pleasure principle. Modernism was an effort to write from and to the id, the mass unconscious.

NOTES

[1] Moretti, *The Way of the World,* pp. 79, 77, 228.

[2] DuPlessis, *Writing Beyond the Ending,* p. 163.

[3] Woolf, *The Years,* p. 190.

[4] Karen Lawrence, *The Odyssey of Styles in 'Ulysses,'* p. 64.

[5] Yeats, "What Is Popular Poetry?" in *Essays and Introductions,* pp. 5, 8.

[6] Ibid., pp. 10-11.

[7] Yeats, "Fighting the Waves," in *Explorations,* p. 373.

[8] Ibid., p. 377.

[9] Yeats, *Autobiography,* pp. 158-59.

[10] Ibid., p. 159.

[11] Woolf, "A Sketch of the Past," in *Moments of Being*, p. 80.

[12] Yeats, *Autobiography*, p. 242.

[13] Pound, *Personae*, p. 111.

[14] Yeats, *Autobiography*, p. 119.

[15] Beer speaks of a "vast, untidy system" of extraparliamentary representation. *Modern British Politics*, p. 337. Maier speaks of "the bleeding away of parliamentary authority." *Recasting Bourgeois Europe*, p. 353.

[16] Joyce, *Letters*, 2: 174.

[17] MacCabe, *James Joyce and the Revolution of the Word.*

[18] Ruotolo, *The Interrupted Moment*, discusses interruptions in the introduction (pp. 1-18) and anarchy in the conclusion (pp. 231-38).

[19] Kermode, *The Sense of an Ending*, p. 100-112. Kermode's analysis is worth looking at in some detail, because in it we can see the way that post-war anticollectivism sought to undo Sorel's arguments. Kermode recognizes that modernism was involved in the development of political myths, but he asserts that this was basically a mistake, an erroneous extension of the act of creating fictions: "Fictions, notably the fiction of apocalypse, turn easily into myths: people with live by that which was designed only to know by" (p. 112). Kermode is in effect denying Sorel's and Le Bon's claims that in the collective mind no one can distinguish fictions from real descriptions or myths. Kermode also inverts Sorel's claim that myths produce change: "Myths are the agents of stability, fictions the agents of change" (p. 39). Kermode tries to restore the liberal belief that the individual, in day-to-day life, can escape totalizing myths: he argues that there is a "common language, the vernacular, by means of which from day to day we deal with reality" (p. 107). Change is, in Kermode's view, due to doubt and challenges posed by "reality," not to passionate belief and mass movements. In such a view, the modernist's search for the springs of mass thinking and of communal passions must seem extremely dangerous.

[20] Eliot, "*Ulysses*, Order and Myth," in *Selected Prose*, p. 177.

[21] Margolis, *T. S. Eliot's Intellectual Development*, p. 43 n.

[22] Gregor, *Italian Fascism*, p. 25.

[23] Ibid., p. 100.

[24] Roberto Michels, *Political Parties*, trans. E. Paul and C. Paul (New York: Dover, 1915), p. 53; quoted in Gregor, *Italian Fascism*, p. 217.

[25] Margolis, *T. S. Eliot's Intellectual Development*, p. 11.

[26] Sorel says that socialism should bring workers to an "enthusiasm similar to that which we find in the lives of certain great artists." *Reflections on Violence*, p. 271.

[27] See, for example, Chadwick, "Violence in Yeats's Later Politics and Poetry"; Freyer, *W. B. Yeats and the Anti-Democratic Tradition*, p. 72; Suheil Badi Bushrui, "The Rhetoric of Terror in the Poetry of W. B. Yeats," in Bramsback and Crogham, eds., *Anglo-Irish and Irish Literature*, pp. 19-38; G. J. Watson, "The Politics of Ulysses," in Newman and Thornton, eds., *Joyce's 'Ulysses': The Larger Perspective*, pp. 39-58.

[28] Said, "Yeats and Decolonization," in Eagleton, Jameson, and Said, *Nationalism, Colonialism, and Literature*, p. 70.

[29] Feroza Jussawalla and Reed Way Dasenbrock, eds., *Interviews with Writers of the Post-Colonial World*, p. 15.

[30] Fanon says of colonialism: "It is violence in its natural state, and it will yield only when confronted with greater violence." *The Wretched of the Earth*, p. 55. He also argues that the notion of transcending nationalism belies colonial liberation movements and that national movements cannot be divided. See pp. 247, 158-62.

[31] Chatterjee, *The Nation and Its Fragments*, p. 13.

[32] Freud, *Group Psychology and the Analysis of the Ego*, pp. 52, 22, 68.

[33] Ibid., p. 39.

[34] Adorno, "Freudian Theory," pp. 118-37.

[35] Harold Laski, reply to Walter Lippmann, *New Republic*, May 31, 1919, p. 149; quoted in Zylstra, *From Pluralism to Collectivism*, p. 46.

[36] Jones, *Social Darwinism and English Thought*, p. 132.

[37] The lines of influence between psychologists and politicians went both ways. As Hearnshaw says, social psychology did not develop in England until the hold of individualism over British political thinking broke in the 1870's. *A Short History of British Psychology*, p. 105.

[38] Woolf, *A Room of One's Own*, pp. 51, 101, 102.

[39] Joyce, *Ulysses*, 8.718.

[40] Prince, *Psychotherapy and Multiple Personality*, pp. 213, 198.

[41] Ibid., p. 193-95.

[42] Woolf, *Three Guineas*, pp. 133, 137.

FURTHER READING

Criticism

Greil, Arthur L. *Georges Sorel and the Sociology of Virtue.* Washington, D.C.: University Press of America, 1981, 249 p.

Examines the consistency of Sorel's ethical arguments and moral positions.

Hughes, Henry Stuart. "Georges Sorel's Search for Reality." In *Consciousness and Society: The Reorientation of European Social Thought 1890-1930.* New York: Vintage, 1958, 433 p.

Explores such influences on Sorel's subjectivism as Friedrich Nietzsche and Henri Bergson.

Humphrey, Richard. *Georges Sorel: Prophet without Honor, A Study in Anti-Intellectualism.* Cambridge, Mass.: Harvard University Press, 1951, 244 p.

Discusses Sorel's work as a unified study of human motivation and political science.

Jennings, J. R. *Georges Sorel: The Character and Development of His Thought.* London: Macmillan, 1985, 209 p.

Considers Sorel as a popularizer of other theorists's works.

Kaplan, Alice Yaeger. "Slogan Text: Sorel." In *Reproductions of Banality: Fascism, Literature, and French Intellectual Life.* Minneapolis: University of Minnesota Press, 1986, 214 p.

Considers Sorel's theories the work of a dilettante.

Meisel, James H. *The Genesis of Georges Sorel: An Account of His Formative Period Followed by a Study of His Influence.* Ann Arbor, Mich.: George Wahr, 1951, 320 p.

Focuses on Sorel's politics and comments on his philosophy, metaphysics, and ethics.

Nye, Robert A. "Two Paths to a Psychology of Social Action: Gustave LeBon and Georges Sorel." *The Journal of Modern History* 45, No. 3 (September 1973): 411-38.

Traces the similarities between the writings of LeBon and Sorel, concentrating on their theories of politics and the masses.

Roth, Jack Joseph. "The Roots of Italian Fascism: Sorel and Sorelismo." *The Journal of Modern History* 39, No. 1 (March 1967): 30-45.

Documents Sorel's development as a revolutionary writer, giving particular attention to his influence on Italian Fascism.

———. *The Cult of Violence: Sorel and the Sorelians.* Berkeley: University of California Press, 1980, 359 p.

Discusses such political movements championed by Sorel as Syndicalism, Nationalism, Bolshevism and Fascism, and the impact of his writing through the 1920s and 1930s.

Schecter, Darrow. "Two Views of the Revolution: Gramsci and Sorel, 1916-1920." *History of European Ideas* 12, No. 5 (1990): 637-53.

Traces Sorel's early affinity and later disenchantment with Marxism.

Stanley, John. *The Political & Social Theories of George Sorel.* Berkeley: University of California Press, 1981, 387 p.

Details Sorel's intellectual development.

Sternhell, Zeev, Mario Sznajder, and Maia Asheri. "Georges Sorel and the Antimaterialist Revision of Marxism." In *The Birth of Fascist Ideology: From Cultural Rebellion to Political Revolution.* Rev. ed. New Jersey: Princeton University Press, 1994, 338 p.

Considers Sorel's views on Marxism.

Vernon, Richard. *Commitment and Change: Georges Sorel and the Idea of Revolution.* Toronto. University of Toronto Press, 1978, 148 p.

Finds Sorel to be an eccentric figure whose writings are still relevant and misunderstood.

Weber, Eugen. "Power and the Producers." *Times Literary Supplement* (20 August 1982): 895-96.

Review of John Stanley's *The Sociology of Virtue: The Political and Social Theories of Georges Sorel* that presents an overview of Sorel's writing and theories.

Graham Wallas

1858-1932

English political scientist and biographer.

INTRODUCTION

Wallas is considered a pioneering figure in the field of political psychology. An early member of the socialist Fabian Society, Wallas is credited with the introduction of human psychology into the field of political science, which had hitherto focused primarily on institutions and the rational factors involved in political choice. Believing that the intellectualist approach of Victorian economists, sociologists, and political theorists represented an incorrect view of political relationships, he offered a critique of the traditional view in his *Human Nature in Politics.* Later, Wallas presented another component of his thought by analyzing modern society and defending liberal democracy from twentieth-century anti-rationalism in his *The Great Society: A Psychological Analysis.*

Biographical Information

Wallas was born in Sunderland, Durham, England on 31 May 1858 to Gilbert Innes Wallas, a clergyman, and his wife Frances Talbot Peacock. Wallas received his early education at Shrewsbury and later studied classical literature at Corpus Christi College, Oxford. He became a schoolmaster in 1881, but left the Highgate School four years later over "a question of religious conformity." In 1886 Wallas made the first of four lecturing visits to the United States and joined the Fabian Society. He contributed "Property under Socialism" to the 1889 collection *Fabian Essays in Socialism.* In 1890 he was engaged as a university extension lecturer. Wallas resigned from the Fabian Society in 1895 and was appointed to a lectureship at the London School of Economics and Political Science, an institution he had helped to found. Wallas retained his position at the London School until 1923, acting as chair of the political science department from 1914. It was during this period that he wrote and published his *The Life of Francis Place, 1771-1854* and the three works of political science for which he is principally noted, *Human Nature in Politics*, *The Great Society: A Psychological Analysis*, and *Our Social Heritage.* Wallas's wrote *The Art of Thought,* which appeared in 1926, and visited the United States in 1928 to lecture at the Williamstown Institute. He was granted honorary doctoral degrees from the University of Manchester in 1922 and Oxford University in 1931. Wallas died on 9 August 1931 at Portloe, Cornwall.

Major Works

Wallas's first book *The Life of Francis Place* is a historical biography of an English labor activist who rose from destitution in a debtor's prison which contains analysis of early nineteenth-century British social reform movements. Like this biography, Wallas's later works also consider sociopolitical issues, though they generally focus on the state of contemporary politics. In *Human Nature in Politics* Wallas criticized the intellectualist assumptions current among Western political theorists and emphasized the importance of psychology in political science. In that work, Wallas observes that political behavior is largely subject to what he called "non-rational inference" and that these patterns comprise a serious threat to contemporary democracy. In *The Great Society* Wallas presents an analysis of social organization within the large, modern state. In contrast to *Human Nature in Politics*, which warns against nineteenth-century intellectualism, *The Great Society* includes a critique of various forms of twentieth-century anti-rationalism. *Our Social Heritage* studies those qualities of human personality acquired through social tradition. In *The Art of Thought* Wallas probes the subconscious determinants of creative thinking. Uncompleted at the time of his death, *Social Judgment* was edited by his daughter May Wallas and published in 1934. The work explores the historical and psychological components of the judgment process and the means by which this process may be improved. Also published posthumously, *Men and Ideas: Essays* contains articles and lectures on political science, social psychology, and education, as well as biographical sketches of several social theorists including Jeremy Bentham and John Ruskin.

Critical Reception

Because Wallas failed to provide a systematic approach in his political thought, critics have tended to view him as an innovative thinker whose valuable critique of modern political theory was not matched by positive contributions to the field. He is frequently remembered for his role with the Fabian Society in the 1890s. Many scholars, however, have since acknowledged that Wallas's early socialist stance did not contradict his support of democracy, but rather reflected his desire to strengthen liberalism through sustained, insightful criticism of the competitive and dehumanizing aspects of capitalism. Thus, while Wallas is often associated with anti-intellectualism, most commentators have continued to consider him a proponent of liberal ideals achieved through rational and collective social action. Despite Wallas's somewhat paradoxical approach to social dynamics and the limits of his influence on twentieth-century political science, critics have generally praised his innovative study of non-rational behavior in politics.

PRINCIPAL WORKS

"Property under Socialism" [published in the collection *Fabian Essays in Socialism*] (essay) 1889
The Life of Francis Place, 1771-1854 (biography) 1898
Human Nature in Politics (political theory) 1908
The Great Society: A Psychological Analysis (political theory) 1914
Our Social Heritage (political theory) 1921
Jeremy Bentham (lecture) 1922
William Johnson Fox (1786-1864) (lecture) 1924
The Art of Thought (political theory) 1926
Physical and Social Science (lecture) 1930
Social Judgment [edited by May Wallas] (political theory) 1934
Men and Ideas: Essays [edited by May Wallas] (essays) 1940

CRITICISM

Edward Porritt (essay date 1897)

SOURCE: A review of *The Life of Francis Place,* by Graham Wallas, in the *American Historical Review,* Vol. III, No. I, October, 1897, pp. 723-25.

[*In the following review, Porritt favorably assesses Wallas's* The Life of Francis Place, *commenting that in the work Wallas "handled admirably the enormous mass of material at his disposal."*]

The special value of Mr. Wallas's ***Life of Francis Place*** is at once obvious to students of English constitutional and party history of the period between the French Revolution and the abolition of the Corn Laws. Biographies and volumes of memoirs and letters coming within these sixty years have been published in large numbers during the last twenty-five years. First-hand material of this kind has been constantly growing in volume; but up to the present time there has been no authoritative book covering that part of the movement for constitutional reform with which Francis Place was so conspicuously identified. Place was never of the House of Commons. Although he began life as a working tailor, quite early in his career he had a shop of his own, and was exceedingly prosperous. In the days of the unreformed Parliament, it would have been easy for a man of his wealth to have bought a seat in the House of Commons, as was done by Hume, Ricardo, Romilly and other men who were on the popular side in the Reform movement. Place never availed himself of this opportunity; yet no man, in or out of Parliament, was more actively concerned in politics than he. His life was largely given up to politics. It was exclusively so from about his forty-sixth year. He was associated with the movement for the repeal of the Combination Laws; from 1807 to 1832 with the movement for the first Reform Bill; later on with the movements for poor-law reform and municipal reform; with the Chartist agitation; with the movement for the repeal of the taxes on newspapers; and finally with the agitation for the repeal of the Corn Laws.

In all these movements, Place was active as an organizer; often as a lobbyist; and continuously as an advocate of reform in any newspaper whose editor would print his letters. New light is thrown by Mr. Wallas's book on the agitation for the repeal of the Combination Laws, and also on the beginnings of the system of elementary education in England; for among his numerous activities, Place took a foremost part in the establishment of the British and Foreign Schools Society, an institution which still exists, and which between 1808 and the Forster Education Act of 1870 did so much good work in promoting unsectarian elementary education. But more than all, Mr. Wallas's book is valuable for that part of it that covers the closing days of the long movement for the first Parliamentary Reform Act. It would have been welcome to students if only for these two chapters. For some years past, there has been no lack of information concerning the ministerial and Parliamentary aspects of the closing year of an agitation for Reform which can be traced back to the time of the Tudors—concerning the fortunes of the struggle, after the first Reform Bill had been introduced by Lord John Russell, had passed the House of Commons, and had been rejected by the House of Lords. The Whig and official side can be traced in detail in Le Marchant's *Life of Althorp*; in Walpole's *Life of Lord John Russell*; in Brougham's *Correspondence*; and from day to day, almost from hour to hour, in Earl Grey's *Correspondence with Princess Lieven.* The Tory side is to be found in Jennings's *Memoirs and Correspondence of Croker,* and in the *Wellington Civil Correspondence.* The part played by William IV. can be followed in his *Letters to Earl Grey.* The demagogic side of the struggle from the beginning of the century is told in Huish's *Life of Hunt* and in the *Memoirs of Cartwright.* But hitherto there has been a lack of first-hand information as to what was doing in the constituencies, especially as to what was doing in London, during the period of tension and crisis which intervened from the 1st of March, 1831, when Lord John Russell introduced his bill, until the second Reform bill was accepted by the House of Lords on June 4, 1832.

The ***Life of Place*** fills this gap, and forms as important a contribution to the literature of the great constitutional crisis as Grey's *Letters to Princess Lieven,* or the *Letters of William IV. to Grey.* It is not possible here to recall, however briefly, the events of that critical period. But it may be stated that Place's story of them brings out two important facts, more or less new. It shows in the first place how greatly and how pleasantly the extent of the reform proposed in Lord John Russell's bill surprised Place, and the cooler heads among the reformers out of Parliament—how greatly it surprised those who, while actively and energetically on the popular side, had no sympathy with Hunt, and with the reception which Hunt gave to the bill in the House of Commons. Place obtained his first news of the bill from a reporter of the *Morning Chronicle.* "It was so very much beyond anything that I had expected," he wrote, "that had it been told me by a person unused to proceedings in the House, I should have supposed that he had made a mistake." In the second place, the narrative quoted by Mr. Wallas from Place's papers show how perilously near to revolution England came, after Earl Grey had resigned. Place's story leaves the impression that had the Duke of Wellington taken office, there must inevitably have been collisions between the troops and the people.

From a student's point of view, Mr. Wallas has handled admirably the enormous mass of material at his disposal. Wherever possible he has allowed Place to tell his own story, and very largely he leaves it to the reader to form his own estimate of Place, and the singularly important, though unobtrusive part Place played in the history of English politics in the first half of the nineteenth century.

Henry Jones Ford (essay date 1909)

SOURCE: A review of *Human Nature in Politics,* by Graham Wallas, in the *Yale Review,* Vol. 18, May, 1909, pp. 101-03.

[*In the following review, Ford considers Wallas's* Human Nature in Politics *as a work of "unique value."*]

This work is a philosophical inquiry by a practical politician into the nature of the forces that shape politics. Books of this class are rare. Few men have the combination of abundant knowledge with power of expression required to produce them. Hence they possess unique value.

The work is in two parts, the first of which may be characterized as a schedule of the bankruptcy of Liberalism as a political philosophy, and the second as a consideration of the possibility of obtaining from science a new system to take over the assets and continue the business as a going concern. The first part is, of course, more solid and complete. It deals with facts which Mr. Wallas illustrates from his own experience. The second part, which speculates on what might be, seems to be a groping in the fog to find a way out. But he does not claim that it is anything more than that. All he contends is that the fog is there and that the exploration is inevitable. He is on his guard against illusions, recalling Napoleon's warning of the pitfalls awaiting ideologues who see things as they wish them to be. He remarks that "if our imaginations ever start on the old road to Utopia, we are checked by remembering that we are blood-relations of the other animals, and that we have no more right than our kinsfolk to suppose that the mind of the universe has contrived that we can find the perfect life by looking for it." If bees should attain self-consciousness, and have dreams of political progress, nevertheless "as long as they were bees their life must remain bewildered and violent and short." Such reflections suggest to Mr. Wallas that perhaps no great improvement in politics is possible until we have altered the human type itself "through the hazardous experiment of selective breeding."

While Mr. Wallas is vague in dealing with what might be, his vision is distinct and clear in considering things as they are. He says (p. 15) that "many of the more systematic books on politics by American university professors are useless" for lack of grasp on reality. The advocates of direct primaries would do well to ponder his remarks on the futility of putting upon the people political tasks beyond human capacity. He mentions (p. 224) that in his own case he found it impossible to "give the time necessary for forming a real opinion on fifteen candidates" in a borough election, so he solved the problem by voting a "straight ticket." He is well aware that this meant that the successful candidates were really the appointees of party managers, and he draws the conclusion that in order that elections shall really elect they shall be few in number and concentrated in effect. Multiplication of elections, instead of increasing control of government by public opinion, destroys it. Mr. Wallas correctly attributes to this cause the prevalence of graft in American politics. In England the present tendency is to reduce the number of elections. Mr. Wallas (p. 226) says that "since 1888, parliament, in reconstructing the system of local government, has steadily diminished the number of elections, with the avowed purpose of increasing their efficiency." In this country we are multiplying them. The avowed purpose of the direct primary system is to strike down bosses and to extirpate corruption by giving the people the means of selecting good men for party offerings of candidacy. But results do not conform to the intentions with which causes are set in operation; they are always determined by the conditions that are actually established. Hence by increasing the complications and by adding to the expense of elections the direct primary system is certain to enlarge professional control of politics and to intensify corruption. It may be set down as an axiom of politics: the greater the number of elective offices, the greater the cost of government. The blunders now made in this country would hardly be possible were it not that political science has been eclipsed by sociology, and what Mr. Wallas characterizes as "non-rational inference" is in vogue. People who mistake feeling for thinking, and who thus impute to their projects the merit of their motives, may find in Mr. Wallas' chapter on "Representative Government" therapeutic aid such as their case requires.

A. D. Lindsay (essay date 1914)

SOURCE: A review of *The Great Society: A Psychological Analysis,* by Graham Wallas, in the *Political Quarterly,* No. 3, September, 1914, pp. 201-04.

[*In the following review, Lindsay offers a positive estimation of* The Great Society, *but observes that certain portions of the book should have been "considered less from the standpoint of psychology and more from that of philosophy."*]

This [volume, ***The Great Society***] is a welcome sequel and complement to that most original and stimulating book ***Human Nature in Politics***. Mr. Wallas is easily the most instructive of our present writers in political theory. This book is as full of enlightening *obiter dicta,* of passages of shrewd observation and of ripe wisdom, as was his earlier work. It is also more important as essaying a much greater task. ***Human Nature in Politics*** was mainly negative in its result. It showed remorselessly how the optimistic democratic theory of the early nineteenth-century Radicals was vitiated by their intellectualism, by their neglect of the part played in man's nature by half-conscious emotional forces, easily exploited for evil ends. No doubt the author held out a hope that if we all became converted to his passionate belief in the importance of psychology we might escape the dangers he had so convincingly described, but his grounds for encouragement were not persuasive. For it was difficult not to be struck by the fact that the insight into politics of which the book showed so much, had almost nothing to do with the study of psychology and everything to do with Mr. Wallas's own wisdom and experience.

In this book Mr. Wallas has essayed the more constructive work at which the earlier book only hinted, and tried to show more definitely what psychology can do for us.

He begins with a picture of the problem created by the existence of what he calls 'the Great Society,' showing how the transformation of the external conditions of civilized life by the inventions of the last hundred years have produced a political situation which is 'without precedent in the history of the world,' how for all our inventions the dominant fact of modern politics is the insecurity of the Great Society and the general failure of mankind to control the conditions they have themselves created. 'We feel that we must reconsider the basis of our organized life because without reconsideration we have no chance of controlling it.' If only this book makes the average man who cares about politics face the problem of civilization as Mr. Wallas has done, it will have done a great service.

The book is 'written with the practical purpose of bringing the knowledge which has been accumulated by psychologists into touch with the actual problems of civilized life.' It may be advisable, therefore, to leave unnoticed the many incidental subjects on which Mr. Wallas touches and consider the main subject of his book, the importance of psychology for politics. The book is divided into two parts. In the first we have an account of the psychological characteristics of the ordinary individual man, which aims at showing us the material from which political organization is formed; in the second a discussion of political organization with a view to asking how it can be better adapted to the facts of human psychology. Actually I think there are two main questions which Mr. Wallas is discussing, though he does not always distinguish them clearly. He begins by presenting us with his psychological account of the ordinary individual with his capacities and his needs, and then asks (1) how fitted are these capacities to solve the problems of 'the Great Society,' and (2) how far does 'the Great Society' satisfy man's ordinary needs.

The first point to be made is that Mr. Wallas follows the method of Hobbes. He begins by examining the nature of the ordinary individual man, assuming that that can be considered by itself, and then asks how men with natures such as he has described can be organized in Society and what Society will do to help them. We have been accustomed to look on this procedure as the typical mistake of the individualist. Mr. Wallas is in some sense an individualist in political theory. He thinks that the State should be described as an organization rather than as an organism; he does not believe in the existence of a common will or consciousness distinct from the wills of the individual members of the State. 'The Organized Will of a modern society only comes into existence as a result of the formation of difficult and always imperfect social machinery.' He has no belief in the psychology of a social self, and little patience with all the pretentious nonsense which has been talked about crowd psychology by Le Bon and others. Yet there can be little doubt that his individualism is justified and necessary. Human nature is not, of course, independent of Society, but nevertheless it remains very much the same through all changes of political organization. The new conditions of life are continually calling for new responses, but the new responses cannot be organic. The process of organic development is much too slow. Human nature is much the same now as it was a hundred or five hundred or a thousand years ago; political problems are quite different; and the new situation must be met not by organic change but by organization. The fact, then, that human nature is infinitely more stable and slow to change than political conditions is a vital fact for the politician which most 'organic' theories of Society neglect, which further justifies us in regarding typical human nature as the material out of which political organizations are made, whose needs are the end such organizations should serve. Knowledge of the ordinary human being then is the foundation-stone of politics. Any political schemes which ignore his limitations are foredoomed to failure, as any that do not serve his happiness are useless.

This position is, I think, fundamentally sound, and it is obviously, as over against all 'organic' and 'common consciousness' theories of the State, very important. Its connexion with psychology is clear if we can from psychology learn what are the enduring elements of human nature. Mr. Wallas holds that we can. For as we are looking for permanent and inherited characteristics, we should be able with the help of physiological psychology to distinguish these 'dispositions,' as Mr. Wallas calls them, from acquired or improvised ways of behaving. Mr. Wallas here bases himself on the study of 'instincts' which has been projected by Mr. Shand and Dr. MacDougall. These dispositions form our political material and their functioning is necessary to happiness. Most of the unhappiness of modern Society is due, Mr. Wallas thinks, to 'baulked dispositions,' and the great problem of Society is to give them free play in an environment totally different from that which produced them. The greater part of the book consists of chapters dealing with dispositions, habit, fear, pleasure-pain and happiness, love, hatred, 'taking a lead' and 'following a lead,' and thought. Most of what Mr. Wallas has to say in these chapters is very instructive, but we doubt whether it is really as certainly based on scientific psychology as he makes out. But that doubt depends on what Mr. Wallas would deem a more serious impiety, the doubt whether any psychology can be scientific in the sense that there can be any classification of 'dispositions' which is not guided by the purpose which these are to serve. A discussion of this point would make this review of inordinate length, and in any case this criticism in no way detracts from the extreme value of Mr. Wallas's work.

In the second part of the book, which is on the whole the more interesting, I think it can be shown that Mr. Wallas's reliance on psychology has led him into a definite error. He is considering three different kinds of organization, and adopts as the basis of his classification the division of the three forms of consciousness, Cognition, Conation, and Feeling. If he was anything like as well read in modern philosophy as he is in modern psychology, he would have had to take notice of the very serious criticism which has been directed, particularly by Croce, against that tripartite division. One thing that criticism has made clear, viz. that Feeling, however it is to be understood, cannot be regarded as co-ordinate, or as Mr. Wallas would say, 'in the same plane with' Cognition and Conation. He distinguishes three kinds of organization—the organization of thought, of will, and of happiness. The distinction between a thought and a will organization in politics is most important, and Mr. Wallas has some most instructive things to say on the subject. But surely it is obvious that he is wrong in talking of an organization of happiness in the same sense. In the first two members of his division thought and will are what is organized, in the third happiness or feeling is the end or purpose of organization. Take Mr. Wallas's own illustration: 'The Organization created by a Shop Hours Regulation Bill aims primarily at securing a feeling of comfort among those employed in retail trades. It is therefore predominantly a Feeling Organization, or, as I shall call it to avoid ambiguity, a Happiness Organization.' But such an organization organizes thought or will in order to provide happiness, and all thought and will organizations have the same end. The criticism may seem pedantic, but it is important, first, because it shows the danger of building too confidently on psychological distinctions, and secondly, because if Mr. Wallas had recognized that the consideration of purpose is distinct from the consideration of material, he would have recognized more generously than he does that though happiness depends on the satisfaction of certain 'dispositions,' it is not merely constituted by such satisfaction and must be considered less from the standpoint of psychology and more from that of philosophy.

It remains that this is a work of classical importance in political theory, the most noteworthy publication since Green's *Principles of Political Obligation.*

Harold J. Laski (essay date 1932)

SOURCE: "Lowes Dickinson and Graham Wallas," in the *Political Quarterly,* Vol. III, No. 4, October-December, 1932, pp. 461-66.

[*In the following excerpt, Laski evaluates Wallas and the significance of his work.*]

Graham Wallas was, I think, the supreme teacher of social philosophy in the last forty years. Other men have left a systematic edifice more likely to have enduring influence—Leonard Hobhouse, Alfred Marshall, Mr. and Mrs. Webb. But Wallas had two gifts of unique quality. He was a magnificent lecturer who, at his best, was one of the most inspiring academic forces of our time. The innumerable students, both in England and America, who went to hear him were different people because they had passed through his lecture-room. And, even more remarkably, he was a very great director of research. I doubt whether anyone I have ever known had quite his faculty for making the young graduate feel the moral urgency and intellectual fascination of digging through the raw material to the principle which emerges. Always full of suggestion, endlessly patient, quick, alert, vivid, he conveyed, as few men conveyed, the sense of the delight of the chase, the immense social importance of the quarry killed. All over the world there are distinguished students of the social sciences upon whose books the vivid impact of his own eager personality has been permanently imprinted.

His own work was of high quality. The ***Francis Place*** may be said, with Mr. and Mrs. Webb's *History of Trade Unionism,* to have begun the serious study of English social evolution in the nineteenth century. The change it effected in the historian's outlook can be seen by anyone who examines the classic work of Sir Leslie Stephen, Mr. and Mrs. Hammond, Professor Élie Halévy. Not less notable was the ***Human Nature in Politics*** which wrought little less than a revolution in the habits of political analysis. Its great achievement was to compel attention to what actually happens in the operation of institutions. Wallas had an ample experience of practical affairs, and he showed a brilliant power to bring its results into the service of doctrine. I am inclined to argue that no English thinker since Hobbes had seen more clearly the importance of the psychological foundations of politics; and since that book, few treatises on this theme have been usefully written that have not been coloured by its conclusions.

Wallas, perhaps, was unsuccessful in bringing his thought into orderly and systematic form. One felt always with him that the very width of the material he commanded made him avoid the necessity of dogmatism. He was, too, a very slow worker, whose passion for revision made him refuse ever to publish until he was satisfied that he had done his utmost for perfection. His books remain, therefore, rather an invaluable series of suggestions which colour the thoughts of every reader than a body of definite principles about which the argument of a period concentrates; they are essays towards a philosophy rather than a philosophy itself. But there have not been half-a-dozen political thinkers in England since John Stuart Mill who have given a more creative impulse to the movement of ideas.

Like Lowes Dickinson, Wallas was a socialist, freethinker, internationalist. With him, I think, the root conviction was a passion for equality. He hated privilege with something of the fine indignation of his own hero, Bentham. He disliked aristocracy and the monarchy because they stood in the path of equality. He disliked the churches because they biased the mind of man against the claims of reason and so gave to ideas an unequal status. He was an internationalist because war gave men power to be the oppressors of man. And because, in his special way, he had the temperament of a fighter, he brought to these principles service of high quality. He was tireless in their promotion. Popular education, law reform, Italian freedom, the insistence on the obligation of the universities to add to the fulness of national life, the removal of all barriers in the way of free expression—on these great themes I can bear testimony to the abounding energy he brought to their aid, his devotion to them, his zest in their victories.

He was a happy person. His enthusiasms were his life, and he saw the full significance of what they might achieve. He had made the service of intelligence a faith, and he never doubted its adequacy or its ultimate triumph. He had a genius for making friends, and few people have ever been able to build contacts so various or so significant. At the London School of Economics, which he helped to found, and where he was one of the four teachers to whom its reputation was first due, he had long been a loved, almost a legendary, figure. He could work with every type of mind and with every condition of man. He retained the eagerness of youth, and he never stopped learning. He gave all his inexhaustible energy to the work of the day, and he loved it for its own sake. No friend of Wallas' will feel that life is quite the same in value without the stimulus of his genius for fellowship in intellectual adventure.

The scholar's life stands apart from the values of the market place. Neither his acts nor his teaching reveal their significance with the immediate pungency characteristic of what is done by the man of affairs. But more surely, I think, than the acts and teaching of other men, they wind themselves into the mind and temper of their generation to bring forth, in the end, a richer fruit. No one would claim for either Lowes Dickinson or Wallas that kind of ultimate significance which belongs to the thinker of the first rank. Yet I think most people who know their work would say that our thoughts are different because of what they thought, our temper more creative because of the fashion in which they did their thinking. And all who knew them will cling to precious memories which they will esteem as part of life's unalterable good.

Leonard Woolf (essay date 1940)

SOURCE: A review of *Men and Ideas: Essays by Graham Wallas,* in the *Political Quarterly,* Vol. XL, No. 3, July-September, 1940, pp. 301-03.

[*In the following review, Woolf comments on Wallas's "extraordinary originality and freshness of mental vision," though he observes that the thinker was hindered by his lack of "a profoundly creative mind."*]

Volumes of essays, which are in fact miscellaneous articles and addresses, are a severe test of the author's worth, particularly if their subject is political or historical. Graham Wallas stands the test so well that it would alone suffice to show that he was a very remarkable man. The selection and editing [of ***Men and Ideas: Essays by Graham Wallas***] has been done by his daughter eight years after his death, but she tells us in an editorial note that, though she is responsible for the selection, it had been her father's intention to publish such a volume. She has done her task extremely well. There is not one essay in the volume which is not of permanent interest and value, and, like everything which Wallas wrote, they have the hall-mark of the 24-carat mind and of his highly individual attitude and method of thought. The book is divided into three parts. The first part contains six biographical essays, two on Bentham and the others on William Johnson Fox, Robert Owen, Ruskin, and Lord Sheffield. The second part contains five essays on social and political subjects. Here the most important is certainly a study of the British Civil Service which he wrote in 1928, and there is also a very interesting paper on Darwinism and social motive, which he read to a Conference of Liberal Churches in 1906. Finally, there are seven essays on his special subject, education.

The outstanding quality of Wallas's mind was its originality, and one may even say that his originality was original. It did not consist in his thinking or saying particularly striking things and it was not the kind of originality which produces what is called brilliance. It came from his ability, to which Professor Gilbert Murray draws attention in his preface, always to observe and think freshly. Every one must have noticed that, if you have a picture on the wall of your room, which you may admire immensely and even consider one of the greatest masterpieces, after a certain time it almost ceases to exist to you. You hardly see it because you are always seeing it and always in the same way. Most people, even very profound and original thinkers, after a certain number of years see the objects of their observation and the subjects of their thought in just the same way. They have looked so often at the same kind of things that they lose the faculty of seeing them freshly or indeed of *seeing* them at all, and everything falls automatically into the pattern of their own thought. Most people would probably say that Mr. Shaw and Mr. Wells, Wallas's most distinguished contemporaries, were far more original and brilliant than he was. In a sense that would be true, and yet in later life for sheer originality and freshness of thought Wallas would beat them every time. If, say in the year 1930, you had presented the three of them with a new social complex or problem, you would have been able to predict with some certainty the kind of way in which Mr. Shaw and Mr. Wells would see it, though you might not be able to predict at all the extremely brilliant, original, or valuable things which they would say about it. On the other hand, it would have been quite impossible to predict how Wallas would see it, because he would see it as if he were looking at that kind of thing or problem for the first time. At first sight what he said might sound to you a little flat; yet if you thought it over, you might see that it was an entirely new way of looking at things and threw new light upon the depths of society and politics.

There is hardly an essay in this book which does not reveal this remarkable quality of Wallas's mind, and it is particularly noticeable in studies of Bentham, Darwinism, the Civil Service, and Froebelian education. It is this characteristic which enabled him to exercise a profound influence upon the readers of his books and upon his pupils. Professor Murray says that he regards Wallas "as one of the most original minds of his generation" and of ***The Great Society*** he says: "That book is one of the very few of which I could say that it made a permanent difference in my outlook on human conduct." These are high claims, but there is no exaggeration in them, and one might add that ***The Art of Thought*** is not unworthy to stand by the side of ***The Great Society***; it makes a permanent difference in one's outlook on human thought and education. Such being Wallas's genius and achievement, it may sound strange to ask why he did not produce an even profounder book and have an even profounder influence upon his generation. Yet, to anyone who has studied his books carefully, the question ought not to seem strange. It is true that they do make a permanent difference in one's outlook on large and important areas of society, that they open new vistas of thought and enquiry. Nevertheless when one gets to the last page of them, one feels a slight sense of disappointment and frustration. The reason is that Wallas, while he had this extraordinary originality and freshness of mental vision, did not have a profoundly creative mind. The difference will be most clearly seen and the consequences apparent, if one compares the mind of Freud with that of Wallas. When you read Freud, you not only feel that he is continually seeing things with a completely fresh and original eye, but that at the same time he is synthesizing and making the most profound discoveries by flashes of creative understanding. With Wallas, you get the freshness and originality of sight and an intense stimulus to thought, but you are left then to think for yourself; the suggestion is analytic, not synthetic; and you are left with the curious feeling that the flash of creative imagination is coming—that it is coming on the next page.

Dwight Waldo (essay date 1942)

SOURCE: "Graham Wallas: Reason and Emotion in Social Change," in *Journal of Social Philosophy & Jurisprudence,* Vol. 7, No. 2, January, 1942, pp. 142-60.

[*In the following essay, Waldo examines Wallas's project of synthesizing reason and emotion in his political theory.*]

The pioneering contributions of Graham Wallas in a number of fields of inquiry, among them social psychology and the study of public opinion, are well known and widely acknowledged. Much less well known, generally disregarded are the reflections upon the nature, function and methods of the social studies, which form the essential matrix of his early works and are the very substance of his later writings. Several years have now passed since the appearance of the posthumous fragment, ***Social Judgment.*** It is the opinion of the writer that meanwhile the main currents of social philosophy in this country have flowed in the direction of the positions which Wallas reached in this and other later speculative writings. If this opinion is true, the setting forth and critical examination of Wallas's reflections is a timely and worthwhile undertaking. It is at least possible that his last two books, ***The Art of Thought*** (1926) and ***Social Judgment*** (1935), judged at the time of their publication as the mere gleanings of a productive intellectual life, were instead a late harvest.

At any event it is desirable, in the interest of truth, to amend a vague but general notion, arising from the popularity of the analytical and critical portions of his early works, that Wallas was skeptical of the efficacy, or opposed to the use of human reason. This conception of Wallas's attitude and contribution is completely in error. For the task in which Wallas was engaged from the time of the publication of ***Human Nature in Politics*** in 1908 until his death was the advocacy of the efficacy and necessity of conscious and creative thought in the management of human affairs. It is possible, indeed probable, judging from the evidence of the written word, that the main result of Wallas's writings has been the strengthening of the currents of irrationalism and defeatism. But it is easily demonstrable that this was not their intent. It is probably true, as one eminent scholar has said, that ***Human Nature in Politics*** "is the classical criticism of rationalism in political conduct," if what is meant is that it thoroughly discredited the sterile intellectualism and simple faith that were then staples of democratic thought. But this work did not deny the need or the efficiency of the rational aspects of mind. In fact, the latter part of ***Human Nature in Politics*** is a plea for the use of reason in effecting social change; and all of Wallas's later works may be most fruitfully interpreted as an attempt, increasingly ardent, to make secure for intelligence the prime rôle denied to it by irrationalist psychology and philosophy.

The key both to the rather widespread misconception of Wallas's purpose and to the peculiar significance of his speculation on reason lies in his writings on the subject of the emotions: to the considerable attention given them in the first instance, and to the attempt to subordinate them to reason or reasonableness in the second. It is the great paradox of his work that it is at once insistent upon the *importance* of the irrational factors and upon the *validity* of the rational factors in man's nature. Accepting the existence of the former and arguing for the reality and the necessity of the latter, he attempted to formulate a psychology and philosophy in which the two were synthesized, each with an independent and legitimate existence, but capable of working together to produce something greater than either alone, and greater than the sum of the two when one is the mere servant of the other—a "something" imperfectly limned but deeply felt—designated in ***Social Judgment*** by the term "wisdom."

It may well be that he attempted the impossible. In the thought most characteristic of the modern era, reason and emotion are assigned to different universes of discourse, whichever is given primacy. Hume's conclusion that "reason is and ought only to be the slave of the passions and can never pretend to any other office than to serve and obey them" has been very widely accepted. Much of modern psychological and social theory has been in the nature of variations upon this fundamental theme.[1] Certainly it is possible to find serious weakness in the particular synthesis that Wallas attempted. But the nobility of the conception warrants examination of an attempt at execution, in the hope that it may at least provide clues for greater success.

In pursuing this inquiry it will be useful to bear in mind this hypothesis: that the effect of a belief in a dichotomy of reason and emotion has been, where it has not resulted simply in pessimism and cynicism, to promote the belief among social students that the way to success is through aping the methods of those whose universe of discourse is inanimate matter or sub-human life. At any event, Wallas's work demonstrates that there is an intimate relation between (a) the theory one entertains as to the relationship of reason and emotion, and (b) the faith one will have in the possibility of making social science a "natural science." Beginning his characteristic work with both a firm belief in the desirability and possibility of uniting reason and emotion to achieve social ends, and an ardent desire to make the social disciplines more "scientific," Wallas was forced in the course of his thinking to the conclusion that the two aims were largely incompatible: that the conception of advance by co-operation of passion and intellect entails opposition to most of the modes of thought currently passing as "scientific." There is now increasing evidence that social thinkers generally are willing to abandon the pursuit of the mirage of a "method" which applied will forthwith transform social studies into Science. It is hardly possible not to conclude from a perusal of the literature of social philosophy of recent years that the tide has not set in another direction.[2] The necessary task, it seems to the writer, for one dissatisfied with "scientific" social science and who is yet not willing merely to till his garden with benevolent skepticism, is to find a psychological theory and a philosophy by which reason and emotion may be reconciled, to the end that the efficiency of reason and the utility of reasonableness may be reasserted.[3]

At the present writing, this country is being forced to make decisions of incalculable importance for its own future and the future of the world. Charges of "emotionalism" (by those obviously under impulsion of strong emotions) fill the air and are deemed a sufficient refutation of opposing views on national policy. It is a general assumption that problems of public policy yield different answers, accordingly as they are approached "intellectually" or "emotionally." There is no indication that our social sciences have contributed anything to the current scene except confusion—opposing sets of dogmas each claiming to be "scientific," and all equally useless to anyone who, honestly trying to face all facts, has a decision to make concerning human lives, values, and the future. A social science that is of no value in the judgment process is at best a secondary tool and at worst a fraud and delusion. This is the conclusion which Graham Wallas reached; in seeking to go beyond it he was led to examine the necessary and desirable relationship of reason and emotion as the very root of the matter. The record is an interesting chapter in the history of recent thought and may indicate new points of attack upon a problem as old as earliest Greek social speculation.

Wallas begins his ***Human Nature in Politics*** with a broadside against the old rationalist psychology: "Whoever sets himself to base his political thinking on a re-examination of the working of human nature, must begin by trying to overcome his own tendency to exaggerate the intellectuality of mankind." Away with the intellectualist assumption that human actions are based on a reasoned calculation of ends and means! Man, a fellow of the lower animals, is a creature of instinctive impulses, and because of his biological history may often be expected to act like them. Such is the tenor of Part One. But Wallas did not adopt the anti-intellectualist conclusions that came to be associated with the line of thought he did so much to stimulate.[4] Instead, the second half of the book, "Possibilities of Progress," is testimony that at no time did he abandon belief in the idea that man may, by taking thought, improve his earthly estate. The defense of this belief, which is the main *motif* of all his work henceforth, can for purposes of convenience be summarized by reviewing his reflections on (1) the psychological bases and cultural improvement of thought, (2) "scientific method" in social science, (3) the "outlooks" of contemporary science and Christianity, and (4) the techniques and institutions through which reason and emotion may be co-ordinated to produce socially valuable thought.

I

Although man as a result of his evolutionary history is an animal of passions, these passions may be controlled by an effort of will, and directed by the faculty of thought. This is the position which is taken in ***Human***

Nature in Politics after the classic demonstration that political conduct in even the best of existing democracies is very largely "irrational." The significant fact is not that political behavior is so largely irrational, but that it contains elements of rationality which can and should be expanded. For, fortunately, man is not dependent wholly, in his political thinking, "upon those forms of inference by immediate association . . . which he shares with the higher brutes."[5] In fact, human civilization "has been made possible by the invention of methods of thought which enable us to interpret and forecast the workings of nature more successfully than we could if we merely followed the line of least resistance in the use of our minds."[6] The study of politics can and should learn from the successes of physical science, and perhaps one of the things which can benefit politics is an extension to the mental processes of certain methods and ideals of behavior. But the extension to politics of the scientific conception of intellectual conduct must fail if it implies a false opposition between "reason" and "emotion." For it simply is not true that "in order to reason men must become passionless."[7] The ideal that should guide us today in our thinking in matters concerned directly with man is that which was expressed by Plato, when in the *Republic* he teaches that "the supreme purpose of the State realizes itself in men's hearts by a 'harmony' which strengthens the motive force of passion, because the separate passions no longer war among themselves, but are concentrated on an end discovered by the intellect."[8] In this return to an ancient ideal there is foreshadowed the development of Wallas's later thought, but the ideal was to prove to be extremely difficult to state and defend when the effect of nearly all contemporary psychological theory was seemingly to demonstrate its invalidity.

If there was work to be done in 1908 in discrediting sterile intellectualism and nineteenth century optimism, so that a realistic attack upon the problems of democracy could be made, by 1914, the year of ***The Great Society***, the currents were moving in the opposite direction. Wallas was impressed by the increasing forces of anti-intellectualism, and in the preface of this work he records that whereas ***Human Nature in Politics*** was an analysis of representative government "which turned into an argument against nineteenth-century intellectualism," the present work is "an analysis . . . which has turned, at times, into an argument against certain forms of twentieth-century anti-intellectualism." In the body of the work Wallas attempts to discover a sound psychological support for the ideal of harmony among the passions and their direction by the intellect. Barring the way to belief in this ideal is the conception of instinct as "drive," and intelligence as "machine," a conception shared by both the Utilitarians and certain of their critics among the social psychologists, since both disparage reason as an independent force, and both think of pain and pleasure as guides to irrational ends. Against all "machine-drive" conceptions Wallas posed the idea that intelligence is an innate diposition on a plane with other so-called instincts, and is capable of independent action or assertion. Purely by accident we have come to regard thought as a "process," and anger as a "drive"; but when all mental phenomena are projected onto one plane and all termed *dispositions*, then thought takes its place among other "dispositions"—*e.g.*, the dispositions to experience fear or anger.[9] Against those who, like James and Bergson, urge the superiority of an emotional "divining power" over reason, he argued that if this "divining power" was other than mere words it was the phenomenon which he treated under the title "instinctive inference," and that while instinctive inference has some advantages in a primitive environment, the very significance of civilization is that we have passed beyond that mode of thought.[10]

In ***Our Social Heritage***, although the efficacy of thought as an agent of social change is for the most part assumed, the argument is carried forward somewhat. Here the idea of "conscious *will*" as a force capable of controlling the mental processes, of directing them into socially profitable channels, is set forth.[11] Here also it is argued that not only the intellectual, but the emotional, relation of the social thinker to his material is important, "for if fertility of association without logical consistency is unsafe, logical consistency without fertility of association is barren.[12]

In ***The Art of Thought***, which is an avowed attempt to make the knowledge accumulated by modern psychology "useful for the thought processes of a working thinker," Wallas undertakes to point out the inadequacy of a mechanistic conception of thought as a basis for social theory, and he attempts again to find a sphere of independence for thought in psychological theory. On the first score he points out that the Communists have adopted the mechanistic conception of the relation of passion to reason, together with a rigid dogma of determinism, to guide them in their own thought, and they have convinced themselves that "unbiased reflection before one's simplest animal instincts, is at the same time not only biologically impossible, but politically and economically inadmissible."[13] On the second score Wallas opposes to all mechanistic theories of intelligence what he calls the "hormic" theory of organic life and co-ordination: a physiological theory which holds that though the parts of a living organism tend toward integrated action, the amount of integration may vary; for all the component parts "possess in varying degrees a force of their own."[14] Mind not only exists apart and in its own right, but can be consciously used to coordinate other forces.

In ***Social Judgment*** Wallas's speculation on the nature of the thought process and of the means by which it may be made more useful in the social change culminates in the idea of "wisdom": an art of consciously harmonizing emotion and reason in the production of valid and socially useful judgments. Judgment may be "natural" or untrained in form; or it may be "artificial," dependent upon socially inherited educational processes and disciplines. As a pattern of behavior that is part of the "social heritage," judgment is subject to change—and to improvement, if we set our minds to the task. The clue to the improvement of the judgment process lies in the coordination of reason and emotion: "human judgment requires a successful co-operation, which is neither inevitable nor impossible, between two imperfectly co-ordinated psychological factors."[15] In way of demonstration of this we may observe that in the past, at places widely separated by time and space, human societies have stumbled upon a mode of life and thought which so successfully united reason and passion that they enjoyed periods of tremendous intellectual fertility and possessed in some sense a "wisdom." It is urgently necessary at this moment in man's history that "the special kind of judgment process which is stimulated by the presence or idea of our fellow-men, and contemplates social action" be made a conscious art.[16]

II

The history of Wallas's thought on the usefulness of "science" to the methods of the social disciplines is a record of enthusiasm followed by increasing skepticism, and in some respects, opposition. This seems to be the inevitable result, as the writer has previously suggested, of the unfolding of the implications of the conception of the co-ordination of reason and emotion as the key to social progress. Wallas always urges the efficacy and desirability of thought, but in his early works he urges what are in fact two different means of increasing the force or usefulness of thought. The first, the adoption of the methods of the natural sciences, he increasingly abandoned and limited in its scope of usefulness. The second, the union of reason and emotion in the production of useful social inventions and valid social judgments, he haltingly developed. The two ideas exist side by side in the early works, before their general incompatibility became apparent.

In ***Human Nature in Politics*** "unscientific" methods of thought about things political are attacked with force—and while he later went beyond his conclusions here, it is undeniable that they contain much of value to anyone whose thinking about things political has not yet reached this level of sophistication. Enthusiasm for the discovery and classification of facts now appears naïve, but the insistence upon plurality of causes and upon the tremendous complexity of an heredity-environment relationship may be of value still. Some political thinkers, for example, still toy with the idea of building a science—or at least a theory—of politics upon the concept of "power," a principle which (as they think) should bear the same relationship to politics as, say, measurement to geometry. This, if accomplished, would have the extremely dubious merit of placing political theory upon a par with economic theory of more than a century ago. There is no reason to believe that a hypothetical political man would be either more real or more useful than an economic man.

In ***The Great Society***, in which Wallas's thought takes a sociological turn, social psychology is advanced as the discipline which "aims at discovering and arranging the knowledge which will enable us to forecast, and therefore to influence, the conduct of large numbers of human beings organized in societies."[17] But the outline for such a science is not so ambitious as that for a science of politics in ***Human Nature in Politics***, and consists for the most part of a mere survey of the most common human dispositions in relation to social environment.

Wallas devoted his Huxley Memorial Lecture, in 1930, explicitly to the problem of the relationship of the physical and the social sciences. He urges an understanding between the two disciplines, else twenty years hence "half the population, and all the accumulated wealth of Europe" may be destroyed.[18] The idea is here developed that the two disciplines are effecting a rapprochement and, in some respects, now overlap. This is not the result of the adoption of the methods of the one by the other; it is rather that recent speculation in many fields has broken down many barriers, so that "physical" and "social" are merely relative terms used for convenience. For example, few now speak of economic "laws," and even the physicists have become chary of the notion; ideas of freedom are replacing the former rigid, fatalistic, conceptions. The implication for the social scientist is that it is plainly his duty, in the twentieth-century crisis, "to invent patterns of social behavior which men may choose to follow, rather than merely to discover laws of social behavior which they must inevitably follow."[19] This is the culmination of a line of thought that insists upon the creativeness of reason. It repudiates the previous speculation in which causality and predictability were regarded as of the essence of science, and "scientific method" in the social sciences was conceived to be a matter of assuming the former and trying to achieve the latter. The significant fact for the social studies is instead the *creativeness* of reason. Man is able, by taking thought, to improve his lot. Mind is not powerless, a slave of man's baser passions. Mind, a guide to the passions and achieving its greatest triumphs in co-ordination with them, *must* be active in adaptation of the social heritage, or this civilization, built in a moment of time by creatures adapted by nature to a primitive environment, will crumble. Man must *invent* new institutions, new patterns of action, and in this task an intimate co-operation of reason and emotion is necessary. Even as early as ***Human Nature in Politics*** emphasis was placed upon the desirability of inventing new social-political institutions and new modes of thought and conduct. Hope is there expressed that the study of human nature might open an "unworked mine of political invention,"[20] and the plea is frequently made for the invention of new entities of mind to correspond more closely to the external political world. Through the pages of all subsequent books the term "invention" is sprinkled liberally, where the author points out the inefficiency or danger of the old and the need of the new. Despite his criticism of Bentham's naïve ideas of human nature, Wallas entertained a very lively respect for Bentham precisely because of his fertility in social invention, due, Wallas held, to a fine harmony of reason and emotion. And he condemned Henry Adams (who came under the influence of the "real sciences") for having been, unlike his grandfather, content with a life of dilettantism. It is important for the student to remember that politics is studied, as

Aristotle said, "for the sake of action rather than knowledge."[21] The realization that the proper end of thought is action, and not simply thought, is itself an aid to the essential harmony of thought and feeling.

III

Developing his thoughts on the possibility and necessity of reconciling reason and emotion brought Wallas to the consideration of two prevailing "world outlooks," both of which claim the ability so to "penetrate and illumine our particular forms of thought and action as to make a good life possible for all mankind."[22] One of these is the empirical and often harsh spirit associated with the science of the days of the billiard-ball atom, with its robust doctrine of physical determinism; the other is the spirit of contemporary Christianity. As indicated above, Wallas, in the Huxley Memorial Lecture, compromised with the chastened spirit of twentieth-century scientific theory, conceding that both physical and social science could learn from each other, since it now appears that the barriers between them are breaking down. His argument was not, then, that social science could not or should not become "scientific." His quarrel was rather with those devotees of the social studies whose conception of scientific method is adherence to popularizations of the scientific theory of the previous decade—or century—in this case nineteenth-century physics and biology. His notion was that the nature of the subject matter and the nature of the task must define the method, and that the imposition of modes of thought appropriate to another subject matter in another era could not be regarded, in any proper sense, as scientific. This, however, is a conclusion arrived at haltingly, as the implications of his philosophy of reason and emotion developed. For he came to maturity in the post-Darwinian period of scientific exuberance, belligerence and confidence, and he became deeply imbued with this spirit. Only an intense feeling of human sympathy, a keen common sense, and the experience of participation in political life enabled him gradually to extricate himself from the restrictions of that spirit; and one cannot escape the feeling that to the very end it imposes limitations on his capacity for constructive thought.

The nature of Wallas's objection to the "scientific outlook" is that it separates "reason" and "science" from "emotion" and "value," and tends to regard the latter as unreal, unimportant, or illegitimate. He tends to attribute this dichotomy in modern thought to the spread of the notion of mechanical causation with its seeming denial of free will, though it must be confessed that he is neither clear nor consistent on the point. Part of this confusion is, no doubt, the result of the difficulty he experienced in formulating his own theory because of the "dogma of determinism." A social analysis that begins by premising, as Wallas does explicitly in ***The Great Society***, that human actions are the result of the interaction of heredity and environment, would seem to deny free will; yet he expounds a philosophy that insists upon the efficacy of thought. In that work he brushed aside the difficulty, saying that, although it has always been objected against the insertion of cause and effect into regions heretofore assigned to free human or superhuman activity, that human energy was thereby paralyzed, the actual practical result of such extension of knowledge of cause and effect has been to increase man's energy and sense of freedom—as in the natural sciences. And he dismisses the subject with the suggestion that the "philosophical answer to this objection may be left to the philosophers."[23] But so crucial a problem could not be left to the philosophers, and in ***Our Social Heritage*** he in effect reverses his previous position, holding that the unfortunate (but not logically inevitable) result of the knowledge of cause and effect, revealed as a result of the work of Darwin, has been to paralyze the sense of personal initiative upon which human progress depends. On the theoretical side, however, a compromise is struck: the seeming dilemma of free will or determinism may be merely an example of the inadequacy of the human mind to comprehend the subtleties of nature, and to a mind higher than or different from our own, events would appear as both free and caused.[24] In the ***Art of Thought*** he again considers the problem and again suggests that "free will" is an anthropomorphic term and the problem may not be a real one. But the balance of the argument is here on the side of free will, so far as human activity is concerned. Even if determinism be true, it is probably true also that because of the complexity of social phenomena more factors may be relevant to a given situation than we can manipulate with the human mind, and hence we cannot "deduce from it reliable predictions as to the future course of social events."[25] There is "nothing in modern physics . . . to prevent the social student from believing and feeling that he is an agent and not a mere spectator of action."[26] And the inverse correlation between the degree of consciousness involved in social phenomena and the predictability of these social phenomena is strong evidence, if not proof, that thought is real.

Whether or not the "dogma of determinism" is at the heart of the matter, as is frequently suggested by Wallas, he would argue that in any event a result of the "scientific outlook" upon the study of the social sciences has been greatly to over-simplify their working conception of human nature, to dismiss "values" or "norms" from consideration, except *à l'exterieur* as modes of behavior, and to paralyze constructive thought and action. The over-simplification of human nature is perhaps the result of emphasis upon measurement, from the fact that it is easier to compare "certain simple facts in human behavior" to the more easily observed evidences of causation in the realm of the natural sciences than it is "other and more complex facts."[27] As early as Hobbes (whose ideal was geometry) there may be observed a tendency to emphasize the simpler and more elemental facts of human nature and to disregard complex and distinctively human factors. Any other political motive than fear in the governed, and desire for power in the governor, seemed to Hobbes to be "unscientific, and therefore, by the subconscious process of psychological logic, either non-existent or existing illegitimately."[28] The effect of excluding the more complex motives from the moral sciences during the past hundred years is readily discernible. The philosophic radicals and the classical economists took over (from French and ecclesiastical sources) as an adequate theory of human nature, the dogmas that all men are governed by a desire to gain pleasure and avoid pain and that pleasure consists in the possession of power and wealth; and the "scientific socialists" reshaped the theory to support a working class argument for revolution. The idea derived from Darwin, that instincts are within the concept of evolution, did but change the nature of the over-simplification. And Bergson's *élan vital,* offered as a means of avoiding the dilemma of determinism, was seized upon by Syndicalists before the war, and Bolshevists after the war, as "one more reason why they should ignore in their own conduct any but the simplest motives."[29] To-day this tendency reflects itself in psychology in the attention given to the observable, measurable, phenomena of the human type. The practical result has been to treat such motives as anger, greed, and sex, "whose muscular results were most obvious, as being the only legitimate subject-matter of science, and to ignore as unscientific more complex motives such as pity and kindness."[30] All conscious preferences are ignored as unreal "epiphenomena." The reflection of this attitude into the social studies, which depend upon the study of psychology for fundamental data, has been the theory that the social sciences should study "reality," irrespective of whether it is "good" or "bad," and that students of social science *qua* students of social science should ignore the realm of value.[31]

The practical effect of this laboratory attitude, which claims the authority of science, is to induce a "harshly empirical" element into judgments that have, or should have, significance in the realm of feeling; to paralyze human energy; and to dissuade the more highly placed minority to whom society nominally looks for guidance, from undertaking the "agony of social invention." Statesmen and manufacturers who accepted the "laws" of political economy assumed, when examining the relationship of the "laws" to their own more complex "human" feelings, that the economic laws were rules of conduct with the authority of "science" back of them, which they could disobey only at a risk, if at all. Hence they deliberately tried to inhibit any feelings on social questions they might otherwise have had.[32] To-day a different (yet strangely similar) situation obtains, but with the same cause—"science" and an acceptance of the dogma of determinism. Gone are the laws of political economy, gone faith in moral laws. In the place of the once confident working generalizations there now reigns an attitude of fatalism, a firm belief that "nothing which any one of us can do will greatly alter that which will happen in the future."[33] The result is to destroy that personal initiative without which democracy "is the worst possible form of government."[34]

If the mental attitude associated with science errs in assigning to separate universes of discourse "reason" and "science" on the one hand, and "emotion" and "value" on the other hand, the mental attitude associated with present-day institutionalized Christianity falls into as grievous an error by making the same separation, but by treating, conversely, the world of science as unreal. Unable or unwilling to harmonize old orthodoxies with new knowledge the church seeks to defend itself by denying the efficacy or reality of knowledge or reason, and by insisting upon the sufficiency of unquestioning faith, the special significance of "religious experience," and the importance of the sacramental aspects of religion.[35] The War of 1914 revealed the inadequacy of reliance upon the church for guidance in social thought, inasmuch as it merely followed dominant public opinion in preserving its own interests. Present attitudes in religious thought are contrary to the all-important harmony of intellect and passion, and it is the special task of this generation to hand on "the heritage of a world-outlook deeper and wider and more helpful than that of modern Christendom."[36]

IV

The idea of social advance by increasing the effectiveness of reason, and of increasing the effectiveness of reason by producing a harmony among man's faculties, did not remain in Wallas's hands a mere theory, for much of his wide-ranging social analysis was an attempt to give it content. To be sure, he regarded his own suggestions as only tentative gropings, but so strongly did he feel the urgency of his argument that he felt bound to illustrate his meaning and indicate the points at which advances might be made. Man's nature and his nurture *must* be adjusted, and since he cannot return to a "state of nature" he must invent the "city of the future";[37] the harmony of reason and emotion is at once a part of a proper adjustment between man and his environment, and the indispensable first step in achieving that adjustment.

First of all, it is suggested in ***Human Nature in Politics***, the integration of the faculties should be conceived of as a moral ideal, becoming, perhaps, an ideal entity such as "science" is to its devotees. Not that there is any procedure known at present by which this ideal may be inculcated; indeed it is a problem upon which "much steady thinking and observation" are still required.[38] Perhaps, Wallas surmises, new standards of mental conduct will result from the mere popularization of psychological theory. As our knowledge of self extends, our ideas of moral conduct may extend themselves naturally to the mental processes, for the "limits of our conscious conduct are fixed by the limits of our self knowledge."[39]

But we dare not wait in passive hope that this will be the case: necessity demands action, and we must be active in inventing institutions that will produce socially valuable thought by uniting reason and passion. Much of Wallas's social analysis, as suggested above, is to be construed as a part of this objective, and it is impossible to summarize these widely scattered suggestions. A few words, however, are appropriate on the subjects of education and the civil service.

As an educator Wallas had a keen professional interest in formal educational arrangements, and because he devoted much space to such subjects he has been accused of being "academic" and out of touch with the "real world." Given his general philosophy, however, the attention to education was inevitable, and at no time did his examination of and recommendations for either English or American education lose touch with reality. He thought, for example, that ideals of intellectual conduct should be inculcated in the schools, but conceded that it is "extraordinarily difficult to discover how this can be done under the actual conditions of school teaching."[40] His own suggestions, scattered over twenty-five years, he regarded only as tentative first steps, not as a miracle-working formula. Academic social scientists in search of a "method" may come at last to regard their students as an important part of the material of their discipline, and not as more or less disagreeable incidents encountered in the search.

In respect of the civil service of the modern state, Wallas was convinced of its strategic importance as an agency of either progress or retrogression. It represents the most significant political "invention" of the nineteenth century, and since it is the institutionalization of the thought of the nation, no effort is too great to insure that it coordinate reason and emotion in the production of socially valuable thought. Disaster is almost certain to overtake us if, now that a civil service exists, it is conceived as an unchanging entity and the greatest effort is not made to secure that it function efficiently as a thought-organization.

V

It is relatively easy, as suggested in the introduction, to make damaging criticisms of this structure which Wallas tried to erect. It is possible, even, only several years after ***Social Judgment*** to look back and to label as museum specimens the lines of thought which flowed through Wallas's mind, to "place" him in his historical intellectual milieu. One can observe, for example, the full impact of Darwinism, which, while he rose above it in some respects, kept him from sympathy with ideas that would have fertilized his own line of thought. There is Wallas the heir of nineteenth-century liberalism, Wallas the disciple of Fabianism; Wallas of the gentlemen's education in the classics—and much more. But his distinctive contribution, outlined above, although it did not suit the temper of his times, is of undoubted importance to any social student trying to re-think his position in the light of recent speculation.

Some lines of criticism may be anticipated. First, the whole notion of change by conscious thought would be denied outright by many. Professor Sait, for example, has recently written a stimulating and useful book,[41] one of the chief purposes of which is to deny the efficacy or usefulness of "excogitated ideas"; intellectuals, he argues, have no more influence over the course of human events than have the shadows of an overhanging tree upon the course of a stream. There is, of course, no way that Mr. Sait can be unquestionably refuted. No doubt it is useful occasionally to prick the bubbles of academic pretension. But he may also be incorrect, and it is not inappropriate to suggest that Mr. Sait, as all who use the intellect to discredit the reality of intellect, has placed himself in a logical dilemma; his thesis may be true, but if it is true all reason for believing it is destroyed. Is his idea of "excogitated ideas," perhaps, a particularly choice example of an excogitated idea?[42]

The notion of "progress," which is both implicit and explicit in Wallas's writings, would undoubtedly be a topic in any extended criticism of his ideas. Undoubtedly there is nineteenth-century optimism in this notion, and Wallas in his expansive moods pictures a vista of human happiness which even the most sanguine do not permit themselves in these times. It is only fair to say, however, that Wallas's notion of progress was not of its inevitability but only of its possibility; and even here he reserved the theoretical possibility that because of the nature of man or the nature of the universe even the possibility of progress might not exist.[43]

Significant and perhaps fatal objections can be raised to Wallas's theories on the philosophical level. Controversy over the nature and the proper spheres of the rational and the non- or ir- rational fills the history of philosophy as well as the history of social and political theory proper. It would be ridiculous to presume that Wallas provides an answer to such questions by his system—if so tentative and incomplete a line of speculation may be called a system.

Perhaps he never really faces up to the question of values. He insists in ***Human Nature in Politics*** that values are dependent upon facts—upon the facts of human nature. But he in fact accepted almost unquestionably the values of the humanitarianism and liberalism of his time. He never faced up to the problem of the relationship of these values to the creative process which would result from the proposed synthesis of reason and emotion. Instead he assumed that the values he accepted were valid for all Men of Good Will, that they would guide the judgment process and that its results would in turn conform to them. Such phrases as "socially valuable thought" and "valid judgment" conceal real difficulties. Obviously what he proposes has affinities with pragmatism with its moral relativism. Yet he opposed pragmatism, in part at least, for this very reason. On the philosophical level also is the objection that no theory is advanced to prove the efficacy of mind, to prove that mind is able to know and to change the existential world. This belief, despite his argument for reason, remains a matter of faith and common sense. Despite these objections—even assuming their validity—Wallas has come to grips with the fundamental problem of any "social science" worthy of the name. He has indicated the direction in which advance must be made if it *is* made.

NOTES

[1] Viewed in broader perspective this is, of course, an extension of the argument that justice exists by convention and not by nature. It is one of the wonders of recent political and legal thought how great a reputation for

emancipation and enlightenment could be secured by paraphrasing the conclusions of the Sophists and presenting them as the imperatives of the currently most popular psychological theory.

[2] Charles A. Beard's *Memorandum on Social Philosophy,* in the Fifth Anniversary number of the JOURNAL OF SOCIAL PHILOSOPHY (October, 1939) may be taken as a summary of recent trends.

[3] The objection may be filed here that the facts of human nature are what they are, and that if it is true that reason has no office but to serve the passions, no "psychological theory" can alter the fact. Quite true, and Wallas reserved the possibility that perhaps since we are "blood relations of the other animals" our lives, as theirs, "must remain bewildered and violent and short." (*Human Nature in Politics,* p. 179). But it is just possible that the facts are other than most of modern psychology has suggested; and so Wallas believed.

On the score of philosophy, it may be worthwhile to remember that Hume not only separated reason and emotion, but demonstrated that belief in causality is (in the words of Bertrand Russell) "little better than a superstition"—yet the physical sciences, acting as if it were true, transformed our external world.

[4] This fact has been noted in passing by a number of commentators, including R. M. McIver, Lewis Mumford, J. A. Hobson, and H. E. Barnes.

[5] *Human Nature in Politics* (London: 1908), p. 114.

[6] *Loc. cit.*

[7] *Ibid.,* p. 187.

[8] *Loc. cit.*

[9] *The Great Society* (New York: 1914), pp. 22-3.

[10] *Ibid.,* p. 218 ff.

[11] New York: 1921, p. 26 ff.

[12] *Ibid.,* p. 28.

[13] New York: 1926, p. 34.

[14] *Ibid.,* p. 38.

[15] *Social Judgment* (New York: 1935), p. 20.

[16] *Ibid.,* p. 23.

[17] Page 20. The difficulties of a philosophy which contemplates no discrepancy between "forecasting" the future of a system and "influencing" the same system will be commented on below.

[18] *Physical and Social Science,* in HUXLEY MEMORIAL LECTURES, 1925-1932 (London: 1932), p. 1.

[19] *Ibid.,* p. 5.

[20] Page 19.

[21] *Ibid.,* p. 168.

[22] *Our Social Heritage,* p. 245.

[23] *The Great Society,* p. 24.

[24] *Our Social Heritage,* pp. 246-48.

[25] *Social Judgment,* p. 141.

[26] *Ibid.,* p. 165.

[27] *Our Social Heritage,* p. 244.

[28] *Loc. cit.*

[29] *Ibid.,* p. 248.

[30] *Social Judgment,* p. 134. The reference here is to Behaviorism, now, happily, as a formal movement dead, but not without its followers among legal and social students.

[31] The great furor but a few years ago over the reception of Pareto is in some measure an indication of the strength of this view, for Pareto was an eminent exponent of the general attitude which Wallas was resisting: " . . . my wish is to construct a system of sociology on the model of celestial mechanics, physics, chemistry . . ." *The Mind and Society* (New York: 1935), ed. Arthur Livingston, trans. Andrew Bongiorno and Arthur Livingston, Vol. I, sec. 20, p. 16. For a many-sided discussion of Pareto's significance for social theory, see JOURNAL OF SOCIAL PHILOSOPHY, Vol. I, No. 1. (October, 1935).

[32] *Our Social Heritage,* p. 246.

[33] *Social Judgment,* p. 141.

[34] *Our Social Heritage,* p. 250.

[35] Discussion of the church may be found in *Our Social Heritage,* ch. XII; *Social Judgment,* ch. VIII.

[36] *Our Social Heritage,* p. 184.

[37] *The Great Society,* p. 67.

[38] *Human Nature in Politics,* p. 190.

[39] *Ibid.,* p. 181. As already indicated Wallas found this hope a vain one. By 1920 he recognized that far from rather naturally bringing the realization of such an ideal, the spread and popularization of psychological terms and concepts was producing the "incidental" and undesirable

effect of "increasing the feeling of helplessness in the individual citizen when faced by great movements of opinion among tens of millions of fellow citizens." *Our Social Heritage,* p. 150. In *Human Nature in Politics* is also expressed the wishful hope that a fusion might take place between the "emotional traditions of religion, and the new conception of intellectual duty introduced by Science" pp. 196-7. But the hope is tempered by fear that the breach is too wide, and he later (as noted in the text) joined issue with both modes of thought.

[40] *Human Nature in Politics,* p. 191.

[41] *Political Institutions: A Preface* (New York: 1938).

[42] There is, curiously, a wide area in which the beliefs of Wallas and Sait overlap, despite what is probably a fundamental disagreement. Wallas would concede that much of the thought product of the "intellectuals" is unreal and sterile, but would deny that it need be; indeed, he thinks that he may be able to suggest a remedy.

[43] For himself, however, he thought it "hardly possible for any one to endure life who does not believe that they [men] will succeed in producing a harmony between themselves and their environment far deeper and wider than anything which we can see to-day." *The Great Society,* p. 68.

Harry Elmer Barnes (essay date 1948)

SOURCE: "Graham Wallas and the Sociopsychological Basis of Politics and Social Reconstruction," in *An Introduction to the History of Sociology,* University of Chicago Press, 1948, pp. 696-716.

[*In the following essay, Barnes analyzes Wallas's theory of political psychology as presented in his* Human Nature in Politics, The Great Society, *and* Our Social Heritage.]

I. THE NATURE AND SCOPE OF THE WRITINGS OF GRAHAM WALLAS

An exceedingly suggestive attempt by an Englishman to apply sociology and psychology to the treatment of public problems is to be found in the works of Graham Wallas (1858-1932), late professor of political science in the University of London. Wallas, like Bagehot, was a happy combination of the student and the practical man of affairs—something that is distressingly rare in America but need not be so if Wallas' suggestions are carried out in the near future. This healthy juncture of the scholar and the observer of practical affairs gives to his works that intellectual flavor so remote from the writings of the agitator and that concreteness and grasp of actual conditions which are so conspicuously absent from most of the academic works upon social and political science.

Wallas entered the field of political literature as one of the authors of the famous ***Fabian Essays*** of 1888. His first extended work, however, was the splendid biography of Francis Place, published in 1897. The works which contain his chief social and political theories are ***Human Nature in Politics***, published in 1908; ***The Great Society***, published in 1914; and his American lectures, ***Our Social Heritage***, published in 1921. As these works will be analyzed below, all that need be mentioned in this place are some of the outstanding general characteristics of his writings.

In the first place, his early training as a classical scholar gave him a thorough grasp of the Platonic and Aristotelian social theories, to which he often recurs for example and comparison. His connections with the Fabian Society generated a rational and conscientious desire for sound social reform. Finally, his interest in that modern functional psychology, of which William James was the first important exponent, led him to think along psychological lines in both his academic studies and his practical relations to political problems and encouraged him to apply psychological principles consistently in formulating plans for social and political betterment.

Important in Wallas' political psychology is his emphasis upon the instinctive and subconscious processes of the mind as important factors in determining conduct. In this regard, he mentions his indebtedness to the suggestive essays of Dr. Trotter. While this is a step in the right direction, it is to be regretted that his first work presents no acknowledged acquaintance with the vast development of this field by psychiatrists like Morton Prince and Boris Sidis, or Sigmund Freud, Karl Jung, and the psychoanalysts. Wallas seems to have reached empirically many of their fundamental doctrines, and in his later books he specifically acknowledges his indebtedness to their conceptions. Yet, despite a courageous attempt to modernize political psychology, some critics have complained that Wallas had not entirely freed himself from some vestiges of the older psychology and logic. Ernest Barker, for example, in discussing ***Human Nature in Politics***, has summarized some of these possible defects:

> Many lines of criticism occur. Something could be said of its sensationalist premises; something of its nominalist philosophy; something of that tendency to explain the higher in terms of the lower, which leads to the explanation of civilised life by the conditions of life in prehistoric times and to the repeated coupling of man with "the other animals." We might urge that reason is none the less reason when it is not conscious inference, and that it is a fallacy to derationalize political society because it is not an explicit organization of conscious reason. Better however than to criticise is to emphasise the truths which Mr. Graham Wallas suggests.[1]

II. THE IRRATIONAL NATURE OF POLITICAL THOUGHT AND BEHAVIOR

In his ***Human Nature in Politics***,[2] Wallas criticizes the defects in the modern psychological interpretations of political processes, outlines a rational method of remedying these defects, and suggests the main improvements which may be hoped for from such procedure. His main thesis is that psychology either is wholly omitted in the modern treatment of politics or, if employed at all, is the old, erroneous hyperintellectual hedonism, coming down from Bentham, which deals with man as a calculating machine, undisturbed by emotion, custom, tradition, and the like. The following passage well indicates the general line of his argument on this point: "For the moment, therefore, nearly all students of politics analyze institutions and avoid the analysis of man. The study of human nature by the psychologists has, it is true, advanced enormously since the discovery of human evolution, but it has advanced without affecting or being affected by the study of politics."[3] Wallas points out the domination of the old-fashioned views about human nature by referring to certain passages by Professors Ostrogorski, Bryce, and Merivale as good examples:

> Apparently Merivale means the same thing by "abstract" political philosophy that Mr. Bryce means by "ideal" democracy. Both refer to a conception of human nature constructed in all good faith by certain eighteenth-century philosophers, which is now no longer exactly believed in, but which, because nothing else has taken its place, still exercises a kind of shadowy authority in a hypothetical universe. . . . [4]

> If so, the passage [by Mr. Bryce] is a good instance of the effect of our traditional course of study in politics. No doctor would now begin a medical treatise by saying "the ideal man requires no food, and is impervious to the action of bacteria, but this ideal is far removed from the actualities of any known population." No modern treatise on pedagogy begins with the statement that "the ideal boy knows things without being taught them, and his sole wish is the advancement of science, but no boys like this have ever existed. . . . [5]

> This essay of mine is offered as a plea that a corresponding change [i.e., corresponding to the revolution of modern criminology and pedagogy by psychology] in the conditions of political science is possible. In the great University whose constituent colleges are the universities of the world, there is a steadily growing body of professors and students of politics who give the whole day to their work. I cannot but think that, as the years go on, more of them will call to their aid that study of mankind which is the ancient ally of the moral sciences.[6]

The fundamental basis of political behavior is to be found in the mental organization of the individual, acted upon by the stimuli of the political environment. The individual is, psychologically considered, a bundle of impulses and potential responses to external stimulation. These impulses are the product of the mental evolution of the race; and the effective functioning of the individual in political society depends upon an adequate stimulation of these impulses and predispositions to thought and action. In analyzing the foundations of individual and social behavior, the first prerequisite is that we give up the old psychology, which maintained that human acts are deliberately calculated means to a preconceived end, and recognize that the majority of human mental processes are subconscious or half-conscious—the result of instinctive or habitual impulses: "Whoever sets himself to base his political thinking on a re-examination of human nature must begin by trying to overcome his own tendency to exaggerate the intellectuality of mankind."[7]

The chief personal impulses which Wallas emphasizes are affection, fear, ridicule, desire for property, pugnacity, suspicion, curiosity, and the desire to excel. Each of these impulses is most effective to the extent that it acts without competition with other impulses, arises from direct stimulation, and results from an appeal to an instinct formed early in the evolution of the race. For this reason the artificial and recently developed stimulation of books and newspapers is superficial and transient in its effect, while the emotions caused by the bodily presence and personal traits and behavior of a political candidate are much more stirring and lasting than reading about politics or an appeal to abstract principles. Political campaigns are planned for the purpose of creating an impulsive personal affection for a candidate rather than a reasoned conclusion as to his personal merits or the excellence of his platform. In contrast to Le Bon, Wallas holds that the frequent repetition of a subject tends to create an impression of unreality upon both speaker and audience; therefore, the successful political leader must vary his appeal. Since the conditions of human evolution have required a mixture of privacy and social intercourse, the individual in modern life thrives best when this proper proportion of both is maintained. But such a pattern of life is difficult for the politician, who is called upon to be in almost perpetual association with his party workers. Finally, all political impulses are likely to be greatly intensified if they are stimulated when individuals are assembled in a crowd. This psychic instability of crowds may result from the fact that a stampede of the primitive social groups was the surest way to safety.

The political environment, as the stimulus which operates upon the impulsive dispositions of men, differs from these dispositions in that it is far more variable. Human nature has apparently changed but little since the beginning of the historic era. Therefore, any great reforms must be based upon the improvement of the political environment rather than upon any hope of a fundamental revolution of human nature. But, even though no considerable change in human nature may be looked for, an understanding of its characteristics and behavior may be able to produce a real transformation in conduct, quite aside from changes in the environment. Now the most significant thing about the political environment is that the great political entities which stimulate mankind are mainly recognized by the human mind through symbols. Some of the most important symbolized political entities are parties, nations, justice, authority, freedom, rights, etc. The mind does not, as a rule, comprehend the whole complex of ideas involved in a political entity but associates this complex with some aspect, image, or interpretation of it which serves as a symbol for the whole. For example, the royal scepter or other insignia of office tend to symbolize the institution of royalty, and the individual is content to let it stop with this rather than proceed to analyze the whole history and psychology of kingship. Even language itself is mainly intelligible to us through its symbolic nature and content, and the reception and interpretation of the symbols which words represent will naturally differ among individuals according to the experiences of their past life. The farther back the origin of the complex of ideas which are thus symbolized, the greater the emotional value that will attach to the symbol. A good example of the necessity for having a deep emotional association for a symbol is to be seen in the difficulty of creating loyalty to a newly constructed nation, dynasty, or aristocracy.

Of all modern political entities which stimulate our individual impulses, the political party is the most important and powerful. While the party may have an intellectual origin and be designed to achieve a definite end, it will have little strength or duration unless it secures sufficient emotional values for its symbols, such as party colors, tunes, names, and the like. A skilful party uses its symbols in the same way that a commercial concern employs its trade-marks and advertisements. The nature and validity of the thing symbolized may vary considerably, but that is not so important to the success of the party as that a high emotional response to the symbol be provided and sustained. If a candidate is not properly symbolized by his party, he has no chance of success. The most insignificant nonentity, properly associated with the party symbols, is much more likely to be successful in an election than the strongest personality in a country, if the latter cuts himself off from all party connections and makes an appeal solely to the intelligence of the voters. The instances of a man's forming a successful political entity in himself are rare. Even in such cases a man must adhere for a long time to a given set of principles, so that his followers may attach a high emotional value to them. This same continuity in doctrine must be observed by every newspaper that desires to be the successful organ of a party.

Wallas next makes a specific inquiry as to the extent to which reason enters into political action. His conclusion is essentially the same as that presented by Benjamin Kidd, namely, that reason plays only a small part in political life. The process by which he reaches this conclusion is quite different, however, from that employed by Kidd. Instead of arbitrary definitions and a priori assumptions, Wallas bases his judgment on an acute psychological analysis of human conduct. While it is difficult to say at just what point instinctive and habitual actions end and reasoned action begins, it is certain that there is a very large range for subconscious, nonrational inference in our mental processes, and it is equally obvious that the majority of our political opinions are reached in a nonrational manner. Men seem to attach greater emotional significance to the opinions which are reached intuitively than to those which are the result of reasoned conclusions. While subconscious impulses may be a fairly satisfactory guide for general affairs, since they are usually the result of several convergent suggestions, such is not the case in the field of our political thoughts and actions. It is the primary purpose of the political art deliberately to exploit our tendency to reach our opinions in a subconscious manner, and it aims so to stimulate our subconscious mind that we will automatically agree with the position taken by the party.

Yet, after all, reasoning in politics may better be described as extremely difficult rather than impossible. The difficulty is twofold. In the first place, man has to create the political entities about which he reasons, and these are, in turn, represented to the mind through symbols, largely subconscious in their psychic operation. In the second place, while reasoning in pure science is based upon the comparison of concrete similar objects or of objects alike in certain abstract qualities, political psychology has never found a satisfactory standard for comparing men. Neither Platonic idealism, Locke's theological ethics, Rousseauan natural rights, or Benthamite hedonism is able to furnish this standard for comparison. As a substitute for the failures of political psychology in the past, Wallas offers a synthetic program for the scientific study of political phenomena which will make reasoning in politics possible. The whole problem is to obtain, arrange, and study as many facts about man as are available. The beginning of this study should be a thorough acquaintance with the facts about human behavior which can be gained from the latest developments in psychology. Little or nothing can be hoped for from the pursuit of formal political science, based upon analyses of constitutions and unreal intellectualistic presuppositions. The only way to get any idea of the human type, with its infinite variations in thought and action, is to measure these variations by the statistical method and thus obtain some conception of the modal type and the nature and extent of the variations from this type. One must get into the habit of thinking in terms of statistical curves. Finally, the environment, natural and social, must be studied in the same manner, with a view to discovering the interaction between the individual and the environment. Most real statesmen now think quantitatively but only roughly and automatically. What is needed is such a cultivation of the scientific method as will enable one to start in political life with that exact quantitative knowledge which is now crudely and subconsciously acquired only after long experience. Wallas finds an indication of a step in the right direction in the present employment of statistics in the governmental bureaus and in the taking of censuses. The information thus compiled enables the citizens to check somewhat upon the wild statements of politicians designed to stir emotions but based on false assumptions and inaccurate information.

Wallas next takes up a consideration of the results which may be expected from the application of his proposed methods of study of political processes. In the first place, the faulty intellectualistic conceptions of political conduct would be abandoned, and the knowledge of actual political methods would provide citizens with the ability to fortify themselves against exploitation by masters of the art of political manipulation and would help them to curb the evils in the present methods of political parties. As soon as men are made conscious of the nature and genesis of the political thoughts and actions which have hitherto been subconscious, they will be able to handle the situation with greater realism and intelligence. In fact, Wallas advocates a sort of general political psychotherapy analogous to developments in psychiatry. He holds that a pathological political system may be reformed if the mass of the citizens are made fully conscious of the actual nature of their malady. Certain half-conscious progress in this direction may be seen in the growing use of such terms as "spellbinder" and "sensational," which make men a little less susceptible to the mental influences thus designated. The extension of this knowledge must, however, be deliberate and vigorous if it is to keep ahead of the constantly improving art of political exploitation and propaganda. While this extension of political knowledge may be aided by intellectual appeals through preaching and teaching, it can never succeed on a large scale until it is given an emotional background. That there may sometime be a co-ordination of thought and feeling, leading to a reformed and purified political system, is indicated by the action of the Japanese as revealed to the world in their struggle with Russia.

The next question that arises is the relation of the foregoing suggestions to the improvement of representative government and democracy, which, while by no means an entire success, may be regarded as the most satisfactory political system yet devised. While the consent of the governed may be accepted as an essential condition of a democratic government, what is most needed at present is a reform in the electoral system—the modern method of registering consent. It is useless to attempt to create a superior governing class which will live apart from the emotions of the world; what is really urgent is to make a political election similar to an English jury trial, namely, designed to obtain the facts in the circumstances and render an intelligent verdict. The pressing need is to improve the methods by which political opinions are formed rather than merely expressed. Encouraging steps have been taken in the English laws against bribery and inordinate expenditures in election. The old tendency to attempt to solve the problem through purely intellectual devices reappears in the proposal of Mill for public voting and that of Lord Courtney for proportional representation. Much more desirable are an abolition of the elements of mob suggestion and intimidation in elections; the spread of education in political methods; and the increase in the number of persons actively interested in the political life of the nation. The greatest improvement in political administration in the nineteenth century was the establishment of a permanent and efficient civil service in England and America. This branch of the government is the really effective "Second Chamber," for the information which it collects leads to the discrediting of the emotional appeals of a political orator which are based upon gross ignorance of facts. A consistent improvement and extension of the civil service is one of the most promising methods of moving toward a better political system.

International politics, like domestic policies, may greatly improve if subjected to a psychological reconstruction: "The future peace of the world turns largely on the question whether we have, as is sometimes said and often assumed, an instinctive affection for those human beings whose features and color are like our own, combined with an instinctive hatred for those who are unlike us." Since the days of Aristotle there has been a great change in the conception of the possible extent of a state. The modern state can no longer be a thing comprehended by direct personal observation; it can exist only as a mental entity, symbol, or abstraction. It was the thesis of Mazzini and Bismarck that no state could be successful unless composed of homogeneous peoples. This view has since been weakened because diverse nationalities have prospered within single successful states, and modern imperialism and colonization have tended politically to unite European and non-European types. What is now most to be desired is not national or imperial egoism but a recognition of the value of national differences. This stage of political thought might have been reached already if it had not been for the misinterpretation of Darwinism, which represented war as the chief source of progress. A healthy sign is the present tendency among biologists and sociologists to represent progress as the result of co-operation quite as much as the outcome of struggle:

> No one now expects an immediate, or prophesies with certainty an ultimate Federation of the Globe; but the consciousness of a common purpose in mankind, or even the acknowledgment that such a common purpose is possible, would alter the face of world politics at once. The discussion at the Hague of a halt in the race of armaments would no longer seem utopian, and the strenuous profession by the colonizing powers that they have no selfish ends in view might be transformed from a sordid and useless hypocrisy into a fact to which each nation might adjust its policy. The irrational race hatred which breaks out from time to time on the fringes of empire, would have little effect in world politics when opposed by a consistent conception of the future of human progress.[8]

The main importance of Wallas' ***Human Nature in Politics*** for social and political theory is that it worked a veritable revolution in political psychology among informed and thoughtful students of the subject. It constituted the *reductio ad absurdum* of the Benthamite felicific calculus, which had dominated political thought from the days of the Utilitarian political philosophers to those of Bryce and Ostrogorski and had affected the thinking of Marx and the radicals as well as that of the liberals. This theory had held that man's political behavior is founded upon rationality, clear perception of individual interests, and deliberate calculation of results. Wallas revealed the far more fundamental importance of irrational traits and emotional forces in behavior, without resorting to any fanciful mysticism or illogical flights, such as those manifested by Kidd.[9]

III. THE SOCIOPSYCHOLOGICAL TRAITS OF THE GREAT SOCIETY

When Wallas' second work, ***The Great Society***, appeared, several new and interesting developments in his general sociological thinking came to light.[10] His first work, while stating that a sound psychology of society and politics must rest upon a consideration of both individual traits and the social environment which stimulates them, had been devoted primarily to an investigation of the manner in which personal traits operate in political life. ***The Great Society*** is logically devoted mainly to a consideration of the social and political environment and of the desirable methods whereby it can be so reconstructed as to provide a more complete set of stimuli for the individual personality. It seems that Wallas may have been affected by the afterthought that he had done his work too well in his earlier book. His clear and convincing demonstration that modern political activities are based upon a distressingly small amount of intelligent action on the part of anyone except the leaders in party exploitation seemed to trouble him. While he had emphatically stated in his ***Human Nature in Politics*** that our only hope lies in increasing the deliberate and intelligent analysis of political institutions and activities, he apparently felt that a better case should be made out for the position and function of rational thought.

The scope of Wallas' second work is considerably broader than that of the first. Instead of devoting his attention primarily to the problems of contemporary politics, he makes a psychological analysis of our modern civilization which has grown up since the industrial revolution. This civilization he designates as "The Great Society." His avowed aim is to suggest a new type of social organization which would produce more of a harmony between human nature and the new material conditions produced by industrialization and urbanization. As, in his first book, he found representative democracy to be an experiment which was not entirely successful, so he discovers in ***The Great Society*** that our modern civilization has developed serious problems. They were, for the most part, unforeseen by the majority of those who witnessed the transformation but are threatening enough to render the question of the ultimate success of urban industrialism problematical rather than assured. To the consideration of these grave problems Wallas brings the same broad conception of psychology that distinguished his earlier work, even improved at certain points. It is particularly refreshing to find an author who attempts an analysis of society upon the basis of modernized dynamic psychology.[11] In ***The Great Society*** Wallas' psychology combines the introspective and the behavioristic theories; he had enriched his knowledge of the unconscious processes in the individual mind by a study of the discoveries made by modern abnormal psychology; and, finally, his social psychology rejects all one-sided explanations and is based upon the broad conception of the reactions of the individual organism to the complex of stimuli from the environment. Again, he has now become an avowed "sociologist." The word was mentioned but once in his earlier book, but now all his analyses are made from the "sociological viewpoint." All in all, it is a more valuable sociological study than ***Human Nature in Politics***.

The society of the present day is to be traced to the great mechanical inventions of the industrial revolution, which gave the material basis for our civilization. The social transformation has been as far-reaching as the industrial and far less happy in its attendant circumstances. Instead of a social system based upon local association and personal relationships, we now have one founded upon world-wide, impersonal, and almost mechanical relations. Those great scientific discoveries, which have made the technical changes in industry possible, have not been accompanied by a parallel and proportionate development of a science of social relationships. Psychological knowledge has been diffused only among a small class of experts and has not permeated society in a manner comparable to the knowledge of technical processes in industry.

It is Wallas' aim to supply this need and to discover how far a realistic psychology of social processes can go toward discovering a way out of our present social dilemma through formulating the outlines of a satisfactory form of social organization for our times. To achieve an acceptable theory of social psychology upon which to base an analysis of our society, Wallas contends that one must accept the doctrine that the type forms of human conduct are the result of both inherited and acquired dispositions to act in a certain manner, stimulated by the experiences of the organism within its environment. The two especially important complex dispositions in mankind are instinct and intelligence, and Wallas, somewhat in opposition to the position taken in his previous work, insists that man is as naturally disposed to thought as he is to instinctive action. But human dispositions, either instinctive or intellectual, cannot function properly unless they are acted upon by the "appropriate stimuli" in the environment. Unstimulated dispositions develop into what he designates as "balked dispositions," or what modern dynamic psychologists would call "repressed complexes." These balked dispositions cause that nervous and mental instability so prevalent in our modern civilization. This has no basis in organic defects of the nervous system, but it is the fundamental pathological characteristic of modern society.[12] The reason for the prevalence of balked dispositions in modern society is that our hereditary natural makeup has changed but little for ages, while the environment which stimulates that nature has been completely revolutionized in the last century. While no one can hope to revive exactly the same set of stimuli as operated in an earlier type of culture, it is the task of modern social reorganization to discover and supply equivalent stimuli to release that repressed energy which has been dammed up by our balked dispositions and make a happy and efficient life once more possible for the majority of the race.

On the basis of such a conception of social psychology Wallas finds that those theories which emphasize but one subjective aspect of the psychology of social processes are inadequate and unsatisfactory. Among the theories of this type which he rejects are those based upon habit, fear, hedonism, love, hatred, and the various psychologies of the crowd, founded on imitation, sympathy, and suggestion. The problems of modern society can be solved only by the application of carefully reasoned thought; and, while thought may have a subconscious basis, it is highly essential that society shall do all in its power to improve and increase those aspects of thought which are amenable to deliberate and conscious operations.

Since all human activities are an expression of thought, will, and emotion, efficient social organization must make provision for bringing all these aspects of human activity into play in an effective and well-balanced manner. The organized activity of society in this direction, however, has thus far been distressingly inadequate. The old method of stimulating thought by oral discussion has been largely displaced in modern society by mechanical devices for imparting information, which, while they are much more efficient in distributing printed or oral information are greatly inferior in originating new thought. Particularly difficult is it for the average workingman to develop any independent or fruitful thought on public affairs, because of the destruction of the close personal relationships that formerly existed in small groups of workmen, and the efforts of the vested interests, political and economic, to exploit the workingman's ignorance by perversions and distortions of the truth in the printed journals that reach the working class. The attempt to create a condition of effective thinking by discussion in modern legislatures has all too often degenerated into a burlesque which makes the members good-natured cynics. This travesty reaches its height in the speeches of American congressmen, written by their secretaries and published, without being delivered, in the *Congressional Record.*

The effective organization of the social will is equally deficient in modern society. The three contending varieties of will organization—individualism, based on the institution of private property; socialism, founded upon the proposition to extend the functions of the democratic state; and syndicalism, demanding a government on the basis of representation by occupations—all possess certain advantages but are equally inadequate when taken alone. The next essential step in political invention is to find by experiment the correct combination of these three contending principles.

As to the organization of society to promote human happiness through a richer emotional life, it seems that, while modern industrialism has tremendously increased the technical devices for producing commodities for human comfort and convenience, it is equally true that the process has failed proportionately to increase the sum total of human happiness. The great advances have been made with the aim of increasing the production of wealth rather than with the aim of securing a greater amount of satisfaction in its consumption. One of the most alarming aspects of the modern social transformation is that society had allowed the process to gain such momentum, before it awakened to what was going on, that the new developments have begun to get beyond the control of society: "That which chiefly angers and excites us now, as we contemplate the society in which we live, is not a conviction that the world is a worse place than it has ever been, but the feeling that we have lost grip over the course of events, and are stupidly wasting the power over nature which might make the world infinitely better."[13]

It will be the test of the success of modern society if it is able to make up by future efforts what it has lost through its lethargy and apathy in the past. The laboring class has been especially unfortunate in this transition. The impersonal, monotonous, large-scale, and highly subdivided and standardized industry of today has destroyed the pleasure of manual labor, and the conditions of urban life among the working classes have made it difficult for them to achieve happiness outside of working hours.

The conclusion of Wallas' work—its constructive program—is its most unsatisfactory part. In his proposals as to how to reorganize society to attain happiness, he mixes many fertile suggestions as to diversifying interests and economizing effort with Aristotle's metaphysical conception of the "mean" as the ideal, and he ends by practically throwing up his hands and passing the problem over to philosophy. As R. M. MacIver well observes: "His discussion of the type of social organization which would bring a new harmony of life and environment did not advance much beyond some luminous suggestions as to the need for it." Fortunately, he had already provided his readers with enough suggestions as to a more practical and promising program so that they need not assent to his conclusions or regret their lack of coherence and precision.

IV. RECONSTRUCTING OUR SOCIAL HERITAGE

Wallas' third sociological treatise—and the logical completion of his body of social theory—was presented in a series of lectures delivered at the New School for Social Research and at Yale University. It was published in 1921, under the title ***Our Social Heritage***. Each of his books seems to have proceeded naturally out of the shortcomings which Wallas recognized in its predecessor. His ***Human Nature in Politics*** attacked the current intellectualism in political, social, and economic theory. His ***Great Society***, while assuming the dominance of subconscious and emotional elements, insisted that improvement could come only through rational thought and conscious effort. But, when it came to showing how rational thought and conscious effort might create a new and more satisfactory social organization, Wallas proved rather feeble and inconclusive. ***Our Social Heritage*** is a well-reasoned analysis of important factors involved in any sound program for the conscious improvement of society. It deals with "the ideas, habits, and institutions directly concerned in the political, economic, and social organization of those modern communities which constitute 'The Great Society.'" It had an immediate pragmatic and remedial purpose, for he believed that, without an adequate understanding of our "socially inherited ways of living and thinking" and a determination to adjust them more closely to the needs of the day, humanity will speedily be confronted with greater disasters than the first World War.

Wallas takes as his starting-point the essential distinction between "nature" and "nurture." Man's nature, or his physiological and neurological equipment, has not changed for thousands of years. Indeed, man may be said to have become "biologically parasitic on his social heritage." The other animals can thrive without a social heritage, but man would soon become extinct without its support. "Nurture," upon which man must depend for his present existence and for his future progress, includes both personal acquisitions and those which come to the individual from society, past and present. The cultural supremacy of man has been primarily, if not wholly, a product of his social heritage, or nurture. Likewise, any hope of future improvement depends upon a better understanding and utilization of our socially inherited culture and institutions. Yet this problem is becoming progressively more difficult, for the great increase of pertinent information is making it more difficult to find the means for an adequate transmission of our social heritage, and the rapid technological changes are necessitating a constant social readjustment.[14]

Any adequate utilization and reconstruction of our social heritage involves sustained muscular and mental effort. Impulses must be to some extent replaced by conscious effort. There must come into being a self-conscious will for improvement. It is not easy, however, to sustain conscious effort. Physiological reactions and instincts have been evolved to meet continuous needs. Higher conscious activity has been produced to serve only occasional wants. Therefore, conscious effort brings a high degree of fatigue. It is doubtful whether either conscious mental or muscular effort can function with great efficiency or persistence unless it is accompanied by a free play of the emotions and the force of the "artistic drive." Conscious intellectual effort has been most successful in pure science and technology and least so in the social sciences; but the improvement of our social heritage depends upon a more scientific and pragmatic social science.[15]

In a very real sense, social reconstruction and the reorganization of our social heritage depend upon devising better ways for the development and organization of various types of co-operation—group, national, and international. There are several forms of co-operation exhibited in the biological world—the leaderless and unorganized co-operation of the ants, the co-operation of cattle under a single leader, and the co-operation of a wolf pack, in which each member is affected by instincts of both leadership and obedience. Mankind exemplifies this last, or wolf, type of the co-operation of a "loosely and intermittently gregarious animal." Man is capable of consciously organized and directed co-operation, but this requires unusual effort and produces an excessive amount of fatigue. Conscious group co-operation has been as yet only imperfectly attained by mankind and tends to break down in times of stress, as proved by the disasters of the British Dardanelles and Mesopotamian expeditions during the first World War.

National co-operation is far more artificial than group co-operation and depends to a much greater extent on socially inherited knowledge and conscious effort. Group co-operation rests to a considerable extent upon personal knowledge and contacts, but "a modern civilized man can never see or hear the nation of which he is a member, and, if he thinks or feels about it, he must do so by employing some acquired entity of the mind." An accurate idea of the nation, then, is essential if we are to have any "reliable stimulus to large-scale coöperative emotion and coöperative action." The average citizen, however, has no systematic method for building up his "idea of the nation." It is the unconscious and carelessly acquired product of his daily experiences. Much of it is due to conscious propaganda by the vested interests, for, though the average citizen may be aimless, careless, and thoughtless, "the controllers of newspapers, especially of the sinister American or British journals whose writers are apparently encouraged to 'color the news' as well as their comments on the news, in accordance with the will of a multi-millionaire proprietor, know pretty exactly what they are doing." Hence, if we are to have any solid basis for national co-operation, we must work out a more scientific method of acquiring our idea of a nation and its accompanying emotions.

Wallas submits some interesting and thoughtful suggestions toward this end. We should start with a Cartesian skepticism and proceed by critical reasoning. Our conclusions must be based upon a careful and patient observation of our fellow-citizens, their type, actions, and aspirations. Such scrutiny of our countrymen will convince us of the wide divergence and variety of type, fitness, tastes, and capacity which exist. The fallacious notion of the uniformity of men has been the curse of modern politics and economics. Yet we can never have a stable national organization or effective national co-operation without a greater degree of common consent to the existing social and economic order than that which now prevails. The problem will probably best be solved by recognizing this diversity of taste and capacity and providing an equality of opportunity for the diversified population to realize their aspirations according to their differing capacities. The better adjustment of individual tasks and responsibilities to individual differences between human beings must become "the conscious, organized and effective purpose of modern civilization."

World co-operation is even more difficult of achievement than national co-operation. If one is to approach intelligently the problem of international relations, he must make the initial admission that "the change of scale from national coöperation to world-coöperation involves a change in the form and character of the coöperative process. It is a change of kind as well as degree." Many of those very instinctive and emotional forces which produce group and national co-operation automatically impel us to hate aliens and induce a combative attitude toward them. Yet world co-operation in certain phases of economic and commercial activity has become a basic fact in modern life, and it is futile to retain Cobden's dream that we can enjoy commercial intercourse without involving political relations. There is little hope of building up a sound internationalism on a purely instinctive or emotional basis. It must be founded on conscious thought and reasoned calculation of results. Especially must we learn to calculate the disastrous results of a world war and obtain therefrom an impulse to avoid war and a willingness to take those steps which are necessary to prevent its recurrence. Woodrow Wilson's "Fourteen Points" once seemed destined to provide a basis for rational international co-operation, but the opportunity was ingloriously lost at Paris in 1919. Certain improvements in international thinking must be made if we are to have any effective world co-operation. We must abandon generalizations about an abstract state which will not apply to any concrete state; we must study history, government, law, and biology from the new problem attitude of world co-operation; we must work out a control of the press which will make it impotent to debase statesmanship and arouse unnecessary international hatred and will make journalism a real force for sound international education; we must reconsider liberty, independence, nationality, and equality from an international point of view and also give them greater recognition at home; we must stimulate political invention, so as to adapt national institutions to supernational needs; and we must co-operate in every way in any procedure which will produce an international outlook. It would even be worthwhile to send representatives to the League of Nations meeting at Geneva, if only to co-operate in an international survey of the heavens.[16]

Since the first World War there have been many appeals from representatives of organized Christianity, and especially from those who come from the more conservative religious circles, to make religion the basis of world union and co-operation. Wallas suggests that it would be most pertinent to inquire what organized religion had contributed during the ten years preceding 1921 to make good its claim to fitness to assume leadership in world unity. His examination of the evidence constitutes an overwhelming indictment of the role of organized Christianity in world affairs. Without notable exceptions, the church has aligned itself with the reactionary and vicious elements in the international situation. The German Lutherans supported Prussian militarism and the invasion of Belgium. The Austrian Catholics were the leaders in the anti-Serbian movement. The Anglican church vigorously favored crushing peace terms for Germany and condoned the Irish policy of the government and the massacres in India. The French Catholic elements have supported the peace of revenge and French postwar diplomacy. Above all, sacramental Christianity lacks the essential ethical element which is necessary for social reconstruction. No group accepts the sacraments with more reverence and enthusiasm than the Spanish brigands. Wallas concludes:

> The special task of our generation might be so to work and think as to be able to hand on to the boys and girls who, fifty years hence, at some other turning-point of world history, may gather in the schools, the heritage of a world-outlook deeper and wider and more helpful than that of modern Christendom.[17]

Science also needs to be revamped before it can be of much assistance in world co-operation. It has been of great aid in technology, but it is indispensable that science be socialized and moralized and that these revamped and broader scientific methods be adopted more rapidly in the moral and social sciences.

In this manner Wallas makes a plea for conscious, rational, and "telic" progress, which entitles him to a place with Comte, Lester F. Ward, Ludwig Stein, and L. T. Hobhouse among social philosophers.

The above summary of the more salient points in Wallas' ***Social Heritage*** gives but a faint impression of the content of the book, with its wealth of concrete illustrative material, but it will probably justify Harold Laski's contention that it is the product of "sober wisdom."[18]

After finishing ***Our Social Heritage***, Wallas appears once more to have had misgivings about the adequacy of a published book, especially about the vagueness of his suggestions concerning the type of education needed to lead society into a more rational form of organization and to put an end to war. At any rate, Wallas produced two later books which revolved around the problem of "how far the knowledge accumulated by modern psychology can be made useful for the improvement of the thought-processes of a working thinker." These books were ***The Art of Thought*** (1926) and the posthumous volume, ***Social Judgment*** (1935).

In these books Wallas argued the theme, already familiar to readers of ***The Great Society*** and ***Our Social Heritage***, that, while we have greatly increased our power over nature, we have failed to guide and utilize this control over nature through a social organization harmonious with an age of applied science and technological efficiency. He stresses the point made in ***Our Social Heritage***, that, while we can wage war ever more effectively, we seem as impotent as ever in preventing war. Wallas agrees with Ward that the only way to assure the type of social program needed to adjust man to an industrial age and to curb war is to create a realistic educational setup. He goes on from there to criticize the archaic content and faulty methods of contemporary education and to suggest how scientific psychology might be exploited to effect a salutary revolution in both pedagogy and the technique of social reconstruction. While Wallas comes out with the same general "telic" philosophy as Ward, his emphasis is more on the methods of education than upon its content and social objectives.

The book on ***Social Judgment***, as published, was an unfinished torso, embodying only the first and introductory portion of what might have been Wallas' most mature and complete contribution to social and political theory. What was published is chiefly prolegomena to systematic theory—wise but rather discursive homilies on history, morals, philosophy, psychology, and education. The unfinished portion was to be the systematic section of the work. As his daughter, who edited the book, tells us: "It appears from his notes and raw material which were among his papers that Part II would have opened with a long chapter on Government, dealing in the main with the problems and institutions of democratic government in the modern world, and that the later chapters would have included one on Private Property and one on International Organization."

Even this brief and inadequate summary of Wallas' works will suffice to convince the reader of their importance. If, as A. A. Tenney once said, the prime end of sociology is a rational criticism of public policy, then few writers have acquitted themselves of the responsibility imposed by their subject in so efficient a manner as has Graham Wallas.

His works represent, in a general way, the best that sociology has to offer in the way of suggestions to political science and practice. He insists that, first of all, political science must be modernized, both in subject matter and in method. It must take account of the vast changes in civilization since the time of Aristotle, or even of Montesquieu and Burke, and must deal effectively with the new problems which these changes have produced. It can no longer afford to concern itself with metaphysical questions about society or with unreal conceptions of human nature but must deal with actual conditions of the present, and deal with them scientifically. By this "scientific" treatment he means that political science must base its generalizations upon the fundamental laws of human psychology, as revealed by careful empirical observation of human conduct, not only in political groupings but in wider forms of association.

To be sure, there are many defects in his books. The professional psychologist would quarrel with him over many points of detail, and he gives little evidence of having read widely in the strictly sociological literature of recent times, but these defects are more than compensated for by the abundance of illuminating concrete illustrations of his main propositions, which a keenly observant and reflective mind had drawn from close contact with many phases of English life in a half-century of active connection with academic and political affairs.

Until students of political science turn their attention from a preponderant concern with formal treatises on their subject, from Pufendorf to Burgess, and deal seriously with those defects in their subject which Wallas has so clearly revealed, there can be little hope that academic political science will have any considerable leavening effect upon modern political life. Likewise, practical democratic politics are likely to go on the rocks unless some method of rational control over political emotionalism and propaganda can be assured. Further, the problem before us is not only that of introducing rationality into democracy; we must also have a democratic program of social reconstruction which will readjust our ways of living and thinking to the realities of the post-industrial revolution age. Such a program must rest upon an up-to-date educational system, not only inspired by realistic social objectives but also guided by the expert techniques which have been provided by scientific psychology.

NOTES

[1] *Political Thought in England from Herbert Spencer to the Present Day* (New York, 1915), p. 156.

[2] This work is well reviewed by another leader in English political thought, J. A. Hobson, in the *Sociological Review*, 1909, pp. 293-94. See also Barker's excellent analysis, *op. cit.*, pp. 153-57.

[3] *Human Nature in Politics*, p. 14.

[4] *Ibid.*, p. 128.

[5] *Ibid.*, p. 127.

[6] *Ibid.*, p. 18.

[7] *Ibid.*, p. 21.

[8] *Ibid.*, pp. 294-95.

[9] Cf. W. C. Mitchell, "Bentham's Felicific Calculus," *Political Science Quarterly*, June, 1918.

[10] This book is reviewed by E. L. Talbert in the *American Journal of Sociology*, March, 1915, pp. 708-11; and by A. B. Wolfe in the *American Economic Review*, June, 1915, pp. 311 ff. The latter is especially to be commended.

[11] A good analysis of Wallas' psychology is to be found in W. C. Mitchell, "Human Behavior and Economics," *Quarterly Journal of Economics*, November, 1914, pp. 12-18.

[12] *The Great Society*, pp. 63 ff.

[13] *Ibid.*, p. 323.

[14] *Our Social Heritage*, chap. i.

[15] *Ibid.*, chap. ii.

[16] *Ibid.*, chaps. iii-iv, ix, xi-xii.

[17] *Ibid.*, p. 291.

[18] It is especially gratifying to note that Wallas apparently escaped the effects of the war hysteria which distorted the writings of so many sociologists and publicists. Yet he relies to a distressing degree upon English data and illustrations, a procedure which is all the more unpardonable in an author with an extensive knowledge of the United States.

Mary Peter Mack (essay date 1958)

SOURCE: "Graham Wallas' New Individualism," in *Western Political Quarterly*, Vol. 11, No. 1, March, 1958, pp. 14-32.

[*In the following essay, Mack follows the development and influence of Wallas's political thought.*]

As he walked with Lowes Dickinson in Cambridge one day, Graham Wallas suddenly stretched his hand out as if trying to seize something, and asked, "Don't you sometimes feel that the solution of the problem of democracy is just *there,* almost within reach, if only you could see more clearly and grasp more firmly?" Dickinson's eyebrows arched ironically.[1] What was Wallas looking for? Did he find it? Or was he a Don Quixote of political science, off on a chivalrous but outmoded mission? Was he seeking the impossible?

In 1908 Wallas published ***Human Nature in Politics***, one of the first books to warn of the monster political force that could spring from manipulated mass opinion and of the small part played by reason in politics. He warned in order to plead for improvement. Most of his later writings are expansions of one sentence in that early book.

> If . . . a conscious moral purpose is to be strong enough to overcome, as a political force, the advancing art of political exploitation, the conception of control from within must be formed into an ideal entity which, like "Science," can appeal to popular imagination, and be spread by an organized system of education.[2]

Wallas' one defense against unreason was a kind of individual moral rearmament. He pleaded with public servants and students of government for special efforts of thought and more thought, illuminated and improved by moral passion. The explosions of the twenty-five years that have passed since he died in 1932 seem, however, to mock his kindly teachings. Many politicians began to think of the psychological facts of nonrational inference which Wallas had uneasily presented, but they often used them for their own purposes and ignored his moral exhortations.

As quixotic as Wallas' defense may now seem, he himself chose it by default. He became the apostle of resurrected individualism only very slowly, after trying and rejecting many alternatives and almost in spite of himself. He was born in 1858, the fifth child of a clergyman, and was educated at Shrewsbury and Corpus Christi, Oxford. He began his career quietly as a classics master at Highgate. In 1885 he resigned over a religious issue.

Like so many of the educated middle class in late Victorian England, Wallas was deeply stirred by social conscience. The same motives which moved Arnold Toynbee to lecture to workingmen and Charles Booth to undertake his laborious survey of the London working classes drove Wallas to join the Fabian Society in 1886. He revolted against conventional liberalism and individualism, which seemed to him to have become insipid and irrelevant, and became a Socialist. He was a Fabian until 1904, at first an ardent, then a lukewarm, and finally a hostile one. He turned from Fabian Socialism to Syndicalism and Guild Socialism, which were then slowly becoming known in England through the writings of Sorel and Gierke.

World War I, however, killed his enthusiasm not only for Syndicalism but for doctrinal approaches to social problems of any kind whatever. Gradually, in all the books which followed ***Human Nature in Politics***,[3] he began to work out a kind of New Individualism which he had first hinted at there. To bring the traditions of Bentham and Mill up-to-date he developed a liberalism-in-reverse, one which began with the facts of modern large-scale economic and social organization and analyzed the structure piece by piece, until the single thinking feeling man could be located in it.

Human Nature in Politics at once made Wallas' reputation as a political thinker. Previously he had published only **"Property Under Socialism,"** one of the ***Fabian Essays in Socialism*** (1889), and his classic biography of Francis Place, the Benthamite tailor (1898). There is irony in the fate his writings have suffered. When ***Human Nature in Politics*** first appeared in 1908 he was already fifty years old. He had been teaching continuously for twenty-seven years, first at Highgate, then as a Fabian soap-box orator, a night school lecturer, and finally as instructor of political science at the new London School of Economics. He had been a member of the Fabian Society for sixteen years, and had had eleven years of experience as a member of the London School Board and London County Council. He had run for office and won, and knew at first-hand the maneuvers and compromises a successful administrator must make. Few political theorists can have been better equipped than he was to understand the actual workings of human nature in politics. No one before him had applied a careful study of modern psychology to politics and no one but he could have corroborated it so fully from the depths of this own experience.

In a way, Wallas' book was altogether too successful. His description of the large part played by nonrational inference in political decision and of the dangers of its unscrupulous cultivation by propagandists was so convincing that it quickly became a platitude. In the process it was ripped from its context and magnified beyond proportion to his larger argument, which was then neglected.

His account of the complexities and undetermined boundaries of the mind was never intended to stand by itself. It was the empirical foundation he needed to support himself both as a critic and as a moralist. From it, he drew the materials for his attack on those reductionist political theories which deduce man's political behavior from oversimplified assumptions about his psychological nature; and on it, he built his own unified normative view of the world. All his books are a blend of descriptive, critical, and normative elements and all of them are attempts to answer the questions he first raised in ***Human Nature in Politics***.

What were Wallas' claims as a critic? What drove him slowly from one position to another? From orthodox liberalism to Fabian Socialism to Syndicalism to New Individualism? Why was he unhappy with each successive doctrine? What was his New Individualism and why did he consider it better than any current alternative political and social theories? Was he right or did his groping development take a wrong direction? Right or wrong, Wallas asked eternally meaningful questions and gave thoughtful sincere answers.

WALLAS THE CRITIC

Wallas saw the world humbly as a giant complex of fast-changing phenomena, and he thought all reductionist monist and dualist explanations of it were follies. The first responsibility of a political thinker was to accept complexity—of the environment, of the individual human mind, and of the relations of men to each other—as empirical fact. He always asked of any theory, what does it leave out? How far does it fall short of a complete *Weltanschauung*, a panoramic view of the world which includes the whole range of man's dispositions, emotions, thoughts, and actions? In one or another of his books, Wallas measured almost every important political and social theory against his own doctrine of psychological diversity and found it wanting.

In ***Social Judgment***, the book he was writing when he died, Wallas finally tied together all the specific criticisms he had been making since ***Human Nature in Politics***. The history of Western thought could ultimately be reduced to a conflict between two and only two ways of looking at the world. There is Science,[4] which represents the world of fact, and Religion, which represents the world of value. The two worlds have never met. The scientific attitude "tends to treat the world of value as unreal, and the 'religious' to treat the world of science as unreal."[5] Wallas believed as John Dewey did, that the urgent job of modern thought is to bring the two worlds together. But it was emphatically not the world of orthodox religion that he wanted to join to science. Nor was it the "science" of conventional political science that he wished to keep.

Organized religion, he felt, had contributed nothing constructive to social thought. By emphasizing dogma it encouraged men to abandon their first duty, to follow arguments wherever they led. This had been disastrous in politics, where references to Providence cloaked every kind of arbitrary action. Political problems were always immediate. They posed active choices and demanded active decisions. Appealing to the foreordained will of God or a "divine hand" at a moment of crisis was more than irresponsible; it was immoral. This is a Wallas ipsedixitism, but he also believed that the disintegration of organized religion was a fact and that our grandchildren "may drop the Palestinian mythology as easily as a worn-out garment."[6] He was premature.

Wallas discussed religious institutions because they were social facts. From his reformer's point of view, religion as an organized institution was an archaic dead weight and evil, but the emotions religion inspired were psychological facts and valuable. He wanted to detach the rich fund of "spiritual" emotions aroused by extra empirical dogmas and transfer them to the secular social world of fact. He wanted to put passion in political science, or in the language of modern ethics, to give emotive meaning to matters of fact. "One would like to hope that a . . . fusion might take place between the emotional and philosophical traditions of religion, and the new conception of intellectual duty by Science. . . . "[7]

By joining facts and values, he hoped to establish an adequate *Weltanschauung*. Though he repudiated orthodox religion as one-sided and parochial, he adopted its occasional evangelist fervor. He cried, " . . . a conviction swept through me that the special task of our generation might be so to work and think as to be able to hand on . . . the heritage of a world outlook deeper and wider and more helpful than modern Christendom."[8] Could science provide this deeper and wider world outlook? Could its disciplines and methods move men to great efforts of social reconstruction? Wallas thought so. "Men will not take up the 'intolerable disease of thought' unless their feelings are first stirred, and the strength of the idea of Science has been that it does touch men's feeling."[9] Nor could they begin too soon. In "politics, economics, literature, religion, and ethics the difficulties arising from the failure of human thought to contrive an adaptation of human society to its new environment are equally obvious. Thought, therefore . . . is now required more urgently than ever before in the history of mankind."[10]

What, then, was wrong with the "science" of classical political science? Since John Stuart Mill's era the only feelings it had provoked were disgust and revulsion, feelings which had driven Wallas himself to Fabian Socialism in the 1880's. Since the time of Newton English political thought had been modeled on the physical sciences. Wallas reviewed its history and found it both an intellectual and emotional failure. It assumed universal laws and there are none. This led to heavy determinism, smothering any efforts at creative reform. It was based on a primitive science of psychology which shrank the operations of the mind to one or two basic impulses and deduced political and social behavior from them. Most thoughtful people agreed that this reductionist procedure was bankrupt because it notoriously underestimated the numberless impulses which actually do move men.

More than that, the political propositions that arose from mechanistic psychological assumptions were disastrous in practice.

> . . . there is one group of thinkers who have in our own time taken the "mechanist" conception of the relation of instinct to reason as a guide for their own intellectual methods. These are the Marxian Communists in Russia and elsewhere. . . . And they seem determined to stamp out among their fellow citizens, with the thoroughness of the Spanish Inquisition, all those methods of inventive thought which originally enabled Marx to think and write *Das Kapital*.[11]

So Wallas spoke in 1926. In 1908 he had begun his career as a critic with an attack on Classical Liberalism. He soon realized he had made a false start. Though his fame rests on ***Human Nature in Politics***, though it contains hints of most of the ideas he developed later, this book is not characteristic Wallas. The focus is wrong. Here the descriptive social psychologist, describing the effects of nonrational inference in politics, is in the foreground. In his later works, the normative moralist stands in front. Here his doctrinal criticism is aimed at the "intellectualist" fallacy which assumes "that every human action is the result of an intellectual process, by which a man first thinks of some end which he desires, and then calculates the means by which that end can be attained."[12] This is the deductive process often attributed to Bentham. Wallas charged Macaulay with it. In his other works, Wallas accepted nonrational inference as a fact and went on from there. It is true that people do not often calculate rationally, but if they do not, they *ought* to and they must be taught to do so.

His argument against the "intellectualist" fallacy was not, of course, that political action is entirely irrational, but that reason is only one impulse among many conflicting and perhaps inseparable impulses. He came to see that by his attack on reason in politics he was fanning the flames of twentieth-century irrationalism. He saw, too, that the fault of Classical Liberalism was not "intellectualism" but reductionism, dividing the mind into a dualism of facts and values and celebrating facts at the total expense of values. By the time Wallas generalized his criticism of Classical Liberalism, he realized that it applied fully as well to Fabian Socialism and wondered whether "the word socialism may go the way of 'natural rights' and 'the greatest happiness principle.'"[13]

He had not always thought so. From 1886 to 1904 he had belonged to the Fabian Society. He had been one of the original triumvirate with George Bernard Shaw and Sidney Webb, a contributor to the ***Fabian Essays***, an enthusiastic platform proselytizer, and a member of the Executive from 1888 to 1895. Apparently he had been committed to the hilt. But already in his article, **"Property Under Socialism"** for the ***Essays***, Wallas seemed to suggest that the Fabian equation of economic security with happiness might be a delusion. "Under the justest possible social system we might still have to face all those vices and diseases which are not the direct result of poverty and overwork; we might still suffer . . . mental anguish and bewilderment. . . . "[14]

Wallas finally broke with the Fabians, ostensibly over tariff reform and education, but actually over the much wider ideological issues which later became the subjects of his books. In his *History of the Fabian Society,* Edward Pease explained that Wallas' resignation "has been followed by . . . [no] personal and political disagreements. . . . Mr. Wallas has remained a Fabian in all except name."[15] This was both true and false. He continued to follow the Fabians as far as they went but determined to go much further.

In a way, the public figure Graham Wallas was a creation of the Fabian Society. He had a lounging, indolent temperament. Without the constant goading of his fellow-Fabians and their mighty example of tireless disinterested labor in social science, he might never have written anything. It was their practice, "Shaw's exacting passion for artistic perfection and Webb's almost incredible force and industry,"[16] which later supplied him with evidence for his philosophy of mental and moral self-development. They also taught him to distrust simplified solutions and to see social problems as questions of more or less. Finally, he praised their call for scientific method in politics, but there his agreement with them ended, for "admirable as that plea is, it will not have its full effect unless the members of the . . . [Fabian Society] learn to avoid the habit of separating the facts of human motive into those which are scientific and those which are not."[17] Here again was reductionism. The Fabians had no vision of a comprehensive social organization which would nourish the whole man, spiritually, economically, culturally, politically. In 1916 Wallas explained why he had left them. Their Tract No. 70 in 1896, "for instance, declared that the Fabian Society 'has no distinctive opinions on the Marriage Question, Religion, Art . . . or any other subject than its own special business of practical Democracy and Socialism'. . . . In my case other things than our own special business were always breaking in. . . ."[18]

Having weighed and disposed of two competing forms of social organization which vied with each other in turn-of-the-century England, Wallas turned to the third, Syndicalism or its variant, Guild Socialism.[19] In one respect, he thought Syndicalism or vocational association was clearly superior to either of the others. It proposed a natural form of political organization based on the common activities and interests of working groups. The political structure of Classical Liberalism and Socialism, on the other hand, corresponded with no known human needs or impulses. It divided society geographically instead of functionally. One-man one-vote territorial democracy was an abstract and arbitrary creation. Wallas admitted that Syndicalism and Guild Socialism arose from legitimate dissatisfaction with parliamentary democracy, its clumsy artificial representative machinery, its emphasis on the rights of property, and its sanction of lop-sided economic inequality.

Unfortunately, in operation Syndicalism took a sinister turn. Wallas had no need to return to the medieval guild economy for evil examples. Twentieth-century England was riddled with small-scale Syndicalist organizations—the trades-unions, the lawyers', teachers', doctors' associations. These professional groups no sooner became organized, he thought, than they began to ossify. They became in-groups with their own vested interests and fixed habits. They were radical levelers. They equalized rates of pay and they operated on the seniority principle. They were always conservative and resisted change.

All this was antithetic to Wallas' whole philosophy, descriptive and normative. It was a fact for him that the human mind is infinitely variable and complex. It was another fact that modern industrial society was a whirling chaos of change. The political scientist should therefore be a kind of juggler who weighed and balanced the varieties of human impulse with one hand and technological changes with the other. He should try to bring as many of these old and new facts as possible into play by inventing, modifying, harmonizing, or adapting old or new social institutions to fit them. Institutions must be kept in motion and they must allow for the natural inequality of their members. Wallas demanded greater economic equality and initial equality of opportunity, but after that, encouraged every mark of uniqueness and creative initiative.

Since none of the three rival forms of social organization satisfied his requirements for a *Weltanschauung,* he arranged a characteristic compromise. He was a sweeping but kindly critic who believed that whatever is, is, though partly wrong, at least partly right. Every institution, however archaic, tyrannical, or otiose, reflected some one or more true human instincts. So it was with Individualism, for example, which was based on a genuine property instinct. That instinct had, however, been adapted by evolution to an environment now obsolete and Socialism was an inevitable reaction. Socialism, in turn, rested on the feeling of resentment aroused by exaggerated privilege, and Syndicalism, on man's gregarious co-operative impulses. If "neither Individualism, therefore, nor Socialism, nor Syndicalism, affords by itself a single sufficient basis for the Will-Organization of the Great Society," social scientists will have to invent a new organization, and "it is clear . . . that it will have to contain all the three elements."[20]

Wallas had come to this equilibrium by 1914. But even had there been no war, he could not have rested content with such an artificial compromise between kinds of *economic* organization. It did not begin to satisfy the full range of spiritual, intellectual, and aesthetic impulses which he himself insisted make up the human mind and which political institutions ought to reflect. Then the war came and exploded his customary ways of thinking in terms of labeled doctrines or institutional formulas. All England had to adapt itself to the sudden national emergency, and Wallas was astounded at the accomplishments in large-scale social reorganization, in heightened national morale, and above all in technical and administrative invention.[21] He mused over the possible explanations of these radical social advances. Had the trades-unions taken the initiative? Or perhaps the Socialist societies? Not at all. Both had been drags on the national effort. The trades-unions had steadily resisted conscription and "dilution" of industry by women. The more ardent Socialists, the members of the I.L.P., had refused to serve in the wartime coalition government.

What was done had been done by individuals with freed hands, either outside experts called in by government or members of the civil service. Here are the seeds of Wallas' New Individualism and of the central problem of all his later writings. How, he asked, can thought and action, reason and emotion, be made to re-enforce each other? Those who think out a policy and those who act on it are usually two different sets of people. How is it possible for each of them to develop the moral and intellectual vision needed to imagine the full social consequences of their decisions? This is, of course, the same old search for a *Weltanschauung,* with the location changed from doctrines and institutions to the individual bureaucrat.

During the war Wallas lingered once again over the ruins of Socialism and asked a rhetorical question which he had long since answered to his own satisfaction. "One wonders . . . now that this war has shifted the centre of gravity in problems of human organization, whether when peace comes, socialism will still seem . . . to be a sufficing *Weltanschauung*? Or will the struggle for economic and political equality . . . come to be looked on . . . as a part only . . . of some larger conception of life?"[22] Sooner or later, consciously or unconsciously, many of Wallas' former fellow Fabians asked themselves the same question, were dissatisfied, and also began to hunger for "some larger conception of life." Already in 1889 Annie Besant had plunged into theosophy. More than forty years later the Webbs found a new spiritual universe in communism, and Shaw, some comfort in the leadership principle. Perhaps because the Webbs held on so long to their faith in political solutions of social problems, they were heavily hit when disillusion set in and reacted drastically. Wallas, who had all along been sceptical, was alone among the Fabians in turning back to tradition. He wanted to bring Individualism up-to-date and to take over where the Utilitarians had left off.

WALLAS AND THE LIBERAL TRADITION

Wallas wanted to do well what the Utilitarians had done badly—to base political science on a genuine science of psychology. "The thinkers of the past, from Plato, to Bentham to Mill, had each his own view of human nature, and they made those views the basis of their speculations on government. But no modern treatise on political science . . . now begins with anything corresponding. . . . "[23] Why? He concluded that Utilitarian psychological theory and its implications in Liberal practice, which ought to have gone hand-in-hand, were hopelessly at odds. Utilitarian psychology gave a Newtonian picture of the mind of man, mechanically operating according to the universal principle of pleasure and pain, and therefore radically equalitarian. Had Utilitarian psychological theory squared with its implied Liberal practice, nineteenth-century British society would have been a marvel of harmonious, automatic, equalitarian efficiency. It was hardly that. The Liberal party eventually wore itself out trying to catch up with massive social movements it often neither understood nor could control, and which made a farce of Utilitarian psychological oversimplifications.

Like Bentham, Wallas believed that the phrase "good in theory, bad in practice" was contradictory. Since Utilitarianism was bad in practice, it was no good in theory. It must be discarded and a new psychology developed which kept in step with the onrush of changing social phenomena. This is what Wallas set out to do. He threw out the old Newtonian analogies and adopted the language of Darwinism instead.

> Can we learn . . . to think of the varying individuals of the whole human race? . . . the publication of the "Origin of Species" in 1859 offered an answer. Since then we have in fact been able to represent the human race to our imagination . . . as a biological group, every individual in which differs from every other not arbitrarily but according to an intelligible process of organic evolution.[24]

Wallas appreciated the fact that the Utilitarians belonged to a pre-Darwinian world which lacked the persuasive mass of biological evidence to support a subtly elaborate psychology. He pitied John Stuart Mill's floundering efforts to reconcile simplified Utilitarian psychological theory with his own complex personality on the one hand, and the turbulent "condition of England question" on the other. According to him, Mill partially succeeded in the first reconciliation and got nowhere in the second.

Mill's famous emotional crisis in the autumn of 1826, when he seemed to have nothing left to live for, supplied Wallas with a parable and he returned to it again and again.[25] If the model Benthamite, nurtured and trained from infancy in the inflexible rational mechanics of Utilitarianism, broke down under the strain, what more dramatic proof could be found of its inadequacy? Mill slumped through the winter and spring of 1827. Then one day tears came to his eyes as he read Marmontel's *Memoires*. He discovered feeling and was saved. He had broken through the monist Utilitarian world of rational calculation to a new dualism, a world of thought and a world of feeling.

This was a step in the right direction but Wallas demanded a higher synthesis which Mill never made except in his appreciation of poetry. In Wallas' psychology, the mind is an elaborate web of thoughts and feelings which interact and intensify each other. Instead of the reductionist static psychology which the Utilitarians adopted, Wallas offered a "hormic" conception of the way the mind works. "Hormé" is the Greek word for "drive" and he used it to cover all the "imperceptible gradations from spontaneous 'urge' to conscious will."[26] A hormic psychology "substitutes the conception of a living and imperfect tendency towards integration for the conception of a mechanical and perfect integration. . . . "[27] Wallas called this special feeling "intimation," the awareness that a thought is coming. It is just here that thought and emotion fuse. It is one stage of the process of creative thinking which a new art of thought ought to control and modify. First come preparation and incubation, then illumination or intimation, and finally verification.[28]

Wallas wanted Mill "to produce a harmony in his soul by the deliberate cultivation and co-ordination both of thought and of feeling,"[29] but "unfortunately, Mill never saw that the due balance among the faculties was a condition of logical thought as well as in other forms of human behavior."[30] In Book VI of *A System of Logic*, Mill rejected the Utilitarian "geometrical method," which held that all social phenomena result from a single property of human nature. His own analysis of social science, however, was caught in the same strait jacket of determinism, "the doctrine of what is called philosophical necessity, [that] weighed on my existence like an incubus,"[31] which he had struggled to escape twenty years earlier. Mill's "physical or concrete deductive method," which deductively "infers the law of each effect from the laws of causation on which that effect depends"[32] allowed equally little scope for the bursts of informed feeling, intuition, imagination which illuminate all creative activity.

If Mill's insight into poetry were true, if his enjoyment did come from the imaginative blend of thought *and* feeling, was this not the key to all creative activity? To all forms of art? To mathematics and ethics? To the physical sciences? Wallas began to study the creative process and to collect testimony from great artists and scientists about their actual moments of creation and discovery. He found confirmation everywhere—in Plato's discussion of the control of the passions by the "spirited" and "rational" principles, in Shelley's call "to feel that which we perceive, and to imagine that which we know,"[33] in the mathematical physicist Poincaré's description of the special feeling which lit up the moment of discovery. The methods of art were the same as those of science. The future of both depended upon the conscious cultivation of a kind of methodical madness by artists and scientists, working alone and making a moral commitment to do their best.

Wallas insisted that political phenomena must be studied scientifically. But he also felt that they are so complex and change so rapidly that they cannot become a "science," that is, a specific body of systematized knowledge. What the political thinker must learn from the scientists is neither laws nor fixed theories but methods of invention. The creative scientist's method is the same as the artist's: both are climaxed by aesthetic illumination, a harmony of idea and impulse. Transferred to social phenomena, Wallas called it "social judgment." Politics is then a branch of morals and invention is an obligation of the political scientist. As early as ***Human Nature in Politics***, Wallas had spoken of "the co-ordination of reason and passion as a moral ideal."[34]

Here we have come to the heart of Wallas' New Individualism, for if his analysis of the creative process were correct for the natural and physical sciences,[35] then any political "scientist" worthy of the name must study it and practice it. The social thinker must become a deliberate inventor. And invention is not a joint enterprise.

> In laboratories and universities and government offices we can test hypotheses and compare results by means of the subdivided labour of hundreds of observers to whom each other's knowledge is un-known. But the formation of the original hypothesis, the inventive moment on which successful action depends, must take place in an individual brain.[36]

The social thinker must give up the chimera of a fixed body of scientific doctrine, as contemporary physicists had already done, and look to science for method only. This is what Mill had never been able to do. He kept the world of value and art strictly separate from the world of fact and science,[37] and showed thereby that he simply did not understand scientific method. He had done no scientific work himself, nor had he studied the accounts of practicing scientists like Faraday and Herschel. He picked up what he knew third-hand from popularizers like Dr. William Whewell.

Mill saved himself from determinism but he left Liberalism inert under it, unable to produce urgently needed programs of social melioration. Liberalism failed because it had taken over Mill's negative conception of liberty, which began and ended with the isolated individual as the prime fact and insisted on "the absolute and essential importance of human development in all its diversity."[38] Wallas stood Liberalism on its head. He called for a positive definition of liberty which began with collective organization as a prime fact, worked to shape each individual uniquely by education, and then encouraged its best members in "the deliberate invention and organization of expedients for making common action effective."[39]

World War I showed what could be done by giving free rein to individual initiative in social reconstruction but, ironically, an even better example could be found in the Utilitarian and Liberal tradition itself. That example was Jeremy Bentham, whose dedicated life of disinterested social invention spread a glow over the dark mixture of oligarchy and anarchy which was early-nineteenth-century England. The Benthamite tradition was carried into government by his disciples, Chadwick, Joseph Hume, and Southwood Smith. Indeed, Liberalism governed England as long as it did only because so many Liberals in government ignored it and did their own inventing.[40]

If Wallas had a hero, that hero was Bentham; for despite his occasional triviality, his rationalism, his naïve psychology, he alone among the great political thinkers practiced that invention which is the heart and life of political science.[41] Mill, for example, had invented nothing. In the image of Bentham's example, Wallas gradually shifted and narrowed the focus of his political investigations. He went from the customary analysis of the meanings of political abstractions like natural rights and liberty in ***Human Nature in Politics*** to the construction of economic institutions which would mirror the whole range of human wants in ***The Great Society*** and finally to the development and organization of effective invention. Again in Bentham's image—the later Bentham of *Chrestomathia* and the *Constitutional Code*—Wallas began to concentrate on the schools and the civil service as the two institutional centers of social invention. An educational system must be developed which singled out talent, stimulated initiative, and gave systematic training in psychology and the processes of thought. The civil service must be made more fluid, so that the best products of the schools were smoothly absorbed into it, given time and opportunity to let their imaginations run in new directions, and encouraged to try their hands at both policy-making and administration.[42]

In still other ways Wallas was Bentham's heir. He, too, was an ardent critic of the conventional vocabulary of politics. Both felt that if abstract terms—such as rights, independence, liberty, power—mean anything, they must ultimately refer to concrete psychological facts. "The political part of our social heritage," Wallas said, "normally reaches us in the form of large vague words."[43] Bentham called himself a lexicographer because he was sure that correct definition was the starting-point of all useful political discussion. Wallas agreed with him. "It is . . . [the] relation between words and things which makes the central difficulty of thought about politics. The words are so rigid, so easily personified, so associated with affection and prejudice; the things symbolized by the words are so unstable."[44]

Wallas thought that Bentham outshone Mill in perhaps an even more fundamental way. He never lay under the curse of determinism. He dismissed the problem briskly, "*Entre nous,* I don't care two straws about liberty and necessity at any time."[45] The uneasy dualist compromise between the world of science and the world of art which Mill evolved was alien to Bentham, who believed all along in a unified world of thought and feeling, knowing and doing, science and art. "As between *art* and *science,* in the whole field of thought and action . . . whatsoever spot is occupied by either, is occupied by both: it is occupied by them in joint-tenancy."[46] According to Bentham, value attaches to any facts the moment we are aware of their use. When we see that something can be done to what is known, science is an art. Wallas was the most undoctrinaire and untheoretical of men, and he was certainly no Utilitarian. Principles did not interest him. He cared about attitudes and methods, not systems or doctrines. What he valued above all in Bentham was neither his marvelous analytic power nor his hedonism, but his fertile inventiveness and his insight into the unity of art and science. "The process of thought," Wallas agreed, "has always been in human life part of the process of action."[47] The very structure of Wallas' books reflects his unceasing insistence on the unity of science and art, thought and action. His works generally have two parts, an opening description and analysis of psychological processes, followed by his application of them to social action.[48]

For all this, Wallas himself was only vaguely an inventor. He made a few suggestions: the staffs of foreign embassies should include cultural and scientific as well as diplomatic attachés; successful civil service appointees should sharpen and prove their capacities by a piece of original social research;[49] desk-bound administrators in the civil service should make occasional tours-of-duty in the field, so they could learn to harmonize their thinking with doing. At bottom, however, Wallas was an old-fashioned moralist, a kind of secular social preacher more concerned to exhort and inspire than to invent.

Nor was Wallas' intended fusion of art and science, thought and emotion, much more satisfactory. Even as inspiration, his discussion was left hanging in the air. He confessed, in the last paragraph of ***The Great Society***:

> But here we reach the point where our examination of the conditions of Happiness, and, indeed, the whole method of psychological analysis, ceases to be a sufficient guide to life. It is rather through Philosophy than Psychology, rather through a general interpretation of the universe than through a detailed study of so small a part of it as our own minds, that the call of the Extreme [a term which Wallas borrowed from Aristotle's *Ethics* to describe the union of thought and passion] makes itself most clearly heard.[50]

This was philosophical limbo. Wallas later pulled himself out of it. The science of psychology was at last beginning to free itself from the mechanical metaphors which had so long hampered it, and he welcomed all the latest developments from Freud to Gestalt psychology. So far as psychologists were no longer bound by dual worlds of thought and emotion, Wallas reassigned the analysis of creative social invention to them. Modern thought depends on knowledge accumulated and arranged by "scientific" methods. "But behind the use by thinkers of rules and materials drawn from the sciences there has always been . . . an unformulated 'mystery' of thought. . . . That 'something' lies in the field now claimed by the science of psychology."[51] Though Wallas relocated the "mystery" with the psychologists, he did not pretend that they had unraveled it. In ***The Art of Thought*** he tried to do it himself by making an analysis of the processes of thought, but he merely succeeded in giving the "mystery" a name—Intimation or Illumination, the feeling that a thought is coming. This was about as helpful to the student or civil servant whom Wallas was exhorting to heroic efforts of *social* invention as an explanation of sleep by a "soporific potency." Intimation of what? Illumination of what? Wallas was treating a question of values as a matter of psychological description and it did not work.

He might better have done as Bentham did: make a frank normative commitment to a general principle, either the Greatest Happiness of the Greatest Number or some other more persuasive and inspirational.

There was one doctrine of Bentham's that Wallas took over intact: the doctrine of individual responsibility. As Bentham would have every man his own lawyer and his own priest, so Wallas would have every man his own moralist, psychologist, inventor. He concluded: "In the end, I should come to the individual trying to regulate his own impulses by his own painfully acquired knowledge of facts, and responsible to his future self for using that knowledge without fear or favor."[52] Bentham spoke to an audience of legislators; Wallas, to students and civil servants. Yet they were individualists of the same kind. Their pleas were prescriptive. Both called on men to help remake outworn social patterns. Both focused on the problem of men in power. How could they be made and kept responsible? Bentham evolved the Principle of Single-Seated Responsibility and Wallas seconded him. "Someone must always, at each crisis, be ready to propose a policy for all the effects of which he is willing to be responsible."[53]

But Wallas was an individualist with a difference. The later Utilitarians, though not Bentham himself, tried to build a laissez-faire society on a leveling psychology in which all men are alike motivated by pleasures and pains. Wallas called for a collective society which consciously hunted for and developed individual differences.

WALLAS AMONG HIS CONTEMPORARIES

Slowly, patiently, genially, single-mindedly, Wallas sought a *Weltanschauung*. He was a thinker in slow motion. He wrote and rewrote his books with painstaking care, anxious that no one misunderstand him. He had been a teacher long before he became a writer and a schoolmaster's tone lingers in his works. They are often bland, didactic, and repetitive. He was always concerned with the same overriding question: how can effective creative thought be organized in modern industrial mass society? The same themes run through his books: the need for international co-operation, the importance and danger of the vocabulary of politics, the fundamental need for good schools and civil service, the facts of psychological diversity and the evils of reductionist explanations.

All his books attempt to dispel dualisms and to harmonize thought and emotion. Sooner or later, the same attempt was taken up elsewhere, in England, France, Spain, the United States, by philosophers, economists, and novelists. Wallas was not unique. His ideas are throughout representative of Western thought in the first half of the twentieth century, and this is one measure of his quality.

Among the earliest of Wallas' colleagues in quest of intellectual and spiritual harmony was H. G. Wells. Though Wells caricatured Wallas rather cruelly as Willersly in *The New Machiavelli,* he shared many of his ideas. Wells' hero tried to develop Wallas' "social judgment."

> You see, I began in my teens by wanting to plan and build cities . . . I ended in the middle thirties by desiring only to serve and increase a general process of thought. . . . With that I felt there must go an emotion. I hit upon a phrase . . . to convey the spirit that I felt was at the very heart of real human progress—love and fine thinking.[54]

The New Machiavelli was published in 1911. Fifteen years later Wells and Wallas were both still wrestling with the same problem. The political world of *The World of William Clissold* was a spiritually empty place, where the men of energy and imagination were driven vicariously into business and money-making because they could find no moving creed elsewhere. Wells, too, asked how public service could be made spiritually significant. Like Wallas, he had long deplored the emotional bankruptcy of Socialism. Wallas' disenchantment with the Fabian Society was a lingering process. Wells charged in and out again like an enraged bull, but he agreed that the Fabians "were neglecting human life altogether in social organization."[55]

Wells conceded how much he and Wallas owed to Ostrogorski. Wallas, he said,

> . . . had been greatly impressed by the book of Professor Ostrogorski on Democracy and the Organization of Political Parties (1902). It was an early break towards realism in political science. It swept aside legist conceptions of government by a frank treatment of parliamentary actuality.
>
> Under this stimulus he produced Human Nature in Politics (1908). W. Lippmann, under [Wallas'] inspiration produced a Preface to Politics and [I] my own Modern Utopia.[56]

Lord Keynes was actually such an inventor as Wallas called for. He, too, was struck by the enormous opportunities for social reorganization opened up by World War I and began to see the problem in terms of individual responsibility. He said: "The next step forward must come, not from political agitation or premature experiments, but from thought. In the field of action, reformers will not be successful until they can steadily pursue a clear and definite object with their intellects and their feelings in tune."[57]

Even Laski, as he jogged along the road from pluralism to Marxism, paused to tell Justice Holmes:

> I felt . . . how much more political questions are moral questions, I mean of character, of *esprit,* and how little questions of machinery and formulae. . . . I have been writing about responsibility and as I have written it has become incredibly more urgent to me to find the secret of the moral tradition which builds responsibility than of the political machinery which secures it. . . . [58]

How can morals and politics, spiritual values and economic and social facts be joined? This was a widely recognized problem, pondered as well among French intellectual mandarins in some of their less ostrich-like moods. It is a recurrent question in Gide's *Journals,* and he agreed with Valery and Wallas that reform must begin in the schools. It was a problem which stirred Ortega y Gasset, and F. S. C. Northrop's *Meeting of East and West* is Wallas' harmony of thought and feeling.

But for the most part, their awareness of the problem was incidental and they dealt with it in fleeting and wistful asides. For Wallas, however, the harmony of thought and emotion was central, the unifying theme of all his writings. It was a matter of fact in his descriptive psychology; it was the armory for his attacks on dualisms and reductionism; its conscious cultivation was a normative aim of his call for educational reform and social invention.

Only for John Dewey did this psychological insight play a role as crucial as with Wallas. Dewey and Wallas drew the same implications from it for their social philosophies. Though Wallas' style was always clear and simple and Dewey's sometimes turgid and involved, they often thought alike. Year in and year out Dewey exploded dualisms as Wallas did: theory-practice, value-science, learning-doing, sensation-thought. They repeatedly warned against false simplifications in psychology and political theory, and criticized Hobbes for basing political organization on fear; the Utilitarians, on pleasures and pains; and the Marxists, on economic determinism. This is Dewey, but Wallas might have written it.

> There are an indefinite number of original or instinctive activities. . . . To increase the creative phase and the humane quality of these activities is an affair of modifying the social conditions which stimulate, select, etc. native activities. The first step in dealing with it is to increase our detailed scientific knowledge. . . . Having the knowledge we may set hopefully at work upon a course of social invention and experimental engineering.[59]

Here in one brief passage are three characteristic Wallas doctrines: the indefinite variety of human instincts, the need for conformable social organizations, and consequently the urgent call for social invention.

Dewey and Wallas believed that the divorce of facts and values so rife through Western history ended in critical spiritual malaise and that "the problem of restoring integration and co-operation between man's beliefs about the world in which he lives and his beliefs about the values and purposes that should direct his conduct is the deepest problem of modern life."[60] They thought that modern scientific method could be restorative, that the testimony of experimental scientists about an emotional-rational integration during their moments of discovery should be taken to heart by social scientists. Because of "the fact that in its experimental procedure science has surrendered the separation between knowing and doing," they hoped it would be possible to extend "the needed integration in the wider field of collective human experience."[61]

One problem was still left dangling. What content was to be given to the values? Dewey tried to tie it down naturalistically, but Wallas left it suspended and unanswered. He was more concerned with persuading people to give up dualisms than he was with ethical analyses, with pointing to examples of successful intellectual-emotional harmony than with verbal definitions. In the end, in ***Social Judgment***, he had to admit that there was as yet no "art of feeling." He ran up against the same "mystery" as he had in ***The Art of Thought***. Yet somewhat vague and tender-minded as Wallas' speculations may have been, they were not quixotic. He early recognized a moral problem which many others after him agreed was genuine and urgent.

But even had he succeeded in giving a concrete meaning to the phrase "social judgment" (that is, the fusion of thought and emotion in social conduct), he would soon have been beset by a barrage of more strictly political questions. The best social invention, the most profound exercise of social judgment, is useless outside a political context. It must first be approved by superiors, translated into commands, passed down the hierarchy of subordinate authorities, and enforced within the framework of existing institutions. Inevitably questions of the organization and distribution of political power, of the structure and function of social institutions, crop up, but Wallas avoided them all. Nor did he face the specific economic causes lying behind the social evils he sought to banish.

Of course Wallas was not an economist. He was a descriptive psychologist, a social reformer, and a moralist. In his writings he switched easily from one role to another. What kind of performance did he give? His integrity and sincerity were perfect, but there were possible interpretations he never made and questions he never asked. The descriptive psychologist might have inquired, if the human psyche is a complex tangle of impulses, how is it possible to measure those which are specifically political? The political reformer might have wondered if his assumption that institutions should adapt themselves to the enormous variety of human impulses was a good one? Is it possible to organize society in such complex and changing patterns? The moralist might have hesitated before this: if all impulses were allowed free rein there would be no society. All would be chaos and anarchy. Who shall decide and how shall he choose which impulses should be encouraged; which, diminished; how much and when? Wallas celebrated inequality and change, but habit and the search for security may be the strongest human motives. He knew this but made little of it.

Though many of Wallas' themes did not change, he did. He played all three parts until he died in 1932, but gradually he became a moralist above all. That he shrank his interest to moral issues was fair enough, but he did it at the risk of turning his audience of students and civil servants into an army of Don Quixotes. If they were converted by Wallas to ride off on a crusade of social invention, he gave them a rousing inspirational send-off, but neither a map of the way nor a plan of strategy.

NOTES

[1] Kingsley Martin, *Harold Laski* (New York: Viking, 1953), pp. 43-44.

[2] *Human Nature in Politics* (3rd ed.; New York: Knopf, 1921), p. 21.

[3] The date first published is in brackets. *The Great Society* [1914] (New York: Macmillan, 1919). *Our Social Heritage* [1921] (New Haven: Yale University Press, 1921). *The Art of Thought* [1926] (New York: Harcourt, Brace, 1926). *Social Judgment* [unfinished at Wallas' death in 1932] (New York: Harcourt, Brace, 1935). *Men and Ideas* [collected essays], ed. May Wallas (London: Allen & Unwin, 1940).

[4] Wallas had an unfortunate habit of capitalizing abstractions which gives them a reified aura he did not perhaps initially intend. In his later writings, however, he often delivered sermons on self-improvement and he may have capitalized by design for inspirational purposes.

[5] *Social Judgment*, p. 145.

[6] *Ibid.*, p. 162.

[7] *Human Nature in Politics*, pp. 212-13.

[8] *Our Social Heritage*, p. 291.

[9] *Human Nature in Politics*, p. 204.

[10] *The Art of Thought*, p. 26.

[11] *Ibid.*, pp. 33-35.

[12] *Human Nature in Politics*, p. 45.

[13] "Socialism and the Fabian Society," *Men and Ideas*, p. 107.

[14] George Bernard Shaw (ed.), *Fabian Essays in Socialism* (London: Walter Scott, 1889), p. 148.

[15] New York: International Publishers, 1926, p. 156.

[16] *Men and Ideas*, p. 105.

[17] *Our Social Heritage*, p. 256.

[18] *Men and Ideas*, p. 106.

[19] For Wallas' fullest discussion and criticism of the competing kinds of social organization, see *The Great Society*.

[20] *Ibid.*, p. 310.

[21] *Our Social Heritage*, p. 120.

[22] *Men and Ideas*, p. 107.

[23] *Human Nature in Politics*, p. 35.

[24] *Ibid.*, p. 298.

[25] For example, *Our Social Heritage*, p. 168; *Social Judgment*, pp. 88 ff.; *Men and Ideas*, p. 206.

[26] *The Art of Thought*, p. 223.

[27] *Ibid.*, p. 38.

[28] *Ibid.*, p. 112.

[29] *Social Judgment*, p. 88.

[30] *Men and Ideas*, p. 206.

[31] J. S. Mill, *Autobiography* (London: Oxford University Press, 1952), p. 143.

[32] J. S. Mill, *A System of Logic* (London: Longmans, Green, 1949), p. 584.

[33] Quoted from *Defence of Poetry* both in *The Art of Thought*, chapter v, and *Social Judgment*, p. 131.

[34] Pp. 204 ff.

[35] The importance he attached to it can be gauged by the fact that he wrote an entire book about it, *The Art of Thought*.

[36] *The Great Society*, p. 16.

[37] It is doubtful whether Wallas made a serious effort to understand Mill. If G. E. Moore is correct, Mill committed the "naturalistic fallacy" by his very inability to keep facts and values apart.

[38] *Our Social Heritage*, p. 168.

[39] *Ibid.*, p. 170.

[40] *Ibid.*, p. 175.

[41] See Wallas' excellent essay on Bentham in *Men and Ideas*.

[42] See his essay, "The British Civil Service," *ibid.*

[43] *Our Social Heritage*, p. 158.

[44] *Human Nature in Politics*, p. 96.

[45] *Jeremy Bentham's Works*, ed. John Bowring (Edinburgh: William Tait, 1843), X, 216.

[46] *Ibid.*, VIII, 27. Quoted approvingly in Wallas' essay, "Physical and Social Science," *Men and Ideas*, p. 206.

[47] *Men and Ideas*, p. 192.

[48] See, for example, *Human Nature in Politics, The Great Society, Social Judgment*.

[49] Here Wallas used himself as an example. He believed that his years of intensive research in the Francis Place mss. were an invaluable intellectual training for all his later work.

[50] P. 369.

[51] *The Art of Thought*, p. 27.

[52] *Our Social Heritage*, p. 202.

[53] *Social Judgment*, p. 30.

[54] H. G. Wells, *The New Machiavelli* (New York: Duffield, 1911), p. 308.

[55] *Ibid.*, p. 307.

[56] H. G. Wells, *Experiment in Autobiography* (New York: Macmillan, 1934), p. 511.

[57] J. M. Keynes, "The End of Laissez Faire," *Essays in Persuasion* (New York: Harcourt, Brace, 1932), p. 321.

[58] *Holmes-Laski Letters*, ed. Mark DeWolfe Howe (Cambridge: Harvard University Press, 1952), I, 531. Laski spoke to Holmes of *The Art of Thought* as "elegant trifling" (II, 840).

[59] John Dewey, *Human Nature in Conduct* (New York: Modern Library, 1930), p. 148.

[60] John Dewey, "The Construction of Good," *Readings in Ethical Theory*, ed. Hospers and Sellars (New York: Appleton-Century Crofts, 1952), p. 273.

[61] *Ibid.*

Robert D. Heslep (essay date 1968)

SOURCE: "Graham Wallas and The Great Society," in *Educational Theory*, Vol. 18, No. 2, Spring, 1968, pp. 151-63.

[*In the following essay, Heslep probes Wallas's normative analysis of the modern "Great Society," particularly as it applies to morality, happiness, and education.*]

I

Graham Wallas is usually recognized as a major contributor to the literature on the Great Society, a term which is again in currency. First, he is commonly acknowledged as the person who initially publicized the term. Before the publication of his book ***The Great Society***,[1] the term was rarely used;[2] and since then it has become a stock item in the vocabulary of social philosophers.

Second, the reference which he gave to the term has been well received. In contrast with the present-day popular reference of the term; his is existential rather than normative. Instead of employing the term to refer to some society which should be created, he used it to name a society which does, in fact, exist, for better or for worse. More precisely, he utilized the term to label the society constituted by the relatively recent world-wide interactions of men in most phases of their lives:

> During the last hundred years the external conditions of civilised life have been transformed by a series of inventions which have abolished the old limits to the creation of mechanical force, the carriage of men and goods, and communication by written and spoken words. One effect of this transformation is a general change of social scale. Men find themselves working and thinking and feeling in relation to an environment, which, both in its worldwide extension and its intimate connection with all sides of human existence, is without precedent in the history of the world.

> Economists have invented the term The Great Industry for the special aspect of this change which is dealt with by their science, and sociologists may conveniently call the whole result The Great Society.[3]

Of those who have borrowed Wallas' reference of "the Great Society," John Dewey[4] and Walter Lippmann[5] are two of the most famous.

Although Wallas has been accorded these two points of recognition, he has not been remembered much for his chief concern with the Great Society. He was not merely interested in identifying and naming the society; rather, he was primarily concerned with a moral examination of it. He concentrated on specifying the troubles of the society and making recommendations for rectifying them. It is his normative investigation of the Great Society which has been generally forgotten. Most social philosophers seem to think that Wallas simply pointed out the presence of the Great Society and that Dewey, as well as others, furnished the proposals for reconstructing it. They do not appear cognizant that he was as concerned with reorganizing the society as anyone else. This neglect is unfortunate, especially for those interested in education. The Great Society as regarded by Wallas still exists and still has problems. Moreover, a number of Wallas' proposals are, in a sense, pertinent to education today.

Although Wallas' normative examination of the Great Society is somewhat exhortative, it is not a preachment: for it rests upon a definite theoretical foundation. The foundation, unfortunately, is conspicuously unsatisfactory; but it is not so inadequate as to keep Wallas' discussion from raising issues which must be taken into account by inquiries into education in the Great Society nowadays.

II

The theoretical basis of Wallas' argument about the Great Society has two aspects, social-psychological and ethical. The former is mainly concerned with man's nature and environment: and the latter is chiefly concerned with a major moral goal of human life in the Great Society, namely, happiness.

By "human nature" Wallas means the "sum-total" of the inherited human dispositions, which are both elementary and complex.[6] The simple ones " . . . include the senses, and such measurable facts as memory and association, habit and fatigue";[7] the complex ones are the instincts and intelligence.[8] According to Wallas, man's nature has not always existed; it evolved ages ago and over a period of millions of years, in response to conditions threatening the balance between man and his environment.[9] It has not changed noticeably since appearing, however. At the birth of any person, human nature is not totally present; man's innate tendencies " . . . reveal themselves . . . gradually during life and growth."[10] Furthermore, human nature as it appears in any person suffers modifications through his experiences. At any given moment, then, a human being " . . . is the result of the action of his experience on his nature."[11] Thus, the members of one culture differ from those of another even though the two groups share a common nature; and, insofar as the members of a same culture have different experiences they, too, vary from one another in interests, talents, etc., despite their possessing a common nature. That man's inborn tendencies are alterable by his experience implies that they are subject to education. When dispositions are not aroused and satisfied, they induce "a state of nervous strain."[12]

According to Wallas, " . . . the normal course by which an instinctive disposition reveals itself is the impact on our nervous system of some appropriate external or internal physical occurence (called the 'stimulus') followed, either simultaneously, or in succession to each other, by conscious feeling and muscular movement."[13] Since each instinct evolved in view of a certain set of environmental objects, it is useful in coping with objects only to the extent that they resemble those with regards to which it developed. And objects are possible stimuli to an instinct only in that they are similar to the objects in view of which it evolved. For instance, a possible stimulus of the human male sexual instinct resembles somehow the human female.[14] An object relevant to an instinct will not excite the instinct just because the object is present to a person; the object must first be recognized by the person as what it is. While the objects pertinent to an instinct differ from one another in special and particular ways, they have common characteristics and, insofar, are the same. That an instinct responds to stimuli with special and particular differences means that it is somewhat, but not highly, "elastic."[15]

When an instinctive action is repeated, it becomes altered: " . . . memory and acquired habit must enter as forces modifying both the action itself and the forms of consciousness which accompany the action. Not long, therefore, after birth, men, and apparently the other higher vertebrates, begin to live in an atmosphere of organised ideas, of memory, that is to say, association and imagination."[16] An outcome of man's living in this "atmosphere" is that his instincts become controlled, through habituation, by his intelligence. For example, the "purely instinctive impulse to hunt" becomes regulated by the process of reflection upon future wants and available ways of satisfying them. When instincts go unstimulated, they do not thereby become dissipated or otiose; or, in contrast with St. Paul's belief, they do not become mortified. As already intimated, they merely engender a state of tension. Finally, the instincts are, to some extent, interactive with one another. For instance, the obstruction of one often stimulates another as in the case of sex-love and pugnacity: and, as with fear and curiosity, instincts may be rivals with one another.[17]

To the degree that intelligence controls instinctive impulses, it acts as an "independent directing force"; it is not just a servant of the instincts. In other parlance, human nature is rational as well as instinctual.[18] Some innate dispositions are distinctly intellectual, viz., thought, which comprehends both daydreaming and inquiry, and language, " . . . our inherited inclination to express and to receive ideas by symbols, . . ."[19] Some inborn dispositions, however, do not seem to be intellectual at times although they appear to be so on occasion. Curiosity and "trial and error," for example, give rise to instinctive as well as intelligent acts.[20] Unlike any one instinct, intelligence is effective with an indefinite variety of environmental objects: it is the most plastic of human dispositions. Since inborn human inclinations are alterable through experience, intelligence may be shaped by man's educational efforts. To quote Wallas: " . . . thought can be fed by deliberately collected material, and stimulated, sustained, and, to a certain extent, controlled by an effort of the will."[21] Because of their variances in experience, different people have diversities in intelligence; they employ sundry methods and information when examining a given subject-matter.

While man's nature has remained relatively constant, his environment has undergone a series of major changes. As a consequence, his instincts, which developed in view of his original surroundings and which he chiefly relied upon in reacting to the latter, have become less and less effective as faculties for maintaining a harmony between himself and his world. The objects relevant to the instincts have become continually harder to recognize as such and, in instances, have vanished. Conditions have appeared which are apparently impertinent to the instincts. And the growing complexity of man's environment has tended to instigate conflicts among the instincts. On the other hand, intelligence, which was not much utilized at first, has steadily increased in significance as a power for securing a balance between man and his environment. It is the faculty whereby man can learn about novel conditions; it is the power whereby man can form habits suitable to his new circumstances and modify the circumstances somewhat to his advantage.[22] Upon entering each new era of his history, man has necessarily faltered somewhat: for in each case he has had to make intellectual adjustments—to gather new knowledge and design new methods—before he has been in a position to decide what new habits and environmental changes have been needed. Until making such adjustments, he has tended, in each instance, to rely upon outmoded habits as a means for responding to his circumstances. Moreover, whenever intelligence has instituted environmental alterations, it has helped foster, thereby, the onset of a new era and, thus, new difficulties.

The harmony between man and his world which was appropriate to his primitive condition was mainly a relationship whereby his instincts were aroused and gratified. His nature and circumstances made little else possible at the time. But, since the increase of the importance of his intelligence and the decline of the effectiveness of his instincts, that is, since the beginning of civilization, the proper balance between man and his world has assumed a new character. This balance, Wallas submits, is a relationship whereby, among other things, man attains happiness. Wallas does not intend that happiness is the only goal which should be fostered by this relationship; he regards it only as one of the major ones. Unfortunately, he does not say what the others are. According to Wallas, happiness is neither pain nor pleasure (although it may contain both).[23] Essentially, it is virtue and a concern with one's "more permanent self." While Wallas is not explicit on what virtue is, he does suggest, in scattered passages, that it implies the willful exercise of one's powers of action in accordance with a mean.[24] Insofar, happiness does not renounce the instincts; it simply demands that they be controlled with a view to temperance. Wallas is also vague about the concern with one's "more permanent self," but he does indicate that it implies one's being aware of the connexion between one's past and present and planning one's future on the basis of all of one's present possibilities.[25] Plainly, then, intelligence is assigned a major role in the attainment of happiness.

The relation between virtue and the interest in one's self is not examined by Wallas; and, regrettably, it is not made very clear by anything which he says. Nonetheless, this much seems evident: Virtue helps the concern with one's self. Moderation means, when opposed to deficiency in conduct, that one will use all of one's powers of action and, insofar, act with respect to all of one's given possibilities. And moderation implies, when opposed to excess in conduct, that one will not dissipate one's powers of action and, inasmuch, will be able to take advantage of present possibilities.

Happiness is ultimately gained by individual effort; however, it cannot be had through such effort alone. Since any person at any given moment is his nature as modified by his experiences and since his experiences are determined, partly, by his environment, he is not likely to achieve a state of happiness unless he lives under conditions conducive to virtuous habits and an interest in his self. In other words, man is dependent, somewhat, upon society for the achievement of his happiness. Happiness, then, is a major, but not *the*, principle to follow in organizing modern society. By making happiness contingent upon a duly ordered society, Wallas places himself in Aristotle's company. However, by not making happiness *the* principle of social organization, he does not identify it with the social good and, inasmuch, puts himself in disagreement with Aristotle: "And yet we cannot . . . be sure that by aiming at Happiness, 'like archers with their mark before them,' we shall attain social good. Conduct, merely passive contemplation for instance, may produce real Happiness without leading to the ultimate good either of society or the race."[26] Unhappily, Wallas does not explain what the social good is.

The Great Society, which includes, among other elements, industrialization, urbanization, and a highly advanced and wide-spread technology, is, by and large, an outgrowth of man's intellectual activities—scientific, technological, economic, and political. And, as far as Wallas is concerned, the society has succeeded greatly " . . . in the removal of certain specific causes of Unhappiness. . . . "[27] It has increased the life span, reduced disease and the ravages of poverty, eliminated slavery and serfdom, and given some dispositions, "like Curiosity and Ambition," a richer satisfaction than they have had before. Nonetheless, the society "... has resulted in a degree of discomfort and uncertainty which was unexpected by those who helped to make it."[28] So, Wallas summarizes his criticism of the Great Society in this fashion: "That, indeed, which chiefly angers and excites us now, as we contemplate the society in which we live, is not a conviction that the world is a worse place than it has ever been, but the feeling that we have lost grip over the course of events, and are stupidly wasting the power over nature which might make the world infinitely better."[29]

There are two chief ways in which the Great Society has failed to promote happiness. First, it has provided many conditions which tend to discourage virtuous conduct.[30] Being devoid of surroundings which are stimulating to numerous instincts and other inherited dispositions, it has not aroused and satisfied the latter and, thereby, has encouraged the intemperance of deficiency. The point has been reflected in employment conditions, which have been established primarily with a view to the efficient production and distribution of commodities, not to happiness. Employees are often confined to highly repetitious operations, which allow for the exercise of only a narrow set of inclinations; they have frequently worked in large groups, which do not encourage friendship, discussion, and other modes of intimate social intercourse; and they have not uncommonly been assigned jobs regardless of their special talents. The point has also been exemplified in the situation of women, who, while relieved of their strictly domestic function, have not been allotted access to roles which can fully make use of their inborn tendencies. And the point has been notoriously reflected in the cities, where conditions of solitude, relaxation, neighborliness, beauty, etc., have gone wanting by and large. By "baulking" inclinations, the Great Society has induced feelings of tension and, inasmuch, has fostered the intemperance of excess. Many people have searched frantically for excitement, taken to drunkenness, and indulged in senseless violence. Second, the Great Society has not helped one to understand and control his situation adequately and, consequently, to be sufficiently concerned with his self.[31] In the society the various environments of people have been, as often as not, remote, obscure, and knowable and controllable only indirectly. But there have been established few customs, institutions, and facilities to help the mass of people discern and regulate their distant and hidden surroundings and, thus, comprehend and plan with respect to all relevant present possibilities. Therefore, at least to the extent that the Great Society has not furnished conditions conducive to happiness, it is in need of reconstruction.

Wallas' specific proposals for re-ordering the Great Society fall into two main groups. One aims at encouraging virtue by giving greater play to man's inborn dispositions (within, of course, the limits of moderation).[32] With regards to employment conditions, it recommends that highly repetitious operations, wherever possible, be assumed by machinery; that routine operations which cannot be mechanized be varied with other labor; that employees work in relatively small groups; that some initiative be permitted all workers; and that employees be assigned jobs according to their special abilities, which can be developed by schools. Respecting women, it calls for their complete enfranchisement—economic and social as well as political. In view of the cities, it prescribes tasteful architecture and easily accessible parks, gymnasia, and forest areas. And, taking into account those instinctive actions which, as in the instances of killing and fighting, are scarcely virtuous now if directed against the objects in response to which they evolved, it proposes the widespread availability of ersatz objects, or "outlets."

The other principal set of Wallas' proposals purports to improve the "organization of thought and will" within the Great Society. If the society is to be altered so as to increase conditions of happiness, it must be changed under the guidance of intelligence. Thus, the society will have to be investigated and planned by experts since, because of its vastness and complexity, it can be adequately comprehended only by those with specialized knowledge and skills. And it, as reported by the experts, will have to be discussed by officials of government and industry, who will decide what policies and programs are desirable. Consequently, there must exist customs, institutions, and facilities which will enable experts and officials, who cannot succeed in their work apart from social forms, to carry on their inquiries and deliberations as well as possible. If, moreover, any member of the society is to act on the basis of all his present possibilities, he must apprehend, to some extent, the remote and obscure environments affecting himself. Hence, there will have to be customs, institutions, and facilities to help him obtain knowledge of such surroundings. It follows, then, that arrangements must be made to disseminate relevant knowledge among experts and officials and among the masses. Such arrangements have been part and parcel of the Great Society. Scholarly tomes, professional journals, research centers, and conventions have abounded for the experts. Advisers and committees have long existed for officials. And mass media of information have been inexpensive and common enough. Just the distribution of knowledge is not sufficient, however. What else is needed, Wallas points out, are elements favorable to "dialectical thought," viz., intimate groups whose purpose is the earnest discussion of issues.[33] Dialectical thought will have distinct advantages. It will help experts to gain insights and clarify their ideas: it will enable officials to deliberate apart from external pressures; and it will enhance appropriate interest as well as communicate knowledge among the masses. In order that the Great Society's non-expert and non-official members will be able to utilize publicized knowledge, there will have to be universal schooling. And, in order that these people will have time and places for serious discussion, there will have to be such mundane conditions as "reasonably short" working hours, spacious housing, club rooms, and park benches.[34]

In making their studies and deliberations about the Great Society, experts and officials will have to listen to the opinions of the society's ordinary members. Otherwise, the experts will overlook ways in which the society affects its members' happiness; and the officials will never adequately know how their policies and programs bear upon the members. In turn, ordinary members of the Great Society will have to report their common problems and express their opinions of given policies and programs. By so doing, of course, the members will not only be co-operating with experts and officials; they will also be exerting a possible influence over their environments and, thus, enhancing the likelihood of their acting with respect to present possibilities. Plainly, therefore, there is a need for agencies in the Great Society whereby the opinions of all its members can be stated and heard. As far as Wallas is concerned, none of the main rival "will" institutions existing in the Great Society will alone be satisfactory. Private property is held by its exponents " . . . not as an expedient to be adapted to varying human needs, but as an indefeasible and unchangeable 'right'."[35] Professions and labor associations tend to identify the general interest with their respective special interests.[36] And elected legislative representation, which has become the most widely used of the three in the Great Society, is encumbered with the ineptitudes and distastefulness of politicking and the nagging questions about the significance of the geographic basis of legislative representation and the meaning of a majority vote.[37] Moreover, Wallas is dubious that a ". . . satisfactory Will-Organisation of human beings with their present limitations, in a society on so vast a scale, is possible. . . . "[38] Even so, he believes that a better "Will-Organisation" than has existed can be had; and he thinks that it should contain all three of the institutions just mentioned.[39] Elected legislative representation ought to be included since it will look after interests in local affairs. The professions and labor associations should be included since they will seek to care for conditions of more than local concern. And private property ought to be included because of the importance of man's property instinct in the Great Society.

III

Upon seeing that Wallas' normative discussion of the Great Society rests, in part, on an instinct psychology, one might be immediately inclined to dismiss the discussion as theoretically inadequate. Instincts have not been used as principles for over a quarter of a century, and the claims of their existence have been favorite targets of experimental psychologists for over a decade. Yet, the theoretical ground of Wallas' argument should not be peremptorily discounted, at least for these reasons. Fashion is not, by itself, a mark of adequacy; and the existence of instincts has not been irrefragably disproven. It must be conceded, however, that one does not need to look long to spot the weaknesses of the argument's theoretical basis.

Wallas' principle of human nature, the "sum-total" of man's inherited dispositions, has a key function in his argument. It is employed to explain, fundamentally, normal human action and, thus, to help indicate measures for controlling such behavior in the Great Society. Plainly, however, the principle is not an instructive statement of any explanation of human conduct. According to the principle, human beings tend to act, in view of given objects, in definite kinds of ways: and they tend to act in those ways *because* they are innately disposed to do so with respect to those objects. Men normally love women *because* they are naturally inclined to love them; people normally eat food *because* they have a natural tendency to eat it; human beings think about problems *because* they are naturally disposed to do so; etc. Yet, to say that people normally act in such and such a fashion in view of given objects *because* they are disposed (naturally or otherwise) to do so is not to explain anything. The "because" clause simply rephrases what is already known: The statement that people tend to act in a certain mode within certain circumstances *implies* that *they are disposed* to do so. In other words, the clause offers as an explanation the effect to be explained and, therefore, involves circular reasoning. To paraphrase Dewey, the clause merely reduplicates " . . . in a so-called causal force the effects to be accounted for." It is " . . . of a piece with the notorious potency of opium to put men to sleep because of its dormitive power."[40] In effect, then, Wallas' principle of human nature, rather than being an account of why people normally behave as they do with regards to given objects, is merely a description of the way that they do behave in view of those objects. Each "inborn inclination" is nothing more than a classification of human acts.

But, even if Wallas' principle of "human nature" does not furnish an explanation of normal human behavior, it still might be helpful as a guide for controlling such behavior in the Great Society. For, if it does indicate how people will usually respond within certain circumstances, it does point to a means for regulating their behavior, viz., the control of their circumstances. However, the principle will be helpful in this respect only to the extent that Wallas makes clear what the various sorts of normal human actions are and what conditions will evoke what normal actions. Unfortunately, he clarifies neither very well. While he lists numerous general sorts of normal human behavior, he rarely examines what they involve; and, when he does attempt to analyze any of them, he often does so superficially and desultorily. Even with regards to the major "disposition" of thought, he says little of substance. Inasmuch as he describes normal human action vaguely, he does not help one to see that the circumstances which, he claims, will induce such action will induce it. Moreover, while Wallas does specify some conditions which, he alleges, will encourage certain specific reactions, he does not enable one to discover what other specific conditions will elicit them and what other specific conditions will arouse and satisfy other specific types of responses. At best, consequently, Wallas' principle of "human nature" seems useful as a guide for controlling normal human action in only a very limited way.

The principle, it well be recalled, also has a lesser function in Wallas' normative discussion of the Great Society: It accounts for nervous tension and, in so doing, helps indicate conditions needed in the society. According to the principle, nervous strain appears because some inherited inclination has not been stimulated or, if it has been, has not been satisfied; and severe nervous stress enhances the likelihood of immoderate conduct. Hence, the Great Society should provide, without fostering excesses or deficiencies in conduct, as many possible stimuli of its members innate tendencies as it can and should furnish whatever conditions it can to help temperate courses of action to be completed. This proposal, however, is vitiated by Wallas' sketchy analysis of normal human behavior. Enabling one to learn of possible stimuli of only a relatively few inborn tendencies, the analysis helps one to establish conditions stimulating to only a small set of such tendencies. And, leaving mostly obscure what the various inherited dispositions involve, the analysis gives few clear directions about which conditions will help which courses of action to be consummated.

Happiness is also a key principle in Wallas' argument. Being a major objective which should be achieved in the Great Society, it is a principal term in view of which the society ought to be organized. Unhappily, it is so fuzzily formulated by Wallas that it provides virtually no guidance. First Wallas barely examines virtue, one of the two elements of happiness. He does not at all discuss what is meant by "the willful exercise of conduct" and makes little more than glib comments about temperance. At best, he says that what is moderation in one situation will not be moderation in another and offers some examples on this point. He never attempts to present a criterion for determining temperance in a situation. As a result, he does not enable one to know if the arrangements which, he proposes, will foster virtuous conduct will do so; and he does not make it possible for one to decide what other conditions might promote virtuous conduct. Second, he examines even less the concern with one's "more permanent self," the other element of happiness. He does not at all explain the significance of being aware of the connexion between one's past and present, and he makes no effort to specify what it means to act "on the basis of" one's present possibilities. Does it signify that one should try to do everything which is possible? Or does it mean that one ought to try to do only some things which are possible? If it signifies the latter, which possible things ought to be done? By not answering these questions, Wallas does not help one to observe if the changes which he recommends for the Great Society will enable its members to act in view of the "right" possibilities; and he does not lead one to perceive what other arrangements should be established so as to help its members to act with respect to such possibilities.

But happiness is not the only term where Wallas proves disappointing when he talks about the proper objective of the Great Society. Contending that happiness is not identical with the social good, he implies that there is much more than the former which should be achieved by the society. Incredibly, however, he leaves the social good obscure; he does not even attempt to explain the concept. More emphatically, he admonishes that happiness is not enough in the Great Society; but he gives no clue as to what else there should be.

IV

Although Wallas' normative examination of the Great Society is, not primarily concerned with education, it is definitely significant for the latter. Allusions to this point have already been made. Furthermore, the Great Society depicted by Wallas is no less important today than it was in his time. In fact, it appears to be more firmly established nowadays than it was then; for, if nothing else has done so, the course of politics, economics, and communications technology since the second world war has greatly enhanced the likelihood that remote and obscure environments are significantly related to all facets of one's life. It may also be noted that the kinds of problems which Wallas attributed to the Great Society in his day are still present. It seems quite appropriate, therefore, to specify what Wallas' argument says about education.

It is especially when the argument is considered in this respect that one regrets that Wallas did not develop his theoretical ideas adequately. On the surface, at least, these ideas indicate that, if they were formulated satisfactorily, they could, perhaps, be very helpful in setting the tasks of education in the Great Society. Wallas' conception of man's nature and environment, if it were fully clear, might importantly contribute to a comprehension of the control of normal human behavior in the Great Society and, thereby, a comprehension of the teaching of students in the society. And his conception of happiness, if it were wholly perspicuous, could possibly be quite valuable in the determination of educational goals in the Great Society. But, even if Wallas' argument is not theoretically sound enough to help much in defining the tasks of education in the Great Society, it makes a certain amount of sense for education in the society; for it raises issues which are pertinent to discussions of such education.

It will be convenient to examine only the major issues, and it will be further convenient to start with the most obvious of these. Wallas, it will be remembered, contends that one of the major goals of life in the Great Society is happiness. And, in view of what he means, albeit vaguely, by "happiness," he holds that it is necessary in this society, through universal schooling and other modes of education, to inform the masses of their respective environmental conditions and to develop fully their talents. Since, however, Wallas fails to analyze his concept of happiness satisfactorily, he does not, as already intimated, provide through this proposal an adequate statement of the goals of education in the Great Society. Nevertheless, in his discussion of the concept he prompts major questions concerning education in the Great Society, Wallas does not allege that happiness is the moral purpose of man: he claims only that it is one of the moral goals appropriate to man's civilized life, including his life in the Great Society. Thereby, he urges the point that some moral aims rather than others are especially relevant to life in this society. So, when he attempts to show what education should do to enable people to attain happiness in the Great Society, he poses this issue: What ought education to do to prepare people to obtain the moral goals especially appropriate to their life in the Great Society? This question, of course, presupposes another issue: What are the moral aims pertinent to life in the Great Society? This issue is clearly a moral one; but, since it is immediately presupposed by a distinctly educational question, it must also be regarded as an educational issue.

While the moral goals of life in the Great Society and education's job in view of these goals are major questions concerning education in the Great Society, they certainly are not the only chief issues posed by Wallas. A point made fairly evident by him in his criticism of the Great Society of his day is that the society was not conducive to the sort of education which, he thought, is desirable. He frequently noted that conditions in the society discouraged universal schooling; and, just as often, he remarked that such conditions inhibited the informal education of adults, which takes place not only by virtue of mass media but also by significant conversation, which Wallas called "dialectical thought." Accordingly, he made numerous proposals for changes in the Great Society which would make it more likely for the task of education to be fulfilled. In one respect, Wallas' criticism is no longer as valid as it once was. At least, the Great Society appears to foster universal schooling more and more. In another respect, of course, Wallas' criticism is as sound as it was during his time. Commuter trains, rush hour traffic, busy offices, noisy factories, and brief lunch periods are discouraging to meaningful conversation. And crowded dwellings, bustling shopping centers, tight schedules, and club meetings are not encouraging either. But whether or not his critical points remain valid is incidental here. What is important about his criticism is that it recognizes that the aim of education in the Great Society—whatever that aim might be—can be realized only to the extent that the society is ordered in a fashion which will favor the realization of the aim. In effect, he prompts the issue of how can the Great Society be organized so that it will help or, at least, not hinder education in the fulfillment of its purpose, whatever that may be.

Finally, Wallas presents the question of how can the Great Society be ordered so that it will enable its members to make complete use of the education which they receive. In his study of the Great Society, Wallas reminds one, again and again, that people are generally prevented by conditions in the society from obtaining as much happiness as they have the capabilities of acquiring. Women in the society are politically, socially, and economically dislocated. The society's urban centers are stifling to many dispositions. The stress on indefinite economic growth in the society leads to a heavy emphasis on efficiency in production and on consumption; and whereas the emphasis on efficiency places severe restrictions upon the worker's dispositions, the stress upon consumption encourages excesses in life. And, last, the fact that the reporting institutions in the society are meager and ineffectual means that the mass of people in the society cannot significantly influence the formulation of political policies, programs, and plans and, thereby, exercise control, in view of their happiness, over their distant and hidden environments. In effect, Wallas is stating that it is not enough for people to be capable of being happy; it is also necessary for them to live in a society which allows them to act according to their virtuous abilities. By making this point, he indicates that it is not sufficient for the inhabitants of the Great Society to have an education which gives them the capabilities for living the good life, whatever it might be. It is also mandatory for this society to be so organized that it will enable them to utilize their capabilities fully. To the extent that conditions in the Great Society do not allow a person to employ the education which he has received (however "right" that education is), they render the education a waste.

Upon inspection these issues may be seen as neither abstruse nor subtle; they might even be recognized as commonsensical. Nevertheless, they do not seem to be appreciated by a large number of current writers on education, in the Great Society. While many of these writers attempt to show what education ought to do in order to achieve assigned goals, they frequently do not consider whether or not these goals are significant of moral aims relevant to human life in the Great Society. Moreover, they usually give no sign of having wondered what such aims might be. While numerous of these writers advance programs and plans for expanding and strengthening education in the Great Society, they often fail to take into account what political, social, and economic changes would favor the expansion and strengthening of education. Furthermore, they usually ignore what modifications must be made in the Great Society so that its members can fully utilize their education once they have received it. So, even though Wallas did not satisfactorily determine the job of education in the Great Society, he did raise questions appropriate to such education which are frequently overlooked today; and for this reason, if no other, he deserves study by those concerned with education in the Great Society.

NOTES

[1] Place unk.: The Macmillan Company, 1914. The work was reprinted in 1928 (New York: The Macmillan Company).

[2] It has been held that the term was used by John Ball, a preacher at the time of the Peasants' Revolt of 1381; and by Wordsworth, Vid. Letters. *Time* (January 29, 1965), p. 4.

[3] Wallas, *op. cit.* (1928), p. 3.

[4] Cf. John Dewey, *The Public and Its Problems* (Denver: Alan Swallow, 1954), p. 96.

[5] Cf. Walter Lippmann, *Public Opinion* (New York: Harcourt, Brace & Co., 1922), p. 370.

[6] Wallas, *op. cit.*, (1928), p. 21.

[7] *Ibid.*, p. 28.

[8] *Ibid.*

[9] *Ibid.*, p. 61.

[10] *Ibid.*, p. 22.

[11] *Ibid.*

[12] *Ibid.*, p. 65.

[13] *Ibid.*, p. 33.

[14] *Ibid.*, pp. 57 & 60.

[15] *Ibid.*, p. 58.

[16] *Ibid.*, p. 36.

[17] *Ibid.*, p. 54.

[18] *Ibid.*, p. 36.

[19] *Ibid.*, p. 51.

[20] *Ibid.*, p. 45.

[21] *Ibid.*, p. 50.

[22] *Ibid.*, p. 61.

[23] *Ibid.*, pp. 95-103.

[24] *Ibid.*, pp. 104 and 348ff.

[25] *Ibid.*, pp. 103-4.

[26] *Ibid.*, p. 320.

[27] *Ibid.*, p. 322.

[28] *Ibid.*

[29] *Ibid.*, p. 323.

[30] *Ibid.*, pp. 4-8, 62-63, 323-69.

[31] *Ibid.*, pp. 4-5.

[32] *Ibid.*, pp. 331-69.

[33] *Ibid.*, pp. 242-8.

[34] *Ibid.*, pp. 285-6.

[35] *Ibid.*, p. 311.

[36] *Ibid.*, pp. 310-11.

[37] *Ibid.*, p. 310.

[38] *Ibid.*, p. 309.

[39] *Ibid.*, pp. 309-10.

[40] Dewey, *op. cit.*, p. 9.

Sugwon Kang (essay date 1979)

SOURCE: "Graham Wallas and Liberal Democracy," in the *Review of Politics,* Vol. 41, No. 4, October, 1979, pp. 536-60.

[In the following essay, Kang studies Wallas's attempts to strengthen and sustain the foundations of liberal democracy.]

During his lifetime (1858-1932) Graham Wallas's pioneering contributions to the study of politics were widely acknowledged. Thus, his ***Human Nature in Politics*** (1908) was rightly acclaimed as a turning point in British and American political science, away from the study of political institutions and toward the study of political behavior. With his later works, notably ***The Great Society*** (1914), ***Our Social Heritage*** (1921) and ***The Art of Thought*** (1926), Wallas's influence spilled over into other fields of social inquiry provoking a chain of serious debates among the pundits of various disciplines. And the term "Great Society," by which Wallas meant a complex, mechanized industrial society, the monster-child of the Industrial Revolution, became a household phrase in the 1930's among the New Deal liberals in the United States, where, according to historian Samuel Eliot Morison, he had been the most influential English political philosopher since Herbert Spencer.[1]

But today, not yet fifty years after his death, Wallas is largely a forgotten name, even among the professional students of politics. He is occasionally mentioned in textbooks, usually in footnotes; otherwise, one will encounter his name in the history books in connection with the Fabian Society, which he helped to guide through its formative years in collaboration with Sidney and Beatrice Webb and George Bernard Shaw. As a living intellectual force Wallas's importance today is decidedly negligible. There is not even a small band of enthusiasts trying to restore the fame of this "great and inadequately honoured man," as George Catlin has described him.[2]

This is all the more regrettable because Wallas had a long and illustrious career as a university teacher. First, he was lecturer of political science at the newly created London School of Economics and Political Science, from its inception in 1895; and, then, between 1914 and his retirement in 1923, he was the first holder of the chair of political science at the same institution.[3] We know from all available accounts that Wallas was a teacher of uncommon gifts,[4] who compares favorably with such legendary figures as John Ruskin of an earlier era, whom Wallas himself greatly admired as an undergraduate in Oxford. Indeed, Wallas was a living mine of suggestions and hints, and through his ability to arouse a sense of suspense and anticipation on the part of his readers and audiences he was able to elicit and sustain their enthusiasm as long as he kept teaching and writing. Yet, his genius lacked that power of construction upon which all thinkers must ultimately stake their claims to lasting fame. Wallas was not noted for the systematic thought for which Freud, Weber, Durkheim and Pareto are remembered, though in varying degrees.

After a careful study of his life and thought, however, one is made to realize that the generations following Wallas may have overlooked one very critical aspect of his work. Carried away as we are with the methodological concerns of political research, we tend to evaluate Wallas's contributions primarily as those of an advocate of a glamorous new science, thus glossing over the larger political lessons that are implicit in his search for methodological refinement. He is remembered as a critic of the "intellectualist fallacies" in political discussion, but seldom is he recalled as the first great diagnostician of the problems of liberal democracy. This neglect of course renders any analysis of Wallas's thought incomplete. But it may also exemplify the appalling lack of historical consciousness on the part of the partisans of liberal democracy today, living in a generation not noted for its thirst for historical knowledge.

Graham Wallas became as potent a critic of liberal democracy as he did, one suspects, partly because he was himself a liberal democrat with unimpeachable credentials. And he never doubted his historical mission: writing in 1908 he observed that the problems of liberal democracy had "in the past been mainly pointed out by the opponents of democracy," whereas, "if democracy is to succeed," these problems "must be frankly considered by the democrats themselves."[5]

The method which Wallas urged upon his fellow democrats to rescue liberal democracy from itself was political psychology; and in this effort he was clearly without equal, if not alone. Speaking of ***Human Nature in Politics*** Harold Laski commented:

> I am inclined to argue that no English thinker since Hobbes had seen more clearly the importance of the psychological foundations of politics; and since that book, few treatises on this theme have been usefully written that have not been coloured by its conclusions.[6]

Elsewhere Laski observed that the historical contribution of that book was nothing less than a "revolution in the methodology of political discussion, both in England and in America."[7] According to Horace Kallen, the "advent" of the "psychological political science" was "signalized with Graham Wallas's ***Human Nature in Politics***." Significantly, Kallen concluded his essay, "Political Science as Psychology," by asking rhetorically: "So, then, if political science is not psychology, what is it?"[8] Harold Lasswell once paid his teacher Charles Merriam the generous tribute that it was he who "first saw the importance of psychology for politics."[9] Merriam, however, passed the honor over to his English colleague Graham Wallas, saying that it was Wallas, not he, who first seriously attempted "to establish the significance of psychology in the domain of political inquiry"[10] and tried to "interpret political phenomena in terms of psychological forces rather than in terms of form and structure."[11]

Of the substantive contribution of ***Human Nature in Politics*** George H. Sabine has said that it was "the classical criticism of rationalism in political conduct."[12] "I tried in 1908 to make two main points clear," Wallas wrote in 1920: the first point had to do with the "danger" of the "intellectualist" assumption "that every human action is the result of an intellectual process, by which a man first thinks of some end which he desires, and then calculates the means by which that end can be attained," and the second point concerned the "need of substituting for that assumption a conscious and systematic effort of thought."[13] Now, twelve years later, he was able to say, confidently:

> In 1920 insistence on my first point is not so necessary as it was in 1908. The assumption that men are automatically guided by "enlightened self-interest" has been discredited by the facts of the war and the peace, the success of an anti-parliamentary and anti-intellectualist revolution in Russia, the British election of 1918. . . . It is my second point which, in the world as the war has left it, is most important. There is no longer much danger that we shall assume that man always and automatically thinks of ends and calculates means. The danger is that we may be too tired or too hopeless to undertake the conscious effort by which alone we can think of ends and calculate means.[14]

It is difficult to determine to what extent Wallas's own efforts had contributed to such a change in the climate of opinion; we are certainly not justified in construing the above passage to imply any such causal connection. Surely, the anti-intellectualist forces which Wallas so penetratingly detected on the eve of the Great War in his ***Great Society*** must have been present in the Western mind when Wallas wrote his ***Human Nature in Politics*** only six years before. Nonetheless, Wallas's sense of relief, coupled with his irritation with the opposite form of reductionism, namely anti-intellectualism, was shared by some of his leading contemporaries. Writing in 1923, the Cambridge psychologist W. H. R. Rivers noted that the pendulum had already swung "too far in the opposite direction, so that there is now a tendency to underestimate the importance of the intellectual factors in the determination of human conduct."[15]

There was one notable exception to the public's judgment that Wallas had written a novel thesis in his refutation of the alleged "intellectualist fallacies" of the nineteenth-century British liberalism grounded in the Benthamite Utilitarian psychology. One reviewer argued that Wallas's campaign against the "intellectualist" political psychology, for all its courage and eloquence, was tantamount to knocking down a straw man, made, as it were, with a language of politics largely restricted to public discussion, which no one of average intelligence ever took very seriously in the first place. The reviewer had no complaints about Wallas's refutation of the alleged intellectualist assumption, according to which "men always act on a reasoned opinion as to their interest"; he only doubted if such an improbable assumption could ever have been "so closely interwoven with our habits of political and economic thought," as Wallas would have us believe. Hardly. "It is an assumption that falls down almost as soon as it is stated," said the critic, but Wallas "has a lively way of battering it."[16] This reviewer went on to argue that there is a wide gap between public talk of politics and private understanding of its realities and that one who destroys public myths will not always surprise, much less enlighten, very many private citizens, for they are seldom as easily fooled as their leaders would like them to be or as their philosophers are inclined to believe.

Had Wallas fooled himself into thinking that people are more foolish than they actually are? The critic thought he had. ***Human Nature in Politics,*** he argued, was "an amusing attempt of a man in political life to find his way back from the public simplicities we all disbelieve to the complexities we are privately aware of. It would be hard to find a public American who was half so frank or a private American who was not more so."[17] The reviewer, however, failed to take the next step by raising the question, If we are, as private individuals, as illusion-free as he would have us believe, what accounts for the practical utility of these public myths? Ought we not to assume that there are enough people out there who take these myths to be true?

At least, Henry Steele Commager did not seem to share this critic's view that "in private life" most of us are hardheaded realists. In discussing Walter Lippmann's essay on *Public Opinion* Commager observed that "practicing politicians had doubtless understood the true nature of public opinion, but scholars and publicists had assumed that it was rational and reliable."[18] That was a distinction worth making. When chided by an old friend for allegedly having written a book merely to explain the obvious, Wallas replied:

> You say that the facts of human life and motive to which the psychology books give names are "perfectly well known to people who have not read them." They are, I believe, very largely well-known to experienced politicians by the time they reach fifty years of age, but I am convinced that they are not known to some of the best of the young men who enter politics each year.[19]

Wallas was not battering a straw man—not, at least, as far as the scholars and publicists were concerned. For many among his contemporaries who had come under the influence of book learning, the shallow rationalism of the Benthamite psychology was worse than a nuisance; to borrow Wallas' own words, it presented a "danger for all human activities, but especially for the working of democracy."[20] In his 1938 reminiscence of the years preceding the world war John Maynard Keynes, no fool by any stretch of the imagination, described himself to be "amongst the first" of his generation "to escape from the Benthamite tradition,"[21] and he called that tradition "the worm which has been gnawing at the insides of modern civilization and is responsible for its present moral decay."[22] He then struck at the heart of the matter:

> As cause and consequence of our general state of mind we completely misunderstood human nature, including our own. The rationality which we attributed to it led to a superficiality, not only of judgment, but also of feeling. It was not only that intellectually we were pre-Freudian, but we had lost something which our predecessors had without replacing it. I still suffer incurably from attributing an unreal rationality to other people's feelings and behaviour (and doubtless to my own, too).[23]

Like Keynes, Bertrand Russell had a hard fight to free himself from a faulty rationalism in which he had been reared, even though he did not associate it specifically with Bentham. But, more definitely than Keynes, Russell traced his intellectual awakening to his experiences during the war. In his autobiography Russell wrote:

> I had supposed until that time that it was quite common for parents to love their children, but the War persuaded me that it is a rare exception. I had supposed that most people liked money better than almost anything else, but I discovered that they liked destruction even better. I had supposed that intellectuals frequently loved truth, but I found here again that not ten per cent of them prefer truth to popularity.
>
> The War of 1914-1918 changed everything for me. I ceased to be academic and took to writing a new kind of books. I changed my whole conception of human nature.[24]

It is a supreme tribute to Wallas's intellectual acumen, then, that long before the outbreak of the world war he was able to see clearly, and also to define, the problems of social and political psychology which some of his most brilliant contemporaries were not able to see until after the war had brought them out in the open. Likewise, Wallas has been credited with having shown a "prophetic power"[25] in his analysis of the problems of the "Great Society" on the eve of the war, demonstrating how fragile was the fabric of modern industrial civilization and how bankrupt were liberal democracy's intellectual premises that had, in part, helped to bring about that civilization.

"To him more than to anyone else in the English tradition," wrote Max Lerner, "we owe our present knowledge that political behavior is irrational, that politics is the business of manipulating and exploiting the basic yet complex drives of men, and that all political progress must reckon with those drives."[26] Indeed, Wallas did view politics in terms of psychological manipulation, as an "empirical art" concerned with "the creation of opinion by the deliberate exploitation of subconscious non-rational inference."[27] And of all the brilliant arguments he presented in ***Human Nature in Politics*** in his effort to discredit the rationalist assumptions of the Benthamite psychology, perhaps none was more so than his memorable characterization of politics as an art of advertisement. He wrote:

> The whole relation between party entities and political impulse can perhaps be best illustrated from the art of advertisement. In advertisement the intellectual process can be watched apart from its ethical implications, and advertisement and party politics are becoming more and more closely assimilated in method. The political poster is placed side by side with the trade or theatrical poster on the hoardings, it is drawn by the same artist, and follows the same empirical rules of art.[28]

Wallas left no doubt as to how he might first have acquired such a vulgar notion of politics, that is, through a politician: "I remember that before my first election my most experienced political friend said to me, 'Remember that you are undertaking a six weeks' advertising campaign.'[29] As long as he [the candidate] is so engaged," Wallas added, "the maxim that it is wrong to appeal to anything but the severest process of logical thought in his constituents will seem to him, if he has time to think of it, not so much untrue as irrelevant."[30]

In his use of advertisement as an analytical model Wallas was without doubt a pioneer, the first one ever to come to grips with the politics of mass society; no one of his generation saw as clearly as he did the relevance of salesmanship for statesmanship in an age of mass media and mass consumption. It was not until five years after the publication of ***Human Nature in Politics*** that the American political scientist A. Lawrence Lowell made the phrases "age of advertisement" and "age of brokers" famous, by presenting an extensive discussion of the politicians' manipulation of a mass electorate through the employment of the art of advertisement. Lowell called these politicians "brokers," who act as middlemen, or "go-betweens," among different social groups with conflicting interests.[31] The idea of brokerage politics, characteristic of a pluralistic society with countervailing powers, has been one of the more distinctly American contributions to political science, originating in James Madison's classical commentary on "factions" (*The Federalist,* No. 10) and more systematically treated in the twentieth century by a group of able political scientists beginning with Arthur Bentley.[32] This idea remained largely outside the purview of Wallas's own intellectual concern, but if anyone should be credited with first having detected the close similarity between political campaigns and commercial advertisement, it was clearly Wallas, and not Lowell.

It is of course something else to suggest, as I think may be said with justice, that Wallas failed to appreciate the fact that the commercialization and vulgarization of the democratic process are only a by-product of brokerage politics. But if Wallas may be criticized on that ground, that would not necessarily detract from the validity of his hypothesis that in his essential behavioral characteristics a politician is a salesman and that he relates himself to his constituents no differently than a manufacturer relates himself to the consumer. That assumption, I think, has been fully borne out in the decades that followed ***Human Nature in Politics***. Some half-century after Wallas had spoken of advertisement and party politics "becoming more and more closely assimilated in method" and of political posters being "drawn by the same artist," following "the same empirical rules of art," as the trade or theatrical posters, both major parties in the United States—the Republican party in 1952 and the Democratic party four years later—turned over their campaign propaganda to the professional public relations firms on Madison Avenue. And today, true to Wallas's prophecy, political candidates are literally "sold" to the public by professional advertising agencies according to "the same empirical rules of art" as those employed, methodically, in the selling of toothpastes, breakfast cereals and ladies' hosiery.[33] These professional agencies endeavor to create in the minds of captive viewers, alternately, a false sense of insecurity and security, a false sense of need and satisfaction.

It may be said, in retrospect, that the single most enduring contribution Wallas made to the study of politics lay in his simple but eloquent plea that a discussion of human nature be made the foundation of all political inquiry—a plea which he himself put into practice with admirable success. "The deepest error of our political thinking," wrote the young Walter Lippmann, six years after the appearance of ***Human Nature in Politics***, was "to talk of politics without reference to human beings." Lippmann believed that Wallas had succeeded in correcting that error by demonstrating how the behavior of concrete human beings could be made "the center of political investigation" and that, in so doing, he had turned the study of politics "back to the humane tradition of Plato to Machiavelli."[34] Harold Lasswell has since spoken of this "humanizing trend" in political science, which "has always been represented in the 'classics,' usually in the form of some theory of 'human nature,'" and has given Wallas and "his students" the credit for having revived that venerable tradition.[35]

The relevance of political psychology for the survival of liberal democracy was not left merely to the reader's imagination. Even though the "main controversy over the best form of government appears to have been finally settled in favor of representative democracy," Wallas noted in his introduction to ***Human Nature in Politics,*** "in the very nations which have most wholeheartedly accepted representative democracy, politicians and political students seem puzzled and disappointed by their experience of it." With the expansion of suffrage the Western societies appeared to have more and more democracy but, somehow, enjoying it less and less. Wallas was particularly disturbed by the fact that in the two most advanced representative democracies, the United States and England, it was "the growing, and not the decaying, forces of society" that seemed to "create the most disquieting problems."[36] Is liberal democracy inherently incompatible with modern society?

Within a few years of the publication of ***Human Nature in Politics*** England witnessed what historian George Dangerfield was later to describe as "the Strange Death of Liberal England," as it plunged into what may have been the most serious domestic political crisis since the Chartist and anti-Corn Law agitations of the late 1830's, under the combined pressures of the suffragette and trade union agitations and the parliamentary dispute over the Irish Home Rule.[37] Compromise, courtesy, good manners, and all the social amenities so closely identified with the British way of life suddenly seemed things of the past. Many were driven into a state of melancholy musing over the death of a tradition. Already in 1905 the Liberal politician C. F. G. Masterman could write that "expectancy and surprise" were the "notes of the age." He would describe himself, in the vein of Matthew Arnold ("Grande Chartreuse," St. 15), as poised in suspension between two worlds divided by a great void: "On the one hand is a past still showing faint survivals of vitality; on the other is the future but hardly coming to birth."[38] Four years later, now a Liberal M.P., Masterman was able to offer a diagnosis that was less prophetic but also less ambiguous: "It is rather in the region of the spirit that the doubts are still disturbing," he declared, noting how over the years "fulness of bread" had been "accompanied with leanness of soul."[39]

This sense of uncertainty, indeed foreboding, so characteristic of the closing years of a protracted garden party called the Edwardian age, was only to prove a signpost to things to come, and to stay, even though there were conflicting voices trying to explain the precise meaning of the malaise. For Graham Wallas, who was less given to prophetic fancy than Masterman and still less liable to fret over a few cracks in the citadel of social conventions, the challenge of the age was more immediately political: to scrutinize the reigning wisdom, that is, liberalism, which had rendered the political system incapable of coping with the unruly forces of modern society.

Wallas became conscious of the troubles of liberalism early in his life as he came under the twin spells of Darwinian biology and Aristotelian politics. In the same year he was born, 1858, the son of an evangelical minister of an orthodox persuasion, the world saw the publication of the joint thesis on "natural selection" by Charles Darwin and Alfred Russel Wallace, which was followed a year later by the historic appearance of Darwin's *Origin of Species*. Wallas first encountered the Darwinian theory when he was a student at Corpus Christi College, Oxford, and he was quickly converted. Once the young Wallas had the temerity to submit a tract in defense of Darwin's theory against what he deemed an unfounded attack made upon it by the resident professor of moral philosophy. Following his years in college Darwinism became something of a religion to Wallas, for during the rest of his life he was to sing the praises of Darwin for having first "demonstrated the blood-relationship of men with the other animals."[40] He argued that "the proved continuity of human and non-human life" demanded "a biological outlook which should study mankind, not in isolation but as one of a member of related species,"[41] and advocated, tirelessly, that political science incorporate the findings of the new biological science as it revises its conception of human nature.

Wallas was not slow to appreciate the social implications of the Darwinian biology but was harshly critical of the vulgar use that was then being made of it under the label of "Social Darwinism"; he condemned it as a thinly disguised apology for militarism, imperialism and racism, characterizing it as "thoroughly unscientific."[42] Rather, the lesson to be drawn from the Darwinian world view, so Wallace believed, was that we must come to terms with the incongruity between man and his environment before we can fully understand the crisis of the modern industrial society. The problem of the modern age, he said, was that "the coming of the Great Society has created an environment in which, for most of us, neither our instinctive nor our intelligent dispositions find it easy to discover their most useful stimuli."[43] Given the conflict between man's nature and his present social environment, leaving the situation where it was would do human nature gross violence. On the other hand, so Wallas argued in his postwar work, ***Our Social Heritage***, given man's helpless dependence on his inherited habits and customs, any attempt at eliminating that social heritage would be suicidal. There is a way out of our predicament: progressive alteration of our social heritage to make that heritage more compatible with our biological nature, particularly to improve our existing modes of cooperation. This is what Wallas meant by his often-repeated phrase "social reconstruction," a phrase very much in vogue in the postwar years.

"My earlier book dealt in the main with the problem of representative government," so wrote Wallas in introducing his ***Great Society***. "This will deal with general social organization, considered with special reference to the difficulties created by the formation of what I have called the Great Society."[44] Wallas had written his new book in part in response to the suggestion of William James that there was a need for a book which would deal specifically with "the diseases of society and their prevention."[45] The continuity from ***Human Nature in Politics*** to ***The Great Society*** was not lost on the reading public, in spite of the author's own attempt to distinguish their aims. Thus, Ernest Barker described the new book as "a treatise on social therapeutics," adding that it was Wallas's intention "in the light of social psychology . . . to diagnose the diseases of our present system of representative government and to suggest their remedies."[46]

Wallas's consciousness of the importance of environment was further heightened by his exposure to the teachings of Aristotle, which came even earlier than his encounter with the Darwinian theory. As a young lad he was trained at Shrewsbury, which was then one of the most prestigious "public schools" in England, particularly distinguished for its curriculum in classics. At the age of nineteen Wallas was sent to Oxford on a classical scholarship, to graduate four years later with "Class II Honours" in *Literae Humaniores,* to embark upon what was to be a brief career as a classical schoolmaster. After all that training in classics, however, Wallas did not become a classicist as such. Rather, the training had the effect of impressing upon him the urgent need to reexamine the moral and intellectual foundations of the contemporary society in the light of the Greek conception of polity as a community of friends engaged in a common task, that is, the pursuit of the good life—which was in sharp contrast with the prevailing liberal conception of society essentially as a legal association. Wallas found the liberal conception hopelessly atomistic.

When Wallas went to Oxford in 1877, the philosophy of John Stuart Mill was the dominant voice there, even though he had been dead for four years. Wallas's tutor, Thomas Case, was himself a great admirer of Mill, the last of the Utilitarians, and under Case's tutelage Wallas devoured *The System of Logic* then considered the most important of Mill's works. In that book Mill complained of the backwardness of the "moral sciences" and urged that the methods of physical sciences be applied to the moral sciences to remedy their sorry state. Wallas could not have agreed with Mill more, and yet Mill's own political views seemed strangely formalistic and dry, seemingly out of touch with what Wallas later came to understand to be the realities of social life. Liberty as defined by Mill in his classic treatise under that title had a certain air of unreality: it seemed at once negative and static. Hobbes's formula of liberty as the "absence of external impediments" had been left intact in its essential components. Wallas viewed this conception of liberty as a serious obstacle to the forces of social change because of its inherent tendency to treat any political action as an infringement upon personal liberties. The problem was particularly serious because, in spite of his unimpressive record as a political inventor, Mill remained the "intellectual autocrat" of British liberalism.[47]

Mill's static conception of liberty was hardly improved upon by the Oxford idealists, Wallas believed. Despite their noble intentions to give liberty some positive and dynamic content, they were powerless to bring about the desired change because, like the German thinkers they were emulating, these idealists went about their business the wrong way, that is, as "metaphysicians" rather than as psychologists. When Wallas was a senior at Corpus Christi, T. H. Green was delivering his lectures on the "Principles of Political Obligation" just a block away at Balliol and was making many converts. Wallas went to hear Green one day and came away quite unimpressed because the eminent professor seemed singularly lacking in biological or psychological insight.[48]

In his own time Wallas found the lingering influence of Mill's negative concept of liberty in Sidney Webb's definition, according to which liberty is the "practical opportunity that we have of exercising our faculties and fulfilling our desires."[49] Wallas argued that this definition was "insufficient," because, as he put it, "it does not recognize that the unfreedom-reaction depends more on the cause of obstruction to impulse than on the mere fact of obstruction."[50] In short, the sense of deprivation of liberty comes not from actually losing the ability to do this or that but, rather, from one's resentment of the perceived causes of that deprivation. This was Aristotle's profound insight,[51] and for Wallas it was but a facet of the "many-sided positive conception"[52] of the ancient Greeks, according to which liberty is closely linked with "the instinct of resentment."[53] Thus, Wallas praised Pericles for having "understood the explosive mine of resentment which may lie beneath the surface of a community that ignores" the sensibilities of ordinary people and, above all, for having realized that "free government means something more subtle and more difficult than the mere avoidance" of what is but an external manifestation of that resentment.[54]

In the final analysis, Wallas argued, again echoing Aristotle, no cooperative effort on a national scale, under whatever label, can satisfy the needs of a modern society unless it is grounded on a firm basis of popular consent. But conscious consent, the secret of political stability, is the child of economic and social equality, and the only thing that will enable a large majority of the population wilfully and consciously to play its part in any cooperative endeavor is "a much nearer approximation to economic and social equality than now exists in any industrial nation."[55] Thus, Wallas's egalitarianism was deeply rooted in his conviction that the social fabric of a complex modern industrial society cannot endure the psychological strains of gross economic and social inequality. "If our civilization is to survive, greater social equality must indeed come," he wrote in 1908. "Men will not continue to live peacefully together," he added, prophetically, "in huge cities under conditions that are intolerable to any sensitive mind, both among those who profit and those who suffer by them."[56]

When the young Wallas left Oxford in 1881, upon graduation, he had become not only a devotee of Aristotle and Darwin but also a convert to the new religion of social conscience. The eighties were a decade of moral agitation spurred by the sight of an enormous and ever-widening gulf between wealth and poverty that appeared literally to tear the English society asunder into "two nations," in the memorable phrase of Disraeli. This alienation of social classes was particularly glaring in London where the division between the wealthy "West End" and the poverty-stricken "East End" seemed complete, neither understanding the life-style of the other. It was the vision of bringing these "two nations" together that inspired the creation of the University Settlements throughout England, beginning with the foundation of Toynbee Hall in East London in 1884, and also the introduction, through

Toynbee Hall, of the Ethical Society movement from the United States shortly thereafter. Wallas was drawn into the Settlement movement from the beginning and took an active part therein for most of his life, as he did in the Ethical Society movement.

But it was the Fabian Society, also founded in 1884, that was to claim the largest share of his energies and talents for many years, both because of the strategic place it was to occupy in British national politics and because of the leadership role he was to play in the society until he resigned his membership twenty years later. Wallas did not join the society until 1886, a year after he had been dismissed from a teaching post for refusing to take Holy Communion; but he had known three of the present members, George Bernard Shaw, Sidney Webb and Sydney Olivier, with whom he was to form the "Fabian Junta."

Within a year of his initiation into the Fabian Society Wallas chose historical research as his particular contribution to the cause of socialism. By 1888 he was delivering a series of lectures on the Chartist movement, which was received as a pioneering contribution to historiography. These lectures "wrought a tremendous disillusion as to the novelty of our [Fabian] own ideas and methods of propaganda," so recalled Shaw afterwards, and "it was in this new frame of mind that the monumental series of works by the Webbs came into existence."[57] It was during his work on Chartism in the British Museum, in the early nineties, that Wallas stumbled upon a huge mass of papers of Francis Place, the English radical reformer and Chartist leader who helped draft the "People's charter." When ***The Life of Francis Place*** appeared later in the decade, it was widely acclaimed as a masterpiece of political biography. "There are perhaps five or six living men who can disentangle the social history of England in the nineteenth century with the same knowledge and wisdom as Mr. Wallas," wrote Harold Laski years later. "That has made him," Laski argued, "in a real sense the parent of what is rapidly becoming the most significant part of modern English historiography."[58] Even though Wallas's reputation as a political theorist was soon to outshine his reputation as a historian, many have continued to rate ***The Life of Francis Place*** as one of the author's finest efforts.[59]

Wallas once said of his work that he had emerged from his research a "different man."[60] Apart from gaining a rich insight into the history of the radical movement in England, Wallas made an important discovery that was to guide and shape his thinking for the rest of his life: the idea of "invention." Throughout his biography Place is portrayed not merely as a supreme political tactician, agitator and lobbyist but also as a "political inventor," in whom the life of thought and the life of action seemed to be joined in a happy blend. It is no coincidence that such a person should have been a friend and pupil of the greatest political inventor of them all, or "by far the most successful political inventor whom we have produced in England,"[61] as Wallas would say of Jeremy Bentham. If, indeed, it had not been for the many daring political inventions of Place and other progenies of Bentham, such as E. Chadwick, Gibbon Wakefield and Rowland Hill, that were brought to bear on the tasks of social reform of the day,[62] British liberalism might have become obsolete in the illustrious hands of John Stuart Mill.

When Wallas brought Bentham into the Fabian discussions Bentham was hardly obscure, but he was distinctly unpopular. He had long since been effectively replaced by the towering figure of Mill, and for a while, at least in Oxford, to be a "Benthamite" was an invitation to ostracism.[63] Wallas could recall that when he was an undergraduate students were "trained to despise Bentham," noting, further, that some of their tutors "made, indeed, a considerable proportion of their income by jeering at those quotations from Bentham's writings which they met with in the manuals of philosophy."[64] By the beginning of the nineties all the leading Fabians, most of whom were still in their early thirties, had contemporary social thinkers whom they would identify as their heroes, though in a rather vague sort of way. Webb was often thought of as a Millite, Shaw a Henry Georgeite, Olivier a Comtean, William Clarke a Mazzinian, and so forth. Wallas alone was without a master in modern social thought, having to make do with the incongruous pair of Aristotle and Darwin. So it was that when he discovered and began preaching Bentham's philosophy of invention—not to be confused with his Utilitarian psychology, which Wallas came to despise heartily—he had made a significant breakthrough not only for the popularization of Bentham's timely philosophy but also for his own sake as a member of the club. Bentham the inventor remained Wallas's hero to the end of his life; Bentham seemed to complete Wallas's "trinity of idolatry," with the other sacred chairs already reserved for Aristotle and Darwin.

In 1888 Wallas was elected into the Fabian Society's executive with Shaw, Webb, Olivier, William Clarke, Annie Besant and Hubert Bland; these were the authors of the celebrated "Fabian Essays," which were published the following year to rousing public acclaim. But in 1895 Wallas resigned from the executive and became deeply involved in the politics of public education, having been elected the previous year to the London School Board, and also, shortly thereafter, in the politics of the London County Council. Nine years later he resigned from the Fabian Society itself when he could not prevail upon the majority to reject Joseph Chamberlain's protective tariff and to reaffirm free trade. Like a good Liberal, though he never was a member of the Liberal party, Wallas had also protested against the expansionist foreign policy of Lord Salisbury's Conservative government; at the outbreak of the Boer War in 1899, he was part of that group which demanded that the Fabian Society "dissociates itself from the imperialism of capitalism and vainglorious nationalism."[65] But nothing could have offended the liberal sensibilities of an agnostic educator more than the reintroduction of religion into public education.[66]

No one in the Fabian Society championed the cause of secularism more passionately than did Wallas. In an article written in 1888 he described his mood as "savagely

Anti-Christian" in matters relating to religious indoctrination "as if I were a Secularist, pure and simple" and expressed his conviction that the country would be better off "if only we disestablished the Church" and "induced a sufficient number of persons to 'make game of the patriarchs.'"[67] It did not take him long, however, to discover that the patriarchs had powerful allies not only in the government but also within the Fabian Society itself.

Sidney Webb, who shared Wallas's distaste for religious interference in education, had his new education act on the drawing board and courted the support of the Conservatives to ensure its adoption. The Conservatives, on the other hand, could not ignore the sentiment of the clergy, their traditional allies, who wanted the school boards abolished, because the school boards were then widely, and correctly, perceived as the bastions of secularism. Furthermore, the clergy insisted that the new law should make a provision whereby the beleaguered sectarian schools would be supported out of the local rates, that is, property tax. Wallas opposed these efforts strenuously and was able to rally the Liberals and the Nonconformists behind the school boards as the last line of defense for freedom in the realm of public education. But, in the end, Webb and the Fabian majority gave in to the Conservative demands. The Education Act of 1902 was a major victory for the Anglican and Catholic clergy, who had been apprehensive lest their schools should go bankrupt, and a major setback for the secularists, who had hoped that they would do so, in order that the elected school boards might take over the entire system of elementary education. Needless to add, it was also a personal defeat for Wallas, who had staked his reputation on the belief that a free society cannot allow its educational process to be dominated by the forces of religious obscurantism.[68]

To be sure, Wallas did not resign from the Fabian Society over the education issue. However, as Edward Pease, the Fabian secretary and historian, later pointed out, Wallas eventually left the society "because in the long controversy over education policy he had found himself constantly in the position of a hostile critic."[69] Shortly after his resignation, in January 1904, Wallas wrote Pease reflecting on his own politics: "On the questions which divide the Liberal and Conservative parties, I am a Liberal."[70] Indeed, in all three disputes Wallas fought on the losing side, the Liberal side, or the anti-Conservative side, invariably crossing swords with his old friends Webb and Shaw, who took turns to lead the majority within the society. Wallas decided to leave, wrote Historian Élie Halévy, because "he felt himself compromised by the deliberately anti-Liberal attitude the heads of the Fabian Society had adopted." Halévy also recorded, again correctly, that Wallas's retirement from the society was "perfectly amicable," adding that he "continued to be the friend and admirer of those with whom he had worked throughout his youth."[71] But one can see, in retrospect, that as their friendships lasted unbroken and undiminished so did their fundamental differences of temperament and outlook.

During the early days of the Fabian Society Beatrice Webb observed that her husband, Sidney, was the "organizer" and giver of "most of the practical initiative," whereas Wallas represented "morality and scrupulousness," which appealed "to those of the upper and educated class who have good intentions." As for Shaw, he "gives the sparkle and flavour" and "leads off the men of straw, men with light heads—the would-be revolutionaries, who are attracted by his wit, his daring onslaughts and amusing paradoxes."[72] The years following the Great War seemed to bring to relief, relentlessly, the political consequences of these temperamental differences among old friends who had been brought together by a common devotion to the cause of social equality. Just as he had found himself outnumbered in the Fabian Society by those willing to abandon liberal principles for reasons of political expediency, so in the postwar years Wallas found himself swimming in a pool full of unfriendly creatures calling themselves "realists."

These were the years that witnessed the rise of communism and fascism, ideologies of violence so different and yet so alike, clamoring at the gate of liberal democracy, trying to lure the uncommitted with promises of equality and efficiency, and testing the souls of liberal democrats who were growing increasingly suspicious that their agreeable form of government might at last have outlived its usefulness. In a state of exhaustion owing to four years of killing and destruction, some people were doubtful whether liberal democracy could ever be repaired; exasperated by the slowness and inefficiency of its ways, some believed that it was time to jump ship.

In 1932 the Webbs paid their visit to the Soviet Union, returning home convinced that communism was the answer to much of what the democratic systems had failed to solve. Three years later they presented their conclusions to a stunned British public in the *Soviet Communism,* in which the doctrine of gradualism, the essence of Fabian Socialism, appeared completely abandoned. Death spared Wallas the embarrassment of reading it. But there was no way Wallas could have avoided getting involved in the debate over fascism in the mid-twenties as Shaw carried on his open love affair with *Il Duce,* agitating a vulnerable British public which was already displaying a penchant for political ruffianism in its toleration of the likes of Winston Churchill.

"Credere, obbedire, combattre" ("have faith, obey, fight") and "Mussolini ha sempre ragione" ("Mussolini is always right"), so the slogans read. But the Abyssinian war was still several years away, and until after Mussolini's defeat in the Second World War not many people could have imagined the true scope of the Fascist inefficiency, which he managed to conceal behind the facade of military discipline. From its inception in 1922 fascism had billed itself as the antithesis of all the governing principles of liberal democracy; yet, to the "realists," fascism appeared to promise the kind of social equality and economic recovery democratic systems could not deliver. Admittedly, Shaw was something of a showman, given to clowning and hyperbole, unafraid to lavish a sense of humor at the expense of the public. But his praises of Mussolini were the confessions of a sober social critic, who was merely echoing a widely held sentiment of his time.

Among those who shared Shaw's pro-Fascist sympathies was Churchill. He had undergone one of his political conversions, departing from his previous Liberal radicalism and now behaving more and more like a regular Tory diehard. During the General Strike of 1926 Churchill was by far the stoutest on Stanley Baldwin's cabinet to oppose a negotiated settlement with labor; to him the strike was communist-inspired blackmail, to which the only workable response was a militant one. It was in this frame of mind that Churchill, while vacationing in Italy, saw fit to declare that Mussolini had "rendered a service to the whole world."

In February of 1927, following a round of public flirtations with fascism, Shaw received a letter from Wallas, which read in part:

> In Vienna last year I watched a body of "Nationalist" (Fascist) ex-officers marching through the streets, and they were a formidable body of men, and I watched Winston Churchill's armoured cars marching last May through London streets, and realised that he and the young members of his defence bodies were probably thinking of the ease with which they could bring about a Fascist coup de main in London.[73]

Shaw had urged that if one could not support fascism one ought at least to hold his tongue and refrain from minding other people's business. Wallas was not impressed by Shaw's sudden plea for international good manners and expressed his sense of dismay: "And your influence all over the world is very great."[74] Even T. S. Eliot, who was then acquiring a reputation as a reactionary, largely through his editorship of the literary quarterly *The Criterion*, echoed this concern two years later when he offered his editorial observation that the "aging Fabians," like Shaw and H. G. Wells, seemed to prefer "some kind of fascism" and "autocracy." He feared that this fascination with dictatorship on the part of the eminent men of letters could "become the instinctive attitude of thousands of unthinking people a few years hence."[75]

Amid all this frenzy over the Fascist movement in Italy Wallas greeted the public with his fifth book, ***The Art of Thought***, a masterpiece in introspective psychology. In it he demonstrated how the nonrational and involuntary forces within the human mind could be rationally guided and coordinated to produce fruitful thought. Having previously written three books diagnosing various aspects of the problems of modern society, Wallas had now shifted his attention to the practical question of how best to make use of our mental faculties in coping with those problems. Max Lerner, who greatly admired the book, described it as "a sort of handbook for political inventors."[76] But, more than that, ***The Art of Thought*** was further testimony to Wallas's enduring attachment to the liberal tradition; the book was, in effect, a reaffirmation of the psychological individualism that is implicit in the entire British liberal tradition, from Hobbes to Mill. Not surprisingly, Wallas has always been an unyielding foe of the "group mind" school of social psychology. He took particular disliking to the doctrine of "imitation," calling Gabriel Tarde's classic *Lois de l'Imitation* "one of the most baffling and unsatisfactory books that I have ever read,"[77] because it tended to legitimate the "group mind" hypothesis. Even the venerable authority of William James seemed powerless to persuade Wallas to modify his dogged stance.[78]

In an age when the leading students of human affairs were prone to seek intellectual respectability by debunking reason's false claims, Wallas sought patiently to maximize the chances for realizing her true possibilities. In an age when self-styled political realism and totalitarian élitism seemed to go hand in hand, both drawing their intellectual sustenance from antirationalism of some kind, Wallas remained unalterably opposed to any easy solution that was incompatible with the ideals of liberty and self-government, because he knew only too well that trading off one type of tyranny for another was hardly a solution. He held firm to his liberal conviction that, for all its failings, liberal democracy must find its own cures for its peculiar problems. When he died in the summer of 1932, at the age of 74, the fateful movements just north of the Alps had begun making Mussolini's experiment seem relatively harmless. Events were soon to turn the fashionable realism of the day on its head.

Today, once again, liberal democracy is on the defensive. Its existence is tenuous in those very nations in which it has survived over the past hundred years or more, though with intermittent success—those countries where it must prove its viability if it is to have a future at all. Under the deceptive veneer of self-confidence born of the industrial growth and technological advancement of the postworld war years, the Western nations are gripped with a mood of uncertainty. Rape of the environment, nuclear proliferation, racial tensions, the energy crisis, terrorism, and a host of other problems have suddenly shaken the liberal democrat's confidence in the continuing validity of his inherited creed: liberty, equality and representative government. Most recently we have been forced to ask the question, What must be the organic deficiency of representative democracy that such large numbers of voters throughout Western Europe should feel the need to embrace communism at the polls, while, admittedly, making it clear that they are in no mood to abandon the basic tenets of parliamentary system?

Shall liberal democracy prove equal to the challenges of the day, or has it become truly obsolete, waiting to be dumped into the ideological graveyard of history? What are the chances of rescuing it from the perplexity of its own divided soul? Should we sing with the poet,

> Vex not his ghost: O, Let him pass! He hates him
> That would upon the rack of this tough world
> Stretch him out longer.
>
> *King Lear,* Act 5, Scene 3

Or should we grant liberal democracy a second medical opinion before rushing to its funeral?

Such questions have been raised before in the troubled career of liberal democracy; they are worth raising again only because they have never been answered satisfactorily. Warnings have been posted and counsels given; the state of perplexity in which we live today may be a measure of our failure to give heed to these past warnings and to profit from the lessons. Graham Wallas was a political philosopher who at another critical juncture in the evolution of liberal democracy sought to stave off the decline of the political system he held dear. He argued that the traditional liberal hostility toward the state and the disbelief in the power of political action to make society more just and more livable had stood in the way of much-needed social change. Later in his life, following the Great War, Wallas was forced to confront a political challenge of an altogether different stripe: the learned infatuation with the cult of "direct action." Both these tendencies, perversions of democratic thought, seemed symptomatic of a deeper malaise: liberal democracy's unconscionable neglect of the human foundation of political and social order.

Wallas did not reject the intellectual tradition of liberal democracy in toto; rather, he sought to repair its troubled foundations by scrutinizing its assumptions that had been taken for granted. Nor did he have answers to all the practical problems he had detected in liberal democracy; as a partial remedy for its impending obsolescence, he merely sought to implant in the minds of the committed an awareness of its mortal ambiguities.

NOTES

[1] Samuel Eliot Morison, *The Oxford History of the American People* (New York, 1965), p.,813.

[2] G. E. G. Catlin, *Systematic Politics: Elementa Politica et Sociologica* (Toronto, 1962), p. 8.

[3] Wallas was succeeded to the Chair by Harold J. Laski, Michael Oakeshott and Maurice Cranston.

[4] See the eulogies of Graham Wallas published as "Graham Wallas" in *Economica,* vol. 12 (November, 1932), reprinted as *Graham Wallas: 1858-1932* (London, 1932).

[5] Graham Wallas, *Human Nature in Politics,* 4th ed. (London, 1948), p. 253 (hereafter HNP.)

[6] Harold J. Laski, "Lowes Dickinson and Graham Wallas," *Political Quarterly,* 3 (1932), 465.

[7] Laski's eulogy of Wallas in *Graham Wallas: 1858-1932,* p. 10.

[8] Horace Kallen, "Political Science as Psychology," *American Political Science Review,* 17 (1923), 194-195; 203.

[9] Quoted in Bernard Crick, *The American Science of Politics: Its Origins and Conditions* (Berkeley, 1959), pp. 137-138.

[10] Charles Merriam, "The Significance of Psychology for the Study of Politics," *American Political Science Review,* 18 (1924), 473.

[11] Charles Merriam and Harry Elmer Barnes, eds., *A History of Political Theories: Recent Times—Essays on Contemporary Developments in Political Theory* (New York, 1924), p. 19.

[12] George H. Sabine, "Political Science and Philosophy," *The Social Sciences and Their Interrelations,* eds. Ogburn and Goldenweiser (New York, 1927), p. 248.

[13] Wallas's preface to the third edition of HNP (1920).

[14] *Ibid.*

[15] W. H. R. Rivers, *Psychology and Politics and Other Essays,* with a prefatory note by G. E. Smith and an appreciation by C. S. Myers (London, 1923), p. 5.

[16] F. M. Colby's review, *Bookman,* 30 (1909-1910), 396.

[17] *Ibid.,* p. 398.

[18] Henry Steele Commager, *The American Mind: An Interpretation of American Thought and Character Since the 1880's* (New Haven, 1950), p. 334. One obvious exception was Lippmann's own teacher, "the brilliant Graham Wallas . . ." (p. 332).

[19] Letter to Hastings Rashdall, 16 January 1909. Bodleian Library, Oxford.

[20] Preface to the third edition of HNP, 1920, p. 5.

[21] John Maynard Keynes, "My Early Beliefs," *Essays and Sketches in Biography* (New York, 1956), p. 251.

[22] *Ibid.*

[23] *Ibid.,* pp. 253-254.

[24] Bertrand Russell, *Autobiography* (Boston, 1968), vol. 2, *1914-1944,* 6 and 36.

[25] G. E. G. Catlin, *A Study of the Principles of Politics: Being an Essay Towards Political Rationalization* (New York, 1930), p. 220.

[26] Max Lerner, *Ideas Are Weapons: The History and Uses of Ideas* (New York, 1939), p. 316.

[27] HNP, p. 18.

[28] *Ibid.,* p. 107.

[29] *Ibid.*, p. 190.

[30] *Ibid.*, p. 191.

[31] A. Lawrence Lowell, *Public Opinion and Popular Government* (New York, 1913), pp. 58-61.

[32] Arthur Bentley, *The Process of Government (1908).*

[33] See Joe McGinnis's insightful analysis of the management of the presidential campaign of Richard Nixon in his *The Selling of the President* (New York, 1968).

[34] Walter Lippmann, *Preface to Politics* (New York, 1913), pp. 32 and 77.

[35] Harold D. Lasswell and Abraham Kaplan, *Power and Society: A Framework for Political Inquiry* (New Haven, 1950), p. 14.

[36] HNP, pp. 25-26 and 27.

[37] George Dangerfield, *The Strange Death of Liberal England* (New York, 1935).

[38] C. F. G. Masterman, *In Peril of Change* (London, 1905), p. xii.

[39] C. F. G. Masterman, *The Condition of England* (London, 1909), p. 208.

[40] See *The Literary Guide and Rationalist Review,* July 1926, p. 126.

[41] Graham Wallas, *The Great Society: A Psychological Analysis* (London, 1914, p. 118. (hereafter GS).

[42] HNP, p. 302.

[43] GS, p. 62.

[44] GS, pp. 18-19.

[45] Letter to Wallas, 8 December 1908. Wallas Papers, L.S.E.

[46] Sir Ernest Barker, *Political Thought in England: 1848-1914* (London, 1959), pp. 204-205.

[47] Graham Wallas, *Our Social Heritage* (New Haven, 1921), p. 176 (hereafter OSH).

[48] See Wallas's review of *L. T. Hobhouse: His Life and Work* by J. A. Hobson and Morris Ginsberg in *The New Statesman and Nation,* 25 April 1931, p. 326.

[49] Quoted in OSH, p. 159.

[50] *Ibid.*, p. 168.

[51] See Aristotle's *Politics* bk. 5, where he drew the important distinction between actual inequality and a perception, or consciousness, of inequality. The latter, not the former, so Aristotle thought, leads to a "sense of injustice," which in turn leads to *stasis,* or a seditious atmosphere.

[52] OSH, p. 166.

[53] *Ibid.*, p. 165.

[54] *Ibid.*, p. 167.

[55] *Ibid.*, p. 88.

[56] HNP, p. 245.

[57] Quoted in Edward R. Pease, *History of the Fabian Society,* 2nd ed. (London, 1925), pp. 277-278.

[58] Harold J. Laski, "A Social Pioneer" (review of *The Life of Francis Place), The Dial,* 68 (May, 1920), 619.

[59] Lord Bertrand Russell believed that *Place* ranked with *Human Nature in Politics* as Wallas's two greatest works. Letters to me, 17 July 1968.

[60] *Men and Ideas: Essays by Graham Wallas,* ed. May Wallas, with a preface by Gilbert Murray (London, 1940), pp. 208-209 (hereafter MI).

[61] MI, p. 45.

[62] OSH, p. 176.

[63] See Robert Louis Stevenson's *The Story of a Lie* and Emery Neff's *Carlyle and Mill: An Introduction to Victorian Thought.*

[64] MI, p. 34.

[65] A. M. McBriar, *Fabian Socialism and English Politics: 1884-1918* (London, 1962), p. 121.

[66] In the last quarter of the nineteenth century there were two different systems of elementary education, one, "denominational schools" run by churches, mostly Anglican, and the other, those run by elected "school boards" of which the London School Board was by far the largest, the most efficient and the most prestigious. As a general rule, the board-supported schools were much superior to the "denominational" ones both in facilities and in the quality of teachers, and even though they were required to provide some type of "undenominational" religious teaching under the Cowper-Temple clause of the Education Act of 1870, they could nevertheless boast of themselves as the bastions of secularism in the realm of education. Originally elected to the London School Board in 1894, Wallas served on the board for 10 years, including the seven years from 1897 to 1904 as chairman of its powerful School Management Committee.

[67] Graham Wallas, "Socialists and the School Boards," *Today,* 10, no. 60 (November, 1888), 130.

[68] Shortly after the passage of the education act, Beatrice Webb made the following entry in her diary: "[Wallas] has a deeply-rooted suspicion that Sidney is playing false with regard to religious education. He wants all religious teaching abolished. As Sidney is not himself a 'religionist,' Graham thinks that he too should wish it swept away. Politically, this seems to Sidney impossible, whilst I do not desire it even if it were possible." (Beatrice Webb, *Our Partnership* [New York, 1948], pp. 256-257)

[69] Pease, *Fabian Society,* p. 156.

[70] Letter to Pease, quoted in May Wallas's letter to me dated 17 February 1972.

[71] Élie Havlévy, *A History of the English People in the Nineteenth Century,* vol. 5 ("Imperialism and the Rise of Labour: 1895-1905, trans. E. I. Watkin (London, 1929), p. 366.

[72] B. Webb, *Our Partnership,* pp. 38-39.

[73] Wallas to Shaw, 13 February 1927, G.B.S. Collection, British Museum.

[74] *Ibid.*

[75] Editorial "Commentary," *The Criterion,* 8, no. 32 (April, 1929), 378-379.

[76] Max Lerner, *Ideas,* p. 317.

[77] GS, pp. 120-121.

[78] James wrote: "I myself see things à la Tarde, perhaps too exclusively." Letter to Wallas, quoted in GS, p. 121.

Stefan Collini (essay date 1980)

SOURCE: "The Fabian Fringe Thinker," in the *Times Literary Supplement,* No. 4035, July 25, 1980, pp. 837-38.

[*In the following review of* Graham Wallas and the Great Society *by Terence H. Qualter, Collini regards Wallas's equivocal influence on modern political science.*]

> Did I remark to you that I am beginning to discover that there is a genuinely English mind? I see that when I talk to Wallas, who is full of real insights, can never concentrate on any subject, never argue about it abstractly, is always driven to the use of concrete illustration, is rarely logical, and about eight times out of ten patently in the right.

Thus Harold Laski in 1920, in one of that endless torrent of breathless letters which made Justice Holmes's old age such hard work. The combination of self-importance and banality in Laski's announcement of his discovery is not very endearing, and those who can now only know Wallas through his published work may also feel that this judgment puts his batting average a bit high. But Laski's remark does point to the central difficulty in obtaining for Wallas his historical due: his writing is informal and unsystematic in manner, and not easily classifiable in content.

Unfortunately for Wallas, authors tend to win a place in the history of social and political thought by making what is usually, and whiggishly, referred to as a "theoretical contribution". The premium on its being recognizably a *theory* is very high. One result of this exaggerated emphasis is that some writers whose basic ideas have been primarily distinguished by their high degree of risibility are accorded a lot of attention in the text-book histories because they attempted to articulate them in an often inappropriately systematic and usually unjustifiably ambitious way. By contrast, figures whose insights and judgments were shrewd, interesting and well-expressed, but who did not attempt to cast their thoughts in the form of a set of abstract propositions of putatively universal applicability get ignored.

Putting this distinction in the required, over-conceptualized, way (it is a game any number can play), one could say that the history of social thought exhibits a contrast between two basic types—the Conqueror and the Pillager. The former possesses unlimited intellectual ambitions, and having, Haussmann-like, driven a few broad, shiny concepts through the warren of historically accumulated details, he begins at once to compile a logically exhaustive Domesday survey: "there lieth within the realm of the socially possible four types of action, three modes of production, two forms of kinship, and one social reality" (best sung to a traditional Christmas air). The Pillager, on the other hand, has the collector's instinct: curious specimens are his prey, and the maxim rather than the treatise is his preferred mode of expression.

Wallas was an inveterate Pillager. His chief methodological injunction was, in effect, "always carry your notebook". In fact, his rather solemn compilation of such recommendations, published in 1926 as ***The Art of Thought,*** might well have been entitled *Teach Yourself Pillaging,* containing as it does so much practical advice about keeping newspaper cuttings and putting one's "fringe thoughts" in square brackets. (He also nicely described newspaper reading, engagingly for one who did so much of it, as "a life-long training in the bad habit of mildly enjoying and completely forgetting an infinite series of disconnected ideas".) However, whereas old Conquerors, having strutted their brief hour upon the fashionable stage, still have homage regularly paid to them in histories of the social sciences, old Pillagers pretty soon fall on hard times. Of course, very narrow criteria of human worth are at work in thus directing posterity's attention; to have worked, as Wallas did, to produce a somewhat more efficient city council or a somewhat more responsible colonial civil service may well be a worthier historical monument than the temples to intellectual megalomania with which the conquerors have cluttered up our cultural landscape. Be that as it may, it is still the fate of the Pillager's books to become the exclusive property of the curators of the museums of intellectual history.

Here, however, the second feature of Wallas's work contributes to its neglect, since it has never been clear in which room of the museum it should be exhibited. He has, to begin with, always had a guaranteed place in the Fabian room as an essayist and, with Webb and Olivier, one of the Fabian Society's "three musketeers" in its more dashing days. Interestingly, the illustration on the dust-jacket of Professor Qualter's book [*Graham Wallas and the Great Society*] reproduces the 1895 newspaper drawing of "The Extreme Left", showing Wallas and the Webbs listening, inevitably, to Shaw while sitting in a field on what looks like a typically Fabian picnic, with notebooks rather than hampers open before them and no food in sight (not even that most Fabian of dishes, the hard-boiled egg).

These days, the Fabians are second only to the Bloomsbury group as the most overstudied set of English intellectuals, and just as one fears a two-volume edition of *The Wit and Wisdom of Saxon Sydney-Turner* in the one case, so in the other a systematic study of *The Social and Political Thought of Hubert Bland* cannot be far off. (Actually, a direct contest between the two teams is hardly fair, since Bloomsbury possess the incomparable advantages of having its offspring as referees, an almost indefinite number of substitutes, and much more sex.) Wallas really only belongs to the Society's early, heroic period, since, after drifting away from it over several years, he resigned in 1904, by which time the "three musketeers", illustrating that obscure Hegelian dictum about quantitative change becoming qualitative change, had become the "old gang". These years are now very well documented, and one can follow Wallas's role in detail in the studies by McBriar, the Mackenzies, and, best of all, Willard Wolfe's *From Radicalism to Socialism.* But since of Wallas's books only the ***Life of Francis Place*** was written during this period, the museum curators still have a problem.

The "Pioneers of Political Science" room is where they have traditionally tended to dump the rest of his work. The prize exhibit here is, quite properly, his best-known book, ***Human Nature in Politics***, published in 1908. This is still widely remembered for its telling indictment of the intellectualism of nineteenth-century political theory, and for its original exploration of the role of non-rational behaviour in politics. This is, however, a rather selective memory of the book—or at least of its first half—which makes Wallas out as far more of an "irrationalist" and "Machiavellian" than he really was. Like several more famous contemporaries, he saw himself as acknowledging man's actual irrationality the better to harness his energies to serve rational purposes. Part Two of the book, revealingly entitled "The Possibilities of Progress", contains some rather feeble remedies for the problems so incisively analysed in Part One, and has consequently been forgotten. But its earnest rationalism and its somewhat pious moralism are more representative of Wallas's enterprise as a whole.

In reflecting upon the reception of the book (in the Preface to its successor, ***The Great Society***, published in 1914), Wallas recognized that, as so often, a realistic assessment of the limits of human rationality had given unintended comfort to reason's enemies: "I may, therefore, say briefly that the earlier book was an analysis of representative government, which turned into an argument against nineteenth-century intellectualism; and that this book is an analysis of the social organization of a large modern state, which has turned, at times, into an argument against certain forms of twentieth-century anti-intellectualism." In short, his complaint about intellectualism was that it gave intellect a bad name.

His chief resource in arriving at a more realistic appraisal of political behaviour was psychology, and particularly the ideas of William James. The "Early Social Psychologists" room is thus another possible home for some of Wallas's writings, especially ***Our Social Heritage*** of 1921. His work has sometimes been regarded as a rather primitive kind of political sociology, shifting the attention away from the aridities of constitution-counting and the abstractions of political theory, and towards the more richly explanatory interplay between a society's politics and other aspects of its collective life. But in fact Wallas's perspective remained stubbornly individualist and asociological: "human nature" has not, after all, been the most favoured concept among sociologists. His theoretical allegiances were rather what might be called "ethological": he was far more interested in what could be learnt about man's inherited responses from comparative studies of animals than he was in, say, questions of class and social structure. In some ways, he belongs more naturally in the company of a social psychologist like McDougall than with political sociologists, like Michels and Mosca, with whom he is more usually bracketed.

This not entirely satisfactory classification of Wallas, as well, perhaps, as the eminently forgettable nature of so much political science (of which he was the first Professor, so designated, in this country), was well caught in a confessional remark of his admirer, Alfred Zimmern: "I can never remember what he is supposed to be Professor of, but if it is not Social Psychology it ought to be". And the fact that he was, from 1914, a professor should remind us that he also figures among the Founding Persons of the LSE (he was, technically, its first director though he never took up the office), and an important force in the development of the University of London.

As all this suggests, Wallas exemplifies a type which is, for obvious reasons, very poorly served by the retrospective tunnel-vision of the social scientist scrutinizing the past for commendable professional predecessors. Instead, he is the kind of figure who most requires and rewards the more catholic and finely-textured approach of the intellectual historian, who can be sufficiently alert to the diverse dimensions of his life and work, and sufficiently at home in their historical setting, to be able to portray their features in the round.

Wallas has, in fact, already been the subject of one such study, namely Martin Wiener's *Between Two Worlds: The*

Political Thought of Graham Wallas, published in 1971. More recently, he has also been one of the central figures in several more wide-ranging pieces of intellectual history, most notably Peter Clarke's *Liberals and Social Democrats.* All this, obviously and rightly, gave Professor Qualter cause for pause. As he disarmingly tells us in his preface, he had for many years nursed the ambition to write "the first book on Graham Wallas". Time alas, waits for no book, and he has had to settle for a more modest aim. He offers a few understandably defensive remarks about the relationship of his study to Wiener's, with which he has "no quarrel" but from which he sees his own as differing in "style" and "emphasis". I fear that there will be a rather small number of people wanting to read *two* books on Graham Wallas, and that those who want to read one will do better with Wiener's. Professor Qualter's is certainly a competent brief study, paraphrasing and quoting extensively from a wide range of Wallas's published writings. But where he writes as a Professor of Political Science, primarily interested in Wallas's "contribution" and its "relevance", Wiener wrote as an historian, more sensitive to the chronology and complexity of Wallas's thought, drawing upon a more diverse selection of sources (especially manuscript sources), and exhibiting a surer grasp of the political and intellectual life of turn-of-the-century Britain.

The attempt to infuse modern industrial civilization with some of the cherished qualities of the ancient city-states is what Professor Qualter sees as the central and enduring theme of Wallas's oeuvre, with a commitment to education in the widest sense as the means by which this was to be most securely effected. Concentration upon this theme does have the merit of putting Wallas's moralism (and, for that matter, his classicism) at the centre of the discussion. And yet it is one of those plausible, nebulous affirmations of good intentions to which almost any social thinker might put his name, without thereby being committed to any of the actual causes which the historical Wallas saw as its corollaries. Professor Qualter writes well about Wallas's expertise in the psychology of education—he must have been a formidable presence on the London School Board—and yet, for all the admirably clear summaries of the "doctrines" and "positions" which he upheld, the distinctive quality of Wallas's mind remains rather elusive.

Two of his own favourite phrases provide suggestive ways of characterizing that quality. He intended his ideas to be useful to what he called "the working thinker", and he repeatedly celebrated Bentham's achievements as "a political inventor". In neither case, it is worth remarking, does the characterization assign primary importance to *writing.* Wallas himself touched upon this in a typical piece of soul-searching: having reached the age of fifty, and having only just published his second book, he wondered, in an unpublished letter to Shaw,

> Whether I have been entirely "futile", and I am blessed if I know. If I had done a day's work every day at writing, I could have produced more books, and perhaps it has been stupid of me not to have done so. But I have never looked upon myself as a professional writer. My "Works of Charles Lamb" have been the bound volumes of committee minutes, and the notebooks of people who have been to my lectures. I have helped to keep the School of Economics going, and every elementary school in London is really different in its looks, the size of its classes, its medical inspector, the selection of its teachers and its general efficiency from what it would have been had I not gone bald-headed into the School Board in 1894. The books which I did not write would, I think, have been about as good as J. A. Hobson's. It may be that I should have got more done by means of them than by direct administration. But I am not at all sure.

Both the self-doubt and the self-congratulation in this testament may strike a responsive chord in some of his readers, though his estimation of the quality of the books he did not write is more accurate than many could manage. Still, maybe the literary and political ambitions which are implicit in this confession have not been entirely frustrated: this *is,* after all, the second book on Graham Wallas, whilst Hobson still awaits his first.

"Political inventor" also conveys something of the Heath Robinson quality of Wallas's work. He was the self-improving industrious artisan of social thought, very much the Aristotle of the evening classes. He was knowledgeable about an impressive range of topics and able to link them up in unpredictable ways, though the image his mind suggests is always that of the cluttered attic rather than the neatly-ordered filing cabinet. He squirrelled pieces of information away on the venerable grounds that "they might come in useful", as they often did. When, for example, he wishes, in developing his version of the distinction between nature and nurture, to underline the fact that non-human animals, too, learn certain patterns of behaviour which are not inherited, he rummages through his mental lumber-room till he finds just the thing: "In New Zealand the 'mountain parrot' apparently hands down by social inheritance the art of attacking sheep's kidneys". *Voilà tout!*

Presumably, political inventors live on, if at all, through their patents, though I doubt if Wallas's descendants are living it up on royalties from grateful governments. Teachers, it is said, live on in the memories—and, after a time, the recorded memories—of their pupils, and there is abundant testimony to Wallas's skills and influence not only as a lecturer and tutor, but also in the exercise of the very peculiar craft of supervising research students. Much of his best writing certainly bears some of the marks of the good lecture—clear, arresting, provocative, but ultimately unsatisfying. In his day, he was regarded as an absolutely outstanding lecturer. "His lecture room at the LSE", Laski recalled, "was an amazing sight. Half the nationalities of the world had their representatives there; and one had only to scan their faces to realize that what he said opened new and attractive horizons to them". For all the celebration of his pedagogic skills, however, it could not be said that he founded a "school", or even that he permanently altered the study of politics. And for all the self-conscious iconoclasm of ***Human Nature in Politics***, from this distance his career looks like another example of the immense resilience of the class of genteel, classically-educated, well-read amateurs in English public life.

As a young man, he had naturally defined himself by what he was against. The son of a clergyman, he was dismissed from schoolmastering in his twenties for refusing to take communion, and thereafter he maintained an implacable anti-clericalism, always, as Beatrice Webb noted, looking for "the priest behind the policy". He was a product of Shrewsbury and Oxford who held by Darwin and Socialism. In "advanced" circles in London in the 1880s this provided a gratifyingly fashionable and radical identity.

But such antagonisms presumed, as always, a sufficiently close community of concerns with those from whom he differed. There was some truth in the jibe that he was "a bishop manqué", and his intellectual tastes were certainly more traditional than his official self-description would lead one to believe. In his writing about the study of politics, for example, Wallas's bogey was always the subject as taught at Oxford. Even in his fifties he could still spit fire at "what passes in Oxford for the study of politics", and how it "represents a conscious or half-conscious attempt to substitute a satisfying picture of that which does not exist, for an unsatisfying picture of that which does exist". And yet his own concerns and points of reference remained very much those of the college tutor. His Fabian essay began by taking issue with Austin's canonical definition of property; thirty years later he still felt compelled to devote several pages of ***Our Social Heritage*** to disputing Mill's account of liberty.

This continuity with the tradition of political thought which he ostensibly rejected was marked, above all, in his preoccupation with Aristotle. He could sneer at how "Aristotle, the student of morals and politics, has occupied in nineteenth and twentieth-century Oxford a position nearly as important as Aristotle, the logician, in the Oxford of the Middle Ages", but in this respect Wallas had what might now be called an ongoing pot-and-kettle-type relationship with Oxford. Aristotle was nearly always the most frequently cited authority in his books, outdoing even Darwin and William James, and one of the most self-congratulatory things he could think to say in his increasingly self-congratulatory old age (according to Laski's unsympathetic and perhaps unreliable report) was that no one had "put psychology in its proper perspective between Aristotle and my Human Nature in Politics". In his earliest substantial publication, in the Socialist journal *Today* in 1888, Wallas had addressed himself to the theme of **"Aristotle on Wealth and Property"**, inquiring, with bland anachronism, "how far Aristotle's study and criticism of the various forms of society which he knew, led him towards a general science of sociology". As it turned out, his preoccupation with Aristotle was to outlast that with sociology, and in that, at least, he may have been representative of one rather localized but enduring manifestation of that "English mind" which Laski thought he had discovered.

FURTHER READING

Bibliography

Moran, Michael G., Michael E. Rukstelis, and Daniel A. Roberts. "Graham Wallas (1858-1932): A Bibliography." *Bulletin of Bibliography* 45, No. 3 (1988): 194-203.

Chronological bibliography of primary and secondary sources preceded by a brief introduction to Wallas's work.

Criticism

Beardsley, Monroe Curtis. "'Rationality' in Conduct: Wallas and Pareto." *Ethics* LIV, No. 2 (January 1944): 79-95.

Disputes several fallacies related to "nonlogical" human conduct presented in the works of Wallas and Vilfredo Pareto.

Bowle, John. "Modern Sociologists: Durkheim on Environment: Graham Wallas and Social Psychology." In *Politics and Opinion in the Nineteenth Century: An Historical Introduction*, pp. 445-64. London: Jonathan Cape, 1954.

Considers Wallas as a pioneer in the study of the sociological effects of the subconscious mind.

Clarke, Peter. "Human Nature in Politics." In *Liberals and Social Democrats*, pp. 128-63. Cambridge: Cambridge University Press, 1978.

Evaluates Wallas's *Human Nature in Politics* within its cultural and historical contexts.

Colby, F. M. Review of *Human Nature in Politics*. *Bookman* 30, No. 4 (December 1909): 396-99.

Dismissive review of Wallas's *Human Nature in Politics*, which finds his observations of irrationality in political behavior to be somewhat obvious.

Dewey, John. Review of *The Art of Thought*. *New Republic* XLVII, No. 602 (16 June 1926): 118-19.

Finds Wallas's *The Art of Thought* to be insightful and useful as a pedagogical text, but in many ways disappointing.

Lerner, Max. "Graham Wallas: The Fabian or the Tiger?" In *Ideas Are Weapons: The History and Uses of Ideas*, pp. 314-18. New York: Viking Press, 1939.

Brief survey of Wallas that sees his thought as poised between belief in rational collectivism and in the irrationality of human beings as social creatures.

Namier, Sir Lewis. "Human Nature in Politics." In *Personalities and Politics*, pp. 1-7. New York: The Macmillan Company, 1955.

Explores Wallas's critique of rational behavior, citing historical examples of political irrationality.

Qualter, T. H. "The Manipulation of Popular Impulse: Graham Wallas Revisited." *The Canadian Journal of Economics and Political Science* XXV, No. 2 (May 1959): 165-73.

Examines Wallas's treatment of the theme of propaganda as a threat to democracy in *The Great Society*.

———. *Graham Wallas and the Great Society*. New York: Macmillan, 1980, 204 p.

Discusses Wallas's contributions and relevance to the field of political science, particularly in relation to his concern with education and classical ethics.

Seligman, Edwin R. A. Review of *The Life of Francis Place: 1771-1854*. *Political Science Quarterly* XIII, No. 3 (September 1898): 572.

Favorable assessment of Wallas's biography *The Life of Francis Place*.

Vincent, George E. Review of *Human Nature in Politics*. *The Hibbert Journal* VII (1909): 930-33.

Regards Wallas's analysis of "non-rational inference" and emphasis on the quantitative estimation of social forces as sagacious, while acknowledging his failure "to appreciate the part which custom and sentiment play in preserving the stability of society."

Wiener, Martin J. *Between Two Worlds: The Political Thought of Graham Wallas*. Oxford: Clarendon Press, 1971, 229 p.

Study of Wallas's ideas and of their immediate and lasting effects.

Twentieth-Century Literary Criticism

Cumulative Indexes
Volumes 1-91

How to Use This Index

The main references

Calvino, Italo 1923–1985 .... **CLC 5, 8, 11, 22, 33, 39, 73; SSC 3**

list all author entries in the following Gale Literary Criticism series:

BLC = *Black Literature Criticism*
CLC = *Contemporary Literary Criticism*
CLR = *Children's Literature Review*
CMLC = *Classical and Medieval Literature Criticism*
DA = *DISCovering Authors*
DAB = *DISCovering Authors: British*
DAC = *DISCovering Authors: Canadian*
DAM = *DISCovering Authors: Modules*
DRAM*: Dramatists Module;* ***MST****: Most-Studied Authors Module;*
MULT*: Multicultural Authors Module;* ***NOV****: Novelists Module;*
POET*: Poets Module;* ***POP****: Popular Fiction and Genre Authors Module*
DC = *Drama Criticism*
HLC = *Hispanic Literature Criticism*
LC = *Literature Criticism from 1400 to 1800*
NCLC = *Nineteenth-Century Literature Criticism*
PC = *Poetry Criticism*
SSC = *Short Story Criticism*
TCLC = *Twentieth-Century Literary Criticism*
WLC = *World Literature Criticism, 1500 to the Present*

The cross-references

See also CANR 23; CA 85-88; obituary CA116

list all author entries in the following Gale biographical and literary sources:

AAYA = *Authors & Artists for Young Adults*
AITN = *Authors in the News*
BEST = *Bestsellers*
BW = *Black Writers*
CA = *Contemporary Authors*
CAAS = *Contemporary Authors Autobiography Series*
CABS = *Contemporary Authors Bibliographical Series*
CANR = *Contemporary Authors New Revision Series*
CAP = *Contemporary Authors Permanent Series*
CDALB = *Concise Dictionary of American Literary Biography*
CDBLB = *Concise Dictionary of British Literary Biography*
DLB = *Dictionary of Literary Biography*
DLBD = *Dictionary of Literary Biography Documentary Series*
DLBY = *Dictionary of Literary Biography Yearbook*
HW = *Hispanic Writers*
JRDA = *Junior DISCovering Authors*
MAICYA = *Major Authors and Illustrators for Children and Young Adults*
MTCW = *Major 20th-Century Writers*
NNAL = *Native North American Literature*
SAAS = *Something about the Author Autobiography Series*
SATA = *Something about the Author*
YABC = *Yesterday's Authors of Books for Children*

Literary Criticism Series Cumulative Author Index

20/1631
See Upward, Allen
A/C Cross
See Lawrence, T(homas) E(dward)
Abasiyanik, Sait Faik 1906-1954
See Sait Faik
See also CA 123
Abbey, Edward 1927-1989 .... **CLC 36, 59**
See also CA 45-48; 128; CANR 2, 41; MTCW 2
Abbott, Lee K(ittredge) 1947- .... **CLC 48**
See also CA 124; CANR 51; DLB 130
Abe, Kobo 1924-1993**CLC 8, 22, 53, 81; DAM NOV**
See also CA 65-68; 140; CANR 24, 60; DLB 182; MTCW 1, 2
Abelard, Peter c. 1079-c. 1142 .... **CMLC 11**
See also DLB 115, 208
Abell, Kjeld 1901-1961 .... **CLC 15**
See also CA 111
Abish, Walter 1931- .... **CLC 22**
See also CA 101; CANR 37; DLB 130
Abrahams, Peter (Henry) 1919- .... **CLC 4**
See also BW 1; CA 57-60; CANR 26; DLB 117; MTCW 1, 2
Abrams, M(eyer) H(oward) 1912- .... **CLC 24**
See also CA 57-60; CANR 13, 33; DLB 67
Abse, Dannie 1923-**CLC 7, 29; DAB; DAM POET**
See also CA 53-56; CAAS 1; CANR 4, 46, 74; DLB 27; MTCW 1
Achebe, (Albert) Chinua(lumogu) 1930-**CLC 1, 3, 5, 7, 11, 26, 51, 75; BLC 1; DA; DAB; DAC; DAM MST, MULT, NOV; WLC**
See also AAYA 15; BW 2, 3; CA 1-4R; CANR 6, 26, 47; CLR 20; DLB 117; MAICYA; MTCW 1, 2; SATA 38, 40; SATA-Brief 38
Acker, Kathy 1948-1997 .... **CLC 45, 111**
See also CA 117; 122; 162; CANR 55
Ackroyd, Peter 1949- .... **CLC 34, 52**
See also CA 123; 127; CANR 51, 74; DLB 155; INT 127; MTCW 1
Acorn, Milton 1923- .... **CLC 15; DAC**
See also CA 103; DLB 53; INT 103
Adamov, Arthur 1908-1970 ..... **CLC 4, 25; DAM DRAM**
See also CA 17-18; 25-28R; CAP 2; MTCW 1
Adams, Alice (Boyd) 1926-**CLC 6, 13, 46; SSC 24**
See also CA 81-84; CANR 26, 53, 75; DLBY 86; INT CANR-26; MTCW 1, 2
Adams, Andy 1859-1935 .... **TCLC 56**
See also YABC 1
Adams, Brooks 1848-1927 .... **TCLC 80**
See also CA 123; DLB 47
Adams, Douglas (Noel) 1952-**CLC 27, 60; DAM POP**
See also AAYA 4; BEST 89:3; CA 106; CANR 34, 64; DLBY 83; JRDA; MTCW 1
Adams, Francis 1862-1893 .... **NCLC 33**
Adams, Henry (Brooks) 1838-1918 **TCLC 4, 52; DA; DAB; DAC; DAM MST**
See also CA 104; 133; CANR 77; DLB 12, 47, 189; MTCW 1
Adams, Richard (George) 1920- .. **CLC 4, 5, 18; DAM NOV**
See also AAYA 16; AITN 1, 2; CA 49-52; CANR 3, 35; CLR 20; JRDA; MAICYA; MTCW 1, 2; SATA 7, 69
Adamson, Joy(-Friederike Victoria) 1910-1980 **CLC 17**
See also CA 69-72; 93-96; CANR 22; MTCW 1; SATA 11; SATA-Obit 22
Adcock, Fleur 1934- .... **CLC 41**
See also CA 25-28R; CAAS 23; CANR 11, 34, 69; DLB 40
Addams, Charles (Samuel) 1912-1988 .. **CLC 30**
See also CA 61-64; 126; CANR 12, 79
Addams, Jane 1860-1945 .... **TCLC 76**
Addison, Joseph 1672-1719 .... **LC 18**
See also CDBLB 1660-1789; DLB 101
Adler, Alfred (F.) 1870-1937 .... **TCLC 61**
See also CA 119; 159
Adler, C(arole) S(chwerdtfeger) 1932- . **CLC 35**
See also AAYA 4; CA 89-92; CANR 19, 40; JRDA; MAICYA; SAAS 15; SATA 26, 63, 102
Adler, Renata 1938- .... **CLC 8, 31**
See also CA 49-52; CANR 5, 22, 52; MTCW 1
Ady, Endre 1877-1919 .... **TCLC 11**
See also CA 107
A.E. 1867-1935 .... **TCLC 3, 10**
See also Russell, George William
Aeschylus 525B.C.-456B.C.**CMLC 11; DA; DAB; DAC; DAM DRAM, MST; DC 8; WLCS**
See also DLB 176
Aesop 620(?)B.C.-564(?)B.C. .... **CMLC 24**
See also CLR 14; MAICYA; SATA 64
Affable Hawk
See MacCarthy, Sir(Charles Otto) Desmond
Africa, Ben
See Bosman, Herman Charles
Afton, Effie
See Harper, Frances Ellen Watkins
Agapida, Fray Antonio
See Irving, Washington
Agee, James (Rufus) 1909-1955 ..... **TCLC 1, 19; DAM NOV**
See also AITN 1; CA 108; 148; CDALB 1941-1968; DLB 2, 26, 152; MTCW 1
Aghill, Gordon
See Silverberg, Robert
Agnon, S(hmuel) Y(osef Halevi) 1888-1970 **CLC 4, 8, 14; SSC 30**
See also CA 17-18; 25-28R; CANR 60; CAP 2; MTCW 1, 2
Agrippa von Nettesheim, Henry Cornelius 1486-1535 .... **LC 27**
Aherne, Owen
See Cassill, R(onald) V(erlin)
Ai 1947- .... **CLC 4, 14, 69**
See also CA 85-88; CAAS 13; CANR 70; DLB 120
Aickman, Robert (Fordyce) 1914-1981 . **CLC 57**
See also CA 5-8R; CANR 3, 72
Aiken, Conrad (Potter) 1889-1973 .. **CLC 1, 3, 5, 10, 52; DAM NOV, POET; PC 26; SSC 9**
See also CA 5-8R; 45-48; CANR 4, 60; CDALB 1929-1941; DLB 9, 45, 102; MTCW 1, 2; SATA 3, 30
Aiken, Joan (Delano) 1924- .... **CLC 35**
See also AAYA 1, 25; CA 9-12R; CANR 4, 23, 34, 64; CLR 1, 19; DLB 161; JRDA; MAICYA; MTCW 1; SAAS 1; SATA 2, 30, 73
Ainsworth, William Harrison 1805-1882 **NCLC 13**
See also DLB 21; SATA 24
Aitmatov, Chingiz (Torekulovich) 1928- **CLC 71**
See also CA 103; CANR 38; MTCW 1; SATA 56
Akers, Floyd
See Baum, L(yman) Frank
Akhmadulina, Bella Akhatovna 1937- **CLC 53; DAM POET**
See also CA 65-68
Akhmatova, Anna 1888-1966**CLC 11, 25, 64; DAM POET; PC 2**
See also CA 19-20; 25-28R; CANR 35; CAP 1; MTCW 1, 2
Aksakov, Sergei Timofeyvich 1791-1859**NCLC 2**
See also DLB 198
Aksenov, Vassily
See Aksyonov, Vassily (Pavlovich)
Akst, Daniel 1956- .... **CLC 109**
See also CA 161
Aksyonov, Vassily (Pavlovich) 1932-**CLC 22, 37, 101**
See also CA 53-56; CANR 12, 48, 77
Akutagawa, Ryunosuke 1892-1927 ..... **TCLC 16**
See also CA 117; 154
Alain 1868-1951 .... **TCLC 41**
See also CA 163
Alain-Fournier .... **TCLC 6**
See also Fournier, Henri Alban
See also DLB 65
Alarcon, Pedro Antonio de 1833-1891 .. **NCLC 1**
Alas (y Urena), Leopoldo (Enrique Garcia) 1852-1901 .... **TCLC 29**
See also CA 113; 131; HW 1
Albee, Edward (Franklin III) 1928-**CLC 1, 2, 3, 5, 9, 11, 13, 25, 53, 86, 113; DA; DAB; DAC; DAM DRAM, MST; DC 11; WLC**
See also AITN 1; CA 5-8R; CABS 3; CANR 8, 54, 74; CDALB 1941-1968; DLB 7; INT CANR-8; MTCW 1, 2
Alberti, Rafael 1902- .... **CLC 7**
See also CA 85-88; CANR 81; DLB 108; HW 2
Albert the Great 1200(?)-1280 .... **CMLC 16**
See also DLB 115
Alcala-Galiano, Juan Valera y
See Valera y Alcala-Galiano, Juan
Alcott, Amos Bronson 1799-1888 .... **NCLC 1**
See also DLB 1
Alcott, Louisa May 1832-1888 **NCLC 6, 58; DA; DAB; DAC; DAM MST, NOV; SSC 27; WLC**
See also AAYA 20; CDALB 1865-1917; CLR 1, 38; DLB 1, 42, 79; DLBD 14; JRDA; MAICYA; SATA 100; YABC 1
Aldanov, M. A.
See Aldanov, Mark (Alexandrovich)
Aldanov, Mark (Alexandrovich) 1886(?)-1957 **TCLC 23**
See also CA 118
Aldington, Richard 1892-1962 .... **CLC 49**
See also CA 85-88; CANR 45; DLB 20, 36, 100, 149
Aldiss, Brian W(ilson) 1925-**CLC 5, 14, 40; DAM NOV**
See also CA 5-8R; CAAS 2; CANR 5, 28, 64; DLB 14; MTCW 1, 2; SATA 34
Alegria, Claribel 1924-**CLC 75; DAM MULT; PC 26**
See also CA 131; CAAS 15; CANR 66; DLB 145; HW 1; MTCW 1
Alegria, Fernando 1918- .... **CLC 57**
See also CA 9-12R; CANR 5, 32, 72; HW 1, 2
Aleichem, Sholom .... **TCLC 1, 35; SSC 33**

See also Rabinovitch, Sholem
Alepoudelis, Odysseus
See Elytis, Odysseus
Aleshkovsky, Joseph 1929-
See Aleshkovsky, Yuz
See also CA 121; 128
Aleshkovsky, Yuz .... **CLC 44**
See also Aleshkovsky, Joseph
Alexander, Lloyd (Chudley) 1924- .... **CLC 35**
See also AAYA 1, 27; CA 1-4R; CANR 1, 24, 38, 55; CLR 1, 5, 48; DLB 52; JRDA; MAICYA; MTCW 1; SAAS 19; SATA 3, 49, 81
Alexander, Meena 1951- .... **CLC 121**
See also CA 115; CANR 38, 70
Alexander, Samuel 1859-1938 .... **TCLC 77**
Alexie, Sherman (Joseph, Jr.) 1966- ... **CLC 96; DAM MULT**
See also AAYA 28; CA 138; CANR 65; DLB 175, 206; MTCW 1; NNAL
Alfau, Felipe 1902- .... **CLC 66**
See also CA 137
Alger, Horatio, Jr. 1832-1899 .... **NCLC 8**
See also DLB 42; SATA 16
Algren, Nelson 1909-1981 **CLC 4, 10, 33; SSC 33**
See also CA 13-16R; 103; CANR 20, 61; CDALB 1941-1968; DLB 9; DLBY 81, 82; MTCW 1, 2
Ali, Ahmed 1910- .... **CLC 69**
See also CA 25-28R; CANR 15, 34
Alighieri, Dante
See Dante
Allan, John B.
See Westlake, Donald E(dwin)
Allan, Sidney
See Hartmann, Sadakichi
Allan, Sydney
See Hartmann, Sadakichi
Allen, Edward 1948- .... **CLC 59**
Allen, Fred 1894-1956 .... **TCLC 87**
Allen, Paula Gunn 1939- . **CLC 84; DAM MULT**
See also CA 112; 143; CANR 63; DLB 175; MTCW 1; NNAL
Allen, Roland
See Ayckbourn, Alan
Allen, Sarah A.
See Hopkins, Pauline Elizabeth
Allen, Sidney H.
See Hartmann, Sadakichi
Allen, Woody 1935- ...... **CLC 16, 52; DAM POP**
See also AAYA 10; CA 33-36R; CANR 27, 38, 63; DLB 44; MTCW 1
Allende, Isabel 1942- **CLC 39, 57, 97; DAM MULT, NOV; HLC; WLCS**
See also AAYA 18; CA 125; 130; CANR 51, 74; DLB 145; HW 1, 2; INT 130; MTCW 1, 2
Alleyn, Ellen
See Rossetti, Christina (Georgina)
Allingham, Margery (Louise) 1904-1966 **CLC 19**
See also CA 5-8R; 25-28R; CANR 4, 58; DLB 77; MTCW 1, 2
Allingham, William 1824-1889 .... **NCLC 25**
See also DLB 35
Allison, Dorothy E. 1949- .... **CLC 78**
See also CA 140; CANR 66; MTCW 1
Allston, Washington 1779-1843 .... **NCLC 2**
See also DLB 1
Almedingen, E. M. .... **CLC 12**
See also Almedingen, Martha Edith von
See also SATA 3
Almedingen, Martha Edith von 1898-1971
See Almedingen, E. M.
See also CA 1-4R; CANR 1
Almodovar, Pedro 1949(?)- ... **CLC 114; HLCS 1**
See also CA 133; CANR 72; HW 2
Almqvist, Carl Jonas Love 1793-1866 . **NCLC 42**
Alonso, Damaso 1898-1990 .... **CLC 14**
See also CA 110; 131; 130; CANR 72; DLB 108; HW 1, 2
Alov
See Gogol, Nikolai (Vasilyevich)
Alta 1942- .... **CLC 19**
See also CA 57-60
Alter, Robert B(ernard) 1935- .... **CLC 34**
See also CA 49-52; CANR 1, 47
Alther, Lisa 1944- .... **CLC 7, 41**
See also CA 65-68; CAAS 30; CANR 12, 30, 51; MTCW 1
Althusser, L.
See Althusser, Louis
Althusser, Louis 1918-1990 .... **CLC 106**
See also CA 131; 132
Altman, Robert 1925- .... **CLC 16, 116**
See also CA 73-76; CANR 43
Alvarez, A(lfred) 1929- .... **CLC 5, 13**
See also CA 1-4R; CANR 3, 33, 63; DLB 14, 40
Alvarez, Alejandro Rodriguez 1903-1965
See Casona, Alejandro
See also CA 131; 93-96; HW 1
Alvarez, Julia 1950- .... **CLC 93; HLCS 1**
See also AAYA 25; CA 147; CANR 69; MTCW 1
Alvaro, Corrado 1896-1956 .... **TCLC 60**
See also CA 163
Amado, Jorge 1912- ..... **CLC 13, 40, 106; DAM MULT, NOV; HLC**
See also CA 77-80; CANR 35, 74; DLB 113; HW 2; MTCW 1, 2
Ambler, Eric 1909-1998 .... **CLC 4, 6, 9**
See also CA 9-12R; 171; CANR 7, 38, 74; DLB 77; MTCW 1, 2
Amichai, Yehuda 1924- .... **CLC 9, 22, 57, 116**
See also CA 85-88; CANR 46, 60; MTCW 1
Amichai, Yehudah
See Amichai, Yehuda
Amiel, Henri Frederic 1821-1881 .... **NCLC 4**
Amis, Kingsley (William) 1922-1995 **CLC 1, 2, 3, 5, 8, 13, 40, 44; DA; DAB; DAC; DAM MST, NOV**
See also AITN 2; CA 9-12R; 150; CANR 8, 28, 54; CDBLB 1945-1960; DLB 15, 27, 100, 139; DLBY 96; INT CANR-8; MTCW 1, 2
Amis, Martin (Louis) 1949- **CLC 4, 9, 38, 62, 101**
See also BEST 90:3; CA 65-68; CANR 8, 27, 54, 73; DLB 14, 194; INT CANR-27; MTCW 1
Ammons, A(rchie) R(andolph) 1926- **CLC 2, 3, 5, 8, 9, 25, 57, 108; DAM POET; PC 16**
See also AITN 1; CA 9-12R; CANR 6, 36, 51, 73; DLB 5, 165; MTCW 1, 2
Amo, Tauraatua i
See Adams, Henry (Brooks)
Amory, Thomas 1691(?)-1788 .... **LC 48**
Anand, Mulk Raj 1905- **CLC 23, 93; DAM NOV**
See also CA 65-68; CANR 32, 64; MTCW 1, 2
Anatol
See Schnitzler, Arthur
Anaximander c. 610B.C.-c. 546B.C. .... **CMLC 22**
Anaya, Rudolfo A(lfonso) 1937- .. **CLC 23; DAM MULT, NOV; HLC**
See also AAYA 20; CA 45-48; CAAS 4; CANR 1, 32, 51; DLB 82, 206; HW 1; MTCW 1, 2
Andersen, Hans Christian 1805-1875 **NCLC 7, 79; DA; DAB; DAC; DAM MST, POP; SSC 6; WLC**
See also CLR 6; MAICYA; SATA 100; YABC 1
Anderson, C. Farley
See Mencken, H(enry) L(ouis); Nathan, George Jean
Anderson, Jessica (Margaret) Queale 1916- **CLC 37**
See also CA 9-12R; CANR 4, 62
Anderson, Jon (Victor) 1940- **CLC 9; DAM POET**
See also CA 25-28R; CANR 20
Anderson, Lindsay (Gordon) 1923-1994 **CLC 20**
See also CA 125; 128; 146; CANR 77
Anderson, Maxwell 1888-1959 ... **TCLC 2; DAM DRAM**
See also CA 105; 152; DLB 7; MTCW 2
Anderson, Poul (William) 1926- .... **CLC 15**
See also AAYA 5; CA 1-4R; CAAS 2; CANR 2, 15, 34, 64; CLR 58; DLB 8; INT CANR-15; MTCW 1, 2; SATA 90; SATA-Brief 39; SATA-Essay 106
Anderson, Robert (Woodruff) 1917- .... **CLC 23; DAM DRAM**
See also AITN 1; CA 21-24R; CANR 32; DLB 7
Anderson, Sherwood 1876-1941 **TCLC 1, 10, 24; DA; DAB; DAC; DAM MST, NOV; SSC 1; WLC**
See also AAYA 30; CA 104; 121; CANR 61; CDALB 1917-1929; DLB 4, 9, 86; DLBD 1; MTCW 1, 2
Andier, Pierre
See Desnos, Robert
Andouard
See Giraudoux, (Hippolyte) Jean
Andrade, Carlos Drummond de .... **CLC 18**
See also Drummond de Andrade, Carlos
Andrade, Mario de 1893-1945 .... **TCLC 43**
Andreae, Johann V(alentin) 1586-1654 ... **LC 32**
See also DLB 164
Andreas-Salome, Lou 1861-1937 .... **TCLC 56**
See also DLB 66
Andress, Lesley
See Sanders, Lawrence
Andrewes, Lancelot 1555-1626 .... **LC 5**
See also DLB 151, 172
Andrews, Cicily Fairfield
See West, Rebecca
Andrews, Elton V.
See Pohl, Frederik
Andreyev, Leonid (Nikolaevich) 1871-1919 **TCLC 3**
See also CA 104
Andric, Ivo 1892-1975 .... **CLC 8**
See also CA 81-84; 57-60; CANR 43, 60; DLB 147; MTCW 1
Androvar
See Prado (Calvo), Pedro
Angelique, Pierre
See Bataille, Georges
Angell, Roger 1920- .... **CLC 26**
See also CA 57-60; CANR 13, 44, 70; DLB 171, 185
Angelou, Maya 1928- **CLC 12, 35, 64, 77; BLC 1; DA; DAB; DAC; DAM MST, MULT, POET, POP; WLCS**
See also AAYA 7, 20; BW 2, 3; CA 65-68; CANR 19, 42, 65; CDALBS; CLR 53; DLB 38; MTCW 1, 2; SATA 49
Anna Comnena 1083-1153 .... **CMLC 25**
Annensky, Innokenty (Fyodorovich) 1856-1909 **TCLC 14**
See also CA 110; 155
Annunzio, Gabriele d'
See D'Annunzio, Gabriele
Anodos
See Coleridge, Mary E(lizabeth)
Anon, Charles Robert
See Pessoa, Fernando (Antonio Nogueira)
Anouilh, Jean (Marie Lucien Pierre) 1910-1987 **CLC 1, 3, 8, 13, 40, 50; DAM DRAM; DC 8**
See also CA 17-20R; 123; CANR 32; MTCW 1, 2
Anthony, Florence
See Ai
Anthony, John
See Ciardi, John (Anthony)
Anthony, Peter
See Shaffer, Anthony (Joshua); Shaffer, Peter (Levin)
Anthony, Piers 1934- .... **CLC 35; DAM POP**
See also AAYA 11; CA 21-24R; CANR 28, 56, 73; DLB 8; MTCW 1, 2; SAAS 22; SATA 84
Anthony, Susan B(rownell) 1916-1991 **TCLC 84**

See also CA 89-92; 134
Antoine, Marc
See Proust, (Valentin-Louis-George-Eugene-) Marcel
Antoninus, Brother
See Everson, William (Oliver)
Antonioni, Michelangelo 1912- .... **CLC 20**
See also CA 73-76; CANR 45, 77
Antschel, Paul 1920-1970
See Celan, Paul
See also CA 85-88; CANR 33, 61; MTCW 1
Anwar, Chairil 1922-1949 .... **TCLC 22**
See also CA 121
Apess, William 1798-1839(?) ... **NCLC 73; DAM MULT**
See also DLB 175; NNAL
Apollinaire, Guillaume 1880-1918**TCLC 3, 8, 51; DAM POET; PC 7**
See also Kostrowitzki, Wilhelm Apollinaris de
See also CA 152; MTCW 1
Appelfeld, Aharon 1932- .... **CLC 23, 47**
See also CA 112; 133
Apple, Max (Isaac) 1941- .... **CLC 9, 33**
See also CA 81-84; CANR 19, 54; DLB 130
Appleman, Philip (Dean) 1926- .... **CLC 51**
See also CA 13-16R; CAAS 18; CANR 6, 29, 56
Appleton, Lawrence
See Lovecraft, H(oward) P(hillips)
Apteryx
See Eliot, T(homas) S(tearns)
Apuleius, (Lucius Madaurensis) 125(?)-175(?) **CMLC 1**
See also DLB 211
Aquin, Hubert 1929-1977 .... **CLC 15**
See also CA 105; DLB 53
Aquinas, Thomas 1224(?)-1274 .... **CMLC 33**
See also DLB 115
Aragon, Louis 1897-1982**CLC 3, 22; DAM NOV, POET**
See also CA 69-72; 108; CANR 28, 71; DLB 72; MTCW 1, 2
Arany, Janos 1817-1882 .... **NCLC 34**
Aranyos, Kakay
See Mikszath, Kalman
Arbuthnot, John 1667-1735 .... **LC 1**
See also DLB 101
Archer, Herbert Winslow
See Mencken, H(enry) L(ouis)
Archer, Jeffrey (Howard) 1940- .. **CLC 28; DAM POP**
See also AAYA 16; BEST 89:3; CA 77-80; CANR 22, 52; INT CANR-22
Archer, Jules 1915- .... **CLC 12**
See also CA 9-12R; CANR 6, 69; SAAS 5; SATA 4, 85
Archer, Lee
See Ellison, Harlan (Jay)
Arden, John 1930- **CLC 6, 13, 15; DAM DRAM**
See also CA 13-16R; CAAS 4; CANR 31, 65, 67; DLB 13; MTCW 1
Arenas, Reinaldo 1943-1990**CLC 41; DAM MULT; HLC**
See also CA 124; 128; 133; CANR 73; DLB 145; HW 1; MTCW 1
Arendt, Hannah 1906-1975 .... **CLC 66, 98**
See also CA 17-20R; 61-64; CANR 26, 60; MTCW 1, 2
Aretino, Pietro 1492-1556 .... **LC 12**
Arghezi, Tudor 1880-1967 .... **CLC 80**
See also Theodorescu, Ion N.
See also CA 167
Arguedas, Jose Maria 1911-1969 .. **CLC 10, 18; HLCS 1**
See also CA 89-92; CANR 73; DLB 113; HW 1
Argueta, Manlio 1936- .... **CLC 31**
See also CA 131; CANR 73; DLB 145; HW 1
Ariosto, Ludovico 1474-1533 .... **LC 6**
Aristides
See Epstein, Joseph
Aristophanes 450B.C.-385B.C. .... **CMLC 4; DA; DAB; DAC; DAM DRAM, MST; DC 2; WLCS**
See also DLB 176
Aristotle 384B.C.-322B.C. **CMLC 31; DA; DAB; DAC; DAM MST; WLCS**
See also DLB 176
Arlt, Roberto (Godofredo Christophersen) 1900-1942 .... **TCLC 29; DAM MULT; HLC**
See also CA 123; 131; CANR 67; HW 1, 2
Armah, Ayi Kwei 1939-**CLC 5, 33; BLC 1; DAM MULT, POET**
See also BW 1; CA 61-64; CANR 21, 64; DLB 117; MTCW 1
Armatrading, Joan 1950- .... **CLC 17**
See also CA 114
Arnette, Robert
See Silverberg, Robert
Arnim, Achim von (Ludwig Joachim von Arnim) 1781-1831 .... **NCLC 5; SSC 29**
See also DLB 90
Arnim, Bettina von 1785-1859 .... **NCLC 38**
See also DLB 90
Arnold, Matthew 1822-1888 .... **NCLC 6, 29; DA; DAB; DAC; DAM MST, POET; PC 5; WLC**
See also CDBLB 1832-1890; DLB 32, 57
Arnold, Thomas 1795-1842 .... **NCLC 18**
See also DLB 55
Arnow, Harriette (Louisa) Simpson 1908-1986 **CLC 2, 7, 18**
See also CA 9-12R; 118; CANR 14; DLB 6; MTCW 1, 2; SATA 42; SATA-Obit 47
Arouet, Francois-Marie
See Voltaire
Arp, Hans
See Arp, Jean
Arp, Jean 1887-1966 .... **CLC 5**
See also CA 81-84; 25-28R; CANR 42, 77
Arrabal
See Arrabal, Fernando
Arrabal, Fernando 1932- .... **CLC 2, 9, 18, 58**
See also CA 9-12R; CANR 15
Arrick, Fran .... **CLC 30**
See also Gaberman, Judie Angell
Artaud, Antonin (Marie Joseph) 1896-1948**TCLC 3, 36; DAM DRAM**
See also CA 104; 149; MTCW 1
Arthur, Ruth M(abel) 1905-1979 .... **CLC 12**
See also CA 9-12R; 85-88; CANR 4; SATA 7, 26
Artsybashev, Mikhail (Petrovich) 1878-1927 **TCLC 31**
See also CA 170
Arundel, Honor (Morfydd) 1919-1973 ... **CLC 17**
See also CA 21-22; 41-44R; CAP 2; CLR 35; SATA 4; SATA-Obit 24
Arzner, Dorothy 1897-1979 .... **CLC 98**
Asch, Sholem 1880-1957 .... **TCLC 3**
See also CA 105
Ash, Shalom
See Asch, Sholem
Ashbery, John (Lawrence) 1927-**CLC 2, 3, 4, 6, 9, 13, 15, 25, 41, 77; DAM POET; PC 26**
See also CA 5-8R; CANR 9, 37, 66; DLB 5, 165; DLBY 81; INT CANR-9; MTCW 1, 2
Ashdown, Clifford
See Freeman, R(ichard) Austin
Ashe, Gordon
See Creasey, John
Ashton-Warner, Sylvia (Constance) 1908-1984 **CLC 19**
See also CA 69-72; 112; CANR 29; MTCW 1, 2
Asimov, Isaac 1920-1992 **CLC 1, 3, 9, 19, 26, 76, 92; DAM POP**
See also AAYA 13; BEST 90:2; CA 1-4R; 137; CANR 2, 19, 36, 60; CLR 12; DLB 8; DLBY 92; INT CANR-19; JRDA; MAICYA; MTCW 1, 2; SATA 1, 26, 74
Assis, Joaquim Maria Machado de
See Machado de Assis, Joaquim Maria
Astley, Thea (Beatrice May) 1925- .... **CLC 41**
See also CA 65-68; CANR 11, 43, 78
Aston, James
See White, T(erence) H(anbury)
Asturias, Miguel Angel 1899-1974**CLC 3, 8, 13; DAM MULT, NOV; HLC**
See also CA 25-28; 49-52; CANR 32; CAP 2; DLB 113; HW 1; MTCW 1, 2
Atares, Carlos Saura
See Saura (Atares), Carlos
Atheling, William
See Pound, Ezra (Weston Loomis)
Atheling, William, Jr.
See Blish, James (Benjamin)
Atherton, Gertrude (Franklin Horn) 1857-1948 **TCLC 2**
See also CA 104; 155; DLB 9, 78, 186
Atherton, Lucius
See Masters, Edgar Lee
Atkins, Jack
See Harris, Mark
Atkinson, Kate .... **CLC 99**
See also CA 166
Attaway, William (Alexander) 1911-1986**CLC 92; BLC 1; DAM MULT**
See also BW 2, 3; CA 143; DLB 76
Atticus
See Fleming, Ian (Lancaster); Wilson, (Thomas) Woodrow
Atwood, Margaret (Eleanor) 1939-**CLC 2, 3, 4, 8, 13, 15, 25, 44, 84; DA; DAB; DAC; DAM MST, NOV, POET; PC 8; SSC 2; WLC**
See also AAYA 12; BEST 89:2; CA 49-52; CANR 3, 24, 33, 59; DLB 53; INT CANR-24; MTCW 1, 2; SATA 50
Aubigny, Pierre d'
See Mencken, H(enry) L(ouis)
Aubin, Penelope 1685-1731(?) .... **LC 9**
See also DLB 39
Auchincloss, Louis (Stanton) 1917- **CLC 4, 6, 9, 18, 45; DAM NOV; SSC 22**
See also CA 1-4R; CANR 6, 29, 55; DLB 2; DLBY 80; INT CANR-29; MTCW 1
Auden, W(ystan) H(ugh) 1907-1973**CLC 1, 2, 3, 4, 6, 9, 11, 14, 43; DA; DAB; DAC; DAM DRAM, MST, POET; PC 1; WLC**
See also AAYA 18; CA 9-12R; 45-48; CANR 5, 61; CDBLB 1914-1945; DLB 10, 20; MTCW 1, 2
Audiberti, Jacques 1900-1965 ..... **CLC 38; DAM DRAM**
See also CA 25-28R
Audubon, John James 1785-1851 .... **NCLC 47**
Auel, Jean M(arie) 1936-**CLC 31, 107; DAM POP**
See also AAYA 7; BEST 90:4; CA 103; CANR 21, 64; INT CANR-21; SATA 91
Auerbach, Erich 1892-1957 .... **TCLC 43**
See also CA 118; 155
Augier, Emile 1820-1889 .... **NCLC 31**
See also DLB 192
August, John
See De Voto, Bernard (Augustine)
Augustine 354-430 . **CMLC 6; DA; DAB; DAC; DAM MST; WLCS**
See also DLB 115
Aurelius
See Bourne, Randolph S(illiman)
Aurobindo, Sri
See Ghose, Aurabinda
Austen, Jane 1775-1817**NCLC 1, 13, 19, 33, 51; DA; DAB; DAC; DAM MST, NOV; WLC**
See also AAYA 19; CDBLB 1789-1832; DLB 116
Auster, Paul 1947- .... **CLC 47**
See also CA 69-72; CANR 23, 52, 75; MTCW 1

Austin, Frank
See Faust, Frederick (Schiller)
Austin, Mary (Hunter) 1868-1934 .... **TCLC 25**
See also CA 109; DLB 9, 78, 206
Autran Dourado, Waldomiro
See Dourado, (Waldomiro Freitas) Autran
Averroes 1126-1198 .... **CMLC 7**
See also DLB 115
Avicenna 980-1037 .... **CMLC 16**
See also DLB 115
Avison, Margaret 1918-**CLC 2, 4, 97; DAC; DAM POET**
See also CA 17-20R; DLB 53; MTCW 1
Axton, David
See Koontz, Dean R(ay)
Ayckbourn, Alan 1939-**CLC 5, 8, 18, 33, 74; DAB; DAM DRAM**
See also CA 21-24R; CANR 31, 59; DLB 13; MTCW 1, 2
Aydy, Catherine
See Tennant, Emma (Christina)
Ayme, Marcel (Andre) 1902-1967 .... **CLC 11**
See also CA 89-92; CANR 67; CLR 25; DLB 72; SATA 91
Ayrton, Michael 1921-1975 .... **CLC 7**
See also CA 5-8R; 61-64; CANR 9, 21
Azorin .... **CLC 11**
See also Martinez Ruiz, Jose
Azuela, Mariano 1873-1952**TCLC 3; DAM MULT; HLC**
See also CA 104; 131; CANR 81; HW 1, 2; MTCW 1, 2
Baastad, Babbis Friis
See Friis-Baastad, Babbis Ellinor
Bab
See Gilbert, W(illiam) S(chwenck)
Babbis, Eleanor
See Friis-Baastad, Babbis Ellinor
Babel, Isaac
See Babel, Isaak (Emmanuilovich)
Babel, Isaak (Emmanuilovich) 1894-1941(?) **TCLC 2, 13; SSC 16**
See also CA 104; 155; MTCW 1
Babits, Mihaly 1883-1941 .... **TCLC 14**
See also CA 114
Babur 1483-1530 .... **LC 18**
Bacchelli, Riccardo 1891-1985 .... **CLC 19**
See also CA 29-32R; 117
Bach, Richard (David) 1936-**CLC 14; DAM NOV, POP**
See also AITN 1; BEST 89:2; CA 9-12R; CANR 18; MTCW 1; SATA 13
Bachman, Richard
See King, Stephen (Edwin)
Bachmann, Ingeborg 1926-1973 .... **CLC 69**
See also CA 93-96; 45-48; CANR 69; DLB 85
Bacon, Francis 1561-1626 .... **LC 18, 32**
See also CDBLB Before 1660; DLB 151
Bacon, Roger 1214(?)-1292 .... **CMLC 14**
See also DLB 115
Bacovia, George .... **TCLC 24**
See also Vasiliu, Gheorghe
Badanes, Jerome 1937- .... **CLC 59**
Bagehot, Walter 1826-1877 .... **NCLC 10**
See also DLB 55
Bagnold, Enid 1889-1981 **CLC 25; DAM DRAM**
See also CA 5-8R; 103; CANR 5, 40; DLB 13, 160, 191; MAICYA; SATA 1, 25
Bagritsky, Eduard 1895-1934 .... **TCLC 60**
Bagrjana, Elisaveta
See Belcheva, Elisaveta
Bagryana, Elisaveta .... **CLC 10**
See also Belcheva, Elisaveta
See also DLB 147
Bailey, Paul 1937- .... **CLC 45**
See also CA 21-24R; CANR 16, 62; DLB 14
Baillie, Joanna 1762-1851 .... **NCLC 71**
See also DLB 93
Bainbridge, Beryl (Margaret) 1933-**CLC 4, 5, 8, 10, 14, 18, 22, 62; DAM NOV**
See also CA 21-24R; CANR 24, 55, 75; DLB 14; MTCW 1, 2
Baker, Elliott 1922- .... **CLC 8**
See also CA 45-48; CANR 2, 63
Baker, Jean H. .... **TCLC 3, 10**
See also Russell, George William
Baker, Nicholson 1957- ..... **CLC 61; DAM POP**
See also CA 135; CANR 63
Baker, Ray Stannard 1870-1946 .... **TCLC 47**
See also CA 118
Baker, Russell (Wayne) 1925- .... **CLC 31**
See also BEST 89:4; CA 57-60; CANR 11, 41, 59; MTCW 1, 2
Bakhtin, M.
See Bakhtin, Mikhail Mikhailovich
Bakhtin, M. M.
See Bakhtin, Mikhail Mikhailovich
Bakhtin, Mikhail
See Bakhtin, Mikhail Mikhailovich
Bakhtin, Mikhail Mikhailovich 1895-1975 **CLC 83**
See also CA 128; 113
Bakshi, Ralph 1938(?)- .... **CLC 26**
See also CA 112; 138
Bakunin, Mikhail (Alexandrovich) 1814-1876 **NCLC 25, 58**
Baldwin, James (Arthur) 1924-1987 **CLC 1, 2, 3, 4, 5, 8, 13, 15, 17, 42, 50, 67, 90; BLC 1; DA; DAB; DAC; DAM MST, MULT, NOV, POP; DC 1; SSC 10, 33; WLC**
See also AAYA 4; BW 1; CA 1-4R; 124; CABS 1; CANR 3, 24; CDALB 1941-1968; DLB 2, 7, 33; DLBY 87; MTCW 1, 2; SATA 9; SATA-Obit 54
Ballard, J(ames) G(raham) 1930- **CLC 3, 6, 14, 36; DAM NOV, POP; SSC 1**
See also AAYA 3; CA 5-8R; CANR 15, 39, 65; DLB 14, 207; MTCW 1, 2; SATA 93
Balmont, Konstantin (Dmitriyevich) 1867-1943 **TCLC 11**
See also CA 109; 155
Baltausis, Vincas
See Mikszath, Kalman
Balzac, Honore de 1799-1850**NCLC 5, 35, 53; DA; DAB; DAC; DAM MST, NOV; SSC 5; WLC**
See also DLB 119
Bambara, Toni Cade 1939-1995**CLC 19, 88; BLC 1; DA; DAC; DAM MST, MULT; SSC 35; WLCS**
See also AAYA 5; BW 2, 3; CA 29-32R; 150; CANR 24, 49, 81; CDALBS; DLB 38; MTCW 1, 2
Bamdad, A.
See Shamlu, Ahmad
Banat, D. R.
See Bradbury, Ray (Douglas)
Bancroft, Laura
See Baum, L(yman) Frank
Banim, John 1798-1842 .... **NCLC 13**
See also DLB 116, 158, 159
Banim, Michael 1796-1874 .... **NCLC 13**
See also DLB 158, 159
Banjo, The
See Paterson, A(ndrew) B(arton)
Banks, Iain
See Banks, Iain M(enzies)
Banks, Iain M(enzies) 1954- .... **CLC 34**
See also CA 123; 128; CANR 61; DLB 194; INT 128
Banks, Lynne Reid .... **CLC 23**
See also Reid Banks, Lynne
See also AAYA 6
Banks, Russell 1940- .... **CLC 37, 72**
See also CA 65-68; CAAS 15; CANR 19, 52, 73; DLB 130
Banville, John 1945- .... **CLC 46, 118**
See also CA 117; 128; DLB 14; INT 128
Banville, Theodore (Faullain) de 1832-1891**NCLC 9**
Baraka, Amiri 1934- **CLC 1, 2, 3, 5, 10, 14, 33, 115; BLC 1; DA; DAC; DAM MST, MULT, POET, POP; DC 6; PC 4; WLCS**
See also Jones, LeRoi
See also BW 2, 3; CA 21-24R; CABS 3; CANR 27, 38, 61; CDALB 1941-1968; DLB 5, 7, 16, 38; DLBD 8; MTCW 1, 2
Barbauld, Anna Laetitia 1743-1825 .... **NCLC 50**
See also DLB 107, 109, 142, 158
Barbellion, W. N. P. .... **TCLC 24**
See also Cummings, Bruce F(rederick)
Barbera, Jack (Vincent) 1945- .... **CLC 44**
See also CA 110; CANR 45
Barbey d'Aurevilly, Jules Amedee 1808-1889 **NCLC 1; SSC 17**
See also DLB 119
Barbour, John c. 1316-1395 .... **CMLC 33**
See also DLB 146
Barbusse, Henri 1873-1935 .... **TCLC 5**
See also CA 105; 154; DLB 65
Barclay, Bill
See Moorcock, Michael (John)
Barclay, William Ewert
See Moorcock, Michael (John)
Barea, Arturo 1897-1957 .... **TCLC 14**
See also CA 111
Barfoot, Joan 1946- .... **CLC 18**
See also CA 105
Barham, Richard Harris 1788-1845 ... **NCLC 77**
See also DLB 159
Baring, Maurice 1874-1945 .... **TCLC 8**
See also CA 105; 168; DLB 34
Baring-Gould, Sabine 1834-1924 .... **TCLC 88**
See also DLB 156, 190
Barker, Clive 1952- .... **CLC 52; DAM POP**
See also AAYA 10; BEST 90:3; CA 121; 129; CANR 71; INT 129; MTCW 1, 2
Barker, George Granville 1913-1991 **CLC 8, 48; DAM POET**
See also CA 9-12R; 135; CANR 7, 38; DLB 20; MTCW 1
Barker, Harley Granville
See Granville-Barker, Harley
See also DLB 10
Barker, Howard 1946- .... **CLC 37**
See also CA 102; DLB 13
Barker, Jane 1652-1732 .... **LC 42**
Barker, Pat(ricia) 1943- .... **CLC 32, 94**
See also CA 117; 122; CANR 50; INT 122
Barlach, Ernst 1870-1938 .... **TCLC 84**
See also DLB 56, 118
Barlow, Joel 1754-1812 .... **NCLC 23**
See also DLB 37
Barnard, Mary (Ethel) 1909- .... **CLC 48**
See also CA 21-22; CAP 2
Barnes, Djuna 1892-1982**CLC 3, 4, 8, 11, 29; SSC 3**
See also CA 9-12R; 107; CANR 16, 55; DLB 4, 9, 45; MTCW 1, 2
Barnes, Julian (Patrick) 1946- .. **CLC 42; DAB**
See also CA 102; CANR 19, 54; DLB 194; DLBY 93; MTCW 1
Barnes, Peter 1931- .... **CLC 5, 56**
See also CA 65-68; CAAS 12; CANR 33, 34, 64; DLB 13; MTCW 1
Barnes, William 1801-1886 .... **NCLC 75**
See also DLB 32
Baroja (y Nessi), Pio 1872-1956 .. **TCLC 8; HLC**
See also CA 104
Baron, David
See Pinter, Harold
Baron Corvo

See Rolfe, Frederick (William Serafino Austin Lewis Mary)
Barondess, Sue K(aufman) 1926-1977 .... **CLC 8**
See also Kaufman, Sue
See also CA 1-4R; 69-72; CANR 1
Baron de Teive
See Pessoa, Fernando (Antonio Nogueira)
Baroness Von S.
See Zangwill, Israel
Barres, (Auguste-) Maurice 1862-1923**TCLC 47**
See also CA 164; DLB 123
Barreto, Afonso Henrique de Lima
See Lima Barreto, Afonso Henrique de
Barrett, (Roger) Syd 1946- .... **CLC 35**
Barrett, William (Christopher) 1913-1992 **CLC 27**
See also CA 13-16R; 139; CANR 11, 67; INT CANR-11
Barrie, J(ames) M(atthew) 1860-1937 **TCLC 2; DAB; DAM DRAM**
See also CA 104; 136; CANR 77; CDBLB 1890-1914; CLR 16; DLB 10, 141, 156; MAICYA; MTCW 1; SATA 100; YABC 1
Barrington, Michael
See Moorcock, Michael (John)
Barrol, Grady
See Bograd, Larry
Barry, Mike
See Malzberg, Barry N(athaniel)
Barry, Philip 1896-1949 .... **TCLC 11**
See also CA 109; DLB 7
Bart, Andre Schwarz
See Schwarz-Bart, Andre
Barth, John (Simmons) 1930-**CLC 1, 2, 3, 5, 7, 9, 10, 14, 27, 51, 89; DAM NOV; SSC 10**
See also AITN 1, 2; CA 1-4R; CABS 1; CANR 5, 23, 49, 64; DLB 2; MTCW 1
Barthelme, Donald 1931-1989**CLC 1, 2, 3, 5, 6, 8, 13, 23, 46, 59, 115; DAM NOV; SSC 2**
See also CA 21-24R; 129; CANR 20, 58; DLB 2; DLBY 80, 89; MTCW 1, 2; SATA 7; SATA-Obit 62
Barthelme, Frederick 1943- .... **CLC 36, 117**
See also CA 114; 122; CANR 77; DLBY 85; INT 122
Barthes, Roland (Gerard) 1915-1980**CLC 24, 83**
See also CA 130; 97-100; CANR 66; MTCW 1, 2
Barzun, Jacques (Martin) 1907- .... **CLC 51**
See also CA 61-64; CANR 22
Bashevis, Isaac
See Singer, Isaac Bashevis
Bashkirtseff, Marie 1859-1884 .... **NCLC 27**
Basho
See Matsuo Basho
Bass, Kingsley B., Jr.
See Bullins, Ed
Bass, Rick 1958- .... **CLC 79**
See also CA 126; CANR 53; DLB 212
Bassani, Giorgio 1916- .... **CLC 9**
See also CA 65-68; CANR 33; DLB 128, 177; MTCW 1
Bastos, Augusto (Antonio) Roa
See Roa Bastos, Augusto (Antonio)
Bataille, Georges 1897-1962 .... **CLC 29**
See also CA 101; 89-92
Bates, H(erbert) E(rnest) 1905-1974 .... **CLC 46; DAB; DAM POP; SSC 10**
See also CA 93-96; 45-48; CANR 34; DLB 162, 191; MTCW 1, 2
Bauchart
See Camus, Albert
Baudelaire, Charles 1821-1867 **NCLC 6, 29, 55; DA; DAB; DAC; DAM MST, POET; PC 1; SSC 18; WLC**
Baudrillard, Jean 1929- .... **CLC 60**
Baum, L(yman) Frank 1856-1919 .... **TCLC 7**
See also CA 108; 133; CLR 15; DLB 22; JRDA; MAICYA; MTCW 1, 2; SATA 18, 100
Baum, Louis F.
See Baum, L(yman) Frank
Baumbach, Jonathan 1933- .... **CLC 6, 23**
See also CA 13-16R; CAAS 5; CANR 12, 66; DLBY 80; INT CANR-12; MTCW 1
Bausch, Richard (Carl) 1945- .... **CLC 51**
See also CA 101; CAAS 14; CANR 43, 61; DLB 130
Baxter, Charles (Morley) 1947-**CLC 45, 78; DAM POP**
See also CA 57-60; CANR 40, 64; DLB 130; MTCW 2
Baxter, George Owen
See Faust, Frederick (Schiller)
Baxter, James K(eir) 1926-1972 .... **CLC 14**
See also CA 77-80
Baxter, John
See Hunt, E(verette) Howard, (Jr.)
Bayer, Sylvia
See Glassco, John
Baynton, Barbara 1857-1929 .... **TCLC 57**
Beagle, Peter S(oyer) 1939- .... **CLC 7, 104**
See also CA 9-12R; CANR 4, 51, 73; DLBY 80; INT CANR-4; MTCW 1; SATA 60
Bean, Normal
See Burroughs, Edgar Rice
Beard, Charles A(ustin) 1874-1948 .... **TCLC 15**
See also CA 115; DLB 17; SATA 18
Beardsley, Aubrey 1872-1898 .... **NCLC 6**
Beattie, Ann 1947- **CLC 8, 13, 18, 40, 63; DAM NOV, POP; SSC 11**
See also BEST 90:2; CA 81-84; CANR 53, 73; DLBY 82; MTCW 1, 2
Beattie, James 1735-1803 .... **NCLC 25**
See also DLB 109
Beauchamp, Kathleen Mansfield 1888-1923
See Mansfield, Katherine
See also CA 104; 134; DA; DAC; DAM MST; MTCW 2
Beaumarchais, Pierre-Augustin Caron de 1732-1799 .... **DC 4**
See also DAM DRAM
Beaumont, Francis 1584(?)-1616 ... **LC 33; DC 6**
See also CDBLB Before 1660; DLB 58, 121
Beauvoir, Simone (Lucie Ernestine Marie Bertrand) de 1908-1986 **CLC 1, 2, 4, 8, 14, 31, 44, 50, 71; DA; DAB; DAC; DAM MST, NOV; SSC 35; WLC**
See also CA 9-12R; 118; CANR 28, 61; DLB 72; DLBY 86; MTCW 1, 2
Becker, Carl (Lotus) 1873-1945 .... **TCLC 63**
See also CA 157; DLB 17
Becker, Jurek 1937-1997 .... **CLC 7, 19**
See also CA 85-88; 157; CANR 60; DLB 75
Becker, Walter 1950- .... **CLC 26**
Beckett, Samuel (Barclay) 1906-1989**CLC 1, 2, 3, 4, 6, 9, 10, 11, 14, 18, 29, 57, 59, 83; DA; DAB; DAC; DAM DRAM, MST, NOV; SSC 16; WLC**
See also CA 5-8R; 130; CANR 33, 61; CDBLB 1945-1960; DLB 13, 15; DLBY 90; MTCW 1, 2
Beckford, William 1760-1844 .... **NCLC 16**
See also DLB 39
Beckman, Gunnel 1910- .... **CLC 26**
See also CA 33-36R; CANR 15; CLR 25; MAICYA; SAAS 9; SATA 6
Becque, Henri 1837-1899 .... **NCLC 3**
See also DLB 192
Beddoes, Thomas Lovell 1803-1849 ...... **NCLC 3**
See also DLB 96
Bede c. 673-735 .... **CMLC 20**
See also DLB 146
Bedford, Donald F.
See Fearing, Kenneth (Flexner)
Beecher, Catharine Esther 1800-1878 **NCLC 30**
See also DLB 1
Beecher, John 1904-1980 .... **CLC 6**
See also AITN 1; CA 5-8R; 105; CANR 8
Beer, Johann 1655-1700 .... **LC 5**
See also DLB 168
Beer, Patricia 1924- .... **CLC 58**
See also CA 61-64; CANR 13, 46; DLB 40
Beerbohm, Max
See Beerbohm, (Henry) Max(imilian)
Beerbohm, (Henry) Max(imilian) 1872-1956 **TCLC 1, 24**
See also CA 104; 154; CANR 79; DLB 34, 100
Beer-Hofmann, Richard 1866-1945 .... **TCLC 60**
See also CA 160; DLB 81
Begiebing, Robert J(ohn) 1946- .... **CLC 70**
See also CA 122; CANR 40
Behan, Brendan 1923-1964**CLC 1, 8, 11, 15, 79; DAM DRAM**
See also CA 73-76; CANR 33; CDBLB 1945-1960; DLB 13; MTCW 1, 2
Behn, Aphra 1640(?)-1689**LC 1, 30, 42; DA; DAB; DAC; DAM DRAM, MST, NOV, POET; DC 4; PC 13; WLC**
See also DLB 39, 80, 131
Behrman, S(amuel) N(athaniel) 1893-1973 **CLC 40**
See also CA 13-16; 45-48; CAP 1; DLB 7, 44
Belasco, David 1853-1931 .... **TCLC 3**
See also CA 104; 168; DLB 7
Belcheva, Elisaveta 1893- .... **CLC 10**
See also Bagryana, Elisaveta
Beldone, Phil "Cheech"
See Ellison, Harlan (Jay)
Beleno
See Azuela, Mariano
Belinski, Vissarion Grigoryevich 1811-1848 **NCLC 5**
See also DLB 198
Belitt, Ben 1911- .... **CLC 22**
See also CA 13-16R; CAAS 4; CANR 7, 77; DLB 5
Bell, Gertrude (Margaret Lowthian) 1868-1926 **TCLC 67**
See also CA 167; DLB 174
Bell, J. Freeman
See Zangwill, Israel
Bell, James Madison 1826-1902**TCLC 43; BLC 1; DAM MULT**
See also BW 1; CA 122; 124; DLB 50
Bell, Madison Smartt 1957- .... **CLC 41, 102**
See also CA 111; CANR 28, 54, 73; MTCW 1
Bell, Marvin (Hartley) 1937- .. **CLC 8, 31; DAM POET**
See also CA 21-24R; CAAS 14; CANR 59; DLB 5; MTCW 1
Bell, W. L. D.
See Mencken, H(enry) L(ouis)
Bellamy, Atwood C.
See Mencken, H(enry) L(ouis)
Bellamy, Edward 1850-1898 .... **NCLC 4**
See also DLB 12
Bellin, Edward J.
See Kuttner, Henry
Belloc, (Joseph) Hilaire (Pierre Sebastien Rene Swanton) 1870-1953 ..... **TCLC 7, 18; DAM POET; PC 24**
See also CA 106; 152; DLB 19, 100, 141, 174; MTCW 1; YABC 1
Belloc, Joseph Peter Rene Hilaire
See Belloc, (Joseph) Hilaire (Pierre Sebastien Rene Swanton)
Belloc, Joseph Pierre Hilaire
See Belloc, (Joseph) Hilaire (Pierre Sebastien Rene Swanton)
Belloc, M. A.
See Lowndes, Marie Adelaide (Belloc)
Bellow, Saul 1915-**CLC 1, 2, 3, 6, 8, 10, 13, 15, 25, 33, 34, 63, 79; DA; DAB; DAC; DAM MST,**

NOV, POP; SSC 14; WLC
See also AITN 2; BEST 89:3; CA 5-8R; CABS 1; CANR 29, 53; CDALB 1941-1968; DLB 2, 28; DLBD 3; DLBY 82; MTCW 1, 2
Belser, Reimond Karel Maria de 1929-
See Ruyslinck, Ward
See also CA 152
Bely, Andrey .... **TCLC 7; PC 11**
See also Bugayev, Boris Nikolayevich
See also MTCW 1
Belyi, Andrei
See Bugayev, Boris Nikolayevich
Benary, Margot
See Benary-Isbert, Margot
Benary-Isbert, Margot 1889-1979 .... **CLC 12**
See also CA 5-8R; 89-92; CANR 4, 72; CLR 12; MAICYA; SATA 2; SATA-Obit 21
Benavente (y Martinez), Jacinto 1866-1954**TCLC 3; DAM DRAM, MULT; HLCS 1**
See also CA 106; 131; CANR 81; HW 1, 2; MTCW 1, 2
Benchley, Peter (Bradford) 1940-**CLC 4, 8; DAM NOV, POP**
See also AAYA 14; AITN 2; CA 17-20R; CANR 12, 35, 66; MTCW 1, 2; SATA 3, 89
Benchley, Robert (Charles) 1889-1945**TCLC 1, 55**
See also CA 105; 153; DLB 11
Benda, Julien 1867-1956 .... **TCLC 60**
See also CA 120; 154
Benedict, Ruth (Fulton) 1887-1948 ..... **TCLC 60**
See also CA 158
Benedict, Saint c. 480-c. 547 .... **CMLC 29**
Benedikt, Michael 1935- .... **CLC 4, 14**
See also CA 13-16R; CANR 7; DLB 5
Benet, Juan 1927- .... **CLC 28**
See also CA 143
Benet, Stephen Vincent 1898-1943**TCLC 7; DAM POET; SSC 10**
See also CA 104; 152; DLB 4, 48, 102; DLBY 97; MTCW 1; YABC 1
Benet, William Rose 1886-1950 **TCLC 28; DAM POET**
See also CA 118; 152; DLB 45
Benford, Gregory (Albert) 1941- .... **CLC 52**
See also CA 69-72, 175; CAAE 175; CAAS 27; CANR 12, 24, 49; DLBY 82
Bengtsson, Frans (Gunnar) 1894-1954 **TCLC 48**
See also CA 170
Benjamin, David
See Slavitt, David R(ytman)
Benjamin, Lois
See Gould, Lois
Benjamin, Walter 1892-1940 .... **TCLC 39**
See also CA 164
Benn, Gottfried 1886-1956 .... **TCLC 3**
See also CA 106; 153; DLB 56
Bennett, Alan 1934-**CLC 45, 77; DAB; DAM MST**
See also CA 103; CANR 35, 55; MTCW 1, 2
Bennett, (Enoch) Arnold 1867-1931 **TCLC 5, 20**
See also CA 106; 155; CDBLB 1890-1914; DLB 10, 34, 98, 135; MTCW 2
Bennett, Elizabeth
See Mitchell, Margaret (Munnerlyn)
Bennett, George Harold 1930-
See Bennett, Hal
See also BW 1; CA 97-100
Bennett, Hal .... **CLC 5**
See also Bennett, George Harold
See also DLB 33
Bennett, Jay 1912- .... **CLC 35**
See also AAYA 10; CA 69-72; CANR 11, 42, 79; JRDA; SAAS 4; SATA 41, 87; SATA-Brief 27
Bennett, Louise (Simone) 1919-**CLC 28; BLC 1; DAM MULT**
See also BW 2, 3; CA 151; DLB 117
Benson, E(dward) F(rederic) 1867-1940**TCLC 27**
See also CA 114; 157; DLB 135, 153
Benson, Jackson J. 1930- .... **CLC 34**
See also CA 25-28R; DLB 111
Benson, Sally 1900-1972 .... **CLC 17**
See also CA 19-20; 37-40R; CAP 1; SATA 1, 35; SATA-Obit 27
Benson, Stella 1892-1933 .... **TCLC 17**
See also CA 117; 155; DLB 36, 162
Bentham, Jeremy 1748-1832 .... **NCLC 38**
See also DLB 107, 158
Bentley, E(dmund) C(lerihew) 1875-1956**TCLC 12**
See also CA 108; DLB 70
Bentley, Eric (Russell) 1916- .... **CLC 24**
See also CA 5-8R; CANR 6, 67; INT CANR-6
Beranger, Pierre Jean de 1780-1857 .. **NCLC 34**
Berdyaev, Nicolas
See Berdyaev, Nikolai (Aleksandrovich)
Berdyaev, Nikolai (Aleksandrovich) 1874-1948 **TCLC 67**
See also CA 120; 157
Berdyayev, Nikolai (Aleksandrovich)
See Berdyaev, Nikolai (Aleksandrovich)
Berendt, John (Lawrence) 1939- .... **CLC 86**
See also CA 146; CANR 75; MTCW 1
Beresford, J(ohn) D(avys) 1873-1947 .. **TCLC 81**
See also CA 112; 155; DLB 162, 178, 197
Bergelson, David 1884-1952 .... **TCLC 81**
Berger, Colonel
See Malraux, (Georges-)Andre
Berger, John (Peter) 1926- .... **CLC 2, 19**
See also CA 81-84; CANR 51, 78; DLB 14, 207
Berger, Melvin H. 1927- .... **CLC 12**
See also CA 5-8R; CANR 4; CLR 32; SAAS 2; SATA 5, 88
Berger, Thomas (Louis) 1924-**CLC 3, 5, 8, 11, 18, 38; DAM NOV**
See also CA 1-4R; CANR 5, 28, 51; DLB 2; DLBY 80; INT CANR-28; MTCW 1, 2
Bergman, (Ernst) Ingmar 1918- ..... **CLC 16, 72**
See also CA 81-84; CANR 33, 70; MTCW 2
Bergson, Henri(-Louis) 1859-1941 ..... **TCLC 32**
See also CA 164
Bergstein, Eleanor 1938- .... **CLC 4**
See also CA 53-56; CANR 5
Berkoff, Steven 1937- .... **CLC 56**
See also CA 104; CANR 72
Bermant, Chaim (Icyk) 1929- .... **CLC 40**
See also CA 57-60; CANR 6, 31, 57
Bern, Victoria
See Fisher, M(ary) F(rances) K(ennedy)
Bernanos, (Paul Louis) Georges 1888-1948 **TCLC 3**
See also CA 104; 130; DLB 72
Bernard, April 1956- .... **CLC 59**
See also CA 131
Berne, Victoria
See Fisher, M(ary) F(rances) K(ennedy)
Bernhard, Thomas 1931-1989 ..... **CLC 3, 32, 61**
See also CA 85-88; 127; CANR 32, 57; DLB 85, 124; MTCW 1
Bernhardt, Sarah (Henriette Rosine) 1844-1923 **TCLC 75**
See also CA 157
Berriault, Gina 1926- ..... **CLC 54, 109; SSC 30**
See also CA 116; 129; CANR 66; DLB 130
Berrigan, Daniel 1921- .... **CLC 4**
See also CA 33-36R; CAAS 1; CANR 11, 43, 78; DLB 5
Berrigan, Edmund Joseph Michael, Jr. 1934-1983
See Berrigan, Ted
See also CA 61-64; 110; CANR 14
Berrigan, Ted .... **CLC 37**
See also Berrigan, Edmund Joseph Michael, Jr.
See also DLB 5, 169
Berry, Charles Edward Anderson 1931-
See Berry, Chuck
See also CA 115
Berry, Chuck .... **CLC 17**
See also Berry, Charles Edward Anderson
Berry, Jonas
See Ashbery, John (Lawrence)
Berry, Wendell (Erdman) 1934- **CLC 4, 6, 8, 27, 46; DAM POET**
See also AITN 1; CA 73-76; CANR 50, 73; DLB 5, 6; MTCW 1
Berryman, John 1914-1972**CLC 1, 2, 3, 4, 6, 8, 10, 13, 25, 62; DAM POET**
See also CA 13-16; 33-36R; CABS 2; CANR 35; CAP 1; CDALB 1941-1968; DLB 48; MTCW 1, 2
Bertolucci, Bernardo 1940- .... **CLC 16**
See also CA 106
Berton, Pierre (Francis Demarigny) 1920- **CLC 104**
See also CA 1-4R; CANR 2, 56; DLB 68; SATA 99
Bertrand, Aloysius 1807-1841 .... **NCLC 31**
Bertran de Born c. 1140-1215 .... **CMLC 5**
Besant, Annie (Wood) 1847-1933 .... **TCLC 9**
See also CA 105
Bessie, Alvah 1904-1985 .... **CLC 23**
See also CA 5-8R; 116; CANR 2, 80; DLB 26
Bethlen, T. D.
See Silverberg, Robert
Beti, Mongo .... **CLC 27; BLC 1; DAM MULT**
See also Biyidi, Alexandre
See also CANR 79
Betjeman, John 1906-1984 **CLC 2, 6, 10, 34, 43; DAB; DAM MST, POET**
See also CA 9-12R; 112; CANR 33, 56; CDBLB 1945-1960; DLB 20; DLBY 84; MTCW 1, 2
Bettelheim, Bruno 1903-1990 .... **CLC 79**
See also CA 81-84; 131; CANR 23, 61; MTCW 1, 2
Betti, Ugo 1892-1953 .... **TCLC 5**
See also CA 104; 155
Betts, Doris (Waugh) 1932- .... **CLC 3, 6, 28**
See also CA 13-16R; CANR 9, 66, 77; DLBY 82; INT CANR-9
Bevan, Alistair
See Roberts, Keith (John Kingston)
Bey, Pilaff
See Douglas, (George) Norman
Bialik, Chaim Nachman 1873-1934 .... **TCLC 25**
See also CA 170
Bickerstaff, Isaac
See Swift, Jonathan
Bidart, Frank 1939- .... **CLC 33**
See also CA 140
Bienek, Horst 1930- .... **CLC 7, 11**
See also CA 73-76; DLB 75
Bierce, Ambrose (Gwinett) 1842-1914(?)**TCLC 1, 7, 44; DA; DAC; DAM MST; SSC 9; WLC**
See also CA 104; 139; CANR 78; CDALB 1865-1917; DLB 11, 12, 23, 71, 74, 186
Biggers, Earl Derr 1884-1933 .... **TCLC 65**
See also CA 108; 153
Billings, Josh
See Shaw, Henry Wheeler
Billington, (Lady) Rachel (Mary) 1942- **CLC 43**
See also AITN 2; CA 33-36R; CANR 44
Binyon, T(imothy) J(ohn) 1936- .... **CLC 34**
See also CA 111; CANR 28
Bioy Casares, Adolfo 1914-1999**CLC 4, 8, 13, 88; DAM MULT; HLC; SSC 17**
See also CA 29-32R; 177; CANR 19, 43, 66; DLB 113; HW 1, 2; MTCW 1, 2
Bird, Cordwainer
See Ellison, Harlan (Jay)
Bird, Robert Montgomery 1806-1854 ... **NCLC 1**
See also DLB 202
Birkerts, Sven 1951- .... **CLC 116**
See also CA 128; 133; 176; CAAS 29; INT 133
Birney, (Alfred) Earle 1904-1995**CLC 1, 4, 6, 11; DAC; DAM MST, POET**

See also CA 1-4R; CANR 5, 20; DLB 88; MTCW 1
Biruni, al 973-1048(?) .... **CMLC 28**
Bishop, Elizabeth 1911-1979 **CLC 1, 4, 9, 13, 15, 32; DA; DAC; DAM MST, POET; PC 3**
See also CA 5-8R; 89-92; CABS 2; CANR 26, 61; CDALB 1968-1988; DLB 5, 169; MTCW 1, 2; SATA-Obit 24
Bishop, John 1935- .... **CLC 10**
See also CA 105
Bissett, Bill 1939- .... **CLC 18; PC 14**
See also CA 69-72; CAAS 19; CANR 15; DLB 53; MTCW 1
Bissoondath, Neil (Devindra) 1955- .. **CLC 120; DAC**
See also CA 136
Bitov, Andrei (Georgievich) 1937- .... **CLC 57**
See also CA 142
Biyidi, Alexandre 1932-
See Beti, Mongo
See also BW 1, 3; CA 114; 124; CANR 81; MTCW 1, 2
Bjarme, Brynjolf
See Ibsen, Henrik (Johan)
Bjoernson, Bjoernstjerne (Martinius) 1832-1910 **TCLC 7, 37**
See also CA 104
Black, Robert
See Holdstock, Robert P.
Blackburn, Paul 1926-1971 .... **CLC 9, 43**
See also CA 81-84; 33-36R; CANR 34; DLB 16; DLBY 81
Black Elk 1863-1950 ..... **TCLC 33; DAM MULT**
See also CA 144; MTCW 1; NNAL
Black Hobart
See Sanders, (James) Ed(ward)
Blacklin, Malcolm
See Chambers, Aidan
Blackmore, R(ichard) D(oddridge) 1825-1900 **TCLC 27**
See also CA 120; DLB 18
Blackmur, R(ichard) P(almer) 1904-1965**CLC 2, 24**
See also CA 11-12; 25-28R; CANR 71; CAP 1; DLB 63
Black Tarantula
See Acker, Kathy
Blackwood, Algernon (Henry) 1869-1951**TCLC 5**
See also CA 105; 150; DLB 153, 156, 178
Blackwood, Caroline 1931-1996 .. **CLC 6, 9, 100**
See also CA 85-88; 151; CANR 32, 61, 65; DLB 14, 207; MTCW 1
Blade, Alexander
See Hamilton, Edmond; Silverberg, Robert
Blaga, Lucian 1895-1961 .... **CLC 75**
See also CA 157
Blair, Eric (Arthur) 1903-1950
See Orwell, George
See also CA 104; 132; DA; DAB; DAC; DAM MST, NOV; MTCW 1, 2; SATA 29
Blair, Hugh 1718-1800 .... **NCLC 75**
Blais, Marie-Claire 1939- .. **CLC 2, 4, 6, 13, 22; DAC; DAM MST**
See also CA 21-24R; CAAS 4; CANR 38, 75; DLB 53; MTCW 1, 2
Blaise, Clark 1940- .... **CLC 29**
See also AITN 2; CA 53-56; CAAS 3; CANR 5, 66; DLB 53
Blake, Fairley
See De Voto, Bernard (Augustine)
Blake, Nicholas
See Day Lewis, C(ecil)
See also DLB 77
Blake, William 1757-1827**NCLC 13, 37, 57; DA; DAB; DAC; DAM MST, POET; PC 12; WLC**
See also CDBLB 1789-1832; CLR 52; DLB 93, 163; MAICYA; SATA 30
Blasco Ibanez, Vicente 1867-1928 **TCLC 12; DAM NOV**
See also CA 110; 131; CANR 81; HW 1, 2; MTCW 1
Blatty, William Peter 1928- . **CLC 2; DAM POP**
See also CA 5-8R; CANR 9
Bleeck, Oliver
See Thomas, Ross (Elmore)
Blessing, Lee 1949- .... **CLC 54**
Blish, James (Benjamin) 1921-1975 ..... **CLC 14**
See also CA 1-4R; 57-60; CANR 3; DLB 8; MTCW 1; SATA 66
Bliss, Reginald
See Wells, H(erbert) G(eorge)
Blixen, Karen (Christentze Dinesen) 1885-1962
See Dinesen, Isak
See also CA 25-28; CANR 22, 50; CAP 2; MTCW 1, 2; SATA 44
Bloch, Robert (Albert) 1917-1994 .... **CLC 33**
See also AAYA 29; CA 5-8R; 146; CAAS 20; CANR 5, 78; DLB 44; INT CANR-5; MTCW 1; SATA 12; SATA-Obit 82
Blok, Alexander (Alexandrovich) 1880-1921 **TCLC 5; PC 21**
See also CA 104
Blom, Jan
See Breytenbach, Breyten
Bloom, Harold 1930- .... **CLC 24, 103**
See also CA 13-16R; CANR 39, 75; DLB 67; MTCW 1
Bloomfield, Aurelius
See Bourne, Randolph S(illiman)
Blount, Roy (Alton), Jr. 1941- .... **CLC 38**
See also CA 53-56; CANR 10, 28, 61; INT CANR-28; MTCW 1, 2
Bloy, Leon 1846-1917 .... **TCLC 22**
See also CA 121; DLB 123
Blume, Judy (Sussman) 1938-**CLC 12, 30; DAM NOV, POP**
See also AAYA 3, 26; CA 29-32R; CANR 13, 37, 66; CLR 2, 15; DLB 52; JRDA; MAICYA; MTCW 1, 2; SATA 2, 31, 79
Blunden, Edmund (Charles) 1896-1974**CLC 2, 56**
See also CA 17-18; 45-48; CANR 54; CAP 2; DLB 20, 100, 155; MTCW 1
Bly, Robert (Elwood) 1926-**CLC 1, 2, 5, 10, 15, 38; DAM POET**
See also CA 5-8R; CANR 41, 73; DLB 5; MTCW 1, 2
Boas, Franz 1858-1942 .... **TCLC 56**
See also CA 115
Bobette
See Simenon, Georges (Jacques Christian)
Boccaccio, Giovanni 1313-1375**CMLC 13; SSC 10**
Bochco, Steven 1943- .... **CLC 35**
See also AAYA 11; CA 124; 138
Bodel, Jean 1167(?)-1210 .... **CMLC 28**
Bodenheim, Maxwell 1892-1954 .... **TCLC 44**
See also CA 110; DLB 9, 45
Bodker, Cecil 1927- .... **CLC 21**
See also CA 73-76; CANR 13, 44; CLR 23; MAICYA; SATA 14
Boell, Heinrich (Theodor) 1917-1985**CLC 2, 3, 6, 9, 11, 15, 27, 32, 72; DA; DAB; DAC; DAM MST, NOV; SSC 23; WLC**
See also CA 21-24R; 116; CANR 24; DLB 69; DLBY 85; MTCW 1, 2
Boerne, Alfred
See Doeblin, Alfred
Boethius 480(?)-524(?) .... **CMLC 15**
See also DLB 115
Bogan, Louise 1897-1970**CLC 4, 39, 46, 93; DAM POET; PC 12**
See also CA 73-76; 25-28R; CANR 33; DLB 45, 169; MTCW 1, 2
Bogarde, Dirk .... **CLC 19**
See also Van Den Bogarde, Derek Jules Gaspard Ulric Niven
See also DLB 14
Bogosian, Eric 1953- .... **CLC 45**
See also CA 138
Bograd, Larry 1953- .... **CLC 35**
See also CA 93-96; CANR 57; SAAS 21; SATA 33, 89
Boiardo, Matteo Maria 1441-1494 .... **LC 6**
Boileau-Despreaux, Nicolas 1636-1711 ..... **LC 3**
Bojer, Johan 1872-1959 .... **TCLC 64**
Boland, Eavan (Aisling) 1944- **CLC 40, 67, 113; DAM POET**
See also CA 143; CANR 61; DLB 40; MTCW 2
Boll, Heinrich
See Boell, Heinrich (Theodor)
Bolt, Lee
See Faust, Frederick (Schiller)
Bolt, Robert (Oxton) 1924-1995 .. **CLC 14; DAM DRAM**
See also CA 17-20R; 147; CANR 35, 67; DLB 13; MTCW 1
Bombet, Louis-Alexandre-Cesar
See Stendhal
Bomkauf
See Kaufman, Bob (Garnell)
Bonaventura .... **NCLC 35**
See also DLB 90
Bond, Edward 1934-**CLC 4, 6, 13, 23; DAM DRAM**
See also CA 25-28R; CANR 38, 67; DLB 13; MTCW 1
Bonham, Frank 1914-1989 .... **CLC 12**
See also AAYA 1; CA 9-12R; CANR 4, 36; JRDA; MAICYA; SAAS 3; SATA 1, 49; SATA-Obit 62
Bonnefoy, Yves 1923-**CLC 9, 15, 58; DAM MST, POET**
See also CA 85-88; CANR 33, 75; MTCW 1, 2
Bontemps, Arna(ud Wendell) 1902-1973 **CLC 1, 18; BLC 1; DAM MULT, NOV, POET**
See also BW 1; CA 1-4R; 41-44R; CANR 4, 35; CLR 6; DLB 48, 51; JRDA; MAICYA; MTCW 1, 2; SATA 2, 44; SATA-Obit 24
Booth, Martin 1944- .... **CLC 13**
See also CA 93-96; CAAS 2
Booth, Philip 1925- .... **CLC 23**
See also CA 5-8R; CANR 5; DLBY 82
Booth, Wayne C(layson) 1921- .... **CLC 24**
See also CA 1-4R; CAAS 5; CANR 3, 43; DLB 67
Borchert, Wolfgang 1921-1947 .... **TCLC 5**
See also CA 104; DLB 69, 124
Borel, Petrus 1809-1859 .... **NCLC 41**
Borges, Jorge Luis 1899-1986**CLC 1, 2, 3, 4, 6, 8, 9, 10, 13, 19, 44, 48, 83; DA; DAB; DAC; DAM MST, MULT; HLC; PC 22; SSC 4; WLC**
See also AAYA 26; CA 21-24R; CANR 19, 33, 75; DLB 113; DLBY 86; HW 1, 2; MTCW 1, 2
Borowski, Tadeusz 1922-1951 .... **TCLC 9**
See also CA 106; 154
Borrow, George (Henry) 1803-1881 ...... **NCLC 9**
See also DLB 21, 55, 166
Bosman, Herman Charles 1905-1951 . **TCLC 49**
See also Malan, Herman
See also CA 160
Bosschere, Jean de 1878(?)-1953 .... **TCLC 19**
See also CA 115
Boswell, James 1740-1795 **LC 4, 50; DA; DAB; DAC; DAM MST; WLC**
See also CDBLB 1660-1789; DLB 104, 142
Bottoms, David 1949- .... **CLC 53**
See also CA 105; CANR 22; DLB 120; DLBY 83
Boucicault, Dion 1820-1890 .... **NCLC 41**
Boucolon, Maryse 1937(?)-
See Conde, Maryse
See also BW 3; CA 110; CANR 30, 53, 76
Bourget, Paul (Charles Joseph) 1852-1935**TCLC 12**
See also CA 107; DLB 123

Author Index

Bourjaily, Vance (Nye) 1922- .... **CLC 8, 62**
See also CA 1-4R; CAAS 1; CANR 2, 72; DLB 2, 143
Bourne, Randolph S(illiman) 1886-1918**TCLC 16**
See also CA 117; 155; DLB 63
Bova, Ben(jamin William) 1932- .... **CLC 45**
See also AAYA 16; CA 5-8R; CAAS 18; CANR 11, 56; CLR 3; DLBY 81; INT CANR-11; MAICYA; MTCW 1; SATA 6, 68
Bowen, Elizabeth (Dorothea Cole) 1899-1973**CLC 1, 3, 6, 11, 15, 22, 118; DAM NOV; SSC 3, 28**
See also CA 17-18; 41-44R; CANR 35; CAP 2; CDBLB 1945-1960; DLB 15, 162; MTCW 1, 2
Bowering, George 1935- .... **CLC 15, 47**
See also CA 21-24R; CAAS 16; CANR 10; DLB 53
Bowering, Marilyn R(uthe) 1949- .... **CLC 32**
See also CA 101; CANR 49
Bowers, Edgar 1924- .... **CLC 9**
See also CA 5-8R; CANR 24; DLB 5
Bowie, David .... **CLC 17**
See also Jones, David Robert
Bowles, Jane (Sydney) 1917-1973 ..... **CLC 3, 68**
See also CA 19-20; 41-44R; CAP 2
Bowles, Paul (Frederick) 1910-**CLC 1, 2, 19, 53; SSC 3**
See also CA 1-4R; CAAS 1; CANR 1, 19, 50, 75; DLB 5, 6; MTCW 1, 2
Box, Edgar
See Vidal, Gore
Boyd, Nancy
See Millay, Edna St. Vincent
Boyd, William 1952- .... **CLC 28, 53, 70**
See also CA 114; 120; CANR 51, 71
Boyle, Kay 1902-1992**CLC 1, 5, 19, 58, 121; SSC 5**
See also CA 13-16R; 140; CAAS 1; CANR 29, 61; DLB 4, 9, 48, 86; DLBY 93; MTCW 1, 2
Boyle, Mark
See Kienzle, William X(avier)
Boyle, Patrick 1905-1982 .... **CLC 19**
See also CA 127
Boyle, T. C. 1948-
See Boyle, T(homas) Coraghessan
Boyle, T(homas) Coraghessan 1948-**CLC 36, 55, 90; DAM POP; SSC 16**
See also BEST 90:4; CA 120; CANR 44, 76; DLBY 86; MTCW 2
Boz
See Dickens, Charles (John Huffam)
Brackenridge, Hugh Henry 1748-1816 **NCLC 7**
See also DLB 11, 37
Bradbury, Edward P.
See Moorcock, Michael (John)
See also MTCW 2
Bradbury, Malcolm (Stanley) 1932-**CLC 32, 61; DAM NOV**
See also CA 1-4R; CANR 1, 33; DLB 14, 207; MTCW 1, 2
Bradbury, Ray (Douglas) 1920-**CLC 1, 3, 10, 15, 42, 98; DA; DAB; DAC; DAM MST, NOV, POP; SSC 29; WLC**
See also AAYA 15; AITN 1, 2; CA 1-4R; CANR 2, 30, 75; CDALB 1968-1988; DLB 2, 8; MTCW 1, 2; SATA 11, 64
Bradford, Gamaliel 1863-1932 .... **TCLC 36**
See also CA 160; DLB 17
Bradley, David (Henry), Jr. 1950- **CLC 23, 118; BLC 1; DAM MULT**
See also BW 1, 3; CA 104; CANR 26, 81; DLB 33
Bradley, John Ed(mund, Jr.) 1958- .... **CLC 55**
See also CA 139
Bradley, Marion Zimmer 1930- .. **CLC 30; DAM POP**
See also AAYA 9; CA 57-60; CAAS 10; CANR 7, 31, 51, 75; DLB 8; MTCW 1, 2; SATA 90
Bradstreet, Anne 1612(?)-1672**LC 4, 30; DA; DAC; DAM MST, POET; PC 10**
See also CDALB 1640-1865; DLB 24
Brady, Joan 1939- .... **CLC 86**
See also CA 141
Bragg, Melvyn 1939- .... **CLC 10**
See also BEST 89:3; CA 57-60; CANR 10, 48; DLB 14
Brahe, Tycho 1546-1601 .... **LC 45**
Braine, John (Gerard) 1922-1986 .. **CLC 1, 3, 41**
See also CA 1-4R; 120; CANR 1, 33; CDBLB 1945-1960; DLB 15; DLBY 86; MTCW 1
Bramah, Ernest 1868-1942 .... **TCLC 72**
See also CA 156; DLB 70
Brammer, William 1930(?)-1978 .... **CLC 31**
See also CA 77-80
Brancati, Vitaliano 1907-1954 .... **TCLC 12**
See also CA 109
Brancato, Robin F(idler) 1936- .... **CLC 35**
See also AAYA 9; CA 69-72; CANR 11, 45; CLR 32; JRDA; SAAS 9; SATA 97
Brand, Max
See Faust, Frederick (Schiller)
Brand, Millen 1906-1980 .... **CLC 7**
See also CA 21-24R; 97-100; CANR 72
Branden, Barbara .... **CLC 44**
See also CA 148
Brandes, Georg (Morris Cohen) 1842-1927**TCLC 10**
See also CA 105
Brandys, Kazimierz 1916- .... **CLC 62**
Branley, Franklyn M(ansfield) 1915- **CLC 21**
See also CA 33-36R; CANR 14, 39; CLR 13; MAICYA; SAAS 16; SATA 4, 68
Brathwaite, Edward (Kamau) 1930- ..... **CLC 11; BLCS; DAM POET**
See also BW 2, 3; CA 25-28R; CANR 11, 26, 47; DLB 125
Brautigan, Richard (Gary) 1935-1984**CLC 1, 3, 5, 9, 12, 34, 42; DAM NOV**
See also CA 53-56; 113; CANR 34; DLB 2, 5, 206; DLBY 80, 84; MTCW 1; SATA 56
Brave Bird, Mary 1953-
See Crow Dog, Mary (Ellen)
See also NNAL
Braverman, Kate 1950- .... **CLC 67**
See also CA 89-92
Brecht, (Eugen) Bertolt (Friedrich) 1898-1956 **TCLC 1, 6, 13, 35; DA; DAB; DAC; DAM DRAM, MST; DC 3; WLC**
See also CA 104; 133; CANR 62; DLB 56, 124; MTCW 1, 2
Brecht, Eugen Berthold Friedrich
See Brecht, (Eugen) Bertolt (Friedrich)
Bremer, Fredrika 1801-1865 .... **NCLC 11**
Brennan, Christopher John 1870-1932**TCLC 17**
See also CA 117
Brennan, Maeve 1917-1993 .... **CLC 5**
See also CA 81-84; CANR 72
Brent, Linda
See Jacobs, Harriet A(nn)
Brentano, Clemens (Maria) 1778-1842 . **NCLC 1**
See also DLB 90
Brent of Bin Bin
See Franklin, (Stella Maria Sarah) Miles (Lampe)
Brenton, Howard 1942- .... **CLC 31**
See also CA 69-72; CANR 33, 67; DLB 13; MTCW 1
Breslin, James 1930-1996
See Breslin, Jimmy
See also CA 73-76; CANR 31, 75; DAM NOV; MTCW 1, 2
Breslin, Jimmy .... **CLC 4, 43**
See also Breslin, James
See also AITN 1; DLB 185; MTCW 2
Bresson, Robert 1901- .... **CLC 16**
See also CA 110; CANR 49
Breton, Andre 1896-1966**CLC 2, 9, 15, 54; PC 15**
See also CA 19-20; 25-28R; CANR 40, 60; CAP 2; DLB 65; MTCW 1, 2
Breytenbach, Breyten 1939(?)-**CLC 23, 37; DAM POET**
See also CA 113; 129; CANR 61
Bridgers, Sue Ellen 1942- .... **CLC 26**
See also AAYA 8; CA 65-68; CANR 11, 36; CLR 18; DLB 52; JRDA; MAICYA; SAAS 1; SATA 22, 90; SATA-Essay 109
Bridges, Robert (Seymour) 1844-1930 **TCLC 1; DAM POET**
See also CA 104; 152; CDBLB 1890-1914; DLB 19, 98
Bridie, James .... **TCLC 3**
See also Mavor, Osborne Henry
See also DLB 10
Brin, David 1950- .... **CLC 34**
See also AAYA 21; CA 102; CANR 24, 70; INT CANR-24; SATA 65
Brink, Andre (Philippus) 1935-**CLC 18, 36, 106**
See also CA 104; CANR 39, 62; INT 103; MTCW 1, 2
Brinsmead, H(esba) F(ay) 1922- .... **CLC 21**
See also CA 21-24R; CANR 10; CLR 47; MAICYA; SAAS 5; SATA 18, 78
Brittain, Vera (Mary) 1893(?)-1970 ...... **CLC 23**
See also CA 13-16; 25-28R; CANR 58; CAP 1; DLB 191; MTCW 1, 2
Broch, Hermann 1886-1951 .... **TCLC 20**
See also CA 117; DLB 85, 124
Brock, Rose
See Hansen, Joseph
Brodkey, Harold (Roy) 1930-1996 .... **CLC 56**
See also CA 111; 151; CANR 71; DLB 130
Brodskii, Iosif
See Brodsky, Joseph
Brodsky, Iosif Alexandrovich 1940-1996
See Brodsky, Joseph
See also AITN 1; CA 41-44R; 151; CANR 37; DAM POET; MTCW 1, 2
Brodsky, Joseph 1940-1996**CLC 4, 6, 13, 36, 100; PC 9**
See also Brodskii, Iosif; Brodsky, Iosif Alexandrovich
See also MTCW 1
Brodsky, Michael (Mark) 1948- .... **CLC 19**
See also CA 102; CANR 18, 41, 58
Bromell, Henry 1947- .... **CLC 5**
See also CA 53-56; CANR 9
Bromfield, Louis (Brucker) 1896-1956**TCLC 11**
See also CA 107; 155; DLB 4, 9, 86
Broner, E(sther) M(asserman) 1930- ... **CLC 19**
See also CA 17-20R; CANR 8, 25, 72; DLB 28
Bronk, William (M.) 1918-1999 .... **CLC 10**
See also CA 89-92; 177; CANR 23; DLB 165
Bronstein, Lev Davidovich
See Trotsky, Leon
Bronte, Anne 1820-1849 .... **NCLC 71**
See also DLB 21, 199
Bronte, Charlotte 1816-1855 **NCLC 3, 8, 33, 58; DA; DAB; DAC; DAM MST, NOV; WLC**
See also AAYA 17; CDBLB 1832-1890; DLB 21, 159, 199
Bronte, Emily (Jane) 1818-1848**NCLC 16, 35; DA; DAB; DAC; DAM MST, NOV, POET; PC 8; WLC**
See also AAYA 17; CDBLB 1832-1890; DLB 21, 32, 199
Brooke, Frances 1724-1789 .... **LC 6, 48**
See also DLB 39, 99
Brooke, Henry 1703(?)-1783 .... **LC 1**
See also DLB 39
Brooke, Rupert (Chawner) 1887-1915**TCLC 2, 7; DA; DAB; DAC; DAM MST, POET; PC 24; WLC**
See also CA 104; 132; CANR 61; CDBLB 1914-

1945; DLB 19; MTCW 1, 2
Brooke-Haven, P.
See Wodehouse, P(elham) G(renville)
Brooke-Rose, Christine 1926(?)- .... **CLC 40**
See also CA 13-16R; CANR 58; DLB 14
Brookner, Anita 1928- ... **CLC 32, 34, 51; DAB; DAM POP**
See also CA 114; 120; CANR 37, 56; DLB 194; DLBY 87; MTCW 1, 2
Brooks, Cleanth 1906-1994 ..... **CLC 24, 86, 110**
See also CA 17-20R; 145; CANR 33, 35; DLB 63; DLBY 94; INT CANR-35; MTCW 1, 2
Brooks, George
See Baum, L(yman) Frank
Brooks, Gwendolyn 1917-**CLC 1, 2, 4, 5, 15, 49; BLC 1; DA; DAC; DAM MST, MULT, POET; PC 7; WLC**
See also AAYA 20; AITN 1; BW 2, 3; CA 1-4R; CANR 1, 27, 52, 75; CDALB 1941-1968; CLR 27; DLB 5, 76, 165; MTCW 1, 2; SATA 6
Brooks, Mel .... **CLC 12**
See also Kaminsky, Melvin
See also AAYA 13; DLB 26
Brooks, Peter 1938- .... **CLC 34**
See also CA 45-48; CANR 1
Brooks, Van Wyck 1886-1963 .... **CLC 29**
See also CA 1-4R; CANR 6; DLB 45, 63, 103
Brophy, Brigid (Antonia) 1929-1995 . **CLC 6, 11, 29, 105**
See also CA 5-8R; 149; CAAS 4; CANR 25, 53; DLB 14; MTCW 1, 2
Brosman, Catharine Savage 1934- .... **CLC 9**
See also CA 61-64; CANR 21, 46
Brossard, Nicole 1943- .... **CLC 115**
See also CA 122; CAAS 16; DLB 53
Brother Antoninus
See Everson, William (Oliver)
The Brothers Quay
See Quay, Stephen; Quay, Timothy
Broughton, T(homas) Alan 1936- .... **CLC 19**
See also CA 45-48; CANR 2, 23, 48
Broumas, Olga 1949- .... **CLC 10, 73**
See also CA 85-88; CANR 20, 69
Brown, Alan 1950- .... **CLC 99**
See also CA 156
Brown, Charles Brockden 1771-1810 **NCLC 22, 74**
See also CDALB 1640-1865; DLB 37, 59, 73
Brown, Christy 1932-1981 .... **CLC 63**
See also CA 105; 104; CANR 72; DLB 14
Brown, Claude 1937- ..... **CLC 30; BLC 1; DAM MULT**
See also AAYA 7; BW 1, 3; CA 73-76; CANR 81
Brown, Dee (Alexander) 1908-**CLC 18, 47; DAM POP**
See also AAYA 30; CA 13-16R; CAAS 6; CANR 11, 45, 60; DLBY 80; MTCW 1, 2; SATA 5
Brown, George
See Wertmueller, Lina
Brown, George Douglas 1869-1902 .... **TCLC 28**
See also CA 162
Brown, George Mackay 1921-1996**CLC 5, 48, 100**
See also CA 21-24R; 151; CAAS 6; CANR 12, 37, 67; DLB 14, 27, 139; MTCW 1; SATA 35
Brown, (William) Larry 1951- .... **CLC 73**
See also CA 130; 134; INT 133
Brown, Moses
See Barrett, William (Christopher)
Brown, Rita Mae 1944- ... **CLC 18, 43, 79; DAM NOV, POP**
See also CA 45-48; CANR 2, 11, 35, 62; INT CANR-11; MTCW 1, 2
Brown, Roderick (Langmere) Haig-
See Haig-Brown, Roderick (Langmere)
Brown, Rosellen 1939- .... **CLC 32**
See also CA 77-80; CAAS 10; CANR 14, 44
Brown, Sterling Allen 1901-1989**CLC 1, 23, 59; BLC 1; DAM MULT, POET**
See also BW 1, 3; CA 85-88; 127; CANR 26; DLB 48, 51, 63; MTCW 1, 2
Brown, Will
See Ainsworth, William Harrison
Brown, William Wells 1813-1884**NCLC 2; BLC 1; DAM MULT; DC 1**
See also DLB 3, 50
Browne, (Clyde) Jackson 1948(?)- .... **CLC 21**
See also CA 120
Browning, Elizabeth Barrett 1806-1861**NCLC 1, 16, 61, 66; DA; DAB; DAC; DAM MST, POET; PC 6; WLC**
See also CDBLB 1832-1890; DLB 32, 199
Browning, Robert 1812-1889 **NCLC 19, 79; DA; DAB; DAC; DAM MST, POET; PC 2; WLCS**
See also CDBLB 1832-1890; DLB 32, 163; YABC 1
Browning, Tod 1882-1962 .... **CLC 16**
See also CA 141; 117
Brownson, Orestes Augustus 1803-1876 **NCLC 50**
See also DLB 1, 59, 73
Bruccoli, Matthew J(oseph) 1931- .... **CLC 34**
See also CA 9-12R; CANR 7; DLB 103
Bruce, Lenny .... **CLC 21**
See also Schneider, Leonard Alfred
Bruin, John
See Brutus, Dennis
Brulard, Henri
See Stendhal
Brulls, Christian
See Simenon, Georges (Jacques Christian)
Brunner, John (Kilian Houston) 1934-1995 **CLC 8, 10; DAM POP**
See also CA 1-4R; 149; CAAS 8; CANR 2, 37; MTCW 1, 2
Bruno, Giordano 1548-1600 .... **LC 27**
Brutus, Dennis 1924- .... **CLC 43; BLC 1; DAM MULT, POET; PC 24**
See also BW 2, 3; CA 49-52; CAAS 14; CANR 2, 27, 42, 81; DLB 117
Bryan, C(ourtlandt) D(ixon) B(arnes) 1936-**CLC 29**
See also CA 73-76; CANR 13, 68; DLB 185; INT CANR-13
Bryan, Michael
See Moore, Brian
Bryant, William Cullen 1794-1878 **NCLC 6, 46; DA; DAB; DAC; DAM MST, POET; PC 20**
See also CDALB 1640-1865; DLB 3, 43, 59, 189
Bryusov, Valery Yakovlevich 1873-1924**TCLC 10**
See also CA 107; 155
Buchan, John 1875-1940 **TCLC 41; DAB; DAM POP**
See also CA 108; 145; DLB 34, 70, 156; MTCW 1; YABC 2
Buchanan, George 1506-1582 .... **LC 4**
See also DLB 152
Buchheim, Lothar-Guenther 1918- .... **CLC 6**
See also CA 85-88
Buchner, (Karl) Georg 1813-1837 ...... **NCLC 26**
Buchwald, Art(hur) 1925- .... **CLC 33**
See also AITN 1; CA 5-8R; CANR 21, 67; MTCW 1, 2; SATA 10
Buck, Pearl S(ydenstricker) 1892-1973 **CLC 7, 11, 18; DA; DAB; DAC; DAM MST, NOV**
See also AITN 1; CA 1-4R; 41-44R; CANR 1, 34; CDALBS; DLB 9, 102; MTCW 1, 2; SATA 1, 25
Buckler, Ernest 1908-1984 **CLC 13; DAC; DAM MST**
See also CA 11-12; 114; CAP 1; DLB 68; SATA 47
Buckley, Vincent (Thomas) 1925-1988 . **CLC 57**
See also CA 101
Buckley, William F(rank), Jr. 1925- **CLC 7, 18, 37; DAM POP**
See also AITN 1; CA 1-4R; CANR 1, 24, 53; DLB 137; DLBY 80; INT CANR-24; MTCW 1, 2
Buechner, (Carl) Frederick 1926-**CLC 2, 4, 6, 9; DAM NOV**
See also CA 13-16R; CANR 11, 39, 64; DLBY 80; INT CANR-11; MTCW 1, 2
Buell, John (Edward) 1927- .... **CLC 10**
See also CA 1-4R; CANR 71; DLB 53
Buero Vallejo, Antonio 1916- .... **CLC 15, 46**
See also CA 106; CANR 24, 49, 75; HW 1; MTCW 1, 2
Bufalino, Gesualdo 1920(?)- .... **CLC 74**
See also DLB 196
Bugayev, Boris Nikolayevich 1880-1934**TCLC 7; PC 11**
See also Bely, Andrey
See also CA 104; 165; MTCW 1
Bukowski, Charles 1920-1994**CLC 2, 5, 9, 41, 82, 108; DAM NOV, POET; PC 18**
See also CA 17-20R; 144; CANR 40, 62; DLB 5, 130, 169; MTCW 1, 2
Bulgakov, Mikhail (Afanas'evich) 1891-1940 **TCLC 2, 16; DAM DRAM, NOV; SSC 18**
See also CA 105; 152
Bulgya, Alexander Alexandrovich 1901-1956 **TCLC 53**
See also Fadeyev, Alexander
See also CA 117
Bullins, Ed 1935- ..... **CLC 1, 5, 7; BLC 1; DAM DRAM, MULT; DC 6**
See also BW 2, 3; CA 49-52; CAAS 16; CANR 24, 46, 73; DLB 7, 38; MTCW 1, 2
Bulwer-Lytton, Edward (George Earle Lytton) 1803-1873 .... **NCLC 1, 45**
See also DLB 21
Bunin, Ivan Alexeyevich 1870-1953**TCLC 6; SSC 5**
See also CA 104
Bunting, Basil 1900-1985 **CLC 10, 39, 47; DAM POET**
See also CA 53-56; 115; CANR 7; DLB 20
Bunuel, Luis 1900-1983**CLC 16, 80; DAM MULT; HLC**
See also CA 101; 110; CANR 32, 77; HW 1
Bunyan, John 1628-1688 **LC 4; DA; DAB; DAC; DAM MST; WLC**
See also CDBLB 1660-1789; DLB 39
Burckhardt, Jacob (Christoph) 1818-1897**NCLC 49**
Burford, Eleanor
See Hibbert, Eleanor Alice Burford
Burgess, Anthony **CLC 1, 2, 4, 5, 8, 10, 13, 15, 22, 40, 62, 81, 94; DAB**
See also Wilson, John (Anthony) Burgess
See also AAYA 25; AITN 1; CDBLB 1960 to Present; DLB 14, 194; DLBY 98; MTCW 1
Burke, Edmund 1729(?)-1797**LC 7, 36; DA; DAB; DAC; DAM MST; WLC**
See also DLB 104
Burke, Kenneth (Duva) 1897-1993 .... **CLC 2, 24**
See also CA 5-8R; 143; CANR 39, 74; DLB 45, 63; MTCW 1, 2
Burke, Leda
See Garnett, David
Burke, Ralph
See Silverberg, Robert
Burke, Thomas 1886-1945 .... **TCLC 63**
See also CA 113; 155; DLB 197
Burney, Fanny 1752-1840 .... **NCLC 12, 54**
See also DLB 39
Burns, Robert 1759-1796**LC 3, 29, 40; DA; DAB; DAC; DAM MST, POET; PC 6; WLC**
See also CDBLB 1789-1832; DLB 109
Burns, Tex
See L'Amour, Louis (Dearborn)
Burnshaw, Stanley 1906- .... **CLC 3, 13, 44**

See also CA 9-12R; DLB 48; DLBY 97
Burr, Anne 1937- .... **CLC 6**
See also CA 25-28R
Burroughs, Edgar Rice 1875-1950 **TCLC 2, 32; DAM NOV**
See also AAYA 11; CA 104; 132; DLB 8; MTCW 1, 2; SATA 41
Burroughs, William S(eward) 1914-1997**CLC 1, 2, 5, 15, 22, 42, 75, 109; DA; DAB; DAC; DAM MST, NOV, POP; WLC**
See also AITN 2; CA 9-12R; 160; CANR 20, 52; DLB 2, 8, 16, 152; DLBY 81, 97; MTCW 1, 2
Burton, SirRichard F(rancis) 1821-1890 **NCLC 42**
See also DLB 55, 166, 184
Busch, Frederick 1941- .... **CLC 7, 10, 18, 47**
See also CA 33-36R; CAAS 1; CANR 45, 73; DLB 6
Bush, Ronald 1946- .... **CLC 34**
See also CA 136
Bustos, F(rancisco)
See Borges, Jorge Luis
Bustos Domecq, H(onorio)
See Bioy Casares, Adolfo; Borges, Jorge Luis
Butler, Octavia E(stelle) 1947- ..... **CLC 38, 121; BLCS; DAM MULT, POP**
See also AAYA 18; BW 2, 3; CA 73-76; CANR 12, 24, 38, 73; DLB 33; MTCW 1, 2; SATA 84
Butler, Robert Olen (Jr.) 1945- .. **CLC 81; DAM POP**
See also CA 112; CANR 66; DLB 173; INT 112; MTCW 1
Butler, Samuel 1612-1680 .... **LC 16, 43**
See also DLB 101, 126
Butler, Samuel 1835-1902**TCLC 1, 33; DA; DAB; DAC; DAM MST, NOV; WLC**
See also CA 143; CDBLB 1890-1914; DLB 18, 57, 174
Butler, Walter C.
See Faust, Frederick (Schiller)
Butor, Michel (Marie Francois) 1926- **CLC 1, 3, 8, 11, 15**
See also CA 9-12R; CANR 33, 66; DLB 83; MTCW 1, 2
Butts, Mary 1892(?)-1937 .... **TCLC 77**
See also CA 148
Buzo, Alexander (John) 1944- .... **CLC 61**
See also CA 97-100; CANR 17, 39, 69
Buzzati, Dino 1906-1972 .... **CLC 36**
See also CA 160; 33-36R; DLB 177
Byars, Betsy (Cromer) 1928- .... **CLC 35**
See also AAYA 19; CA 33-36R; CANR 18, 36, 57; CLR 1, 16; DLB 52; INT CANR-18; JRDA; MAICYA; MTCW 1; SAAS 1; SATA 4, 46, 80; SATA-Essay 108
Byatt, A(ntonia) S(usan Drabble) 1936- **CLC 19, 65; DAM NOV, POP**
See also CA 13-16R; CANR 13, 33, 50, 75; DLB 14, 194; MTCW 1, 2
Byrne, David 1952- .... **CLC 26**
See also CA 127
Byrne, John Keyes 1926-
See Leonard, Hugh
See also CA 102; CANR 78; INT 102
Byron, George Gordon (Noel) 1788-1824**NCLC 2, 12; DA; DAB; DAC; DAM MST, POET; PC 16; WLC**
See also CDBLB 1789-1832; DLB 96, 110
Byron, Robert 1905-1941 .... **TCLC 67**
See also CA 160; DLB 195
C. 3. 3.
See Wilde, Oscar
Caballero, Fernan 1796-1877 .... **NCLC 10**
Cabell, Branch
See Cabell, James Branch
Cabell, James Branch 1879-1958 .... **TCLC 6**
See also CA 105; 152; DLB 9, 78; MTCW 1
Cable, George Washington 1844-1925 **TCLC 4; SSC 4**
See also CA 104; 155; DLB 12, 74; DLBD 13
Cabral de Melo Neto, Joao 1920- **CLC 76; DAM MULT**
See also CA 151
Cabrera Infante, G(uillermo) 1929-**CLC 5, 25, 45, 120; DAM MULT; HLC**
See also CA 85-88; CANR 29, 65; DLB 113; HW 1, 2; MTCW 1, 2
Cade, Toni
See Bambara, Toni Cade
Cadmus and Harmonia
See Buchan, John
Caedmon fl. 658-680 .... **CMLC 7**
See also DLB 146
Caeiro, Alberto
See Pessoa, Fernando (Antonio Nogueira)
Cage, John (Milton, Jr.) 1912-1992 .... **CLC 41**
See also CA 13-16R; 169; CANR 9, 78; DLB 193; INT CANR-9
Cahan, Abraham 1860-1951 .... **TCLC 71**
See also CA 108; 154; DLB 9, 25, 28
Cain, G.
See Cabrera Infante, G(uillermo)
Cain, Guillermo
See Cabrera Infante, G(uillermo)
Cain, James M(allahan) 1892-1977**CLC 3, 11, 28**
See also AITN 1; CA 17-20R; 73-76; CANR 8, 34, 61; MTCW 1
Caine, Mark
See Raphael, Frederic (Michael)
Calasso, Roberto 1941- .... **CLC 81**
See also CA 143
Calderon de la Barca, Pedro 1600-1681 . **LC 23; DC 3; HLCS 1**
Caldwell, Erskine (Preston) 1903-1987**CLC 1, 8, 14, 50, 60; DAM NOV; SSC 19**
See also AITN 1; CA 1-4R; 121; CAAS 1; CANR 2, 33; DLB 9, 86; MTCW 1, 2
Caldwell, (Janet Miriam) Taylor (Holland) 1900-1985 .... **CLC 2, 28, 39; DAM NOV, POP**
See also CA 5-8R; 116; CANR 5; DLBD 17
Calhoun, John Caldwell 1782-1850 ..... **NCLC 15**
See also DLB 3
Calisher, Hortense 1911- **CLC 2, 4, 8, 38; DAM NOV; SSC 15**
See also CA 1-4R; CANR 1, 22, 67; DLB 2; INT CANR-22; MTCW 1, 2
Callaghan, Morley Edward 1903-1990**CLC 3, 14, 41, 65; DAC; DAM MST**
See also CA 9-12R; 132; CANR 33, 73; DLB 68; MTCW 1, 2
Callimachus c. 305B.C.-c. 240B.C. ..... **CMLC 18**
See also DLB 176
Calvin, John 1509-1564 .... **LC 37**
Calvino, Italo 1923-1985**CLC 5, 8, 11, 22, 33, 39, 73; DAM NOV; SSC 3**
See also CA 85-88; 116; CANR 23, 61; DLB 196; MTCW 1, 2
Cameron, Carey 1952- .... **CLC 59**
See also CA 135
Cameron, Peter 1959- .... **CLC 44**
See also CA 125; CANR 50
Campana, Dino 1885-1932 .... **TCLC 20**
See also CA 117; DLB 114
Campanella, Tommaso 1568-1639 .... **LC 32**
Campbell, John W(ood, Jr.) 1910-1971 . **CLC 32**
See also CA 21-22; 29-32R; CANR 34; CAP 2; DLB 8; MTCW 1
Campbell, Joseph 1904-1987 .... **CLC 69**
See also AAYA 3; BEST 89:2; CA 1-4R; 124; CANR 3, 28, 61; MTCW 1, 2
Campbell, Maria 1940- .... **CLC 85; DAC**
See also CA 102; CANR 54; NNAL
Campbell, (John) Ramsey 1946-**CLC 42; SSC 19**
See also CA 57-60; CANR 7; INT CANR-7
Campbell, (Ignatius) Roy (Dunnachie) 1901-1957 .... **TCLC 5**
See also CA 104; 155; DLB 20; MTCW 2
Campbell, Thomas 1777-1844 .... **NCLC 19**
See also DLB 93; 144
Campbell, Wilfred .... **TCLC 9**
See also Campbell, William
Campbell, William 1858(?)-1918
See Campbell, Wilfred
See also CA 106; DLB 92
Campion, Jane .... **CLC 95**
See also CA 138
Campos, Alvaro de
See Pessoa, Fernando (Antonio Nogueira)
Camus, Albert 1913-1960 **CLC 1, 2, 4, 9, 11, 14, 32, 63, 69; DA; DAB; DAC; DAM DRAM, MST, NOV; DC 2; SSC 9; WLC**
See also CA 89-92; DLB 72; MTCW 1, 2
Canby, Vincent 1924- .... **CLC 13**
See also CA 81-84
Cancale
See Desnos, Robert
Canetti, Elias 1905-1994 .. **CLC 3, 14, 25, 75, 86**
See also CA 21-24R; 146; CANR 23, 61, 79; DLB 85, 124; MTCW 1, 2
Canfield, Dorothea F.
See Fisher, Dorothy (Frances) Canfield
Canfield, Dorothea Frances
See Fisher, Dorothy (Frances) Canfield
Canfield, Dorothy
See Fisher, Dorothy (Frances) Canfield
Canin, Ethan 1960- .... **CLC 55**
See also CA 131; 135
Cannon, Curt
See Hunter, Evan
Cao, Lan 1961- .... **CLC 109**
See also CA 165
Cape, Judith
See Page, P(atricia) K(athleen)
Capek, Karel 1890-1938 **TCLC 6, 37; DA; DAB; DAC; DAM DRAM, MST, NOV; DC 1; WLC**
See also CA 104; 140; MTCW 1
Capote, Truman 1924-1984**CLC 1, 3, 8, 13, 19, 34, 38, 58; DA; DAB; DAC; DAM MST, NOV, POP; SSC 2; WLC**
See also CA 5-8R; 113; CANR 18, 62; CDALB 1941-1968; DLB 2, 185; DLBY 80, 84; MTCW 1, 2; SATA 91
Capra, Frank 1897-1991 .... **CLC 16**
See also CA 61-64; 135
Caputo, Philip 1941- .... **CLC 32**
See also CA 73-76; CANR 40
Caragiale, Ion Luca 1852-1912 .... **TCLC 76**
See also CA 157
Card, Orson Scott 1951- **CLC 44, 47, 50; DAM POP**
See also AAYA 11; CA 102; CANR 27, 47, 73; INT CANR-27; MTCW 1, 2; SATA 83
Cardenal, Ernesto 1925- . **CLC 31; DAM MULT, POET; HLC; PC 22**
See also CA 49-52; CANR 2, 32, 66; HW 1, 2; MTCW 1, 2
Cardozo, Benjamin N(athan) 1870-1938**TCLC 65**
See also CA 117; 164
Carducci, Giosue (Alessandro Giuseppe) 1835-1907 .... **TCLC 32**
See also CA 163
Carew, Thomas 1595(?)-1640 .... **LC 13**
See also DLB 126
Carey, Ernestine Gilbreth 1908- .... **CLC 17**
See also CA 5-8R; CANR 71; SATA 2
Carey, Peter 1943- .... **CLC 40, 55, 96**
See also CA 123; 127; CANR 53, 76; INT 127; MTCW 1, 2; SATA 94
Carleton, William 1794-1869 .... **NCLC 3**
See also DLB 159
Carlisle, Henry (Coffin) 1926- .... **CLC 33**

See also CA 13-16R; CANR 15
Carlsen, Chris
See Holdstock, Robert P.
Carlson, Ron(ald F.) 1947- .... **CLC 54**
See also CA 105; CANR 27
Carlyle, Thomas 1795-1881**NCLC 70; DA; DAB; DAC; DAM MST**
See also CDBLB 1789-1832; DLB 55; 144
Carman, (William) Bliss 1861-1929**TCLC 7; DAC**
See also CA 104; 152; DLB 92
Carnegie, Dale 1888-1955 .... **TCLC 53**
Carossa, Hans 1878-1956 .... **TCLC 48**
See also CA 170; DLB 66
Carpenter, Don(ald Richard) 1931-1995 **CLC 41**
See also CA 45-48; 149; CANR 1, 71
Carpenter, Edward 1844-1929 .... **TCLC 88**
See also CA 163
Carpentier (y Valmont), Alejo 1904-1980 **CLC 8, 11, 38, 110; DAM MULT; HLC; SSC 35**
See also CA 65-68; 97-100; CANR 11, 70; DLB 113; HW 1, 2
Carr, Caleb 1955(?)- .... **CLC 86**
See also CA 147; CANR 73
Carr, Emily 1871-1945 .... **TCLC 32**
See also CA 159; DLB 68
Carr, John Dickson 1906-1977 .... **CLC 3**
See also Fairbairn, Roger
See also CA 49-52; 69-72; CANR 3, 33, 60; MTCW 1, 2
Carr, Philippa
See Hibbert, Eleanor Alice Burford
Carr, Virginia Spencer 1929- .... **CLC 34**
See also CA 61-64; DLB 111
Carrere, Emmanuel 1957- .... **CLC 89**
Carrier, Roch 1937- ... **CLC 13, 78; DAC; DAM MST**
See also CA 130; CANR 61; DLB 53; SATA 105
Carroll, James P. 1943(?)- .... **CLC 38**
See also CA 81-84; CANR 73; MTCW 1
Carroll, Jim 1951- .... **CLC 35**
See also AAYA 17; CA 45-48; CANR 42
Carroll, Lewis .... **NCLC 2, 53; PC 18; WLC**
See also Dodgson, Charles Lutwidge
See also CDBLB 1832-1890; CLR 2, 18; DLB 18, 163, 178; DLBY 98; JRDA
Carroll, Paul Vincent 1900-1968 .... **CLC 10**
See also CA 9-12R; 25-28R; DLB 10
Carruth, Hayden 1921-**CLC 4, 7, 10, 18, 84; PC 10**
See also CA 9-12R; CANR 4, 38, 59; DLB 5, 165; INT CANR-4; MTCW 1, 2; SATA 47
Carson, Rachel Louise 1907-1964**CLC 71; DAM POP**
See also CA 77-80; CANR 35; MTCW 1, 2; SATA 23
Carter, Angela (Olive) 1940-1992**CLC 5, 41, 76; SSC 13**
See also CA 53-56; 136; CANR 12, 36, 61; DLB 14, 207; MTCW 1, 2; SATA 66; SATA-Obit 70
Carter, Nick
See Smith, Martin Cruz
Carver, Raymond 1938-1988 **CLC 22, 36, 53, 55; DAM NOV; SSC 8**
See also CA 33-36R; 126; CANR 17, 34, 61; DLB 130; DLBY 84, 88; MTCW 1, 2
Cary, Elizabeth, Lady Falkland 1585-1639 **LC 30**
Cary, (Arthur) Joyce (Lunel) 1888-1957**TCLC 1, 29**
See also CA 104; 164; CDBLB 1914-1945; DLB 15, 100; MTCW 2
Casanova de Seingalt, Giovanni Jacopo 1725-1798 **LC 13**
Casares, Adolfo Bioy
See Bioy Casares, Adolfo
Casely-Hayford, J(oseph) E(phraim) 1866-1930 **TCLC 24; BLC 1; DAM MULT**
See also BW 2; CA 123; 152
Casey, John (Dudley) 1939- .... **CLC 59**
See also BEST 90:2; CA 69-72; CANR 23
Casey, Michael 1947- .... **CLC 2**
See also CA 65-68; DLB 5
Casey, Patrick
See Thurman, Wallace (Henry)
Casey, Warren (Peter) 1935-1988 .... **CLC 12**
See also CA 101; 127; INT 101
Casona, Alejandro .... **CLC 49**
See also Alvarez, Alejandro Rodriguez
Cassavetes, John 1929-1989 .... **CLC 20**
See also CA 85-88; 127
Cassian, Nina 1924- .... **PC 17**
Cassill, R(onald) V(erlin) 1919- .... **CLC 4, 23**
See also CA 9-12R; CAAS 1; CANR 7, 45; DLB 6
Cassirer, Ernst 1874-1945 .... **TCLC 61**
See also CA 157
Cassity, (Allen) Turner 1929- .... **CLC 6, 42**
See also CA 17-20R; CAAS 8; CANR 11; DLB 105
Castaneda, Carlos (Cesar Aranha) 1931(?)-1998 **CLC 12, 119**
See also CA 25-28R; CANR 32, 66; HW 1; MTCW 1
Castedo, Elena 1937- .... **CLC 65**
See also CA 132
Castedo-Ellerman, Elena
See Castedo, Elena
Castellanos, Rosario 1925-1974 . **CLC 66; DAM MULT; HLC**
See also CA 131; 53-56; CANR 58; DLB 113; HW 1; MTCW 1
Castelvetro, Lodovico 1505-1571 .... **LC 12**
Castiglione, Baldassare 1478-1529 .... **LC 12**
Castle, Robert
See Hamilton, Edmond
Castro, Guillen de 1569-1631 .... **LC 19**
Castro, Rosalia de 1837-1885**NCLC 3, 78; DAM MULT**
Cather, Willa
See Cather, Willa Sibert
Cather, Willa Sibert 1873-1947 **TCLC 1, 11, 31; DA; DAB; DAC; DAM MST, NOV; SSC 2; WLC**
See also AAYA 24; CA 104; 128; CDALB 1865-1917; DLB 9, 54, 78; DLBD 1; MTCW 1, 2; SATA 30
Catherine, Saint 1347-1380 .... **CMLC 27**
Cato, Marcus Porcius 234B.C.-149B.C.**CMLC 21**
See also DLB 211
Catton, (Charles) Bruce 1899-1978 ...... **CLC 35**
See also AITN 1; CA 5-8R; 81-84; CANR 7, 74; DLB 17; SATA 2; SATA-Obit 24
Catullus c. 84B.C.-c. 54B.C. .... **CMLC 18**
See also DLB 211
Cauldwell, Frank
See King, Francis (Henry)
Caunitz, William J. 1933-1996 .... **CLC 34**
See also BEST 89:3; CA 125; 130; 152; CANR 73; INT 130
Causley, Charles (Stanley) 1917- .... **CLC 7**
See also CA 9-12R; CANR 5, 35; CLR 30; DLB 27; MTCW 1; SATA 3, 66
Caute, (John) David 1936- . **CLC 29; DAM NOV**
See also CA 1-4R; CAAS 4; CANR 1, 33, 64; DLB 14
Cavafy, C(onstantine) P(eter) 1863-1933**TCLC 2, 7; DAM POET**
See also Kavafis, Konstantinos Petrou
See also CA 148; MTCW 1
Cavallo, Evelyn
See Spark, Muriel (Sarah)
Cavanna, Betty .... **CLC 12**
See also Harrison, Elizabeth Cavanna
See also JRDA; MAICYA; SAAS 4; SATA 1, 30
Cavendish, Margaret Lucas 1623-1673 ... **LC 30**
See also DLB 131
Caxton, William 1421(?)-1491(?) .... **LC 17**
See also DLB 170
Cayer, D. M.
See Duffy, Maureen
Cayrol, Jean 1911- .... **CLC 11**
See also CA 89-92; DLB 83
Cela, Camilo Jose 1916- .. **CLC 4, 13, 59; DAM MULT; HLC**
See also BEST 90:2; CA 21-24R; CAAS 10; CANR 21, 32, 76; DLBY 89; HW 1; MTCW 1, 2
Celan, Paul .... **CLC 10, 19, 53, 82; PC 10**
See also Antschel, Paul
See also DLB 69
Celine, Louis-Ferdinand **CLC 1, 3, 4, 7, 9, 15, 47**
See also Destouches, Louis-Ferdinand
See also DLB 72
Cellini, Benvenuto 1500-1571 .... **LC 7**
Cendrars, Blaise 1887-1961 .... **CLC 18, 106**
See also Sauser-Hall, Frederic
Cernuda (y Bidon), Luis 1902-1963**CLC 54; DAM POET**
See also CA 131; 89-92; DLB 134; HW 1
Cervantes (Saavedra), Miguel de 1547-1616**LC 6, 23; DA; DAB; DAC; DAM MST, NOV; SSC 12; WLC**
Cesaire, Aime (Fernand) 1913-**CLC 19, 32, 112; BLC 1; DAM MULT, POET; PC 25**
See also BW 2, 3; CA 65-68; CANR 24, 43, 81; MTCW 1, 2
Chabon, Michael 1963- .... **CLC 55**
See also CA 139; CANR 57
Chabrol, Claude 1930- .... **CLC 16**
See also CA 110
Challans, Mary 1905-1983
See Renault, Mary
See also CA 81-84; 111; CANR 74; MTCW 2; SATA 23; SATA-Obit 36
Challis, George
See Faust, Frederick (Schiller)
Chambers, Aidan 1934- .... **CLC 35**
See also AAYA 27; CA 25-28R; CANR 12, 31, 58; JRDA; MAICYA; SAAS 12; SATA 1, 69, 108
Chambers, James 1948-
See Cliff, Jimmy
See also CA 124
Chambers, Jessie
See Lawrence, D(avid) H(erbert Richards)
Chambers, Robert W(illiam) 1865-1933**TCLC 41**
See also CA 165; DLB 202; SATA 107
Chandler, Raymond (Thornton) 1888-1959**TCLC 1, 7; SSC 23**
See also AAYA 25; CA 104; 129; CANR 60; CDALB 1929-1941; DLBD 6; MTCW 1, 2
Chang, Eileen 1920-1995 .... **SSC 28**
See also CA 166
Chang, Jung 1952- .... **CLC 71**
See also CA 142
Chang Ai-Ling
See Chang, Eileen
Channing, William Ellery 1780-1842 . **NCLC 17**
See also DLB 1, 59
Chao, Patricia 1955- .... **CLC 119**
See also CA 163
Chaplin, Charles Spencer 1889-1977 ... **CLC 16**
See also Chaplin, Charlie
See also CA 81-84; 73-76
Chaplin, Charlie
See Chaplin, Charles Spencer
See also DLB 44
Chapman, George 1559(?)-1634 .... **LC 22; DAM DRAM**
See also DLB 62, 121
Chapman, Graham 1941-1989 .... **CLC 21**
See also Monty Python
See also CA 116; 129; CANR 35
Chapman, John Jay 1862-1933 .... **TCLC 7**
See also CA 104

Author Index

Chapman, Lee
See Bradley, Marion Zimmer
Chapman, Walker
See Silverberg, Robert
Chappell, Fred (Davis) 1936- .... **CLC 40, 78**
See also CA 5-8R; CAAS 4; CANR 8, 33, 67; DLB 6, 105
Char, Rene(-Emile) 1907-1988**CLC 9, 11, 14, 55; DAM POET**
See also CA 13-16R; 124; CANR 32; MTCW 1, 2
Charby, Jay
See Ellison, Harlan (Jay)
Chardin, Pierre Teilhard de
See Teilhard de Chardin, (Marie Joseph) Pierre
Charles I 1600-1649 .... **LC 13**
Charriere, Isabelle de 1740-1805 .... **NCLC 66**
Charyn, Jerome 1937- .... **CLC 5, 8, 18**
See also CA 5-8R; CAAS 1; CANR 7, 61; DLBY 83; MTCW 1
Chase, Mary (Coyle) 1907-1981 .... **DC 1**
See also CA 77-80; 105; SATA 17; SATA-Obit 29
Chase, Mary Ellen 1887-1973 .... **CLC 2**
See also CA 13-16; 41-44R; CAP 1; SATA 10
Chase, Nicholas
See Hyde, Anthony
Chateaubriand, Francois Rene de 1768-1848 **NCLC 3**
See also DLB 119
Chatterje, Sarat Chandra 1876-1936(?)
See Chatterji, Saratchandra
See also CA 109
Chatterji, Bankim Chandra 1838-1894**NCLC 19**
Chatterji, Saratchandra .... **TCLC 13**
See also Chatterje, Sarat Chandra
Chatterton, Thomas 1752-1770**LC 3; DAM POET**
See also DLB 109
Chatwin, (Charles) Bruce 1940-1989**CLC 28, 57, 59; DAM POP**
See also AAYA 4; BEST 90:1; CA 85-88; 127; DLB 194, 204
Chaucer, Daniel
See Ford, Ford Madox
Chaucer, Geoffrey 1340(?)-1400**LC 17; DA; DAB; DAC; DAM MST, POET; PC 19; WLCS**
See also CDBLB Before 1660; DLB 146
Chaviaras, Strates 1935-
See Haviaras, Stratis
See also CA 105
Chayefsky, Paddy .... **CLC 23**
See also Chayefsky, Sidney
See also DLB 7, 44; DLBY 81
Chayefsky, Sidney 1923-1981
See Chayefsky, Paddy
See also CA 9-12R; 104; CANR 18; DAM DRAM
Chedid, Andree 1920- .... **CLC 47**
See also CA 145
Cheever, John 1912-1982**CLC 3, 7, 8, 11, 15, 25, 64; DA; DAB; DAC; DAM MST, NOV, POP; SSC 1; WLC**
See also CA 5-8R; 106; CABS 1; CANR 5, 27, 76; CDALB 1941-1968; DLB 2, 102; DLBY 80, 82; INT CANR-5; MTCW 1, 2
Cheever, Susan 1943- .... **CLC 18, 48**
See also CA 103; CANR 27, 51; DLBY 82; INT CANR-27
Chekhonte, Antosha
See Chekhov, Anton (Pavlovich)
Chekhov, Anton (Pavlovich) 1860-1904 **TCLC 3, 10, 31, 55; DA; DAB; DAC; DAM DRAM, MST; DC 9; SSC 2, 28; WLC**
See also CA 104; 124; SATA 90
Chernyshevsky, Nikolay Gavrilovich 1828-1889 **NCLC 1**
Cherry, Carolyn Janice 1942-
See Cherryh, C. J.
See also CA 65-68; CANR 10
Cherryh, C. J. .... **CLC 35**
See also Cherry, Carolyn Janice
See also AAYA 24; DLBY 80; SATA 93
Chesnutt, Charles W(addell) 1858-1932**TCLC 5, 39; BLC 1; DAM MULT; SSC 7**
See also BW 1, 3; CA 106; 125; CANR 76; DLB 12, 50, 78; MTCW 1, 2
Chester, Alfred 1929(?)-1971 .... **CLC 49**
See also CA 33-36R; DLB 130
Chesterton, G(ilbert) K(eith) 1874-1936**TCLC 1, 6, 64; DAM NOV, POET; SSC 1**
See also CA 104; 132; CANR 73; CDBLB 1914-1945; DLB 10, 19, 34, 70, 98, 149, 178; MTCW 1, 2; SATA 27
Chiang, Pin-chin 1904-1986
See Ding Ling
See also CA 118
Ch'ien Chung-shu 1910- .... **CLC 22**
See also CA 130; CANR 73; MTCW 1, 2
Child, L. Maria
See Child, Lydia Maria
Child, Lydia Maria 1802-1880 .... **NCLC 6, 73**
See also DLB 1, 74; SATA 67
Child, Mrs.
See Child, Lydia Maria
Child, Philip 1898-1978 .... **CLC 19, 68**
See also CA 13-14; CAP 1; SATA 47
Childers, (Robert) Erskine 1870-1922 **TCLC 65**
See also CA 113; 153; DLB 70
Childress, Alice 1920-1994 **CLC 12, 15, 86, 96; BLC 1; DAM DRAM, MULT, NOV; DC 4**
See also AAYA 8; BW 2, 3; CA 45-48; 146; CANR 3, 27, 50, 74; CLR 14; DLB 7, 38; JRDA; MAICYA; MTCW 1, 2; SATA 7, 48, 81
Chin, Frank (Chew, Jr.) 1940- .... **DC 7**
See also CA 33-36R; CANR 71; DAM MULT; DLB 206
Chislett, (Margaret) Anne 1943- .... **CLC 34**
See also CA 151
Chitty, Thomas Willes 1926- .... **CLC 11**
See also Hinde, Thomas
See also CA 5-8R
Chivers, Thomas Holley 1809-1858 .... **NCLC 49**
See also DLB 3
Choi, Susan .... **CLC 119**
Chomette, Rene Lucien 1898-1981
See Clair, Rene
See also CA 103
Chopin, Kate**TCLC 5, 14; DA; DAB; SSC 8; WLCS**
See also Chopin, Katherine
See also CDALB 1865-1917; DLB 12, 78
Chopin, Katherine 1851-1904
See Chopin, Kate
See also CA 104; 122; DAC; DAM MST, NOV
Chretien de Troyes c. 12th cent. - ..... **CMLC 10**
See also DLB 208
Christie
See Ichikawa, Kon
Christie, Agatha (Mary Clarissa) 1890-1976**CLC 1, 6, 8, 12, 39, 48, 110; DAB; DAC; DAM NOV**
See also AAYA 9; AITN 1, 2; CA 17-20R; 61-64; CANR 10, 37; CDBLB 1914-1945; DLB 13, 77; MTCW 1, 2; SATA 36
Christie, (Ann) Philippa
See Pearce, Philippa
See also CA 5-8R; CANR 4
Christine de Pizan 1365(?)-1431(?) .... **LC 9**
See also DLB 208
Chubb, Elmer
See Masters, Edgar Lee
Chulkov, Mikhail Dmitrievich 1743-1792 . **LC 2**
See also DLB 150
Churchill, Caryl 1938- .... **CLC 31, 55; DC 5**
See also CA 102; CANR 22, 46; DLB 13; MTCW 1
Churchill, Charles 1731-1764 .... **LC 3**
See also DLB 109
Chute, Carolyn 1947- .... **CLC 39**
See also CA 123
Ciardi, John (Anthony) 1916-1986 . **CLC 10, 40, 44; DAM POET**
See also CA 5-8R; 118; CAAS 2; CANR 5, 33; CLR 19; DLB 5; DLBY 86; INT CANR-5; MAICYA; MTCW 1, 2; SAAS 26; SATA 1, 65; SATA-Obit 46
Cicero, Marcus Tullius 106B.C.-43B.C.**CMLC 3**
See also DLB 211
Cimino, Michael 1943- .... **CLC 16**
See also CA 105
Cioran, E(mil) M. 1911-1995 .... **CLC 64**
See also CA 25-28R; 149
Cisneros, Sandra 1954- ..... **CLC 69, 118; DAM MULT; HLC; SSC 32**
See also AAYA 9; CA 131; CANR 64; DLB 122, 152; HW 1, 2; MTCW 2
Cixous, Helene 1937- .... **CLC 92**
See also CA 126; CANR 55; DLB 83; MTCW 1, 2
Clair, Rene .... **CLC 20**
See also Chomette, Rene Lucien
Clampitt, Amy 1920-1994 .... **CLC 32; PC 19**
See also CA 110; 146; CANR 29, 79; DLB 105
Clancy, Thomas L., Jr. 1947-
See Clancy, Tom
See also CA 125; 131; CANR 62; INT 131; MTCW 1, 2
Clancy, Tom .... **CLC 45, 112; DAM NOV, POP**
See also Clancy, Thomas L., Jr.
See also AAYA 9; BEST 89:1, 90:1; MTCW 2
Clare, John 1793-1864 ..... **NCLC 9; DAB; DAM POET; PC 23**
See also DLB 55, 96
Clarin
See Alas (y Urena), Leopoldo (Enrique Garcia)
Clark, Al C.
See Goines, Donald
Clark, (Robert) Brian 1932- .... **CLC 29**
See also CA 41-44R; CANR 67
Clark, Curt
See Westlake, Donald E(dwin)
Clark, Eleanor 1913-1996 .... **CLC 5, 19**
See also CA 9-12R; 151; CANR 41; DLB 6
Clark, J. P.
See Clark, John Pepper
See also DLB 117
Clark, John Pepper 1935-**CLC 38; BLC 1; DAM DRAM, MULT; DC 5**
See also Clark, J. P.
See also BW 1; CA 65-68; CANR 16, 72; MTCW 1
Clark, M. R.
See Clark, Mavis Thorpe
Clark, Mavis Thorpe 1909- .... **CLC 12**
See also CA 57-60; CANR 8, 37; CLR 30; MAICYA; SAAS 5; SATA 8, 74
Clark, Walter Van Tilburg 1909-1971 .. **CLC 28**
See also CA 9-12R; 33-36R; CANR 63; DLB 9, 206; SATA 8
Clark Bekederemo, J(ohnson) P(epper)
See Clark, John Pepper
Clarke, Arthur C(harles) 1917-**CLC 1, 4, 13, 18, 35; DAM POP; SSC 3**
See also AAYA 4; CA 1-4R; CANR 2, 28, 55, 74; JRDA; MAICYA; MTCW 1, 2; SATA 13, 70
Clarke, Austin 1896-1974**CLC 6, 9; DAM POET**
See also CA 29-32; 49-52; CAP 2; DLB 10, 20
Clarke, Austin C(hesterfield) 1934- **CLC 8, 53; BLC 1; DAC; DAM MULT**
See also BW 1; CA 25-28R; CAAS 16; CANR 14, 32, 68; DLB 53, 125
Clarke, Gillian 1937- .... **CLC 61**
See also CA 106; DLB 40
Clarke, Marcus (Andrew Hislop) 1846-1881 **NCLC 19**
Clarke, Shirley 1925- .... **CLC 16**

Clash, The
See Headon, (Nicky) Topper; Jones, Mick; Simonon, Paul; Strummer, Joe
Claudel, Paul (Louis Charles Marie) 1868-1955 **TCLC 2, 10**
See also CA 104; 165; DLB 192
Claudius, Matthias 1740-1815 .... **NCLC 75**
See also DLB 97
Clavell, James (duMaresq) 1925-1994**CLC 6, 25, 87; DAM NOV, POP**
See also CA 25-28R; 146; CANR 26, 48; MTCW 1, 2
Cleaver, (Leroy) Eldridge 1935-1998**CLC 30, 119; BLC 1; DAM MULT**
See also BW 1, 3; CA 21-24R; 167; CANR 16, 75; MTCW 2
Cleese, John (Marwood) 1939- .... **CLC 21**
See also Monty Python
See also CA 112; 116; CANR 35; MTCW 1
Cleishbotham, Jebediah
See Scott, Walter
Cleland, John 1710-1789 .... **LC 2, 48**
See also DLB 39
Clemens, Samuel Langhorne 1835-1910
See Twain, Mark
See also CA 104; 135; CDALB 1865-1917; DA; DAB; DAC; DAM MST, NOV; DLB 11, 12, 23, 64, 74, 186, 189; JRDA; MAICYA; SATA 100; YABC 2
Cleophil
See Congreve, William
Clerihew, E.
See Bentley, E(dmund) C(lerihew)
Clerk, N. W.
See Lewis, C(live) S(taples)
Cliff, Jimmy .... **CLC 21**
See also Chambers, James
Cliff, Michelle 1946- .... **CLC 120; BLCS**
See also BW 2; CA 116; CANR 39, 72; DLB 157
Clifton, (Thelma) Lucille 1936-**CLC 19, 66; BLC 1; DAM MULT, POET; PC 17**
See also BW 2, 3; CA 49-52; CANR 2, 24, 42, 76; CLR 5; DLB 5, 41; MAICYA; MTCW 1, 2; SATA 20, 69
Clinton, Dirk
See Silverberg, Robert
Clough, Arthur Hugh 1819-1861 .... **NCLC 27**
See also DLB 32
Clutha, Janet Paterson Frame 1924-
See Frame, Janet
See also CA 1-4R; CANR 2, 36, 76; MTCW 1, 2
Clyne, Terence
See Blatty, William Peter
Cobalt, Martin
See Mayne, William (James Carter)
Cobb, Irvin S(hrewsbury) 1876-1944 ... **TCLC 77**
See also CA 175; DLB 11, 25, 86
Cobbett, William 1763-1835 .... **NCLC 49**
See also DLB 43, 107, 158
Coburn, D(onald) L(ee) 1938- .... **CLC 10**
See also CA 89-92
Cocteau, Jean (Maurice Eugene Clement) 1889-1963**CLC 1, 8, 15, 16, 43; DA; DAB; DAC; DAM DRAM, MST, NOV; WLC**
See also CA 25-28; CANR 40; CAP 2; DLB 65; MTCW 1, 2
Codrescu, Andrei 1946- ..... **CLC 46, 121; DAM POET**
See also CA 33-36R; CAAS 19; CANR 13, 34, 53, 76; MTCW 2
Coe, Max
See Bourne, Randolph S(illiman)
Coe, Tucker
See Westlake, Donald E(dwin)
Coen, Ethan 1958- .... **CLC 108**
See also CA 126
Coen, Joel 1955- .... **CLC 108**
See also CA 126
The Coen Brothers
See Coen, Ethan; Coen, Joel
Coetzee, J(ohn) M(ichael) 1940-**CLC 23, 33, 66, 117; DAM NOV**
See also CA 77-80; CANR 41, 54, 74; MTCW 1, 2
Coffey, Brian
See Koontz, Dean R(ay)
Coffin, Robert P(eter) Tristram 1892-1955**TCLC 95**
See also CA 123; 169; DLB 45
Cohan, George M(ichael) 1878-1942 ... **TCLC 60**
See also CA 157
Cohen, Arthur A(llen) 1928-1986 ..... **CLC 7, 31**
See also CA 1-4R; 120; CANR 1, 17, 42; DLB 28
Cohen, Leonard (Norman) 1934-**CLC 3, 38; DAC; DAM MST**
See also CA 21-24R; CANR 14, 69; DLB 53; MTCW 1
Cohen, Matt 1942- .... **CLC 19; DAC**
See also CA 61-64; CAAS 18; CANR 40; DLB 53
Cohen-Solal, Annie 19(?)- .... **CLC 50**
Colegate, Isabel 1931- .... **CLC 36**
See also CA 17-20R; CANR 8, 22, 74; DLB 14; INT CANR-22; MTCW 1
Coleman, Emmett
See Reed, Ishmael
Coleridge, M. E.
See Coleridge, Mary E(lizabeth)
Coleridge, Mary E(lizabeth) 1861-1907**TCLC 73**
See also CA 116; 166; DLB 19, 98
Coleridge, Samuel Taylor 1772-1834**NCLC 9, 54; DA; DAB; DAC; DAM MST, POET; PC 11; WLC**
See also CDBLB 1789-1832; DLB 93, 107
Coleridge, Sara 1802-1852 .... **NCLC 31**
See also DLB 199
Coles, Don 1928- .... **CLC 46**
See also CA 115; CANR 38
Coles, Robert (Martin) 1929- .... **CLC 108**
See also CA 45-48; CANR 3, 32, 66, 70; INT CANR-32; SATA 23
Colette, (Sidonie-Gabrielle) 1873-1954**TCLC 1, 5, 16; DAM NOV; SSC 10**
See also CA 104; 131; DLB 65; MTCW 1, 2
Collett, (Jacobine) Camilla (Wergeland) 1813-1895 **NCLC 22**
Collier, Christopher 1930- .... **CLC 30**
See also AAYA 13; CA 33-36R; CANR 13, 33; JRDA; MAICYA; SATA 16, 70
Collier, James L(incoln) 1928- ... **CLC 30; DAM POP**
See also AAYA 13; CA 9-12R; CANR 4, 33, 60; CLR 3; JRDA; MAICYA; SAAS 21; SATA 8, 70
Collier, Jeremy 1650-1726 .... **LC 6**
Collier, John 1901-1980 .... **SSC 19**
See also CA 65-68; 97-100; CANR 10; DLB 77
Collingwood, R(obin) G(eorge) 1889(?)-1943 **TCLC 67**
See also CA 117; 155
Collins, Hunt
See Hunter, Evan
Collins, Linda 1931- .... **CLC 44**
See also CA 125
Collins, (William) Wilkie 1824-1889**NCLC 1, 18**
See also CDBLB 1832-1890; DLB 18, 70, 159
Collins, William 1721-1759**LC 4, 40; DAM POET**
See also DLB 109
Collodi, Carlo 1826-1890 .... **NCLC 54**
See also Lorenzini, Carlo
See also CLR 5
Colman, George 1732-1794
See Glassco, John
Colt, Winchester Remington
See Hubbard, L(afayette) Ron(ald)
Colter, Cyrus 1910- .... **CLC 58**
See also BW 1; CA 65-68; CANR 10, 66; DLB 33
Colton, James
See Hansen, Joseph
Colum, Padraic 1881-1972 .... **CLC 28**
See also CA 73-76; 33-36R; CANR 35; CLR 36; MAICYA; MTCW 1; SATA 15
Colvin, James
See Moorcock, Michael (John)
Colwin, Laurie (E.) 1944-1992 **CLC 5, 13, 23, 84**
See also CA 89-92; 139; CANR 20, 46; DLBY 80; MTCW 1
Comfort, Alex(ander) 1920- . **CLC 7; DAM POP**
See also CA 1-4R; CANR 1, 45; MTCW 1
Comfort, Montgomery
See Campbell, (John) Ramsey
Compton-Burnett, I(vy) 1884(?)-1969 .. **CLC 1, 3, 10, 15, 34; DAM NOV**
See also CA 1-4R; 25-28R; CANR 4; DLB 36; MTCW 1
Comstock, Anthony 1844-1915 .... **TCLC 13**
See also CA 110; 169
Comte, Auguste 1798-1857 .... **NCLC 54**
Conan Doyle, Arthur
See Doyle, Arthur Conan
Conde, Maryse 1937- **CLC 52, 92; BLCS; DAM MULT**
See also Boucolon, Maryse
See also BW 2; MTCW 1
Condillac, Etienne Bonnot de 1714-1780 . **LC 26**
Condon, Richard (Thomas) 1915-1996**CLC 4, 6, 8, 10, 45, 100; DAM NOV**
See also BEST 90:3; CA 1-4R; 151; CAAS 1; CANR 2, 23; INT CANR-23; MTCW 1, 2
Confucius 551B.C.-479B.C.**CMLC 19; DA; DAB; DAC; DAM MST; WLCS**
Congreve, William 1670-1729**LC 5, 21; DA; DAB; DAC; DAM DRAM, MST, POET; DC 2; WLC**
See also CDBLB 1660-1789; DLB 39, 84
Connell, Evan S(helby), Jr. 1924- **CLC 4, 6, 45; DAM NOV**
See also AAYA 7; CA 1-4R; CAAS 2; CANR 2, 39, 76; DLB 2; DLBY 81; MTCW 1, 2
Connelly, Marc(us Cook) 1890-1980 .... **CLC 7**
See also CA 85-88; 102; CANR 30; DLB 7; DLBY 80; SATA-Obit 25
Connor, Ralph .... **TCLC 31**
See also Gordon, Charles William
See also DLB 92
Conrad, Joseph 1857-1924**TCLC 1, 6, 13, 25, 43, 57; DA; DAB; DAC; DAM MST, NOV; SSC 9; WLC**
See also AAYA 26; CA 104; 131; CANR 60; CDBLB 1890-1914; DLB 10, 34, 98, 156; MTCW 1, 2; SATA 27
Conrad, Robert Arnold
See Hart, Moss
Conroy, Pat
See Conroy, (Donald) Pat(rick)
See also MTCW 2
Conroy, (Donald) Pat(rick) 1945- .. **CLC 30, 74; DAM NOV, POP**
See also Conroy, Pat
See also AAYA 8; AITN 1; CA 85-88; CANR 24, 53; DLB 6; MTCW 1
Constant (de Rebecque), (Henri) Benjamin 1767-1830 .... **NCLC 6**
See also DLB 119
Conybeare, Charles Augustus
See Eliot, T(homas) S(tearns)
Cook, Michael 1933- .... **CLC 58**
See also CA 93-96; CANR 68; DLB 53
Cook, Robin 1940- .... **CLC 14; DAM POP**
See also BEST 90:2; CA 108; 111; CANR 41; INT 111
Cook, Roy
See Silverberg, Robert

Cooke, Elizabeth 1948- .... **CLC 55**
See.also CA 129
Cooke, John Esten 1830-1886 .... **NCLC 5**
See also DLB 3
Cooke, John Estes
See Baum, L(yman) Frank
Cooke, M. E.
See Creasey, John
Cooke, Margaret
See Creasey, John
Cook-Lynn, Elizabeth 1930-**CLC 93; DAM MULT**
See also CA 133; DLB 175; NNAL
Cooney, Ray .... **CLC 62**
Cooper, Douglas 1960- .... **CLC 86**
Cooper, Henry St. John
See Creasey, John
Cooper, J(oan) California (?)- .... **CLC 56; DAM MULT**
See also AAYA 12; BW 1; CA 125; CANR 55; DLB 212
Cooper, James Fenimore 1789-1851**NCLC 1, 27, 54**
See also AAYA 22; CDALB 1640-1865; DLB 3; SATA 19
Coover, Robert (Lowell) 1932- **CLC 3, 7, 15, 32, 46, 87; DAM NOV; SSC 15**
See also CA 45-48; CANR 3, 37, 58; DLB 2; DLBY 81; MTCW 1, 2
Copeland, Stewart (Armstrong) 1952- . **CLC 26**
Copernicus, Nicolaus 1473-1543 .... **LC 45**
Coppard, A(lfred) E(dgar) 1878-1957**TCLC 5; SSC 21**
See also CA 114; 167; DLB 162; YABC 1
Coppee, Francois 1842-1908 .... **TCLC 25**
See also CA 170
Coppola, Francis Ford 1939- .... **CLC 16**
See also CA 77-80; CANR 40, 78; DLB 44
Corbiere, Tristan 1845-1875 .... **NCLC 43**
Corcoran, Barbara 1911- .... **CLC 17**
See also AAYA 14; CA 21-24R; CAAS 2; CANR 11, 28, 48; CLR 50; DLB 52; JRDA; SAAS 20; SATA 3, 77
Cordelier, Maurice
See Giraudoux, (Hippolyte) Jean
Corelli, Marie 1855-1924 .... **TCLC 51**
See also Mackay, Mary
See also DLB 34, 156
Corman, Cid 1924- .... **CLC 9**
See also Corman, Sidney
See also CAAS 2; DLB 5, 193
Corman, Sidney 1924-
See Corman, Cid
See also CA 85-88; CANR 44; DAM POET
Cormier, Robert (Edmund) 1925-**CLC 12, 30; DA; DAB; DAC; DAM MST, NOV**
See also AAYA 3, 19; CA 1-4R; CANR 5, 23, 76; CDALB 1968-1988; CLR 12, 55; DLB 52; INT CANR-23; JRDA; MAICYA; MTCW 1, 2; SATA 10, 45, 83
Corn, Alfred (DeWitt III) 1943- .... **CLC 33**
See also CA 104; CAAS 25; CANR 44; DLB 120; DLBY 80
Corneille, Pierre 1606-1684 **LC 28; DAB; DAM MST**
Cornwell, David (John Moore) 1931- **CLC 9, 15; DAM POP**
See also le Carre, John
See also CA 5-8R; CANR 13, 33, 59; MTCW 1, 2
Corso, (Nunzio) Gregory 1930- .... **CLC 1, 11**
See also CA 5-8R; CANR 41, 76; DLB 5, 16; MTCW 1, 2
Cortazar, Julio 1914-1984**CLC 2, 3, 5, 10, 13, 15, 33, 34, 92; DAM MULT, NOV; HLC; SSC 7**
See also CA 21-24R; CANR 12, 32, 81; DLB 113; HW 1, 2; MTCW 1, 2
Cortes, Hernan 1484-1547 .... **LC 31**
Corvinus, Jakob
See Raabe, Wilhelm (Karl)
Corwin, Cecil
See Kornbluth, C(yril) M.
Cosic, Dobrica 1921- .... **CLC 14**
See also CA 122; 138; DLB 181
Costain, Thomas B(ertram) 1885-1965 . **CLC 30**
See also CA 5-8R; 25-28R; DLB 9
Costantini, Humberto 1924(?)-1987 ...... **CLC 49**
See also CA 131; 122; HW 1
Costello, Elvis 1955- .... **CLC 21**
Costenoble, Philostene
See Ghelderode, Michel de
Cotes, Cecil V.
See Duncan, Sara Jeannette
Cotter, Joseph Seamon Sr. 1861-1949 **TCLC 28; BLC 1; DAM MULT**
See also BW 1; CA 124; DLB 50
Couch, Arthur Thomas Quiller
See Quiller-Couch, SirArthur (Thomas)
Coulton, James
See Hansen, Joseph
Couperus, Louis (Marie Anne) 1863-1923**TCLC 15**
See also CA 115
Coupland, Douglas 1961- . **CLC 85; DAC; DAM POP**
See also CA 142; CANR 57
Court, Wesli
See Turco, Lewis (Putnam)
Courtenay, Bryce 1933- .... **CLC 59**
See also CA 138
Courtney, Robert
See Ellison, Harlan (Jay)
Cousteau, Jacques-Yves 1910-1997 .... **CLC 30**
See also CA 65-68; 159; CANR 15, 67; MTCW 1; SATA 38, 98
Coventry, Francis 1725-1754 .... **LC 46**
Cowan, Peter (Walkinshaw) 1914- .... **SSC 28**
See also CA 21-24R; CANR 9, 25, 50
Coward, Noel (Peirce) 1899-1973**CLC 1, 9, 29, 51; DAM DRAM**
See also AITN 1; CA 17-18; 41-44R; CANR 35; CAP 2; CDBLB 1914-1945; DLB 10; MTCW 1, 2
Cowley, Abraham 1618-1667 .... **LC 43**
See also DLB 131, 151
Cowley, Malcolm 1898-1989 .... **CLC 39**
See also CA 5-8R; 128; CANR 3, 55; DLB 4, 48; DLBY 81, 89; MTCW 1, 2
Cowper, William 1731-1800**NCLC 8; DAM POET**
See also DLB 104, 109
Cox, William Trevor 1928- **CLC 9, 14, 71; DAM NOV**
See also Trevor, William
See also CA 9-12R; CANR 4, 37, 55, 76; DLB 14; INT CANR-37; MTCW 1, 2
Coyne, P. J.
See Masters, Hilary
Cozzens, James Gould 1903-1978**CLC 1, 4, 11, 92**
See also CA 9-12R; 81-84; CANR 19; CDALB 1941-1968; DLB 9; DLBD 2; DLBY 84, 97; MTCW 1, 2
Crabbe, George 1754-1832 .... **NCLC 26**
See also DLB 93
Craddock, Charles Egbert
See Murfree, Mary Noailles
Craig, A. A.
See Anderson, Poul (William)
Craik, Dinah Maria (Mulock) 1826-1887 **NCLC 38**
See also DLB 35, 163; MAICYA; SATA 34
Cram, Ralph Adams 1863-1942 .... **TCLC 45**
See also CA 160
Crane, (Harold) Hart 1899-1932 **TCLC 2, 5, 80; DA; DAB; DAC; DAM MST, POET; PC 3; WLC**
See also CA 104; 127; CDALB 1917-1929; DLB 4, 48; MTCW 1, 2
Crane, R(onald) S(almon) 1886-1967**CLC 27**
See also CA 85-88; DLB 63
Crane, Stephen (Townley) 1871-1900**TCLC 11, 17, 32; DA; DAB; DAC; DAM MST, NOV, POET; SSC 7; WLC**
See also AAYA 21; CA 109; 140; CDALB 1865-1917; DLB 12, 54, 78; YABC 2
Cranshaw, Stanley
See Fisher, Dorothy (Frances) Canfield
Crase, Douglas 1944- .... **CLC 58**
See also CA 106
Crashaw, Richard 1612(?)-1649 .... **LC 24**
See also DLB 126
Craven, Margaret 1901-1980 .... **CLC 17; DAC**
See also CA 103
Crawford, F(rancis) Marion 1854-1909**TCLC 10**
See also CA 107; 168; DLB 71
Crawford, Isabella Valancy 1850-1887 **NCLC 12**
See also DLB 92
Crayon, Geoffrey
See Irving, Washington
Creasey, John 1908-1973 .... **CLC 11**
See also CA 5-8R; 41-44R; CANR 8, 59; DLB 77; MTCW 1
Crebillon, Claude Prosper Jolyot de (fils) 1707-1777 .... **LC 1, 28**
Credo
See Creasey, John
Credo, Alvaro J. de
See Prado (Calvo), Pedro
Creeley, Robert (White) 1926-**CLC 1, 2, 4, 8, 11, 15, 36, 78; DAM POET**
See also CA 1-4R; CAAS 10; CANR 23, 43; DLB 5, 16, 169; DLBD 17; MTCW 1, 2
Crews, Harry (Eugene) 1935- ..... **CLC 6, 23, 49**
See also AITN 1; CA 25-28R; CANR 20, 57; DLB 6, 143, 185; MTCW 1, 2
Crichton, (John) Michael 1942-**CLC 2, 6, 54, 90; DAM NOV, POP**
See also AAYA 10; AITN 2; CA 25-28R; CANR 13, 40, 54, 76; DLBY 81; INT CANR-13; JRDA; MTCW 1, 2; SATA 9, 88
Crispin, Edmund .... **CLC 22**
See also Montgomery, (Robert) Bruce
See also DLB 87
Cristofer, Michael 1945(?)-**CLC 28; DAM DRAM**
See also CA 110; 152; DLB 7
Croce, Benedetto 1866-1952 .... **TCLC 37**
See also CA 120; 155
Crockett, David 1786-1836 .... **NCLC 8**
See also DLB 3, 11
Crockett, Davy
See Crockett, David
Crofts, Freeman Wills 1879-1957 ...... **TCLC 55**
See also CA 115; DLB 77
Croker, John Wilson 1780-1857 .... **NCLC 10**
See also DLB 110
Crommelynck, Fernand 1885-1970 .... **CLC 75**
See also CA 89-92
Cromwell, Oliver 1599-1658 .... **LC 43**
Cronin, A(rchibald) J(oseph) 1896-1981 **CLC 32**
See also CA 1-4R; 102; CANR 5; DLB 191; SATA 47; SATA-Obit 25
Cross, Amanda
See Heilbrun, Carolyn G(old)
Crothers, Rachel 1878(?)-1958 .... **TCLC 19**
See also CA 113; DLB 7
Croves, Hal
See Traven, B.
Crow Dog, Mary (Ellen) (?)- .... **CLC 93**
See also Brave Bird, Mary
See also CA 154
Crowfield, Christopher
See Stowe, Harriet (Elizabeth) Beecher
Crowley, Aleister .... **TCLC 7**
See also Crowley, Edward Alexander

Crowley, Edward Alexander 1875-1947
See Crowley, Aleister
See also CA 104
Crowley, John 1942- .... **CLC 57**
See also CA 61-64; CANR 43; DLBY 82; SATA 65
Crud
See Crumb, R(obert)
Crumarums
See Crumb, R(obert)
Crumb, R(obert) 1943- .... **CLC 17**
See also CA 106
Crumbum
See Crumb, R(obert)
Crumski
See Crumb, R(obert)
Crum the Bum
See Crumb, R(obert)
Crunk
See Crumb, R(obert)
Crustt
See Crumb, R(obert)
Cryer, Gretchen (Kiger) 1935- .... **CLC 21**
See also CA 114; 123
Csath, Geza 1887-1919 .... **TCLC 13**
See also CA 111
Cudlip, David R(ockwell) 1933- .... **CLC 34**
See also CA 177
Cullen, Countee 1903-1946 **TCLC 4, 37; BLC 1; DA; DAC; DAM MST, MULT, POET; PC 20; WLCS**
See also BW 1; CA 108; 124; CDALB 1917-1929; DLB 4, 48, 51; MTCW 1, 2; SATA 18
Cum, R.
See Crumb, R(obert)
Cummings, Bruce F(rederick) 1889-1919
See Barbellion, W. N. P.
See also CA 123
Cummings, E(dward) E(stlin) 1894-1962**CLC 1, 3, 8, 12, 15, 68; DA; DAB; DAC; DAM MST, POET; PC 5; WLC**
See also CA 73-76; CANR 31; CDALB 1929-1941; DLB 4, 48; MTCW 1, 2
Cunha, Euclides (Rodrigues Pimenta) da 1866-1909 **TCLC 24**
See also CA 123
Cunningham, E. V.
See Fast, Howard (Melvin)
Cunningham, J(ames) V(incent) 1911-1985 **CLC 3, 31**
See also CA 1-4R; 115; CANR 1, 72; DLB 5
Cunningham, Julia (Woolfolk) 1916- .. **CLC 12**
See also CA 9-12R; CANR 4, 19, 36; JRDA; MAICYA; SAAS 2; SATA 1, 26
Cunningham, Michael 1952- .... **CLC 34**
See also CA 136
Cunninghame Graham, R(obert) B(ontine) 1852-1936 .... **TCLC 19**
See also Graham, R(obert) B(ontine) Cunninghame
See also CA 119; DLB 98
Currie, Ellen 19(?)- .... **CLC 44**
Curtin, Philip
See Lowndes, Marie Adelaide (Belloc)
Curtis, Price
See Ellison, Harlan (Jay)
Cutrate, Joe
See Spiegelman, Art
Cynewulf c. 770-c. 840 .... **CMLC 23**
Czaczkes, Shmuel Yosef
See Agnon, S(hmuel) Y(osef Halevi)
Dabrowska, Maria (Szumska) 1889-1965**CLC 15**
See also CA 106
Dabydeen, David 1955- .... **CLC 34**
See also BW 1; CA 125; CANR 56
Dacey, Philip 1939- .... **CLC 51**
See also CA 37-40R; CAAS 17; CANR 14, 32, 64; DLB 105
Dagerman, Stig (Halvard) 1923-1954 **TCLC 17**
See also CA 117; 155
Dahl, Roald 1916-1990 .. **CLC 1, 6, 18, 79; DAB; DAC; DAM MST, NOV, POP**
See also AAYA 15; CA 1-4R; 133; CANR 6, 32, 37, 62; CLR 1, 7, 41; DLB 139; JRDA; MAICYA; MTCW 1, 2; SATA 1, 26, 73; SATA-Obit 65
Dahlberg, Edward 1900-1977 .... **CLC 1, 7, 14**
See also CA 9-12R; 69-72; CANR 31, 62; DLB 48; MTCW 1
Daitch, Susan 1954- .... **CLC 103**
See also CA 161
Dale, Colin .... **TCLC 18**
See also Lawrence, T(homas) E(dward)
Dale, George E.
See Asimov, Isaac
Daly, Elizabeth 1878-1967 .... **CLC 52**
See also CA 23-24; 25-28R; CANR 60; CAP 2
Daly, Maureen 1921- .... **CLC 17**
See also AAYA 5; CANR 37; JRDA; MAICYA; SAAS 1; SATA 2
Damas, Leon-Gontran 1912-1978 .... **CLC 84**
See also BW 1; CA 125; 73-76
Dana, Richard Henry Sr. 1787-1879 ... **NCLC 53**
Daniel, Samuel 1562(?)-1619 .... **LC 24**
See also DLB 62
Daniels, Brett
See Adler, Renata
Dannay, Frederic 1905-1982 **CLC 11; DAM POP**
See also Queen, Ellery
See also CA 1-4R; 107; CANR 1, 39; DLB 137; MTCW 1
D'Annunzio, Gabriele 1863-1938 .... **TCLC 6, 40**
See also CA 104; 155
Danois, N. le
See Gourmont, Remy (-Marie-Charles) de
Dante 1265-1321 **CMLC 3, 18; DA; DAB; DAC; DAM MST, POET; PC 21; WLCS**
d'Antibes, Germain
See Simenon, Georges (Jacques Christian)
Danticat, Edwidge 1969- .... **CLC 94**
See also AAYA 29; CA 152; CANR 73; MTCW 1
Danvers, Dennis 1947- .... **CLC 70**
Danziger, Paula 1944- .... **CLC 21**
See also AAYA 4; CA 112; 115; CANR 37; CLR 20; JRDA; MAICYA; SATA 36, 63, 102; SATA-Brief 30
Da Ponte, Lorenzo 1749-1838 .... **NCLC 50**
Dario, Ruben 1867-1916 . **TCLC 4; DAM MULT; HLC; PC 15**
See also CA 131; CANR 81; HW 1, 2; MTCW 1, 2
Darley, George 1795-1846 .... **NCLC 2**
See also DLB 96
Darrow, Clarence (Seward) 1857-1938 **TCLC 81**
See also CA 164
Darwin, Charles 1809-1882 .... **NCLC 57**
See also DLB 57, 166
Daryush, Elizabeth 1887-1977 .... **CLC 6, 19**
See also CA 49-52; CANR 3, 81; DLB 20
Dasgupta, Surendranath 1887-1952 ... **TCLC 81**
See also CA 157
Dashwood, Edmee Elizabeth Monica de la Pasture 1890-1943
See Delafield, E. M.
See also CA 119; 154
Daudet, (Louis Marie) Alphonse 1840-1897**NCLC 1**
See also DLB 123
Daumal, Rene 1908-1944 .... **TCLC 14**
See also CA 114
Davenant, William 1606-1668 .... **LC 13**
See also DLB 58, 126
Davenport, Guy (Mattison, Jr.) 1927- **CLC 6, 14, 38; SSC 16**
See also CA 33-36R; CANR 23, 73; DLB 130
Davidson, Avram (James) 1923-1993
See Queen, Ellery
See also CA 101; 171; CANR 26; DLB 8
Davidson, Donald (Grady) 1893-1968 **CLC 2, 13, 19**
See also CA 5-8R; 25-28R; CANR 4; DLB 45
Davidson, Hugh
See Hamilton, Edmond
Davidson, John 1857-1909 .... **TCLC 24**
See also CA 118; DLB 19
Davidson, Sara 1943- .... **CLC 9**
See also CA 81-84; CANR 44, 68; DLB 185
Davie, Donald (Alfred) 1922-1995**CLC 5, 8, 10, 31**
See also CA 1-4R; 149; CAAS 3; CANR 1, 44; DLB 27; MTCW 1
Davies, Ray(mond Douglas) 1944- .... **CLC 21**
See also CA 116; 146
Davies, Rhys 1901-1978 .... **CLC 23**
See also CA 9-12R; 81-84; CANR 4; DLB 139, 191
Davies, (William) Robertson 1913-1995**CLC 2, 7, 13, 25, 42, 75, 91; DA; DAB; DAC; DAM MST, NOV, POP; WLC**
See also BEST 89:2; CA 33-36R; 150; CANR 17, 42; DLB 68; INT CANR-17; MTCW 1, 2
Davies, W(illiam) H(enry) 1871-1940 ... **TCLC 5**
See also CA 104; DLB 19, 174
Davies, Walter C.
See Kornbluth, C(yril) M.
Davis, Angela (Yvonne) 1944- ..... **CLC 77; DAM MULT**
See also BW 2, 3; CA 57-60; CANR 10, 81
Davis, B. Lynch
See Bioy Casares, Adolfo; Borges, Jorge Luis
Davis, B. Lynch
See Bioy Casares, Adolfo
Davis, Harold Lenoir 1894-1960 .... **CLC 49**
See also CA 89-92; DLB 9, 206
Davis, Rebecca (Blaine) Harding 1831-1910 **TCLC 6**
See also CA 104; DLB 74
Davis, Richard Harding 1864-1916 ..... **TCLC 24**
See also CA 114; DLB 12, 23, 78, 79, 189; DLBD 13
Davison, Frank Dalby 1893-1970 .... **CLC 15**
See also CA 116
Davison, Lawrence H.
See Lawrence, D(avid) H(erbert Richards)
Davison, Peter (Hubert) 1928- .... **CLC 28**
See also CA 9-12R; CAAS 4; CANR 3, 43; DLB 5
Davys, Mary 1674-1732 .... **LC 1, 46**
See also DLB 39
Dawson, Fielding 1930- .... **CLC 6**
See also CA 85-88; DLB 130
Dawson, Peter
See Faust, Frederick (Schiller)
Day, Clarence (Shepard, Jr.) 1874-1935**TCLC 25**
See also CA 108; DLB 11
Day, Thomas 1748-1789 .... **LC 1**
See also DLB 39; YABC 1
Day Lewis, C(ecil) 1904-1972**CLC 1, 6, 10; DAM POET; PC 11**
See also Blake, Nicholas
See also CA 13-16; 33-36R; CANR 34; CAP 1; DLB 15, 20; MTCW 1, 2
Dazai Osamu 1909-1948 .... **TCLC 11**
See also Tsushima, Shuji
See also CA 164; DLB 182
de Andrade, Carlos Drummond 1892-1945
See Drummond de Andrade, Carlos
Deane, Norman
See Creasey, John
de Beauvoir, Simone (Lucie Ernestine Marie Bertrand)
See Beauvoir, Simone (Lucie Ernestine Marie

Bertrand) de
de Beer, P.
See Bosman, Herman Charles
de Brissac, Malcolm
See Dickinson, Peter (Malcolm)
de Chardin, Pierre Teilhard
See Teilhard de Chardin, (Marie Joseph) Pierre
Dee, John 1527-1608 .... **LC 20**
Deer, Sandra 1940- .... **CLC 45**
De Ferrari, Gabriella 1941- .... **CLC 65**
See also CA 146
Defoe, Daniel 1660(?)-1731 **LC 1, 42; DA; DAB; DAC; DAM MST, NOV; WLC**
See also AAYA 27; CDBLB 1660-1789; DLB 39, 95, 101; JRDA; MAICYA; SATA 22
de Gourmont, Remy(-Marie-Charles)
See Gourmont, Remy (-Marie-Charles) de
de Hartog, Jan 1914- .... **CLC 19**
See also CA 1-4R; CANR 1
de Hostos, E. M.
See Hostos (y Bonilla), Eugenio Maria de
de Hostos, Eugenio M.
See Hostos (y Bonilla), Eugenio Maria de
Deighton, Len .... **CLC 4, 7, 22, 46**
See also Deighton, Leonard Cyril
See also AAYA 6; BEST 89:2; CDBLB 1960 to Present; DLB 87
Deighton, Leonard Cyril 1929-
See Deighton, Len
See also CA 9-12R; CANR 19, 33, 68; DAM NOV, POP; MTCW 1, 2
Dekker, Thomas 1572(?)-1632 ...... **LC 22; DAM DRAM**
See also CDBLB Before 1660; DLB 62, 172
Delafield, E. M. 1890-1943 .... **TCLC 61**
See also Dashwood, Edmee Elizabeth Monica de la Pasture
See also DLB 34
de la Mare, Walter (John) 1873-1956**TCLC 4, 53; DAB; DAC; DAM MST, POET; SSC 14; WLC**
See also CA 163; CDBLB 1914-1945; CLR 23; DLB 162; MTCW 1; SATA 16
Delaney, Franey
See O'Hara, John (Henry)
Delaney, Shelagh 1939- .. **CLC 29; DAM DRAM**
See also CA 17-20R; CANR 30, 67; CDBLB 1960 to Present; DLB 13; MTCW 1
Delany, Mary (Granville Pendarves) 1700-1788 **LC 12**
Delany, Samuel R(ay, Jr.) 1942- . **CLC 8, 14, 38; BLC 1; DAM MULT**
See also AAYA 24; BW 2, 3; CA 81-84; CANR 27, 43; DLB 8, 33; MTCW 1, 2
De La Ramee, (Marie) Louise 1839-1908
See Ouida
See also SATA 20
de la Roche, Mazo 1879-1961 .... **CLC 14**
See also CA 85-88; CANR 30; DLB 68; SATA 64
De La Salle, Innocent
See Hartmann, Sadakichi
Delbanco, Nicholas (Franklin) 1942- **CLC 6, 13**
See also CA 17-20R; CAAS 2; CANR 29, 55; DLB 6
del Castillo, Michel 1933- .... **CLC 38**
See also CA 109; CANR 77
Deledda, Grazia (Cosima) 1875(?)-1936**TCLC 23**
See also CA 123
Delibes, Miguel .... **CLC 8, 18**
See also Delibes Setien, Miguel
Delibes Setien, Miguel 1920-
See Delibes, Miguel
See also CA 45-48; CANR 1, 32; HW 1; MTCW 1
DeLillo, Don 1936-**CLC 8, 10, 13, 27, 39, 54, 76; DAM NOV, POP**
See also BEST 89:1; CA 81-84; CANR 21, 76; DLB 6, 173; MTCW 1, 2
de Lisser, H. G.
See De Lisser, H(erbert) G(eorge)
See also DLB 117
De Lisser, H(erbert) G(eorge) 1878-1944 **TCLC 12**
See also de Lisser, H. G.
See also BW 2; CA 109; 152
Deloney, Thomas 1560(?)-1600 .... **LC 41**
See also DLB 167
Deloria, Vine (Victor), Jr. 1933- **CLC 21; DAM MULT**
See also CA 53-56; CANR 5, 20, 48; DLB 175; MTCW 1; NNAL; SATA 21
Del Vecchio, John M(ichael) 1947- ...... **CLC 29**
See also CA 110; DLBD 9
de Man, Paul (Adolph Michel) 1919-1983**CLC 55**
See also CA 128; 111; CANR 61; DLB 67; MTCW 1, 2
De Marinis, Rick 1934- .... **CLC 54**
See also CA 57-60; CAAS 24; CANR 9, 25, 50
Dembry, R. Emmet
See Murfree, Mary Noailles
Demby, William 1922- ... **CLC 53; BLC 1; DAM MULT**
See also BW 1, 3; CA 81-84; CANR 81; DLB 33
de Menton, Francisco
See Chin, Frank (Chew, Jr.)
Demijohn, Thom
See Disch, Thomas M(ichael)
de Montherlant, Henry (Milon)
See Montherlant, Henry (Milon) de
Demosthenes 384B.C.-322B.C. .... **CMLC 13**
See also DLB 176
de Natale, Francine
See Malzberg, Barry N(athaniel)
Denby, Edwin (Orr) 1903-1983 .... **CLC 48**
See also CA 138; 110
Denis, Julio
See Cortazar, Julio
Denmark, Harrison
See Zelazny, Roger (Joseph)
Dennis, John 1658-1734 .... **LC 11**
See also DLB 101
Dennis, Nigel (Forbes) 1912-1989 .... **CLC 8**
See also CA 25-28R; 129; DLB 13, 15; MTCW 1
Dent, Lester 1904(?)-1959 .... **TCLC 72**
See also CA 112; 161
De Palma, Brian (Russell) 1940- .... **CLC 20**
See also CA 109
De Quincey, Thomas 1785-1859 .... **NCLC 4**
See also CDBLB 1789-1832; DLB 110; 144
Deren, Eleanora 1908(?)-1961
See Deren, Maya
See also CA 111
Deren, Maya 1917-1961 .... **CLC 16, 102**
See also Deren, Eleanora
Derleth, August (William) 1909-1971 .. **CLC 31**
See also CA 1-4R; 29-32R; CANR 4; DLB 9; DLBD 17; SATA 5
Der Nister 1884-1950 .... **TCLC 56**
de Routisie, Albert
See Aragon, Louis
Derrida, Jacques 1930- .... **CLC 24, 87**
See also CA 124; 127; CANR 76; MTCW 1
Derry Down Derry
See Lear, Edward
Dersonnes, Jacques
See Simenon, Georges (Jacques Christian)
Desai, Anita 1937- **CLC 19, 37, 97; DAB; DAM NOV**
See also CA 81-84; CANR 33, 53; MTCW 1, 2; SATA 63
Desai, Kiran 1971- .... **CLC 119**
See also CA 171
de Saint-Luc, Jean
See Glassco, John
de Saint Roman, Arnaud
See Aragon, Louis
Descartes, Rene 1596-1650 .... **LC 20, 35**
De Sica, Vittorio 1901(?)-1974 .... **CLC 20**
See also CA 117
Desnos, Robert 1900-1945 .... **TCLC 22**
See also CA 121; 151
Destouches, Louis-Ferdinand 1894-1961 **CLC 9, 15**
See also Celine, Louis-Ferdinand
See also CA 85-88; CANR 28; MTCW 1
de Tolignac, Gaston
See Griffith, D(avid Lewelyn) W(ark)
Deutsch, Babette 1895-1982 .... **CLC 18**
See also CA 1-4R; 108; CANR 4, 79; DLB 45; SATA 1; SATA-Obit 33
Devenant, William 1606-1649 .... **LC 13**
Devkota, Laxmiprasad 1909-1959 .... **TCLC 23**
See also CA 123
De Voto, Bernard (Augustine) 1897-1955 **TCLC 29**
See also CA 113; 160; DLB 9
De Vries, Peter 1910-1993**CLC 1, 2, 3, 7, 10, 28, 46; DAM NOV**
See also CA 17-20R; 142; CANR 41; DLB 6; DLBY 82; MTCW 1, 2
Dewey, John 1859-1952 .... **TCLC 95**
See also CA 114; 170
Dexter, John
See Bradley, Marion Zimmer
Dexter, Martin
See Faust, Frederick (Schiller)
Dexter, Pete 1943- .... **CLC 34, 55; DAM POP**
See also BEST 89:2; CA 127; 131; INT 131; MTCW 1
Diamano, Silmang
See Senghor, Leopold Sedar
Diamond, Neil 1941- .... **CLC 30**
See also CA 108
Diaz del Castillo, Bernal 1496-1584**LC 31; HLCS 1**
di Bassetto, Corno
See Shaw, George Bernard
Dick, Philip K(indred) 1928-1982**CLC 10, 30, 72; DAM NOV, POP**
See also AAYA 24; CA 49-52; 106; CANR 2, 16; DLB 8; MTCW 1, 2
Dickens, Charles (John Huffam) 1812-1870 **NCLC 3, 8, 18, 26, 37, 50; DA; DAB; DAC; DAM MST, NOV; SSC 17; WLC**
See also AAYA 23; CDBLB 1832-1890; DLB 21, 55, 70, 159, 166; JRDA; MAICYA; SATA 15
Dickey, James (Lafayette) 1923-1997**CLC 1, 2, 4, 7, 10, 15, 47, 109; DAM NOV, POET, POP**
See also AITN 1, 2; CA 9-12R; 156; CABS 2; CANR 10, 48, 61; CDALB 1968-1988; DLB 5, 193; DLBD 7; DLBY 82, 93, 96, 97, 98; INT CANR-10; MTCW 1, 2
Dickey, William 1928-1994 .... **CLC 3, 28**
See also CA 9-12R; 145; CANR 24, 79; DLB 5
Dickinson, Charles 1951- .... **CLC 49**
See also CA 128
Dickinson, Emily (Elizabeth) 1830-1886**NCLC 21, 77; DA; DAB; DAC; DAM MST, POET; PC 1; WLC**
See also AAYA 22; CDALB 1865-1917; DLB 1; SATA 29
Dickinson, Peter (Malcolm) 1927- . **CLC 12, 35**
See also AAYA 9; CA 41-44R; CANR 31, 58; CLR 29; DLB 87, 161; JRDA; MAICYA; SATA 5, 62, 95
Dickson, Carr
See Carr, John Dickson
Dickson, Carter
See Carr, John Dickson
Diderot, Denis 1713-1784 .... **LC 26**
Didion, Joan 1934-**CLC 1, 3, 8, 14, 32; DAM NOV**
See also AITN 1; CA 5-8R; CANR 14, 52, 76;

CDALB 1968-1988; DLB 2, 173, 185; DLBY 81, 86; MTCW 1, 2
Dietrich, Robert
See Hunt, E(verette) Howard, (Jr.)
Difusa, Pati
See Almodovar, Pedro
Dillard, Annie 1945-**CLC 9, 60, 115; DAM NOV**
See also AAYA 6; CA 49-52; CANR 3, 43, 62; DLBY 80; MTCW 1, 2; SATA 10
Dillard, R(ichard) H(enry) W(ilde) 1937- **CLC 5**
See also CA 21-24R; CAAS 7; CANR 10; DLB 5
Dillon, Eilis 1920-1994 .... **CLC 17**
See also CA 9-12R; 147; CAAS 3; CANR 4, 38, 78; CLR 26; MAICYA; SATA 2, 74; SATA-Essay 105; SATA-Obit 83
Dimont, Penelope
See Mortimer, Penelope (Ruth)
Dinesen, Isak .... **CLC 10, 29, 95; SSC 7**
See also Blixen, Karen (Christentze Dinesen)
See also MTCW 1
Ding Ling .... **CLC 68**
See also Chiang, Pin-chin
Diphusa, Patty
See Almodovar, Pedro
Disch, Thomas M(ichael) 1940- .... **CLC 7, 36**
See also AAYA 17; CA 21-24R; CAAS 4; CANR 17, 36, 54; CLR 18; DLB 8; MAICYA; MTCW 1, 2; SAAS 15; SATA 92
Disch, Tom
See Disch, Thomas M(ichael)
d'Isly, Georges
See Simenon, Georges (Jacques Christian)
Disraeli, Benjamin 1804-1881 . **NCLC 2, 39, 79**
See also DLB 21, 55
Ditcum, Steve
See Crumb, R(obert)
Dixon, Paige
See Corcoran, Barbara
Dixon, Stephen 1936- .... **CLC 52; SSC 16**
See also CA 89-92; CANR 17, 40, 54; DLB 130
Doak, Annie
See Dillard, Annie
Dobell, Sydney Thompson 1824-1874 .. **NCLC 43**
See also DLB 32
Doblin, Alfred .... **TCLC 13**
See also Doeblin, Alfred
Dobrolyubov, Nikolai Alexandrovich 1836-1861 **NCLC 5**
Dobson, Austin 1840-1921 .... **TCLC 79**
See also DLB 35; 144
Dobyns, Stephen 1941- .... **CLC 37**
See also CA 45-48; CANR 2, 18
Doctorow, E(dgar) L(aurence) 1931- . **CLC 6, 11, 15, 18, 37, 44, 65, 113; DAM NOV, POP**
See also AAYA 22; AITN 2; BEST 89:3; CA 45-48; CANR 2, 33, 51, 76; CDALB 1968-1988; DLB 2, 28, 173; DLBY 80; MTCW 1, 2
Dodgson, Charles Lutwidge 1832-1898
See Carroll, Lewis
See also CLR 2; DA; DAB; DAC; DAM MST, NOV, POET; MAICYA; SATA 100; YABC 2
Dodson, Owen (Vincent) 1914-1983**CLC 79; BLC 1; DAM MULT**
See also BW 1; CA 65-68; 110; CANR 24; DLB 76
Doeblin, Alfred 1878-1957 .... **TCLC 13**
See also Doblin, Alfred
See also CA 110; 141; DLB 66
Doerr, Harriet 1910- .... **CLC 34**
See also CA 117; 122; CANR 47; INT 122
Domecq, H(onorio Bustos)
See Bioy Casares, Adolfo
Domecq, H(onorio) Bustos
See Bioy Casares, Adolfo; Borges, Jorge Luis
Domini, Rey
See Lorde, Audre (Geraldine)
Dominique
See Proust, (Valentin-Louis-George-Eugene-) Marcel
Don, A
See Stephen, Sir Leslie
Donaldson, Stephen R. 1947-**CLC 46; DAM POP**
See also CA 89-92; CANR 13, 55; INT CANR-13
Donleavy, J(ames) P(atrick) 1926- . **CLC 1, 4, 6, 10, 45**
See also AITN 2; CA 9-12R; CANR 24, 49, 62, 80; DLB 6, 173; INT CANR-24; MTCW 1, 2
Donne, John 1572-1631 .... **LC 10, 24; DA; DAB; DAC; DAM MST, POET; PC 1; WLC**
See also CDBLB Before 1660; DLB 121, 151
Donnell, David 1939(?)- .... **CLC 34**
Donoghue, P. S.
See Hunt, E(verette) Howard, (Jr.)
Donoso (Yanez), Jose 1924-1996**CLC 4, 8, 11, 32, 99; DAM MULT; HLC; SSC 34**
See also CA 81-84; 155; CANR 32, 73; DLB 113; HW 1, 2; MTCW 1, 2
Donovan, John 1928-1992 .... **CLC 35**
See also AAYA 20; CA 97-100; 137; CLR 3; MAICYA; SATA 72; SATA-Brief 29
Don Roberto
See Cunninghame Graham, R(obert) B(ontine)
Doolittle, Hilda 1886-1961**CLC 3, 8, 14, 31, 34, 73; DA; DAC; DAM MST, POET; PC 5; WLC**
See also H. D.
See also CA 97-100; CANR 35; DLB 4, 45; MTCW 1, 2
Dorfman, Ariel 1942- **CLC 48, 77; DAM MULT; HLC**
See also CA 124; 130; CANR 67, 70; HW 1, 2; INT 130
Dorn, Edward (Merton) 1929- .... **CLC 10, 18**
See also CA 93-96; CANR 42, 79; DLB 5; INT 93-96
Dorris, Michael (Anthony) 1945-1997 **CLC 109; DAM MULT, NOV**
See also AAYA 20; BEST 90:1; CA 102; 157; CANR 19, 46, 75; CLR 58; DLB 175; MTCW 2; NNAL; SATA 75; SATA-Obit 94
Dorris, Michael A.
See Dorris, Michael (Anthony)
Dorsan, Luc
See Simenon, Georges (Jacques Christian)
Dorsange, Jean
See Simenon, Georges (Jacques Christian)
Dos Passos, John (Roderigo) 1896-1970**CLC 1, 4, 8, 11, 15, 25, 34, 82; DA; DAB; DAC; DAM MST, NOV; WLC**
See also CA 1-4R; 29-32R; CANR 3; CDALB 1929-1941; DLB 4, 9; DLBD 1, 15; DLBY 96; MTCW 1, 2
Dossage, Jean
See Simenon, Georges (Jacques Christian)
Dostoevsky, Fedor Mikhailovich 1821-1881**NCLC 2, 7, 21, 33, 43; DA; DAB; DAC; DAM MST, NOV; SSC 2, 33; WLC**
Doughty, Charles M(ontagu) 1843-1926**TCLC 27**
See also CA 115; DLB 19, 57, 174
Douglas, Ellen .... **CLC 73**
See also Haxton, Josephine Ayres; Williamson, Ellen Douglas
Douglas, Gavin 1475(?)-1522 .... **LC 20**
See also DLB 132
Douglas, George
See Brown, George Douglas
Douglas, Keith (Castellain) 1920-1944 **TCLC 40**
See also CA 160; DLB 27
Douglas, Leonard
See Bradbury, Ray (Douglas)
Douglas, Michael
See Crichton, (John) Michael
Douglas, (George) Norman 1868-1952 **TCLC 68**
See also CA 119; 157; DLB 34, 195
Douglas, William
See Brown, George Douglas
Douglass, Frederick 1817(?)-1895 . **NCLC 7, 55; BLC 1; DA; DAC; DAM MST, MULT; WLC**
See also CDALB 1640-1865; DLB 1, 43, 50, 79; SATA 29
Dourado, (Waldomiro Freitas) Autran 1926-**CLC 23, 60**
See also CA 25-28R; CANR 34, 81; DLB 145; HW 2
Dourado, Waldomiro Autran
See Dourado, (Waldomiro Freitas) Autran
Dove, Rita (Frances) 1952- . **CLC 50, 81; BLCS; DAM MULT, POET; PC 6**
See also BW 2; CA 109; CAAS 19; CANR 27, 42, 68, 76; CDALBS; DLB 120; MTCW 1
Doveglion
See Villa, Jose Garcia
Dowell, Coleman 1925-1985 .... **CLC 60**
See also CA 25-28R; 117; CANR 10; DLB 130
Dowson, Ernest (Christopher) 1867-1900**TCLC 4**
See also CA 105; 150; DLB 19, 135
Doyle, A. Conan
See Doyle, Arthur Conan
Doyle, Arthur Conan 1859-1930 .. **TCLC 7; DA; DAB; DAC; DAM MST, NOV; SSC 12; WLC**
See also AAYA 14; CA 104; 122; CDBLB 1890-1914; DLB 18, 70, 156, 178; MTCW 1, 2; SATA 24
Doyle, Conan
See Doyle, Arthur Conan
Doyle, John
See Graves, Robert (von Ranke)
Doyle, Roddy 1958(?)- .... **CLC 81**
See also AAYA 14; CA 143; CANR 73; DLB 194
Doyle, Sir A. Conan
See Doyle, Arthur Conan
Doyle, Sir Arthur Conan
See Doyle, Arthur Conan
Dr. A
See Asimov, Isaac; Silverstein, Alvin
Drabble, Margaret 1939- **CLC 2, 3, 5, 8, 10, 22, 53; DAB; DAC; DAM MST, NOV, POP**
See also CA 13-16R; CANR 18, 35, 63; CDBLB 1960 to Present; DLB 14, 155; MTCW 1, 2; SATA 48
Drapier, M. B.
See Swift, Jonathan
Drayham, James
See Mencken, H(enry) L(ouis)
Drayton, Michael 1563-1631 **LC 8; DAM POET**
See also DLB 121
Dreadstone, Carl
See Campbell, (John) Ramsey
Dreiser, Theodore (Herman Albert) 1871-1945 **TCLC 10, 18, 35, 83; DA; DAC; DAM MST, NOV; SSC 30; WLC**
See also CA 106; 132; CDALB 1865-1917; DLB 9, 12, 102, 137; DLBD 1; MTCW 1, 2
Drexler, Rosalyn 1926- .... **CLC 2, 6**
See also CA 81-84; CANR 68
Dreyer, Carl Theodor 1889-1968 .... **CLC 16**
See also CA 116
Drieu la Rochelle, Pierre(-Eugene) 1893-1945 **TCLC 21**
See also CA 117; DLB 72
Drinkwater, John 1882-1937 .... **TCLC 57**
See also CA 109; 149; DLB 10, 19, 149
Drop Shot
See Cable, George Washington
Droste-Hulshoff, Annette Freiin von 1797-1848 **NCLC 3**
See also DLB 133
Drummond, Walter
See Silverberg, Robert
Drummond, William Henry 1854-1907 **TCLC 25**
See also CA 160; DLB 92

Drummond de Andrade, Carlos 1902-1987 **CLC 18**
See also Andrade, Carlos Drummond de
See also CA 132; 123
Drury, Allen (Stuart) 1918-1998 .... **CLC 37**
See also CA 57-60; 170; CANR 18, 52; INT CANR-18
Dryden, John 1631-1700 .... **LC 3, 21; DA; DAB; DAC; DAM DRAM, MST, POET; DC 3; PC 25; WLC**
See also CDBLB 1660-1789; DLB 80, 101, 131
Duberman, Martin (Bauml) 1930- .... **CLC 8**
See also CA 1-4R; CANR 2, 63
Dubie, Norman (Evans) 1945- .... **CLC 36**
See also CA 69-72; CANR 12; DLB 120
Du Bois, W(illiam) E(dward) B(urghardt) 1868-1963**CLC 1, 2, 13, 64, 96; BLC 1; DA; DAC; DAM MST, MULT, NOV; WLC**
See also BW 1, 3; CA 85-88; CANR 34; CDALB 1865-1917; DLB 47, 50, 91; MTCW 1, 2; SATA 42
Dubus, Andre 1936-1999**CLC 13, 36, 97; SSC 15**
See also CA 21-24R; 177; CANR 17; DLB 130; INT CANR-17
Duca Minimo
See D'Annunzio, Gabriele
Ducharme, Rejean 1941- .... **CLC 74**
See also CA 165; DLB 60
Duclos, Charles Pinot 1704-1772 .... **LC 1**
Dudek, Louis 1918- .... **CLC 11, 19**
See also CA 45-48; CAAS 14; CANR 1; DLB 88
Duerrenmatt, Friedrich 1921-1990 . **CLC 1, 4, 8, 11, 15, 43, 102; DAM DRAM**
See also CA 17-20R; CANR 33; DLB 69, 124; MTCW 1, 2
Duffy, Bruce 1953(?)- .... **CLC 50**
See also CA 172
Duffy, Maureen 1933- .... **CLC 37**
See also CA 25-28R; CANR 33, 68; DLB 14; MTCW 1
Dugan, Alan 1923- .... **CLC 2, 6**
See also CA 81-84; DLB 5
du Gard, Roger Martin
See Martin du Gard, Roger
Duhamel, Georges 1884-1966 .... **CLC 8**
See also CA 81-84; 25-28R; CANR 35; DLB 65; MTCW 1
Dujardin, Edouard (Emile Louis) 1861-1949 **TCLC 13**
See also CA 109; DLB 123
Dulles, John Foster 1888-1959 .... **TCLC 72**
See also CA 115; 149
Dumas, Alexandre (pere)
See Dumas, Alexandre (Davy de la Pailleterie)
Dumas, Alexandre (Davy de la Pailleterie) 1802-1870**NCLC 11; DA; DAB; DAC; DAM MST, NOV; WLC**
See also DLB 119, 192; SATA 18
Dumas, Alexandre (fils) 1824-1895**NCLC 71; DC 1**
See also AAYA 22; DLB 192
Dumas, Claudine
See Malzberg, Barry N(athaniel)
Dumas, Henry L. 1934-1968 .... **CLC 6, 62**
See also BW 1; CA 85-88; DLB 41
du Maurier, Daphne 1907-1989 .. **CLC 6, 11, 59; DAB; DAC; DAM MST, POP; SSC 18**
See also CA 5-8R; 128; CANR 6, 55; DLB 191; MTCW 1, 2; SATA 27; SATA-Obit 60
Dunbar, Paul Laurence 1872-1906 . **TCLC 2, 12; BLC 1; DA; DAC; DAM MST, MULT, POET; PC 5; SSC 8; WLC**
See also BW 1, 3; CA 104; 124; CANR 79; CDALB 1865-1917; DLB 50, 54, 78; SATA 34
Dunbar, William 1460(?)-1530(?) .... **LC 20**
See also DLB 132, 146
Duncan, Dora Angela
See Duncan, Isadora
Duncan, Isadora 1877(?)-1927 .... **TCLC 68**
See also CA 118; 149
Duncan, Lois 1934- .... **CLC 26**
See also AAYA 4; CA 1-4R; CANR 2, 23, 36; CLR 29; JRDA; MAICYA; SAAS 2; SATA 1, 36, 75
Duncan, Robert (Edward) 1919-1988 **CLC 1, 2, 4, 7, 15, 41, 55; DAM POET; PC 2**
See also CA 9-12R; 124; CANR 28, 62; DLB 5, 16, 193; MTCW 1, 2
Duncan, Sara Jeannette 1861-1922 .... **TCLC 60**
See also CA 157; DLB 92
Dunlap, William 1766-1839 .... **NCLC 2**
See also DLB 30, 37, 59
Dunn, Douglas (Eaglesham) 1942- ... **CLC 6, 40**
See also CA 45-48; CANR 2, 33; DLB 40; MTCW 1
Dunn, Katherine (Karen) 1945- .... **CLC 71**
See also CA 33-36R; CANR 72; MTCW 1
Dunn, Stephen 1939- .... **CLC 36**
See also CA 33-36R; CANR 12, 48, 53; DLB 105
Dunne, Finley Peter 1867-1936 .... **TCLC 28**
See also CA 108; DLB 11, 23
Dunne, John Gregory 1932- .... **CLC 28**
See also CA 25-28R; CANR 14, 50; DLBY 80
Dunsany, Edward John Moreton Drax Plunkett 1878-1957
See Dunsany, Lord
See also CA 104; 148; DLB 10; MTCW 1
Dunsany, Lord .... **TCLC 2, 59**
See also Dunsany, Edward John Moreton Drax Plunkett
See also DLB 77, 153, 156
du Perry, Jean
See Simenon, Georges (Jacques Christian)
Durang, Christopher (Ferdinand) 1949-**CLC 27, 38**
See also CA 105; CANR 50, 76; MTCW 1
Duras, Marguerite 1914-1996**CLC 3, 6, 11, 20, 34, 40, 68, 100**
See also CA 25-28R; 151; CANR 50; DLB 83; MTCW 1, 2
Durban, (Rosa) Pam 1947- .... **CLC 39**
See also CA 123
Durcan, Paul 1944- ... **CLC 43, 70; DAM POET**
See also CA 134
Durkheim, Emile 1858-1917 .... **TCLC 55**
Durrell, Lawrence (George) 1912-1990**CLC 1, 4, 6, 8, 13, 27, 41; DAM NOV**
See also CA 9-12R; 132; CANR 40, 77; CDBLB 1945-1960; DLB 15, 27, 204; DLBY 90; MTCW 1, 2
Durrenmatt, Friedrich
See Duerrenmatt, Friedrich
Dutt, Toru 1856-1877 .... **NCLC 29**
Dwight, Timothy 1752-1817 .... **NCLC 13**
See also DLB 37
Dworkin, Andrea 1946- .... **CLC 43**
See also CA 77-80; CAAS 21; CANR 16, 39, 76; INT CANR-16; MTCW 1, 2
Dwyer, Deanna
See Koontz, Dean R(ay)
Dwyer, K. R.
See Koontz, Dean R(ay)
Dwyer, Thomas A. 1923- .... **CLC 114**
See also CA 115
Dye, Richard
See De Voto, Bernard (Augustine)
Dylan, Bob 1941- .... **CLC 3, 4, 6, 12, 77**
See also CA 41-44R; DLB 16
E. V. L.
See Lucas, E(dward) V(errall)
Eagleton, Terence (Francis) 1943-
See Eagleton, Terry
See also CA 57-60; CANR 7, 23, 68; MTCW 1, 2
Eagleton, Terry .... **CLC 63**
See also Eagleton, Terence (Francis)
See also MTCW 1
Early, Jack
See Scoppettone, Sandra
East, Michael
See West, Morris L(anglo)
Eastaway, Edward
See Thomas, (Philip) Edward
Eastlake, William (Derry) 1917-1997 ..... **CLC 8**
See also CA 5-8R; 158; CAAS 1; CANR 5, 63; DLB 6, 206; INT CANR-5
Eastman, Charles A(lexander) 1858-1939 **TCLC 55; DAM MULT**
See also DLB 175; NNAL; YABC 1
Eberhart, Richard (Ghormley) 1904- **CLC 3, 11, 19, 56; DAM POET**
See also CA 1-4R; CANR 2; CDALB 1941-1968; DLB 48; MTCW 1
Eberstadt, Fernanda 1960- .... **CLC 39**
See also CA 136; CANR 69
Echegaray (y Eizaguirre), Jose (Maria Waldo) 1832-1916 .... **TCLC 4; HLCS 1**
See also CA 104; CANR 32; HW 1; MTCW 1
Echeverria, (Jose) Esteban (Antonino) 1805-1851 **NCLC 18**
Echo
See Proust, (Valentin-Louis-George-Eugene-) Marcel
Eckert, Allan W. 1931- .... **CLC 17**
See also AAYA 18; CA 13-16R; CANR 14, 45; INT CANR-14; SAAS 21; SATA 29, 91; SATA-Brief 27
Eckhart, Meister 1260(?)-1328(?) .... **CMLC 9**
See also DLB 115
Eckmar, F. R.
See de Hartog, Jan
Eco, Umberto 1932-**CLC 28, 60; DAM NOV, POP**
See also BEST 90:1; CA 77-80; CANR 12, 33, 55; DLB 196; MTCW 1, 2
Eddison, E(ric) R(ucker) 1882-1945 .... **TCLC 15**
See also CA 109; 156
Eddy, Mary (Ann Morse) Baker 1821-1910**TCLC 71**
See also CA 113; 174
Edel, (Joseph) Leon 1907-1997 .... **CLC 29, 34**
See also CA 1-4R; 161; CANR 1, 22; DLB 103; INT CANR-22
Eden, Emily 1797-1869 .... **NCLC 10**
Edgar, David 1948- .... **CLC 42; DAM DRAM**
See also CA 57-60; CANR 12, 61; DLB 13; MTCW 1
Edgerton, Clyde (Carlyle) 1944- .... **CLC 39**
See also AAYA 17; CA 118; 134; CANR 64; INT 134
Edgeworth, Maria 1768-1849 .... **NCLC 1, 51**
See also DLB 116, 159, 163; SATA 21
Edmonds, Paul
See Kuttner, Henry
Edmonds, Walter D(umaux) 1903-1998 . **CLC 35**
See also CA 5-8R; CANR 2; DLB 9; MAICYA; SAAS 4; SATA 1, 27; SATA-Obit 99
Edmondson, Wallace
See Ellison, Harlan (Jay)
Edson, Russell .... **CLC 13**
See also CA 33-36R
Edwards, Bronwen Elizabeth
See Rose, Wendy
Edwards, G(erald) B(asil) 1899-1976 ..... **CLC 25**
See also CA 110
Edwards, Gus 1939- .... **CLC 43**
See also CA 108; INT 108
Edwards, Jonathan 1703-1758 . **LC 7; DA; DAC; DAM MST**
See also DLB 24
Efron, Marina Ivanovna Tsvetaeva
See Tsvetaeva (Efron), Marina (Ivanovna)
Ehle, John (Marsden, Jr.) 1925- .... **CLC 27**

See also CA 9-12R
Ehrenbourg, Ilya (Grigoryevich)
See Ehrenburg, Ilya (Grigoryevich)
Ehrenburg, Ilya (Grigoryevich) 1891-1967 **CLC 18, 34, 62**
See also CA 102; 25-28R
Ehrenburg, Ilyo (Grigoryevich)
See Ehrenburg, Ilya (Grigoryevich)
Ehrenreich, Barbara 1941- .... **CLC 110**
See also BEST 90:4; CA 73-76; CANR 16, 37, 62; MTCW 1, 2
Eich, Guenter 1907-1972 .... **CLC 15**
See also CA 111; 93-96; DLB 69, 124
Eichendorff, Joseph Freiherr von 1788-1857 **NCLC 8**
See also DLB 90
Eigner, Larry .... **CLC 9**
See also Eigner, Laurence (Joel)
See also CAAS 23; DLB 5
Eigner, Laurence (Joel) 1927-1996
See Eigner, Larry
See also CA 9-12R; 151; CANR 6; DLB 193
Einstein, Albert 1879-1955 .... **TCLC 65**
See also CA 121; 133; MTCW 1, 2
Eiseley, Loren Corey 1907-1977 .... **CLC 7**
See also AAYA 5; CA 1-4R; 73-76; CANR 6; DLBD 17
Eisenstadt, Jill 1963- .... **CLC 50**
See also CA 140
Eisenstein, Sergei (Mikhailovich) 1898-1948 **TCLC 57**
See also CA 114; 149
Eisner, Simon
See Kornbluth, C(yril) M.
Ekeloef, (Bengt) Gunnar 1907-1968 .... **CLC 27; DAM POET; PC 23**
See also CA 123; 25-28R
Ekelof, (Bengt) Gunnar
See Ekeloef, (Bengt) Gunnar
Ekelund, Vilhelm 1880-1949 .... **TCLC 75**
Ekwensi, C. O. D.
See Ekwensi, Cyprian (Odiatu Duaka)
Ekwensi, Cyprian (Odiatu Duaka) 1921- **CLC 4; BLC 1; DAM MULT**
See also BW 2, 3; CA 29-32R; CANR 18, 42, 74; DLB 117; MTCW 1, 2; SATA 66
Elaine .... **TCLC 18**
See also Leverson, Ada
El Crummo
See Crumb, R(obert)
Elder, Lonne III 1931-1996 .... **DC 8**
See also BLC 1; BW 1, 3; CA 81-84; 152; CANR 25; DAM MULT; DLB 7, 38, 44
Elia
See Lamb, Charles
Eliade, Mircea 1907-1986 .... **CLC 19**
See also CA 65-68; 119; CANR 30, 62; MTCW 1
Eliot, A. D.
See Jewett, (Theodora) Sarah Orne
Eliot, Alice
See Jewett, (Theodora) Sarah Orne
Eliot, Dan
See Silverberg, Robert
Eliot, George 1819-1880 **NCLC 4, 13, 23, 41, 49; DA; DAB; DAC; DAM MST, NOV; PC 20; WLC**
See also CDBLB 1832-1890; DLB 21, 35, 55
Eliot, John 1604-1690 .... **LC 5**
See also DLB 24
Eliot, T(homas) S(tearns) 1888-1965 **CLC 1, 2, 3, 6, 9, 10, 13, 15, 24, 34, 41, 55, 57, 113; DA; DAB; DAC; DAM DRAM, MST, POET; PC 5; WLC**
See also AAYA 28; CA 5-8R; 25-28R; CANR 41; CDALB 1929-1941; DLB 7, 10, 45, 63; DLBY 88; MTCW 1, 2
Elizabeth 1866-1941 .... **TCLC 41**
Elkin, Stanley L(awrence) 1930-1995 **CLC 4, 6, 9, 14, 27, 51, 91; DAM NOV, POP; SSC 12**
See also CA 9-12R; 148; CANR 8, 46; DLB 2, 28; DLBY 80; INT CANR-8; MTCW 1, 2
Elledge, Scott .... **CLC 34**
Elliot, Don
See Silverberg, Robert
Elliott, Don
See Silverberg, Robert
Elliott, George P(aul) 1918-1980 .... **CLC 2**
See also CA 1-4R; 97-100; CANR 2
Elliott, Janice 1931- .... **CLC 47**
See also CA 13-16R; CANR 8, 29; DLB 14
Elliott, Sumner Locke 1917-1991 .... **CLC 38**
See also CA 5-8R; 134; CANR 2, 21
Elliott, William
See Bradbury, Ray (Douglas)
Ellis, A. E. .... **CLC 7**
Ellis, Alice Thomas .... **CLC 40**
See also Haycraft, Anna
See also DLB 194; MTCW 1
Ellis, Bret Easton 1964- **CLC 39, 71, 117; DAM POP**
See also AAYA 2; CA 118; 123; CANR 51, 74; INT 123; MTCW 1
Ellis, (Henry) Havelock 1859-1939 ...... **TCLC 14**
See also CA 109; 169; DLB 190
Ellis, Landon
See Ellison, Harlan (Jay)
Ellis, Trey 1962- .... **CLC 55**
See also CA 146
Ellison, Harlan (Jay) 1934- **CLC 1, 13, 42; DAM POP; SSC 14**
See also AAYA 29; CA 5-8R; CANR 5, 46; DLB 8; INT CANR-5; MTCW 1, 2
Ellison, Ralph (Waldo) 1914-1994 **CLC 1, 3, 11, 54, 86, 114; BLC 1; DA; DAB; DAC; DAM MST, MULT, NOV; SSC 26; WLC**
See also AAYA 19; BW 1, 3; CA 9-12R; 145; CANR 24, 53; CDALB 1941-1968; DLB 2, 76; DLBY 94; MTCW 1, 2
Ellmann, Lucy (Elizabeth) 1956- .... **CLC 61**
See also CA 128
Ellmann, Richard (David) 1918-1987 ..... **CLC 50**
See also BEST 89:2; CA 1-4R; 122; CANR 2, 28, 61; DLB 103; DLBY 87; MTCW 1, 2
Elman, Richard (Martin) 1934-1997 ..... **CLC 19**
See also CA 17-20R; 163; CAAS 3; CANR 47
Elron
See Hubbard, L(afayette) Ron(ald)
Eluard, Paul .... **TCLC 7, 41**
See also Grindel, Eugene
Elyot, Sir Thomas 1490(?)-1546 .... **LC 11**
Elytis, Odysseus 1911-1996 .... **CLC 15, 49, 100; DAM POET; PC 21**
See also CA 102; 151; MTCW 1, 2
Emecheta, (Florence Onye) Buchi 1944- **CLC 14, 48; BLC 2; DAM MULT**
See also BW 2, 3; CA 81-84; CANR 27, 81; DLB 117; MTCW 1, 2; SATA 66
Emerson, Mary Moody 1774-1863 .... **NCLC 66**
Emerson, Ralph Waldo 1803-1882 . **NCLC 1, 38; DA; DAB; DAC; DAM MST, POET; PC 18; WLC**
See also CDALB 1640-1865; DLB 1, 59, 73
Eminescu, Mihail 1850-1889 .... **NCLC 33**
Empson, William 1906-1984 **CLC 3, 8, 19, 33, 34**
See also CA 17-20R; 112; CANR 31, 61; DLB 20; MTCW 1, 2
Enchi, Fumiko (Ueda) 1905-1986 .... **CLC 31**
See also CA 129; 121; DLB 182
Ende, Michael (Andreas Helmuth) 1929-1995 **CLC 31**
See also CA 118; 124; 149; CANR 36; CLR 14; DLB 75; MAICYA; SATA 61; SATA-Brief 42; SATA-Obit 86
Endo, Shusaku 1923-1996 **CLC 7, 14, 19, 54, 99; DAM NOV**
See also CA 29-32R; 153; CANR 21, 54; DLB 182; MTCW 1, 2
Engel, Marian 1933-1985 .... **CLC 36**
See also CA 25-28R; CANR 12; DLB 53; INT CANR-12
Engelhardt, Frederick
See Hubbard, L(afayette) Ron(ald)
Enright, D(ennis) J(oseph) 1920- .. **CLC 4, 8, 31**
See also CA 1-4R; CANR 1, 42; DLB 27; SATA 25
Enzensberger, Hans Magnus 1929- ...... **CLC 43**
See also CA 116; 119
Ephron, Nora 1941- .... **CLC 17, 31**
See also AITN 2; CA 65-68; CANR 12, 39
Epicurus 341B.C.-270B.C. .... **CMLC 21**
See also DLB 176
Epsilon
See Betjeman, John
Epstein, Daniel Mark 1948- .... **CLC 7**
See also CA 49-52; CANR 2, 53
Epstein, Jacob 1956- .... **CLC 19**
See also CA 114
Epstein, Jean 1897-1953 .... **TCLC 92**
Epstein, Joseph 1937- .... **CLC 39**
See also CA 112; 119; CANR 50, 65
Epstein, Leslie 1938- .... **CLC 27**
See also CA 73-76; CAAS 12; CANR 23, 69
Equiano, Olaudah 1745(?)-1797 .. **LC 16; BLC 2; DAM MULT**
See also DLB 37, 50
ER .... **TCLC 33**
See also CA 160; DLB 85
Erasmus, Desiderius 1469(?)-1536 .... **LC 16**
Erdman, Paul E(mil) 1932- .... **CLC 25**
See also AITN 1; CA 61-64; CANR 13, 43
Erdrich, Louise 1954- .. **CLC 39, 54, 120; DAM MULT, NOV, POP**
See also AAYA 10; BEST 89:1; CA 114; CANR 41, 62; CDALBS; DLB 152, 175, 206; MTCW 1; NNAL; SATA 94
Erenburg, Ilya (Grigoryevich)
See Ehrenburg, Ilya (Grigoryevich)
Erickson, Stephen Michael 1950-
See Erickson, Steve
See also CA 129
Erickson, Steve 1950- .... **CLC 64**
See also Erickson, Stephen Michael
See also CANR 60, 68
Ericson, Walter
See Fast, Howard (Melvin)
Eriksson, Buntel
See Bergman, (Ernst) Ingmar
Ernaux, Annie 1940- .... **CLC 88**
See also CA 147
Erskine, John 1879-1951 .... **TCLC 84**
See also CA 112; 159; DLB 9, 102
Eschenbach, Wolfram von
See Wolfram von Eschenbach
Eseki, Bruno
See Mphahlele, Ezekiel
Esenin, Sergei (Alexandrovich) 1895-1925 **TCLC 4**
See also CA 104
Eshleman, Clayton 1935- .... **CLC 7**
See also CA 33-36R; CAAS 6; DLB 5
Espriella, Don Manuel Alvarez
See Southey, Robert
Espriu, Salvador 1913-1985 .... **CLC 9**
See also CA 154; 115; DLB 134
Espronceda, Jose de 1808-1842 .... **NCLC 39**
Esse, James
See Stephens, James
Esterbrook, Tom
See Hubbard, L(afayette) Ron(ald)
Estleman, Loren D. 1952- .. **CLC 48; DAM NOV,**

POP
See also AAYA 27; CA 85-88; CANR 27, 74; INT CANR-27; MTCW 1, 2
Euclid 306B.C.-283B.C. .... **CMLC 25**
Eugenides, Jeffrey 1960(?)- .... **CLC 81**
See also CA 144
Euripides c. 485B.C.-406B.C.**CMLC 23; DA; DAB; DAC; DAM DRAM, MST; DC 4; WLCS**
See also DLB 176
Evan, Evin
See Faust, Frederick (Schiller)
Evans, Caradoc 1878-1945 .... **TCLC 85**
Evans, Evan
See Faust, Frederick (Schiller)
Evans, Marian
See Eliot, George
Evans, Mary Ann
See Eliot, George
Evarts, Esther
See Benson, Sally
Everett, Percival L. 1956- .... **CLC 57**
See also BW 2; CA 129
Everson, R(onald) G(ilmour) 1903- .... **CLC 27**
See also CA 17-20R; DLB 88
Everson, William (Oliver) 1912-1994**CLC 1, 5, 14**
See also CA 9-12R; 145; CANR 20; DLB 212; MTCW 1
Evtushenko, Evgenii Aleksandrovich
See Yevtushenko, Yevgeny (Alexandrovich)
Ewart, Gavin (Buchanan) 1916-1995 **CLC 13, 46**
See also CA 89-92; 150; CANR 17, 46; DLB 40; MTCW 1
Ewers, Hanns Heinz 1871-1943 .... **TCLC 12**
See also CA 109; 149
Ewing, Frederick R.
See Sturgeon, Theodore (Hamilton)
Exley, Frederick (Earl) 1929-1992 ..... **CLC 6, 11**
See also AITN 2; CA 81-84; 138; DLB 143; DLBY 81
Eynhardt, Guillermo
See Quiroga, Horacio (Sylvestre)
Ezekiel, Nissim 1924- .... **CLC 61**
See also CA 61-64
Ezekiel, Tish O'Dowd 1943- .... **CLC 34**
See also CA 129
Fadeyev, A.
See Bulgya, Alexander Alexandrovich
Fadeyev, Alexander .... **TCLC 53**
See also Bulgya, Alexander Alexandrovich
Fagen, Donald 1948- .... **CLC 26**
Fainzilberg, Ilya Arnoldovich 1897-1937
See Ilf, Ilya
See also CA 120; 165
Fair, Ronald L. 1932- .... **CLC 18**
See also BW 1; CA 69-72; CANR 25; DLB 33
Fairbairn, Roger
See Carr, John Dickson
Fairbairns, Zoe (Ann) 1948- .... **CLC 32**
See also CA 103; CANR 21
Falco, Gian
See Papini, Giovanni
Falconer, James
See Kirkup, James
Falconer, Kenneth
See Kornbluth, C(yril) M.
Falkland, Samuel
See Heijermans, Herman
Fallaci, Oriana 1930- .... **CLC 11, 110**
See also CA 77-80; CANR 15, 58; MTCW 1
Faludy, George 1913- .... **CLC 42**
See also CA 21-24R
Faludy, Gyoergy
See Faludy, George
Fanon, Frantz 1925-1961 **CLC 74; BLC 2; DAM MULT**
See also BW 1; CA 116; 89-92
Fanshawe, Ann 1625-1680 .... **LC 11**
Fante, John (Thomas) 1911-1983 ..... **CLC 60**
See also CA 69-72; 109; CANR 23; DLB 130; DLBY 83
Farah, Nuruddin 1945- .. **CLC 53; BLC 2; DAM MULT**
See also BW 2, 3; CA 106; CANR 81; DLB 125
Fargue, Leon-Paul 1876(?)-1947 ... **TCLC 11**
See also CA 109
Farigoule, Louis
See Romains, Jules
Farina, Richard 1936(?)-1966 .... **CLC 9**
See also CA 81-84; 25-28R
Farley, Walter (Lorimer) 1915-1989 ..... **CLC 17**
See also CA 17-20R; CANR 8, 29; DLB 22; JRDA; MAICYA; SATA 2, 43
Farmer, Philip Jose 1918- .... **CLC 1, 19**
See also AAYA 28; CA 1-4R; CANR 4, 35; DLB 8; MTCW 1; SATA 93
Farquhar, George 1677-1707**LC 21; DAM DRAM**
See also DLB 84
Farrell, J(ames) G(ordon) 1935-1979 ...... **CLC 6**
See also CA 73-76; 89-92; CANR 36; DLB 14; MTCW 1
Farrell, James T(homas) 1904-1979 **CLC 1, 4, 8, 11, 66; SSC 28**
See also CA 5-8R; 89-92; CANR 9, 61; DLB 4, 9, 86; DLBD 2; MTCW 1, 2
Farren, Richard J.
See Betjeman, John
Farren, Richard M.
<indSee Betjeman, John
Fassbinder, Rainer Werner 1946-1982 . **CLC 20**
See also CA 93-96; 106; CANR 31
Fast, Howard (Melvin) 1914-**CLC 23; DAM NOV**
See also AAYA 16; CA 1-4R; CAAS 18; CANR 1, 33, 54, 75; DLB 9; INT CANR-33; MTCW 1; SATA 7; SATA-Essay 107
Faulcon, Robert
See Holdstock, Robert P.
Faulkner, William (Cuthbert) 1897-1962**CLC 1, 3, 6, 8, 9, 11, 14, 18, 28, 52, 68; DA; DAB; DAC; DAM MST, NOV; SSC 1, 35; WLC**
See also AAYA 7; CA 81-84; CANR 33; CDALB 1929-1941; DLB 9, 11, 44, 102; DLBD 2; DLBY 86, 97; MTCW 1, 2
Fauset, Jessie Redmon 1884(?)-1961**CLC 19, 54; BLC 2; DAM MULT**
See also BW 1; CA 109; DLB 51
Faust, Frederick (Schiller) 1892-1944(?) **TCLC 49; DAM POP**
See also CA 108; 152
Faust, Irvin 1924- .... **CLC 8**
See also CA 33-36R; CANR 28, 67; DLB 2, 28; DLBY 80
Fawkes, Guy
See Benchley, Robert (Charles)
Fearing, Kenneth (Flexner) 1902-1961 . **CLC 51**
See also CA 93-96; CANR 59; DLB 9
Fecamps, Elise
See Creasey, John
Federman, Raymond 1928- .... **CLC 6, 47**
See also CA 17-20R; CAAS 8; CANR 10, 43; DLBY 80
Federspiel, J(uerg) F. 1931- .... **CLC 42**
See also CA 146
Feiffer, Jules (Ralph) 1929- **CLC 2, 8, 64; DAM DRAM**
See also AAYA 3; CA 17-20R; CANR 30, 59; DLB 7, 44; INT CANR-30; MTCW 1; SATA 8, 61
Feige, Hermann Albert Otto Maximilian
See Traven, B.
Feinberg, David B. 1956-1994 .... **CLC 59**
See also CA 135; 147
Feinstein, Elaine 1930- .... **CLC 36**
See also CA 69-72; CAAS 1; CANR 31, 68; DLB 14, 40; MTCW 1
Feldman, Irving (Mordecai) 1928- ..... **CLC 7**
See also CA 1-4R; CANR 1; DLB 169
Felix-Tchicaya, Gerald
See Tchicaya, Gerald Felix
Fellini, Federico 1920-1993 .... **CLC 16, 85**
See also CA 65-68; 143; CANR 33
Felsen, Henry Gregor 1916- .... **CLC 17**
See also CA 1-4R; CANR 1; SAAS 2; SATA 1
Fenno, Jack
See Calisher, Hortense
Fenollosa, Ernest (Francisco) 1853-1908**TCLC 91**
Fenton, James Martin 1949- .... **CLC 32**
See also CA 102; DLB 40
Ferber, Edna 1887-1968 .... **CLC 18, 93**
See also AITN 1; CA 5-8R; 25-28R; CANR 68; DLB 9, 28, 86; MTCW 1, 2; SATA 7
Ferguson, Helen
See Kavan, Anna
Ferguson, Samuel 1810-1886 .... **NCLC 33**
See also DLB 32
Fergusson, Robert 1750-1774 .... **LC 29**
See also DLB 109
Ferling, Lawrence
See Ferlinghetti, Lawrence (Monsanto)
Ferlinghetti, Lawrence (Monsanto) 1919(?)-**CLC 2, 6, 10, 27, 111; DAM POET; PC 1**
See also CA 5-8R; CANR 3, 41, 73; CDALB 1941-1968; DLB 5, 16; MTCW 1, 2
Fernandez, Vicente Garcia Huidobro
See Huidobro Fernandez, Vicente Garcia
Ferrer, Gabriel (Francisco Victor) Miro
See Miro (Ferrer), Gabriel (Francisco Victor)
Ferrier, Susan (Edmonstone) 1782-1854**NCLC 8**
See also DLB 116
Ferrigno, Robert 1948(?)- .... **CLC 65**
See also CA 140
Ferron, Jacques 1921-1985 .... **CLC 94; DAC**
See also CA 117; 129; DLB 60
Feuchtwanger, Lion 1884-1958 .... **TCLC 3**
See also CA 104; DLB 66
Feuillet, Octave 1821-1890 .... **NCLC 45**
See also DLB 192
Feydeau, Georges (Leon Jules Marie) 1862-1921 **TCLC 22; DAM DRAM**
See also CA 113; 152; DLB 192
Fichte, Johann Gottlieb 1762-1814 ...... **NCLC 62**
See also DLB 90
Ficino, Marsilio 1433-1499 .... **LC 12**
Fiedeler, Hans
See Doeblin, Alfred
Fiedler, Leslie A(aron) 1917- ...... **CLC 4, 13, 24**
See also CA 9-12R; CANR 7, 63; DLB 28, 67; MTCW 1, 2
Field, Andrew 1938- .... **CLC 44**
See also CA 97-100; CANR 25
Field, Eugene 1850-1895 .... **NCLC 3**
See also DLB 23, 42, 140; DLBD 13; MAICYA; SATA 16
Field, Gans T.
See Wellman, Manly Wade
Field, Michael 1915-1971 .... **TCLC 43**
See also CA 29-32R
Field, Peter
See Hobson, Laura Z(ametkin)
Fielding, Henry 1707-1754 **LC 1, 46; DA; DAB; DAC; DAM DRAM, MST, NOV; WLC**
See also CDBLB 1660-1789; DLB 39, 84, 101
Fielding, Sarah 1710-1768 .... **LC 1, 44**
See also DLB 39
Fields, W. C. 1880-1946 .... **TCLC 80**
See also DLB 44
Fierstein, Harvey (Forbes) 1954- **CLC 33; DAM DRAM, POP**
See also CA 123; 129
Figes, Eva 1932- .... **CLC 31**
See also CA 53-56; CANR 4, 44; DLB 14
Finch, Anne 1661-1720 .... **LC 3; PC 21**

See also DLB 95
Finch, Robert (Duer Claydon) 1900- .... **CLC 18**
See also CA 57-60; CANR 9, 24, 49; DLB 88
Findley, Timothy 1930-**CLC 27, 102; DAC; DAM MST**
See also CA 25-28R; CANR 12, 42, 69; DLB 53
Fink, William
See Mencken, H(enry) L(ouis)
Firbank, Louis 1942-
See Reed, Lou
See also CA 117
Firbank, (Arthur Annesley) Ronald 1886-1926 **TCLC 1**
See also CA 104; 177; DLB 36
Fisher, Dorothy (Frances) Canfield 1879-1958 **TCLC 87**
See also CA 114; 136; CANR 80; DLB 9, 102; MAICYA; YABC 1
Fisher, M(ary) F(rances) K(ennedy) 1908-1992 **CLC 76, 87**
See also CA 77-80; 138; CANR 44; MTCW 1
Fisher, Roy 1930- .... **CLC 25**
See also CA 81-84; CAAS 10; CANR 16; DLB 40
Fisher, Rudolph 1897-1934**TCLC 11; BLC 2; DAM MULT; SSC 25**
See also BW 1, 3; CA 107; 124; CANR 80; DLB 51, 102
Fisher, Vardis (Alvero) 1895-1968 .... **CLC 7**
See also CA 5-8R; 25-28R; CANR 68; DLB 9, 206
Fiske, Tarleton
See Bloch, Robert (Albert)
Fitch, Clarke
See Sinclair, Upton (Beall)
Fitch, John IV
See Cormier, Robert (Edmund)
Fitzgerald, Captain Hugh
See Baum, L(yman) Frank
FitzGerald, Edward 1809-1883 .... **NCLC 9**
See also DLB 32
Fitzgerald, F(rancis) Scott (Key) 1896-1940 **TCLC 1, 6, 14, 28, 55; DA; DAB; DAC; DAM MST, NOV; SSC 6, 31; WLC**
See also AAYA 24; AITN 1; CA 110; 123; CDALB 1917-1929; DLB 4, 9, 86; DLBD 1, 15, 16; DLBY 81, 96; MTCW 1, 2
Fitzgerald, Penelope 1916- .... **CLC 19, 51, 61**
See also CA 85-88; CAAS 10; CANR 56; DLB 14, 194; MTCW 2
Fitzgerald, Robert (Stuart) 1910-1985 .. **CLC 39**
See also CA 1-4R; 114; CANR 1; DLBY 80
FitzGerald, Robert D(avid) 1902-1987 ... **CLC 19**
See also CA 17-20R
Fitzgerald, Zelda (Sayre) 1900-1948 ... **TCLC 52**
See also CA 117; 126; DLBY 84
Flanagan, Thomas (James Bonner) 1923- .. **CLC 25, 52**
See also CA 108; CANR 55; DLBY 80; INT 108; MTCW 1
Flaubert, Gustave 1821-1880**NCLC 2, 10, 19, 62, 66; DA; DAB; DAC; DAM MST, NOV; SSC 11; WLC**
See also DLB 119
Flecker, Herman Elroy
See Flecker, (Herman) James Elroy
Flecker, (Herman) James Elroy 1884-1915**TCLC 43**
See also CA 109; 150; DLB 10, 19
Fleming, Ian (Lancaster) 1908-1964 **CLC 3, 30; DAM POP**
See also AAYA 26; CA 5-8R; CANR 59; CDBLB 1945-1960; DLB 87, 201; MTCW 1, 2; SATA 9
Fleming, Thomas (James) 1927- .... **CLC 37**
See also CA 5-8R; CANR 10; INT CANR-10; SATA 8
Fletcher, John 1579-1625 .... **LC 33; DC 6**
See also CDBLB Before 1660; DLB 58
Fletcher, John Gould 1886-1950 .... **TCLC 35**
See also CA 107; 167; DLB 4, 45
Fleur, Paul
See Pohl, Frederik
Flooglebuckle, Al
See Spiegelman, Art
Flying Officer X
See Bates, H(erbert) E(rnest)
Fo, Dario 1926-**CLC 32, 109; DAM DRAM; DC 10**
See also CA 116; 128; CANR 68; DLBY 97; MTCW 1, 2
Fogarty, Jonathan Titulescu Esq.
See Farrell, James T(homas)
Folke, Will
See Bloch, Robert (Albert)
Follett, Ken(neth Martin) 1949- .. **CLC 18; DAM NOV, POP**
See also AAYA 6; BEST 89:4; CA 81-84; CANR 13, 33, 54; DLB 87; DLBY 81; INT CANR-33; MTCW 1
Fontane, Theodor 1819-1898 .... **NCLC 26**
See also DLB 129
Foote, Horton 1916- .. **CLC 51, 91; DAM DRAM**
See also CA 73-76; CANR 34, 51; DLB 26; INT CANR-34
Foote, Shelby 1916- .. **CLC 75; DAM NOV, POP**
See also CA 5-8R; CANR 3, 45, 74; DLB 2, 17; MTCW 2
Forbes, Esther 1891-1967 .... **CLC 12**
See also AAYA 17; CA 13-14; 25-28R; CAP 1; CLR 27; DLB 22; JRDA; MAICYA; SATA 2, 100
Forche, Carolyn (Louise) 1950- **CLC 25, 83, 86; DAM POET; PC 10**
See also CA 109; 117; CANR 50, 74; DLB 5, 193; INT 117; MTCW 1
Ford, Elbur
See Hibbert, Eleanor Alice Burford
Ford, Ford Madox 1873-1939**TCLC 1, 15, 39, 57; DAM NOV**
See also CA 104; 132; CANR 74; CDBLB 1914-1945; DLB 162; MTCW 1, 2
Ford, Henry 1863-1947 .... **TCLC 73**
See also CA 115; 148
Ford, John 1586-(?) .... **DC 8**
See also CDBLB Before 1660; DAM DRAM; DLB 58
Ford, John 1895-1973 .... **CLC 16**
See also CA 45-48
Ford, Richard 1944- .... **CLC 46, 99**
See also CA 69-72; CANR 11, 47; MTCW 1
Ford, Webster
See Masters, Edgar Lee
Foreman, Richard 1937- .... **CLC 50**
See also CA 65-68; CANR 32, 63
Forester, C(ecil) S(cott) 1899-1966 .... **CLC 35**
See also CA 73-76; 25-28R; DLB 191; SATA 13
Forez
See Mauriac, Francois (Charles)
Forman, James Douglas 1932- .... **CLC 21**
See also AAYA 17; CA 9-12R; CANR 4, 19, 42; JRDA; MAICYA; SATA 8, 70
Fornes, Maria Irene 1930- **CLC 39, 61; DC 10; HLCS 1**
See also CA 25-28R; CANR 28, 81; DLB 7; HW 1, 2; INT CANR-28; MTCW 1
Forrest, Leon (Richard) 1937-1997**CLC 4; BLCS**
See also BW 2; CA 89-92; 162; CAAS 7; CANR 25, 52; DLB 33
Forster, E(dward) M(organ) 1879-1970 **CLC 1, 2, 3, 4, 9, 10, 13, 15, 22, 45, 77; DA; DAB; DAC; DAM MST, NOV; SSC 27; WLC**
See also AAYA 2; CA 13-14; 25-28R; CANR 45; CAP 1; CDBLB 1914-1945; DLB 34, 98, 162, 178, 195; DLBD 10; MTCW 1, 2; SATA 57
Forster, John 1812-1876 .... **NCLC 11**
See also DLB 144, 184
Forsyth, Frederick 1938-**CLC 2, 5, 36; DAM NOV, POP**
See also BEST 89:4; CA 85-88; CANR 38, 62; DLB 87; MTCW 1, 2
Forten, Charlotte L. .... **TCLC 16; BLC 2**
See also Grimke, Charlotte L(ottie) Forten
See also DLB 50
Foscolo, Ugo 1778-1827 .... **NCLC 8**
Fosse, Bob .... **CLC 20**
See also Fosse, Robert Louis
Fosse, Robert Louis 1927-1987
See Fosse, Bob
See also CA 110; 123
Foster, Stephen Collins 1826-1864 ..... **NCLC 26**
Foucault, Michel 1926-1984 ...... **CLC 31, 34, 69**
See also CA 105; 113; CANR 34; MTCW 1, 2
Fouque, Friedrich (Heinrich Karl) de la Motte 1777-1843 .... **NCLC 2**
See also DLB 90
Fourier, Charles 1772-1837 .... **NCLC 51**
Fournier, Henri Alban 1886-1914
See Alain-Fournier
See also CA 104
Fournier, Pierre 1916- .... **CLC 11**
See also Gascar, Pierre
See also CA 89-92; CANR 16, 40
Fowles, John (Philip) 1926-**CLC 1, 2, 3, 4, 6, 9, 10, 15, 33, 87; DAB; DAC; DAM MST; SSC 33**
See also CA 5-8R; CANR 25, 71; CDBLB 1960 to Present; DLB 14, 139, 207; MTCW 1, 2; SATA 22
Fox, Paula 1923- .... **CLC 2, 8, 121**
See also AAYA 3; CA 73-76; CANR 20, 36, 62; CLR 1, 44; DLB 52; JRDA; MAICYA; MTCW 1; SATA 17, 60
Fox, William Price (Jr.) 1926- .... **CLC 22**
See also CA 17-20R; CAAS 19; CANR 11; DLB 2; DLBY 81
Foxe, John 1516(?)-1587 .... **LC 14**
See also DLB 132
Frame, Janet 1924-**CLC 2, 3, 6, 22, 66, 96; SSC 29**
See also Clutha, Janet Paterson Frame
France, Anatole .... **TCLC 9**
See also Thibault, Jacques Anatole Francois
See also DLB 123; MTCW 1
Francis, Claude 19(?)- .... **CLC 50**
Francis, Dick 1920- . **CLC 2, 22, 42, 102; DAM POP**
See also AAYA 5, 21; BEST 89:3; CA 5-8R; CANR 9, 42, 68; CDBLB 1960 to Present; DLB 87; INT CANR-9; MTCW 1, 2
Francis, Robert (Churchill) 1901-1987 **CLC 15**
See also CA 1-4R; 123; CANR 1
Frank, Anne(lies Marie) 1929-1945**TCLC 17; DA; DAB; DAC; DAM MST; WLC**
See also AAYA 12; CA 113; 133; CANR 68; MTCW 1, 2; SATA 87; SATA-Brief 42
Frank, Bruno 1887-1945 .... **TCLC 81**
See also DLB 118
Frank, Elizabeth 1945- .... **CLC 39**
See also CA 121; 126; CANR 78; INT 126
Frankl, Viktor E(mil) 1905-1997 .... **CLC 93**
See also CA 65-68; 161
Franklin, Benjamin
See Hasek, Jaroslav (Matej Frantisek)
Franklin, Benjamin 1706-1790**LC 25; DA; DAB; DAC; DAM MST; WLCS**
See also CDALB 1640-1865; DLB 24, 43, 73
Franklin, (Stella Maria Sarah) Miles (Lampe) 1879-1954 .... **TCLC 7**
See also CA 104; 164
Fraser, (Lady) Antonia (Pakenham) 1932- . **CLC 32, 107**
See also CA 85-88; CANR 44, 65; MTCW 1, 2; SATA-Brief 32
Fraser, George MacDonald 1925- .... **CLC 7**

See also CA 45-48; CANR 2, 48, 74; MTCW 1
Fraser, Sylvia 1935- .... **CLC 64**
See also CA 45-48; CANR 1, 16, 60
Frayn, Michael 1933- ... **CLC 3, 7, 31, 47; DAM DRAM, NOV**
See also CA 5-8R; CANR 30, 69; DLB 13, 14, 194; MTCW 1, 2
Fraze, Candida (Merrill) 1945- .... **CLC 50**
See also CA 126
Frazer, J(ames) G(eorge) 1854-1941 ... **TCLC 32**
See also CA 118
Frazer, Robert Caine
See Creasey, John
Frazer, Sir James George
See Frazer, J(ames) G(eorge)
Frazier, Charles 1950- .... **CLC 109**
See also CA 161
Frazier, Ian 1951- .... **CLC 46**
See also CA 130; CANR 54
Frederic, Harold 1856-1898 .... **NCLC 10**
See also DLB 12, 23; DLBD 13
Frederick, John
See Faust, Frederick (Schiller)
Frederick the Great 1712-1786 .... **LC 14**
Fredro, Aleksander 1793-1876 .... **NCLC 8**
Freeling, Nicolas 1927- .... **CLC 38**
See also CA 49-52; CAAS 12; CANR 1, 17, 50; DLB 87
Freeman, Douglas Southall 1886-1953 **TCLC 11**
See also CA 109; DLB 17; DLBD 17
Freeman, Judith 1946- .... **CLC 55**
See also CA 148
Freeman, Mary Eleanor Wilkins 1852-1930 **TCLC 9; SSC 1**
See also CA 106; 177; DLB 12, 78
Freeman, R(ichard) Austin 1862-1943 **TCLC 21**
See also CA 113; DLB 70
French, Albert 1943- .... **CLC 86**
See also BW 3; CA 167
French, Marilyn 1929- ... **CLC 10, 18, 60; DAM DRAM, NOV, POP**
See also CA 69-72; CANR 3, 31; INT CANR-31; MTCW 1, 2
French, Paul
See Asimov, Isaac
Freneau, Philip Morin 1752-1832 .... **NCLC 1**
See also DLB 37, 43
Freud, Sigmund 1856-1939 .... **TCLC 52**
See also CA 115; 133; CANR 69; MTCW 1, 2
Friedan, Betty (Naomi) 1921- .... **CLC 74**
See also CA 65-68; CANR 18, 45, 74; MTCW 1, 2
Friedlander, Saul 1932- .... **CLC 90**
See also CA 117; 130; CANR 72
Friedman, B(ernard) H(arper) 1926- ...... **CLC 7**
See also CA 1-4R; CANR 3, 48
Friedman, Bruce Jay 1930- .... **CLC 3, 5, 56**
See also CA 9-12R; CANR 25, 52; DLB 2, 28; INT CANR-25
Friel, Brian 1929- ..... **CLC 5, 42, 59, 115; DC 8**
See also CA 21-24R; CANR 33, 69; DLB 13; MTCW 1
Friis-Baastad, Babbis Ellinor 1921-1970**CLC 12**
See also CA 17-20R; 134; SATA 7
Frisch, Max (Rudolf) 1911-1991**CLC 3, 9, 14, 18, 32, 44; DAM DRAM, NOV**
See also CA 85-88; 134; CANR 32, 74; DLB 69, 124; MTCW 1, 2
Fromentin, Eugene (Samuel Auguste) 1820-1876 **NCLC 10**
See also DLB 123
Frost, Frederick
See Faust, Frederick (Schiller)
Frost, Robert (Lee) 1874-1963**CLC 1, 3, 4, 9, 10, 13, 15, 26, 34, 44; DA; DAB; DAC; DAM MST, POET; PC 1; WLC**
See also AAYA 21; CA 89-92; CANR 33; CDALB 1917-1929; DLB 54; DLBD 7; MTCW 1, 2; SATA 14
Froude, James Anthony 1818-1894 ..... **NCLC 43**
See also DLB 18, 57, 144
Froy, Herald
See Waterhouse, Keith (Spencer)
Fry, Christopher 1907- ..... **CLC 2, 10, 14; DAM DRAM**
See also CA 17-20R; CAAS 23; CANR 9, 30, 74; DLB 13; MTCW 1, 2; SATA 66
Frye, (Herman) Northrop 1912-1991 **CLC 24, 70**
See also CA 5-8R; 133; CANR 8, 37; DLB 67, 68; MTCW 1, 2
Fuchs, Daniel 1909-1993 .... **CLC 8, 22**
See also CA 81-84; 142; CAAS 5; CANR 40; DLB 9, 26, 28; DLBY 93
Fuchs, Daniel 1934- .... **CLC 34**
See also CA 37-40R; CANR 14, 48
Fuentes, Carlos 1928-**CLC 3, 8, 10, 13, 22, 41, 60, 113; DA; DAB; DAC; DAM MST, MULT, NOV; HLC; SSC 24; WLC**
See also AAYA 4; AITN 2; CA 69-72; CANR 10, 32, 68; DLB 113; HW 1, 2; MTCW 1, 2
Fuentes, Gregorio Lopez y
See Lopez y Fuentes, Gregorio
Fugard, (Harold) Athol 1932-**CLC 5, 9, 14, 25, 40, 80; DAM DRAM; DC 3**
See also AAYA 17; CA 85-88; CANR 32, 54; MTCW 1
Fugard, Sheila 1932- .... **CLC 48**
See also CA 125
Fuller, Charles (H., Jr.) 1939- **CLC 25; BLC 2; DAM DRAM, MULT; DC 1**
See also BW 2; CA 108; 112; DLB 38; INT 112; MTCW 1
Fuller, John (Leopold) 1937- .... **CLC 62**
See also CA 21-24R; CANR 9, 44; DLB 40
Fuller, Margaret .... **NCLC 5, 50**
See also Ossoli, Sarah Margaret (Fuller marchesa d')
Fuller, Roy (Broadbent) 1912-1991 ... **CLC 4, 28**
See also CA 5-8R; 135; CAAS 10; CANR 53; DLB 15, 20; SATA 87
Fulton, Alice 1952- .... **CLC 52**
See also CA 116; CANR 57; DLB 193
Furphy, Joseph 1843-1912 .... **TCLC 25**
See also CA 163
Fussell, Paul 1924- .... **CLC 74**
See also BEST 90:1; CA 17-20R; CANR 8, 21, 35, 69; INT CANR-21; MTCW 1, 2
Futabatei, Shimei 1864-1909 .... **TCLC 44**
See also CA 162; DLB 180
Futrelle, Jacques 1875-1912 .... **TCLC 19**
See also CA 113; 155
Gaboriau, Emile 1835-1873 .... **NCLC 14**
Gadda, Carlo Emilio 1893-1973 .... **CLC 11**
See also CA 89-92; DLB 177
Gaddis, William 1922-1998**CLC 1, 3, 6, 8, 10, 19, 43, 86**
See also CA 17-20R; 172; CANR 21, 48; DLB 2; MTCW 1, 2
Gage, Walter
See Inge, William (Motter)
Gaines, Ernest J(ames) 1933-**CLC 3, 11, 18, 86; BLC 2; DAM MULT**
See also AAYA 18; AITN 1; BW 2, 3; CA 9-12R; CANR 6, 24, 42, 75; CDALB 1968-1988; DLB 2, 33, 152; DLBY 80; MTCW 1, 2; SATA 86
Gaitskill, Mary 1954- .... **CLC 69**
See also CA 128; CANR 61
Galdos, Benito Perez
See Perez Galdos, Benito
Gale, Zona 1874-1938 ...... **TCLC 7; DAM DRAM**
See also CA 105; 153; DLB 9, 78
Galeano, Eduardo (Hughes) 1940-**CLC 72; HLCS 1**
See also CA 29-32R; CANR 13, 32; HW 1
Galiano, Juan Valera y Alcala
See Valera y Alcala-Galiano, Juan
Galilei, Galileo 1546-1642 .... **LC 45**
Gallagher, Tess 1943- **CLC 18, 63; DAM POET; PC 9**
See also CA 106; DLB 212
Gallant, Mavis 1922-**CLC 7, 18, 38; DAC; DAM MST; SSC 5**
See also CA 69-72; CANR 29, 69; DLB 53; MTCW 1, 2
Gallant, Roy A(rthur) 1924- .... **CLC 17**
See also CA 5-8R; CANR 4, 29, 54; CLR 30; MAICYA; SATA 4, 68
Gallico, Paul (William) 1897-1976 .... **CLC 2**
See also AITN 1; CA 5-8R; 69-72; CANR 23; DLB 9, 171; MAICYA; SATA 13
Gallo, Max Louis 1932- .... **CLC 95**
See also CA 85-88
Gallois, Lucien
See Desnos, Robert
Gallup, Ralph
See Whitemore, Hugh (John)
Galsworthy, John 1867-1933 .. **TCLC 1, 45; DA; DAB; DAC; DAM DRAM, MST, NOV; SSC 22; WLC**
See also CA 104; 141; CANR 75; CDBLB 1890-1914; DLB 10, 34, 98, 162; DLBD 16; MTCW 1
Galt, John 1779-1839 .... **NCLC 1**
See also DLB 99, 116, 159
Galvin, James 1951- .... **CLC 38**
See also CA 108; CANR 26
Gamboa, Federico 1864-1939 .... **TCLC 36**
See also CA 167; HW 2
Gandhi, M. K.
See Gandhi, Mohandas Karamchand
Gandhi, Mahatma
See Gandhi, Mohandas Karamchand
Gandhi, Mohandas Karamchand 1869-1948**TCLC 59; DAM MULT**
See also CA 121; 132; MTCW 1, 2
Gann, Ernest Kellogg 1910-1991 .... **CLC 23**
See also AITN 1; CA 1-4R; 136; CANR 1
Garcia, Cristina 1958- .... **CLC 76**
See also CA 141; CANR 73; HW 2
Garcia Lorca, Federico 1898-1936**TCLC 1, 7, 49; DA; DAB; DAC; DAM DRAM, MST, MULT, POET; DC 2; HLC; PC 3; WLC**
See also CA 104; 131; CANR 81; DLB 108; HW 1, 2; MTCW 1, 2
Garcia Marquez, Gabriel (Jose) 1928-**CLC 2, 3, 8, 10, 15, 27, 47, 55, 68; DA; DAB; DAC; DAM MST, MULT, NOV, POP; HLC; SSC 8; WLC**
See also AAYA 3; BEST 89:1, 90:4; CA 33-36R; CANR 10, 28, 50, 75; DLB 113; HW 1, 2; MTCW 1, 2
Gard, Janice
See Latham, Jean Lee
Gard, Roger Martin du
See Martin du Gard, Roger
Gardam, Jane 1928- .... **CLC 43**
See also CA 49-52; CANR 2, 18, 33, 54; CLR 12; DLB 14, 161; MAICYA; MTCW 1; SAAS 9; SATA 39, 76; SATA-Brief 28
Gardner, Herb(ert) 1934- .... **CLC 44**
See also CA 149
Gardner, John (Champlin), Jr. 1933-1982**CLC 2, 3, 5, 7, 8, 10, 18, 28, 34; DAM NOV, POP; SSC 7**
See also AITN 1; CA 65-68; 107; CANR 33, 73; CDALBS; DLB 2; DLBY 82; MTCW 1; SATA 40; SATA-Obit 31
Gardner, John (Edmund) 1926- ... **CLC 30; DAM POP**
See also CA 103; CANR 15, 69; MTCW 1
Gardner, Miriam
See Bradley, Marion Zimmer
Gardner, Noel

See Kuttner, Henry
Gardons, S. S.
See Snodgrass, W(illiam) D(e Witt)
Garfield, Leon 1921-1996 .... **CLC 12**
See also AAYA 8; CA 17-20R; 152; CANR 38, 41, 78; CLR 21; DLB 161; JRDA; MAICYA; SATA 1, 32, 76; SATA-Obit 90
Garland, (Hannibal) Hamlin 1860-1940 **TCLC 3; SSC 18**
See also CA 104; DLB 12, 71, 78, 186
Garneau, (Hector de) Saint-Denys 1912-1943 **TCLC 13**
See also CA 111; DLB 88
Garner, Alan 1934- .. **CLC 17; DAB; DAM POP**
See also AAYA 18; CA 73-76; CANR 15, 64; CLR 20; DLB 161; MAICYA; MTCW 1, 2; SATA 18, 69; SATA-Essay 108
Garner, Hugh 1913-1979 .... **CLC 13**
See also CA 69-72; CANR 31; DLB 68
Garnett, David 1892-1981 .... **CLC 3**
See also CA 5-8R; 103; CANR 17, 79; DLB 34; MTCW 2
Garos, Stephanie
See Katz, Steve
Garrett, George (Palmer) 1929- **CLC 3, 11, 51; SSC 30**
See also CA 1-4R; CAAS 5; CANR 1, 42, 67; DLB 2, 5, 130, 152; DLBY 83
Garrick, David 1717-1779 . **LC 15; DAM DRAM**
See also DLB 84
Garrigue, Jean 1914-1972 .... **CLC 2, 8**
See also CA 5-8R; 37-40R; CANR 20
Garrison, Frederick
See Sinclair, Upton (Beall)
Garth, Will
See Hamilton, Edmond; Kuttner, Henry
Garvey, Marcus (Moziah, Jr.) 1887-1940 . **TCLC 41; BLC 2; DAM MULT**
See also BW 1; CA 120; 124; CANR 79
Gary, Romain .... **CLC 25**
See also Kacew, Romain
See also DLB 83
Gascar, Pierre .... **CLC 11**
See also Fournier, Pierre
Gascoyne, David (Emery) 1916- .... **CLC 45**
See also CA 65-68; CANR 10, 28, 54; DLB 20; MTCW 1
Gaskell, Elizabeth Cleghorn 1810-1865**NCLC 70; DAB; DAM MST; SSC 25**
See also CDBLB 1832-1890; DLB 21, 144, 159
Gass, William H(oward) 1924-**CLC 1, 2, 8, 11, 15, 39; SSC 12**
See also CA 17-20R; CANR 30, 71; DLB 2; MTCW 1, 2
Gasset, Jose Ortega y
See Ortega y Gasset, Jose
Gates, Henry Louis, Jr. 1950- .. **CLC 65; BLCS; DAM MULT**
See also BW 2, 3; CA 109; CANR 25, 53, 75; DLB 67; MTCW 1
Gautier, Theophile 1811-1872**NCLC 1, 59; DAM POET; PC 18; SSC 20**
See also DLB 119
Gawsworth, John
See Bates, H(erbert) E(rnest)
Gay, John 1685-1732 .... **LC 49; DAM DRAM**
See also DLB 84, 95
Gay, Oliver
See Gogarty, Oliver St. John
Gaye, Marvin (Penze) 1939-1984 .... **CLC 26**
See also CA 112
Gebler, Carlo (Ernest) 1954- .... **CLC 39**
See also CA 119; 133
Gee, Maggie (Mary) 1948- .... **CLC 57**
See also CA 130; DLB 207
Gee, Maurice (Gough) 1931- .... **CLC 29**
See also CA 97-100; CANR 67; CLR 56; SATA 46, 101
Gelbart, Larry (Simon) 1923- .... **CLC 21, 61**
See also CA 73-76; CANR 45
Gelber, Jack 1932- .... **CLC 1, 6, 14, 79**
See also CA 1-4R; CANR 2; DLB 7
Gellhorn, Martha (Ellis) 1908-1998 **CLC 14, 60**
See also CA 77-80; 164; CANR 44; DLBY 82, 98
Genet, Jean 1910-1986**CLC 1, 2, 5, 10, 14, 44, 46; DAM DRAM**
See also CA 13-16R; CANR 18; DLB 72; DLBY 86; MTCW 1, 2
Gent, Peter 1942- .... **CLC 29**
See also AITN 1; CA 89-92; DLBY 82
Gentlewoman in New England, A
See Bradstreet, Anne
Gentlewoman in Those Parts, A
See Bradstreet, Anne
George, Jean Craighead 1919- .... **CLC 35**
See also AAYA 8; CA 5-8R; CANR 25; CLR 1; DLB 52; JRDA; MAICYA; SATA 2, 68
George, Stefan (Anton) 1868-1933 .. **TCLC 2, 14**
See also CA 104
Georges, Georges Martin
See Simenon, Georges (Jacques Christian)
Gerhardi, William Alexander
See Gerhardie, William Alexander
Gerhardie, William Alexander 1895-1977**CLC 5**
See also CA 25-28R; 73-76; CANR 18; DLB 36
Gerstler, Amy 1956- .... **CLC 70**
See also CA 146
Gertler, T. .... **CLC 34**
See also CA 116; 121; INT 121
Ghalib .... **NCLC 39, 78**
See also Ghalib, Hsadullah Khan
Ghalib, Hsadullah Khan 1797-1869
See Ghalib
See also DAM POET
Ghelderode, Michel de 1898-1962**CLC 6, 11; DAM DRAM**
See also CA 85-88; CANR 40, 77
Ghiselin, Brewster 1903- .... **CLC 23**
See also CA 13-16R; CAAS 10; CANR 13
Ghose, Aurabinda 1872-1950 .... **TCLC 63**
See also CA 163
Ghose, Zulfikar 1935- .... **CLC 42**
See also CA 65-68; CANR 67
Ghosh, Amitav 1956- .... **CLC 44**
See also CA 147; CANR 80
Giacosa, Giuseppe 1847-1906 .... **TCLC 7**
See also CA 104
Gibb, Lee
See Waterhouse, Keith (Spencer)
Gibbon, Lewis Grassic .... **TCLC 4**
See also Mitchell, James Leslie
Gibbons, Kaye 1960- ..... **CLC 50, 88; DAM POP**
See also CA 151; CANR 75; MTCW 1
Gibran, Kahlil 1883-1931**TCLC 1, 9; DAM POET, POP; PC 9**
See also CA 104; 150; MTCW 2
Gibran, Khalil
See Gibran, Kahlil
Gibson, William 1914-**CLC 23; DA; DAB; DAC; DAM DRAM, MST**
See also CA 9-12R; CANR 9, 42, 75; DLB 7; MTCW 1; SATA 66
Gibson, William (Ford) 1948-**CLC 39, 63; DAM POP**
See also AAYA 12; CA 126; 133; CANR 52; MTCW 1
Gide, Andre (Paul Guillaume) 1869-1951**TCLC 5, 12, 36; DA; DAB; DAC; DAM MST, NOV; SSC 13; WLC**
See also CA 104; 124; DLB 65; MTCW 1, 2
Gifford, Barry (Colby) 1946- .... **CLC 34**
See also CA 65-68; CANR 9, 30, 40
Gilbert, Frank
See De Voto, Bernard (Augustine)
Gilbert, W(illiam) S(chwenck) 1836-1911 **TCLC 3; DAM DRAM, POET**
See also CA 104; 173; SATA 36
Gilbreth, Frank B., Jr. 1911- .... **CLC 17**
See also CA 9-12R; SATA 2
Gilchrist, Ellen 1935- . **CLC 34, 48; DAM POP; SSC 14**
See also CA 113; 116; CANR 41, 61; DLB 130; MTCW 1, 2
Giles, Molly 1942- .... **CLC 39**
See also CA 126
Gill, Eric 1882-1940 .... **TCLC 85**
Gill, Patrick
See Creasey, John
Gilliam, Terry (Vance) 1940- .... **CLC 21**
See also Monty Python
See also AAYA 19; CA 108; 113; CANR 35; INT 113
Gillian, Jerry
See Gilliam, Terry (Vance)
Gilliatt, Penelope (Ann Douglass) 1932-1993**CLC 2, 10, 13, 53**
See also AITN 2; CA 13-16R; 141; CANR 49; DLB 14
Gilman, Charlotte (Anna) Perkins (Stetson) 1860-1935 .... **TCLC 9, 37; SSC 13**
See also CA 106; 150; MTCW 1
Gilmour, David 1949- .... **CLC 35**
See also CA 138, 147
Gilpin, William 1724-1804 .... **NCLC 30**
Gilray, J. D.
See Mencken, H(enry) L(ouis)
Gilroy, Frank D(aniel) 1925- .... **CLC 2**
See also CA 81-84; CANR 32, 64; DLB 7
Gilstrap, John 1957(?)- .... **CLC 99**
See also CA 160
Ginsberg, Allen 1926-1997 **CLC 1, 2, 3, 4, 6, 13, 36, 69, 109; DA; DAB; DAC; DAM MST, POET; PC 4; WLC**
See also AITN 1; CA 1-4R; 157; CANR 2, 41, 63; CDALB 1941-1968; DLB 5, 16, 169; MTCW 1, 2
Ginzburg, Natalia 1916-1991 . **CLC 5, 11, 54, 70**
See also CA 85-88; 135; CANR 33; DLB 177; MTCW 1, 2
Giono, Jean 1895-1970 .... **CLC 4, 11**
See also CA 45-48; 29-32R; CANR 2, 35; DLB 72; MTCW 1
Giovanni, Nikki 1943-**CLC 2, 4, 19, 64, 117; BLC 2; DA; DAB; DAC; DAM MST, MULT, POET; PC 19; WLCS**
See also AAYA 22; AITN 1; BW 2, 3; CA 29-32R; CAAS 6; CANR 18, 41, 60; CDALBS; CLR 6; DLB 5, 41; INT CANR-18; MAICYA; MTCW 1, 2; SATA 24, 107
Giovene, Andrea 1904- .... **CLC 7**
See also CA 85-88
Gippius, Zinaida (Nikolayevna) 1869-1945
See Hippius, Zinaida
See also CA 106
Giraudoux, (Hippolyte) Jean 1882-1944**TCLC 2, 7; DAM DRAM**
See also CA 104; DLB 65
Gironella, Jose Maria 1917- .... **CLC 11**
See also CA 101
Gissing, George (Robert) 1857-1903**TCLC 3, 24, 47**
See also CA 105; 167; DLB 18, 135, 184
Giurlani, Aldo
See Palazzeschi, Aldo
Gladkov, Fyodor (Vasilyevich) 1883-1958**TCLC 27**
See also CA 170
Glanville, Brian (Lester) 1931- .... **CLC 6**
See also CA 5-8R; CAAS 9; CANR 3, 70; DLB 15, 139; SATA 42
Glasgow, Ellen (Anderson Gholson) 1873-1945

TCLC 2, 7; SSC 34
See also CA 104; 164; DLB 9, 12; MTCW 2
Glaspell, Susan 1882(?)-1948 . **TCLC 55; DC 10**
See also CA 110; 154; DLB 7, 9, 78; YABC 2
Glassco, John 1909-1981 .... **CLC 9**
See also CA 13-16R; 102; CANR 15; DLB 68
Glasscock, Amnesia
See Steinbeck, John (Ernst)
Glasser, Ronald J. 1940(?)- .... **CLC 37**
Glassman, Joyce
See Johnson, Joyce
Glendinning, Victoria 1937- .... **CLC 50**
See also CA 120; 127; CANR 59; DLB 155
Glissant, Edouard 1928-**CLC 10, 68; DAM MULT**
See also CA 153
Gloag, Julian 1930- .... **CLC 40**
See also AITN 1; CA 65-68; CANR 10, 70
Glowacki, Aleksander
See Prus, Boleslaw
Gluck, Louise (Elisabeth) 1943-**CLC 7, 22, 44, 81; DAM POET; PC 16**
See also CA 33-36R; CANR 40, 69; DLB 5; MTCW 2
Glyn, Elinor 1864-1943 .... **TCLC 72**
See also DLB 153
Gobineau, Joseph Arthur (Comte) de 1816-1882 **NCLC 17**
See also DLB 123
Godard, Jean-Luc 1930- .... **CLC 20**
See also CA 93-96
Godden, (Margaret) Rumer 1907-1998 . **CLC 53**
See also AAYA 6; CA 5-8R; 172; CANR 4, 27, 36, 55, 80; CLR 20; DLB 161; MAICYA; SAAS 12; SATA 3, 36; SATA-Obit 109
Godoy Alcayaga, Lucila 1889-1957
See Mistral, Gabriela
See also BW 2; CA 104; 131; CANR 81; DAM MULT; HW 1, 2; MTCW 1, 2
Godwin, Gail (Kathleen) 1937- **CLC 5, 8, 22, 31, 69; DAM POP**
See also CA 29-32R; CANR 15, 43, 69; DLB 6; INT CANR-15; MTCW 1, 2
Godwin, William 1756-1836 .... **NCLC 14**
See also CDBLB 1789-1832; DLB 39, 104, 142, 158, 163
Goebbels, Josef
See Goebbels, (Paul) Joseph
Goebbels, (Paul) Joseph 1897-1945 ..... **TCLC 68**
See also CA 115; 148
Goebbels, Joseph Paul
See Goebbels, (Paul) Joseph
Goethe, Johann Wolfgang von 1749-1832**NCLC 4, 22, 34; DA; DAB; DAC; DAM DRAM, MST, POET; PC 5; WLC**
See also DLB 94
Gogarty, Oliver St. John 1878-1957 .... **TCLC 15**
See also CA 109; 150; DLB 15, 19
Gogol, Nikolai (Vasilyevich) 1809-1852**NCLC 5, 15, 31; DA; DAB; DAC; DAM DRAM, MST; DC 1; SSC 4, 29; WLC**
See also DLB 198
Goines, Donald 1937(?)-1974 ... **CLC 80; BLC 2; DAM MULT, POP**
See also AITN 1; BW 1, 3; CA 124; 114; DLB 33
Gold, Herbert 1924- .... **CLC 4, 7, 14, 42**
See also CA 9-12R; CANR 17, 45; DLB 2; DLBY 81
Goldbarth, Albert 1948- .... **CLC 5, 38**
See also CA 53-56; CANR 6, 40; DLB 120
Goldberg, Anatol 1910-1982 .... **CLC 34**
See also CA 131; 117
Goldemberg, Isaac 1945- .... **CLC 52**
See also CA 69-72; CAAS 12; CANR 11, 32; HW 1
Golding, William (Gerald) 1911-1993**CLC 1, 2, 3, 8, 10, 17, 27, 58, 81; DA; DAB; DAC; DAM MST, NOV; WLC**
See also AAYA 5; CA 5-8R; 141; CANR 13, 33, 54; CDBLB 1945-1960; DLB 15, 100; MTCW 1, 2
Goldman, Emma 1869-1940 .... **TCLC 13**
See also CA 110; 150
Goldman, Francisco 1954- .... **CLC 76**
See also CA 162
Goldman, William (W.) 1931- ...... **CLC 1, 48**
See also CA 9-12R; CANR 29, 69; DLB 44
Goldmann, Lucien 1913-1970 .... **CLC 24**
See also CA 25-28; CAP 2
Goldoni, Carlo 1707-1793 .... **LC 4; DAM DRAM**
Goldsberry, Steven 1949- .... **CLC 34**
See also CA 131
Goldsmith, Oliver 1728-1774**LC 2, 48; DA; DAB; DAC; DAM DRAM, MST, NOV, POET; DC 8; WLC**
See also CDBLB 1660-1789; DLB 39, 89, 104, 109, 142; SATA 26
Goldsmith, Peter
See Priestley, J(ohn) B(oynton)
Gombrowicz, Witold 1904-1969**CLC 4, 7, 11, 49; DAM DRAM**
See also CA 19-20; 25-28R; CAP 2
Gomez de la Serna, Ramon 1888-1963 .... **CLC 9**
See also CA 153; 116; CANR 79; HW 1, 2
Goncharov, Ivan Alexandrovich 1812-1891**NCLC 1, 63**
Goncourt, Edmond (Louis Antoine Huot) de 1822-1896 .... **NCLC 7**
See also DLB 123
Goncourt, Jules (Alfred Huot) de 1830-1870 **NCLC 7**
See also DLB 123
Gontier, Fernande 19(?)- .... **CLC 50**
Gonzalez Martinez, Enrique 1871-1952**TCLC 72**
See also CA 166; CANR 81; HW 1, 2
Goodman, Paul 1911-1972 .... **CLC 1, 2, 4, 7**
See also CA 19-20; 37-40R; CANR 34; CAP 2; DLB 130; MTCW 1
Gordimer, Nadine 1923- **CLC 3, 5, 7, 10, 18, 33, 51, 70; DA; DAB; DAC; DAM MST, NOV; SSC 17; WLCS**
See also CA 5-8R; CANR 3, 28, 56; INT CANR-28; MTCW 1, 2
Gordon, Adam Lindsay 1833-1870 ...... **NCLC 21**
Gordon, Caroline 1895-1981 **CLC 6, 13, 29, 83; SSC 15**
See also CA 11-12; 103; CANR 36; CAP 1; DLB 4, 9, 102; DLBD 17; DLBY 81; MTCW 1, 2
Gordon, Charles William 1860-1937
See Connor, Ralph
See also CA 109
Gordon, Mary (Catherine) 1949- .... **CLC 13, 22**
See also CA 102; CANR 44; DLB 6; DLBY 81; INT 102; MTCW 1
Gordon, N. J.
See Bosman, Herman Charles
Gordon, Sol 1923- .... **CLC 26**
See also CA 53-56; CANR 4; SATA 11
Gordone, Charles 1925-1995 .... **CLC 1, 4; DAM DRAM; DC 8**
See also BW 1, 3; CA 93-96; 150; CANR 55; DLB 7; INT 93-96; MTCW 1
Gore, Catherine 1800-1861 .... **NCLC 65**
See also DLB 116
Gorenko, Anna Andreevna
See Akhmatova, Anna
Gorky, Maxim 1868-1936**TCLC 8; DAB; SSC 28; WLC**
See also Peshkov, Alexei Maximovich
See also MTCW 2
Goryan, Sirak
See Saroyan, William
Gosse, Edmund (William) 1849-1928 .. **TCLC 28**
See also CA 117; DLB 57, 144, 184
Gotlieb, Phyllis Fay (Bloom) 1926- .... **CLC 18**
See also CA 13-16R; CANR 7; DLB 88
Gottesman, S. D.
See Kornbluth, C(yril) M.; Pohl, Frederik
Gottfried von Strassburg fl. c. 1210- . **CMLC 10**
See also DLB 138
Gould, Lois .... **CLC 4, 10**
See also CA 77-80; CANR 29; MTCW 1
Gourmont, Remy (-Marie-Charles) de 1858-1915 .... **TCLC 17**
See also CA 109; 150; MTCW 2
Govier, Katherine 1948- .... **CLC 51**
See also CA 101; CANR 18, 40
Goyen, (Charles) William 1915-1983 . **CLC 5, 8, 14, 40**
See also AITN 2; CA 5-8R; 110; CANR 6, 71; DLB 2; DLBY 83; INT CANR-6
Goytisolo, Juan 1931-**CLC 5, 10, 23; DAM MULT; HLC**
See also CA 85-88; CANR 32, 61; HW 1, 2; MTCW 1, 2
Gozzano, Guido 1883-1916 .... **PC 10**
See also CA 154; DLB 114
Gozzi, (Conte) Carlo 1720-1806 .... **NCLC 23**
Grabbe, Christian Dietrich 1801-1836 . **NCLC 2**
See also DLB 133
Grace, Patricia Frances 1937- .... **CLC 56**
See also CA 176
Gracian y Morales, Baltasar 1601-1658 .. **LC 15**
Gracq, Julien .... **CLC 11, 48**
See also Poirier, Louis
See also DLB 83
Grade, Chaim 1910-1982 .... **CLC 10**
See also CA 93-96; 107
Graduate of Oxford, A
See Ruskin, John
Grafton, Garth
See Duncan, Sara Jeannette
Graham, John
See Phillips, David Graham
Graham, Jorie 1951- .... **CLC 48, 118**
See also CA 111; CANR 63; DLB 120
Graham, R(obert) B(ontine) Cunninghame
See Cunninghame Graham, R(obert) B(ontine)
See also DLB 98, 135, 174
Graham, Robert
See Haldeman, Joe (William)
Graham, Tom
See Lewis, (Harry) Sinclair
Graham, W(illiam) S(ydney) 1918-1986 **CLC 29**
See also CA 73-76; 118; DLB 20
Graham, Winston (Mawdsley) 1910- .... **CLC 23**
See also CA 49-52; CANR 2, 22, 45, 66; DLB 77
Grahame, Kenneth 1859-1932 ... **TCLC 64; DAB**
See also CA 108; 136; CANR 80; CLR 5; DLB 34, 141, 178; MAICYA; MTCW 2; SATA 100; YABC 1
Granovsky, Timofei Nikolaevich 1813-1855 **NCLC 75**
See also DLB 198
Grant, Skeeter
See Spiegelman, Art
Granville-Barker, Harley 1877-1946 ... **TCLC 2; DAM DRAM**
See also Barker, Harley Granville
See also CA 104
Grass, Guenter (Wilhelm) 1927- **CLC 1, 2, 4, 6, 11, 15, 22, 32, 49, 88; DA; DAB; DAC; DAM MST, NOV; WLC**
See also CA 13-16R; CANR 20, 75; DLB 75, 124; MTCW 1, 2
Gratton, Thomas
See Hulme, T(homas) E(rnest)
Grau, Shirley Ann 1929- .... **CLC 4, 9; SSC 15**
See also CA 89-92; CANR 22, 69; DLB 2; INT CANR-22; MTCW 1
Gravel, Fern
See Hall, James Norman

Graver, Elizabeth 1964- .... **CLC 70**
See also CA 135; CANR 71
Graves, Richard Perceval 1945- .... **CLC 44**
See also CA 65-68; CANR 9, 26, 51
Graves, Robert (von Ranke) 1895-1985 **CLC 1, 2, 6, 11, 39, 44, 45; DAB; DAC; DAM MST, POET; PC 6**
See also CA 5-8R; 117; CANR 5, 36; CDBLB 1914-1945; DLB 20, 100, 191; DLBD 18; DLBY 85; MTCW 1, 2; SATA 45
Graves, Valerie
See Bradley, Marion Zimmer
Gray, Alasdair (James) 1934- .... **CLC 41**
See also CA 126; CANR 47, 69; DLB 194; INT 126; MTCW 1, 2
Gray, Amlin 1946- .... **CLC 29**
See also CA 138
Gray, Francine du Plessix 1930- . **CLC 22; DAM NOV**
See also BEST 90:3; CA 61-64; CAAS 2; CANR 11, 33, 75, 81; INT CANR-11; MTCW 1, 2
Gray, John (Henry) 1866-1934 .... **TCLC 19**
See also CA 119; 162
Gray, Simon (James Holliday) 1936- **CLC 9, 14, 36**
See also AITN 1; CA 21-24R; CAAS 3; CANR 32, 69; DLB 13; MTCW 1
Gray, Spalding 1941- **CLC 49, 112; DAM POP; DC 7**
See also CA 128; CANR 74; MTCW 2
Gray, Thomas 1716-1771 ... **LC 4, 40; DA; DAB; DAC; DAM MST; PC 2; WLC**
See also CDBLB 1660-1789; DLB 109
Grayson, David
See Baker, Ray Stannard
Grayson, Richard (A.) 1951- .... **CLC 38**
See also CA 85-88; CANR 14, 31, 57
Greeley, Andrew M(oran) 1928- . **CLC 28; DAM POP**
See also CA 5-8R; CAAS 7; CANR 7, 43, 69; MTCW 1, 2
Green, Anna Katharine 1846-1935 ..... **TCLC 63**
See also CA 112; 159; DLB 202
Green, Brian
See Card, Orson Scott
Green, Hannah
See Greenberg, Joanne (Goldenberg)
Green, Hannah 1927(?)-1996 .... **CLC 3**
See also CA 73-76; CANR 59
Green, Henry 1905-1973 .... **CLC 2, 13, 97**
See also Yorke, Henry Vincent
See also CA 175; DLB 15
Green, Julian (Hartridge) 1900-1998
See Green, Julien
See also CA 21-24R; 169; CANR 33; DLB 4, 72; MTCW 1
Green, Julien .... **CLC 3, 11, 77**
See also Green, Julian (Hartridge)
See also MTCW 2
Green, Paul (Eliot) 1894-1981 ..... **CLC 25; DAM DRAM**
See also AITN 1; CA 5-8R; 103; CANR 3; DLB 7, 9; DLBY 81
Greenberg, Ivan 1908-1973
See Rahv, Philip
See also CA 85-88
Greenberg, Joanne (Goldenberg) 1932- . **CLC 7, 30**
See also AAYA 12; CA 5-8R; CANR 14, 32, 69; SATA 25
Greenberg, Richard 1959(?)- .... **CLC 57**
See also CA 138
Greene, Bette 1934- .... **CLC 30**
See also AAYA 7; CA 53-56; CANR 4; CLR 2; JRDA; MAICYA; SAAS 16; SATA 8, 102
Greene, Gael .... **CLC 8**
See also CA 13-16R; CANR 10
Greene, Graham (Henry) 1904-1991 **CLC 1, 3, 6, 9, 14, 18, 27, 37, 70, 72; DA; DAB; DAC; DAM MST, NOV; SSC 29; WLC**
See also AITN 2; CA 13-16R; 133; CANR 35, 61; CDBLB 1945-1960; DLB 13, 15, 77, 100, 162, 201, 204; DLBY 91; MTCW 1, 2; SATA 20
Greene, Robert 1558-1592 .... **LC 41**
See also DLB 62, 167
Greer, Richard
See Silverberg, Robert
Gregor, Arthur 1923- .... **CLC 9**
See also CA 25-28R; CAAS 10; CANR 11; SATA 36
Gregor, Lee
See Pohl, Frederik
Gregory, Isabella Augusta (Persse) 1852-1932 **TCLC 1**
See also CA 104; DLB 10
Gregory, J. Dennis
See Williams, John A(lfred)
Grendon, Stephen
See Derleth, August (William)
Grenville, Kate 1950- .... **CLC 61**
See also CA 118; CANR 53
Grenville, Pelham
See Wodehouse, P(elham) G(renville)
Greve, Felix Paul (Berthold Friedrich) 1879-1948
See Grove, Frederick Philip
See also CA 104; 141, 175; CANR 79; DAC; DAM MST
Grey, Zane 1872-1939 .... **TCLC 6; DAM POP**
See also CA 104; 132; DLB 212; MTCW 1, 2
Grieg, (Johan) Nordahl (Brun) 1902-1943 **TCLC 10**
See also CA 107
Grieve, C(hristopher) M(urray) 1892-1978 **CLC 11, 19; DAM POET**
See also MacDiarmid, Hugh; Pteleon
See also CA 5-8R; 85-88; CANR 33; MTCW 1
Griffin, Gerald 1803-1840 .... **NCLC 7**
See also DLB 159
Griffin, John Howard 1920-1980 .... **CLC 68**
See also AITN 1; CA 1-4R; 101; CANR 2
Griffin, Peter 1942- .... **CLC 39**
See also CA 136
Griffith, D(avid Lewelyn) W(ark) 1875(?)-1948 **TCLC 68**
See also CA 119; 150; CANR 80
Griffith, Lawrence
See Griffith, D(avid Lewelyn) W(ark)
Griffiths, Trevor 1935- .... **CLC 13, 52**
See also CA 97-100; CANR 45; DLB 13
Griggs, Sutton Elbert 1872-1930(?) .... **TCLC 77**
See also CA 123; DLB 50
Grigson, Geoffrey (Edward Harvey) 1905-1985 **CLC 7, 39**
See also CA 25-28R; 118; CANR 20, 33; DLB 27; MTCW 1, 2
Grillparzer, Franz 1791-1872 .... **NCLC 1**
See also DLB 133
Grimble, Reverend Charles James
See Eliot, T(homas) S(tearns)
Grimke, Charlotte L(ottie) Forten 1837(?)-1914
See Forten, Charlotte L.
See also BW 1; CA 117; 124; DAM MULT, POET
Grimm, Jacob Ludwig Karl 1785-1863 **NCLC 3, 77**
See also DLB 90; MAICYA; SATA 22
Grimm, Wilhelm Karl 1786-1859 ... **NCLC 3, 77**
See also DLB 90; MAICYA; SATA 22
Grimmelshausen, Johann Jakob Christoffel von 1621-1676 .... **LC 6**
See also DLB 168
Grindel, Eugene 1895-1952
See Eluard, Paul
See also CA 104
Grisham, John 1955- .... **CLC 84; DAM POP**
See also AAYA 14; CA 138; CANR 47, 69; MTCW 2
Grossman, David 1954- .... **CLC 67**
See also CA 138
Grossman, Vasily (Semenovich) 1905-1964 **CLC 41**
See also CA 124; 130; MTCW 1
Grove, Frederick Philip .... **TCLC 4**
See also Greve, Felix Paul (Berthold Friedrich)
See also DLB 92
Grubb
See Crumb, R(obert)
Grumbach, Doris (Isaac) 1918- . **CLC 13, 22, 64**
See also CA 5-8R; CAAS 2; CANR 9, 42, 70; INT CANR-9; MTCW 2
Grundtvig, Nicolai Frederik Severin 1783-1872 **NCLC 1**
Grunge
See Crumb, R(obert)
Grunwald, Lisa 1959- .... **CLC 44**
See also CA 120
Guare, John 1938- **CLC 8, 14, 29, 67; DAM DRAM**
See also CA 73-76; CANR 21, 69; DLB 7; MTCW 1, 2
Gudjonsson, Halldor Kiljan 1902-1998
See Laxness, Halldor
See also CA 103; 164
Guenter, Erich
See Eich, Guenter
Guest, Barbara 1920- .... **CLC 34**
See also CA 25-28R; CANR 11, 44; DLB 5, 193
Guest, Edgar A(lbert) 1881-1959 .... **TCLC 95**
See also CA 112; 168
Guest, Judith (Ann) 1936- **CLC 8, 30; DAM NOV, POP**
See also AAYA 7; CA 77-80; CANR 15, 75; INT CANR-15; MTCW 1, 2
Guevara, Che .... **CLC 87; HLC**
See also Guevara (Serna), Ernesto
Guevara (Serna), Ernesto 1928-1967
See Guevara, Che
See also CA 127; 111; CANR 56; DAM MULT; HW 1
Guicciardini, Francesco 1483-1540 .... **LC 49**
Guild, Nicholas M. 1944- .... **CLC 33**
See also CA 93-96
Guillemin, Jacques
See Sartre, Jean-Paul
Guillen, Jorge 1893-1984 **CLC 11; DAM MULT, POET; HLCS 1**
See also CA 89-92; 112; DLB 108; HW 1
Guillen, Nicolas (Cristobal) 1902-1989 **CLC 48, 79; BLC 2; DAM MST, MULT, POET; HLC; PC 23**
See also BW 2; CA 116; 125; 129; HW 1
Guillevic, (Eugene) 1907- .... **CLC 33**
See also CA 93-96
Guillois
See Desnos, Robert
Guillois, Valentin
See Desnos, Robert
Guiney, Louise Imogen 1861-1920 ...... **TCLC 41**
See also CA 160; DLB 54
Guiraldes, Ricardo (Guillermo) 1886-1927 **TCLC 39**
See also CA 131; HW 1; MTCW 1
Gumilev, Nikolai (Stepanovich) 1886-1921 **TCLC 60**
See also CA 165
Gunesekera, Romesh 1954- .... **CLC 91**
See also CA 159
Gunn, Bill .... **CLC 5**
See also Gunn, William Harrison
See also DLB 38
Gunn, Thom(son William) 1929- **CLC 3, 6, 18, 32, 81; DAM POET; PC 26**
See also CA 17-20R; CANR 9, 33; CDBLB 1960 to Present; DLB 27; INT CANR-33; MTCW 1

Author Index

Gunn, William Harrison 1934(?)-1989
See Gunn, Bill
See also AITN 1; BW 1, 3; CA 13-16R; 128; CANR 12, 25, 76
Gunnars, Kristjana 1948- .... **CLC 69**
See also CA 113; DLB 60
Gurdjieff, G(eorgei) I(vanovich) 1877(?)-1949 **TCLC 71**
See also CA 157
Gurganus, Allan 1947- .... **CLC 70; DAM POP**
See also BEST 90:1; CA 135
Gurney, A(lbert) R(amsdell), Jr. 1930- **CLC 32, 50, 54; DAM DRAM**
See also CA 77-80; CANR 32, 64
Gurney, Ivor (Bertie) 1890-1937 .... **TCLC 33**
See also CA 167
Gurney, Peter
See Gurney, A(lbert) R(amsdell), Jr.
Guro, Elena 1877-1913 .... **TCLC 56**
Gustafson, James M(oody) 1925- .... **CLC 100**
See also CA 25-28R; CANR 37
Gustafson, Ralph (Barker) 1909- .... **CLC 36**
See also CA 21-24R; CANR 8, 45; DLB 88
Gut, Gom
See Simenon, Georges (Jacques Christian)
Guterson, David 1956- .... **CLC 91**
See also CA 132; CANR 73; MTCW 2
Guthrie, A(lfred) B(ertram), Jr. 1901-1991 **CLC 23**
See also CA 57-60; 134; CANR 24; DLB 212; SATA 62; SATA-Obit 67
Guthrie, Isobel
See Grieve, C(hristopher) M(urray)
Guthrie, Woodrow Wilson 1912-1967
See Guthrie, Woody
See also CA 113; 93-96
Guthrie, Woody .... **CLC 35**
See also Guthrie, Woodrow Wilson
Guy, Rosa (Cuthbert) 1928- .... **CLC 26**
See also AAYA 4; BW 2; CA 17-20R; CANR 14, 34; CLR 13; DLB 33; JRDA; MAICYA; SATA 14, 62
Gwendolyn
See Bennett, (Enoch) Arnold
H. D. .... **CLC 3, 8, 14, 31, 34, 73; PC 5**
See also Doolittle, Hilda
H. de V.
See Buchan, John
Haavikko, Paavo Juhani 1931- .... **CLC 18, 34**
See also CA 106
Habbema, Koos
See Heijermans, Herman
Habermas, Juergen 1929- .... **CLC 104**
See also CA 109
Habermas, Jurgen
See Habermas, Juergen
Hacker, Marilyn 1942- **CLC 5, 9, 23, 72, 91; DAM POET**
See also CA 77-80; CANR 68; DLB 120
Haeckel, Ernst Heinrich (Philipp August) 1834-1919 .... **TCLC 83**
See also CA 157
Hafiz c. 1326-1389(?) .... **CMLC 34**
Haggard, H(enry) Rider 1856-1925 ..... **TCLC 11**
See also CA 108; 148; DLB 70, 156, 174, 178; MTCW 2; SATA 16
Hagiosy, L.
See Larbaud, Valery (Nicolas)
Hagiwara Sakutaro 1886-1942 **TCLC 60; PC 18**
Haig, Fenil
See Ford, Ford Madox
Haig-Brown, Roderick (Langmere) 1908-1976 **CLC 21**
See also CA 5-8R; 69-72; CANR 4, 38; CLR 31; DLB 88; MAICYA; SATA 12
Hailey, Arthur 1920- .. **CLC 5; DAM NOV, POP**
See also AITN 2; BEST 90:3; CA 1-4R; CANR 2, 36, 75; DLB 88; DLBY 82; MTCW 1, 2
Hailey, Elizabeth Forsythe 1938- .... **CLC 40**
See also CA 93-96; CAAS 1; CANR 15, 48; INT CANR-15
Haines, John (Meade) 1924- .... **CLC 58**
See also CA 17-20R; CANR 13, 34; DLB 212
Hakluyt, Richard 1552-1616 .... **LC 31**
Haldeman, Joe (William) 1943- .... **CLC 61**
See also CA 53-56; CAAS 25; CANR 6, 70, 72; DLB 8; INT CANR-6
Hale, Sarah Josepha (Buell) 1788-1879 **NCLC 75**
See also DLB 1, 42, 73
Haley, Alex(ander Murray Palmer) 1921-1992 **CLC 8, 12, 76; BLC 2; DA; DAB; DAC; DAM MST, MULT, POP**
See also AAYA 26; BW 2, 3; CA 77-80; 136; CANR 61; CDALBS; DLB 38; MTCW 1, 2
Haliburton, Thomas Chandler 1796-1865 **NCLC 15**
See also DLB 11, 99
Hall, Donald (Andrew, Jr.) 1928- **CLC 1, 13, 37, 59; DAM POET**
See also CA 5-8R; CAAS 7; CANR 2, 44, 64; DLB 5; MTCW 1; SATA 23, 97
Hall, Frederic Sauser
See Sauser-Hall, Frederic
Hall, James
See Kuttner, Henry
Hall, James Norman 1887-1951 .... **TCLC 23**
See also CA 123; 173; SATA 21
Hall, Radclyffe
See Hall, (Marguerite) Radclyffe
See also MTCW 2
Hall, (Marguerite) Radclyffe 1886-1943 **TCLC 12**
See also CA 110; 150; DLB 191
Hall, Rodney 1935- .... **CLC 51**
See also CA 109; CANR 69
Halleck, Fitz-Greene 1790-1867 .... **NCLC 47**
See also DLB 3
Halliday, Michael
See Creasey, John
Halpern, Daniel 1945- .... **CLC 14**
See also CA 33-36R
Hamburger, Michael (Peter Leopold) 1924- **CLC 5, 14**
See also CA 5-8R; CAAS 4; CANR 2, 47; DLB 27
Hamill, Pete 1935- .... **CLC 10**
See also CA 25-28R; CANR 18, 71
Hamilton, Alexander 1755(?)-1804 ...... **NCLC 49**
See also DLB 37
Hamilton, Clive
See Lewis, C(live) S(taples)
Hamilton, Edmond 1904-1977 .... **CLC 1**
See also CA 1-4R; CANR 3; DLB 8
Hamilton, Eugene (Jacob) Lee
See Lee-Hamilton, Eugene (Jacob)
Hamilton, Franklin
See Silverberg, Robert
Hamilton, Gail
See Corcoran, Barbara
Hamilton, Mollie
See Kaye, M(ary) M(argaret)
Hamilton, (Anthony Walter) Patrick 1904-1962 **CLC 51**
See also CA 176; 113; DLB 191
Hamilton, Virginia 1936- **CLC 26; DAM MULT**
See also AAYA 2, 21; BW 2, 3; CA 25-28R; CANR 20, 37, 73; CLR 1, 11, 40; DLB 33, 52; INT CANR-20; JRDA; MAICYA; MTCW 1, 2; SATA 4, 56, 79
Hammett, (Samuel) Dashiell 1894-1961 **CLC 3, 5, 10, 19, 47; SSC 17**
See also AITN 1; CA 81-84; CANR 42; CDALB 1929-1941; DLBD 6; DLBY 96; MTCW 1, 2
Hammon, Jupiter 1711(?)-1800(?) **NCLC 5; BLC 2; DAM MULT, POET; PC 16**
See also DLB 31, 50
Hammond, Keith
See Kuttner, Henry
Hamner, Earl (Henry), Jr. 1923- .... **CLC 12**
See also AITN 2; CA 73-76; DLB 6
Hampton, Christopher (James) 1946- .... **CLC 4**
See also CA 25-28R; DLB 13; MTCW 1
Hamsun, Knut .... **TCLC 2, 14, 49**
See also Pedersen, Knut
Handke, Peter 1942- **CLC 5, 8, 10, 15, 38; DAM DRAM, NOV**
See also CA 77-80; CANR 33, 75; DLB 85, 124; MTCW 1, 2
Hanley, James 1901-1985 .... **CLC 3, 5, 8, 13**
See also CA 73-76; 117; CANR 36; DLB 191; MTCW 1
Hannah, Barry 1942- .... **CLC 23, 38, 90**
See also CA 108; 110; CANR 43, 68; DLB 6; INT 110; MTCW 1
Hannon, Ezra
See Hunter, Evan
Hansberry, Lorraine (Vivian) 1930-1965 **CLC 17, 62; BLC 2; DA; DAB; DAC; DAM DRAM, MST, MULT; DC 2**
See also AAYA 25; BW 1, 3; CA 109; 25-28R; CABS 3; CANR 58; CDALB 1941-1968; DLB 7, 38; MTCW 1, 2
Hansen, Joseph 1923- .... **CLC 38**
See also CA 29-32R; CAAS 17; CANR 16, 44, 66; INT CANR-16
Hansen, Martin A(lfred) 1909-1955 .... **TCLC 32**
See also CA 167
Hanson, Kenneth O(stlin) 1922- .... **CLC 13**
See also CA 53-56; CANR 7
Hardwick, Elizabeth (Bruce) 1916- **CLC 13; DAM NOV**
See also CA 5-8R; CANR 3, 32, 70; DLB 6; MTCW 1, 2
Hardy, Thomas 1840-1928 **TCLC 4, 10, 18, 32, 48, 53, 72; DA; DAB; DAC; DAM MST, NOV, POET; PC 8; SSC 2; WLC**
See also CA 104; 123; CDBLB 1890-1914; DLB 18, 19, 135; MTCW 1, 2
Hare, David 1947- .... **CLC 29, 58**
See also CA 97-100; CANR 39; DLB 13; MTCW 1
Harewood, John
See Van Druten, John (William)
Harford, Henry
See Hudson, W(illiam) H(enry)
Hargrave, Leonie
See Disch, Thomas M(ichael)
Harjo, Joy 1951- .... **CLC 83; DAM MULT**
See also CA 114; CANR 35, 67; DLB 120, 175; MTCW 2; NNAL
Harlan, Louis R(udolph) 1922- .... **CLC 34**
See also CA 21-24R; CANR 25, 55, 80
Harling, Robert 1951(?)- .... **CLC 53**
See also CA 147
Harmon, William (Ruth) 1938- .... **CLC 38**
See also CA 33-36R; CANR 14, 32, 35; SATA 65
Harper, F. E. W.
See Harper, Frances Ellen Watkins
Harper, Frances E. W.
See Harper, Frances Ellen Watkins
Harper, Frances E. Watkins
See Harper, Frances Ellen Watkins
Harper, Frances Ellen
See Harper, Frances Ellen Watkins
Harper, Frances Ellen Watkins 1825-1911 **TCLC 14; BLC 2; DAM MULT, POET; PC 21**
See also BW 1, 3; CA 111; 125; CANR 79; DLB 50
Harper, Michael S(teven) 1938- .... **CLC 7, 22**
See also BW 1; CA 33-36R; CANR 24; DLB 41
Harper, Mrs. F. E. W.
See Harper, Frances Ellen Watkins
Harris, Christie (Lucy) Irwin 1907- ..... **CLC 12**

See also CA 5-8R; CANR 6; CLR 47; DLB 88; JRDA; MAICYA; SAAS 10; SATA 6, 74
Harris, Frank 1856-1931 .... **TCLC 24**
See also CA 109; 150; CANR 80; DLB 156, 197
Harris, George Washington 1814-1869**NCLC 23**
See also DLB 3, 11
Harris, Joel Chandler 1848-1908**TCLC 2; SSC 19**
See also CA 104; 137; CANR 80; CLR 49; DLB 11, 23, 42, 78, 91; MAICYA; SATA 100; YABC 1
Harris, John (Wyndham Parkes Lucas) Beynon 1903-1969
See Wyndham, John
See also CA 102; 89-92
Harris, MacDonald .... **CLC 9**
See also Heiney, Donald (William)
Harris, Mark 1922- .... **CLC 19**
See also CA 5-8R; CAAS 3; CANR 2, 55; DLB 2; DLBY 80
Harris, (Theodore) Wilson 1921- .... **CLC 25**
See also BW 2, 3; CA 65-68; CAAS 16; CANR 11, 27, 69; DLB 117; MTCW 1
Harrison, Elizabeth Cavanna 1909-
See Cavanna, Betty
See also CA 9-12R; CANR 6, 27
Harrison, Harry (Max) 1925- .... **CLC 42**
See also CA 1-4R; CANR 5, 21; DLB 8; SATA 4
Harrison, James (Thomas) 1937-**CLC 6, 14, 33, 66; SSC 19**
See also CA 13-16R; CANR 8, 51, 79; DLBY 82; INT CANR-8
Harrison, Jim
See Harrison, James (Thomas)
Harrison, Kathryn 1961- .... **CLC 70**
See also CA 144; CANR 68
Harrison, Tony 1937- .... **CLC 43**
See also CA 65-68; CANR 44; DLB 40; MTCW 1
Harriss, Will(ard Irvin) 1922- .... **CLC 34**
See also CA 111
Harson, Sley
See Ellison, Harlan (Jay)
Hart, Ellis
See Ellison, Harlan (Jay)
Hart, Josephine 1942(?)- .... **CLC 70; DAM POP**
See also CA 138; CANR 70
Hart, Moss 1904-1961 ..... **CLC 66; DAM DRAM**
See also CA 109; 89-92; DLB 7
Harte, (Francis) Bret(t) 1836(?)-1902**TCLC 1, 25; DA; DAC; DAM MST; SSC 8; WLC**
See also CA 104; 140; CANR 80; CDALB 1865-1917; DLB 12, 64, 74, 79, 186; SATA 26
Hartley, L(eslie) P(oles) 1895-1972 ... **CLC 2, 22**
See also CA 45-48; 37-40R; CANR 33; DLB 15, 139; MTCW 1, 2
Hartman, Geoffrey H. 1929- .... **CLC 27**
See also CA 117; 125; CANR 79; DLB 67
Hartmann, Sadakichi 1867-1944 .... **TCLC 73**
See also CA 157; DLB 54
Hartmann von Aue c. 1160-c. 1205 ..... **CMLC 15**
See also DLB 138
Hartmann von Aue 1170-1210 .... **CMLC 15**
Haruf, Kent 1943- .... **CLC 34**
See also CA 149
Harwood, Ronald 1934- .. **CLC 32; DAM DRAM, MST**
See also CA 1-4R; CANR 4, 55; DLB 13
Hasegawa Tatsunosuke
See Futabatei, Shimei
Hasek, Jaroslav (Matej Frantisek) 1883-1923 **TCLC 4**
See also CA 104; 129; MTCW 1, 2
Hass, Robert 1941- .... **CLC 18, 39, 99; PC 16**
See also CA 111; CANR 30, 50, 71; DLB 105, 206; SATA 94
Hastings, Hudson
See Kuttner, Henry
Hastings, Selina .... **CLC 44**
Hathorne, John 1641-1717 .... **LC 38**
Hatteras, Amelia
See Mencken, H(enry) L(ouis)
Hatteras, Owen .... **TCLC 18**
See also Mencken, H(enry) L(ouis); Nathan, George Jean
Hauptmann, Gerhart (Johann Robert) 1862-1946 **TCLC 4; DAM DRAM**
See also CA 104; 153; DLB 66, 118
Havel, Vaclav 1936-**CLC 25, 58, 65; DAM DRAM; DC 6**
See also CA 104; CANR 36, 63; MTCW 1, 2
Haviaras, Stratis .... **CLC 33**
See also Chaviaras, Strates
Hawes, Stephen 1475(?)-1523(?) .... **LC 17**
See also DLB 132
Hawkes, John (Clendennin Burne, Jr.) 1925-1998 **CLC 1, 2, 3, 4, 7, 9, 14, 15, 27, 49**
See also CA 1-4R; 167; CANR 2, 47, 64; DLB 2, 7; DLBY 80, 98; MTCW 1, 2
Hawking, S. W.
See Hawking, Stephen W(illiam)
Hawking, Stephen W(illiam) 1942-**CLC 63, 105**
See also AAYA 13; BEST 89:1; CA 126; 129; CANR 48; MTCW 2
Hawkins, Anthony Hope
See Hope, Anthony
Hawthorne, Julian 1846-1934 .... **TCLC 25**
See also CA 165
Hawthorne, Nathaniel 1804-1864 **NCLC 39; DA; DAB; DAC; DAM MST, NOV; SSC 3, 29; WLC**
See also AAYA 18; CDALB 1640-1865; DLB 1, 74; YABC 2
Haxton, Josephine Ayres 1921-
See Douglas, Ellen
See also CA 115; CANR 41
Hayaseca y Eizaguirre, Jorge
See Echegaray (y Eizaguirre), Jose (Maria Waldo)
Hayashi, Fumiko 1904-1951 .... **TCLC 27**
See also CA 161; DLB 180
Haycraft, Anna
See Ellis, Alice Thomas
See also CA 122; MTCW 2
Hayden, Robert E(arl) 1913-1980**CLC 5, 9, 14, 37; BLC 2; DA; DAC; DAM MST, MULT, POET; PC 6**
See also BW 1, 3; CA 69-72; 97-100; CABS 2; CANR 24, 75; CDALB 1941-1968; DLB 5, 76; MTCW 1, 2; SATA 19; SATA-Obit 26
Hayford, J(oseph) E(phraim) Casely
See Casely-Hayford, J(oseph) E(phraim)
Hayman, Ronald 1932- .... **CLC 44**
See also CA 25-28R; CANR 18, 50; DLB 155
Haywood, Eliza (Fowler) 1693(?)-1756 . **LC 1, 44**
See also DLB 39
Hazlitt, William 1778-1830 .... **NCLC 29**
See also DLB 110, 158
Hazzard, Shirley 1931- .... **CLC 18**
See also CA 9-12R; CANR 4, 70; DLBY 82; MTCW 1
Head, Bessie 1937-1986**CLC 25, 67; BLC 2; DAM MULT**
See also BW 2, 3; CA 29-32R; 119; CANR 25; DLB 117; MTCW 1, 2
Headon, (Nicky) Topper 1956(?)- .... **CLC 30**
Heaney, Seamus (Justin) 1939-**CLC 5, 7, 14, 25, 37, 74, 91; DAB; DAM POET; PC 18; WLCS**
See also CA 85-88; CANR 25, 48, 75; CDBLB 1960 to Present; DLB 40; DLBY 95; MTCW 1, 2
Hearn, (Patricio) Lafcadio (Tessima Carlos) 1850-1904 .... **TCLC 9**
See also CA 105; 166; DLB 12, 78, 189
Hearne, Vicki 1946- .... **CLC 56**
See also CA 139
Hearon, Shelby 1931- .... **CLC 63**
See also AITN 2; CA 25-28R; CANR 18, 48
Heat-Moon, William Least .... **CLC 29**
See also Trogdon, William (Lewis)
See also AAYA 9
Hebbel, Friedrich 1813-1863 .... **NCLC 43; DAM DRAM**
See also DLB 129
Hebert, Anne 1916-**CLC 4, 13, 29; DAC; DAM MST, POET**
See also CA 85-88; CANR 69; DLB 68; MTCW 1, 2
Hecht, Anthony (Evan) 1923-**CLC 8, 13, 19; DAM POET**
See also CA 9-12R; CANR 6; DLB 5, 169
Hecht, Ben 1894-1964 .... **CLC 8**
See also CA 85-88; DLB 7, 9, 25, 26, 28, 86
Hedayat, Sadeq 1903-1951 .... **TCLC 21**
See also CA 120
Hegel, Georg Wilhelm Friedrich 1770-1831 **NCLC 46**
See also DLB 90
Heidegger, Martin 1889-1976 .... **CLC 24**
See also CA 81-84; 65-68; CANR 34; MTCW 1, 2
Heidenstam, (Carl Gustaf) Verner von 1859-1940 **TCLC 5**
See also CA 104
Heifner, Jack 1946- .... **CLC 11**
See also CA 105; CANR 47
Heijermans, Herman 1864-1924 .... **TCLC 24**
See also CA 123
Heilbrun, Carolyn G(old) 1926- .... **CLC 25**
See also CA 45-48; CANR 1, 28, 58
Heine, Heinrich 1797-1856 . **NCLC 4, 54; PC 25**
See also DLB 90
Heinemann, Larry (Curtiss) 1944- .... **CLC 50**
See also CA 110; CAAS 21; CANR 31, 81; DLBD 9; INT CANR-31
Heiney, Donald (William) 1921-1993
See Harris, MacDonald
See also CA 1-4R; 142; CANR 3, 58
Heinlein, Robert A(nson) 1907-1988**CLC 1, 3, 8, 14, 26, 55; DAM POP**
See also AAYA 17; CA 1-4R; 125; CANR 1, 20, 53; DLB 8; JRDA; MAICYA; MTCW 1, 2; SATA 9, 69; SATA-Obit 56
Helforth, John
See Doolittle, Hilda
Hellenhofferu, Vojtech Kapristian z
See Hasek, Jaroslav (Matej Frantisek)
Heller, Joseph 1923- **CLC 1, 3, 5, 8, 11, 36, 63; DA; DAB; DAC; DAM MST, NOV, POP; WLC**
See also AAYA 24; AITN 1; CA 5-8R; CABS 1; CANR 8, 42, 66; DLB 2, 28; DLBY 80; INT CANR-8; MTCW 1, 2
Hellman, Lillian (Florence) 1906-1984**CLC 2, 4, 8, 14, 18, 34, 44, 52; DAM DRAM; DC 1**
See also AITN 1, 2; CA 13-16R; 112; CANR 33; DLB 7; DLBY 84; MTCW 1, 2
Helprin, Mark 1947- .. **CLC 7, 10, 22, 32; DAM NOV, POP**
See also CA 81-84; CANR 47, 64; CDALBS; DLBY 85; MTCW 1, 2
Helvetius, Claude-Adrien 1715-1771 .... **LC 26**
Helyar, Jane Penelope Josephine 1933-
See Poole, Josephine
See also CA 21-24R; CANR 10, 26; SATA 82
Hemans, Felicia 1793-1835 .... **NCLC 71**
See also DLB 96
Hemingway, Ernest (Miller) 1899-1961**CLC 1, 3, 6, 8, 10, 13, 19, 30, 34, 39, 41, 44, 50, 61, 80; DA; DAB; DAC; DAM MST, NOV; SSC 1, 25; WLC**
See also AAYA 19; CA 77-80; CANR 34; CDALB 1917-1929; DLB 4, 9, 102, 210; DLBD 1, 15, 16; DLBY 81, 87, 96, 98; MTCW 1, 2

Hempel, Amy 1951- .... **CLC 39**
See also CA 118; 137; CANR 70; MTCW 2
Henderson, F. C.
See Mencken, H(enry) L(ouis)
Henderson, Sylvia
See Ashton-Warner, Sylvia (Constance)
Henderson, Zenna (Chlarson) 1917-1983**SSC 29**
See also CA 1-4R; 133; CANR 1; DLB 8; SATA 5
Henkin, Joshua .... **CLC 119**
See also CA 161
Henley, Beth .... **CLC 23; DC 6**
See also Henley, Elizabeth Becker
See also CABS 3; DLBY 86
Henley, Elizabeth Becker 1952-
See Henley, Beth
See also CA 107; CANR 32, 73; DAM DRAM, MST; MTCW 1, 2
Henley, William Ernest 1849-1903 .... **TCLC 8**
See also CA 105; DLB 19
Hennissart, Martha
See Lathen, Emma
See also CA 85-88; CANR 64
Henry, O. .... **TCLC 1, 19; SSC 5; WLC**
See also Porter, William Sydney
Henry, Patrick 1736-1799 .... **LC 25**
Henryson, Robert 1430(?)-1506(?) .... **LC 20**
See also DLB 146
Henry VIII 1491-1547 .... **LC 10**
See also DLB 132
Henschke, Alfred
See Klabund
Hentoff, Nat(han Irving) 1925- .... **CLC 26**
See also AAYA 4; CA 1-4R; CAAS 6; CANR 5, 25, 77; CLR 1, 52; INT CANR-25; JRDA; MAICYA; SATA 42, 69; SATA-Brief 27
Heppenstall, (John) Rayner 1911-1981 . **CLC 10**
See also CA 1-4R; 103; CANR 29
Heraclitus c. 540B.C.-c. 450B.C. .... **CMLC 22**
See also DLB 176
Herbert, Frank (Patrick) 1920-1986**CLC 12, 23, 35, 44, 85; DAM POP**
See also AAYA 21; CA 53-56; 118; CANR 5, 43; CDALBS; DLB 8; INT CANR-5; MTCW 1, 2; SATA 9, 37; SATA-Obit 47
Herbert, George 1593-1633 . **LC 24; DAB; DAM POET; PC 4**
See also CDBLB Before 1660; DLB 126
Herbert, Zbigniew 1924-1998 . **CLC 9, 43; DAM POET**
See also CA 89-92; 169; CANR 36, 74; MTCW 1
Herbst, Josephine (Frey) 1897-1969 ..... **CLC 34**
See also CA 5-8R; 25-28R; DLB 9
Hergesheimer, Joseph 1880-1954 .... **TCLC 11**
See also CA 109; DLB 102, 9
Herlihy, James Leo 1927-1993 .... **CLC 6**
See also CA 1-4R; 143; CANR 2
Hermogenes fl. c. 175- .... **CMLC 6**
Hernandez, Jose 1834-1886 .... **NCLC 17**
Herodotus c. 484B.C.-429B.C. .... **CMLC 17**
See also DLB 176
Herrick, Robert 1591-1674 ... **LC 13; DA; DAB; DAC; DAM MST, POP; PC 9**
See also DLB 126
Herring, Guilles
See Somerville, Edith
Herriot, James 1916-1995 .. **CLC 12; DAM POP**
See also Wight, James Alfred
See also AAYA 1; CA 148; CANR 40; MTCW 2; SATA 86
Herrmann, Dorothy 1941- .... **CLC 44**
See also CA 107
Herrmann, Taffy
See Herrmann, Dorothy
Hersey, John (Richard) 1914-1993**CLC 1, 2, 7, 9, 40, 81, 97; DAM POP**
See also AAYA 29; CA 17-20R; 140; CANR 33; CDALBS; DLB 6, 185; MTCW 1, 2; SATA 25; SATA-Obit 76
Herzen, Aleksandr Ivanovich 1812-1870 . **NCLC 10, 61**
Herzl, Theodor 1860-1904 .... **TCLC 36**
See also CA 168
Herzog, Werner 1942- .... **CLC 16**
See also CA 89-92
Hesiod c. 8th cent. B.C.- .... **CMLC 5**
See also DLB 176
Hesse, Hermann 1877-1962**CLC 1, 2, 3, 6, 11, 17, 25, 69; DA; DAB; DAC; DAM MST, NOV; SSC 9; WLC**
See also CA 17-18; CAP 2; DLB 66; MTCW 1, 2; SATA 50
Hewes, Cady
See De Voto, Bernard (Augustine)
Heyen, William 1940- .... **CLC 13, 18**
See also CA 33-36R; CAAS 9; DLB 5
Heyerdahl, Thor 1914- .... **CLC 26**
See also CA 5-8R; CANR 5, 22, 66, 73; MTCW 1, 2; SATA 2, 52
Heym, Georg (Theodor Franz Arthur) 1887-1912 **TCLC 9**
See also CA 106
Heym, Stefan 1913- .... **CLC 41**
See also CA 9-12R; CANR 4; DLB 69
Heyse, Paul (Johann Ludwig von) 1830-1914 **TCLC 8**
See also CA 104; DLB 129
Heyward, (Edwin) DuBose 1885-1940 .. **TCLC 59**
See also CA 108; 157; DLB 7, 9, 45; SATA 21
Hibbert, Eleanor Alice Burford 1906-1993**CLC 7; DAM POP**
See also BEST 90:4; CA 17-20R; 140; CANR 9, 28, 59; MTCW 2; SATA 2; SATA-Obit 74
Hichens, Robert (Smythe) 1864-1950 . **TCLC 64**
See also CA 162; DLB 153
Higgins, George V(incent) 1939-**CLC 4, 7, 10, 18**
See also CA 77-80; CAAS 5; CANR 17, 51; DLB 2; DLBY 81, 98; INT CANR-17; MTCW 1
Higginson, Thomas Wentworth 1823-1911**TCLC 36**
See also CA 162; DLB 1, 64
Highet, Helen
See MacInnes, Helen (Clark)
Highsmith, (Mary) Patricia 1921-1995 **CLC 2, 4, 14, 42, 102; DAM NOV, POP**
See also CA 1-4R; 147; CANR 1, 20, 48, 62; MTCW 1, 2
Highwater, Jamake (Mamake) 1942(?)- **CLC 12**
See also AAYA 7; CA 65-68; CAAS 7; CANR 10, 34; CLR 17; DLB 52; DLBY 85; JRDA; MAICYA; SATA 32, 69; SATA-Brief 30
Highway, Tomson 1951- .... **CLC 92; DAC; DAM MULT**
See also CA 151; CANR 75; MTCW 2; NNAL
Higuchi, Ichiyo 1872-1896 .... **NCLC 49**
Hijuelos, Oscar 1951-**CLC 65; DAM MULT, POP; HLC**
See also AAYA 25; BEST 90:1; CA 123; CANR 50, 75; DLB 145; HW 1, 2; MTCW 2
Hikmet, Nazim 1902(?)-1963 .... **CLC 40**
See also CA 141; 93-96
Hildegard von Bingen 1098-1179 .... **CMLC 20**
See also DLB 148
Hildesheimer, Wolfgang 1916-1991 ...... **CLC 49**
See also CA 101; 135; DLB 69, 124
Hill, Geoffrey (William) 1932- **CLC 5, 8, 18, 45; DAM POET**
See also CA 81-84; CANR 21; CDBLB 1960 to Present; DLB 40; MTCW 1
Hill, George Roy 1921- .... **CLC 26**
See also CA 110; 122
Hill, John
See Koontz, Dean R(ay)
Hill, Susan (Elizabeth) 1942- **CLC 4, 113; DAB; DAM MST, NOV**
See also CA 33-36R; CANR 29, 69; DLB 14, 139; MTCW 1
Hillerman, Tony 1925- .... **CLC 62; DAM POP**
See also AAYA 6; BEST 89:1; CA 29-32R; CANR 21, 42, 65; DLB 206; SATA 6
Hillesum, Etty 1914-1943 .... **TCLC 49**
See also CA 137
Hilliard, Noel (Harvey) 1929- .... **CLC 15**
See also CA 9-12R; CANR 7, 69
Hillis, Rick 1956- .... **CLC 66**
See also CA 134
Hilton, James 1900-1954 .... **TCLC 21**
See also CA 108; 169; DLB 34, 77; SATA 34
Himes, Chester (Bomar) 1909-1984 **CLC 2, 4, 7, 18, 58, 108; BLC 2; DAM MULT**
See also BW 2; CA 25-28R; 114; CANR 22; DLB 2, 76, 143; MTCW 1, 2
Hinde, Thomas .... **CLC 6, 11**
See also Chitty, Thomas Willes
Hindin, Nathan
See Bloch, Robert (Albert)
Hine, (William) Daryl 1936- .... **CLC 15**
See also CA 1-4R; CAAS 15; CANR 1, 20; DLB 60
Hinkson, Katharine Tynan
See Tynan, Katharine
Hinton, S(usan) E(loise) 1950-**CLC 30, 111; DA; DAB; DAC; DAM MST, NOV**
See also AAYA 2; CA 81-84; CANR 32, 62; CDALBS; CLR 3, 23; JRDA; MAICYA; MTCW 1, 2; SATA 19, 58
Hippius, Zinaida .... **TCLC 9**
See also Gippius, Zinaida (Nikolayevna)
Hiraoka, Kimitake 1925-1970
See Mishima, Yukio
See also CA 97-100; 29-32R; DAM DRAM; MTCW 1, 2
Hirsch, E(ric) D(onald), Jr. 1928- .... **CLC 79**
See also CA 25-28R; CANR 27, 51; DLB 67; INT CANR-27; MTCW 1
Hirsch, Edward 1950- .... **CLC 31, 50**
See also CA 104; CANR 20, 42; DLB 120
Hitchcock, Alfred (Joseph) 1899-1980 .. **CLC 16**
See also AAYA 22; CA 159; 97-100; SATA 27; SATA-Obit 24
Hitler, Adolf 1889-1945 .... **TCLC 53**
See also CA 117; 147
Hoagland, Edward 1932- .... **CLC 28**
See also CA 1-4R; CANR 2, 31, 57; DLB 6; SATA 51
Hoban, Russell (Conwell) 1925-**CLC 7, 25; DAM NOV**
See also CA 5-8R; CANR 23, 37, 66; CLR 3; DLB 52; MAICYA; MTCW 1, 2; SATA 1, 40, 78
Hobbes, Thomas 1588-1679 .... **LC 36**
See also DLB 151
Hobbs, Perry
See Blackmur, R(ichard) P(almer)
Hobson, Laura Z(ametkin) 1900-1986 **CLC 7, 25**
See also CA 17-20R; 118; CANR 55; DLB 28; SATA 52
Hochhuth, Rolf 1931-**CLC 4, 11, 18; DAM DRAM**
See also CA 5-8R; CANR 33, 75; DLB 124; MTCW 1, 2
Hochman, Sandra 1936- .... **CLC 3, 8**
See also CA 5-8R; DLB 5
Hochwaelder, Fritz 1911-1986 ..... **CLC 36; DAM DRAM**
See also CA 29-32R; 120; CANR 42; MTCW 1
Hochwalder, Fritz
See Hochwaelder, Fritz
Hocking, Mary (Eunice) 1921- .... **CLC 13**
See also CA 101; CANR 18, 40
Hodgins, Jack 1938- .... **CLC 23**
See also CA 93-96; DLB 60
Hodgson, William Hope 1877(?)-1918 **TCLC 13**

See also CA 111; 164; DLB 70, 153, 156, 178; MTCW 2
Hoeg, Peter 1957- .... **CLC 95**
See also CA 151; CANR 75; MTCW 2
Hoffman, Alice 1952- .... **CLC 51; DAM NOV**
See also CA 77-80; CANR 34, 66; MTCW 1, 2
Hoffman, Daniel (Gerard) 1923- . **CLC 6, 13, 23**
See also CA 1-4R; CANR 4; DLB 5
Hoffman, Stanley 1944- .... **CLC 5**
See also CA 77-80
Hoffman, William M(oses) 1939- .... **CLC 40**
See also CA 57-60; CANR 11, 71
Hoffmann, E(rnst) T(heodor) A(madeus) 1776-1822 **NCLC 2; SSC 13**
See also DLB 90; SATA 27
Hofmann, Gert 1931- .... **CLC 54**
See also CA 128
Hofmannsthal, Hugo von 1874-1929 ... **TCLC 11; DAM DRAM; DC 4**
See also CA 106; 153; DLB 81, 118
Hogan, Linda 1947- .... **CLC 73; DAM MULT**
See also CA 120; CANR 45, 73; DLB 175; NNAL
Hogarth, Charles
See Creasey, John
Hogarth, Emmett
See Polonsky, Abraham (Lincoln)
Hogg, James 1770-1835 .... **NCLC 4**
See also DLB 93, 116, 159
Holbach, Paul Henri Thiry Baron 1723-1789 **L C 14**
Holberg, Ludvig 1684-1754 .... **LC 6**
Holden, Ursula 1921- .... **CLC 18**
See also CA 101; CAAS 8; CANR 22
Holderlin, (Johann Christian) Friedrich 1770-1843 **NCLC 16; PC 4**
Holdstock, Robert
See Holdstock, Robert P.
Holdstock, Robert P. 1948- .... **CLC 39**
See also CA 131; CANR 81
Holland, Isabelle 1920- .... **CLC 21**
See also AAYA 11; CA 21-24R; CANR 10, 25, 47; CLR 57; JRDA; MAICYA; SATA 8, 70; SATA-Essay 103
Holland, Marcus
See Caldwell, (Janet Miriam) Taylor (Holland)
Hollander, John 1929- .... **CLC 2, 5, 8, 14**
See also CA 1-4R; CANR 1, 52; DLB 5; SATA 13
Hollander, Paul
See Silverberg, Robert
Holleran, Andrew 1943(?)- .... **CLC 38**
See also CA 144
Hollinghurst, Alan 1954- .... **CLC 55, 91**
See also CA 114; DLB 207
Hollis, Jim
See Summers, Hollis (Spurgeon, Jr.)
Holly, Buddy 1936-1959 .... **TCLC 65**
Holmes, Gordon
See Shiel, M(atthew) P(hipps)
Holmes, John
See Souster, (Holmes) Raymond
Holmes, John Clellon 1926-1988 .... **CLC 56**
See also CA 9-12R; 125; CANR 4; DLB 16
Holmes, Oliver Wendell, Jr. 1841-1935**TCLC 77**
See also CA 114
Holmes, Oliver Wendell 1809-1894 .... **NCLC 14**
See also CDALB 1640-1865; DLB 1, 189; SATA 34
Holmes, Raymond
See Souster, (Holmes) Raymond
Holt, Victoria
See Hibbert, Eleanor Alice Burford
Holub, Miroslav 1923-1998 .... **CLC 4**
See also CA 21-24R; 169; CANR 10
Homer c. 8th cent. B.C.- **CMLC 1, 16; DA; DAB; DAC; DAM MST, POET; PC 23; WLCS**
See also DLB 176
Hongo, Garrett Kaoru 1951- .... **PC 23**
See also CA 133; CAAS 22; DLB 120
Honig, Edwin 1919- .... **CLC 33**
See also CA 5-8R; CAAS 8; CANR 4, 45; DLB 5
Hood, Hugh (John Blagdon) 1928- .. **CLC 15, 28**
See also CA 49-52; CAAS 17; CANR 1, 33; DLB 53
Hood, Thomas 1799-1845 .... **NCLC 16**
See also DLB 96
Hooker, (Peter) Jeremy 1941- .... **CLC 43**
See also CA 77-80; CANR 22; DLB 40
hooks, bell .... **CLC 94; BLCS**
See also Watkins, Gloria
See also MTCW 2
Hope, A(lec) D(erwent) 1907- .... **CLC 3, 51**
See also CA 21-24R; CANR 33, 74; MTCW 1, 2
Hope, Anthony 1863-1933 .... **TCLC 83**
See also CA 157; DLB 153, 156
Hope, Brian
See Creasey, John
Hope, Christopher (David Tully) 1944- . **CLC 52**
See also CA 106; CANR 47; SATA 62
Hopkins, Gerard Manley 1844-1889 . **NCLC 17; DA; DAB; DAC; DAM MST, POET; PC 15; WLC**
See also CDBLB 1890-1914; DLB 35, 57
Hopkins, John (Richard) 1931-1998 .... **CLC 4**
See also CA 85-88; 169
Hopkins, Pauline Elizabeth 1859-1930**TCLC 28; BLC 2; DAM MULT**
See also BW 2, 3; CA 141; DLB 50
Hopkinson, Francis 1737-1791 .... **LC 25**
See also DLB 31
Hopley-Woolrich, Cornell George 1903-1968
See Woolrich, Cornell
See also CA 13-14; CANR 58; CAP 1; MTCW 2
Horatio
See Proust, (Valentin-Louis-George-Eugene-) Marcel
Horgan, Paul (George Vincent O'Shaughnessy) 1903-1995 .... **CLC 9, 53; DAM NOV**
See also CA 13-16R; 147; CANR 9, 35; DLB 212; DLBY 85; INT CANR-9; MTCW 1, 2; SATA 13; SATA-Obit 84
Horn, Peter
See Kuttner, Henry
Hornem, Horace Esq.
See Byron, George Gordon (Noel)
Horney, Karen (Clementine Theodore Danielsen) 1885-1952 .... **TCLC 71**
See also CA 114; 165
Hornung, E(rnest) W(illiam) 1866-1921**TCLC 59**
See also CA 108; 160; DLB 70
Horovitz, Israel (Arthur) 1939- .. **CLC 56; DAM DRAM**
See also CA 33-36R; CANR 46, 59; DLB 7
Horvath, Odon von
See Horvath, Oedoen von
See also DLB 85, 124
Horvath, Oedoen von 1901-1938 .... **TCLC 45**
See also Horvath, Odon von
See also CA 118
Horwitz, Julius 1920-1986 .... **CLC 14**
See also CA 9-12R; 119; CANR 12
Hospital, Janette Turner 1942- .... **CLC 42**
See also CA 108; CANR 48
Hostos, E. M. de
See Hostos (y Bonilla), Eugenio Maria de
Hostos, Eugenio M. de
See Hostos (y Bonilla), Eugenio Maria de
Hostos, Eugenio Maria
See Hostos (y Bonilla), Eugenio Maria de
Hostos (y Bonilla), Eugenio Maria de 1839-1903 **TCLC 24**
See also CA 123; 131; HW 1
Houdini
See Lovecraft, H(oward) P(hillips)
Hougan, Carolyn 1943- .... **CLC 34**
See also CA 139
Household, Geoffrey (Edward West) 1900-1988 **CLC 11**
See also CA 77-80; 126; CANR 58; DLB 87; SATA 14; SATA-Obit 59
Housman, A(lfred) E(dward) 1859-1936 **TCLC 1, 10; DA; DAB; DAC; DAM MST, POET; PC 2; WLCS**
See also CA 104; 125; DLB 19; MTCW 1, 2
Housman, Laurence 1865-1959 .... **TCLC 7**
See also CA 106; 155; DLB 10; SATA 25
Howard, Elizabeth Jane 1923- .... **CLC 7, 29**
See also CA 5-8R; CANR 8, 62
Howard, Maureen 1930- .... **CLC 5, 14, 46**
See also CA 53-56; CANR 31, 75; DLBY 83; INT CANR-31; MTCW 1, 2
Howard, Richard 1929- .... **CLC 7, 10, 47**
See also AITN 1; CA 85-88; CANR 25, 80; DLB 5; INT CANR-25
Howard, Robert E(rvin) 1906-1936 .... **TCLC 8**
See also CA 105; 157
Howard, Warren F.
See Pohl, Frederik
Howe, Fanny (Quincy) 1940- .... **CLC 47**
See also CA 117; CAAS 27; CANR 70; SATA-Brief 52
Howe, Irving 1920-1993 .... **CLC 85**
See also CA 9-12R; 141; CANR 21, 50; DLB 67; MTCW 1, 2
Howe, Julia Ward 1819-1910 .... **TCLC 21**
See also CA 117; DLB 1, 189
Howe, Susan 1937- .... **CLC 72**
See also CA 160; DLB 120
Howe, Tina 1937- .... **CLC 48**
See also CA 109
Howell, James 1594(?)-1666 .... **LC 13**
See also DLB 151
Howells, W. D.
See Howells, William Dean
Howells, William D.
See Howells, William Dean
Howells, William Dean 1837-1920**TCLC 7, 17, 41**
See also CA 104; 134; CDALB 1865-1917; DLB 12, 64, 74, 79, 189; MTCW 2
Howes, Barbara 1914-1996 .... **CLC 15**
See also CA 9-12R; 151; CAAS 3; CANR 53; SATA 5
Hrabal, Bohumil 1914-1997 .... **CLC 13, 67**
See also CA 106; 156; CAAS 12; CANR 57
Hroswitha of Gandersheim c. 935-c. 1002 **CMLC 29**
See also DLB 148
Hsun, Lu
See Lu Hsun
Hubbard, L(afayette) Ron(ald) 1911-1986**CLC 43; DAM POP**
See also CA 77-80; 118; CANR 52; MTCW 2
Huch, Ricarda (Octavia) 1864-1947 .... **TCLC 13**
See also CA 111; DLB 66
Huddle, David 1942- .... **CLC 49**
See also CA 57-60; CAAS 20; DLB 130
Hudson, Jeffrey
See Crichton, (John) Michael
Hudson, W(illiam) H(enry) 1841-1922 **TCLC 29**
See also CA 115; DLB 98, 153, 174; SATA 35
Hueffer, Ford Madox
See Ford, Ford Madox
Hughart, Barry 1934- .... **CLC 39**
See also CA 137
Hughes, Colin
See Creasey, John
Hughes, David (John) 1930- .... **CLC 48**
See also CA 116; 129; DLB 14
Hughes, Edward James
See Hughes, Ted
See also DAM MST, POET
Hughes, (James) Langston 1902-1967 **CLC 1, 5,**

10, 15, 35, 44, 108; BLC 2; DA; DAB; DAC; DAM DRAM, MST, MULT, POET; DC 3; PC 1; SSC 6; WLC
See also AAYA 12; BW 1, 3; CA 1-4R; 25-28R; CANR 1, 34; CDALB 1929-1941; CLR 17; DLB 4, 7, 48, 51, 86; JRDA; MAICYA; MTCW 1, 2; SATA 4, 33
Hughes, Richard (Arthur Warren) 1900-1976 **CLC 1, 11; DAM NOV**
See also CA 5-8R; 65-68; CANR 4; DLB 15, 161; MTCW 1; SATA 8; SATA-Obit 25
Hughes, Ted 1930-1998 **CLC 2, 4, 9, 14, 37, 119; DAB; DAC; PC 7**
See also Hughes, Edward James
See also CA 1-4R; 171; CANR 1, 33, 66; CLR 3; DLB 40, 161; MAICYA; MTCW 1, 2; SATA 49; SATA-Brief 27; SATA-Obit 107
Hugo, Richard F(ranklin) 1923-1982 **CLC 6, 18, 32; DAM POET**
See also CA 49-52; 108; CANR 3; DLB 5, 206
Hugo, Victor (Marie) 1802-1885**NCLC 3, 10, 21; DA; DAB; DAC; DAM DRAM, MST, NOV, POET; PC 17; WLC**
See also AAYA 28; DLB 119, 192; SATA 47
Huidobro, Vicente
See Huidobro Fernandez, Vicente Garcia
Huidobro Fernandez, Vicente Garcia 1893-1948 **TCLC 31**
See also CA 131; HW 1
Hulme, Keri 1947- .... **CLC 39**
See also CA 125; CANR 69; INT 125
Hulme, T(homas) E(rnest) 1883-1917 . **TCLC 21**
See also CA 117; DLB 19
Hume, David 1711-1776 .... **LC 7**
See also DLB 104
Humphrey, William 1924-1997 .... **CLC 45**
See also CA 77-80; 160; CANR 68; DLB 212
Humphreys, Emyr Owen 1919- .... **CLC 47**
See also CA 5-8R; CANR 3, 24; DLB 15
Humphreys, Josephine 1945- .... **CLC 34, 57**
See also CA 121; 127; INT 127
Huneker, James Gibbons 1857-1921 ... **TCLC 65**
See also DLB 71
Hungerford, Pixie
See Brinsmead, H(esba) F(ay)
Hunt, E(verette) Howard, (Jr.) 1918- .... **CLC 3**
See also AITN 1; CA 45-48; CANR 2, 47
Hunt, Kyle
See Creasey, John
Hunt, (James Henry) Leigh 1784-1859 **NCLC 1, 70; DAM POET**
See also DLB 96, 110, 144
Hunt, Marsha 1946- .... **CLC 70**
See also BW 2, 3; CA 143; CANR 79
Hunt, Violet 1866(?)-1942 .... **TCLC 53**
See also DLB 162, 197
Hunter, E. Waldo
See Sturgeon, Theodore (Hamilton)
Hunter, Evan 1926- .... **CLC 11, 31; DAM POP**
See also CA 5-8R; CANR 5, 38, 62; DLBY 82; INT CANR-5; MTCW 1; SATA 25
Hunter, Kristin (Eggleston) 1931- .... **CLC 35**
See also AITN 1; BW 1; CA 13-16R; CANR 13; CLR 3; DLB 33; INT CANR-13; MAICYA; SAAS 10; SATA 12
Hunter, Mollie 1922- .... **CLC 21**
See also McIlwraith, Maureen Mollie Hunter
See also AAYA 13; CANR 37, 78; CLR 25; DLB 161; JRDA; MAICYA; SAAS 7; SATA 54, 106
Hunter, Robert (?)-1734 .... **LC 7**
Hurston, Zora Neale 1903-1960 . **CLC 7, 30, 61; BLC 2; DA; DAC; DAM MST, MULT, NOV; SSC 4; WLCS**
See also AAYA 15; BW 1, 3; CA 85-88; CANR 61; CDALBS; DLB 51, 86; MTCW 1, 2
Huston, John (Marcellus) 1906-1987 .... **CLC 20**
See also CA 73-76; 123; CANR 34; DLB 26
Hustvedt, Siri 1955- .... **CLC 76**
See also CA 137
Hutten, Ulrich von 1488-1523 .... **LC 16**
See also DLB 179
Huxley, Aldous (Leonard) 1894-1963**CLC 1, 3, 4, 5, 8, 11, 18, 35, 79; DA; DAB; DAC; DAM MST, NOV; WLC**
See also AAYA 11; CA 85-88; CANR 44; CDBLB 1914-1945; DLB 36, 100, 162, 195; MTCW 1, 2; SATA 63
Huxley, T(homas) H(enry) 1825-1895 **NCLC 67**
See also DLB 57
Huysmans, Joris-Karl 1848-1907 ... **TCLC 7, 69**
See also CA 104; 165; DLB 123
Hwang, David Henry 1957-**CLC 55; DAM DRAM; DC 4**
See also CA 127; 132; CANR 76; DLB 212; INT 132; MTCW 2
Hyde, Anthony 1946- .... **CLC 42**
See also CA 136
Hyde, Margaret O(ldroyd) 1917- .... **CLC 21**
See also CA 1-4R; CANR 1, 36; CLR 23; JRDA; MAICYA; SAAS 8; SATA 1, 42, 76
Hynes, James 1956(?)- .... **CLC 65**
See also CA 164
Ian, Janis 1951- .... **CLC 21**
See also CA 105
Ibanez, Vicente Blasco
See Blasco Ibanez, Vicente
Ibarguengoitia, Jorge 1928-1983 .... **CLC 37**
See also CA 124; 113; HW 1
Ibsen, Henrik (Johan) 1828-1906**TCLC 2, 8, 16, 37, 52; DA; DAB; DAC; DAM DRAM, MST; DC 2; WLC**
See also CA 104; 141
Ibuse, Masuji 1898-1993 .... **CLC 22**
See also CA 127; 141; DLB 180
Ichikawa, Kon 1915- .... **CLC 20**
See also CA 121
Idle, Eric 1943- .... **CLC 21**
See also Monty Python
See also CA 116; CANR 35
Ignatow, David 1914-1997 .... **CLC 4, 7, 14, 40**
See also CA 9-12R; 162; CAAS 3; CANR 31, 57; DLB 5
Ihimaera, Witi 1944- .... **CLC 46**
See also CA 77-80
Ilf, Ilya .... **TCLC 21**
See also Fainzilberg, Ilya Arnoldovich
Illyes, Gyula 1902-1983 .... **PC 16**
See also CA 114; 109
Immermann, Karl (Lebrecht) 1796-1840**NCLC 4, 49**
See also DLB 133
Ince, Thomas H. 1882-1924 .... **TCLC 89**
Inchbald, Elizabeth 1753-1821 .... **NCLC 62**
See also DLB 39, 89
Inclan, Ramon (Maria) del Valle
See Valle-Inclan, Ramon (Maria) del
Infante, G(uillermo) Cabrera
See Cabrera Infante, G(uillermo)
Ingalls, Rachel (Holmes) 1940- .... **CLC 42**
See also CA 123; 127
Ingamells, Reginald Charles
See Ingamells, Rex
Ingamells, Rex 1913-1955 .... **TCLC 35**
See also CA 167
Inge, William (Motter) 1913-1973 **CLC 1, 8, 19; DAM DRAM**
See also CA 9-12R; CDALB 1941-1968; DLB 7; MTCW 1, 2
Ingelow, Jean 1820-1897 .... **NCLC 39**
See also DLB 35, 163; SATA 33
Ingram, Willis J.
See Harris, Mark
Innaurato, Albert (F.) 1948(?)- .... **CLC 21, 60**
See also CA 115; 122; CANR 78; INT 122
Innes, Michael
See Stewart, J(ohn) I(nnes) M(ackintosh)
Innis, Harold Adams 1894-1952 .... **TCLC 77**
See also DLB 88
Ionesco, Eugene 1909-1994**CLC 1, 4, 6, 9, 11, 15, 41, 86; DA; DAB; DAC; DAM DRAM, MST; WLC**
See also CA 9-12R; 144; CANR 55; MTCW 1, 2; SATA 7; SATA-Obit 79
Iqbal, Muhammad 1873-1938 .... **TCLC 28**
Ireland, Patrick
See O'Doherty, Brian
Iron, Ralph
See Schreiner, Olive (Emilie Albertina)
Irving, John (Winslow) 1942- .. **CLC 13, 23, 38, 112; DAM NOV, POP**
See also AAYA 8; BEST 89:3; CA 25-28R; CANR 28, 73; DLB 6; DLBY 82; MTCW 1, 2
Irving, Washington 1783-1859 **NCLC 2, 19; DA; DAB; DAC; DAM MST; SSC 2; WLC**
See also CDALB 1640-1865; DLB 3, 11, 30, 59, 73, 74, 186; YABC 2
Irwin, P. K.
See Page, P(atricia) K(athleen)
Isaacs, Jorge Ricardo 1837-1895 .... **NCLC 70**
Isaacs, Susan 1943- .... **CLC 32; DAM POP**
See also BEST 89:1; CA 89-92; CANR 20, 41, 65; INT CANR-20; MTCW 1, 2
Isherwood, Christopher (William Bradshaw) 1904-1986**CLC 1, 9, 11, 14, 44; DAM DRAM, NOV**
See also CA 13-16R; 117; CANR 35; DLB 15, 195; DLBY 86; MTCW 1, 2
Ishiguro, Kazuo 1954-**CLC 27, 56, 59, 110; DAM NOV**
See also BEST 90:2; CA 120; CANR 49; DLB 194; MTCW 1, 2
Ishikawa, Hakuhin
See Ishikawa, Takuboku
Ishikawa, Takuboku 1886(?)-1912**TCLC 15; DAM POET; PC 10**
See also CA 113; 153
Iskander, Fazil 1929- .... **CLC 47**
See also CA 102
Isler, Alan (David) 1934- .... **CLC 91**
See also CA 156
Ivan IV 1530-1584 .... **LC 17**
Ivanov, Vyacheslav Ivanovich 1866-1949**TCLC 33**
See also CA 122
Ivask, Ivar Vidrik 1927-1992 .... **CLC 14**
See also CA 37-40R; 139; CANR 24
Ives, Morgan
See Bradley, Marion Zimmer
Izumi Shikibu c. 973-c. 1034 .... **CMLC 33**
J. R. S.
See Gogarty, Oliver St. John
Jabran, Kahlil
See Gibran, Kahlil
Jabran, Khalil
See Gibran, Kahlil
Jackson, Daniel
See Wingrove, David (John)
Jackson, Jesse 1908-1983 .... **CLC 12**
See also BW 1; CA 25-28R; 109; CANR 27; CLR 28; MAICYA; SATA 2, 29; SATA-Obit 48
Jackson, Laura (Riding) 1901-1991
See Riding, Laura
See also CA 65-68; 135; CANR 28; DLB 48
Jackson, Sam
See Trumbo, Dalton
Jackson, Sara
See Wingrove, David (John)
Jackson, Shirley 1919-1965**CLC 11, 60, 87; DA; DAC; DAM MST; SSC 9; WLC**
See also AAYA 9; CA 1-4R; 25-28R; CANR 4, 52; CDALB 1941-1968; DLB 6; MTCW 2; SATA 2

Jacob, (Cyprien-)Max 1876-1944 .... **TCLC 6**
See also CA 104
Jacobs, Harriet A(nn) 1813(?)-1897 ... **NCLC 67**
Jacobs, Jim 1942- .... **CLC 12**
See also CA 97-100; INT 97-100
Jacobs, W(illiam) W(ymark) 1863-1943**TCLC 22**
See also CA 121; 167; DLB 135
Jacobsen, Jens Peter 1847-1885 .... **NCLC 34**
Jacobsen, Josephine 1908- .... **CLC 48, 102**
See also CA 33-36R; CAAS 18; CANR 23, 48
Jacobson, Dan 1929- .... **CLC 4, 14**
See also CA 1-4R; CANR 2, 25, 66; DLB 14, 207; MTCW 1
Jacqueline
See Carpentier (y Valmont), Alejo
Jagger, Mick 1944- .... **CLC 17**
Jahiz, al- c. 780-c. 869 .... **CMLC 25**
Jakes, John (William) 1932-**CLC 29; DAM NOV, POP**
See also BEST 89:4; CA 57-60; CANR 10, 43, 66; DLBY 83; INT CANR-10; MTCW 1, 2; SATA 62
James, Andrew
See Kirkup, James
James, C(yril) L(ionel) R(obert) 1901-1989 **CLC 33; BLCS**
See also BW 2; CA 117; 125; 128; CANR 62; DLB 125; MTCW 1
James, Daniel (Lewis) 1911-1988
See Santiago, Danny
See also CA 174; 125
James, Dynely
See Mayne, William (James Carter)
James, Henry Sr. 1811-1882 .... **NCLC 53**
James, Henry 1843-1916**TCLC 2, 11, 24, 40, 47, 64; DA; DAB; DAC; DAM MST, NOV; SSC 8, 32; WLC**
See also CA 104; 132; CDALB 1865-1917; DLB 12, 71, 74, 189; DLBD 13; MTCW 1, 2
James, M. R.
See James, Montague (Rhodes)
See also DLB 156
James, Montague (Rhodes) 1862-1936 . **TCLC 6; SSC 16**
See also CA 104; DLB 201
James, P. D. 1920- .... **CLC 18, 46**
See also White, Phyllis Dorothy James
See also BEST 90:2; CDBLB 1960 to Present; DLB 87; DLBD 17
James, Philip
See Moorcock, Michael (John)
James, William 1842-1910 .... **TCLC 15, 32**
See also CA 109
James I 1394-1437 .... **LC 20**
Jameson, Anna 1794-1860 .... **NCLC 43**
See also DLB 99, 166
Jami, Nur al-Din 'Abd al-Rahman 1414-1492**LC 9**
Jammes, Francis 1868-1938 .... **TCLC 75**
Jandl, Ernst 1925- .... **CLC 34**
Janowitz, Tama 1957- .... **CLC 43; DAM POP**
See also CA 106; CANR 52
Japrisot, Sebastien 1931- .... **CLC 90**
Jarrell, Randall 1914-1965**CLC 1, 2, 6, 9, 13, 49; DAM POET**
See also CA 5-8R; 25-28R; CABS 2; CANR 6, 34; CDALB 1941-1968; CLR 6; DLB 48, 52; MAICYA; MTCW 1, 2; SATA 7
Jarry, Alfred 1873-1907 .... **TCLC 2, 14; DAM DRAM; SSC 20**
See also CA 104; 153; DLB 192
Jarvis, E. K.
See Bloch, Robert (Albert); Ellison, Harlan (Jay); Silverberg, Robert
Jeake, Samuel, Jr.
See Aiken, Conrad (Potter)
Jean Paul 1763-1825 .... **NCLC 7**
Jefferies, (John) Richard 1848-1887 .. **NCLC 47**
See also DLB 98, 141; SATA 16
Jeffers, (John) Robinson 1887-1962**CLC 2, 3, 11, 15, 54; DA; DAC; DAM MST, POET; PC 17; WLC**
See also CA 85-88; CANR 35; CDALB 1917-1929; DLB 45, 212; MTCW 1, 2
Jefferson, Janet
See Mencken, H(enry) L(ouis)
Jefferson, Thomas 1743-1826 .... **NCLC 11**
See also CDALB 1640-1865; DLB 31
Jeffrey, Francis 1773-1850 .... **NCLC 33**
See also DLB 107
Jelakowitch, Ivan
See Heijermans, Herman
Jellicoe, (Patricia) Ann 1927- .... **CLC 27**
See also CA 85-88; DLB 13
Jen, Gish .... **CLC 70**
See also Jen, Lillian
Jen, Lillian 1956(?)-
See Jen, Gish
See also CA 135
Jenkins, (John) Robin 1912- .... **CLC 52**
See also CA 1-4R; CANR 1; DLB 14
Jennings, Elizabeth (Joan) 1926- ..... **CLC 5, 14**
See also CA 61-64; CAAS 5; CANR 8, 39, 66; DLB 27; MTCW 1; SATA 66
Jennings, Waylon 1937- .... **CLC 21**
Jensen, Johannes V. 1873-1950 .... **TCLC 41**
See also CA 170
Jensen, Laura (Linnea) 1948- .... **CLC 37**
See also CA 103
Jerome, Jerome K(lapka) 1859-1927 .. **TCLC 23**
See also CA 119; 177; DLB 10, 34, 135
Jerrold, Douglas William 1803-1857 ... **NCLC 2**
See also DLB 158, 159
Jewett, (Theodora) Sarah Orne 1849-1909**TCLC 1, 22; SSC 6**
See also CA 108; 127; CANR 71; DLB 12, 74; SATA 15
Jewsbury, Geraldine (Endsor) 1812-1880 **NCLC 22**
See also DLB 21
Jhabvala, Ruth Prawer 1927- . **CLC 4, 8, 29, 94; DAB; DAM NOV**
See also CA 1-4R; CANR 2, 29, 51, 74; DLB 139, 194; INT CANR-29; MTCW 1, 2
Jibran, Kahlil
See Gibran, Kahlil
Jibran, Khalil
See Gibran, Kahlil
Jiles, Paulette 1943- .... **CLC 13, 58**
See also CA 101; CANR 70
Jimenez (Mantecon), Juan Ramon 1881-1958 **TCLC 4; DAM MULT, POET; HLC; PC 7**
See also CA 104; 131; CANR 74; DLB 134; HW 1; MTCW 1, 2
Jimenez, Ramon
See Jimenez (Mantecon), Juan Ramon
Jimenez Mantecon, Juan
See Jimenez (Mantecon), Juan Ramon
Jin, Ha 1956- .... **CLC 109**
See also CA 152
Joel, Billy .... **CLC 26**
See also Joel, William Martin
Joel, William Martin 1949-
See Joel, Billy
See also CA 108
John, Saint 7th cent. - .... **CMLC 27**
John of the Cross, St. 1542-1591 .... **LC 18**
Johnson, B(ryan) S(tanley William) 1933-1973 **CLC 6, 9**
See also CA 9-12R; 53-56; CANR 9; DLB 14, 40
Johnson, Benj. F. of Boo
See Riley, James Whitcomb
Johnson, Benjamin F. of Boo
See Riley, James Whitcomb
Johnson, Charles (Richard) 1948-**CLC 7, 51, 65; BLC 2; DAM MULT**
See also BW 2, 3; CA 116; CAAS 18; CANR 42, 66; DLB 33; MTCW 2
Johnson, Denis 1949- .... **CLC 52**
See also CA 117; 121; CANR 71; DLB 120
Johnson, Diane 1934- .... **CLC 5, 13, 48**
See also CA 41-44R; CANR 17, 40, 62; DLBY 80; INT CANR-17; MTCW 1
Johnson, Eyvind (Olof Verner) 1900-1976**CLC 14**
See also CA 73-76; 69-72; CANR 34
Johnson, J. R.
See James, C(yril) L(ionel) R(obert)
Johnson, James Weldon 1871-1938 **TCLC 3, 19; BLC 2; DAM MULT, POET; PC 24**
See also BW 1, 3; CA 104; 125; CDALB 1917-1929; CLR 32; DLB 51; MTCW 1, 2; SATA 31
Johnson, Joyce 1935- .... **CLC 58**
See also CA 125; 129
Johnson, Judith (Emlyn) 1936- .... **CLC 7, 15**
See also CA 25-28R, 153; CANR 34
Johnson, Lionel (Pigot) 1867-1902 ..... **TCLC 19**
See also CA 117; DLB 19
Johnson, Marguerite (Annie)
See Angelou, Maya
Johnson, Mel
See Malzberg, Barry N(athaniel)
Johnson, Pamela Hansford 1912-1981 **CLC 1, 7, 27**
See also CA 1-4R; 104; CANR 2, 28; DLB 15; MTCW 1, 2
Johnson, Robert 1911(?)-1938 .... **TCLC 69**
See also BW 3; CA 174
Johnson, Samuel 1709-1784 .. **LC 15; DA; DAB; DAC; DAM MST; WLC**
See also CDBLB 1660-1789; DLB 39, 95, 104, 142
Johnson, Uwe 1934-1984 .... **CLC 5, 10, 15, 40**
See also CA 1-4R; 112; CANR 1, 39; DLB 75; MTCW 1
Johnston, George (Benson) 1913- .... **CLC 51**
See also CA 1-4R; CANR 5, 20; DLB 88
Johnston, Jennifer 1930- .... **CLC 7**
See also CA 85-88; DLB 14
Jolley, (Monica) Elizabeth 1923-**CLC 46; SSC 19**
See also CA 127; CAAS 13; CANR 59
Jones, Arthur Llewellyn 1863-1947
See Machen, Arthur
See also CA 104
Jones, D(ouglas) G(ordon) 1929- .... **CLC 10**
See also CA 29-32R; CANR 13; DLB 53
Jones, David (Michael) 1895-1974**CLC 2, 4, 7, 13, 42**
See also CA 9-12R; 53-56; CANR 28; CDBLB 1945-1960; DLB 20, 100; MTCW 1
Jones, David Robert 1947-
See Bowie, David
See also CA 103
Jones, Diana Wynne 1934- .... **CLC 26**
See also AAYA 12; CA 49-52; CANR 4, 26, 56; CLR 23; DLB 161; JRDA; MAICYA; SAAS 7; SATA 9, 70, 108
Jones, Edward P. 1950- .... **CLC 76**
See also BW 2, 3; CA 142; CANR 79
Jones, Gayl 1949-**CLC 6, 9; BLC 2; DAM MULT**
See also BW 2, 3; CA 77-80; CANR 27, 66; DLB 33; MTCW 1, 2
Jones, James 1921-1977 .... **CLC 1, 3, 10, 39**
See also AITN 1, 2; CA 1-4R; 69-72; CANR 6; DLB 2, 143; DLBD 17; DLBY 98; MTCW 1
Jones, John J.
See Lovecraft, H(oward) P(hillips)
Jones, LeRoi .... **CLC 1, 2, 3, 5, 10, 14**
See also Baraka, Amiri
See also MTCW 2
Jones, Louis B. 1953- .... **CLC 65**
See also CA 141; CANR 73
Jones, Madison (Percy, Jr.) 1925- .... **CLC 4**
See also CA 13-16R; CAAS 11; CANR 7, 54; DLB

152
Jones, Mervyn 1922- .... **CLC 10, 52**
See also CA 45-48; CAAS 5; CANR 1; MTCW 1
Jones, Mick 1956(?)- .... **CLC 30**
Jones, Nettie (Pearl) 1941- .... **CLC 34**
See also BW 2; CA 137; CAAS 20
Jones, Preston 1936-1979 .... **CLC 10**
See also CA 73-76; 89-92; DLB 7
Jones, Robert F(rancis) 1934- .... **CLC 7**
See also CA 49-52; CANR 2, 61
Jones, Rod 1953- .... **CLC 50**
See also CA 128
Jones, Terence Graham Parry 1942- ... **CLC 21**
See also Jones, Terry; Monty Python
See also CA 112; 116; CANR 35; INT 116
Jones, Terry
See Jones, Terence Graham Parry
See also SATA 67; SATA-Brief 51
Jones, Thom 1945(?)- .... **CLC 81**
See also CA 157
Jong, Erica 1942-**CLC 4, 6, 8, 18, 83; DAM NOV, POP**
See also AITN 1; BEST 90:2; CA 73-76; CANR 26, 52, 75; DLB 2, 5, 28, 152; INT CANR-26; MTCW 1, 2
Jonson, Ben(jamin) 1572(?)-1637 **LC 6, 33; DA; DAB; DAC; DAM DRAM, MST, POET; DC 4; PC 17; WLC**
See also CDBLB Before 1660; DLB 62, 121
Jordan, June 1936-. **CLC 5, 11, 23, 114; BLCS; DAM MULT, POET**
See also AAYA 2; BW 2, 3; CA 33-36R; CANR 25, 70; CLR 10; DLB 38; MAICYA; MTCW 1; SATA 4
Jordan, Neil (Patrick) 1950- .... **CLC 110**
See also CA 124; 130; CANR 54; INT 130
Jordan, Pat(rick M.) 1941- .... **CLC 37**
See also CA 33-36R
Jorgensen, Ivar
See Ellison, Harlan (Jay)
Jorgenson, Ivar
See Silverberg, Robert
Josephus, Flavius c. 37-100 .... **CMLC 13**
Josipovici, Gabriel 1940- .... **CLC 6, 43**
See also CA 37-40R; CAAS 8; CANR 47; DLB 14
Joubert, Joseph 1754-1824 .... **NCLC 9**
Jouve, Pierre Jean 1887-1976 .... **CLC 47**
See also CA 65-68
Jovine, Francesco 1902-1950 .... **TCLC 79**
Joyce, James (Augustine Aloysius) 1882-1941 **TCLC 3, 8, 16, 35, 52; DA; DAB; DAC; DAM MST, NOV, POET; PC 22; SSC 3, 26; WLC**
See also CA 104; 126; CDBLB 1914-1945; DLB 10, 19, 36, 162; MTCW 1, 2
Jozsef, Attila 1905-1937 .... **TCLC 22**
See also CA 116
Juana Ines de la Cruz 1651(?)-1695**LC 5; HLCS 1; PC 24**
Judd, Cyril
See Kornbluth, C(yril) M.; Pohl, Frederik
Julian of Norwich 1342(?)-1416(?) .... **LC 6**
See also DLB 146
Junger, Sebastian 1962- .... **CLC 109**
See also AAYA 28; CA 165
Juniper, Alex
See Hospital, Janette Turner
Junius
See Luxemburg, Rosa
Just, Ward (Swift) 1935- .... **CLC 4, 27**
See also CA 25-28R; CANR 32; INT CANR-32
Justice, Donald (Rodney) 1925- **CLC 6, 19, 102; DAM POET**
See also CA 5-8R; CANR 26, 54, 74; DLBY 83; INT CANR-26; MTCW 2
Juvenal c. 60-c. 13 .... **CMLC 8**
See also Juvenalis, Decimus Junius
See also DLB 211
Juvenalis, Decimus Junius 55(?)-c. 127(?)
See Juvenal
Juvenis
See Bourne, Randolph S(illiman)
Kacew, Romain 1914-1980
See Gary, Romain
See also CA 108; 102
Kadare, Ismail 1936- .... **CLC 52**
See also CA 161
Kadohata, Cynthia .... **CLC 59**
See also CA 140
Kafka, Franz 1883-1924**TCLC 2, 6, 13, 29, 47, 53; DA; DAB; DAC; DAM MST, NOV; SSC 5, 29, 35; WLC**
See also CA 105; 126; DLB 81; MTCW 1, 2
Kahanovitsch, Pinkhes
See Der Nister
Kahn, Roger 1927- .... **CLC 30**
See also CA 25-28R; CANR 44, 69; DLB 171; SATA 37
Kain, Saul
See Sassoon, Siegfried (Lorraine)
Kaiser, Georg 1878-1945 .... **TCLC 9**
See also CA 106; DLB 124
Kaletski, Alexander 1946- .... **CLC 39**
See also CA 118; 143
Kalidasa fl. c. 400- .... **CMLC 9; PC 22**
Kallman, Chester (Simon) 1921-1975 ..... **CLC 2**
See also CA 45-48; 53-56; CANR 3
Kaminsky, Melvin 1926-
See Brooks, Mel
See also CA 65-68; CANR 16
Kaminsky, Stuart M(elvin) 1934- .... **CLC 59**
See also CA 73-76; CANR 29, 53
Kandinsky, Wassily 1866-1944 .... **TCLC 92**
See also CA 118; 155
Kane, Francis
See Robbins, Harold
Kane, Paul
See Simon, Paul (Frederick)
Kane, Wilson
See Bloch, Robert (Albert)
Kanin, Garson 1912-1999 .... **CLC 22**
See also AITN 1; CA 5-8R; 177; CANR 7, 78; DLB 7
Kaniuk, Yoram 1930- .... **CLC 19**
See also CA 134
Kant, Immanuel 1724-1804 .... **NCLC 27, 67**
See also DLB 94
Kantor, MacKinlay 1904-1977 .... **CLC 7**
See also CA 61-64; 73-76; CANR 60, 63; DLB 9, 102; MTCW 2
Kaplan, David Michael 1946- .... **CLC 50**
Kaplan, James 1951- .... **CLC 59**
See also CA 135
Karageorge, Michael
See Anderson, Poul (William)
Karamzin, Nikolai Mikhailovich 1766-1826 **NCLC 3**
See also DLB 150
Karapanou, Margarita 1946- .... **CLC 13**
See also CA 101
Karinthy, Frigyes 1887-1938 .... **TCLC 47**
See also CA 170
Karl, Frederick R(obert) 1927- .... **CLC 34**
See also CA 5-8R; CANR 3, 44
Kastel, Warren
See Silverberg, Robert
Kataev, Evgeny Petrovich 1903-1942
See Petrov, Evgeny
See also CA 120
Kataphusin
See Ruskin, John
Katz, Steve 1935- .... **CLC 47**
See also CA 25-28R; CAAS 14, 64; CANR 12; DLBY 83
Kauffman, Janet 1945- .... **CLC 42**
See also CA 117; CANR 43; DLBY 86
Kaufman, Bob (Garnell) 1925-1986 .... **CLC 49**
See also BW 1; CA 41-44R; 118; CANR 22; DLB 16, 41
Kaufman, George S. 1889-1961 ... **CLC 38; DAM DRAM**
See also CA 108; 93-96; DLB 7; INT 108; MTCW 2
Kaufman, Sue .... **CLC 3, 8**
See also Barondess, Sue K(aufman)
Kavafis, Konstantinos Petrou 1863-1933
See Cavafy, C(onstantine) P(eter)
See also CA 104
Kavan, Anna 1901-1968 .... **CLC 5, 13, 82**
See also CA 5-8R; CANR 6, 57; MTCW 1
Kavanagh, Dan
See Barnes, Julian (Patrick)
Kavanagh, Julie 1952- .... **CLC 119**
See also CA 163
Kavanagh, Patrick (Joseph) 1904-1967 **CLC 22**
See also CA 123; 25-28R; DLB 15, 20; MTCW 1
Kawabata, Yasunari 1899-1972 . **CLC 2, 5, 9, 18, 107; DAM MULT; SSC 17**
See also CA 93-96; 33-36R; DLB 180; MTCW 2
Kaye, M(ary) M(argaret) 1909- .... **CLC 28**
See also CA 89-92; CANR 24, 60; MTCW 1, 2; SATA 62
Kaye, Mollie
See Kaye, M(ary) M(argaret)
Kaye-Smith, Sheila 1887-1956 .... **TCLC 20**
See also CA 118; DLB 36
Kaymor, Patrice Maguilene
See Senghor, Leopold Sedar
Kazan, Elia 1909- .... **CLC 6, 16, 63**
See also CA 21-24R; CANR 32, 78
Kazantzakis, Nikos 1883(?)-1957 **TCLC 2, 5, 33**
See also CA 105; 132; MTCW 1, 2
Kazin, Alfred 1915-1998 .... **CLC 34, 38, 119**
See also CA 1-4R; CAAS 7; CANR 1, 45, 79; DLB 67
Keane, Mary Nesta (Skrine) 1904-1996
See Keane, Molly
See also CA 108; 114; 151
Keane, Molly .... **CLC 31**
See also Keane, Mary Nesta (Skrine)
See also INT 114
Keates, Jonathan 1946(?)- .... **CLC 34**
See also CA 163
Keaton, Buster 1895-1966 .... **CLC 20**
Keats, John 1795-1821 .. **NCLC 8, 73; DA; DAB; DAC; DAM MST, POET; PC 1; WLC**
See also CDBLB 1789-1832; DLB 96, 110
Keene, Donald 1922- .... **CLC 34**
See also CA 1-4R; CANR 5
Keillor, Garrison .... **CLC 40, 115**
See also Keillor, Gary (Edward)
See also AAYA 2; BEST 89:3; DLBY 87; SATA 58
Keillor, Gary (Edward) 1942-
See Keillor, Garrison
See also CA 111; 117; CANR 36, 59; DAM POP; MTCW 1, 2
Keith, Michael
See Hubbard, L(afayette) Ron(ald)
Keller, Gottfried 1819-1890 .... **NCLC 2; SSC 26**
See also DLB 129
Keller, Nora Okja .... **CLC 109**
Kellerman, Jonathan 1949- **CLC 44; DAM POP**
See also BEST 90:1; CA 106; CANR 29, 51; INT CANR-29
Kelley, William Melvin 1937- .... **CLC 22**
See also BW 1; CA 77-80; CANR 27; DLB 33
Kellogg, Marjorie 1922- .... **CLC 2**
See also CA 81-84
Kellow, Kathleen
See Hibbert, Eleanor Alice Burford
Kelly, M(ilton) T(erry) 1947- .... **CLC 55**

See also CA 97-100; CAAS 22; CANR 19, 43
Kelman, James 1946- .... **CLC 58, 86**
See also CA 148; DLB 194
Kemal, Yashar 1923- .... **CLC 14, 29**
See also CA 89-92; CANR 44
Kemble, Fanny 1809-1893 .... **NCLC 18**
See also DLB 32
Kemelman, Harry 1908-1996 .... **CLC 2**
See also AITN 1; CA 9-12R; 155; CANR 6, 71; DLB 28
Kempe, Margery 1373(?)-1440(?) .... **LC 6**
See also DLB 146
Kempis, Thomas a 1380-1471 .... **LC 11**
Kendall, Henry 1839-1882 .... **NCLC 12**
Keneally, Thomas (Michael) 1935- **CLC 5, 8, 10, 14, 19, 27, 43, 117; DAM NOV**
See also CA 85-88; CANR 10, 50, 74; MTCW 1, 2
Kennedy, Adrienne (Lita) 1931- **CLC 66; BLC 2; DAM MULT; DC 5**
See also BW 2, 3; CA 103; CAAS 20; CABS 3; CANR 26, 53; DLB 38
Kennedy, John Pendleton 1795-1870 ..... **NCLC 2**
See also DLB 3
Kennedy, Joseph Charles 1929-
See Kennedy, X. J.
See also CA 1-4R; CANR 4, 30, 40; SATA 14, 86
Kennedy, William 1928- **CLC 6, 28, 34, 53; DAM NOV**
See also AAYA 1; CA 85-88; CANR 14, 31, 76; DLB 143; DLBY 85; INT CANR-31; MTCW 1, 2; SATA 57
Kennedy, X. J. .... **CLC 8, 42**
See also Kennedy, Joseph Charles
See also CAAS 9; CLR 27; DLB 5; SAAS 22
Kenny, Maurice (Francis) 1929- . **CLC 87; DAM MULT**
See also CA 144; CAAS 22; DLB 175; NNAL
Kent, Kelvin
See Kuttner, Henry
Kenton, Maxwell
See Southern, Terry
Kenyon, Robert O.
See Kuttner, Henry
Kepler, Johannes 1571-1630 .... **LC 45**
Kerouac, Jack .... **CLC 1, 2, 3, 5, 14, 29, 61**
See also Kerouac, Jean-Louis Lebris de
See also AAYA 25; CDALB 1941-1968; DLB 2, 16; DLBD 3; DLBY 95; MTCW 2
Kerouac, Jean-Louis Lebris de 1922-1969
See Kerouac, Jack
See also AITN 1; CA 5-8R; 25-28R; CANR 26, 54; DA; DAB; DAC; DAM MST, NOV, POET, POP; MTCW 1, 2; WLC
Kerr, Jean 1923- .... **CLC 22**
See also CA 5-8R; CANR 7; INT CANR-7
Kerr, M. E. .... **CLC 12, 35**
See also Meaker, Marijane (Agnes)
See also AAYA 2, 23; CLR 29; SAAS 1
Kerr, Robert .... **CLC 55**
Kerrigan, (Thomas) Anthony 1918- .... **CLC 4, 6**
See also CA 49-52; CAAS 11; CANR 4
Kerry, Lois
See Duncan, Lois
Kesey, Ken (Elton) 1935- **CLC 1, 3, 6, 11, 46, 64; DA; DAB; DAC; DAM MST, NOV, POP; WLC**
See also AAYA 25; CA 1-4R; CANR 22, 38, 66; CDALB 1968-1988; DLB 2, 16, 206; MTCW 1, 2; SATA 66
Kesselring, Joseph (Otto) 1902-1967 .. **CLC 45; DAM DRAM, MST**
See also CA 150
Kessler, Jascha (Frederick) 1929- .... **CLC 4**
See also CA 17-20R; CANR 8, 48
Kettelkamp, Larry (Dale) 1933- .... **CLC 12**
See also CA 29-32R; CANR 16; SAAS 3; SATA 2
Key, Ellen 1849-1926 .... **TCLC 65**
Keyber, Conny
See Fielding, Henry
Keyes, Daniel 1927- .. **CLC 80; DA; DAC; DAM MST, NOV**
See also AAYA 23; CA 17-20R; CANR 10, 26, 54, 74; MTCW 2; SATA 37
Keynes, John Maynard 1883-1946 ...... **TCLC 64**
See also CA 114; 162, 163; DLBD 10; MTCW 2
Khanshendel, Chiron
See Rose, Wendy
Khayyam, Omar 1048-1131 **CMLC 11; DAM POET; PC 8**
Kherdian, David 1931- .... **CLC 6, 9**
See also CA 21-24R; CAAS 2; CANR 39, 78; CLR 24; JRDA; MAICYA; SATA 16, 74
Khlebnikov, Velimir .... **TCLC 20**
See also Khlebnikov, Viktor Vladimirovich
Khlebnikov, Viktor Vladimirovich 1885-1922
See Khlebnikov, Velimir
See also CA 117
Khodasevich, Vladislav (Felitsianovich) 1886-1939 **TCLC 15**
See also CA 115
Kielland, Alexander Lange 1849-1906 .. **TCLC 5**
See also CA 104
Kiely, Benedict 1919- .... **CLC 23, 43**
See also CA 1-4R; CANR 2; DLB 15
Kienzle, William X(avier) 1928- . **CLC 25; DAM POP**
See also CA 93-96; CAAS 1; CANR 9, 31, 59; INT CANR-31; MTCW 1, 2
Kierkegaard, Soren 1813-1855 ..... **NCLC 34, 78**
Kieslowski, Krzysztof 1941-1996 .... **CLC 120**
See also CA 147; 151
Killens, John Oliver 1916-1987 .... **CLC 10**
See also BW 2; CA 77-80; 123; CAAS 2; CANR 26; DLB 33
Killigrew, Anne 1660-1685 .... **LC 4**
See also DLB 131
Kim
See Simenon, Georges (Jacques Christian)
Kincaid, Jamaica 1949- **CLC 43, 68; BLC 2; DAM MULT, NOV**
See also AAYA 13; BW 2, 3; CA 125; CANR 47, 59; CDALBS; DLB 157; MTCW 2
King, Francis (Henry) 1923- .. **CLC 8, 53; DAM NOV**
See also CA 1-4R; CANR 1, 33; DLB 15, 139; MTCW 1
King, Kennedy
See Brown, George Douglas
King, Martin Luther, Jr. 1929-1968 **CLC 83; BLC 2; DA; DAB; DAC; DAM MST, MULT; WLCS**
See also BW 2, 3; CA 25-28; CANR 27, 44; CAP 2; MTCW 1, 2; SATA 14
King, Stephen (Edwin) 1947- **CLC 12, 26, 37, 61, 113; DAM NOV, POP; SSC 17**
See also AAYA 1, 17; BEST 90:1; CA 61-64; CANR 1, 30, 52, 76; DLB 143; DLBY 80; JRDA; MTCW 1, 2; SATA 9, 55
King, Steve
See King, Stephen (Edwin)
King, Thomas 1943- **CLC 89; DAC; DAM MULT**
See also CA 144; DLB 175; NNAL; SATA 96
Kingman, Lee .... **CLC 17**
See also Natti, (Mary) Lee
See also SAAS 3; SATA 1, 67
Kingsley, Charles 1819-1875 .... **NCLC 35**
See also DLB 21, 32, 163, 190; YABC 2
Kingsley, Sidney 1906-1995 .... **CLC 44**
See also CA 85-88; 147; DLB 7
Kingsolver, Barbara 1955- **CLC 55, 81; DAM POP**
See also AAYA 15; CA 129; 134; CANR 60; CDALBS; DLB 206; INT 134; MTCW 2
Kingston, Maxine (Ting Ting) Hong 1940- **CLC 12, 19, 58, 121; DAM MULT, NOV; WLCS**
See also AAYA 8; CA 69-72; CANR 13, 38, 74; CDALBS; DLB 173, 212; DLBY 80; INT CANR-13; MTCW 1, 2; SATA 53
Kinnell, Galway 1927- **CLC 1, 2, 3, 5, 13, 29; PC 26**
See also CA 9-12R; CANR 10, 34, 66; DLB 5; DLBY 87; INT CANR-34; MTCW 1, 2
Kinsella, Thomas 1928- .... **CLC 4, 19**
See also CA 17-20R; CANR 15; DLB 27; MTCW 1, 2
Kinsella, W(illiam) P(atrick) 1935- . **CLC 27, 43; DAC; DAM NOV, POP**
See also AAYA 7; CA 97-100; CAAS 7; CANR 21, 35, 66, 75; INT CANR-21; MTCW 1, 2
Kinsey, Alfred C(harles) 1894-1956 ... **TCLC 91**
See also CA 115; 170; MTCW 2
Kipling, (Joseph) Rudyard 1865-1936 **TCLC 8, 17; DA; DAB; DAC; DAM MST, POET; PC 3; SSC 5; WLC**
See also CA 105; 120; CANR 33; CDBLB 1890-1914; CLR 39; DLB 19, 34, 141, 156; MAICYA; MTCW 1, 2; SATA 100; YABC 2
Kirkup, James 1918- .... **CLC 1**
See also CA 1-4R; CAAS 4; CANR 2; DLB 27; SATA 12
Kirkwood, James 1930(?)-1989 .... **CLC 9**
See also AITN 2; CA 1-4R; 128; CANR 6, 40
Kirshner, Sidney
See Kingsley, Sidney
Kis, Danilo 1935-1989 .... **CLC 57**
See also CA 109; 118; 129; CANR 61; DLB 181; MTCW 1
Kivi, Aleksis 1834-1872 .... **NCLC 30**
Kizer, Carolyn (Ashley) 1925- . **CLC 15, 39, 80; DAM POET**
See also CA 65-68; CAAS 5; CANR 24, 70; DLB 5, 169; MTCW 2
Klabund 1890-1928 .... **TCLC 44**
See also CA 162; DLB 66
Klappert, Peter 1942- .... **CLC 57**
See also CA 33-36R; DLB 5
Klein, A(braham) M(oses) 1909-1972 .. **CLC 19; DAB; DAC; DAM MST**
See also CA 101; 37-40R; DLB 68
Klein, Norma 1938-1989 .... **CLC 30**
See also AAYA 2; CA 41-44R; 128; CANR 15, 37; CLR 2, 19; INT CANR-15; JRDA; MAICYA; SAAS 1; SATA 7, 57
Klein, T(heodore) E(ibon) D(onald) 1947- **CLC 34**
See also CA 119; CANR 44, 75
Kleist, Heinrich von 1777-1811 **NCLC 2, 37; DAM DRAM; SSC 22**
See also DLB 90
Klima, Ivan 1931- .... **CLC 56; DAM NOV**
See also CA 25-28R; CANR 17, 50
Klimentov, Andrei Platonovich 1899-1951
See Platonov, Andrei
See also CA 108
Klinger, Friedrich Maximilian von 1752-1831 **NCLC 1**
See also DLB 94
Klingsor the Magician
See Hartmann, Sadakichi
Klopstock, Friedrich Gottlieb 1724-1803 **NCLC 11**
See also DLB 97
Knapp, Caroline 1959- .... **CLC 99**
See also CA 154
Knebel, Fletcher 1911-1993 .... **CLC 14**
See also AITN 1; CA 1-4R; 140; CAAS 3; CANR 1, 36; SATA 36; SATA-Obit 75
Knickerbocker, Diedrich
See Irving, Washington
Knight, Etheridge 1931-1991 ... **CLC 40; BLC 2; DAM POET; PC 14**
See also BW 1, 3; CA 21-24R; 133; CANR 23; DLB 41; MTCW 2
Knight, Sarah Kemble 1666-1727 .... **LC 7**

See also DLB 24, 200

Knister, Raymond 1899-1932 .... **TCLC 56**
See also DLB 68

Knowles, John 1926-**CLC 1, 4, 10, 26; DA; DAC; DAM MST, NOV**
See also AAYA 10; CA 17-20R; CANR 40, 74, 76; CDALB 1968-1988; DLB 6; MTCW 1, 2; SATA 8, 89

Knox, Calvin M.
See Silverberg, Robert

Knox, John c. 1505-1572 .... **LC 37**
See also DLB 132

Knye, Cassandra
See Disch, Thomas M(ichael)

Koch, C(hristopher) J(ohn) 1932- .... **CLC 42**
See also CA 127

Koch, Christopher
See Koch, C(hristopher) J(ohn)

Koch, Kenneth 1925- **CLC 5, 8, 44; DAM POET**
See also CA 1-4R; CANR 6, 36, 57; DLB 5; INT CANR-36; MTCW 2; SATA 65

Kochanowski, Jan 1530-1584 .... **LC 10**

Kock, Charles Paul de 1794-1871 .... **NCLC 16**

Koda Shigeyuki 1867-1947
See Rohan, Koda
See also CA 121

Koestler, Arthur 1905-1983**CLC 1, 3, 6, 8, 15, 33**
See also CA 1-4R; 109; CANR 1, 33; CDBLB 1945-1960; DLBY 83; MTCW 1, 2

Kogawa, Joy Nozomi 1935- **CLC 78; DAC; DAM MST, MULT**
See also CA 101; CANR 19, 62; MTCW 2; SATA 99

Kohout, Pavel 1928- .... **CLC 13**
See also CA 45-48; CANR 3

Koizumi, Yakumo
See Hearn, (Patricio) Lafcadio (Tessima Carlos)

Kolmar, Gertrud 1894-1943 .... **TCLC 40**
See also CA 167

Komunyakaa, Yusef 1947- ... **CLC 86, 94; BLCS**
See also CA 147; DLB 120

Konrad, George
See Konrad, Gyoergy

Konrad, Gyoergy 1933- .... **CLC 4, 10, 73**
See also CA 85-88

Konwicki, Tadeusz 1926- .... **CLC 8, 28, 54, 117**
See also CA 101; CAAS 9; CANR 39, 59; MTCW 1

Koontz, Dean R(ay) 1945- .. **CLC 78; DAM NOV, POP**
See also AAYA 9; BEST 89:3, 90:2; CA 108; CANR 19, 36, 52; MTCW 1; SATA 92

Kopernik, Mikolaj
See Copernicus, Nicolaus

Kopit, Arthur (Lee) 1937- **CLC 1, 18, 33; DAM DRAM**
See also AITN 1; CA 81-84; CABS 3; DLB 7; MTCW 1

Kops, Bernard 1926- .... **CLC 4**
See also CA 5-8R; DLB 13

Kornbluth, C(yril) M. 1923-1958 .... **TCLC 8**
See also CA 105; 160; DLB 8

Korolenko, V. G.
See Korolenko, Vladimir Galaktionovich

Korolenko, Vladimir
See Korolenko, Vladimir Galaktionovich

Korolenko, Vladimir G.
See Korolenko, Vladimir Galaktionovich

Korolenko, Vladimir Galaktionovich 1853-1921 **TCLC 22**
See also CA 121

Korzybski, Alfred (Habdank Skarbek) 1879-1950 **TCLC 61**
See also CA 123; 160

Kosinski, Jerzy (Nikodem) 1933-1991 **CLC 1, 2, 3, 6, 10, 15, 53, 70; DAM NOV**
See also CA 17-20R; 134; CANR 9, 46; DLB 2; DLBY 82; MTCW 1, 2

Kostelanetz, Richard (Cory) 1940- .... **CLC 28**
See also CA 13-16R; CAAS 8; CANR 38, 77

Kostrowitzki, Wilhelm Apollinaris de 1880-1918
See Apollinaire, Guillaume
See also CA 104

Kotlowitz, Robert 1924- .... **CLC 4**
See also CA 33-36R; CANR 36

Kotzebue, August (Friedrich Ferdinand) von 1761-1819 .... **NCLC 25**
See also DLB 94

Kotzwinkle, William 1938- .... **CLC 5, 14, 35**
See also CA 45-48; CANR 3, 44; CLR 6; DLB 173; MAICYA; SATA 24, 70

Kowna, Stancy
See Szymborska, Wislawa

Kozol, Jonathan 1936- .... **CLC 17**
See also CA 61-64; CANR 16, 45

Kozoll, Michael 1940(?)- .... **CLC 35**

Kramer, Kathryn 19(?)- .... **CLC 34**

Kramer, Larry 1935- **CLC 42; DAM POP; DC 8**
See also CA 124; 126; CANR 60

Krasicki, Ignacy 1735-1801 .... **NCLC 8**

Krasinski, Zygmunt 1812-1859 .... **NCLC 4**

Kraus, Karl 1874-1936 .... **TCLC 5**
See also CA 104; DLB 118

Kreve (Mickevicius), Vincas 1882-1954**TCLC 27**
See also CA 170

Kristeva, Julia 1941- .... **CLC 77**
See also CA 154

Kristofferson, Kris 1936- .... **CLC 26**
See also CA 104

Krizanc, John 1956- .... **CLC 57**

Krleza, Miroslav 1893-1981 .... **CLC 8, 114**
See also CA 97-100; 105; CANR 50; DLB 147

Kroetsch, Robert 1927-**CLC 5, 23, 57; DAC; DAM POET**
See also CA 17-20R; CANR 8, 38; DLB 53; MTCW 1

Kroetz, Franz
See Kroetz, Franz Xaver

Kroetz, Franz Xaver 1946- .... **CLC 41**
See also CA 130

Kroker, Arthur (W.) 1945- .... **CLC 77**
See also CA 161

Kropotkin, Peter (Aleksieevich) 1842-1921**TCLC 36**
See also CA 119

Krotkov, Yuri 1917- .... **CLC 19**
See also CA 102

Krumb
See Crumb, R(obert)

Krumgold, Joseph (Quincy) 1908-1980 **CLC 12**
See also CA 9-12R; 101; CANR 7; MAICYA; SATA 1, 48; SATA-Obit 23

Krumwitz
See Crumb, R(obert)

Krutch, Joseph Wood 1893-1970 .... **CLC 24**
See also CA 1-4R; 25-28R; CANR 4; DLB 63, 206

Krutzch, Gus
See Eliot, T(homas) S(tearns)

Krylov, Ivan Andreevich 1768(?)-1844 .. **NCLC 1**
See also DLB 150

Kubin, Alfred (Leopold Isidor) 1877-1959 **TCLC 23**
See also CA 112; 149; DLB 81

Kubrick, Stanley 1928-1999 .... **CLC 16**
See also AAYA 30; CA 81-84; 177; CANR 33; DLB 26

Kumin, Maxine (Winokur) 1925-**CLC 5, 13, 28; DAM POET; PC 15**
See also AITN 2; CA 1-4R; CAAS 8; CANR 1, 21, 69; DLB 5; MTCW 1, 2; SATA 12

Kundera, Milan 1929-**CLC 4, 9, 19, 32, 68, 115; DAM NOV; SSC 24**
See also AAYA 2; CA 85-88; CANR 19, 52, 74; MTCW 1, 2

Kunene, Mazisi (Raymond) 1930- .... **CLC 85**
See also BW 1, 3; CA 125; CANR 81; DLB 117

Kunitz, Stanley (Jasspon) 1905-**CLC 6, 11, 14; PC 19**
See also CA 41-44R; CANR 26, 57; DLB 48; INT CANR-26; MTCW 1, 2

Kunze, Reiner 1933- .... **CLC 10**
See also CA 93-96; DLB 75

Kuprin, Aleksandr Ivanovich 1870-1938**TCLC 5**
See also CA 104

Kureishi, Hanif 1954(?)- .... **CLC 64**
See also CA 139; DLB 194

Kurosawa, Akira 1910-1998 **CLC 16, 119; DAM MULT**
See also AAYA 11; CA 101; 170; CANR 46

Kushner, Tony 1957(?)-**CLC 81; DAM DRAM; DC 10**
See also CA 144; CANR 74; MTCW 2

Kuttner, Henry 1915-1958 .... **TCLC 10**
See also Vance, Jack
See also CA 107; 157; DLB 8

Kuzma, Greg 1944- .... **CLC 7**
See also CA 33-36R; CANR 70

Kuzmin, Mikhail 1872(?)-1936 .... **TCLC 40**
See also CA 170

Kyd, Thomas 1558-1594**LC 22; DAM DRAM; DC 3**
See also DLB 62

Kyprianos, Iossif
See Samarakis, Antonis

La Bruyere, Jean de 1645-1696 .... **LC 17**

Lacan, Jacques (Marie Emile) 1901-1981**CLC 75**
See also CA 121; 104

Laclos, Pierre Ambroise Francois Choderlos de 1741-1803 .... **NCLC 4**

La Colere, Francois
See Aragon, Louis

Lacolere, Francois
See Aragon, Louis

La Deshabilleuse
See Simenon, Georges (Jacques Christian)

Lady Gregory
See Gregory, Isabella Augusta (Persse)

Lady of Quality, A
See Bagnold, Enid

La Fayette, Marie (Madelaine Pioche de la Vergne Comtes 1634-1693 .... **LC 2**

Lafayette, Rene
See Hubbard, L(afayette) Ron(ald)

Laforgue, Jules 1860-1887 **NCLC 5, 53; PC 14; SSC 20**

Lagerkvist, Paer (Fabian) 1891-1974 **CLC 7, 10, 13, 54; DAM DRAM, NOV**
See also Lagerkvist, Par
See also CA 85-88; 49-52; MTCW 1, 2

Lagerkvist, Par .... **SSC 12**
See also Lagerkvist, Paer (Fabian)
See also MTCW 2

Lagerloef, Selma (Ottiliana Lovisa) 1858-1940 **TCLC 4, 36**
See also Lagerlof, Selma (Ottiliana Lovisa)
See also CA 108; MTCW 2; SATA 15

Lagerlof, Selma (Ottiliana Lovisa)
See Lagerloef, Selma (Ottiliana Lovisa)
See also CLR 7; SATA 15

La Guma, (Justin) Alex(ander) 1925-1985 .. **CLC 19; BLCS; DAM NOV**
See also BW 1, 3; CA 49-52; 118; CANR 25, 81; DLB 117; MTCW 1, 2

Laidlaw, A. K.
See Grieve, C(hristopher) M(urray)

Lainez, Manuel Mujica
See Mujica Lainez, Manuel
See also HW 1

Laing, R(onald) D(avid) 1927-1989 .... **CLC 95**
See also CA 107; 129; CANR 34; MTCW 1

Lamartine, Alphonse (Marie Louis Prat) de 1790-1869**NCLC 11; DAM POET; PC 16**
Lamb, Charles 1775-1834..... **NCLC 10; DA; DAB; DAC; DAM MST; WLC**
See also CDBLB 1789-1832; DLB 93, 107, 163; SATA 17
Lamb, Lady Caroline 1785-1828 .... **NCLC 38**
See also DLB 116
Lamming, George (William) 1927-**CLC 2, 4, 66; BLC 2; DAM MULT**
See also BW 2, 3; CA 85-88; CANR 26, 76; DLB 125; MTCW 1, 2
L'Amour, Louis (Dearborn) 1908-1988 **C L C 25, 55; DAM NOV, POP**
See also AAYA 16; AITN 2; BEST 89:2; CA 1-4R; 125; CANR 3, 25, 40; DLB 206; DLBY 80; MTCW 1, 2
Lampedusa, Giuseppe (Tomasi) di 1896-1957 **TCLC 13**
See also Tomasi di Lampedusa, Giuseppe
See also CA 164; DLB 177; MTCW 2
Lampman, Archibald 1861-1899 .... **NCLC 25**
See also DLB 92
Lancaster, Bruce 1896-1963 .... **CLC 36**
See also CA 9-10; CANR 70; CAP 1; SATA 9
Lanchester, John .... **CLC 99**
Landau, Mark Alexandrovich
See Aldanov, Mark (Alexandrovich)
Landau-Aldanov, Mark Alexandrovich
See Aldanov, Mark (Alexandrovich)
Landis, Jerry
See Simon, Paul (Frederick)
Landis, John 1950- .... **CLC 26**
See also CA 112; 122
Landolfi, Tommaso 1908-1979 .... **CLC 11, 49**
See also CA 127; 117; DLB 177
Landon, Letitia Elizabeth 1802-1838 ... **NCLC 15**
See also DLB 96
Landor, Walter Savage 1775-1864 ...... **NCLC 14**
See also DLB 93, 107
Landwirth, Heinz 1927-
See Lind, Jakov
See also CA 9-12R; CANR 7
Lane, Patrick 1939- .... **CLC 25; DAM POET**
See also CA 97-100; CANR 54; DLB 53; INT 97-100
Lang, Andrew 1844-1912 .... **TCLC 16**
See also CA 114; 137; DLB 98, 141, 184; MAICYA; SATA 16
Lang, Fritz 1890-1976 .... **CLC 20, 103**
See also CA 77-80; 69-72; CANR 30
Lange, John
See Crichton, (John) Michael
Langer, Elinor 1939- .... **CLC 34**
See also CA 121
Langland, William 1330(?)-1400(?) **LC 19; DA; DAB; DAC; DAM MST, POET**
See also DLB 146
Langstaff, Launcelot
See Irving, Washington
Lanier, Sidney 1842-1881 **NCLC 6; DAM POET**
See also DLB 64; DLBD 13; MAICYA; SATA 18
Lanyer, Aemilia 1569-1645 .... **LC 10, 30**
See also DLB 121
Lao-Tzu
See Lao Tzu
Lao Tzu fl. 6th cent. B.C.- .... **CMLC 7**
Lapine, James (Elliot) 1949- .... **CLC 39**
See also CA 123; 130; CANR 54; INT 130
Larbaud, Valery (Nicolas) 1881-1957 .... **TCLC 9**
See also CA 106; 152
Lardner, Ring
See Lardner, Ring(gold) W(ilmer)
Lardner, Ring W., Jr.
See Lardner, Ring(gold) W(ilmer)
Lardner, Ring(gold) W(ilmer) 1885-1933**TCLC 2, 14; SSC 32**
See also CA 104; 131; CDALB 1917-1929; DLB 11, 25, 86; DLBD 16; MTCW 1, 2
Laredo, Betty
See Codrescu, Andrei
Larkin, Maia
See Wojciechowska, Maia (Teresa)
Larkin, Philip (Arthur) 1922-1985**CLC 3, 5, 8, 9, 13, 18, 33, 39, 64; DAB; DAM MST, POET; PC 21**
See also CA 5-8R; 117; CANR 24, 62; CDBLB 1960 to Present; DLB 27; MTCW 1, 2
Larra (y Sanchez de Castro), Mariano Jose de 1809-1837 .... **NCLC 17**
Larsen, Eric 1941- .... **CLC 55**
See also CA 132
Larsen, Nella 1891-1964 **CLC 37; BLC 2; DAM MULT**
See also BW 1; CA 125; DLB 51
Larson, Charles R(aymond) 1938- .... **CLC 31**
See also CA 53-56; CANR 4
Larson, Jonathan 1961-1996 .... **CLC 99**
See also AAYA 28; CA 156
Las Casas, Bartolome de 1474-1566 .... **LC 31**
Lasch, Christopher 1932-1994 .... **CLC 102**
See also CA 73-76; 144; CANR 25; MTCW 1, 2
Lasker-Schueler, Else 1869-1945 .... **TCLC 57**
See also DLB 66, 124
Laski, Harold 1893-1950 .... **TCLC 79**
Latham, Jean Lee 1902-1995 .... **CLC 12**
See also AITN 1; CA 5-8R; CANR 7; CLR 50; MAICYA; SATA 2, 68
Latham, Mavis
See Clark, Mavis Thorpe
Lathen, Emma .... **CLC 2**
See also Hennissart, Martha; Latsis, Mary J(ane)
Lathrop, Francis
See Leiber, Fritz (Reuter, Jr.)
Latsis, Mary J(ane) 1927(?)-1997
See Lathen, Emma
See also CA 85-88; 162
Lattimore, Richmond (Alexander) 1906-1984**CLC 3**
See also CA 1-4R; 112; CANR 1
Laughlin, James 1914-1997 .... **CLC 49**
See also CA 21-24R; 162; CAAS 22; CANR 9, 47; DLB 48; DLBY 96, 97
Laurence, (Jean) Margaret (Wemyss) 1926-1987 **CLC 3, 6, 13, 50, 62; DAC; DAM MST; SSC 7**
See also CA 5-8R; 121; CANR 33; DLB 53; MTCW 1, 2; SATA-Obit 50
Laurent, Antoine 1952- .... **CLC 50**
Lauscher, Hermann
See Hesse, Hermann
Lautreamont, Comte de 1846-1870**NCLC 12; SSC 14**
Laverty, Donald
See Blish, James (Benjamin)
Lavin, Mary 1912-1996 .... **CLC 4, 18, 99; SSC 4**
See also CA 9-12R; 151; CANR 33; DLB 15; MTCW 1
Lavond, Paul Dennis
See Kornbluth, C(yril) M.; Pohl, Frederik
Lawler, Raymond Evenor 1922- .... **CLC 58**
See also CA 103
Lawrence, D(avid) H(erbert Richards) 1885-1930 **TCLC 2, 9, 16, 33, 48, 61, 93; DA; DAB; DAC; DAM MST, NOV, POET; SSC 4, 19; WLC**
See also CA 104; 121; CDBLB 1914-1945; DLB 10, 19, 36, 98, 162, 195; MTCW 1, 2
Lawrence, T(homas) E(dward) 1888-1935 **TCLC 18**
See also Dale, Colin
See also CA 115; 167; DLB 195
Lawrence of Arabia
See Lawrence, T(homas) E(dward)
Lawson, Henry (Archibald Hertzberg) 1867-1922 .... **TCLC 27; SSC 18**
See also CA 120
Lawton, Dennis
See Faust, Frederick (Schiller)
Laxness, Halldor .... **CLC 25**
See also Gudjonsson, Halldor Kiljan
Layamon fl. c. 1200- .... **CMLC 10**
See also DLB 146
Laye, Camara 1928-1980**CLC 4, 38; BLC 2; DAM MULT**
See also BW 1; CA 85-88; 97-100; CANR 25; MTCW 1, 2
Layton, Irving (Peter) 1912- .. **CLC 2, 15; DAC; DAM MST, POET**
See also CA 1-4R; CANR 2, 33, 43, 66; DLB 88; MTCW 1, 2
Lazarus, Emma 1849-1887 .... **NCLC 8**
Lazarus, Felix
See Cable, George Washington
Lazarus, Henry
See Slavitt, David R(ytman)
Lea, Joan
See Neufeld, John (Arthur)
Leacock, Stephen (Butler) 1869-1944 . **TCLC 2; DAC; DAM MST**
See also CA 104; 141; CANR 80; DLB 92; MTCW 2
Lear, Edward 1812-1888 .... **NCLC 3**
See also CLR 1; DLB 32, 163, 166; MAICYA; SATA 18, 100
Lear, Norman (Milton) 1922- .... **CLC 12**
See also CA 73-76
Leautaud, Paul 1872-1956 .... **TCLC 83**
See also DLB 65
Leavis, F(rank) R(aymond) 1895-1978 .. **CLC 24**
See also CA 21-24R; 77-80; CANR 44; MTCW 1, 2
Leavitt, David 1961- .... **CLC 34; DAM POP**
See also CA 116; 122; CANR 50, 62; DLB 130; INT 122; MTCW 2
Leblanc, Maurice (Marie Emile) 1864-1941**TCLC 49**
See also CA 110
Lebowitz, Fran(ces Ann) 1951(?)- .... **CLC 11, 36**
See also CA 81-84; CANR 14, 60, 70; INT CANR-14; MTCW 1
Lebrecht, Peter
See Tieck, (Johann) Ludwig
le Carre, John .... **CLC 3, 5, 9, 15, 28**
See also Cornwell, David (John Moore)
See also BEST 89:4; CDBLB 1960 to Present; DLB 87; MTCW 2
Le Clezio, J(ean) M(arie) G(ustave) 1940- . **C L C 31**
See also CA 116; 128; DLB 83
Leconte de Lisle, Charles-Marie-Rene 1818-1894 **NCLC 29**
Le Coq, Monsieur
See Simenon, Georges (Jacques Christian)
Leduc, Violette 1907-1972 .... **CLC 22**
See also CA 13-14; 33-36R; CANR 69; CAP 1
Ledwidge, Francis 1887(?)-1917 .... **TCLC 23**
See also CA 123; DLB 20
Lee, Andrea 1953-**CLC 36; BLC 2; DAM MULT**
See also BW 1, 3; CA 125
Lee, Andrew
See Auchincloss, Louis (Stanton)
Lee, Chang-rae 1965- .... **CLC 91**
See also CA 148
Lee, Don L. .... **CLC 2**
See also Madhubuti, Haki R.
Lee, George W(ashington) 1894-1976 . **CLC 52; BLC 2; DAM MULT**
See also BW 1; CA 125; DLB 51
Lee, (Nelle) Harper 1926-**CLC 12, 60; DA; DAB; DAC; DAM MST, NOV; WLC**

See also AAYA 13; CA 13-16R; CANR 51; CDALB 1941-1968; DLB 6; MTCW 1, 2; SATA 11

Lee, Helen Elaine 1959(?)- .... **CLC 86**
See also CA 148

Lee, Julian
See Latham, Jean Lee

Lee, Larry
See Lee, Lawrence

Lee, Laurie 1914-1997**CLC 90; DAB; DAM POP**
See also CA 77-80; 158; CANR 33, 73; DLB 27; MTCW 1

Lee, Lawrence 1941-1990 .... **CLC 34**
See also CA 131; CANR 43

Lee, Li-Young 1957- .... **PC 24**
See also CA 153; DLB 165

Lee, Manfred B(ennington) 1905-1971 .. **CLC 11**
See also Queen, Ellery
See also CA 1-4R; 29-32R; CANR 2; DLB 137

Lee, Shelton Jackson 1957(?)-**CLC 105; BLCS; DAM MULT**
See also Lee, Spike
See also BW 2, 3; CA 125; CANR 42

Lee, Spike
See Lee, Shelton Jackson
See also AAYA 4, 29

Lee, Stan 1922- .... **CLC 17**
See also AAYA 5; CA 108; 111; INT 111

Lee, Tanith 1947- .... **CLC 46**
See also AAYA 15; CA 37-40R; CANR 53; SATA 8, 88

Lee, Vernon .... **TCLC 5; SSC 33**
See also Paget, Violet
See also DLB 57, 153, 156, 174, 178

Lee, William
See Burroughs, William S(eward)

Lee, Willy
See Burroughs, William S(eward)

Lee-Hamilton, Eugene (Jacob) 1845-1907 **TCLC 22**
See also CA 117

Leet, Judith 1935- .... **CLC 11**

Le Fanu, Joseph Sheridan 1814-1873**NCLC 9, 58; DAM POP; SSC 14**
See also DLB 21, 70, 159, 178

Leffland, Ella 1931- .... **CLC 19**
See also CA 29-32R; CANR 35, 78; DLBY 84; INT CANR-35; SATA 65

Leger, Alexis
See Leger, (Marie-Rene Auguste) Alexis Saint-Leger

Leger, (Marie-Rene Auguste) Alexis Saint-Leger 1887-1975**CLC 4, 11, 46; DAM POET; PC 23**
See also CA 13-16R; 61-64; CANR 43; MTCW 1

Leger, Saintleger
See Leger, (Marie-Rene Auguste) Alexis Saint-Leger

Le Guin, Ursula K(roeber) 1929- **CLC 8, 13, 22, 45, 71; DAB; DAC; DAM MST, POP; SSC 12**
See also AAYA 9, 27; AITN 1; CA 21-24R; CANR 9, 32, 52, 74; CDALB 1968-1988; CLR 3, 28; DLB 8, 52; INT CANR-32; JRDA; MAICYA; MTCW 1, 2; SATA 4, 52, 99

Lehmann, Rosamond (Nina) 1901-1990 .. **CLC 5**
See also CA 77-80; 131; CANR 8, 73; DLB 15; MTCW 2

Leiber, Fritz (Reuter, Jr.) 1910-1992 .... **CLC 25**
See also CA 45-48; 139; CANR 2, 40; DLB 8; MTCW 1, 2; SATA 45; SATA-Obit 73

Leibniz, Gottfried Wilhelm von 1646-1716**LC 35**
See also DLB 168

Leimbach, Martha 1963-
See Leimbach, Marti
See also CA 130

Leimbach, Marti .... **CLC 65**
See also Leimbach, Martha

Leino, Eino .... **TCLC 24**
See also Loennbohm, Armas Eino Leopold

Leiris, Michel (Julien) 1901-1990 .... **CLC 61**
See also CA 119; 128; 132

Leithauser, Brad 1953- .... **CLC 27**
See also CA 107; CANR 27, 81; DLB 120

Lelchuk, Alan 1938- .... **CLC 5**
See also CA 45-48; CAAS 20; CANR 1, 70

Lem, Stanislaw 1921- .... **CLC 8, 15, 40**
See also CA 105; CAAS 1; CANR 32; MTCW 1

Lemann, Nancy 1956- .... **CLC 39**
See also CA 118; 136

Lemonnier, (Antoine Louis) Camille 1844-1913 **TCLC 22**
See also CA 121

Lenau, Nikolaus 1802-1850 .... **NCLC 16**

L'Engle, Madeleine (Camp Franklin) 1918- **CLC 12; DAM POP**
See also AAYA 28; AITN 2; CA 1-4R; CANR 3, 21, 39, 66; CLR 1, 14, 57; DLB 52; JRDA; MAICYA; MTCW 1, 2; SAAS 15; SATA 1, 27, 75

Lengyel, Jozsef 1896-1975 .... **CLC 7**
See also CA 85-88; 57-60; CANR 71

Lenin 1870-1924
See Lenin, V. I.
See also CA 121; 168

Lenin, V. I. .... **TCLC 67**
See also Lenin

Lennon, John (Ono) 1940-1980 .... **CLC 12, 35**
See also CA 102

Lennox, Charlotte Ramsay 1729(?)-1804**NCLC 23**
See also DLB 39

Lentricchia, Frank (Jr.) 1940- .... **CLC 34**
See also CA 25-28R; CANR 19

Lenz, Siegfried 1926- .... **CLC 27; SSC 33**
See also CA 89-92; CANR 80; DLB 75

Leonard, Elmore (John, Jr.) 1925- . **CLC 28, 34, 71, 120; DAM POP**
See also AAYA 22; AITN 1; BEST 89:1, 90:4; CA 81-84; CANR 12, 28, 53, 76; DLB 173; INT CANR-28; MTCW 1, 2

Leonard, Hugh .... **CLC 19**
See also Byrne, John Keyes
See also DLB 13

Leonov, Leonid (Maximovich) 1899-1994**CLC 92; DAM NOV**
See also CA 129; CANR 74, 76; MTCW 1, 2

Leopardi, (Conte) Giacomo 1798-1837 **NCLC 22**

Le Reveler
See Artaud, Antonin (Marie Joseph)

Lerman, Eleanor 1952- .... **CLC 9**
See also CA 85-88; CANR 69

Lerman, Rhoda 1936- .... **CLC 56**
See also CA 49-52; CANR 70

Lermontov, Mikhail Yuryevich 1814-1841 **NCLC 47; PC 18**
See also DLB 205

Leroux, Gaston 1868-1927 .... **TCLC 25**
See also CA 108; 136; CANR 69; SATA 65

Lesage, Alain-Rene 1668-1747 .... **LC 2, 28**

Leskov, Nikolai (Semyonovich) 1831-1895**NCLC 25; SSC 34**

Lessing, Doris (May) 1919-**CLC 1, 2, 3, 6, 10, 15, 22, 40, 94; DA; DAB; DAC; DAM MST, NOV; SSC 6; WLCS**
See also CA 9-12R; CAAS 14; CANR 33, 54, 76; CDBLB 1960 to Present; DLB 15, 139; DLBY 85; MTCW 1, 2

Lessing, Gotthold Ephraim 1729-1781 .... **LC 8**
See also DLB 97

Lester, Richard 1932- .... **CLC 20**

Lever, Charles (James) 1806-1872 ...... **NCLC 23**
See also DLB 21

Leverson, Ada 1865(?)-1936(?) .... **TCLC 18**
See also Elaine
See also CA 117; DLB 153

Levertov, Denise 1923-1997**CLC 1, 2, 3, 5, 8, 15, 28, 66; DAM POET; PC 11**
See also CA 1-4R; 163; CAAS 19; CANR 3, 29, 50; CDALBS; DLB 5, 165; INT CANR-29; MTCW 1, 2

Levi, Jonathan .... **CLC 76**

Levi, Peter (Chad Tigar) 1931- .... **CLC 41**
See also CA 5-8R; CANR 34, 80; DLB 40

Levi, Primo 1919-1987 ...... **CLC 37, 50; SSC 12**
See also CA 13-16R; 122; CANR 12, 33, 61, 70; DLB 177; MTCW 1, 2

Levin, Ira 1929- .... **CLC 3, 6; DAM POP**
See also CA 21-24R; CANR 17, 44, 74; MTCW 1, 2; SATA 66

Levin, Meyer 1905-1981 .... **CLC 7; DAM POP**
See also AITN 1; CA 9-12R; 104; CANR 15; DLB 9, 28; DLBY 81; SATA 21; SATA-Obit 27

Levine, Norman 1924- .... **CLC 54**
See also CA 73-76; CAAS 23; CANR 14, 70; DLB 88

Levine, Philip 1928- **CLC 2, 4, 5, 9, 14, 33, 118; DAM POET; PC 22**
See also CA 9-12R; CANR 9, 37, 52; DLB 5

Levinson, Deirdre 1931- .... **CLC 49**
See also CA 73-76; CANR 70

Levi-Strauss, Claude 1908- .... **CLC 38**
See also CA 1-4R; CANR 6, 32, 57; MTCW 1, 2

Levitin, Sonia (Wolff) 1934- .... **CLC 17**
See also AAYA 13; CA 29-32R; CANR 14, 32, 79; CLR 53; JRDA; MAICYA; SAAS 2; SATA 4, 68

Levon, O. U.
See Kesey, Ken (Elton)

Levy, Amy 1861-1889 .... **NCLC 59**
See also DLB 156

Lewes, George Henry 1817-1878 .... **NCLC 25**
See also DLB 55, 144

Lewis, Alun 1915-1944 .... **TCLC 3**
See also CA 104; DLB 20, 162

Lewis, C. Day
See Day Lewis, C(ecil)

Lewis, C(live) S(taples) 1898-1963**CLC 1, 3, 6, 14, 27; DA; DAB; DAC; DAM MST, NOV, POP; WLC**
See also AAYA 3; CA 81-84; CANR 33, 71; CDBLB 1945-1960; CLR 3, 27; DLB 15, 100, 160; JRDA; MAICYA; MTCW 1, 2; SATA 13, 100

Lewis, Janet 1899-1998 .... **CLC 41**
See also Winters, Janet Lewis
See also CA 9-12R; 172; CANR 29, 63; CAP 1; DLBY 87

Lewis, Matthew Gregory 1775-1818**NCLC 11, 62**
See also DLB 39, 158, 178

Lewis, (Harry) Sinclair 1885-1951 **TCLC 4, 13, 23, 39; DA; DAB; DAC; DAM MST, NOV; WLC**
See also CA 104; 133; CDALB 1917-1929; DLB 9, 102; DLBD 1; MTCW 1, 2

Lewis, (Percy) Wyndham 1882(?)-1957**TCLC 2, 9; SSC 34**
See also CA 104; 157; DLB 15; MTCW 2

Lewisohn, Ludwig 1883-1955 .... **TCLC 19**
See also CA 107; DLB 4, 9, 28, 102

Lewton, Val 1904-1951 .... **TCLC 76**

Leyner, Mark 1956- .... **CLC 92**
See also CA 110; CANR 28, 53; MTCW 2

Lezama Lima, Jose 1910-1976 . **CLC 4, 10, 101; DAM MULT; HLCS 2**
See also CA 77-80; CANR 71; DLB 113; HW 1, 2

L'Heureux, John (Clarke) 1934- .... **CLC 52**
See also CA 13-16R; CANR 23, 45

Liddell, C. H.
See Kuttner, Henry

Lie, Jonas (Lauritz Idemil) 1833-1908(?)**TCLC 5**
See also CA 115

Lieber, Joel 1937-1971 .... **CLC 6**

See also CA 73-76; 29-32R
Lieber, Stanley Martin
See Lee, Stan
Lieberman, Laurence (James) 1935- **CLC 4, 36**
See also CA 17-20R; CANR 8, 36
Lieh Tzu fl. 7th cent. B.C.-5th cent. B.C.**CMLC 27**
Lieksman, Anders
See Haavikko, Paavo Juhani
Li Fei-kan 1904-
See Pa Chin
See also CA 105
Lifton, Robert Jay 1926- .... **CLC 67**
See also CA 17-20R; CANR 27, 78; INT CANR-27; SATA 66
Lightfoot, Gordon 1938- .... **CLC 26**
See also CA 109
Lightman, Alan P(aige) 1948- .... **CLC 81**
See also CA 141; CANR 63
Ligotti, Thomas (Robert) 1953-**CLC 44; SSC 16**
See also CA 123; CANR 49
Li Ho 791-817 .... **PC 13**
Liliencron, (Friedrich Adolf Axel) Detlev von 1844-1909 .... **TCLC 18**
See also CA 117
Lilly, William 1602-1681 .... **LC 27**
Lima, Jose Lezama
See Lezama Lima, Jose
Lima Barreto, Afonso Henrique de 1881-1922 **TCLC 23**
See also CA 117
Limonov, Edward 1944- .... **CLC 67**
See also CA 137
Lin, Frank
See Atherton, Gertrude (Franklin Horn)
Lincoln, Abraham 1809-1865 .... **NCLC 18**
Lind, Jakov .... **CLC 1, 2, 4, 27, 82**
See also Landwirth, Heinz
See also CAAS 4
Lindbergh, Anne (Spencer) Morrow 1906- **CLC 82; DAM NOV**
See also CA 17-20R; CANR 16, 73; MTCW 1, 2; SATA 33
Lindsay, David 1878-1945 .... **TCLC 15**
See also CA 113
Lindsay, (Nicholas) Vachel 1879-1931 **TCLC 17; DA; DAC; DAM MST, POET; PC 23; WLC**
See also CA 114; 135; CANR 79; CDALB 1865-1917; DLB 54; SATA 40
Linke-Poot
See Doeblin, Alfred
Linney, Romulus 1930- .... **CLC 51**
See also CA 1-4R; CANR 40, 44, 79
Linton, Eliza Lynn 1822-1898 .... **NCLC 41**
See also DLB 18
Li Po 701-763 .... **CMLC 2**
Lipsius, Justus 1547-1606 .... **LC 16**
Lipsyte, Robert (Michael) 1938- ... **CLC 21; DA; DAC; DAM MST, NOV**
See also AAYA 7; CA 17-20R; CANR 8, 57; CLR 23; JRDA; MAICYA; SATA 5, 68
Lish, Gordon (Jay) 1934- .... **CLC 45; SSC 18**
See also CA 113; 117; CANR 79; DLB 130; INT 117
Lispector, Clarice 1925(?)-1977**CLC 43; HLCS 2; SSC 34**
See also CA 139; 116; CANR 71; DLB 113; HW 2
Littell, Robert 1935(?)- .... **CLC 42**
See also CA 109; 112; CANR 64
Little, Malcolm 1925-1965
See Malcolm X
See also BW 1, 3; CA 125; 111; DA; DAB; DAC; DAM MST, MULT; MTCW 1, 2
Littlewit, Humphrey Gent.
See Lovecraft, H(oward) P(hillips)
Litwos
See Sienkiewicz, Henryk (Adam Alexander Pius)
Liu, E 1857-1909 .... **TCLC 15**
See also CA 115
Lively, Penelope (Margaret) 1933- **CLC 32, 50; DAM NOV**
See also CA 41-44R; CANR 29, 67, 79; CLR 7; DLB 14, 161, 207; JRDA; MAICYA; MTCW 1, 2; SATA 7, 60, 101
Livesay, Dorothy (Kathleen) 1909-**CLC 4, 15, 79; DAC; DAM MST, POET**
See also AITN 2; CA 25-28R; CAAS 8; CANR 36, 67; DLB 68; MTCW 1
Livy c. 59B.C.-c. 17 .... **CMLC 11**
See also DLB 211
Lizardi, Jose Joaquin Fernandez de 1776-1827 **NCLC 30**
Llewellyn, Richard
See Llewellyn Lloyd, Richard Dafydd Vivian
See also DLB 15
Llewellyn Lloyd, Richard Dafydd Vivian 1906-1983 **CLC 7, 80**
See also Llewellyn, Richard
See also CA 53-56; 111; CANR 7, 71; SATA 11; SATA-Obit 37
Llosa, (Jorge) Mario (Pedro) Vargas
See Vargas Llosa, (Jorge) Mario (Pedro)
Lloyd, Manda
See Mander, (Mary) Jane
Lloyd Webber, Andrew 1948-
See Webber, Andrew Lloyd
See also AAYA 1; CA 116; 149; DAM DRAM; SATA 56
Llull, Ramon c. 1235-c. 1316 .... **CMLC 12**
Lobb, Ebenezer
See Upward, Allen
Locke, Alain (Le Roy) 1886-1954**TCLC 43; BLCS**
See also BW 1, 3; CA 106; 124; CANR 79; DLB 51
Locke, John 1632-1704 .... **LC 7, 35**
See also DLB 101
Locke-Elliott, Sumner
See Elliott, Sumner Locke
Lockhart, John Gibson 1794-1854 .... **NCLC 6**
See also DLB 110, 116, 144
Lodge, David (John) 1935- .. **CLC 36; DAM POP**
See also BEST 90:1; CA 17-20R; CANR 19, 53; DLB 14, 194; INT CANR-19; MTCW 1, 2
Lodge, Thomas 1558-1625 .... **LC 41**
Lodge, Thomas 1558-1625 .... **LC 41**
See also DLB 172
Loennbohm, Armas Eino Leopold 1878-1926
See Leino, Eino
See also CA 123
Loewinsohn, Ron(ald William) 1937- ... **CLC 52**
See also CA 25-28R; CANR 71
Logan, Jake
See Smith, Martin Cruz
Logan, John (Burton) 1923-1987 .... **CLC 5**
See also CA 77-80; 124; CANR 45; DLB 5
Lo Kuan-chung 1330(?)-1400(?) .... **LC 12**
Lombard, Nap
See Johnson, Pamela Hansford
London, Jack ...... **TCLC 9, 15, 39; SSC 4; WLC**
See also London, John Griffith
See also AAYA 13; AITN 2; CDALB 1865-1917; DLB 8, 12, 78, 212; SATA 18
London, John Griffith 1876-1916
See London, Jack
See also CA 110; 119; CANR 73; DA; DAB; DAC; DAM MST, NOV; JRDA; MAICYA; MTCW 1, 2
Long, Emmett
See Leonard, Elmore (John, Jr.)
Longbaugh, Harry
See Goldman, William (W.)
Longfellow, Henry Wadsworth 1807-1882 **NCLC 2, 45; DA; DAB; DAC; DAM MST, POET; WLCS**
See also CDALB 1640-1865; DLB 1, 59; SATA 19
Longinus c. 1st cent. - .... **CMLC 27**
See also DLB 176
Longley, Michael 1939- .... **CLC 29**
See also CA 102; DLB 40
Longus fl. c. 2nd cent. - .... **CMLC 7**
Longway, A. Hugh
See Lang, Andrew
Lonnrot, Elias 1802-1884 .... **NCLC 53**
Lopate, Phillip 1943- .... **CLC 29**
See also CA 97-100; DLBY 80; INT 97-100
Lopez Portillo (y Pacheco), Jose 1920- . **CLC 46**
See also CA 129; HW 1
Lopez y Fuentes, Gregorio 1897(?)-1966**CLC 32**
See also CA 131; HW 1
Lorca, Federico Garcia
See Garcia Lorca, Federico
Lord, Bette Bao 1938- .... **CLC 23**
See also BEST 90:3; CA 107; CANR 41, 79; INT 107; SATA 58
Lord Auch
See Bataille, Georges
Lord Byron
See Byron, George Gordon (Noel)
Lorde, Audre (Geraldine) 1934-1992**CLC 18, 71; BLC 2; DAM MULT, POET; PC 12**
See also BW 1, 3; CA 25-28R; 142; CANR 16, 26, 46; DLB 41; MTCW 1, 2
Lord Houghton
See Milnes, Richard Monckton
Lord Jeffrey
See Jeffrey, Francis
Lorenzini, Carlo 1826-1890
See Collodi, Carlo
See also MAICYA; SATA 29, 100
Lorenzo, Heberto Padilla
See Padilla (Lorenzo), Heberto
Loris
See Hofmannsthal, Hugo von
Loti, Pierre .... **TCLC 11**
See also Viaud, (Louis Marie) Julien
See also DLB 123
Louie, David Wong 1954- .... **CLC 70**
See also CA 139
Louis, Father M.
See Merton, Thomas
Lovecraft, H(oward) P(hillips) 1890-1937**TCLC 4, 22; DAM POP; SSC 3**
See also AAYA 14; CA 104; 133; MTCW 1, 2
Lovelace, Earl 1935- .... **CLC 51**
See also BW 2; CA 77-80; CANR 41, 72; DLB 125; MTCW 1
Lovelace, Richard 1618-1657 .... **LC 24**
See also DLB 131
Lowell, Amy 1874-1925 **TCLC 1, 8; DAM POET; PC 13**
See also CA 104; 151; DLB 54, 140; MTCW 2
Lowell, James Russell 1819-1891 .... **NCLC 2**
See also CDALB 1640-1865; DLB 1, 11, 64, 79, 189
Lowell, Robert (Traill Spence, Jr.) 1917-1977 **CLC 1, 2, 3, 4, 5, 8, 9, 11, 15, 37; DA; DAB; DAC; DAM MST, NOV; PC 3; WLC**
See also CA 9-12R; 73-76; CABS 2; CANR 26, 60; CDALBS; DLB 5, 169; MTCW 1, 2
Lowenthal, Michael (Francis) 1969- .... **CLC 119**
See also CA 150
Lowndes, Marie Adelaide (Belloc) 1868-1947 **TCLC 12**
See also CA 107; DLB 70
Lowry, (Clarence) Malcolm 1909-1957 **TCLC 6, 40; SSC 31**
See also CA 105; 131; CANR 62; CDBLB 1945-1960; DLB 15; MTCW 1, 2
Lowry, Mina Gertrude 1882-1966
See Loy, Mina
See also CA 113

Loxsmith, John
See Brunner, John (Kilian Houston)
Loy, Mina .... **CLC 28; DAM POET; PC 16**
See also Lowry, Mina Gertrude
See also DLB 4, 54
Loyson-Bridet
See Schwob, Marcel (Mayer Andre)
Lucan 39-65 .... **CMLC 33**
See also DLB 211
Lucas, Craig 1951- .... **CLC 64**
See also CA 137; CANR 71
Lucas, E(dward) V(errall) 1868-1938 **TCLC 73**
See also CA 176; DLB 98, 149, 153; SATA 20
Lucas, George 1944- .... **CLC 16**
See also AAYA 1, 23; CA 77-80; CANR 30; SATA 56
Lucas, Hans
See Godard, Jean-Luc
Lucas, Victoria
See Plath, Sylvia
Lucian c. 120-c. 180 .... **CMLC 32**
See also DLB 176
Ludlam, Charles 1943-1987 .... **CLC 46, 50**
See also CA 85-88; 122; CANR 72
Ludlum, Robert 1927- . **CLC 22, 43; DAM NOV, POP**
See also AAYA 10; BEST 89:1, 90:3; CA 33-36R; CANR 25, 41, 68; DLBY 82; MTCW 1, 2
Ludwig, Ken .... **CLC 60**
Ludwig, Otto 1813-1865 .... **NCLC 4**
See also DLB 129
Lugones, Leopoldo 1874-1938**TCLC 15; HLCS 2**
See also CA 116; 131; HW 1
Lu Hsun 1881-1936 .... **TCLC 3; SSC 20**
See also Shu-Jen, Chou
Lukacs, George .... **CLC 24**
See also Lukacs, Gyorgy (Szegeny von)
Lukacs, Gyorgy (Szegeny von) 1885-1971
See Lukacs, George
See also CA 101; 29-32R; CANR 62; MTCW 2
Luke, Peter (Ambrose Cyprian) 1919-1995 **CLC 38**
See also CA 81-84; 147; CANR 72; DLB 13
Lunar, Dennis
See Mungo, Raymond
Lurie, Alison 1926- .... **CLC 4, 5, 18, 39**
See also CA 1-4R; CANR 2, 17, 50; DLB 2; MTCW 1; SATA 46
Lustig, Arnost 1926- .... **CLC 56**
See also AAYA 3; CA 69-72; CANR 47; SATA 56
Luther, Martin 1483-1546 .... **LC 9, 37**
See also DLB 179
Luxemburg, Rosa 1870(?)-1919 .... **TCLC 63**
See also CA 118
Luzi, Mario 1914- .... **CLC 13**
See also CA 61-64; CANR 9, 70; DLB 128
Lyly, John 1554(?)-1606**LC 41; DAM DRAM; DC 7**
See also DLB 62, 167
L'Ymagier
See Gourmont, Remy (-Marie-Charles) de
Lynch, B. Suarez
See Bioy Casares, Adolfo; Borges, Jorge Luis
Lynch, B. Suarez
See Bioy Casares, Adolfo
Lynch, David (K.) 1946- .... **CLC 66**
See also CA 124; 129
Lynch, James
See Andreyev, Leonid (Nikolaevich)
Lynch Davis, B.
See Bioy Casares, Adolfo; Borges, Jorge Luis
Lyndsay, Sir David 1490-1555 .... **LC 20**
Lynn, Kenneth S(chuyler) 1923- .... **CLC 50**
See also CA 1-4R; CANR 3, 27, 65
Lynx
See West, Rebecca
Lyons, Marcus
See Blish, James (Benjamin)
Lyre, Pinchbeck
See Sassoon, Siegfried (Lorraine)
Lytle, Andrew (Nelson) 1902-1995 .... **CLC 22**
See also CA 9-12R; 150; CANR 70; DLB 6; DLBY 95
Lyttelton, George 1709-1773 .... **LC 10**
Maas, Peter 1929- .... **CLC 29**
See also CA 93-96; INT 93-96; MTCW 2
Macaulay, Rose 1881-1958 .... **TCLC 7, 44**
See also CA 104; DLB 36
Macaulay, Thomas Babington 1800-1859 **NCLC 42**
See also CDBLB 1832-1890; DLB 32, 55
MacBeth, George (Mann) 1932-1992 **CLC 2, 5, 9**
See also CA 25-28R; 136; CANR 61, 66; DLB 40; MTCW 1; SATA 4; SATA-Obit 70
MacCaig, Norman (Alexander) 1910- . **CLC 36; DAB; DAM POET**
See also CA 9-12R; CANR 3, 34; DLB 27
MacCarthy, Sir(Charles Otto) Desmond 1877-1952 **TCLC 36**
See also CA 167
MacDiarmid, Hugh .. **CLC 2, 4, 11, 19, 63; PC 9**
See also Grieve, C(hristopher) M(urray)
See also CDBLB 1945-1960; DLB 20
MacDonald, Anson
See Heinlein, Robert A(nson)
Macdonald, Cynthia 1928- .... **CLC 13, 19**
See also CA 49-52; CANR 4, 44; DLB 105
MacDonald, George 1824-1905 .... **TCLC 9**
See also CA 106; 137; CANR 80; DLB 18, 163, 178; MAICYA; SATA 33, 100
Macdonald, John
See Millar, Kenneth
MacDonald, John D(ann) 1916-1986 . **CLC 3, 27, 44; DAM NOV, POP**
See also CA 1-4R; 121; CANR 1, 19, 60; DLB 8; DLBY 86; MTCW 1, 2
Macdonald, John Ross
See Millar, Kenneth
Macdonald, Ross .... **CLC 1, 2, 3, 14, 34, 41**
See also Millar, Kenneth
See also DLBD 6
MacDougal, John
See Blish, James (Benjamin)
MacEwen, Gwendolyn (Margaret) 1941-1987**CLC 13, 55**
See also CA 9-12R; 124; CANR 7, 22; DLB 53; SATA 50; SATA-Obit 55
Macha, Karel Hynek 1810-1846 .... **NCLC 46**
Machado (y Ruiz), Antonio 1875-1939 .. **TCLC 3**
See also CA 104; 174; DLB 108; HW 2
Machado de Assis, Joaquim Maria 1839-1908 **TCLC 10; BLC 2; HLCS 2; SSC 24**
See also CA 107; 153
Machen, Arthur .... **TCLC 4; SSC 20**
See also Jones, Arthur Llewellyn
See also DLB 36, 156, 178
Machiavelli, Niccolo 1469-1527 .. **LC 8, 36; DA; DAB; DAC; DAM MST; WLCS**
MacInnes, Colin 1914-1976 .... **CLC 4, 23**
See also CA 69-72; 65-68; CANR 21; DLB 14; MTCW 1, 2
MacInnes, Helen (Clark) 1907-1985**CLC 27, 39; DAM POP**
See also CA 1-4R; 117; CANR 1, 28, 58; DLB 87; MTCW 1, 2; SATA 22; SATA-Obit 44
Mackenzie, Compton (Edward Montague) 1883-1972 .... **CLC 18**
See also CA 21-22; 37-40R; CAP 2; DLB 34, 100
Mackenzie, Henry 1745-1831 .... **NCLC 41**
See also DLB 39
Mackintosh, Elizabeth 1896(?)-1952
See Tey, Josephine
See also CA 110
MacLaren, James
See Grieve, C(hristopher) M(urray)
Mac Laverty, Bernard 1942- .... **CLC 31**
See also CA 116; 118; CANR 43; INT 118
MacLean, Alistair (Stuart) 1922(?)-1987 **CLC 3, 13, 50, 63; DAM POP**
See also CA 57-60; 121; CANR 28, 61; MTCW 1; SATA 23; SATA-Obit 50
Maclean, Norman (Fitzroy) 1902-1990 . **CLC 78; DAM POP; SSC 13**
See also CA 102; 132; CANR 49; DLB 206
MacLeish, Archibald 1892-1982**CLC 3, 8, 14, 68; DAM POET**
See also CA 9-12R; 106; CANR 33, 63; CDALBS; DLB 4, 7, 45; DLBY 82; MTCW 1, 2
MacLennan, (John) Hugh 1907-1990 **CLC 2, 14, 92; DAC; DAM MST**
See also CA 5-8R; 142; CANR 33; DLB 68; MTCW 1, 2
MacLeod, Alistair 1936- .. **CLC 56; DAC; DAM MST**
See also CA 123; DLB 60; MTCW 2
Macleod, Fiona
See Sharp, William
MacNeice, (Frederick) Louis 1907-1963**CLC 1, 4, 10, 53; DAB; DAM POET**
See also CA 85-88; CANR 61; DLB 10, 20; MTCW 1, 2
MacNeill, Dand
See Fraser, George MacDonald
Macpherson, James 1736-1796 .... **LC 29**
See also Ossian
See also DLB 109
Macpherson, (Jean) Jay 1931- .... **CLC 14**
See also CA 5-8R; DLB 53
MacShane, Frank 1927- .... **CLC 39**
See also CA 9-12R; CANR 3, 33; DLB 111
Macumber, Mari
See Sandoz, Mari(e Susette)
Madach, Imre 1823-1864 .... **NCLC 19**
Madden, (Jerry) David 1933- .... **CLC 5, 15**
See also CA 1-4R; CAAS 3; CANR 4, 45; DLB 6; MTCW 1
Maddern, Al(an)
See Ellison, Harlan (Jay)
Madhubuti, Haki R. 1942- ... **CLC 6, 73; BLC 2; DAM MULT, POET; PC 5**
See also Lee, Don L.
See also BW 2, 3; CA 73-76; CANR 24, 51, 73; DLB 5, 41; DLBD 8; MTCW 2
Maepenn, Hugh
See Kuttner, Henry
Maepenn, K. H.
See Kuttner, Henry
Maeterlinck, Maurice 1862-1949 **TCLC 3; DAM DRAM**
See also CA 104; 136; CANR 80; DLB 192; SATA 66
Maginn, William 1794-1842 .... **NCLC 8**
See also DLB 110, 159
Mahapatra, Jayanta 1928- **CLC 33; DAM MULT**
See also CA 73-76; CAAS 9; CANR 15, 33, 66
Mahfouz, Naguib (Abdel Aziz Al-Sabilgi) 1911(?)-
See Mahfuz, Najib
See also BEST 89:2; CA 128; CANR 55; DAM NOV; MTCW 1, 2
Mahfuz, Najib .... **CLC 52, 55**
See also Mahfouz, Naguib (Abdel Aziz Al-Sabilgi)
See also DLBY 88
Mahon, Derek 1941- .... **CLC 27**
See also CA 113; 128; DLB 40
Mailer, Norman 1923-**CLC 1, 2, 3, 4, 5, 8, 11, 14, 28, 39, 74, 111; DA; DAB; DAC; DAM MST, NOV, POP**
See also AITN 2; CA 9-12R; CABS 1; CANR 28,

74, 77; CDALB 1968-1988; DLB 2, 16, 28, 185; DLBD 3; DLBY 80, 83; MTCW 1, 2
Maillet, Antonine 1929- ...... **CLC 54, 118; DAC**
See also CA 115; 120; CANR 46, 74, 77; DLB 60; INT 120; MTCW 2
Mais, Roger 1905-1955 .... **TCLC 8**
See also BW 1, 3; CA 105; 124; DLB 125; MTCW 1
Maistre, Joseph de 1753-1821 .... **NCLC 37**
Maitland, Frederic 1850-1906 .... **TCLC 65**
Maitland, Sara (Louise) 1950- .... **CLC 49**
See also CA 69-72; CANR 13, 59
Major, Clarence 1936- .. **CLC 3, 19, 48; BLC 2; DAM MULT**
See also BW 2, 3; CA 21-24R; CAAS 6; CANR 13, 25, 53; DLB 33
Major, Kevin (Gerald) 1949- .... **CLC 26; DAC**
See also AAYA 16; CA 97-100; CANR 21, 38; CLR 11; DLB 60; INT CANR-21; JRDA; MAICYA; SATA 32, 82
Maki, James
See Ozu, Yasujiro
Malabaila, Damiano
See Levi, Primo
Malamud, Bernard 1914-1986**CLC 1, 2, 3, 5, 8, 9, 11, 18, 27, 44, 78, 85; DA; DAB; DAC; DAM MST, NOV, POP; SSC 15; WLC**
See also AAYA 16; CA 5-8R; 118; CABS 1; CANR 28, 62; CDALB 1941-1968; DLB 2, 28, 152; DLBY 80, 86; MTCW 1, 2
Malan, Herman
See Bosman, Herman Charles; Bosman, Herman Charles
Malaparte, Curzio 1898-1957 .... **TCLC 52**
Malcolm, Dan
See Silverberg, Robert
Malcolm X .... **CLC 82, 117; BLC 2; WLCS**
See also Little, Malcolm
Malherbe, Francois de 1555-1628 .... **LC 5**
Mallarme, Stephane 1842-1898**NCLC 4, 41; DAM POET; PC 4**
Mallet-Joris, Francoise 1930- .... **CLC 11**
See also CA 65-68; CANR 17; DLB 83
Malley, Ern
See McAuley, James Phillip
Mallowan, Agatha Christie
See Christie, Agatha (Mary Clarissa)
Maloff, Saul 1922- .... **CLC 5**
See also CA 33-36R
Malone, Louis
See MacNeice, (Frederick) Louis
Malone, Michael (Christopher) 1942- .. **CLC 43**
See also CA 77-80; CANR 14, 32, 57
Malory, (Sir) Thomas 1410(?)-1471(?)**LC 11; DA; DAB; DAC; DAM MST; WLCS**
See also CDBLB Before 1660; DLB 146; SATA 59; SATA-Brief 33
Malouf, (George Joseph) David 1934-**CLC 28, 86**
See also CA 124; CANR 50, 76; MTCW 2
Malraux, (Georges-)Andre 1901-1976**CLC 1, 4, 9, 13, 15, 57; DAM NOV**
See also CA 21-22; 69-72; CANR 34, 58; CAP 2; DLB 72; MTCW 1, 2
Malzberg, Barry N(athaniel) 1939- .... **CLC 7**
See also CA 61-64; CAAS 4; CANR 16; DLB 8
Mamet, David (Alan) 1947-**CLC 9, 15, 34, 46, 91; DAM DRAM; DC 4**
See also AAYA 3; CA 81-84; CABS 3; CANR 15, 41, 67, 72; DLB 7; MTCW 1, 2
Mamoulian, Rouben (Zachary) 1897-1987**CLC 16**
See also CA 25-28R; 124
Mandelstam, Osip (Emilievich) 1891(?)-1938(?) **TCLC 2, 6; PC 14**
See also CA 104; 150; MTCW 2
Mander, (Mary) Jane 1877-1949 .... **TCLC 31**
See also CA 162
Mandeville, John fl. 1350- .... **CMLC 19**
See also DLB 146
Mandiargues, Andre Pieyre de .... **CLC 41**
See also Pieyre de Mandiargues, Andre
See also DLB 83
Mandrake, Ethel Belle
See Thurman, Wallace (Henry)
Mangan, James Clarence 1803-1849 .. **NCLC 27**
Maniere, J.-E.
See Giraudoux, (Hippolyte) Jean
Mankiewicz, Herman (Jacob) 1897-1953**TCLC 85**
See also CA 120; 169; DLB 26
Manley, (Mary) Delariviere 1672(?)-1724**LC 1, 42**
See also DLB 39, 80
Mann, Abel
See Creasey, John
Mann, Emily 1952- .... **DC 7**
See also CA 130; CANR 55
Mann, (Luiz) Heinrich 1871-1950 .... **TCLC 9**
See also CA 106; 164; DLB 66, 118
Mann, (Paul) Thomas 1875-1955**TCLC 2, 8, 14, 21, 35, 44, 60; DA; DAB; DAC; DAM MST, NOV; SSC 5; WLC**
See also CA 104; 128; DLB 66; MTCW 1, 2
Mannheim, Karl 1893-1947 .... **TCLC 65**
Manning, David
See Faust, Frederick (Schiller)
Manning, Frederic 1887(?)-1935 .... **TCLC 25**
See also CA 124
Manning, Olivia 1915-1980 .... **CLC 5, 19**
See also CA 5-8R; 101; CANR 29; MTCW 1
Mano, D. Keith 1942- .... **CLC 2, 10**
See also CA 25-28R; CAAS 6; CANR 26, 57; DLB 6
Mansfield, Katherine**TCLC 2, 8, 39; DAB; SSC 9, 23; WLC**
See also Beauchamp, Kathleen Mansfield
See also DLB 162
Manso, Peter 1940- .... **CLC 39**
See also CA 29-32R; CANR 44
Mantecon, Juan Jimenez
See Jiménez (Mantecon), Juan Ramon
Manton, Peter
See Creasey, John
Man Without a Spleen, A
See Chekhov, Anton (Pavlovich)
Manzoni, Alessandro 1785-1873 .... **NCLC 29**
Map, Walter 1140-1209 .... **CMLC 32**
Mapu, Abraham (ben Jekutiel) 1808-1867**NCLC 18**
Mara, Sally
See Queneau, Raymond
Marat, Jean Paul 1743-1793 .... **LC 10**
Marcel, Gabriel Honore 1889-1973 .... **CLC 15**
See also CA 102; 45-48; MTCW 1, 2
Marchbanks, Samuel
See Davies, (William) Robertson
Marchi, Giacomo
See Bassani, Giorgio
Margulies, Donald .... **CLC 76**
Marie de France c. 12th cent. - **CMLC 8; PC 22**
See also DLB 208
Marie de l'Incarnation 1599-1672 .... **LC 10**
Marier, Captain Victor
See Griffith, D(avid Lewelyn) W(ark)
Mariner, Scott
See Pohl, Frederik
Marinetti, Filippo Tommaso 1876-1944 **TCLC 10**
See also CA 107; DLB 114
Marivaux, Pierre Carlet de Chamblain de 1688-1763 .... **LC 4; DC 7**
Markandaya, Kamala .... **CLC 8, 38**
See also Taylor, Kamala (Purnaiya)
Markfield, Wallace 1926- .... **CLC 8**
See also CA 69-72; CAAS 3; DLB 2, 28
Markham, Edwin 1852-1940 .... **TCLC 47**
See also CA 160; DLB 54, 186
Markham, Robert
See Amis, Kingsley (William)
Marks, J
See Highwater, Jamake (Mamake)
Marks-Highwater, J
See Highwater, Jamake (Mamake)
Markson, David M(errill) 1927- .... **CLC 67**
See also CA 49-52; CANR 1
Marley, Bob .... **CLC 17**
See also Marley, Robert Nesta
Marley, Robert Nesta 1945-1981
See Marley, Bob
See also CA 107; 103
Marlowe, Christopher 1564-1593**LC 22, 47; DA; DAB; DAC; DAM DRAM, MST; DC 1; WLC**
See also CDBLB Before 1660; DLB 62
Marlowe, Stephen 1928-
See Queen, Ellery
See also CA 13-16R; CANR 6, 55
Marmontel, Jean-Francois 1723-1799 .... **LC 2**
Marquand, John P(hillips) 1893-1960 **CLC 2, 10**
See also CA 85-88; CANR 73; DLB 9, 102; MTCW 2
Marques, Rene 1919-1979**CLC 96; DAM MULT; HLC**
See also CA 97-100; 85-88; CANR 78; DLB 113; HW 1, 2
Marquez, Gabriel (Jose) Garcia
See Garcia Marquez, Gabriel (Jose)
Marquis, Don(ald Robert Perry) 1878-1937**TCLC 7**
See also CA 104; 166; DLB 11, 25
Marric, J. J.
See Creasey, John
Marryat, Frederick 1792-1848 .... **NCLC 3**
See also DLB 21, 163
Marsden, James
See Creasey, John
Marsh, (Edith) Ngaio 1899-1982**CLC 7, 53; DAM POP**
See also CA 9-12R; CANR 6, 58; DLB 77; MTCW 1, 2
Marshall, Garry 1934- .... **CLC 17**
See also AAYA 3; CA 111; SATA 60
Marshall, Paule 1929-**CLC 27, 72; BLC 3; DAM MULT; SSC 3**
See also BW 2, 3; CA 77-80; CANR 25, 73; DLB 157; MTCW 1, 2
Marshallik
See Zangwill, Israel
Marsten, Richard
See Hunter, Evan
Marston, John 1576-1634 .. **LC 33; DAM DRAM**
See also DLB 58, 172
Martha, Henry
See Harris, Mark
Marti (y Perez), Jose (Julian) 1853-1895 **NCLC 63; DAM MULT; HLC**
See also HW 2
Martial c. 40-c. 104 .... **PC 10**
See also DLB 211
Martin, Ken
See Hubbard, L(afayette) Ron(ald)
Martin, Richard
See Creasey, John
Martin, Steve 1945- .... **CLC 30**
See also CA 97-100; CANR 30; MTCW 1
Martin, Valerie 1948- .... **CLC 89**
See also BEST 90:2; CA 85-88; CANR 49
Martin, Violet Florence 1862-1915 ..... **TCLC 51**
Martin, Webber
See Silverberg, Robert
Martindale, Patrick Victor
See White, Patrick (Victor Martindale)
Martin du Gard, Roger 1881-1958 ...... **TCLC 24**
See also CA 118; DLB 65
Martineau, Harriet 1802-1876 .... **NCLC 26**
See also DLB 21, 55, 159, 163, 166, 190; YABC 2

Author Index

Martines, Julia
See O'Faolain, Julia
Martinez, Enrique Gonzalez
See Gonzalez Martinez, Enrique
Martinez, Jacinto Benavente y
See Benavente (y Martinez), Jacinto
Martinez Ruiz, Jose 1873-1967
See Azorin; Ruiz, Jose Martinez
See also CA 93-96; HW 1
Martinez Sierra, Gregorio 1881-1947 .. **TCLC 6**
See also CA 115
Martinez Sierra, Maria (de la O'LeJarraga) 1874-1974 .... **TCLC 6**
See also CA 115
Martinsen, Martin
See Follett, Ken(neth Martin)
Martinson, Harry (Edmund) 1904-1978 **CLC 14**
See also CA 77-80; CANR 34
Marut, Ret
See Traven, B.
Marut, Robert
See Traven, B.
Marvell, Andrew 1621-1678 **LC 4, 43; DA; DAB; DAC; DAM MST, POET; PC 10; WLC**
See also CDBLB 1660-1789; DLB 131
Marx, Karl (Heinrich) 1818-1883 .... **NCLC 17**
See also DLB 129
Masaoka Shiki .... **TCLC 18**
See also Masaoka Tsunenori
Masaoka Tsunenori 1867-1902
See Masaoka Shiki
See also CA 117
Masefield, John (Edward) 1878-1967 **CLC 11, 47; DAM POET**
See also CA 19-20; 25-28R; CANR 33; CAP 2; CDBLB 1890-1914; DLB 10, 19, 153, 160; MTCW 1, 2; SATA 19
Maso, Carole 19(?)- .... **CLC 44**
See also CA 170
Mason, Bobbie Ann 1940- **CLC 28, 43, 82; SSC 4**
See also AAYA 5; CA 53-56; CANR 11, 31, 58; CDALBS; DLB 173; DLBY 87; INT CANR-31; MTCW 1, 2
Mason, Ernst
See Pohl, Frederik
Mason, Lee W.
See Malzberg, Barry N(athaniel)
Mason, Nick 1945- .... **CLC 35**
Mason, Tally
See Derleth, August (William)
Mass, William
See Gibson, William
Master Lao
See Lao Tzu
Masters, Edgar Lee 1868-1950 **TCLC 2, 25; DA; DAC; DAM MST, POET; PC 1; WLCS**
See also CA 104; 133; CDALB 1865-1917; DLB 54; MTCW 1, 2
Masters, Hilary 1928- .... **CLC 48**
See also CA 25-28R; CANR 13, 47
Mastrosimone, William 19(?)- .... **CLC 36**
Mathe, Albert
See Camus, Albert
Mather, Cotton 1663-1728 .... **LC 38**
See also CDALB 1640-1865; DLB 24, 30, 140
Mather, Increase 1639-1723 .... **LC 38**
See also DLB 24
Matheson, Richard Burton 1926- .... **CLC 37**
See also CA 97-100; DLB 8, 44; INT 97-100
Mathews, Harry 1930- .... **CLC 6, 52**
See also CA 21-24R; CAAS 6; CANR 18, 40
Mathews, John Joseph 1894-1979 **CLC 84; DAM MULT**
See also CA 19-20; 142; CANR 45; CAP 2; DLB 175; NNAL
Mathias, Roland (Glyn) 1915- .... **CLC 45**
See also CA 97-100; CANR 19, 41; DLB 27
Matsuo Basho 1644-1694 .... **PC 3**
See also DAM POET
Mattheson, Rodney
See Creasey, John
Matthews, Brander 1852-1929 .... **TCLC 95**
See also DLB 71, 78; DLBD 13
Matthews, Greg 1949- .... **CLC 45**
See also CA 135
Matthews, William (Procter, III) 1942-1997 **CLC 40**
See also CA 29-32R; 162; CAAS 18; CANR 12, 57; DLB 5
Matthias, John (Edward) 1941- .... **CLC 9**
See also CA 33-36R; CANR 56
Matthiessen, Peter 1927- **CLC 5, 7, 11, 32, 64; DAM NOV**
See also AAYA 6; BEST 90:4; CA 9-12R; CANR 21, 50, 73; DLB 6, 173; MTCW 1, 2; SATA 27
Maturin, Charles Robert 1780(?)-1824 **NCLC 6**
See also DLB 178
Matute (Ausejo), Ana Maria 1925- .... **CLC 11**
See also CA 89-92; MTCW 1
Maugham, W. S.
See Maugham, W(illiam) Somerset
Maugham, W(illiam) Somerset 1874-1965 **CLC 1, 11, 15, 67, 93; DA; DAB; DAC; DAM DRAM, MST, NOV; SSC 8; WLC**
See also CA 5-8R; 25-28R; CANR 40; CDBLB 1914-1945; DLB 10, 36, 77, 100, 162, 195; MTCW 1, 2; SATA 54
Maugham, William Somerset
See Maugham, W(illiam) Somerset
Maupassant, (Henri Rene Albert) Guy de 1850-1893 .. **NCLC 1, 42; DA; DAB; DAC; DAM MST; SSC 1; WLC**
See also DLB 123
Maupin, Armistead 1944- ... **CLC 95; DAM POP**
See also CA 125; 130; CANR 58; INT 130; MTCW 2
Maurhut, Richard
See Traven, B.
Mauriac, Claude 1914-1996 .... **CLC 9**
See also CA 89-92; 152; DLB 83
Mauriac, Francois (Charles) 1885-1970 **CLC 4, 9, 56; SSC 24**
See also CA 25-28; CAP 2; DLB 65; MTCW 1, 2
Mavor, Osborne Henry 1888-1951
See Bridie, James
See also CA 104
Maxwell, William (Keepers, Jr.) 1908- **CLC 19**
See also CA 93-96; CANR 54; DLBY 80; INT 93-96
May, Elaine 1932- .... **CLC 16**
See also CA 124; 142; DLB 44
Mayakovski, Vladimir (Vladimirovich) 1893-1930 **TCLC 4, 18**
See also CA 104; 158; MTCW 2
Mayhew, Henry 1812-1887 .... **NCLC 31**
See also DLB 18, 55, 190
Mayle, Peter 1939(?)- .... **CLC 89**
See also CA 139; CANR 64
Maynard, Joyce 1953- .... **CLC 23**
See also CA 111; 129; CANR 64
Mayne, William (James Carter) 1928- **CLC 12**
See also AAYA 20; CA 9-12R; CANR 37, 80; CLR 25; JRDA; MAICYA; SAAS 11; SATA 6, 68
Mayo, Jim
See L'Amour, Louis (Dearborn)
Maysles, Albert 1926- .... **CLC 16**
See also CA 29-32R
Maysles, David 1932- .... **CLC 16**
Mazer, Norma Fox 1931- .... **CLC 26**
See also AAYA 5; CA 69-72; CANR 12, 32, 66; CLR 23; JRDA; MAICYA; SAAS 1; SATA 24, 67, 105
Mazzini, Guiseppe 1805-1872 .... **NCLC 34**
McAuley, James Phillip 1917-1976 .... **CLC 45**
See also CA 97-100
McBain, Ed
See Hunter, Evan
McBrien, William Augustine 1930- ..... **CLC 44**
See also CA 107
McCaffrey, Anne (Inez) 1926- ..... **CLC 17; DAM NOV, POP**
See also AAYA 6; AITN 2; BEST 89:2; CA 25-28R; CANR 15, 35, 55; CLR 49; DLB 8; JRDA; MAICYA; MTCW 1, 2; SAAS 11; SATA 8, 70
McCall, Nathan 1955(?)- .... **CLC 86**
See also BW 3; CA 146
McCann, Arthur
See Campbell, John W(ood, Jr.)
McCann, Edson
See Pohl, Frederik
McCarthy, Charles, Jr. 1933-
See McCarthy, Cormac
See also CANR 42, 69; DAM POP; MTCW 2
McCarthy, Cormac 1933- .... **CLC 4, 57, 59, 101**
See also McCarthy, Charles, Jr.
See also DLB 6, 143; MTCW 2
McCarthy, Mary (Therese) 1912-1989 **CLC 1, 3, 5, 14, 24, 39, 59; SSC 24**
See also CA 5-8R; 129; CANR 16, 50, 64; DLB 2; DLBY 81; INT CANR-16; MTCW 1, 2
McCartney, (James) Paul 1942- ..... **CLC 12, 35**
See also CA 146
McCauley, Stephen (D.) 1955- .... **CLC 50**
See also CA 141
McClure, Michael (Thomas) 1932- ... **CLC 6, 10**
See also CA 21-24R; CANR 17, 46, 77; DLB 16
McCorkle, Jill (Collins) 1958- .... **CLC 51**
See also CA 121; DLBY 87
McCourt, Frank 1930- .... **CLC 109**
See also CA 157
McCourt, James 1941- .... **CLC 5**
See also CA 57-60
McCourt, Malachy 1932- .... **CLC 119**
McCoy, Horace (Stanley) 1897-1955 ... **TCLC 28**
See also CA 108; 155; DLB 9
McCrae, John 1872-1918 .... **TCLC 12**
See also CA 109; DLB 92
McCreigh, James
See Pohl, Frederik
McCullers, (Lula) Carson (Smith) 1917-1967 **CLC 1, 4, 10, 12, 48, 100; DA; DAB; DAC; DAM MST, NOV; SSC 9, 24; WLC**
See also AAYA 21; CA 5-8R; 25-28R; CABS 1, 3; CANR 18; CDALB 1941-1968; DLB 2, 7, 173; MTCW 1, 2; SATA 27
McCulloch, John Tyler
See Burroughs, Edgar Rice
McCullough, Colleen 1938(?)- **CLC 27, 107; DAM NOV, POP**
See also CA 81-84; CANR 17, 46, 67; MTCW 1, 2
McDermott, Alice 1953- .... **CLC 90**
See also CA 109; CANR 40
McElroy, Joseph 1930- .... **CLC 5, 47**
See also CA 17-20R
McEwan, Ian (Russell) 1948- **CLC 13, 66; DAM NOV**
See also BEST 90:4; CA 61-64; CANR 14, 41, 69; DLB 14, 194; MTCW 1, 2
McFadden, David 1940- .... **CLC 48**
See also CA 104; DLB 60; INT 104
McFarland, Dennis 1950- .... **CLC 65**
See also CA 165
McGahern, John 1934- .... **CLC 5, 9, 48; SSC 17**
See also CA 17-20R; CANR 29, 68; DLB 14; MTCW 1
McGinley, Patrick (Anthony) 1937- ..... **CLC 41**
See also CA 120; 127; CANR 56; INT 127
McGinley, Phyllis 1905-1978 .... **CLC 14**
See also CA 9-12R; 77-80; CANR 19; DLB 11, 48; SATA 2, 44; SATA-Obit 24
McGinniss, Joe 1942- .... **CLC 32**

See also AITN 2; BEST 89:2; CA 25-28R; CANR 26, 70; DLB 185; INT CANR-26
McGivern, Maureen Daly
See Daly, Maureen
McGrath, Patrick 1950- ..... **CLC 55**
See also CA 136; CANR 65
McGrath, Thomas (Matthew) 1916-1990**CLC 28, 59; DAM POET**
See also CA 9-12R; 132; CANR 6, 33; MTCW 1; SATA 41; SATA-Obit 66
McGuane, Thomas (Francis III) 1939- **CLC 3, 7, 18, 45**
See also AITN 2; CA 49-52; CANR 5, 24, 49; DLB 2, 212; DLBY 80; INT CANR-24; MTCW 1
McGuckian, Medbh 1950- ..... **CLC 48; DAM POET**
See also CA 143; DLB 40
McHale, Tom 1942(?)-1982 ..... **CLC 3, 5**
See also AITN 1; CA 77-80; 106
McIlvanney, William 1936- ..... **CLC 42**
See also CA 25-28R; CANR 61; DLB 14, 207
McIlwraith, Maureen Mollie Hunter
See Hunter, Mollie
See also SATA 2
McInerney, Jay 1955- . **CLC 34, 112; DAM POP**
See also AAYA 18; CA 116; 123; CANR 45, 68; INT 123; MTCW 2
McIntyre, Vonda N(eel) 1948- ..... **CLC 18**
See also CA 81-84; CANR 17, 34, 69; MTCW 1
McKay, Claude TCLC 7, 41; BLC 3; DAB; PC 2
See also McKay, Festus Claudius
See also DLB 4, 45, 51, 117
McKay, Festus Claudius 1889-1948
See McKay, Claude
See also BW 1, 3; CA 104; 124; CANR 73; DA; DAC; DAM MST, MULT, NOV, POET; MTCW 1, 2; WLC
McKuen, Rod 1933- ..... **CLC 1, 3**
See also AITN 1; CA 41-44R; CANR 40
McLoughlin, R. B.
See Mencken, H(enry) L(ouis)
McLuhan, (Herbert) Marshall 1911-1980**CLC 37, 83**
See also CA 9-12R; 102; CANR 12, 34, 61; DLB 88; INT CANR-12; MTCW 1, 2
McMillan, Terry (L.) 1951- .... **CLC 50, 61, 112; BLCS; DAM MULT, NOV, POP**
See also AAYA 21; BW 2, 3; CA 140; CANR 60; MTCW 2
McMurtry, Larry (Jeff) 1936-**CLC 2, 3, 7, 11, 27, 44; DAM NOV, POP**
See also AAYA 15; AITN 2; BEST 89:2; CA 5-8R; CANR 19, 43, 64; CDALB 1968-1988; DLB 2, 143; DLBY 80, 87; MTCW 1, 2
McNally, T. M. 1961- ..... **CLC 82**
McNally, Terrence 1939-**CLC 4, 7, 41, 91; DAM DRAM**
See also CA 45-48; CANR 2, 56; DLB 7; MTCW 2
McNamer, Deirdre 1950- ..... **CLC 70**
McNeal, Tom ..... **CLC 119**
McNeile, Herman Cyril 1888-1937
See Sapper
See also DLB 77
McNickle, (William) D'Arcy 1904-1977**CLC 89; DAM MULT**
See also CA 9-12R; 85-88; CANR 5, 45; DLB 175, 212; NNAL; SATA-Obit 22
McPhee, John (Angus) 1931- ..... **CLC 36**
See also BEST 90:1; CA 65-68; CANR 20, 46, 64, 69; DLB 185; MTCW 1, 2
McPherson, James Alan 1943- ..... **CLC 19, 77; BLCS**
See also BW 1, 3; CA 25-28R; CAAS 17; CANR 24, 74; DLB 38; MTCW 1, 2
McPherson, William (Alexander) 1933- **CLC 34**
See also CA 69-72; CANR 28; INT CANR-28
Mead, George Herbert 1873-1958 ..... **TCLC 89**
Mead, Margaret 1901-1978 ..... **CLC 37**
See also AITN 1; CA 1-4R; 81-84; CANR 4; MTCW 1, 2; SATA-Obit 20
Meaker, Marijane (Agnes) 1927-
See Kerr, M. E.
See also CA 107; CANR 37, 63; INT 107; JRDA; MAICYA; MTCW 1; SATA 20, 61, 99
Medoff, Mark (Howard) 1940- **CLC 6, 23; DAM DRAM**
See also AITN 1; CA 53-56; CANR 5; DLB 7; INT CANR-5
Medvedev, P. N.
See Bakhtin, Mikhail Mikhailovich
Meged, Aharon
See Megged, Aharon
Meged, Aron
See Megged, Aharon
Megged, Aharon 1920- ..... **CLC 9**
See also CA 49-52; CAAS 13; CANR 1
Mehta, Ved (Parkash) 1934- ..... **CLC 37**
See also CA 1-4R; CANR 2, 23, 69; MTCW 1
Melanter
See Blackmore, R(ichard) D(oddridge)
Melies, Georges 1861-1938 ..... **TCLC 81**
Melikow, Loris
See Hofmannsthal, Hugo von
Melmoth, Sebastian
See Wilde, Oscar
Meltzer, Milton 1915- ..... **CLC 26**
See also AAYA 8; CA 13-16R; CANR 38; CLR 13; DLB 61; JRDA; MAICYA; SAAS 1; SATA 1, 50, 80
Melville, Herman 1819-1891**NCLC 3, 12, 29, 45, 49; DA; DAB; DAC; DAM MST, NOV; SSC 1, 17; WLC**
See also AAYA 25; CDALB 1640-1865; DLB 3, 74; SATA 59
Menander c. 342B.C.-c. 292B.C. **CMLC 9; DAM DRAM; DC 3**
See also DLB 176
Mencken, H(enry) L(ouis) 1880-1956 . **TCLC 13**
See also CA 105; 125; CDALB 1917-1929; DLB 11, 29, 63, 137; MTCW 1, 2
Mendelsohn, Jane 1965(?)- ..... **CLC 99**
See also CA 154
Mercer, David 1928-1980 .. **CLC 5; DAM DRAM**
See also CA 9-12R; 102; CANR 23; DLB 13; MTCW 1
Merchant, Paul
See Ellison, Harlan (Jay)
Meredith, George 1828-1909**TCLC 17, 43; DAM POET**
See also CA 117; 153; CANR 80; CDBLB 1832-1890; DLB 18, 35, 57, 159
Meredith, William (Morris) 1919-**CLC 4, 13, 22, 55; DAM POET**
See also CA 9-12R; CAAS 14; CANR 6, 40; DLB 5
Merezhkovsky, Dmitry Sergeyevich 1865-1941 **TCLC 29**
See also CA 169
Merimee, Prosper 1803-1870**NCLC 6, 65; SSC 7**
See also DLB 119, 192
Merkin, Daphne 1954- ..... **CLC 44**
See also CA 123
Merlin, Arthur
See Blish, James (Benjamin)
Merrill, James (Ingram) 1926-1995**CLC 2, 3, 6, 8, 13, 18, 34, 91; DAM POET**
See also CA 13-16R; 147; CANR 10, 49, 63; DLB 5, 165; DLBY 85; INT CANR-10; MTCW 1, 2
Merriman, Alex
See Silverberg, Robert
Merriman, Brian 1747-1805 ..... **NCLC 70**
Merritt, E. B.
See Waddington, Miriam
Merton, Thomas 1915-1968**CLC 1, 3, 11, 34, 83; PC 10**
See also CA 5-8R; 25-28R; CANR 22, 53; DLB 48; DLBY 81; MTCW 1, 2
Merwin, W(illiam) S(tanley) 1927-**CLC 1, 2, 3, 5, 8, 13, 18, 45, 88; DAM POET**
See also CA 13-16R; CANR 15, 51; DLB 5, 169; INT CANR-15; MTCW 1, 2
Metcalf, John 1938- ..... **CLC 37**
See also CA 113; DLB 60
Metcalf, Suzanne
See Baum, L(yman) Frank
Mew, Charlotte (Mary) 1870-1928 ..... **TCLC 8**
See also CA 105; DLB 19, 135
Mewshaw, Michael 1943- ..... **CLC 9**
See also CA 53-56; CANR 7, 47; DLBY 80
Meyer, June
See Jordan, June
Meyer, Lynn
See Slavitt, David R(ytman)
Meyer-Meyrink, Gustav 1868-1932
See Meyrink, Gustav
See also CA 117
Meyers, Jeffrey 1939- ..... **CLC 39**
See also CA 73-76; CANR 54; DLB 111
Meynell, Alice (Christina Gertrude Thompson) 1847-1922 ..... **TCLC 6**
See also CA 104; 177; DLB 19, 98
Meyrink, Gustav ..... **TCLC 21**
See also Meyer-Meyrink, Gustav
See also DLB 81
Michaels, Leonard 1933- .... **CLC 6, 25; SSC 16**
See also CA 61-64; CANR 21, 62; DLB 130; MTCW 1
Michaux, Henri 1899-1984 ..... **CLC 8, 19**
See also CA 85-88; 114
Micheaux, Oscar (Devereaux) 1884-1951 **TCLC 76**
See also BW 3; CA 174; DLB 50
Michelangelo 1475-1564 ..... **LC 12**
Michelet, Jules 1798-1874 ..... **NCLC 31**
Michels, Robert 1876-1936 ..... **TCLC 88**
Michener, James A(lbert) 1907(?)-1997**CLC 1, 5, 11, 29, 60, 109; DAM NOV, POP**
See also AAYA 27; AITN 1; BEST 90:1; CA 5-8R; 161; CANR 21, 45, 68; DLB 6; MTCW 1, 2
Mickiewicz, Adam 1798-1855 ..... **NCLC 3**
Middleton, Christopher 1926- ..... **CLC 13**
See also CA 13-16R; CANR 29, 54; DLB 40
Middleton, Richard (Barham) 1882-1911**TCLC 56**
See also DLB 156
Middleton, Stanley 1919- ..... **CLC 7, 38**
See also CA 25-28R; CAAS 23; CANR 21, 46, 81; DLB 14
Middleton, Thomas 1580-1627 ..... **LC 33; DAM DRAM, MST; DC 5**
See also DLB 58
Migueis, Jose Rodrigues 1901- ..... **CLC 10**
Mikszath, Kalman 1847-1910 ..... **TCLC 31**
See also CA 170
Miles, Jack ..... **CLC 100**
Miles, Josephine (Louise) 1911-1985 . **CLC 1, 2, 14, 34, 39; DAM POET**
See also CA 1-4R; 116; CANR 2, 55; DLB 48
Militant
See Sandburg, Carl (August)
Mill, John Stuart 1806-1873 ..... **NCLC 11, 58**
See also CDBLB 1832-1890; DLB 55, 190
Millar, Kenneth 1915-1983 . **CLC 14; DAM POP**
See also Macdonald, Ross
See also CA 9-12R; 110; CANR 16, 63; DLB 2; DLBD 6; DLBY 83; MTCW 1, 2
Millay, E. Vincent
See Millay, Edna St. Vincent
Millay, Edna St. Vincent 1892-1950 **TCLC 4, 49; DA; DAB; DAC; DAM MST, POET; PC 6;**

WLCS
See also CA 104; 130; CDALB 1917-1929; DLB 45; MTCW 1, 2
Miller, Arthur 1915-**CLC 1, 2, 6, 10, 15, 26, 47, 78; DA; DAB; DAC; DAM DRAM, MST; DC 1; WLC**
See also AAYA 15; AITN 1; CA 1-4R; CABS 3; CANR 2, 30, 54, 76; CDALB 1941-1968; DLB 7; MTCW 1, 2
Miller, Henry (Valentine) 1891-1980**CLC 1, 2, 4, 9, 14, 43, 84; DA; DAB; DAC; DAM MST, NOV; WLC**
See also CA 9-12R; 97-100; CANR 33, 64; CDALB 1929-1941; DLB 4, 9; DLBY 80; MTCW 1, 2
Miller, Jason 1939(?)- .... **CLC 2**
See also AITN 1; CA 73-76; DLB 7
Miller, Sue 1943- .... **CLC 44; DAM POP**
See also BEST 90:3; CA 139; CANR 59; DLB 143
Miller, Walter M(ichael, Jr.) 1923-**CLC 4, 30**
See also CA 85-88; DLB 8
Millett, Kate 1934- .... **CLC 67**
See also AITN 1; CA 73-76; CANR 32, 53, 76; MTCW 1, 2
Millhauser, Steven (Lewis) 1943-**CLC 21, 54, 109**
See also CA 110; 111; CANR 63; DLB 2; INT 111; MTCW 2
Millin, Sarah Gertrude 1889-1968 .... **CLC 49**
See also CA 102; 93-96
Milne, A(lan) A(lexander) 1882-1956**TCLC 6, 88; DAB; DAC; DAM MST**
See also CA 104; 133; CLR 1, 26; DLB 10, 77, 100, 160; MAICYA; MTCW 1, 2; SATA 100; YABC 1
Milner, Ron(ald) 1938- .. **CLC 56; BLC 3; DAM MULT**
See also AITN 1; BW 1; CA 73-76; CANR 24, 81; DLB 38; MTCW 1
Milnes, Richard Monckton 1809-1885 **NCLC 61**
See also DLB 32, 184
Milosz, Czeslaw 1911-**CLC 5, 11, 22, 31, 56, 82; DAM MST, POET; PC 8; WLCS**
See also CA 81-84; CANR 23, 51; MTCW 1, 2
Milton, John 1608-1674**LC 9, 43; DA; DAB; DAC; DAM MST, POET; PC 19; WLC**
See also CDBLB 1660-1789; DLB 131, 151
Min, Anchee 1957- .... **CLC 86**
See also CA 146
Minehaha, Cornelius
See Wedekind, (Benjamin) Frank(lin)
Miner, Valerie 1947- .... **CLC 40**
See also CA 97-100; CANR 59
Minimo, Duca
See D'Annunzio, Gabriele
Minot, Susan 1956- .... **CLC 44**
See also CA 134
Minus, Ed 1938- .... **CLC 39**
Miranda, Javier
See Bioy Casares, Adolfo
Miranda, Javier
See Bioy Casares, Adolfo
Mirbeau, Octave 1848-1917 .... **TCLC 55**
See also DLB 123, 192
Miro (Ferrer), Gabriel (Francisco Victor) 1879-1930 .... **TCLC 5**
See also CA 104
Mishima, Yukio 1925-1970**CLC 2, 4, 6, 9, 27; DC 1; SSC 4**
See also Hiraoka, Kimitake
See also DLB 182; MTCW 2
Mistral, Frederic 1830-1914 .... **TCLC 51**
See also CA 122
Mistral, Gabriela .... **TCLC 2; HLC**
See also Godoy Alcayaga, Lucila
See also MTCW 2
Mistry, Rohinton 1952- .... **CLC 71; DAC**
See also CA 141
Mitchell, Clyde
See Ellison, Harlan (Jay); Silverberg, Robert
Mitchell, James Leslie 1901-1935
See Gibbon, Lewis Grassic
See also CA 104; DLB 15
Mitchell, Joni 1943- .... **CLC 12**
See also CA 112
Mitchell, Joseph (Quincy) 1908-1996 ... **CLC 98**
See also CA 77-80; 152; CANR 69; DLB 185; DLBY 96
Mitchell, Margaret (Munnerlyn) 1900-1949 **TCLC 11; DAM NOV, POP**
See also AAYA 23; CA 109; 125; CANR 55; CDALBS; DLB 9; MTCW 1, 2
Mitchell, Peggy
See Mitchell, Margaret (Munnerlyn)
Mitchell, S(ilas) Weir 1829-1914 ... **TCLC 36**
See also CA 165; DLB 202
Mitchell, W(illiam) O(rmond) 1914-1998**CLC 25; DAC; DAM MST**
See also CA 77-80; 165; CANR 15, 43; DLB 88
Mitchell, William 1879-1936 .... **TCLC 81**
Mitford, Mary Russell 1787-1855 .... **NCLC 4**
See also DLB 110, 116
Mitford, Nancy 1904-1973 .... **CLC 44**
See also CA 9-12R; DLB 191
Miyamoto, (Chujo) Yuriko 1899-1951 . **TCLC 37**
See also CA 170, 174; DLB 180
Miyazawa, Kenji 1896-1933 .... **TCLC 76**
See also CA 157
Mizoguchi, Kenji 1898-1956 .... **TCLC 72**
See also CA 167
Mo, Timothy (Peter) 1950(?)- .... **CLC 46**
See also CA 117; DLB 194; MTCW 1
Modarressi, Taghi (M.) 1931- .... **CLC 44**
See also CA 121; 134; INT 134
Modiano, Patrick (Jean) 1945- .... **CLC 18**
See also CA 85-88; CANR 17, 40; DLB 83
Moerck, Paal
See Roelvaag, O(le) E(dvart)
Mofolo, Thomas (Mokopu) 1875(?)-1948**TCLC 22; BLC 3; DAM MULT**
See also CA 121; 153; MTCW 2
Mohr, Nicholasa 1938-**CLC 12; DAM MULT; HLC**
See also AAYA 8; CA 49-52; CANR 1, 32, 64; CLR 22; DLB 145; HW 1, 2; JRDA; SAAS 8; SATA 8, 97
Mojtabai, A(nn) G(race) 1938- **CLC 5, 9, 15, 29**
See also CA 85-88
Moliere 1622-1673 **LC 10, 28; DA; DAB; DAC; DAM DRAM, MST; WLC**
Molin, Charles
See Mayne, William (James Carter)
Molnar, Ferenc 1878-1952**TCLC 20; DAM DRAM**
See also CA 109; 153
Momaday, N(avarre) Scott 1934- **CLC 2, 19, 85, 95; DA; DAB; DAC; DAM MST, MULT, NOV, POP; PC 25; WLCS**
See also AAYA 11; CA 25-28R; CANR 14, 34, 68; CDALBS; DLB 143, 175; INT CANR-14; MTCW 1, 2; NNAL; SATA 48; SATA-Brief 30
Monette, Paul 1945-1995 .... **CLC 82**
See also CA 139; 147
Monroe, Harriet 1860-1936 .... **TCLC 12**
See also CA 109; DLB 54, 91
Monroe, Lyle
See Heinlein, Robert A(nson)
Montagu, Elizabeth 1720-1800 .... **NCLC 7**
Montagu, Mary (Pierrepont) Wortley 1689-1762 **LC 9; PC 16**
See also DLB 95, 101
Montagu, W. H.
See Coleridge, Samuel Taylor
Montague, John (Patrick) 1929- ..... **CLC 13, 46**
See also CA 9-12R; CANR 9, 69; DLB 40; MTCW 1
Montaigne, Michel (Eyquem) de 1533-1592**LC 8; DA; DAB; DAC; DAM MST; WLC**
Montale, Eugenio 1896-1981**CLC 7, 9, 18; PC 13**
See also CA 17-20R; 104; CANR 30; DLB 114; MTCW 1
Montesquieu, Charles-Louis de Secondat 1689-1755 .... **LC 7**
Montgomery, (Robert) Bruce 1921-1978
See Crispin, Edmund
See also CA 104
Montgomery, L(ucy) M(aud) 1874-1942**TCLC 51; DAC; DAM MST**
See also AAYA 12; CA 108; 137; CLR 8; DLB 92; DLBD 14; JRDA; MAICYA; MTCW 2; SATA 100; YABC 1
Montgomery, Marion H., Jr. 1925- .... **CLC 7**
See also AITN 1; CA 1-4R; CANR 3, 48; DLB 6
Montgomery, Max
See Davenport, Guy (Mattison, Jr.)
Montherlant, Henry (Milon) de 1896-1972**CLC 8, 19; DAM DRAM**
See also CA 85-88; 37-40R; DLB 72; MTCW 1
Monty Python
See Chapman, Graham; Cleese, John (Marwood); Gilliam, Terry (Vance); Idle, Eric; Jones, Terence Graham Parry; Palin, Michael (Edward)
See also AAYA 7
Moodie, Susanna (Strickland) 1803-1885 **NCLC 14**
See also DLB 99
Mooney, Edward 1951-
See Mooney, Ted
See also CA 130
Mooney, Ted .... **CLC 25**
See also Mooney, Edward
Moorcock, Michael (John) 1939- **CLC 5, 27, 58**
See also Bradbury, Edward P.
See also AAYA 26; CA 45-48; CAAS 5; CANR 2, 17, 38, 64; DLB 14; MTCW 1, 2; SATA 93
Moore, Brian 1921-1999**CLC 1, 3, 5, 7, 8, 19, 32, 90; DAB; DAC; DAM MST**
See also CA 1-4R; 174; CANR 1, 25, 42, 63; MTCW 1, 2
Moore, Edward
See Muir, Edwin
Moore, G. E. 1873-1958 .... **TCLC 89**
Moore, George Augustus 1852-1933**TCLC 7; SSC 19**
See also CA 104; 177; DLB 10, 18, 57, 135
Moore, Lorrie .... **CLC 39, 45, 68**
See also Moore, Marie Lorena
Moore, Marianne (Craig) 1887-1972**CLC 1, 2, 4, 8, 10, 13, 19, 47; DA; DAB; DAC; DAM MST, POET; PC 4; WLCS**
See also CA 1-4R; 33-36R; CANR 3, 61; CDALB 1929-1941; DLB 45; DLBD 7; MTCW 1, 2; SATA 20
Moore, Marie Lorena 1957-
See Moore, Lorrie
See also CA 116; CANR 39
Moore, Thomas 1779-1852 .... **NCLC 6**
See also DLB 96, 144
Morand, Paul 1888-1976 .... **CLC 41; SSC 22**
See also CA 69-72; DLB 65
Morante, Elsa 1918-1985 .... **CLC 8, 47**
See also CA 85-88; 117; CANR 35; DLB 177; MTCW 1, 2
Moravia, Alberto 1907-1990**CLC 2, 7, 11, 27, 46; SSC 26**
See also Pincherle, Alberto
See also DLB 177; MTCW 2
More, Hannah 1745-1833 .... **NCLC 27**
See also DLB 107, 109, 116, 158
More, Henry 1614-1687 .... **LC 9**
See also DLB 126
More, Sir Thomas 1478-1535 .... **LC 10, 32**
Moreas, Jean .... **TCLC 18**

See also Papadiamantopoulos, Johannes
Morgan, Berry 1919- .... **CLC 6**
See also CA 49-52; DLB 6
Morgan, Claire
See Highsmith, (Mary) Patricia
Morgan, Edwin (George) 1920- .... **CLC 31**
See also CA 5-8R; CANR 3, 43; DLB 27
Morgan, (George) Frederick 1922- ...... **CLC 23**
See also CA 17-20R; CANR 21
Morgan, Harriet
See Mencken, H(enry) L(ouis)
Morgan, Jane
See Cooper, James Fenimore
Morgan, Janet 1945- .... **CLC 39**
See also CA 65-68
Morgan, Lady 1776(?)-1859 .... **NCLC 29**
See also DLB 116, 158
Morgan, Robin (Evonne) 1941- .... **CLC 2**
See also CA 69-72; CANR 29, 68; MTCW 1; SATA 80
Morgan, Scott
See Kuttner, Henry
Morgan, Seth 1949(?)-1990 .... **CLC 65**
See also CA 132
Morgenstern, Christian 1871-1914 ...... **TCLC 8**
See also CA 105
Morgenstern, S.
See Goldman, William (W.)
Moricz, Zsigmond 1879-1942 .... **TCLC 33**
<indeSee also CA 165
Morike, Eduard (Friedrich) 1804-1875 **NCLC 10**
See also DLB 133
Moritz, Karl Philipp 1756-1793 .... **LC 2**
See also DLB 94
Morland, Peter Henry
See Faust, Frederick (Schiller)
Morley, Christopher (Darlington) 1890-1957 **TCLC 87**
See also CA 112; DLB 9
Morren, Theophil
See Hofmannsthal, Hugo von
Morris, Bill 1952- .... **CLC 76**
Morris, Julian
See West, Morris L(anglo)
Morris, Steveland Judkins 1950(?)-
See Wonder, Stevie
See also CA 111
Morris, William 1834-1896 .... **NCLC 4**
See also CDBLB 1832-1890; DLB 18, 35, 57, 156, 178, 184
Morris, Wright 1910-1998 .. **CLC 1, 3, 7, 18, 37**
See also CA 9-12R; 167; CANR 21, 81; DLB 2, 206; DLBY 81; MTCW 1, 2
Morrison, Arthur 1863-1945 .... **TCLC 72**
See also CA 120; 157; DLB 70, 135, 197
Morrison, Chloe Anthony Wofford
See Morrison, Toni
Morrison, James Douglas 1943-1971
See Morrison, Jim
See also CA 73-76; CANR 40
Morrison, Jim .... CLC 17
See also Morrison, James Douglas
Morrison, Toni 1931- **CLC 4, 10, 22, 55, 81, 87; BLC 3; DA; DAB; DAC; DAM MST, MULT, NOV, POP**
See also AAYA 1, 22; BW 2, 3; CA 29-32R; CANR 27, 42, 67; CDALB 1968-1988; DLB 6, 33, 143; DLBY 81; MTCW 1, 2; SATA 57
Morrison, Van 1945- .... **CLC 21**
See also CA 116; 168
Morrissy, Mary 1958- .... **CLC 99**
Mortimer, John (Clifford) 1923- .... **CLC 28, 43; DAM DRAM, POP**
See also CA 13-16R; CANR 21, 69; CDBLB 1960 to Present; DLB 13; INT CANR-21; MTCW 1, 2
Mortimer, Penelope (Ruth) 1918- .... **CLC 5**
See also CA 57-60; CANR 45
Morton, Anthony
See Creasey, John
Mosca, Gaetano 1858-1941 .... **TCLC 75**
Mosher, Howard Frank 1943- .... **CLC 62**
See also CA 139; CANR 65
Mosley, Nicholas 1923- .... **CLC 43, 70**
See also CA 69-72; CANR 41, 60; DLB 14, 207
Mosley, Walter 1952- ..... **CLC 97; BLCS; DAM MULT, POP**
See also AAYA 17; BW 2; CA 142; CANR 57; MTCW 2
Moss, Howard 1922-1987**CLC 7, 14, 45, 50; DAM POET**
See also CA 1-4R; 123; CANR 1, 44; DLB 5
Mossgiel, Rab
See Burns, Robert
Motion, Andrew (Peter) 1952- .... **CLC 47**
See also CA 146; DLB 40
Motley, Willard (Francis) 1909-1965 .... **CLC 18**
See also BW 1; CA 117; 106; DLB 76, 143
Motoori, Norinaga 1730-1801 .... **NCLC 45**
Mott, Michael (Charles Alston) 1930-**CLC 15, 34**
See also CA 5-8R; CAAS 7; CANR 7, 29
Mountain Wolf Woman 1884-1960 .... **CLC 92**
See also CA 144; NNAL
Moure, Erin 1955- .... **CLC 88**
See also CA 113; DLB 60
Mowat, Farley (McGill) 1921- .... **CLC 26; DAC; DAM MST**
See also AAYA 1; CA 1-4R; CANR 4, 24, 42, 68; CLR 20; DLB 68; INT CANR-24; JRDA; MAICYA; MTCW 1, 2; SATA 3, 55
Mowatt, Anna Cora 1819-1870 .... **NCLC 74**
Moyers, Bill 1934- .... **CLC 74**
See also AITN 2; CA 61-64; CANR 31, 52
Mphahlele, Es'kia
See Mphahlele, Ezekiel
See also DLB 125
Mphahlele, Ezekiel 1919-**CLC 25; BLC 3; DAM MULT**
See also Mphahlele, Es'kia
See also BW 2, 3; CA 81-84; CANR 26, 76; MTCW 2
Mqhayi, S(amuel) E(dward) K(rune Loliwe) 1875-1945 .... **TCLC 25; BLC 3; DAM MULT**
See also CA 153
Mrozek, Slawomir 1930- .... **CLC 3, 13**
See also CA 13-16R; CAAS 10; CANR 29; MTCW 1
Mrs. Belloc-Lowndes
See Lowndes, Marie Adelaide (Belloc)
Mtwa, Percy (?)- .... **CLC 47**
Mueller, Lisel 1924- .... **CLC 13, 51**
See also CA 93-96; DLB 105
Muir, Edwin 1887-1959 .... **TCLC 2, 87**
See also CA 104; DLB 20, 100, 191
Muir, John 1838-1914 .... **TCLC 28**
See also CA 165; DLB 186
Mujica Lainez, Manuel 1910-1984 .... **CLC 31**
See also Lainez, Manuel Mujica
See also CA 81-84; 112; CANR 32; HW 1
Mukherjee, Bharati 1940- . **CLC 53, 115; DAM NOV**
See also BEST 89:2; CA 107; CANR 45, 72; DLB 60; MTCW 1, 2
Muldoon, Paul 1951- . **CLC 32, 72; DAM POET**
See also CA 113; 129; CANR 52; DLB 40; INT 129
Mulisch, Harry 1927- .... **CLC 42**
See also CA 9-12R; CANR 6, 26, 56
Mull, Martin 1943- .... **CLC 17**
See also CA 105
Muller, Wilhelm .... NCLC 73
Mulock, Dinah Maria
See Craik, Dinah Maria (Mulock)
Munford, Robert 1737(?)-1783 .... **LC 5**
See also DLB 31
Mungo, Raymond 1946- .... **CLC 72**
See also CA 49-52; CANR 2
Munro, Alice 1931-**CLC 6, 10, 19, 50, 95; DAC; DAM MST, NOV; SSC 3; WLCS**
See also AITN 2; CA 33-36R; CANR 33, 53, 75; DLB 53; MTCW 1, 2; SATA 29
Munro, H(ector) H(ugh) 1870-1916
See Saki
See also CA 104; 130; CDBLB 1890-1914; DA; DAB; DAC; DAM MST, NOV; DLB 34, 162; MTCW 1, 2; WLC
Murdoch, (Jean) Iris 1919-**CLC 1, 2, 3, 4, 6, 8, 11, 15, 22, 31, 51; DAB; DAC; DAM MST, NOV**
See also CA 13-16R; CANR 8, 43, 68; CDBLB 1960 to Present; DLB 14, 194; INT CANR-8; MTCW 1, 2
Murfree, Mary Noailles 1850-1922 ... **SSC 22**
See also CA 122; 176; DLB 12, 74
Murnau, Friedrich Wilhelm
See Plumpe, Friedrich Wilhelm
Murphy, Richard 1927- .... **CLC 41**
See also CA 29-32R; DLB 40
Murphy, Sylvia 1937- .... **CLC 34**
See also CA 121
Murphy, Thomas (Bernard) 1935- .... **CLC 51**
See also CA 101
Murray, Albert L. 1916- .... **CLC 73**
See also BW 2; CA 49-52; CANR 26, 52, 78; DLB 38
Murray, Judith Sargent 1751-1820 ..... **NCLC 63**
See also DLB 37, 200
Murray, Les(lie) A(llan) 1938- .... **CLC 40; DAM POET**
See also CA 21-24R; CANR 11, 27, 56
Murry, J. Middleton
See Murry, John Middleton
Murry, John Middleton 1889-1957 ...... **TCLC 16**
See also CA 118; DLB 149
Musgrave, Susan 1951- .... **CLC 13, 54**
See also CA 69-72; CANR 45
Musil, Robert (Edler von) 1880-1942**TCLC 12, 68; SSC 18**
See also CA 109; CANR 55; DLB 81, 124; MTCW 2
Muske, Carol 1945- .... **CLC 90**
See also Muske-Dukes, Carol (Anne)
Muske-Dukes, Carol (Anne) 1945-
See Muske, Carol
See also CA 65-68; CANR 32, 70
Musset, (Louis Charles) Alfred de 1810-1857 **NCLC 7**
See also DLB 192
My Brother's Brother
See Chekhov, Anton (Pavlovich)
Myers, L(eopold) H(amilton) 1881-1944**TCLC 59**
See also CA 157; DLB 15
Myers, Walter Dean 1937-**CLC 35; BLC 3; DAM MULT, NOV**
See also AAYA 4, 23; BW 2, 3; CA 33-36R; CANR 20, 42, 67; CLR 4, 16, 35; DLB 33; INT CANR-20; JRDA; MAICYA; MTCW 2; SAAS 2; SATA 41, 71, 109; SATA-Brief 27
Myers, Walter M.
See Myers, Walter Dean
Myles, Symon
See Follett, Ken(neth Martin)
Nabokov, Vladimir (Vladimirovich) 1899-1977 **CLC 1, 2, 3, 6, 8, 11, 15, 23, 44, 46, 64; DA; DAB; DAC; DAM MST, NOV; SSC 11; WLC**
See also CA 5-8R; 69-72; CANR 20; CDALB 1941-1968; DLB 2; DLBD 3; DLBY 80, 91; MTCW 1, 2
Nagai Kafu 1879-1959 .... **TCLC 51**
See also Nagai Sokichi
See also DLB 180
Nagai Sokichi 1879-1959

See Nagai Kafu
See also CA 117
Nagy, Laszlo 1925-1978 .... **CLC 7**
See also CA 129; 112
Naidu, Sarojini 1879-1943 .... **TCLC 80**
Naipaul, Shiva(dhar Srinivasa) 1945-1985 . **CLC 32, 39; DAM NOV**
See also CA 110; 112; 116; CANR 33; DLB 157; DLBY 85; MTCW 1, 2
Naipaul, V(idiadhar) S(urajprasad) 1932-**CLC 4, 7, 9, 13, 18, 37, 105; DAB; DAC; DAM MST, NOV**
See also CA 1-4R; CANR 1, 33, 51; CDBLB 1960 to Present; DLB 125, 204, 206; DLBY 85; MTCW 1, 2
Nakos, Lilika 1899(?)- .... **CLC 29**
Narayan, R(asipuram) K(rishnaswami) 1906- **CLC 7, 28, 47, 121; DAM NOV; SSC 25**
See also CA 81-84; CANR 33, 61; MTCW 1, 2; SATA 62
Nash, (Frediric) Ogden 1902-1971**CLC 23; DAM POET; PC 21**
See also CA 13-14; 29-32R; CANR 34, 61; CAP 1; DLB 11; MAICYA; MTCW 1, 2; SATA 2, 46
Nashe, Thomas 1567-1601(?) .... **LC 41**
See also DLB 167
Nashe, Thomas 1567-1601 .... **LC 41**
Nathan, Daniel
See Dannay, Frederic
Nathan, George Jean 1882-1958 .... **TCLC 18**
See also Hatteras, Owen
See also CA 114; 169; DLB 137
Natsume, Kinnosuke 1867-1916
See Natsume, Soseki
See also CA 104
Natsume, Soseki 1867-1916 .... **TCLC 2, 10**
See also Natsume, Kinnosuke
See also DLB 180
Natti, (Mary) Lee 1919-
See Kingman, Lee
See also CA 5-8R; CANR 2
Naylor, Gloria 1950- .. **CLC 28, 52; BLC 3; DA; DAC; DAM MST, MULT, NOV, POP; WLCS**
See also AAYA 6; BW 2, 3; CA 107; CANR 27, 51, 74; DLB 173; MTCW 1, 2
Neihardt, John Gneisenau 1881-1973 ... **CLC 32**
See also CA 13-14; CANR 65; CAP 1; DLB 9, 54
Nekrasov, Nikolai Alekseevich 1821-1878**NCLC 11**
Nelligan, Emile 1879-1941 .... **TCLC 14**
See also CA 114; DLB 92
Nelson, Willie 1933- .... **CLC 17**
See also CA 107
Nemerov, Howard (Stanley) 1920-1991**CLC 2, 6, 9, 36; DAM POET; PC 24**
See also CA 1-4R; 134; CABS 2; CANR 1, 27, 53; DLB 5, 6; DLBY 83; INT CANR-27; MTCW 1, 2
Neruda, Pablo 1904-1973**CLC 1, 2, 5, 7, 9, 28, 62; DA; DAB; DAC; DAM MST, MULT, POET; HLC; PC 4; WLC**
See also CA 19-20; 45-48; CAP 2; HW 1; MTCW 1, 2
Nerval, Gerard de 1808-1855**NCLC 1, 67; PC 13; SSC 18**
Nervo, (Jose) Amado (Ruiz de) 1870-1919 **TCLC 11; HLCS 2**
See also CA 109; 131; HW 1
Nessi, Pio Baroja y
See Baroja (y Nessi), Pio
Nestroy, Johann 1801-1862 .... **NCLC 42**
See also DLB 133
Netterville, Luke
See O'Grady, Standish (James)
Neufeld, John (Arthur) 1938- .... **CLC 17**
See also AAYA 11; CA 25-28R; CANR 11, 37, 56; CLR 52; MAICYA; SAAS 3; SATA 6, 81
Neville, Emily Cheney 1919- .... **CLC 12**
See also CA 5-8R; CANR 3, 37; JRDA; MAICYA; SAAS 2; SATA 1
Newbound, Bernard Slade 1930-
See Slade, Bernard
See also CA 81-84; CANR 49; DAM DRAM
Newby, P(ercy) H(oward) 1918-1997 . **CLC 2, 13; DAM NOV**
See also CA 5-8R; 161; CANR 32, 67; DLB 15; MTCW 1
Newlove, Donald 1928- .... **CLC 6**
See also CA 29-32R; CANR 25
Newlove, John (Herbert) 1938- .... **CLC 14**
See also CA 21-24R; CANR 9, 25
Newman, Charles 1938- .... **CLC 2, 8**
See also CA 21-24R
Newman, Edwin (Harold) 1919- .... **CLC 14**
See also AITN 1; CA 69-72; CANR 5
Newman, John Henry 1801-1890 .... **NCLC 38**
See also DLB 18, 32, 55
Newton, (Sir)Isaac 1642-1727 .... **LC 35**
Newton, Suzanne 1936- .... **CLC 35**
See also CA 41-44R; CANR 14; JRDA; SATA 5, 77
Nexo, Martin Andersen 1869-1954 ..... **TCLC 43**
Nezval, Vitezslav 1900-1958 .... **TCLC 44**
See also CA 123
Ng, Fae Myenne 1957(?)- .... **CLC 81**
See also CA 146
Ngema, Mbongeni 1955- .... **CLC 57**
See also BW 2; CA 143
Ngugi, James T(hiong'o) .... **CLC 3, 7, 13**
See also Ngugi wa Thiong'o
Ngugi wa Thiong'o 1938-**CLC 36; BLC 3; DAM MULT, NOV**
See also Ngugi, James T(hiong'o)
See also BW 2; CA 81-84; CANR 27, 58; DLB 125; MTCW 1, 2
Nichol, B(arrie) P(hillip) 1944-1988 ..... **CLC 18**
See also CA 53-56; DLB 53; SATA 66
Nichols, John (Treadwell) 1940- .... **CLC 38**
See also CA 9-12R; CAAS 2; CANR 6, 70; DLBY 82
Nichols, Leigh
See Koontz, Dean R(ay)
Nichols, Peter (Richard) 1927- ... **CLC 5, 36, 65**
See also CA 104; CANR 33; DLB 13; MTCW 1
Nicolas, F. R. E.
See Freeling, Nicolas
Niedecker, Lorine 1903-1970 **CLC 10, 42; DAM POET**
See also CA 25-28; CAP 2; DLB 48
Nietzsche, Friedrich (Wilhelm) 1844-1900**TCLC 10, 18, 55**
See also CA 107; 121; DLB 129
Nievo, Ippolito 1831-1861 .... **NCLC 22**
Nightingale, Anne Redmon 1943-
See Redmon, Anne
See also CA 103
Nightingale, Florence 1820-1910 .... **TCLC 85**
See also DLB 166
Nik. T. O.
See Annensky, Innokenty (Fyodorovich)
Nin, Anais 1903-1977**CLC 1, 4, 8, 11, 14, 60; DAM NOV, POP; SSC 10**
See also AITN 2; CA 13-16R; 69-72; CANR 22, 53; DLB 2, 4, 152; MTCW 1, 2
Nishida, Kitaro 1870-1945 .... **TCLC 83**
Nishiwaki, Junzaburo 1894-1982 .... **PC 15**
See also CA 107
Nissenson, Hugh 1933- .... **CLC 4, 9**
See also CA 17-20R; CANR 27; DLB 28
Niven, Larry .... **CLC 8**
See also Niven, Laurence Van Cott
See also AAYA 27; DLB 8
Niven, Laurence Van Cott 1938-
See Niven, Larry
See also CA 21-24R; CAAS 12; CANR 14, 44, 66; DAM POP; MTCW 1, 2; SATA 95
Nixon, Agnes Eckhardt 1927- .... **CLC 21**
See also CA 110
Nizan, Paul 1905-1940 .... **TCLC 40**
See also CA 161; DLB 72
Nkosi, Lewis 1936-**CLC 45; BLC 3; DAM MULT**
See also BW 1, 3; CA 65-68; CANR 27, 81; DLB 157
Nodier, (Jean) Charles (Emmanuel) 1780-1844 **NCLC 19**
See also DLB 119
Noguchi, Yone 1875-1947 .... **TCLC 80**
Nolan, Christopher 1965- .... **CLC 58**
See also CA 111
Noon, Jeff 1957- .... **CLC 91**
See also CA 148
Norden, Charles
See Durrell, Lawrence (George)
Nordhoff, Charles (Bernard) 1887-1947**TCLC 23**
See also CA 108; DLB 9; SATA 23
Norfolk, Lawrence 1963- .... **CLC 76**
See also CA 144
Norman, Marsha 1947-**CLC 28; DAM DRAM; DC 8**
See also CA 105; CABS 3; CANR 41; DLBY 84
Normyx
See Douglas, (George) Norman
Norris, Frank 1870-1902 .... **SSC 28**
See also Norris, (Benjamin) Frank(lin, Jr.)
See also CDALB 1865-1917; DLB 12, 71, 186
Norris, (Benjamin) Frank(lin, Jr.) 1870-1902 **TCLC 24**
See also Norris, Frank
See also CA 110; 160
Norris, Leslie 1921- .... **CLC 14**
See also CA 11-12; CANR 14; CAP 1; DLB 27
North, Andrew
See Norton, Andre
North, Anthony
See Koontz, Dean R(ay)
North, Captain George
See Stevenson, Robert Louis (Balfour)
North, Milou
See Erdrich, Louise
Northrup, B. A.
See Hubbard, L(afayette) Ron(ald)
North Staffs
See Hulme, T(homas) E(rnest)
Norton, Alice Mary
See Norton, Andre
See also MAICYA; SATA 1, 43
Norton, Andre 1912- .... **CLC 12**
See also Norton, Alice Mary
See also AAYA 14; CA 1-4R; CANR 68; CLR 50; DLB 8, 52; JRDA; MTCW 1; SATA 91
Norton, Caroline 1808-1877 .... **NCLC 47**
See also DLB 21, 159, 199
Norway, Nevil Shute 1899-1960
See Shute, Nevil
See also CA 102; 93-96; MTCW 2
Norwid, Cyprian Kamil 1821-1883 ...... **NCLC 17**
Nosille, Nabrah
See Ellison, Harlan (Jay)
Nossack, Hans Erich 1901-1978 .... **CLC 6**
See also CA 93-96; 85-88; DLB 69
Nostradamus 1503-1566 .... **LC 27**
Nosu, Chuji
See Ozu, Yasujiro
Notenburg, Eleanora (Genrikhovna) von
See Guro, Elena
Nova, Craig 1945- .... **CLC 7, 31**
See also CA 45-48; CANR 2, 53
Novak, Joseph
See Kosinski, Jerzy (Nikodem)
Novalis 1772-1801 .... **NCLC 13**
See also DLB 90

Novis, Emile
See Weil, Simone (Adolphine)
Nowlan, Alden (Albert) 1933-1983**CLC 15; DAC; DAM MST**
See also CA 9-12R; CANR 5; DLB 53
Noyes, Alfred 1880-1958 .... **TCLC 7**
See also CA 104; DLB 20
Nunn, Kem .... **CLC 34**
See also CA 159
Nye, Robert 1939- .... **CLC 13, 42; DAM NOV**
See also CA 33-36R; CANR 29, 67; DLB 14; MTCW 1; SATA 6
Nyro, Laura 1947- .... **CLC 17**
Oates, Joyce Carol 1938-**CLC 1, 2, 3, 6, 9, 11, 15, 19, 33, 52, 108; DA; DAB; DAC; DAM MST, NOV, POP; SSC 6; WLC**
See also AAYA 15; AITN 1; BEST 89:2; CA 5-8R; CANR 25, 45, 74; CDALB 1968-1988; DLB 2, 5, 130; DLBY 81; INT CANR-25; MTCW 1, 2
O'Brien, Darcy 1939-1998 .... **CLC 11**
See also CA 21-24R; 167; CANR 8, 59
O'Brien, E. G.
See Clarke, Arthur C(harles)
O'Brien, Edna 1936-**CLC 3, 5, 8, 13, 36, 65, 116; DAM NOV; SSC 10**
See also CA 1-4R; CANR 6, 41, 65; CDBLB 1960 to Present; DLB 14; MTCW 1, 2
O'Brien, Fitz-James 1828-1862 .... **NCLC 21**
See also DLB 74
O'Brien, Flann .... **CLC 1, 4, 5, 7, 10, 47**
See also O Nuallain, Brian
O'Brien, Richard 1942- .... **CLC 17**
See also CA 124
O'Brien, (William) Tim(othy) 1946- **CLC 7, 19, 40, 103; DAM POP**
See also AAYA 16; CA 85-88; CANR 40, 58; CDALBS; DLB 152; DLBD 9; DLBY 80; MTCW 2
Obstfelder, Sigbjoern 1866-1900 .... **TCLC 23**
See also CA 123
O'Casey, Sean 1880-1964**CLC 1, 5, 9, 11, 15, 88; DAB; DAC; DAM DRAM, MST; WLCS**
See also CA 89-92; CANR 62; CDBLB 1914-1945; DLB 10; MTCW 1, 2
O'Cathasaigh, Sean
See O'Casey, Sean
Ochs, Phil 1940-1976 .... **CLC 17**
See also CA 65-68
O'Connor, Edwin (Greene) 1918-1968 .. **CLC 14**
See also CA 93-96; 25-28R
O'Connor, (Mary) Flannery 1925-1964**CLC 1, 2, 3, 6, 10, 13, 15, 21, 66, 104; DA; DAB; DAC; DAM MST, NOV; SSC 1, 23; WLC**
See also AAYA 7; CA 1-4R; CANR 3, 41; CDALB 1941-1968; DLB 2, 152; DLBD 12; DLBY 80; MTCW 1, 2
O'Connor, Frank .... **CLC 23; SSC 5**
See also O'Donovan, Michael John
See also DLB 162
O'Dell, Scott 1898-1989 .... **CLC 30**
See also AAYA 3; CA 61-64; 129; CANR 12, 30; CLR 1, 16; DLB 52; JRDA; MAICYA; SATA 12, 60
Odets, Clifford 1906-1963 **CLC 2, 28, 98; DAM DRAM; DC 6**
See also CA 85-88; CANR 62; DLB 7, 26; MTCW 1, 2
O'Doherty, Brian 1934- .... **CLC 76**
See also CA 105
O'Donnell, K. M.
See Malzberg, Barry N(athaniel)
O'Donnell, Lawrence
See Kuttner, Henry
O'Donovan, Michael John 1903-1966 ... **CLC 14**
See also O'Connor, Frank
See also CA 93-96
Oe, Kenzaburo 1935- **CLC 10, 36, 86; DAM NOV; SSC 20**
See also CA 97-100; CANR 36, 50, 74; DLB 182; DLBY 94; MTCW 1, 2
O'Faolain, Julia 1932- .... **CLC 6, 19, 47, 108**
See also CA 81-84; CAAS 2; CANR 12, 61; DLB 14; MTCW 1
O'Faolain, Sean 1900-1991 **CLC 1, 7, 14, 32, 70; SSC 13**
See also CA 61-64; 134; CANR 12, 66; DLB 15, 162; MTCW 1, 2
O'Flaherty, Liam 1896-1984 .. **CLC 5, 34; SSC 6**
See also CA 101; 113; CANR 35; DLB 36, 162; DLBY 84; MTCW 1, 2
Ogilvy, Gavin
See Barrie, J(ames) M(atthew)
O'Grady, Standish (James) 1846-1928**TCLC 5**
See also CA 104; 157
O'Grady, Timothy 1951- .... **CLC 59**
See also CA 138
O'Hara, Frank 1926-1966**CLC 2, 5, 13, 78; DAM POET**
See also CA 9-12R; 25-28R; CANR 33; DLB 5, 16, 193; MTCW 1, 2
O'Hara, John (Henry) 1905-1970 **CLC 1, 2, 3, 6, 11, 42; DAM NOV; SSC 15**
See also CA 5-8R; 25-28R; CANR 31, 60; CDALB 1929-1941; DLB 9, 86; DLBD 2; MTCW 1, 2
O Hehir, Diana 1922- .... **CLC 41**
See also CA 93-96
Okigbo, Christopher (Ifenayichukwu) 1932-1967 **CLC 25, 84; BLC 3; DAM MULT, POET; PC 7**
See also BW 1, 3; CA 77-80; CANR 74; DLB 125; MTCW 1, 2
Okri, Ben 1959- .... **CLC 87**
See also BW 2, 3; CA 130; 138; CANR 65; DLB 157; INT 138; MTCW 2
Olds, Sharon 1942-**CLC 32, 39, 85; DAM POET; PC 22**
See also CA 101; CANR 18, 41, 66; DLB 120; MTCW 2
Oldstyle, Jonathan
See Irving, Washington
Olesha, Yuri (Karlovich) 1899-1960 .... **CLC 8**
See also CA 85-88
Oliphant, Laurence 1829(?)-1888 .... **NCLC 47**
See also DLB 18, 166
Oliphant, Margaret (Oliphant Wilson) 1828-1897 **NCLC 11, 61; SSC 25**
See also DLB 18, 159, 190
Oliver, Mary 1935- .... **CLC 19, 34, 98**
See also CA 21-24R; CANR 9, 43; DLB 5, 193
Olivier, Laurence (Kerr) 1907-1989 ..... **CLC 20**
See also CA 111; 150; 129
Olsen, Tillie 1912- . **CLC 4, 13, 114; DA; DAB; DAC; DAM MST; SSC 11**
See also CA 1-4R; CANR 1, 43, 74; CDALBS; DLB 28, 206; DLBY 80; MTCW 1, 2
Olson, Charles (John) 1910-1970**CLC 1, 2, 5, 6, 9, 11, 29; DAM POET; PC 19**
See also CA 13-16; 25-28R; CABS 2; CANR 35, 61; CAP 1; DLB 5, 16, 193; MTCW 1, 2
Olson, Toby 1937- .... **CLC 28**
See also CA 65-68; CANR 9, 31
Olyesha, Yuri
See Olesha, Yuri (Karlovich)
Ondaatje, (Philip) Michael 1943-**CLC 14, 29, 51, 76; DAB; DAC; DAM MST**
See also CA 77-80; CANR 42, 74; DLB 60; MTCW 2
Oneal, Elizabeth 1934-
See Oneal, Zibby
See also CA 106; CANR 28; MAICYA; SATA 30, 82
Oneal, Zibby .... **CLC 30**
See also Oneal, Elizabeth
See also AAYA 5; CLR 13; JRDA
O'Neill, Eugene (Gladstone) 1888-1953**TCLC 1, 6, 27, 49; DA; DAB; DAC; DAM DRAM, MST; WLC**
See also AITN 1; CA 110; 132; CDALB 1929-1941; DLB 7; MTCW 1, 2
Onetti, Juan Carlos 1909-1994 **CLC 7, 10; DAM MULT, NOV; HLCS 2; SSC 23**
See also CA 85-88; 145; CANR 32, 63; DLB 113; HW 1, 2; MTCW 1, 2
O Nuallain, Brian 1911-1966
See O'Brien, Flann
See also CA 21-22; 25-28R; CAP 2
Ophuls, Max 1902-1957 .... **TCLC 79**
See also CA 113
Opie, Amelia 1769-1853 .... **NCLC 65**
See also DLB 116, 159
Oppen, George 1908-1984 ...... **CLC 7, 13, 34**
See also CA 13-16R; 113; CANR 8; DLB 5, 165
Oppenheim, E(dward) Phillips 1866-1946 **TCLC 45**
See also CA 111; DLB 70
Opuls, Max
See Ophuls, Max
Origen c. 185-c. 254 .... **CMLC 19**
Orlovitz, Gil 1918-1973 .... **CLC 22**
See also CA 77-80; 45-48; DLB 2, 5
Orris
See Ingelow, Jean
Ortega y Gasset, Jose 1883-1955 **TCLC 9; DAM MULT; HLC**
See also CA 106; 130; HW 1, 2; MTCW 1, 2
Ortese, Anna Maria 1914- .... **CLC 89**
See also DLB 177
Ortiz, Simon J(oseph) 1941- .... **CLC 45; DAM MULT, POET; PC 17**
See also CA 134; CANR 69; DLB 120, 175; NNAL
Orton, Joe .... **CLC 4, 13, 43; DC 3**
See also Orton, John Kingsley
See also CDBLB 1960 to Present; DLB 13; MTCW 2
Orton, John Kingsley 1933-1967
See Orton, Joe
See also CA 85-88; CANR 35, 66; DAM DRAM; MTCW 1, 2
Orwell, George **TCLC 2, 6, 15, 31, 51; DAB; WLC**
See also Blair, Eric (Arthur)
See also CDBLB 1945-1960; DLB 15, 98, 195
Osborne, David
See Silverberg, Robert
Osborne, George
See Silverberg, Robert
Osborne, John (James) 1929-1994**CLC 1, 2, 5, 11, 45; DA; DAB; DAC; DAM DRAM, MST; WLC**
See also CA 13-16R; 147; CANR 21, 56; CDBLB 1945-1960; DLB 13; MTCW 1, 2
Osborne, Lawrence 1958- .... **CLC 50**
Osbourne, Lloyd 1868-1947 .... **TCLC 93**
Oshima, Nagisa 1932- .... **CLC 20**
See also CA 116; 121; CANR 78
Oskison, John Milton 1874-1947**TCLC 35; DAM MULT**
See also CA 144; DLB 175; NNAL
Ossian c. 3rd cent. - .... **CMLC 28**
See also Macpherson, James
Ossoli, Sarah Margaret (Fuller marchesa d') 1810-1850
See Fuller, Margaret
See also SATA 25
Ostrovsky, Alexander 1823-1886 .. **NCLC 30, 57**
Otero, Blas de 1916-1979 .... **CLC 11**
See also CA 89-92; DLB 134
Otto, Rudolf 1869-1937 .... **TCLC 85**
Otto, Whitney 1955- .... **CLC 70**

Author Index

See also CA 140
Ouida .... **TCLC 43**
See also De La Ramee, (Marie) Louise
See also DLB 18, 156
Ousmane, Sembene 1923- .... **CLC 66; BLC 3**
See also BW 1, 3; CA 117; 125; CANR 81; MTCW 1
Ovid 43B.C.-17 .... **CMLC 7; DAM POET; PC 2**
See also DLB 211
Owen, Hugh
See Faust, Frederick (Schiller)
Owen, Wilfred (Edward Salter) 1893-1918 **TCLC 5, 27; DA; DAB; DAC; DAM MST, POET; PC 19; WLC**
See also CA 104; 141; CDBLB 1914-1945; DLB 20; MTCW 2
Owens, Rochelle 1936- .... **CLC 8**
See also CA 17-20R; CAAS 2; CANR 39
Oz, Amos 1939- **CLC 5, 8, 11, 27, 33, 54; DAM NOV**
See also CA 53-56; CANR 27, 47, 65; MTCW 1, 2
Ozick, Cynthia 1928- **CLC 3, 7, 28, 62; DAM NOV, POP; SSC 15**
See also BEST 90:1; CA 17-20R; CANR 23, 58; DLB 28, 152; DLBY 82; INT CANR-23; MTCW 1, 2
Ozu, Yasujiro 1903-1963 .... **CLC 16**
See also CA 112
Pacheco, C.
See Pessoa, Fernando (Antonio Nogueira)
Pa Chin .... **CLC 18**
See also Li Fei-kan
Pack, Robert 1929- .... **CLC 13**
See also CA 1-4R; CANR 3, 44; DLB 5
Padgett, Lewis
See Kuttner, Henry
Padilla (Lorenzo), Heberto 1932- .... **CLC 38**
See also AITN 1; CA 123; 131; HW 1
Page, Jimmy 1944- .... **CLC 12**
Page, Louise 1955- .... **CLC 40**
See also CA 140; CANR 76
Page, P(atricia) K(athleen) 1916- .... **CLC 7, 18; DAC; DAM MST; PC 12**
See also CA 53-56; CANR 4, 22, 65; DLB 68; MTCW 1
Page, Thomas Nelson 1853-1922 .... **SSC 23**
See also CA 118; 177; DLB 12, 78; DLBD 13
Pagels, Elaine Hiesey 1943- .... **CLC 104**
See also CA 45-48; CANR 2, 24, 51
Paget, Violet 1856-1935
See Lee, Vernon
See also CA 104; 166
Paget-Lowe, Henry
See Lovecraft, H(oward) P(hillips)
Paglia, Camille (Anna) 1947- .... **CLC 68**
See also CA 140; CANR 72; MTCW 2
Paige, Richard
See Koontz, Dean R(ay)
Paine, Thomas 1737-1809 .... **NCLC 62**
See also CDALB 1640-1865; DLB 31, 43, 73, 158
Pakenham, Antonia
See Fraser, (Lady) Antonia (Pakenham)
Palamas, Kostes 1859-1943 .... **TCLC 5**
See also CA 105
Palazzeschi, Aldo 1885-1974 .... **CLC 11**
See also CA 89-92; 53-56; DLB 114
Paley, Grace 1922- **CLC 4, 6, 37; DAM POP; SSC 8**
See also CA 25-28R; CANR 13, 46, 74; DLB 28; INT CANR-13; MTCW 1, 2
Palin, Michael (Edward) 1943- .... **CLC 21**
See also Monty Python
See also CA 107; CANR 35; SATA 67
Palliser, Charles 1947- .... **CLC 65**
See also CA 136; CANR 76
Palma, Ricardo 1833-1919 .... **TCLC 29**
See also CA 168
Pancake, Breece Dexter 1952-1979
See Pancake, Breece D'J
See also CA 123; 109
Pancake, Breece D'J .... **CLC 29**
See also Pancake, Breece Dexter
See also DLB 130
Panko, Rudy
See Gogol, Nikolai (Vasilyevich)
Papadiamantis, Alexandros 1851-1911 **TCLC 29**
See also CA 168
Papadiamantopoulos, Johannes 1856-1910
See Moreas, Jean
See also CA 117
Papini, Giovanni 1881-1956 .... **TCLC 22**
See also CA 121
Paracelsus 1493-1541 .... **LC 14**
See also DLB 179
Parasol, Peter
See Stevens, Wallace
Pardo Bazan, Emilia 1851-1921 .... **SSC 30**
Pareto, Vilfredo 1848-1923 .... **TCLC 69**
See also CA 175
Parfenie, Maria
See Codrescu, Andrei
Parini, Jay (Lee) 1948- .... **CLC 54**
See also CA 97-100; CAAS 16; CANR 32
Park, Jordan
See Kornbluth, C(yril) M.; Pohl, Frederik
Park, Robert E(zra) 1864-1944 .... **TCLC 73**
See also CA 122; 165
Parker, Bert
See Ellison, Harlan (Jay)
Parker, Dorothy (Rothschild) 1893-1967 **CLC 15, 68; DAM POET; SSC 2**
See also CA 19-20; 25-28R; CAP 2; DLB 11, 45, 86; MTCW 1, 2
Parker, Robert B(rown) 1932- .... **CLC 27; DAM NOV, POP**
See also AAYA 28; BEST 89:4; CA 49-52; CANR 1, 26, 52; INT CANR-26; MTCW 1
Parkin, Frank 1940- .... **CLC 43**
See also CA 147
Parkman, Francis, Jr. 1823-1893 .... **NCLC 12**
See also DLB 1, 30, 186
Parks, Gordon (Alexander Buchanan) 1912- **CLC 1, 16; BLC 3; DAM MULT**
See also AITN 2; BW 2, 3; CA 41-44R; CANR 26, 66; DLB 33; MTCW 2; SATA 8, 108
Parmenides c. 515B.C.-c. 450B.C. .... **CMLC 22**
See also DLB 176
Parnell, Thomas 1679-1718 .... **LC 3**
See also DLB 94
Parra, Nicanor 1914- **CLC 2, 102; DAM MULT; HLC**
See also CA 85-88; CANR 32; HW 1; MTCW 1
Parrish, Mary Frances
See Fisher, M(ary) F(rances) K(ennedy)
Parson
See Coleridge, Samuel Taylor
Parson Lot
See Kingsley, Charles
Partridge, Anthony
See Oppenheim, E(dward) Phillips
Pascal, Blaise 1623-1662 .... **LC 35**
Pascoli, Giovanni 1855-1912 .... **TCLC 45**
See also CA 170
Pasolini, Pier Paolo 1922-1975 **CLC 20, 37, 106; PC 17**
See also CA 93-96; 61-64; CANR 63; DLB 128, 177; MTCW 1
Pasquini
See Silone, Ignazio
Pastan, Linda (Olenik) 1932- .... **CLC 27; DAM POET**
See also CA 61-64; CANR 18, 40, 61; DLB 5
Pasternak, Boris (Leonidovich) 1890-1960 **CLC 7, 10, 18, 63; DA; DAB; DAC; DAM MST, NOV, POET; PC 6; SSC 31; WLC**
See also CA 127; 116; MTCW 1, 2
Patchen, Kenneth 1911-1972 **CLC 1, 2, 18; DAM POET**
See also CA 1-4R; 33-36R; CANR 3, 35; DLB 16, 48; MTCW 1
Pater, Walter (Horatio) 1839-1894 .... **NCLC 7**
See also CDBLB 1832-1890; DLB 57, 156
Paterson, A(ndrew) B(arton) 1864-1941 **TCLC 32**
See also CA 155; SATA 97
Paterson, Katherine (Womeldorf) 1932- **CLC 12, 30**
See also AAYA 1; CA 21-24R; CANR 28, 59; CLR 7, 50; DLB 52; JRDA; MAICYA; MTCW 1; SATA 13, 53, 92
Patmore, Coventry Kersey Dighton 1823-1896 **NCLC 9**
See also DLB 35, 98
Paton, Alan (Stewart) 1903-1988 **CLC 4, 10, 25, 55, 106; DA; DAB; DAC; DAM MST, NOV; WLC**
See also AAYA 26; CA 13-16; 125; CANR 22; CAP 1; DLBD 17; MTCW 1, 2; SATA 11; SATA-Obit 56
Paton Walsh, Gillian 1937-
See Walsh, Jill Paton
See also CANR 38; JRDA; MAICYA; SAAS 3; SATA 4, 72, 109
Patton, George S. 1885-1945 .... **TCLC 79**
Paulding, James Kirke 1778-1860 .... **NCLC 2**
See also DLB 3, 59, 74
Paulin, Thomas Neilson 1949-
See Paulin, Tom
See also CA 123; 128
Paulin, Tom .... **CLC 37**
See also Paulin, Thomas Neilson
See also DLB 40
Paustovsky, Konstantin (Georgievich) 1892-1968 **CLC 40**
See also CA 93-96; 25-28R
Pavese, Cesare 1908-1950 **TCLC 3; PC 13; SSC 19**
See also CA 104; 169; DLB 128, 177
Pavic, Milorad 1929- .... **CLC 60**
See also CA 136; DLB 181
Pavlov, Ivan Petrovich 1849-1936 .... **TCLC 91**
See also CA 118
Payne, Alan
See Jakes, John (William)
Paz, Gil
See Lugones, Leopoldo
Paz, Octavio 1914-1998 **CLC 3, 4, 6, 10, 19, 51, 65, 119; DA; DAB; DAC; DAM MST, MULT, POET; HLC; PC 1; WLC**
See also CA 73-76; 165; CANR 32, 65; DLBY 90, 98; HW 1, 2; MTCW 1, 2
p'Bitek, Okot 1931-1982 **CLC 96; BLC 3; DAM MULT**
See also BW 2, 3; CA 124; 107; DLB 125; MTCW 1, 2
Peacock, Molly 1947- .... **CLC 60**
See also CA 103; CAAS 21; CANR 52; DLB 120
Peacock, Thomas Love 1785-1866 .... **NCLC 22**
See also DLB 96, 116
Peake, Mervyn 1911-1968 .... **CLC 7, 54**
See also CA 5-8R; 25-28R; CANR 3; DLB 15, 160; MTCW 1; SATA 23
Pearce, Philippa .... **CLC 21**
See also Christie, (Ann) Philippa
See also CLR 9; DLB 161; MAICYA; SATA 1, 67
Pearl, Eric
See Elman, Richard (Martin)
Pearson, T(homas) R(eid) 1956- .... **CLC 39**
See also CA 120; 130; INT 130
Peck, Dale 1967- .... **CLC 81**
See also CA 146; CANR 72
Peck, John 1941- .... **CLC 3**
See also CA 49-52; CANR 3

Peck, Richard (Wayne) 1934- .... **CLC 21**
See also AAYA 1, 24; CA 85-88; CANR 19, 38; CLR 15; INT CANR-19; JRDA; MAICYA; SAAS 2; SATA 18, 55, 97
Peck, Robert Newton 1928- **CLC 17; DA; DAC; DAM MST**
See also AAYA 3; CA 81-84; CANR 31, 63; CLR 45; JRDA; MAICYA; SAAS 1; SATA 21, 62; SATA-Essay 108
Peckinpah, (David) Sam(uel) 1925-1984 **CLC 20**
See also CA 109; 114
Pedersen, Knut 1859-1952
See Hamsun, Knut
See also CA 104; 119; CANR 63; MTCW 1, 2
Peeslake, Gaffer
See Durrell, Lawrence (George)
Peguy, Charles Pierre 1873-1914 .... **TCLC 10**
See also CA 107
Peirce, Charles Sanders 1839-1914 **TCLC 81**
Pena, Ramon del Valle y
See Valle-Inclan, Ramon (Maria) del
Pendennis, Arthur Esquir
See Thackeray, William Makepeace
Penn, William 1644-1718 .... **LC 25**
See also DLB 24
Pepece
See Prado (Calvo), Pedro
Pepys, Samuel 1633-1703**LC 11; DA; DAB; DAC; DAM MST; WLC**
See also CDBLB 1660-1789; DLB 101
Percy, Walker 1916-1990 **CLC 2, 3, 6, 8, 14, 18, 47, 65; DAM NOV, POP**
See also CA 1-4R; 131; CANR 1, 23, 64; DLB 2; DLBY 80, 90; MTCW 1, 2
Percy, William Alexander 1885-1942 . **TCLC 84**
See also CA 163; MTCW 2
Perec, Georges 1936-1982 .... **CLC 56, 116**
See also CA 141; DLB 83
Pereda (y Sanchez de Porrua), Jose Maria de 1833-1906 .... **TCLC 16**
See also CA 117
Pereda y Porrua, Jose Maria de
See Pereda (y Sanchez de Porrua), Jose Maria de
Peregoy, George Weems
See Mencken, H(enry) L(ouis)
Perelman, S(idney) J(oseph) 1904-1979**CLC 3, 5, 9, 15, 23, 44, 49; DAM DRAM; SSC 32**
See also AITN 1, 2; CA 73-76; 89-92; CANR 18; DLB 11, 44; MTCW 1, 2
Peret, Benjamin 1899-1959 .... **TCLC 20**
See also CA 117
Peretz, Isaac Loeb 1851(?)-1915**TCLC 16; SSC 26**
See also CA 109
Peretz, Yitzkhok Leibush
See Peretz, Isaac Loeb
Perez Galdos, Benito 1843-1920**TCLC 27; HLCS 2**
See also CA 125; 153; HW 1
Perrault, Charles 1628-1703 .... **LC 2**
See also MAICYA; SATA 25
Perry, Brighton
See Sherwood, Robert E(mmet)
Perse, St.-John
See Leger, (Marie-Rene Auguste) Alexis Saint-Leger
Perutz, Leo(pold) 1882-1957 .... **TCLC 60**
See also CA 147; DLB 81
Peseenz, Tulio F.
See Lopez y Fuentes, Gregorio
Pesetsky, Bette 1932- .... **CLC 28**
See also CA 133; DLB 130
Peshkov, Alexei Maximovich 1868-1936
See Gorky, Maxim
See also CA 105; 141; DA; DAC; DAM DRAM, MST, NOV; MTCW 2
Pessoa, Fernando (Antonio Nogueira) 1888-1935 **TCLC 27; DAM MULT; HLC; PC 20**
See also CA 125
Peterkin, Julia Mood 1880-1961 .... **CLC 31**
See also CA 102; DLB 9
Peters, Joan K(aren) 1945- .... **CLC 39**
See also CA 158
Peters, Robert L(ouis) 1924- .... **CLC 7**
See also CA 13-16R; CAAS 8; DLB 105
Petofi, Sandor 1823-1849 .... **NCLC 21**
Petrakis, Harry Mark 1923- .... **CLC 3**
See also CA 9-12R; CANR 4, 30
Petrarch 1304-1374**CMLC 20; DAM POET; PC 8**
Petrov, Evgeny .... **TCLC 21**
See also Kataev, Evgeny Petrovich
Petry, Ann (Lane) 1908-1997 .... **CLC 1, 7, 18**
See also BW 1, 3; CA 5-8R; 157; CAAS 6; CANR 4, 46; CLR 12; DLB 76; JRDA; MAICYA; MTCW 1; SATA 5; SATA-Obit 94
Petursson, Halligrimur 1614-1674 .... **LC 8**
Peychinovich
See Vazov, Ivan (Minchov)
Phaedrus c. 18B.C.-c. 50 .... **CMLC 25**
See also DLB 211
Philips, Katherine 1632-1664 .... **LC 30**
See also DLB 131
Philipson, Morris H. 1926- .... **CLC 53**
See also CA 1-4R; CANR 4
Phillips, Caryl 1958-**CLC 96; BLCS; DAM MULT**
See also BW 2; CA 141; CANR 63; DLB 157; MTCW 2
Phillips, David Graham 1867-1911 ...... **TCLC 44**
See also CA 108; 176; DLB 9, 12
Phillips, Jack
See Sandburg, Carl (August)
Phillips, Jayne Anne 1952-**CLC 15, 33; SSC 16**
See also CA 101; CANR 24, 50; DLBY 80; INT CANR-24; MTCW 1, 2
Phillips, Richard
See Dick, Philip K(indred)
Phillips, Robert (Schaeffer) 1938- .... **CLC 28**
See also CA 17-20R; CAAS 13; CANR 8; DLB 105
Phillips, Ward
See Lovecraft, H(oward) P(hillips)
Piccolo, Lucio 1901-1969 .... **CLC 13**
See also CA 97-100; DLB 114
Pickthall, Marjorie L(owry) C(hristie) 1883-1922 **TCLC 21**
See also CA 107; DLB 92
Pico della Mirandola, Giovanni 1463-1494**LC 15**
Piercy, Marge 1936- .... **CLC 3, 6, 14, 18, 27, 62**
See also CA 21-24R; CAAS 1; CANR 13, 43, 66; DLB 120; MTCW 1, 2
Piers, Robert
See Anthony, Piers
Pieyre de Mandiargues, Andre 1909-1991
See Mandiargues, Andre Pieyre de
See also CA 103; 136; CANR 22
Pilnyak, Boris .... **TCLC 23**
See also Vogau, Boris Andreyevich
Pincherle, Alberto 1907-1990 **CLC 11, 18; DAM NOV**
See also Moravia, Alberto
See also CA 25-28R; 132; CANR 33, 63; MTCW 1
Pinckney, Darryl 1953- .... **CLC 76**
See also BW 2, 3; CA 143; CANR 79
Pindar 518B.C.-446B.C. .... **CMLC 12; PC 19**
See also DLB 176
Pineda, Cecile 1942- .... **CLC 39**
See also CA 118
Pinero, Arthur Wing 1855-1934**TCLC 32; DAM DRAM**
See also CA 110; 153; DLB 10
Pinero, Miguel (Antonio Gomez) 1946-1988**CLC 4, 55**
See also CA 61-64; 125; CANR 29; HW 1
Pinget, Robert 1919-1997 .... **CLC 7, 13, 37**
See also CA 85-88; 160; DLB 83
Pink Floyd
See Barrett, (Roger) Syd; Gilmour, David; Mason, Nick; Waters, Roger; Wright, Rick
Pinkney, Edward 1802-1828 .... **NCLC 31**
Pinkwater, Daniel Manus 1941- .... **CLC 35**
See also Pinkwater, Manus
See also AAYA 1; CA 29-32R; CANR 12, 38; CLR 4; JRDA; MAICYA; SAAS 3; SATA 46, 76
Pinkwater, Manus
See Pinkwater, Daniel Manus
See also SATA 8
Pinsky, Robert 1940-**CLC 9, 19, 38, 94, 121; DAM POET**
See also CA 29-32R; CAAS 4; CANR 58; DLBY 82, 98; MTCW 2
Pinta, Harold
See Pinter, Harold
Pinter, Harold 1930-**CLC 1, 3, 6, 9, 11, 15, 27, 58, 73; DA; DAB; DAC; DAM DRAM, MST; WLC**
See also CA 5-8R; CANR 33, 65; CDBLB 1960 to Present; DLB 13; MTCW 1, 2
Piozzi, Hester Lynch (Thrale) 1741-1821 **NCLC 57**
See also DLB 104, 142
Pirandello, Luigi 1867-1936 ... **TCLC 4, 29; DA; DAB; DAC; DAM DRAM, MST; DC 5; SSC 22; WLC**
See also CA 104; 153; MTCW 2
Pirsig, Robert M(aynard) 1928- .. **CLC 4, 6, 73; DAM POP**
See also CA 53-56; CANR 42, 74; MTCW 1, 2; SATA 39
Pisarev, Dmitry Ivanovich 1840-1868 .. **NCLC 25**
Pix, Mary (Griffith) 1666-1709 .... **LC 8**
See also DLB 80
Pixerecourt, (Rene Charles) Guilbert de 1773-1844 **NCLC 39**
See also DLB 192
Plaatje, Sol(omon) T(shekisho) 1876-1932**TCLC 73; BLCS**
See also BW 2, 3; CA 141; CANR 79
Plaidy, Jean
See Hibbert, Eleanor Alice Burford
Planche, James Robinson 1796-1880 .. **NCLC 42**
Plant, Robert 1948- .... **CLC 12**
Plante, David (Robert) 1940-**CLC 7, 23, 38; DAM NOV**
See also CA 37-40R; CANR 12, 36, 58; DLBY 83; INT CANR-12; MTCW 1
Plath, Sylvia 1932-1963 **CLC 1, 2, 3, 5, 9, 11, 14, 17, 50, 51, 62, 111; DA; DAB; DAC; DAM MST, POET; PC 1; WLC**
See also AAYA 13; CA 19-20; CANR 34; CAP 2; CDALB 1941-1968; DLB 5, 6, 152; MTCW 1, 2; SATA 96
Plato 428(?)B.C.-348(?)B.C. **CMLC 8; DA; DAB; DAC; DAM MST; WLCS**
See also DLB 176
Platonov, Andrei .... **TCLC 14**
See also Klimentov, Andrei Platonovich
Platt, Kin 1911- .... **CLC 26**
See also AAYA 11; CA 17-20R; CANR 11; JRDA; SAAS 17; SATA 21, 86
Plautus c. 251B.C.-184B.C. ...... **CMLC 24; DC 6**
See also DLB 211
Plick et Plock
See Simenon, Georges (Jacques Christian)
Plimpton, George (Ames) 1927- .... **CLC 36**
See also AITN 1; CA 21-24R; CANR 32, 70; DLB 185; MTCW 1, 2; SATA 10
Pliny the Elder c. 23-79 .... **CMLC 23**
See also DLB 211
Plomer, William Charles Franklin 1903-1973 **CLC 4, 8**
See also CA 21-22; CANR 34; CAP 2; DLB 20,

162, 191; MTCW 1; SATA 24
Plowman, Piers
See Kavanagh, Patrick (Joseph)
Plum, J.
See Wodehouse, P(elham) G(renville)
Plumly, Stanley (Ross) 1939- .... **CLC 33**
See also CA 108; 110; DLB 5, 193; INT 110
Plumpe, Friedrich Wilhelm 1888-1931 **TCLC 53**
See also CA 112
Po Chu-i 772-846 .... **CMLC 24**
Poe, Edgar Allan 1809-1849 **NCLC 1, 16, 55, 78; DA; DAB; DAC; DAM MST, POET; PC 1; SSC 34; WLC**
See also AAYA 14; CDALB 1640-1865; DLB 3, 59, 73, 74; SATA 23
Poet of Titchfield Street, The
See Pound, Ezra (Weston Loomis)
Pohl, Frederik 1919- .... **CLC 18; SSC 25**
See also AAYA 24; CA 61-64; CAAS 1; CANR 11, 37, 81; DLB 8; INT CANR-11; MTCW 1, 2; SATA 24
Poirier, Louis 1910-
See Gracq, Julien
See also CA 122; 126
Poitier, Sidney 1927- .... **CLC 26**
See also BW 1; CA 117
Polanski, Roman 1933- .... **CLC 16**
See also CA 77-80
Poliakoff, Stephen 1952- .... **CLC 38**
See also CA 106; DLB 13
Police, The
See Copeland, Stewart (Armstrong); Summers, Andrew James; Sumner, Gordon Matthew
Polidori, John William 1795-1821 ...... **NCLC 51**
See also DLB 116
Pollitt, Katha 1949- .... **CLC 28**
See also CA 120; 122; CANR 66; MTCW 1, 2
Pollock, (Mary) Sharon 1936- ... **CLC 50; DAC; DAM DRAM, MST**
See also CA 141; DLB 60
Polo, Marco 1254-1324 .... **CMLC 15**
Polonsky, Abraham (Lincoln) 1910- ..... **CLC 92**
See also CA 104; DLB 26; INT 104
Polybius c. 200B.C.-c. 118B.C. .... **CMLC 17**
See also DLB 176
Pomerance, Bernard 1940- **CLC 13; DAM DRAM**
See also CA 101; CANR 49
Ponge, Francis (Jean Gaston Alfred) 1899-1988 **CLC 6, 18; DAM POET**
See also CA 85-88; 126; CANR 40
Pontoppidan, Henrik 1857-1943 .... **TCLC 29**
See also CA 170
Poole, Josephine .... **CLC 17**
See also Helyar, Jane Penelope Josephine
See also SAAS 2; SATA 5
Popa, Vasko 1922-1991 .... **CLC 19**
See also CA 112; 148; DLB 181
Pope, Alexander 1688-1744 **LC 3; DA; DAB; DAC; DAM MST, POET; PC 26; WLC**
See also CDBLB 1660-1789; DLB 95, 101
Porter, Connie (Rose) 1959(?)- .... **CLC 70**
See also BW 2, 3; CA 142; SATA 81
Porter, Gene(va Grace) Stratton 1863(?)-1924 **TCLC 21**
See also CA 112
Porter, Katherine Anne 1890-1980 . **CLC 1, 3, 7, 10, 13, 15, 27, 101; DA; DAB; DAC; DAM MST, NOV; SSC 4, 31**
See also AITN 2; CA 1-4R; 101; CANR 1, 65; CDALBS; DLB 4, 9, 102; DLBD 12; DLBY 80; MTCW 1, 2; SATA 39; SATA-Obit 23
Porter, Peter (Neville Frederick) 1929- . **CLC 5, 13, 33**
See also CA 85-88; DLB 40
Porter, William Sydney 1862-1910
See Henry, O.
See also CA 104; 131; CDALB 1865-1917; DA; DAB; DAC; DAM MST; DLB 12, 78, 79; MTCW 1, 2; YABC 2
Portillo (y Pacheco), Jose Lopez
See Lopez Portillo (y Pacheco), Jose
Post, Melville Davisson 1869-1930...... **TCLC 39**
See also CA 110
Potok, Chaim 1929- **CLC 2, 7, 14, 26, 112; DAM NOV**
See also AAYA 15; AITN 1, 2; CA 17-20R; CANR 19, 35, 64; DLB 28, 152; INT CANR-19; MTCW 1, 2; SATA 33, 106
Potter, (Helen) Beatrix 1866-1943
See Webb, (Martha) Beatrice (Potter)
See also MAICYA; MTCW 2
Potter, Dennis (Christopher George) 1935-1994 **CLC 58, 86**
See also CA 107; 145; CANR 33, 61; MTCW 1
Pound, Ezra (Weston Loomis) 1885-1972 **CLC 1, 2, 3, 4, 5, 7, 10, 13, 18, 34, 48, 50, 112; DA; DAB; DAC; DAM MST, POET; PC 4; WLC**
See also CA 5-8R; 37-40R; CANR 40; CDALB 1917-1929; DLB 4, 45, 63; DLBD 15; MTCW 1, 2
Povod, Reinaldo 1959-1994 .... **CLC 44**
See also CA 136; 146
Powell, Adam Clayton, Jr. 1908-1972 ... **CLC 89; BLC 3; DAM MULT**
See also BW 1, 3; CA 102; 33-36R
Powell, Anthony (Dymoke) 1905- **CLC 1, 3, 7, 9, 10, 31**
See also CA 1-4R; CANR 1, 32, 62; CDBLB 1945-1960; DLB 15; MTCW 1, 2
Powell, Dawn 1897-1965 .... **CLC 66**
See also CA 5-8R; DLBY 97
Powell, Padgett 1952- .... **CLC 34**
See also CA 126; CANR 63
Power, Susan 1961- .... **CLC 91**
Powers, J(ames) F(arl) 1917- ... **CLC 1, 4, 8, 57; SSC 4**
See also CA 1-4R; CANR 2, 61; DLB 130; MTCW 1
Powers, John J(ames) 1945-
See Powers, John R.
See also CA 69-72
Powers, John R. .... **CLC 66**
See also Powers, John J(ames)
Powers, Richard (S.) 1957- .... **CLC 93**
See also CA 148; CANR 80
Pownall, David 1938- .... **CLC 10**
See also CA 89-92; CAAS 18; CANR 49; DLB 14
Powys, John Cowper 1872-1963 **CLC 7, 9, 15, 46**
See also CA 85-88; DLB 15; MTCW 1, 2
Powys, T(heodore) F(rancis) 1875-1953 **TCLC 9**
See also CA 106; DLB 36, 162
Prado (Calvo), Pedro 1886-1952 .... **TCLC 75**
See also CA 131; HW 1
Prager, Emily 1952- .... **CLC 56**
Pratt, E(dwin) J(ohn) 1883(?)-1964 **CLC 19; DAC; DAM POET**
See also CA 141; 93-96; CANR 77; DLB 92
Premchand .... **TCLC 21**
See also Srivastava, Dhanpat Rai
Preussler, Otfried 1923- .... **CLC 17**
See also CA 77-80; SATA 24
Prevert, Jacques (Henri Marie) 1900-1977 **CLC 15**
See also CA 77-80; 69-72; CANR 29, 61; MTCW 1; SATA-Obit 30
Prevost, Abbe (Antoine Francois) 1697-1763 **LC 1**
Price, (Edward) Reynolds 1933- **CLC 3, 6, 13, 43, 50, 63; DAM NOV; SSC 22**
See also CA 1-4R; CANR 1, 37, 57; DLB 2; INT CANR-37
Price, Richard 1949- .... **CLC 6, 12**
See also CA 49-52; CANR 3; DLBY 81
Prichard, Katharine Susannah 1883-1969 . **CLC 46**
See also CA 11-12; CANR 33; CAP 1; MTCW 1; SATA 66
Priestley, J(ohn) B(oynton) 1894-1984 **CLC 2, 5, 9, 34; DAM DRAM, NOV**
See also CA 9-12R; 113; CANR 33; CDBLB 1914-1945; DLB 10, 34, 77, 100, 139; DLBY 84; MTCW 1, 2
Prince 1958(?)- .... **CLC 35**
Prince, F(rank) T(empleton) 1912- ...... **CLC 22**
See also CA 101; CANR 43, 79; DLB 20
Prince Kropotkin
See Kropotkin, Peter (Aleksieevich)
Prior, Matthew 1664-1721 .... **LC 4**
See also DLB 95
Prishvin, Mikhail 1873-1954 .... **TCLC 75**
Pritchard, William H(arrison) 1932- ... **CLC 34**
See also CA 65-68; CANR 23; DLB 111
Pritchett, V(ictor) S(awdon) 1900-1997 **CLC 5, 13, 15, 41; DAM NOV; SSC 14**
See also CA 61-64; 157; CANR 31, 63; DLB 15, 139; MTCW 1, 2
Private 19022
See Manning, Frederic
Probst, Mark 1925- .... **CLC 59**
See also CA 130
Prokosch, Frederic 1908-1989 .... **CLC 4, 48**
See also CA 73-76; 128; DLB 48; MTCW 2
Propertius, Sextus c. 50B.C.-c. 16B.C. **CMLC 32**
See also DLB 211
Prophet, The
See Dreiser, Theodore (Herman Albert)
Prose, Francine 1947- .... **CLC 45**
See also CA 109; 112; CANR 46; SATA 101
Proudhon
See Cunha, Euclides (Rodrigues Pimenta) da
Proulx, Annie
See Proulx, E(dna) Annie
Proulx, E(dna) Annie 1935- **CLC 81; DAM POP**
See also CA 145; CANR 65; MTCW 2
Proust, (Valentin-Louis-George-Eugene-) Marcel 1871-1922 **TCLC 7, 13, 33; DA; DAB; DAC; DAM MST, NOV; WLC**
See also CA 104; 120; DLB 65; MTCW 1, 2
Prowler, Harley
See Masters, Edgar Lee
Prus, Boleslaw 1845-1912 .... **TCLC 48**
Pryor, Richard (Franklin Lenox Thomas) 1940- **CLC 26**
See also CA 122; 152
Przybyszewski, Stanislaw 1868-1927 . **TCLC 36**
See also CA 160; DLB 66
Pteleon
See Grieve, C(hristopher) M(urray)
See also DAM POET
Puckett, Lute
See Masters, Edgar Lee
Puig, Manuel 1932-1990 ... **CLC 3, 5, 10, 28, 65; DAM MULT; HLC**
See also CA 45-48; CANR 2, 32, 63; DLB 113; HW 1, 2; MTCW 1, 2
Pulitzer, Joseph 1847-1911 .... **TCLC 76**
See also CA 114; DLB 23
Purdy, A(lfred) W(ellington) 1918- **CLC 3, 6, 14, 50; DAC; DAM MST, POET**
See also CA 81-84; CAAS 17; CANR 42, 66; DLB 88
Purdy, James (Amos) 1923- **CLC 2, 4, 10, 28, 52**
See also CA 33-36R; CAAS 1; CANR 19, 51; DLB 2; INT CANR-19; MTCW 1
Pure, Simon
See Swinnerton, Frank Arthur
Pushkin, Alexander (Sergeyevich) 1799-1837 **NCLC 3, 27; DA; DAB; DAC; DAM DRAM, MST, POET; PC 10; SSC 27; WLC**
See also DLB 205; SATA 61
P'u Sung-ling 1640-1715 .... **LC 49; SSC 31**

Putnam, Arthur Lee
See Alger, Horatio, Jr.
Puzo, Mario 1920-1999**CLC 1, 2, 6, 36, 107; DAM NOV, POP**
See also CA 65-68; CANR 4, 42, 65; DLB 6; MTCW 1, 2
Pygge, Edward
See Barnes, Julian (Patrick)
Pyle, Ernest Taylor 1900-1945
See Pyle, Ernie
See also CA 115; 160
Pyle, Ernie 1900-1945 .... **TCLC 75**
See also Pyle, Ernest Taylor
See also DLB 29; MTCW 2
Pyle, Howard 1853-1911 .... **TCLC 81**
See also CA 109; 137; CLR 22; DLB 42, 188; DLBD 13; MAICYA; SATA 16, 100
Pym, Barbara (Mary Crampton) 1913-1980 **CLC 13, 19, 37, 111**
See also CA 13-14; 97-100; CANR 13, 34; CAP 1; DLB 14, 207; DLBY 87; MTCW 1, 2
Pynchon, Thomas (Ruggles, Jr.) 1937-**CLC 2, 3, 6, 9, 11, 18, 33, 62, 72; DA; DAB; DAC; DAM MST, NOV, POP; SSC 14; WLC**
See also BEST 90:2; CA 17-20R; CANR 22, 46, 73; DLB 2, 173; MTCW 1, 2
Pythagoras c. 570B.C.-c. 500B.C. .... **CMLC 22**
See also DLB 176
Q
See Quiller-Couch, SirArthur (Thomas)
Qian Zhongshu
See Ch'ien Chung-shu
Qroll
See Dagerman, Stig (Halvard)
Quarrington, Paul (Lewis) 1953- .... **CLC 65**
See also CA 129; CANR 62
Quasimodo, Salvatore 1901-1968 .... **CLC 10**
See also CA 13-16; 25-28R; CAP 1; DLB 114; MTCW 1
Quay, Stephen 1947- .... **CLC 95**
Quay, Timothy 1947- .... **CLC 95**
Queen, Ellery .... **CLC 3, 11**
See also Dannay, Frederic; Davidson, Avram (James); Lee, Manfred B(ennington); Marlowe, Stephen; Sturgeon, Theodore (Hamilton); Vance, John Holbrook
Queen, Ellery, Jr.
See Dannay, Frederic; Lee, Manfred B(ennington)
Queneau, Raymond 1903-1976 **CLC 2, 5, 10, 42**
See also CA 77-80; 69-72; CANR 32; DLB 72; MTCW 1, 2
Quevedo, Francisco de 1580-1645 .... **LC 23**
Quiller-Couch, SirArthur (Thomas) 1863-1944 **TCLC 53**
See also CA 118; 166; DLB 135, 153, 190
Quin, Ann (Marie) 1936-1973 .... **CLC 6**
See also CA 9-12R; 45-48; DLB 14
Quinn, Martin
See Smith, Martin Cruz
Quinn, Peter 1947- .... **CLC 91**
Quinn, Simon
See Smith, Martin Cruz
Quiroga, Horacio (Sylvestre) 1878-1937 . **TCLC 20; DAM MULT; HLC**
See also CA 117; 131; HW 1; MTCW 1
Quoirez, Francoise 1935- .... **CLC 9**
See also Sagan, Francoise
See also CA 49-52; CANR 6, 39, 73; MTCW 1, 2
Raabe, Wilhelm (Karl) 1831-1910 ...... **TCLC 45**
See also CA 167; DLB 129
Rabe, David (William) 1940-**CLC 4, 8, 33; DAM DRAM**
See also CA 85-88; CABS 3; CANR 59; DLB 7
Rabelais, Francois 1483-1553 . **LC 5; DA; DAB; DAC; DAM MST; WLC**
Rabinovitch, Sholem 1859-1916
See Aleichem, Sholom
See also CA 104
Rabinyan, Dorit 1972- .... **CLC 119**
See also CA 170
Rachilde 1860-1953 .... **TCLC 67**
See also DLB 123, 192
Racine, Jean 1639-1699**LC 28; DAB; DAM MST**
Radcliffe, Ann (Ward) 1764-1823 .... **NCLC 6, 55**
See also DLB 39, 178
Radiguet, Raymond 1903-1923 .... **TCLC 29**
See also CA 162; DLB 65
Radnoti, Miklos 1909-1944 .... **TCLC 16**
See also CA 118
Rado, James 1939- .... **CLC 17**
See also CA 105
Radvanyi, Netty 1900-1983
See Seghers, Anna
See also CA 85-88; 110
Rae, Ben
See Griffiths, Trevor
Raeburn, John (Hay) 1941- .... **CLC 34**
See also CA 57-60
Ragni, Gerome 1942-1991 .... **CLC 17**
See also CA 105; 134
Rahv, Philip 1908-1973 .... **CLC 24**
See also Greenberg, Ivan
See also DLB 137
Raimund, Ferdinand Jakob 1790-1836 **NCLC 69**
See also DLB 90
Raine, Craig 1944- .... **CLC 32, 103**
See also CA 108; CANR 29, 51; DLB 40
Raine, Kathleen (Jessie) 1908- .... **CLC 7, 45**
See also CA 85-88; CANR 46; DLB 20; MTCW 1
Rainis, Janis 1865-1929 .... **TCLC 29**
See also CA 170
Rakosi, Carl 1903- .... **CLC 47**
See also Rawley, Callman
See also CAAS 5; DLB 193
Raleigh, Richard
See Lovecraft, H(oward) P(hillips)
Raleigh, Sir Walter 1554(?)-1618 ...... **LC 31, 39**
See also CDBLB Before 1660; DLB 172
Rallentando, H. P.
See Sayers, Dorothy L(eigh)
Ramal, Walter
See de la Mare, Walter (John)
Ramana Maharshi 1879-1950 .... **TCLC 84**
Ramoacn y Cajal, Santiago 1852-1934 **TCLC 93**
Ramon, Juan
See Jimenez (Mantecon), Juan Ramon
Ramos, Graciliano 1892-1953 .... **TCLC 32**
See also CA 167; HW 2
Rampersad, Arnold 1941- .... **CLC 44**
See also BW 2, 3; CA 127; 133; CANR 81; DLB 111; INT 133
Rampling, Anne
See Rice, Anne
Ramsay, Allan 1684(?)-1758 .... **LC 29**
See also DLB 95
Ramuz, Charles-Ferdinand 1878-1947 **TCLC 33**
See also CA 165
Rand, Ayn 1905-1982**CLC 3, 30, 44, 79; DA; DAC; DAM MST, NOV, POP; WLC**
See also AAYA 10; CA 13-16R; 105; CANR 27, 73; CDALBS; MTCW 1, 2
Randall, Dudley (Felker) 1914- **CLC 1; BLC 3; DAM MULT**
See also BW 1, 3; CA 25-28R; CANR 23; DLB 41
Randall, Robert
See Silverberg, Robert
Ranger, Ken
See Creasey, John
Ransom, John Crowe 1888-1974 **CLC 2, 4, 5, 11, 24; DAM POET**
See also CA 5-8R; 49-52; CANR 6, 34; CDALBS; DLB 45, 63; MTCW 1, 2
Rao, Raja 1909- .... **CLC 25, 56; DAM NOV**
See also CA 73-76; CANR 51; MTCW 1, 2
Raphael, Frederic (Michael) 1931- ... **CLC 2, 14**
See also CA 1-4R; CANR 1; DLB 14
Ratcliffe, James P.
See Mencken, H(enry) L(ouis)
Rathbone, Julian 1935- .... **CLC 41**
See also CA 101; CANR 34, 73
Rattigan, Terence (Mervyn) 1911-1977 .. **CLC 7; DAM DRAM**
See also CA 85-88; 73-76; CDBLB 1945-1960; DLB 13; MTCW 1, 2
Ratushinskaya, Irina 1954- .... **CLC 54**
See also CA 129; CANR 68
Raven, Simon (Arthur Noel) 1927- .... **CLC 14**
See also CA 81-84
Ravenna, Michael
See Welty, Eudora
Rawley, Callman 1903-
See Rakosi, Carl
See also CA 21-24R; CANR 12, 32
Rawlings, Marjorie Kinnan 1896-1953**TCLC 4**
See also AAYA 20; CA 104; 137; CANR 74; DLB 9, 22, 102; DLBD 17; JRDA; MAICYA; MTCW 2; SATA 100; YABC 1
Ray, Satyajit 1921-1992**CLC 16, 76; DAM MULT**
See also CA 114; 137
Read, Herbert Edward 1893-1968 .... **CLC 4**
See also CA 85-88; 25-28R; DLB 20, 149
Read, Piers Paul 1941- .... **CLC 4, 10, 25**
See also CA 21-24R; CANR 38; DLB 14; SATA 21
Reade, Charles 1814-1884 .... **NCLC 2, 74**
See also DLB 21
Reade, Hamish
See Gray, Simon (James Holliday)
Reading, Peter 1946- .... **CLC 47**
See also CA 103; CANR 46; DLB 40
Reaney, James 1926- **CLC 13; DAC; DAM MST**
See also CA 41-44R; CAAS 15; CANR 42; DLB 68; SATA 43
Rebreanu, Liviu 1885-1944 .... **TCLC 28**
See also CA 165
Rechy, John (Francisco) 1934- **CLC 1, 7, 14, 18, 107; DAM MULT; HLC**
See also CA 5-8R; CAAS 4; CANR 6, 32, 64; DLB 122; DLBY 82; HW 1, 2; INT CANR-6
Redcam, Tom 1870-1933 .... **TCLC 25**
Reddin, Keith .... **CLC 67**
Redgrove, Peter (William) 1932- ...... **CLC 6, 41**
See also CA 1-4R; CANR 3, 39, 77; DLB 40
Redmon, Anne .... **CLC 22**
See also Nightingale, Anne Redmon
See also DLBY 86
Reed, Eliot
See Ambler, Eric
Reed, Ishmael 1938- . **CLC 2, 3, 5, 6, 13, 32, 60; BLC 3; DAM MULT**
See also BW 2, 3; CA 21-24R; CANR 25, 48, 74; DLB 2, 5, 33, 169; DLBD 8; MTCW 1, 2
Reed, John (Silas) 1887-1920 .... **TCLC 9**
See also CA 106
Reed, Lou .... **CLC 21**
See also Firbank, Louis
Reeve, Clara 1729-1807 .... **NCLC 19**
See also DLB 39
Reich, Wilhelm 1897-1957 .... **TCLC 57**
Reid, Christopher (John) 1949- .... **CLC 33**
See also CA 140; DLB 40
Reid, Desmond
See Moorcock, Michael (John)
Reid Banks, Lynne 1929-
See Banks, Lynne Reid
See also CA 1-4R; CANR 6, 22, 38; CLR 24; JRDA; MAICYA; SATA 22, 75
Reilly, William K.
See Creasey, John

Reiner, Max
See Caldwell, (Janet Miriam) Taylor (Holland)
Reis, Ricardo
See Pessoa, Fernando (Antonio Nogueira)
Remarque, Erich Maria 1898-1970 **CLC 21; DA; DAB; DAC; DAM MST, NOV**
See also AAYA 27; CA 77-80; 29-32R; DLB 56; MTCW 1, 2
Remington, Frederic 1861-1909 .... **TCLC 89**
See also CA 108; 169; DLB 12, 186, 188; SATA 41
Remizov, A.
See Remizov, Aleksei (Mikhailovich)
Remizov, A. M.
See Remizov, Aleksei (Mikhailovich)
Remizov, Aleksei (Mikhailovich) 1877-1957 **TCLC 27**
See also CA 125; 133
Renan, Joseph Ernest 1823-1892 .... **NCLC 26**
Renard, Jules 1864-1910 .... **TCLC 17**
See also CA 117
Renault, Mary .... **CLC 3, 11, 17**
See also Challans, Mary
See also DLBY 83; MTCW 2
Rendell, Ruth (Barbara) 1930- **CLC 28, 48; DAM POP**
See also Vine, Barbara
See also CA 109; CANR 32, 52, 74; DLB 87; INT CANR-32; MTCW 1, 2
Renoir, Jean 1894-1979 .... **CLC 20**
See also CA 129; 85-88
Resnais, Alain 1922- .... **CLC 16**
Reverdy, Pierre 1889-1960 .... **CLC 53**
See also CA 97-100; 89-92
Rexroth, Kenneth 1905-1982 **CLC 1, 2, 6, 11, 22, 49, 112; DAM POET; PC 20**
See also CA 5-8R; 107; CANR 14, 34, 63; CDALB 1941-1968; DLB 16, 48, 165, 212; DLBY 82; INT CANR-14; MTCW 1, 2
Reyes, Alfonso 1889-1959 ... **TCLC 33; HLCS 2**
See also CA 131; HW 1
Reyes y Basoalto, Ricardo Eliecer Neftali
See Neruda, Pablo
Reymont, Wladyslaw (Stanislaw) 1868(?)-1925 **TCLC 5**
See also CA 104
Reynolds, Jonathan 1942- .... **CLC 6, 38**
See also CA 65-68; CANR 28
Reynolds, Joshua 1723-1792 .... **LC 15**
See also DLB 104
Reynolds, Michael Shane 1937- .... **CLC 44**
See also CA 65-68; CANR 9
Reznikoff, Charles 1894-1976 .... **CLC 9**
See also CA 33-36; 61-64; CAP 2; DLB 28, 45
Rezzori (d'Arezzo), Gregor von 1914-1998 **CLC 25**
See also CA 122; 136; 167
Rhine, Richard
See Silverstein, Alvin
Rhodes, Eugene Manlove 1869-1934 ... **TCLC 53**
Rhodius, Apollonius c. 3rd cent. B.C.- **CMLC 28**
See also DLB 176
R'hoone
See Balzac, Honore de
Rhys, Jean 1890(?)-1979 **CLC 2, 4, 6, 14, 19, 51; DAM NOV; SSC 21**
See also CA 25-28R; 85-88; CANR 35, 62; CDBLB 1945-1960; DLB 36, 117, 162; MTCW 1, 2
Ribeiro, Darcy 1922-1997 .... **CLC 34**
See also CA 33-36R; 156
Ribeiro, Joao Ubaldo (Osorio Pimentel) 1941- **CLC 10, 67**
See also CA 81-84
Ribman, Ronald (Burt) 1932- .... **CLC 7**
See also CA 21-24R; CANR 46, 80
Ricci, Nino 1959- .... **CLC 70**
See also CA 137
Rice, Anne 1941- .... **CLC 41; DAM POP**
See also AAYA 9; BEST 89:2; CA 65-68; CANR 12, 36, 53, 74; MTCW 2
Rice, Elmer (Leopold) 1892-1967 **CLC 7, 49; DAM DRAM**
See also CA 21-22; 25-28R; CAP 2; DLB 4, 7; MTCW 1, 2
Rice, Tim(othy Miles Bindon) 1944- .... **CLC 21**
See also CA 103; CANR 46
Rich, Adrienne (Cecile) 1929- **CLC 3, 6, 7, 11, 18, 36, 73, 76; DAM POET; PC 5**
See also CA 9-12R; CANR 20, 53, 74; CDALBS; DLB 5, 67; MTCW 1, 2
Rich, Barbara
See Graves, Robert (von Ranke)
Rich, Robert
See Trumbo, Dalton
Richard, Keith .... **CLC 17**
See also Richards, Keith
Richards, David Adams 1950- ..... **CLC 59; DAC**
See also CA 93-96; CANR 60; DLB 53
Richards, I(vor) A(rmstrong) 1893-1979 **CLC 14, 24**
See also CA 41-44R; 89-92; CANR 34, 74; DLB 27; MTCW 2
Richards, Keith 1943-
See Richard, Keith
See also CA 107; CANR 77
Richardson, Anne
See Roiphe, Anne (Richardson)
Richardson, Dorothy Miller 1873-1957 **TCLC 3**
See also CA 104; DLB 36
Richardson, Ethel Florence (Lindesay) 1870-1946
See Richardson, Henry Handel
See also CA 105
Richardson, Henry Handel .... **TCLC 4**
See also Richardson, Ethel Florence (Lindesay)
See also DLB 197
Richardson, John 1796-1852 .... **NCLC 55; DAC**
See also DLB 99
Richardson, Samuel 1689-1761 ... **LC 1, 44; DA; DAB; DAC; DAM MST, NOV; WLC**
See also CDBLB 1660-1789; DLB 39
Richler, Mordecai 1931- **CLC 3, 5, 9, 13, 18, 46, 70; DAC; DAM MST, NOV**
See also AITN 1; CA 65-68; CANR 31, 62; CLR 17; DLB 53; MAICYA; MTCW 1, 2; SATA 44, 98; SATA-Brief 27
Richter, Conrad (Michael) 1890-1968 ... **CLC 30**
See also AAYA 21; CA 5-8R; 25-28R; CANR 23; DLB 9, 212; MTCW 1, 2; SATA 3
Ricostranza, Tom
See Ellis, Trey
Riddell, Charlotte 1832-1906 .... **TCLC 40**
See also CA 165; DLB 156
Ridgway, Keith 1965- .... **CLC 119**
See also CA 172
Riding, Laura .... **CLC 3, 7**
See also Jackson, Laura (Riding)
Riefenstahl, Berta Helene Amalia 1902-
See Riefenstahl, Leni
See also CA 108
Riefenstahl, Leni .... **CLC 16**
See also Riefenstahl, Berta Helene Amalia
Riffe, Ernest
See Bergman, (Ernst) Ingmar
Riggs, (Rolla) Lynn 1899-1954 . **TCLC 56; DAM MULT**
See also CA 144; DLB 175; NNAL
Riis, Jacob A(ugust) 1849-1914 .... **TCLC 80**
See also CA 113; 168; DLB 23
Riley, James Whitcomb 1849-1916 .... **TCLC 51; DAM POET**
See also CA 118; 137; MAICYA; SATA 17
Riley, Tex
See Creasey, John
Rilke, Rainer Maria 1875-1926 . **TCLC 1, 6, 19; DAM POET; PC 2**
See also CA 104; 132; CANR 62; DLB 81; MTCW 1, 2
Rimbaud, (Jean Nicolas) Arthur 1854-1891 **NCLC 4, 35; DA; DAB; DAC; DAM MST, POET; PC 3; WLC**
Rinehart, Mary Roberts 1876-1958 .... **TCLC 52**
See also CA 108; 166
Ringmaster, The
See Mencken, H(enry) L(ouis)
Ringwood, Gwen(dolyn Margaret) Pharis 1910-1984 **CLC 48**
See also CA 148; 112; DLB 88
Rio, Michel 19(?)- .... **CLC 43**
Ritsos, Giannes
See Ritsos, Yannis
Ritsos, Yannis 1909-1990 .... **CLC 6, 13, 31**
See also CA 77-80; 133; CANR 39, 61; MTCW 1
Ritter, Erika 1948(?)- .... **CLC 52**
Rivera, Jose Eustasio 1889-1928 .... **TCLC 35**
See also CA 162; HW 1, 2
Rivers, Conrad Kent 1933-1968 .... **CLC 1**
See also BW 1; CA 85-88; DLB 41
Rivers, Elfrida
See Bradley, Marion Zimmer
Riverside, John
See Heinlein, Robert A(nson)
Rizal, Jose 1861-1896 .... **NCLC 27**
Roa Bastos, Augusto (Antonio) 1917- . **CLC 45; DAM MULT; HLC**
See also CA 131; DLB 113; HW 1
Robbe-Grillet, Alain 1922- **CLC 1, 2, 4, 6, 8, 10, 14, 43**
See also CA 9-12R; CANR 33, 65; DLB 83; MTCW 1, 2
Robbins, Harold 1916-1997 .. **CLC 5; DAM NOV**
See also CA 73-76; 162; CANR 26, 54; MTCW 1, 2
Robbins, Thomas Eugene 1936-
See Robbins, Tom
See also CA 81-84; CANR 29, 59; DAM NOV, POP; MTCW 1, 2
Robbins, Tom .... **CLC 9, 32, 64**
See also Robbins, Thomas Eugene
See also BEST 90:3; DLBY 80; MTCW 2
Robbins, Trina 1938- .... **CLC 21**
See also CA 128
Roberts, Charles G(eorge) D(ouglas) 1860-1943 **TCLC 8**
See also CA 105; CLR 33; DLB 92; SATA 88; SATA-Brief 29
Roberts, Elizabeth Madox 1886-1941 .. **TCLC 68**
See also CA 111; 166; DLB 9, 54, 102; SATA 33; SATA-Brief 27
Roberts, Kate 1891-1985 .... **CLC 15**
See also CA 107; 116
Roberts, Keith (John Kingston) 1935- . **CLC 14**
See also CA 25-28R; CANR 46
Roberts, Kenneth (Lewis) 1885-1957 .. **TCLC 23**
See also CA 109; DLB 9
Roberts, Michele (B.) 1949- .... **CLC 48**
See also CA 115; CANR 58
Robertson, Ellis
See Ellison, Harlan (Jay); Silverberg, Robert
Robertson, Thomas William 1829-1871 **NCLC 35; DAM DRAM**
Robeson, Kenneth
See Dent, Lester
Robinson, Edwin Arlington 1869-1935 . **TCLC 5; DA; DAC; DAM MST, POET; PC 1**
See also CA 104; 133; CDALB 1865-1917; DLB 54; MTCW 1, 2
Robinson, Henry Crabb 1775-1867 ..... **NCLC 15**
See also DLB 107
Robinson, Jill 1936- .... **CLC 10**
See also CA 102; INT 102
Robinson, Kim Stanley 1952- .... **CLC 34**
See also AAYA 26; CA 126; SATA 109

Robinson, Lloyd
See Silverberg, Robert
Robinson, Marilynne 1944- .... **CLC 25**
See also CA 116; CANR 80; DLB 206
Robinson, Smokey .... **CLC 21**
See also Robinson, William, Jr.
Robinson, William, Jr. 1940-
See Robinson, Smokey
See also CA 116
Robison, Mary 1949- .... **CLC 42, 98**
See also CA 113; 116; DLB 130; INT 116
Rod, Edouard 1857-1910 .... **TCLC 52**
Roddenberry, Eugene Wesley 1921-1991
See Roddenberry, Gene
See also CA 110; 135; CANR 37; SATA 45; SATA-Obit 69
Roddenberry, Gene .... **CLC 17**
See also Roddenberry, Eugene Wesley
See also AAYA 5; SATA-Obit 69
Rodgers, Mary 1931- .... **CLC 12**
See also CA 49-52; CANR 8, 55; CLR 20; INT CANR-8; JRDA; MAICYA; SATA 8
Rodgers, W(illiam) R(obert) 1909-1969 . **CLC 7**
See also CA 85-88; DLB 20
Rodman, Eric
See Silverberg, Robert
<indexbody>**Rodman, Howard** 1920(?)-1985 **CLC 65**
See also CA 118
Rodman, Maia
See Wojciechowska, Maia (Teresa)
Rodriguez, Claudio 1934- .... **CLC 10**
See also DLB 134
Roelvaag, O(le) E(dvart) 1876-1931 ..... **TCLC 17**
See also CA 117; 171; DLB 9
Roethke, Theodore (Huebner) 1908-1963**CLC 1, 3, 8, 11, 19, 46, 101; DAM POET; PC 15**
See also CA 81-84; CABS 2; CDALB 1941-1968; DLB 5, 206; MTCW 1, 2
Rogers, Samuel 1763-1855 .... **NCLC 69**
See also DLB 93
Rogers, Thomas Hunton 1927- .... **CLC 57**
See also CA 89-92; INT 89-92
Rogers, Will(iam Penn Adair) 1879-1935 **TCLC 8, 71; DAM MULT**
See also CA 105; 144; DLB 11; MTCW 2; NNAL
Rogin, Gilbert 1929- .... **CLC 18**
See also CA 65-68; CANR 15
Rohan, Koda .... **TCLC 22**
See also Koda Shigeyuki
Rohlfs, Anna Katharine Green
See Green, Anna Katharine
Rohmer, Eric .... **CLC 16**
See also Scherer, Jean-Marie Maurice
Rohmer, Sax .... **TCLC 28**
See also Ward, Arthur Henry Sarsfield
See also DLB 70
Roiphe, Anne (Richardson) 1935- .... **CLC 3, 9**
See also CA 89-92; CANR 45, 73; DLBY 80; INT 89-92
Rojas, Fernando de 1465-1541 .. **LC 23; HLCS 1**
Rolfe, Frederick (William Serafino Austin Lewis Mary) 1860-1913 .... **TCLC 12**
See also CA 107; DLB 34, 156
Rolland, Romain 1866-1944 .... **TCLC 23**
See also CA 118; DLB 65
Rolle, Richard c. 1300-c. 1349 .... **CMLC 21**
See also DLB 146
Rolvaag, O(le) E(dvart)
See Roelvaag, O(le) E(dvart)
Romain Arnaud, Saint
See Aragon, Louis
Romains, Jules 1885-1972 .... **CLC 7**
See also CA 85-88; CANR 34; DLB 65; MTCW 1
Romero, Jose Ruben 1890-1952 .... **TCLC 14**
See also CA 114; 131; HW 1
Ronsard, Pierre de 1524-1585 .... **LC 6; PC 11**
Rooke, Leon 1934- .. **CLC 25, 34; DAM POP**
See also CA 25-28R; CANR 23, 53
Roosevelt, Franklin Delano 1882-1945 **TCLC 93**
See also CA 116; 173
Roosevelt, Theodore 1858-1919 .... **TCLC 69**
See also CA 115; 170; DLB 47, 186
Roper, William 1498-1578 .... **LC 10**
Roquelaure, A. N.
See Rice, Anne
Rosa, Joao Guimaraes 1908-1967**CLC 23; HLCS 1**
See also CA 89-92; DLB 113
Rose, Wendy 1948-**CLC 85; DAM MULT; PC 13**
See also CA 53-56; CANR 5, 51; DLB 175; NNAL; SATA 12
Rosen, R. D.
See Rosen, Richard (Dean)
Rosen, Richard (Dean) 1949- .... **CLC 39**
See also CA 77-80; CANR 62; INT CANR-30
Rosenberg, Isaac 1890-1918 .... **TCLC 12**
See also CA 107; DLB 20
Rosenblatt, Joe .... **CLC 15**
See also Rosenblatt, Joseph
Rosenblatt, Joseph 1933-
See Rosenblatt, Joe
See also CA 89-92; INT 89-92
Rosenfeld, Samuel
See Tzara, Tristan
Rosenstock, Sami
See Tzara, Tristan
Rosenstock, Samuel
See Tzara, Tristan
Rosenthal, M(acha) L(ouis) 1917-1996 . **CLC 28**
See also CA 1-4R; 152; CAAS 6; CANR 4, 51; DLB 5; SATA 59
Ross, Barnaby
See Dannay, Frederic
Ross, Bernard L.
See Follett, Ken(neth Martin)
Ross, J. H.
See Lawrence, T(homas) E(dward)
Ross, John Hume
See Lawrence, T(homas) E(dward)
Ross, Martin
See Martin, Violet Florence
See also DLB 135
Ross, (James) Sinclair 1908-1996**CLC 13; DAC; DAM MST; SSC 24**
See also CA 73-76; CANR 81; DLB 88
Rossetti, Christina (Georgina) 1830-1894**NCLC 2, 50, 66; DA; DAB; DAC; DAM MST, POET; PC 7; WLC**
See also DLB 35, 163; MAICYA; SATA 20
Rossetti, Dante Gabriel 1828-1882 **NCLC 4, 77; DA; DAB; DAC; DAM MST, POET; WLC**
See also CDBLB 1832-1890; DLB 35
Rossner, Judith (Perelman) 1935- . **CLC 6, 9, 29**
See also AITN 2; BEST 90:3; CA 17-20R; CANR 18, 51, 73; DLB 6; INT CANR-18; MTCW 1, 2
Rostand, Edmond (Eugene Alexis) 1868-1918 **TCLC 6, 37; DA; DAB; DAC; DAM DRAM, MST; DC 10**
See also CA 104; 126; DLB 192; MTCW 1
Roth, Henry 1906-1995 .... **CLC 2, 6, 11, 104**
See also CA 11-12; 149; CANR 38, 63; CAP 1; DLB 28; MTCW 1, 2
Roth, Philip (Milton) 1933-**CLC 1, 2, 3, 4, 6, 9, 15, 22, 31, 47, 66, 86, 119; DA; DAB; DAC; DAM MST, NOV, POP; SSC 26; WLC**
See also BEST 90:3; CA 1-4R; CANR 1, 22, 36, 55; CDALB 1968-1988; DLB 2, 28, 173; DLBY 82; MTCW 1, 2
Rothenberg, Jerome 1931- .... **CLC 6, 57**
See also CA 45-48; CANR 1; DLB 5, 193
Roumain, Jacques (Jean Baptiste) 1907-1944 **TCLC 19; BLC 3; DAM MULT**
See also BW 1; CA 117; 125
Rourke, Constance (Mayfield) 1885-1941 **TCLC 12**
See also CA 107; YABC 1
Rousseau, Jean-Baptiste 1671-1741 .... **LC 9**
Rousseau, Jean-Jacques 1712-1778 . **LC 14, 36; DA; DAB; DAC; DAM MST; WLC**
Roussel, Raymond 1877-1933 .... **TCLC 20**
See also CA 117
Rovit, Earl (Herbert) 1927- .... **CLC 7**
See also CA 5-8R; CANR 12
Rowe, Elizabeth Singer 1674-1737 .... **LC 44**
See also DLB 39, 95
Rowe, Nicholas 1674-1718 .... **LC 8**
See also DLB 84
Rowley, Ames Dorrance
See Lovecraft, H(oward) P(hillips)
Rowson, Susanna Haswell 1762(?)-1824**NCLC 5, 69**
See also DLB 37, 200
Roy, Arundhati 1960(?)- .... **CLC 109**
See also CA 163; DLBY 97
Roy, Gabrielle 1909-1983 **CLC 10, 14; DAB; DAC; DAM MST**
See also CA 53-56; 110; CANR 5, 61; DLB 68; MTCW 1; SATA 104
Royko, Mike 1932-1997 .... **CLC 109**
See also CA 89-92; 157; CANR 26
Rozewicz, Tadeusz 1921-**CLC 9, 23; DAM POET**
See also CA 108; CANR 36, 66; MTCW 1, 2
Ruark, Gibbons 1941- .... **CLC 3**
See also CA 33-36R; CAAS 23; CANR 14, 31, 57; DLB 120
Rubens, Bernice (Ruth) 1923- .... **CLC 19, 31**
See also CA 25-28R; CANR 33, 65; DLB 14, 207; MTCW 1
Rubin, Harold
See Robbins, Harold
Rudkin, (James) David 1936- .... **CLC 14**
See also CA 89-92; DLB 13
Rudnik, Raphael 1933- .... **CLC 7**
See also CA 29-32R
Ruffian, M.
See Hasek, Jaroslav (Matej Frantisek)
Ruiz, Jose Martinez .... **CLC 11**
See also Martinez Ruiz, Jose
Rukeyser, Muriel 1913-1980 **CLC 6, 10, 15, 27; DAM POET; PC 12**
See also CA 5-8R; 93-96; CANR 26, 60; DLB 48; MTCW 1, 2; SATA-Obit 22
Rule, Jane (Vance) 1931- .... **CLC 27**
See also CA 25-28R; CAAS 18; CANR 12; DLB 60
Rulfo, Juan 1918-1986 **CLC 8, 80; DAM MULT; HLC; SSC 25**
See also CA 85-88; 118; CANR 26; DLB 113; HW 1, 2; MTCW 1, 2
Rumi, Jalal al-Din 1297-1373 .... **CMLC 20**
Runeberg, Johan 1804-1877 .... **NCLC 41**
Runyon, (Alfred) Damon 1884(?)-1946 **TCLC 10**
See also CA 107; 165; DLB 11, 86, 171; MTCW 2
Rush, Norman 1933- .... **CLC 44**
See also CA 121; 126; INT 126
Rushdie, (Ahmed) Salman 1947-**CLC 23, 31, 55, 100; DAB; DAC; DAM MST, NOV, POP; WLCS**
See also BEST 89:3; CA 108; 111; CANR 33, 56; DLB 194; INT 111; MTCW 1, 2
Rushforth, Peter (Scott) 1945- .... **CLC 19**
See also CA 101
Ruskin, John 1819-1900 .... **TCLC 63**
See also CA 114; 129; CDBLB 1832-1890; DLB 55, 163, 190; SATA 24
Russ, Joanna 1937- .... **CLC 15**
See also CANR 11, 31, 65; DLB 8; MTCW 1
Russell, George William 1867-1935
See Baker, Jean H.
See also CA 104; 153; CDBLB 1890-1914; DAM

POET
Russell, (Henry) Ken(neth Alfred) 1927-**CLC 16**
See also CA 105
Russell, William Martin 1947- .... **CLC 60**
See also CA 164
Rutherford, Mark .... **TCLC 25**
See also White, William Hale
See also DLB 18
Ruyslinck, Ward 1929- .... **CLC 14**
See also Belser, Reimond Karel Maria de
Ryan, Cornelius (John) 1920-1974 .... **CLC 7**
See also CA 69-72; 53-56; CANR 38
Ryan, Michael 1946- .... **CLC 65**
See also CA 49-52; DLBY 82
Ryan, Tim
See Dent, Lester
Rybakov, Anatoli (Naumovich) 1911-1998**CLC 23, 53**
See also CA 126; 135; 172; SATA 79; SATA-Obit 108
Ryder, Jonathan
See Ludlum, Robert
Ryga, George 1932-1987 .. **CLC 14; DAC; DAM MST**
See also CA 101; 124; CANR 43; DLB 60
S. H.
See Hartmann, Sadakichi
S. S.
See Sassoon, Siegfried (Lorraine)
Saba, Umberto 1883-1957 .... **TCLC 33**
See also CA 144; CANR 79; DLB 114
Sabatini, Rafael 1875-1950 .... **TCLC 47**
See also CA 162
Sabato, Ernesto (R.) 1911- ... **CLC 10, 23; DAM MULT; HLC**
See also CA 97-100; CANR 32, 65; DLB 145; HW 1, 2; MTCW 1, 2
Sa-Carniero, Mario de 1890-1916 .... **TCLC 83**
Sacastru, Martin
See Bioy Casares, Adolfo
Sacastru, Martin
See Bioy Casares, Adolfo
Sacher-Masoch, Leopold von 1836(?)-1895**NCLC 31**
Sachs, Marilyn (Stickle) 1927- .... **CLC 35**
See also AAYA 2; CA 17-20R; CANR 13, 47; CLR 2; JRDA; MAICYA; SAAS 2; SATA 3, 68
Sachs, Nelly 1891-1970 .... **CLC 14, 98**
See also CA 17-18; 25-28R; CAP 2; MTCW 2
Sackler, Howard (Oliver) 1929-1982 ..... **CLC 14**
See also CA 61-64; 108; CANR 30; DLB 7
Sacks, Oliver (Wolf) 1933- .... **CLC 67**
See also CA 53-56; CANR 28, 50, 76; INT CANR-28; MTCW 1, 2
Sadakichi
See Hartmann, Sadakichi
Sade, Donatien Alphonse Francois, Comte de 1740-1814 .... **NCLC 47**
Sadoff, Ira 1945- .... **CLC 9**
See also CA 53-56; CANR 5, 21; DLB 120
Saetone
See Camus, Albert
Safire, William 1929- .... **CLC 10**
See also CA 17-20R; CANR 31, 54
Sagan, Carl (Edward) 1934-1996 .... **CLC 30, 112**
See also AAYA 2; CA 25-28R; 155; CANR 11, 36, 74; MTCW 1, 2; SATA 58; SATA-Obit 94
Sagan, Francoise .... **CLC 3, 6, 9, 17, 36**
See also Quoirez, Francoise
See also DLB 83; MTCW 2
Sahgal, Nayantara (Pandit) 1927- .... **CLC 41**
See also CA 9-12R; CANR 11
Saint, H(arry) F. 1941- .... **CLC 50**
See also CA 127
St. Aubin de Teran, Lisa 1953-
See Teran, Lisa St. Aubin de
See also CA 118; 126; INT 126
Saint Birgitta of Sweden c. 1303-1373**CMLC 24**
Sainte-Beuve, Charles Augustin 1804-1869 **NCLC 5**
Saint-Exupery, Antoine (Jean Baptiste Marie Roger) de 1900-1944**TCLC 2, 56; DAM NOV; WLC**
See also CA 108; 132; CLR 10; DLB 72; MAICYA; MTCW 1, 2; SATA 20
St. John, David
See Hunt, E(verette) Howard, (Jr.)
Saint-John Perse
See Leger, (Marie-Rene Auguste) Alexis Saint-Leger
Saintsbury, George (Edward Bateman) 1845-1933 **TCLC 31**
See also CA 160; DLB 57, 149
Sait Faik .... **TCLC 23**
See also Abasiyanik, Sait Faik
Saki .... **TCLC 3; SSC 12**
See also Munro, H(ector) H(ugh)
See also MTCW 2
Sala, George Augustus .... **NCLC 46**
Salama, Hannu 1936- .... **CLC 18**
Salamanca, J(ack) R(ichard) 1922-**CLC 4, 15**
See also CA 25-28R
Sale, J. Kirkpatrick
See Sale, Kirkpatrick
Sale, Kirkpatrick 1937- .... **CLC 68**
See also CA 13-16R; CANR 10
Salinas, Luis Omar 1937-**CLC 90; DAM MULT; HLC**
See also CA 131; CANR 81; DLB 82; HW 1, 2
Salinas (y Serrano), Pedro 1891(?)-1951**TCLC 17**
See also CA 117; DLB 134
Salinger, J(erome) D(avid) 1919-**CLC 1, 3, 8, 12, 55, 56; DA; DAB; DAC; DAM MST, NOV, POP; SSC 2, 28; WLC**
See also AAYA 2; CA 5-8R; CANR 39; CDALB 1941-1968; CLR 18; DLB 2, 102, 173; MAICYA; MTCW 1, 2; SATA 67
Salisbury, John
See Caute, (John) David
Salter, James 1925- .... **CLC 7, 52, 59**
See also CA 73-76; DLB 130
Saltus, Edgar (Everton) 1855-1921 .... **TCLC 8**
See also CA 105; DLB 202
Saltykov, Mikhail Evgrafovich 1826-1889 **NCLC 16**
Samarakis, Antonis 1919- .... **CLC 5**
See also CA 25-28R; CAAS 16; CANR 36
Sanchez, Florencio 1875-1910 .... **TCLC 37**
See also CA 153; HW 1
Sanchez, Luis Rafael 1936- .... **CLC 23**
See also CA 128; DLB 145; HW 1
Sanchez, Sonia 1934-**CLC 5, 116; BLC 3; DAM MULT; PC 9**
See also BW 2, 3; CA 33-36R; CANR 24, 49, 74; CLR 18; DLB 41; DLBD 8; MAICYA; MTCW 1, 2; SATA 22
Sand, George 1804-1876 ... **NCLC 2, 42, 57; DA; DAB; DAC; DAM MST, NOV; WLC**
See also DLB 119, 192
Sandburg, Carl (August) 1878-1967**CLC 1, 4, 10, 15, 35; DA; DAB; DAC; DAM MST, POET; PC 2; WLC**
See also AAYA 24; CA 5-8R; 25-28R; CANR 35; CDALB 1865-1917; DLB 17, 54; MAICYA; MTCW 1, 2; SATA 8
Sandburg, Charles
See Sandburg, Carl (August)
Sandburg, Charles A.
See Sandburg, Carl (August)
Sanders, (James) Ed(ward) 1939- **CLC 53; DAM POET**
See also CA 13-16R; CAAS 21; CANR 13, 44, 78; DLB 16
Sanders, Lawrence 1920-1998**CLC 41; DAM POP**
See also BEST 89:4; CA 81-84; 165; CANR 33, 62; MTCW 1
Sanders, Noah
See Blount, Roy (Alton), Jr.
Sanders, Winston P.
See Anderson, Poul (William)
Sandoz, Mari(e Susette) 1896-1966 ...... **CLC 28**
See also CA 1-4R; 25-28R; CANR 17, 64; DLB 9, 212; MTCW 1, 2; SATA 5
Saner, Reg(inald Anthony) 1931- .... **CLC 9**
See also CA 65-68
Sankara 788-820 .... **CMLC 32**
Sannazaro, Jacopo 1456(?)-1530 .... **LC 8**
Sansom, William 1912-1976**CLC 2, 6; DAM NOV; SSC 21**
See also CA 5-8R; 65-68; CANR 42; DLB 139; MTCW 1
Santayana, George 1863-1952 .... **TCLC 40**
See also CA 115; DLB 54, 71; DLBD 13
Santiago, Danny .... **CLC 33**
See also James, Daniel (Lewis)
See also DLB 122
Santmyer, Helen Hoover 1895-1986 ...... **CLC 33**
See also CA 1-4R; 118; CANR 15, 33; DLBY 84; MTCW 1
Santoka, Taneda 1882-1940 .... **TCLC 72**
Santos, Bienvenido N(uqui) 1911-1996 **CLC 22; DAM MULT**
See also CA 101; 151; CANR 19, 46
Sapper .... **TCLC 44**
See also McNeile, Herman Cyril
Sapphire
See Sapphire, Brenda
Sapphire, Brenda 1950- .... **CLC 99**
Sappho fl. 6th cent. B.C.- **CMLC 3; DAM POET; PC 5**
See also DLB 176
Saramago, Jose 1922- .... **CLC 119; HLCS 1**
See also CA 153
Sarduy, Severo 1937-1993 .. **CLC 6, 97; HLCS 1**
See also CA 89-92; 142; CANR 58, 81; DLB 113; HW 1, 2
Sargeson, Frank 1903-1982 .... **CLC 31**
See also CA 25-28R; 106; CANR 38, 79
Sarmiento, Felix Ruben Garcia
See Dario, Ruben
Saro-Wiwa, Ken(ule Beeson) 1941-1995**CLC 114**
See also BW 2; CA 142; 150; CANR 60; DLB 157
Saroyan, William 1908-1981**CLC 1, 8, 10, 29, 34, 56; DA; DAB; DAC; DAM DRAM, MST, NOV; SSC 21; WLC**
See also CA 5-8R; 103; CANR 30; CDALBS; DLB 7, 9, 86; DLBY 81; MTCW 1, 2; SATA 23; SATA-Obit 24
Sarraute, Nathalie 1900-**CLC 1, 2, 4, 8, 10, 31, 80**
See also CA 9-12R; CANR 23, 66; DLB 83; MTCW 1, 2
Sarton, (Eleanor) May 1912-1995 **CLC 4, 14, 49, 91; DAM POET**
See also CA 1-4R; 149; CANR 1, 34, 55; DLB 48; DLBY 81; INT CANR-34; MTCW 1, 2; SATA 36; SATA-Obit 86
Sartre, Jean-Paul 1905-1980 . **CLC 1, 4, 7, 9, 13, 18, 24, 44, 50, 52; DA; DAB; DAC; DAM DRAM, MST, NOV; DC 3; SSC 32; WLC**
See also CA 9-12R; 97-100; CANR 21; DLB 72; MTCW 1, 2
Sassoon, Siegfried (Lorraine) 1886-1967 .. **CLC 36; DAB; DAM MST, NOV, POET; PC 12**
See also CA 104; 25-28R; CANR 36; DLB 20, 191; DLBD 18; MTCW 1, 2
Satterfield, Charles
See Pohl, Frederik
Saul, John (W. III) 1942- ... **CLC 46; DAM NOV, POP**

See also AAYA 10; BEST 90:4; CA 81-84; CANR 16, 40, 81; SATA 98
Saunders, Caleb
See Heinlein, Robert A(nson)
Saura (Atares), Carlos 1932- .... **CLC 20**
See also CA 114; 131; CANR 79; HW 1
Sauser-Hall, Frederic 1887-1961 .... **CLC 18**
See also Cendrars, Blaise
See also CA 102; 93-96; CANR 36, 62; MTCW 1
Saussure, Ferdinand de 1857-1913 ..... **TCLC 49**
Savage, Catharine
See Brosman, Catharine Savage
Savage, Thomas 1915- .... **CLC 40**
See also CA 126; 132; CAAS 15; INT 132
Savan, Glenn 19(?)- .... **CLC 50**
Sayers, Dorothy L(eigh) 1893-1957 **TCLC 2, 15; DAM POP**
See also CA 104; 119; CANR 60; CDBLB 1914-1945; DLB 10, 36, 77, 100; MTCW 1, 2
Sayers, Valerie 1952- .... **CLC 50**
See also CA 134; CANR 61
Sayles, John (Thomas) 1950- ...... **CLC 7, 10, 14**
See also CA 57-60; CANR 41; DLB 44
Scammell, Michael 1935- .... **CLC 34**
See also CA 156
Scannell, Vernon 1922- .... **CLC 49**
See also CA 5-8R; CANR 8, 24, 57; DLB 27; SATA 59
Scarlett, Susan
See Streatfeild, (Mary) Noel
Scarron
See Mikszath, Kalman
Schaeffer, Susan Fromberg 1941- **CLC 6, 11, 22**
See also CA 49-52; CANR 18, 65; DLB 28; MTCW 1, 2; SATA 22
Schary, Jill
See Robinson, Jill
Schell, Jonathan 1943- .... **CLC 35**
See also CA 73-76; CANR 12
Schelling, Friedrich Wilhelm Joseph von 1775-1854 .... **NCLC 30**
See also DLB 90
Schendel, Arthur van 1874-1946 .... **TCLC 56**
Scherer, Jean-Marie Maurice 1920-
See Rohmer, Eric
See also CA 110
Schevill, James (Erwin) 1920- .... **CLC 7**
See also CA 5-8R; CAAS 12
Schiller, Friedrich 1759-1805 **NCLC 39, 69; DAM DRAM**
See also DLB 94
Schisgal, Murray (Joseph) 1926- .... **CLC 6**
See also CA 21-24R; CANR 48
Schlee, Ann 1934- .... **CLC 35**
See also CA 101; CANR 29; SATA 44; SATA-Brief 36
Schlegel, August Wilhelm von 1767-1845 **NCLC 15**
See also DLB 94
Schlegel, Friedrich 1772-1829 .... **NCLC 45**
See also DLB 90
Schlegel, Johann Elias (von) 1719(?)-1749 **LC 5**
Schlesinger, Arthur M(eier), Jr. 1917- **CLC 84**
See also AITN 1; CA 1-4R; CANR 1, 28, 58; DLB 17; INT CANR-28; MTCW 1, 2; SATA 61
Schmidt, Arno (Otto) 1914-1979 .... **CLC 56**
See also CA 128; 109; DLB 69
Schmitz, Aron Hector 1861-1928
See Svevo, Italo
See also CA 104; 122; MTCW 1
Schnackenberg, Gjertrud 1953- .... **CLC 40**
See also CA 116; DLB 120
Schneider, Leonard Alfred 1925-1966
See Bruce, Lenny
See also CA 89-92
Schnitzler, Arthur 1862-1931 **TCLC 4; SSC 15**
See also CA 104; DLB 81, 118
Schoenberg, Arnold 1874-1951 ...... **TCLC 75**
See also CA 109
Schonberg, Arnold
See Schoenberg, Arnold
Schopenhauer, Arthur 1788-1860 .... **NCLC 51**
See also DLB 90
Schor, Sandra (M.) 1932(?)-1990 .... **CLC 65**
See also CA 132
Schorer, Mark 1908-1977 .... **CLC 9**
See also CA 5-8R; 73-76; CANR 7; DLB 103
Schrader, Paul (Joseph) 1946- .... **CLC 26**
See also CA 37-40R; CANR 41; DLB 44
Schreiner, Olive (Emilie Albertina) 1855-1920 **TCLC 9**
See also CA 105; 154; DLB 18, 156, 190
Schulberg, Budd (Wilson) 1914- ...... **CLC 7, 48**
See also CA 25-28R; CANR 19; DLB 6, 26, 28; DLBY 81
Schulz, Bruno 1892-1942 . **TCLC 5, 51; SSC 13**
See also CA 115; 123; MTCW 2
Schulz, Charles M(onroe) 1922- .... **CLC 12**
See also CA 9-12R; CANR 6; INT CANR-6; SATA 10
Schumacher, E(rnst) F(riedrich) 1911-1977 **CLC 80**
See also CA 81-84; 73-76; CANR 34
Schuyler, James Marcus 1923-1991 **CLC 5, 23; DAM POET**
See also CA 101; 134; DLB 5, 169; INT 101
Schwartz, Delmore (David) 1913-1966 **CLC 2, 4, 10, 45, 87; PC 8**
See also CA 17-18; 25-28R; CANR 35; CAP 2; DLB 28, 48; MTCW 1, 2
Schwartz, Ernst
See Ozu, Yasujiro
Schwartz, John Burnham 1965- .... **CLC 59**
See also CA 132
Schwartz, Lynne Sharon 1939- .... **CLC 31**
See also CA 103; CANR 44; MTCW 2
Schwartz, Muriel A.
See Eliot, T(homas) S(tearns)
Schwarz-Bart, Andre 1928- .... **CLC 2, 4**
See also CA 89-92
Schwarz-Bart, Simone 1938- ...... **CLC 7; BLCS**
See also BW 2; CA 97-100
Schwitters, Kurt (Hermann Edward Karl Julius) 1887-1948 .... **TCLC 95**
See also CA 158
Schwob, Marcel (Mayer Andre) 1867-1905 **TCLC 20**
See also CA 117; 168; DLB 123
Sciascia, Leonardo 1921-1989 .... **CLC 8, 9, 41**
See also CA 85-88; 130; CANR 35; DLB 177; MTCW 1
Scoppettone, Sandra 1936- .... **CLC 26**
See also AAYA 11; CA 5-8R; CANR 41, 73; SATA 9, 92
Scorsese, Martin 1942- .... **CLC 20, 89**
See also CA 110; 114; CANR 46
Scotland, Jay
See Jakes, John (William)
Scott, Duncan Campbell 1862-1947 **TCLC 6; DAC**
See also CA 104; 153; DLB 92
Scott, Evelyn 1893-1963 .... **CLC 43**
See also CA 104; 112; CANR 64; DLB 9, 48
Scott, F(rancis) R(eginald) 1899-1985 .. **CLC 22**
See also CA 101; 114; DLB 88; INT 101
Scott, Frank
See Scott, F(rancis) R(eginald)
Scott, Joanna 1960- .... **CLC 50**
See also CA 126; CANR 53
Scott, Paul (Mark) 1920-1978 .... **CLC 9, 60**
See also CA 81-84; 77-80; CANR 33; DLB 14, 207; MTCW 1
Scott, Sarah 1723-1795 .... **LC 44**
See also DLB 39
Scott, Walter 1771-1832 **NCLC 15, 69; DA; DAB; DAC; DAM MST, NOV, POET; PC 13; SSC 32; WLC**
See also AAYA 22; CDBLB 1789-1832; DLB 93, 107, 116, 144, 159; YABC 2
Scribe, (Augustin) Eugene 1791-1861 **NCLC 16; DAM DRAM; DC 5**
See also DLB 192
Scrum, R.
See Crumb, R(obert)
Scudery, Madeleine de 1607-1701 .... **LC 2**
Scum
See Crumb, R(obert)
Scumbag, Little Bobby
See Crumb, R(obert)
Seabrook, John
See Hubbard, L(afayette) Ron(ald)
Sealy, I. Allan 1951- .... **CLC 55**
Search, Alexander
See Pessoa, Fernando (Antonio Nogueira)
Sebastian, Lee
See Silverberg, Robert
Sebastian Owl
See Thompson, Hunter S(tockton)
Sebestyen, Ouida 1924- .... **CLC 30**
See also AAYA 8; CA 107; CANR 40; CLR 17; JRDA; MAICYA; SAAS 10; SATA 39
Secundus, H. Scriblerus
See Fielding, Henry
Sedges, John
See Buck, Pearl S(ydenstricker)
Sedgwick, Catharine Maria 1789-1867 **NCLC 19**
See also DLB 1, 74
Seelye, John (Douglas) 1931- .... **CLC 7**
See also CA 97-100; CANR 70; INT 97-100
Seferiades, Giorgos Stylianou 1900-1971
See Seferis, George
See also CA 5-8R; 33-36R; CANR 5, 36; MTCW 1
Seferis, George .... **CLC 5, 11**
See also Seferiades, Giorgos Stylianou
Segal, Erich (Wolf) 1937- **CLC 3, 10; DAM POP**
See also BEST 89:1; CA 25-28R; CANR 20, 36, 65; DLBY 86; INT CANR-20; MTCW 1
Seger, Bob 1945- .... **CLC 35**
Seghers, Anna .... **CLC 7**
See also Radvanyi, Netty
See also DLB 69
Seidel, Frederick (Lewis) 1936- .... **CLC 18**
See also CA 13-16R; CANR 8; DLBY 84
Seifert, Jaroslav 1901-1986 .... **CLC 34, 44, 93**
See also CA 127; MTCW 1, 2
Sei Shonagon c. 966-1017(?) .... **CMLC 6**
Séjour, Victor 1817-1874 .... **DC 10**
See also DLB 50
Sejour Marcou et Ferrand, Juan Victor
See Séjour, Victor
Selby, Hubert, Jr. 1928- **CLC 1, 2, 4, 8; SSC 20**
See also CA 13-16R; CANR 33; DLB 2
Selzer, Richard 1928- .... **CLC 74**
See also CA 65-68; CANR 14
Sembene, Ousmane
See Ousmane, Sembene
Senancour, Etienne Pivert de 1770-1846 **NCLC 16**
See also DLB 119
Sender, Ramon (Jose) 1902-1982 .. **CLC 8; DAM MULT; HLC**
See also CA 5-8R; 105; CANR 8; HW 1; MTCW 1
Seneca, Lucius Annaeus c. 1-c. 65 **CMLC 6; DAM DRAM; DC 5**
See also DLB 211
Senghor, Leopold Sedar 1906- **CLC 54; BLC 3; DAM MULT, POET; PC 25**
See also BW 2, 3; CA 116; 125; CANR 47, 74; MTCW 1, 2
Senna, Danzy 1970- .... **CLC 119**
See also CA 169

Serling, (Edward) Rod(man) 1924-1975 **CLC 30**
See also AAYA 14; AITN 1; CA 162; 57-60; DLB 26
Serna, Ramon Gomez de la
See Gomez de la Serna, Ramon
Serpieres
See Guillevic, (Eugene)
Service, Robert
See Service, Robert W(illiam)
See also DAB; DLB 92
Service, Robert W(illiam) 1874(?)-1958 **TCLC 15; DA; DAC; DAM MST, POET; WLC**
See also Service, Robert
See also CA 115; 140; SATA 20
Seth, Vikram 1952- ... **CLC 43, 90; DAM MULT**
See also CA 121; 127; CANR 50, 74; DLB 120; INT 127; MTCW 2
Seton, Cynthia Propper 1926-1982 .... **CLC 27**
See also CA 5-8R; 108; CANR 7
Seton, Ernest (Evan) Thompson 1860-1946 **TCLC 31**
See also CA 109; CLR 59; DLB 92; DLBD 13; JRDA; SATA 18
Seton-Thompson, Ernest
See Seton, Ernest (Evan) Thompson
Settle, Mary Lee 1918- .... **CLC 19, 61**
See also CA 89-92; CAAS 1; CANR 44; DLB 6; INT 89-92
Seuphor, Michel
See Arp, Jean
Sevigne, Marie (de Rabutin-Chantal) Marquise de 1626-1696 .... **LC 11**
Sewall, Samuel 1652-1730 .... **LC 38**
See also DLB 24
Sexton, Anne (Harvey) 1928-1974 **CLC 2, 4, 6, 8, 10, 15, 53; DA; DAB; DAC; DAM MST, POET; PC 2; WLC**
See also CA 1-4R; 53-56; CABS 2; CANR 3, 36; CDALB 1941-1968; DLB 5, 169; MTCW 1, 2; SATA 10
Shaara, Jeff 1952- .... **CLC 119**
See also CA 163
Shaara, Michael (Joseph, Jr.) 1929-1988 **CLC 15; DAM POP**
See also AITN 1; CA 102; 125; CANR 52; DLBY 83
Shackleton, C. C.
See Aldiss, Brian W(ilson)
Shacochis, Bob .... **CLC 39**
See also Shacochis, Robert G.
Shacochis, Robert G. 1951-
See Shacochis, Bob
See also CA 119; 124; INT 124
Shaffer, Anthony (Joshua) 1926- **CLC 19; DAM DRAM**
See also CA 110; 116; DLB 13
Shaffer, Peter (Levin) 1926- **CLC 5, 14, 18, 37, 60; DAB; DAM DRAM, MST; DC 7**
See also CA 25-28R; CANR 25, 47, 74; CDBLB 1960 to Present; DLB 13; MTCW 1, 2
Shakey, Bernard
See Young, Neil
Shalamov, Varlam (Tikhonovich) 1907(?)-1982 **CLC 18**
See also CA 129; 105
Shamlu, Ahmad 1925- .... **CLC 10**
Shammas, Anton 1951- .... **CLC 55**
Shange, Ntozake 1948- **CLC 8, 25, 38, 74; BLC 3; DAM DRAM, MULT; DC 3**
See also AAYA 9; BW 2; CA 85-88; CABS 3; CANR 27, 48, 74; DLB 38; MTCW 1, 2
Shanley, John Patrick 1950- .... **CLC 75**
See also CA 128; 133
Shapcott, Thomas W(illiam) 1935- .... **CLC 38**
See also CA 69-72; CANR 49
Shapiro, Jane .... **CLC 76**
Shapiro, Karl (Jay) 1913- **CLC 4, 8, 15, 53; PC 25**
See also CA 1-4R; CAAS 6; CANR 1, 36, 66; DLB 48; MTCW 1, 2
Sharp, William 1855-1905 .... **TCLC 39**
See also CA 160; DLB 156
Sharpe, Thomas Ridley 1928-
See Sharpe, Tom
See also CA 114; 122; INT 122
Sharpe, Tom .... **CLC 36**
See also Sharpe, Thomas Ridley
See also DLB 14
Shaw, Bernard .... **TCLC 45**
See also Shaw, George Bernard
See also BW 1; MTCW 2
Shaw, G. Bernard
See Shaw, George Bernard
Shaw, George Bernard 1856-1950 **TCLC 3, 9, 21; DA; DAB; DAC; DAM DRAM, MST; WLC**
See also Shaw, Bernard
See also CA 104; 128; CDBLB 1914-1945; DLB 10, 57, 190; MTCW 1, 2
Shaw, Henry Wheeler 1818-1885 .... **NCLC 15**
See also DLB 11
Shaw, Irwin 1913-1984 **CLC 7, 23, 34; DAM DRAM, POP**
See also AITN 1; CA 13-16R; 112; CANR 21; CDALB 1941-1968; DLB 6, 102; DLBY 84; MTCW 1, 21
Shaw, Robert 1927-1978 .... **CLC 5**
See also AITN 1; CA 1-4R; 81-84; CANR 4; DLB 13, 14
Shaw, T. E.
See Lawrence, T(homas) E(dward)
Shawn, Wallace 1943- .... **CLC 41**
See also CA 112
Shea, Lisa 1953- .... **CLC 86**
See also CA 147
Sheed, Wilfrid (John Joseph) 1930- **CLC 2, 4, 10, 53**
See also CA 65-68; CANR 30, 66; DLB 6; MTCW 1, 2
Sheldon, Alice Hastings Bradley 1915(?)-1987
See Tiptree, James, Jr.
See also CA 108; 122; CANR 34; INT 108; MTCW 1
Sheldon, John
See Bloch, Robert (Albert)
Shelley, Mary Wollstonecraft (Godwin) 1797-1851 **NCLC 14, 59; DA; DAB; DAC; DAM MST, NOV; WLC**
See also AAYA 20; CDBLB 1789-1832; DLB 110, 116, 159, 178; SATA 29
Shelley, Percy Bysshe 1792-1822 **NCLC 18; DA; DAB; DAC; DAM MST, POET; PC 14; WLC**
See also CDBLB 1789-1832; DLB 96, 110, 158
Shepard, Jim 1956- .... **CLC 36**
See also CA 137; CANR 59; SATA 90
Shepard, Lucius 1947- .... **CLC 34**
See also CA 128; 141; CANR 81
Shepard, Sam 1943- **CLC 4, 6, 17, 34, 41, 44; DAM DRAM; DC 5**
See also AAYA 1; CA 69-72; CABS 3; CANR 22; DLB 7, 212; MTCW 1, 2
Shepherd, Michael
See Ludlum, Robert
Sherburne, Zoa (Lillian Morin) 1912-1995 **CLC 30**
See also AAYA 13; CA 1-4R; 176; CANR 3, 37; MAICYA; SAAS 18; SATA 3
Sheridan, Frances 1724-1766 .... **LC 7**
See also DLB 39, 84
Sheridan, Richard Brinsley 1751-1816 **NCLC 5; DA; DAB; DAC; DAM DRAM, MST; DC 1; WLC**
See also CDBLB 1660-1789; DLB 89
Sherman, Jonathan Marc .... **CLC 55**
Sherman, Martin 1941(?)- .... **CLC 19**
See also CA 116; 123
Sherwin, Judith Johnson
See Johnson, Judith (Emlyn)
Sherwood, Frances 1940- .... **CLC 81**
See also CA 146
Sherwood, Robert E(mmet) 1896-1955 . **TCLC 3; DAM DRAM**
See also CA 104; 153; DLB 7, 26
Shestov, Lev 1866-1938 .... **TCLC 56**
Shevchenko, Taras 1814-1861 .... **NCLC 54**
Shiel, M(atthew) P(hipps) 1865-1947 .... **TCLC 8**
See also Holmes, Gordon
See also CA 106; 160; DLB 153; MTCW 2
Shields, Carol 1935- .... **CLC 91, 113; DAC**
See also CA 81-84; CANR 51, 74; MTCW 2
Shields, David 1956- .... **CLC 97**
See also CA 124; CANR 48
Shiga, Naoya 1883-1971 .... **CLC 33; SSC 23**
See also CA 101; 33-36R; DLB 180
Shikibu, Murasaki c. 978-c. 1014 .... **CMLC 1**
Shilts, Randy 1951-1994 .... **CLC 85**
See also AAYA 19; CA 115; 127; 144; CANR 45; INT 127; MTCW 2
Shimazaki, Haruki 1872-1943
See Shimazaki Toson
See also CA 105; 134
Shimazaki Toson 1872-1943 .... **TCLC 5**
See also Shimazaki, Haruki
See also DLB 180
Sholokhov, Mikhail (Aleksandrovich) 1905-1984 **CLC 7, 15**
See also CA 101; 112; MTCW 1, 2; SATA-Obit 36
Shone, Patric
See Hanley, James
Shreve, Susan Richards 1939- .... **CLC 23**
See also CA 49-52; CAAS 5; CANR 5, 38, 69; MAICYA; SATA 46, 95; SATA-Brief 41
Shue, Larry 1946-1985 ... **CLC 52; DAM DRAM**
See also CA 145; 117
Shu-Jen, Chou 1881-1936
See Lu Hsun
See also CA 104
Shulman, Alix Kates 1932- .... **CLC 2, 10**
See also CA 29-32R; CANR 43; SATA 7
Shuster, Joe 1914- .... **CLC 21**
Shute, Nevil .... **CLC 30**
See also Norway, Nevil Shute
See also MTCW 2
Shuttle, Penelope (Diane) 1947- .... **CLC 7**
See also CA 93-96; CANR 39; DLB 14, 40
Sidney, Mary 1561-1621 .... **LC 19, 39**
Sidney, Sir Philip 1554-1586 **LC 19, 39; DA; DAB; DAC; DAM MST, POET**
See also CDBLB Before 1660; DLB 167
Siegel, Jerome 1914-1996 .... **CLC 21**
See also CA 116; 169; 151
Siegel, Jerry
See Siegel, Jerome
Sienkiewicz, Henryk (Adam Alexander Pius) 1846-1916 .... **TCLC 3**
See also CA 104; 134
Sierra, Gregorio Martinez
See Martinez Sierra, Gregorio
Sierra, Maria (de la O'LeJarraga) Martinez
See Martinez Sierra, Maria (de la O'LeJarraga)
Sigal, Clancy 1926- .... **CLC 7**
See also CA 1-4R
Sigourney, Lydia Howard (Huntley) 1791-1865 **NCLC 21**
See also DLB 1, 42, 73
Siguenza y Gongora, Carlos de 1645-1700 **LC 8; HLCS 2**
Sigurjonsson, Johann 1880-1919 .... **TCLC 27**
See also CA 170
Sikelianos, Angelos 1884-1951 .... **TCLC 39**

Silkin, Jon 1930- .... **CLC 2, 6, 43**
See also CA 5-8R; CAAS 5; DLB 27
Silko, Leslie (Marmon) 1948- **CLC 23, 74, 114; DA; DAC; DAM MST, MULT, POP; WLCS**
See also AAYA 14; CA 115; 122; CANR 45, 65; DLB 143, 175; MTCW 2; NNAL
Sillanpaa, Frans Eemil 1888-1964 .... **CLC 19**
See also CA 129; 93-96; MTCW 1
Sillitoe, Alan 1928- .... **CLC 1, 3, 6, 10, 19, 57**
See also AITN 1; CA 9-12R; CAAS 2; CANR 8, 26, 55; CDBLB 1960 to Present; DLB 14, 139; MTCW 1, 2; SATA 61
Silone, Ignazio 1900-1978 .... **CLC 4**
See also CA 25-28; 81-84; CANR 34; CAP 2; MTCW 1
Silver, Joan Micklin 1935- .... **CLC 20**
See also CA 114; 121; INT 121
Silver, Nicholas
See Faust, Frederick (Schiller)
Silverberg, Robert 1935- ...... **CLC 7; DAM POP**
See also AAYA 24; CA 1-4R; CAAS 3; CANR 1, 20, 36; CLR 59; DLB 8; INT CANR-20; MAICYA; MTCW 1, 2; SATA 13, 91; SATA-Essay 104
Silverstein, Alvin 1933- .... **CLC 17**
See also CA 49-52; CANR 2; CLR 25; JRDA; MAICYA; SATA 8, 69
Silverstein, Virginia B(arbara Opshelor) 1937- **CLC 17**
See also CA 49-52; CANR 2; CLR 25; JRDA; MAICYA; SATA 8, 69
Sim, Georges
See Simenon, Georges (Jacques Christian)
Simak, Clifford D(onald) 1904-1988 . **CLC 1, 55**
See also CA 1-4R; 125; CANR 1, 35; DLB 8; MTCW 1; SATA-Obit 56
Simenon, Georges (Jacques Christian) 1903-1989 **CLC 1, 2, 3, 8, 18, 47; DAM POP**
See also CA 85-88; 129; CANR 35; DLB 72; DLBY 89; MTCW 1, 2
Simic, Charles 1938-**CLC 6, 9, 22, 49, 68; DAM POET**
See also CA 29-32R; CAAS 4; CANR 12, 33, 52, 61; DLB 105; MTCW 2
Simmel, Georg 1858-1918 .... **TCLC 64**
See also CA 157
Simmons, Charles (Paul) 1924- .... **CLC 57**
See also CA 89-92; INT 89-92
Simmons, Dan 1948- .... **CLC 44; DAM POP**
See also AAYA 16; CA 138; CANR 53, 81
Simmons, James (Stewart Alexander) 1933-**CLC 43**
See also CA 105; CAAS 21; DLB 40
Simms, William Gilmore 1806-1870 .... **NCLC 3**
See also DLB 3, 30, 59, 73
Simon, Carly 1945- .... **CLC 26**
See also CA 105
Simon, Claude 1913-1984**CLC 4, 9, 15, 39; DAM NOV**
See also CA 89-92; CANR 33; DLB 83; MTCW 1
Simon, (Marvin) Neil 1927-**CLC 6, 11, 31, 39, 70; DAM DRAM**
See also AITN 1; CA 21-24R; CANR 26, 54; DLB 7; MTCW 1, 2
Simon, Paul (Frederick) 1941(?)- .... **CLC 17**
See also CA 116; 153
Simonon, Paul 1956(?)- .... **CLC 30**
Simpson, Harriette
See Arnow, Harriette (Louisa) Simpson
Simpson, Louis (Aston Marantz) 1923-**CLC 4, 7, 9, 32; DAM POET**
See also CA 1-4R; CAAS 4; CANR 1, 61; DLB 5; MTCW 1, 2
Simpson, Mona (Elizabeth) 1957- .... **CLC 44**
See also CA 122; 135; CANR 68
Simpson, N(orman) F(rederick) 1919- . **CLC 29**
See also CA 13-16R; DLB 13
Sinclair, Andrew (Annandale) 1935- . **CLC 2, 14**
See also CA 9-12R; CAAS 5; CANR 14, 38; DLB 14; MTCW 1
Sinclair, Emil
See Hesse, Hermann
Sinclair, Iain 1943- .... **CLC 76**
See also CA 132; CANR 81
Sinclair, Iain MacGregor
See Sinclair, Iain
Sinclair, Irene
See Griffith, D(avid Lewelyn) W(ark)
Sinclair, Mary Amelia St. Clair 1865(?)-1946
See Sinclair, May
See also CA 104
Sinclair, May 1863-1946 .... **TCLC 3, 11**
See also Sinclair, Mary Amelia St. Clair
See also CA 166; DLB 36, 135
Sinclair, Roy
See Griffith, D(avid Lewelyn) W(ark)
Sinclair, Upton (Beall) 1878-1968 **CLC 1, 11, 15, 63; DA; DAB; DAC; DAM MST, NOV; WLC**
See also CA 5-8R; 25-28R; CANR 7; CDALB 1929-1941; DLB 9; INT CANR-7; MTCW 1, 2; SATA 9
Singer, Isaac
See Singer, Isaac Bashevis
Singer, Isaac Bashevis 1904-1991**CLC 1, 3, 6, 9, 11, 15, 23, 38, 69, 111; DA; DAB; DAC; DAM MST, NOV; SSC 3; WLC**
See also AITN 1, 2; CA 1-4R; 134; CANR 1, 39; CDALB 1941-1968; CLR 1; DLB 6, 28, 52; DLBY 91; JRDA; MAICYA; MTCW 1, 2; SATA 3, 27; SATA-Obit 68
Singer, Israel Joshua 1893-1944 .... **TCLC 33**
See also CA 169
Singh, Khushwant 1915- .... **CLC 11**
See also CA 9-12R; CAAS 9; CANR 6
Singleton, Ann
See Benedict, Ruth (Fulton)
Sinjohn, John
See Galsworthy, John
Sinyavsky, Andrei (Donatevich) 1925-1997**CLC 8**
See also CA 85-88; 159
Sirin, V.
See Nabokov, Vladimir (Vladimirovich)
Sissman, L(ouis) E(dward) 1928-1976 **CLC 9, 18**
See also CA 21-24R; 65-68; CANR 13; DLB 5
Sisson, C(harles) H(ubert) 1914- .... **CLC 8**
See also CA 1-4R; CAAS 3; CANR 3, 48; DLB 27
Sitwell, Dame Edith 1887-1964**CLC 2, 9, 67; DAM POET; PC 3**
See also CA 9-12R; CANR 35; CDBLB 1945-1960; DLB 20; MTCW 1, 2
Siwaarmill, H. P.
See Sharp, William
Sjoewall, Maj 1935- .... **CLC 7**
See also CA 65-68; CANR 73
Sjowall, Maj
See Sjoewall, Maj
Skelton, John 1463-1529 .... **PC 25**
Skelton, Robin 1925-1997 .... **CLC 13**
See also AITN 2; CA 5-8R; 160; CAAS 5; CANR 28; DLB 27, 53
Skolimowski, Jerzy 1938- .... **CLC 20**
See also CA 128
Skram, Amalie (Bertha) 1847-1905 .... **TCLC 25**
See also CA 165
Skvorecky, Josef (Vaclav) 1924-**CLC 15, 39, 69; DAC; DAM NOV**
See also CA 61-64; CAAS 1; CANR 10, 34, 63; MTCW 1, 2
Slade, Bernard .... **CLC 11, 46**
See also Newbound, Bernard Slade
See also CAAS 9; DLB 53
Slaughter, Carolyn 1946- .... **CLC 56**
See also CA 85-88
Slaughter, Frank G(ill) 1908- .... **CLC 29**
See also AITN 2; CA 5-8R; CANR 5; INT CANR-5
Slavitt, David R(ytman) 1935- .... **CLC 5, 14**
See also CA 21-24R; CAAS 3; CANR 41; DLB 5, 6
Slesinger, Tess 1905-1945 .... **TCLC 10**
See also CA 107; DLB 102
Slessor, Kenneth 1901-1971 .... **CLC 14**
See also CA 102; 89-92
Slowacki, Juliusz 1809-1849 .... **NCLC 15**
Smart, Christopher 1722-1771**LC 3; DAM POET; PC 13**
See also DLB 109
Smart, Elizabeth 1913-1986 .... **CLC 54**
See also CA 81-84; 118; DLB 88
Smiley, Jane (Graves) 1949- **CLC 53, 76; DAM POP**
See also CA 104; CANR 30, 50, 74; INT CANR-30
Smith, A(rthur) J(ames) M(arshall) 1902-1980 **CLC 15; DAC**
See also CA 1-4R; 102; CANR 4; DLB 88
Smith, Adam 1723-1790 .... **LC 36**
See also DLB 104
Smith, Alexander 1829-1867 .... **NCLC 59**
See also DLB 32, 55
Smith, Anna Deavere 1950- .... **CLC 86**
See also CA 133
Smith, Betty (Wehner) 1896-1972 .... **CLC 19**
See also CA 5-8R; 33-36R; DLBY 82; SATA 6
Smith, Charlotte (Turner) 1749-1806 . **NCLC 23**
See also DLB 39, 109
Smith, Clark Ashton 1893-1961 .... **CLC 43**
See also CA 143; CANR 81; MTCW 2
Smith, Dave .... **CLC 22, 42**
See also Smith, David (Jeddie)
See also CAAS 7; DLB 5
Smith, David (Jeddie) 1942-
See Smith, Dave
See also CA 49-52; CANR 1, 59; DAM POET
Smith, Florence Margaret 1902-1971
See Smith, Stevie
See also CA 17-18; 29-32R; CANR 35; CAP 2; DAM POET; MTCW 1, 2
Smith, Iain Crichton 1928-1998 .... **CLC 64**
See also CA 21-24R; 171; DLB 40, 139
Smith, John 1580(?)-1631 .... **LC 9**
See also DLB 24, 30
Smith, Johnston
See Crane, Stephen (Townley)
Smith, Joseph, Jr. 1805-1844 .... **NCLC 53**
Smith, Lee 1944- .... **CLC 25, 73**
See also CA 114; 119; CANR 46; DLB 143; DLBY 83; INT 119
Smith, Martin
See Smith, Martin Cruz
Smith, Martin Cruz 1942-**CLC 25; DAM MULT, POP**
See also BEST 89:4; CA 85-88; CANR 6, 23, 43, 65; INT CANR-23; MTCW 2; NNAL
Smith, Mary-Ann Tirone 1944- .... **CLC 39**
See also CA 118; 136
Smith, Patti 1946- .... **CLC 12**
See also CA 93-96; CANR 63
Smith, Pauline (Urmson) 1882-1959 ... **TCLC 25**
Smith, Rosamond
See Oates, Joyce Carol
Smith, Sheila Kaye
See Kaye-Smith, Sheila
Smith, Stevie .... **CLC 3, 8, 25, 44; PC 12**
See also Smith, Florence Margaret
See also DLB 20; MTCW 2
Smith, Wilbur (Addison) 1933- .... **CLC 33**
See also CA 13-16R; CANR 7, 46, 66; MTCW 1, 2
Smith, William Jay 1918- .... **CLC 6**
See also CA 5-8R; CANR 44; DLB 5; MAICYA;

SAAS 22; SATA 2, 68
Smith, Woodrow Wilson
See Kuttner, Henry
Smolenskin, Peretz 1842-1885 .... **NCLC 30**
Smollett, Tobias (George) 1721-1771 ... **LC 2, 46**
See also CDBLB 1660-1789; DLB 39, 104
Snodgrass, W(illiam) D(e Witt) 1926- **CLC 2, 6, 10, 18, 68; DAM POET**
See also CA 1-4R; CANR 6, 36, 65; DLB 5; MTCW 1, 2
Snow, C(harles) P(ercy) 1905-1980 **CLC 1, 4, 6, 9, 13, 19; DAM NOV**
See also CA 5-8R; 101; CANR 28; CDBLB 1945-1960; DLB 15, 77; DLBD 17; MTCW 1, 2
Snow, Frances Compton
See Adams, Henry (Brooks)
Snyder, Gary (Sherman) 1930- **CLC 1, 2, 5, 9, 32, 120; DAM POET; PC 21**
See also CA 17-20R; CANR 30, 60; DLB 5, 16, 165, 212; MTCW 2
Snyder, Zilpha Keatley 1927- .... **CLC 17**
See also AAYA 15; CA 9-12R; CANR 38; CLR 31; JRDA; MAICYA; SAAS 2; SATA 1, 28, 75
Soares, Bernardo
See Pessoa, Fernando (Antonio Nogueira)
Sobh, A.
See Shamlu, Ahmad
Sobol, Joshua .... **CLC 60**
Socrates 469B.C.-399B.C. .... **CMLC 27**
Soderberg, Hjalmar 1869-1941 .... **TCLC 39**
Sodergran, Edith (Irene)
See Soedergran, Edith (Irene)
Soedergran, Edith (Irene) 1892-1923 .. **TCLC 31**
Softly, Edgar
See Lovecraft, H(oward) P(hillips)
Softly, Edward
See Lovecraft, H(oward) P(hillips)
Sokolov, Raymond 1941- .... **CLC 7**
See also CA 85-88
Solo, Jay
See Ellison, Harlan (Jay)
Sologub, Fyodor .... **TCLC 9**
See also Teternikov, Fyodor Kuzmich
Solomons, Ikey Esquir
See Thackeray, William Makepeace
Solomos, Dionysios 1798-1857 .... **NCLC 15**
Solwoska, Mara
See French, Marilyn
Solzhenitsyn, Aleksandr I(sayevich) 1918- **CLC 1, 2, 4, 7, 9, 10, 18, 26, 34, 78; DA; DAB; DAC; DAM MST, NOV; SSC 32; WLC**
See also AITN 1; CA 69-72; CANR 40, 65; MTCW 1, 2
Somers, Jane
See Lessing, Doris (May)
Somerville, Edith 1858-1949 .... **TCLC 51**
See also DLB 135
Somerville & Ross
See Martin, Violet Florence; Somerville, Edith
Sommer, Scott 1951- .... **CLC 25**
See also CA 106
Sondheim, Stephen (Joshua) 1930- **CLC 30, 39; DAM DRAM**
See also AAYA 11; CA 103; CANR 47, 68
Song, Cathy 1955- .... **PC 21**
See also CA 154; DLB 169
Sontag, Susan 1933- **CLC 1, 2, 10, 13, 31, 105; DAM POP**
See also CA 17-20R; CANR 25, 51, 74; DLB 2, 67; MTCW 1, 2
Sophocles 496(?)B.C.-406(?)B.C. . **CMLC 2; DA; DAB; DAC; DAM DRAM, MST; DC 1; WLCS**
See also DLB 176
Sordello 1189-1269 .... **CMLC 15**
Sorel, Georges 1847-1922 .... **TCLC 91**
See also CA 118
Sorel, Julia
See Drexler, Rosalyn
Sorrentino, Gilbert 1929- . **CLC 3, 7, 14, 22, 40**
See also CA 77-80; CANR 14, 33; DLB 5, 173; DLBY 80; INT CANR-14
Soto, Gary 1952- **CLC 32, 80; DAM MULT; HLC**
See also AAYA 10; CA 119; 125; CANR 50, 74; CLR 38; DLB 82; HW 1, 2; INT 125; JRDA; MTCW 2; SATA 80
Soupault, Philippe 1897-1990 .... **CLC 68**
See also CA 116; 147; 131
Souster, (Holmes) Raymond 1921- ... **CLC 5, 14; DAC; DAM POET**
See also CA 13-16R; CAAS 14; CANR 13, 29, 53; DLB 88; SATA 63
Southern, Terry 1924(?)-1995 .... **CLC 7**
See also CA 1-4R; 150; CANR 1, 55; DLB 2
Southey, Robert 1774-1843 .... **NCLC 8**
See also DLB 93, 107, 142; SATA 54
Southworth, Emma Dorothy Eliza Nevitte 1819-1899 .... **NCLC 26**
Souza, Ernest
See Scott, Evelyn
Soyinka, Wole 1934- **CLC 3, 5, 14, 36, 44; BLC 3; DA; DAB; DAC; DAM DRAM, MST, MULT; DC 2; WLC**
See also BW 2, 3; CA 13-16R; CANR 27, 39; DLB 125; MTCW 1, 2
Spackman, W(illiam) M(ode) 1905-1990 **CLC 46**
See also CA 81-84; 132
Spacks, Barry (Bernard) 1931- .... **CLC 14**
See also CA 154; CANR 33; DLB 105
Spanidou, Irini 1946- .... **CLC 44**
Spark, Muriel (Sarah) 1918- **CLC 2, 3, 5, 8, 13, 18, 40, 94; DAB; DAC; DAM MST, NOV; SSC 10**
See also CA 5-8R; CANR 12, 36, 76; CDBLB 1945-1960; DLB 15, 139; INT CANR-12; MTCW 1, 2
Spaulding, Douglas
See Bradbury, Ray (Douglas)
Spaulding, Leonard
See Bradbury, Ray (Douglas)
Spence, J. A. D.
See Eliot, T(homas) S(tearns)
Spencer, Elizabeth 1921- .... **CLC 22**
See also CA 13-16R; CANR 32, 65; DLB 6; MTCW 1; SATA 14
Spencer, Leonard G.
See Silverberg, Robert
Spencer, Scott 1945- .... **CLC 30**
See also CA 113; CANR 51; DLBY 86
Spender, Stephen (Harold) 1909-1995 **CLC 1, 2, 5, 10, 41, 91; DAM POET**
See also CA 9-12R; 149; CANR 31, 54; CDBLB 1945-1960; DLB 20; MTCW 1, 2
Spengler, Oswald (Arnold Gottfried) 1880-1936 **TCLC 25**
See also CA 118
Spenser, Edmund 1552(?)-1599 ... **LC 5, 39; DA; DAB; DAC; DAM MST, POET; PC 8; WLC**
See also CDBLB Before 1660; DLB 167
Spicer, Jack 1925-1965 .... **CLC 8, 18, 72; DAM POET**
See also CA 85-88; DLB 5, 16, 193
Spiegelman, Art 1948- .... **CLC 76**
See also AAYA 10; CA 125; CANR 41, 55, 74; MTCW 2; SATA 109
Spielberg, Peter 1929- .... **CLC 6**
See also CA 5-8R; CANR 4, 48; DLBY 81
Spielberg, Steven 1947- .... **CLC 20**
See also AAYA 8, 24; CA 77-80; CANR 32; SATA 32
Spillane, Frank Morrison 1918-
See Spillane, Mickey
See also CA 25-28R; CANR 28, 63; MTCW 1, 2; SATA 66
Spillane, Mickey .... **CLC 3, 13**
See also Spillane, Frank Morrison
See also MTCW 2
Spinoza, Benedictus de 1632-1677 .... **LC 9**
Spinrad, Norman (Richard) 1940- .... **CLC 46**
See also CA 37-40R; CAAS 19; CANR 20; DLB 8; INT CANR-20
Spitteler, Carl (Friedrich Georg) 1845-1924 **TCLC 12**
See also CA 109; DLB 129
Spivack, Kathleen (Romola Drucker) 1938- **CLC 6**
See also CA 49-52
Spoto, Donald 1941- .... **CLC 39**
See also CA 65-68; CANR 11, 57
Springsteen, Bruce (F.) 1949- .... **CLC 17**
See also CA 111
Spurling, Hilary 1940- .... **CLC 34**
See also CA 104; CANR 25, 52
Spyker, John Howland
See Elman, Richard (Martin)
Squires, (James) Radcliffe 1917-1993 .. **CLC 51**
See also CA 1-4R; 140; CANR 6, 21
Srivastava, Dhanpat Rai 1880(?)-1936
See Premchand
See also CA 118
Stacy, Donald
See Pohl, Frederik
Stael, Germaine de 1766-1817
See Stael-Holstein, Anne Louise Germaine Necker Baronn
See also DLB 119
Stael-Holstein, Anne Louise Germaine Necker Baronn 1766-1817 .... **NCLC 3**
See also Stael, Germaine de
See also DLB 192
Stafford, Jean 1915-1979 **CLC 4, 7, 19, 68; SSC 26**
See also CA 1-4R; 85-88; CANR 3, 65; DLB 2, 173; MTCW 1, 2; SATA-Obit 22
Stafford, William (Edgar) 1914-1993 .. **CLC 4, 7, 29; DAM POET**
See also CA 5-8R; 142; CAAS 3; CANR 5, 22; DLB 5, 206; INT CANR-22
Stagnelius, Eric Johan 1793-1823 ...... **NCLC 61**
Staines, Trevor
See Brunner, John (Kilian Houston)
Stairs, Gordon
See Austin, Mary (Hunter)
Stalin, Joseph 1879-1953 .... **TCLC 92**
Stannard, Martin 1947- .... **CLC 44**
See also CA 142; DLB 155
Stanton, Elizabeth Cady 1815-1902 ..... **TCLC 73**
See also CA 171; DLB 79
Stanton, Maura 1946- .... **CLC 9**
See also CA 89-92; CANR 15; DLB 120
Stanton, Schuyler
See Baum, L(yman) Frank
Stapledon, (William) Olaf 1886-1950 .. **TCLC 22**
See also CA 111; 162; DLB 15
Starbuck, George (Edwin) 1931-1996 .. **CLC 53; DAM POET**
See also CA 21-24R; 153; CANR 23
Stark, Richard
See Westlake, Donald E(dwin)
Staunton, Schuyler
See Baum, L(yman) Frank
Stead, Christina (Ellen) 1902-1983 . **CLC 2, 5, 8, 32, 80**
See also CA 13-16R; 109; CANR 33, 40; MTCW 1, 2
Stead, William Thomas 1849-1912 ..... **TCLC 48**
See also CA 167
Steele, Richard 1672-1729 .... **LC 18**
See also CDBLB 1660-1789; DLB 84, 101
Steele, Timothy (Reid) 1948- .... **CLC 45**
See also CA 93-96; CANR 16, 50; DLB 120
Steffens, (Joseph) Lincoln 1866-1936 . **TCLC 20**

See also CA 117
Stegner, Wallace (Earle) 1909-1993 . **CLC 9, 49, 81; DAM NOV; SSC 27**
See also AITN 1; BEST 90:3; CA 1-4R; 141; CAAS 9; CANR 1, 21, 46; DLB 9, 206; DLBY 93; MTCW 1, 2
Stein, Gertrude 1874-1946**TCLC 1, 6, 28, 48; DA; DAB; DAC; DAM MST, NOV, POET; PC 18; WLC**
See also CA 104; 132; CDALB 1917-1929; DLB 4, 54, 86; DLBD 15; MTCW 1, 2
Steinbeck, John (Ernst) 1902-1968 . **CLC 1, 5, 9, 13, 21, 34, 45, 75; DA; DAB; DAC; DAM DRAM, MST, NOV; SSC 11; WLC**
See also AAYA 12; CA 1-4R; 25-28R; CANR 1, 35; CDALB 1929-1941; DLB 7, 9, 212; DLBD 2; MTCW 1, 2; SATA 9
Steinem, Gloria 1934- .... **CLC 63**
See also CA 53-56; CANR 28, 51; MTCW 1, 2
Steiner, George 1929- .... **CLC 24; DAM NOV**
See also CA 73-76; CANR 31, 67; DLB 67; MTCW 1, 2; SATA 62
Steiner, K. Leslie
See Delany, Samuel R(ay, Jr.)
Steiner, Rudolf 1861-1925 .... **TCLC 13**
See also CA 107
Stendhal 1783-1842**NCLC 23, 46; DA; DAB; DAC; DAM MST, NOV; SSC 27; WLC**
See also DLB 119
Stephen, Adeline Virginia
See Woolf, (Adeline) Virginia
Stephen, SirLeslie 1832-1904 .... **TCLC 23**
See also CA 123; DLB 57, 144, 190
Stephen, Sir Leslie
See Stephen, SirLeslie
Stephen, Virginia
See Woolf, (Adeline) Virginia
Stephens, James 1882(?)-1950 .... **TCLC 4**
See also CA 104; DLB 19, 153, 162
Stephens, Reed
See Donaldson, Stephen R.
Steptoe, Lydia
See Barnes, Djuna
Sterchi, Beat 1949- .... **CLC 65**
Sterling, Brett
See Bradbury, Ray (Douglas); Hamilton, Edmond
Sterling, Bruce 1954- .... **CLC 72**
See also CA 119; CANR 44
Sterling, George 1869-1926 .... **TCLC 20**
See also CA 117; 165; DLB 54
Stern, Gerald 1925- .... **CLC 40, 100**
See also CA 81-84; CANR 28; DLB 105
Stern, Richard (Gustave) 1928- .... **CLC 4, 39**
See also CA 1-4R; CANR 1, 25, 52; DLBY 87; INT CANR-25
Sternberg, Josef von 1894-1969 .... **CLC 20**
See also CA 81-84
Sterne, Laurence 1713-1768**LC 2, 48; DA; DAB; DAC; DAM MST, NOV; WLC**
See also CDBLB 1660-1789; DLB 39
Sternheim, (William Adolf) Carl 1878-1942 **TCLC 8**
See also CA 105; DLB 56, 118
Stevens, Mark 1951- .... **CLC 34**
See also CA 122
Stevens, Wallace 1879-1955**TCLC 3, 12, 45; DA; DAB; DAC; DAM MST, POET; PC 6; WLC**
See also CA 104; 124; CDALB 1929-1941; DLB 54; MTCW 1, 2
Stevenson, Anne (Katharine) 1933- . **CLC 7, 33**
See also CA 17-20R; CAAS 9; CANR 9, 33; DLB 40; MTCW 1
Stevenson, Robert Louis (Balfour) 1850-1894 **NCLC 5, 14, 63; DA; DAB; DAC; DAM MST, NOV; SSC 11; WLC**
See also AAYA 24; CDBLB 1890-1914; CLR 10, 11; DLB 18, 57, 141, 156, 174; DLBD 13; JRDA; MAICYA; SATA 100; YABC 2
Stewart, J(ohn) I(nnes) M(ackintosh) 1906-1994 **CLC 7, 14, 32**
See also CA 85-88; 147; CAAS 3; CANR 47; MTCW 1, 2
Stewart, Mary (Florence Elinor) 1916-**CLC 7, 35, 117; DAB**
See also AAYA 29; CA 1-4R; CANR 1, 59; SATA 12
Stewart, Mary Rainbow
See Stewart, Mary (Florence Elinor)
Stifle, June
See Campbell, Maria
Stifter, Adalbert 1805-1868 .. **NCLC 41; SSC 28**
See also DLB 133
Still, James 1906- .... **CLC 49**
See also CA 65-68; CAAS 17; CANR 10, 26; DLB 9; SATA 29
Sting 1951-
See Sumner, Gordon Matthew
See also CA 167
Stirling, Arthur
See Sinclair, Upton (Beall)
Stitt, Milan 1941- .... **CLC 29**
See also CA 69-72
Stockton, Francis Richard 1834-1902
See Stockton, Frank R.
See also CA 108; 137; MAICYA; SATA 44
Stockton, Frank R. .... **TCLC 47**
See also Stockton, Francis Richard
See also DLB 42, 74; DLBD 13; SATA-Brief 32
Stoddard, Charles
See Kuttner, Henry
Stoker, Abraham 1847-1912
See Stoker, Bram
See also CA 105; 150; DA; DAC; DAM MST, NOV; SATA 29
Stoker, Bram 1847-1912 . **TCLC 8; DAB; WLC**
See also Stoker, Abraham
See also AAYA 23; CDBLB 1890-1914; DLB 36, 70, 178
Stolz, Mary (Slattery) 1920- .... **CLC 12**
See also AAYA 8; AITN 1; CA 5-8R; CANR 13, 41; JRDA; MAICYA; SAAS 3; SATA 10, 71
Stone, Irving 1903-1989 .... **CLC 7; DAM POP**
See also AITN 1; CA 1-4R; 129; CAAS 3; CANR 1, 23; INT CANR-23; MTCW 1, 2; SATA 3; SATA-Obit 64
Stone, Oliver (William) 1946- .... **CLC 73**
See also AAYA 15; CA 110; CANR 55
Stone, Robert (Anthony) 1937- ... **CLC 5, 23, 42**
See also CA 85-88; CANR 23, 66; DLB 152; INT CANR-23; MTCW 1
Stone, Zachary
See Follett, Ken(neth Martin)
Stoppard, Tom 1937-**CLC 1, 3, 4, 5, 8, 15, 29, 34, 63, 91; DA; DAB; DAC; DAM DRAM, MST; DC 6; WLC**
See also CA 81-84; CANR 39, 67; CDBLB 1960 to Present; DLB 13; DLBY 85; MTCW 1, 2
Storey, David (Malcolm) 1933- ... **CLC 2, 4, 5, 8; DAM DRAM**
See also CA 81-84; CANR 36; DLB 13, 14, 207; MTCW 1
Storm, Hyemeyohsts 1935- **CLC 3; DAM MULT**
See also CA 81-84; CANR 45; NNAL
Storm, Theodor 1817-1888 .... **SSC 27**
Storm, (Hans) Theodor (Woldsen) 1817-1888 **NCLC 1; SSC 27**
See also DLB 129
Storni, Alfonsina 1892-1938**TCLC 5; DAM MULT; HLC**
See also CA 104; 131; HW 1
Stoughton, William 1631-1701 .... **LC 38**
See also DLB 24
Stout, Rex (Todhunter) 1886-1975 .... **CLC 3**
See also AITN 2; CA 61-64; CANR 71
Stow, (Julian) Randolph 1935- .. **CLC 23, 48**
See also CA 13-16R; CANR 33; MTCW 1
Stowe, Harriet (Elizabeth) Beecher 1811-1896 **NCLC 3, 50; DA; DAB; DAC; DAM MST, NOV; WLC**
See also CDALB 1865-1917; DLB 1, 12, 42, 74, 189; JRDA; MAICYA; YABC 1
Strachey, (Giles) Lytton 1880-1932 ..... **TCLC 12**
See also CA 110; DLB 149; DLBD 10; MTCW 2
Strand, Mark 1934- .... **CLC 6, 18, 41, 71; DAM POET**
See also CA 21-24R; CANR 40, 65; DLB 5; SATA 41
Straub, Peter (Francis) 1943-**CLC 28, 107; DAM POP**
See also BEST 89:1; CA 85-88; CANR 28, 65; DLBY 84; MTCW 1, 2
Strauss, Botho 1944- .... **CLC 22**
See also CA 157; DLB 124
Streatfeild, (Mary) Noel 1895(?)-1986 .. **CLC 21**
See also CA 81-84; 120; CANR 31; CLR 17; DLB 160; MAICYA; SATA 20; SATA-Obit 48
Stribling, T(homas) S(igismund) 1881-1965**CLC 23**
See also CA 107; DLB 9
Strindberg, (Johan) August 1849-1912**TCLC 1, 8, 21, 47; DA; DAB; DAC; DAM DRAM, MST; WLC**
See also CA 104; 135; MTCW 2
Stringer, Arthur 1874-1950 .... **TCLC 37**
See also CA 161; DLB 92
Stringer, David
See Roberts, Keith (John Kingston)
Stroheim, Erich von 1885-1957 .... **TCLC 71**
Strugatskii, Arkadii (Natanovich) 1925-1991 **CLC 27**
See also CA 106; 135
Strugatskii, Boris (Natanovich) 1933- . **CLC 27**
See also CA 106
Strummer, Joe 1953(?)- .... **CLC 30**
Strunk, William, Jr. 1869-1946 .... **TCLC 92**
See also CA 118; 164
Stuart, Don A.
See Campbell, John W(ood, Jr.)
Stuart, Ian
See MacLean, Alistair (Stuart)
Stuart, Jesse (Hilton) 1906-1984**CLC 1, 8, 11, 14, 34; SSC 31**
See also CA 5-8R; 112; CANR 31; DLB 9, 48, 102; DLBY 84; SATA 2; SATA-Obit 36
Sturgeon, Theodore (Hamilton) 1918-1985 **CLC 22, 39**
See also Queen, Ellery
See also CA 81-84; 116; CANR 32; DLB 8; DLBY 85; MTCW 1, 2
Sturges, Preston 1898-1959 .... **TCLC 48**
See also CA 114; 149; DLB 26
Styron, William 1925- . **CLC 1, 3, 5, 11, 15, 60; DAM NOV, POP; SSC 25**
See also BEST 90:4; CA 5-8R; CANR 6, 33, 74; CDALB 1968-1988; DLB 2, 143; DLBY 80; INT CANR-6; MTCW 1, 2
Su, Chien 1884-1918
See Su Man-shu
See also CA 123
Suarez Lynch, B.
See Bioy Casares, Adolfo; Borges, Jorge Luis
Suckow, Ruth 1892-1960 .... **SSC 18**
See also CA 113; DLB 9, 102
Sudermann, Hermann 1857-1928 .... **TCLC 15**
See also CA 107; DLB 118
Sue, Eugene 1804-1857 .... **NCLC 1**
See also DLB 119
Sueskind, Patrick 1949- .... **CLC 44**
See also Suskind, Patrick
Sukenick, Ronald 1932- .... **CLC 3, 4, 6, 48**
See also CA 25-28R; CAAS 8; CANR 32; DLB

173; DLBY 81
Suknaski, Andrew 1942- .... **CLC 19**
See also CA 101; DLB 53
Sullivan, Vernon
See Vian, Boris
Sully Prudhomme 1839-1907 .... **TCLC 31**
Su Man-shu .... **TCLC 24**
See also Su, Chien
Summerforest, Ivy B.
See Kirkup, James
Summers, Andrew James 1942- .... **CLC 26**
Summers, Andy
See Summers, Andrew James
Summers, Hollis (Spurgeon, Jr.) 1916- **CLC 10**
See also CA 5-8R; CANR 3; DLB 6
Summers, (Alphonsus Joseph-Mary Augustus) Montague 1880-1948 .... **TCLC 16**
See also CA 118; 163
Sumner, Gordon Matthew .... **CLC 26**
See also Sting
Surtees, Robert Smith 1803-1864 .... **NCLC 14**
See also DLB 21
Susann, Jacqueline 1921-1974 .... **CLC 3**
See also AITN 1; CA 65-68; 53-56; MTCW 1, 2
Su Shih 1036-1101 .... **CMLC 15**
Suskind, Patrick
See Sueskind, Patrick
See also CA 145
Sutcliff, Rosemary 1920-1992 .... **CLC 26; DAB; DAC; DAM MST, POP**
See also AAYA 10; CA 5-8R; 139; CANR 37; CLR 1, 37; JRDA; MAICYA; SATA 6, 44, 78; SATA-Obit 73
Sutro, Alfred 1863-1933 .... **TCLC 6**
See also CA 105; DLB 10
Sutton, Henry
See Slavitt, David R(ytman)
Svevo, Italo 1861-1928 .... **TCLC 2, 35; SSC 25**
See also Schmitz, Aron Hector
Swados, Elizabeth (A.) 1951- .... **CLC 12**
See also CA 97-100; CANR 49; INT 97-100
Swados, Harvey 1920-1972 .... **CLC 5**
See also CA 5-8R; 37-40R; CANR 6; DLB 2
Swan, Gladys 1934- .... **CLC 69**
See also CA 101; CANR 17, 39
Swarthout, Glendon (Fred) 1918-1992 .. **CLC 35**
See also CA 1-4R; 139; CANR 1, 47; SATA 26
Sweet, Sarah C.
See Jewett, (Theodora) Sarah Orne
Swenson, May 1919-1989**CLC 4, 14, 61, 106; DA; DAB; DAC; DAM MST, POET; PC 14**
See also CA 5-8R; 130; CANR 36, 61; DLB 5; MTCW 1, 2; SATA 15
Swift, Augustus
See Lovecraft, H(oward) P(hillips)
Swift, Graham (Colin) 1949- .... **CLC 41, 88**
See also CA 117; 122; CANR 46, 71; DLB 194; MTCW 2
Swift, Jonathan 1667-1745 **LC 1, 42; DA; DAB; DAC; DAM MST, NOV, POET; PC 9; WLC**
See also CDBLB 1660-1789; CLR 53; DLB 39, 95, 101; SATA 19
Swinburne, Algernon Charles 1837-1909 **TCLC 8, 36; DA; DAB; DAC; DAM MST, POET; PC 24; WLC**
See also CA 105; 140; CDBLB 1832-1890; DLB 35, 57
Swinfen, Ann .... **CLC 34**
Swinnerton, Frank Arthur 1884-1982 .. **CLC 31**
See also CA 108; DLB 34
Swithen, John
See King, Stephen (Edwin)
Sylvia
See Ashton-Warner, Sylvia (Constance)
Symmes, Robert Edward
See Duncan, Robert (Edward)
Symonds, John Addington 1840-1893 . **NCLC 34**
See also DLB 57, 144
Symons, Arthur 1865-1945 .... **TCLC 11**
See also CA 107; DLB 19, 57, 149
Symons, Julian (Gustave) 1912-1994 **CLC 2, 14, 32**
See also CA 49-52; 147; CAAS 3; CANR 3, 33, 59; DLB 87, 155; DLBY 92; MTCW 1
Synge, (Edmund) J(ohn) M(illington) 1871-1909 **TCLC 6, 37; DAM DRAM; DC 2**
See also CA 104; 141; CDBLB 1890-1914; DLB 10, 19
Syruc, J.
See Milosz, Czeslaw
Szirtes, George 1948- .... **CLC 46**
See also CA 109; CANR 27, 61
Szymborska, Wislawa 1923- .... **CLC 99**
See also CA 154; DLBY 96; MTCW 2
T. O., Nik
See Annensky, Innokenty (Fyodorovich)
Tabori, George 1914- .... **CLC 19**
See also CA 49-52; CANR 4, 69
Tagore, Rabindranath 1861-1941 ... **TCLC 3, 53; DAM DRAM, POET; PC 8**
See also CA 104; 120; MTCW 1, 2
Taine, Hippolyte Adolphe 1828-1893 ... **NCLC 15**
Talese, Gay 1932- .... **CLC 37**
See also AITN 1; CA 1-4R; CANR 9, 58; DLB 185; INT CANR-9; MTCW 1, 2
Tallent, Elizabeth (Ann) 1954- .... **CLC 45**
See also CA 117; CANR 72; DLB 130
Tally, Ted 1952- .... **CLC 42**
See also CA 120; 124; INT 124
Talvik, Heiti 1904-1947 .... **TCLC 87**
Tamayo y Baus, Manuel 1829-1898 .... **NCLC 1**
Tammsaare, A(nton) H(ansen) 1878-1940 **TCLC 27**
See also CA 164
Tam'si, Tchicaya U
See Tchicaya, Gerald Felix
Tan, Amy (Ruth) 1952-**CLC 59, 120; DAM MULT, NOV, POP**
See also AAYA 9; BEST 89:3; CA 136; CANR 54; CDALBS; DLB 173; MTCW 2; SATA 75
Tandem, Felix
See Spitteler, Carl (Friedrich Georg)
Tanizaki, Jun'ichiro 1886-1965 . **CLC 8, 14, 28; SSC 21**
See also CA 93-96; 25-28R; DLB 180; MTCW 2
Tanner, William
See Amis, Kingsley (William)
Tao Lao
See Storni, Alfonsina
Tarassoff, Lev
See Troyat, Henri
Tarbell, Ida M(inerva) 1857-1944 .... **TCLC 40**
See also CA 122; DLB 47
Tarkington, (Newton) Booth 1869-1946 **TCLC 9**
See also CA 110; 143; DLB 9, 102; MTCW 2; SATA 17
Tarkovsky, Andrei (Arsenyevich) 1932-1986**CLC 75**
See also CA 127
Tartt, Donna 1964(?)- .... **CLC 76**
See also CA 142
Tasso, Torquato 1544-1595 .... **LC 5**
Tate, (John Orley) Allen 1899-1979**CLC 2, 4, 6, 9, 11, 14, 24**
See also CA 5-8R; 85-88; CANR 32; DLB 4, 45, 63; DLBD 17; MTCW 1, 2
Tate, Ellalice
See Hibbert, Eleanor Alice Burford
Tate, James (Vincent) 1943- .... **CLC 2, 6, 25**
See also CA 21-24R; CANR 29, 57; DLB 5, 169
Tavel, Ronald 1940- .... **CLC 6**
See also CA 21-24R; CANR 33
Taylor, C(ecil) P(hilip) 1929-1981 .... **CLC 27**
See also CA 25-28R; 105; CANR 47
Taylor, Edward 1642(?)-1729 ..... **LC 11; DA; DAB; DAC; DAM MST, POET**
See also DLB 24
Taylor, Eleanor Ross 1920- .... **CLC 5**
See also CA 81-84; CANR 70
Taylor, Elizabeth 1912-1975 .... **CLC 2, 4, 29**
See also CA 13-16R; CANR 9, 70; DLB 139; MTCW 1; SATA 13
Taylor, Frederick Winslow 1856-1915 **TCLC 76**
Taylor, Henry (Splawn) 1942- .... **CLC 44**
See also CA 33-36R; CAAS 7; CANR 31; DLB 5
Taylor, Kamala (Purnaiya) 1924-
See Markandaya, Kamala
See also CA 77-80
Taylor, Mildred D. .... **CLC 21**
See also AAYA 10; BW 1; CA 85-88; CANR 25; CLR 9, 59; DLB 52; JRDA; MAICYA; SAAS 5; SATA 15, 70
Taylor, Peter (Hillsman) 1917-1994**CLC 1, 4, 18, 37, 44, 50, 71; SSC 10**
See also CA 13-16R; 147; CANR 9, 50; DLBY 81, 94; INT CANR-9; MTCW 1, 2
Taylor, Robert Lewis 1912-1998 .... **CLC 14**
See also CA 1-4R; 170; CANR 3, 64; SATA 10
Tchekhov, Anton
See Chekhov, Anton (Pavlovich)
Tchicaya, Gerald Felix 1931-1988 .. **CLC 101**
See also CA 129; 125; CANR 81
Tchicaya U Tam'si
See Tchicaya, Gerald Felix
Teasdale, Sara 1884-1933 .... **TCLC 4**
See also CA 104; 163; DLB 45; SATA 32
Tegner, Esaias 1782-1846 .... **NCLC 2**
Teilhard de Chardin, (Marie Joseph) Pierre 1881-1955 .... **TCLC 9**
See also CA 105
Temple, Ann
See Mortimer, Penelope (Ruth)
Tennant, Emma (Christina) 1937- .. **CLC 13, 52**
See also CA 65-68; CAAS 9; CANR 10, 38, 59; DLB 14
Tenneshaw, S. M.
See Silverberg, Robert
Tennyson, Alfred 1809-1892 . **NCLC 30, 65; DA; DAB; DAC; DAM MST, POET; PC 6; WLC**
See also CDBLB 1832-1890; DLB 32
Teran, Lisa St. Aubin de .... **CLC 36**
See also St. Aubin de Teran, Lisa
Terence c. 184B.C.-c. 159B.C. . **CMLC 14; DC 7**
See also DLB 211
Teresa de Jesus, St. 1515-1582 .... **LC 18**
Terkel, Louis 1912-
See Terkel, Studs
See also CA 57-60; CANR 18, 45, 67; MTCW 1, 2
Terkel, Studs .... **CLC 38**
See also Terkel, Louis
See also AITN 1; MTCW 2
Terry, C. V.
See Slaughter, Frank G(ill)
Terry, Megan 1932- .... **CLC 19**
See also CA 77-80; CABS 3; CANR 43; DLB 7
Tertullian c. 155-c. 245 .... **CMLC 29**
Tertz, Abram
See Sinyavsky, Andrei (Donatevich)
Tesich, Steve 1943(?)-1996 .... **CLC 40, 69**
See also CA 105; 152; DLBY 83
Tesla, Nikola 1856-1943 .... **TCLC 88**
Teternikov, Fyodor Kuzmich 1863-1927
See Sologub, Fyodor
See also CA 104
Tevis, Walter 1928-1984 .... **CLC 42**
See also CA 113
Tey, Josephine .... **TCLC 14**
See also Mackintosh, Elizabeth
See also DLB 77
Thackeray, William Makepeace 1811-1863**NCLC 5, 14, 22, 43; DA; DAB; DAC; DAM MST,**

NOV; WLC
See also CDBLB 1832-1890; DLB 21, 55, 159, 163; SATA 23
Thakura, Ravindranatha
See Tagore, Rabindranath
Tharoor, Shashi 1956- .... **CLC 70**
See also CA 141
Thelwell, Michael Miles 1939- .... **CLC 22**
See also BW 2; CA 101
Theobald, Lewis, Jr.
See Lovecraft, H(oward) P(hillips)
Theodorescu, Ion N. 1880-1967
See Arghezi, Tudor
See also CA 116
Theriault, Yves 1915-1983 **CLC 79; DAC; DAM MST**
See also CA 102; DLB 88
Theroux, Alexander (Louis) 1939- .... **CLC 2, 25**
See also CA 85-88; CANR 20, 63
Theroux, Paul (Edward) 1941- **CLC 5, 8, 11, 15, 28, 46; DAM POP**
See also AAYA 28; BEST 89:4; CA 33-36R; CANR 20, 45, 74; CDALBS; DLB 2; MTCW 1, 2; SATA 44, 109
Thesen, Sharon 1946- .... **CLC 56**
See also CA 163
Thevenin, Denis
See Duhamel, Georges
Thibault, Jacques Anatole Francois 1844-1924
See France, Anatole
See also CA 106; 127; DAM NOV; MTCW 1, 2
Thiele, Colin (Milton) 1920- .... **CLC 17**
See also CA 29-32R; CANR 12, 28, 53; CLR 27; MAICYA; SAAS 2; SATA 14, 72
Thomas, Audrey (Callahan) 1935-**CLC 7, 13, 37, 107; SSC 20**
See also AITN 2; CA 21-24R; CAAS 19; CANR 36, 58; DLB 60; MTCW 1
Thomas, D(onald) M(ichael) 1935-**CLC 13, 22, 31**
See also CA 61-64; CAAS 11; CANR 17, 45, 75; CDBLB 1960 to Present; DLB 40, 207; INT CANR-17; MTCW 1, 2
Thomas, Dylan (Marlais) 1914-1953 **TCLC 1, 8, 45; DA; DAB; DAC; DAM DRAM, MST, POET; PC 2; SSC 3; WLC**
See also CA 104; 120; CANR 65; CDBLB 1945-1960; DLB 13, 20, 139; MTCW 1, 2; SATA 60
Thomas, (Philip) Edward 1878-1917 ... **TCLC 10; DAM POET**
See also CA 106; 153; DLB 98
Thomas, Joyce Carol 1938- .... **CLC 35**
See also AAYA 12; BW 2, 3; CA 113; 116; CANR 48; CLR 19; DLB 33; INT 116; JRDA; MAICYA; MTCW 1, 2; SAAS 7; SATA 40, 78
Thomas, Lewis 1913-1993 .... **CLC 35**
See also CA 85-88; 143; CANR 38, 60; MTCW 1, 2
Thomas, M. Carey 1857-1935 .... **TCLC 89**
Thomas, Paul
See Mann, (Paul) Thomas
Thomas, Piri 1928- .... **CLC 17; HLCS 2**
See also CA 73-76; HW 1
Thomas, R(onald) S(tuart) 1913- **CLC 6, 13, 48; DAB; DAM POET**
See also CA 89-92; CAAS 4; CANR 30; CDBLB 1960 to Present; DLB 27; MTCW 1
Thomas, Ross (Elmore) 1926-1995 .... **CLC 39**
See also CA 33-36R; 150; CANR 22, 63
Thompson, Francis Clegg
See Mencken, H(enry) L(ouis)
Thompson, Francis Joseph 1859-1907 .. **TCLC 4**
See also CA 104; CDBLB 1890-1914; DLB 19
Thompson, Hunter S(tockton) 1939- **CLC 9, 17, 40, 104; DAM POP**
See also BEST 89:1; CA 17-20R; CANR 23, 46, 74, 77; DLB 185; MTCW 1, 2
Thompson, James Myers
See Thompson, Jim (Myers)
Thompson, Jim (Myers) 1906-1977(?) .. **CLC 69**
See also CA 140
Thompson, Judith .... **CLC 39**
Thomson, James 1700-1748 **LC 16, 29, 40; DAM POET**
See also DLB 95
Thomson, James 1834-1882 **NCLC 18; DAM POET**
See also DLB 35
Thoreau, Henry David 1817-1862 **NCLC 7, 21, 61; DA; DAB; DAC; DAM MST; WLC**
See also CDALB 1640-1865; DLB 1
Thornton, Hall
See Silverberg, Robert
Thucydides c. 455B.C.-399B.C. .... **CMLC 17**
See also DLB 176
Thurber, James (Grover) 1894-1961 . **CLC 5, 11, 25; DA; DAB; DAC; DAM DRAM, MST, NOV; SSC 1**
See also CA 73-76; CANR 17, 39; CDALB 1929-1941; DLB 4, 11, 22, 102; MAICYA; MTCW 1, 2; SATA 13
Thurman, Wallace (Henry) 1902-1934 . **TCLC 6; BLC 3; DAM MULT**
See also BW 1, 3; CA 104; 124; CANR 81; DLB 51
Ticheburn, Cheviot
See Ainsworth, William Harrison
Tieck, (Johann) Ludwig 1773-1853 **NCLC 5, 46; SSC 31**
See also DLB 90
Tiger, Derry
See Ellison, Harlan (Jay)
Tilghman, Christopher 1948(?)- .... **CLC 65**
See also CA 159
Tillinghast, Richard (Williford) 1940- **CLC 29**
See also CA 29-32R; CAAS 23; CANR 26, 51
Timrod, Henry 1828-1867 .... **NCLC 25**
See also DLB 3
Tindall, Gillian (Elizabeth) 1938- .... **CLC 7**
See also CA 21-24R; CANR 11, 65
Tiptree, James, Jr. .... **CLC 48, 50**
See also Sheldon, Alice Hastings Bradley
See also DLB 8
Titmarsh, Michael Angelo
See Thackeray, William Makepeace
Tocqueville, Alexis (Charles Henri Maurice Clerel, Comte) de 1805-1859 .... **NCLC 7, 63**
Tolkien, J(ohn) R(onald) R(euel) 1892-1973 **CLC 1, 2, 3, 8, 12, 38; DA; DAB; DAC; DAM MST, NOV, POP; WLC**
See also AAYA 10; AITN 1; CA 17-18; 45-48; CANR 36; CAP 2; CDBLB 1914-1945; CLR 56; DLB 15, 160; JRDA; MAICYA; MTCW 1, 2; SATA 2, 32, 100; SATA-Obit 24
Toller, Ernst 1893-1939 .... **TCLC 10**
See also CA 107; DLB 124
Tolson, M. B.
See Tolson, Melvin B(eaunorus)
Tolson, Melvin B(eaunorus) 1898(?)-1966 .. **CLC 36, 105; BLC 3; DAM MULT, POET**
See also BW 1, 3; CA 124; 89-92; CANR 80; DLB 48, 76
Tolstoi, Aleksei Nikolaevich
See Tolstoy, Alexey Nikolaevich
Tolstoy, Alexey Nikolaevich 1882-1945 **TCLC 18**
See also CA 107; 158
Tolstoy, Count Leo
See Tolstoy, Leo (Nikolaevich)
Tolstoy, Leo (Nikolaevich) 1828-1910 **TCLC 4, 11, 17, 28, 44, 79; DA; DAB; DAC; DAM MST, NOV; SSC 9, 30; WLC**
See also CA 104; 123; SATA 26
Tomasi di Lampedusa, Giuseppe 1896-1957
See Lampedusa, Giuseppe (Tomasi) di
See also CA 111
Tomlin, Lily .... **CLC 17**
See also Tomlin, Mary Jean
Tomlin, Mary Jean 1939(?)-
See Tomlin, Lily
See also CA 117
Tomlinson, (Alfred) Charles 1927- **CLC 2, 4, 6, 13, 45; DAM POET; PC 17**
See also CA 5-8R; CANR 33; DLB 40
Tomlinson, H(enry) M(ajor) 1873-1958 **TCLC 71**
See also CA 118; 161; DLB 36, 100, 195
Tonson, Jacob
See Bennett, (Enoch) Arnold
Toole, John Kennedy 1937-1969 ...... **CLC 19, 64**
See also CA 104; DLBY 81; MTCW 2
Toomer, Jean 1894-1967 **CLC 1, 4, 13, 22; BLC 3; DAM MULT; PC 7; SSC 1; WLCS**
See also BW 1; CA 85-88; CDALB 1917-1929; DLB 45, 51; MTCW 1, 2
Torley, Luke
See Blish, James (Benjamin)
Tornimparte, Alessandra
See Ginzburg, Natalia
Torre, Raoul della
See Mencken, H(enry) L(ouis)
Torrey, E(dwin) Fuller 1937- .... **CLC 34**
See also CA 119; CANR 71
Torsvan, Ben Traven
See Traven, B.
Torsvan, Benno Traven
See Traven, B.
Torsvan, Berick Traven
See Traven, B.
Torsvan, Berwick Traven
See Traven, B.
Torsvan, Bruno Traven
See Traven, B.
Torsvan, Traven
See Traven, B.
Tournier, Michel (Edouard) 1924-**CLC 6, 23, 36, 95**
See also CA 49-52; CANR 3, 36, 74; DLB 83; MTCW 1, 2; SATA 23
Tournimparte, Alessandra
See Ginzburg, Natalia
Towers, Ivar
See Kornbluth, C(yril) M.
Towne, Robert (Burton) 1936(?)- .... **CLC 87**
See also CA 108; DLB 44
Townsend, Sue .... **CLC 61**
See also Townsend, Susan Elaine
See also AAYA 28; SATA 55, 93; SATA-Brief 48
Townsend, Susan Elaine 1946-
See Townsend, Sue
See also CA 119; 127; CANR 65; DAB; DAC; DAM MST
Townshend, Peter (Dennis Blandford) 1945-**CLC 17, 42**
See also CA 107
Tozzi, Federigo 1883-1920 .... **TCLC 31**
See also CA 160
Traill, Catharine Parr 1802-1899 .... **NCLC 31**
See also DLB 99
Trakl, Georg 1887-1914 .... **TCLC 5; PC 20**
See also CA 104; 165; MTCW 2
Transtroemer, Tomas (Goesta) 1931-**CLC 52, 65; DAM POET**
See also CA 117; 129; CAAS 17
Transtromer, Tomas Gosta
See Transtroemer, Tomas (Goesta)
Traven, B. (?)-1969 .... **CLC 8, 11**
See also CA 19-20; 25-28R; CAP 2; DLB 9, 56; MTCW 1
Treitel, Jonathan 1959- .... **CLC 70**
Tremain, Rose 1943- .... **CLC 42**
See also CA 97-100; CANR 44; DLB 14
Tremblay, Michel 1942-**CLC 29, 102; DAC; DAM MST**
See also CA 116; 128; DLB 60; MTCW 1, 2

Trevanian .... **CLC 29**
See also Whitaker, Rod(ney)
Trevor, Glen
See Hilton, James
Trevor, William 1928-**CLC 7, 9, 14, 25, 71, 116; SSC 21**
See also Cox, William Trevor
See also DLB 14, 139; MTCW 2
Trifonov, Yuri (Valentinovich) 1925-1981**CLC 45**
See also CA 126; 103; MTCW 1
Trilling, Lionel 1905-1975 .... **CLC 9, 11, 24**
See also CA 9-12R; 61-64; CANR 10; DLB 28, 63; INT CANR-10; MTCW 1, 2
Trimball, W. H.
See Mencken, H(enry) L(ouis)
Tristan
See Gomez de la Serna, Ramon
Tristram
See Housman, A(lfred) E(dward)
Trogdon, William (Lewis) 1939-
See Heat-Moon, William Least
See also CA 115; 119; CANR 47; INT 119
Trollope, Anthony 1815-1882 .. **NCLC 6, 33; DA; DAB; DAC; DAM MST, NOV; SSC 28; WLC**
See also CDBLB 1832-1890; DLB 21, 57, 159; SATA 22
Trollope, Frances 1779-1863 .... **NCLC 30**
See also DLB 21, 166
Trotsky, Leon 1879-1940 .... **TCLC 22**
See also CA 118; 167
Trotter (Cockburn), Catharine 1679-1749 **LC 8**
See also DLB 84
Trout, Kilgore
See Farmer, Philip Jose
Trow, George W. S. 1943- .... **CLC 52**
See also CA 126
Troyat, Henri 1911- .... **CLC 23**
See also CA 45-48; CANR 2, 33, 67; MTCW 1
Trudeau, G(arretson) B(eekman) 1948-
See Trudeau, Garry B.
See also CA 81-84; CANR 31; SATA 35
Trudeau, Garry B. .... **CLC 12**
See also Trudeau, G(arretson) B(eekman)
See also AAYA 10; AITN 2
Truffaut, Francois 1932-1984 .... **CLC 20, 101**
See also CA 81-84; 113; CANR 34
Trumbo, Dalton 1905-1976 .... **CLC 19**
See also CA 21-24R; 69-72; CANR 10; DLB 26
Trumbull, John 1750-1831 .... **NCLC 30**
See also DLB 31
Trundlett, Helen B.
See Eliot, T(homas) S(tearns)
Tryon, Thomas 1926-1991 **CLC 3, 11; DAM POP**
See also AITN 1; CA 29-32R; 135; CANR 32, 77; MTCW 1
Tryon, Tom
See Tryon, Thomas
Ts'ao Hsueh-ch'in 1715(?)-1763 .... **LC 1**
Tsushima, Shuji 1909-1948
See Dazai Osamu
See also CA 107
Tsvetaeva (Efron), Marina (Ivanovna) 1892-1941 **TCLC 7, 35; PC 14**
See also CA 104; 128; CANR 73; MTCW 1, 2
Tuck, Lily 1938- .... **CLC 70**
See also CA 139
Tu Fu 712-770 .... **PC 9**
See also DAM MULT
Tunis, John R(oberts) 1889-1975 .... **CLC 12**
See also CA 61-64; CANR 62; DLB 22, 171; JRDA; MAICYA; SATA 37; SATA-Brief 30
Tuohy, Frank .... **CLC 37**
See also Tuohy, John Francis
See also DLB 14, 139
Tuohy, John Francis 1925-
See Tuohy, Frank
See also CA 5-8R; CANR 3, 47
Turco, Lewis (Putnam) 1934- ...... **CLC 11, 63**
See also CA 13-16R; CAAS 22; CANR 24, 51; DLBY 84
Turgenev, Ivan 1818-1883 **NCLC 21; DA; DAB; DAC; DAM MST, NOV; DC 7; SSC 7; WLC**
Turgot, Anne-Robert-Jacques 1727-1781 **LC 26**
Turner, Frederick 1943- .... **CLC 48**
See also CA 73-76; CAAS 10; CANR 12, 30, 56; DLB 40
Tutu, Desmond M(pilo) 1931- .. **CLC 80; BLC 3; DAM MULT**
See also BW 1, 3; CA 125; CANR 67, 81
Tutuola, Amos 1920-1997**CLC 5, 14, 29; BLC 3; DAM MULT**
See also BW 2, 3; CA 9-12R; 159; CANR 27, 66; DLB 125; MTCW 1, 2
Twain, Mark TCLC 6, 12, 19, 36, 48, 59; SSC 34; WLC
See also Clemens, Samuel Langhorne
See also AAYA 20; CLR 58; DLB 11, 12, 23, 64, 74
Tyler, Anne 1941-**CLC 7, 11, 18, 28, 44, 59, 103; DAM NOV, POP**
See also AAYA 18; BEST 89:1; CA 9-12R; CANR 11, 33, 53; CDALBS; DLB 6, 143; DLBY 82; MTCW 1, 2; SATA 7, 90
Tyler, Royall 1757-1826 .... **NCLC 3**
See also DLB 37
Tynan, Katharine 1861-1931 .... **TCLC 3**
See also CA 104; 167; DLB 153
Tyutchev, Fyodor 1803-1873 .... **NCLC 34**
Tzara, Tristan 1896-1963 **CLC 47; DAM POET**
See also CA 153; 89-92; MTCW 2
Uhry, Alfred 1936- **CLC 55; DAM DRAM, POP**
See also CA 127; 133; INT 133
Ulf, Haerved
See Strindberg, (Johan) August
Ulf, Harved
See Strindberg, (Johan) August
Ulibarri, Sabine R(eyes) 1919- ... **CLC 83; DAM MULT; HLCS 2**
See also CA 131; CANR 81; DLB 82; HW 1, 2
Unamuno (y Jugo), Miguel de 1864-1936**TCLC 2, 9; DAM MULT, NOV; HLC; SSC 11**
See also CA 104; 131; CANR 81; DLB 108; HW 1, 2; MTCW 1, 2
Undercliffe, Errol
See Campbell, (John) Ramsey
Underwood, Miles
See Glassco, John
Undset, Sigrid 1882-1949 ... **TCLC 3; DA; DAB; DAC; DAM MST, NOV; WLC**
See also CA 104; 129; MTCW 1, 2
Ungaretti, Giuseppe 1888-1970 ... **CLC 7, 11, 15**
See also CA 19-20; 25-28R; CAP 2; DLB 114
Unger, Douglas 1952- .... **CLC 34**
See also CA 130
Unsworth, Barry (Forster) 1930- .... **CLC 76**
See also CA 25-28R; CANR 30, 54; DLB 194
Updike, John (Hoyer) 1932- **CLC 1, 2, 3, 5, 7, 9, 13, 15, 23, 34, 43, 70; DA; DAB; DAC; DAM MST, NOV, POET, POP; SSC 13, 27; WLC**
See also CA 1-4R; CABS 1; CANR 4, 33, 51; CDALB 1968-1988; DLB 2, 5, 143; DLBD 3; DLBY 80, 82, 97; MTCW 1, 2
Upshaw, Margaret Mitchell
See Mitchell, Margaret (Munnerlyn)
Upton, Mark
See Sanders, Lawrence
Upward, Allen 1863-1926 .... **TCLC 85**
See also CA 117; DLB 36
Urdang, Constance (Henriette) 1922- .. **CLC 47**
See also CA 21-24R; CANR 9, 24
Uriel, Henry
See Faust, Frederick (Schiller)
Uris, Leon (Marcus) 1924-**CLC 7, 32; DAM NOV, POP**
See also AITN 1, 2; BEST 89:2; CA 1-4R; CANR 1, 40, 65; MTCW 1, 2; SATA 49
Urmuz
See Codrescu, Andrei
Urquhart, Jane 1949- .... **CLC 90; DAC**
See also CA 113; CANR 32, 68
Ustinov, Peter (Alexander) 1921- .... **CLC 1**
See also AITN 1; CA 13-16R; CANR 25, 51; DLB 13; MTCW 2
U Tam'si, Gerald Felix Tchicaya
See Tchicaya, Gerald Felix
U Tam'si, Tchicaya
See Tchicaya, Gerald Felix
Vachss, Andrew (Henry) 1942- .... **CLC 106**
See also CA 118; CANR 44
Vachss, Andrew H.
See Vachss, Andrew (Henry)
Vaculik, Ludvik 1926- .... **CLC 7**
See also CA 53-56; CANR 72
Vaihinger, Hans 1852-1933 .... **TCLC 71**
See also CA 116; 166
Valdez, Luis (Miguel) 1940-**CLC 84; DAM MULT; DC 10; HLC**
See also CA 101; CANR 32, 81; DLB 122; HW 1
Valenzuela, Luisa 1938- ..... **CLC 31, 104; DAM MULT; HLCS 2; SSC 14**
See also CA 101; CANR 32, 65; DLB 113; HW 1, 2
Valera y Alcala-Galiano, Juan 1824-1905 **TCLC 10**
See also CA 106
Valery, (Ambroise) Paul (Toussaint Jules) 1871-1945 .... **TCLC 4, 15; DAM POET; PC 9**
See also CA 104; 122; MTCW 1, 2
Valle-Inclan, Ramon (Maria) del 1866-1936**TCLC 5; DAM MULT; HLC**
See also CA 106; 153; CANR 80; DLB 134; HW 2
Vallejo, Antonio Buero
See Buero Vallejo, Antonio
Vallejo, Cesar (Abraham) 1892-1938**TCLC 3, 56; DAM MULT; HLC**
See also CA 105; 153; HW 1
Valles, Jules 1832-1885 .... **NCLC 71**
See also DLB 123
Vallette, Marguerite Eymery
See Rachilde
Valle Y Pena, Ramon del
See Valle-Inclan, Ramon (Maria) del
Van Ash, Cay 1918- .... **CLC 34**
Vanbrugh, Sir John 1664-1726 ..... **LC 21; DAM DRAM**
See also DLB 80
Van Campen, Karl
See Campbell, John W(ood, Jr.)
Vance, Gerald
See Silverberg, Robert
Vance, Jack .... **CLC 35**
See also Kuttner, Henry; Vance, John Holbrook
See also DLB 8
Vance, John Holbrook 1916-
See Queen, Ellery; Vance, Jack
See also CA 29-32R; CANR 17, 65; MTCW 1
Van Den Bogarde, Derek Jules Gaspard Ulric Niven 1921-
See Bogarde, Dirk
See also CA 77-80
Vandenburgh, Jane .... **CLC 59**
See also CA 168
Vanderhaeghe, Guy 1951- .... **CLC 41**
See also CA 113; CANR 72
van der Post, Laurens (Jan) 1906-1996 .. **CLC 5**
See also CA 5-8R; 155; CANR 35; DLB 204
van de Wetering, Janwillem 1931- .... **CLC 47**
See also CA 49-52; CANR 4, 62
Van Dine, S. S. .... **TCLC 23**
See also Wright, Willard Huntington
Van Doren, Carl (Clinton) 1885-1950 . **TCLC 18**
See also CA 111; 168

Van Doren, Mark 1894-1972 .... **CLC 6, 10**
See also CA 1-4R; 37-40R; CANR 3; DLB 45; MTCW 1, 2
Van Druten, John (William) 1901-1957 **TCLC 2**
See also CA 104; 161; DLB 10
Van Duyn, Mona (Jane) 1921-**CLC 3, 7, 63, 116; DAM POET**
See also CA 9-12R; CANR 7, 38, 60; DLB 5
Van Dyne, Edith
See Baum, L(yman) Frank
van Itallie, Jean-Claude 1936- .... **CLC 3**
See also CA 45-48; CAAS 2; CANR 1, 48; DLB 7
van Ostaijen, Paul 1896-1928 .... **TCLC 33**
See also CA 163
Van Peebles, Melvin 1932-**CLC 2, 20; DAM MULT**
See also BW 2, 3; CA 85-88; CANR 27, 67
Vansittart, Peter 1920- .... **CLC 42**
See also CA 1-4R; CANR 3, 49
Van Vechten, Carl 1880-1964 .... **CLC 33**
See also CA 89-92; DLB 4, 9, 51
Van Vogt, A(lfred) E(lton) 1912- .... **CLC 1**
See also CA 21-24R; CANR 28; DLB 8; SATA 14
Varda, Agnes 1928- .... **CLC 16**
See also CA 116; 122
Vargas Llosa, (Jorge) Mario (Pedro) 1936- **C L C 3, 6, 9, 10, 15, 31, 42, 85; DA; DAB; DAC; DAM MST, MULT, NOV; HLC**
See also CA 73-76; CANR 18, 32, 42, 67; DLB 145; HW 1, 2; MTCW 1, 2
Vasiliu, Gheorghe 1881-1957
See Bacovia, George
See also CA 123
Vassa, Gustavus
See Equiano, Olaudah
Vassilikos, Vassilis 1933- .... **CLC 4, 8**
See also CA 81-84; CANR 75
Vaughan, Henry 1621-1695 .... **LC 27**
See also DLB 131
Vaughn, Stephanie .... **CLC 62**
Vazov, Ivan (Minchov) 1850-1921 .... **TCLC 25**
See also CA 121; 167; DLB 147
Veblen, Thorstein B(unde) 1857-1929 **TCLC 31**
See also CA 115; 165
Vega, Lope de 1562-1635 .... **LC 23; HLCS 2**
Venison, Alfred
See Pound, Ezra (Weston Loomis)
Verdi, Marie de
See Mencken, H(enry) L(ouis)
Verdu, Matilde
See Cela, Camilo Jose
Verga, Giovanni (Carmelo) 1840-1922 . **TCLC 3; SSC 21**
See also CA 104; 123
Vergil 70B.C.-19B.C. **CMLC 9; DA; DAB; DAC; DAM MST, POET; PC 12; WLCS**
See also Virgil
Verhaeren, Emile (Adolphe Gustave) 1855-1916 **TCLC 12**
See also CA 109
Verlaine, Paul (Marie) 1844-1896 .. **NCLC 2, 51; DAM POET; PC 2**
Verne, Jules (Gabriel) 1828-1905 ... **TCLC 6, 52**
See also AAYA 16; CA 110; 131; DLB 123; JRDA; MAICYA; SATA 21
Very, Jones 1813-1880 .... **NCLC 9**
See also DLB 1
Vesaas, Tarjei 1897-1970 .... **CLC 48**
See also CA 29-32R
Vialis, Gaston
See Simenon, Georges (Jacques Christian)
Vian, Boris 1920-1959 .... **TCLC 9**
See also CA 106; 164; DLB 72; MTCW 2
Viaud, (Louis Marie) Julien 1850-1923
See Loti, Pierre
See also CA 107
Vicar, Henry
See Felsen, Henry Gregor
Vicker, Angus
See Felsen, Henry Gregor
Vidal, Gore 1925- **CLC 2, 4, 6, 8, 10, 22, 33, 72; DAM NOV, POP**
See also AITN 1; BEST 90:2; CA 5-8R; CANR 13, 45, 65; CDALBS; DLB 6, 152; INT CANR-13; MTCW 1, 2
Viereck, Peter (Robert Edwin) 1916- ..... **CLC 4**
See also CA 1-4R; CANR 1, 47; DLB 5
Vigny, Alfred (Victor) de 1797-1863 .... **NCLC 7; DAM POET; PC 26**
See also DLB 119, 192
Vilakazi, Benedict Wallet 1906-1947 . **TCLC 37**
See also CA 168
Villa, Jose Garcia 1904-1997 .... **PC 22**
See also CA 25-28R; CANR 12
Villaurrutia, Xavier 1903-1950 .... **TCLC 80**
See also HW 1
Villiers de l'Isle Adam, Jean Marie Mathias Philippe Auguste, Comte de 1838-1889 **NCLC 3; SSC 14**
See also DLB 123
Villon, Francois 1431-1463(?) .... **PC 13**
See also DLB 208
Vinci, Leonardo da 1452-1519 .... **LC 12**
Vine, Barbara .... **CLC 50**
See also Rendell, Ruth (Barbara)
See also BEST 90:4
Vinge, Joan (Carol) D(ennison) 1948- **CLC 30; SSC 24**
See also CA 93-96; CANR 72; SATA 36
Violis, G.
See Simenon, Georges (Jacques Christian)
Virgil 70B.C.-19B.C.
See Vergil
See also DLB 211
Visconti, Luchino 1906-1976 .... **CLC 16**
See also CA 81-84; 65-68; CANR 39
Vittorini, Elio 1908-1966 .... **CLC 6, 9, 14**
See also CA 133; 25-28R
Vivekananda, Swami 1863-1902 .... **TCLC 88**
Vizenor, Gerald Robert 1934- .. **CLC 103; DAM MULT**
See also CA 13-16R; CAAS 22; CANR 5, 21, 44, 67; DLB 175; MTCW 2; NNAL
Vizinczey, Stephen 1933- .... **CLC 40**
See also CA 128; INT 128
Vliet, R(ussell) G(ordon) 1929-1984 ..... **CLC 22**
See also CA 37-40R; 112; CANR 18
Vogau, Boris Andreyevich 1894-1937(?)
See Pilnyak, Boris
See also CA 123
Vogel, Paula A(nne) 1951- .... **CLC 76**
See also CA 108
Voigt, Cynthia 1942- .... **CLC 30**
See also AAYA 3, 30; CA 106; CANR 18, 37, 40; CLR 13, 48; INT CANR-18; JRDA; MAICYA; SATA 48, 79; SATA-Brief 33
Voigt, Ellen Bryant 1943- .... **CLC 54**
See also CA 69-72; CANR 11, 29, 55; DLB 120
Voinovich, Vladimir (Nikolaevich) 1932-**CLC 10, 49**
See also CA 81-84; CAAS 12; CANR 33, 67; MTCW 1
Vollmann, William T. 1959-**CLC 89; DAM NOV, POP**
See also CA 134; CANR 67; MTCW 2
Voloshinov, V. N.
See Bakhtin, Mikhail Mikhailovich
Voltaire 1694-1778**LC 14; DA; DAB; DAC; DAM DRAM, MST; SSC 12; WLC**
von Aschendrof, BaronIgnatz
See Ford, Ford Madox
von Daeniken, Erich 1935- .... **CLC 30**
See also AITN 1; CA 37-40R; CANR 17, 44
von Daniken, Erich
See von Daeniken, Erich
von Heidenstam, (Carl Gustaf) Verner
See Heidenstam, (Carl Gustaf) Verner von
von Heyse, Paul (Johann Ludwig)
See Heyse, Paul (Johann Ludwig von)
von Hofmannsthal, Hugo
See Hofmannsthal, Hugo von
von Horvath, Odon
See Horvath, Oedoen von
von Horvath, Oedoen
See Horvath, Oedoen von
von Liliencron, (Friedrich Adolf Axel) Detlev
See Liliencron, (Friedrich Adolf Axel) Detlev von
Vonnegut, Kurt, Jr. 1922-**CLC 1, 2, 3, 4, 5, 8, 12, 22, 40, 60, 111; DA; DAB; DAC; DAM MST, NOV, POP; SSC 8; WLC**
See also AAYA 6; AITN 1; BEST 90:4; CA 1-4R; CANR 1, 25, 49, 75; CDALB 1968-1988; DLB 2, 8, 152; DLBD 3; DLBY 80; MTCW 1, 2
Von Rachen, Kurt
See Hubbard, L(afayette) Ron(ald)
von Rezzori (d'Arezzo), Gregor
See Rezzori (d'Arezzo), Gregor von
von Sternberg, Josef
See Sternberg, Josef von
Vorster, Gordon 1924- .... **CLC 34**
See also CA 133
Vosce, Trudie
See Ozick, Cynthia
Voznesensky, Andrei (Andreievich) 1933-**CLC 1, 15, 57; DAM POET**
See also CA 89-92; CANR 37; MTCW 1
Waddington, Miriam 1917- .... **CLC 28**
See also CA 21-24R; CANR 12, 30; DLB 68
Wagman, Fredrica 1937- .... **CLC 7**
See also CA 97-100; INT 97-100
Wagner, Linda W.
See Wagner-Martin, Linda (C.)
Wagner, Linda Welshimer
See Wagner-Martin, Linda (C.)
Wagner, Richard 1813-1883 .... **NCLC 9**
See also DLB 129
Wagner-Martin, Linda (C.) 1936- .... **CLC 50**
See also CA 159
Wagoner, David (Russell) 1926- .... **CLC 3, 5, 15**
See also CA 1-4R; CAAS 3; CANR 2, 71; DLB 5; SATA 14
Wah, Fred(erick James) 1939- .... **CLC 44**
See also CA 107; 141; DLB 60
Wahloo, Per 1926-1975 .... **CLC 7**
See also CA 61-64; CANR 73
Wahloo, Peter
See Wahloo, Per
Wain, John (Barrington) 1925-1994 . **CLC 2, 11, 15, 46**
See also CA 5-8R; 145; CAAS 4; CANR 23, 54; CDBLB 1960 to Present; DLB 15, 27, 139, 155; MTCW 1, 2
Wajda, Andrzej 1926- .... **CLC 16**
See also CA 102
Wakefield, Dan 1932- .... **CLC 7**
See also CA 21-24R; CAAS 7
Wakoski, Diane 1937-**CLC 2, 4, 7, 9, 11, 40; DAM POET; PC 15**
See also CA 13-16R; CAAS 1; CANR 9, 60; DLB 5; INT CANR-9; MTCW 2
Wakoski-Sherbell, Diane
See Wakoski, Diane
Walcott, Derek (Alton) 1930-**CLC 2, 4, 9, 14, 25, 42, 67, 76; BLC 3; DAB; DAC; DAM MST, MULT, POET; DC 7**
See also BW 2; CA 89-92; CANR 26, 47, 75, 80; DLB 117; DLBY 81; MTCW 1, 2
Waldman, Anne (Lesley) 1945- .... **CLC 7**
See also CA 37-40R; CAAS 17; CANR 34, 69; DLB 16
Waldo, E. Hunter
See Sturgeon, Theodore (Hamilton)

Waldo, Edward Hamilton
See Sturgeon, Theodore (Hamilton)
Walker, Alice (Malsenior) 1944-**CLC 5, 6, 9, 19, 27, 46, 58, 103; BLC 3; DA; DAB; DAC; DAM MST, MULT, NOV, POET, POP; SSC 5; WLCS**
See also AAYA 3; BEST 89:4; BW 2, 3; CA 37-40R; CANR 9, 27, 49, 66; CDALB 1968-1988; DLB 6, 33, 143; INT CANR-27; MTCW 1, 2; SATA 31
Walker, David Harry 1911-1992 .... **CLC 14**
See also CA 1-4R; 137; CANR 1; SATA 8; SATA-Obit 71
Walker, Edward Joseph 1934-
See Walker, Ted
See also CA 21-24R; CANR 12, 28, 53
Walker, George F. 1947-**CLC 44, 61; DAB; DAC; DAM MST**
See also CA 103; CANR 21, 43, 59; DLB 60
Walker, Joseph A. 1935- **CLC 19; DAM DRAM, MST**
See also BW 1, 3; CA 89-92; CANR 26; DLB 38
Walker, Margaret (Abigail) 1915-1998**CLC 1, 6; BLC; DAM MULT; PC 20**
See also BW 2, 3; CA 73-76; 172; CANR 26, 54, 76; DLB 76, 152; MTCW 1, 2
Walker, Ted .... **CLC 13**
See also Walker, Edward Joseph
See also DLB 40
Wallace, David Foster 1962- .... **CLC 50, 114**
See also CA 132; CANR 59; MTCW 2
Wallace, Dexter
See Masters, Edgar Lee
Wallace, (Richard Horatio) Edgar 1875-1932 **TCLC 57**
See also CA 115; DLB 70
Wallace, Irving 1916-1990**CLC 7, 13; DAM NOV, POP**
See also AITN 1; CA 1-4R; 132; CAAS 1; CANR 1, 27; INT CANR-27; MTCW 1, 2
Wallant, Edward Lewis 1926-1962 .... **CLC 5, 10**
See also CA 1-4R; CANR 22; DLB 2, 28, 143; MTCW 1, 2
Wallas, Graham 1858-1932 .... **TCLC 91**
Walley, Byron
See Card, Orson Scott
Walpole, Horace 1717-1797 .... **LC 49**
See also DLB 39, 104
Walpole, Hugh (Seymour) 1884-1941 ... **TCLC 5**
See also CA 104; 165; DLB 34; MTCW 2
Walser, Martin 1927- .... **CLC 27**
See also CA 57-60; CANR 8, 46, DLB 75, 124
Walser, Robert 1878-1956 .... **TCLC 18; SSC 20**
See also CA 118; 165; DLB 66
Walsh, Jill Paton .... **CLC 35**
See also Paton Walsh, Gillian
See also AAYA 11; CLR 2; DLB 161; SAAS 3
Walter, Villiam Christian
See Andersen, Hans Christian
Wambaugh, Joseph (Aloysius, Jr.) 1937-**CLC 3, 18; DAM NOV, POP**
See also AITN 1; BEST 89:3; CA 33-36R; CANR 42, 65; DLB 6; DLBY 83; MTCW 1, 2
Wang Wei 699(?)-761(?) .... **PC 18**
Ward, Arthur Henry Sarsfield 1883-1959
See Rohmer, Sax
See also CA 108; 173
Ward, Douglas Turner 1930- .... **CLC 19**
See also BW 1; CA 81-84; CANR 27; DLB 7, 38
Ward, E. D.
See Lucas, E(dward) V(errall)
Ward, Mary Augusta
See Ward, Mrs. Humphry
Ward, Mrs. Humphry 1851-1920 .... **TCLC 55**
See also DLB 18
Ward, Peter
See Faust, Frederick (Schiller)
Warhol, Andy 1928(?)-1987 .... **CLC 20**
See also AAYA 12; BEST 89:4; CA 89-92; 121; CANR 34
Warner, Francis (Robert le Plastrier) 1937-**CLC 14**
See also CA 53-56; CANR 11
Warner, Marina 1946- .... **CLC 59**
See also CA 65-68; CANR 21, 55; DLB 194
Warner, Rex (Ernest) 1905-1986 .... **CLC 45**
See also CA 89-92; 119; DLB 15
Warner, Susan (Bogert) 1819-1885 .... **NCLC 31**
See also DLB 3, 42
Warner, Sylvia (Constance) Ashton
See Ashton-Warner, Sylvia (Constance)
Warner, Sylvia Townsend 1893-1978 **CLC 7, 19; SSC 23**
See also CA 61-64; 77-80; CANR 16, 60; DLB 34, 139; MTCW 1, 2
Warren, Mercy Otis 1728-1814 .... **NCLC 13**
See also DLB 31, 200
Warren, Robert Penn 1905-1989 . **CLC 1, 4, 6, 8, 10, 13, 18, 39, 53, 59; DA; DAB; DAC; DAM MST, NOV, POET; SSC 4; WLC**
See also AITN 1; CA 13-16R; 129; CANR 10, 47; CDALB 1968-1988; DLB 2, 48, 152; DLBY 80, 89; INT CANR-10; MTCW 1, 2; SATA 46; SATA-Obit 63
Warshofsky, Isaac
See Singer, Isaac Bashevis
Warton, Thomas 1728-1790 **LC 15; DAM POET**
See also DLB 104, 109
Waruk, Kona
See Harris, (Theodore) Wilson
Warung, Price 1855-1911 .... **TCLC 45**
Warwick, Jarvis
See Garner, Hugh
Washington, Alex
See Harris, Mark
Washington, Booker T(aliaferro) 1856-1915 **TCLC 10; BLC 3; DAM MULT**
See also BW 1; CA 114; 125; SATA 28
Washington, George 1732-1799 .... **LC 25**
See also DLB 31
Wassermann, (Karl) Jakob 1873-1934 . **TCLC 6**
See also CA 104; 163; DLB 66
Wasserstein, Wendy 1950-**CLC 32, 59, 90; DAM DRAM; DC 4**
See also CA 121; 129; CABS 3; CANR 53, 75; INT 129; MTCW 2; SATA 94
Waterhouse, Keith (Spencer) 1929- ..... **CLC 47**
See also CA 5-8R; CANR 38, 67; DLB 13, 15; MTCW 1, 2
Waters, Frank (Joseph) 1902-1995 .... **CLC 88**
See also CA 5-8R; 149; CAAS 13; CANR 3, 18, 63; DLB 212; DLBY 86
Waters, Roger 1944- .... **CLC 35**
Watkins, Frances Ellen
See Harper, Frances Ellen Watkins
Watkins, Gerrold
See Malzberg, Barry N(athaniel)
Watkins, Gloria 1955(?)-
See hooks, bell
See also BW 2; CA 143; MTCW 2
Watkins, Paul 1964- .... **CLC 55**
See also CA 132; CANR 62
Watkins, Vernon Phillips 1906-1967 .... **CLC 43**
See also CA 9-10; 25-28R; CAP 1; DLB 20
Watson, Irving S.
See Mencken, H(enry) L(ouis)
Watson, John H.
See Farmer, Philip Jose
Watson, Richard F.
See Silverberg, Robert
Waugh, Auberon (Alexander) 1939- .... **CLC 7**
See also CA 45-48; CANR 6, 22; DLB 14, 194
Waugh, Evelyn (Arthur St. John) 1903-1966**CLC 1, 3, 8, 13, 19, 27, 44, 107; DA; DAB; DAC; DAM MST, NOV, POP; WLC**
See also CA 85-88; 25-28R; CANR 22; CDBLB 1914-1945; DLB 15, 162, 195; MTCW 1, 2
Waugh, Harriet 1944- .... **CLC 6**
See also CA 85-88; CANR 22
Ways, C. R.
See Blount, Roy (Alton), Jr.
Waystaff, Simon
See Swift, Jonathan
Webb, (Martha) Beatrice (Potter) 1858-1943 **TCLC 22**
See also Potter, (Helen) Beatrix
See also CA 117; DLB 190
Webb, Charles (Richard) 1939- .... **CLC 7**
See also CA 25-28R
Webb, James H(enry), Jr. 1946- .... **CLC 22**
See also CA 81-84
Webb, Mary (Gladys Meredith) 1881-1927 **TCLC 24**
See also CA 123; DLB 34
Webb, Mrs. Sidney
See Webb, (Martha) Beatrice (Potter)
Webb, Phyllis 1927- .... **CLC 18**
See also CA 104; CANR 23; DLB 53
Webb, Sidney (James) 1859-1947 .... **TCLC 22**
See also CA 117; 163; DLB 190
Webber, Andrew Lloyd .... **CLC 21**
See also Lloyd Webber, Andrew
Weber, Lenora Mattingly 1895-1971 ..... **CLC 12**
See also CA 19-20; 29-32R; CAP 1; SATA 2; SATA-Obit 26
Weber, Max 1864-1920 .... **TCLC 69**
See also CA 109
Webster, John 1579(?)-1634(?)**LC 33; DA; DAB; DAC; DAM DRAM, MST; DC 2; WLC**
See also CDBLB Before 1660; DLB 58
Webster, Noah 1758-1843 .... **NCLC 30**
See also DLB 1, 37, 42, 43, 73
Wedekind, (Benjamin) Frank(lin) 1864-1918 **TCLC 7; DAM DRAM**
See also CA 104; 153; DLB 118
Weidman, Jerome 1913-1998 .... **CLC 7**
See also AITN 2; CA 1-4R; 171; CANR 1; DLB 28
Weil, Simone (Adolphine) 1909-1943 .. **TCLC 23**
See also CA 117; 159; MTCW 2
Weininger, Otto 1880-1903 .... **TCLC 84**
Weinstein, Nathan
See West, Nathanael
Weinstein, Nathan von Wallenstein
See West, Nathanael
Weir, Peter (Lindsay) 1944- .... **CLC 20**
See also CA 113; 123
Weiss, Peter (Ulrich) 1916-1982 **CLC 3, 15, 51; DAM DRAM**
See also CA 45-48; 106; CANR 3; DLB 69, 124
Weiss, Theodore (Russell) 1916- .. **CLC 3, 8, 14**
See also CA 9-12R; CAAS 2; CANR 46; DLB 5
Welch, (Maurice) Denton 1915-1948 .. **TCLC 22**
See also CA 121; 148
Welch, James 1940-**CLC 6, 14, 52; DAM MULT, POP**
See also CA 85-88; CANR 42, 66; DLB 175; NNAL
Weldon, Fay 1931-**CLC 6, 9, 11, 19, 36, 59; DAM POP**
See also CA 21-24R; CANR 16, 46, 63; CDBLB 1960 to Present; DLB 14, 194; INT CANR-16; MTCW 1, 2
Wellek, Rene 1903-1995 .... **CLC 28**
See also CA 5-8R; 150; CAAS 7; CANR 8; DLB 63; INT CANR-8
Weller, Michael 1942- .... **CLC 10, 53**
See also CA 85-88
Weller, Paul 1958- .... **CLC 26**
Wellershoff, Dieter 1925- .... **CLC 46**
See also CA 89-92; CANR 16, 37

Welles, (George) Orson 1915-1985**CLC 20, 80**
See also CA 93-96; 117
Wellman, John McDowell 1945-
See Wellman, Mac
See also CA 166
Wellman, Mac 1945- .... **CLC 65**
See also Wellman, John McDowell; Wellman, John McDowell
Wellman, Manly Wade 1903-1986 .... **CLC 49**
See also CA 1-4R; 118; CANR 6, 16, 44; SATA 6; SATA-Obit 47
Wells, Carolyn 1869(?)-1942 .... **TCLC 35**
See also CA 113; DLB 11
Wells, H(erbert) G(eorge) 1866-1946**TCLC 6, 12, 19; DA; DAB; DAC; DAM MST, NOV; SSC 6; WLC**
See also AAYA 18; CA 110; 121; CDBLB 1914-1945; DLB 34, 70, 156, 178; MTCW 1, 2; SATA 20
Wells, Rosemary 1943- .... **CLC 12**
See also AAYA 13; CA 85-88; CANR 48; CLR 16; MAICYA; SAAS 1; SATA 18, 69
Welty, Eudora 1909-**CLC 1, 2, 5, 14, 22, 33, 105; DA; DAB; DAC; DAM MST, NOV; SSC 1, 27; WLC**
See also CA 9-12R; CABS 1; CANR 32, 65; CDALB 1941-1968; DLB 2, 102, 143; DLBD 12; DLBY 87; MTCW 1, 2
Wen I-to 1899-1946 .... **TCLC 28**
Wentworth, Robert
See Hamilton, Edmond
Werfel, Franz (Viktor) 1890-1945 .... **TCLC 8**
See also CA 104; 161; DLB 81, 124
Wergeland, Henrik Arnold 1808-1845 . **NCLC 5**
Wersba, Barbara 1932- .... **CLC 30**
See also AAYA 2, 30; CA 29-32R; CANR 16, 38; CLR 3; DLB 52; JRDA; MAICYA; SAAS 2; SATA 1, 58; SATA-Essay 103
Wertmueller, Lina 1928- .... **CLC 16**
See also CA 97-100; CANR 39, 78
Wescott, Glenway 1901-1987 .. **CLC 13; SSC 35**
See also CA 13-16R; 121; CANR 23, 70; DLB 4, 9, 102
Wesker, Arnold 1932-**CLC 3, 5, 42; DAB; DAM DRAM**
See also CA 1-4R; CAAS 7; CANR 1, 33; CDBLB 1960 to Present; DLB 13; MTCW 1
Wesley, Richard (Errol) 1945- .... **CLC 7**
See also BW 1; CA 57-60; CANR 27; DLB 38
Wessel, Johan Herman 1742-1785 .... **LC 7**
West, Anthony (Panther) 1914-1987 ..... **CLC 50**
See also CA 45-48; 124; CANR 3, 19; DLB 15
West, C. P.
See Wodehouse, P(elham) G(renville)
West, (Mary) Jessamyn 1902-1984 ... **CLC 7, 17**
See also CA 9-12R; 112; CANR 27; DLB 6; DLBY 84; MTCW 1, 2; SATA-Obit 37
West, Morris L(anglo) 1916- .... **CLC 6, 33**
See also CA 5-8R; CANR 24, 49, 64; MTCW 1, 2
West, Nathanael 1903-1940**TCLC 1, 14, 44; SSC 16**
See also CA 104; 125; CDALB 1929-1941; DLB 4, 9, 28; MTCW 1, 2
West, Owen
See Koontz, Dean R(ay)
West, Paul 1930- .... **CLC 7, 14, 96**
See also CA 13-16R; CAAS 7; CANR 22, 53, 76; DLB 14; INT CANR-22; MTCW 2
West, Rebecca 1892-1983 .... **CLC 7, 9, 31, 50**
See also CA 5-8R; 109; CANR 19; DLB 36; DLBY 83; MTCW 1, 2
Westall, Robert (Atkinson) 1929-1993 . **CLC 17**
See also AAYA 12; CA 69-72; 141; CANR 18, 68; CLR 13; JRDA; MAICYA; SAAS 2; SATA 23, 69; SATA-Obit 75
Westermarck, Edward 1862-1939 .... **TCLC 87**
Westlake, Donald E(dwin) 1933-**CLC 7, 33; DAM POP**
See also CA 17-20R; CAAS 13; CANR 16, 44, 65; INT CANR-16; MTCW 2
Westmacott, Mary
See Christie, Agatha (Mary Clarissa)
Weston, Allen
See Norton, Andre
Wetcheek, J. L.
See Feuchtwanger, Lion
Wetering, Janwillem van de
See van de Wetering, Janwillem
Wetherald, Agnes Ethelwyn 1857-1940**TCLC 81**
See also DLB 99
Wetherell, Elizabeth
See Warner, Susan (Bogert)
Whale, James 1889-1957 .... **TCLC 63**
Whalen, Philip 1923- .... **CLC 6, 29**
See also CA 9-12R; CANR 5, 39; DLB 16
Wharton, Edith (Newbold Jones) 1862-1937**TCLC 3, 9, 27, 53; DA; DAB; DAC; DAM MST, NOV; SSC 6; WLC**
See also AAYA 25; CA 104; 132; CDALB 1865-1917; DLB 4, 9, 12, 78, 189; DLBD 13; MTCW 1, 2
Wharton, James
See Mencken, H(enry) L(ouis)
Wharton, William (a pseudonym) CLC 18, 37
See also CA 93-96; DLBY 80; INT 93-96
Wheatley (Peters), Phillis 1754(?)-1784**LC 3, 50; BLC 3; DA; DAC; DAM MST, MULT, POET; PC 3; WLC**
See also CDALB 1640-1865; DLB 31, 50
Wheelock, John Hall 1886-1978 .... **CLC 14**
See also CA 13-16R; 77-80; CANR 14; DLB 45
White, E(lwyn) B(rooks) 1899-1985 **CLC 10, 34, 39; DAM POP**
See also AITN 2; CA 13-16R; 116; CANR 16, 37; CDALBS; CLR 1, 21; DLB 11, 22; MAICYA; MTCW 1, 2; SATA 2, 29, 100; SATA-Obit 44
White, Edmund (Valentine III) 1940-**CLC 27, 110; DAM POP**
See also AAYA 7; CA 45-48; CANR 3, 19, 36, 62; MTCW 1, 2
White, Patrick (Victor Martindale) 1912-1990 **CLC 3, 4, 5, 7, 9, 18, 65, 69**
See also CA 81-84; 132; CANR 43; MTCW 1
White, Phyllis Dorothy James 1920-
See James, P. D.
See also CA 21-24R; CANR 17, 43, 65; DAM POP; MTCW 1, 2
White, T(erence) H(anbury) 1906-1964 **CLC 30**
See also AAYA 22; CA 73-76; CANR 37; DLB 160; JRDA; MAICYA; SATA 12
White, Terence de Vere 1912-1994 .... **CLC 49**
See also CA 49-52; 145; CANR 3
White, Walter
See White, Walter F(rancis)
See also BLC; DAM MULT
White, Walter F(rancis) 1893-1955 .... **TCLC 15**
See also White, Walter
See also BW 1; CA 115; 124; DLB 51
White, William Hale 1831-1913
See Rutherford, Mark
See also CA 121
Whitehead, E(dward) A(nthony) 1933- .... **CLC 5**
See also CA 65-68; CANR 58
Whitemore, Hugh (John) 1936- .... **CLC 37**
See also CA 132; CANR 77; INT 132
Whitman, Sarah Helen (Power) 1803-1878**NCLC 19**
See also DLB 1
Whitman, Walt(er) 1819-1892 **NCLC 4, 31; DA; DAB; DAC; DAM MST, POET; PC 3; WLC**
See also CDALB 1640-1865; DLB 3, 64; SATA 20
Whitney, Phyllis A(yame) 1903- . **CLC 42; DAM POP**
See also AITN 2; BEST 90:3; CA 1-4R; CANR 3, 25, 38, 60; CLR 59; JRDA; MAICYA; MTCW 2; SATA 1, 30
Whittemore, (Edward) Reed (Jr.) 1919- .. **CLC 4**
See also CA 9-12R; CAAS 8; CANR 4; DLB 5
Whittier, John Greenleaf 1807-1892**NCLC 8, 59**
See also DLB 1
Whittlebot, Hernia
See Coward, Noel (Peirce)
Wicker, Thomas Grey 1926-
See Wicker, Tom
See also CA 65-68; CANR 21, 46
Wicker, Tom .... **CLC 7**
See also Wicker, Thomas Grey
Wideman, John Edgar 1941- **CLC 5, 34, 36, 67; BLC 3; DAM MULT**
See also BW 2, 3; CA 85-88; CANR 14, 42, 67; DLB 33, 143; MTCW 2
Wiebe, Rudy (Henry) 1934-**CLC 6, 11, 14; DAC; DAM MST**
See also CA 37-40R; CANR 42, 67; DLB 60
Wieland, Christoph Martin 1733-1813 **NCLC 17**
See also DLB 97
Wiene, Robert 1881-1938 .... **TCLC 56**
Wieners, John 1934- .... **CLC 7**
See also CA 13-16R; DLB 16
Wiesel, Elie(zer) 1928- ... **CLC 3, 5, 11, 37; DA; DAB; DAC; DAM MST, NOV; WLCS**
See also AAYA 7; AITN 1; CA 5-8R; CAAS 4; CANR 8, 40, 65; CDALBS; DLB 83; DLBY 87; INT CANR-8; MTCW 1, 2; SATA 56
Wiggins, Marianne 1947- .... **CLC 57**
See also BEST 89:3; CA 130; CANR 60
Wight, James Alfred 1916-1995
See Herriot, James
See also CA 77-80; SATA 55; SATA-Brief 44
Wilbur, Richard (Purdy) 1921- **CLC 3, 6, 9, 14, 53, 110; DA; DAB; DAC; DAM MST, POET**
See also CA 1-4R; CABS 2; CANR 2, 29, 76; CDALBS; DLB 5, 169; INT CANR-29; MTCW 1, 2; SATA 9, 108
Wild, Peter 1940- .... **CLC 14**
See also CA 37-40R; DLB 5
Wilde, Oscar 1854(?)-1900**TCLC 1, 8, 23, 41; DA; DAB; DAC; DAM DRAM, MST, NOV; SSC 11; WLC**
See also CA 104; 119; CDBLB 1890-1914; DLB 10, 19, 34, 57, 141, 156, 190; SATA 24
Wilder, Billy .... **CLC 20**
See also Wilder, Samuel
See also DLB 26
Wilder, Samuel 1906-
See Wilder, Billy
See also CA 89-92
Wilder, Thornton (Niven) 1897-1975**CLC 1, 5, 6, 10, 15, 35, 82; DA; DAB; DAC; DAM DRAM, MST, NOV; DC 1; WLC**
See also AAYA 29; AITN 2; CA 13-16R; 61-64; CANR 40; CDALBS; DLB 4, 7, 9; DLBY 97; MTCW 1, 2
Wilding, Michael 1942- .... **CLC 73**
See also CA 104; CANR 24, 49
Wiley, Richard 1944- .... **CLC 44**
See also CA 121; 129; CANR 71
Wilhelm, Kate .... **CLC 7**
See also Wilhelm, Katie Gertrude
See also AAYA 20; CAAS 5; DLB 8; INT CANR-17
Wilhelm, Katie Gertrude 1928-
See Wilhelm, Kate
See also CA 37-40R; CANR 17, 36, 60; MTCW 1
Wilkins, Mary
See Freeman, Mary Eleanor Wilkins
Willard, Nancy 1936- .... **CLC 7, 37**
See also CA 89-92; CANR 10, 39, 68; CLR 5; DLB 5, 52; MAICYA; MTCW 1; SATA 37, 71; SATA-Brief 30
William of Ockham 1285-1347 .... **CMLC 32**

Williams, Ben Ames 1889-1953 ..... **TCLC 89**
See also DLB 102
Williams, C(harles) K(enneth) 1936-**CLC 33, 56; DAM POET**
See also CA 37-40R; CAAS 26; CANR 57; DLB 5
Williams, Charles
See Collier, James L(incoln)
Williams, Charles (Walter Stansby) 1886-1945 **TCLC 1, 11**
See also CA 104; 163; DLB 100, 153
Williams, (George) Emlyn 1905-1987 .. **CLC 15; DAM DRAM**
See also CA 104; 123; CANR 36; DLB 10, 77; MTCW 1
Williams, Hank 1923-1953 .... **TCLC 81**
Williams, Hugo 1942- .... **CLC 42**
See also CA 17-20R; CANR 45; DLB 40
Williams, J. Walker
See Wodehouse, P(elham) G(renville)
Williams, John A(lfred) 1925-**CLC 5, 13; BLC 3; DAM MULT**
See also BW 2, 3; CA 53-56; CAAS 3; CANR 6, 26, 51; DLB 2, 33; INT CANR-6
Williams, Jonathan (Chamberlain) 1929-**CLC 13**
See also CA 9-12R; CAAS 12; CANR 8; DLB 5
Williams, Joy 1944- .... **CLC 31**
See also CA 41-44R; CANR 22, 48
Williams, Norman 1952- .... **CLC 39**
See also CA 118
Williams, Sherley Anne 1944- **CLC 89; BLC 3; DAM MULT, POET**
See also BW 2, 3; CA 73-76; CANR 25; DLB 41; INT CANR-25; SATA 78
Williams, Shirley
See Williams, Sherley Anne
Williams, Tennessee 1911-1983**CLC 1, 2, 5, 7, 8, 11, 15, 19, 30, 39, 45, 71, 111; DA; DAB; DAC; DAM DRAM, MST; DC 4; WLC**
See also AITN 1, 2; CA 5-8R; 108; CABS 3; CANR 31; CDALB 1941-1968; DLB 7; DLBD 4; DLBY 83; MTCW 1, 2
Williams, Thomas (Alonzo) 1926-1990 **CLC 14**
See also CA 1-4R; 132; CANR 2
Williams, William C.
See Williams, William Carlos
Williams, William Carlos 1883-1963**CLC 1, 2, 5, 9, 13, 22, 42, 67; DA; DAB; DAC; DAM MST, POET; PC 7; SSC 31**
See also CA 89-92; CANR 34; CDALB 1917-1929; DLB 4, 16, 54, 86; MTCW 1, 2
Williamson, David (Keith) 1942- .... **CLC 56**
See also CA 103; CANR 41
Williamson, Ellen Douglas 1905-1984
See Douglas, Ellen
See also CA 17-20R; 114; CANR 39
Williamson, Jack .... **CLC 29**
See also Williamson, John Stewart
See also CAAS 8; DLB 8
Williamson, John Stewart 1908-
See Williamson, Jack
See also CA 17-20R; CANR 23, 70
Willie, Frederick
See Lovecraft, H(oward) P(hillips)
Willingham, Calder (Baynard, Jr.) 1922-1995 **CLC 5, 51**
See also CA 5-8R; 147; CANR 3; DLB 2, 44; MTCW 1
Willis, Charles
See Clarke, Arthur C(harles)
Willis, Fingal O'Flahertie
See Wilde, Oscar
Willy
See Colette, (Sidonie-Gabrielle)
Willy, Colette
See Colette, (Sidonie-Gabrielle)
Wilson, A(ndrew) N(orman) 1950- .... **CLC 33**
See also CA 112; 122; DLB 14, 155, 194; MTCW 2
Wilson, Angus (Frank Johnstone) 1913-1991 **CLC 2, 3, 5, 25, 34; SSC 21**
See also CA 5-8R; 134; CANR 21; DLB 15, 139, 155; MTCW 1, 2
Wilson, August 1945-**CLC 39, 50, 63, 118; BLC 3; DA; DAB; DAC; DAM DRAM, MST, MULT; DC 2; WLCS**
See also AAYA 16; BW 2, 3; CA 115; 122; CANR 42, 54, 76; MTCW 1, 2
Wilson, Brian 1942- .... **CLC 12**
Wilson, Colin 1931- .... **CLC 3, 14**
See also CA 1-4R; CAAS 5; CANR 1, 22, 33, 77; DLB 14, 194; MTCW 1
Wilson, Dirk
See Pohl, Frederik
Wilson, Edmund 1895-1972 ... **CLC 1, 2, 3, 8, 24**
See also CA 1-4R; 37-40R; CANR 1, 46; DLB 63; MTCW 1, 2
Wilson, Ethel Davis (Bryant) 1888(?)-1980 **CLC 13; DAC; DAM POET**
See also CA 102; DLB 68; MTCW 1
Wilson, John 1785-1854 .... **NCLC 5**
Wilson, John (Anthony) Burgess 1917-1993
See Burgess, Anthony
See also CA 1-4R; 143; CANR 2, 46; DAC; DAM NOV; MTCW 1, 2
Wilson, Lanford 1937- **CLC 7, 14, 36; DAM DRAM**
See also CA 17-20R; CABS 3; CANR 45; DLB 7
Wilson, Robert M. 1944- .... **CLC 7, 9**
See also CA 49-52; CANR 2, 41; MTCW 1
Wilson, Robert McLiam 1964- .... **CLC 59**
See also CA 132
Wilson, Sloan 1920- .... **CLC 32**
See also CA 1-4R; CANR 1, 44
Wilson, Snoo 1948- .... **CLC 33**
See also CA 69-72
Wilson, William S(mith) 1932- .... **CLC 49**
See also CA 81-84
Wilson, (Thomas) Woodrow 1856-1924**TCLC 79**
See also CA 166; DLB 47
Winchilsea, Anne (Kingsmill) Finch Counte 1661-1720
See Finch, Anne
Windham, Basil
See Wodehouse, P(elham) G(renville)
Wingrove, David (John) 1954- .... **CLC 68**
See also CA 133
Winnemucca, Sarah 1844-1891 .... **NCLC 79**
Wintergreen, Jane
See Duncan, Sara Jeannette
Winters, Janet Lewis .... **CLC 41**
See also Lewis, Janet
See also DLBY 87
Winters, (Arthur) Yvor 1900-1968 . **CLC 4, 8, 32**
See also CA 11-12; 25-28R; CAP 1; DLB 48; MTCW 1
Winterson, Jeanette 1959- . **CLC 64; DAM POP**
See also CA 136; CANR 58; DLB 207; MTCW 2
Winthrop, John 1588-1649 .... **LC 31**
See also DLB 24, 30
Wirth, Louis 1897-1952 .... **TCLC 92**
Wiseman, Frederick 1930- .... **CLC 20**
See also CA 159
Wister, Owen 1860-1938 .... **TCLC 21**
See also CA 108; 162; DLB 9, 78, 186; SATA 62
Witkacy
See Witkiewicz, Stanislaw Ignacy
Witkiewicz, Stanislaw Ignacy 1885-1939**TCLC 8**
See also CA 105; 162
Wittgenstein, Ludwig (Josef Johann) 1889-1951 **TCLC 59**
See also CA 113; 164; MTCW 2
Wittig, Monique 1935(?)- .... **CLC 22**
See also CA 116; 135; DLB 83
Wittlin, Jozef 1896-1976 .... **CLC 25**
See also CA 49-52; 65-68; CANR 3
Wodehouse, P(elham) G(renville) 1881-1975**CLC 1, 2, 5, 10, 22; DAB; DAC; DAM NOV; SSC 2**
See also AITN 2; CA 45-48; 57-60; CANR 3, 33; CDBLB 1914-1945; DLB 34, 162; MTCW 1, 2; SATA 22
Woiwode, L.
See Woiwode, Larry (Alfred)
Woiwode, Larry (Alfred) 1941- .... **CLC 6, 10**
See also CA 73-76; CANR 16; DLB 6; INT CANR-16
Wojciechowska, Maia (Teresa) 1927- .. **CLC 26**
See also AAYA 8; CA 9-12R; CANR 4, 41; CLR 1; JRDA; MAICYA; SAAS 1; SATA 1, 28, 83; SATA-Essay 104
Wolf, Christa 1929- .... **CLC 14, 29, 58**
See also CA 85-88; CANR 45; DLB 75; MTCW 1
Wolfe, Gene (Rodman) 1931-**CLC 25; DAM POP**
See also CA 57-60; CAAS 9; CANR 6, 32, 60; DLB 8; MTCW 2
Wolfe, George C. 1954- .... **CLC 49; BLCS**
See also CA 149
Wolfe, Thomas (Clayton) 1900-1938**TCLC 4, 13, 29, 61; DA; DAB; DAC; DAM MST, NOV; SSC 33; WLC**
See also CA 104; 132; CDALB 1929-1941; DLB 9, 102; DLBD 2, 16; DLBY 85, 97; MTCW 1, 2
Wolfe, Thomas Kennerly, Jr. 1930-
See Wolfe, Tom
See also CA 13-16R; CANR 9, 33, 70; DAM POP; DLB 185; INT CANR-9; MTCW 1, 2
Wolfe, Tom .... **CLC 1, 2, 9, 15, 35, 51**
See also Wolfe, Thomas Kennerly, Jr.
See also AAYA 8; AITN 2; BEST 89:1; DLB 152
Wolff, Geoffrey (Ansell) 1937- .... **CLC 41**
See also CA 29-32R; CANR 29, 43, 78
Wolff, Sonia
See Levitin, Sonia (Wolff)
Wolff, Tobias (Jonathan Ansell) 1945-**CLC 39, 64**
See also AAYA 16; BEST 90:2; CA 114; 117; CAAS 22; CANR 54, 76; DLB 130; INT 117; MTCW 2
Wolfram von Eschenbach c. 1170-c. 1220**CMLC 5**
See also DLB 138
Wolitzer, Hilma 1930- .... **CLC 17**
See also CA 65-68; CANR 18, 40; INT CANR-18; SATA 31
Wollstonecraft, Mary 1759-1797 .... **LC 5, 50**
See also CDBLB 1789-1832; DLB 39, 104, 158
Wonder, Stevie .... **CLC 12**
See also Morris, Steveland Judkins
Wong, Jade Snow 1922- .... **CLC 17**
See also CA 109
Woodberry, George Edward 1855-1930 **TCLC 73**
See also CA 165; DLB 71, 103
Woodcott, Keith
See Brunner, John (Kilian Houston)
Woodruff, Robert W.
See Mencken, H(enry) L(ouis)
Woolf, (Adeline) Virginia 1882-1941 **TCLC 1, 5, 20, 43, 56; DA; DAB; DAC; DAM MST, NOV; SSC 7; WLC**
See also Woolf, Virginia Adeline
See also CA 104; 130; CANR 64; CDBLB 1914-1945; DLB 36, 100, 162; DLBD 10; MTCW 1
Woolf, Virginia Adeline
See Woolf, (Adeline) Virginia
See also MTCW 2
Woollcott, Alexander (Humphreys) 1887-1943 **TCLC 5**
See also CA 105; 161; DLB 29
Woolrich, Cornell 1903-1968 .... **CLC 77**
See also Hopley-Woolrich, Cornell George
Wordsworth, Dorothy 1771-1855 .... **NCLC 25**
See also DLB 107

Wordsworth, William 1770-1850 .. **NCLC 12, 38; DA; DAB; DAC; DAM MST, POET; PC 4; WLC**
See also CDBLB 1789-1832; DLB 93, 107
Wouk, Herman 1915- **CLC 1, 9, 38; DAM NOV, POP**
See also CA 5-8R; CANR 6, 33, 67; CDALBS; DLBY 82; INT CANR-6; MTCW 1, 2
Wright, Charles (Penzel, Jr.) 1935- **CLC 6, 13, 28, 119**
See also CA 29-32R; CAAS 7; CANR 23, 36, 62; DLB 165; DLBY 82; MTCW 1, 2
Wright, Charles Stevenson 1932- **CLC 49; BLC 3; DAM MULT, POET**
See also BW 1; CA 9-12R; CANR 26; DLB 33
Wright, Frances 1795-1852 .... **NCLC 74**
See also DLB 73
Wright, Frank Lloyd 1867-1959 .... **TCLC 95**
See also CA 174
Wright, Jack R.
See Harris, Mark
Wright, James (Arlington) 1927-1980 **CLC 3, 5, 10, 28; DAM POET**
See also AITN 2; CA 49-52; 97-100; CANR 4, 34, 64; CDALBS; DLB 5, 169; MTCW 1, 2
Wright, Judith (Arandell) 1915- **CLC 11, 53; PC 14**
See also CA 13-16R; CANR 31, 76; MTCW 1, 2; SATA 14
Wright, L(aurali) R. 1939- .... **CLC 44**
See also CA 138
Wright, Richard (Nathaniel) 1908-1960 **CLC 1, 3, 4, 9, 14, 21, 48, 74; BLC 3; DA; DAB; DAC; DAM MST, MULT, NOV; SSC 2; WLC**
See also AAYA 5; BW 1; CA 108; CANR 64; CDALB 1929-1941; DLB 76, 102; DLBD 2; MTCW 1, 2
Wright, Richard B(ruce) 1937- .... **CLC 6**
See also CA 85-88; DLB 53
Wright, Rick 1945- .... **CLC 35**
Wright, Rowland
See Wells, Carolyn
Wright, Stephen 1946- .... **CLC 33**
Wright, Willard Huntington 1888-1939
See Van Dine, S. S.
See also CA 115; DLBD 16
Wright, William 1930- .... **CLC 44**
See also CA 53-56; CANR 7, 23
Wroth, Lady Mary 1587-1653(?) .... **LC 30**
See also DLB 121
Wu Ch'eng-en 1500(?)-1582(?) .... **LC 7**
Wu Ching-tzu 1701-1754 .... **LC 2**
Wurlitzer, Rudolph 1938(?)- .... **CLC 2, 4, 15**
See also CA 85-88; DLB 173
Wycherley, William 1641-1715 . **LC 8, 21; DAM DRAM**
See also CDBLB 1660-1789; DLB 80
Wylie, Elinor (Morton Hoyt) 1885-1928 **TCLC 8; PC 23**
See also CA 105; 162; DLB 9, 45
Wylie, Philip (Gordon) 1902-1971 .... **CLC 43**
See also CA 21-22; 33-36R; CAP 2; DLB 9
Wyndham, John .... **CLC 19**
See also Harris, John (Wyndham Parkes Lucas) Beynon
Wyss, Johann David Von 1743-1818 ... **NCLC 10**
See also JRDA; MAICYA; SATA 29; SATA-Brief 27
Xenophon c. 430B.C.-c. 354B.C. .... **CMLC 17**
See also DLB 176
Yakumo Koizumi
See Hearn, (Patricio) Lafcadio (Tessima Carlos)
Yamamoto, Hisaye 1921- . **SSC 34; DAM MULT**
Yanez, Jose Donoso
See Donoso (Yanez), Jose
Yanovsky, Basile S.
See Yanovsky, V(assily) S(emenovich)
Yanovsky, V(assily) S(emenovich) 1906-1989 **CLC 2, 18**
See also CA 97-100; 129
Yates, Richard 1926-1992 .... **CLC 7, 8, 23**
See also CA 5-8R; 139; CANR 10, 43; DLB 2; DLBY 81, 92; INT CANR-10
Yeats, W. B.
See Yeats, William Butler
Yeats, William Butler 1865-1939 **TCLC 1, 11, 18, 31, 93; DA; DAB; DAC; DAM DRAM, MST, POET; PC 20; WLC**
See also CA 104; 127; CANR 45; CDBLB 1890-1914; DLB 10, 19, 98, 156; MTCW 1, 2
Yehoshua, A(braham) B. 1936- .... **CLC 13, 31**
See also CA 33-36R; CANR 43
Yep, Laurence Michael 1948- .... **CLC 35**
See also AAYA 5; CA 49-52; CANR 1, 46; CLR 3, 17, 54; DLB 52; JRDA; MAICYA; SATA 7, 69
Yerby, Frank G(arvin) 1916-1991 . **CLC 1, 7, 22; BLC 3; DAM MULT**
See also BW 1, 3; CA 9-12R; 136; CANR 16, 52; DLB 76; INT CANR-16; MTCW 1
Yesenin, Sergei Alexandrovich
See Esenin, Sergei (Alexandrovich)
Yevtushenko, Yevgeny (Alexandrovich) 1933- **CLC 1, 3, 13, 26, 51; DAM POET**
See also CA 81-84; CANR 33, 54; MTCW 1
Yezierska, Anzia 1885(?)-1970 .... **CLC 46**
See also CA 126; 89-92; DLB 28; MTCW 1
Yglesias, Helen 1915- .... **CLC 7, 22**
See also CA 37-40R; CAAS 20; CANR 15, 65; INT CANR-15; MTCW 1
Yokomitsu Riichi 1898-1947 .... **TCLC 47**
See also CA 170
Yonge, Charlotte (Mary) 1823-1901 .... **TCLC 48**
See also CA 109; 163; DLB 18, 163; SATA 17
York, Jeremy
See Creasey, John
York, Simon
See Heinlein, Robert A(nson)
Yorke, Henry Vincent 1905-1974 .... **CLC 13**
See also Green, Henry
See also CA 85-88; 49-52
Yosano Akiko 1878-1942 .... **TCLC 59; PC 11**
See also CA 161
Yoshimoto, Banana .... **CLC 84**
See also Yoshimoto, Mahoko
Yoshimoto, Mahoko 1964-
See Yoshimoto, Banana
See also CA 144
Young, Al(bert James) 1939- .. **CLC 19; BLC 3; DAM MULT**
See also BW 2, 3; CA 29-32R; CANR 26, 65; DLB 33
Young, Andrew (John) 1885-1971 .... **CLC 5**
See also CA 5-8R; CANR 7, 29
Young, Collier
See Bloch, Robert (Albert)
Young, Edward 1683-1765 .... **LC 3, 40**
See also DLB 95
Young, Marguerite (Vivian) 1909-1995 . **CLC 82**
See also CA 13-16; 150; CAP 1
Young, Neil 1945- .... **CLC 17**
See also CA 110
Young Bear, Ray A. 1950- **CLC 94; DAM MULT**
See also CA 146; DLB 175; NNAL
Yourcenar, Marguerite 1903-1987 **CLC 19, 38, 50, 87; DAM NOV**
See also CA 69-72; CANR 23, 60; DLB 72; DLBY 88; MTCW 1, 2
Yurick, Sol 1925- .... **CLC 6**
See also CA 13-16R; CANR 25
Zabolotsky, Nikolai Alekseevich 1903-1958 **TCLC 52**
See also CA 116; 164
Zamiatin, Yevgenii
See Zamyatin, Evgeny Ivanovich
Zamora, Bernice (B. Ortiz) 1938- .. **CLC 89; DAM MULT; HLC**
See also CA 151; CANR 80; DLB 82; HW 1, 2
Zamyatin, Evgeny Ivanovich 1884-1937 **TCLC 8, 37**
See also CA 105; 166
Zangwill, Israel 1864-1926 .... **TCLC 16**
See also CA 109; 167; DLB 10, 135, 197
Zappa, Francis Vincent, Jr. 1940-1993
See Zappa, Frank
See also CA 108; 143; CANR 57
Zappa, Frank .... **CLC 17**
See also Zappa, Francis Vincent, Jr.
Zaturenska, Marya 1902-1982 .... **CLC 6, 11**
See also CA 13-16R; 105; CANR 22
Zeami 1363-1443 .... **DC 7**
Zelazny, Roger (Joseph) 1937-1995 ...... **CLC 21**
See also AAYA 7; CA 21-24R; 148; CANR 26, 60; DLB 8; MTCW 1, 2; SATA 57; SATA-Brief 39
Zhdanov, Andrei Alexandrovich 1896-1948 **TCLC 18**
See also CA 117; 167
Zhukovsky, Vasily (Andreevich) 1783-1852 **NCLC 35**
See also DLB 205
Ziegenhagen, Eric .... **CLC 55**
Zimmer, Jill Schary
See Robinson, Jill
Zimmerman, Robert
See Dylan, Bob
Zindel, Paul 1936- **CLC 6, 26; DA; DAB; DAC; DAM DRAM, MST, NOV; DC 5**
See also AAYA 2; CA 73-76; CANR 31, 65; CDALBS; CLR 3, 45; DLB 7, 52; JRDA; MAICYA; MTCW 1, 2; SATA 16, 58, 102
Zinov'Ev, A. A.
See Zinoviev, Alexander (Aleksandrovich)
Zinoviev, Alexander (Aleksandrovich) 1922- **CLC 19**
See also CA 116; 133; CAAS 10
Zoilus
See Lovecraft, H(oward) P(hillips)
Zola, Emile (Edouard Charles Antoine) 1840-1902 **TCLC 1, 6, 21, 41; DA; DAB; DAC; DAM MST, NOV; WLC**
See also CA 104; 138; DLB 123
Zoline, Pamela 1941- .... **CLC 62**
See also CA 161
Zorrilla y Moral, Jose 1817-1893 .... **NCLC 6**
Zoshchenko, Mikhail (Mikhailovich) 1895-1958 **TCLC 15; SSC 15**
See also CA 115; 160
Zuckmayer, Carl 1896-1977 .... **CLC 18**
See also CA 69-72; DLB 56, 124
Zuk, Georges
See Skelton, Robin
Zukofsky, Louis 1904-1978 **CLC 1, 2, 4, 7, 11, 18; DAM POET; PC 11**
See also CA 9-12R; 77-80; CANR 39; DLB 5, 165; MTCW 1
Zweig, Paul 1935-1984 .... **CLC 34, 42**
See also CA 85-88; 113
Zweig, Stefan 1881-1942 .... **TCLC 17**
See also CA 112; 170; DLB 81, 118
Zwingli, Huldreich 1484-1531 .... **LC 37**
See also DLB 179

Literary Criticism Series Cumulative Topic Index

This index lists all topic entries in Gale's *Classical and Medieval Literature Criticism, Contemporary Literary Criticism, Literature Criticism from 1400 to 1800, Nineteenth-Century Literature Criticism,* and *Twentieth-Century Literary Criticism.*

Age of Johnson LC 15: 1-87
Johnson's London, 3-15
aesthetics of neoclassicism, 15-36
"age of prose and reason," 36-45
clubmen and bluestockings, 45-56
printing technology, 56-62
periodicals: "a map of busy life," 62-74
transition, 74-86

Age of Spenser LC 39: 1-70
Overviews, 2-21
Literary Style, 22-34
Poets and the Crown, 34-70

AIDS in Literature CLC 81: 365-416

Alcohol and Literature TCLC 70: 1-58
overview, 2-8
fiction, 8-48
poetry and drama, 48-58

American Abolitionism NCLC 44: 1-73
overviews, 2-26
abolitionist ideals, 26-46
the literature of abolitionism, 46-72

American Autobiography TCLC 86: 1-115
overviews, 3-36
American authors and autobiography, 36-82
African-American autobiography, 82-114

American Black Humor Fiction TCLC 54: 1-85
characteristics of black humor, 2-13
origins and development, 13-38
black humor distinguished from related literary trends, 38-60
black humor and society, 60-75
black humor reconsidered, 75-83

American Civil War in Literature NCLC 32: 1-109
overviews, 2-20
regional perspectives, 20-54
fiction popular during the war, 54-79
the historical novel, 79-108

American Frontier in Literature NCLC 28: 1-103
definitions, 2-12
development, 12-17
nonfiction writing about the frontier, 17-30
frontier fiction, 30-45
frontier protagonists, 45-66
portrayals of Native Americans, 66-86
feminist readings, 86-98
twentieth-century reaction against frontier literature, 98-100

American Humor Writing NCLC 52: 1-59
overviews, 2-12
the Old Southwest, 12-42
broader impacts, 42-5
women humorists, 45-58

***American Mercury*, The** TCLC 74: 1-80

American Popular Song, Golden Age of TCLC 42: 1-49
background and major figures, 2-34
the lyrics of popular songs, 34-47

American Proletarian Literature TCLC 54: 86-175
overviews, 87-95
American proletarian literature and the American Communist Party, 95-111
ideology and literary merit, 111-7
novels, 117-36
Gastonia, 136-48
drama, 148-54
journalism, 154-9
proletarian literature in the United States, 159-74

American Romanticism NCLC 44: 74-138
overviews, 74-84
sociopolitical influences, 84-104
Romanticism and the American frontier, 104-15
thematic concerns, 115-37

American Western Literature TCLC 46: 1-100
definition and development of American Western literature, 2-7
characteristics of the Western novel, 8-23
Westerns as history and fiction, 23-34
critical reception of American Western literature, 34-41
the Western hero, 41-73
women in Western fiction, 73-91
later Western fiction, 91-9

Art and Literature TCLC 54: 176-248
overviews, 176-93
definitions, 193-219
influence of visual arts on literature, 219-31
spatial form in literature, 231-47

Arthurian Literature CMLC 10: 1-127
historical context and literary beginnings, 2-27
development of the legend through Malory, 27-64
development of the legend from Malory to the Victorian Age, 65-81
themes and motifs, 81-95
principal characters, 95-125

Arthurian Revival NCLC 36: 1-77
overviews, 2-12
Tennyson and his influence, 12-43
other leading figures, 43-73
the Arthurian legend in the visual arts, 73-6

Australian Literature TCLC 50: 1-94
origins and development, 2-21
characteristics of Australian literature, 21-33
historical and critical perspectives, 33-41
poetry, 41-58
fiction, 58-76
drama, 76-82
Aboriginal literature, 82-91

Beat Generation, Literature of the TCLC 42: 50-102
overviews, 51-9
the Beat generation as a social phenomenon, 59-62
development, 62-5
Beat literature, 66-96
influence, 97-100

The Bell Curve Controversy CLC 91: 281-330

***Bildungsroman* in Nineteenth-Century Literature** NCLC 20: 92-168
surveys, 93-113
in Germany, 113-40
in England, 140-56
female *Bildungsroman,* 156-67

Bloomsbury Group TCLC 34: 1-73
history and major figures, 2-13
definitions, 13-7
influences, 17-27
thought, 27-40
prose, 40-52
and literary criticism, 52-4
political ideals, 54-61
response to, 61-71

The Blues in Literature TCLC 82: 1-71

Bly, Robert, *Iron John: A Book about Men and Men's Work* CLC 70: 414-62

The Book of J CLC 65: 289-311

Buddhism and Literature TCLC 70: 59-164
eastern literature, 60-113
western literature, 113-63

Businessman in American Literature TCLC 26: 1-48
portrayal of the businessman, 1-32
themes and techniques in business fiction, 32-47

Catholicism in Nineteenth-Century American Literature NCLC 64: 1-58
overviews, 3-14
polemical literature, 14-46
Catholicism in literature, 47-57

Celtic Mythology CMLC 26: 1-111
overviews, 2-22
Celtic myth as literature and history, 22-48
Celtic religion: Druids and divinities, 48-80
Fionn MacCuhaill and the Fenian cycle, 80-111

Celtic Twilight
See **Irish Literary Renaissance**

Chartist Movement and Literature, The NCLC 60: 1-84
overview: nineteenth-century working-class fiction, 2-19
Chartist fiction and poetry, 19-73
the Chartist press, 73-84

Children's Literature, Nineteenth-Century NCLC 52: 60-135
overviews, 61-72
moral tales, 72-89
fairy tales and fantasy, 90-119
making men/making women, 119-34

The City and Literature TCLC 90: 1-124
overviews, 2-9
the city in American literature, 9-86
the city in European literature, 86-124

Civic Critics, Russian NCLC 20: 402-46
principal figures and background, 402-9
and Russian Nihilism, 410-6
aesthetic and critical views, 416-45

The Cockney School NCLC 68: 1-64
overview, 2-7
Blackwood's Magazine and the contemporary critical response, 7-24
the political and social import of the Cockneys and their critics, 24-63

Colonial America: The Intellectual Background LC 25: 1-98
overviews, 2-17
philosophy and politics, 17-31
early religious influences in Colonial America, 31-60
consequences of the Revolution, 60-78
religious influences in post-revolutionary America, 78-87
colonial literary genres, 87-97

Colonialism in Victorian English Literature NCLC 56: 1-77
overviews, 2-34
colonialism and gender, 34-51
monsters and the occult, 51-76

Columbus, Christopher, Books on the Quincentennial of His Arrival in the New World CLC 70: 329-60

Comic Books TCLC 66: 1-139
historical and critical perspectives, 2-48
superheroes, 48-67
underground comix, 67-88
comic books and society, 88-122
adult comics and graphic novels, 122-36

Connecticut Wits NCLC 48: 1-95
general overviews, 2-40
major works, 40-76
intellectual context, 76-95

Crime in Literature TCLC 54: 249-307
evolution of the criminal figure in literature, 250-61
crime and society, 261-77
literary perspectives on crime and punishment, 277-88
writings by criminals, 288-306

Czechoslovakian Literature of the Twentieth Century TCLC 42: 103-96
through World War II, 104-35
de-Stalinization, the Prague Spring, and contemporary literature, 135-72
Slovak literature, 172-85
Czech science fiction, 185-93

Dadaism TCLC 46: 101-71
background and major figures, 102-16
definitions, 116-26
manifestos and commentary by Dadaists, 126-40
theater and film, 140-58
nature and characteristics of Dadaist writing, 158-70

Darwinism and Literature NCLC 32: 110-206
background, 110-31
direct responses to Darwin, 131-71
collateral effects of Darwinism, 171-205

Death in Nineteenth-Century British Literature NCLC 68: 65-142
overviews, 66-92
responses to death, 92-102
feminist perspectives, 103-17
striving for immortality, 117-41

Death in Literature TCLC 78:1-183
fiction, 2-115
poetry, 115-46
drama, 146-81

de Man, Paul, Wartime Journalism of CLC 55: 382-424

Detective Fiction, Nineteenth-Century NCLC 36: 78-148
origins of the genre, 79-100
history of nineteenth-century detective fiction, 101-33
significance of nineteenth-century detective fiction, 133-46

Detective Fiction, Twentieth-Century TCLC 38: 1-96
genesis and history of the detective story, 3-22
defining detective fiction, 22-32
evolution and varieties, 32-77
the appeal of detective fiction, 77-90

Disease and Literature TCLC 66: 140-283
overviews, 141-65
disease in nineteenth-century literature, 165-81
tuberculosis and literature, 181-94
women and disease in literature, 194-221
plague literature, 221-53
AIDS in literature, 253-82

The Double in Nineteenth-Century Literature NCLC 40: 1-95
genesis and development of the theme, 2-15
the double and Romanticism, 16-27
sociological views, 27-52
psychological interpretations, 52-87
philosophical considerations, 87-95

Dramatic Realism NCLC 44: 139-202
overviews, 140-50
origins and definitions, 150-66
impact and influence, 166-93
realist drama and tragedy, 193-201

Drugs and Literature TCLC 78: 184-282
overviews, 185-201
pre-twentieth-century literature, 201-42
twentieth-century literature, 242-82

Eastern Mythology CMLC 26: 112-92
heroes and kings, 113-51
cross-cultural perspective, 151-69

relations to history and society, 169-92

Electronic "Books": Hypertext and Hyperfiction CLC 86: 367-404
books vs. CD-ROMS, 367-76
hypertext and hyperfiction, 376-95
implications for publishing, libraries, and the public, 395-403

Eliot, T. S., Centenary of Birth CLC 55: 345-75

Elizabethan Drama LC 22: 140-240
origins and influences, 142-67
characteristics and conventions, 167-83
theatrical production, 184-200
histories, 200-12
comedy, 213-20
tragedy, 220-30

Elizabethan Prose Fiction LC 41: 1-70
overviews, 1-15
origins and influences, 15-43
style and structure, 43-69

The Encyclopedists LC 26: 172-253
overviews, 173-210
intellectual background, 210-32
views on esthetics, 232-41
views on women, 241-52

English Caroline Literature LC 13: 221-307
background, 222-41
evolution and varieties, 241-62
the Cavalier mode, 262-75
court and society, 275-91
politics and religion, 291-306

English Decadent Literature of the 1890s NCLC 28: 104-200
fin de siècle: the Decadent period, 105-19
definitions, 120-37
major figures: "the tragic generation," 137-50
French literature and English literary Decadence, 150-7
themes, 157-61
poetry, 161-82
periodicals, 182-96

English Essay, Rise of the LC 18: 238-308
definitions and origins, 236-54
influence on the essay, 254-69
historical background, 269-78
the essay in the seventeenth century, 279-93
the essay in the eighteenth century, 293-307

English Mystery Cycle Dramas LC 34: 1-88
overviews, 1-27
the nature of dramatic performances, 27-42
the medieval worldview and the mystery cycles, 43-67
the doctrine of repentance and the mystery cycles, 67-76
the fall from grace in the mystery cycles, 76-88

English Revolution, Literature of the LC 43: 1-58
overviews, 2-24
pamphlets of the English Revolution, 24-38
political Sermons of the English Revolution, 38-48
poetry of the English Revolution, 48-57

English Romantic Hellenism NCLC 68: 143-250
overviews, 144-69
historical development of English Romantic Hellenism, 169-91
inflience of Greek mythology on the Romantics, 191-229
influence of Greek literature, art, and culture on the Romantics, 229-50

English Romantic Poetry NCLC 28: 201-327
overviews and reputation, 202-37
major subjects and themes, 237-67
forms of Romantic poetry, 267-78
politics, society, and Romantic poetry, 278-99
philosophy, religion, and Romantic poetry, 299-324

Espionage Literature TCLC 50: 95-159
overviews, 96-113
espionage fiction/formula fiction, 113-26
spies in fact and fiction, 126-38
the female spy, 138-44
social and psychological perspectives, 144-58

European Romanticism NCLC 36: 149-284
definitions, 149-77
origins of the movement, 177-82
Romantic theory, 182-200
themes and techniques, 200-23
Romanticism in Germany, 223-39
Romanticism in France, 240-61
Romanticism in Italy, 261-4
Romanticism in Spain, 264-8
impact and legacy, 268-82

Existentialism and Literature TCLC 42: 197-268
overviews and definitions, 198-209
history and influences, 209-19
Existentialism critiqued and defended, 220-35
philosophical and religious perspectives, 235-41
Existentialist fiction and drama, 241-67

Familiar Essay NCLC 48: 96-211
definitions and origins, 97-130
overview of the genre, 130-43
elements of form and style, 143-59
elements of content, 159-73
the Cockneys: Hazlitt, Lamb, and Hunt, 173-91
status of the genre, 191-210

The Faust Legend LC 47: 1-117

Fear in Literature TCLC 74: 81-258
overviews, 81
pre-twentieth-century literature, 123
twentieth-century literature, 182

Feminism in the 1990s: Commentary on Works by Naomi Wolf, Susan Faludi, and Camille Paglia CLC 76: 377-415

Feminist Criticism in 1990 CLC 65: 312-60

Fifteenth-Century English Literature LC 17: 248-334
background, 249-72
poetry, 272-315
drama, 315-23
prose, 323-33

Film and Literature TCLC 38: 97-226
overviews, 97-119
film and theater, 119-34
film and the novel, 134-45
the art of the screenplay, 145-66
genre literature/genre film, 167-79
the writer and the film industry, 179-90
authors on film adaptations of their works, 190-200
fiction into film: comparative essays, 200-23

Folklore and Literature TCLC 86: 116-293
overviews, 118-144
Native American literature, 144-67
African-American literature, 167-238
Folklore and the American West, 238-57
Modern and postmodern literature, 257-91

French Drama in the Age of Louis XIV LC 28: 94-185
overview, 95-127
tragedy, 127-46
comedy, 146-66
tragicomedy, 166-84

French Enlightenment LC 14: 81-145
the question of definition, 82-9
Le siècle des lumières, 89-94
women and the salons, 94-105
censorship, 105-15
the philosophy of reason, 115-31
influence and legacy, 131-44

French Realism NCLC 52: 136-216
origins and definitions, 137-70
issues and influence, 170-98
realism and representation, 198-215

French Revolution and English Literature NCLC 40: 96-195
history and theory, 96-123

romantic poetry, 123-50
the novel, 150-81
drama, 181-92
children's literature, 192-5

Futurism, Italian TCLC 42: 269-354
principles and formative influences, 271-9
manifestos, 279-88
literature, 288-303
theater, 303-19
art, 320-30
music, 330-6
architecture, 336-9
and politics, 339-46
reputation and significance, 346-51

Gaelic Revival
See **Irish Literary Renaissance**

Gates, Henry Louis, Jr., and African-American Literary Criticism CLC 65: 361-405

Gay and Lesbian Literature CLC 76: 416-39

German Exile Literature TCLC 30: 1-58
the writer and the Nazi state, 1-10
definition of, 10-4
life in exile, 14-32
surveys, 32-50
Austrian literature in exile, 50-2
German publishing in the United States, 52-7

German Expressionism TCLC 34: 74-160
history and major figures, 76-85
aesthetic theories, 85-109
drama, 109-26
poetry, 126-38
film, 138-42
painting, 142-7
music, 147-53
and politics, 153-8

***Glasnost* and Contemporary Soviet Literature** CLC 59: 355-97

Gothic Novel NCLC 28: 328-402
development and major works, 328-34
definitions, 334-50
themes and techniques, 350-78
in America, 378-85
in Scotland, 385-91
influence and legacy, 391-400

Graphic Narratives CLC 86: 405-32
history and overviews, 406-21
the "Classics Illustrated" series, 421-2
reviews of recent works, 422-32

Greek Historiography CMLC 17: 1-49

Greek Mythology CMLC-26 193-320
overviews, 194-209
origins and development of Greek mythology, 209-29
cosmogonies and divinities in Greek mythology, 229-54
heroes and heroines in Greek mythology, 254-80
women in Greek mythology, 280-320

Harlem Renaissance TCLC 26: 49-125
principal issues and figures, 50-67
the literature and its audience, 67-74
theme and technique in poetry, fiction, and drama, 74-115
and American society, 115-21
achievement and influence, 121-2

Havel, Václav, Playwright and President CLC 65: 406-63

Historical Fiction, Nineteenth-Century NCLC 48: 212-307
definitions and characteristics, 213-36
Victorian historical fiction, 236-65
American historical fiction, 265-88
realism in historical fiction, 288-306

Holocaust and the Atomic Bomb: Fifty Years Later CLC 91: 331-82
the Holocaust remembered, 333-52
Anne Frank revisited, 352-62
the atomic bomb and American memory, 362-81

Holocaust Denial Literature TCLC 58: 1-110
overviews, 1-30
Robert Faurisson and Noam Chomsky, 30-52
Holocaust denial literature in America, 52-71
library access to Holocaust denial literature, 72-5
the authenticity of Anne Frank's diary, 76-90
David Irving and the "normalization" of Hitler, 90-109

Holocaust, Literature of the TCLC 42: 355-450
historical overview, 357-61
critical overview, 361-70
diaries and memoirs, 370-95
novels and short stories, 395-425
poetry, 425-41
drama, 441-8

Homosexuality in Nineteenth-Century Literature NCLC 56: 78-182
defining homosexuality, 80-111
Greek love, 111-44
trial and danger, 144-81

Hungarian Literature of the Twentieth Century TCLC 26: 126-88
surveys of, 126-47
Nyugat and early twentieth-century literature, 147-56
mid-century literature, 156-68
and politics, 168-78
since the 1956 revolt, 178-87

Hysteria in Nineteenth-Century Literature NCLC 64: 59-184
the history of hysteria, 60-75
the gender of hysteria, 75-103
hysteria and women's narratives, 103-57
hysteria in nineteenth-century poetry, 157-83

Imagism TCLC 74: 259-454
history and development, 260
major figures, 288
sources and influences, 352
Imagism and other movements, 397
influence and legacy, 431

Indian Literature in English TCLC 54: 308-406
overview, 309-13
origins and major figures, 313-25
the Indo-English novel, 325-55
Indo-English poetry, 355-67
Indo-English drama, 367-72
critical perspectives on Indo-English literature, 372-80
modern Indo-English literature, 380-9
Indo-English authors on their work, 389-404

Industrial Revolution in Literature, The NCLC 56: 183-273
historical and cultural perspectives, 184-201
contemporary reactions to the machine, 201-21
themes and symbols in literature, 221-73

The Irish Famine as Represented in Nineteenth-Century Literature NCLC 64: 185-261
overviews, 187-98
historical background, 198-212
famine novels, 212-34
famine poetry, 234-44
famine letters and eye-witness accounts, 245-61

Irish Literary Renaissance TCLC 46: 172-287
overview, 173-83
development and major figures, 184-202
influence of Irish folklore and mythology, 202-22
Irish poetry, 222-34
Irish drama and the Abbey Theatre, 234-56
Irish fiction, 256-86

Irish Nationalism and Literature NCLC 44: 203-73
the Celtic element in literature, 203-19
anti-Irish sentiment and the Celtic response, 219-34
literary ideals in Ireland, 234-45
literary expressions, 245-73

Italian Futurism
See **Futurism, Italian**

Italian Humanism LC 12: 205-77
origins and early development, 206-18
revival of classical letters, 218-23
humanism and other philosophies, 224-39
humanisms and humanists, 239-46
the plastic arts, 246-57
achievement and significance, 258-76

Italian Romanticism NCLC 60: 85-145
origins and overviews, 86-101
Italian Romantic theory, 101-25
the language of Romanticism, 125-45

Jacobean Drama LC 33: 1-37
the Jacobean worldview: an era of transition, 2-14
the moral vision of Jacobean drama, 14-22
Jacobean tragedy, 22-3
the Jacobean masque, 23-36

Jewish-American Fiction TCLC 62: 1-181
overviews, 2-24
major figures, 24-48
Jewish writers and American life, 48-78
Jewish characters in American fiction, 78-108
themes in Jewish-American fiction, 108-43
Jewish-American women writers, 143-59
the Holocaust and Jewish-American fiction, 159-81

Knickerbocker Group, The NCLC 56: 274-341
overviews, 276-314
Knickerbocker periodicals, 314-26
writers and artists, 326-40

Lake Poets, The NCLC 52: 217-304
characteristics of the Lake Poets and their works, 218-27
literary influences and collaborations, 227-66
defining and developing Romantic ideals, 266-84
embracing Conservatism, 284-303

Larkin, Philip, Controversy CLC 81: 417-64

Latin American Literature, Twentieth-Century TCLC 58: 111-98
historical and critical perspectives, 112-36
the novel, 136-45
the short story, 145-9
drama, 149-60
poetry, 160-7
the writer and society, 167-86
Native Americans in Latin American literature, 186-97

Literature and Millenial Lists CLC 119: 431-67
criticism, 434-67
introduction, 431-33
The Modern Library list, 433
The Waterstone list, 438-439

Madness in Twentieth-Century Literature TCLC 50: 160-225
overviews, 161-71
madness and the creative process, 171-86
suicide, 186-91
madness in American literature, 191-207
madness in German literature, 207-13
madness and feminist artists, 213-24

Memoirs of Trauma CLC 109: 419-466
overview, 420
criticism, 429

Metaphysical Poets LC 24: 356-439
early definitions, 358-67
surveys and overviews, 367-92
cultural and social influences, 392-406
stylistic and thematic variations, 407-38

Modern Essay, The TCLC 58: 199-273
overview, 200-7
the essay in the early twentieth century, 207-19
characteristics of the modern essay, 219-32
modern essayists, 232-45
the essay as a literary genre, 245-73

Modern Japanese Literature TCLC 66: 284-389
poetry, 285-305
drama, 305-29
fiction, 329-61
western influences, 361-87

Modernism TCLC 70: 165-275
definitions, 166-184
Modernism and earlier influences, 184-200
stylistic and thematic traits, 200-229
poetry and drama, 229-242
redefining Modernism, 242-275

Muckraking Movement in American Journalism TCLC 34: 161-242
development, principles, and major figures, 162-70
publications, 170-9
social and political ideas, 179-86
targets, 186-208
fiction, 208-19
decline, 219-29
impact and accomplishments, 229-40

Multiculturalism in Literature and Education CLC 70: 361-413

Music and Modern Literature TCLC 62: 182-329
overviews, 182-211
musical form/literary form, 211-32
music in literature, 232-50
the influence of music on literature, 250-73
literature and popular music, 273-303
jazz and poetry, 303-28

Native American Literature CLC 76: 440-76

Natural School, Russian NCLC 24: 205-40
history and characteristics, 205-25
contemporary criticism, 225-40

Naturalism NCLC 36: 285-382
definitions and theories, 286-305
critical debates on Naturalism, 305-16
Naturalism in theater, 316-32
European Naturalism, 332-61
American Naturalism, 361-72
the legacy of Naturalism, 372-81

Negritude TCLC 50: 226-361
origins and evolution, 227-56
definitions, 256-91
Negritude in literature, 291-343
Negritude reconsidered, 343-58

New Criticism TCLC 34: 243-318
development and ideas, 244-70
debate and defense, 270-99
influence and legacy, 299-315

The New World in Renaissance Literature LC 31: 1-51
overview, 1-18
utopia vs. terror, 18-31
explorers and Native Americans, 31-51

New York Intellectuals and *Partisan Review* TCLC 30: 117-98
development and major figures, 118-28
influence of Judaism, 128-39
Partisan Review, 139-57
literary philosophy and practice, 157-75
political philosophy, 175-87
achievement and significance, 187-97

The New Yorker TCLC 58: 274-357
overviews, 274-95
major figures, 295-304
New Yorker style, 304-33
fiction, journalism, and humor at *The New Yorker*, 333-48
the new *New Yorker*, 348-56

Newgate Novel NCLC 24: 166-204
development of Newgate literature, 166-73
Newgate Calendar, 173-7
Newgate fiction, 177-95
Newgate drama, 195-204

Nigerian Literature of the Twentieth Century TCLC 30: 199-265
surveys of, 199-227
English language and African life, 227-45
politics and the Nigerian writer, 245-54
Nigerian writers and society, 255-62

Nineteenth-Century Native American

Autobiography NCLC 64: 262-389
overview, 263-8
problems of authorship, 268-81
the evolution of Native American autobiography, 281-304
political issues, 304-15
gender and autobiography, 316-62
autobiographical works during the turn of the century, 362-88

Norse Mythology CMLC-26: 321-85
history and mythological tradition, 322-44
Eddic poetry, 344-74
Norse mythology and other traditions, 374-85

Northern Humanism LC 16: 281-356
background, 282-305
precursor of the Reformation, 305-14
the Brethren of the Common Life, the Devotio Moderna, and education, 314-40
the impact of printing, 340-56

Novel of Manners, The NCLC 56: 342-96
social and political order, 343-53
domestic order, 353-73
depictions of gender, 373-83
the American novel of manners, 383-95

Nuclear Literature: Writings and Criticism in the Nuclear Age TCLC 46: 288-390
overviews, 290-301
fiction, 301-35
poetry, 335-8
nuclear war in Russo-Japanese literature, 338-55
nuclear war and women writers, 355-67
the nuclear referent and literary criticism, 367-88

Occultism in Modern Literature TCLC 50: 362-406
influence of occultism on literature, 363-72
occultism, literature, and society, 372-87
fiction, 387-96
drama, 396-405

Opium and the Nineteenth-Century Literary Imagination NCLC 20: 250-301
original sources, 250-62
historical background, 262-71
and literary society, 271-9
and literary creativity, 279-300

The Oxford Movement NCLC 72: 1-197
overviews, 2-24
background, 24-59
and education, 59-69
religious responses, 69-128
literary aspects, 128-178
political implications, 178-196

The Parnassian Movement NCLC 72: 198-241
overviews, 199-231
and epic form, 231-38
and positivism, 238-41

Periodicals, Nineteenth-Century British NCLC 24: 100-65
overviews, 100-30
in the Romantic Age, 130-41
in the Victorian era, 142-54
and the reviewer, 154-64

Plath, Sylvia, and the Nature of Biography CLC 86: 433-62
the nature of biography, 433-52
reviews of *The Silent Woman,* 452-61

Political Theory from the 15th to the 18th Century LC 36: 1-55
Overview, 1-26
Natural Law, 26-42
Empiricism, 42-55

Polish Romanticism NCLC 52: 305-71
overviews, 306-26
major figures, 326-40
Polish Romantic drama, 340-62
influences, 362-71

Popular Literature TCLC 70: 279-382
overviews, 280-324
"formula" fiction, 324-336
readers of popular literature, 336-351
evolution of popular literature, 351-382

The Portrayal of Jews in Nineteenth-Century English Literature NCLC 72: 242-368
overviews, 244-77
Anglo-Jewish novels, 277-303
depictions by non-Jewish writers, 303-44
Hebraism versus Hellenism, 344-67

Postmodernism TCLC 90:125-307
overview, 126-166
criticism , 166-224
fiction, 224-282
poetry, 282-300
drama, 300-307

Pre-Raphaelite Movement NCLC 20: 302-401
overview, 302-4
genesis, 304-12
Germ and *Oxford and Cambridge Magazine,* 312-20
Robert Buchanan and the "Fleshly School of Poetry," 320-31
satires and parodies, 331-4
surveys, 334-51
aesthetics, 351-75
sister arts of poetry and painting, 375-94
influence, 394-9

Preromanticism LC 40: 1-56
overviews, 2-14
defining the period, 14-23
new directions in poetry and prose, 23-45
the focus on the self, 45-56

Presocratic Philosophy CMLC 22: 1-56
overviews, 3-24
the Ionians and the Pythagoreans, 25-35
Heraclitus, the Eleatics, and the Atomists, 36-47
the Sophists, 47-55

Protestant Reformation, Literature of the LC 37: 1-83
overviews, 1-49
humanism and scholasticism, 49-69
the reformation and literature, 69-82

Psychoanalysis and Literature TCLC 38: 227-338
overviews, 227-46
Freud on literature, 246-51
psychoanalytic views of the literary process, 251-61
psychoanalytic theories of response to literature, 261-88
psychoanalysis and literary criticism, 288-312
psychoanalysis as literature/literature as psychoanalysis, 313-34

Rap Music CLC 76: 477-50

Renaissance Natural Philosophy LC 27: 201-87
cosmology, 201-28
astrology, 228-54
magic, 254-86

Restoration Drama LC 21: 184-275
general overviews, 185-230
Jeremy Collier stage controversy, 230-9
other critical interpretations, 240-75

Revising the Literary Canon CLC 81: 465-509

Robin Hood, Legend of LC 19: 205-58
origins and development of the Robin Hood legend, 206-20
representations of Robin Hood, 220-44
Robin Hood as hero, 244-56

Rushdie, Salman, *Satanic Verses* Controversy CLC 55 214-63; 59: 404-56

Russian Nihilism NCLC 28: 403-47
definitions and overviews, 404-17
women and Nihilism, 417-27
literature as reform: the Civic Critics, 427-33
Nihilism and the Russian novel: Turgenev and Dostoevsky, 433-47

Russian Thaw TCLC 26: 189-247
literary history of the period, 190-206
theoretical debate of socialist realism, 206-11
Novy Mir, 211-7
Literary Moscow, 217-24
Pasternak, *Zhivago,* and the Nobel

Prize, 224-7
poetry of liberation, 228-31
Brodsky trial and the end of the Thaw, 231-6
achievement and influence, 236-46

Salem Witch Trials LC-38: 1-145
overviews, 2-30
historical background, 30-65
judicial background, 65-78
the search for causes, 78-115
the role of women in the trials, 115-44

Salinger, J. D., Controversy Surrounding *In Search of J. D. Salinger* CLC 55: 325-44

Science and Modern Literature TCLC 90: 308-419
overviews, 295-333
fiction, 333-395
poetry, 395-405
drama, 405-419

Science Fiction, Nineteenth-Century NCLC 24: 241-306
background, 242-50
definitions of the genre, 251-6
representative works and writers, 256-75
themes and conventions, 276-305

Scottish Chaucerians LC 20: 363-412

Scottish Poetry, Eighteenth-Century LC 29: 95-167
overviews, 96-114
the Scottish Augustans, 114-28
the Scots Vernacular Revival, 132-63
Scottish poetry after Burns, 163-6

Sea in Literature, The TCLC 82: 72-191
drama, 73-79
poetry, 79-119
fiction, 119-191

Sentimental Novel, The NCLC 60: 146-245
overviews, 147-58
the politics of domestic fiction, 158-79
a literature of resistance and repression, 179-212
the reception of sentimental fiction, 213-44

Sex and Literature TCLC 82: 192-434
overviews, 193-216
drama, 216-263
poetry, 263-287
fiction, 287-431

Sherlock Holmes Centenary TCLC 26: 248-310
Doyle's life and the composition of the Holmes stories, 248-59
life and character of Holmes, 259-78
method, 278-9
Holmes and the Victorian world, 279-92
Sherlockian scholarship, 292-301
Doyle and the development of the detective story, 301-7
Holmes's continuing popularity, 307-9

Slave Narratives, American NCLC 20: 1-91
background, 2-9
overviews, 9-24
contemporary responses, 24-7
language, theme, and technique, 27-70
historical authenticity, 70-5
antecedents, 75-83
role in development of Black American literature, 83-8

Spanish Civil War Literature TCLC 26: 311-85
topics in, 312-33
British and American literature, 333-59
French literature, 359-62
Spanish literature, 362-73
German literature, 373-5
political idealism and war literature, 375-83

Spanish Golden Age Literature LC 23: 262-332
overviews, 263-81
verse drama, 281-304
prose fiction, 304-19
lyric poetry, 319-31

Spasmodic School of Poetry NCLC 24: 307-52
history and major figures, 307-21
the Spasmodics on poetry, 321-7
Firmilian and critical disfavor, 327-39
theme and technique, 339-47
influence, 347-51

Sports in Literature TCLC 86: 294-445
overviews, 295-324
major writers and works, 324-402
sports, literature, and social issues, 402-45

Steinbeck, John, Fiftieth Anniversary of *The Grapes of Wrath* CLC 59: 311-54

Sturm und Drang NCLC 40: 196-276
definitions, 197-238
poetry and poetics, 238-58
drama, 258-75

Supernatural Fiction in the Nineteenth Century NCLC 32: 207-87
major figures and influences, 208-35
the Victorian ghost story, 236-54
the influence of science and occultism, 254-66
supernatural fiction and society, 266-86

Supernatural Fiction, Modern TCLC 30: 59-116
evolution and varieties, 60-74
"decline" of the ghost story, 74-86
as a literary genre, 86-92
technique, 92-101
nature and appeal, 101-15

Surrealism TCLC 30: 334-406
history and formative influences, 335-43
manifestos, 343-54
philosophic, aesthetic, and political principles, 354-75
poetry, 375-81
novel, 381-6
drama, 386-92
film, 392-8
painting and sculpture, 398-403
achievement, 403-5

Symbolism, Russian TCLC 30: 266-333
doctrines and major figures, 267-92
theories, 293-8
and French Symbolism, 298-310
themes in poetry, 310-4
theater, 314-20
and the fine arts, 320-32

Symbolist Movement, French NCLC 20: 169-249
background and characteristics, 170-86
principles, 186-91
attacked and defended, 191-7
influences and predecessors, 197-211
and Decadence, 211-6
theater, 216-26
prose, 226-33
decline and influence, 233-47

Television and Literature TCLC 78: 283-426
television and literacy, 283-98
reading vs. watching, 298-341
adaptations, 341-62
literary genres and television, 362-90
television genres and literature, 390-410
children's literature/children's television, 410-25

Theater of the Absurd TCLC 38: 339-415
"The Theater of the Absurd," 340-7
major plays and playwrights, 347-58
and the concept of the absurd, 358-86
theatrical techniques, 386-94
predecessors of, 394-402
influence of, 402-13

Tin Pan Alley
See **American Popular Song, Golden Age of**

Transcendentalism, American NCLC 24: 1-99
overviews, 3-23
contemporary documents, 23-41
theological aspects of, 42-52
and social issues, 52-74
literature of, 74-96

Travel Writing in the Nineteenth Century NCLC 44: 274-392
the European grand tour, 275-303
the Orient, 303-47
North America, 347-91

Travel Writing in the Twentieth Century TCLC 30: 407-56
conventions and traditions, 407-27
and fiction writing, 427-43
comparative essays on travel writers, 443-54

True-Crime Literature CLC 99: 333-433
history and analysis, 334-407
reviews of true-crime publications, 407-23
writing instruction, 424-29
author profiles, 429-33

***Ulysses* and the Process of Textual Reconstruction** TCLC 26: 386-416
evaluations of the new *Ulysses,* 386-94
editorial principles and procedures, 394-401
theoretical issues, 401-16

Utopian Literature, Nineteenth-Century NCLC 24: 353-473
definitions, 354-74
overviews, 374-88
theory, 388-408
communities, 409-26
fiction, 426-53
women and fiction, 454-71

Utopian Literature, Renaissance LC-32: 1-63
overviews, 2-25
classical background, 25-33
utopia and the social contract, 33-9
origins in mythology, 39-48
utopia and the Renaissance country house, 48-52
influence of millenarianism, 52-62

Vampire in Literature TCLC 46: 391-454
origins and evolution, 392-412
social and psychological perspectives, 413-44
vampire fiction and science fiction, 445-53

Victorian Autobiography NCLC 40: 277-363
development and major characteristics, 278-88
themes and techniques, 289-313
the autobiographical tendency in Victorian prose and poetry, 313-47
Victorian women's autobiographies, 347-62

Victorian Fantasy Literature NCLC 60: 246-384
overviews, 247-91
major figures, 292-366
women in Victorian fantasy literature, 366-83

Victorian Hellenism NCLC 68: 251-376
overviews, 252-78
the meanings of Hellenism, 278-335
the literary influence, 335-75

Victorian Novel NCLC 32: 288-454
development and major characteristics, 290-310
themes and techniques, 310-58
social criticism in the Victorian novel, 359-97
urban and rural life in the Victorian novel, 397-406
women in the Victorian novel, 406-25
Mudie's Circulating Library, 425-34
the late-Victorian novel, 434-51

Vietnam War in Literature and Film CLC 91: 383-437
overview, 384-8
prose, 388-412
film and drama, 412-24
poetry, 424-35

Vorticism TCLC 62: 330-426
Wyndham Lewis and Vorticism, 330-8
characteristics and principles of Vorticism, 338-65
Lewis and Pound, 365-82
Vorticist writing, 382-416
Vorticist painting, 416-26

Women's Diaries, Nineteenth-Century NCLC 48: 308-54
overview, 308-13
diary as history, 314-25
sociology of diaries, 325-34
diaries as psychological scholarship, 334-43
diary as autobiography, 343-8
diary as literature, 348-53

Women Writers, Seventeenth-Century LC 30: 2-58
overview, 2-15
women and education, 15-9
women and autobiography, 19-31
women's diaries, 31-9
early feminists, 39-58

World War I Literature TCLC 34: 392-486
overview, 393-403
English, 403-27
German, 427-50
American, 450-66
French, 466-74
and modern history, 474-82

Yellow Journalism NCLC 36: 383-456
overviews, 384-96
major figures, 396-413

Young Playwrights Festival
1988—CLC 55: 376-81
1989—CLC 59: 398-403
1990—CLC 65: 444-8

Twentieth-Century Literary Criticism Cumulative Nationality Index

AMERICAN
Adams, Andy **56**
Adams, Brooks **80**
Adams, Henry (Brooks) **4, 52**
Addams, Jane **76**
Agee, James (Rufus) **1, 19**
Allen, Fred **87**
Anderson, Maxwell **2**
Anderson, Sherwood **1, 10, 24**
Anthony, Susan B(rownell) **84**
Atherton, Gertrude (Franklin Horn) **2**
Austin, Mary (Hunter) **25**
Baker, Ray Stannard **47**
Barry, Philip **11**
Baum, L(yman) Frank **7**
Beard, Charles A(ustin) **15**
Becker, Carl (Lotus) **63**
Belasco, David **3**
Bell, James Madison **43**
Benchley, Robert (Charles) **1, 55**
Benedict, Ruth (Fulton) **60**
Benet, Stephen Vincent **7**
Benet, William Rose **28**
Bierce, Ambrose (Gwinett) **1, 7, 44**
Biggers, Earl Derr **65**
Black Elk **33**
Boas, Franz **56**
Bodenheim, Maxwell **44**
Bourne, Randolph S(illiman) **16**
Bradford, Gamaliel **36**
Brennan, Christopher John **17**
Bromfield, Louis (Brucker) **11**
Burroughs, Edgar Rice **2, 32**
Cabell, James Branch **6**
Cable, George Washington **4**
Cahan, Abraham **71**
Cardozo, Benjamin N(athan) **65**
Carnegie, Dale **53**
Cather, Willa Sibert **1, 11, 31**
Chambers, Robert W(illiam) **41**
Chandler, Raymond (Thornton) **1, 7**
Chapman, John Jay **7**
Chesnutt, Charles W(addell) **5, 39**
Chopin, Kate **5, 14**
Cobb, Irvin S. **77**
Cohan, George M(ichael) **60**
Comstock, Anthony **13**
Cotter, Joseph Seamon Sr. **28**
Cram, Ralph Adams **45**
Crane, (Harold) Hart **2, 5, 80**
Crane, Stephen (Townley) **11, 17, 32**
Crawford, F(rancis) Marion **10**
Crothers, Rachel **19**
Cullen, Countee **4, 37**
Darrow, Clarence (Seward) **81**
Davis, Rebecca (Blaine) Harding **6**
Davis, Richard Harding **24**
Day, Clarence (Shepard Jr.) **25**
Dent, Lester **72**
De Voto, Bernard (Augustine) **29**
Dreiser, Theodore (Herman Albert) **10, 18, 35, 83**
Dulles, John Foster **72**
Dunbar, Paul Laurence **2, 12**
Duncan, Isadora **68**
Dunne, Finley Peter **28**
Eastman, Charles A(lexander) **55**
Eddy, Mary (Morse) Baker **71**
Einstein, Albert **65**
Erskine, John **84**
Faust, Frederick (Schiller) **49**
Fenollosa, Ernest (Francisco) **91**
Fields, W. C. **80**
Fisher, Dorothy (Frances) Canfield **87**
Fisher, Rudolph **11**
Fitzgerald, F(rancis) Scott (Key) **1, 6, 14, 28, 55**
Fitzgerald, Zelda (Sayre) **52**
Flecker, (Herman) James Elroy **43**
Fletcher, John Gould **35**
Ford, Henry **73**
Forten, Charlotte L. **16**
Freeman, Douglas Southall **11**
Freeman, Mary Eleanor Wilkins **9**
Futrelle, Jacques **19**
Gale, Zona **7**
Garland, (Hannibal) Hamlin **3**
Gilman, Charlotte (Anna) Perkins (Stetson) **9, 37**
Glasgow, Ellen (Anderson Gholson) **2, 7**
Glaspell, Susan **55**
Goldman, Emma **13**
Green, Anna Katharine **63**
Grey, Zane **6**
Griffith, D(avid Lewelyn) W(ark) **68**
Griggs, Sutton Elbert **77**
Guiney, Louise Imogen **41**
Hall, James Norman **23**
Harper, Frances Ellen Watkins **14**
Harris, Joel Chandler **2**
Harte, (Francis) Bret(t) **1, 25**
Hartmann, Sadakichi **73**
Hatteras, Owen **18**
Hawthorne, Julian **25**
Hearn, (Patricio) Lafcadio (Tessima Carlos) **9**
Henry, O. **1, 19**
Hergesheimer, Joseph **11**
Higginson, Thomas Wentworth **36**
Holly, Buddy **65**
Holmes, Oliver Wendell Jr. **77**
Hopkins, Pauline Elizabeth **28**
Horney, Karen (Clementine Theodore Danielsen) **71**
Howard, Robert E(rvin) **8**
Howe, Julia Ward **21**
Howells, William Dean **7, 17, 41**
Huneker, James Gibbons **65**
Ince, Thomas H. **89**
James, Henry **2, 11, 24, 40, 47, 64**
James, William **15, 32**
Jewett, (Theodora) Sarah Orne **1, 22**
Johnson, James Weldon **3, 19**
Johnson, Robert **69**
Kinsey, Alfred C(harles) **91**
Kornbluth, C(yril) M. **8**
Korzybski, Alfred (Habdank Skarbek) **61**
Kuttner, Henry **10**
Lardner, Ring(gold) W(ilmer) **2, 14**
Lewis, (Harry) Sinclair **4, 13, 23, 39**
Lewisohn, Ludwig **19**
Lewton, Val **76**
Lindsay, (Nicholas) Vachel **17**
Locke, Alain (Le Roy) **43**
London, Jack **9, 15, 39**
Lovecraft, H(oward) P(hillips) **4, 22**
Lowell, Amy **1, 8**
Mankiewicz, Herman (Jacob) **85**
Markham, Edwin **47**
Marquis, Don(ald Robert Perry) **7**
Masters, Edgar Lee **2, 25**
McCoy, Horace (Stanley) **28**
McKay, Claude **7, 41**
Mead, George Herbert **89**
Mencken, H(enry) L(ouis) **13**
Micheaux, Oscar **76**
Millay, Edna St. Vincent **4, 49**
Mitchell, Margaret (Munnerlyn) **11**
Mitchell, S(ilas) Weir **36**
Mitchell, William **81**
Monroe, Harriet **12**
Morley, Christopher (Darlington) **87**
Muir, John **28**
Nathan, George Jean **18**
Nordhoff, Charles (Bernard) **23**
Norris, (Benjamin) Frank(lin Jr.) **24**
O'Neill, Eugene (Gladstone) **1, 6, 27, 49**
Oskison, John Milton **35**
Park, Robert E(zra) **73**
Patton, George S. **79**
Peirce, Charles Sanders **81**
Percy, William Alexander **84**
Phillips, David Graham **44**
Porter, Gene(va Grace) Stratton **21**
Post, Melville Davisson **39**
Pulitzer, Joseph **76**
Pyle, Ernie **75**
Pyle, Howard **81**
Rawlings, Marjorie Kinnan **4**
Reed, John (Silas) **9**
Reich, Wilhelm **57**
Remington, Frederic **89**
Rhodes, Eugene Manlove **53**
Riggs, (Rolla) Lynn **56**
Riis, Jacob A(ugust) **80**
Riley, James Whitcomb **51**
Rinehart, Mary Roberts **52**
Roberts, Elizabeth Madox **68**
Roberts, Kenneth (Lewis) **23**

Robinson, Edwin Arlington **5**
Roelvaag, O(le) E(dvart) **17**
Rogers, Will(iam Penn Adair) **8, 71**
Roosevelt, Theodore **69**
Rourke, Constance (Mayfield) **12**
Runyon, (Alfred) Damon **10**
Saltus, Edgar (Everton) **8**
Santayana, George **40**
Schoenberg, Arnold **75**
Sherwood, Robert E(mmet) **3**
Slesinger, Tess **10**
Stanton, Elizabeth Cady **73**
Steffens, (Joseph) Lincoln **20**
Stein, Gertrude **1, 6, 28, 48**
Sterling, George **20**
Stevens, Wallace **3, 12, 45**
Stockton, Frank R. **47**
Stroheim, Erich von **71**
Sturges, Preston **48**
Tarbell, Ida M(inerva) **40**
Tarkington, (Newton) Booth **9**
Taylor, Frederick Winslow **76**
Teasdale, Sara **4**
Tesla, Nikola **88**
Thomas, M. Carey **89**
Thurman, Wallace (Henry) **6**
Twain, Mark **6, 12, 19, 36, 48, 59**
Van Dine, S. S. **23**
Van Doren, Carl (Clinton) **18**
Veblen, Thorstein B(unde) **31**
Washington, Booker T(aliaferro) **10**
Wells, Carolyn **35**
West, Nathanael **1, 14, 44**
Whale, James **63**
Wharton, Edith (Newbold Jones) **3, 9, 27, 53**
White, Walter F(rancis) **15**
Williams, Ben Ames **89**
Williams, Hank **81**
Wilson, (Thomas) Woodrow **79**
Wister, Owen **21**
Wolfe, Thomas (Clayton) **4, 13, 29, 61**
Woodberry, George Edward **73**
Woollcott, Alexander (Humphreys) **5**
Wylie, Elinor (Morton Hoyt) **8**

ARGENTINIAN
Arlt, Roberto (Godofredo Christophersen) **29**
Guiraldes, Ricardo (Guillermo) **39**
Hudson, W(illiam) H(enry) **29**
Lugones, Leopoldo **15**
Storni, Alfonsina **5**

AUSTRALIAN
Baynton, Barbara **57**
Franklin, (Stella Maria Sarah) Miles (Lampe) **7**
Furphy, Joseph **25**
Ingamells, Rex **35**
Lawson, Henry (Archibald Hertzberg) **27**
Paterson, A(ndrew) B(arton) **32**
Richardson, Henry Handel **4**
Warung, Price **45**

AUSTRIAN
Beer-Hofmann, Richard **60**
Broch, Hermann **20**
Freud, Sigmund **52**
Hofmannsthal, Hugo von **11**
Kafka, Franz **2, 6, 13, 29, 47, 53**
Kraus, Karl **5**
Kubin, Alfred (Leopold Isidor) **23**
Meyrink, Gustav **21**
Musil, Robert (Edler von) **12, 68**
Perutz, Leo(pold) **60**
Roth, (Moses) Joseph **33**
Schnitzler, Arthur **4**
Steiner, Rudolf **13**
Stroheim, Erich von **71**
Trakl, Georg **5**
Weininger, Otto **84**
Werfel, Franz (Viktor) **8**
Zweig, Stefan **17**

BELGIAN
Bosschere, Jean de **19**
Lemonnier, (Antoine Louis) Camille **22**
Maeterlinck, Maurice **3**
van Ostaijen, Paul **33**
Verhaeren, Emile (Adolphe Gustave) **12**

BRAZILIAN
Andrade, Mario de **43**
Cunha, Euclides (Rodrigues Pimenta) da **24**
Lima Barreto, Afonso Henrique de **23**
Machado de Assis, Joaquim Maria **10**
Ramos, Graciliano **32**

BULGARIAN
Vazov, Ivan (Minchov) **25**

CANADIAN
Campbell, Wilfred **9**
Carman, (William) Bliss **7**
Carr, Emily **32**
Connor, Ralph **31**
Drummond, William Henry **25**
Duncan, Sara Jeannette **60**
Garneau, (Hector de) Saint-Denys **13**
Grove, Frederick Philip **4**
Innis, Harold Adams **77**
Knister, Raymond **56**
Leacock, Stephen (Butler) **2**
McCrae, John **12**
Montgomery, L(ucy) M(aud) **51**
Nelligan, Emile **14**
Pickthall, Marjorie L(owry) C(hristie) **21**
Roberts, Charles G(eorge) D(ouglas) **8**
Scott, Duncan Campbell **6**
Service, Robert W(illiam) **15**
Seton, Ernest (Evan) Thompson **31**
Stringer, Arthur **37**
Wetherald, Agnes Ethelwyn **81**

CHILEAN
Huidobro Fernandez, Vicente Garcia **31**
Mistral, Gabriela **2**
Prado (Calvo), Pedro **75**

CHINESE
Liu, E **15**
Lu Hsun **3**
Su Man-shu **24**
Wen I-to **28**

COLOMBIAN
Rivera, Jose Eustasio **35**

CZECH
Capek, Karel **6, 37**
Freud, Sigmund **52**
Hasek, Jaroslav (Matej Frantisek) **4**
Kafka, Franz **2, 6, 13, 29, 47, 53**
Nezval, Vitezslav **44**

DANISH
Brandes, Georg (Morris Cohen) **10**
Hansen, Martin A(lfred) **32**
Jensen, Johannes V. **41**
Nexo, Martin Andersen **43**
Pontoppidan, Henrik **29**

DUTCH
Couperus, Louis (Marie Anne) **15**
Frank, Anne(lies Marie) **17**
Heijermans, Herman **24**
Hillesum, Etty **49**
Schendel, Arthur van **56**

ENGLISH
Alexander, Samuel **77**
Barbellion, W. N. P. **24**
Baring, Maurice **8**
Baring-Gould, Sabine **88**
Beerbohm, (Henry) Max(imilian) **1, 24**
Bell, Gertrude (Margaret Lowthian) **67**
Belloc, (Joseph) Hilaire (Pierre Sebastien Rene Swanton) **7, 18**
Bennett, (Enoch) Arnold **5, 20**
Benson, E(dward) F(rederic) **27**
Benson, Stella **17**
Bentley, E(dmund) C(lerihew) **12**
Beresford, J(ohn) D(avys) **81**
Besant, Annie (Wood) **9**
Blackmore, R(ichard) D(oddridge) **27**
Blackwood, Algernon (Henry) **5**
Bramah, Ernest **72**
Bridges, Robert (Seymour) **1**
Brooke, Rupert (Chawner) **2, 7**
Burke, Thomas **63**
Butler, Samuel **1, 33**
Butts, Mary **77**
Byron, Robert **67**
Carpenter, Edward **88**
Chesterton, G(ilbert) K(eith) **1, 6, 64**
Childers, (Robert) Erskine **65**
Coleridge, Mary E(lizabeth) **73**
Collingwood, R(obin) G(eorge) **67**
Conrad, Joseph **1, 6, 13, 25, 43, 57**
Coppard, A(lfred) E(dgar) **5**
Corelli, Marie **51**
Crofts, Freeman Wills **55**
Crowley, Aleister **7**
Dale, Colin **18**
Delafield, E. M. **61**
de la Mare, Walter (John) **4, 53**
Dobson, Austin **79**
Doughty, Charles M(ontagu) **27**
Douglas, Keith (Castellain) **40**
Dowson, Ernest (Christopher) **4**
Doyle, Arthur Conan **7**
Drinkwater, John **57**
Eddison, E(ric) R(ucker) **15**
Elaine **18**
Elizabeth **41**
Ellis, (Henry) Havelock **14**
Firbank, (Arthur Annesley) Ronald **1**
Ford, Ford Madox **1, 15, 39, 57**
Freeman, R(ichard) Austin **21**
Galsworthy, John **1, 45**
Gilbert, W(illiam) S(chwenck) **3**
Gill, Eric **85**
Gissing, George (Robert) **3, 24, 47**
Glyn, Elinor **72**
Gosse, Edmund (William) **28**
Grahame, Kenneth **64**
Granville-Barker, Harley **2**
Gray, John (Henry) **19**
Gurney, Ivor (Bertie) **33**
Haggard, H(enry) Rider **11**
Hall, (Marguerite) Radclyffe **12**

Hardy, Thomas **4, 10, 18, 32, 48, 53, 72**
Henley, William Ernest **8**
Hilton, James **21**
Hodgson, William Hope **13**
Hope, Anthony **83**
Housman, A(lfred) E(dward) **1, 10**
Housman, Laurence **7**
Hudson, W(illiam) H(enry) **29**
Hulme, T(homas) E(rnest) **21**
Hunt, Violet **53**
Jacobs, W(illiam) W(ymark) **22**
James, Montague (Rhodes) **6**
Jerome, Jerome K(lapka) **23**
Johnson, Lionel (Pigot) **19**
Kaye-Smith, Sheila **20**
Keynes, John Maynard **64**
Kipling, (Joseph) Rudyard **8, 17**
Laski, Harold **79**
Lawrence, D(avid) H(erbert Richards) **2, 9, 16, 33, 48, 61**
Lawrence, T(homas) E(dward) **18**
Lee, Vernon **5**
Lee-Hamilton, Eugene (Jacob) **22**
Leverson, Ada **18**
Lewis, (Percy) Wyndham **2, 9**
Lindsay, David **15**
Lowndes, Marie Adelaide (Belloc) **12**
Lowry, (Clarence) Malcolm **6, 40**
Lucas, E(dward) V(errall) **73**
Macaulay, Rose **7, 44**
MacCarthy, (Charles Otto) Desmond **36**
Maitland, Frederic **65**
Manning, Frederic **25**
Meredith, George **17, 43**
Mew, Charlotte (Mary) **8**
Meynell, Alice (Christina Gertrude Thompson) **6**
Middleton, Richard (Barham) **56**
Milne, A(lan) A(lexander) **6, 88**
Moore, G. E. **89**
Morrison, Arthur **72**
Murry, John Middleton **16**
Nightingale, Florence **85**
Noyes, Alfred **7**
Oppenheim, E(dward) Phillips **45**
Orwell, George **2, 6, 15, 31, 51**
Ouida **43**
Owen, Wilfred (Edward Salter) **5, 27**
Pinero, Arthur Wing **32**
Powys, T(heodore) F(rancis) **9**
Quiller-Couch, Arthur (Thomas) **53**
Richardson, Dorothy Miller **3**
Rohmer, Sax **28**
Rolfe, Frederick (William Serafino Austin Lewis Mary) **12**
Rosenberg, Isaac **12**
Ruskin, John **20**
Rutherford, Mark **25**
Sabatini, Rafael **47**
Saintsbury, George (Edward Bateman) **31**
Saki **3**
Sapper **44**
Sayers, Dorothy L(eigh) **2, 15**
Shiel, M(atthew) P(hipps) **8**
Sinclair, May **3, 11**
Stapledon, (William) Olaf **22**
Stead, William Thomas **48**
Stephen, Leslie **23**
Strachey, (Giles) Lytton **12**
Summers, (Alphonsus Joseph-Mary Augustus) Montague **16**
Sutro, Alfred **6**
Swinburne, Algernon Charles **8, 36**
Symons, Arthur **11**
Thomas, (Philip) Edward **10**
Thompson, Francis Joseph **4**
Tomlinson, H(enry) M(ajor) **71**
Upward, Allen **85**
Van Druten, John (William) **2**
Wallace, (Richard Horatio) Edgar **57**
Wallas, Graham **91**
Walpole, Hugh (Seymour) **5**
Ward, Mrs. Humphry **55**
Warung, Price **45**
Webb, (Martha) Beatrice (Potter) **22**
Webb, Mary (Gladys Meredith) **24**
Webb, Sidney (James) **22**
Welch, (Maurice) Denton **22**
Wells, H(erbert) G(eorge) **6, 12, 19**
Williams, Charles (Walter Stansby) **1, 11**
Woolf, (Adeline) Virginia **1, 5, 20, 43, 56**
Yonge, Charlotte (Mary) **48**
Zangwill, Israel **16**

ESTONIAN
Talvik, Heiti **87**
Tammsaare, A(nton) H(ansen) **27**

FINNISH
Leino, Eino **24**
Soedergran, Edith (Irene) **31**
Westermarck, Edward **87**

FRENCH
Alain **41**
Alain-Fournier **6**
Apollinaire, Guillaume **3, 8, 51**
Artaud, Antonin (Marie Joseph) **3, 36**
Barbusse, Henri **5**
Barres, (Auguste-) Maurice **47**
Benda, Julien **60**
Bergson, Henri(-Louis) **32**
Bernanos, (Paul Louis) Georges **3**
Bernhardt, Sarah (Henriette Rosine) **75**
Bloy, Leon **22**
Bourget, Paul (Charles Joseph) **12**
Claudel, Paul (Louis Charles Marie) **2, 10**
Colette, (Sidonie-Gabrielle) **1, 5, 16**
Coppee, Francois **25**
Daumal, Rene **14**
Desnos, Robert **22**
Drieu la Rochelle, Pierre(-Eugene) **21**
Dujardin, Edouard (Emile Louis) **13**
Durkheim, Emile **55**
Eluard, Paul **7, 41**
Fargue, Leon-Paul **11**
Feydeau, Georges (Leon Jules Marie) **22**
France, Anatole **9**
Gide, Andre (Paul Guillaume) **5, 12, 36**
Giraudoux, (Hippolyte) Jean **2, 7**
Gourmont, Remy (-Marie-Charles) de **17**
Huysmans, Joris-Karl **7, 69**
Jacob, (Cyprien-)Max **6**
Jammes, Francis **75**
Jarry, Alfred **2, 14**
Larbaud, Valery (Nicolas) **9**
Leautaud, Paul **83**
Leblanc, Maurice (Marie Emile) **49**
Leroux, Gaston **25**
Loti, Pierre **11**
Martin du Gard, Roger **24**
Melies, Georges **81**
Mirbeau, Octave **55**
Mistral, Frederic **51**
Moreas, Jean **18**
Nizan, Paul **40**
Peguy, Charles Pierre **10**
Peret, Benjamin **20**
Proust, (Valentin-Louis-George-Eugene-) Marcel **7, 13, 33**
Rachilde **67**
Radiguet, Raymond **29**
Renard, Jules **17**
Rolland, Romain **23**
Rostand, Edmond (Eugene Alexis) **6, 37**
Roussel, Raymond **20**
Saint-Exupery, Antoine (Jean Baptiste Marie Roger) de **2, 56**
Schwob, Marcel (Mayer Andre) **20**
Sorel, Georges **91**
Sully Prudhomme **31**
Teilhard de Chardin, (Marie Joseph) Pierre **9**
Valery, (Ambroise) Paul (Toussaint Jules) **4, 15**
Verne, Jules (Gabriel) **6, 52**
Vian, Boris **9**
Weil, Simone (Adolphine) **23**
Zola, Emile (Edouard Charles Antoine) **1, 6, 21, 41**

GERMAN
Andreas-Salome, Lou **56**
Auerbach, Erich **43**
Barlach, Ernst **84**
Benjamin, Walter **39**
Benn, Gottfried **3**
Borchert, Wolfgang **5**
Brecht, (Eugen) Bertolt (Friedrich) **1, 6, 13, 35**
Carossa, Hans **48**
Cassirer, Ernst **61**
Doblin, Alfred **13**
Doeblin, Alfred **13**
Einstein, Albert **65**
Ewers, Hanns Heinz **12**
Feuchtwanger, Lion **3**
Frank, Bruno **81**
George, Stefan (Anton) **2, 14**
Goebbels, (Paul) Joseph **68**
Haeckel, Ernst Heinrich (Philipp August) **83**
Hauptmann, Gerhart (Johann Robert) **4**
Heym, Georg (Theodor Franz Arthur) **9**
Heyse, Paul (Johann Ludwig von) **8**
Hitler, Adolf **53**
Horney, Karen (Clementine Theodore Danielsen) **71**
Huch, Ricarda (Octavia) **13**
Kaiser, Georg **9**
Klabund **44**
Kolmar, Gertrud **40**
Lasker-Schueler, Else **57**
Liliencron, (Friedrich Adolf Axel) Detlev von **18**
Luxemburg, Rosa **63**
Mann, (Luiz) Heinrich **9**
Mann, (Paul) Thomas **2, 8, 14, 21, 35, 44, 60**
Mannheim, Karl **65**
Michels, Robert **88**
Morgenstern, Christian **8**
Nietzsche, Friedrich (Wilhelm) **10, 18, 55**
Ophuls, Max **79**
Otto, Rudolf **85**
Plumpe, Friedrich Wilhelm **53**
Raabe, Wilhelm (Karl) **45**
Rilke, Rainer Maria **1, 6, 19**
Simmel, Georg **64**
Spengler, Oswald (Arnold Gottfried) **25**
Sternheim, (William Adolf) Carl **8**
Sudermann, Hermann **15**
Toller, Ernst **10**
Vaihinger, Hans **71**
Wassermann, (Karl) Jakob **6**
Weber, Max **69**

Wedekind, (Benjamin) Frank(lin) **7**
Wiene, Robert **56**

GHANIAN
Casely-Hayford, J(oseph) E(phraim) **24**

GREEK
Cavafy, C(onstantine) P(eter) **2, 7**
Kazantzakis, Nikos **2, 5, 33**
Palamas, Kostes **5**
Papadiamantis, Alexandros **29**
Sikelianos, Angelos **39**

HAITIAN
Roumain, Jacques (Jean Baptiste) **19**

HUNGARIAN
Ady, Endre **11**
Babits, Mihaly **14**
Csath, Geza **13**
Herzl, Theodor **36**
Horvath, Oedoen von **45**
Jozsef, Attila **22**
Karinthy, Frigyes **47**
Mikszath, Kalman **31**
Molnar, Ferenc **20**
Moricz, Zsigmond **33**
Radnoti, Miklos **16**

ICELANDIC
Sigurjonsson, Johann **27**

INDIAN
Chatterji, Saratchandra **13**
Dasgupta, Surendranath **81**
Gandhi, Mohandas Karamchand **59**
Ghose, Aurabinda **63**
Iqbal, Muhammad **28**
Naidu, Sarojini **80**
Premchand **21**
Ramana Maharshi **84**
Tagore, Rabindranath **3, 53**
Vivekananda, Swami **88**

INDONESIAN
Anwar, Chairil **22**

IRANIAN
Hedayat, Sadeq **21**

IRISH
A.E. **3, 10**
Baker, Jean H. **3, 10**
Cary, (Arthur) Joyce (Lunel) **1, 29**
Dunsany, Lord **2, 59**
Gogarty, Oliver St. John **15**
Gregory, Isabella Augusta (Persse) **1**
Harris, Frank **24**
Joyce, James (Augustine Aloysius) **3, 8, 16, 35, 52**
Ledwidge, Francis **23**
Martin, Violet Florence **51**
Moore, George Augustus **7**
O'Grady, Standish (James) **5**
Shaw, Bernard **45**
Shaw, George Bernard **3, 9, 21**
Somerville, Edith **51**
Stephens, James **4**
Stoker, Bram **8**
Synge, (Edmund) J(ohn) M(illington) **6, 37**
Tynan, Katharine **3**
Wilde, Oscar **1, 8, 23, 41**
Yeats, William Butler **1, 11, 18, 31**

ITALIAN
Alvaro, Corrado **60**
Betti, Ugo **5**
Brancati, Vitaliano **12**
Campana, Dino **20**
Carducci, Giosue (Alessandro Giuseppe) **32**
Croce, Benedetto **37**
D'Annunzio, Gabriele **6, 40**
Deledda, Grazia (Cosima) **23**
Giacosa, Giuseppe **7**
Jovine, Francesco **79**
Lampedusa, Giuseppe (Tomasi) di **13**
Malaparte, Curzio **52**
Marinetti, Filippo Tommaso **10**
Mosca, Gaetano **75**
Papini, Giovanni **22**
Pareto, Vilfredo **69**
Pascoli, Giovanni **45**
Pavese, Cesare **3**
Pirandello, Luigi **4, 29**
Saba, Umberto **33**
Svevo, Italo **2, 35**
Tozzi, Federigo **31**
Verga, Giovanni (Carmelo) **3**

JAMAICAN
De Lisser, H(erbert) G(eorge) **12**
Garvey, Marcus (Moziah Jr.) **41**
Mais, Roger **8**
McKay, Claude **7, 41**
Redcam, Tom **25**

JAPANESE
Akutagawa, Ryunosuke **16**
Dazai Osamu **11**
Futabatei, Shimei **44**
Hagiwara Sakutaro **60**
Hayashi, Fumiko **27**
Ishikawa, Takuboku **15**
Masaoka Shiki **18**
Miyamoto, Yuriko **37**
Miyazawa, Kenji **76**
Mizoguchi, Kenji **72**
Nagai Kafu **51**
Natsume, Soseki **2, 10**
Nishida, Kitaro **83**
Noguchi, Yone **80**
Rohan, Koda **22**
Santoka, Taneda **72**
Shimazaki Toson **5**
Yokomitsu Riichi **47**
Yosano Akiko **59**

LATVIAN
Rainis, Janis **29**

LEBANESE
Gibran, Kahlil **1, 9**

LESOTHAN
Mofolo, Thomas (Mokopu) **22**

LITHUANIAN
Kreve (Mickevicius), Vincas **27**

MEXICAN
Azuela, Mariano **3**
Gamboa, Federico **36**
Gonzalez Martinez, Enrique **72**
Nervo, (Jose) Amado (Ruiz de) **11**
Reyes, Alfonso **33**
Romero, Jose Ruben **14**
Villaurrutia, Xavier **80**

NEPALI
Devkota, Laxmiprasad **23**

NEW ZEALANDER
Mander, (Mary) Jane **31**
Mansfield, Katherine **2, 8, 39**

NICARAGUAN
Dario, Ruben **4**

NORWEGIAN
Bjoernson, Bjoernstjerne (Martinius) **7, 37**
Bojer, Johan **64**
Grieg, (Johan) Nordahl (Brun) **10**
Hamsun, Knut **2, 14, 49**
Ibsen, Henrik (Johan) **2, 8, 16, 37, 52**
Kielland, Alexander Lange **5**
Lie, Jonas (Lauritz Idemil) **5**
Obstfelder, Sigbjoern **23**
Skram, Amalie (Bertha) **25**
Undset, Sigrid **3**

PAKISTANI
Iqbal, Muhammad **28**

PERUVIAN
Palma, Ricardo **29**
Vallejo, Cesar (Abraham) **3, 56**

POLISH
Asch, Sholem **3**
Borowski, Tadeusz **9**
Conrad, Joseph **1, 6, 13, 25, 43, 57**
Peretz, Isaac Loeb **16**
Prus, Boleslaw **48**
Przybyszewski, Stanislaw **36**
Reymont, Wladyslaw (Stanislaw) **5**
Schulz, Bruno **5, 51**
Sienkiewicz, Henryk (Adam Alexander Pius) **3**
Singer, Israel Joshua **33**
Witkiewicz, Stanislaw Ignacy **8**

PORTUGUESE
Pessoa, Fernando (Antonio Nogueira) **27**
Sa-Carniero, Mario de **83**

PUERTO RICAN
Hostos (y Bonilla), Eugenio Maria de **24**

ROMANIAN
Bacovia, George **24**
Caragiale, Ion Luca **76**
Rebreanu, Liviu **28**

RUSSIAN
Aldanov, Mark (Alexandrovich) **23**
Andreyev, Leonid (Nikolaevich) **3**
Annensky, Innokenty (Fyodorovich) **14**
Artsybashev, Mikhail (Petrovich) **31**
Babel, Isaak (Emmanuilovich) **2, 13**
Bagritsky, Eduard **60**
Balmont, Konstantin (Dmitriyevich) **11**
Bely, Andrey **7**
Berdyaev, Nikolai (Aleksandrovich) **67**
Bergelson, David **81**
Blok, Alexander (Alexandrovich) **5**
Bryusov, Valery Yakovlevich **10**
Bulgakov, Mikhail (Afanas'evich) **2, 16**
Bulgya, Alexander Alexandrovich **53**
Bunin, Ivan Alexeyevich **6**
Chekhov, Anton (Pavlovich) **3, 10, 31, 55**
Der Nister **56**
Eisenstein, Sergei (Mikhailovich) **57**

Esenin, Sergei (Alexandrovich) **4**
Fadeyev, Alexander **53**
Gladkov, Fyodor (Vasilyevich) **27**
Gorky, Maxim **8**
Gumilev, Nikolai (Stepanovich) **60**
Gurdjieff, G(eorgei) I(vanovich) **71**
Guro, Elena **56**
Hippius, Zinaida **9**
Ilf, Ilya **21**
Ivanov, Vyacheslav Ivanovich **33**
Khlebnikov, Velimir **20**
Khodasevich, Vladislav (Felitsianovich) **15**
Korolenko, Vladimir Galaktionovich **22**
Kropotkin, Peter (Aleksieevich) **36**
Kuprin, Aleksandr Ivanovich **5**
Kuzmin, Mikhail **40**
Lenin, V. I. **67**
Mandelstam, Osip (Emilievich) **2, 6**
Mayakovski, Vladimir (Vladimirovich) **4, 18**
Merezhkovsky, Dmitry Sergeyevich **29**
Pavlov, Ivan Petrovich **91**
Petrov, Evgeny **21**
Pilnyak, Boris **23**
Platonov, Andrei **14**
Prishvin, Mikhail **75**
Remizov, Aleksei (Mikhailovich) **27**
Shestov, Lev **56**
Sologub, Fyodor **9**
Tolstoy, Alexey Nikolaevich **18**
Tolstoy, Leo (Nikolaevich) **4, 11, 17, 28, 44, 79**
Trotsky, Leon **22**
Tsvetaeva (Efron), Marina (Ivanovna) **7, 35**
Zabolotsky, Nikolai Alekseevich **52**
Zamyatin, Evgeny Ivanovich **8, 37**
Zhdanov, Andrei Alexandrovich **18**
Zoshchenko, Mikhail (Mikhailovich) **15**

SCOTTISH
Barrie, J(ames) M(atthew) **2**
Bridie, James **3**
Brown, George Douglas **28**
Buchan, John **41**
Cunninghame Graham, R(obert) B(ontine) **19**
Davidson, John **24**
Frazer, J(ames) G(eorge) **32**
Gibbon, Lewis Grassic **4**
Lang, Andrew **16**
MacDonald, George **9**
Muir, Edwin **2, 87**
Sharp, William **39**
Tey, Josephine **14**

SOUTH AFRICAN
Bosman, Herman Charles **49**
Campbell, (Ignatius) Roy (Dunnachie) **5**
Mqhayi, S(amuel) E(dward) K(rune Loliwe) **25**
Plaatje, Sol(omon) T(shekisho) **73**
Schreiner, Olive (Emilie Albertina) **9**
Smith, Pauline (Urmson) **25**
Vilakazi, Benedict Wallet **37**

SPANISH
Alas (y Urena), Leopoldo (Enrique Garcia) **29**
Barea, Arturo **14**
Baroja (y Nessi), Pio **8**
Benavente (y Martinez), Jacinto **3**
Blasco Ibanez, Vicente **12**
Echegaray (y Eizaguirre), Jose (Maria Waldo) **4**
Garcia Lorca, Federico **1, 7, 49**
Jimenez (Mantecon), Juan Ramon **4**
Machado (y Ruiz), Antonio **3**
Martinez Sierra, Gregorio **6**
Martinez Sierra, Maria (de la O'LeJarraga) **6**
Miro (Ferrer), Gabriel (Francisco Victor) **5**
Ortega y Gasset, Jose **9**
Pereda (y Sanchez de Porrua), Jose Maria de **16**
Perez Galdos, Benito **27**
Salinas (y Serrano), Pedro **17**
Unamuno (y Jugo), Miguel de **2, 9**
Valera y Alcala-Galiano, Juan **10**
Valle-Inclan, Ramon (Maria) del **5**

SWEDISH
Bengtsson, Frans (Gunnar) **48**
Dagerman, Stig (Halvard) **17**
Ekelund, Vilhelm **75**
Heidenstam, (Carl Gustaf) Verner von **5**
Key, Ellen **65**
Lagerloef, Selma (Ottiliana Lovisa) **4, 36**
Soderberg, Hjalmar **39**
Strindberg, (Johan) August **1, 8, 21, 47**

SWISS
Ramuz, Charles-Ferdinand **33**
Rod, Edouard **52**
Saussure, Ferdinand de **49**
Spitteler, Carl (Friedrich Georg) **12**
Walser, Robert **18**

SYRIAN
Gibran, Kahlil **1, 9**

TURKISH
Sait Faik **23**

UKRAINIAN
Aleichem, Sholom **1, 35**
Bialik, Chaim Nachman **25**

URUGUAYAN
Quiroga, Horacio (Sylvestre) **20**
Sanchez, Florencio **37**

WELSH
Davies, W(illiam) H(enry) **5**
Evans, Caradoc **85**
Lewis, Alun **3**
Machen, Arthur **4**
Thomas, Dylan (Marlais) **1, 8, 45**

TCLC-91 Title Index

L'Ancienne et la nouvelle metaphysique (Sorel) **91**:321
"Aristotle on Wealth and Property" (Wallas) **91**:404
The Art of Thought (Wallas) **91**:357, 359, 361, 372, 380-1, 390, 398, 401
L'avenir socialiste des syndicats (Sorel) **91**:332
"The Chorius of Slaves" (Talvik) **87**:320
See "The Chorus of Slaves"
Conception materialististe de l'Histoire (Sorel) **91**:197
Conditioned Reflexes: An Investigation of the Physiological Activity of the Cerebral Cortex (Pavlov) **91**:102
Confessions (Sorel) **91**:193
"The Contemporary Unification in Experiment of the Main Aspects of Medicine, as Exemplified by Digestion" (Pavlov) **91**:150
Contribution a l'etude profane de la Bible (Sorel) **91**:233, 321, 329
La Decomposition du Marxisme (Sorel) **91**:332
"The Discovery of America" (Fenollosa) **91**:2
The Dreyfus Revolution (Sorel)
See *Revolution Dreyfusienne*
East and West: The Discovery of America, and Other Poems (Fenollosa) **91**:2
Epochs of Chinese and Japanese Art: An Outline of East Asiatic Design (Fenollosa) **91**:3
"An Essay on the Chinese Written Character as a Medium for Poetry" (Fenollosa) **91**:7, 15
Experimental Psychology and Other Essays (Pavlov) **91**:
Fabian Essays in Socialism (Wallas) **91**:365, 374, 376
La fin du monde antique (Sorel) **91**:193, 197, 213, 233, 301, 321-2, 329
"Fuji at Sunrise" (Fenollosa) **91**:3
"The Future Union of East and WEst" (Fenollosa) **91**:2
The Great Society: A Psychological Analysis (Wallas) **91**:354, 357, 359-61, 365, 369-70, 372, 379-80, 383, 390-1, 394, 402
"Himalya" (Fenollosa) **91**:3
Human Nature in Politics (Wallas) **91**:354-5, 357-60, 362-3, 365, 368-70, 374-6, 378-9, 390-4, 402, 404
Les Illusions du progres (Sorel) **91**:188, 193, 198, 200, 219, 224-5, 227, 295, 316, 332
The Illusions of Progress (Sorel)
See *Les Illusions du progres*
Insegnamenti sociali della economia contemporanea (Sorel) **91**:296-301, 303, 305
L'Introduction a l'Economie Moderne (Sorel) **91**:205, 209, 332
The Kinsey Report (Kinsey) **91**:42
Lectures on Conditioned Reflexes (Pavlov) **91**:123
Lectures on the Work of the Main Digestive Glands (Pavlov)
See *The Work of the Digestive Glands*
The Life of Francis Place (Wallas) **91**:352, 355, 396, 402
De l'utilite du pragmatisme (Sorel) **91**:194, 307
"M AA l'anti-philosophe" (Tzara)
See "M AA l'anti-philosophe"
materials for a Theory of the Proletariat (Sorel)
See *Materiaux d'une theorie du proletariat*
Materiaux d'une theorie du proletariat (Sorel) **91**:184, 201, 332
Men and Ideas: Essays (Wallas) **91**:356
Noh, or Accomplishment: A Study of the Classical Stage of Japan (Fenollosa) **91**:5
"Notes from Outside Sources" (Fenollosa) **91**:23
"On the Mutual Relations of Physiology and Medicine in Questions of Digestion" (Pavlov) **91**:150
"On the Surgical Method of Incestigation of the Secretory Phenomena of the Stomach" (Pavlov) **91**:150
Our Social Heritage (Wallas) **91**:359, 361, 365, 370, 372, 390, 394, 402, 404
"Physiological Surgery of the Digestive Canal" (Pavlov) **91**:150
Pour Lénine (Sorel) **91**:293
"The Present Meeting of East and WEst" (Fenollosa) **91**:2
Le proces de Socrate (Sorel) **91**:193, 205, 209, 213-4, 233, 291, 295, 321, 329
"Property Under Socialism" (Wallas) **91**:374, 376
"The Psychical Secretion of the Salivary Glands (Complex Nervous Phenomena in the Work of the Salivary Glands)" (Pavlov) **91**:150
Reflections on Violence (Sorel)
See *Reflexions sur la violence*
Reflexions sur la violence (Sorel) **91**:173, 176-8, 183-4, 188, 190, 193, 195, 199, 204-5, 209-10, 213-4, 219, 225, 233, 257, 263, 267, 272-4, 277, 291-3, 295-6, 301, 303, 305, 307-8, 311, 322, 332, 336, 344
"The Reply of a Physiologist to Psychologists" (Pavlov) **91**:84
"Le Reveil de l'ame francaise, le Mystere de la Charite de Jeanne de'Arc" (Sorel) **91**:241
Revolution Dreyfusienne (Sorel) **91**:188, 334
La ruine du monde antique (Sorel)
See *La fin du monde antique*
Saggi di critica del Marxismo (Sorel) **91**:332
"The Separated East" (Fenollosa) **91**:2
"The Separated West" (Fenollosa) **91**:2
Sexual Behavior in the Human Female (Kinsey) **91**:58, 68
Sexual Behavior in the Human Male (Kinsey) **91**:41, 44, 46, 68-70
Social Foundations of Contemporary Economics (Sorel)
See *Insegnamenti sociali della economia contemporanea*
Social Judgment (Wallas) **91**:357-9, 363, 372, 375, 381
Le systeme historique de Renan (Sorel) **91**:260-2, 329
"Vivisection" (Pavlov) **91**:150
The Work of the Digestive Glands (Pavlov) **91**:146, 150, 154-5, 157, 162-3

Title Index

ISBN 0-7876-2021-1

9 780787 620219 90000